7/01

Encyclopedia of
Paleontology

Encyclopedia of
Paleontology

Volume 1
A – L

Editor
Ronald Singer
The R.R. Bensley Professor of Biology and Medical Sciences
University of Chicago

FITZROY DEARBORN PUBLISHERS
CHICAGO · LONDON

FITZROY DEARBORN PUBLISHERS
919 North Michigan Avenue, Suite 760
Chicago, IL 60611
USA

or

FITZROY DEARBORN PUBLISHERS
310 Regent Street
London W1R 5AJ
England

British Library and Library of Congress Cataloguing in Publication Data are available.

ISBN 1–884964–96–6

First published in the USA and UK 1999

Interior Design and Typeset by Print Means Inc., New York, New York

Printed by Edwards Brothers, Ann Arbor, Michigan

Cover design by Peter Aristedes, Chicago Advertising and Design, Chicago, Illinois

Cover illustration: Reconstruction of a Pennsylvanian swamp with a diverse chelicerate fauna, illustration by Lonny Stark

CONTENTS

INTRODUCTION

People are drawn to fossils. All over the world, enthusiastic nonprofessionals soak up the latest news about remarkable fossil discoveries and often try to discover their own. The fossil halls of natural history museums are always packed with visitors. Paleontology is hot, and there is always a need for an up-to-date, accessible reference.

One factor that persuaded me to undertake this project was the concern that when many people hear the word "paleontology," they conjure an immediate association with dinosaurs. This almost visceral linkage leaves out innumerable other vertebrate taxa, as well as invertebrates belonging to more than 35 phyla, the other kingdoms of life—plants, fungi, "algae," protists—and the vast array of concerns that extend beyond the identification of individual organisms. Paleontologists—who often prefer to be called paleobiologists—seek to understand the entire fabric of lost worlds. This, of course, includes the identification of species and tracing their evolutionary relationships. It also includes reconstructions of these animals' basic biology, behavior, and ecology. It calls for the reconstruction of ancient climates, atmospheric and ocean chemistries, continental boundaries and positions, sea levels, and now-vanished terrains and environments.

The distant past is not simply a strangely vegetated theme park populated by extinct animals: its entire fabric is eerily unfamiliar and dimly understood. Entire ecosystems wholly alien to our experience must be rebuilt on the basis of carefully collected facts and testable theories. Windows need to be fashioned in order to observe phenomena that unfold over immense spans of time, phenomena that may otherwise escape our attention.

Today there are more than 1.5 million named and described species of plants and animals on our planet and perhaps 4 to 5 million more that have never been identified. If one makes a crude estimate that the average species lasts a million years, this would indicate that somewhere around 2.7 *billion* species have come and gone since the start of the Cambrian period, some 540 million years ago. The fossil record has yielded only a minute fraction of this number, and the sample is a biased one. Biases arise from the composition and size of organisms, the environment they inhabited, the collecting biases of investigators, and the accessibility of fossil-bearing rocks. Soft-bodied forms are poorly represented and are only glimpsed in widely separated windows afforded by rare Lagerstaaten (preserved-intact former environments and their inhabitants), such as the Canadian Burgess Shale. Many environments are not conducive to fossilization: forms that lived in the deep ocean and in mountainous areas are rarely preserved. Some time periods are under-represented, due to unusually low geological activity, lack of surface exposure of the sediments, or widespread alteration of the rocks by heat and pressure. Despite these and other biasing factors, the fossil record has managed to record evidence of most major taxa.

This encyclopedia attempts to cover all major groups of fossil organisms, but inevitably, some groups will be given more space than others. Extent of coverage has been tempered by space considerations, the availability of specialists to write about them, public fascination for certain groups, and my personal preferences. For example, there is one article on sponges and spongelike organisms. While sponges may not excite the average layperson, they have been important components of marine faunas since the late Precambrian. By far the most primitive of the metazoans, they may represent an independent experiment in the formation of multicellular animal life. Their morphological diversity is impressive and their importance as reef-builders cannot be overlooked.

Some practitioners of the "hard sciences" have mischaracterized paleontologists as "bone hunters" indulging a pursuit akin to stamp collecting. In fact, a practicing paleontologist requires a broader knowledge base and a greater diversity of skills than perhaps any other profession. New techniques are constantly being developed or improved in order to extract every scintilla of useful information. Today we can reliably estimate global temperatures using oxygen isotope ratios locked in the skeletons of marine microfossils. We can reconstruct the diets of extinct animals using carbon isotope ratios and trace elements stacked in bone. The techniques of molecular biology allow us to isolate the DNA from certain extinct organisms and compare it to the DNA of suspected modern relatives. New dating techniques appear with regularity and allow precise correlation and sequencing of sedimentary deposits worldwide. Systematics—the study of evolutionary relationships—has undergone a revolution in the last 30 years, and many unexpected connections have been found between animals as disparate as whales and cattle. Paleontology has unambiguously demonstrated that you cannot accurately reconstruct evolutionary patterns without bringing fossils into the picture. Many major evolutionary changes can *only* be traced through the rock record.

Paleontology is not only relevant to the past but is essential for understanding the history of life and for imagining the future we are creating for ourselves, our descendants, and our planet. Studies of paleoclimate show that the last 10,000 years have been unusually stable, which leaves open the possibility that climatic instability could return, with catastrophic consequences for modern civilizations. Past mass extinctions demonstrate how, and at what speed, the earth rebounds from devastation. By the time it runs its course, the current, human-mediated mass extinction may shape up to be as profound as the one that wiped out the dinosaurs. Just after the Cretaceous extinction, ferns became the dominant plant form and it took a few million years for a very different world to arise from the ashes of that global catastrophe. What will happen if humans do not reverse the current trends of deforestation, habitat fragmentation, and overpopulation?

While the major portion of this encyclopedia surveys the current state of knowledge, I wanted to include a little bit of the history of paleontology. This rich legacy is contained in many of the articles dealing with major taxa, the several regional profiles, and in biographies of some of the major historical figures. I have included energetic fieldworkers, individuals whose strengths lay in reconstruction and description, and scientists who revolutionized theory and analysis. In order to present complete profiles of these historical figures, it was decided that only deceased individuals would be the subjects of their own entries; the contributions of living workers in the field can be assessed through the ample citation of current scholarship in each essay.

Thanks go to the many individuals who have created illustrations for this project or have granted permission for their reproduction. Where no credit line is given, an illustration may be assumed to be the work of the essay's author. Special thanks go to Catherine P. Sexton, who reworked many illustrations for us and helped unify the style of our cladistic diagrams.

The articles in this encyclopedia have been written by authoritative scholars, in prose that is informal yet informative. It is my hope that they convey the excitement and ever-changing nature of paleontology and stimulate active contemplation of its many corners.

RONALD SINGER

ADVISERS

Edouard L. Boné
Université Catholique de Louvain

James A. Hopson
University of Chicago

Charles S. Churcher
University of Toronto

Ronald G. Wolff
University of Florida

CONTRIBUTORS

Josep Antoni Alcover
R. McNeill Alexander
Josephine Y. Aller
Edgar F. Allin
Robert Asher
Catherine Badgley
Steven Beaupre
Michael A. Bell
Stefan Bengtson
S. Christopher Bennett
Gale A. Bishop
José F. Bonaparte
Edouard L. Boné
Elizabeth L. Brainerd
Danita S. Brandt
Christopher B. Braun
Emily S. Bray
Derek E.G. Briggs
John C. Briggs
Brooks B. Britt
Christopher A. Brochu
Luis A. Buatois
Eric Buffetaut
Robyn J. Burnham
Carole J. Burrow
Jack M. Callaway
Brian Callender
Kathleen A. Campbell
Kenneth Carpenter
Matthew T. Carrano
Anusuya Chinsamy
Andreas Christian
Roberto Cipriani
E.N.K. Clarkson
W.A. Clemens

Richard Cloutier
Edwin H. Colbert
Allen G. Collins
H.B.S. Cooke
Paul Copper
Rodolfo A. Coria
Robert S. Corruccini
Robert Samuel Craig
Darin A. Croft
Roger J. Cuffey
Gilles Cuny
Stanislaw Czarniecki
Paul G. Davis
Mary R. Dawson
Eric Delson
Michael K. Diamond
David Dilcher
David W. Dilkes
William A. DiMichele
Daryl P. Domning
Philip C.J. Donoghue
Stephen K. Donovan
James A. Doyle
Elise Dufour
Gareth J. Dyke
Robert B. Eckhardt
Scott A. Elias
Julie Englander
Janie A. Enter
Joseph A. Ezzo
David E. Fastovsky
Lawrence J. Flynn
Susan M. Ford
Ann Forsten
Catherine A. Forster

Pierre-Yves Gagnier
Peter M. Galton
James D. Gardner
Timothy J. Gaudin
Dana H. Geary
Nicholas R. Geist
Patricia G. Gensel
Denis Geraads
Gerd Geyer
Emmanuel Gheerbrant
William R. Hammer
P.J. Hancox
David A.T. Harper
S. Blair Hedges
Robert S. Hill
James A. Hopson
Stéphane Hua
John P. Hunter
Christine Janis
Philippe Janvier
Paul A. Johnston
Roger G. Johnston
Anne Kemp
Margaret Jane Knaus
Eva Bundgaard Koppelhus
Dieter Korn
David W. Krause
Wolfram Michael Kürschner
Conrad C. Labandeira
W. David Lambert
Brigitte Lange-Badré
Michael S.Y. Lee
Ben A. LePage
Margaret E. Lewis
Anne-Marie Lézine
John A. Long
Spencer G. Lucas
R.D.E. MacPhee
Michael W. Maisch
Jon Mallatt
M. Gabriela Mángano
John Martin
Thomas Martin
Valérie Martin-Rolland
Judy A. Massare
W. Desmond Maxwell
Jenny C. McElwain
Michael L. McKinney
Mark A.S. McMenamin
Kenneth J. McNamara
Christopher A. McRoberts
Sara J. Metcalf
Desui Miao
Roger Miles
Angela C. Milner
Marisol Montellano Ballesteros

E.M.V. Nambudiri
Karl J. Niklas
R. Glenn Northcutt
Michael J. Novacek
J. Michael Parrish
Kevin J. Peterson
Paul David Polly
Mary F. Poteet
Donald R. Prothero
Mark A. Purnell
Jean-Claude Rage
D. Tab Rasmussen
Robert R. Reisz
Thomas H. Rich
Olivier Rieppel
Kenneth D. Rose
Charles A. Ross
Gar W. Rothwell
John Ruben
Manfred Ruddat
Michael Ruse
Scott D. Sampson
Ivan J. Sansom
Eric J. Sargis
William A.S. Sarjeant
Stephen E. Scheckler
Judith A. Schiebout
Robert M. Schoch
Stephan Schultka
Hans-Peter Schultze
Mary H. Schweitzer
Gustavo J. Scillato-Yané
Colin T. Scrutton
Adolf Seilacher
Rudolph Serbet
Brian T. Shea
Degan Shu
Neil H. Shubin
Judith E. Skog
Gerald R. Smith
Giles Smith
Jodie E. Smith
John J. Socha
David A.E. Spalding
Brian R. Speer
Fred Spoor
Brian J. Stafford
Glenn W. Storrs
Hans-Dieter Sues
Stuart S. Sumida
Frederick S. Szalay
Ian Tattersall
Bert Theunissen
J.G.M Thewissen
Jeff Thomason
Suyin Ting

Phillip V. Tobias

Tim T. Tokaryk

Haiyan Tong

Susan Turner

Russell H. Tuttle

Richard J. Twitchett

Peter S. Ungar

John E. Utgaard

Johan van der Burgh

Sergio F. Vizcaíno

Emilia I. Vorobyeva

Ben Waggoner

Michael W. Webb

Lars Werdelin

H.B. Whittington

Nic A. Williams

Brian J. Willis

Matthew A. Wills

Scott L. Wing

Ronald G. Wolff

Anthony D. Wright

J.J. Wymer

Ellis L. Yochelson

Gavin C. Young

ALPHABETICAL LIST OF ENTRIES

THEMATIC OUTLINE OF ENTRIES

This outline is divided into the following 12 sections:

ANALYTICAL APPROACHES
BIOLOGY AND BEHAVIOR
EVOLUTIONARY CONCEPTS
GEOGRAPHY AND ENVIRONMENT
INDIVIDUALS
MORPHOLOGY
PALEONTOLOGY AS A DISCIPLINE
PATTERNS IN THE HISTORY OF LIFE
PRACTICAL APPROACHES
REGIONAL OVERVIEWS
STRATIGRAPHIC AND FOSSIL RECORD
TAXA

The section on taxa is further divided into subsections.

ANALYTICAL APPROACHES

Biomass and Productivity Estimates
Biomechanics
Comparative Anatomy
Functional Morphology
Statistical Techniques
Molecular Paleontology

BIOLOGY AND BEHAVIOR

Aerial Locomotion
Aquatic Invertebrates, Adaptive Strategies
  of
Aquatic Locomotion
Burrowing Adaptations in Vertebrates
Diet
Feeding Adaptations: Invertebrates
Feeding Adaptations: Vertebrates
Gastroliths
Growth, Postembryonic
Paleoethology
Reproductive Strategies: Plants

Reproductive Strategies: Vertebrates
Respiration
Terrestrial Locomotion in Vertebrates
Thermoregulation

EVOLUTIONARY CONCEPTS

Adaptation
Allometry
Coevolutionary Relationships
Diversity
Evolutionary Novelty
Evolutionary Theory
Evolutionary Trends
Extinction
Growth, Development, and
  Evolution
Heterochrony
Homology
Phyletic Dwarfism and Gigantism
Selection
Speciation and Morphological
  Change

Systematics
Variation

GEOGRAPHY AND ENVIRONMENT

Atmospheric Environment
Global Environment
Ocean Environment
Paleoclimatology
Plate Tectonics and Continental Drift
Seas, Ancient
Terrestrial Environment

INDIVIDUALS

Abel, Othenio
Agassiz, Jean Louis Rudolphe
Ameghino, Carlos
Ameghino, Florentino
Andrews, Roy Chapman
Anning, Mary

MORPHOLOGY

PALEONTOLOGY AS A DISCIPLINE

PATTERNS IN THE HISTORY OF LIFE

PRACTICAL APPROACHES

REGIONAL OVERVIEWS

A

AARDVARKS

The eutherian (placental) order Tubulidentata includes a single family, Orycteropodidae; there is one extant (present-day) species, *Orycteropus afer* (aardvark). Usually described as being somewhat piglike in external form, *Orycteropus* dwells in bushlands and open forest where it feeds principally on social insects (although it occasionally consumes other foods). The morphological distinctiveness of Tubulidentata implies that the order is ancient, but the oldest fossils that can be placed securely in this family on the basis of shared derived features are only Early Miocene in age (Patterson 1975, 1978). Efforts to refer various early Tertiary European, North American, and Asian taxa (groups; singular, taxon) to Tubulidentata have not achieved wide acceptance.

The oldest and least likely view of tubulidentate systematics is that aardvarks are closely related to Xenarthra + Pholidota (parts of the nineteenth-century French scientist Georges Cuvier's original "Edentata"). No shared derived traits have been identified that support this view, now abandoned by virtually all scientists. Nineteenth-century investigations of the brain, somatic musculature, and other soft-tissue structures of aardvarks suggested a possible link with ungulates (hoofed, typically herbivorous quadrupedal mammals, such as pigs, sheep, deer, horses, and tapirs). This view gained support in the early twentieth century with the proposal that tubulidentates were related to early Tertiary condylarthrans (a paraphyletic group of primitive ungulates). A condylarthran heritage for aardvarks and their relatives was endorsed most recently by B. Patterson (1975, 1978). M.C. McKenna and S.K. Bell (1997) placed Tubulidentata in Ungulata *incertae sedis*.

Although tubulidentates provisionally may be considered part of the great ungulate lineage, the evidence for this placement remains far from satisfactory. J.G.M. Thewissen (1985) raised doubts about the utility of cerebral and cranial characters previously used to associate aardvarks with ungulates, noting that some of them were exceptionally primitive. In a study by M.J. Novacek and colleagues (1988), Tubulidentata was found to occupy a branch on the eutherian cladogram (family tree) that also supported Insectivora (e.g., moles, shrews, hedgehogs) and Carnivora (e.g., cats, dogs, hyenas, weasels, seals), although character support

for this arrangement was poor. In a restudy of the same character set, R.D.E. MacPhee (1994) found that deletion of only two characters caused this branch to collapse (in the resulting strict consensus diagram, *Orycteropus* and *Plesiorycteropus* brigaded with Xenarthra and Pholidota—Cuvier's Edentata!). Molecular evidence for the placement of *Orycteropus* has not yet been published.

Cranially, the living aardvark combines very primitive basicranial and neurocranial organization with highly derived (specialized) features of the face and the dentition (Thewissen 1985). Peglike and enamelless, aardvark teeth are composed of a specialized tissue descriptively identified as "tubulodentine." E. Lönnberg (1906) considered aardvark teeth to be the morphological equivalent of roots (i.e., teeth that had evolutionarily lost their enamel crowns). However, the histological (minute structural) organization of tubulodentine differs from typical dentine: In magnified cross section, an aardvark tooth is seen to consist of numerous small polygons, each polygon being comprised of a slender pulp cavity surrounded by a bundle of radiating tubules. The teeth of no other mammals have such an appearance, even in cases in which the teeth are composed mostly or solely of dentine (e.g., epoicotheres, phyllophages).

The only genera that Patterson (1975) included in Tubulidentata are exclusively Neogene (Miocene and later): these include *Orycteropus* (Late Miocene–Recent of East Africa, South Africa, West Asia), *Leptorycteropus* (Late Miocene of East Africa), *Myorycteropus* (Early Miocene of East Africa), and *Plesiorycteropus* (Recent of Madagascar). The first three have distinctively tubulidentate teeth and therefore share a critical derived trait. (Supposed Paleogene tubulidentates, such as *Archaeorycteropus, Palaeorycteropus,* and *Leptomanis* were considered to be either dubious or too poorly known to evaluate.) Neogene aardvarks were distributed over a wide swath of the Old World, fossils having been found in western Europe, the Indian subcontinent, the Caucasus, and several parts of eastern and southern Africa. Cranially they differ little from the surviving species, although postcrania (skeletons) are often distinctive. The best known of the extinct tubulidentates is *Orycteropus gaudryi,* a Miocene (Turonian) species from western

Asia. Patterson (1978) noted that Plio-Pleistocene African aardvarks (conventionally included in *Orycteropus* by most authors) are more diverse than their formal nomenclature implies, but this group still awaits revision. All accepted tubulidentates appear to have been insectivorous.

By any definition, *Plesiorycteropus,* from the late Quaternary of Madagascar, is an extreme outlier within Tubulidentata. The skeleton of this genus is known in considerable detail, although unfortunately no complete faces or jaws have yet been recognized. Most scholars, including Patterson (1975, 1978), have unhesitatingly referred *Plesiorycteropus* to Orycteropodidae (subfamily Plesiorycteropodinae), but, as MacPhee (1994) showed, there is little evidence to support this allocation. In fact, *Plesiorycteropus* is not very much like any Recent eutherian, although it bears isolated, convergent resemblances to several widely separated groups, including dasypodids (armadillos) and manids (pangolins) as well as orycteropodids. In recognition of the distinctiveness of *Plesiorycteropus,* MacPhee (1994) created the separate order Bibymalagasia (Eutheria *incertae sedis*) for its reception.

R.D.E. MacPhee

See also Ungulates, Archaic

Works Cited

Lönnberg, E. 1906. On a new *Orycteropus* from northern Congo and some remarks on the dentition of the Tubulidentata. *Arkiv för Zoologi, Stockholm* 3:1–35.

MacPhee, R.D.E. 1994. *Morphology, Adaptations, and Relationships of Plesiorycteropus, with a Diagnosis of a New Order of Eutherian Mammals.* Bulletin of the American Museum of Natural History, 220. New York: American Museum of Natural History.

McKenna, M.C., and S.K. Bell. 1997. *Classification of Mammals above the Species Level.* New York: Columbia University Press.

Novacek, M.J., A.R. Wyss, and M.C. McKenna. 1988. The major groups of eutherian mammals. *In* M. Benton (ed.), *The Phylogeny and Classification of the Tetrapods.* Vol. 2, *Mammals.* Oxford: Clarendon Press; New York: Oxford University Press.

Patterson, B. 1975. The fossil aardvarks (Mammalia: Tubulidentata). *Bulletin of the Museum of Comparative Zoology, Harvard University* 147:185–237.

———. 1978. Pholidota and Tubulidentata. *In* V. Maglio and H.S.B. Cook (eds.), *Evolution of African Mammals.* Cambridge, Massachusetts: Harvard University Press.

Thewissen, J.G.M. 1985. Cephalic evidence for the affinities of Tubulidentata. *Mammalia* 49:257–84.

Further Reading

McKenna, M.C., and S.K. Bell. 1997. *Classification of Mammals above the Species Level.* New York: Columbia University Press.

Novacek, M.J., A.R. Wyss, and M.C. McKenna. 1988. The major groups of eutherian mammals. *In* M. Benton (ed.), *The Phylogeny and Classification of the Tetrapods.* Vol. 2, *Mammals.* Oxford: Clarendon Press; New York: Oxford University Press.

Patterson, B. 1975. The fossil aardvarks (Mammalia: Tubulidentata). *Bulletin of the Museum of Comparative Zoology, Harvard University* 147:185–237.

———. 1978. Pholidota and Tubulidentata. *In* V. Maglio and H.S.B. Cook (eds.), *Evolution of African Mammals.* Cambridge, Massachusetts: Harvard University Press.

ABEL, OTHENIO

Austrian, 1875–1946

Othenio Abel was born on 20 June 1875 in Vienna, Austria. The son of a teacher in the horticulture school and the descendant of several generations of gardeners, Abel was exposed to botany and biology at an early age. This exposure was certainly influential in contributing to Abel's most significant scientific achievement: the founding of paleobiology. During his career Abel published 275 works, received a variety of honors, and led several paleontological expeditions on three continents. He died on 4 July 1946 in Pichl am Mondsee, Austria.

Although Abel attended the Faculty of Law of the University of Vienna, his interest in the natural sciences was apparent; he collected fossils, and his first publications were on orchids. In 1898 Abel was appointed assistant at the Geological Institute of the University of Vienna. A year later, in 1899, he received his Ph.D. in geology and paleontology from the University of Vienna. Afterwards, he briefly attended the school of mining in Leoben, and then, in 1900, he became *mitarbeiten* at the Imperial Royal Geological State Institute in Vienna. Abel remained active at this position until 1907, during which time he published his study on the Cetacea "Untersuchungen uber die fossilen Platanistiden des wiener Beckens."

Following this publication, Abel was invited to Belgium to study fossil whales. In 1900 he was appointed foreign collaborator of the Royal Museum of Natural History of Belgium, where he befriended Louis Dollo. Dollo became Abel's teacher of paleontology, and his teachings were influential in the founding of paleobiology.

Although he was appointed to various positions throughout his career, Abel was most closely associated with the University of Vienna and produced the majority of his work while there. In 1901 he became *Privatdozent* in paleontology. In 1907 he was appointed associate professor, and in 1912 he received full professorship. Then, in 1917, he became professor of paleobiology and director of the paleobiology department, which would later become the Paleobiological Institute of the University of Vienna. Abel also served as dean in 1927/28 and rector in 1932/33.

During his years with the University of Vienna, Abel produced his most important works. In 1912 *Grundzuge der Palaobiologie der Wirbeltiere* appeared, followed in 1914 by *Die vorzeitlichen Saugetiere* and in 1916 by *Palaobiologie der Cepha-*

lopoden. Later works include *Die Stamme der Wirbeltiere* in 1919, *Lehrbuch der Palaozoologie* in 1920, *Lebensbilder aus der Tierwelt der Vorzeit* in 1922, and *Geschichte und Methode der Rekonstruktion vorzeitlicher Wirbeltiere* in 1925. In 1928 Abel founded the journal *Palaeobiologica,* in which many of his shorter papers appeared.

During his years with the University of Vienna, Abel also was in charge of several important paleozoological expeditions including excavations in the Pontian site of Pikermi in Greece, the Drachenhohle near Mixnitz, Styria (a region in Austria), America (1925), and South Africa (1929). His expeditions helped garner honorary doctorates from the universities of Cape Town and Athens.

For his work and contribution, Abel was recognized with numerous awards and honors. He was awarded the Bigsby Medal of the Geological Society of London (1911), the Elliot Medal of the National Academy of Sciences in Washington (1922), and the Rainer Medal of the Zoological-Botanical Society of Vienna. Abel also received honorary member status of various scientific academies, and in 1921 he served as the president of the Paleontological Society.

After spending most of his career with the University of Vienna, Abel was appointed professor of paleontology at the University of Gottingen. For five years, from 1935 to 1940, Abel amassed new collections and continued to investigate newer subdivisions of paleontology. Then, in 1940, Abel retired and returned to Austria, where he continued with his scientific activities. Othenio Abel died on 4 July 1946 in Pichl am Mondsee, Austria.

EDOUARD L. BONÉ AND BRIAN CALLENDER

Biography

Born in Vienna, Austria, 20 June 1875. Received Ph.D., University of Vienna 1899. Appointed foreign collaborator of Royal Museum of Natural History of Belgium, 1900; assistant professor, University of Vienna, 1907; received Bigsby Medal of the Geological Society of London, 1911; professor, University of Vienna, 1912; professor of paleobiology and director of paleobiology department, University of Vienna, 1917; president of the Paleontological Society, 1921; received Elliot Medal of the National Academy of Sciences in Washington, 1922; received the Rainer Medal of the Zoological-Botanical Society of Vienna, 1922; dean, University of Vienna, 1927/28; rector, University of Vienna, 1932/33; professor, University of Gottingen, 1935. Died 4 July 1946 in Pichl am Mondsee, Austria.

Major Publications

1912. *Grundzüge der Paläobiologie der Wirbeltiere.* Stuttgart: Schweizerbart.

1914. *Die vorzeitlichen Säugetiere.* Jena: Fischer.

1916. *Paläobiologie der Cephalopoden.* Jena: Fischer.

1919. *Die Stämme der Wirbeltiere.* Berlin: Gruyter.

1920. *Lehrbuch der Paläozoologie* 1st ed. Jena: Fischer; 2nd ed., Jena: Fischer, 1924.

1922. *Lebensbilder aus der Tierwelt der Vorzeit.* Jena: Fischer; 2nd ed., Jena: Fischer, 1927.

1925. *Geschichte und Methode der Rekonstruktion vorzeitlicher Wirbeltiere.* Jena: Fischer.

Further Reading

Ehrenberg, K. 1949. Othenio Abel, sein Werden und Wirken. *Neues Jahrbuch fur Mineralogie, Geologie und Paläontologie* 11/12:325–28.

ACANTHODIANS

The acanthodians are an extinct group of fossil fishes that lived for at least 150 million years during the Paleozoic era (from the Ordovician to the Permian periods). The name comes from the Greek word *Acanthos* (spine or thorn), because acanthodians are characterized by a sharp spine at the leading edge of each fin (Figure 1).

Scholars have known that isolated spines of acanthodians belonged to fishes for more than 160 years, since the group was first established by the great Swiss scientist Louis Agassiz in 1833. He erected the genus and species *"Acanthodes bronni"* for some well-preserved fossil fish, up to 50 centimeters long, found in ironstone nodules of Early Permian age around Saarbruck in Germany. Agassiz also described acanthodians from another famous fossil fish locality, the Devonian "Old Red Sandstone" of Scotland (Agassiz 1833–44). In recent times, well-preserved complete fishes have been discovered at various new localities, including Arctic Canada (Northwest Territories), southeastern Australia (Gippsland, Victoria) and Siberia (Severnaya Zemlya).

Acanthodians represent one of the four major groups of gnathostome (jawed) fishes. They may be the oldest gnathostomes known from the fossil record, with fragmentary remains recorded from the Lower Silurian of the United States and China and recent reports of scales typical of acanthodians in Ordovician strata. Acanthodians flourished during the Devonian and Carboniferous periods, when they attained a worldwide distribution. Devonian acanthodians existed from Antarctica in the south, to Greenland and Arctic Canada in the north. They have been described in many localities in Europe and North America and are also recorded from Russia, Siberia, China, the Middle East, Australia, Africa, and South America. Important scientific accounts of the group published during this century include Watson (1937), Miles (1973a, 1973b), and Denison (1979). So far over 60 genera (groups; singular, genus) and 150 species of acanthodians have been described, but many are known only by isolated spines, teeth, or scales. Most researchers recognize three major acanthodian subgroups (the Climatiiformes, Ischnacanthiformes, and Acanthodiformes).

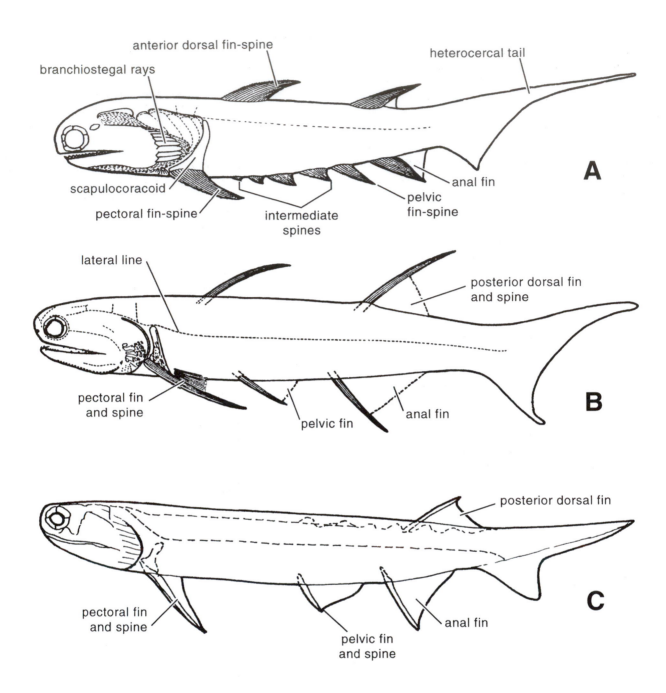

Figure 1. Representatives of the three orders of acanthodian fishes. *A*, the climatiiform *Climatius reticulatus* (length to 20 centimeters) from the Early Devonian of Scotland; *B*, the ischnacanthiform *Ischnacanthus gracilis* (length to 16 centimeters) from the Early Devonian of Scotland; *C*, the acanthodiform *Howittacanthus kentoni* (length to 25 centimeters) from the Middle-Late Devonian of Gippsland, Victoria. *A, B*, after Watson (1937), and Denison (1979); *C*, modified from Long (1986a).

Morphology

Apart from isolated spines, scales, and teeth, along with general body shape (when whole fish are preserved), few details of acanthodian morphology are known in most forms, because the skeleton readily fell apart before it could fossilize. Much of our knowledge of acanthodian structure is based on one species, *Acanthodes bronni* from the Early Permian. However, this is one of the latest members of the group, so it may not represent the morphology (shape and structure) of primitive acanthodians.

Most acanthodians were small fishes, up to 25 centimeters long, with a fusiform body shape (tapered at each end), terminal mouth, large eyes, and a heterocercal (strongly upturned) tail (Figure 1). A few evolved a deeper body form (e.g., *Brochoadmones, Culmacanthus*) (Figure 2D) or exceptionally large size (*Xylacanthus* and

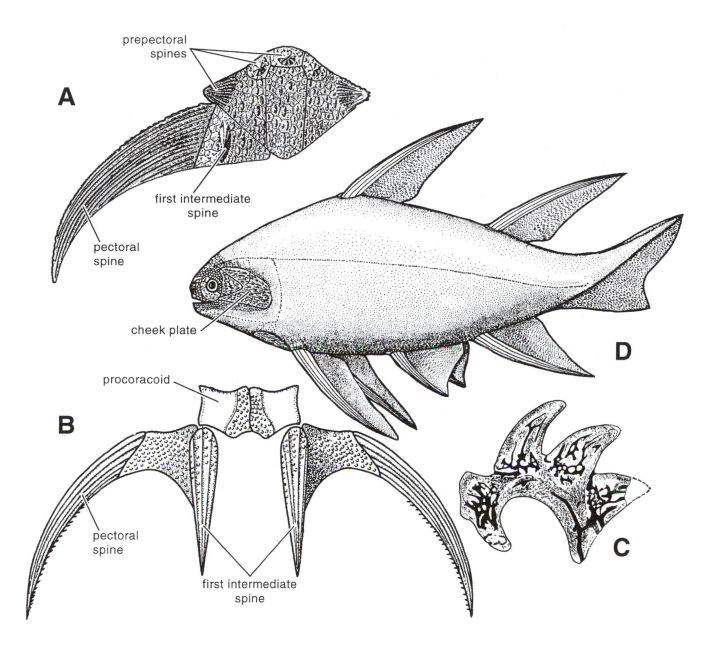

Figure 2. Examples of the dermal skeleton in acanthodians. *A, B,* pattern of dermal plates and attached spines of the pectoral girdle (ventral view) in the climatiiform acanthodians *Climatius* and *Diplacanthus* from Scotland; *C,* section through a tooth spiral of *Nostolepis* (×33); *D,* restoration of *Culmacanthus stewarti* (left side) from Victoria, showing the large dermal cheek plate (actual length, approximately 14 centimeters). *A, B,* from Miles (1973a); *C,* from Ørvig (1973), Denison (1979); *D,* from Long (1983), Young (1989).

Gyracanthus, up to 2.5 meters long). The whole body, including the fin webs, was covered with closely packed, tiny, studlike scales. Spines precede all of the fins, including paired fins (this is never the case in cartilaginous fishes). Some acanthodians also have intermediate spines between the pectoral and pelvic fins, located below and to the rear of the gills and near the anus, respectively (Figure 1A), but these never carry a fin web. The large eyes were located at the front of the snout, suggesting that the nasal capsules were small. In a few species, nostrils have been identified as small openings lying close to the midline (center of the "face") immediately above the edge (margin) of the mouth. Posterior or excurrent nostrils may have been located in the front corner of the orbit (opening for the eye), as in some early actinopterygians. Acanthodians had a sensory system that ran along the sides of the body, with an associated pattern of sensory grooves over the head and cheek. Similar grooves are seen in other primitive gnathostomes.

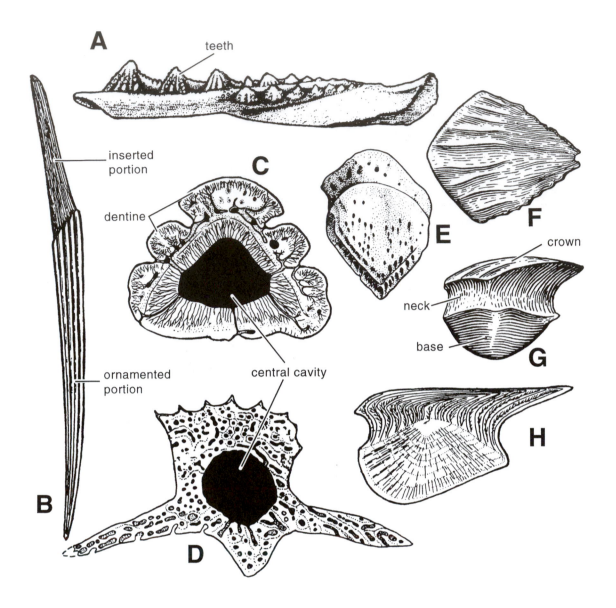

Figure 3. Isolated dentigerous jawbones, fin spines, and scales of various acanthodians. *A, Taemasacanthus erroli* jawbone (actual length 4 centimeters); *B, Onchus overathensis* fin spine, complete (actual length 14 centimeters); *C, Gomphonchus* fin spine, cross section (×60); *D, Machaeracanthus* fin spine, cross section (×10); *E, Poracanthodes punctatus* scale, crown view (×60); *F, G, Haplacanthus* scales, crown and side views (×75); *H, Gomphonchus* scale, cross section (×90). *A*, from Long (1986b); *B, C, E, F*, and *G*, from Denison (1979); *D*, from Young (1992); *H*, from Gross (1971).

Like other early vertebrates, the acanthodian skeleton comprises two independent systems: the external "dermal skeleton" of bones, teeth, scales, and fin spines, all located in the skin; and the internal skeleton, or "endoskeleton." The dermal skeleton of acanthodians is said to be "micromeric," because it is made up mainly of small elements and scales, rather than the large sutured (joined, or grown together) bones enclosing the front of the body, as developed in the osteichthyans and placoderms (the "macromeric" condition). In most cases, the acanthodian head is covered by tiny scales, similar to those on the body surface, but some forms had enlarged bones in the cheek and shoulder girdle (Figure 2). Most

acanthodians had a ring of five or six bones around the eye (possibly differently developed in climatiiforms and acanthodiforms), and enlarged scales attached to a structure called the hyoid arch to form the hyoid gill cover. Apart from fin spines, the only other large dermal elements are the mandibular bone, a bone which underlies and strengthens the lower jaw, and the actual upper and lower tooth-bearing (dentigerous) jaw bones (Figure 3A), which occur in one acanthodian subgroup (the ischnacanthiforms).

The fin spines that characterize the Acanthodii have varied development within the group. In Climatiidae, they are short and stout, heavily ornamented with ribs and tubercles (small, bony

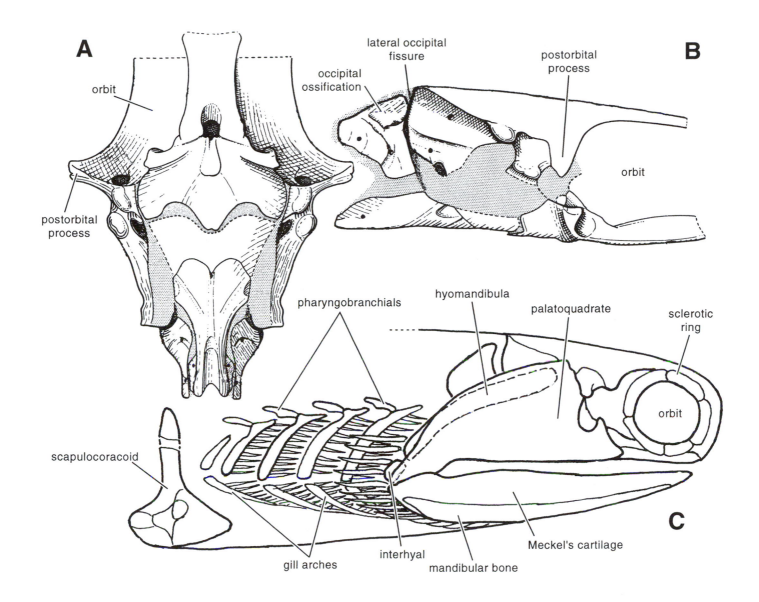

Figure 4. Internal morphology of the head skeleton in *Acanthodes*. *A, B,* restored braincase (neurocranium) in ventral and right lateral views; *C,* restoration in right lateral view, showing neurocranium, jaws, branchial arches, and scapulocoracoid. *A, B,* after Miles (1973b); *C,* modified from Watson (1937), Nelson (1968), Miles (1973a, 1973b).

protuberances), and are only superficially inserted in the skin (Figure 1A). The more slender spines of the Diplacanthidae have a long base of insertion, and the external portion is often ribbed (Figure 1B). Gyracanthidae had coarse, obliquely arranged, ornamented ridges on the spines, and typical ischnacanthiform and acanthodiform spines are slender, occasionally flattened, and either smooth or having only a few longitudinal ribs (Figure 1C). Cross sections of spines show a central cavity surrounded by dentinous tissue, sometimes with cellular bone (Figure 3C, D). Some of these cross sections are unique to certain genera and can be used in identification.

The small scales of acanthodians typically grew when new materials were deposited periodically around the scale, such that each time it occurred the crown and base were covered completely with a new layer (Figure 3H). The minute internal structure of each scale varies considerably, but generally the crown is formed of dentine or "mesodentine" (a tissue intermediate between dentine and bone) and the base of cellular or acellular bone. Small canals for blood vessels pass through the scales, and some forms have a more extensive "pore-canal" system, probably for sensory purposes (e.g., *Poracanthodes*, Figure 3E). Isolated scales of this type were previously thought to be specialized scales of the sensory grooves, but recently discovered, relatively intact specimens show that such grooves covered the whole body surface. In general, primitive acanthodians had ornamented scales (Figure 3F), but in the more derived (specialized) acanthodiforms the scale crowns are smooth.

In all vertebrates, the various components of the endoskeleton form initially as cartilage. In acanthodians, some of these internal elements became enveloped by a thin surface layer of perichondral (layered) bone, which, when preserved, shows the internal structure. The vertebrate endoskeleton includes the braincase, jaw cartilages, gill skeleton, vertebral column, and the internal pectoral and pelvic girdles and fin supports. In acanthodians, the braincase is well known only in the genus *Acanthodes,* where it is preserved as several separate perichondral structures (Figure 4A, B). The prominent postorbital processes (large, bony projection behind the eye socket) and narrow region between the orbits gives a close resemblance to one group of osteichthyans (bony fishes), called the actinopterygians (ray-finned fishes). Both had short, separately-boned occipital regions. The space between the two—the "lateral occipital fissure"—was connected by cartilage and provided a passage for the tenth cranial (vagus) nerve.

As in other jawed fishes, the mouth was formed internally by two structures that together form the "mandibular arch": the palatoquadrate above, and Meckel's cartilage below (Figure 4C). Behind the mandibular arch is the "hyoid arch," which in all known gnathostome fishes is modified to support the jaws. At one time, scholars believed that acanthodians had a normal gill slit behind the mandibular arch (with the hyoid an unmodified branchial, or gill, arch). However, in *Acanthodes* the hyomandibula fitted in a groove inside the lower back edge of the palatoquadrate, with gill openings farther back, between the five branchial arches (Figure 4C). This is a typical gnathostome arrangement, as seen in primitive osteichthyans.

In *Acanthodes* the endoskeleton of the shoulder girdle, which carried the pectoral fin and dermal spine, was ossified (turned into bone by calcium deposits) in three portions (scapular, coracoid, and procoracoid). The internal skeleton of acanthodian fins is known in only a few species, which show short bases of perichondral bone beneath the skin covering of scales and fin rays. The vertebral column of acanthodians is poorly known, but the notochord (a rigid, fiber-wound structure composed of collegan and other connective tissue that lies below the backbone) persisted in the body during development, with other structures, such as ossified neural arches and spines and hemal arches (found in front of the tail vertebrae).

Mode of Life

The general acanthodian body shape suggests an active swimming lifestyle. It has been argued that since no members of the group are known to have developed a flattened, broad body form, they may have possessed a swim bladder (a gas-filled sac that provides buoyancy) to help maintain body orientation in the water. This adaptation did not occur in chondrichthyans and placoderms, in which the flattened body form evolved several times as an adaptation for living on the sea floor. However, trace fossils from Early Devonian sediments in Nova Scotia have been attributed to acanthodians that rested or swam across a muddy bottom.

The large eyes of acanthodians indicate a primary reliance on sight to detect both prey and predators. The climatiiforms, with simple teeth, probably fed on small invertebrates; on the other hand, the ischnacanthids, with their well-developed tooth and jaw structure, were probably highly efficient predators. Many

acanthodiforms may have been specialized filter feeders, and gut contents preserved inside *Acanthodes* specimens show that they consumed crustaceans and other small invertebrates that inhabited mid-level and surface waters. However, one specimen also includes a small palaeoniscoid fish (primitive ray-fin) in the gut, showing that acanthodians both competed with, and sometimes preyed upon, this similarly adapted fish group. The spines of acanthodians no doubt afforded some protection from predators, but these fish are known to have been eaten by other groups—preserved acanthodian remains have been found in coprolites (fossilized dung), and in the gut contents of Devonian placoderms and of larger palaeoniscoids in the Carboniferous and Permian.

Acanthodians remains are encountered in the sediments of most Paleozoic fossil fish deposits of the appropriate age, but early representatives of the group seem to have been restricted to marine (salt water) environments. They were evidently never the dominant members of any fauna, but by Early and Middle Devonian time they had invaded fresh water and are commonly a minor element in most Devonian fossil fish assemblages (groupings of a wide variety of types of animals), represented by isolated spines and scales (Figure 3). Some of the best localities—those that yield complete acanthodians—seem to be fine-grained sediments deposited in freshwater lakes (e.g., the middle Old Red Sandstone deposits of Scotland or the Mount Howitt occurrence in Victoria, Australia). In certain residues from marine limestones that have been processed in acid to extract microfossils, acanthodian scales are often common and are sometimes the most abundant component.

Classification and Evolutionary Relationships

Three major acanthodian subgroups are generally recognized. The Climatiiformes (Early Silurian–Early Carboniferous) include the most primitive acanthodians, and may be paraphyletic (at most, only distantly related to each other). Climatiids are characterized by two dorsal fins, ornamented scales and fin spines (usually with a shallow insertion), and up to six intermediate spines (Figure 1A). The lower jaw lacks a mandibular bone, and the single teeth along the length of the jaws were attached directly to the jaw cartilages. Typically, the shoulder girdle is covered by ornamented dermal plates (Figure 2). Recently, however, R.H. Denison's view (1979), that this characteristic is not primitive for acanthodians, has gained support with the discovery of Arctic Canadian acanthodians (brochoadmonoids), which lack a dermal cover to the shoulder girdle.

The Ischnacanthiformes (Late Silurian–Late Carboniferous) also had two dorsal fins (Figure 1B), but the fin spines are slender and deeply inserted and are usually smooth or marked only with simple grooves. There are no dermal bones on the shoulder girdle, and intermediate spines are usually absent. The long mouth was equipped with upper and lower gnathal bones, which bear ankylosed teeth (teeth fused to bone) (Figure 3A).

The Acanthodiformes (Early Devonian–Early Permian) are readily recognized because they have only one dorsal fin (fin along the backbone) (Figure 1C). The body tends to be elongate, sometimes reaching eel-like proportions (*Traquairichthys*). The deeply inserted fin spines are slender and smooth, sometimes with a single rib. Acanthodiforms had a long mouth but no teeth, and in forms such as *Acanthodes* (Figure 4C) the elongate gill chamber and gill rakers suggest that they were primarily filter-feeders. Most acanthodiform genera had smooth, unornamented scales, and advanced members showed a tendency to reduce the squamation (scale cover) to a row along the sensory canals of the lateral line system.

The interrelationships between acanthodians are not well understood, but acanthodiforms and ischnacanthiforms seem to be monophyletic groups (groups having a single line of descent) characterized by shared specializations (Figure 5). It is possible, however, that climatiiforms constitute a paraphyletic group—primitive forms lack a dermal shoulder girdle, and advanced members like *Culmacanthus* (Figure 2D) may be more closely related to ischnacanthiforms and acanthodiforms than to other climatiiforms.

Regarding the relationship of acanthodians to other fish groups, different scholars have proposed both of the extant (modern-day) gnathostome fishes (osteichthyans and chondrichthyans) as closest relatives. There is a general resemblance between acanthodians and chondrichthyans—both have a micromeric dermal skeleton. For this reason, acanthodians have often been referred to as "spiny sharks." However, it is likely that the absence of large dermal bones is a primitive characteristic, and, therefore, not an indicator of evolutionary relationship. The main modern evidence that acanthodians are immediately related to chondrichthyans derives from the observation that, in *Acanthodes*, the gill elements at the top of the gill arches are directed toward the body trunk (Figure 4C), which also occurs in the cartilaginous fishes (Nelson 1968), but not in bony fishes. (In bony fishes the gill elements are directed toward the head.) However, *Acanthodes* is one of the most recently evolved acanthodians, so this evidence needs to be tested with more primitive examples, in which gill structure is still poorly known.

Another proof for relationships rests on mouth and gill structures. Both acanthodians and placoderms had an unmodified hyoid arch separated from the mandibular arch by a complete gill slit, a condition that some scholars presumed to be an "intermediate" condition between jawless and jawed fishes. As a result, D.M.S. Watson erected a "class Aphetophyoidea" for both groups (1937). But the morphology of *Acanthodes* (Figure 4) shows this to be wrong. A third possibility is that acanthodians are the sister group to both chondrichthyans and osteichthyans, since all share complexities of the fin endoskeleton, endochondral bone formation, and one-to-one tooth replacement in the jaws. In ischnacanthid, the teeth are firmly attached to gnathal bones, so the teeth could not have been replaced in the manner seen in extant gnathostomes. Some scholars have proposed that ischnacanthids periodically shed the entire gnathal (jaw) bone, but growth pattern studies suggest that teeth and supporting bone were continually formed at the front end of the jaw and worn down at the back end. This is not clearly a primitive condition. In fact, it could be a specialization that evolved within the acanthodians from a more normal type of tooth replacement, as is suggested by tooth spirals (Figure 2C), found in both climatiiforms and ischnacanthiforms.

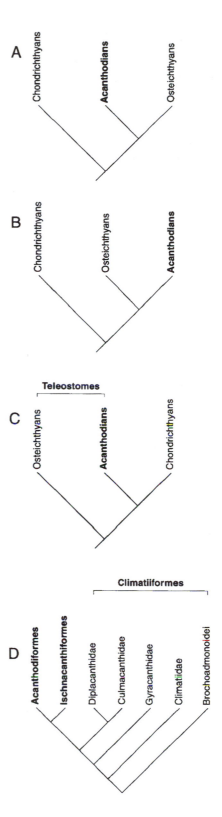

Figure 5. Acanthodian relationships. *A, B,* and *C,* three possible arrangements of relationship between acanthodians and the two extant groups of gnathostome fishes. The "teleostome" grouping, which places acanthodians with osteichthyans, is best supported by current evidence; *D,* possible scheme of interrelationships of acanthodians, which assumes that the Climatiiformes is paraphyletic (i.e., not a natural group).

Stronger evidence, based on a range of morphological characters, supports the teleostome hypothesis of R.S. Miles (1973b), which places the Acanthodii and the Osteichthyes as sister groups (Figure 5C). This suggests that the two share derived characters, including a fully developed operculo-gular series (in acanthodians represented by branchiostegal rays), a dermal shoulder girdle (if primitive for acanthodians), and a similarly shaped ossified palato-quadrate and Meckelian bone. On the evidence of *Acanthodes,* both groups also share elements in the hyoid arch, and the bone deposition pattern in the acanthodian neurocranium resembles that of primitive actinopterygians. Again, the problem lies in the shortage of evidence about the detailed morphology of primitive acanthodians. Future fossil discoveries must arise before acanthodian relationships can be established.

GAVIN C. YOUNG

See also Micropaleontology, Vertebrate

Works Cited

Agassiz, L. 1833–43. *Recherches sur les poissons fossiles.* 5 vols. Neufchatel: Nicolet and Petitpierre.

Denison, R.H. 1979. Acanthodii. *In* H.-P. Schultze (ed.), *Handbook of Paleoichthyology.* Vol. 5, Stuttgart and New York: Fischer.

Gross, W. 1971. Downtonische und Dittonische Acanthodier-Reste des Ostseegebietes. *Palaeontographica,* abt. A, 136:1–82.

Long, J.A. 1983. A new diplacanthoid acanthodian from the Late Devonian of Victoria. *Memoir of the Association of Australasian Palaeontologists* 1:51–65.

———. 1986a. A new Late Devonian acanthodian fish from Mt. Howitt, Victoria, Australia, with remarks on acanthodian biogeography. *Proceedings of the Royal Society of Victoria* 98:1–17.

———. 1986b. New ischnacanthid acanthodians from the Early Devonian of Australia, with comments on acanthodian interrelationships. *Zoological Journal of the Linnean Society of London* 87:321–39.

Miles, R.S. 1973a. Articulated acanthodian fishes from the Old Red Sandstone of England, with a review of the structure and evolution of the acanthodian shoulder-girdle. *Bulletin of the British Museum (Natural History), Geology* 24:113–213.

———. 1973b. Relationships of acanthodians. *Zoological Journal of the Linnean Society of London* 53, Supplement 1:63–103.

Nelson, G.J. 1968. Gill-arch structure in *Acanthodes. In* T. Ørvig (ed.), *Current Problems in Lower Vertebrate Phylogeny.* Proceedings of the Fourth Nobel Symposium. Stockholm: Almqvist and Wiksell; London and New York: Interscience.

Ørvig, T. 1973. Acanthodian dentition and its bearing on the relationships of the group. *Palaeontographica,* abt. A, 143:119–50.

Watson, D.M.S. 1937. The acanthodian fishes. *Philosophical Transactions of the Royal Society of London,* ser. B, 228:49–146.

Young, G.C. 1989. New occurrences of culmacanthid acanthodians (Pisces, Devonian) from Antarctica and southeastern Australia. *Proceedings of the Linnean Society of New South Wales* 111:12–25.

———. 1992. Description of the fish spine. *In* G.F. Webers, C. Craddock, and J.F. Splettstoesser (eds.), *Geology and Paleontology of the Ellsworth Mountains, West Antarctica.* Geological Society of America, Memoir 170. Boulder, Colorado: Geological Society of America.

Further Reading

Gagnier, P.Y. 1996. Acanthodii. *In* H.-P. Schultze and R. Cloutier (eds.), *Devonian Fishes and Plants of Miguasha, Quebec, Canada.* Munich: Pfeil.

Gagnier, P.Y., and M.V.H. Wilson. 1996. Early Devonian acanthodians from northern Canada. *Palaeontology* 39:241–58.

Gross, W. 1971. Downtonische und Dittonische Acanthodier-Reste des Ostseegebietes. *Palaeontographica,* abt. A, 136:1–82.

Long, J.A. 1983. A new diplacanthoid acanthodian from the Late Devonian of Victoria. *Memoir of the Association of Australasian Palaeontologists* 1:51–65.

———. 1986a. A new Late Devonian acanthodian fish from Mt. Howitt, Victoria, Australia, with remarks on acanthodian biogeography. *Proceedings of the Royal Society of Victoria* 98:1–17.

———. 1986b. New ischnacanthid acanthodians from the Early Devonian of Australia, with comments on acanthodian interrelationships. *Zoological Journal of the Linnean Society of London* 87:321–39.

———. 1995. *The Rise of Fishes.* Sydney: University of NSW Press; Baltimore, Maryland: Johns Hopkins University Press.

Ørvig, T. 1973. Acanthodian dentition and its bearing on the relationships of the group. *Palaeontographica,* abt. A, 143:119–50.

Valiukevicius, J. 1992. First articulated *Poracanthodes* from the Lower Devonian of Severnaya Zemlya. *In* E. Mark-Kurik (ed.), *Fossil Fishes as Living Animals.* Tallinn: Academy of Sciences of Estonia.

Young, G.C. 1989. New occurrences of culmacanthid acanthodians (Pisces, Devonian) from Antarctica and southeastern Australia. *Proceedings of the Linnean Society of New South Wales* 111:12–25.

———. 1992. Description of the fish spine. *In* G.F. Webers, C. Craddock, and J.F. Splettstoesser (eds.), *Geology and Paleontology of the Ellsworth Mountains, West Antarctica.* Geological Society of America, Memoir 170. Boulder, Colorado: Geological Society of America.

Zidek, J. 1976. *Kansas Hamilton Quarry (Upper Pennsylvanian) Acanthodes, with remarks on the previously reported North American occurrences of the genus.* University of Kansas Paleontological Contributions, 83. Lawrence: University of Kansas.

ACTINOPTERYGIANS

These bony fishes represent the most diversified group of living vertebrates. With more than 29,000 extant species, actinopterygians represent half of all vertebrate species. It is believed that at least an equal number of extinct species have been discovered from the fossil record. The actinopterygians were originally named the Actinopteri, meaning "ray-finned." In 1871, the famous American paleontologist, Edward D. Cope, gave these fishes their name with reference to their fins, which are webs of skin supported by bony or horny spines—fin rays. In 1891, the British paleontologist, Arthur Smith Woodward, keeper of Palaeontology at the British Museum (Natural History) in London, coined the term *Actinopterygii* in his classic *Catalogue of the Fossil Fishes in the British Museum (Natural History)*. The British zoologist, Edwin Stephen Goodrich, likewise adopted this term.

Although the group was formally named only by the end of the nineteenth century, references to specific actinopterygians date back to ancient Greece. The Greek philosopher Aristotle is credited with giving one of the oldest scientific names to an actinopterygian, the living moray eel, in his *Historia Animalium*. However, it was not until the beginning of the nineteenth century that the first scientific name was given to a fossil actinopterygian. In his masterpiece, *Recherches sur les Poissons fossiles* (1833–44), the Swiss-American naturalist Jean Louis Rodolphe Agassiz (1807–73), founder of early vertebrate paleontology, described fossil and living ray-finned fishes, which he classified into three groups—Chondrostei, Holostei, and Teleostei. Although his classifications are still used by some systematists, the first two of these taxa (groups; singular, taxon) are paraphyletic (i.e., fail to include all their descendants) and should not be used as valid taxa. Today, Chondrostei are referred to as basal actinopterygians (most primitive), whereas higher actinopterygians, or Neopterygii, include Holostei and Teleostei. Traditionally, the Chondrostei have contained numerous extinct species assigned to the grade Palaeonisciformes (genera from the Triassic), the Polypteriformes (Cladistia-bichirs), and the Acipenseriformes (sturgeons and paddlefishes). Some 270 fossil genera (singular, genus) of basal actinopterygians, which used to be classified within the Chondrostei, have been described, and there are seven extant (present-day) genera (the bichir *Polypterus,* the reedfish *Erpetoichthys,* the sturgeon *Acipenser,* the beluga *Huso,* the shovel-nosed sturgeon *Scaphirhynchus,* the North American paddlefish *Polyodon,* and the Chinese paddlefish *Psephurus*).

The oldest group of neopterygians is the Semionotidae, which originated during the Upper Permian. Approximately 120 genera of holosteans (meaning Ginglymodi plus Halecostomi, other than Teleostei) have been described, of which three survive to the present day—the gar (elongate fish with a long, narrow jaw) *Lepisosteus,* the alligator gar *Atractosteus,* and the bowfin *Amia.* There are relatively few genera of fossil sturgeons and paddlefishes ranging from the Upper Jurassic to the Pleistocene. Halecomorphs are first known from Lower Triassic deposits and include about 50 genera. Most current hypotheses concerning the earliest known teleosts concentrate upon either small Late Triassic fishes in the order Pholidophoriformes (Patterson and Rosen 1977) or the Early Jurassic *Leptolepis coryphaenoides* from Germany (Arratia 1997). Of about 450 living teleostean families, only 15 are present in the Cretaceous. The largest taxon of teleosts is the acanthomorphs, represented by about 15,000 living species. Modern family-level acanthomorph diversity is rooted in the Early Eocene. This diversification corresponds to the teleost explosion, which was the most dramatic evolutionary radiation ever seen in vertebrate history. The main distinctive feature of the acanthomorphs is the presence of defensive, sharp, bony spines at the anterior part of all fins but the tail.

Evolutionary Relationships

Actinopterygians form a natural or monophyletic group closely related to the lobe-finned sarcopterygians (lungfishes, coelacanths, and their extinct relatives). Together, these two groups form the osteichthyans (bony fishes), which are more closely related to acanthodians ("spiny sharks") than to any other primitive vertebrates. The fossil record of ray-finned fishes and lobe-finned fishes extend back to the Upper Silurian, thus both groups must have shared a common ancestor approximately 420 million years ago. There is very little controversy concerning the monophyly (origin from a common ancestor) of the Actinopterygii; only a few authors have suggested that some basal actinopterygians were related more closely to acanthodians. However, the monophyly is corroborated by a few morphological characters unique to the group.

Owing to the large number of species, actinopterygian interrelationships are still a highly debated topic among ichthyologists (zoologists specializing in fishes) and paleoichthyologists. Although stem Siluro-Devonian actinopterygians represent a very low percentage of the total diversity of ray-finned fishes, they are most significant in order to understand the group's relationships with other osteichthyans and to diagnose the Actinopterygii. Numerous authors have hypothesized that the Middle-Late Devonian paleoniscoid *Cheirolepis* is the sister group (the closest related group) of the all other actinopterygians, or is the most primitive of ray-finned fishes. The living cladistians, *Polypterus* and *Erpetoichthys* from central Africa, frequently are considered to be a basal taxon of the Actinopterygii. Polypterids (bichirs) are easily recognizable by their series of dorsal finlets, pectoral fins with fleshy lobe, an elongate body encased by thick bony scales, and a heavily armored, bony skull. The phylogenetic (evolutionary) position of the cladistians or polypteriforms has been debated for more than a century; alternately it has been considered either as closely related to actinopterygians or to sarcopterygians. Some paleontologists even created a separate order—the Brachiopterygii—with an intermediate status between ray-finned and lobed-finned fishes. Until recently, the cladistian fossil record was known only to go as far back as the Cretaceous; however, although it remains poorly documented, it has been recently extended to the Carboniferous (Lund et al. 1995). With the exception of fragmentary fossils from the Upper Cretaceous and the Paleocene of Bolivia, all the Mesozoic and Recent polypterid fossils come from Africa.

Ichthyologists and paleoichthyologists have been among the first systematists to analyze relationships and classify fishes using the principles of Hennigian cladistics (a method of defining taxa based on shared characteristics). In 1984, Brian Gardiner presented one of the first phylogenetic hypotheses of basal actinopterygians as a conclusion to his exhaustive morphological description of the Late Devonian *Mimia* and *Moythomasia* from Gogo in Australia. In Gardiner's tree, *Cheirolepis* was hypothesized to be the sister group of the other actinopterygians, while the Cladistia, represented by *Polypterus,* was suggested to be the extant sister group of the remaining actinopterygians. Various authors subsequently used Gardiner's (1984) and Gardiner and B. Schaeffer's (1989) hypotheses as the basic topology to which new forms are added. Until the early 1990s, most analyses of stem actinopterygians always included the same Devonian taxa and traditional anatomical characters. In 1992, Hans-Peter Schultze produced their first phyletic scheme that included all the Late Silurian to Middle Devonian genera. Another contribution of Schultze's analysis is the emphasis on the histological (microscopic structures) and morphological characters of the scales, primarily because most of these taxa are known exclusively from isolated scales. Characters were defined in terms of the histological composition of the scales, such as whether one or multiple layers of dentine (hard calcerous tissues) is present, and whether ganoine (enamel-like tissue) is present directly on the dentine or not.

With the recent publication of *Interrelationships of Fishes* (Stiassny et al. 1996), phylogenies (evolutionary histories) dealing with all major groups of actinopterygians are proposed in a cladistic framework. Actinopterygians, and more specifically teleosts, have been at the center of the debate on the best way to use fossils in phylogenetic reconstruction or cladistics. In their 1977 review of Mesozoic teleosts, Colin Patterson, from the Natural History Museum in London, and Don E. Rosen, from the American Museum of Natural History in New York, suggested that fossils cannot overturn a classification based on living species. In 1997, the neo- and paleoichthyologist Gloria Arratia, from the Museum für Naturkunde der Humboldt-Universität in Berlin, demonstrated clearly that both living and fossil taxa should be included in a cladistic analysis in order to obtain the most accurate phylogeny.

Morphological Diversity

A general description of actinopterygian morphology is complex, owing to the extreme taxonomic and anatomical diversity of the group. In primitive forms, the skull is heavily ossified with very large orbits (eye sockets) situated laterally (on the sides of the head). The eyes were surrounded externally by four sclerotic plates. The cheek region is most characteristic: One cheek bone, the squamosal, is absent, and the preopercular is a long and narrow inclined bone. The maxilla (upper jaw) has a well-developed dorsal (upward pointing) process, and the jugal bone (found near the orbit) is crescent-shaped.

The skull roof incorporates a few large bones; the central series is composed of pairs of parietals bones and postparietals; numerous ichthyologists, however, prefer to use the terms "frontals" and "parietals," respectively. A bony covering over the gills, called the opercular series, consists of a large operculum and suboperculum. The operculum is a platelike bone covering the gills; this structure is an evolutionary novelty present uniquely in ray-finned fishes and lobe-finned fishes. Below the operculum are a number of narrow branchiostegal rays that shield the throat yet permit its expansion. The mandible (lower jaw) bears externally two infradentaries that are found below a bone that holds the fish's teeth. This long bone, called a dentary, also carries the mandibular sensory canal. Internal to the dentary are several bones studded with denticles. The roof of the mouth is covered with small denticles. The braincase is well ossified and is divided by a ventral (belly-side) fissure and an otico-occipital fissure. The branchial gill apparatus is composed of five arches, as in other jawed fishes. The hyoid (second branchial) arch includes a long and straight hyomandibula, an interhyal, a ceratohyal, and a hypohyal.

A typical actinopterygian body has paired pectoral fins (just behind the gills) and pelvic fins, and the median (midline) fins include a single dorsal and an anal fin. The primitive pectoral girdle is formed by a series of four bones: a dorsal presupracleithrum, a supracleithrum, a cleithrum, and a ventral clavicle. (The clavicle is lost in advanced actinopterygians.) The tail (caudal) fin of basal actinopterygians is heterocercal—the fin has an upper lobe that is larger than the lower lobe. The larger upper lobe is supported by a strong supporting rod consisting of the notochord and the vertebrae, both of which extend into the elongate upper lobe of the fin. (This structure is also seen in the tail of today's sharks.) In later forms, this condition is modified into a homocercal tail, one that is nearly symmetrical about the midline. All fins are composed of numerous lepidotrichia (rays derived from body scales). Dorsally situated neural arches (through which the spinal cord passes) and ventrally situated haemal arches (through which the main trunk artery passes) extend from the vertebrae. In primitive forms the rhombic scales, which imbricate with each other by narrow peg-and-socket articulation, cover the whole body. During the evolution of the group, scales became thin, rounded (cycloid and ctenoid), and overlapped each other. The lateral line system is part of the fish's sensory system. This long canal runs down each side of the body and forms branches on the skull. This complex sensory canal protects hundreds of mechanoreceptors, called "neuromasts," which detect water movements and changes in water pressure. Throughout the evolution of actinopterygians, every one of these characters changed.

On morphological grounds, actinopterygians can be distinguished from other fishes based on a series of uniquely derived (specialized) characters that are transformed subsequently within the history of the group (Arratia and Cloutier 1996; Patterson 1982). Cranial (skull) characters concern the morphology of the dermal bones (bones that form in the skin). The snout of the primitive actinopterygians is made of a large compound bone referred to as the premaxillo-antorbital. At the intersection of the skull table and the cheek, a T-shaped bone—the dermosphenotic—forms the dorsal border of the orbit. Three dermal bones—dermosphenotic, supratemporal, and the intertemporal—surrounded the spiracular opening, a gill opening that precedes the normal five. On the cheek region, the preopercular sensory canal is carried by a single element, the preoperculum; the squamosal is absent in actinopterygians. Hard ganoine tissue, which share some affinities with enamel, covers the scales and external dermal bones. Recent studies on living actinopterygians reveal that ganoine differs from enamel on histological (structural) grounds. A single dorsal fin is present, instead of two dorsal fins, as in sarcopterygians and basal acanthodians. The fin-rays of the pectoral fin are supported by a plate called a propterygium. Median small bony plates, known as basal fulcra, cover the dorsal side of the caudal fin. Fulcra are present in most Paleozoic actinopterygians and are found at the base of the dorsal, anal, as well as the ventral part of the caudal fin. Fringing fulcra are present on the anterior edge of all fins; they most likely correspond to modified terminal segments of lepidotrichia.

Functional and Evolutionary Morphology

The actinopterygian evolutionary success could be attributed to the diversification of the group into different modes of feeding and locomotion. Both the jaw apparatus and the appendicular (body) skeleton have shown a great deal of versatility for adaptation.

In primitive ray-finned fishes, the jaw joint is a simple hinge between the mandible and the quadrate, a skull bone that forms the jaw's suspension system. The jaws are primitively propped against the side of the braincase by a large first gill arcs element called the hyomandibula. In most primitive living and fossil actinopterygians, cheek dermal bones overlying the jaw bones are attached to the braincase, which limits the range of movement of the jaws. Among higher ray-finned fishes, there has been a tendency for some of the cheek bones to become mobile, allowing the mouth to expand laterally as it opens. This novelty creates a drop in pressure so that water and food are sucked into the mouth cavity. Throughout the evolution of teleosts, this mode of feeding will be exploited. In order to increase the mouth's mobility, the bones of the upper jaw—the premaxillae and maxillae, which form the upper dental arcade in most fishes—became detached from the cheekbones.

Major modifications of the appendicular skeleton occur during the evolution of the teleosts and more specifically among acanthomorphs. The following trends most likely are related to the evolutionary success of the group: migration toward the front of the pelvic girdle and fins and its subsequent linkage with the pectoral girdle, a dorsal placement of the pectoral fins, a reduction in number of pectoral radials (support rods) and pelvic fin rays, and the development of pelvic, dorsal, and anal fin spines.

Temporal and Spatial Distribution

With the exception of the Early Devonian *Dialipina* from Siberia (Schultze 1992) and northern Canada, the oldest actinopterygians (Late Silurian *Andreolepis, Lophosteus,* and *Naxilepis*) are known only from scales. Other early Devonian scales associated with basal actinopterygians include *Ligulalepis, Orvikuina,* and *Terenolepis.*

During the Middle-Late Devonian, actinopterygians were still poorly diversified. The following are the genera known today: *Cheirolepis* (Eifelian-Frasnian of Nevada, Québec, Scotland, and Germany), *Howqualepis* (Frasnian of Australia), *Kentuckia* (Famennian of Ohio, U.S.), *Mimia* (Frasnian of Australia), *Moythomasia* (Frasnian of Europe, U.S., and Western Australia), *Osorioichthys* (Famennian of Belgium), *Stegotrachelus* (Middle Devonian of Shetlands, U.K.), and *Tegeolepis* (Famennian of Ohio, U.S.). This brief survey accounts for the complete Devonian actinopterygian diversity, which demonstrates the morphological homogeneity.

Shortly after their origin, actinopterygians were distributed worldwide. Ray-finned fishes also have been identified as isolated scales found in microvertebrate assemblages all over the world. Already in the Devonian, isolated scales identified as *Moythomasia* have been reported from Europe, North America, north Africa, and Australia. None of the Devonian families survived into the Carboniferous, with the exception of the stegotrachelids, which have been identified through isolated scales in the Viséan of Belgium.

From the Carboniferous to the Triassic, the dominant ray-finned fishes belong to a diverse, paraphylic grouping known as the palaeoniscoids. The paleoniscoid group contains more than 30 families and over 120 genera. Generally small fishes (less than 30 centimeters in length), palaeoniscoids bore rhombic scales covered with shiny ganoine. Most of the Carboniferous actinopterygians are built on a similar body plan to their Devonian relatives with a few exceptions, such as the deep-bodied amphicentrids *(Cheirodopsis),* the curious eel-like tarrasiiforms platysomids (e.g., *Platysomus*), with a single continuous median fin (e.g., Carboniferous *Tarassimius* from the Bear Gulch fauna of Montana), and the deep-scaled phanerorhynchids (e.g., *Phanerorhynchus* from the Middle Coal Measures of Lancashire, U.K.). Although poorly defined, *Elonichthys* and *Rhadinichthys* are generalized (fairly typical) Carboniferous actinopterygians. Many palaeoniscoids superficially resembled the actinopterygians of today, ranging from elongate eel-like forms to compressed forms similar to living angelfishes.

At the dawn of the Triassic, a new group of ray-finned fishes originated that was to become the most dominant group of vertebrates—the *Teleostei.* As indicated, teleosts are the most diverse group in terms of number of species and their spatial distribution. A great many Tertiary fishes are represented in the fossil record simply by the otoliths (earstones) found in marine sediments.

Environment

Living actinopterygians have been reported from elevations ranging from the deep abyss of the Marianas Trench (11 kilometers below sea level) up to lakes and rivers in the highest mountains, such as Lake Chungara in Chile (+4.5 kilometers above sea level). Likewise, the range of environments spans steaming hot volcanic springs (43 degrees centigrade) or desert springs (40 degrees centigrade) to the freezing Antarctic waters (−1.8 degrees centigrade). These extreme habitats are rarely encountered in paleontology, although Carboniferous paleoniscoids were found associated with hot volcanic springs in the East Kirkton site of Scotland. In this case, however, the hot water was most likely the cause of death rather than the locale of their habitat. Recent actinopterygians are found in marine, brackish, and freshwater habitats. Similar environments have been recorded through geological time. Approximately 40 percent of fish species live in freshwater, which represents approximately 2.5 percent of all water in the world. During the Devonian, actinopterygians have been associated with aqueous environments including: a hypersaline lake (*Cheirolepis* from Achanarras beds), a lake (*Howqualepis* from Mt. Howitt), an estuary (*Cheirolepis* from the Escuminac Formation), an inter-reef environment (*Moythomasia* and *Mimia* from Gogo Formation), and open seas (*Kentuckia* from the Cleveland Shale). During the Carboniferous, actinopterygians invaded and exploited the diversity of freshwater habitats. Of the 27 Carboniferous families, 14 are assumed to have occurred in freshwater. Although living holosteans inhabit freshwater, their Mesozoic relatives invaded and diversified extensively in the seas.

A number of ray-finned fishes migrate between freshwater and the sea. Fishes such as salmon are said to be "anadromous" because they live in a marine habitat but return to freshwater for spawning. On the other hand, catadromous fishes, such as eel, live in freshwater but reproduce in the sea. Some researchers suggest that migratory behavior accounts for the great diversity of brackish habitats since the Paleozoic.

Fishes are not only adapted to various levels of salinity; representatives of more than 46 families have adapted to air-breathing, by gulping air into their lungs (e.g., *Polypterus*), by using their gas bladder, or by using novel air-breathing organs (ABO's) located variously in the head, throat, stomach, or intestines. The amphibious mudskipper *Periophthalmus,* demonstrating a wide range of adaptation for active life on land, is most notable among air-breathing actinopterygians.

Biology and Behavior

Ray-finned fishes generally are built on the same basic body plan, but they display an important range of sizes, shapes, and color patterns. The need to find food and mates, as well as the necessity to avoid predators, have governed behavior since the origin of the group.

The Middle Jurassic pachychormid *Leedsichthys* from England reached up to 12 meters long, making it the largest teleost ever to have lived. The adults of some living gobies, *Heterandria formosa,* measure up to eight milimeters in length, making them the smallest vertebrate. Size variation within species frequently is interpreted as representing growth series. A complete growth series of the Eocene *Diplomystus* from Green River has been described, including an embryo found in the egg to a specimen reaching almost 50 centimeters.

Extant and extinct actinopterygians occupy every possible level on the food chain from scavenger to carnivore. Evidence of piscivorous (fish-eating) behavior is well recorded throughout the actinopterygians' history. The Canadian *Cheirolepis* from the Upper Devonian of Miguasha provides the first evidence of predation. Acanthodians and small *Cheirolepis* have been found in the digestive track of this actinopterygian, which accounts for one of the oldest vertebrate examples of cannibalism. One of the most famous examples of predation is the large ichthyodectiform *Xiphactinus audax* (four meters long) with a complete two-meter-long *Gillicus arcuatus* in its abdomen. This impressive specimen of a Bulldog fish comes from the Upper Cretaceous marine Niobrara Chalk in Kansas, U.S.

Some of the mass mortality of actinopterygians found in the fossil record have been interpreted as evidence of schooling, such as the Eocene herring *Knightia* from Green River, or spawning, such as the Pleistocene capelin *Mallotus* from the deposits of the Champlain and Goldwaith Seas in eastern Canada.

Important Sites around the World

Most of our knowledge of actinopterygian diversity over the past 400 million years comes from just a few famous fossil localities around the world. Some of these fossil sites are considered Fossil-Lagerstätten, places that are rich in amazingly well-preserved fossils.

In contrast to post-Devonian localities, Devonian actinopterygian sites are rare and poorly diversified in terms of ray-finned fishes. For the Devonian, four world famous localities deserve to be mentioned. A newly discovered locality in the District of Mackenzie in northwestern Canada has yielded numerous articulated specimens of the primitive Early Devonian *Dialipina*. During the Middle to Upper Devonian, the classic localities of the Achanarras Fish Beds in Scotland and the Escuminac Formation (known in older literature as the Scaumenac Bay) in eastern Québec, Canada are the most prestigious. In 1835, Louis Agassiz described *Cheirolepis trailli* from Scotland as an acanthodian while the Canadian geologist, Joseph F. Whiteaves, described *C. canadensis* in 1881 without a comment on its taxonomy. In both fauna, the actinopterygian *Cheirolepis* is relatively scarce (approximately 10 and 2 percent of the assemblage, respectively). Until the recent discovery of *Dialipina, Cheirolepis* was the oldest, best-preserved Devonian actinopterygian. Discovered in 1967, but not extensively described until 1984 by Brian G. Gardiner, the well-preserved actinopterygians from the Gogo Formation of Western Australia—*Mimia toombsi* and *Moythomasia durgaringa*—are the best Paleozoic actinopterygians in which the whole skeleton can be studied. In these Early Frasnian, inter-reef ray-finned fishes, the neurocranium is preserved in three dimensions. All these Devonian paleoniscids are interpreted as marine, with the possible exception of the Scottish *Cheirolepis*.

Among the hundreds of Carboniferous localities in which actinopterygian remains have been found, only a few can be considered to be exceptional in terms of diversity and quality of preservation. Most noteworthy are Namurian Bear Gulch Limestone (Heath Formation, Montana), Westphalian Mazon Creek fauna (Carbondale Formation, Illinois), and Tournaisian Glencartholm (Cemenstone Group, Eskdale, Scotland).

In terms of numbers of species, the actinopterygian material from the Bear Gulch Limestone far exceeds that of any other Paleozoic deposit in the world (approximately 35–38 species). This locality also exceeds all others in terms of number of specimens (more than 3700 specimens) and quality of preservation. Ramsay Heatley Traquair (1840–1913) first described the actinopterygians from Glencartholm in 1881, and subsequently Moy-Thomas and

Dyne revised them in the 1930s, followed by B.G. Gardiner in the 1960s. Approximately 20 different species belonging to 11 families of ray-finned fishes are known, including some worldwide genera such as *Rhadinichthys* and *Elonichthys*. Although the Mazon Creek fish fauna is not as diverse as the other two locales, some of the 13 species classified in seven genera are useful in providing information on the stages of juvenile development. Both the Bear Gulch Limestone and the Mazon Creek fauna are Lagerstätten.

Late Jurassic marine actinopterygians are best represented by the famous lithographic limestones of Germany (Solnhofen, where 100 species have been classified in 18 families) and France (Cerin), and a few deposits in Chile and Cuba. The Bavarian lithographic limestones have been quarried since the Stone Age. In the 1730s, the first fossil fishes from the Solnhofen Lagerstätte were noted in the literature. In 1755, D. Knorr and D. Walck illustrated and described some of the most common fishes from Solnhofen, but did not provide names. In 1818, the Frenchman Henri Ducrotay de Blainville (1777–1850), successor of Georges Cuvier at the Muséum National d'Histoire Naturelle in Paris, was the first naturalist to assign the fossil forms of Solnhofen-to-Recent genera such as the herring *Clupea,* the pike *Esox,* and the butterfish *Stromateus.* The ray-finned fish assemblage was living in warm shallow lagoons and was composed of rare coccolepids, semionotiforms represented mainly by *Lepidotes,* macrosemiids, pycnodontids, amiiforms, caturids, ophiopsids, ionoscopids, aspidorhynchids, pleuropholids, pholidophorids, and several small teleosts. Although relatively rare, the fossil fishes show exceptional preservation. In terms of generic diversity, the fish fauna of the French and German lithographic limestones are comparable.

The Lower Cretaceous Santana Formation of northeastern Brazil (27 species have been classified in 13 families) includes both marine and freshwater teleosts. The fishes of this assemblage generally are preserved with excellent anatomical data. The Santana fish fauna includes representatives of gars, amiids, and teleosts, with the exception of osteoglossomorphs (Maisey 1991). This marine and freshwater Early Cretaceous fish fauna is characteristic of Gondwana, the Earth's southern landmass at that time.

The Middle Cretaceous fish fauna from Lebanon is known from three classic fish localities—Hakel, Hadjula, and Sakel Alma. The Lebanese fossil fishes have been recognized since antiquity, as evidenced in a mention by the Greek historian Herodotus as early as 450 B.C. However, the studies of ray-finned fishes did not begin until the mid–1800s. Although more diverse than the Santana Formation (with 54 genera classified in 22 families), the anatomy of the fossils from Lebanon remains poorly known owing to the poorer state of preservation. One of the leading actinopterygian systematists, Colin Patterson, provided revisions of the Cretaceous salmoniform and berycoid fishes from Lebanon. At Hajula, the salmoniform *Gaudryella* is the most common fish, whereas at Hakel that title belongs to the clupeomorph *Diplomystus.*

For the Eocene, Monte Bolca from northern Italy (more than 160 species) is the best marine fossil site. The best lacustrine locality is that of the Green River Formation from Wyoming where 28 species have been classified in 15 families. The botanist A. Mattioli's mention of the Monte Bolca site in 1552 may be the oldest historical record of ray-finned fishes. The so-called petrified fishes from Monte Bolca thereafter became treasures for the nobles from Verona. More than four centuries ago, the exact nature of these fishes was not understood. They were simply considered to be curiosities of nature. As early as 1584, perfectly preserved actinopterygians from Monte Bolca were displayed in museums, such as the Francesco Calceolari Museum, and in university collections. Over time, specimens from Monte Bolca found their way to museums around the world, including the prestigious collections at the Muséum National d'Histoire Naturelle in Paris where they were studied by the French paleoichthyologist Jacques Blot, and in the United States at the Carnegie Museum and the Museum of Comparative Zoology where they were investigated by C.R. Eastman. Not known for as long as the Monte Bolca fishes, the first record of fossil fishes from the Green River Formation dates back to 1856, when Joseph Leidy identified a fossil as a herring, subsequently named *Knightia eocoena.* Since then, this Green River herring has been found by the thousands. In 1871, E.D. Cope described some of the actinopterygians, which were known to come from the "Petrified Fish Cut." Subsequently, he described major discoveries in his monograph entitled *The Vertebrata of the Tertiary Formations of the West* (1884). Since then, the American paleoichthyologist Lance Grande from the Field Museum of Natural History in Chicago has excavated and studied extensively the Green River fossil fishes. The Green River system was composed of three Eocene intermontane lakes under warm, temperate to subtropical conditions. This Eocene fish fauna is most interesting in its similarities to contemporary Chinese assemblages, suggesting an inter-pacific paleogeographic connection. The fossils of Monte Bolca and Green River demonstrate that many of the modern families of actinopterygians had appeared already by the Early Eocene.

RICHARD CLOUTIER

Works Cited

Arratia, G. 1997. Basal teleosts and teleostean phylogeny. *Palaeo Ichthyologica* 7:5–168.

Arratia, G., and R. Cloutier. 1996. Reassessment of the morphology of *Cheirolepis canadensis* (Actinopterygii). *In* H.-P. Schultze and R. Cloutier (eds.), *Devonian Fishes and Plants of Miguasha, Quebec, Canada.* Munich: Pfeil.

Cope, E.D. 1871. Contribution to the ichthyology of the Lesser Antilles. *Transaction of the American Philosophical Society* 14:445–83.

Gardiner, B.G. 1984. The relationships of the palaeoniscid fishes, a review based on new specimens of *Mimia* and *Moythomasia* from the Upper Devonian of Western Australia. *Bulletin of the British Museum (Natural History), Geology* 37:173–428.

Gardiner, B.G., and B. Schaeffer. 1989. Interrelationships of lower actinopterygian fishes. *Zoological Journal of the Linnean Society* 97:135–87.

Grande, L. 1984. *Paleontology of the Green River Formation, with a Review of the Fish Fauna.* Bulletin 63, 2nd ed., Geological Survey of Wyoming.

Lund, R., C. Poplin, and K. McCarthy. 1995. Preliminary analysis of the interrelationships of some Paleozoic Actinopterygii. *Géobios, mémoire spécial* 19:215–20.

Maisey, J.G. (ed.). 1991. *Santana Fossils: An Illustrated Atlas.* Neptune, New Jersey: T.F.H. Publications.

Patterson, C. 1982. Morphology and interrelationships of primitive actinopterygian fishes. *American Zoologist* 22:241–59.

Patterson, C., and D.E. Rosen. 1977. Review of ichthyodectiform and other Mesozoic teleost fishes and the theory and practice of classifying fossils. *Bulletin of the American Museum of Natural History* 158:85–172.

Schultze, H.-P. 1992. Early Devonian actinopterygians (Osteichthyes, Pisces) from Siberia. *In* E. Mark-Kurik (ed.), *Fossil Fishes as Living Animals*. Academia 1. Tallinn: Academy of Sciences of Estonia.

Stiassny, M.L.J., L.R. Parenti, and G.D. Johnson (eds.). 1996. *Interrelationships of Fishes*. San Diego, California: Academic Press.

Further Reading

Maisey, J.G. 1996. *Discovering Fossil Fishes*. New York: Holt.

Paxton, J.R., and W.N. Eschmeyer (eds.). 1994. *Encyclopedia of Fishes*. Sydney: University of New South Wales Press; San Diego, California: Academic Press, 1995.

ADAPTATION

An "adaptation" is a feature of an organism that has become established in a population by preferential selection because it performs or facilitates a specific function and thereby enhances the organism's chance of survival. The prevailing view is that adaptations develop as solutions to problems that are posed by the organism's environment. The term adaptation is also used to describe the process that results in the development of these beneficial characters: Adaptation produces adaptations. These adaptations are relatively permanent in that they are present across many generations of species, although they may be subjected to some measure of refinement. This specialized use of the term differs markedly from using it to describe the responses of an individual to an immediate problem in its lifetime, such as a fluctuation in temperature, food supply, or some other fundamental aspect of a life process.

In 1859 Charles Darwin described adaptations as useful variations of a character. In his view, the best adapted individuals were those that possessed character variations that were most useful in permitting the organism to perform its basic life functions, such as feeding and reproducing. In Darwin's opinion, such beneficial characters would tend to be favored by natural selection and would become established in a population by preferential survival. Twentieth-century evolutionary biologists modified this early view of adaptations and the way they are perpetuated from one generation to the next. Proponents of the "Neo-Darwinian synthesis" refined Darwin's theory of natural selection and redefined adaptation strictly in terms of selection. They regarded an adaptation as the result of natural selection acting on one or more physical characters of an organism in the context of a particular function. In their view, these physical characters are the manifestations of genes in the genotype. ("Genotype" is an organism's genetic inheritance, "phenotype" is the inexact physical expression of those genes.)

Using this amended definition, evolutionary biologists argued that adaptations must be examined in terms of the effect that they have on the reproductive success ("fitness") of an organism. If selection (e.g., environmental conditions such as a receding ocean) is acting on a beneficial character (an adaptation, such as the ability to breathe air) to increase its representation in a subsequent generation, then the adaptation is truly beneficial and will promote the organism's reproductive success, or fitness. Therefore, in order to show that a character is an adaptation, it is necessary to demonstrate how it enhances the organism's chance of survival and reproductive success. Furthermore, the character or feature only can be identified as an adaptation if it is the product of selection for the character in question. It is not sufficient to merely show that the character has the ability to perform a task efficiently, nor is it adequate to demonstrate a good fit between the organism and the environment (Burian 1992; West-Eberhard 1990).

Adaptation in Paleontology

It is rather difficult to determine in a fossil form if a character enhanced its fitness. The imperfections of the fossil record are well known to biologists and paleontologists. Conducting meaningful population studies using fossils is a hazardous task, although it has been attempted in a few cases, with limited success. Paleontologists, then, are forced to use other criteria, as summarized by P.W. Skelton (1990), to identify characters that were adaptations in fossilized organisms: First, the scholar must establish a function for the character. This is achieved by examining the feature in light of the organism's construction, postulating its mode of life, and by making comparisons with living organisms. The process also serves to establish whether or not the feature was an incidental structure resulting from the construction of another feature, and therefore not an adaptation. Next, one tests the suitability of the feature for the posited function and its effectiveness by comparing the feature to an idealized version modeled for the particular function. Finally—and fundamental to the identification of an adaptation—one must demonstrate a history of a preexisting feature that, over time, shows modifications toward the form of the idealized model (Skelton 1990). Demonstrating such a history is the purview of paleontology, using intermediary stages in an evolutionary sequence preserved in the rock record. Unfortunately, it is rare for adequate numbers of individuals to be preserved as fossils over the required time span, thereby hampering rigorous attempts to identify adaptations.

Not All Characters are Adaptations

Not every feature of an organism has a function, and yet for a long time there was a tendency in biology to atomize every creature into its component characters and to prescribe a function to each—to identify an adaptation. This tendency followed from the mistaken belief that all characters of an organism are established by direct natural selection of the most beneficial state. S.J. Gould and R.C. Lewontin (1979) demonstrated in their famous paper on the Spandrels of San Marco that this "adaptationist programme" was not valid. Biologists today are less willing to follow the adaptationist program, preferring to begin their analyses with careful consideration of the origin of specific features. This usually provides a good basis for deciding if the character in question has a function before any attempt is made to identify it as an adaptation. Lewontin (1978) uses the human chin as a fine example. The chin is not seen in other primates, so it might be tempting to prescribe an adaptive function to this unique morphological (structural) feature. Yet, the chin results solely because two growth fields located in the lower jaw—the dentary (bone) field and the alveolar (tooth) field—proceed at different rates. The chin is only an "accidental" byproduct. Since it has no function, it is not an adaptation.

The example of the human chin illustrates why scholars should exercise caution when attempting to assign a function, and therefore adaptive status, to a character in a fossil form. What may seem to be the most parsimonious (simplest) explanation for the presence of a character may not always be correct. There are limits to the criteria outlined above. The most pervasive problem in the study of fossils is the absence of preserved ancestral forms. This lack makes it impossible to identify a history of modification for a preexisting feature. Take, for example, the large paired horns on the skull of the theropod dinosaur *Carnotaurus*. Other theropod dinosaurs developed small horns, but none reach the size seen in *Carnotaurus*. The horns may possibly have functioned for sexual display, species recognition, or thermoregulatory control (if they were covered with a highly vascular tissue). They may also have been used for less likely functions, such as defense. The most economical explanation, based on comparison with living organisms, would suggest that the large horns are a species-specific (limited to a particular species) character to facilitate recognition of potential breeding partners. However, *Carnotaurus* is an isolated fossil, so there are no preserved examples of its immediate ancestors to illustrate a history of modification of the horns. That means we have no evidence that will support such a determination. Accordingly, it would be presumptuous to declare the skull horns of *Carnotaurus* as an adaptation for species recognition, no matter how rational it might seem to do so.

Origin of Adaptations

How do adaptations arise in the first place? Natural selection will work to modify and refine a feature once its function is established, but the selective process provides no explanation for the origin of the feature. Darwin (1859) noted it is probable that a feature will convert from one function to another during the process of adaptation. Therefore, the current function of a feature provides no ready insight into its history or into the process of modification that led to its current functional status.

There is a possibility that a feature might have its origin in a macromutation (the sudden appearance of a major novelty), but the probability of a macromutation producing an efficient character is slight at best. Regardless, this notion of origin for adaptations cannot be tested, as Skelton (1990) noted. The testable theory suggests that a precursor to the feature under study was modified in some way or was placed in a different environment, and then showed evidence of suitability for the eventual function. The feature then was modified further by natural selection: That is to say, it was adapted for that function it came to perform (Skelton 1990). Such a precursor is termed a "preadaptation" because it assumed a new function before it became modified. Feathers are an example of a preadaptation. Their original function was display, thermoregulation, prey procurement, or simply increase of surface area (Futuyma 1998). Only later were feathers adapted to facilitate flight in birds.

The classic picture of the origin of adaptations is one in which an organism modifies a suitable character by natural selection in order to solve a problem set by its environment. However, Lewontin (1978) has argued that organisms are more likely to make their own environment rather than respond to it, citing as an example the way that trees alter the soil by putting down roots and dropping leaves. There is no doubt that there is constant interaction between organism and environment, but organisms are incapable of controlling many aspects of their environment. Natural selection is brought to bear in order to modify certain features that will allow the organism to "adapt" to the changes.

Summary

Adaptation is a complex concept. The tangled semantics associated with the process of adaptation and the definition of an adaptation are appropriate for a theory that has been redefined and manipulated to work in the context early biologists, Neo-Darwinists, paleontologists, and others required of it. In general, an adaptation might best be described as a trait that has been developed and modified by natural selection in order to perform or facilitate a specific function in order to enhance the bearer's chance for survival and for reproductive success.

W. DESMOND MAXWELL

See also Evolutionary Novelty; Functional Morphology; Selection; Speciation and Morphological Changes; Variation

Works Cited

Burian, R.M. 1992. Adaptation: Historical perspectives. *In* E.F. Keller and E.A. Lloyd (eds.), *Keywords in Evolutionary Biology*. Cambridge, Massachusetts: Harvard University Press.

Darwin, C. 1859. *On the Origin of Species by Means of Natural Selection, or the Preservation of Favoured Races in the Struggle for Life*. London: Murray; New York: Appleton, 1860.

Futuyma, D.J. 1998. *Evolutionary Biology*. 3rd ed., Sunderland, Massachusetts: Sinauer.

Gould, S.J., and R.C. Lewontin. 1979. The spandrels of San Marco and the Panglossian paradigm: A critique of the adaptationist programme. *Proceedings of the Royal Society of London*, ser. B, 205:581–98.

Lewontin, R.C. 1978. Adaptation. *Scientific American* 239 (3):212–30.

Skelton, P.W. 1990. Adaptation. *In* D.E.G. Briggs and P.R. Crowther (eds.), *Palaeobiology: A Synthesis*. Oxford and Boston: Blackwell Scientific.

West-Eberhard, M.J. 1990. Adaptation: Current usages. *In* E.F. Keller and E.A. Lloyds (eds.), *Keywords in Evolutionary Biology.* Cambridge, Massachusetts: Harvard University Press.

Further Reading

Futuyma, D.J. 1979. *Evolutionary Biology.* Sunderland, Massachusetts: Sinauer; 3rd ed., 1998.
Lewontin, R.C. 1978. Adaptation. *Scientific American* 239 (3):212–30.

AERIAL LOCOMOTION

Flight is a major evolutionary innovation that has appeared in many different groups of animals. A flying animal typically has one or two pairs of wings that support the animal's weight as it moves through the air. The wings are shaped so that, when air flows over them, they produce lift, an upward force perpendicular to the direction of airflow. At the same time, wings produce drag, a retarding force that opposes the forward movement of the animal.

The simplest form of flight is gliding, in which the animal moves forward and downward in unpowered flight. The flight path is tilted forward from horizontal, so the lift force from the wings is also tilted forward and is composed of a vertical component that supports the animal's weight and a horizontal component that opposes drag forces and maintains the forward speed. In this way, as the animal descends, the structure and position of the wing converts the potential energy of gravity into forward movement. Soaring is a special form of gliding in which the animal glides through rising air, which enables the animal to maintain or increase its altitude without wing flapping. Soaring is generally used by larger flying animals to save energy and has permitted the evolution of larger body sizes than would have been possible if the animals had to flap continuously to fly.

In active, powered flight the animal flaps its wings up and down. As a wing is flapped downward, airflow over the wing is upward and backward, which tilts the resulting lift force forward. Again, that lift force can be resolved into a vertical component that supports the animal and a horizontal component that opposes drag and maintains the forward speed. However, because the animal's muscles provide the energy rather than gravity's potential energy, the animal does not descend and can either maintain level flight or gain altitude.

Insects were the first animals to evolve flight. Flying insects first appear in the fossil record in the Carboniferous (Pennsylvanian, approximately 320 million years ago), giving rise to a diversity of flying insects in the Paleozoic, with some 20 orders known (Wootton 1981; Carpenter and Burnham 1985). Living flying insects have one or two pairs of wings extending from their thorax, which is the middle of the three chief divisions of an insect's body. Some Paleozoic insects had three or more pairs of wings and winglike structures (Kukalova-Peck 1978). The prevailing theory about the origin of wings in insects is that they evolved by enlargement and modification of movable respiratory appendages on the thorax and abdomen (Kingsolver and Koehl 1994; Averof and Cohen 1997). Although various theories have been proposed to explain this evolutionary change (e.g., for courtship display, thermoregulation, improved respiration, parachuting and gliding), none has gained consensus. However, it is possible that the winglike respiratory structures were greatly enlarged for one function (such as display or thermoregulation) and were selected for flight only after becoming just large enough to function aerodynamically. The pathway to flight is also controversial (Kingsolver and Koehl 1994); some scholars have proposed parachuting and gliding, but others have also suggested that wings first were used to provide thrust for skimming along the surface of water (as in living stoneflies), and that only after their flapping aerodynamics were perfected did the wings enlarge for flight (Marden and Kramer 1994; Kramer and Marden 1997). Facing no competition or predation from flying vertebrates, insects reached considerable size in the Paleozoic; the dragonfly-like insects *Meganeura* from the Carboniferous of France and *Meganeuropsis* from the Pennsylvania of Kansas reached wingspans of 65 and 70 centimeters.

Gliding flight was evolved independently in at least four lines of ancient reptiles in the Permian and Triassic. The first was the primitive *Coelurosauravus* from the Permian of England, Germany, and Madagascar (Carroll 1978; Evans and Haubold 1987; Frey et al. 1997) (Figure 1A). It had broad wings of skin that extended laterally from the sides of the trunk between, but not attached to, the fore and hind limbs. The wings were supported by 22 pairs of elongate bony rods arranged in a radiating pattern, which permitted the wings to be folded backward when not in use. The bony rods have been interpreted as new elements of dermal bone, unrelated to the ribs.

A second line of gliding reptiles were the kuehneosaurids, primitive scale-covered animals from the Triassic of Europe and North America (Robinson 1962; Colbert 1966, 1970; Evans 1982) (Figure 1B,C). Like *Coelurosauravus,* kuehneosaurids had broad wings of skin that extended in a lateral line from the sides of the trunk between the fore and hind limbs. However, in this line the wings were supported by 10 or 11 pairs of elongate ribs. These ribs articulated (connected) with elongate vertebral processes that project laterally from each side of the trunk, permitting the wings to be folded back above the hind limbs when not in use. Essentially the same sort of adaptation to gliding evolved independently in the present-day lizard *Draco* (Colbert 1967), and based on its habits, we can infer that these Paleozoic and Mesozoic gliding reptiles probably lived in trees and used gliding flight to escape predators, reducing the amount of energy required to transport from tree to tree. Today's gliding animals, such as *Draco* and flying squirrels, are able to glide many tens of meters from tree to tree, and it is probable that early gliders could do so as well. However, it also has been suggested that *Kuehneosaurus,* which had rather long hind limbs, might have run on its two hind legs over rocky ground and leaped into the air from the rocks to initiate a glide to evade predators or chase prey (Robinson 1962).

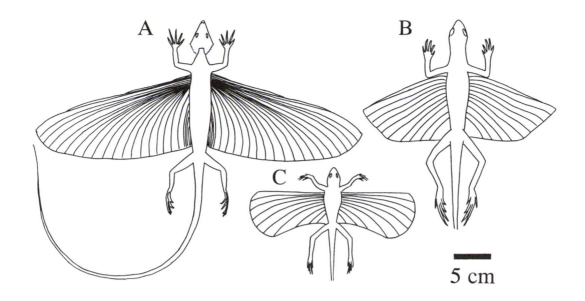

Figure 1. Early wings for gliding flight. *A, Coelurosauravus; B,* the kuehneosaurid *Kuehneosaurus; C,* the keuhneosaurid *Icarosaurus. A* after Frey at al. (1997); *B* and *C* after Carroll (1978).

Different adaptations to gliding flight occurred in *Sharovipteryx* (Sharov 1971; Gans et al. 1987; Tatarinov 1989) and *Longisquama* (Sharov 1970; Haubold and Buffetaut 1987). *Sharovipteryx* had very short forelimbs and extremely elongate hind limbs. It had small, probably immovable gliding membranes extending to the sides from its trunk, and larger membranes between the hind limbs and the tail. Extending the hind limbs forward and to the side would spread the larger gliding membranes. Experiments with a model of *Sharovipteryx* suggest that it could glide well (Gans et al. 1987); however, it is unclear whether it was arboreal and glided from trees (Gans et al. 1987) or was a terrestrial running and leaping animal that used gliding to extend its leaps (Tatarinov 1989). *Longisquama* had eight to ten pairs of elongate feather-shaped structures arising along its spine (Haubold and Buffetaut 1987). The structures were probably highly modified scales that could be extended to the side to form wings for gliding and could be folded up and back when not in use, much like the wings of *Coelurosauravus* and kuehneosaurids.

Pterosaurs were the first vertebrates to evolve active, flapping flight. They appeared in the fossil record in the Upper Triassic and survived until the end of the Mesozoic Era. Their wings consisted of a broad expanse of membranous skin, called a "patagium," spread between the fore and hind limbs and the tail (Figure 2A). The bones of the forelimb were very elongate, and the fourth finger was extremely elongate so that it formed the leading edge of the part of the wing that extended outward, beyond the hand. The first three fingers of the hand were of normal length and bore large claws—they do not appear to have been involved in flight. Pterosaurs had a large and broad, bony sternum to which were attached the large muscles that flapped the wings. Likewise, the humerus (upper arm bone) had a very large crest, where the flight muscles inserted. The hip joint allowed a wide range of movement, permitting the hind limb to be directed to the side as part of the wing in flight and to be brought under the body for walking. The bones of the pterosaur skeleton were very lightly constructed, with thin walls, and they often were pneumatic, containing air spaces connected to the respiratory system.

No intermediates are known between pterosaurs and their nonflying ancestors. The earliest known and most primitive pterosaur, *Preondactylus* (Wild 1984), was already a fully developed pterosaur—it differed from later species primarily in the proportions of the wings and limbs. In early pterosaurs, the patagium attached down the length of the hind limb to the ankle, and the uropatagium (that part of the patagium between the hind limb and tail) was large. In more advanced pterosaurs, the patagium attached to only the thigh, not the entire hind limb, and the uropatagium was smaller. These changes suggest that advanced pterosaurs were better fliers than the early ones.

The way in which pterosaurs evolved flight is controversial. Three theories have been proposed: Parachuting from trees led to gliding and eventually to powered flight (Wild 1978); bipedal running and leaping from the ground led directly to powered flight without passing through a gliding stage (Padian 1983, 1985); and active arboreal leaping between branches and trees led to gliding and powered flight (Bennett 1997). The theory that flight evolved by running and leaping up from the ground is not well supported. It would require a ground-living bipedal ancestor with a high metabolic rate and the ability to run very fast, then make a single leap to considerable heights (Rayner 1985a, 1985b, 1988, 1991). The available evidence suggests that the early pterosaurs and their immediate ancestors were quadrupeds well suited to arboreal climbing and leaping, but were not suited to bipedal running (Bennett 1997). Therefore, an arboreal origin of flight is most probable. The patagium probably was evolved to increase the

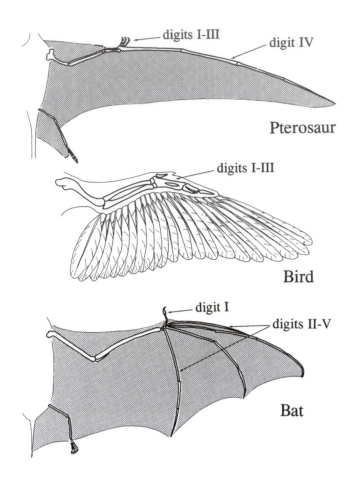

Figure 2. Comparison of the wing structure in a pterosaur, bird, and bat. For pterosaur and bat, wing membrane consists of a stippled spread controlled by the fore and hind limbs and the tail; for the bird, the wing consists of feathers (here, flight feathers) spread and controlled by forelimb alone, supplemented by tail feathers that provide additional lift and directional control.

surface area of the body and limbs for gliding or aerodynamic control while leaping. Selection for improved gliding and control would have led to increased forelimb length, increased wing area, and eventually to flapping flight.

Early pterosaurs were of moderate size with wingspans of 50 centimeters to 2 meters, but in the Cretaceous some genera (groups; singular, genus) evolved great size with wingspans of up to 6 meters in *Pteranodon* and 11 meters in *Quetzalcoatlus*. These animals were too large to sustain powered flapping flight, so they must have been primarily soaring animals.

Birds were the second group of vertebrates to evolve active, flapping flight. They appeared in the fossil record in the Upper Jurassic (approximately 160 million years ago) and have survived until the present day (Feduccia 1996). In birds, the functions of the limbs in locomotion are separate. The forelimb is used only for flight, and the hind limb is used only for terrestrial locomotion. The shoulder girdle is modified so that the glenoid fossa (shoulder socket for arm bone) faces outward to the side, permitting the

forelimb to be directed laterally and flapped up and down in flight. The bones of the forelimb are very elongate and support a series of long feathers (Figure 2B), which are modified scales. It has been suggested that feathers were evolved for thermoregulation and only later were modified for an aerodynamic function (Regal 1975); however, there is no direct evidence of that. The feathers of the earliest known bird, *Archaeopteryx*, were asymmetrical, like the flight feathers of living birds (Feduccia and Tordoff 1979), and would have permitted gliding and flapping flight.

Archaeopteryx, from the Upper Jurassic Solnhofen Limestone of southern Germany, was structurally intermediate between its nonflying, theropod ancestor and later birds. Like the nonflying, theropod ancestor (and unlike later birds), its sternum (breast bone) was small or unossified (non-calcified), the coracoid bones (part of the shoulder girdle joining the scapula, or shoulder blade, in front, near the glenoid fossa) were short and broad, it had three long fingers bearing claws, and it had a long bony tail. In later birds, the sternum was large and bore a keel (extended blade along the sternum) to provide the point of attachment for powerful flight muscles. The coracoids were long and strutlike. The fingers were reduced and fused together and lacked claws, and the bony tail was reduced to a short stumplike pygostyle that supported long tail feathers.

The way in which birds evolved flight is controversial. Two main theories about the pathway to flight in birds have been proposed: Parachuting from trees led to gliding and eventually to powered flight (Bock 1986; Pennycuick 1986; Feduccia 1996); and running and leaping from the ground led directly to powered flight (Ostrom 1974, 1976, 1979, 1985). Both theories have some problems. While theropods had large claws and could have been able to climb trees, there is no direct evidence that any theropods did so. Likewise, although theropods were capable of running fast, there is no evidence that they had a high metabolic rate or were capable of running very fast and leaping to considerable heights in a single bound; the ground-up theory requires both abilities (Rayner 1985a, 1985b, 1988, 1991). At present there is no convincing argument for either theory.

Early birds were of modest size; *Achaeopteryx* and other Mesozoic birds had wingspans of 1 meter or less. However, in the Tertiary era (from 65 to 1 million years ago), some giant birds evolved. Like the giant pterosaurs, these birds must have relied primarily on soaring flight. The largest were the pseudodontorns such as *Osteodontornis* from the Miocene of California, with an estimated wingspan of 6 meters, and the giant vulturelike teratorn, *Argentavis*, from the Miocene of South America, which had an estimated wingspan of 7.5 meters.

Gliding flight was evolved by various lines of arboreal mammals including modern-day dermopterans such as *Cynocephalus*; gliding marsupials such as the living *Petauris*, *Schoinobates*, and *Acrobates*; and flying squirrels such as the living *Glaucomys* and *Petaurista*. All glide from tree to tree using broad membranes of skin spread between the fore and hind limbs and the tail. Dermopterans are found in the fossil record of the Paleocene and Eocene, gliding marsupials are found from the Pliocene through Holocene, and flying squirrels are found from the Miocene to Holocene. However, the fossil record of these gliding mammals consists entirely of only jaws and teeth.

Bats were the third and last group of vertebrates to evolve active, flapping flight. They appeared in the fossil record in the Eocene and have survived until the present day (Jepsen 1970). The wing of the bat consists of a membranous patagium spread between the fore and hind limbs and the tail (Figure 2C). The bones of the forelimb are elongate, the ulna is reduced, digits two through five are very elongate to spread and control the outer part of the patagium, and digit one is of normal size and bears a claw for climbing. The hind limb is elongate and slender, and the foot has strongly curved claws that permit the bat to hang by its feet when not flying. Thus, like pterosaurs and unlike birds, both limbs of bats are involved in flight and in terrestrial locomotion, although most bats are not good at walking on the ground—the hind limb is not strong enough (Howell and Pylka 1977).

The earliest known fossil bat, *Icaronycteris*, is known from an articulated (preserved in anatomical position) skeleton from the Eocene of Wyoming (Jepsen 1966, 1970). It is virtually indistinguishable from later bats in regard to its flight adaptation. There are no known intermediates between bats and their nonflying ancestors, although it has been suggested that bats are closely related to dermopterans (Simmons 1995). It is accepted generally that bats evolved flight from arboreal ancestors, but two different theories of the origin of flight in bats have been proposed. According to one theory, the patagium of bats was first evolved to assist in catching insects and was further developed initially to permit hovering flight (Jepsen 1970; Simmons 1995). According to the second theory, bat ancestors passed through a gliding stage. This latter view is supported by the fact that bats are thought to be closely related to dermopterans (Simmons 1995).

S. CHRISTOPHER BENNETT

See also Bats; Biomechanics; Birds; Pterosaurs; Functional Morphology

Works Cited

Averof, M., and S.M. Cohen. 1997. Evolutionary origin of insect wings from ancestral gills. *Nature* 385:627–30.

Bennett, S.C. 1997. The arboreal leaping theory of the origin of pterosaur flight. *Historical Biology* 12:265–90.

Bock, W.J. 1986. The arboreal origin of avian flight. *In* K. Padian (ed.), *The Origin of Birds and the Evolution of Flight.* Memoirs of the California Academy of Sciences, #8. San Francisco: California Academy of Sciences.

Carpenter, F.M., and L. Burham. 1985. The geological record of insects. *Annual Review of Earth and Planetary Sciences* 13:297–314.

Carroll, R.L. 1978. Permo-Triassic "lizards" from the Karoo System. Part II. A gliding reptile from the Upper Permian of Madagascar. *Palaeontologia Africana* 21:143–59.

Colbert, E.H. 1966. A gliding reptile from the Triassic of New Jersey. *American Museum Novitates* 2246.

———. 1967. Adaptations for gliding in the lizard *Draco. American Museum Novitates* 2283.

———. 1970. The Triassic gliding reptile *Icarosaurus. Bulletin of the American Museum of Natural History* 143:85–142.

Evans, S.E. 1982. The gliding reptiles of the Upper Permian. *Zoological Journal of the Linnean Society* 76:97–123.

Evans, S.E., and H. Haubold. 1987. A review of the Upper Permian genera *Coelurosauravus, Weigeltisaurus,* and *Gracilisaurus* (Reptilia, Diapsida). *Zoological Journal of the Linnean Society* 90:275–303.

Feduccia, A. 1996. *The Origin and Evolution of Birds.* New Haven: Yale University Press.

Feduccia, A., and H.B. Tordoff. 1979. Feathers of *Archaeopteryx:* Asymmetric vanes indicate aerodynamic function. *Science* 203:1021–22.

Frey, E., H.D. Sues, and W. Munk. 1997. Gliding mechanism in the Late Permian reptile *Coelurosauravus. Science* 275:1450–52.

Gans, C., I. Darevski, and L.P. Tatarinov. 1987. *Sharovipteryx,* a reptilian glider? *Paleobiology* 13:415–26.

Haubold, H., and E. Buffetaut. 1987. Une nouvelle interprétation de *Longisquama insignis,* reptile énigmatique du Trias supérieur d'Asie centrale. *Comptes Rendus de l'Académie des Sciences,* ser. 2, 305:65–70.

Howell, D.J., and J. Pylka. 1977. Why bats hang upside down: A biochemical hypothesis. *Journal of Experimental Biology* 69:625–31.

Jepsen, G.L. 1966. Early Eocene bat from Wyoming. *Science* 154:1333–39.

———. 1970. Bat origins and evolution. *In* W.A. Wimsatt (ed.), *Biology of Bats,* Vol. 1. New York: Academic Press.

Kingsolver, J.G., and M.A.R. Koehl. 1994. Selective factors in the evolution of insect wings. *Annual Review of Entomology* 39:425–51.

Kramer, M.G., and J.H. Marden. 1997. Almost airborne. *Nature* 385:403–4.

Kukalova-Peck, J. 1978. Origin and evolution of insect wings and their relation to metamorphosis as documented by the fossil record. *Journal of Morphology* 156:53–125.

Marden, J.H., and M.G. Kramer. 1994. Surface-skimming stoneflies: A possible intermediate stage in insect flight evolution. *Science* 266:427–30.

Ostrom, J.H. 1974. *Archaeopteryx* and the origin of flight. *Quarterly Review of Biology* 49:27–47.

———. 1976. Some hypothetical anatomical stages in the evolution of avian flight. *Smithsonian Contributions to Paleobiology* 21:1–27.

———. 1979. Bird flight: How did it begin? *American Scientist* 67:46–56.

———. 1985. The cursorial origin of avian flight. *In* M.K. Hecht, J.H. Ostrom, G. Viohl, and P. Wellnhofer (eds.), *The Beginnings of Birds: Proceedings of the International Archaeopteryx Conference Eichstätt 1984.* Willibaldsburg, Germany: Freunde des Jura-Museums Eichstätt.

Padian, K. 1983. A functional analysis of flying and walking in pterosaurs. *Paleobiology* 9:218–39.

———. 1984. The origin of pterosaurs. *In* W.E. Reif and F. Westphal (eds.), *Third Symposium on Mesozoic Terrestrial Ecosystems.* Tübingen: Attempto Verlag.

———. 1985. The origin and aerodynamics of flight in extinct vertebrates. *Paleontology* 28:413–33.

Pennycuick, C.J. 1986. Mechanical constraints on the evolution of flight. *In* K. Padian (ed.), *The Origin of Birds and the Evolution of Flight.* Memoirs of the California Academy of Sciences, #8. San Francisco: California Academy of Sciences.

Rayner, J.M.V. 1985a. Mechanical and ecological constraints on flight evolution. *In* M.K. Hecht, J.H. Ostrom, G. Viohl, and P.

Wellnhofer (eds.), *The Beginnings of Birds: Proceedings of the International Archaeopteryx Conference Eichstätt 1984.* Willibaldsburg, Germany: Freunde des Jura-Museums Eichstätt.

———. 1985b. Cursorial gliding in proto-birds, an expanded version of a discussion contribution. *In* M.K. Hecht, J.H. Ostrom, G. Viohl, and P. Wellnhofer (eds.), *The Beginnings of Birds: Proceedings of the International Archaeopteryx Conference Eichstätt 1984.* Willibaldsburg, Germany: Freunde des Jura-Museums Eichstätt.

———. 1988. The evolution of vertebrate flight. *Biological Journal of the Linnean Society* 34:269–87.

———. 1991. Avian flight evolution and the problem of *Archaeopteryx*. *In* J.M.V. Rayner and R.J. Wootton (eds.), *Biomechanics in Evolution.* New York and Cambridge: Cambridge University Press.

Regal, P.J. 1975. The evolutionary origin of feathers. *Quarterly Review of Biology* 50:35–66.

Robinson, P.L. 1962. Gliding lizards from the Upper Keuper of Great Britain. *Proceedings of the Geological Society of London* 1601:137–46.

Sharov, A.G. 1970. An unusual reptile from the Lower Triassic of Fergana. *Paleontological Journal* 1970:112–16.

———. 1971. New flying reptiles from the Mesozoic of Kazakhstan and Kirghizia. *Trudy of the Paleontological Institute, Akademia Nauk, USSR* 130:104–13.

Simmons, N.B. 1995. Bat relationships and the origin of flight. *Symposia of the Zoological Society of London* 67:27–43.

Tatarinov, L.P. 1989. The systematic position and way of life of the problematical Upper Triassic reptile *Sharovipteryx mirabilis*. *Paleontological Journal* 23(2):107–10.

Wild, R. 1978. Die Flugsaurier (Reptilia, Pterosauria) aus der Oberen Trias von Cene bei Bergamo, Italien. *Bollettino della Società Paleontologica Italiana* 17:176–256.

———. 1984. A new pterasaur (Reptilia, Pterosauria) from the Upper Triassic (Norian) of Friuli, Italy. *Gortania. Atti del Museo Friulano di Storia Naturale* 5:45–62.

Wootton, R.J. 1981. Paleozoic insects. *Annual Review of Entomology* 26:319–44.

Further Reading

Norberg, U.M. 1985. Flying, gliding, and soaring. *In* M. Hildebrand, D.M. Bramble, K.F. Liem, and D.B. Wake (eds.), *Functional Vertebrate Morphology.* Cambridge, Massachusetts: Belknap Press of Harvard University Press.

Padian, K. 1985. The origins and aerodynamics of flight in extinct vertebrates. *Palaeontology* 28:413–33.

Rayner, J.M.V. 1981. Flight adaptations in vertebrates. *Symposia of the Zoological Society of London* 48:137–72.

———. 1988. The evolution of vertebrate flight. *Biological Journal of the Linnean Society* 34:269–87.

AFRICA: NORTH AFRICA AND THE MIDDLE EAST

The continents of the Earth ride upon masses of rock called "tectonic plates." They have shifted position over millions of years, coming together and splitting apart, often producing geologic processes and formations, such as earthquakes and mountains. Ever since Africa split from South America in Middle Cretaceous times, the continent has experienced a relatively quiet geological history. This is reflected in the extensive occurrences of Precambrian and Paleozoic rocks, and in the almost complete lack of important orogenic (mountain building) activity. The major exception is the Atlas range in the northwest. A part of the Alpine system, it uplifted in the Early Tertiary following its incipient collision with the Eurasian tectonic plate. The Afro-Arabian plate, roughly with its present-day outline, drifted slowly northward during the Tertiary, remaining more or less separated from Eurasia by a large sea called the Tethys Sea. (This body of water [no longer existent] was located in a place similar to the Mediterranean Sea.) Marine encroachment on the northern border occurred in Morocco in the Paleocene, but was more extensive in the Eocene and Oligocene, occurring from Algeria to Arabia. From these periods, most terrestrial mammals are found close to the seashore. The mammal-bearing layers of rock strata often are intermingled with marine ones, yielding fishes, cetaceans (whales), or sirenians (manatees). Continental-marine associations tend to be less close to each other in the Late Cenozoic, yet there are relatively few purely freshwater, detrital fossil-bearing deposits of the kind that are so common in Europe or Eastern Africa. Figure 1 presents major North African sites.

Mesozoic mammals have been found in North Africa only recently. The locality of Anoual, Morocco, probably of Early Cretaceous age, has yielded a few mammalian teeth. According to D. Sigogneau-Russell of the Paris Museum (1995), some of these teeth document an early stage in the evolution of the tribosphenic molar (one that is triangular and has three cusps), with an incipient protocone (internal cusp) on the upper molars but still without an entoconid (corresponding lower cusp) on the lower ones. Their affinities (relationships) are still uncertain (they may be neither marsupials nor placentals). Although they are probably closer to Laurasiatic forms (organisms that lived on a large continent that later split into Europe and Africa), such as *Aegialodon,* than to South American ones, it is too early to draw paleogeographic conclusions.

A long time gap separates Anoual from the next mammalian fauna, which is also the earliest Tertiary fauna of Africa. It comes from a locality of Upper Paleocene age, Adrar Mgorn near Ouarzazate, Morocco, worked from 1977 onward by French paleontologists and studied mostly by E. Gheerbrant (e.g., 1990). According to Gheerbrant, this fauna shares some features and perhaps some taxa (groups; singular, taxon) with those of the northern areas, Eurasia and North America. As in the latter continents during Late Cretaceous and Early Tertiary times, paleoryctids (small insectivores) are quite diverse, while *Afrodon* and *Adapisoriculus* are

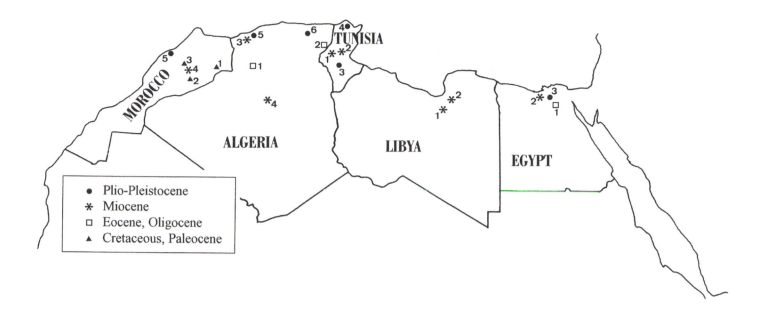

Figure 1. Main Cenozoic Mammalian localities of North Africa. *Morocco: 1,* Anoual; *2,* Adrar Mgorn; *3,* phosphates basin; *4,* Beni Mellal; *5,* Casablanca (Ahl al Oughlam, Thomas and Oulad Hamida quarries). *Algeria: 1,* El Kohol; *2,* Bir el Ater; *3,* Bou Hanifia; *4,* Oued Mya; *5,* Tighenif; *6,* Aïn Boucherit, Aïn Hanech. *Tunisia: 1,* Bled Douarah; *2,* Gebel Krechem; *3,* Aïn Brimba; *4,* Garaet Ichkeul. *Libya: 1,* Gebel Zelten; *2,* Sahabi. *Egypt: 1,* Fayum; *2,* Moghara; *3,* Wadi Natrun.

little different from European species. These finds strongly suggest that there still was some effective continental connection between North Africa and Laurasia through the Tethys, at some time before the Late Paleocene. The Cretaceous–Tertiary boundary could have been a significant period for mammalian exchange between the two regions because there was a well-known ocean regression (drop in sea level). (This regression may be linked to dinosaur extinction.) However, precise dating still is impossible.

Another major discovery at Adrar Mgorn is that of a primate, perhaps an omomyid. True primates (not including plesiadapiforms, which have a reduced number of rodentlike teeth) suddenly appear in the Early Eocene of northern continents, but their center of origin is disputed. *Altiatlasius* from Adrar Mgorn makes Africa a serious candidate, again implying a trans-Tethysian connection near the Paleocene–Eocene boundary. Another mammalian order recently shown to be of African origin are the proboscideans (animals with trunks, such as elephants). Gheerbrant and colleagues (1996) have recognized *Phosphatherium,* recognized as an early member of the elephant group despite its small size, from phosphate layers roughly contemporaneous with Adrar Mgorn. The find is well dated by its Selachian (a type of shark) teeth.

The main result of recent discoveries in the Cretaceous and Paleocene of Morocco is that they necessitate a reevaluation of Africa's role in the early diversification of mammals. We can no longer envision this part of its history as a kind of "splendid isolation" parallel to that of South America. Africa was doubtless the cradle of several mammalian orders and was already part of the realm of several others at that time.

Most of the important Eocene localities of Africa are found in the Maghreb. These have been studied chiefly during the last two decades at the University of Montpellier, France. The richest one, El Kohol in western Algeria, was discovered by M. Mahboubi. It is of Late Early Eocene age. Two other Algerian sites, Glib Zegdou, also found by M. Mahboubi, and Gour Lazib, found by J. Sudre, are roughly the same age. Bir el Ater in eastern Algeria, found by P.E. Coiffait, is of Upper Eocene age. Some of their faunal elements may be descended from those of Adrar Mgorn and some of them, like the marsupial *Garatherium,* may even be rooted in Mesozoic groups that lived on the large continent known as Gondwana. These evolved separately, later in South America and Africa. Others, like the Phiomyid rodents, provide evidence of communication between Africa and southern Asia. There are also some groups for which these early occurrences in Africa pre-date the earliest records in Eurasia, demanding a complete reevaluation of their early biogeographic history. Hyracoids (hyraxes), which today are a vestigial order, were the dominant ungulates (hoofed mammals) during the first part of the African Tertiary. They first are recorded from Gour Lazib and El Kohol. The latter site also has yielded *Numidotherium.* Until recently, this was the earliest known proboscidean. Today, although it is antedated by *Phosphatherium, Numidotherium* still is much better known, thanks to several skulls. Finally, *Algeripithecus* and *Tabelia* from Glib Zegdou and *Biretia* from Bir el Ater are the earliest known Anthropoidea, the group to which all monkeys, apes, and humans belong. None of these groups left Africa before the Early Miocene, remaining African endemics until at least 20 million years ago.

The richest fossiliferous sites of the whole Tertiary of North Africa are those of the Fayum depression near Cairo, whose age is close to the Eocene–Oligocene boundary. Following G. Schweinfurth's early recognition of a whale in 1879, numerous paleontological expeditions, often with the purpose of collecting specimens for museum display, were active mainly between 1900 and 1910. The names of H.J.L. Beadnell, C.W. Andrews, H.F. Osborn, and R. Markgraf are associated with this early phase of collecting, which brought to light many large mammals new to science. After this period of great enthusiasm, interest decreased until E.L. Simons from Yale University described a primate skull fragment, then the earliest known in Africa. This prompted him to organize his first expedition in 1961, the start of a long-term study that lasted more than 35 years. Simon's work provided most fruitful results, especially for smaller mammals (e.g., 1968). The Fayum association of early primates, which now totals more than 10 species, is thus the most diverse from any single location in the Old World (even though they come from various quarries and levels).

The whole Fayum section (lower Qasr el Sagha and overlying Gebel el Qatrani Formations) covers about 2.5 million years, but for biogeographic comparisons, the faunas can be considered as a single unit. While there still are no true carnivores, the region has yielded several creodonts (a suborder of carnivorous mammals), as well as primitive proboscideans (Moeritherium, Phiomia, Palaeomastodon), a great number of hyracoids, and the strange, two-horned Arsinoitherium. The great diversity of these African endemics (animals found only in a particular region) points toward some isolation of the continent during the Late Eocene and Early Oligocene. However, the anthracotheres, of which several species are also present, certainly originated in Eurasia, while the occurrence of phiomyid rodents in southern Asia and of relatives of Arsinoitherium in Romania and Turkey also suggests some connection with extra-African areas.

The Fayum primates, besides a few taxa certainly of Eurasian origin, include mainly early anthropoids. Some of these are primitive, with 36 teeth, but there are also some true Catarrhini, or Old World monkeys, with only 32 teeth (Oligopithecus). The only other early anthropoids are the Algerian ones mentioned above and some specimens recently found in Oman. Therefore, it follows that this group diversified exclusively within the Afro-Arabic plate. The remaining part of the Oligocene is documented by a few localities in Libya (Dor el Tahla) and Tunisia (Gebel bou Gobrine), which have yielded only a few fossils.

The Miocene period is well represented in North Africa, although the handful of important sites from this area do not compare with the hundreds of sites located in the northern Mediterranean. The earliest discovery of Miocene vertebrates, written about by C.W. Andrews in 1899 and M. Blanckenhorn in 1901, was made a century ago by Egyptian geologists at Hateyet el Moghara, near Alexandria. Further collecting by British soldiers during the World War I allowed R. Fourtau (1920) to publish a detailed study. The fauna, probably of early Middle Miocene age, consists mainly of aquatic vertebrates, such as Euthecodon, a fish-eating crocodile with a long slender snout, which lasted until the Pleistocene in East Africa, and several anthracotheres (related to pigs), plus a proboscidean not unlike Eurasian ones. Prohylobates is a cercopithecid primate (Old World monkey) endemic to North Africa, although it is close to Victoriapithecus from farther south. All other specimens of Prohylobates are found only in Gebel Zelten, Libya. This latter locality, surveyed by Italian geologists before World War II, did not yield

vertebrate fossils until 1960, when the French oil geologist M. Magnier explored the area. C. Arambourg, from the Paris Museum, briefly described some specimens, especially the strange Prolibytherium, a ruminant with "antlers" resembling butterfly wings (1959).

R.J.G. Savage and W.R. Hamilton (1973) from Bristol, U.K., made larger collections from Gebel Zelten from 1964 to 1968. The fauna is similar to that of Moghara but richer. It includes various ruminants, suids (Libycochoerus), and anthracotheres (Sivameryx, Afromeryx), a rhino, proboscideans (Choerolophodon and Dinotheres), and a true felid (cat). These taxa are also present in East Africa. Many of them are also very similar to those found in the Indian subcontinent, showing that, by that time, around 16 to 17 million years ago, major exchanges with Eurasia were possible owing to a continental corridor across the Tethys, which closed the connection between the forming Mediterranean Sea and the Indian Ocean. However, neither cervids (deer) nor the equid (horses) Anchitherium, entered Africa. An ecological or geographical barrier must have been effective between the main Eurasian domain and the Arabian peninsula, perhaps the uplifting of the Taurus-Zagros range. On the western side, Arabia progressively became more isolated from Africa by the Red Sea rift through the tectonic plate called the Arabo-Nubian shield. Ecological conditions may have been different. For instance, the few Middle Miocene faunas in Israel and Arabia lack the anthracotheres that are so common in North Africa.

Some authors (e.g., Thomas 1985) have attempted to recognize several dispersal phases at this period. Although the imperfect dating of the few relevant African and Arabian sites hampers such a detailed analysis, it is certainly true that exchanges were episodic rather than continuous. At Beni Mellal, a site in Eastern Morocco first excavated by R. Lavocat in 1951 and dated to perhaps 12 million years ago, there are some European immigrants, such as Listriodon, a suid with tapirlike molars, and some carnivores. However, the lack of cervids and paucity of bovids (cows and their relatives) make the region unlike Europe, and snakes and rabbits are also of African type.

About 11 million years ago, the immigration into the Old World of the North American equid Hipparion marks the limit between Middle and Upper Miocene. Its open-country adaptations—much reduced lateral digits, hypsodont (high crowned) teeth—suggest that this event is related to some changes in climate, but the spread of Hipparion is certainly faster than any simple relation of this kind would imply. Two North African localities have long been thought to document the earliest occurrences of this "guide-fossil." One is Bled Douarah in Central Tunisia, where P. Robinson from the University of Colorado worked from 1967 to 1969. Others include several sites in the Beglia formation (1969), where M. Solignac reported mammalian remains in 1931. No Hipparion was found in its lower levels, which are thus supposed to be of Middle Miocene age, but one cannot completely rule out that this absence is the result of ecological rather than chronological factors.

Some other mammals, especially the ruminants, are reminiscent of well-known eastern Mediterranean Upper Miocene types, while the suid Nyanzachoerus and the early hippopotamid Kenyapotamus clearly demonstrate African affinities. Other exposures in Central Tunisia (Gebel Krechem, worked by the author, and near Chott el Djerid, first mentioned by M. Boule in 1910) are likely to be of more recent age within the Upper Miocene. They all yielded more fragmentary remains. The second important early Upper Miocene locality is Bou Hanifia (Oued el Hammam) in Western Algeria, discovered in 1932 during work on the Bou Hanifia dam. This site was excavated by C. Arambourg in 1951 and published by him in 1959. An underlying tuff (rock composed of material extruded in a volcanic eruption) has been dated to approximately 12.8 to 10.3 million years ago (the only absolute dating for the whole Neogene of North Africa), but the site itself could be significantly more recent. Its fauna, including the early Murid rodent *Progonomys*, is not much different from that found on the northern bank of the Mediterranean. The fauna also foreshadow the typical modern African faunas, with an ostrich, a two-horned rhino, an aardvark, a long-limbed giraffe, and perhaps an early member of the hartebeest-wildebeest group (Alcelaphinae). Oued Mya in the Sahara is of similar age.

This African character is even more conspicuous at Sahabi in Libya, of Late Miocene age (perhaps 6 to 7 million years ago). Vertebrate fossils there were first mentioned by d'Erasmo in 1934, and in the same year C. Petrocchi began extensive surveying and collecting, leading to the discovery of 62 fossil localities and some well-preserved fossils, such as the complete skull of *Stegotetrabelodon*, a forerunner of the African elephant. Further research, conducted by N.T. Boaz from the Virginia Museum, greatly increased our knowledge of the fauna. The many genera (groups of species; singular, genus) that it shares with eastern African and even southern African sites demonstrate the biogeographic unity of the African continent. However, North Africa still harbors some survivors that had become extinct in the southeastern half of the continent by that time, such as the hippolike anthracotheres and brachypothere rhinos, known until the latest Miocene of Douaria in northern Tunisia.

Still, Africa did receive some immigrants from Eurasia in the Late Miocene, like the bear *Agriotherium* (present at Menacer, Algeria) and a boselaphine antelope (at Sahabi). At least one more immigrant arrived in the Early Pliocene, the camel. Its earliest African occurrence is at Wadi Natrun, a site close to Moghara in Egypt and discovered at the same time, but only published by E. Stromer between 1913 and 1920. There is little doubt that these connections between North Africa and Eurasia were facilitated by a salinity crisis, which gradually dried up the Mediterranean Sea in the Late Miocene, but it is not easy to identify the migration routes. The occurrence of a camel in the Late Miocene of Spain would argue in favor of an occidental route (one directly from Europe), but the many similarities with southern Asia imply a communication through the Middle East. Unfortunately, no significant fauna is known in Arabia or the Near East in the Upper Miocene. A trans-Mediterranean passage between Tunisia and Sicily even has been suggested by the discovery of an alcelaphine, a typically African group, in Italy. Micromammals offer more definite answers because they are more easily assigned down even to the level of genera. Some rodents known in the Maghreb near the Miocene–Pliocene boundary are best known from Spain, and their migration certainly followed an occidental route. Gibraltar was certainly not a serious barrier for them, and their spreading or extinction in North Africa was probably controlled by ecological factors.

The Plio-Pleistocene, formerly called Villafranchian by European paleontologists, is not documented in Libya and is almost unknown in Egypt. In the Maghreb, it was first described in 1884 by a French geologist, P. Thomas, shortly before he discovered the Tunisian phosphates. At Aïn (spring) Jourdel in Algeria, he found the first fossil suid, *Sus phacochoeroides*, and the first fossil primate, *Cynocephalus atlanticus*, ever named from Africa. He also named two antelopes, *Palaeoreas gaudryi* and *Antilope tournoueri*. These species, respectively included today in the genera *Kolpochoerus*, *Theropithecus*, *Tragelaphus*, and *Oreonagor/Connochaetes*, are typically African. They are commonly found on the whole continent, but are present only very marginally elsewhere, in Spain or the Middle East.

Most other "villafranchian" sites in the Maghreb are associated with the name of Camille Arambourg, who was mentioned earlier. Born in 1885, he intended to be a farmer in Algeria (then part of France) and studied agronomy, but circumstances allowed him to apply his knowledge for a few years only. In 1915, soon after Arambourg discovered his first fossil fishes while looking for irrigation water, he was sent as an officer to northern Greece (where, incidentally, he found the rich Upper Miocene sites near Thessaloniki). Back in Algeria, he received a position as professor of geology and started paleontological excavations in the Maghreb (and also in the Omo Valley of Ethiopia, where he returned but a few weeks before his death in 1969). The main villafranchian sites that Arambourg excavated span the whole of this period: Garaet Ichkeul and Aïn Brimba in Tunisia are of Lower Pliocene age, while Aïn Boucherit and overlying Aïn Hanech in Algeria are of Lower Pleistocene age. However, the richest locality of this period, Ahl al Oughlam near Casablanca in Morocco, was discovered only in 1985. Excavated by the present author since 1989, the site dates to 2.5 million years ago and has yielded at least 55 species of mammals.

All these sites confirm the zoogeographical homogeneity of the continent at this time. They include some widespread taxa, known both in Eurasia and the rest of Africa, such as most of the carnivores, the mastodont *Anancus*, hippos, and camels. Many of them, however, became extinct in Eurasia earlier than in Africa (especially in North Africa, which acted as a refuge, as already noted above, for some Late Miocene forms). Besides these taxa, Villafranchian North African faunas share with East and/or South Africa a number of exclusively African forms: the giant baboon *Theropithecus*, the elephant *Loxodonta*, equids (*Hipparion* followed by *Equus*), the suid *Kolpochoerus*, the giant giraffe *Sivatherium (Libytherium)*, and most of the antelopes (alcelaphines, reduncines, hippotragines). Very few taxa, on the contrary, are not found south of the Sahara: *Macaca*, *Ursus*, the rodent *Paraethomys*, and one shrew. On the other hand, many East African mammals are absent in the north where the ungulate fauna is always less diverse. Australopithecines, for instance, probably never reached the Maghreb. The most conspicuous differences with Eurasia are the complete lack of *Sus* (swine) and cervids, which usually make up the bulk of the fauna in the Palearctics. Thus, it is clear that most of the faunal exchanges at that time occurred within Africa, with certainly no continuous barrier like the present-day Sahara. Although we have very little direct data about the vegetation, the diversity of the fauna at Ahl al Oughlam suggests a mosaic of grasslands and woodlands. There are indications that it was relatively cold but was still humid, with murid rodents more common and more diverse than gerbils. The latter are indicators of arid environments.

A single site is known in the Middle East near Bethlehem. It has no cervids, but a Eurasian antelope is present. Later, in Lower Pleistocene times, some African elements migrated into the Middle East, where they were recorded at Ubeidiya, a site in Israel excavated by G. Haas in the sixties and more thoroughly exploited recently under the leadership of E. Tchernov (e.g., 1988). While the taxa include the long-horned buffalo *Pelorovis,* the suid *Kolpochoerus* and *Homo,* the Ubeidiya fauna remains dominated by Eurasian species.

For the second half of the Pleistocene, the documentation is quite abundant but often of poor quality because of the lack of adequate dating of rock strata for old collections. Fossil mammals in North Africa (and probably in the whole of Africa) were first recorded in 1837 by H.M. Edwards (a French naturalist like most later paleontologists in the Maghreb) from a cave near Oran. A. Pomel is responsible for most other early discoveries of Middle and Upper Pleistocene faunas. Pomel was first interested in fossils from Central France. He was exiled in Algeria, as a socialist, after the coup d'état of December 1851. After his amnesty in 1859, he began collecting fossil material, in addition to his involvement in administration and politics. This allowed him to publish his famous series of 13 monographs after his retirement, from 1893 to 1898, dealing with all types of large fossil mammals of Algeria. Many of these came from the Lower and Middle Pleistocene locality of Palikao (now Tighenif), which he discovered in 1872. C. Arambourg and R. Hoffstetter excavated this locality again in 1954–56, finding some *Homo erectus* remains.

North Africa received some newcomers from East Africa at that time, such as a second species of *Theropithecus* (which even crossed the Gibraltar straits, reaching Spain), and the suid *Metridiochoerus.* More immigrants, such as the warthog and an alcelaphine antelope, arrived slightly later and are found in later Middle Pleistocene sites, such as the rhino cave near Casablanca. A savanna or steppe environment may have been more extensive than in the Pliocene, as abundant gerbils and a vole immigrated from the Middle East.

The setting of the modern fauna of large mammals occurs only during the later part of the Pleistocene, both by immigration of Eurasian taxa and by extinction of animals now restricted to the sub-Saharan zone. This wave of extinctions, which lasted until historic times, affected mainly large mammals (elephants, rhinos, zebras, hippos, many antelopes, and carnivores), which were partly replaced by a few Eurasian species. These include a lynx, probably from Spain, a cervid close to the red deer (a good swimmer), wild boar (also known in the Nile Valley and probably of Middle Eastern origin), and the aurochs (European bison). The present-day fauna is sadly impoverished. Except for the wild boar, most of these animals are extinct, or almost extinct.

DENIS GERAADS

See also Africa: Sub-Saharan Africa

Works Cited

Andrews, C.W. 1906. *A Descriptive Catalogue of the Tertiary Vertebrata of the Fayûm, Egypt.* London: British Museum.

Arambourg, C. 1959. *Vertébrés continentaux du miocène supérieur de l'Afrique du Nord.* Publications du Service de la Carte Géologique de l'Algérie (N.S., Paléontologie), 4. Alger: Fontana.

Fourtau, R. 1920. *Contribution à l'étude des Vertébrés miocènes de l'Egypte.* Cairo: Government Press.

Geraads, D. 1989. Dating the Northern African Cercopithecid fossil record. *Human Evolution* 2 (1):19–27.

Gheerbrant, E. 1990. On the early biogeographical history of the African Placentals. *Historical Biology* 4:107–16.

Gheerbrant, E., J. Sudre, and H. Cappetta. 1996. A Palaeocene proboscidean from Morocco. *Nature* 383:68–70.

Pomel, A. 1893–98. Paléontologie—Monographies. *Publications du Service de la carte géologique de l'Algérie.* Alger: Fontana.

Robinson, P., and C.C. Black. 1969. Note préliminaire sur les vertébrés fossiles du Vindobonien (formation Béglia) du Bled Douarah, Gouvernorat de Gafsa, Tunisie. *Notes du Service Géologique de Tunisie* 31:67–70.

Savage, R.J.G., and W.R. Hamilton. 1973. Introduction to the Miocene Mammal faunas of Gebel Zelten, Libya. *Bulletin of the British Museum (Natural History) Geology* 22 (8):513–27.

Sigogneau-Russell, D. 1995. Further data and reflections on the tribosphenid mammals (Tribotheria) from the early Cretaceous of Morocco. *Bulletin du Muséum National d'Histoire Naturelle, Paris* C, sér. 4, 16 (2/4):291–312.

Stromer, E. 1913. Mitteilungen über die Wirbeltierreste aus dem Mittelpliozän des Natrontales (Aegypten). *Zeitschrift der Deutschen Geologischen Gesellschaft* 65:350–72; 66:1–33.

Simons, E.L. 1968. Early Cenozoic Mammalian faunas Fayum Province, Egypt. *Peabody Museum of Natural History, Yale University, Bulletin* 28:1–21.

Tchernov, E. 1988. The biogeographical history of the southern Levant. *In* Y. Yom-Tov and E. Tchernov (eds.), *The Zoogeography of Israel.* Monographiae biologicae, 62. Dordrecht: Junk.

Thomas, H. 1985. The early and middle Miocene land connection of the Afro-Arabian plateau and Asia: A major event for hominoid dispersal? *In* E. Delson (ed.), *Ancestors: The Hard Evidence.* New York: Liss.

Thomas, P. 1884. Recherches stratigraphiques et paléontologiques sur quelques formations d'eau douce de l'Algérie. *Mémoires de la Société Géologique de France,* sér. 3, 3:1–80.

Further Reading

Arambourg, C. 1970. Les vertébrés du Pléistocène de l'Afrique du Nord. *Mémoires du Muséum National d'Histoire Naturelle,* sér. 7, 10:1–126.

———. 1979. *Vertébrés villafranchiens d'Afrique du Nord.* Paris: Fondation Singer-Polignac.

Boaz, N.T., A. El Arnauti, A. Gaziry, J. de Heinzelin, and D.D. Boaz. 1987. *Neogene Paleontology and Geology of Sahabi.* New York: Liss.

Fleagle, J.G., and R. Kay (eds.). 1994. *Anthropoid Origins.* New York: Plenum.

Geraads, D. 1997. Carnivores du Pliocène terminal de Ahl al Oughlam (Casablanca, Maroc). *Géobios* 30 (1):127–64.

Maglio, V.J., and H.B.S. Cooke. 1978. *Evolution of African Mammals.* Cambridge, Massachusetts: Harvard University Press.

AFRICA: SUB-SAHARAN AFRICA

Africa is a continent of contrasts, religious, cultural, and political, as well as geographical and geological. Beginning at the Mediterranean, the northern half of the continent is dominated by the great Sahara desert, which effectively divides Africa into North Africa and the sub-Saharan regions. Sub-Saharan Africa (Figure 1) therefore lies between approximately 4 degrees north and 28 degrees south latitude and covers an area of some 16 million square kilometers (excluding Madagascar). Topographic features range from mountain peaks more than 5,000 meters high to depressions 100 meters below sea level. The varied climates of these regions are reflected in the vegetation patterns, with environments ranging from tropical rain forests to semiarid scrub and coastal deserts.

A Precambrian crystalline basement (Figure 2) underlies much of the present day surface of sub-Saharan Africa. In the tropical regions of the west and northwest, the ground is covered by dense vegetation that weathers to form deep lateritic profiles, which do not preserve fossil material. For this reason, the paleontological heritage of these regions is poorly known.

The elevated interior plateau is drier. Its greatest height is in the east, and it tilts down to its lowest point in the west. The uplifted eastern region in particular preserves several sedimentary basins which were both cut and formed by the extensional system known as the African Rift Valley. The southern parts of sub-Saharan Africa are also much drier. They are deeply incised in places, which allows for glimpses of the geological past. It is only in these drier climates of east, central, and southern Africa that substantial sequences of fossiliferous sedimentary rock strata have accumulated and been preserved. Most fossil collecting therefore has concentrated on these drier areas.

Fossils occur in strata ranging in age from the Precambrian until the present; however, the best-known time periods are the Paleozoic–Mesozoic and the Late Cenozoic. Fossils from these three eras provide information on important evolutionary periods, including the transition from reptiles to mammals, the early evolution of dinosaurs and mammals, and the advent of modern mammals and man. Few creatures fire our imaginations as fiercely as do the dinosaurs, and for this reason they are documented in as much detail as possible, although they are not well known from sub-Saharan Africa.

The Paleozoic–Mesozoic rocks (Figure 2) include the continental "Karoo" aged strata of sub-Saharan Africa (Figure 3), as well as the marine and marginal marine Cretaceous deposits. During its Paleozoic–Mesozoic geological and paleontological history, Africa was part of the southern landmass of Gondwana. The continent therefore shares numerous paleontological similarities with other countries that made up Gondwana and Laurasia (the northern supercontinent), including South America, Antarctica, Australia, India, Russia, and China.

The early part of the Cenozoic is poorly documented in sub-Saharan Africa, with Paleocene, Eocene, and Oligocene strata almost unknown. The Miocene is, however, far better documented, with faunas known from Langebaanweg in South Africa, numerous

sites in Namibia and Kenya, as well as Malembe in the Congo and Karugamania in Zaire (Cooke 1963; Savage and Russell 1983).

Of all Cenozoic strata, the Plio-Pleistocene deposits are probably the best documented in sub-Saharan Africa. Sites are known from all along the Great Rift Valley, including the classic hominid sites of East Africa, such as Laetoli, Omo, Olduvai, Hadar, Awash, Afar, Lake Turkana, as well as in Malawi (Mwimbi North) and Zambia (Broken Hill). In South Africa, Plio-Pleistocene fossils are known from the world famous cave sites at Makapansgat, Sterkfontein, Swartkrans, Kromdraai, Drimolen, and Gladysvale, as well as from the paleo-floodplain sites at Cornelia and Mara, along the Modder River, at a spring site at Florisbad, and at a number of coastal sites (Gore 1997). Plio-Pleistocene fossils from karst infills are also documented from Namibia, Botswana, and Angola (Pickford et al. 1994). These various sites are famous throughout the world for their contribution to our knowledge of the evolution of modern mammals and our own hominid lineage.

History of Paleontological Research in Sub-Saharan Africa

The early history of paleontological research in sub-Saharan Africa is inextricably linked to the political history of the subcontinent. Most of the early collecting occurred in the late 1800s and early to mid-1900s, when the region was under colonial occupation by Britain, Germany, France, Belgium, and Portugal. The nineteenth century in particular was a period of exploration and colonization, and many Europeans (mainly doctors, soldiers, engineers, and missionaries) in newly established territories were interested in fossils. For this reason, many of the fossils collected during this period now reside in institutions throughout Europe. After independence, many of the new African states paid little attention to their paleontological heritage. Also, the logistical and political difficulties associated with such work precluded extensive collecting in these countries. Subsequently, during the period from the 1950s until the present, little information has been gathered for a vast number of the countries in sub-Saharan Africa.

For the sake of clarity, the geographical areas of southern, eastern, and west-northwest Africa are treated separately here. The history of paleontological research, major discoveries, and the main geological periods from which fossils have been discovered in each of these regions are assessed individually.

South Africa

South Africa is a country of geological and paleontological superlatives. It possesses one of the richest and most diverse fossil heritages of any African country. Fossils range from the remains of the simplest, unicellular, blue-green algae and bacterial microfossils (which lived more than 3 billion years ago) to the advent of hominids and modern humans. Despite the relatively small number of paleontologists who have worked in South Africa, discoveries

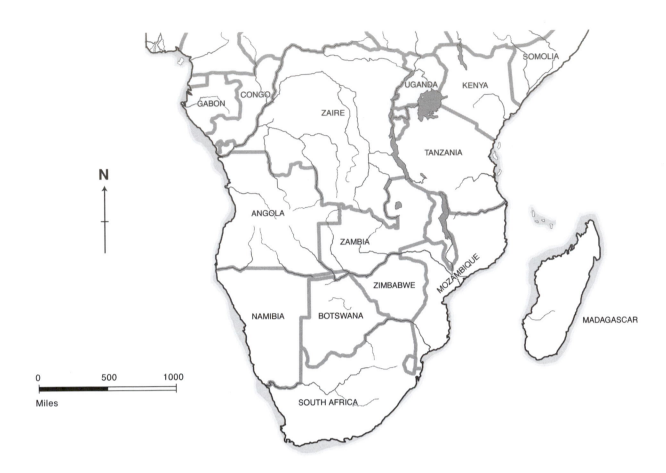

Figure 1. The main fossiliferous countries in Africa, south of the Sahara. Illustration by Tom Willcockson.

made in this country have greatly enhanced the understanding of the development of life on Earth, particularly with respect to the origin of mammals, dinosaurs, and humans.

The Devonian to Jurassic strata of the Cape and Karoo Supergroups contain some of the most extensive and well-exposed Paleozoic–Mesozoic sequences in the world. The rocks of the Cape Supergroup preserve a diverse assortment of Ordovician–Devonian marine invertebrates (Theron 1972; Hiller 1990) and fishes. The strata of the Bokkeveld Group (Reed 1925; Chaloner et al. 1980; Oosthuizen 1984) also preserves fossil plants (Plumstead 1967).

The Karoo Supergroup in South Africa covers an area of approximately 300,000 square kilometers and contains a spectacular fossil fauna dominated by mammal-like reptiles (therapsids), amphibians, archosauriforms, and fishes (Kitching 1977; Oelofsen 1981a). The paleoflora of the Karoo is equally as important as its famous tetrapod fauna. The Permian *Glossopteris* flora gained international importance through the collections of S.F. LeRoux between 1946–55 and the publications of E.P. Plumstead between 1952–62. The recognition of this flora on many of the southern continents gave credence to the emerging theory of continental drift and led to the recognition of the "Greening of Gondwana" (White 1986). The Triassic *Dicroidium* flora is well known thanks to the collecting efforts of J.M. Anderson and H.M. Anderson in the last three decades (Ander-

son and Anderson 1995). This flora is globally important, since it provides an unparalleled window into Late Triassic plant and insect communities at a time where elsewhere in the world deposits record the emergence of the first mammals, dinosaurs, and birds. The Andersons (1985) provide a thorough review of the history of plant collecting in South Africa prior to the early 1980s, eliminating the need to repeat it here.

Like most other sub-Saharan African countries, the Cretaceous and Early Cenozoic (Paleocene–Miocene) record of South Africa is not well preserved. Cretaceous deposits are limited mainly to the coastal plains of the Algoa and Zululand Basins. Early Cenozoic deposits are unknown except for a very patchy Miocene record. The best known of the Cenozoic deposits are the Plio-Pleistocene deposits of the past 5 million years.

Although older fossils are known, South Africa's fossil heritage, and the history of its collection, may be divided broadly into two main geological timeframes: the Paleozoic–Mesozoic and the Late Cenozoic.

Paleozoic–Mesozoic

In South Africa, fossil-bearing deposits of this age range from the Ordovician through the Cretaceous and include rocks of the Cape and Karoo Supergroups, as well as the Algoa and Zululand Groups. A series of biographical sketches follows, allowing for a

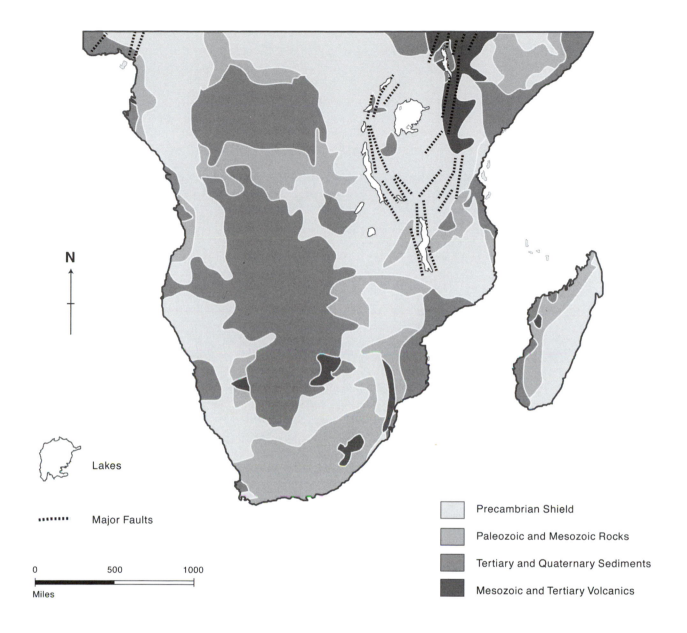

Figure 2. Generalized geology of sub-Saharan Africa. Illustration by Tom Willcockson.

succinct history of fossil collecting from the Paleozoic–Mesozoic rocks of South Africa.

Historical Overview of the Cape Supergroup. In a 1930 article in the *South African Quarterly Journal* (reprinted in Rogers 1937), Dr. George Thom enlisted Mr. Enislie, a Cape Town merchant, to be the first person to collect fossils in the Cape Supergroup, in 1804. Thom himself later collected numerous bivalves, trilobites, and crinoids from the Cape Supergroup. J.W. Salter (1856) collected and described the Bokkeveld Group material. A.R. Rogers and E.H.L. Schwarz pioneered geological surveys of the supergroup, which led to the discovery of numerous fossil localities. In his 1906 publication, Schwarz provides the earliest descriptions and illustrations of plants from the Cape Supergroup.

Sporadic collecting continued during the early to mid–1900s; however, one of the most spectacular collections of fossils from the Bokkeveld Group was not made until the 1960s. R.D.F. Oosthuizen, a farmer and amateur fossil collector, began his collection in the late 1960s and to date has amassed more than 3,000 Cape Supergroup fossils. The significance of this collection is evidenced by the number of forms that bear his name, including the trilobite *Oosthuisenella ocellus.*

In 1985, a highway cut through the Devonian Witteberg Group and led to the discovery of one of the newest localities in the

Figure 3. Distribution of Karoo Supergroup–aged rocks in sub-Saharan Africa. Illustration by Tom Willcockson after Falcon and Ham (1988).

Cape Supergroup (Gess 1996). In 1990, extensive collecting began in earnest. To date, some eleven fish types have been discovered, including members of the earliest known jawed fishes, acanthodians ("spiny sharks"), armored placoderms, and crossopterygians (tassle fins related to the coelacanth) (Anderson and Long 1996). Fossil collecting continues today in the Cape Supergroup with numerous students undertaking projects involving these strata.

Historical Overview of the Karoo Supergroup. The oldest print record of tetrapod fossils in the rocks of the Karoo Supergroup can be dated to 1831 in a letter written by C.H. Crisbrook and published in the *South African Quarterly Journal* under the title, "Organic Remains in the Karoo" (Rogers 1937). The locality from which the cited material was recovered, and its ultimate fate, is unknown. The first documented discovery of fossil reptiles in

Karoo strata is of a herbivorous therapsid found in 1838 by Andrew Geddes Bain near Fort Beaufort (Bain 1857). Bain called these reptiles "bidentals," as they had only two teeth. Today we know them as "dicynodonts," the most abundant tetrapod taxon (group; plural, taxa) from the Beaufort Group.

The early period (1845–99) of paleontological research in the Karoo was dominated by a few key men, including A.G. Bain, W.G. Atherstone, K.D. Kannemeyer, and A. Brown. They were all proverbial Renaissance men, coming from different backgrounds and a diverse set of interests. All were self-taught, amateur natural historians. Of these men, A.G. Bain and W.G. Atherstone deserve special mention for the role they played in molding South African geological and paleontological research.

Bain was a frontier road builder. In 1837, at the age of 40, he moved to Grahamstown to be the military road engineer on the eastern frontier. This move was fortuitous as it led to a meeting with Captain C. Campbell, who lent Bain a copy of Lyell's *Principles of Geology*. This work had such an influence on Bain that he thereafter turned his attention to all matters geological. Subsequently, he collected hundreds of fossils and has been heralded as the father of South African geology and paleontology. In Europe, Bain's Karoo fossils aroused further interest in the Cape colony's geology, leading to much of the later research and collecting in the Karoo, despite the many frontier wars in the region. The difficulty of collecting during this time is summed up in the title of one of Bain's early works, "Reminiscences and Anecdotes Connected with the History of Geology in South Africa; or the Pursuit of Knowledge under Difficulties" (Bain 1857).

Atherstone was a medical doctor. In 1844 he became interested in fossils after meeting Bain at a fossil exhibition. Thereafter, Atherstone often teamed up with Bain to collect numerous therapsids, fishes, and plant fossils from the Karoo, as well as dinosaur remains from the Cretaceous Algoa Basin. His collecting skills are commemorated in the names of many of his finds, such as the Karoo fish, *Atherstonia*.

The middle period (1900–45) was dominated by the efforts of men such as A.W. Rogers, E.H.L. Schwarz, C.J.M. Kitching, A.L. DuToit, S.H. Haughton, and R. Broom. Most of these men were British or British-trained, and apart from Kitching and Broom, all were fully trained geologists involved in the pioneer mapping of South Africa. Of these, Kitching, Broom, Haughton, and DuToit deserve special mention for their contributions.

Prior to the outset of the Second World War, S.H. Rubidge had begun to collect Karoo fossil reptiles on his farm, Wellwood, in the Eastern Cape. Kitching was a road party overseer in this area and collected fossils for Rubidge. Today, this collection is world famous and contains numerous type specimens of Karoo reptiles (Haughton 1965). Kitching's contribution to paleontology was, unfortunately, interrupted by service in Egypt during the Second World War, then terminated by his untimely death in 1943. The words of Rubidge, for whom he collected so many of his fossils, can best summarize Kitching's contribution: "As a fossil hunter he achieved a record unequaled and unapproached. He was the discoverer of many hundreds of reptile fossil skulls in the Karoo and revealed more type specimens than any individual in the annals of South African history."

Perhaps more than any other individual, the name Broom is most often associated with South African paleontology. Broom arrived in South Africa in January of 1897 and devoted the early part of his career to the collection and study of the reptiles of the Karoo. The evidence he collected convinced the world that all higher mammals descended from a therapsid ancestor of the Karoo. In a bibliography he prepared in 1948 for a commemorative volume in his honor (Broom 1948), Broom lists over 400 publications on topics as diverse as "the volume of mixed liquids" to philatelic papers covering old Transvaal stamps. Broom also had occasion to work with and describe specimens collected by Kitching, whom he lauded as "the world's greatest fossil finder."

Broom also had a great influence on the life of Haughton who, between 1915 and 1932 collected many Karoo fossils. He published a steady flow of descriptions of the new reptiles and amphibians from the Karoo, including the now classic "Fauna and Stratigraphy of the Stormberg Series" (Haughton 1924). His work was also the first publication on the stratigraphic history of Africa south of the Sahara (Haughton 1963).

DuToit is often referred to as "the world's greatest field geologist," a title he achieved by spending numerous years in the field, including sixteen mapping the Karoo. Although his main field of interest was geology, he also collected numerous fossils. These finds originally were described by other scholars, but later DuToit did so as well.

Until the 1940s, the most important paleontological collections in South Africa were housed at the South African Museum (Cape Town), Albany Museum (Grahamstown), the National Museum (Bloemfontein), and the Transvaal Museum (Pretoria). Several overseas institutions housed relevant collections as well. In 1945 the Bernard Price Institute (BPI) was established, with Kitching's son, J.W. Kitching, appointed as the first (and sole) member of staff. This one man has dominated the postwar period (1945–70). In the half century since the inception of the BPI, he has amassed a huge number of Karoo fossils. Nobody actually has counted the number of specimens J.W. Kitching has collected, but it must run into the several thousands. His specimens come not only from South Africa, but also East Africa and the Antarctic, a feat that inspired Broom to call him the "world's greatest vertebrate fossil finder."

For the last 30 years, numerous scholars have been active in the Karoo. New research has been conducted, and many new fossils have been discovered (Kitching 1977; Rubidge 1987, 1990; Hancox and Rubidge 1994, 1996). Today, trained professionals with a formal education in geology, zoology, botany, and paleontology undertake most of the research and collecting, although amateurs and farmers still often add exciting new discoveries.

Historical Overview of the Cretaceous Deposits of South Africa. The earliest record of fossils from the Cretaceous of South Africa are writings by C.I. Latrobe (1818) on "screw shaped" marine invertebrates from the Cretaceous rocks of the Algoa Basin. In 1845, W.G. Atherstone and Bain discovered the first dinosaur known from South Africa in these rocks. This specimen was described by R. Owen, some 30 years later, as the "Cape Iguanodon"; however, it now is known to be the world's oldest stegosaur, *Paranthrodon*.

Atherstone (circa 1857) also collected numerous fossil plants from several localities in the Algoa Basin. He was the first to name the Cretaceous sequence in the Algoa Basin. These deposits were virtually ignored by vertebrate paleontologists for more than a hundred years until W. de Klerk revived interest in them in the late 1980s. Since then, they once again have begun to provide fossil sites, including a find of a new Lower Cretaceous theropod dinosaur, affectionately called "Kirky" after the Kirkwood Formation in which it was discovered (de Klerk 1997).

The Zululand Group of Natal also preserves a Cretaceous fauna, which has been known since W.H. Bailey's descriptions in 1855. This marine fauna is composed predominantly of ammonites (snail-shaped cephalopods) of the subfamily Texanitinae and has been well documented over the past 20 years by H.C. Klinger of the South African Museum (Klinger 1980).

South Africa's interior experienced a period of major denudation during the Cretaceous, which resulted in the African Land Surface (King 1962; Partridge and Maud 1987). The only record of life in the interior during this period comes from a Late Cretaceous (approximately 70 million years ago) crater lake fill. Haughton originally studied this site, followed by R.M.H. Smith in the early 1980s. To date, the site yielded fossils of fishes, frogs, mussels, snails, insects, ostracods, and a possible bird (Smith 1996).

Cenozoic

Although the Cenozoic is not as well documented as the Paleozoic, Cenozoic marine invertebrates were the first fossils found in South Africa (Paterson 1790). However, the Cenozoic is poorly preserved and to date, no Paleocene fossils have been discovered. The Neogene record is patchy: It is represented only by a poor Miocene and a better Pliocene record. The Quaternary record is far better known and includes both extinct and extant fossil forms.

The first evidence of the Miocene of South Africa was discovered only in 1958, during phosphate mining operations at the west coast estuary site of Langebaanweg. At first, only two fossils were discovered: an elephant tooth and a short-necked giraffe (Hendey 1981). In 1968, these discoveries led to the initiation of the South African Museum's Langebaanweg Research project. The project has uncovered numerous fossils that point to life in the Miocene of South Africa, including shark teeth, shelled invertebrates, and the three-toed horse *Hipparion*. This latter discovery was of prime importance as it showed for the first time that the widespread forests and woodlands of the Late Oligocene and Early Miocene were in the process of being replaced by savanna and open grasslands during the mid-Miocene.

Plio-Pleistocene fossil assemblages are known from a number of cave and floodplain sites in South Africa. The history of their discovery mostly stretches back to the period between 1930 and 1970. In the mid–1930s, Broom accepted a post at the Transvaal Museum, which changed the thrust of his research and collecting from the Karoo to the Pleistocene mammals of the Transvaal. His work was rewarded in 1930s with the discovery of the first adult australopithecine skulls at Swartkrans and Sterkfontein. Apart from these two sites, the caves and limeworks in the Makapansgat Valley have been the site of most Plio-Pleistocene paleontological research (Kitching 1953, 1965, 1980; Wells and Cooke 1956).

Knowledge of the bone-breccia deposits from the Makapan Valley probably dates back to the turn of the century; however, it was W.I. Eitzman's visit in the middle 1920s that first alerted R.A. Dart to the significance of the limeworks as a fossil site. The British and South African Associations for the Advancement of Science (1929) and C. Van Riet Louw and B.D. Malan in 1936–37 visited the limestones, leading to the recognition of this as a hominid site. P.V. Tobias worked the site in July and September 1945 and in January 1946, leading to Dart's visit in April 1946. J.W. Kitching entered the picture in July 1946, when he and his brother accompanied a group of students from the Witwatersand University's departments of Anatomy and Zoology to the caves. In September 1947, this flurry of activity at the caves finally led to the discovery of australopithecine remains.

In a remarkable series of 39 papers published in the 1950s and 1960s, Dart proposed and propounded his osteodontokeratic (bone-tooth-horn) culture theory (Dart 1957). He painted these early australopithecines as ferocious hunters and killers. It was these papers and Dart's eloquent prose that provoked C.K. Brain into beginning taphonomic (study of events prior to fossilization) investigations of the Swartkrans site. Between 1968–91, Brain undertook a meticulous excavation at Swartkrans, which not only dispelled the myth of the hunter australopithecine, but placed them on the hunted list instead (Brain 1981). He also provided evidence of the earliest management of fire. Together with R. Clarke, their work at the Sterkfontein site across the valley reminded the world that South Africa has much to offer in terms of understanding human origins.

Botswana

Although Karoo-aged strata are known from the eastern margin of Botswana and Plio-Pleistocene karst fills lie in the northwest, most potentially fossiliferous deposits are obscured by a thick cover of Holocene Kalahari sands. For this reason, the paleontology of the country is poorly known. No tetrapod fossils of Karoo age have yet to be discovered, and only a meager Plio-Pleistocene assemblage is known.

Probably the single most remarkable paleontological site in Botswana is the Middle Cretaceous crater lake deposit at Orapa. At this locality, a unique assemblage of more than 6,000 exquisitely preserved fossils have been found. The preservation is so good that they are referred to as "Lagerstäten," or jewels of the fossil record (Rayner 1993). The finds here include some of the earliest flowering plants (angiosperms) (Bamford 1990), as well as numerous insects (McKay and Rayner 1986). At Orapa, structurally advanced flowers appear in the geological record some 15 million years before their Northern Hemisphere counterparts (Rayner 1993). Therefore, this site is of global importance, as it shows that southern Gondwana was a center for diversification of both angiosperms and insects.

Namibia

Prior to the First World War, Namibia was a German colony; however, its paleontological heritage did not receive the attention paid to German East Africa. Following the war, Namibia became a South African protectorate; most of the early collecting was undertaken by South Africans. At present, Karoo, Cretaceous, and Cenozoic fossiliferous deposits are known (Oelofsen 1981b; Pickford 1995; Senut and Pickford 1995), as well as a unique Precambrian Nama fauna (Brain 1996, 1998). The logistical difficulties of working in the desert have, however, precluded conducting large excavations in the area.

In the period between 1908 to 1914, P. Range, H. Schneiderhöhn, and H. von Staff first discovered the Nama fauna in the Nama quartzites of southern Namibia. Even though five of these fossil forms were new to science at the time, little attention was paid to these sites until the late 1960s, when H.D. Pflug began reinvestigating them (Pflug 1972). G.J.B. Germs followed this work between 1967 and 1970, with a major stratigraphic and paleontological investigation of the Lower Nama Group (Germs 1972). Most recently, numerous scholars have been studying these forms (Brain 1998), which are proving to be vital for the understanding of metazoan origins.

Although the entire Karoo succession is not preserved in Namibia, Karoo-aged strata outcrop fairly extensively (Figure 4). A.W. Keyser's collection from the 1970s was the earliest systematic collection of comparable tetrapod fossils (Keyser 1973). Until the early 1990s, not much attention was devoted to these deposits. The renewed interest in Namibia's Karoo-aged reptiles led to M. Pickford's collecting efforts (Pickford 1995), and more recently, to those by a team from the South African Museum (Cape Town), under the guidance of Smith.

The Cenozoic paleontology of Namibia is best known from the summary and work of B. Senut and Pickford (1995) and Pickford and colleagues (1994, 1995). Lower Miocene aeolianite (cemented windblown sediments) deposits have preserved fossils of the giant bird *Diamontornis* (Pickford and Dauphin 1993), as well as various micromammals and ostrich eggshells (Senut and Pickford 1995; Pickford et al. 1995). E.F.F. Sauer (1966) first documented fossil ostrich eggshells from a borehole in northern Namibia. Since this discovery, some seventy localities have been identified, from strata spanning most of the Miocene–Pleistocene (Senut and Pickford 1995).

Zimbabwe

The fossil record of Zimbabwe is not as spectacular as that of South Africa or Namibia. Over half of Zimbabwe's land surface is composed of Archaen igneous and metamorphic rocks. Also, a tenth of the land is covered by the sands of the Kalahari Desert. Despite these geological limitations, and despite limited funding and infrastructure, Zimbabwe boasts a proud heritage of Precambrian to Recent fossils, including representatives of the Karoo, Cretaceous, and Cenozoic. The most fossiliferous rocks are, however, those of the Karoo-aged strata.

In a lecture delivered to the Rhodesia Scientific Association in 1901, A.J.C. Molyneux exhibited a number of Karoo fossils, including fishes, molluscs, and plants, that he had collected from sixteen localities. In 1914, dinosaur remains were first discovered on farms 40 kilometers northeast of Bulawayo (Maufe 1916). Most of the early finds found their way to the British Museum (Natural History), or to one of the Zimbabwean Museums. Since 1936, however, the collection and export of fossils has been under tight control. Now, most of Zimbabwe's fossil heritage can be found in the National Museum of Zimbabwe in Bulawayo.

G. Bond (1973) gives a complete account of the history of fossil discoveries in Zimbabwe up until 1970. Since this time, numerous new sites have been discovered, including richly fossiliferous dinosaur sites on the Chitake River (Forest Sandstone Formation) (Raath et al. 1972). M.A. Raath has since collected numerous other specimens in Zimbabwe, including the first cranial remains of Triassic rhynchosaurs (Raath et al. 1992). D. Munyikwa currently is working on the Cretaceous rocks in Zimbabwe and has made new discoveries of dinosaurs in the Limpopo Valley.

Mozambique

Sedimentary deposits in Mozambique dating from the Karoo to Cenozoic occur in two distinct, marginal, and shallow marine-dominated basins: the southern Mozambique and the northern Rovuma Basin. These basins preserve similar histories of Mesozoic and Cenozoic deposition related to the breakup of Gondwana. Due to the extensive Quaternary cover, a general lack of outcrop, and the political upheaval and civil war of the past twenty years, the paleontological signatures of these two basins remain poorly documented.

In the southern Mozambique basin, a number of localities have been discovered that preserve Karoo-aged strata, yet fossils are rare. In 1956, however, Dr. F. Mouta collected several specimens of the lower Beaufort Group therapsid *Endothiodon* from the Lugno of Niassa Province (Latimer et al. 1995).

Cretaceous deposits are more widespread; however, they are mostly marine. Only a single dinosaur leg bone is known from deposits of this age in Mozambique (Jacobs 1993). G. Civitelli (1988) notes the occurrence of foraminifera (microscopic shelled protists), ammonites, and belemnites (squidlike molluscs) in Lower Cretaceous deposits of Mozambique, along with rare vertebrate remains and silicified fossil wood. The Upper Cretaceous deposits in the Rovuma Basin contain numerous species of the planktonic foraminiferan genus *Globutruncana* (Civitelli 1988).

Cenozoic terrains outcrop all along the southern and northeastern coast and are characterized by the presence of abundant nautiloids (cephalopods with coiled shells), as well as common bivalves (clams) and gastropods (snails) (Civitelli 1988). The Miocene strata of the Rovuma Basin are predominantly calcarenites and contain a paleontological signature including corallinaceous algae, echinoids (sea urchins), bryozoans ("moss animals"), bivalves, benthoic foraminifera, and rare fish teeth.

East Africa

East Africa is dominated by the Great Rift Valley, the only geological feature on Earth that is clearly visible from the moon. This complex system of extensional faults has been evolving for

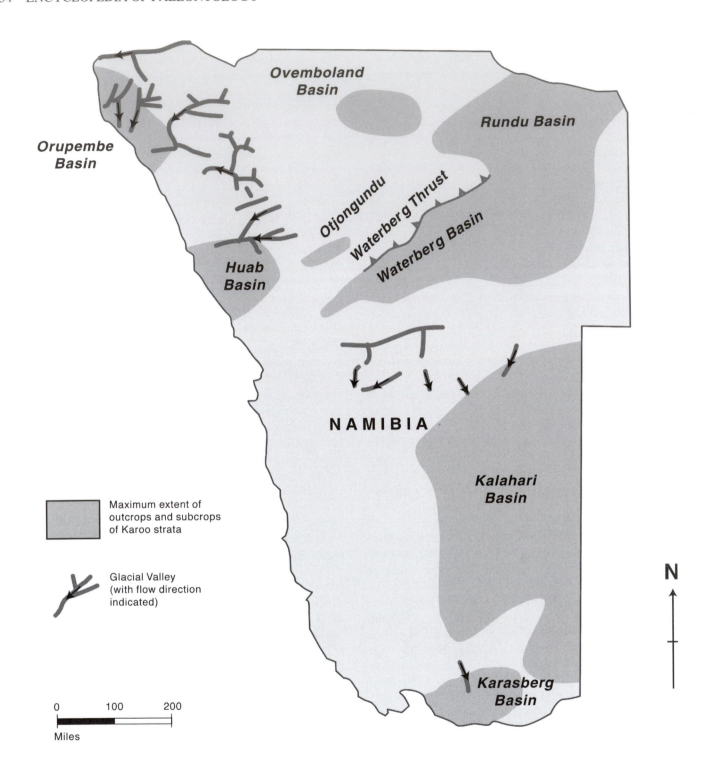

Figure 4. Karoo-aged basins of Namibia. Karoo outcrops and subcrops occur widely in Namibia, with the various basins being separated by areas of nondeposition and/or erosion. Numerous glacial valleys of Late Carboniferous age occur in the northwest of the country. Illustration by Tom Willcockson after Pickford (1995).

the past 40 million years and preserves a thick Cenozoic sequence. Older rocks along the rift valley also preserve a magnificent assemblage of Permo-Triassic Karoo and Cretaceous fossils.

Sedimentary strata containing a Karoo fauna in East Africa occur in Zambia, Malawi, Tanzania, and Kenya: They have been known since the investigations of F. Dixey (1927, 1928, 1937)

and G.M. Stockley (1936). These pioneers traveled around the country by porter safari and often risked life and limb in hostile conditions. They were, however, highly mobile and could set up camp at any locality they wished to investigate.

In 1963 four London-based paleontologists (A.J. Charig, H.W. Ball, C.B. Cox, and J. Attridge) spent five months in East

Africa collecting Permo-Triassic fossils from Zambia and Tanzania. Unlike the early pioneers, this party was mechanized and also enjoyed the conveniences of refrigerators, regular receipt of supplies and mail, sterilized water, and snakebite serum. Despite these comforts, their mobility was hindered by the lack of roads and infrastructure. Ball had to return to England prematurely, owing to injury. The remaining three were joined by three new members: A.W. Crompton (South African Museum, Cape Town), A.R.I. Cruickshank (University of Edinburgh), and Dr. B. Hirschson, who acted as medical officer. This group found 35 new localities, which yielded numerous fossils. Of these some 27 were within the Triassic Manda Formation of Tanzania. Most of the fossils that were collected could be allocated to four reptile groups: archosaurs ("ruling reptiles"), rhynchosaurs (lumbering, beaked, herbivorous archosauromorphs), dicynodonts, and cynodont therapsids (Attridge et al. 1963). Joining this party was J.W. Kitching, who earlier had done work in the region with A.R. Drysdall (Drysdall and Kitching 1962).

Zambia

Karoo-aged fossils in Zambia are known from the Luangwa Valley, where sedimentary strata have been incised deeply by the Luangwa River and its tributaries. The Luangwa is a major tributary of the mighty Zambezi River and is the main river in the eastern portion of Zambia. The area is mostly remote, uninhabited, and devoid of roads, making collecting a difficult task.

R. Prentice first discovered fossils in the upper Luangwa Valley in 1915. F. Dixey surveyed the area in 1928 and 1935 (Dixey 1937), and also collected a number of Permo-Triassic tetrapod fossils. L.D. Boonstra (1938) originally described this collection, which is currently housed in the South African Museum (Cape Town). No further investigations were undertaken in this area until 1960–61 when J.W. Kitching and Drysdall revisited the area. During their four month stay, they collected almost 500 vertebrate fossils, mainly therapsids, from the Permian Madumabisa Mudstone and the Triassic N'tawere Formations. This material is housed in the Bernard Price Institute for Paleontological Research, Johannesburg.

Malawi

In 1883, ten years after Livingstone's death, Henry Drummond first discovered fossils in Malawi (then part of British Central Africa). No other discoveries were made until the early 1900s when a British planter uncovered some dinosaur bones. This discovery prompted the British Museum to send an expedition, led by F.W.H. Migeod and F.R. Parrington, to the northwest of Malawi in 1930. They not only found dinosaur-bearing strata, but also older and younger fossils.

Activity in the area ceased until 1984 when Louis Jacobs led an expedition. Subsequent expeditions over the next six years led to the discovery of a new Cretaceous fauna in the Luwonya Hills area. New fossil finds include five different species of dinosaurs, three types of crocodiles, and various frogs (Jacobs 1993). Jacobs also collected a number of Karoo-aged reptiles from one of F.

Migeod's localities, near the village of Chiweta, overlooking Lake Malawi (Jacobs 1993).

Tanzania

The occurrence of rocks of Karoo age (Permo–Carboniferous–Triassic) in Tanzania has been known since the time of Livingstone's travels, as he is reported to have discovered coal in the Ruhuhu Valley of southwest Tanzania.

In the 1920s, Stockley made the first systematic collection of Permo–Triassic fossils in Tanzania, while surveying the coal-bearing strata reported by Livingstone. Stockley documented at least 35 localities, which produced mainly mammal-like reptiles (therapsids), as well as archosauriforms, amphibians, rare plants, and mollusc fossils (Stockley 1936).

In 1933 Parrington collected from these strata and sent the material back to the Museum of Zoology at Cambridge University. From 1934 to 1936, E. Nowack also collected in this region. Of his collections, the therapsid material was dispatched to Cambridge. The diapsid material was sent to the Institut für Geologie und Pälaeontologie at Tübingen, Germany, and was described by F. von Huene (1942). A few fossils also were sent to Munich, but unfortunately, these were destroyed during the Second World War.

Cox (Cox 1959) and Cruickshank (Cruickshank 1965, 1967) described the material sent to Cambridge. In 1963 these two authors' interest in East Africa was partly responsible for a joint expedition headed by the University of London and the British Museum (Natural History). In contrast to Zambia, where scholars investigated the Permian, the collecting in the Ruhuhu Valley centered on the Triassic exposures. This material is now housed in the British Museum (Natural History).

O. Hankel (1987) is responsible for the most current work on the fossils of the Karoo succession of Tanzania. He described the biostratigraphy of the Luwegu Basin based on vertebrates, fossil wood, and the macro- and microflora. He also documented the discovery of dinosaur (sauropod) bones in Jurassic deposits.

However, dinosaurs in Tanzania are not restricted to the Jurassic. The Cretaceous strata preserve one of the most acclaimed dinosaur sites in Africa, Tendaguru. Dinosaur fossils were first discovered at this locality in 1907 by a German mining engineer, in what was then Deutsch Ostafrika (German East Africa). Excavations continued at this site from 1909 to 1914, until the First World War reached East Africa. At the end of the war, Germany lost its African colonies and German East Africa became Tanganyika Territory, under British protection. Tendaguru, therefore, also became a British possession. In 1924, work continued under the guidance of W.E. Cutler and L. Leakey; however, within nine months of his arrival, Cutler died from malaria. He was succeeded by F. Migeod and Parrington. In 1931, the British Museum abandoned work at Tendaguru and the site has not been worked since (Jacobs 1993).

Uganda

Karoo-aged rocks are known only from three small occurrences on or near the north shore of Lake Victoria. These strata attain a thickness of up to 350 meters and are predominantly gray-to-black siltstones and mudstones that contain a *Glossopteris* flora.

Kenya

A belt about 55 kilometers wide that runs parallel to and near the coast of Kenya contains sedimentary strata known as the Durumana sandstones. The strata have been assigned to the Karoo. These exposures continue southward to link up with strata in the Tanga area. This region has only a sparse Karoo-aged fauna, including numerous invertebrates and the Lower Triassic eosuchian reptile *Kenyasaurus* (Harris and Carrol 1977).

Madagascar

Madagascar is the world's fourth largest island. It lies some 400 kilometers off the east coast of Mozambique. Although Madagascar is located within the tropics, most of the island today is covered by depauperate (impoverished) grassland. Best known for its unique fauna, Madagascar also has an interesting fossil record (Battail et al. 1987). Unfortunately, this history is not well known due to the country's poor infrastructure and the fact that most collecting is done by private individuals.

The Paleozoic–Holocene stratigraphic succession and paleontological history of Madagascar are related directly to the progressive breakup of Gondwana and the subsequent dismemberment of Eastern Gondwana. Much of the Cretaceous and Cenozoic, therefore, corresponds to a period of slow deposition, coincident with the separation of Madagascar and India from Australia and Antarctica.

Karoo-aged strata occur mainly in the southwest of the island and are predominantly continental clastics (erosional deposits), with a single major incursion of seawater over the land. The earliest collecting of Karoo-aged fossil reptiles may be traced back to Colcanap. In 1908, he collected numerous fossils of the eosuchian reptiles *Thadeosaurus* and *Hovosaurus,* as well as plants *(Glossopteris)* and fishes *(Atherstonia)* from a single locality in the Sakemena River Valley (Piveteau 1926; Currie 1981). These fossils now are housed in the Muséum National d'Histoire Naturelle in Paris. In 1995 a team led by Smith and the author collected numerous fossils from the Lower Sakemena, including the first skulls of the eosuchian reptile *Hovosaurus.*

Although Cenozoic strata are plentiful, the fossils of the Cenozoic of Madagascar are not as well documented as the Karoo-aged forms. As most of Madagascar's large vertebrates have become extinct in the last 2,000 years (MacPhee 1986), a good Holocene record is preserved, including numerous eggshells and bones of the elephant bird *Aepyornis,* the largest bird ever known.

West and Northwest Africa

Compared to the southern and eastern parts of the continent, the paleontology of the west and northwest of sub-Saharan Africa is poorly known, based primarily on patchy records, mostly from obscure journals.

Angola

Due to the thick vegetation cover in all but the south of the country, lack of road infrastructure, and political unrest and civil war for the past thirty years, Angola has one of the least well-documented paleontological histories of any country in sub-Saharan Africa. Although a Karoo-aged fauna is believed to be present, no documentation of this material could be found for this study. Only the Cretaceous and Plio-Pleistocene are known in any significant way (Cooper 1976; Pickford et al. 1994). O. Haas (1942) first described Cretaceous ammonites and nautiloids from Angola. Klinger (1980) also describes the ammonites of this region and ascribed them to a Late Cretaceous age. Plio-Pleistocene cave and karst infill deposits have been known since the 1940s (Dart 1950). These deposits, however, remained poorly known until 1989 when the Angola Paleontology Expedition spent three weeks in southern Angola, discovering numerous new localities and abundant fossil remains (Pickford et al. 1994).

Cameroons

Like most of west Africa, Cameroon has a tropical climate, thick lateritic soils, and an impoverished fossil record. The best fossiliferous strata occur in the dry northern half of the country. Of the periods dealt with, only the Cretaceous is known, with ammonite-bearing deposits in the south (Reyment 1995), and dinosaurs in the north of the country (Jacobs 1993). In 1985, a joint French, British, American, and Cameroonian paleontological project began in the north of the country. A year later, in 1986, L. Jacobs joined this team, subsequently finding Cretaceous dinosaur, insect, amphibian, and mammal fossils in the Koum Basin (Jacobs 1993).

Conclusion

During the time of the ancient Greeks and Romans, Pliny the Elder is attributed with writing that "out of Africa there is always something new." This applies equally well today, especially to the paleontology of the continent, which is continuously becoming better known as more discoveries are made. Africa also has long been known as the "Dark Continent," but as the politics of the region change, new light is being shed on the paleontological diversity there. Sub-Saharan Africa's paleontological heritage is particularly important for the wealth of information it supplies regarding the beginnings of metazoan life, the evolution of plants, the origin of mammals, and the ancestry of humans. At present, the best known periods are the Paleozoic–Mesozoic, and the Late Cenozoic, especially in the countries of south and east Africa. With time, the Precambrian and Cambrian are becoming better known.

P.J. Hancox

See also Africa: North Africa and the Middle East

Works Cited

Anderson, E., and J. Long. 1996. The ancient lagoon fishes of Grahamstown. *Phoenix,* Albany Museum Grahamstown, 23–25.

Anderson, J.M., and H.M. Anderson. 1985. *Palaeoflora of Southern Africa: Prodromus of South African Megafloras Devonian to Lower Cretaceous.* Rotterdam: Balkema.

———. 1995. The Molteno Formation: Window onto Late Triassic floral diversity. *In* D.D. Pant (ed.), *Proceedings of the International Conference on Global Environment and Diversification of Plants through Geological Time.* Allahabad: Society of Indian Plant Taxonomists.

Attridge, J., H.W. Ball, A.J. Charig, and C.B. Cox. 1964. The British Museum (Natural History)—University of London joint palaeontological expedition to Northern Rhodesia and Tanganyika. *Nature* 201:445–49.

Bain, A.G. 1857. Geology of South Africa: Reminiscences and anecdotes connected with the history of geology in South Africa; or, the pursuit of knowledge under difficulties. *Eastern Province Monthly Magazine* 1 (1):7–20.

Bamford, M.K. 1990. The Angiosperm Palaeoflora from the Orapa Pipe, Botswana. Ph.D. diss., University of the Witwatersrand, Johannesburg.

Battail, B., L. Beltan, and J. DuTuit. 1987. Africa and Madagascar during Permo-Triassic time: The evidence of the vertebrate faunas. *American Geophysical Union Geophysical Monograph* 41:147-54.

Bond, G. 1973. *The Paleontology of Rhodesia.* Bulletin of the Geological Survey of Rhodesia 70. Zimbabwe: Geological Survey of Rhodesia.

Boonstra, L.D. 1938. A report on some Karroo reptiles from the Luangwa Valley, Northern Rhodesia. *Quarterly Journal of the Geological Society of London* 94:371-84.

Brain, C.K. 1981. *The Hunters or the Hunted? An Introduction to African Cave Taphonomy.* Chicago: University of Chicago Press.

———. 1996. The relevance of Naman and Ediacaran fossil assemblages to the early evolution of animals. Abstract: Ninth Biennial Palaeontological Society of South Africa Conference, Stellenbosch, South Africa.

———. 1998. The importance of Nama Group sediments and fossils to the debate about animal origins. *Palaeontologia africana* 34:1–13.

Broom, R. 1948. Bibliography of R. Broom, M.D., D.Sc., F.R.S. *In* A.L. DuToit (ed.), *Robert Broom Commemorative Volume.* Special publication of the Royal Society of South Africa.

Chaloner, W.G., P.L. Forey, B.G. Gardiner, A.J. Hill, and V.T. Young. 1980. Devonian fish and plants from the Bokkeveld Series of South Africa. *Annals of the South African Museum* 81:127–57.

Civitelli, G. 1988. The Meso-Cenozoic Sedimentary Sequence of the Cabo Delgado Province, Mozambique. *Journal of African Earth Science* 7 (4):629–39.

Cooke, H.B.S. 1963. Pleistocene mammal faunas of Africa, with particular reference to southern Africa. *In* F.C. Howell and F. Bouliere (eds.), *African Ecology and Human Evolution.* London: Methuen; New York: Wenner Gren Foundation for Anthropological Research; Chicago: Aldine.

Cooper, M.R. 1976. The Cretaceous palaeontology and stratigraphy of Angola. D.Sc. diss., University of Oxford.

Cox, C.B. 1959. On the anatomy of a new dicynodont genus with evidence for the position of the tympanum. *Proceedings of the Zoological Society, London* 132:321–67.

Cruickshank, A.R.I. 1965. On a specimen of the anomodont reptile *Kannemeyeria latifrons* (Broom) from the Manda Formation of Tanganyika, Tanzania. *Proceedings Linnean Society, London* 176 (2):149–57.

———. 1967. A new dicynodont from the Manda Formation of Tanzania (Tanganyika). *Journal of Zoology, London* 153:163–208.

Currie, P.J. 1981. *Hovosaurus boulei,* an aquatic Eosuchian from the Upper Permian of Madagascar. *Palaeontologia africana* 24:99–168.

Dart, R.A. 1950. A note on the limestone caverns of Leba, near Humpata, Angola. *South African Archaeological Bulletin* 5 (20):149–51.

———. 1957. The osteodontokeratic culture of *Australopithecus prometheus.* Memoirs of the Transvaal Museum 10:1–105.

Dixey, F. 1927. Notes on the Karroo sequence north-west of Lake Nyasa. *Transactions of the Geological Society of South Africa* 29:59–68.

———. 1928. The dinosaur beds of Lake Nyasa. *Transactions of the Royal Society of South Africa* 16:55–66.

———. 1937. The geology of part of the upper Luangwa valley, North-Eastern Rhodesia. *Quarterly Journal of the Geological Society of London* 93:52–76.

Drysdall, A.R., and J.W. Kitching. 1962. The Karroo Succession of the Upper Luangwa Valley, Northern Rhodesia. *Transactions of the Geological Society of South Africa* 65 (1):75–90.

Falcon, R., and A.J. Ham. 1988. The characteristics of southern African coals. *Journal of the South African Institute of Mining and Metallurgy* 88 (5):145–61.

Germs, G.J.B. 1972. The stratigraphy and palaeontology of the lower Nama group, South West Africa. *Bulletin of the Chamber of Mines Pre-Cambrian Research Unit,* University of Cape Town 12:1–250.

Gess, R. 1996. Taking the lid off a geological plant press. *Phoenix,* Albany Museum Grahamstown, 18–22.

Gore, R. 1997. The dawn of humans: The first steps. *National Geographic* 191 (2):72–99.

Haas, O. 1942. *Some Upper Cretaceous Ammonites from Angola.* American Museum Novitates, 1182. New York: American Museum of Natural History.

Hancox, P.J., and B.S. Rubidge. 1994. A new dicynodont therapsid from South Africa: Implications for the biostratigraphy of the Upper Beaufort (*Cynognathus* Assemblage Zone). *South African Journal of Science* 90:98–99.

———. 1996. The first specimen of the Mid-Triassic dicynodont *Angonisaurus* from the Karoo of South Africa: Implications for the dating and biostratigraphy of the *Cynognathus* Assemblage Zone, Upper Beaufort Group. *South African Journal of Science* 92:391–92.

Hankel, O. 1987. Lithostratigraphic subdivision of the Karoo rocks of the Luwegu Basin (Tanzania) and their biostratigraphic classification based on microfloras, macrofloras, fossil woods and vertebrates. *Geologische Rundschau* 76 (2):539–65.

Harris, J.M., and R.L. Carrol. 1977. *Kenyasaurus,* a new eosuchian reptile from the Early Triassic of Kenya. *Journal of Paleontology* 51:139–49.

Haughton, S.H. 1924. The fauna and stratigraphy of the Stormberg Series. *Annals of the South African Museum* 12 (8):323–497.

———. 1963. *The Stratigraphic History of Africa South of the Sahara.* Edinburgh: Oliver and Boyd; New York: Hafner.

———. 1965. The Rubidge collection of fossil Karroo vertebrates. *Palaeontologia africana* 9:1–17.

Hendey, Q.B. 1981. The geological succession at Langebaanweg Cape Province, and global events of the late Tertiary. *South African Journal of Science* 77:33–38.

Hiller, N. 1990. Lower Devonian Hyoltihs in South Africa and their palaeoenvironmental significance. *Palaeontologia africana* 27:5–8.

Huene, F. von. 1942. Die Anomodontier des Ruhuhu-Gebiets in der Tübingen Sammlung. *Palaeontographica Abt. A* 94:154–84.

Jacobs, L. 1993. *Quest for the African Dinosaurs.* New York: Villard.

Keyser, A.W. 1973. A new Triassic vertebrate fauna from South West Africa. *Palaeontologia africana* 16:1–15.

King, L.C. 1962. *Morphology of the Earth*. Edinburgh: Oliver and Boyd; New York: Hafner.

Kitching, J.W. 1953. A new species of fossil baboon from Potgietersrus. *South African Journal of Science* 50:66–69.

———. 1965. A giant hyracoid from the Limeworks Quarry, Makapansgat, Potgietersrus. *Palaeontologia africana* 9:91–96.

———. 1977. *The Distribution of the Karroo Vertebrate Fauna*. Memoir 1. Johannesburg: Bernard Price Institute for Palaeontological Research.

———. 1980. On some fossil Arthropoda from the Limeworks, Makapansgat, Potgietersrus. *Palaeontologia africana* 23:63–68.

Klerk, W. de. 1997. News from the Albany Museum. *Pal News* 11 (3):13–15.

Klinger, H.C. 1980. Cretaceous Faunas from Zululand and Natal, South Africa. The Ammonite Subfamily Texanitinae Collingnon, 1948. *Annals of the South African Museum* 80:1–357.

Latimer, E.M., C.E. Gow, and B.S. Rubidge. 1995. Dentition and feeding niche of *Endothiodon* (Synapsida, Anomodontia). *Palaeontologia africana* 32:75–82.

Latrobe, C.I. 1818. *Journal of a Visit to South Africa*. Vols. 1 and 2. London: Seely and Ackermann; New York: Eastburn.

MacPhee, R.D.E. 1986. Environment, extinction, and Holocene vertebrate localities in southern Madagascar. *National Geographic Research* 2 (4):441–55.

Maufe, H.B. 1916. Letter to the Honourable Secretary of the Geological Society of South Africa. *Proceedings of the Geological Society of South Africa* 18:33–34.

McKay, I.S., and R.J. Rayner. 1986. Cretaceous fossil insects from Orapa, Botswana. *Journal of the Entomological Society of South Africa* 49:7–17.

Oelofsen, B.W. 1981a. The fossil record of the Class Chondrichthyes in southern Africa. *Palaeontologia africana* 24:11–13.

———. 1981b. An anatomical and systematic study of the family Mesosauridae (Reptilia; Proganosauria) with special reference to its associated fauna and palaeoecological environment in the Whitehill sea. Ph.D. diss., University of Stellenbosch, South Africa.

Oosthuizen, R.D.F. 1984. Preliminary catalogue and report on the biostratigraphy and palaeogeographic distribution of the Bokkeveld fauna. *Transactions of the Geological Society of South Africa* 87:125–40.

Partridge, T.C., and R.R. Maud. 1987. Geomorphic evolution of southern Africa since the Mesozoic. *Transactions of the Geological Society of South Africa* 90:179–208.

Paterson, W. 1790. *Narrative of Four Journeys into the Country of the Hottentots and Caffraria*. 2nd ed., London: Johnson.

Pflug, H.D. 1972. Zur Fauna der Nama-Schichten in Südwest-Afrika. III. Erniettomorpha, Bau und Systematik. *Palaeontographica Abt. A* 139:134–70.

Pickford, M. 1995. Karoo Supergroup Palaeontology of Namibia and brief description of a thecodont from Omingonde. *Palaeontologia africana* 32:51–66.

Pickford, M., and Y. Dauphin. 1993. *Diamantornis wardi* nov. gen., nov. sp., giant extinct bird from Rooilepel, Lower Miocene, Namibia. *Contributions of the Royal Academy of Science, Paris* 316:1643–50.

Pickford, M., P. Mein, and B. Senut. 1994. Fossiliferous Neogene karst fillings in Angola, Botswana and Namibia. *South African Journal of Science* 90:227–30.

Pickford, M., B. Senut, and Y. Dauphin. 1995. Biostratigraphy of the Tsondab Sandstone (Namibia) based on gigantic avian eggshells. *Geóbios* 28 (1):85–98.

Piveteau, J. 1926. Paléontologie de Madagascar. Part 12, Amphibiens et reptiles permiens. *Annals of Palaeontology* 15:53–180.

Plumstead, E.P. 1967. A general review of the Devonian fossil plants found in the Cape System of South Africa. *Palaeontologia africana* 10:1–83.

Raath, M.A. 1977. The anatomy of the Triassic theropod Syntarsus rhodesiensis (Saurischia: Podokesauridae) and a consideration of its biology. Ph.D. diss., Rhodes University.

Raath, M.A., P.M. Oesterlen, and J.W. Kitching. 1992. First record of Triassic Rhynchosauria (Reptilia: Diapsida) from the Lower Zambezi Valley, Zimbabwe. *Palaeontologia africana* 29:1–10.

Raath, M.A., C.C. Smith, and G. Bond. 1972. A new Upper Karroo dinosaur locality on the lower Angwa River Sipolilo District, Rhodesia. *Arnoldia (Rhodesia)* 43:1–10.

Rayner, R.J. 1993. Fossils from a Middle Cretaceous crater lake: Biology and geology. *Kaupia* 2:5–12.

Reed, F.R.C. 1925. Revision of the fauna from the Bokkeveld Beds. *Annals of the South African Museum* 22:27–225.

Reyment, R.A. 1995. The Cretaceous Ammonoidea of southern Nigeria and the southern Cameroons. *Bulletin Geological Survey of Nigeria* 25:1–112.

Rogers, A.W. 1937. The pioneers in South African geology and their work. *Transactions of the Geological Society of South Africa*, Annexure to Volume 39.

Rubidge, B.S. 1987. South Africa's oldest land-living reptiles from the Ecca-Beaufort transition in the southern Karoo. *South African Journal of Science* 83:165–66.

———. 1990. A new vertebrate biozone at the base of the Beaufort Group, Karoo Sequence (South Africa). *Palaeontologia africana* 27:17–20.

Salter, J.W. 1856. Description of Palaeozoic Crustacea and Radiata from South Africa. *Transactions of the Geological Society of London* 2 (7):215–24.

Sauer, E.F.F. 1966. Fossil eggshell fragments of a giant struthious bird (*Struthio oshasai* sp. nov.) from Etosha Pan, South West Africa. *Cimbebasia* 14:1–51.

Savage, D.E., and D.E. Russell. 1983. *Mammalian Paleofaunas of the World*. Reading, Massachusetts: Anderson-Wesley.

Schwarz, E.H.L. 1906. South African Paleozoic fossils. *Records of the Albany Museum* 1:348–60.

Senut, B., and M. Pickford. 1995. Fossil eggs and the Cenozoic continental biostratigraphy of Namibia. *Palaeontologia africana* 32:33–37.

Smith, R.M.H. 1996. Life in a prehistoric crater-lake. *Phoenix*, Albany Museum, Grahamstown, 4–6.

Stockley, G.M. 1936. A further contribution to the Karroo rocks of Tanganyika territory. *Quarterly Journal of the Geological Society of London* 152 (1):1–131.

Theron, J.N. 1972. The stratigraphy and sedimentology of the Bokkeveld Group. D.Sc. diss., University of Stellenbosch, South Africa.

Welles, L.H., and H.B.S. Cooke. 1956. Fossil bovidae from the limeworks Quarry, Makapansgat, Potgietersrus. *Palaeontologia africana* 4:1–55.

White, M.E. 1986. *The Greening of Gondwana*. New South Wales: Reed Books; as *The Flowering of Gondwana*, Princeton, New Jersey: Princeton University Press, 1990.

Further Reading

Armstrong, S. 1996. Fossil hunter of the Karoo. *New Scientist* 2015:36–40.

Bishop, W.W., and J.D. Clark. 1967. *Background to Evolution in Africa*. Chicago: University of Chicago Press.

Brink, A.S. 1981. An illustrated bibliographical catalogue of the synapsida. *Palaeontologia africana* 24:23–26.

Brink, J.S. 1987. The archaeozoology of Florisbad, Orange Free State. *Memoirs of the National Museum Bloemfontein* 24:1–151.

Cluver, M.A., and T.H. Barry. 1977. Advances in South African vertebrate palaeontology. *In* A.C. Brown (ed.), *A History of Scientific Endeavour in South Africa*. Capetown: Royal Society of South Africa.

Haughton, S.H. 1963. *The Stratigraphic History of Africa South of the Sahara*. Edinburgh: Oliver and Boyd; New York: Hafner.

Jacobs, L. 1993. *Quest for the African Dinosaurs*. New York: Villard.

Raath, M.A. 1984. In Memmorium—Sydney Henry Haughton. *Palaeontologia africana* 25:1–3.

———. 1990. Tribute to James W. Kitching. *Palaeontologia africana* 27:1–3.

Rogers, A.W. 1937. The pioneers in South African geology and their work. *Transactions of the Geological Society of South Africa*. Annexure to Volume 39.

Tobias, P.V. 1977. A century of research in human biology and palaeoanthropology in southern Africa. *In* A.C. Brown (ed.), *A History of Scientific Endeavour in South Africa*. Cape Town: Royal Society of South Africa.

AGASSIZ, JEAN LOUIS RUDOLPHE

Swiss/American 1807–73

Jean Louis Rudolphe Agassiz was born on 28 May 1807 in Motier-en-Vuly, Switzerland. Born into a family of wealth and status, Agassiz was expected to succeed as a merchant or physician, but having grown up in the splendors of the Swiss countryside, he was attracted to the natural sciences. Agassiz received his initial academic training at the universities of Zurich, Heidelberg, and Munich, and in 1829 he received his doctorate in philosophy from the University of Erlangen. That same year Agassiz published *Selecta genera et species piscium quas itinere per Brasilian 1817–1820,* a monograph on the fishes of Brazil. In 1830 he received his doctorate of medicine from the University of Munich and afterward briefly studied under Georges Cuvier.

In 1832 Agassiz was appointed professor at the College of Neuchâtel and began important geological work on glaciation, work that would expand the concept of the Ice Age. For a decade, from 1835 to 1845, Agassiz measured and studied the glacial formations of Switzerland and made broad geological comparisons with England and central Europe. From this study Agassiz proposed that in past eras glaciers covered most of northern Europe, and during warming periods the withdrawal of ice created upheaval and left discernible marks in the earth and rocks of glaciated regions. From these marks Agassiz could trace glacial movement to Switzerland and concluded that countries in which unstratified gravel is found were once covered by glaciers. Although not the first study of glaciation, Agassiz's work was novel because it incorporated a broad continental approach to local geology.

Beyond geology, Agassiz also concentrated on ichthyology and paleontology during his tenure at Neuchâtel. Between 1833 and 1844 he published a five-volume monograph, *Recherches sur les poissons fossiles,* that encompassed marine biology, freshwater fishes, embryology, and fossil fishes. In this work Agassiz provided detailed descriptions of over 1,700 extinct species, including illustrated reconstructions within a framework of comparative anatomy. Agassiz also published *Monographies d'échinodermes vivants et fossiles,* a four-volume work.

Following Agassiz's success in Europe, in 1846 he traveled to the United States with the intention of studying the natural history and geology there. That same year he gave a successful series of lectures in eastern cities that conveyed both his excitement for and interest in the natural sciences. He also was invited to the lecture at the Lowell Institute in Boston. Then, in 1847, Agassiz entered a new phase in his scientific career. That year Cécile Braun, his first wife, died, and Agassiz accepted a professorship of zoology at the Lawrence Scientific School at Harvard University. Although he only had intended a temporary stay to compare the natural history of America with that of Europe, Agassiz remained in the United States because he was dutifully in love with Elizabeth Cabot Cary, whom he married in 1850. Elizabeth Cabot Cary was a well-known writer and promoter of women's education, and together they traveled on scientific expeditions, wrote scholarly works, and founded the Anderson School of Natural History. Following Louis' death, she would go on to serve as the first president of Radcliffe College.

Whereas Agassiz's career in Europe heavily concentrated on the scholastic aspect of science, his career in America took a public approach. Agassiz had announced in 1855 his intentions to publish a ten-volume study on the natural environment of the United States, but he only was able to complete four volumes, published as *Contributions to the Natural History of the United States*. While these volumes were beautifully illustrated, they did not as a whole capture a wide public or scientific audience; the notable exception was the one on the embryology of turtles. Agassiz also applied his glacial theory to North America and conducted research in marine biology, but his interests were turning toward establishing scientific institutions. With Agassiz's help, Harvard University established the Museum of Comparative Zoology in 1859. As Agassiz conceived it, the museum brought together graduate studies, fieldwork, research, and publishing and was supported by public and private funds, $600,000 of which was raised by Agassiz during his lifetime. Agassiz also helped found the National Academy of Sciences in 1863 and the Anderson School of Natural History in 1873, which, given Agassiz's reputation, had the greatest influence on scientific teaching in the United States. He also advised the Smithsonian Institution and the U.S. Coast Survey.

In 1865 Agassiz traveled to Brazil. Three years later, he published, with his wife, an account of their expedition, *A Journey in*

Brazil (1868). In 1871 Agassiz took an extensive expedition to California that included travels along both shores of South America.

Agassiz was also a devoted teacher, and his pedagogical methods would revolutionize the teaching of the natural sciences in the United States. Agassiz discouraged the use of books and instead, promoted a method that entailed the acquisition of facts and knowledge from interactions with nature. As a testimony to his methods, every notable teacher of the latter half of the nineteenth century was either taught by Agassiz or one of his students.

Given his influential public status and differing views on evolution, Agassiz became a leading opponent of Darwin and theories of evolution. Growing up in a religious atmosphere (his father was a minister), Agassiz, although not devoutly religious, espoused a theory of natural history in which all flora and fauna were created by a divine being. According to Agassiz, extant flora and fauna did not have any historical or genetic relation to extinct species, but rather, extinct species were created and destroyed by a divine power during a separate period of creation. Those creatures that exhibited little change over time were examples of perfect species. Whereas Charles Darwin and Charles Lyell used glaciation and theories of the Ice Age to explain the existence of related species in different locations, Agassiz believed that the Ice Age was a catastrophe created by a deity. It was a debate that Agassiz brought to the public via popular journals, but it was a battle Agassiz would eventually lose, and one that took away from his scientific interests. Louis Agassiz died on 14 December 1873 in Cambridge, Massachusetts, of a cerebral hemorrhage.

EDOUARD L. BONÉ AND BRIAN CALLENDER

Biography

Born in Motier-en-Vuly, Switzerland, 28 May 1807. Received Ph.D. in philosophy, Universities of Munich and Erlangen, 1829; M.D., University of Munich, 1830. Professor of natural history, College of Neuchâtel, 1832–46; lecturer, Lowell Institute, 1846; professor of zoology and geology, Lawrence Scientific School, Harvard University, 1847–73; curator, Museum of Comparative Zoology, Cambridge, Massachusetts, 1859–73. Extensive expeditions through central Europe, Swiss Alps, eastern United States, trans-Mississippi American west, and South America. Expanded the concept of the Ice Age; helped establish numerous scientific institutions in the United States. Admitted to Royal Society of London, 1838; admitted to French Académie de Sciences, 1839; awarded Prize in Physical Sciences, Académie de Sciences, 1859; cofounder, National Academy of Sciences, 1863; awarded Wollaston Medal, Geological Society of London, 1863; founded Anderson School of Natural History, Penikese Island, Buzzard's Bay, Massachusetts, 1873; named to Hall of Fame for Great Americans, 1915. Died in Cambridge, Massachusetts, 14 December 1873.

Major Publications

1829. *Selecta genera et species piscium quas in itinere per Brasilian 1817–1820*. Munich: Wolf.

1833–44. *Recherches sur les poissons fossiles*. 5 vols. Neuchâtel: Imprimerie de Petitpierre and Nicolet.

1838–42. *Monographies d'échinodermes vivants et fossiles*. 4 vols. Neuchâtel: L'auteur.

1840. *Études sur les glaciers*. Neuchâtel: Jent et Gassmann.

1849. *Twelve Lectures on Comparative Embryology*. Boston: Henry Flanders; Redding, New York: Dewitt and Davenport.

1857–62. *Contributions to the Natural History of the United States*. 4 vols. Boston: Little, Brown; London: Trubner.

1866. *Geological Sketches*. Boston: Ticknor and Fields, and Osgood; London: Trubner.

1874. Evolution and permanence of type. *Atlantic Monthly* 33:94–101.

1876. *Geological Sketches, Second Series*. Boston: Osgood.

Further Reading

Agassiz, E.C.G. 1885. *Louis Agassiz: His Life and Correspondence*. London: Macmillan; Boston: Houghton Mifflin, 10th ed.; Boston: Houghton Mifflin, 1895.

Holder, C.F. 1893. *Louis Agassiz: His Life and Work*. New York: Putnam.

———. 1910. Louis Agassiz. *In* D.S. Jordan (ed.), *Leading American Men of Science*. New York: Holt.

Livingstone, D. 1996. Jean Louis Agassiz. *In* J. Prescott (ed.), *One Hundred Explorers Who Shaped World History*. San Francisco: Bluewood.

Lurie, E. 1960. *Louis Agassiz: A Life in Science*. Chicago: University of Chicago Press.

———. 1974. *Nature and the American Mind: Louis Agassiz and the Culture of Science*. New York: Science History Publications.

Lyman, T. 1873. Commemorative notice of Louis Agassiz. *Annual Report of the Council of American Academy of Arts and Sciences*: 1–13.

Marcou, L. 1895. *Life, Letters, and Works of Louis Agassiz*. 2 vols. New York and London: Macmillan.

Mayr, E. 1959. Agassiz, Darwin, and Evolution. *Harvard Library Bulletin* 13:165–94.

AGNATHANS

See Jawless Fishes

ALGAE

What is an alga? The term "alga" includes most aquatic and photosynthetic organisms, whether massive seaweeds or microscopic forms. They are of enormous importance as the primary food source in most aquatic environments, and as both the original source and primary replenishers of the oxygen in Earth's atmosphere.

The term algae includes both prokaryotes (cellular organisms without a distinct nucleus) and eukaryotes (organisms with distinct nuclei and organelles in their cells). That is, the algae are not recognized as a formal scientific taxon (group; plural, taxa) because they include a mix of organisms from bacteria to close relatives of plants. Rather, they are an ecological grade that share many convergent features. In previous centuries, algae were considered "lower plants." It is now known that most algae are no more closely related to plants than to animals or fungi—there are at least seven separate origins of "algae" among the eukaryotes alone (Figure 1). What does unite all eukaryotic algae is the presence of a plastid, an organelle ultimately the result of an endosymbiotic pairing between a photosynthetic cyanobacterium (blue-green alga) and a eukaryotic cell. All algae thus share certain chemical and physiological characteristics that the bacterial partner brings to the relationship, including chlorophyll, photosynthesis, and glucose compounds. The specific expressions of these traits vary enormously between algal groups, and are important in recognizing those groups.

Algal Ecology

As in plants and some protists, and unlike animals, the products of meiosis (type of cell division in which chromosome numbers are halved) in algae are not always gametes, but sometimes take the form of genetically and morphologically distinct stages in the algal life cycle. Common among these are various types of spores, designed either to disperse to a new location or to survive the parent through harsh environmental conditions. These spores may be flagellated (zoospores) or nonflagellated (aplanospores), and both may be found in the fossil record as acritarchs (fossilized spore casings). Spores may undergo mitotic divisions to create a colony or multicellular individual with a different genetic structure than the parent organism, and they may have an entirely different ecology. Of the various algal groups, the Rhodophyta (red algae) have the most complex life cycle, often involving three or more distinct phases. Some of these algae are known to spend part of their life history burrowing into the shells of gastropods before mating to reproduce the parental form. Also important to many algae is vegetative fragmentation. Colonies or individuals may fragment, either naturally or under stress, to produce propagules that disperse asexually.

Algae are of tremendous importance in aquatic communities as primary producers. Most of the energy put into marine food webs comes in the form of sunlight captured by algal photosynthesis used to manufacture carbohydrates. A by-product of this manufacture is the production of molecular oxygen. In fact, planktonic algae, not land plants, are the primary renewing source of atmospheric oxygen. Algae also play an important role in the physical structuring of communities, serving as cover or substrate for a variety of aquatic organisms, especially their larval forms.

In addition to serving as food and shelter for other organisms, algae often play an important role as symbiotes with fungi and animals. Lichens are a pairing of fungal filaments and algal cells, usually a cyanobacterium or pleurastrophycean alga, in which the fungal partner provides physical structure and nutrients, while the algal cells manufacture food. Zooxanthellae are a similar pairing in which chlorophycean algae (green algae) or dinoflagellates live within the tissues of sponges, cnidrians (radially symmetric invertebrates such as coral and jellyfishes), ciliates, or foraminifera.

Perhaps the most significant historical role of algae is the oxygenation of Earth's atmosphere. During the Proterozoic, oxygen relaeased via cyanobacterial photosynthesis accumulated in the atmosphere and oceans, converting them from a reducing environment to an oxidizing one. This had profound implications for life on this planet, making the world favorable to aerobic organisms. Further consequences of this oxygenation were the creation of an ozone layer in the upper atmosphere, which filtered out harmful radiation for the first time, and a chemical alteration of the Earth's oceans.

Algae also play a role in mineral cycling, as a number of groups deposit mineral plates or skeletons. These include calcite and lime (both calcium carbonates) and silica. Diatoms are very efficient at pulling silica from the surrounding water; their appearance in the later Mesozoic and continued dominance in the ocean has greatly affected global chemistry. Upon the death of these and other skeleton-forming organisms, vast benthic deposits of their mineral skeletons may accumulate to form organically derived limestone and diatomite. The fine grain of these sediments often traps and preserves other kinds of fossils.

Algal Morphology

Because "algae" include such a wide array of organisms, they occur in a variety of sizes and forms. Some are microscopic, while others grow to more than 30 meters in length. Despite these enormous differences, most algae share a common structural limitation of cell walls, which delimit each cell and restrict its shape and growth.

Within this basic limitation exist a variety of body plans. All algal groups include some unicellular species in which a single cell will carry on all the functions necessary for the organism. Most groups include some colonial forms as well, where clusters of cells exist as a single unit, with or without specialization of the individual members. More complex morphologies exist among most eukaryotic algae, including both true multicellularity and other forms, such as coenocytes (tubular or network forms in which many nuclei exist within a single large unit of cytoplasm).

True multicellularity is primarily found in the red, brown, and green algae. The simplest form of multicellularity is growth as filaments, or chains of cells attached end to end and perhaps with occasional branching. Two-dimensional growths of cells are termed membranes and are generally only one or two cells thick. Parenchyma and pseudoparenchyma are three-dimensional growths of cells and result in some of the most complex morphologies.

The convergent unity of morphological forms across algal groups combined with their structural simplicity can make it very difficult to assign a fossil alga to a particular taxonomic group. Because of this, many algal fossils are described morphologically rather than taxonomically.

Algal Systematics

There are more than 120,000 living species of algae, and many thousands more are known only as fossils. In many cases, the fossil record is not sufficient to resolve their relationships; rather, our understanding of algal phylogeny (evolutionary history) has come from work on the myriad extant (present-day) forms, especially in the form of chemical and ultrastructural research. It is only in the 1980s and 1990s, with the rise of molecular phylogenetics, that a reasonably clear picture of relationships developed.

There are six major lines of algal evolution, each with an origin independent of the others. These are the Cyanobacteria, Euglenids, Dinoflagellata, Rhodophyta, Chlorophyta, and Chromista. Of these, only the Chlorophyta (green algae) are closely related to plants, and indeed are believed to be their ancestors. The remaining algal lines are no more closely related to plants than they are to animals or fungi (Figure 1) and most are treated as members of Kingdom Protoctista. As such, "algae" is a grossly polyphyletic group (i.e., derived from many different ancestral stocks) and is no longer recognized taxonomically. However, the algae share many ecological convergences, so it is convenient to talk about them together.

Chromista is the most recently recognized lineage among the algae and so deserves additional explanation. The Chromista is recognized as a kingdom-level taxon and may be the sister group to the combined clade (group with a common ancestor) comprising plants, animals, and fungi. It includes several well-known algal groups: kelps, diatoms, silicoflagellates, and haptophytes, as well as several nonphotosynthetic groups previously classified as fungi, such as the water molds and slime nets. With the exception of the haptophytes, all chromists possess two dissimilar flagella, one covered with uniquely stiffened hairs called mastigonemes. For this reason, this subgroup of the Chromista is termed Heterokonta, or sometimes Stramenopiles. All algal heterokonts possess a unique membrane system enveloping the plastid and nucleus, as well as chlorophyll c, fucoxanthins, and chrysolaminarin; they also lack chlorophyll b and true starch, which are found in green algae and plants. Many chromists produce a skeleton of calcium carbonate, so their evolutionary radiation can reliably be dated to the Late Jurassic.

One of the persistent questions in algal phylogeny is understanding how so many groups independently acquired plastids, and thereby photosynthesis. The current hypothesis is for multiple endosymbiotic events. Fossil, chemical, and cladistic evidence suggests that the chemical pathways of photosynthesis originated in cyanobacteria some 3.8 billion years ago. The groups of eukaryotic algae arose each time a cyanobacterium was engulfed and incorporated into a eukaryote's cytoplasm as a symbiont. Thus, the plastids within plants and algae have a phylogeny independent of their eukaryotic hosts, and it is possible to reconstruct this phylogeny from plastid DNA sequences. This situation is complicated by the fact that plastids in the Euglenids and Dinoflagellata appear to be the result of secondary endosymbiotic events, in which a eukaryotic alga was ingested and incorporated. Evidence for this lies in the multiple layers of membranes surrounding their plastids and in molecular phylogenies of plastid DNA. The complete picture of plastid relationships is still under investigation.

Fossils of Algae

The most frustrating aspect of paleoalgology is to be aware of the enormous phyletic diversity of extant taxa and yet be unable to place some fossils even at the level of division. Almost never are the important features of plastid structure, pigmentation, storge products, flagellar arrangement, reproductive structures, or cell wall composition preserved by the fossilization process. Rather, surrogate features must be employed to identify and classify such fossils.

This problem is felt most acutely when working with macroalgal fossils—those large, soft-bodied seaweeds which are preserved merely as outlines, as carbon films, and only rarely as silicifications within chert or as highly detailed fossils in diatomite. Red algae and green algae in particular have produced many convergent forms, and both are known to have existed since at least the Late Proterozoic. In most cases, the identity of their fossils cannot be judged because of their superficial resemblance. Many of these early fossils also have been hypothesized to be kelps, but the sister groups of the brown algae do not appear in the fossil record until the Late Jurassic, suggesting that the kelps did not appear before that time.

Even sponges and foraminifera have at times been misidentified as algae. The lack of available clues to systematic affinities have led some researchers to examine instead the "level of complexity" and sequence of appearance of traits in the fossil record, but these analyses presuppose that algae are a monophyletic or at least closely related assemblage. As has been pointed out, this is not the case, and so such studies are of limited value for understanding the evolution of algae except in the most gross fashion. However, in the absence of additional systematic data, this is perhaps the best that can be done.

In contrast to the unidentifiability of soft-bodied algae, encrusted and skeletized groups often can be identified with great precision. These algae occur across a range of systematic groups and have developed different and independent methods of creating hard parts. For this reason, the processes will be discussed here with only secondary reference to their systematic affinities.

Calcareous algae secrete calcium carbonate either in the form of calcite or aragonite crystals (depending upon the taxon) to create a rigid or segmented skeleton or a nonskeletal substrate. The process has not been studied in every group in which it occurs, and the mechanisms of precipitation are not fully known, but calcification is rather well characterized in cyanobacteria and in red and green algae. Neither is the function of the calcium products fully understood, although it generally is believed that they perform a protective function in most cases.

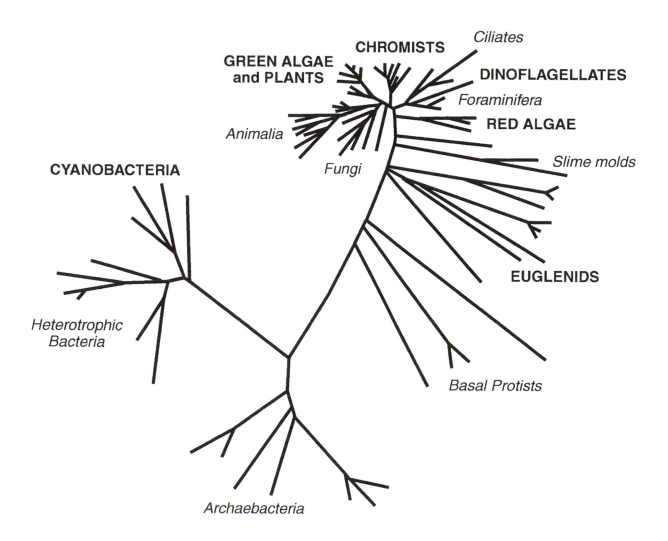

Figure 1. Diagram showing the relationships of the major groups of living organisms. Major groups that have been called "algae" are listed in capital letters; notice that there are several and that they are not closely related at all. The diagram was constructed from DNA sequences coding for ribosomal RNA, and the length of the branches is proportional to differences between the sequences of the organisms. This diagram is based on the works of M.L. Sogin of the Woods Hole Marine Biological Laboratory.

In haptophytes, the calcium carbonate is deposited within the cells, encased in a thin organic layer, then exocytosed (released outside the cell) through the cell membrane. By contrast, most green algae deposit carbonates extracellularly, often in a mucilage. Some calcifying red algae do this as well, although in many the carbonates are incorporated into or otherwise associated with the cell walls. Cyanobacteria generally precipitate carbonates extracellularly as a natural consequence of producing a gelatinous matrix; particles are passively trapped, rather than actively deposited. These differences in deposition, and in the nature of the carbonate crystals, serve to differentiate the major groups of calcareous algae.

The distributions of most calcareous algae are limited by factors of temperature, depth, substrate, and water chemistry. Because of this, these algae provide important information for reconstructing aquatic paleoenvironments. Depth is particularly important, since this affects the amount and wavelength of light available for photosynthesis, and each major group of algae possesses a different range of pigments. As well, the morphology of deposition is often affected by current and turbidity such that conditions of the microenvironment also are recorded.

Calcareous algae were important builders of reefs and bioherms long before the rise of sponges and corals. Although reef-building algae began to wane in the Paleozoic, many modern tropical reefs are still dominated by calcareous red algae.

In addition to the calcareous algae, some algae produce fossilizable hard parts in the form of silica or resistant organic-walled spores. The latter are often termed acritarchs, and are most often produced by green algae, or by dinoflagellates, the latter of which produce a cellulosic wall within their own cell membrane.

Among the silica-depositing category are diatoms, which exist as phytoplankton both in freshwater and in marine systems. They are able to extract silica from solution, depositing it within their Golgi apparatus and sealing it within a thin organic layer to prevent redissolution. Diatoms extract silica from the surrounding water so efficiently that they can demonstrably weaken the walls of glass beakers in which they are cultured. They exist in enormous diversity and large numbers and are arguably the most important primary producers on the planet. The vast quantities of silica they incorporate into their skeletons accumulates in a "benthic ooze" as they die and settle to the ocean floor. When found exposed in terrestrial deposits, this is called diatomite and is of considerable economic importance in abrasives, paints, cosmetics, toothpaste, and filtration.

BRIAN R. SPEER

See also Skeletized Microorganisms: Algae

Further Reading

Carr, N.G., and B.A. Whitton (eds.). 1982. *The Biology of Cyanobacteria*. Botanical Monographs, 19. Oxford and Boston: Blackwell Scientific.

Fensome, R.A. 1993. *A Classification of Living and Fossil Dinoflagellates*. American Museum of Natural History, Micropaleontology Special Publication No. 7. New York: American Museum of Natural History.

Flügel, E. (ed.). 1977. *Fossil Algae: Recent Results and Developments*. Berlin and New York: Springer-Verlag.

Ginsburg, R., R. Rezak, and J.L. Wray. 1972. *Geology of Calcareous Algae: Notes for a Short Course*. Sedimenta 1. Miami, Florida: Comparative Sedimentology Laboratory, University of Miami.

Green, J.C., and B.S.C. Leadbeater (eds.). 1994. *The Haptophyte Algae*. Systematics Association, Special Vol. 51. Oxford: Clarendon; New York: Oxford University Press.

Johnson, J.H. 1961. *Limestone-Building Algae and Algal Limestones*. Golden: Colorado School of Mines.

Lipps, J.H. 1993. *Fossil Prokaryotes and Protists*. Boston: Blackwell Scientific.

Round, F.E., R.M. Crawford, and D.G. Mann. 1990. *The Diatoms: Biology and Morphology of the Genera*. Cambridge and New York: Cambridge University Press.

Tappan, H.N. 1980. *The Paleobiology of Plant Protists*. San Francisco: Freeman.

Taylor, T.N. 1981. *The Biology and Evolution of Fossil Plants*. New York: McGraw-Hill; 2nd ed., with E.L. Taylor. Englewood Cliffs, New Jersey: Prentice-Hall.

Toomey, D.F., and M.H. Nitecki (eds.). 1985. *Paleoalgology: Contemporary Research and Applications*. Berlin and New York: Springer-Verlag.

Van den Hoek, C., D.G. Mann, and H.M. Jahns. 1995. *Algae: An Introduction to Phycology*. Cambridge and New York: Cambridge University Press.

ALLOMETRY

The term "allometry" comes from Greek roots meaning "of different measure" or shape. Allometry has been broadly defined as the study of size and its consequences; more specifically, allometric changes are those that are causally related to shifts in overall or regional size among a series of organisms. The field of allometry has traditionally been associated with morphological patterning and therefore can be viewed as a component of the much broader study of scaling in biology, which encompasses size-related phenomena in ecology, life history, and behavior as well. For the paleontologist dealing with fragmentary fossils, scaling issues have almost exclusively focused on allometric patterns.

Allometry has traditionally been studied on various levels, including ontogenetic (i.e., developmental) growth series, static adult intraspecific series, static interspecific series (e.g., the typical mouse-to-elephant mammal curves or the mouse lemur–to–gorilla primate curves), and hypothesized evolutionary series. Each of these levels of analyses presents particular issues, and several levels may be examined simultaneously, as in cases where partial or full ontogenies are available for a series of species taken to represent an "evolutionary series."

Allometric investigations in the paleontological literature have assumed a central place in discussions of evolutionary trends. Well-known examples include the relatively enlarged antlers of the extinct Irish Elk, relative horn length in titanotheres, coiling and sutural complexity in ammonoids, relative facial length in horses, and relative brain size and body proportions in many other groups thought to have undergone rapid size diversification, such as the gigantism and dwarfism characteristic of many Pleistocene mammalian lineages. Allometric patterning has played a key role in interpreting the postcranial, neural, and dietary adaptions of early hominid taxa. Allometry has also frequently been used as a taxonomic and systematic tool in assessing the variation presented by fossil assemblages and sequences. For example, allometric growth has clarified the minimum number of taxa present in fossil series of lambeosaurine hadrosaurs, of *Protoceratops* and *Diademodon*, and of *Archaeopteryx*, among other extinct forms.

Any biometrical approach to the measurement of size and shape can be justified in assessing allometric phenomena of differential growth or size change. Traditionally, and particularly within the paleontological realm, bivariate analyses of linear dimensions have dominated allometric investigations. In such cases, Huxley's power function, $y = bx^k$, is utilized, relating the two variables y and x, where x is typically some measurement of regional or overall body size. The log-transformed version, or $\log_y = k \log_x + \log_b$, usually allows for more simple linear statistical analysis and accords with notions of growth through cell multiplication. In such cases, when x and y are both linear dimensions, a slope of 1.0 in log-transformed space represents "isometry" (nonallometry) or geometric similarity; a slope significantly greater then 1.0 is described as "positive allometry" and tracks the regular increase in the ratio $y{:}x$. Correspondingly, a

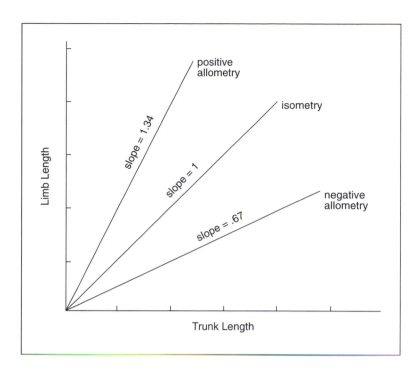

Figure 1. Allometric regression lines of limb length plotted against trunk length. The steeply rising line (slope = 1.34) shows positive allometry. In other words, larger animals (with longer trunks) will have relatively longer limbs. The shallowly rising line (slope = .67) shows negative allometry. Larger animals will have relatively shorter limbs. The intermediate isometric regression line (slope = 1) indicates that relative limb length remains constant at all body sizes. Illustration by Catherine Sexton.

slope less then 1.0 is labeled "negative allometry" and records the progressive diminution of the ratio *y:x*. Multivariate approaches to allometry often have centered on use of principal components analysis, which permits an assessment of differential growth and proportion changes through the relative contribution to character variance and covariance.

Such simple statistical description of crude linear dimensions can of course provide only a tiny window into the underlying regularity of the complex processes of cell division, growth controls, and the genetics of evolutionary size diversification. Nevertheless, recent studies of genetic mutants, transgenic animals, and other experimental models have begun to provide insights into the links between the growth factors and hormones modulating systemic and local growth processes and the morphological patterns that we measure in allometric studies. Additional advances can be expected in this area from the burgeoning field of molecular genetics.

A fundamental issue not widely appreciated is that the mere correlation (however strong) of shape change with size change provides no direct evidence of allometric influences. Needless to say, in any series of forms differing in size, all shape changes will *a priori* be correlated with such size variance. To substantiate a claim of allometry, we need to establish plausible causality through a biologically defensible "linking argument." This linkage is essentially a testable hypothesis that makes predictions that may be directly observed and experimentally verified. For example, patterning of bone diameters and cross sections hypothesized to be size-required (e.g., large animals such

as elephants with disproportionately thick leg bones) may be tested by directly assessing levels of bone strain and loading stresses in animals of varying body sizes.

There are, in fact, two somewhat distinct senses in which intergroup morphological patterning may result from regional or overall size variance. The pioneering work of Julian Huxley established the role of differential growth and size change in producing allometric trends in evolution. The term "ontogenetic scaling" is now often used to characterize those cases where intergroup adult shape differences are allometric owing to the differential extension (gigantism) or truncation (dwarfism) of common underlying patterns of allometric (differential) growth. In the case of biomechanical scaling, intergroup adult shape differences are seen to be "bioengineered" in order to maintain functional equivalence of some specified physiological parameter at different body sizes. In such cases, underlying trajectories of allometric growth for the species comprising the sample typically differ, reflecting the need for selection to alter expected proportions in order to maintain such functional equivalence over broader size ranges than those typically observed in ontogeny.

An appreciation of the distinctive allometric influences of ontogenetic and biomechanical scaling permits the application of a hierarchical approach to form differences across groups of related species. Such shape differences may be dissected into, first, those resulting from the extension/truncation of inherited patterns of allometric growth (via ontogenetic scaling); second, those resulting from selection for altered proportions to maintain functional equivalence in the new size range (via biome-

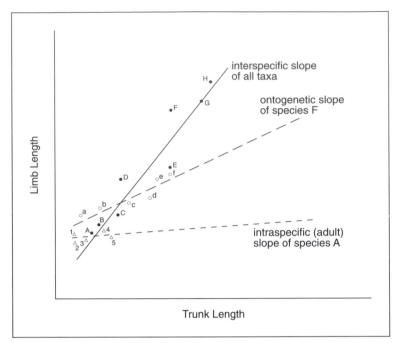

Figure 2. Three different allometric regression lines. Lines are drawn through a scatter of data points. The curve with the steepest slope shows positive allometry of limbs versus trunks in a sampling of taxa. In the sample all specimens (indicated by filled circles and denoted by capital letters) are adults. The intermediate curve shows growth allometry within a single species (E). Open circles (denoted by lowercase letters) on the left side represent very immature individuals, while the open circle farthest to the right (f) represents an adult. The very weakly rising curve is the intraspecific regression line for species A. All specimens, represented by triangles and denoted by numbers, are adults. These plots show that, along with variation in slope, y-intercept values also can also vary. In other words, even lines with identical slopes can intersect the vertical axis (y-intercept) at very different points. Provided that body size is similar, differences in y-intercept values can reflect fundamental differences in proportion that cannot be erased even with identical allometric slope coefficients. In other words, a dachshund will remain a dachshund even if it follows the same ontogenetic regression line as a poodle. Illustration by Catherine P. Sexton.

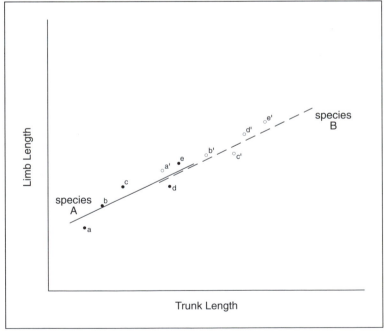

Figure 3. Ontogenetic scaling. Two different but overlapping growth trajectories that follow the same allometric slope. Species A (denoted by filled circles and lowercase letters) follows an ontogenetic slope that has as its endpoint adult e. In species B (denoted by open circles and primed letters), juvenile a' is at the same ontogenetic stage as juvenile a but is just slightly smaller than adult e. Because the slope is less than one (negative allometry), species of adult B will have relatively shorter limbs than adults of species A. Illustration by Catherine P. Sexton.

chanical scaling); and finally, those not causally related to the observed size differences (true nonallometric shape differences). This sequential approach offers both the paleontologist and neontologist a systematic methodology for recognizing allometric and nonallometric inputs into observed morphological diversity.

BRIAN T. SHEA

See also Evolutionary Trends; Growth, Development, and Evolution; Heterochrony; Phyletic Dwarfism and Gigantism

Further Reading

Cock, A.G. 1966. Genetical aspects of metrical growth and form in animals. *Quarter's Review of Biology* 41:131–90.
Gould, S.J. 1966. Allometry and size in ontogeny and phylogeny. *Biology Review of the Cambridge Philosophical Society* 41:587–640.
Huxley, J.S. 1932. *Problems of Relative Growth.* New York: Dial; London: Methuen; rev. ed., Baltimore, Maryland: Johns Hopkins University Press, 1993.
Jungers, W.L. 1985. *Size and Scaling in Primate Biology.* New York: Plenum.
Martin, R.D. 1989. Size, shape and evolution. *In* M. Keynes and G.H. Harrison (eds.), *Evolutionary Studies: A Centenary Celebration of the Life of Julian Huxley, Proceedings of the 24th Annual Symposium of the Eugenics Society of London, 1987.* London: Macmillan.
McMahon, T.A., and J.T. Bonner. 1983. *On Size and Life.* New York: Scientific American Books.

AMEGHINO, CARLOS

Argentinean, 1865–1936

The work of Carlos Ameghino, one of the main representatives of the natural sciences of Argentina, is intimately linked to that of his older brother Florentino. Their collaboration represents one of the most notable examples of complementary cooperation in the history of science. Carlos dedicated himself to matters that Florentino could not perform because of his character and, perhaps, health. Until Florentino's death in 1911, Carlos served as his personal traveling naturalist. Thus, it was Carlos' efforts and sacrifices on numerous difficult field trips that provided Florentino with most of the specimens on which he established more than one thousand fossil vertebrates (mainly mammals). Following Florentino's death, Carlos dedicated himself to organizing the immense collection he had accumulated and training a group of young disciples: Lucas Kraglievich, Alfredo Castellanos, Carlos Rusconi, and Lorenzo Parodi. By 1924, his health began to suffer and he slowly abandoned his work, leaving fewer than 30 papers.

Without doubt, Carlos Ameghino was a great scientist, methodologically rigorous and able to express and formulate original ideas. He clearly demonstrated these qualities by his observations and comments in a very abundant body of correspondence with his brother. Unfortunately, Florentino did not always accept his suggestions, and in many cases subsequent research proved that Carlos' unpublished views had been correct. For example, in one of his trips to Patagonia (1890–91), Carlos discovered fossils that he theorized belonged to a primitive monkey. Florentino disagreed and declared that it was a primate (Homunculidae) with clearly advanced features and ancestral to the Hominidae, later postulating that humans originated in South America. In 1904 Carlos found a very peculiar marsupial in Monte Hermoso, Buenos Aires Province. In a letter to Florentino, he correctly noted that it was a rodentlike marsupial related to others already known from Patagonia. Nevertheless, in the same year Florentino established a new genus of Lagomorpha, *Argyrolagus,* based on that material. Again, Carlos was correct—representatives of this order apparently only reached South America very recently.

Carlos began to help Florentino with his fieldwork in 1876, at the age of 11. His first forays were in the deposits of the Late Pleistocene of Río Luján and Arroyo Frías (between the towns of Mercedes and Luján in Buenos Aires Province). Carlos was already a traveling naturalist of the Museo de la Plata when he made his first trip to Patagonia in 1887. He crisscrossed the territory of Santa Cruz and collected more than two thousand specimens from the then poorly known Miocene "Santacrucian" deposits; Florentino classified them in 83 genera and 144 species, most of them new (Simpson 1984).

In 12 subsequent trips to Patagonia, Carlos discovered four major successive "faunas" known in the Ameghinian nomenclature as the "Notostylopense," "Astraponotense," "Pyrotheriense," and "Colpodonense." They revealed the general aspects of mammalian evolution of Patagonia during the Lower Eocene to Lower Miocene. During these trips Carlos made very important geological observations and interpretations, including maps and profiles of the main rock strata of the Cenozoic units of Patagonia. He also recognized local and regional discordances, places where ocean shorelines had expanded over the land at one time, and numerous other geological features. This information permitted Florentino to prepare a complete stratigraphic scheme for Patagonia, one that remains essentially valid. Florentino published these maps in 1906. This "Bible" of the Cenozoic geology and paleontology of Patagonia would never have been completed were it not for Carlos' fieldwork, ideas, and interpretations.

During his trips Carlos also collected material and information on other fields of study, such as malacology (study of molluscs), linguistics, archaeology, and botany, much of which was published for specialists. His scientific merits long have been recognized by the most prominent naturalists of Argentina and other countries (e.g., George Gaylord Simpson). This recognition led to his appointment in 1913 as chief of the Paleontological Section of the Museo Nacional de Historia Natural de Buenos Aires (now the Museo Argentino de Ciencias Naturales "Bernardino Rivadavia"). In 1919 he became the museum's director. His published works deal with diverse topics, such as the geology and paleontology of Patagonia, Miocene and Pliocene rodents, the fossil canids, the dental characteristics of fossil ursids, the Mio-Pliocene deposits of the Santa María Valley in northwestern Argentina, and a detailed description of *Megatherium gallardoi* (1921).

SERGIO F. VIZCAÍNO AND GUSTAVO J. SCILLATO-YANÉ

Biography

Born in Luján, Buenos Aires Province, Argentina, 18 June 1865. Self-educated. Began fieldwork near Mercedes, Buenos Aires Province, 1876; traveling naturalist of the Museo de La Plata, 1886–89; appointed chief, Paleontological Section, Museo Nacional de Historia Natural de Buenos Aires, 1913; director, Museo Nacional de Historia Natural de Buenos Aires, 1919–24; conducted 13 geological and paleontological field trips to Patagonia, 1887–1903; discovered the first remains of several mammalian taxa (later named by Florentino Ameghino): *Microbiotherium, Proborhyaena, Adinotherium, Theosodon, Eucholoeops, Hapalops, Entelops, Peltephilus, Stegotherium, Proeutatus, Stenotatus,* and *Prozaedyus* (first trip, 1887); *Homunculus* (the first fossil monkey from South America; fourth trip, 1890–91); *Orophodon, Octodontotherium* (seventh trip, 1893–94); *Notostylops* (ninth trip, 1896–98); *Caroloameghinia, Astraponotus* (eleventh trip, 1899); *Argyrolagus* (trip to Monte Hermoso, Buenos Aires Province, 1904); description of *Neotamandua magna* (the largest anteater known, 1919); *Megatherium gallardoi* (with Lucas Kraglievich, 1921). Died in Buenos Aires, 12 April 1936.

Major Publications

1913–36. *Obras completas y correspondencia científica de Florentino Ameghino,* edited by A. Torcelli. 24 vols. La Plata: Taller de Impresiones Oficiales.

1921. With L. Kraglievich. Descripción del "Megatherium Gallardoi" C. Ameghino descubierto en el Panpeano inferior de la ciudad de Buenos Aires. *Anales del Museo Nacional de Historia Natural de Buenos Aires* 31:135–56.

Further Reading

Ameghino, F. 1906. *Les formations sédimentaires du Crétacé supérieur et du Tertiaire de Patagonie, avec un parallèle entre leurs faunes mammalogiques et celles de l'ancien continent.* Anales del Museo Nacional de Historia Natural de Buenos Aires, 15, serie 3ra. Buenos Aires: Museo Nacional de Historia Natural.

Rusconi, C. 1959. Carlos Ameghino y la expedición al Chaco, 1885. *Revista del Museo de Historia Natural de Mendoza* 13:155–64.

———. 1965. Carlos Ameghino: Rasgos de su vida y su obra. *Revista del Museo de Historia Natural de Mendoza* 17:1–162.

Simpson, G.G. 1984. *Discoverers of the Lost World.* New Haven, Connecticut: Yale University Press.

AMEGHINO, FLORENTINO

Argentinean, 1853/4–1911

The tremendous energy of Florentino Ameghino was focused on three main scientific disciplines: paleontology, geology, and anthropology. He published 185 papers, including several extensive monographs. His first paper, published in Paris in 1875, was on the discovery of human and archaeological remains, presumably associated with skeletons of extinct megafauna (large animals) in Quaternary sediments of Buenos Aires Province, Argentina. In his 1880–81 volumes (the first work of Argentinian prehistory) he insisted that humans and the large extinct mammals lived at the same time in the Pampean region of Argentina. Ameghino's 1884 publication was a theoretical analysis of evolutionary processes and a classification system for vertebrates that strikingly includes concepts that fit modern phylogenetic systematics. His 1889 publication was perhaps his magnum opus. In it, he completely revised all the fossil mammals then recognized in Argentina and neighboring countries, with detailed descriptions, classifications, and phylogenies in a geographic and stratigraphic setting. In 1906 he published a geological study of the Cretaceous and Cenozoic of Patagonia based on paleontological data. The faunal successions he established in this work are still valid at present.

Florentino's studies were extraordinary in quality, quantity, and scope. After his death in 1911, his complete works and scientific correspondence were published in 24 volumes. He also expressed his creative genius in other fields related to the sciences.

He developed his own tachygraphic method, published in 1880, and his brother Carlos used it extensively. In 1884 Florentino published a paper on the problem of drought and flooding in Buenos Aires Province—his ingenious solution employed a water storage and drainage system. In his 1906 paper ("Mi Credo") and several posthumous publications, Ameghino expressed his concept of the universe within the limits of the positivism, scientificism, and materialism of the nineteenth century.

Florentino Ameghino pioneered evolutionary studies in Argentina. For this reason he was attacked by prominent traditional scientists, such as German Burmeister (then director of the Museo Público de Buenos Aires), as well as representatives of the Catholic Church. Ameghino's work shows also a high level of theorization. His concept of paleontology was very innovative for the standards of the scientific community of the day. He went beyond descriptive empiricism, considering data as sources for interpretive theories.

His theories can be divided into three groups. The first consists of the many that have been largely accepted, mainly paleontological and geological. Included in this group is Ameghino's contention that humans and large extinct fossil mammals lived at the same time in the South American Late Pleistocene-Early Holocene. The second group consists of ideas, such as the South American origin of humans and the presence of humans during the Tertiary in South America, that were rejected. He was also wrong in his belief that many of the Cenozoic stratigraphic units of Argentina were older than they actually are; this misconception conditioned his theories on the age of humans. Finally, there are theories that, so far, have not been proved or rejected, particularly those proposing a South American origin for some groups of mammals. Paradoxically, these ideas were discarded totally 30 to 40 years ago but have been resurrected by recent research and evidence.

Florentino Ameghino began the systematic collection of fossils in 1869. This first collection grew to more than 40,000 specimens and was sold at a bargain price to the La Plata Museum when Florentino was designated as secretary-subdirector in 1886. The most significant specimens include almost-complete skeletons mounted under his supervision. He also improved the museum's collections by bringing in casts of fossils of an important archaeological collection from the European classic sites, mainly French. Some he gathered for the museum; others he purchased with his own money. When Florentino abandoned the Museo de la Plata in 1888, he lost contact with that first collection and organized a second one by supporting the fieldwork of his youngest brother, Carlos, mostly in Patagonia. This collection is housed at the Museo Argentino de Ciencias Naturales "Bernardino Rivadavia." The importance of both collections is demonstrated by the fact that they are studied continuously by paleontologists from around the world.

SERGIO F. VIZCAÍNO AND GUSTAVO J. SCILLATO-YANÉ

Biography

Born either in Luján, Buenos Aires Province, 18 September 1854, or in Tessi, San Saturnino di Moneglia, Ligure, Italy, 19 September 1853. Self-educated. Teacher, Escuela Normal de Preceptores, Buenos Aires, 1869; began fieldwork near Luján and Mercedes, Buenos Aires Province, 1869; professor of zoology, Universidad Nacional de Córdoba, 1884; subdirector of the Museo de La Plata, 1886–87; académico, faculty of physical sciences and mathematics, Universidad de La Plata, 1887-88; académico and vicedecano, faculty of agronomy and veterinary science, Universidad de La Plata, 1897; professor of geology, faculty of natural sciences, Universidad de La Plata, 1906-11; director of the Museo Nacional de Historia Natural de Buenos Aires (now the Museo Argentino de Ciencias Naturales "Bernardino Rivadavia"),

1902–11. Recipient, Gold Medal, Paris Exposition, 1889; Gold Medal, Chicago Exposition, 1892. Died in La Playa, Buenos Aires Province, 6 August 1911.

Major Publications

1875. Nouveaux débris de l'homme et de son industrie mêlés d'ossements d'animaux quaternaires recueillis auprès de Mercedes. *Journal de Zoologie* 4:527.

1880–81. *La antigüedad del hombre en el Plata.* 2 vols., Buenos Aires: Igon; Paris: Masson.

1884a. *Filogenia: Principios de clasificación transformista basados sobre leyes naturales y proporciones matemáticas.* Buenos Aires: Lajonane; Paris: Tignol.

1884b. Las secas y las inundaciones en la provincia de Buenos Aires. *Boletín del Instituto Geográfico Argentino* 5:113–24.

1889. *Contribución al conocimiento de los mamíferos fósiles de la República Argentina.* Actas de la Academia Nacional de Ciencias de Córdoba, 6. Buenos Aires: Coni.

1906. *Les formations sédimentaires du crétacé supérieur et du tertiaire de Patagonie, avec un parallèle entre leurs faunes mammalogiques et celles de l'ancien continent.* Annales del Museo Nacional de Historia Natural de Buenos Aires, 15, serie 3ra. Buenos Aires: Museo Nacional de Historia Natural.

1906. Mi Credo. *Anales de la Sociedad Científica Argentina* 62:64–95.

1913–36. *Obras completas y correspondencia científica de Florentino Ameghino,* edited by A. Torcelli. 24 vols. La Plata: Taller de Impresiones Oficiales.

Further Reading

Ingenieros, J. 1919. *Las doctrinas de Ameghino: La tierra, la vida y el hombre.* Buenos Aires: Talleres gráficos Argentinos de L.J. Rosso y Cía.

Márquez Miranda, F. 1951. *Ameghino: Una vida heroica.* Colección "Los hombres representativos." Buenos Aires: Nova.

Paoli, A.R.J. 1960. Sobre el lugar de nacimiento del paleontólogo Florentino Ameghino. *Ameghiniana* 2 (2):21–28.

Simpson, G.G. 1984. *Discoverers of the Lost World.* New Haven, Connecticut: Yale University Press.

Tonni, E.P., and A.L. Cione. Florentino Ameghino: Una semblanza personal. *Museo* (Universidad Nacional de La Plata, Museo de La Plata, Facultad de Ciencias Naturales), 2 (9):35–39.

AMNIOTES

An amniote is a vertebrate that has three specialized extraembryonic (lying outside the body of the embryo) membranes known as the "amnion," "chorion," and "allantois" (Figure 1). They provide the embryo with protection, gas exchange, a water source, waste storage, and an environment conducive for development. Lizards, snakes, crocodiles, turtles, mammals, and birds are all amniotes. In contrast, the eggs of amphibians (e.g., frogs) lack these specialized membranes. Their young typically hatch at an immature or larval stage; continued development usually takes place in water.

Amniotes are the most ecologically and taxonomically diverse of all the major groups of vertebrates, with a rich fossil record over the past 320 million years. Most attempts to explain their evolutionary success invoke the reproductive innovation of the amniote egg, with its large amount of yolk and three specialized membranes. The evolution of the amniote egg supposedly broke the vertebrates' dependence upon free bodies of water in order to reproduce. As a result, amniotes were able to exploit the terrestrial (land-based) habitat more efficiently than amphibians.

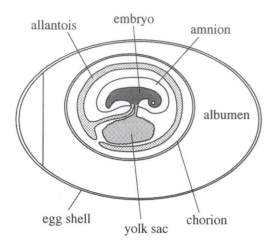

Figure 1. Schematic drawing of an amniote egg.

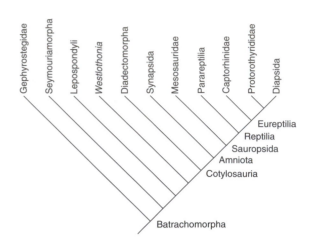

Figure 2. Phylogeny of basal amniotes and near-amniote tetrapods. Derived from Laurin and Reisz (1995, 1997); position of *Westlothonia* based upon Smithson et al. (1994).

Unlike other important evolutionary events that can be documented in fossilized skeletons, such as the emergence of land vertebrates and the origin of mammals, reproductive modes involve soft tissue structures that are highly unlikely to be preserved or leave any clear osteological (bony) correlates in the skeleton. Despite the spectacular records of dinosaur eggs in the Cretaceous, the fossil record of eggs for Paleozoic amniotes is virtually nonexistent. An egg-shaped object from the Early Permian of Texas has been reported to be the oldest vertebrate egg with a calcareous (calcium-embedded) shell, but it may be only a soft-shelled egg (Hirsch 1979).

Given the inability to determine whether or not a particular fossil tetrapod (four-legged vertebrate) laid an amniote egg, paleontologists have turned to the skeleton, searching for definitive reptilian features that could identify the oldest known reptile and, hence, pinpoint the time when the amniotic egg evolved. Consequently, the traditional approach to this evolutionary question has fused the issues of the origin of amniotes and the origin of reptiles. In modern taxonomic (classification) practice, the two issues are quite separate because the groups are not identical (Figure 2), despite the fact that each has an equally long fossil record dating back to the Carboniferous (Figure 3). Reptiles are only one group of tetrapods that is nested within the larger group of Amniota. Explicitly phylogenetic (genetic history) definitions of Amniota and Reptilia are used here, based upon the principles of phylogenetic taxonomy (Queiroz and Gauthier 1994). Clades (groups) of taxa are defined in terms of common ancestry, and taxon names are applied only to monophyletic clades (common ancestor and all of its descendants), not to those that are paraphyletic (common ancestor and some, but not all, of its descendants) or polyphyletic (common ancestor is in another taxon).

It has long been accepted that the non-amniotic condition of amphibians is primitive (a time very early in the evolutionary history of a group) relative to amniotes, which implies that amniotes most likely evolved from early amphibians. Among known groups of extinct amphibians, only the lizardlike microsaurs and anthracosaurs were considered seriously as plausibly ancestral to reptiles. Then, a long history of confusion between

microsaurs and reptiles was resolved finally (Carroll and Baird 1968), and microsaurs now are no longer considered to be ancestral to amniotes. Nonetheless, microsaurs and other lepospondyl tetrapods (Paleozoic amphibians) appear to be nested among those groups related closely to amniotes and should be included in any phylogenetic hypothesis (one relating to a group's evolutionary history) of the origin of amniotes (Laurin and Reisz 1997) (Figure 2). Anthracosaurs have been viewed traditionally as a paraphyletic group of early amphibians, more closely related to amniotes than to modern amphibians. Attention has been focused on three taxa of anthracosaurs: Gephyrostegidae, *Solenodonsaurus janenschi,* and Seymouriamorpha.

At the base of the clade Batrachomorpha (Figure 2) is Gephyrostegidae. There are three known gephyrostegids from the Early and Late Pennsylvanian of Europe and North America; the best known is *Gephyrostegus bohemicus* (Carroll 1970) from the Late Pennsylvanian (upper Westphalian) coal swamp deposits near Nýřany, Czech Republic (Figure 4A). The earliest known gephyrostegid is a virtually complete skeleton of *Bruktererpeton fiebigi* from the Early Pennsylvanian marine shales in the Ruhr area of Germany. All three gephyrostegids are small, possibly terrestrial animals with a total body length of probably less than 400 millimeters, relatively slender limb proportions, and short trunk region, in contrast to the much longer bodies of aquatic anthracosaurs such as *Archeria* and *Eogyrinus.* The diet of gephyrostegids was probably insects and other small animals. *Solenodonsaurus,* also from the coal strata of Nýřany, is a large terrestrial batrachomorph that exceeded 600 millimeters in body length (Carroll 1970). *Solenodonsaurus* is not included in the cladogram in Figure 2 because further study is needed to resolve how it is related to other batrachomorphs.

Seymouriamorphs have been considered by nearly all paleontologists to be very close to the boundary between amphibians

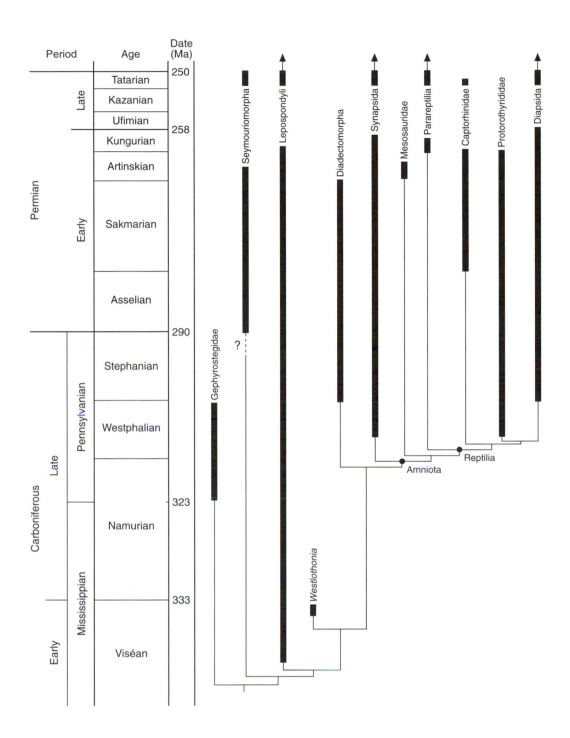

Figure 3. Amniote phylogeny and the fossil record. Symbols: *black bars,* known fossil record; *lines connecting taxa,* follows phylogeny in Figure 2; *arrows,* continuation of taxa to younger than 250 million years; *?,* a possible Late Carboniferous age for the discosauriscid seymouriamorph of Kazakhstan.

and reptiles. The best-known seymouriamorph is *Seymouria* (Figure 4B), found primarily in the Early Permian of the southwestern United States. Additional records are in the Early Permian of Prince Edward Island in eastern Canada and the first discovery outside of North America in the Early Permian of the Thuringian Forest, central Germany. Viewed alternatively as an anthracosau-

rian amphibian or a primitive reptile, *Seymouria* was the centerpiece of speculations on the origin of amniotes until the focus shifted to the Pennsylvanian gephyrostegids and *Solenodonsaurus.* However, more recent work has reaffirmed the phylogenetic importance of seymouriamorphs and shown that they are related more closely to amniotes than the gephyrostegids (Laurin and

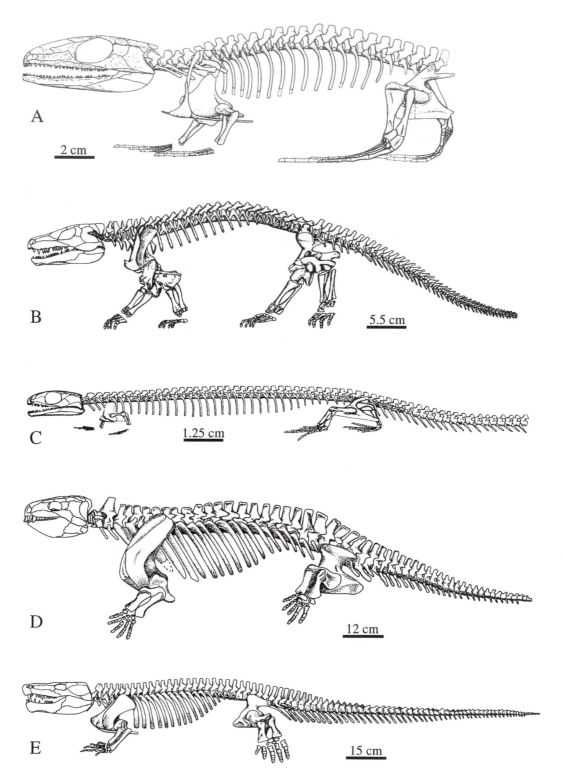

Figure 4. Near-amniote tetrapods. *A, Gephyrostegus bohemicus; B, Seymouria baylorensis; C, Westlothonia lizziae; D, Diadectes tenui-tectes; E, Limnoscelis paludis.* From: *A,* Carroll (1970); drawings *B, D,* and *E,* modified from VERTEBRATE PALEONTOLOGY AND EVOLU-TION by Robert L. Carroll, ©1988 by W.W. Freeman and Company, Used with permission; *C,* from Smithson et al. (1994), reproduced by permission of the Royal Society of Edinburgh and T.R. Smithson, R.L. Carroll, A.L. Panchen, and S.M. Andrews.

Reisz 1997). *Seymouria* is a robust ("hefty"), terrestrial tetrapod that averaged 500 centimeters in body length. It most likely fed upon small vertebrates and insects. All other seymouriamorphs are aquatic and include the kotlassiids from the Late Permian of east-ern Europe and a number of larval and juvenile individuals collec-tively referred to as discosauriscids, found in the Late

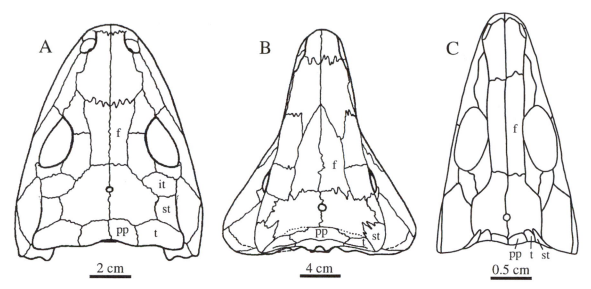

Figure 5. Dorsal view of skulls of two near-amniote tetrapods and an early reptile. *A,* seymouriamorph *Seymouria; B,* diadectomorph *Limnoscelis; C,* protorothyridid reptile *Paleothyris.* Key: *f,* frontal; *pp,* postparietal; *st,* supratemporal; *t,* tabular. Drawings *A* and *B,* modified from Laurin and Reisz (1995); drawing *C,* modified from VERTEBRATE PALEONTOLOGY AND EVOLUTION by Robert L. Carroll, ©1988 by W.W. Freeman and Company, Used with permission.

Carboniferous or Early Permian of Kazakhstan of the former USSR and the Early Permian of the Czech Republic, Germany, and China. Ontogenetic series of discosauriscids include larval forms (intermediate forms between egg and adult form, such as the tadpole) with external gills and lateral-line organs for detection of other animals in water, evidence that demonstrated convincingly the non-amniote nature of seymouriamorphs.

One of the most important recent discoveries of a near-amniote tetrapod is *Westlothonia lizziae* from the Viséan (Late Mississippian) East Kirkton Quarry near Bathgate, Scotland (Figure 4C). Announced originally as the oldest known reptile, a reexamination refuted the reported amniote features and demonstrated that this animal is more likely the sister taxon (closest related group) of the clade of amniotes and diadectomorphs (Smithson et al. 1994). It should be noted, however, that the single known specimen of *Westlothonia* has a skull that is very poorly preserved, and many features are difficult to interpret. (Discovery of additional specimens may alter the phylogenetic hypothesis in Figure 2.) *Westlothonia* has a body length of approximately 300 millimeters, with an unusually elongate trunk region and shortened forelimb that is shorter than the hind limb, in comparison to seymouriamorphs, gephyrostegids, and *Solenodonsaurus.* The small body size, elongate trunk, and shortened forelimbs of *Westlothonia* may be an adaptation for moving close to the ground in dense vegetation and feeding on small animals.

The next major clade is Cotylosauria defined as the most recent common ancestor of diadectomorphs and amniotes and all of its descendants. This definition replaces the historical usage of cotylosaurs as the earliest reptiles, a paraphyletic assemblage of near-amniote tetrapods and primitive reptiles from which all other reptiles were derived. Cotylosaurs lack the "intertemporal bone"—one of a trio of bones (intertemporal, supratemporal, and tabular) that form the edge of the side of the skull table in primitive tetrapods (Figure 5A). In addition, the postparietals, which form the rear of the skull table in primitive tetrapods, shifts onto the occiput (back of the skull) in cotylosaurs (Figures 5B, 5C).

Once thought to be early reptiles but now interpreted as the sister taxon to amniotes, Diadectomorpha is crucial for deciphering the origin of amniotes. Three groups comprise Diadectomorpha: Diadectidae, Tseajaiidae, and Limnoscelidae. Diadectids appeared first in the Late Pennsylvanian of North America and extended their range into Europe during the Early Permian. The most studied diadectid is *Diadectes,* an exceptionally large early tetrapod from the Late Pennsylvanian and Early Permian of the southwestern United States. This animal reached nearly two meters in body length (Figure 4D). The skull is highly specialized, with transversely (side to side) expanded tricuspid cheek teeth and chisel-like anterior (front) teeth.

Bones of the skull roof of *Diadectes* are thick and porous with a series of deep, U-shaped grooves that obscure sutures (places where bones abut, then grow together). This condition makes it difficult to determine how bones joined. As a result, scholars have produced numerous, often quite variant, reconstructions of the skull roof and, consequently, led to differing interpretations of *Diadectes* as an amphibian or reptile. Both the dentition (teeth) and barrel-shaped body suggest that *Diadectes* was a herbivore that ingested high fiber plants and probably employed endosymbionts (bacteria that live within the body) in the digestive tract to aid digestion. Along with edaphosaurid synapsids, the Late Carboniferous diadectids provide the earliest evidence for herbivory among terrestrial vertebrates.

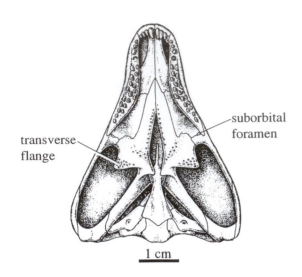

Figure 6. Ventral view of skull of captorhinid reptile. Modified from VERTEBRATE PALEONTOLOGY AND EVOLUTION by Robert L. Carroll, ©1988 by W.W. Freeman and Company, Used with permission.

Tseajaiids are known only from the single sample fossil of the species *Tseajaia campi* from the Late Pennsylvanian–Early Permian of New Mexico and the Early Permian of Utah. Limnoscelids, characterized best by *Limnoscelis paludis* from the Late Pennsylvanian of New Mexico and Colorado, have long been viewed as the most primitive early reptiles and more recently as primitive diadectomorphs. *Limnoscelis* is nearly two meters in

length (Figure 4E), with a broad, triangular skull; enlarged anterior teeth on the upper and lower jaws; and robust limbs and girdles. It was most likely a carnivore, although its level of terrestriality is debatable.

"Amniota" is defined as the most recent common ancestor of Synapsida (mammals and their extinct relatives), Testudines (turtles), Diapsida (lizards, snakes, birds, crocodiles, and their extinct relatives such as dinosaurs and pterosaurs), and all of its descendants. One consequence of this precise definition of Amniota is that all taxa that fall within it have the amniotic condition, even if scholars cannot demonstrate it in the fossil record. The skull of basal amniotes retains many of the same set of bones as in near-amniote tetrapods, but with several modifications. The frontal bones contact the orbit (eye sockets) in basal amniotes (Figure 5C) whereas in seymouriamorphs and diadectomorphs they are excluded (Figures 5A, 5B). The posterior margin of the skull of basal amniotes lacks an otic (ear) notch for a tympanic membrane. An extension of the "pterygoid" bone of the palate (known as the "transverse flange") is present and covered with teeth (Figure 6), and the skull lacks the fanglike teeth on the palate and infolding of the teeth found in most near-amniote tetrapods. Basal amniotes have three ossifications in the pectoral girdle and a single ossification that forms the astragalus (talus) bone in the ankle.

Traditionally, amniotes have been classified into groups according to the pattern of temporal openings in the dermal skull behind the orbit (Figure 7). The most primitive group was assumed to be the one that lacked any temporal openings, a pattern known as "anapsid" (Figure 7A) and presumably inherited from their anthracosaurian ancestors. This group is Anapsida; turtles are the sole extant (present-day) representatives. The

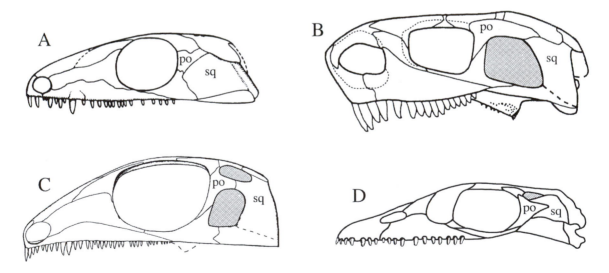

Figure 7. Temporal fenestration of early amniotes. *A*, anapsid *Paleothyris*; *B*, synapsid *Cotylorhynchus*; *C*, diapsid *Petrolacosaurus*; *D*, euryapsid nothosaur *Neusticosaurus*. Identification of a fenestra as upper or lower is determined in relation to contact between postorbital and squamosal. Key: *po*, postorbital; *sq*, squamosal. Skulls are not drawn to scale. Symbols: *stippling*, temporal fenestrae. From: drawings *A*, *C*, and *D*, modified from VERTEBRATE PALEONTOLOGY AND EVOLUTION by Robert L. Carroll, ©1988 by W.W. Freeman and Company, Used with permission; *B*, modified from Laurin and Reisz (1995), with kind permission of Elsevier Science - NL, Sara Burgerhartstraat 25, 1055 KV Amsterdam, The Netherlands.

remaining amniotes have either one or two temporal openings. Synapsids have a single temporal opening, that is set low on the skull and bordered dorsally by contact between the postorbital and squamosal (Figure 7B). Diapsids have a pair of temporal openings that are separated by the postorbital and squamosal (Figure 7C).

A fourth group known as Euryapsida, which supposedly evolved independently from anapsids, has a single temporal opening with its lower border formed by the postorbital (to the rear of the eye) and squamosal (cheek) bones (Figure 7D), similar to the upper temporal opening in diapsids. Euryapsids are all extinct marine reptiles and include the ichthyosaurs (marine reptiles), placodonts (turtlelike animals), plesiosaurs (long-necked animals), and nothosaurs (another long-necked group). The disparate morphologies of euryapsids have continually raised questions of this group's validity, and several independent studies have demonstrated that euryapsids are actually modified diapsids.

The traditional scheme of classification based upon temporal fenestration (openings) has been superseded by one based upon explicit phylogenetic statements. It now is recognized that rather than a series of independent originations of amniote groups from anapsids, there was an initial dichotomy with the appearance of Synapsida and Sauropsida (reptiles and their extinct relatives) (Figure 2). The evidence for this dichotomy appears within the basal Westphalian (Carboniferous) deposits at the sites of Joggins and Florence in Nova Scotia, Canada. Joggins is the more famous of these sites. Fossil reptiles were first found there in 1852 by Sir Charles Lyell and the Canadian geologist and paleontologist Sir William Dawson, during a field trip along the cliffs by the Bay of Fundy. A unique preservational environment is revealed at these sites, in which upright stumps of large, treelike "lycopods" occasionally contain the disarticulated (scattered) skeletons of small vertebrates.

Lycopods, giant relatives of the more familiar club mosses, reached several meters in height. Forests of lycopods, gymnosperms, and ferns dominated lowland wetlands during the Late Carboniferous and formed classic coal swamps and flood plain environments of that period. Episodic flooding of the land from nearby rivers would bury the bases of the lycopods, leading to their eventual death. A stump would remain after the trunk fell, and the inner pith would rot to produce a deep hollow. These hollows acted as natural traps for small terrestrial amphibians and reptiles or as refuges where they later died. Within these stumps the oldest known amniotes, the synapsid *Protoclepsydrops haplous* and the protorothyridid *Hylonomus lyelli,* have been discovered. Both amniotes at the lycopod stump assemblages are small, lizardlike in general morphology, and averaged 200 millimeters from the tip of the snout to the base of the tail.

From their initial appearance in the Westphalian of Nova Scotia, synapsids radiated (diversified and spread geographically) extensively into several groups that adapted to carnivorous, insectivorous, and herbivorous habits. The first major assemblage is the paraphyletic pelycosaurs, known primarily from the Late Pennsylvanian to the Late Permian of North America, followed by the therapsids in the richly fossiliferous (fossil-laden) Late Permian

and Triassic deposits of Russia and South Africa. Mammals are a derived (specialized) group of therapsids.

Sauropsids have a new foramen (small opening) in the palate beneath the orbit; this opening, known as the suborbital foramen, provides a channel for nerves and blood vessels (Figure 6). The most basal group of sauropsids is Mesosauridae from the Early Permian of South America and South Africa. Mesosaurs are the oldest known group of marine amniotes and have a highly derived skeleton indicative of obligatory aquatic locomotion. Up to one meter in body length, mesosaurs have a greatly elongate skull and an array of delicate, needlelike teeth held at different angles along the jaw for filtering small crustaceans from the water (Figure 8). Propulsion was provided by the large, laterally compressed (flattened from side to side) tail. Trunk ribs are enlarged and banana-shaped, a condition known as "pachyostosis"; this condition may be an adaptation to increase the weight of the animal to allow it to maintain a specific depth in the water with minimal muscular effort. The presence of mesosaurids only in South America and South Africa implies that the two southern continents had fit together like pieces of a gigantic jigsaw puzzle during the Paleozoic. Mesosaurids inhabited a narrow sea that separated these two continents. Alfred Wegner viewed the restricted geographic distribution of this unique reptile as one of the strongest pieces of paleontologic evidence in favor of the theory of continental drift.

The next major group above mesosaurs is "Reptilia," defined as the common ancestor of turtles (and other parareptiles) and diapsids and all of its descendants. Reptiles have a modified occiput (back of the skull), with a narrow supraoccipital plate, large post-temporal fenestrae, and reduction of the tabular to a small bone restricted to the occiput (Figure 5C).

A second dichotomy occurs at the base of Reptilia with the appearance of Parareptilia and Eureptilia. Parareptilia is a morphologically heterogeneous group (one with mixed body shapes and structures) that includes the extinct small, insectivorous millerettids and procolophonids and the large herbivorous pareiasaurs, which reached 2.5 meters in body length. Parareptiles have gained renewed importance due to a growing consensus that turtles may be extant parareptiles (Laurin and Reisz 1995), although a recent paper (Rieppel and deBraga 1996) suggested that turtles may be yet another group of modified diapsids. Clearly, the origin of turtles is far from resolved.

Eureptilia (true reptiles) includes diapsids and all other amniotes more closely related to them than to parareptiles. The supratemporal of eureptiles is much smaller than in other tetrapods, forming part of the posterolateral (rear, side) corner of the skull table (Figure 5C). Among primitive eureptiles, the protorothyridids and captorhinids (two early lizardlike reptiles) have attracted considerable attention because they predated all other fossil reptiles. The oldest known reptiles are components of the lycopod tree stump fauna from the Westphalian of Nova Scotia. They are the protorothyridids *Hylonomus* from Joggins (Figure 9A) and the slightly younger *Paleothyris* from Florence. Their small size, morphological similarity to extant iguanid lizards and to the New Zealand tuatara *Sphenodon,* and great stratigraphic age have granted protorothyridids a key position in hypotheses of amniote origins.

Figure 8. Mesosaurid *Stereosternum tumidum* from the Irati Formation (Early Permian), Paraná Basin, Brazil. Photo courtesy of Drs. Robert Reisz and Sean Modesto.

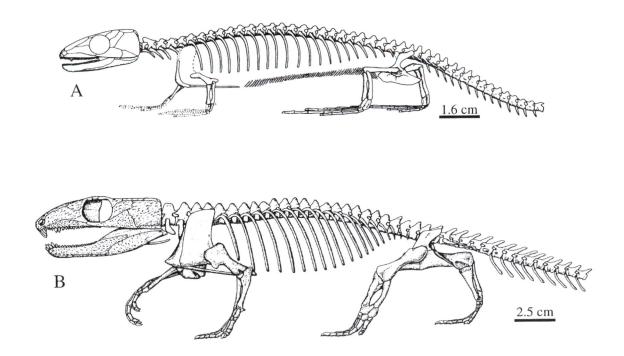

Figure 9. Primitive eureptiles. *A,* protorothyridid *Hylonomus lyelli; B,* Early Permian captorhinid *Captorhinus laticeps* from Texas and Oklahoma. From VERTEBRATE PALEONTOLOGY AND EVOLUTION by Robert L. Carroll, ©1988 by W.W. Freeman and Company, Used with permission.

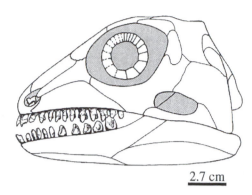

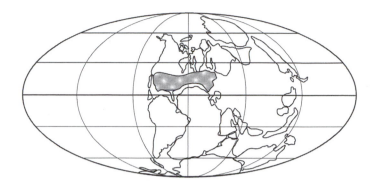

Figure 10. Skull of *Bolosaurus striatus*. Modified from VERTEBRATE PALEONTOLOGY AND EVOLUTION by Robert L. Carroll, ©1988 by W.W. Freeman and Company, Used with permission.

Figure 12. Known distribution of fossil tetrapods during the Westphalian (Late Carboniferous). Symbol: *stippling,* fossil tetrapods. From: map redrawn, Scotese (1994); range of fossil tetrapods, Milner (1993).

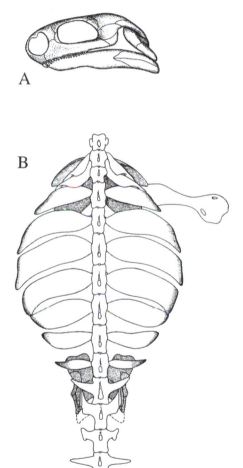

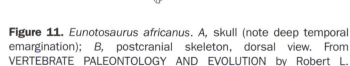

Figure 11. *Eunotosaurus africanus. A,* skull (note deep temporal emargination); *B,* postcranial skeleton, dorsal view. From VERTEBRATE PALEONTOLOGY AND EVOLUTION by Robert L. Carroll, ©1988 by W.W. Freeman and Company, Used with permission.

However, since protorothyridids are more closely related to diapsids, paradoxically it is the large (three-meter long) herbivorous diadectomorphs, primitive synapsids, and the aquatic mesosaurs that reveal more about the common ancestor of amniotes. Protorothyridids are also found in the Late Carboniferous of Illinois, Ohio, and the Czech Republic and the Early Permian of Texas and West Virginia. A probable Early Permian protorothyridid has been found at the same German site that yielded *Seymouria.* Captorhinids appear first in the Early Permian of Texas and Oklahoma and then spread across North America to achieve a cosmopolitan distribution in the Late Permian, with records in North America, Russia, India, and northern and southern Africa. Basal captorhinids have similar body sizes to those of the contemporaneous protorothyridids but clearly are differentiated by their triangular skull with wider temple region, sharply downturned snout, and more robust skeletal system in the limbs (Figure 9B). There was an increase in body size in many derived captorhinids, and multiple rows of teeth on the upper and lower jaws evolved in several large and small taxa.

Diapsida extends from the oldest and most primitive known member *Petrolacosaurus kansensis* (Stephanian; Late Pennsylvanian) from Garnett, Kansas, to the present. Most basal diapsids are small, terrestrial forms with elongate necks and slender bodies not markedly different from protorothyridids. Conventional opinion was that diapsids did not diversify until the Late Permian, but a rare aquatically adapted diapsid with a tall, laterally compressed tail from the Hamilton Quarry (Late Pennsylvanian) in Kansas indicates that diapsids diversified in the Late Carboniferous (deBraga and Reisz 1995).

In addition to those groups mentioned above, other early amniotes known from the Permian have unknown phylogenetic relationships. *Bolosaurus striatus* from the Early Permian of Texas, New Mexico, and Oklahoma (Figure 10), and related taxa from the Late Permian of Russia have highly specialized teeth, consisting of procumbent (forward angled), chisel-shaped front teeth and teeth farther back that are bulbous, with a single major cusp. Although the front teeth are similar to those of *Diadectes* and may have been used to break off vegetation, it is likely that the diet of *Bolosaurus* included insects. *Bolosaurus* has a small lower temporal fenestra in the same position as that of synapsids but otherwise shares no derived features with this group. Another unique Permian amniote is *Eunotosaurus africanus* from the Late Permian of South Africa (Figure 11). At one time thought to be related to turtles due to a superficial similarity between its expanded ribs and the carapace (shell) of turtles, *Eunotosaurus* has been argued recently to be either an aberrant basal synapsid or parareptile.

The combination of the phylogenetic relationships of known early amniotes and near-amniote tetrapods and their fossil records suggests that Amniota's common ancestor existed no later than the Westphalian and perhaps even earlier, in the Carboniferous (Figure 3). Unfortunately, all known tetrapods of the Westphalian are derived from localities restricted to a narrow band along the equator, from the southwestern United States to the Czech Republic (Figure 12). In addition to their geographic restriction, the majority of known Westphalian localities preserve predominantly aquatic faunas from coal swamp and flood plain environments. Faunas of other environments, including terrestrial ones, are virtually unknown for the Westphalian. The narrow environmental and geographic ranges for this critical period in the evolutionary history of vertebrates continues to confound the search for early amniotes.

DAVID W. DILKES

See also Aquatic Reptiles; Egg, Amniote; Sauropsids; Synapsids; Tetrapods: Near-Amniote Tetrapods

Works Cited

Carroll, R.L. 1970. The ancestry of reptiles. *Philosophical Transactions of the Royal Society of London,* ser. B, 257:267–308.
———. 1988. *Vertebrate Paleontology and Evolution.* New York: Freeman.
Carroll, R.L., and D. Baird. 1968. *The Carboniferous Amphibian* Tuditanus [Eosauravus] *and the Distinction between Microsaurs and Reptiles.* American Museum Novitates, 2337. New York: American Museum of Natural History.
deBraga, M., and R.R. Reisz. 1995. A new diapsid reptile from the uppermost Carboniferous (Stephanian) of Kansas. *Palaeontology* 38:199–212.
Hirsch, K.F. 1979. The oldest vertebrate egg? *Journal of Paleontology* 53:1068–84.
Laurin, M., and R.R. Reisz. 1995. A reevaluation of early amniote phylogeny. *Zoological Journal of the Linnean Society* 113:165–223.
———. 1997. A new perspective on tetrapod phylogeny. *In* K.L.M. Martin and S.S. Sumida (eds.), *Amniote Origins.* San Diego, California: Academic Press.
Milner, A.R. 1993. Biogeography of Palaeozoic tetrapods. *In* J.A. Long (ed.), *Palaeozoic Vertebrate Biostratigraphy and Biogeography.* London: Belhaven; Baltimore, Maryland: Johns Hopkins University Press, 1994.
Queiroz, K.D., and J. Gauthier. 1994. Toward a phylogenetic system of biological nomenclature. *Trends in Ecology and Evolution* 9:27–31.
Rieppel, O., and M. deBraga. 1996. Turtles as diapsid reptiles. *Nature* 384:453–55.
Scotese, C.R. 1994. Late Carboniferous paleogeographic map. *In* G.D. Klein (ed.), *Pangea: Paleoclimate, Tectonics, and Sedimentation during Accretion, Zenith, and Breakup of a Supercontinent.* Geological Society of America Special Paper 288. Boulder, Colorado: Geological Society of America.
Smithson, T.R., R.L. Carroll, A.L. Panchen, and S.M. Andrews. 1994. *Westlothiana lizziae* from the Viséan of East Kirkton, West Lothian, Scotland, and the amniote stem. *Transactions of the Royal Society of Edinburgh, Earth Sciences* 84:383–412.

Further Reading

Case, G.R. 1982. *A Pictorial Guide to Fossils.* New York: Van Nostrand Reinhold.
Cooper Jr., S.F. 1996. Origins: The backbone of evolution. *Natural History* 105 (6):30–43.
DiMichele, W.A., and R.W. Hook. 1992. Paleozoic terrestrial ecosystems. *In* A.K. Behrensmeyer, J.D. Damuth, W.A. DiMichele, R. Potts, H.-D. Sues, and S.L. Wing (eds.), *Terrestrial Ecosystems through Time: Evolutionary Paleoecology of Terrestrial Plants and Animals.* Chicago: University of Chicago Press.
Ferguson, L. 1988. *The Fossil Cliffs of Joggins.* Halifax: Nova Scotia Museum.
Reisz, R.R. 1997. The origin and early evolutionary history of amniotes. *Trends in Ecology and Evolution* 12:218–22.

ANAPSIDS

See Sauropsids

ANDREWS, ROY CHAPMAN

American, 1884–1960

Roy Chapman Andrews spent most of his working life associated with the American Museum of Natural History in New York. He gained fame in paleontological circles as the organizer and leader of the American Museum's Central Asiatic Expeditions, which made phenomenal fossil discoveries in the Gobi Desert of Mongolia-China during the 1920s and 1930s.

Born in Beloit, Wisconsin, Andrews was educated at Beloit College. He began work at the American Museum of Natural History, New York, collecting marine mammals in expeditions to Alaska, Indonesia, and Korea between 1908 and 1913. In 1912, Andrews first went to China on behalf of the American Museum of Natural History to collect recent mammals for its Department of Mammalogy. The expedition was very successful, and in 1915 Andrews proposed a series of expeditions to China to explore its zoology over ten years. In 1916–17, the First Asiatic Expedition recovered large numbers of animals in Yunnan and Tibet for the American Museum's collection.

After a stint in the U.S. military during World War I, Andrews returned to Asia in 1919 for the Second Asiatic Expedition, which went to Mongolia. However, earlier that year, in January 1919, Andrews met the Swedish geologist J. Gunnar Andersson in Beijing and became aware of Andersson's success in collecting fossil mammals in eastern and northern China. At the meeting, Andrews offered to fund Andersson's collecting efforts if the fossils were turned over to the American Museum of Natural History. Andersson refused, so early in 1920 Andrews approached Henry Fairfield Osborn (1857–1935), world-renowned vertebrate paleontologist and director of the American Museum of Natural History, with plans for a new expedition, this one to northern China and Mongolia, to collect fossil mammals. Andrews proposed to uncover the fossil evidence to support Osborn's (and other paleontologists') belief that the origin of mammals and of humankind lay in Asia. Osborn backed the idea, and Andrews assembled a team of natural scientists—such as geologists, paleontologists, cartographers, mammalogists, botanists, and entomologists—to explore vast areas aided by a new invention—gasoline-powered vehicles.

To that end, Andrews raised more than $500,000 from some 600 individuals and institutions and secured a fleet of Dodge automobiles. Five Central Asiatic expeditions followed (in 1922, 1923, 1925, 1928, and 1930), headquartered in Beijing and mostly focused on what is now Mongolia, although some collecting took place in China as well. Andrews overcame tremendous logistical difficulties to pull off the five expeditions amid the political and economic chaos of China during the 1920s and 1930s.

Ironically, one of the original scientific purposes of the expeditions was not fulfilled—Andrews found no fossils shedding light on human ancestry. Nevertheless, some of the fossils he did discover—especially the dinosaur eggs found at Flaming Cliffs locality in Mongolia—are legendary. The effect of the Central Asiatic Expeditions on vertebrate paleontology is inestimable. Not only did the scientific discoveries—volumes of technical literature have been written about them—provide the first look at many important facets of the Asian fossil record, but the legendary expeditions also inspired many youngsters to pursue careers in vertebrate paleontology.

After the expeditions ended, Andrews became director of the American Museum of Natural History, but he resigned in 1941. Evidently his talents for organizing expeditions to the remote and dangerous regions of Asia did not guarantee success as a museum administrator. Andrews spent the remaining years of his life largely writing about paleontology and his life and adventures. He died in Carmel, California, in 1960.

SPENCER G. LUCAS

Biography

Born in Beloit, Wisconsin, 26 January 1884. Received B.A., Beloit College, 1906; M.A., Columbia University, 1913. Employed by American Museum of Natural History, 1908–41 (director, 1935–41); naturalist aboard U.S.S. *Albatross,* Netherlands East Indies, 1909–10; explored northern Korea, 1911–12; member, Border Alaska Expedition, 1913; led several Asiatic Expeditions, 1916–17, 1919, 1922, 1923, 1925, 1928, 1930. Received numerous awards, including honorary Sc.D., Brown University, 1926; honorary Sc.D., Beloit College, 1928; Elisha Kent Kane Gold Medal, Philadelphia Geographic Society, 1929; Hubbard Gold Medal, National Geographic Society, 1931; Explorers' Club Medal, 1932; Charles P. Daly Gold Medal, American Geographic Society; Vega Gold Medal, Royal Swedish Anthropological and Geographic Society, 1937; Loczy Medal, Hungarian Geographic Society, 1937; Silver Buffalo Award, National Council, Boy Scouts of America, 1952. Member of numerous scholarly and professional associations, including American Association for the Advancement of Science; American Geographic Society; American Philosophical Society; National Geographic Society; New York Academy of Sciences; Phi Beta Kappa. Best known as leader of Central Asiatic Expeditions, 1920s, 1930s; discovered many famous fossils, most notably dinosaur eggs. Died in Carmel, California, 11 March 1960.

Major Publications

1926. *On the Trail of Ancient Man.* New York: Garden City; London: Putnam, 1927.
1929. *Ends of the Earth.* New York and London: Putnam.
1932. With W. Grange, C.H. Pope, and N.C. Nelson. *The New Conquest of Central Asia.* New York: American Museum of Natural History.
1940. *This Amazing Planet.* New York: Putnam.
1943. *Under a Lucky Star.* New York: Viking.
1953. *All about Dinosaurs.* New York: Random House.
1956. *All about Strange Beasts of the Past.* New York: Random House.
1959. *In the Days of the Dinosaurs.* New York: Random House.

Further Reading

Mateer, N.J., and S.G. Lucas. 1985. Swedish vertebrate palaeontology in China: A history of the Lagrelius Collection. *Bulletin of the Geological Institutions of the University of Uppsala,* new series, 11:1–24.
Preston, D.J. 1987. A daring gamble in the Gobi Desert took the jackpot. *Smithsonian* 18 (9):94–105.
———. 1986. *Dinosaurs in the Attic.* New York: Ballantine.

ANGIOSPERMS

Angiosperms, also known as flowering plants, are the most familiar plant group. They have dominated most terrestrial ecosystems since the Late Cretaceous, except for conifer forests, and form almost the entire basis of human agriculture. Consisting of some 250,000 species, angiosperms are assigned to several hundred families, which vary in growth habit from some of the largest trees to lianas (vines), epiphytes (plants that grow on other plants), herbs (such as grasses), parasites, insectivorous plants, and aquatics (including minute, almost algalike duckweeds). In climate, flowering plants range from the tropical rainforest to extreme deserts and tundras.

In phylogenetic terms, angiosperms are a subgroup of seed plants. They share with other seed plants (traditionally termed "gymnosperms") such advances as the seed and its associated life cycle, with the haploid male and female gametophytes packaged inside the pollen grains and ovules (future seeds), respectively, plus vegetative features such as axillary branching (from a bud above the point of attachment of the leaf) and secondary growth (producing wood, except where this was lost in herbaceous groups, an event that occurred many times in angiosperm evolution). However, angiosperms show several major advances over other seed plants. Such shared advances argue that angiosperms are a monophyletic group (a natural group, i.e., one that has arisen from a single common ancestor), and this has been confirmed by all analyses based on both morphological (shape and structure) and molecular data.

Reproductive advances of angiosperms include the flower—a special reproductive shoot typically bearing a perianth of sepals and petals, then pollen-producing stamens, then carpels, which contain the ovules. Some of these parts may be lost or fused to one another. The flower is basically a device for attracting insects for cross-pollination; in contrast, most other seed plants are wind-pollinated. However, there are many angiosperms that have reverted to wind pollination, a change usually associated with loss of parts. Examples of this phenomenon include grasses and Amentiferae, the main deciduous trees of the temperate zone, such as oaks, birches, and walnuts.

The carpel, illustrated by a pea pod, differs from the female structures of other seed plants in completely enclosing the ovules (angiospermy). As a result, the pollen germinates on a special receptive surface, the stigma, rather than in a pollen chamber of the ovule itself. At maturity, a carpel or several fused carpels form the fruit, which often is specialized for dispersal. The "stamen" is also distinctive. It has four microsporangia (pollen sacs), in two pairs.

Inside the pollen grain and ovule, the male gametophyte is reduced to three nuclei, the female gametophyte to eight (the embryo sac). As in other seed plants, one of the two sperm produced by the male gametophyte fuses with the egg. However, angiosperms are unique in that the second sperm fuses with two other nuclei of the female gametophyte (double fertilization) to form the triploid endosperm. It is usually the main nourishing tissue of the seed. These advances result in a reproductive cycle that is more efficient than other seed plants. Paleobotanists associate this efficiency with origin under unstable environmental conditions that favor rapid reproduction.

Among vegetative organs, the leaves, although highly varied in form and the pattern of major veins, are advanced over those of most other seed plants—there are several orders or size classes of veins, which usually branch out to form a reticulate (netlike) pattern. In most cases, the wood contains vessels for more efficient water conduction, consisting of a row of cells (vessel members) with perforations at their ends, rather than tracheids. The latter, which are the basic conducting cells of other vascular plants, have pits with a primary cell wall. To get from one tracheid to the next, water must pass through the pits. The combination of broad, reticulate-veined leaves and vessels may have contributed to the unequaled success and diversity of angiosperms in the tropics, in the face of conditions of high evaporation and potential overheating. Before the rise of angiosperms in the Mid-Cretaceous, the tropics were dominated by conifers with no vessels and much smaller leaves (Cheirolepidiaceae, Araucariaceae).

Relationships between angiosperms and other seed plants have long been controversial and still are far from resolved. Among living groups, angiosperms have often been linked with the small order Gnetales. Members of this group resemble angiosperms in having vessels in the wood and (in the genus *Gnetum*) leaves with reticulate venation (vein pattern), and radiated in the tropics at the same time as angiosperms. Older arguments for this relationship were based on now-obsolete comparisons between the strobili (cones) of Gnetales, which consist of simple, unisexual, flowerlike units, and the superficially similar catkins of Amentiferae. Botanists now know from fossil and molecular evidence that these catkins are derived within angiosperms. However, the two groups still share many cryptic characters. For example, Gnetales have part of the process of double fertilization: both sperm fuse with nuclei in the female gametophyte, but the second fusion forms an extra zygote rather than triploid endosperm.

Angiosperms also have been linked with Mesozoic Bennettitales (Cycadeoidales), which had large, often bisexual flowerlike structures. However, Bennettitales differed in having single ovules packed among protective scales, suggesting that if the two groups are related, they are each specialized in their own way. The Mesozoic "seed fern" *Caytonia* had female structures consisting of a rachis (axis) with two rows of "cupules" containing several ovules. These cupules have been homologized with angiosperm ovules, which have a second integument that might be derived from the cupule wall. The carpel might be derived from the rachis. The Permian glossopterids of Gondwana (one of the two large continental landmasses that gave rise to today's southern continents) had a simple fertile leaf (bract) bearing one or more "cupules" (sporophylls), which have also been homologized with bitegmic ovules. Phylogenetic analyses of living and fossil seed plants based on morphology (shape and structure) indicate that angiosperms,

Gnetales, and Bennettitales (termed "anthophytes") are all related. Some link anthophytes with glossopterids and *Caytonia,* but others link them with conifers. Figure 1 shows a tree found in one recent analysis, which moved *Caytonia* onto the line to angiosperms; this implies that *Caytonia* cupules and bitegmic ovules were derived from the cupules of glossopterids; the carpel derived from the associated leaf. Two analyses indicate that angiosperms are nested within (derived from) Gnetales, but this conflicts with strong molecular evidence that both taxa are monophyletic. In other respects, molecular analyses have given inconsis-

tent indications on relationships between angiosperms and other living groups.

Systematics of angiosperms has been based largely on the living members, including recent phylogenetic analyses of both morphological and molecular data. The relative lack of paleobotanical input may be less detrimental here than, for example, in seed plants as a whole, since angiosperms include more surviving links between subgroups and fewer major extinct lineages, presumably because of their relatively young age. Traditionally, angiosperms are divided into monocotyledons (monocots) and

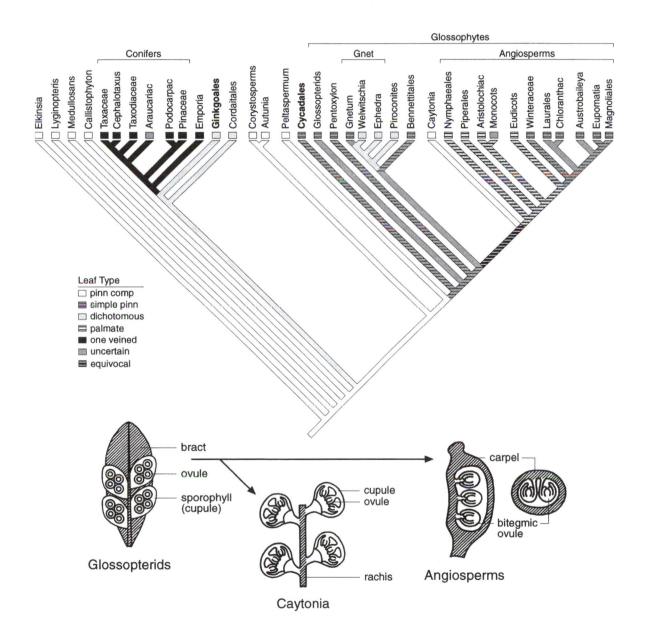

Figure 1. Relationships found in a recent phylogenetic analysis of living and fossil seed plants. Shown are evolution of leaf type, and the inferred derivation of the carpel of angiosperms from the bract-cupule complex of Permian glossopterid. Cupules of the Mesozoic seed plant *Caytonia* and bitegmic ovules of angiosperms derived from glossopterid cupules. Redrawn by Catherine P. Sexton after Doyle (1996).

dicotyledons (dicots), which often are treated as classes (Liliopsida, Magnoliopsida). Monocots, which have only one cotyledon (seed leaf) and have leaves with parallel (actually converging at the tip) venation, appear to be monophyletic. Dicots are a paraphyletic group, of which monocots are actually a derived subgroup. The widely used classification systems of Armen Takhtajan and Arthur Cronquist, first proposed in the 1960s, further divide angiosperms into 10 to 17 subclasses, but the naturalness of many of these (especially Hamamelidae, Dilleniidae, Rosidae, Liliidae, and Arecidae) has been challenged by phylogenetic analyses, especially those based on molecular data. All analyses agree that the subclass Magnoliidae forms a paraphyletic basal grade, although they disagree on which of the many diverse magnoliid groups are most basal: Magnoliales, which are woody plants, usually with bisexual flowers; Chloranthaceae, which have extremely simple flowers; the aquatic genus *Ceratophyllum*; "paleoherbs" such as Nymphaeales (waterlilies), Piperales (black peppers), and monocots, all of which have creeping or climbing stems and little or no secondary growth; or a mixture of woody and herbaceous groups. There is increasing evidence that the 95 percent of dicots (other than Magnoliidae) form a natural group called "eudicots." Their most obvious unifying feature is possession of tricolpate pollen—it has three furrows for germination of the pollen tube, and derived pollen types. Magnoliids and monocots retain the primitive monosulcate pollen type—it has one furrow, as seen in other seed plants.

Although the oldest generally accepted angiosperms are Early Cretaceous, there have been repeated reports of older fossils that may be angiosperms or their precursors. Cladistic analyses (based upon shared characteristics) imply that the line leading to the angiosperms (though not necessarily all modern angiosperm features) existed since the Late Triassic, since the oldest records of potential angiosperm sister groups (Bennettitales, Gnetales, *Caytonia*) go back to this time. One of the most intriguing is *Sanmiguelia*, described by Roland Brown from the Upper Triassic of Colorado. This group had large, pleated leaves with parallel venation suggestive of monocots. Bruce Cornet has associated Texas samples of *Sanmiguelia* with reproductive structures that he interpreted as male and female flowers. However, others have questioned whether the structures making up the flowers are comparable to stamens and carpels, suggesting that if *Sanmiguelia* is related to angiosperms, it may be on the stem-lineage leading to them, rather than a fully modern (crown-group) angiosperm. The same may be said of monosulcate pollen, which Cornet described from the Upper Triassic Newark sequence of Virginia as the Crinopolles group. In this group, the exine (the resistant pollen wall preserved in fossils) consists of an outer reticulate layer (tectum) held up by columellae (features now restricted to angiosperms) and a thick inner layer resembling the endexine of other seed plants (gymnosperms). Until these pollen grains are associated with other plant parts, their affinities will remain controversial.

For many years, most known Early Cretaceous angiosperm fossils were leaves, which were identified or compared with diverse modern taxa. This led to the view that angiosperms originated and began to diversify long before the Cretaceous in some area not represented in the fossil record, such as the tropical uplands, as proposed by Daniel Axelrod. However, since the 1960s, worldwide

studies of fossil pollen, which can be extracted from many otherwise unfossiliferous (fossil-poor) sediments by palynological techniques (those designed to study fossil pollen and spores), and reassessment of the leaf record have revealed a pattern of morphological diversification through the Cretaceous, suggesting instead that angiosperms were radiating during this interval (Figure 2). Most recently, studies pioneered by P.R. Crane, E.M. Friis, and K.R. Pedersen (1995) have shown that angiosperm reproductive structures (flowers, floral parts, fruits) are common in Cretaceous sediments, preserved in compressed form (lignite) or converted to charcoal (fusain) by forest fires, and can be isolated by dissolving and sieving the sediment. These studies have led to more precise hypotheses of relationships between early angiosperms and modern groups, which generally confirm the broad picture based on pollen. Early angiosperms were more abundant and diverse at lower latitudes and appeared later at higher latitudes, a pattern first noted by Axelrod based on the leaf record and documented with palynology by Gilbert Brenner, James A. Doyle, Leo Hickey, Serge Jardiné, Peter Crane, and Scott Lidgard. This favors the view that angiosperms originally were adapted to tropical conditions (although it is uncertain whether these were wet or dry) and spread toward the poles.

The oldest recognizable Cretaceous angiosperm fossils are monosulcate and related types of pollen grains, usually distinguished from the monosulcate pollen of other seed plants by their reticulate tectum and columellae. These early angiosperms are best known from the Wealden and overlying marine beds in England (studied by Norman Hughes, Elizabeth Kemp, Jenny Chapman, and others); the Potomac Group of Delaware, Maryland, and Virginia (Brenner, Doyle, James Walker); coastal basins formed during rifting of the South Atlantic in Gabon (Eugene Boltenhagen, Jardiné, Antoine Doerenkamp, Doyle) and Brazil (Marilia Regali, Murilo de Lima, Waldemar Herngreen); and coastal plain deposits in Egypt (Eckart Schrank, James Penny) and Israel (Brenner, Pieter De Haan). Early angiosperms were fairly diverse (though not common) by the Barremian and Aptian stages (Figure 2), and rare specimens are as old as the Hauterivian of England and Israel and as the Valanginian of Italy. Some groups have been compared with living magnoliid taxa, particularly Chloranthaceae (*Clavatipollenites*: monosulcate pollen with a sculptured sulcus and spin reticulum), the Southern Hemisphere family Winteraceae (*Walkeripollis*: arrangements of four pollen grains with one round pore), and Magnoliales (*Lethomasites*: monosulcates with granules below the tectum rather than columellae but an angiosperm-like inner layer), and others with monocots (*Liliacidites*: reticulate monosulcates with finer sculpture at the ends of the grain). In general, early angiosperm pollen is most diverse in South America, Africa, and the Middle East, or the Northern Gondwana province of Brenner; such types as *Walkeripollis*, possible chloranthaceous relatives with a continuous tectum *(Tucanopollis)*, and problematical extinct types such as *Afropollis* are limited largely or entirely to these areas. An exception is probable monocot pollen *(Liliacidites)*, which so far seems restricted to Laurasia (the Northern Hemisphere landmass of the period) at the early stages of the record.

A major event in the early angiosperm pollen record is the appearance of tricolpate pollen, representing primitive eudicots. These are seen first in most areas in the Albian, but they are com-

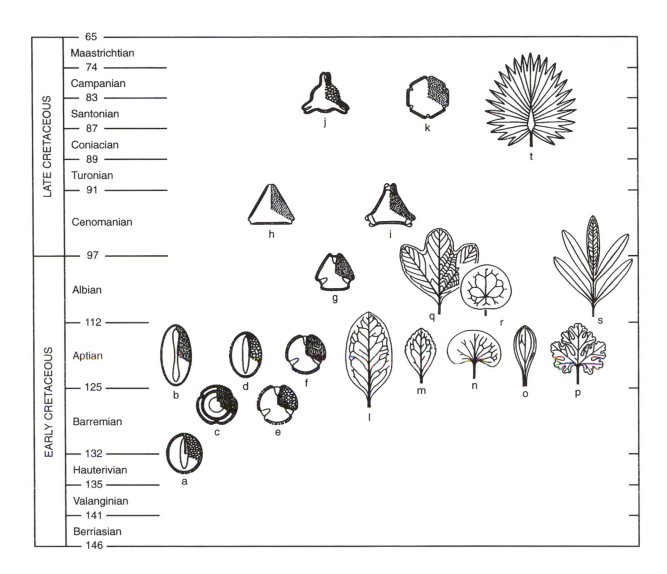

Figure 2. Important Cretaceous angiosperm pollen and leaf types (absolute ages of subdivisions of the Cretaceous in million years). Pollen: *a, Clavatipollenites; b, Lethomasites; c, Walkeripollis; d, Liliacidites; e,* reticulate tricolpate; *f,* striate tricolpate; *g,* triangular tricolporate; *h, Proteacidites; i,* Normapolles; *j, Aquilapollenites; k, Nothofagus.* Leaves: *l, Ficophyllum; m,* leaf with chloranthoid teeth; *n,* reniform leaf; *o, Acaciaephyllum* (monocot?); *p, Vitiphyllum; q, Nelumbites; r, Araliopsoides* (platanoid); *s, Sapindopsis; t,* palm. After Harland et al. (1990), reprinted with permission of Cambridge University Press.

mon in the Aptian of Northern Gondwana, and rare specimens have been reported down to the Late Barremian of both Northern Gondwana and England.

Pre-Albian angiosperm leaves are best known from the Lower Potomac Group of Maryland and Virginia (Aptian). These floras first were described near the turn of the century by William Fontaine, Lester Ward, and Edward Berry and reinvestigated by Jack A. Wolfe, Doyle, and Hickey in the 1970s, with observations on epidermal (cuticle) structure by Garland R. Upchurch (1989). Angiosperm leaves also were described from the Aptian of Portugal by Gaston Saporta in the 1890s and Carlos Teixeira in the 1940s. These leaves are simple (having a single blade, as opposed to compound) and have more irregular venation and stomata (pores for gas exchange) than most modern angiosperms. These are believed to be primitive features. Other such features include pinnately veined leaves (one primary vein gives off two rows of secondary veins) with smooth margins, much like woody magnoliids *(Ficophyllum, Rogersia);* leaves with toothed margins and stomata similar to Chloranthaceae; palmately veined leaves (those with several radiating primary veins), suggestive of herbaceous magnoliids *(Proteaephyllum, Nymphaeites);* a possible monocot with apically converging venation *(Acaciaephyllum);* and palmately lobed leaves that may represent an early eudicot *(Vitiphyllum).* Friis and other have described some fruits from Portugal and the lower Potomac that are comparable to Chloranthaceae; others appear to be magnoliids of uncertain affinities.

During the Albian and Cenomanian stages, tricolpate eud-icot pollen radiated (diversified) explosively, giving rise near the end of the Albian to more advanced tricolporate pollen, with a pore in the middle of each furrow, the most common type in eudicots today. Geographic sampling for this part of the angiosperm pollen record includes not only the British, Poto-mac, and African-South American sections mentioned above but also Oklahoma and Kansas (Richard Hedlund and Geoffrey Norris, Satish Srivastava, Jerome Ward), western Canada (Nor-ris, Chaitanya Singh), the Peruc Formation of the Czech Repub-lic (Blanka Pacltová), and Australia (Mary Dettmann, Dennis Burger). The pollen radiation is associated with major new leaf types (which are the oldest angiosperm macrofossils in many rock strata sequences), and increasing diversity of fossil flowers. Leaf floras with angiosperms include the upper Potomac and Portugal sections, studied by the authors cited above, plus floras in Kansas (Berry), western Canada (Walter Bell), and Kazakh-stan, Siberia, and the Russian Far East (Vsevolod Vakhrameev, Valentina Samylina, Valentin Krassilov). Three large, angiosperm-dominated leaf floras of Cenomanian age are from the Dakota Group of Kansas and Nebraska, first studied by Leo Lesquereux in the 1890s and more recently by David Dilcher, Crane, and Upchurch; the Raritan Formation of New Jersey (John New-berry, Arthur Hollick, Berry); and the Peruc Formation (Josef Velenovský and Ladislav Viniklár).

Many Albian macrofossils can be linked with modern taxa that molecular phylogenetic analyses place near the very begin-nings of the eudicots. Among these are peltate leaves *(Nelumbites)* having the petiole (leaf stalk) attached to the middle of a round blade and associated floral parts related to the genus *Nelumbo* (lotus). This plant superficially resembles waterlilies (Nymphae-ales, an herbaceous magnoliid group) but has tricolpate pollen. These fossils indicate an early movement into aquatic habitats. Relatives of *Platanus* (sycamore) are represented by palmately lobed "platanoid" leaves (e.g., *Araliopsoides*) and pinnately lobed and compound leaves *(Sapindopsis),* which are associated with pompomlike inflorescences (clusters) of small, unisexual flowers with tricolpate pollen. *Sapindopsis*-like leaves are not found in modern *Platanus,* indicating that the platanoid line was much more diverse than it is today. The flowers had a better-developed perianth than *Platanus,* which is wind-pollinated, suggesting that this line underwent a trend from insect to wind pollination. *Plata-nus* is common along the edges (margins) of streams today, and from the Albian through the Late Cretaceous and Tertiary, pla-tanoids were especially abundant in sediments that line stream margins, such as the sandstones that yielded the classic Dakota flora of Kansas. Another very early eudicot group, Buxaceae (box-wood), is represented by inflorescences of unisexual flowers *(Span-omera)* containing tricolpate pollen with striate sculpture, a pollen type found in rock strata down to the Aptian in Northern Gond-wana. The Albian-Cenomanian floral record also documents con-tinued diversification of magnoliids, including relatives of Magnoliaceae *(Archaeanthus)*, Chloranthaceae, Lauraceae (laurels, such as avocado, one of the largest groups in tropical and subtrop-ical forests to the present day), and Calycanthaceae (spice bush). The most common angiosperm woods in the upper Potomac,

described by Patrick S. Herendeen, may also be related to Lau-raceae *(Paraphyllanthoxylon)* and Platanaceae *(Icacinoxylon)*.

Triporate pollen, which has three round pores, appeared in the Cenomanian. Triporates from the Cenomanian of Africa and South America *(Proteacidites)* may represent Proteaceae, one of the most characteristic "Gondwanan" angiosperm groups from the Late Cretaceous to today (found in Australia, Africa, and South America). Another major triporate group is the Normapolles, which were abundant throughout the Late Cretaceous of Europe and eastern North America. Working on rich flower and fruit assemblages from the Santonian-Campanian of Sweden, Friis asso-ciated Normapolles pollen with flowers that can be linked with the wind-pollinated Amentiferae, particularly Juglandaceae (walnut family), but were more primitive in being bisexual. This confirms the view that the unisexual flowers of modern Amentiferae were reduced as a result of specialization for wind pollination.

Late Cretaceous floras illustrate continued diversification of angiosperms and show significant latitudinal differentiation (i.e., certain types were found more often at some latitudes than oth-ers), even though global climates were generally mild. In addition to those from Sweden, Late Cretaceous angiosperm flowers and fruits appeared in the Atlantic Coastal Plain of New Jersey (Rari-tan Formation) and Georgia, studied by William Crepet, Kevin Nixon, Herendeen, and Crane. These include additional magnol-ids and more advanced eudicot groups, such as Fagaceae (oak fam-ily) and Ericaceae (heath family). An important feature of most of these fossils is their small size. To the north, in Siberia, Canada, and Alaska, angiosperms were less diverse; noteworthy elements were platanoid leaves and the extinct *Aquilapollenites* pollen group, of unknown affinities. Near the equator, in Africa and South America, there was a conspicuous radiation of monosulcate and related pollen types comparable to palms, a group of advanced monocots that reach tree size without producing secondary wood. Palm leaves and stems are also known from the Santonian of New Jersey, an indication that near-tropical climates extended to mid-dle latitudes (those between 30 degrees and 60 degrees). At this time in southern South America, Australia, and Antarctica, Pro-teaceae were joined by pollen of *Nothofagus* (southern beech), another dominant element in parts of temperate South America and Australasia today, which has been traditionally placed in Fagaceae but may not be directly related to that Laurasian family.

As elsewhere in paleontology, there has been much contro-versy concerning the existence, magnitude, and long-range effects of extinctions in angiosperms at the end of the Cretaceous. In the western United States, changes in pollen and leaf floras across the Cretaceous-Tertiary boundary have been studied by Robert Tschudy, Douglas Nichols, Wolfe, Upchurch, Hickey, and Kirk Johnson. Many groups typical of the Late Cretaceous, such as *Aquilapollenites* and various magnoliid leaf types, either became extinct or were highly reduced in diversity at the boundary, marked by a bed containing an iridium anomaly attributed to fall-out from an asteroid impact and an interval dominated by ferns, which often colonize areas where vegetation has been destroyed. In New Mexico and Colorado, Early Paleocene floras indicate a shift from open tropical forest, suggesting dry conditions, to closed-canopy tropical rainforest. Further north, evergreen subtropical angiosperms suffered selective extinction, so that deciduous taxa, including many familiar Amentiferae (e.g., Juglandaceae; Betulaceae, birch family; Ulmaceae, elm family), were more highly represented in the Paleocene, although other evidence implies that temperatures were not lower. However, effects in other areas, especially the Southern Hemisphere, are less obvious. Wolfe has proposed that selective extinction of evergreen angiosperm taxa in the Northern Hemisphere is the reason that even today deciduous trees are more dominant in the north temperate zone than they are under similar temperatures in the Southern Hemisphere.

Tertiary angiosperm floras are extremely widespread, and they document in detail the great climatic changes leading to the geographically differentiated floras and vegetation types of the present day. Traditionally, studies of these floras have emphasized implications for plant geography and paleoclimates, but as in the Cretaceous, there is now a tendency for reconstruction of whole plants by association of flowers and other plant parts, allowing more precise hypotheses on affinities with modern taxa and documenting the evolutionary changes leading to modern plants. For example, Steven Manchester showed that Eocene Platanaceae (*Macginitiea*) were more primitive than living *Platanus* because the Eocene group lacked hairs on the carpels and had regular numbers of floral parts, like platanoids in the Cretaceous.

In the Early Tertiary, tropical climates were still more widespread than they are today, so the angiosperm-dominated floras at middle latitudes contained many taxa now restricted to the tropics. A famous example is the Early Eocene London Clay flora of England, composed of pyritized fruits and seeds described in the 1930s by Eleanor M. Reid and Margorie E.J. Chandler and more recently by Margaret Collinson. Important elements in this deposit include the palm *Nypa*, which grows today in mangrove swamps in southeast Asia, rainforest lianas such as Menispermaceae and Icacinaceae, and rainforest trees such as Lauraceae and Annonaceae. Asian rainforest plants also occur in the Clarno fruit and seed flora of Oregon, studied by Richard Scott and Manchester, and leaf floras from the western United States, studied by Ralph Chaney, Harry MacGinitie, and Wolfe. These floras illustrate a general increase in propagule (fruit or seed) size after the Cretaceous-Tertiary boundary. Upchurch and Wolfe ascribe this increase to a shift from dry to wet tropical climate and closed rainforest vegetation. However, Scott L. Wing and Bruce Tiffney consider the change a consequence of changes in the vertebrate herbivore fauna: from large dinosaurs that kept the vegetation in a state of disturbance and played little role in fruit and seed dispersal, to smaller and more selective mammals and birds, many of which acted as dispersal agents. Eocene floras of the Gulf Coast were studied by Berry in the 1920s and more recently reinvestigated by Dilcher, Crepet, and Herendeen, aided by cuticle analysis and discoveries of flowers and fruits. These floras indicate seasonally dry tropical conditions, with, for example, many legumes (Leguminosae), one of the dominant taxa in tropical deciduous forests and savannas today.

In the Early Tertiary of Canada, Alaska, and Siberia, angiosperms were associated with conifers such as the deciduous genus *Metasequoia*. A curious vegetation type dominated by deciduous angiosperms with unusually large leaves occurred near the North Pole; deciduousness in these plants may have been more an adaptation to prolonged winter darkness than to low temperatures. Floras dominated by conifers but also containing diverse, mostly deciduous angiosperms also occurred at higher elevations in middle latitudes, preserved in upland basins in the northwestern United States and adjacent Canada and studied by Axelrod, Wolfe, Wesley Wehr, and Ruth A. Stockey. As was first recognized by Brown, a prominent group all around the Northern Hemisphere consisted of relatives of *Cercidiphyllum* (katsura), a primitive eudicot tree now endemic to east Asia, assigned by Crane and Stockey (1985) to the extinct genus *Joffrea*. *Joffrea* had elongate inflorescences of many flowers, which are reduced small clusters of carpels in *Cercidiphyllum*. From the Paleocene of Alberta, Stockey and colleagues (1997) have described floating aquatics (*Limnobiophyllum*) that are intermediate between the monocot family Araceae (e.g., philodendrons) and the highly reduced Lemnaceae (duckweeds), confirming that Lemnaceae are actually a subgroup of Araceae. Other important groups include Platanaceae; relatives of *Trochodendron* (*Nordenskioldia*), another primitive eudicot group now confined to eastern Asia; Amentiferae; and, especially in upland floras in the later Eocene, the important temperate family Rosaceae (e.g., roses, apples).

Global climatic deterioration in the Early Oligocene had great effects on the geographic distribution and evolution of angiosperms and the origin of familiar modern vegetation types. Late Tertiary floras in the western United States have been studied especially by Chaney, MacGinitie, Axelrod, Estella Leopold, Alan Graham, and Wolfe. Colder and more seasonal climates led to the first appearance of typical deciduous forests at middle latitudes, dominated by such trees as oaks (*Quercus*), birches (*Betula*), and maples (*Acer*). In addition, widespread drying led to the radiation of advanced herbaceous monocots, such as grasses (Gramineae), and eudicots, such as Umbelliferae (carrot family) and Compositae (daisy family), and the expansion new vegetation types dominated by herbs, including both temperate and tropical grasslands. Because of the low preservation potential of the soft stems and leaves of herbs and the dearth of suitable sites of deposition in dry areas, this radiation is best seen in the pollen, fruit, and seed records. Many herbaceous taxa apparently originated in the Late Tertiary, but others (such as grasses) existed earlier, at least back to the Paleocene, as minor elements. By the Middle Miocene, continued cooling of high latitude areas and drying of the continental interiors led to the present disjunct distributions of many angiosperm groups in the temperate forests of Europe, North America, and eastern Asia. During the Pleistocene, glacial and interglacial cycles caused repeated decimation and reexpansion of vegetation types, best revealed in the pollen record. Extinctions of woody angiosperm taxa were most severe in Europe, least so in eastern Asia.

JAMES A. DOYLE

See also Defensive Structures: Plants; Plants: Adaptive Strategies; Plants: Mechanical Plant Design; Plants: Vegetative Features; Reproductive Strategies: Plants

Works Cited

Crane, P.R., E.M. Friis, and K.R. Pedersen. 1995. The origin and early diversification of angiosperms. *Nature* 374:27–33.

Crane, P.R., and R.A. Stockey. 1985. Growth and reproductive biology of *Joffrea speirsii* gen. et sp. nov., a *Cercidiphyllum*-like plant from the Late Paleocene of Alberta, Canada. *Canadian Journal of Botany* 63:340–64.

Doyle, J.A. 1996. Seed plant phylogeny and the relationships of Gnetales. *International Journal of Plant Sciences* 157 (6, Supplement):S3–S39.

Harland, W.B., R.L. Armstrong, A.V. Cox, L.E. Craig, A.G. Smith, and D.G. Smith. 1990. *A Geologic Time Scale 1989.* Cambridge: Cambridge University Press.

Reid, E.M., and M.E.J. Chandler. 1933. *The London Clay Flora.* London: British Museum (Natural History).

Stockey, R.A., G.L. Hoffman, and G.W. Rothwell. 1997. The fossil monocot *Limnobiophyllum scutatum:* Resolving the phylogeny of Lemnaceae. *American Journal of Botany* 84:355–68.

Upchurch Jr., G.R. 1989. Terrestrial environmental changes and extinction patterns at the Cretaceous-Tertiary boundary, North America. *In* S.K. Donovan (ed.), *Mass Extinctions: Processes and Evidence.* New York: Columbia University Press; London: Belhaven.

Wolfe, J.A. 1985. Distribution of major vegetation types during the Tertiary. *In* E.T. Sundquist and W.S. Broecker (eds.), *The Carbon Cycle and Atmospheric CO_2: Natural Variations Archean to Present.* Washington, D.C.: American Geophysical Union.

Further Reading

Beck, C.B. (ed.). 1976. *Origin and Early Evolution of Angiosperms.* New York: Columbia University Press.

Behrensmeyer, A.K., J.D. Damuth, W.A. DiMichele, R. Potts, H.-D. Sues, and S.L. Wing (eds.). 1992. *Terrestrial Ecosystems through Time.* Chicago: University of Chicago Press.

Doyle, J.A., and M.J. Donoghue. 1993. Phylogenies and angiosperm diversification. *Paleobiology* 19:141–67.

Doyle, J.A., and C.L. Hotton. 1991. Diversification of early angiosperm pollen in a cladistic context. *In* S. Blackmore and S.H. Barnes (eds.), *Pollen and Spores: Patterns of Diversification.* Oxford: Clarendon Press; New York: Oxford University Press.

Endress, P.K., and E.M. Friis (eds.). 1994. Early evolution of flowers. *Plant Systematics and Evolution Supplement 8.* Vienna and New York: Springer-Verlag.

Friis, E.M., W.G. Chaloner, and P.R. Crane (eds.). 1987. *The Origins of Angiosperms and Their Biological Consequences.* Cambridge and New York: Cambridge University Press.

Herendeen, P.S., and P.R. Crane. 1995. The fossil history of the monocotyledons. *In* P.J. Rudall, P.J. Cribb, D.F. Cutler, and C.J. Humphries (eds.), *Monocotyledons: Systematics and Evolution.* 2 vols. London and Kew: Royal Botanic Gardens.

Muller, J. 1981. Fossil pollen records of extant angiosperms. *Botanical Review* 47:1–142.

ANKYLOSAURS

Ankylosaurs first appeared during the Middle Jurassic and became extinct at the end of the Cretaceous, a span of about 115 million years. They are small-headed, quadrupedal (i.e., they walked on four legs), short-legged, armor-plated ornithischian, or bird-hipped, dinosaurs (Figure 1). Their skeletons have been modified considerably over the basic ornithischian design, such as typified by *Hypsilophodon*. Although ankylosaurs are advanced reptiles (diapsids), unlike diapsids, in the low ankylosaur skull, two or more of the typical diapsid skull openings are closed in the temple region and around the eyes. The skull also has a low profile, and sheets of bone armor are fused to the surface of the skull. Although the teeth remain small and leaflike, they may have a rim around their base called a "cingulum," or the base of the crown may be swollen. Ankylosaurs have abandoned the bipedal (two-legged) walk of the primitive ornithischian for quadrupedal locomotion. As a result, the limbs are modified for weight-bearing and typically are stocky, rather than long and slender—they certainly were not graceful runners. The pelvis has been modified considerably with upper pelvic bone, the ilium, extending out nearly horizontally. This modification provides enormous areas for leg muscles. The most characteristic feature of ankylosaurs is armor arranged in rows across the neck, back, and tail. Most of this armor consists of disks of bone embedded in the skin, much like that of crocodiles. Some ankylosaurs also sported spines and spikes on the neck, while others sport a mace-like tail club.

Ankylosaurs were one of the earliest dinosaurs to be scientifically named, with *Hylaeosaurus* being named only seven years after the ornithopod *Iguanodon* and 10 years before the name "dinosaur" was coined by Richard Owen in 1841. *Hylaeosaurus* also has the distinction of being one of three life restorations of a dinosaur displayed at the first World's Fair at Crystal Palace, England, in 1854. Since those early days, ankylosaurs have been found on all of the continents, including Antarctica (Gasparini et al. 1987) and Australia (Molnar 1980). They are not common as fossils except in Asia and North America, where they occur along with ceratopsians (group with a bony frill about the rear of the skull) and pachycephalosaurs (group with domed skulls).

Ankylosaurs are believed to have descended from the Late Triassic–Early Jurassic thyreophorans, a group of primitive armored dinosaurs related to both stegosaurs and ankylosaurs (Coombs et al. 1990). Thyreophorans include the small (two meters) bipedal *Scutellosaurus* from the Lower Jurassic of the American Southwest and the large (four meters) quadrupedal *Scelidosaurus* from the Lower Jurassic of England (Figure 2). Armor development in thyreophorans is not as extensive nor as diverse as in ankylosaurs. The teeth are small, leaf-shaped, and generally resemble those of other primitive ornithischians. *Scelidosaurus* is the most ankylosaur-like of all the thyreophorans and is thought to be most closely related to primitive ankylosaurs. *Scelidosaurus* differs from the ankylosaurs in that it still retains numerous primitive characters, such as a tall, narrow skull, the presence

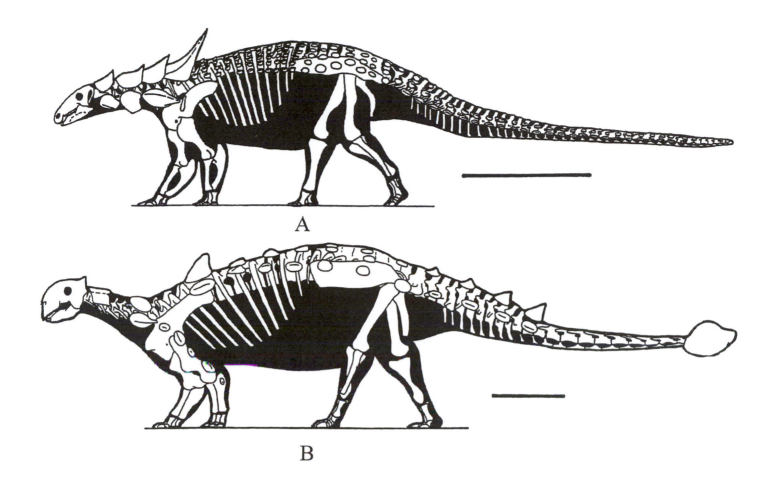

Figure 1. Examples of the two families of Ankylosauria. *A,* Nodosauridae *(Sauropelta); B,* Ankylosauridae *(Euoplocephalus).* Scale: line equals one meter.

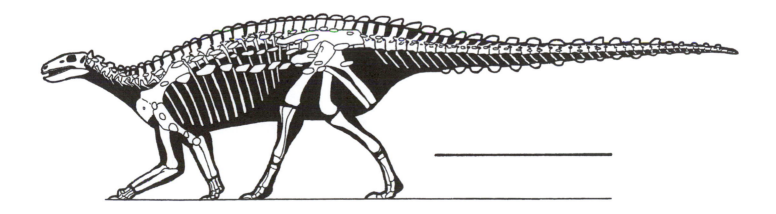

Figure 2. The most ankylosaur-like thyreophoran, *Scelidosaurus.* Scale: line equals one meter.

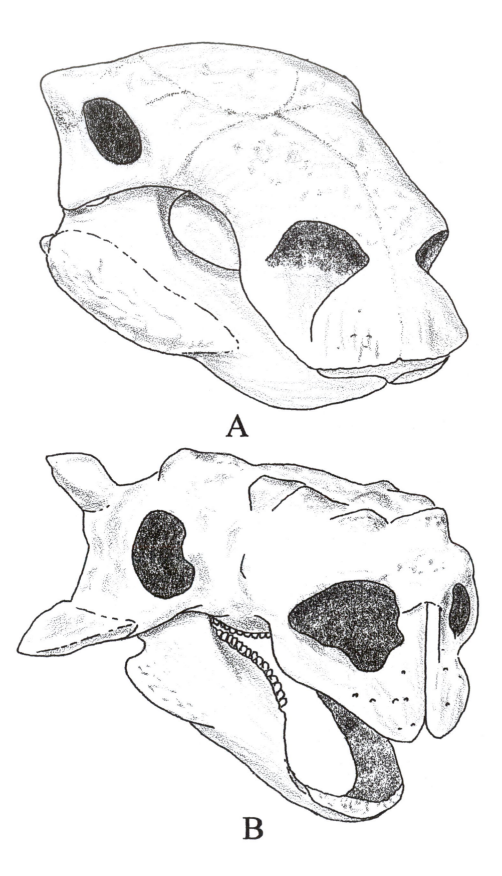

Figure 3. Skulls of two ankylosaurians. *A,* nodosaurid *Edmontonia;* note that the armor fused to the skull consists of a few large pieces; an oval cheek plate is also present; *B, Tarchia;* note the prominent armor "horns" at the rear corners of the head and the large forward-facing nostril openings.

Figure 4. Life reconstructions of the armored dinosaur. Edmontonia and the tyrannosaur Gorgosaurus. Southern Alberta, 78 million years ago.

of all of the skull openings, and an unmodified pelvis. In addition, only a few thin sheets of armor are fused to the skull.

Ankylosaurs can be divided into two families, the Nodosauridae and the Ankylosauridae (Coombs 1978; Coombs and Maryanska 1990). The nodosaurids characteristically have a skull that looks like a pear when viewed from above. On the rear sides of the skull, fenestrae (openings) in the temple region of the skull are visible, whereas fenestrae in front of the eyes and high above the temples are fused shut and covered by armor that also is fused to the skull. This armor is large and symmetrically arranged on both sides of the midline (the imaginary line that runs through the center of the "face," bisecting the eyes, nose, mouth, and the rest of the skull) (Figure 3A). Sometimes a large oval plate covers the cheek region (Figure 3A), which is rather odd since there is little there for a carnivore to bite. The neck armor typically consists of large plates supplemented by spines that project outward or upward (Figure 1A), while the back and tail armor consists mostly of bands of small, keeled disks arranged in transverse rows and a single row of tall, keeled armor projecting from the sides (Carpenter 1984, 1990). The earliest nodosaur occurs in the Middle Jurassic of England. Unfortunately, the specimen, named *Sarcolestes* in 1893, only consists of a lower jaw (Galton 1983). The jaw's overall shape is similar to that seen in later nodosaurids, but otherwise the specimen tells us little about early nodosaurid evolution. The slightly younger *Mymoorapelta* from the Late Jurassic of the western United States is more informative. The ilium is transitional between the fully modified form seen in all ankylosaurs and the unmodified form seen in *Scelidosaurus*. The neck armor consists of outwardly projecting triangular spines. Similar neck armor is seen in *Sauropelta,* an Early Cretaceous nodosaurid from western North America (Figure 1A).

Sauropelta is the best known early nodosaurid. It is a large dinosaur, 5.2 meters long, with an estimated weight of 3 tons.

The tail is long, which seems to be typical of nodosaurids. Footprints thought to be of *Sauropelta* show that the feet were near the midline of the body, placing them below it, not off to the sides. Another larger nodosaurid, *Edmontonia,* found in the Late Cretaceous of Western North America, was 6 meters long. The most characteristic feature of *Edmontonia* is a pair of very large, forward-projecting spikes on the shoulder. This animal was one of the last nodosaurids, but it apparently became extinct before the end of the Cretaceous (Carpenter and Breithaupt 1986).

Ankylosaurids are the better known ankylosaurs. At the end of the tail, this group has a large bone club formed by several large pieces of armor that have fused together around the tail vertebrae. To increase the club's effectiveness, the latter half of the tail forms a club "handle" through the fusion of the vertebrae and by a casing of bony tendons (much like the long bony rods in the drumstick of a turkey). The ankylosaur skull is triangular, being wider than it is long. Except for the eye sockets and nostril openings, all of the skull openings are closed. The skull armor is smaller than that of nodosaurids and is arranged asymmetrically. Prominent armor "horns" are found at the corners of the head (Figure 3B). The neck armor typically consists of two rings of keeled armor fused to an underlying band of bone. The body and tail armor usually consists of hollow, cone-shaped structures that run from the neck to the tail. The oldest ankylosaurid, from the Late Jurassic, has only recently been discovered and has not yet been named (Carpenter et al. 1996). The skull shows many of the features of later ankylosaurids, although numerous primitive features are present as well, such as the presence of premaxillary teeth (in a bone at the front of the upper jaw) and fenestra in the temple region.

Shamosaurus is known from the Lower Cretaceous of Mongolia (Tumanova 1987). Its skull is unusual in that the armor has fused together so that no discernible pattern is visible. The side fenestra has closed. The best-known ankylosaurid is *Euoplocephalus* (Figure 1B), found in the Upper Cretaceous of western North America. It is a large animal, about six meters long, and has very distinctive conical armor on the shoulder and middle of the tail. The club is sometimes spherical (Figure 1B) but sometimes more compressed horizontally. In the skull, the nasal cavity contains an S-shaped loop (Coombs 1978), the purpose of which is unknown. Several other ankylosaurids also have this feature, but not all. *Saichania* is a seven-meter long ankylosaurid from the Upper Cretaceous of Mongolia (Maryanska 1977). It has large nostril openings that face forward, as also happens in *Tarchia* (Figure 3B), also from Mongolia. *Pinacosaurus,* another ankylosaurid from Mongolia, is unusual in that it has lost most of its skull armor. This secondary loss (loss of a specialized adaptation) is important because it shows that loss of the skull openings in ankylosaurids (and probably in nodosaurids as well) is owing to expansion of the surrounding bones, not just the formation of armor to cover the openings. The most popular ankylosaurid is *Ankylosaurus,* which dates from the Latest Cretaceous of North America. Over 10 meters long, it is the largest ankylosaur known, yet it has never been described adequately. It is the last ankylosaurid known—as far as scholars know, no more new species arose after *Ankylosaurus.* Like *Edmontonia, Ankylosaurus* apparently became extinct before the end of the Cretaceous.

The diversity of armor in ankylosaurs raises the question of what the armor was for. The most obvious reason is protection against large predators, especially tyrannosaurids. Certainly the bone disks in the skin would resist piercing by the predator's teeth, and the heavy club on the end of the ankylosaurid tail would keep a predator at a distance. However, some of the armor does not seem to be for defense or offense. For example, the neck spines of *Sauropelta* (Figure 1A) could protect the neck from the bites of a predator, but because they project backwards they cannot be used offensively against the predator, as the shoulder spine in *Edmontonia* could. Furthermore, the tall conical armor on the back and tail of *Euoplocephalus* is even harder to explain as defensive structures.

An alternative hypothesis states that some armor may be display structures, much like the horns of antelopes (Leuthold 1977), or that they were used in fights between members of the same species for territory or mates. That being the case, the prongs on the shoulder spikes of *Edmontonia* suggests that they were also used in shoving contests between males. Indeed, females appear to have smaller shoulder spikes (Carpenter 1990). As for *Euoplocephalus,* the cones on the back are very visible, as would be expected if they were for display. Perhaps this armor could "blush" by increasing the blood flow to the surface of the armor. A bright pink would certainly stand out against the greens of the forest or tans of the desert, making this a reasonable hypothesis.

The small teeth of ankylosaurs show that they were herbivores (plant eaters) because the teeth lacked the piercing and cutting characters of carnivorous (meat-eating) dinosaurs. In North America, where two ankylosaur families occurred together during the Late Cretaceous, the two apparently did not compete for the same food resources because of niche partitioning (i.e., the two families fed on different types of plants). Based on the feeding behavior of large mammals today, the narrow-muzzled nodosaurids were selective feeders, browsing leaves off plants. The broad-muzzled ankylosaurids (except primitive forms) were nonselective grazers, cropping low-growing vegetation indiscriminately (Carpenter 1982). It may be the nonselective feeding of ankylosaurids that made them so successful in the arid and semiarid environments of Asia during the Cretaceous. They could take advantage of any vegetation they found. On the other hand, the wetter, more lush regions of the European Archipelago during the Jurassic and Cretaceous would have had ample supplies of individual types of food, which may explain the selective browsing of the nodosaurids.

The geographical distribution of ankylosaurs during the Mesozoic is interesting and peculiar. Most are northern hemisphere, or Laurasian, dinosaurs. Nodosaurids occur in the Jurassic and Cretaceous of Europe and North America, whereas ankylosaurids occur in the Jurassic and Cretaceous of Asia and North America. The reason why the two families only overlap in North America may be related partially to diet. The southern hemisphere ankylosaurs are enigmatic. *Minmi* from Australia is a blend of nodosaurid and ankylosaurid features, plus several unique features as well. It is possible that the southern hemisphere ankylosaurs represent a third family derived from some as yet unknown basal ankylosaur.

Ankylosaurs were a successful group of dinosaurs, surviving shifting tectonic plates and changing environments for over 115 million years. However, based on the stratigraphic distribution of their bones and teeth in the Earth's rock strata, ankylosaurs apparently became extinct in North America before the end of the Cretaceous (Carpenter and Breithaupt 1986). Elsewhere in the world, the scarcity of terrestrial sediments at the Cretaceous-Tertiary boundary has made it difficult to determine whether the same extinction pattern occurs elsewhere.

KENNETH CARPENTER

See also Skeleton: Dermal Postcranial Skeleton

Works Cited

Carpenter, K. 1982. Skeletal and dermal armor reconstruction of *Euoplocephalus tutus* (Ornithischia: Ankylosauridae) from the Late Cretaceous Oldman Formation of Alberta. *Canadian Journal of Earth Sciences* 19:689–97.

——. 1984. Skeletal reconstruction and life restoration of *Sauropelta* (Ankylosauria: Nodosauridae) from the Cretaceous of North America. *Canadian Journal of Earth Sciences* 21:1491–98.

——. 1990. Ankylosaur systematics: Example using *Panoplosaurus* and *Edmontonia* (Ankylosauria: Nodosauridae). *In* K. Carpenter and P. Currie (eds.), *Dinosaur Systematics: Approaches and Perspectives.* Cambridge and New York: Cambridge University Press.

Carpenter, K., and B. Breithaupt. 1986. Latest Cretaceous occurrences of nodosaurid ankylosaurs (Dinosauria: Ornithischia) in western North America and the gradual extinction of the dinosaurs. *Journal of Vertebrate Paleontology* 6:251–57.

Carpenter, K., J. Kirkland, C. Miles, K. Cloward, and D. Burge. 1996. Evolutionary significance of new ankylosaurs (Dinosauria) from the Upper Jurassic and Lower Cretaceous, Western Interior. *Journal of Vertebrate Paleontology, Abstracts and Program* 19(3):25A.

Coombs, W.P. 1978. The families of the ornithischian dinosaur order Ankylosauria. *Paleontology* 21:143–70.

Coombs, W.P., and T. Maryanska. 1990. Ankylosauria. *In* D. Weishampel, P. Dodson, and H. Osmoloska (eds.), *The Dinosauria.* Berkeley: University of California Press.

Coombs, W.P., D. Weishampel, and L. Witmer. 1990. Basal Thyreophora. *In* D. Weishampel, P. Dodson, and H. Osmoloska (eds.), *The Dinosauria.* Berkeley: University of California Press.

Galton, P.M. 1983. Armoured dinosaurs (Ornithischia: Ankylosauria) from the Middle and Upper Jurassic of Europe. *Palaeontographica. A, Palaeozoologie-Stratigraphie* 182:1–25.

Gasparini, Z., E. Olivero, R. Scasso, and C. Rinaldi. 1987. *Un Ankylosaurio (Reptilia, Ornithischia) Campanio en el Continente Anartico.* Anais do X Congresso Brasileiro de Paleontologia, 131–41.

Leuthold, W. 1977. *African Ungulates.* Berlin and New York: Springer-Verlag.

Maryanska, T. 1977. Ankylosauridae (Dinosauria) from Mongolia. *Paleontologia Polonica* 37:85–151.

Molnar, R. 1980. An ankylosaur (Ornithischia: Reptilia) from the Lower Cretaceous of Southern Queensland. *Memoirs of the Queensland Museum* 20:77–87.

Tumanova, T.A. 1987. Mongol orn' Ankylozavruutz. *Zevlvt-Mongol'yn. Dalyeontolo'yyn Khpmtarsan Zkspyelipi* 32:1–76.

Further Reading

Currie, P., and K. Padian (eds.). 1997. *The Encyclopedia of Dinosaurs.* San Diego, California: Academic Press.

Farlow, J.O., and M.K. Brett-Surman (eds.). 1997. *The Complete Dinosaur.* Bloomington: University of Indiana Press.

ANNELIDS

The elongate body of annelid worms is typically cylindrical, but it has become flattened in some forms, notably the leeches. Annelids are divided into as many as 700 segments, or "metameres," although in most taxa this number is markedly reduced by fusion. In fact, some aberrant forms have lost all traces of segmentation (Fauchald 1977). The head, which is not segmented (Figure 1), is composed of a "prostomium" (which may bear feeding "palps," tentacles, and simple eyes) and a "peristomium" surrounding the mouth (sometimes with tentacle-like "cirri"). Some groups have also recruited body segments into the head.

The trunk metameres are separated by dividing membranes, or "septa"; the membranes are visible externally as "annuli." In primitive forms, each compartment contains a division of the circulatory, excretory, and nervous systems; in more derived (specialized) groups, organs have been regionalized. A central gut, dorsal blood vessel, and ventral nerve cord run the length of the body (Figure 2). The mouth is located anteriorly, while the anus is situated in a "pygidium," a terminal structure found behind the segments. The gut is separated from the body wall by a sealed cavity, or coelom. The body wall itself is composed of an inner layer of longitudinal muscles (for shortening the animal), and an outer layer of circular muscles (for constricting and elongating). These muscles operate in conjunction with the fluid-filled coelom to produce a "hydrostatic skeleton," i.e., one that is maintained, in large part, by fluid pressure. Firm purchase on the substrate is often enhanced by small, sclerotized spines ("setae" or "chaetae") that can be projected or withdrawn into small pits in the body wall. Many annelids burrow using peristaltic waves of contraction that pass down the length of the animal, using the setae as anchors. There are four annelid classes: Polychaeta, Oligochaeta, Hirudinida, and the aberrant Myzostomida.

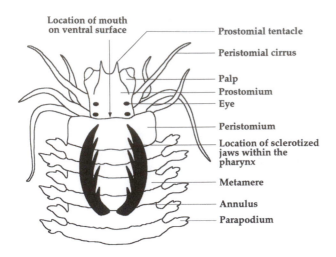

Figure 1. Dorsal view of the anterior end of a polychaete (*Nereis diversicolor*).

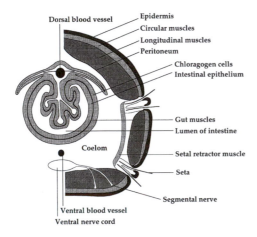

Figure 2. Schematic, transverse section through the body of an annelid, showing the locations of principal tissues and organs.

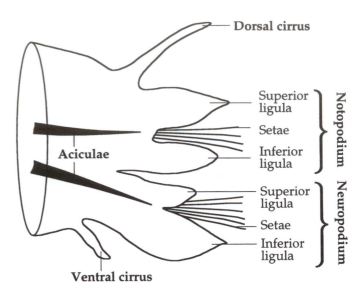

Figure 3. Schematic diagram of a parapodium.

Polychaeta

Polychaetes are predominantly marine and live in a wide range of habitats. The trunk segments may all be similar ("homonomous") or variously differentiated ("heteronomous"). Each segment typically bears a pair of lateral appendages ("parapodia") with two rami (branches)—a ventral neuropodium and dorsal notopodium —and bundles of setae (Figure 3). Parapodia are modified in various ways and perform a range of functions (locomotion, gas exchange, ventilation, anchorage, protection). Predatory polychaetes have sclerotized jaws in a muscular pharynx that can be everted (turned inside out) to capture prey. Other groups are sedentary and partially secrete a tube from which they extend a filtering apparatus or other feeding structures.

The record of polychaetes extends throughout the Phanerozoic, but entire body fossils are comparatively rare. An excellent review is provided by Briggs and Kear (1993). Some have speculated that several Precambrian fossils (e.g., *Spriggina*) might be polychaetes, but the evidence is equivocal. The oldest undisputed specimens are from the Early Cambrian Buen Formation of Peary Land, Greenland (Conway Morris and Peel 1990). The enigmatic *Wiwaxia,* from the Middle Cambrian Spence and Burgess Shales (Canada), and *Canadia,* from the latter location, are now thought to be members of the order Phyllodocida (Butterfield 1990). The Burgess Shale has also yielded fossils of a number of other families (Burgessochaetidae, Peronochaetidae, Insolicoryphidae, and Stephenoscolecidae) (Conway Morris 1979). Other significant finds include the Mississippian Bear Gulch Limestone of Montana (Goniadidae, Nephtyidae, and Lumbrineridae) (Schram 1979), the Moscovian Mazon Creek of Illinois (at least eleven families) (Thompson 1979), the Middle Triassic Grès à Voltzia, near Vosges in northern France (Aphroditidae, Eunicidae, and Spirorbidae) (Gall 1971), as well as several Jurassic sites, such as Voulte-sur-Rhône (Arduini et al. 1982) and Solnhoffen (Barthel et al. 1990). Mazon Creek, Grès à Voltzia, and the Burgess Shale are exceptional deposits that have preserved organic or mineralized traces of the gut and body cuticle. Other sites merely preserve some indication of the outline of the body.

Isolated jaws ("scolecodonts" as fossils), setae and tubes, as well as burrows and castings constitute the vast majority of polychaete finds (Wills 1993). Trace fossils are usually difficult to ascribe to particular taxa, although some tubes (e.g., serpulids) are unmistakable. Scolecodonts are far more useful, but classification is confused since several common groups (e.g., eunicids) have as many as five pairs of jaws, and these are often dissociated. Much elegant work has been done on Ordovician and Silurian scolecodont material from Eastern Europe (e.g., Kielan-Jaworowska 1966).

Oligochaeta

Most oligochaetes live in terrestrial or freshwater environments, although a few have invaded brackish and marine waters. Oligochaetes lack parapodia and usually bear fewer and less elaborate head appendages and fewer setae than polychaetes. The body may be homonomous or divided into specialized regions. A few segments are modified as a "clitellum," a secretory region that functions in reproduction. Most oligochaetes are burrowers, although some live among detritus (decomposing organic matter) or algal filaments. Fossils are rare and often are disputed. The oldest identified with reasonable certainty (tubificids) date from the Upper Carboniferous. *Protoscolex,* found in Upper Ordovician to Upper Silurian marine deposits, may also be an oligochaete.

Hirudinida

The Class Hirudinida includes the leeches (Hirudinia) and some less well-known relatives (Branchiobdellida and Acanthobdellida). All are clitellate (possessing a clitellium). The body is dorsoventrally flattened and composed of a determinate number of segments. The coelom is reduced, internal septa and parapodia are lacking, and paired lateral setae occur in only one group. Anteriorly and posteriorly hirudinids are armed with suckers. Leeches occur in marine and freshwater environments, with a small number of species living in moist terrestrial habitats. Many are active, free-living predators or scavengers. Others feed on the body fluids of a variety of vertebrate and invertebrate hosts. Fossil leeches are extremely rare, the oldest being an unnamed species dating from the Lower Silurian of Waukesha County, near Milwaukee. Two other fossil hirudineans (*Epitrachys rugosus* and *Palaeohirudo eichstaettensis*) have been described from the Upper Jurassic "Lithographen-Scheifer" of Kehlheim and Eichstätt (Bavaria) (Kozur 1970).

Myzostomida

Myzostomids are all symbiotic or parasitic annelids; most live on echinoderms, particularly the arms of crinoids, where they may form gall-like cysts. Their bodies are flattened, annuli are absent, and there are setal hooks on their parapodia for attachment to their hosts. Only one family has a fossil record, dating back to the Ordovician.

MATTHEW A. WILLS

See also Terrestrialization of Animals

Works Cited

Arduini, P., G. Pinna, and G. Teruzzi. 1982. Melanoraphia maculata. n.g. n.sp., a new fossil polychaete of the Sinemurian of Ostcno in Lombardy. *Atti della Società Italiana di Scienze Naturali e del Museo Civica di Storia Naturale, Milano* 123:462–68.

Barthel, K.W., N.H.M. Swinburne, and S. Conway Morris. 1990. *Solnhofen, a Study in Mesozoic Palaeontology.* Cambridge and New York: Cambridge University Press.

Briggs, D.E.G., and A.J. Kear. 1993. Decay and preservation of polychaetes: Taphonomic thresholds in soft-bodied organisms. *Paleobiology* 19:107–35.

Butterfield, N.J. 1990. A reassessment of the enigmatic Burgess Shale fossil *Wiwaxia corrugata* (Matthew) and its relationship to the polychaete Canadia spinosa *Walcott. Paleobiology* 16:287–303.

Conway Morris, S.C. 1979. Middle Cambrian polychaetes from the Burgess Shale of British Columbia. *Philosophical Transactions of the Royal Society of London,* ser. B, 285:227–74.

Conway Morris, S.C., and J.S. Peel. 1990. Articulated halkieriids from the Lower Cambrian of north Greenland. *Nature* 345:802–5.

Fauchald, K. 1977. *The Polychaete Worms: Definitions and Keys to the Orders, Families and Genera.* Natural History Museum of Los Angeles Series, 28. Los Angeles: Natural History Museum of Los Angeles County.

Gall, J.-C. 1971. Faunes et paysages du Grès à Voltzia du nord de Vosges. Essai paléoécologique sur le Buntsandstein supérieur. *Mémoires du Service de la Carte Géologique d'Alsace et de Lorraine* 34.

Kielan-Jaworowska, Z. 1966. Polychaete jaw apparatuses from the Ordovician and Silurian of Poland and a comparison with modern forms. *Palaeontologica Polonica* 16:1–152.

Kozur, H. 1970. Zur Klassifikation und phylogenetischen Entwicklung der fossilen Phyllodocida und Eunicida (Polychaeta). *Freiberger Forschungshefte, Paläontologie,* ser. C, 260:35–81.

Schram, F.R. 1979. Worms of the Mississippian Bear Gulch Limestone of central Montana, USA. *Transactions of the San Diego Society of Natural History* 19:107–20.

Thompson, E.H. 1979. Errant polychaetes (Annelida) from the Pennsylvanian Essex fauna of northern Illinois. *Palaeontographica Abteilung* A163:169–99.

Wills, M.A. 1993. Annelida. *In* M.J. Benton (ed.), *The Fossil Record 2.* London and New York: Chapman and Hall.

Further Reading

Brasier, M.D. 1979. The Cambrian radiation event. *In* M.R. House (ed.), *The Origin of Major Invertebrate Groups.* London and New York: Academic Press.

Brusca, R.C., and G.J. Brusca. 1990. *Invertebrates.* Sunderland, Massachusetts: Sinauer.

Conway Morris, S. 1985. Non-skeletized lower invertebrate fossils: A review. *In* S. Conway Morris, J.D. George, R. Gibson, and H.M. Platt (eds.), *The Origins and Relationships of Lower Invertebrates.* The Systematics Association Special Volume, 28. Oxford: Clarendon.

Mettam, C. 1985. Functional constraints in the evolution of the Annelida *In* S. Conway Morris, J.D. George, R. Gibson, and H.M. Platt (eds.), *The Origins and Relationships of Lower Invertebrates.* The Systematics Association Special Volume, 28. Oxford: Clarendon.

ANNING, MARY

English, 1799–1847

The woman described as "the greatest fossilist the world ever knew" showed signs of perseverance from an early age. Caught in a severe rainstorm in 1800, a nurse led 14-month-old Mary Anning and two other children to an apparent refuge under an elm tree. Lightning struck, and only Mary survived. Her family life was similarly fraught with drama. Of perhaps 10 siblings, only Mary and her older brother Joseph survived to maturity.

Their father Richard, a cabinet maker and carpenter who collected fossils to earn extra money, taught both children the techniques involved in identifying and collecting fossils from the rich limestone cliffs near their home in Lyme Regis, on the southwest coast of England. Richard died when the children were young, leaving his working-class family in debt. The skills he had taught his children would be put to use soon after his death, when Mary was able to extract a large fishlike reptile fossil that Joseph had found in the nearby cliffs. The specimen was sold, bringing aid to the family in a time of need. Although the fossil was not the first of its kind (they also were found in Germany in the eighteenth century), it was by far the most complete found to date in England. More important, this specimen, unlike others, was brought to the attention of scientists, who formally described it and named it *Ichthyosaurus* ("fish-lizard"). This major achievement came when Mary was only 10 or 12 years old, bringing credit to her and the small town of Lyme Regis.

This find was only the first of many in a prolific life of collecting. Anning continued hunting fossils and selling them in her local shop throughout her life, facing much danger from the winter storms that were the best source of new material. In 1823 she discovered a virtually complete skeleton of *Plesiosaurus*, an extinct marine reptile. Of all her finds, this was perhaps her most important contribution to science; according to William Buckland, who later described the first identified dinosaur, "The discovery of this genus forms one of the most important additions that Geology has made to comparative anatomy. It is of the *Plesiosaurus* that [Georges] Cuvier asserts the structure to have been . . . altogether the most monstrous, that have been yet found amid the ruins of a former world. To the head of a Lizard, it united the teeth of a Crocodile; a neck of enormous length, resembling the body of a Serpent; a trunk and tail having the proportions of an ordinary quadruped, the ribs of a Chameleon, and the paddles of a Whale" (quoted in Torrens 1995).

In 1828 Anning found the first complete pterosaur from Britain, *Dimorphodon macronyx*. Not only did it intrigue scientists as England's first fossil flying reptile, but the creature—referred to by Buckland as "a monster resembling nothing that has ever been seen or heard-of upon earth, excepting the dragons of romance and heraldry"—captured the imagination of the public. Tourists flocked to Lyme Regis to see the fossil curios in Anning's shop and to see in person the marvel of a woman who put them there. Even the king of Saxony paid a visit to purchase a specimen for his collection. Her 1829 discovery of *Squaloraja*, a chondrichthyan fish

seen as a link between sharks and rays, further piqued the interest of scientists and the public alike.

In addition to unearthing strange vertebrates, Anning also collected invertebrate fossils. In 1828 she discovered the anterior sheath and ink bag of *Belemnosepia*, an extinct cephalopod. Soft parts such as these are seldom preserved in fossils; those that are preserved give a rare glimpse of how the whole animal was composed.

Anning's fossil finding ability was only a part of her scientific skills. She was also an expert at delicately extracting and preparing the (often large) fossils she found, which required precision handiwork and knowledge of comparative anatomy. In this regard, she was as knowledgeable as her male counterparts in academia, a particularly impressive feat in light of her lack of formal training (which was generally unavailable to working-class women in nineteenth-century England). In addition, Anning aided Buckland in the emerging science of coprology, the study of the fossil remains of coprolites (animal feces). She was able to both identify coprolites and then match them with the fossil animals from which they had come. This science had an influence on the debate as to whether fossils had been created or had evolved.

Although she is regarded today by many as the first female paleontologist, she also has been described by Stephen J. Gould as "the most unsung (or inadequately sung) collecting force in the history of paleontology." Anning was able to collect and sell fossils her entire life, but the findings were not frequent enough to bring financial stability. Much of the money she did earn went toward acts of philanthropy to her townspeople. Honors in her lifetime were few. Sir Everard Home established an unfortunate tradition when he failed to give her credit in his 1814 description of the Lyme Regis ichthyosaur. Although such men as Richard Owen, Thomas Birch, Adam Sedgwick, Georges Cuvier, William Conybeare, and Henry de la Beche used her specimens in their work, rarely was the collector of the fossils acknowledged. It was not until 1828 that she was acknowledged in the scientific literature for her work, although not everyone thereafter followed suit. Even as late as 1995, the British Museum of Natural History still displayed the first ichthyosaur from Lyme Regis with no mention of the young girl who brought it to light. Toward the end of her life, however, the importance of her work began to be recognized. When she contracted breast cancer in 1845, the Geological Society of London elected to provide an annuity for her support, which continued until her early death in 1847.

The fish species *Acrodus anningiae* and *Belenostomus anningiae,* the ostracod species *Cytherelloidea anningi,* the therapsid genus *Anningia,* and the molluscan bivalve genus *Anningella* have been named in her honor. It is believed that the phrase "She sells sea shells at the sea shore" refers to her.

JOHN J. SOCHA

Work Cited

Torrens, H.S. 1995. Mary Anning (1799–1847) of Lyme: "The greatest fossilist the world ever knew." *British Journal for the History of Science* 28:257–84.

Biography

Born in Lyme Regis, England, May 1799. Professional fossil collector. Major discoveries (all from Lyme Regis): first complete ichthyosaur to come to scientists' attention (codiscovered with her brother Joseph), 1809–11?; first complete plesiosaur, 1823; anterior sheath and ink bag of the cephalopod *Belemnosepia,* 1828; first British pterosaur, 1828; fossil chondrichthyan fish *Squaloraja,* 1829; *Plesiosaurus macrocephalus,* 1830. Died in Lyme Regis, 9 March 1847.

Further Reading

de la Beche, H. 1848. Obituary of Mary Anning. *Quarterly Journal of the Geological Society of London* 4:xxiv–xxv.

Lang, W.D. 1939. Mary Anning (1799–1847) and the pioneer geologists of Lyme. *Proceedings of the Dorset Natural History and Archaeological Society* 60:142–64.

McGowan, C. 1983. *The Successful Dragons.* Toronto and Sarasota, Florida: Stevens; updated and revised as *Dinosaurs, Spitfires, and Sea Dragons.* Cambridge, Massachusetts: Harvard University Press, 1991; London: Harvard University Press, 1992.

Ogilvie, M.B. 1986. *Women in Science.* Cambridge, Massachusetts: Massachusetts Institute of Technology Press.

Taylor, M.A. 1994. The plesiosaur's birthplace: The Bristol Institution and its contribution to vertebrate palaeontology. *Zoological Journal of the Linnean Society* 112:179–96.

Taylor, M.A., and H.S. Torrens. 1986. Saleswoman to a new science: Mary Anning and the fossil fish *squaloraja* from the Lias of Lyme Regis. *Proceedings of the Dorset Natural History and Archaeological Society* 108:135–48.

Torrens, H.S. 1995. Mary Anning (1799–1847) of Lyme: "The greatest fossilist the world ever knew." *British Journal for the History of Science* 28:257–84.

Wellnhofer, P. 1991. *The Illustrated Encyclopedia of Pterosaurs.* London: Salamander; New York: Crescent.

ANTARCTICA

Fewer fossils are known from Antarctica than from any other continent, largely because of the inaccessible nature of Antarctica and the fact that 98 percent of its surface area is covered with glacial ice, leaving few rock units available for paleontologists to search. The earliest fossils from Antarctica were collected during the expeditions of the early twentieth century. These include Cambrian archeocyathids (problematic filter-feeding organisms) and trilobite (primitive marine arthropods) fragments from limestone glacial erratics and Permian glossopterid (a type of seed fern) plant material from exposures along the Beardmore Glacier. However, the vast majority of Antarctic fossils have been collected since the late 1960s.

The first Antarctic terrestrial (land) vertebrate fossil, a jaw from an Early Triassic temnospondyl amphibian (an extinct subaquatic relative of modern frogs and salamanders), was collected in 1967 from Graphite Peak between the Beardmore and Shackleton Glaciers. This discovery, from the lower part of the Fremouw Formation, led to several paleontological expeditions to the southern portion of the Transantarctic Mountains (approximately 300 to 400 miles from the geographic South Pole) during the 1970s and early 1980s. During the first of these expeditions (austral summer of 1969–70), specimens of the herbivorous synapsid ("mammal-like" reptile) *Lystrosaurus* were collected from Coalsack Bluff near the Beardmore Glacier. At the time this find added substantial support to the then-emerging theory of plate tectonics (Kitching et al. 1971).

Since the discovery of *Lystrosaurus,* numerous additional taxa of other herbivorous and carnivorous synapsids, procolophonids (small primitive "stem" reptiles), eosuchians (ancient relatives of modern lizards), and temnospondyl amphibians have been added to this fauna. During the 1985–86 Antarctic field season a new fauna of late Early to early Middle Triassic animals was found in the upper portion of the Fremouw Formation along the Gordon Valley near the Beardmore Glacier. This fauna includes large herbivorous (kannemeyeriid) and carnivorous (cynognathid) synapsids as well as capitosaurid temnospondyl amphibians. Second only to one of the dinosaurs mentioned below, these capitosaurs are the largest fossil terrestrial animals known from Antarctica, with skull lengths approaching one meter (Hammer 1990).

The first dinosaurs from Antarctica were collected from two islands off the Antarctic Peninsula during the late 1980s. Only two partial specimens were found, both in Cretaceous marine units. The first specimen is of a fragmentary nodosaurid (armored dinosaur) collected by a group from Argentina in 1986. Two years later a research team from the British Antarctic Survey discovered a partial skeleton of a hypsilophodontid (small ornithopod dinosaur; Hooker et al. 1991).

Dinosaurs first were found on the Antarctic mainland in 1990–91. This fauna, which is Early Jurassic in age, is from the upper portion of the Falla Formation on Mt. Kirkpatrick near the Beardmore Glacier (Hammer and Hickerson 1994). It includes much of the skeleton of a large crested carnivorous theropod dinosaur, *Cryolophosaurus,* teeth from small- to medium-sized scavenging theropods, postcranial elements of a large plateosaurid prosauropod (herbivorous predecessors to large sauropods), a portion of the arm of a primitive pterosaur (flying reptile), and a tooth from a large tritylodont ("mammal-like" reptile that resembles rodents). This fauna still represents the only dinosaur fauna of any age from the mainland of Antarctica. Near the site where the dinosaurs were collected there are also Jurassic fish known from lake bed deposits at Storm Peak.

Many discoveries of fossil plant material from the Permian and Triassic rocks of the Transantarctic Mountains were made beginning in the 1960s. These included glossopterid floras and silicified peat from various Permian units as well as anatomically well preserved plant fossils in silicified peat and *Dicroidium* from the Triassic formations (Taylor and Taylor 1990). While these floras are mainly from the southern portion of the range, unlike the vertebrates they also occur further north at localities near the Dry Valleys, in the Alan Hills, and in Northern Victoria Land. Fossil pollens are also abundant in these units.

In addition to the collections made by early explorers, more recent finds of Paleozoic invertebrates include archeocyathids, trilobites, and brachiopods from Cambrian units in the Transantarctic Mountains and trilobites and brachiopods from the Ellsworth Mountains near the Antarctic Peninsula. Paleozoic fish are known from marine Devonian rocks in the Transantarctic Mountains. Ichnofossils also have been documented from a number of units in the Transantarctic Mountains, including crayfish burrows (Miller and Collinson 1994). Specimens of fossil crayfish from the Triassic have been reported as well.

Beginning in the 1980s a number of expeditions studying Cretaceous and early Tertiary sediments on islands off the Antarctic Peninsula made new paleontological finds. In addition to the two dinosaurs mentioned above, the Cretaceous units have produced a diverse fauna of invertebrates, marine vertebrates, such as plesiosaurs and pliosaurs, and fish. Eocene deposits resting on top of the Cretaceous have yielded a few fragments of fossil marsupials. These represent the only fossil mammals known from the Antarctic.

Some of the most interesting fossils recovered after the early 1980s were from the pre-Pleistocene age Sirius Formation in the Transantarctic Mountains. This unit has produced well-preserved *Nothofagus* (Southern Beech) leaves, unmineralized moss, well-preserved wood, and recycled marine microfossils of Pliocene age (Webb and Harwood 1987). These represent the youngest terrestrial fossils known from the continent.

WILLIAM R. HAMMER

Works Cited

Hammer, W.R. 1990. Triassic terrestrial vertebrate faunas of Antarctica. *In* T.N. Taylor and E.L. Taylor (eds.), *Antarctic Paleobiology: Its Role in the Reconstruction of Gondwanaland*. New York: Springer-Verlag.

Hammer, W.R., and W.J. Hickerson. 1994. A crested theropod dinosaur from Antarctica. *Science* 264:828–30.

Hooker, J.J., A.C. Milner, and S.E.K. Sequeira. 1991. An ornithopod dinosaur from the Late Cretaceous of West Antarctica. *Antarctic Science* 3(3):331–32.

Kitching, J.W., J.W. Collinson, D.H. Elliot, and E.H. Colbert. 1971. *Lystrosaurus* Zone (Triassic) fauna from Antarctica. *Science* 175:524–27.

Miller, M.F., and J.W. Collinson. 1994. Trace fossils from Permian and Triassic sandy braided stream deposits, Central Transantarctic Mountains. *Palaios* 9:605–10.

Taylor T.N., and E.L. Taylor (eds.). 1990. *Antarctic Paleobiology: Its Role in the Reconstruction of Gondwanaland*. New York: Springer-Verlag.

Webb, P.N., and D.M. Harwood. 1987. The terrestrial flora of the Sirius Formation: Its significance in interpreting Late Cenozoic glacial history. *Antarctic Journal of the United States* 22:7–11.

ANTHOZOANS

The Anthozoa, which includes the corals and anemones, is one of the three main classes of the phylum Cnidaria. Although anemones are very rare as fossils because of the preponderance of soft tissues in their bodies, the calcareous (calcium-carbonate) skeletons of corals have a high preservation potential, making them the most common and important of the fossil cnidarians.

Anthozoan Anatomy and Classification

Anthozoans are exclusively polypoid in form—that is, they have a hollow cylindrical body and a central mouth opening surrounded by tentacles. Anthozoans differ from the polyps of other cnidarians principally through the presence of a tube (the "stomodaeum") which extends down from the mouth into the enteron (gut), and in the nature and complexity of radial partitions called "mesenteries," which subdivide the enteron (Wells and Hill 1956) (Figure 1). Digestion, absorption, excretion, and gonad development all take place on the mesenteries. Those that attach to the stomodaeum are said to be "complete."

The Anthozoa are divided into three subclasses. The Ceriantipatharia is a small group of solitary and colonial polyps with 6, 10, or 12 complete mesenteries, 6 of which are considered primary. Two vertical grooves, siphonoglyphs, on opposite sides of the stomodaeum define a so-called "dorsoventral plane." The Octocorallia, a much larger group (including the sea pens, sea fans, soft corals, and precious coral), have eight complete mesenteries and a single siphonoglyph on the ventral (sulcal) side of the stomodaeum. The Zoantharia is the subclass containing the corals and true anemones and is particularly distinguished by having paired mesenteries, of which a first cycle of eight complete and four incomplete are arranged in six pairs. Normally, additional pairs are inserted following various patterns, distinguishing different groups within the subclass. The mesenteries have muscular pleats on one side, facing each other in all pairs except two, which are opposite each other and define the dorsoventral axis. These are known as the "directive pairs." They are associated with either a single ventral siphonogylph (Zoanthiniaria) or a pair of siphonoglyphs (Corallimorpharia/Actiniaria) in the stomodaeum.

Data about the earliest remains of anthozoans and the fossil record of all but the corals throw little light on relationships within the Anthozoa. Scholars base hypotheses on the morphology (shape and structure) and development of living forms, which sug-

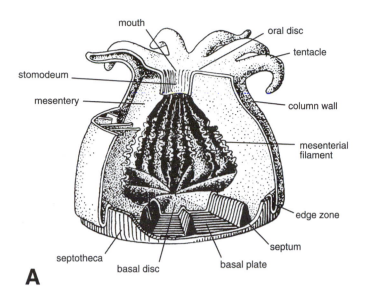

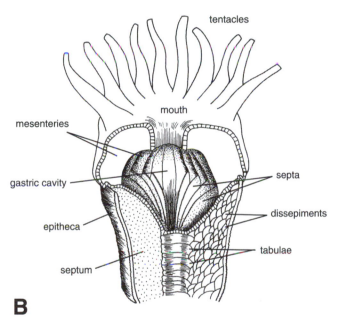

Figure 1. A, a newly settled scleractinian coral polyp and its skeleton. The polyp secretes a basal plate on which the septa are initiated. The septa are secreted in infolds of the basal disc of the polyp between the mesenteries that subdivide the gut, or enteron. As the skeleton is built up, the polyp lifts itself off the basal plate by hydrostatic forces, and the basal disc usually begins to secrete horizontal plates between the septa. B, a reconstruction of a rugose coral polyp and its relationship to its skeleton. The polyp sits on top of its skeleton in the calice. The corallum has an external wall (the epitheca), common to almost all rugosans, within which radially disposed, vertical plates (the septa) alternate with mesenteries in the enteron. The base of the polyp is supported by inclined and horizontal plates, a peripheral series of small dissepiments, and an axial series of larger tabulae. From: *1A,* modified from Wells (1956), *Treatise on Invertebrate Paleontology,* courtesy of and ©1956 The Geological Society of America and The University of Kansas Press. *1B,* reproduced with permission of the Yorkshire Geological Society, from Scrutton (1998).

gests that an anthozoan "stem form" (ancestral group) with six unpaired complete mesenteries gave rise to the Ceriantipatharia on the one hand and to an octocoral/zoantharian stem form on the other. The latter, with eight unpaired complete mesenteries, gave rise to the Octocorallia and, with the addition of four incomplete mesenteries and the arrangement of the mesenteries into pairs, formed the ancestral stock for the Zoantharia.

Geological Record

Essentially, the corals are anemones that have the ability to secrete a calcium carbonate skeleton beneath themselves. This ability evolved independently on several occasions in different groups of anemones (Figure 2). The first corals appear in the Lower Cambrian, where six genera (groups of species; singular, genus) are now recognized (Scrutton 1997). Although most of these show some similarities to the main groups of Paleozoic corals (the orders Rugosa and Tabulata), they lack attributes that would help to clarify their relationships fully. These Cambrian corals appear to have been short-lived, and had disappeared by the mid-Middle Cambrian. After that, no accepted corals are known until the first undisputed "tabulate coral," *Lichenaria,* in the Early Ordovician. Records remain sparse until the Middle Ordovician, when the diversification of the tabulates accelerated and they were joined by the first of the Rugosa. By the end of the Ordovician, before the extinction event, the Rugosa and the Tabulata were represented by approximately 40 and 60 genera, respectively. A third, very small order, the Kilbuchophyllida, also made its appearance in the Middle Ordovician. So far, members of this group appear to have been restricted to a brief interval of time in the area of Scotland and Ireland.

The Rugosa and Tabulata persisted throughout the Paleozoic. After the Late Ordovician extinction event, which affected the Tabulata more severely than the Rugosa, the Rugosa always dominated Paleozoic coral faunas in terms of generic diversity, although the Tabulata remained an important bulk contributor until the Late Devonian, particularly to biohermal (reefs) and perireefal environments. Generic diversity in both groups peaked in the Middle Devonian, and both were affected severely by a series of extinction pulses beginning at the end of the Middle Devonian and continuing until the end of the Upper Devonian. Subsequently, the tabulates remained relatively unimportant, although in the Mississippian the Rugosa recovered to very nearly their peak diversity. Both show the effects of extinctions at the Mississippian/Pennsylvanian boundary before steadily reducing in diversity, until they finally became extinct at the end of the Paleozoic. Two other orders of corals also contributed to faunas during the Paleozoic. The Heterocorallia appeared in the Devonian and became extinct at the end of the Mississippian, while a very small order, the Numidiaphyllida, made a brief appearance in the Late Permian.

No corals are known from the Early Triassic. It appears that all remaining Paleozoic coral groups were wiped out in the great extinctions at the end of the Permian. Anemones must have survived, however, and an Early Triassic trace fossil, *Dolopichnus,* is interpreted as an anemone burrow. Corals reappeared in the Middle Triassic with the order Scleractinia. Scleractinians steadily diversified through the Mesozoic, and following losses in the end

Cretaceous extinction event, they rediversified to produce the rich coral faunas of the present day, well known as the builders of modern coral reefs. No other group of true, zoantharian corals is recognized post-Paleozoic.

Corals are of limited value in biostratigraphy—that is, a given type of coral cannot be used as a "marker" that indicates the age of rock strata. This is because certain types of corals are not confined to only one period of time. However, corals are useful locally, particularly at times in the Paleozoic.

Structure and Relationships of Zoantharian Corals

Each coral polyp, whether it exists as a solitary organism or as a member (module) in a colony, secretes beneath itself a calcium carbonate skeleton, the "corallite." This structure may vary from a cylindrical tube to a virtually flat disc and may consist of discrete plates or spines arranged in horizontal, vertical, or inclined series (Figure 1). Of these characteristics, the most important for determining relationships are the vertical, radiating plates or spines (termed "septa"), that in living corals are known to mirror the arrangement of the polyp's mesenteries (Figure 3). Septa are well developed in the Rugosa (Figures 4F through 4O), Kilbuchophyllida (Figure 4E), Heterocorallia (Figures 4P and 4Q), Numidiaphyllida, and Scleractinia (Figures 4AA through 4JJ). Septa are weak to absent in most Tabulata (Figures 4R through 4Z) and most Lower Cambrian corals (i.e., Figure 4D). In the Scleractinian

polyp, after the first cycle of 6 mesenterial pairs characteristic of all zoantharians has appeared, new cycles are inserted between all the existing pairs, so that the second cycle consists also of 6 pairs, the third cycle of 12 pairs, the fourth of 24 pairs and so on (Figure 3). In the skeleton (although cycles of septa may sometimes appear before the corresponding cycle of mesenteries when complex patterns can arise), this sequence of 6, 6, 12, 24, etc., is reproduced in the insertion of the septa, which normally develop in the space between the mesenteries in a pair. Also, the sequence of insertion is often (but not always) reflected in their relative lengths, so that the first cycle, called "protosepta," are the longest and subsequent cycles, the "metasepta," are progressively shorter.

In the rugose corals, septal insertion is significantly different. Here six protosepta also are recognized, but subsequent septa are inserted serially in only four of the sextants thus defined. No extant (present-day) corals are known with this arrangement, so deductions about development are indirect. However, the Rugosa and the Scleractinia are superficially very similar. Both include solitary and colonial corals and have similar growth forms and well-developed septa. One popular hypothesis was that the Rugosa evolved into the Scleractinia during the Late Permian to Mid-Triassic interval, and intermediate septal arrangements have been claimed. However, these intermediates have not been substantiated (Oliver 1980). Also, most, if not all, Rugosa have a second order of septa, the minor septa, which alternate with the main (major) septa described above (Figure 3). In addition, the rugosan

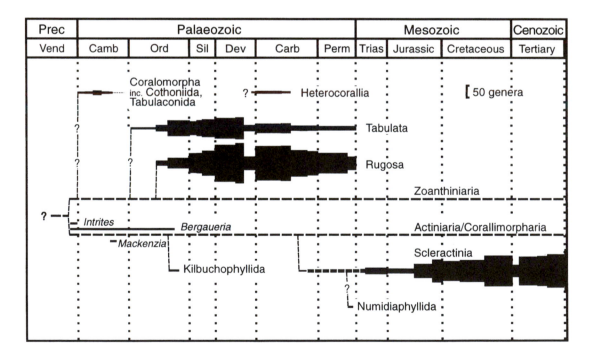

Figure 2. Generalized phylogeny of the subclass Zoantharia of the Anthozoa, which contains the true corals and anemones. The scale in numbers of genera applies to the coral groups only, based on data from Hill (1981) and Wells (1956); horizontal scale proportional to time. Position of the Heterocorallia is arbitrary. *Intrites* and *Bergaueria* are considered to be actinian trace fossils, and *Mackenzia* is a possible fossil actinian anemone. Other anemone trace fossils are known later, in the Phanerozoic, but not shown here. Symbols: *dashed lines,* anemone stocks. Polyphyletic origins of the Scleractinia shown schematically. Reproduced from Scrutton (1997), with permission of the Yorkshire Geological Society.

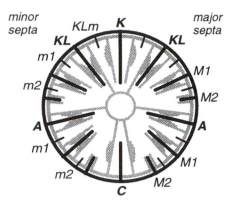

A Rugosa: conjectural mesenterial plan

C Scleractinia: mesenterial plan

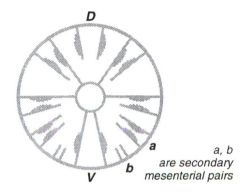

B Zoanthiniaria: mesenterial plan

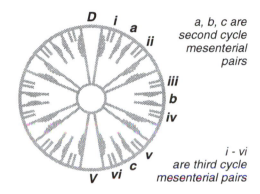

D Corallimorpharia: mesenterial plan

Figure 3. Arrangements of mesenterial pairs and patterns of septal insertion in some corals and anemones. *A,* serial septal insertion in Rugosa, together with conjectural mesenterial pattern, which reflects possible descent from a zoanthiniarian ancestor; minor septa are interpreted as forming between mesenterial pairs. *B,* mesenterial pattern in the Zoanthiniaria, with serial insertion of new pairs in two sextants only, adjacent to the ventral directive couple. *C,* cyclic septal insertion and mesenterial pattern in Scleractinia (lacking septal substitution). *D,* mesenterial pattern in the Corallimorpharia, the anemone group considered to be ancestral to the Scleractinia and the Kilbuchophyllida. Symbols: *black,* septa; *gray,* mesenteries with muscular pleats; *D,* dorsal; *V,* ventral. Protosepta in Rugosa: *K,* counter; *KL,* counter lateral; *A,* alar; *d,* cardinal; *M,* major septa; *m,* minor septa. Based on Scrutton (1997).

skeleton was calcitic, whereas that of the scleractinians is aragonitic (a different type of calcium carbonate), thus requiring a change in skeletal mineralogy that coincided with the change in septal insertion. Furthermore, this does not explain the lack of corals in the Lower Triassic. The Scleractinia and Rugosa now are considered not to be directly related.

The alternative view is that the Scleractinia evolved in the Mid-Triassic from anemone ancestors. The pattern of mesenterial insertion in scleractinian polyps is identical to that in anemones of the Corallimorpharia/Actiniaria group, and the antiquity of this group has been indicated by the discovery of the Ordovician Kilbuchophyllida (which followed the scleractinian septal insertion plan) (Oliver 1996; Scrutton 1997) (Figures 2, 3, 4E). Recent DNA studies suggest that the Scleractinia appeared following multiple skeletonization events in a stock of anemones that evolved from the long-lived corallimorpharian/actiniarian stock in the Late Paleozoic (Veron et al. 1996, Romano and Palumbi 1996).

Scholars infer that the Corallimorpharia/Actiniaria group was ancestral to the Kilbuchophyllida (and probably the Numidiaphyllida, which less certainly has scleractinian septal insertion), as well as the Scleractinia. This interpretation is strengthened by the fact that the kilbuchophyllids and numidiaphyllids had aragonitic skeletons, as in the Scleractinia, whereas those Paleozoic corals in which the skeleton is sufficiently well-preserved utilized calcite. Most anemone trace fossils also are interpreted as actinian burrows, thus extending the history of the Corallimorpharia/Actiniaria group back to the latest Precambrian.

Clues to the origins of the Rugosa must be sought elsewhere. In one group of extant anemones, the Zoanthiniaria, after the first cycle of six mesenterial pairs appear, new pairs are inserted serially in two of the sextants only, flanking the ventral end of the dorsoventral axis (Figure 3). The living zoanthids are a small group of mostly colonial anemones that lack a calcareous skeleton and have no fossil record. However, scholars do assume that these are

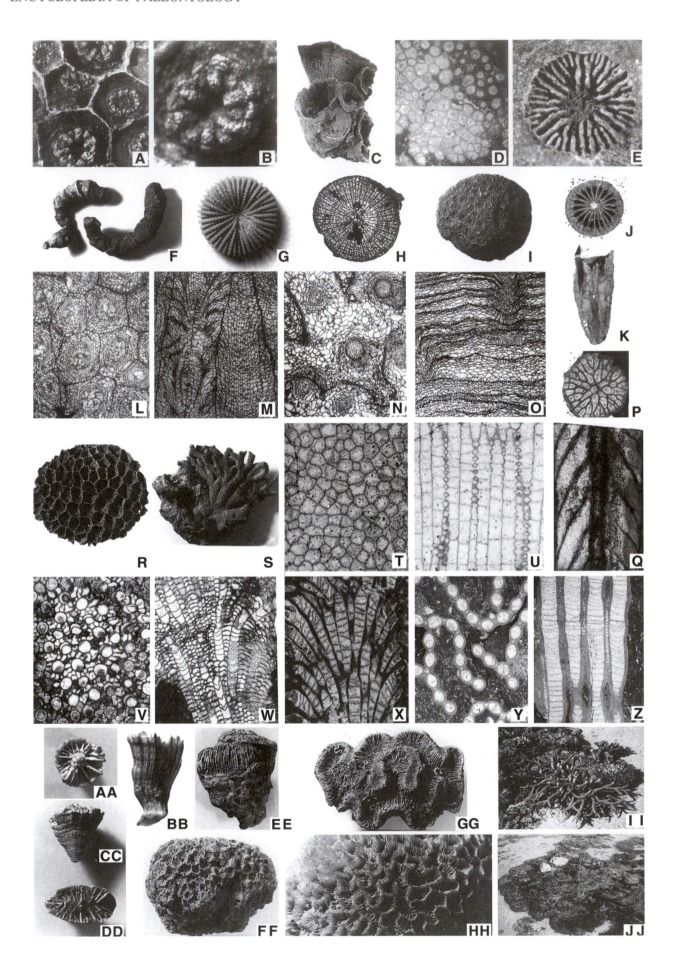

Figure 4. *A, B,* the preservation of fossil polyps in the calices of the tabulate coral *Favosites* sp. (Lower Silurian, Anticosti Island, Quebec.) Scale: *Figure 4A,* ×6; *Figure 4B,* ×25. Reproduced with permission of Paul Copper and the Yorkshire Geological Society, from Scrutton (1997). *C, Cothonion sympomatum.* A cluster of conical corallites, the lower one with operculum in place. This Cambrian coral has some similarities with the Rugosa, which didn't appear until the Middle Ordovician. (Early Middle Cambrian, New South Wales.) Scale: ×3.5. Reproduced with permission of John Jell, the Australasian Association of Palaeontologists, and the Yorkshire Geological Society, from Scrutton (1997). *D, Moorowipora chamberensis.* A cross section of a colony showing corallites close packed *(below left)* but becoming isolated *(top right).* This Cambrian coral has some similarities with later coral groups that appeared in the Ordovician. (Lower Cambrian, South Australia.) Scale: ×1.5. Reproduced with permission of Margaret Fuller, the Royal Society of South Australia, and the Yorkshire Geological Society, from Scrutton (1997). *E, Kilbuchophyllia discoidea.* A mold of a juvenile specimen of this coral in which the characteristic septal arrangement of a scleractinian coral can be clearly seen (compare with Figure 3C). (Middle Ordovician, Scotland.) Scale: ×7. Reproduced with permission of the Yorkshire Geological Society, from Scrutton (1997). *F,* two solitary rugose corals that show curved and geniculate growth resulting from instability on the substrate. Note the external walls to the coralla, the epitheca, and the presence a very small attachment scar at the tip of the left hand coral. (Middle Silurian, Canada.) Scale: ×0.2. *G,* calical view of *Palaeocyclus porpita.* Note that the septa are not perfectly radially disposed but still reflect the pattern of their insertion (compare with Figure 3A). This is a small discoidal rugose coral that in life rested free on a calcareous mud substrate. (Lower Silurian, Gotland.) Scale: ×2. Reproduced with permission of the Yorkshire Geological Society, from Scrutton (1997). *H,* cross section of a typical solitary rugose coral, *Heliophyllum halli.* Note the well-developed radiating septa, with alternating long major septa and shorter minor septa. (Middle Devonian, New York.) Scale: ×0.7. Reproduced with permission of the Yorkshire Geological Society, from Scrutton (1997, Figure 5C). *I,* upper surface of a domal colony of the rugose coral *Acervularia ananas.* The close-packed, polygonal, constituent corallites can be seen clearly. (Middle Silurian, England.) Scale: ×0.25. *J, K,* cross and longitudinal sections of a small, solitary rugose coral *Syringaxon siluriensis.* This is typical of the group of rugose corals characteristic of more marginal environments, such as deeper, cooler, possibly aphotic and dysaerobic waters. (Middle Silurian, England.) Scale: ×2.5. *L, M,* cross and longitudinal sections of the colonial rugose coral *Lithostrotion araneum.* Each corallite is surrounded by a well-developed wall, indicating little communication between adjacent polyps in the colony. (Lower Carboniferous, England.) Scale: ×1.2. *N, O,* cross and longitudinal sections of the colonial rugose coral *Arachnophyllum murchisoni.* Polyps sat on the colony surface directly above the circular structures in Figure 4N. There are no true walls between the corallites, only ridges formed by the vesicular dissepimental tissue, indicating that the polyps were in communication across the colony surface. (Middle Silurian, England.) Scale: ×1.3. *P, Q,* cross and longitudinal sections of a solitary heterocoral, *Heterophyllia grandis.* The heterocorals have well-developed septa like the Rugosa, but they are inserted in a completely different way. They may have evolved from a group of anemones now extinct. (Lower Carboniferous, England.) Scale: ×3. *R,* view of upper surface of colony of the tabulate coral *Michelinia favosa.* The walls of the corallites are marked strongly, but there is no sign of any septa. (Lower Carboniferous, Mississippian, Belgium.) Scale: ×0.3. *S,* side view of the tabulate coral *Cladopora expatiata.* The branching colony is supported by a basal expansion. Each branch consists of many small corallites and in section would look similar to *Thamnopora cervicornis* in Figure 4X. Although these two Paleozoic corals are not themselves reef builders, they belong to the group that in terms of structure is closest to the successful living reef-building coral *Acropora.* (Middle Devonian, Kentucky.) Scale: ×0.2. *T, U,* cross and longitudinal sections of the tabulate coral *Paleofavosites asper.* The corallites are very small and lack well-developed septa. The small circles in Figure 4U are the sections of pores that allow communication between adjacent polyps. (Upper Silurian, England.) Scale: ×3. *V, W,* cross and longitudinal sections of the heliolitid tabulate coral *Propora edwardsi.* The corallites, which lack septa, are set in colonial tissue called coenenchyme; this is equivalent to the coenosteum of some living scleractinian corals. The structure suggests complete integration between polyps in the colony. (Lower Silurian, Scotland.) Scale: ×3. *X,* longitudinal section of a branch of the ramose tabulate coral *Thamnopora cervicornis.* See comments under Figure 4S. (Middle Devonian, England.) Scale: ×1.5. *Y, Z,* cross and longitudinal sections of the tabulate coral *Halysites catenularius.* The corallites, with no septa but strong horizontal tabulae, are arranged like posts along a fence, an arrangement known as cateniform. Note that each corallite is separated by small tubules, which are equivalent to the coenenchyme in Figures 4V, 4W. (Middle Silurian, England.) Scale: ×2.2. *AA, BB,* calical and side views of the solitary, ahermatypic scleractinian coral *Parasmilia* sp. The side view shows strong septal ridges of the first and second order, with weaker third-order ridges in between. There is an attachment scar at the base of the corallum. (Upper Cretaceous, England.) Scale: ×2. *CC, DD,* side and calical views of the solitary, ahermatypic scleractinian coral *Flabellum cuneiforme.* The corallum is elongated along the dorsoventral axis. Four orders of septa are visible in the calice. (Eocene, United States.) Scale: ×1.5. *EE,* side view of the solitary scleractinian coral *Montlivaltia* sp. Traces of epitheca are visible, and many orders of septa. The coral diameter is constricted at the top, and division into two offsets is beginning. (Middle Jurassic, England.) Scale: ×0.6. *FF,* view of upper surface of the colonial hermatypic scleractinian coral *Isastraea limitata.* The colony consists of many small polygonal corallites with well-developed walls. (Middle Jurassic, England.) Scale: ×0.7. *GG,* upper surface of the flabellate hermatypic scleractinian coral *Manicina areolata.* The coral consists of one long elongate meandering corallite, reflecting a single tentacular ring enclosing many mouths arranged along the axis of the corallite. (Recent, Caribbean.) Scale: ×0.4. *HH,* upper surface of the meandroid hermatypic scleractinian coral *Platygyra sinensis.* In this case, each corallite is elongate and complexly intertwined with its neighbors. (Recent, Indo-Pacific.) Scale: ×0.8. *II,* a cluster of scleractinian corals on a reef flat with the Stag's Horn coral *Acropora cervicornis,* about one meter across, prominent at the front (Heron Island, Great Barrier Reef.). *JJ,* a microatoll constructed of a single colony of the hermatypic scleractinian coral *Porites,* about two meters across. (Heron Island, Great Barrier Reef.)

the survivors of a long-lived group of anemones which could have given rise to the Rugosa, either directly or indirectly, by extending serial insertion to another pair of sextants, adjacent and bilaterally symmetrical with the first, together with acquiring a skeleton.

The other major Paleozoic coral group, the Tabulata, were exclusively colonial and also had a calcitic skeleton, but generally the septa are weak to absent so that it is difficult to determine their pattern of insertion. Tabulate corals, with their relatively simple skeletal structure, have had a checkered history (Scrutton 1997). Superficially, some appear similar to the calcareous basal skeletons of demosponges, and indeed, several sponges, particularly the Chaetetida, have been classified with the tabulates in the past. A minority view is that all tabulates were sponges, but various claims that spicules (small, spiny support structures in sponges) have been found in tabulate coral skeletons have been refuted.

On the other hand, unusual preservation in some colonies of *Favosites* from the Silurian of Anticosti Island, Canada, show the remains of very convincing polyps in many of the calices (Copper 1985) (Figures 4A, 4B). Skeletal characteristics in detail are identical also to those in other corals, rather than to the calcareous skeletons of sponges. Finally, recent work on a small group of tabulate corals with well-developed septa has demonstrated an insertion pattern similar to that in rugose corals (Plusquellec et al. 1990). So, assuming this pattern to be characteristic of all tabulates, the likelihood is that the Tabulata could have evolved from an anemone group similar to the ancestor of the Rugosa.

The small group of Cambrian corals includes one genus, *Cothonion,* of solitary-to-clustered small conical individuals with well-developed septa on the underside of an operculum (lid; Figure 4C). Despite this, no clear pattern of septal insertion can be deduced, although in other ways *Cothonion* is similar to the Rugosa. The other genera are colonial and lack well-developed septa, which suggests a similarity to the Tabulata (Figure 4D), even though in some of these, new corallites in the colony are initiated in a way characteristic of rugose rather than tabulate corals. Nonetheless, there is no evidence of direct descent between any of the Cambrian corals and the main coral groups in the Ordovician. Instead, Cambrian corals represent a series of short-lived stocks that became extinct in the Cambrian. Such similarities suggest, at most, possible descent from the same or similar anemone groups as those that gave rise to the Tabulata and Rugosa.

A number of other calcareous structures in the Cambrian are not accepted as corals but have some similarities to anthozoans or other cnidarians. The more coralline of these are placed in an informal category, the Coralomorpha. Further work may clarify their affinities, and some may be related to anemone groups now extinct.

One final group remains to be considered, the Heterocorallia (Figures 4P, 4Q). Members of this group are mainly long, slender corals, mostly solitary but with a few simple branching colonies. Heterocorallia have been placed more or less close to the Rugosa, largely because of their predominantly solitary form and well-developed septa (Hill 1981). However, their skeletal structures, such as the wall and the shape of the calice, are distinct, and their pattern of septal insertion, albeit much disputed, is quite different to that of the Rugosa or indeed any other corals (Scrutton 1997). At the moment, it seems most likely that heterocorallia

evolved from a group of anemones distinct from the two major stocks discussed above and are now extinct.

Coral Classification
Skeletal Structure
Within each order, the classification of corals is based on a range of factors, principally (a) the details of the form and arrangement of the skeletal structures from which the corallite is constructed, (b) skeletal microstructure, and (c) external growth form. Fundamental septal arrangement has been reviewed above, but much additional variation is possible, including the strength of the septa (solid plates, perforate plates, discrete spines, or absent), surface architecture (e.g., smooth, granular), radial or bilateral disposition, thickness, length, and internal microstructure. Septa at or near their outer ends may thicken and meet laterally to form a cylindrical wall (septotheca), with or without the help of other elements. Also, in some cases, one or more (or all) of their inner ends may be modified to form some sort of axial structure. Some corals have a separate external wall (the epitheca), or, a single external wall (holotheca) surrounds all the corallites in a colony. Inclined-to-horizontal plates usually subdivide the corallite transversely (from side to side) and reflect previous positions of the base of the polyp and thus the profile of the calical floor. These may vary from a single series of horizontal plates to a complex pattern of an external series of small, blisterlike plates that are axially inclined, arched, or more rarely peripherally inclined. All have an inner, axial series of larger blisters, or complete or incomplete saucer-shaped, mesashaped, or flat plates (Figure 1B). If an axial structure is developed, there may be yet another axial zone of plates or platelets, which usually form a domelike structure. Unfortunately, terminology tends to differ among the major coral groups, so that Scleractinia possess "vesicular and tabular dissepiments, which may be endothecal (within the theca) or exothecal." In the Rugosa, on the other hand, the outer zone of vesicular plates are "dissepiments," while the inner zone of flatter plates are "tabulae." And, tabulate corals have only "tabulae," which may be flat or vesicular. A very few corals may have no transverse structures at all.

Microstructure
The study of coral microstructure presents various problems and has been a contentious issue. First of all, original microstructure is seldom preserved in those corals with aragonitic skeletons. In most cases, the aragonite has been replaced by calcite, often in large crystals, or the fossil may be an external mold from which the skeletal carbonate has been leached. In the case of the Paleozoic calcitic corals, there has been much dispute as to which microstructures are original and which are secondary. Some scholars have even argued that these corals were also originally aragonitic, but there is now little support for this view. Overall, the result is that scholars make less use of microstructure in classification than might be expected, although the situation is improving. Mesostructural features, such as the characteristics and disposition of "trabeculae" (slender rods of varying microstructure, which are the basic building blocks of the septa) have been of value in classification.

Growth Form

Corals may be either solitary or colonial. Colonies are formed by a founder polyp that duplicates itself by budding, either forming new individuals from tissue outside the crown of the tentacles or by subdivision of the polyp, with new mouths formed inside the tentacular crown. These contrasting methods can be recognized in fossil forms because they result in characteristic structural changes in the skeleton, termed "increase." Solitary and colonial corals can develop with a wide range of external form, which can be useful in classification. In colonial corals, form depends on where new buds and corallites are formed within the colony, the extent to which they develop as discrete individuals, and whether these individuals remain in contact as they continue to grow. Branching corals, in which each branch is a single corallite (fasciculate), are formed by buds that separate completely into isolated polyps, connected only by the skeleton secreted beneath them; in effect, this skeleton records the process of colony development (astogeny).

Alternatively, the buds, although fully individualized, may remain in contact, forming a massive skeleton of close-packed corallites of polygonal (dominantly hexagonal) cross section (Figures 4L, 4M, 4R, 4T, 4U). In others, the buds do not separate completely, and there is a range of increasing integration, from those with simple neural connectivity all the way through to a condition where multiple mouths lead into a single enteron surrounded by an undivided tentacular ring. The level of integration is more or less well reflected in the individuality of the corallites and can, thus, be recognized with reasonable certainty in fossil corals (Coates and Oliver 1973). Most of these forms produce massive colonies (Figures 4N, 4O, 4V, 4W, 4FF, 4JJ), but also ramose (Figures 4S, 4X) and foliaceous forms (where each branch or plate is formed by many corallites), as well as meandroid and flabellate forms (Figures 4GG through 4HH). In the last two, highly elongate corallites complexly intertwine, reflecting linear arrangements of multiple mouths feeding a single enteron.

Overall, scleractinian corals are about 65 percent colonial by genus, but the percentages contrast markedly when broken down between their two major ecological groups. Rugose corals, on the other hand, are about 35 percent colonial by genus, while all tabulate corals are colonial. Most coral species and genera are either solitary or colonial, and within the latter category there are a variety of levels of colonial integration. A number of solitary and colonial corals may have characteristic growth forms. However, growth form results from the interaction of genetic programming and external environmental influences, and the balance shows considerable variation. As a result, a few species include both solitary and colonial individuals with a wide range of growth forms.

Overall, considerable difficulties exist in coral classification within each order, largely because many species have been established with little regard for variation within species. Also, as the coral skeleton is a relatively simple structure, the same components appear over and over again, and it can be difficult to determine which indicate genetic relationship and which have been evolved repeatedly in different lineages (Webb 1996). A recent classification of the Rugosa and Tabulata is contained in Hill (1981) and, although more recent work has proposed many modifications, this major work is still broadly acceptable to most spe-

cialists. In the case of the Scleractinia, several different classifications have been proposed over the last 40 years. The system devised by Wells (1956) has been particularly influential. However, there is much less agreement as to how this group should be subdivided. More recent detailed work on fossil material in which the original aragonite is preserved, along with DNA sequencing analyses of living corals, has highlighted the need for a thorough revision of the classification.

Coral Ecology and Paleoecology
Scleractinia

Living corals play an important ecological role in the construction of tropical coral reefs. However, it is not as well known that corals can also be found at abyssal depths and at latitudes as high as 75 degrees. There are two ecological groups among living Scleractinia, defined by the presence or absence of symbiotic dinoflagellate algae called "zooxanthellae" in the tissues of the polyp (Figures 5, 7). The zooxanthellae play an important, although still not fully understood, role in the metabolism of the coral, principally in the conservation of energy. In simple terms, the waste products of the coral polyp provide food for the algae; the algae, in turn, fix the carbon used by the coral as food and in building its skeleton. Whether or not the coral polyps can ever use the algae directly as food is doubtful, but the algae indirectly provide more than 98 percent of their host's food requirements. The usual action of zooxanthellate corals under stress is to discharge their algae into the surrounding water. The waste disposal activities of the algae promote colonial development and allow coral colonies made up of very small polyps, some only 1 millimeter diameter, to grow very large total area, up to 10 meters or so across. In turn, the algae exert a strong influence on the production of calcium carbonate for the coral's skeleton. As photosynthesizers, algae are dependent on light to function, so there is a strong correlation between light intensity and calcification in zooxanthellate corals. The algae probably help to accelerate calcification in some living corals, such as *Acropora,* which can achieve astounding linear growth rates of up to 270 millimeters per year. However, growth rates in many massive colonies are not particularly fast—on the order of 10 to 15 millimeters per year—and are comparable to growth rates in some corals without symbionts. Recent work has shown that at least in some living corals, the algae act to switch calcification on and off, thus conserving energy, rather than accelerating it (Marshall 1996).

It is the zooxanthellate corals that are the main constructors of living coral reefs; that is to say they are mainly "hermatypic." Confusion has arisen in the past through the application of the term hermatypic (reef-building) to indicate the presence of algal symbionts in corals (zooxanthellate), but the two conditions are not exactly synonymous and should be kept distinct. Most zooxanthellate corals, about 95 percent by genus, are colonial. They are restricted to shallow waters, because of the light requirements of the algae, and to water temperatures of about 16 to 40 degrees Centigrade. It is these constraints that determine the distribution of living reefs. Azooxanthellate corals (those without algae) are not constrained in this way, and although some occur in reefs, most are ahermatypic. Only 30 percent by genus of this group are colo-

Figure 5 Scleractinia	
Zooxanthellate	*Azooxanthellate*
Symbiosis: dinoflagellate algae	Symbiosis: no symbiotic algae
Epitheca: mostly lacking	Epitheca: present in some
Solitary forms <1 meter+ diameter	Mainly small solitary forms

Colonial forms: 95 percent colonial
    large, <10 meters+; mainly massive
    corallites often very small (approximately 1–50
        millimeters)
    close-packed
	Colonial forms: 30 percent colonial
	    corallites: well-spaced, medium-sized
	    mainly dendroidal

Growth rates:
    Acropora 100–150, <270 millimeters/year
    massive forms, 5–15 millimeters/year
    Porites 9 millimeters/year on average
	Growth rates:
	    5–15 millimeters/year
	    <40 millimeters/year in shallow-water
	        branching forms (limited data);
	        calcification rates in some similar to
	        co-occurring zooxanthellates

Skeleton: often light, porous	Skeleton: usually solid nonporous
Temperature: –1° to 29° C	Temperature: 16° to 40° C optimum

Depth
    most 0190 meters
    abundant <70 meters
    optimum 1–25 meters
	Depth
	    0–620 meters; most <800 meters

	Mainly ahermatypic, but fasciculate forms often constructional between depths of 100–150 meters
Most hermatypic	

Figure 5. Summary of the main paleoecological characteristics of Scleractinian corals. Reproduced with permission of the Yorkshire Geological Society, from Scrutton(1998).

nial, and most of these are fasciculate colonies composed of relatively large, well-spaced corallites. However, members of this group can form structures of their own, generally constructed of one or two species of fasciculate corals that form thickets and banks up to several kilometers in length and about 50 meters high. They are found in waters of 100 to 1,500 meters in depth, from equatorial to high latitudes (Stanley and Cairns 1988).

The success of scleractinian corals in building rigid framework reefs, and indeed deep-water banks, lies in their ability to encrust securely onto hard substrates. This facility is due to the lack of an external wall (the "epitheca") and the presence in most scleractinians of an extensive edge-zone to the polyp, active in cementing skeletons together. The resulting framework is very strong and can resist considerable wave energy. Scleractinian corals have played an increasingly important role in reef-building from the Jurassic onwards, although some of the most successful genera on living reefs, such as the stag's-horn coral *Acropora* and the massive-to-ramose *Porites* (Figures 4II, 4JJ), did not evolve until the Tertiary. However, the earliest constructions involving scleractinians were built by azooxanthellate corals, and the first deep-water banks have been identified in the Triassic (Stanley and Cairns

1988). The ecological division between zooxanthellate and azooxanthellate corals appears to have evolved in the very early Jurassic.

Paleozoic Corals

It has been common practice in the past to equate the presence of rich and diverse Paleozoic coral faunas with the development of ancient reefs. However, in contrast to scleractinian corals, both the tabulate and particularly the rugose corals had limited reef-building potential (Figures 6, 7). This was because of the almost universal lack of an edge-zone in the polyps of these corals. Instead, the vast majority had an epitheca or holotheca surrounding the corallum (Figure 4F). Although structure did not preclude the ability to encrust, in most cases attachment scars were small to absent. Adaptations in Paleozoic corals were directed generally to success on soft rather than hard substrates (Scrutton 1998). Furthermore (although this has been disputed), there is no convincing evidence that any Paleozoic corals possessed symbiotic algae. Massive corals remained small, probably no more than two meters maximum diameter, and growth rates and growth forms show little change with depth. Under the influence of light, some zooxanthellate scler-

---

Figure 6 Paleozoic Corals

Rugosa	*Tabulata*
Symbiosis: lacking	Symbiosis: lacking
Epitheca: almost universal	Epitheca: almost universal; restricted to small basal area in some (i.e., ramose colonies)
Solitary forms: approximately 4–14 millimeters diameter	Solitary forms: none

Colonial forms: 36 percent colonial
    colonies mainly small, 30–400 millimeters,
    some <1 meters; massive rarely; <2 meters
    fasciculate rarely larger
    only 16 percent of colonies lack epithecal
        separation of corallites
    corallites approximately 4–50 millimeters diameter
	Colonial forms: 95 percent colonial
	    some level of intracolonial integration
	colonies mainly small, 30–600 millimeters, but some <2
	    meters
	mainly fasciculate, massive

Growth rates: low to moderate; 3–10 (massive); <27 (solitary) millimeters/year; —exceptionally <60–70 millimeters/year	Growth rates: low; 2–9, <20 millimeters/year
Skeleton: usually solid, rarely porous	Skeleton: usually solid, nonporous
Temperature: most tropical-temperate	Temperature: most tropical-temperate

Depth: common <approximately 60+ meters;
    recorded <120 meters, probably extending much
        deeper**
	Depth: common <approximately 60+ meters;
	    probably extending much deeper**

Common in shelf carbonate environments,
    particularly biostromes and some bioherms;
    relatively minor components of reefs
	Common in shelf carbonate environments,
	    particularly biostromes and some bioherms;
	    locally significant contributors of reefs

*Laccophyllid fauna regarded as characteristic of marginal, usually dysphotic/aphobic and/or dysaerobic environments.
**Laccophyllid fauna tolerant of cool, deeper water.

Figure 6. Summary of the main paleoecological characteristics of Paleozoic corals. Reproduced with permission of the Yorkshire Geological Society, from Scrutton (1998) .

---

actinian corals have been shown to reduce their growth rates by 75 percent between surface waters and 30 meters depth, while the colony form changes from dome-shaped to a flat sheet. The main reef builders of the Paleozoic were the stromatoporoids, the basal calcareous skeletons of demosponges, aided by calcareous algae. Corals, particularly the tabulates, played a subsidiary role in these reefs and were common contributors in peri-reefal environments, but corals did not themselves construct significant frameworks.

Paleozoic corals were most important in shallow water bioherms and biostromes, often associated with mud-grade carbonate environments. Fasciculate and some solitary corals were effective sediment bafflers, and many massive corals acted as sediment binders. Thus, numerically rich and diverse faunas were capable of building up the substrate and often provided the foundation subsequently colonized by stromatoporoids. Paleozoic corals favored shallow shelf environments and tropical latitudes, although less diverse faunas are recorded from higher latitudes and deeper, cooler waters. A distinctive fauna of small, simple, solitary rugose corals (e.g., Figures 4J, 4K) and small tabulate coral colonies was associated with dysphotic (low light) and dysaerobic (low oxygen) environments from the Silurian to the Late Permian. This fauna was also able to colonize marginal environments in shallow waters

(Figures 6, 7). This fauna was characteristically cosmopolitan (widespread), in contrast to the changing faunal provincialism displayed by normal shelf faunas.

Ecological and Paleoecological Adaptations

Solitary corals that remained attached throughout life, as with many ahermatypic scleractinians, tend to have small, conical coralla (Figure 4AA, 4BB). Those unattached as adults were often dome- or disc-shaped, with flat bases capable of spreading the weight of the coral on the substrate (snowshoe strategy). Some solitary rugose corals have this form (Figure 4G), but the majority were conical or cylindrical (Figures 4F, 4K). Long, straight, cylindrical coralla could develop in locations where supporting sediment built up around them. Without this support, or where moderate current activity winnowed the sediment, conical corals grew on their sides and developed a characteristic horn-shape as accretion at the calical rim caused it to sink under the influence of gravity, while the polyp continued to grow away from the substrate. In many cases, there is a consistent orientation of the coral's internal structure with respect to the plane of curvature, and some solitary Rugosa developed non-circular cross-sectional shapes that aided lateral stability. The degree

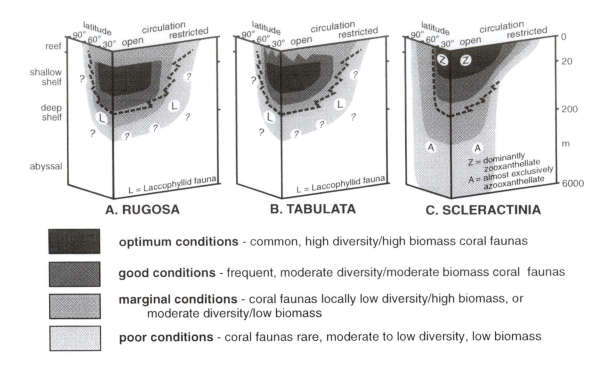

Figure 7. Generalized ecological and paleoecological ranges of the major coral groups in carbonate and fine clastic environments. The reef division is diagrammatic. In *A* and *B*, depth distribution (which often is expressed vaguely for fossil groups) is based on limited evidence. The Laccophyllid fauna *(L)* is generally regarded as deeper, basinal, dysphotic-aphotic, and/or dysaerobic. Most occurrences are probably deep shelf, although there is evidence that this fauna can also occur in some shallower, marginal environments (e.g., arenaceous/terrigenous) or as a pioneer community following a crisis. In *B*, tabulates may make locally important contributions to framework reefs. In *C*, the field labeled *Z* above the line is occupied predominantly by zooxanthellate corals, although azooxanthellates may be present locally as a significant component in nonrestricted reef environments. The field below the line, labeled *A*, is almost exclusively occupied by azooxanthellate corals, although on rare occasions zooxanthellates have been reported to a depth of 460 meters. Adapted with permission of the Yorkshire Geological Society, from Scrutton (1998).

of curvature of horn corals appears to have been related to current strength, with stronger curvature associated with more energetic conditions (stronger currents). On the other hand, short-lived high-energy events, such as storms, could scour away sediment and topple coralla. In some cases this resulted in death, but in others the coral had the ability to grow away from the substrate after such a disturbance, resulting in a corallite with sharp geniculations (bends) along its length (Figure 4F).

In colonial corals, growth forms result from the manner in which new corallites are placed and spaced within the colony, which is genetically controlled, and the influence of a range of environmental variables. If new corallites are produced predominantly at the margins of the colony (peripheral growth), low, spreading growth-forms (e.g., domes, discs, plates, and brackets) develop. At the other extreme, new corallites that develop between older diverging corallites (medial growth), result in taller growth forms, including high domes, bulbous colonies, and ramose colonies, such as the highly successful extant reef-building coral *Acropora* and its closest Paleozoic equivalent, the tabulate coral *Thamnopora* (Figures 4X, 4II). If new corallites do not remain in contact, fasciculate colonies develop, a growth form more common in Paleozoic corals than among the Scleractinia. Almost all

colonial scleractinian corals were attached to a hard substrate in life, and the main environmental controls on growth form appear to be wave energy and light intensity. Delicately branching ramose corals may develop thicker and stubbier branches (or even be reduced to a knobbly surface on the basal expansion cementing the colony to the substrate) as wave energy increases. However, it is now known that some of this apparent variation is associated with a modified gene pool within the species.

Massive corals in shallow water may show the influence of exposure killing off the central areas of the colony while growth continues around the periphery, resulting in the formation of micro-atolls (Figure 4JJ). Under the influence of light levels, colony form (and internal corallite disposition) may change from high domal or bulbous in shallow, well-illuminated situations to flat, platy growth forms in darker, deeper waters. In some cases, such as in certain species of *Porites,* these two growth forms may occur in the same colony as the result of subtle microenvironmental influences. Meandroid and flabellate growth forms, which result from incomplete budding, are unique to the Scleractinia (Figures 4GG, 4HH).

In Paleozoic corals, most colonial forms lived free on soft substrates, when the movement and buildup of sediment was a major factor influencing growth form. Low, spreading growth forms were suited particularly to spreading weight on soft substrates with little or no net sedimentation. Where sediment did accumulate but not to a degree that was lethal to the entire colony, corallites at the margin or over some part of the colony surface might be killed off, followed by renewed lateral spread of the colony over the new sediment surface. Those colonies in which corallites were not in contact (fasciculate) or arranged in series that resembled posts in a fence (cateniform) (Figures 4Y, 4Z) were better able to cope with sedimentation. Indeed, these types of coral relied on sediment accumulating around the lower parts of the colony for stability. Colonies resulting from medial growth achieved higher rates of upward growth, not outward growth, and were particularly suited to conditions of continuing sedimentation. Colony forms included narrow-based, bulbous growth forms, which required sediment buildup around them for stability. Some ramose colonies were attached or stabilized by basal expansions (Figure 4S); otherwise, the alternation of two contrasting growth forms in the same colony was very rare in Paleozoic corals. Only a few tabulates appear to have been obligate encrusters (had a lifestyle that required encrusting) among Paleozoic corals.

COLIN T. SCRUTTON

See also Aquatic Invertebrates, Adaptive Strategies of; Feeding Adaptations: Invertebrates; Reefs and Reef-Building Organisms

Works Cited

Coates, A.G., and W.A. Oliver Jr. 1973. Coloniality in zoantharian corals. *In* R.S. Boardman, A.H. Cheetham, and W.A. Oliver Jr. (eds.), *Animal Colonies, Development and Function through Time.* Stroudsburg, Pennsylvania: Dowden, Hutchinson and Ross.

Copper, P. 1985. Fossilized polyps in 430-Myr-old *Favosites* corals. *Nature* 316:142–44.

Hill, D. 1981. Rugosa and Tabulata. *In* C. Teichert (ed.), *Treatise on Invertebrate Paleontology.* Part F, *Coelenterata* (Supplement 1). Boulder, Colorado: Geological Society of America; Lawrence: University of Kansas Press.

Marshall, A.T. 1996. Calcification in hermatypic and ahermatypic corals. *Science* 271:637–39.

Moore, R.C. (ed.). 1956. *Treatise on Invertebrate Paleontology.* Part F, *Coelenterata.* Boulder, Colorado: Geological Society of America; Lawrence: University of Kansas Press.

Oliver Jr., W.A. 1980. The relationship of the scleractinian corals to the rugose corals. *Paleobiology* 6:146–60.

———. 1996. Origins and relationships of Paleozoic coral groups and the origin of the Scleractinia. *In* G.D. Stanley Jr. (ed.), *Paleobiology and Biology of Corals.* Paleontological Society Papers 1. Columbia, Ohio, and Pittsburgh, Pennsylvania: Paleontological Society.

Plusquellec, Y., J. Lafuste, and G.E. Webb. 1990. Organisation de type tétracoralliaire de rides septales de *Palaeacis* (Cnidaria, Carboniferous). *Lethaia* 23:385–97.

Romano, S.L., and S.R. Palumbi. 1996. Evolution of scleractinian corals inferred from molecular systematics. *Science* 271:640–42.

Scrutton, C.T. 1978. Periodic growth features in fossil organisms and the length of the day and the month. *In* P. Brosche and J. Sünderman (eds.), *Tidal Friction and the Earth's Rotation.* Berlin and New York: Springer-Verlag.

———. 1997. The Palaeozoic corals. Part 1, Origins and relationships. *Proceedings of the Yorkshire Geological Society* 51:177–208.

———.1998. The Palaeozoic corals. Part 2, Structure, variation and palaeoecology. *Proceedings of the Yorkshire Geological Society* 52:1–57.

Scrutton, C.T., and B.R. Rosen. 1985. Cnidaria. *In* J.W. Murray (ed.), *Atlas of Invertebrate Macrofossils.* Harlow: Longman; New York: Wiley.

Sorauf, J.E. 1993. The coral skeleton: Analogy and comparisons, Scleractinia, Rugosa and Tabulata. *Courier Forschungsinstitut Senckenberg* 164:63–70.

Stanley Jr., G.D., and S.D. Cairns. 1988. Constructional azooxanthellate coral communities: An overview with implications for the fossil record. *Palaios* 3:233–42.

Veron, J.E.N., D.M. Odorico, C.A. Chen, and D.J. Miller. 1996. Reassessing evolutionary relationships of scleractinian corals. *Coral Reefs* 15:1–9.

Webb, G.E. 1996. Morphological variation and homoplasy: The challenge of Paleozoic coral systematics. *In* G.D. Stanley Jr. (ed.), *Paleobiology and Biology of Corals.* Paleontological Society Papers 1. Columbia, Ohio, and Pittsburgh, Pennsylvania: Paleontological Society.

Wells, J.W. 1956. Scleractinia. *In* R.C. Moore (ed.), *Treatise on Invertebrate Paleontology, Part F. Coelenterate.* Boulder, Colorado: Geological Society of America; Lawrence: University of Kansas Press.

Wells, J.W., and D. Hill. 1956. Anthozoa—general features. *In* R.C. Moore (ed.), *Treatise on Invertebrate Paleontology, Part F. Coelenterata.* Boulder, Colorado: Geological Society of America; Lawrence: University of Kansas Press.

Further Reading

Hill, D. 1981. Rugosa and Tabulata. *In* C. Teichert (ed.), *Invertebrate Paleontology.* Part F, *Coelenterata* (Supplement 1). Boulder, Colorado: Geological Society of America; Lawrence: University of Kansas Press.

Moore, R.C. (ed.). 1956. *Treatise on Invertebrate Paleontology,* Part F, *Coelenterata.* Boulder, Colorado: Geological Society of America; Lawrence: University of Kansas Press.

Stanley Jr., G.D. (ed.). 1996. *Paleobiology and Biology of Corals.* Paleontological Society Papers 1. Columbia, Ohio, and Pittsburgh, Pennsylvania: Paleontological Society.

Veron, J.E.N. 1995. *Corals in Space and Time: Biogeography and Evolution of the Scleractinia.* Ithaca, New York, and London: Cornell University Press.

AQUATIC INVERTEBRATES, ADAPTIVE STRATEGIES OF

Organisms are intimately linked to their environment. Over the history of a species, the members become adapted to the conditions of their specific environment. If the environment were to change faster than the species could adapt, the species would face extinction. Charles Darwin recognized this complex interrelationship between animals and their environment, and it formed the foundation for his ideas on evolution by natural selection. Natural selection operates as the environment imposes conditions (selection pressures) to which organisms must adapt or perish. These selection pressures include aspects of an organism's physical environment as well as its biological relationships. In marine environments, invertebrates face the physical selection pressures of water temperature, salinity, depth, oxygen content, turbulence, sediment content, and substrate consistency. The main biological selection pressures faced by marine invertebrates are predation and competition for space and food between members of the same species (intraspecific competition) or between different species (interspecific competition).

Marine invertebrates occupying similar ecological niches (e.g., immobile filter-feeders) face similar selection pressures. Specific adaptations to a particular selection pressure (e.g., predation) may be shared by organisms as disparate as clams and trilobites. The adaptations considered here are those that produce specific features of morphology that can be preserved in the fossilized remains (usually the hard outer shell or exoskeleton) of the marine organism.

This discussion of adaptations of marine invertebrates is organized around the animal's environmental niches as defined by their relationship to the water column. These niches are pelagic or planktic (floating passively in the water column), nektic (actively swimming in the water column), and benthic (dwelling at the seafloor). The benthic niche may be further subdivided into epifaunal (living on the top of the seafloor) and infaunal (living within the seafloor).

Pelagic/Planktonic Adaptations

The "plankton" are floaters, and this niche is dominated by unicellular eucaryotes (those with a nucleus), such as foraminifers, radiolaria, and tintinnids. Adaptations to this niche are dominated by designs that enable the organism to remain afloat in the water column. Strategies to accomplish this goal include reducing specific gravity (density) and increasing surface-area-to-volume ratios. In plankton, recurring morphologic designs that help to attain this goal include lacy, delicate tests (skeletons), which reduce specific gravity; globular-shaped tests, which resist settling through the water column; and spines, which increase surface area and thus buoyancy.

Nektic Adaptations

Buoyancy, stability, and either speed or protection are the goals of nektic adaptation. There are only two major groups (phyla) of marine invertebrates that have nektic representatives—(1) arthropods, including crustaceans (ostracodes, crabs, shrimp, and lobsters), chelicerates (horseshoe crabs and the extinct eurypterids) and some members of the extinct Trilobita, and (2) one class of mollusc, the cephalopods (e.g., cuttlefish, squid, octopus, and the extinct ammonites). Two objectives—armor and speed—are mutually at odds in adaptive design, so in the nektic environment there is an adaptive trade-off between the two; that is, heavily armored organisms generally are not fast swimmers, and fast swimmers are usually not heavily armored. Many arthropods, especially the larger ones (chelicerates, crabs, lobsters, and trilobites), are (or were) only occasional swimmers, spending most of their time on the seafloor, and accordingly were well armored. As a result, they were awkward swimmers (watching the horseshoe crab *Limulus* in an aquarium illustrates this point).

Most cephalopods, however, spent the majority of their time in the water column, actively swimming in pursuit of prey or in avoidance of predators. Cephalopods show elaborate adaptations for maintaining buoyancy, stability, and speed. Ancient cephalopods possessed an external chambered shell, either coiled or uncoiled (the modern *Nautilus* is the only living representative with this morphology). These cephalopods achieved neutral buoyancy through careful distribution of their body mass (soft tissue) relative to their shell's center of gravity. This was accomplished in various ways in different cephalopods groups: through adding weight (in the form of endocones or cameral deposits); shedding early formed, gas-filled chambers; or changing the shell shape or coiling pattern during growth.

Other cephalopods, including the modern squid, abandoned the chambered shell for a lightweight, streamlined internal support (the cuttlebone). In return, they achieved greater speed and agility—the better for pursuing prey and dodging predators.

Benthic: Epifaunal

The "benthos" (bottom dwellers) may be divided into two behavioral niches on the basis of whether they are free to move about (mobile), or fixed and immobile (sessile). Both groups face the similar challenge of avoiding predators, exposed as they are on the seafloor, but the two life habits produce different selection pressures, which are reflected in a host of adaptations.

The "mobile benthos" consist primarily of marine invertebrates from two phyla: molluscs (specifically, snails) and arthropods (specifically, trilobites, crustaceans, and chelicerates). These animals face the challenges of moving about the sea floor, capturing prey (or food), and avoiding predators. These two phyla address the challenge of locomotion in very different ways: snails crawl about on a fleshy foot (the extension of the molluscan mantle) and arthropods walk on paired, jointed, armored legs. These basic differences are historical artifacts of their respective evolutionary lineages.

Both groups, however, evolved similar solutions to the selection pressure of predation: they have evolved a protective outer shell, or "exoskeleton." The morphology of snail shells reflects protective adaptations to both physical and biological environmental conditions. Snails living in high-energy environments (e.g., intertidal zones, with heavy wave action) are characterized by thick, wave-resistant shells and tend to be low-spired. Snails living in calmer, deeper water have antipredator spines, while others possess greatly elongated siphonal canals, the better to protect the fleshy siphon (a tubelike organ that draws in or ejects water).

Unlike the snails, who carry their entire life history on their backs as a result of the accretionary growth of their shells, arthropods periodically shed their exoskeletons (molt), rendering them especially vulnerable to predators between the time the old exoskeleton is shed and the new one hardens. Molting is a fundamental, defining character of arthropods. The differential success of the major groups of arthropods may indicate just how critical molting adaptations were in the evolution of this group.

Through the Paleozoic Era (from about 540 to 250 million years ago) the fossil record of arthropods is dominated by a single group, the trilobites. However, this group became extinct by the end of the Paleozoic. The subsequent fossil record of arthropods is neither as abundant nor as diverse and contains mainly crustaceans (crabs, shrimp, lobsters). Trilobites constituted an extremely successful group in most evolutionary measures (e.g., the great number of trilobite taxa, the variety of ecological niches occupied by trilobites, and their considerable range of morphological diversity). Their demise is not satisfactorily explained by the usual extinction mechanism of environmental change.

An alternative explanation arises from a comparison of molting adaptations of the extinct trilobites and those of extant crustaceans. Modern marine arthropods have a single molting pattern. The exoskeleton opens along the same suture(s), and the animal quickly emerges. Trilobite molts show a wide variation in molt habit and indicate that trilobites did not have a single "set" style of molting. The fossils show that trilobites sometimes shed bits and pieces of the exoskeleton, not necessarily all of a piece nor all at one time. Thus, trilobite molting was possibly more prolonged than modern crustacean molting, and the longer molt would increase the danger from potential predators. Trilobites also may have incurred greater mortality during molting by shedding individual pieces of the exoskeleton rather than the entire exoskeleton, as in modern arthropods. This inefficient molt habit was not a problem until the evolution and diversification of trilobite predators. As these predators appeared during the Paleozoic Era, the diversity of trilobites declined to the point of extinction. Modern arthropods appeared during the Mesozoic Era, and their evolution was marked by adaptations that facilitated molting and enabled these animals to elude predators better.

Other features demonstrate the importance of predation as a selection pressure in shaping the adaptations of marine arthropods. Enrollment—the ability to roll up, shielding the vulnerable belly and exposing only the armored back—probably evolved as an antipredator device. Trilobites evolved a variety of enrollment mechanisms, termed "coaptations," that worked in concert to help secure the head shield (cephalon) to the tail shield (pygidium), thus protecting the soft underside of the trilobite.

Spines are also possible antipredatory adaptations, although the function of spines in arthropods is not as clear as in other groups of marine invertebrates—they may be sensory or antipredatory, or they may function as stabilizers for swimming arthropods (as they appear to do in *Limulus,* the horseshoe crab).

Complicating the interpretation of adaptations in the extinct arthropods (or any extinct group) is the fact that different members of the group may have occupied different environmental niches and that some members may have occupied multiple niches (e.g., trilobites that may have swum, walked, and burrowed).

Adaptations among the "sessile (immobile) benthos" are largely a response to two environmental pressures: the nature of the substrate and the challenge of capturing food from a fixed position. The sessile marine invertebrate benthos include sponges, corals, bryozoans, brachiopods, and some echinoderms (e.g., stalked crinoids) and clams.

Generally, the sessile benthos cannot actively pursue prey. Instead, they capture food particles suspended in the water, either as passive filter feeders (sponges) or more selective suspension feeders (crinoids, brachiopods, bryozoans, and clams). Corals, although sessile, are capable of active prey capture with their tentacles.

Because the sessile benthos predominantly feed passively from suspension or by filtering, they are acutely sensitive to the amount of suspended matter in the water column, which is a function of seafloor cohesiveness, energy of the environment, and sedimentation rate. To thrive on a muddy, soupy seafloor, sessile benthos require adaptations that keep the animal from sinking into the mud and keep the feeding apparatus clear. On such types of substrate, the bivalved (two-shelled) brachiopods and clams may develop spines on their lowermost valves or develop a wide, flat shell (the "snowshoe effect"). Either adaptation creates additional surface area that keeps the animals from sinking. Some bivalves achieve an "iceberg" effect by having a massive, elongate lower valve that sinks into the mud, leaving a less massive upper valve (and gape for feeding) above the interface between the sediment and the water.

In high-energy, rocky environments, sessile benthos cement themselves to a surface such as a rock or another shell (clams, barnacles), or attach themselves by means of a threadlike byssus (anchorage fibers, as in mussels). Sponges and corals also tend to be free-living in lower-energy environments but are attached or encrusting in high-energy environments.

Although taxonomically unrelated, the epifauna that form colonies (including sponges, corals, and bryozoans) show similar morphologic responses to environmental conditions. Colonial organisms tend to exhibit plasticity in their colony form—the colony assumes different shapes in different environments. Among colonial organisms there is a tendency toward delicate, twig- or fanlike colonies under low-energy conditions and massive or encrusting growth in high-energy environments.

Benthic: Infaunal

The Paleozoic fossil record of infaunal marine invertebrate benthos is meager, comprising some clams and trilobites. There undoubtedly were many other infaunal dwellers in the Paleozoic, but these probably were unskeletalized and thus left no body fossil record. Evidence of soft-bodied animals is preserved, however, as trace fossils—burrows, feeding structures, tracks, and trails.

During the Mesozoic, occupation of the infaunal niche by skeletal taxa increased dramatically as several major groups developed morphologic innovations that permitted their members to live infaunally (e.g., the development of siphons in clams). The resulting shallow marine invertebrate fauna was so different from its Paleozoic precursor that the event is termed the Mesozoic revolution. This ecologic revolution was marked by a dramatic increase in the diversity of clams and in the appearance of new infaunal groups, including decapod arthropods (crabs, shrimp, and lobsters) and burrowing echinoderms (e.g., sand dollars).

The explosion in clam diversity after the Mesozoic revolution resulted in a wide range of shell forms as clams adapted to the new infaunal niche. Shell outline, convexity, ornament (e.g., ridges and growth lines), and thickness change systematically along an infaunal depth gradient. Shallow-burrowing clams are more globose (convex) and thicker-shelled than deep-burrowing forms. Deeper-burrowing clams are more streamlined (elongate), thin-shelled, and very smooth. This morphology is taken to an extreme by the deep-burrowing "razor clam," *Ensis*.

What Constitutes an Adaptive Strategy

Implicit in the previous discussion is the "adaptationist interpretation": the notion that individual morphologic features are adapted to serve a specific function. However, morphology is more than the sum of individual parts adapted to current needs. It is the result of the interplay of at least three factors: adaptation of the *whole* organism to its environment, the genetic history or evolutionary history of the organism, and constraints imposed by the organism's mode of growth (e.g., the construction of the organism). Therefore, it may not be correct to interpret individual morphologic features solely as adaptations to some current environmental selection pressure. Further complicating adaptationist interpretations is the possibility that a structure serves mul-

tiple functions (e.g., arthropod spines) or that an organism occupies multiple environmental niches (e.g., some trilobites).

Attempts to reduce complex organisms to their constituent parts and to place them neatly into clearly demarcated niches cannot be totally successful, because classification schemes cannot yet capture the full complexity of biological systems. Nevertheless, reasonable adaptive interpretations can be made, and they are strengthened by comparisons between unrelated taxa living in similar environments. Recurrent morphologic patterns across taxonomic boundaries (e.g., the flat shells of the unrelated clams and brachiopods among individuals living on soft seafloors) emerge as common responses—adaptations—to specific environmental conditions. Adaptationist interpretations may be valid but need to be made in their proper context, with full knowledge of the evolutionary and constructional constraints of the organism.

DANITA S. BRANDT

See also Defensive Structures: Invertebrates; Feeding Adaptations: Invertebrates; Ornamentation: Invertebrates; Trophic Groups and Levels

Further Reading

Darwin, C. 1859. *On the Origin of Species by Means of Natural Selection; or, the Preservation of Favoured Races in the Struggle for Life.* London: Murray; 7th ed., London: Murray, 1884; New York: Humboldt, 1884.
Lewontin, R.C. 1978. Adaptation. *Scientific American* 239:212–30.
McMenamin, M.A.S., and D.L.S. McMenamin. 1990. *The Emergence of Animals: The Cambrian Breakthrough.* New York: Columbia University Press.
Palumbi, S.R. 1986. How body plans limit acclimation: Responses of a demosponge to wave force. *Ecology* 67:208–14.
Seilacher, A. 1972. Divaricate patterns in pelecypod shells. *Lethaia* 5:325–43.
Svitil, K. 1997. The trouble with trilobites. *Discover* September, 1997:24.
Vermeij, G.J. 1987. *Evolution and Escalation: An Ecological History of Life.* Princeton, New Jersey: Princeton University Press.

AQUATIC LOCOMOTION

Two important categories can be distinguished among aquatic vertebrates. Primary swimmers refer to animals with aquatic ancestors such as osteichthyans (bony fishes) and chondrichthyans (cartilaginous fishes). Secondary swimmers are aquatic or semiaquatic and descended from a terrestrial ancestor.

Biomechanics

An animal moving in water has to produce a forward force called "thrust." As every action produces a reaction, thrust produces an antagonistic force of water resistance on the body, the "drag." But

in fact, drag can be divided into various components, of which the two most important are the friction drag and the pressure drag. The friction drag corresponds to friction forces of the fluid exercised on the body. The pressure drag refers to the pressure difference between the two extremities of the animal.

A useful measurement for the study of swimming is the fineness ratio (Alexander 1968): FR = total length ÷ maximum diameter (Figure 1). This ratio allows one to characterize "sustained" swimmers, those able to travel and to perform sustained muscular effort over long distances, such as tunas or dolphins. Their fineness ratio is near 4.5.

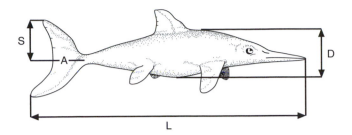

Figure 1. Ichthyosaur (Mesozoic marine reptile). A, area; D, diameter; L, length; S, span; fineness ratio = L/D; aspect ratio = S^2/A. Illustration by Catherine P. Sexton.

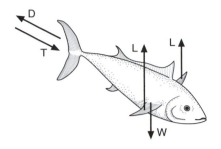

Figure 3. Forces acting on a tuna swimming. D, drag; L, lift; T, thrust; and W, weight. Modified after Lecurn-Renous (1994). Illustration by Catherine P. Sexton.

The aspect ratio (span² ÷ area) quantifies the efficiency of fins, especially the caudal (tail) fin. Fast swimmers have a ratio close to five. Slower swimmers have lower ratios; the butterfly fish, for example, has a ratio of two.

The Reynolds number (water density × length × speed ÷ water viscosity) implies the ratio between speed and viscosity, varying with temperature. A small, slowly swimming animal like a bacterium has a Reynolds number below one. Essentially it fights against viscosity forces. An animal moving with a Reynolds number between 1 and 5.10^5 swims without creating turbulence along its boundary layer (the transition zone where fluid speed is equal to body speed). The most important fast-moving aquatic vertebrates have a Reynolds number exceeding 10^5.

Swimming

The state of equilibrium in the aquatic medium is characterized by the simple equation: thrust = drag. To break this state and propel themselves, organisms must furnish a thrust greater than the drag by using their body or their limbs.

Axial Locomotion

The term "axial locomotion" refers to motion created by propellers situated in the axis of symmetry of the animal's body (Figure 2.1–2.2). The axial locomotion required for propulsion is continuous when all phases of the motion are propulsive. This kind of swimming (used by eels, for example, Figure 2.2) is practiced by an undulatory propeller, such as the trunk or caudal fin. (The expres-

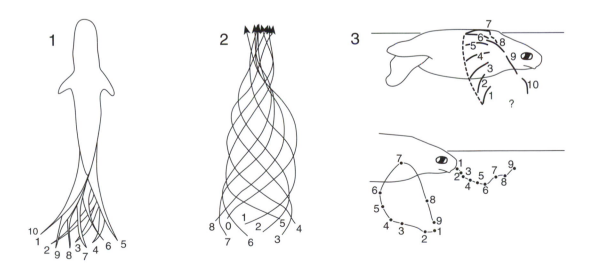

Figure 2. Different kinds of swimming. 1, carangiform swimming (whiting, after Lecurn-Renous 1994); 2, anguilliform swimming (eel, modified after Webb and Blake 1985); 3, subaqueous flight (leatherback turtle, modified after Davenport 1987). Illustration by Catherine P. Sexton.

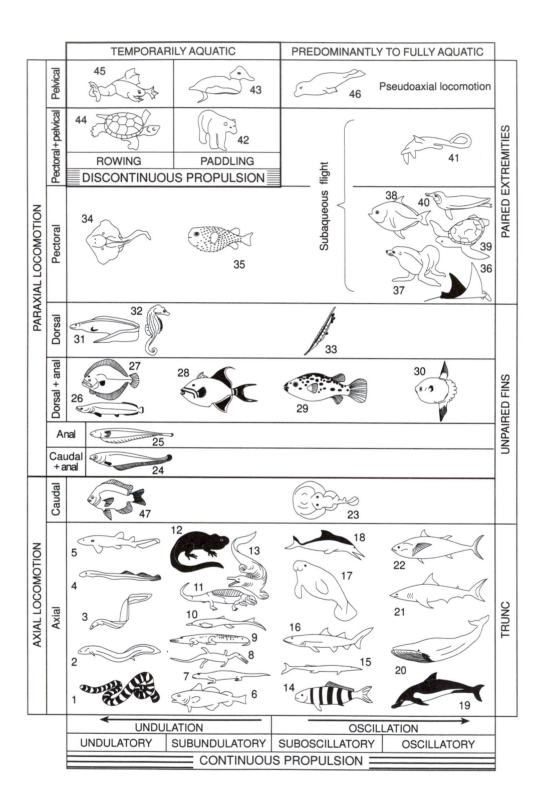

Figure 4. Classification of Braun and Reif (1985). *1, Laticauda* sp. (Hydrophiinae)—sea snake; *2, Lepidosiren* sp. (Lepidosirenidae)—South American lungfish; *3, Anguilla* sp. (Anguillidae)—eel; *4, Petromyzon* sp. (Petromyzonidae)—lamprey; *5, Ginglymostoma* sp. (Ginglymostomatidae)—shark; *6, Gadus* sp. (Gadidae)—cod; *7, Triturus* sp. (Salamandridae)—salamander; *8, Mesosaurus* sp. (Mesosauridae, Lower Permian); *9, Alligator* sp. (Alligatoridae); *10, Cymbospondylus* sp. (Shastasauridae, Upper Triassic)—ichthyosaur; *11, Placodus* sp. (Placodontidae, Upper Triassic)—placodont; *12, Amblyrhynchus* sp. (Iguanidae)—iguana; *13, Clidastes* sp. (Mosasauridae, Upper Cretaceous)—mosasaur; *14, Naucrates* sp. (Carangidae)—advanced teleost fish; *15, Metriorhynchus* sp. (Metriorhynchidae, Middle and Upper Jurassic)—crocodilian; *16, Odontaspis* sp. (Odontaspidae)—shark; *17, Trichechus* sp. (Trichechidae)—manatee; *18, Ophthalmosaurus* sp. (Ichthyosauridae, Upper Jurassic)—ichthyosaur; *19, Delphinus* sp. (Delphinidae)—dolphin; *20, Balaenoptera* sp. (Balaenopteridae)—baleen whale; *21, Carcharodon* sp. (Lamnidae)—shark; *22, Thunnus* sp. (Scombroidea)—tuna; *23, Torpedo* sp. (Torpedinidae—ray; *24, Xenomystus* sp. (Notopteridae)—primitive teleost fish; *25, Apteronotus* sp. (Aptenopteridae)—primitive teleost fish (knife fish); *26, Arapaima* sp. (Osteoglossidae)—primitive teleost fish; *27, Scophthalmus* sp. (Bothidae)—flounder; *28, Balistes* sp. (Balistidae)—advanced teleost fish; *29, Tetraodon* sp. (Tetraodontidae)—puffer (advanced teleost); *30, Mola* sp. (Molidae)—mola; *31, Gymnarchus* sp. (Gymnarchidae)—primitive teleost; *32, Hippocampus* sp. (Syngnathidae)—sea horse (advanced teleost); *33, Aeoliscus* sp. (Centriscidae)—advanced teleost; *34, Raja* sp. (Rajidae)—skate; *35, Diodon* sp. (Diodontidae)—porcupine fish; *36, Manta* sp. (Mobilidae)—ray; *37, Zalophus* sp. (Otariidae)—sea lion; *38, Lampris* sp. (Lampridaie); *39, Eretmochelys* sp. (Cheloniidae)—sea turtle; *40, Sphenicus* sp. (Spheniscidae); *41, Elasmosaurus* sp. (Elasmosauridae, Upper Cretaceous)—plesiosaur; *42, Thalassarctos* sp. (Ursidae)—bear; *43, Podiceps* sp. (Podicepidae); *44, Sternotherus* sp. (Kinosternidae); *45, Xenopus* sp. (Pipidae)—frog; *46, Phoca* sp. (Phocidae)—seal; *47, Abudefduf* sp. (Pomacentridae). Illustration by Catherine P. Sexton.

sion "undulation" refers to motions made by the body and/or unpaired fins; "oscillation" refers to paired fins making a seesaw or cycling motion.) Axial locomotion can be compared with a wave, with its speed of propagation, wavelength, and period. The length of the animal is one of the most important factors in this form of locomotion.

Paraxial Locomotion

Paraxial locomotion needs only the appendicular skeleton, limbs and/or dorsal, pectoral, and anal fins. Propulsion is continuous among aquatic secondary swimmers and discontinuous among semiaquatic or terrestrial vertebrates. For secondary swimmers, propellers always are oscillating.

Discontinuous propulsion consists of a propulsive phase and a repositioning phase (also called "recovery phase"). The latter must avoid generating a negative thrust that would counteract the thrust generated by the propulsive phase. This kind of motion uses resistance during motions to propel the animals, with appendages acting as paddles. This swimming is called either paddling or rowing, depending on whether motions take place in a vertical or horizontal plane, respectively.

Continuous propulsion of paraxial secondary swimmers such as penguins, the leatherback turtle, and plesiosaurs is a kind of swimming belonging to a special category: "subaqueous flight" (Figure 2.3). The paddles of these animals have a hydroplane shape. These hydroplanes have hydrodynamic profiles that, when oriented according to some angle (called the "attack" angle) in a fluid stream, have a lift greater than the drag.

Hydrostatic Control in the Water Column

To control their depth, primary and secondary swimmers exert an active control during locomotion by altering their axial or paraxial motions. To avoid diving, they generate vertical thrust (Figure 3). Dense animals like sharks use their pectoral fins as hydroplanes to generate a lift counterbalancing their density, which is naturally

greater than the density of water. There are other, less demanding ways to move vertically, however, using simple physical principles. Primary swimmers can actually adjust their body density. Stores of fat in the liver (in sharks, coelacanths, and cod, for example) or in tissues help some animals decrease their density. However, in most primary swimmers the principal organ to adjust density is the gas bladder.

The first principle of depth control among secondary swimmers, which is by far the simplest, is the regulation of pulmonary volume, as in marine snakes, the Hydrophiinae, and the marine iguana, *Amblyrhynchus cristatus*, which adjust their buoyancy according to depth. This iguana is neutrally buoyant at a depth of 4.6 meters. Secondary swimmers have improved the vertical position adjustment by playing on three factors in addition to pulmonary regulation: degree of bone density, ingestion of gastroliths (stomach stones), and incorporation of fat in tissues.

In terms of bone density, coastal forms are relatively not well adapted to fast swimming in an open environment; many of these coastal secondary swimmers show a local or general weighting down of their skeleton due to increased bone density (generally termed pachyostosis). Pachyostosis occurs among mammals (notably sirenians and primitive whales, the archeocetes), among birds (sphenicids and alcids—penguins and auks, respectively), many reptilian taxa (pachypleurosaurs, mesosaurs, placodonts, champsosaurs, and snakelike cenomanian squamates), and among several amphibians (stegocephalians). Pachyostosis is encountered among slow swimmers browsing or hunting stationary prey near the bottom. Their negative buoyancy helps these benthic (deep-sea dwelling) animals to "anchor" themselves.

A second structural bone specialization occurs among marine predators able to swim fast over long distances. It consists of lightening of the skeleton (osteoporosis). It is found mainly among cetaceans (whales) and ichthyosaurs. The skeleton of certain secondary swimmers has lost its supporting function in order to develop its new function of depth control.

Many living and fossil secondary swimmer groups such as plesiosaurs, penguins, otarids (eared seals, fur seals, and sea lions),

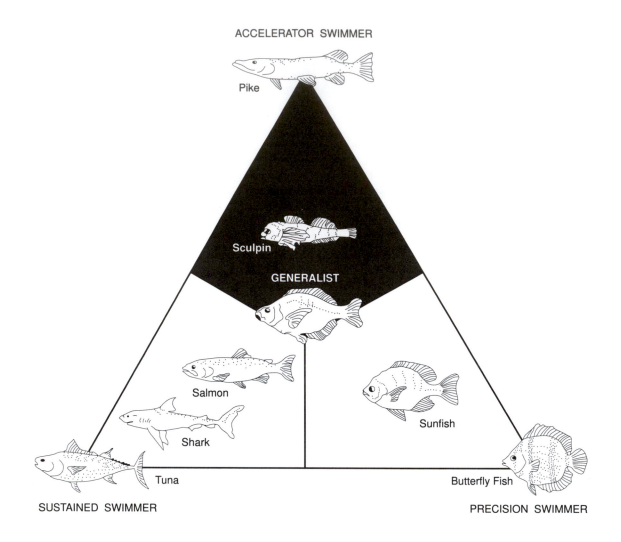

Figure 5. Classification of Webb (1984). Illustration by Catherine P. Sexton.

and crocodilians ingest gastroliths. Secondary swimmers using gastroliths as ballast swim by subaqueous flight or axial undulations. According to M.A. Taylor (1994), this kind of buoyancy control seems to be typical of predator hunting by ambush.

Mammals control their buoyancy using the fat beneath their skin. These tissues also reduce heat loss, increase skin flexibility, and help water to flow along their body. This kind of buoyancy regulation is used by deep divers such as sperm whales.

Maneuverability and Stability

One of the most important locomotion independent factors affecting stability is the relative position of the center of balance, also called center of buoyancy (Hildebrand 1974) in contrast to the center of gravity. Two forces act on a submerged body: the weight, which acts on the center of gravity, and the Archimed thrust (buoyancy), which acts on the center of balance. The first makes the body dive and the second lifts it. The "trim" (attitude with respect to fore-and-aft horizontal plane) therefore depends on

the relative position of these two points. The maneuverability problem is difficult for evolution to solve. Large secondary swimmers are less maneuverable and have less accelerory ability and so have a tendency to hunt much slower prey.

Jet Propulsion

Most invertebrates move by axial undulations or by cyclic beats of their appendages or limbs. Nevertheless, one group can be distinguished from the rest of the animal kingdom: the cephalopods. Their swimming is based on reaction motion or "jet propulsion." The animal violently throws back inhaled water through a tube called a funnel. The animal is then propelled in the opposite direction and can direct itself by orienting its funnel.

Two groups can be distinguished: the most "primitive" ones with an external shell, such as ammonites (fossil) or nautiloids, and those with an internal shell, such as belemnites (fossil), squids, and octopuses. Cephalopods with an external shell act like a reaction submarine. Their shell is constituted of chambers linked by a siphon. The latter fills or empties the chambers, which act like the "ballast" of a submarine, allowing the animal to rise or dive. Cephalopods with an internal shell have more diverse shapes. The more efficient of them, cuttlefish, are able to leap in the air over a distance of 50 meters at a height of 7 meters. They can swim at speeds up to 72 kilometers per hour (Mangold and Bidder 1989).

Vertebrate Aquatic Locomotion: Main Classifications and Morphological Analysis

Primary swimmers group together organisms having a large diversity of shapes and sizes corresponding to distinct ecological niches. Some of them are even shared with some secondary swimmers. There are many systems of classification including primary and/or secondary swimmers (for example, Nopcsa and Heidseck 1934). But, among them, the following two are especially representative of classifications correlating shape to function.

Classification of Braun and Reif (1985)

This system is based on the locomotor apparatus and the kind of locomotion used (Figure 4), and it has the advantage of including all living and fossil organisms, whether they are primary or secondary swimmers.

J. Braun and W.E. Reif emphasize the gradation that exists from anguilliform swimming (the entire body undulates, more than one motion wavelength is seen, Figure 2.2) to carangiform (stiff hydrodynamic body, motion strictly restricted to the caudal area, Figure 2.1) and thunniform swimming (that practiced by the fastest swimmers, such as tunas or dolphins). Thunniform swimming is considered to be the most efficient and evolved style because of its hydrodynamical performance. Animals using this style have a stiff elliptical trunk to avoid lateral drag. Their hydrodynamic body limits friction. Their caudal peduncle (stalk attaching the caudal fin) is narrow, thus avoiding unnecessary oscillations of the body. Their caudal fin is seleniform (crescent shaped), a compromise between maximal thrust and drag reduction.

Classification of Webb (1984)

P. Webb (1984) has proposed a morphofunctional classification based on the type of swimming of living osteichthyans and chondrichthyans (Figure 5). Three categories are distinguished:

Accelerator swimmer (body/caudal fin transient propulsion). This kind of propulsion is typical of a hunter in ambush, able to accelerate suddenly in areas rich with prey. The shape of their body allows them to make motions of large amplitude. The pro-

pulsive elements are located toward the rear. The pike is one of these fishes.

Sustained swimmer (body/caudal fin periodic propulsion). This type of swimming is typical of long-range swimmers searching for scattered prey. They have low accelerating capacities. They have the morphology of carangiform and thunniform swimmers such as marlins.

Precision swimmer (median/paired fin propulsion). These fishes are able to swim at low speed in a complex and rich environment. The animal generally has to hide itself. It is not necessary for them to travel far for feeding or to accelerate suddenly. The paired and unpaired fins are well developed and placed near the center of gravity, allowing the fish to swim in any direction. These features are seen, for example, in the butterfly fish.

Most fishes share characteristics belonging to the various categories; trout, for instance, belong to a generalist category.

STÉPHANE HUA

See also Aquatic Invertebrates, Adaptive Strategies of; Aquatic Reptiles; Biomechanics; Functional Morphology

Works Cited

Alexander, R.McN. 1968. *Animal Mechanics.* Seattle, Washington: University of Washington Press; London: Sidgwick and Jackson.
Braun, J., and W.E. Reif. 1985. A survey of aquatic locomotion in fishes and tetrapods. *Neues Jahrbuch für Geologie und Paläontologie Abhandlungen* 169(3):307–32.
Davenport, J. 1987. Locomotion in hatchling leatherback turtles *Dermochelys coriacea. Journal of Zoology* 212:85–101.
Hildebrand, M. 1974. *Analysis of Vertebrate Structure.* 1st ed., New York: Wiley.
Lecurn-Renous, S. 1994. *Locomotion.* Paris: Dunod.
Mangold, K., and M. Bidder. 1989. Flottabilité et locomotion. *In* Pierre Grassé (ed.), *Traité de Zoologie.* Tome 5, fasc. 4, *Céphalopodes.* Paris: Masson.
Nopcsa, F., and E. Heidseck. 1934. Über eine pachyostotische Rippe aus der Kreide Rüns. *Acta Zoologica* 15:431–55.
Taylor, M.A. 1994. Stone, bone or blubber? Buoyancy control strategies in aquatic tetrapods. *In* L. Maddock, Q. Bone, and J.M.V. Rayner (eds.), *Mechanics and Physiology of Animal Swimming.* Cambridge and New York: Cambridge University Press.
Webb, P. 1984. Body form, locomotion and foraging in aquatic vertebrates. *American Zoologist* 24:107–20.
Webb, P., and R. Blake. 1985. Swimming. *In* M. Hildebrand, D.M. Bramble, K.F. Liem, and D.B. Wake (eds.), *Functional Vertebrate Morphology.* Cambridge, Massachusetts: Harvard University Press.

AQUATIC REPTILES

Reptiles evolved and initially radiated (diversified and spread geographically) in terrestrial habitats, but numerous lineages have reentered the water, becoming largely or completely aquatic. Ichthyosaurs, placodonts, crocodilians, and sauropterygians (plesiosaurs, pliosaurs, and nothosaurs) are the most well known groups. The interrelationships among the major lineages of aquatic reptiles, as well as between them and their nearest terrestrial relatives, are shown in Figure 1. Despite having very distinct terrestrial ancestors, the different groups of aquatic reptiles have evolved very similar adaptations for locomotion under water, buoyancy control, feeding, respiration, and reproduction.

The tail is almost always deep and laterally compressed, with tall, bony arches that provided passageways for neurons and blood vessels. The proximal limbs are flipperlike, with short flat bones (humerus, radius, ulna, femur, tibia, fibula), and there are extra bones in each digit (hyperphalangy) and/or extra digits (hyperdactyly). Aquatic animals must counteract their tendency to float when diving with a lungful of air. Slow-swimming forms often achieved this via hydrostatic methods (ballast), such as increased ossification of the skeletal elements (pachyostosis) or the ingestion of stomach stones (gastroliths). In more active swimmers, hydrodynamic methods (hydrofoils, such as flippers) use energy more efficiently. The support that water provides means that the limbs and girdles no longer need to bear weight. Contact between the hip socket and the ball of the femur is frequently reduced, the limbs poorly ossified, and the elbow and knee joints straightened.

Many groups exhibit gigantism. Long thin necks and small skulls have evolved repeatedly. This structure reduces the amount of water resistance encountered during rapid lunges ("strikes") at prey items. In predatory forms, long narrow snouts often have evolved, allowing the jaws to snap shut quickly with minimal resistance from water. These forms also often have widely spaced, conical stabbing teeth to impale prey, preventing them from swimming or floating away. The external nostrils often shift towards the top of the skull, facilitating breathing at the surface. Finally, many forms are viviparous (bear live young), and thus do not need to return to land to reproduce. The membrane that surrounds an amniotic egg cannot maintain the proportion of water required for a developing embryo to survive underwater. Therefore, oviparous (egg-laying) marine reptiles (such as living sea turtles and sea kraits) must struggle ashore to deposit eggs.

Despite their numerous common adaptations, the morphology (shape and structure) of aquatic reptiles is still diverse. Eight major body forms can be recognized (Figure 2), representing different solutions to the common problem of moving through water. These categories are modified from Carroll (1985) and Massare (1994).

Type 1

The Type 1 body characterizes mosasauroids (marine lizards), thalattosuchians (marine archosaurs), and the primitive ichthyosaur

Chensaurus. The trunk region is cylindrical and of intermediate length, there are two pairs of short webbed feet or flippers (all approximately equal in size), the head is large and narrow, and the neck relatively short. The tail is paddlelike and usually expanded into a tail "fin." These animals move through the water by undulating the trunk and tail; the flippers are used more for orientation or extra thrust during lunges.

Mosasauroids (Figure 2A) include the medium-sized, semi-aquatic aigialosaurs (Upper Jurassic to Mid-Cretaceous) and their descendants, the fully marine, large-to-gigantic mosasaurs (Upper Cretaceous). All mosasauroids had long narrow snouts and highly flexible jaws with numerous sharp conical teeth, and they clearly were fierce predators (Russell 1967). Mosasaurs differ from aigialosaurs, possessing more extensive bodily adaptations for an aquatic existence. The limbs were true flippers rather than webbed feet, the dorsal ribs near the hips were shortened, and the tail was taller, with sides that were more compressed. Mosasaurs frequently exceeded 10 meters in length and included the largest marine reptiles ever (Lingham-Soliar 1995). They were a diverse, abundant, and worldwide group and include three principal lineages (Russell 1967; Bell 1997). Mosasaurines have long bodies and short, flared tails: they lack an overhanging snout (rostrum). Plioplatecarpines and tylosaurines are closely related to one another. Both have short bodies and long narrow tails. Although plioplatecarpines lack a rostrum, tylosaurines possess a large one. Viviparity recently has been recognized in mosasaurs (Bell et al. 1996). The origin of mosasauroids is controversial; the most recent work suggests that they are closely related to snakes (Lee 1997).

Thalattosuchians (Early Jurassic to Mid-Cretaceous) are marine archosaurs (Figure 2B). They consist of two major groups, teleosaurs and metriorhynchids. Teleosaurs have webbed feet, dermal armor (bony plates that originate in the skin), and a tapering tail. They appear to have been bottom-dwelling predators that hunted in coastal waters. Metriorhynchids have flippers, lack dermal armor, and have an expansion of the end of the tail. They appear to have favored pelagic (open-water), offshore waters (Hua and Buffrénil 1996). Previously considered very primitive members of Crocodyliformes and, thus, only distantly related to eusuchians (living crocodilians), thalattosuchians might actually be quite closely related to eusuchians (Clarke 1994).

The primitive ichthyosaur *Chensaurus* differs from all later ichthyosaurs in having a slender body, a constriction in the neck region, and a long slender tail (Figure 2C). Comparisons with extant (modern-day) sharks suggests that, like other Type 1 taxa (groups, singular taxon), *Chensaurus* swam by axially undulating the body and tail (Montani et al. 1996). However, this animal already has most of the traits of later ichthyosaurs, namely the long pointed snout, huge orbits (eye sockets), well-formed flippers, and dorsal fin. So, even though it is a primitive form, it has not shed much light on ancestry of ichthyosaurs. While there is now a consensus that ichthyosaurs are diapsid reptiles (the group that includes the dinosaurs), their position within Diapsida remains

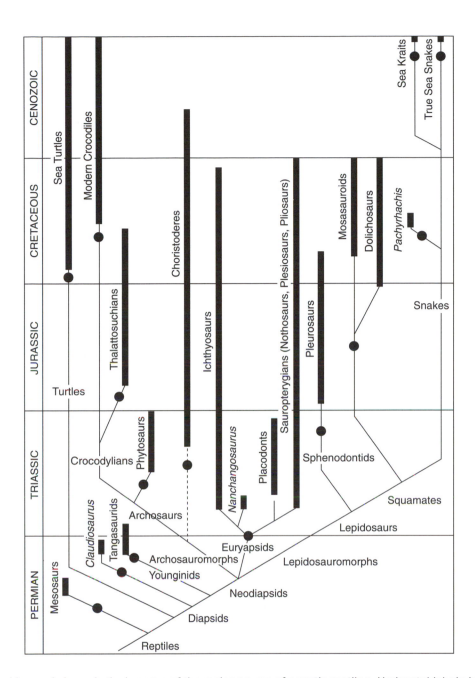

Figure 1. Interrelationships and chronological ranges of the major groups of aquatic reptiles. Horizontal labels indicate more inclusive groups (e.g., *Pachyrhachis* belongs within these successively more inclusive groups: snakes, squamates, lepidosauromorphs, neodiapsids, diapsids, and reptiles). Black circles denote each independent evolution of aquatic adaptations.

uncertain. The most recent analysis (Caldwell 1996) tentatively places them with placodonts and sauropterygians.

Type 2

Type 2 body shape characterizes all ichthyosaurs (except the primitive *Chensaurus*) and *Nanchangosaurus*. The overall shape is very "fishlike" (thunniform) and streamlined (Figure 2D). The head has a narrow, pointed snout that merges smoothly into a spindle-shaped body; there is no narrow neck region. There are two pairs of flippers, the hind pair typically being smaller. Loco-

motion involved mainly the tail, with little or no contribution from body undulations.

Ichthyosaurs above *Chensaurus* are the most highly specialized of all marine reptiles. They range from the Early Triassic, reached a diversity peak in the Early Jurassic, and then gradually declined, vanishing by the Mid-Cretaceous. In addition to the above Type 2 adaptations, these icthyosaurs possessed fleshy dorsal and caudal fins. The limbs are reduced to small steering fins. Later forms have even more streamlined bodies and symmetrical tail fins. The skull is very distinctive, bearing a huge orbit and a large upper temporal fenestra (open area in the temple region of the

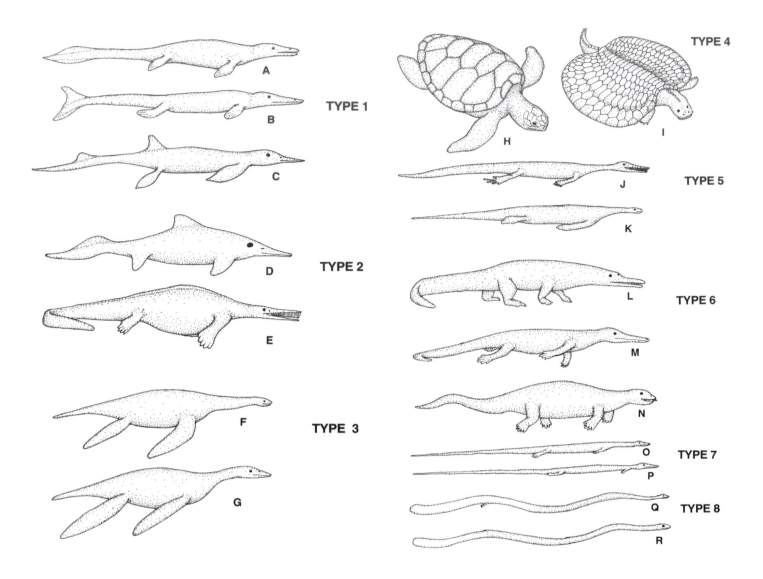

Figure 2. The eight main body types of aquatic reptiles, with two or three representatives of each type. *Type 1, A, mosasaur (Tylosaurus); B, thalattosuchian (Geosaurus); C, primitive ichthyosaur (Chensaurus). Type 2, D, typical ichthyosaur (Mixosaurus); E, Nanchangosaurus. Type 3, F, plesiosaur (Cryptocleidus); G, pliosaur (Peloneustes).* **Figure 2 (continued).** *Type 4, H, sea turtle (Dermochelys); I, advanced placodont (Henodus). Type 5, J, mesosaur (Mesosaurus); K, nothosaur (Nothosaurus). Type 6, L, phytosaur (Rutiodon); M, choristoderan (Champsosaurus); N, primitive placodont (Placodus). Type 7, O, dolichosaur (Dolichosaurus); P, pleurosaur (Pleurosaurus). Type 8, Q, primitive snake (Pachyrhachis); R, sea krait (Laticauda).*

skull). Although they possess 40 to 50 vertebrae, the body is short. This pattern has been attributed to their evolution from longer-bodied ancestors such as *Chensaurus:* advanced ichthyosaurs presumably shortened their bodies by reducing the length of each vertebra, rather than by losing them (Montani et al. 1996). Many fossils of ichthyosaurs with young in utero or even in the process of birth have been found in deposits of the Lower Jurassic of Germany, providing striking proof that they were viviparous and did not return to land to reproduce.

Nanchangosaurus (Hupehsuchus) is an engimatic animal from the Early Triassic of China (Figure 2E). It is similar in shape and body proportions to Triassic ichthyosaurs, but its limbs are more primitive, and it has a completely toothless beak and a row

of dermal armor above the vertebral column that is reminiscent of archosauromorphs (Carroll and Dong 1990).

Type 3

The Type 3 body characterizes advanced sauropterygians (plesiosaurs and pliosaurs). Both plesiosaurs and pliosaurs ranged from the Lower Jurassic until the end of the Cretaceous. The trunk region is short and broad and dorsoventrally compressed (the distance between the belly and the backbone is diminished, forcing the sides outward, such as seen in sharks). The ventral (belly-side) plates of the pectoral and pelvic girdles also are stretched toward the front and back, and the gastralia (ventral ribs) are very massive.

These factors all make the trunk very rigid. The animal is propelled forward entirely by a distinct type of underwater flight, using four long, narrow flippers (Halstead 1989; Massare 1994). (Present-day penguins also use this technique.) Presumably, the short tail was used for steering.

Plesiosaurs have small heads with numerous pointed recurved (curved back toward the throat) teeth, and long, slender necks with up to 76 vertebrae (Figure 2F). The jaws and teeth and the stomach contents suggest that plesiosaurs preyed on fish, pterodactyls, thin-shelled ammonites (molluscs, such as snails, mussels, clams, and nautiluses), and other small prey (Massare 1987), which were caught by rapid lunges of the neck and head. The forelimbs are usually very slightly larger than the hind limbs.

Pliosaurs have large heads with more massive teeth and short necks with as few as 13 vertebrae (Figure 2G). They have been interpreted as opportunistic predators, taking other marine reptiles as well as fish and cephalopods (Massare 1987). Unlike plesiosaurs, they were probably pursuit predators. The forelimbs are usually very slightly smaller than the hind limbs.

Type 4

The Type 4 body characterizes sea turtles and certain advanced placodonts. It appears to be an elaboration of Type 3. The trunk is very short, very broad, dorsoventrally compressed, and encased in a rigid shell. The number of vertebrae in the abbreviated trunk region is reduced. The neck and tail are both short. There are four flippers, the front pair usually being larger and providing most propulsive force.

Sea turtles (cheloniids) date from the Early Cretaceous onward, but were most diverse during Late Cretaceous (Figure 2H). The anterior flippers are used in underwater flight. Unlike typical turtles, cheloniids rely partly on speed to escape predators. Accordingly, they have lost the ability to retract the skull and limbs and have reduced the shell. Today's leatherback turtle (*Dermochelys*) and the related Cretaceous forms *Protostega* and *Archelon* reach nearly four meters in length.

The advanced, turtlelike placodonts are restricted to the Late Triassic and include forms such as *Henodus, Placochelys, Cyamodus,* and *Psephoderma* (Figure 2I). The entire body is covered by a rigid carapace (shell) consisting of polygonal ossicles (bony plates). Some forms even have lost the anterior (front) teeth, instead possessing a turtlelike beak. Their crushing posterior (back) teeth suggest they fed on hard-shelled prey.

Type 5

The Type 5 body characterizes mesosaurs, primitive sauropterygians (nothosaurs), hovasaurids, and *Claudiosaurus*. The trunk region is short to moderate in length and slightly laterally compressed, the tail is very long, and the sides are greatly compressed. The skull is relatively small and the neck relatively long and narrow. Four limbs (webbed feet), approximately equal in size, are retained. They moved rapidly by undulating the tail (and, to a lesser extent, the body) laterally. The prominent limbs may have been used for steering, bottom walking, and slow swimming.

Apart from sea turtles, mesosaurs are the only group of anapsid-grade reptiles (primitive reptiles) to become totally aquatic (Figure 2J). They are found in the Mid-Permian of South Africa and South America. Though aquatic, the mesosaurs' small size and weak swimming specializations would not have allowed them to cross the Atlantic Ocean, so scholars have viewed their distribution as early evidence for continental drift. Mesosaurs have long narrow snouts with needlelike teeth, presumably for trapping very small aquatic prey. The ribs and vertebrae are greatly swollen (pachyostotic). The tail vertebrae have obvious fracture planes, suggesting that mesosaurs could have shed their tails when distressed (caudal autotomy). This is surprising, considering the tail appears to have been their main locomotory organ.

Hovasaurids (*Tangasaurus* and *Hovasaurus*) are aquatic younginids (lizardlike reptiles), a group of primitive diapsids from the Upper Permian. They differ from typical terrestrial younginids in possessing an extremely deep tail and incorporating stomach stones for ballast. *Claudiosaurus* is another diapsid from the Upper Permian of Madagascar. Like mesosaurs, it has pachyostotic vertebrae. The tail, though long, is not dorsoventrally expanded, unlike most long-tailed aquatic taxa. Although previously argued to be ancestral to sauropterygians, recent studies demonstrate that it is in fact a very primitive diapsid, not closely related to any other aquatic taxa (Rieppel 1994).

Nothosaurs (Middle Triassic), as traditionally defined, are primitive sauropterygians, ancestral to plesiosaurs and pliosaurs (Figure 2K). They share many features with plesiosaurs and pliosaurs, such as a large, tooth-bearing bone that forms the front end of the upper jaw (premaxilla), loss of a bone in front of the eye socket (lacrimal) in the snout, loss of the lower (temporal) arch that formed a cheek area, and an elongate region of the skull, in the area behind the eye socket (Rieppel 1994). However, aquatic adaptations to the body skeleton are very different. Small nothosaurs such as pachypleurosaurs swam mainly by undulating the tail laterally. Larger nothosaurs, such as *Corosaurus* and *Simosaurus*, presumably used the limbs as well as the trunk for locomotion, foreshadowing the limb-driven pattern in plesiosaurs and pliosaurs (Storrs 1991).

Type 6

The Type 6 body characterizes modern crocodilians (eusuchians), phytosaurs (parasuchians), choristodirans (champsosaurs), and primitive placodonts. The trunk is stiff and stocky, and the tail is laterally compressed and of moderate length. The limbs are small but well-ossified and capable of terrestrial locomotion. This body form characterizes relatively large, semiaquatic predators.

Placodonts (Middle to Late Triassic) have very robust, solid skulls (Figure 2N). They presumably fed on hard-shelled invertebrates found in shallow water, using their chisel-like front teeth to dislodge prey and broad teeth farther back in the jaw to crush them. Primitive forms had a Type 6 body with a row of dermal armor over the middle of the back. In some later forms, the dermal armor becomes elaborated into a turtlelike carapace, resulting in a Type 4 body. The most recent work suggests that placodonts are related to sauropterygians (Rieppel 1994).

Choristodirans (Figure 2M) are a long-lived lineage of crocodile-like animals known from the Early Triassic to the Oligocene (Storrs and Gower 1993; Evans and Hecht 1993). Except for the primitive *Lazarussuchus,* they have very distinct flat skulls with slender snouts that resemble those of an extant fish-eating crocodile of India, cheek regions that are expanded out to the sides. The ribs are pachyostotic. Their precise affinities with other diapsids long have been problematical; recent work tentatively links them with archosauromorphs (Storrs and Gower 1993; Rieppel 1994).

Phytosaurs (Late Triassic) are archosaurs distantly related to extant modern crocodilians (Figure 2L). They have flat triangular skulls. The snout is elongate, unlike all other long-snouted archosaurs, however, this elongation is achieved by telescoping the region in front of the nostrils, rather than behind them. The nostrils, therefore, remain situated near the eye sockets (rather than at the tip of the snout), and have raised rims, which facilitate breathing while submerged.

Eusuchians (modern crocodilians) consist of crocodylids, alligatorids, gavials, and the "false" gavial. Their osteoderms (bony elements that develop within the dermis) are bound firmly to one another, unlike the overlapping arrangement found in more primitive crocodyliforms (Clark 1994). All are flat-skulled predators that live in freshwater or in estuaries. However, specialized salt-excreting glands (analogous to those of seabirds) suggest that their ancestors might have been marine. Alligatorids are the most primitive eusuchians, and the gavials and "false" gavials are actually closely related to each other (Poe 1996).

Type 7

The Type 7 body characterizes dolichosaurs and most pleurosaurs. The body is elongate and flexible (but not as greatly as in Type 8), all four limbs are present but greatly reduced, and the tail is long and tapering. Locomotion is by undulations of the body and tail.

Dolichosaurs (Early Cretaceous) are marine squamates (lizards and snakes) related to mosasauroids (Figure 2O). They have long, narrow, highly flexible skulls like mosasauroids but differ in being smaller and having longer bodies (especially the neck and tail) and reduced limbs (Caldwell, work in progress).

Pleurosaurs (Early Jurassic to Early Cretaceous) are marine relatives of the extant Tuatara *(Sphenodon)* (Figure 2P). Despite their marine adaptations, pleurosaurs have most of the features of typical sphenodontids: the teeth are fused to the jaw and the teeth at the front are enlarged and chisel-like. In a few early forms, the snout is short (as in terrestrial sphenodontids) and the body only slightly elongate. In later forms, the snout is long and narrow and the body longer (Carroll and Wild 1994). Unlike dolichosaurs, however, only the trunk and tail are elongate; the neck remains short. Consequently, the small forelimbs are positioned quite near the front of the body.

Type 8

The Type 8 body characterizes the three groups of highly aquatic snakes: *Pachyrhachis,* sea kraits (laticaudines), and true sea snakes

(hydrophiines). This body type represents a further development of Type 7. The body is greatly elongate and highly flexible, with a round, whiplike shape in front and flattened with sideways projections at the back. Limbs are greatly reduced or absent. All move like eels.

Pachyrhachis is known from two specimens from the Middle Cretaceous. It is more primitive than all other snakes—it retains a jugal (cheek) bone in the skull and a normal (though small) pelvis and hind limb (Figure 2Q). *Pachyrhachis* resembles certain living sea snakes, having a small skull and narrow neck, but differs markedly from all other snakes, having very broad mid-dorsal vertebrae and ribs (Caldwell and Lee 1997).

The remaining two groups of sea snakes are extant and represent two separate marine radiations of terrestrial (land-based) front-fanged snakes. The sea kraits (Figure 2R) are oviparous, return to shore to lay eggs, and retain the broad ventral scales (gastrosteges) that terrestrial snakes use for locomotion. Hydropheines are viviparous and thus completely aquatic. Their ventral scales are highly fragmented.

MICHAEL S.Y. LEE

See also Aquatic Locomotion; Archosauromorphs; Ichthyosaurs; Lepidosauromorphs; Placodonts; Sauropterygians; Turtles

Works Cited

Bell, G. 1997. A phylogenetic revision of North American and Adriatic Mosasauroidea. *In* J.M. Callaway and E.L. Nicholls (eds.), *Ancient Marine Reptiles.* New York and San Diego, California: Academic Press.

Bell, G., A.M. Sheldon, J.P. Lamb, and J.E. Martin. 1996. The first direct evidence of live birth in Mosasauridae (Squamata): Exceptional preservation in the Cretaceous Pierre Shale of South Dakota. *Journal of Vertebrate Paleontology (Supplement)* 16 (3):21A–22A.

Caldwell, M.W. 1996. Ichthyosauria: A preliminary phylogenetic analysis of diapsid affinities. *Neues Jahrbuch für Geologie und Paläontologie Abhandlungen* 200:361–86.

Caldwell, M.W., and M.S.Y. Lee. 1997. A snake with legs from the marine Cretaceous of the Middle East. *Nature* 386:705–9.

Carroll, R.L. 1985. Evolutionary constraints in aquatic diapsid reptiles. *Special Papers in Paleontology* 33:145–55.

Carroll, R.L., and Z.I. Dong. 1991. *Hupehsuchus,* an enigmatic reptile from the Triassic of China, and the problem of establishing relationships. *Philosophical Transactions of the Royal Society of London: Biological Sciences* 331:131–53.

Carroll, R.L., and R. Wild. 1994. Marine members of the Sphenodontia. *In* N.C. Fraser and H.D. Sues (eds.), *In the Shadow of the Dinosaurs: Early Mesozoic Tetrapods.* Cambridge: Cambridge University Press.

Clark, J.M. 1994. Patterns of evolution in Mesozoic Crocodyliformes. *In* N.C. Fraser and H.D. Sues (eds.), *In the Shadow of the Dinosaurs: Early Mesozoic Tetrapods.* Cambridge and New York: Cambridge University Press.

Evans, S.E., and M.K. Hecht. 1993. A history of an extinct reptilian clade, the Choristodera: Longevity. Lazarus-taxa, and the fossil record. *Evolutionary Biology* 27:323–38.

Halstead, L.B. 1989. Plesiosaur locomotion. *Journal of the Geological Society, London* 146:37–40.

Hua, S., and V. de Buffrénil. 1996. Bone histology as a clue in the interpretation of functional adaptations in the Thalattosuchia (Reptilia, Crocodylia). *Journal of Vertebrate Paleontology* 16:703–17.

Lee, M.S.Y. 1997. The phylogeny of varanoid lizards and the affinities of snakes. *Philosophical Transactions of the Royal Society of London: Biological Sciences* 352:53–91.

Lingham-Soliar, T. 1995. Anatomy and functional morphology of the largest marine reptile known, *Mosasaurus hoffmani* (Mosasauridae, Reptilia) from the Upper Cretaceous, Upper Maastrichtian of the Netherlands. *Philosophical Transactions of the Royal Society of London: Biological Sciences* 347:155–80.

Massare, J.A. 1987. Tooth morphology and prey preference of Mesozoic marine reptiles. *Journal of Vertebrate Paleontology* 7:121–37.

———. 1994. Swimming capabilities of Mesozoic marine reptiles: A review. *In* L. Maddock, Q. Bone, and J.M.V. Rayner (eds.), *Mechanics and Physiology of Animal Swimming.* Cambridge and New York: Cambridge University Press.

Montani, R., H. You, and C. McGowan. 1996. Eel-like swimming in the earliest ichthyosaurs. *Nature* 382:347–48.

Poe, S. 1996. Data set incongruence and the phylogeny of crocodilians. *Systematic Biology* 45:393–414.

Rieppel, O. 1994. Osteology of *Simosaurus gaillardoti* and the relationships of stem-group Sauropterygia. *Fieldiana: Geology,* new ser., 28:1–85.

Russell, D.A. 1967. *Systematics and Morphology of American Mosasaurs (Reptilia Sauria).* Bulletin of the Peabody Museum of Natural History, 23. New Haven, Connecticut: Peabody Museum of Natural History.

Storrs, G.W. 1991. *Anatomy and Relationships of Corosaurus alcovensis (Diapsida: Sauropterygia) and the Triassic Alcova Limestone of Wyoming.* Bulletin of the Peabody Museum of Natural History, 44. New Haven, Connecticut: Peabody Museum of Natural History.

Storrs, G.W., and D.J. Gower. 1993. The earliest possible choristodere (Diapsida) and gaps in the fossil record of semi-aquatic reptiles. *Journal of the Geological Society, London* 150:1103–7.

Further Reading

McGowan, C. 1983. *The Successful Dragons: A Natural History of Extinct Reptiles.* Sarasota, Florida: Stevens; rev. ed., *Dinosaurs, Spitfires and Sea Dragons,* Cambridge, Massachusetts: Harvard University Press, 1992.

Callaway, J.M., and E.L. Nicholls (eds.). 1997. *Ancient Marine Reptiles.* New York and San Diego, California: Academic Press.

ARAMBOURG, CAMILLE LOUIS JOSEPH

French, 1885–1969

As a vertebrate paleontologist, Camille Arambourg is world-renowned for his work in paleoichthyology (the study of ancient fish) and paleoanthropology (the study of ancient humans). He was a true and indefatigable field researcher in the uneasy conditions of his times, especially in Africa. Though officially retired from the Paris Museum in 1955, there was no year between this date and his death in 1969 that did not see him in the field. His successes there resulted from broad knowledge encompassing geology, hydrogeology (study of water in Earth's ecology), pedology (study of soil), paleontology, and even paleobotany (study of ancient plants), making him a true "naturalist," today an extinct species.

Arambourg worked mainly in areas on the perimeter of the Mediterranean Sea, especially in North Africa, but also in East Africa. His competence in vertebrate paleontology extended from fishes to man: He was especially interested in Cretaceous and Tertiary fishes, Plio-Pleistocene hominids, and Neogene and Quaternary mammals—proboscideans (animals related to modern elephants), artiodactyls (even-toed hooved animals such as pigs), perissodactyls (odd-toed hooved animals such as horses), and carnivores. Arambourg was not only interested in classification and phylogenetics, but also in paleobiogeography (of fishes and mammals), paleoecology (e.g., the climatic and depth information that can be learned from fossil fishes), and biostratigraphy (using fossils to determine the age of the rocks they are found in). He published prolifically—some 230 papers since 1912, 150 of which deal with Africa and 72 with hominids.

Arambourg's passion for paleontology led him to work in unusual circumstances. In 1916, during World War I, he was mobilized at the head of a Zouave military company. In trenches near Salonica (Vadar Valley, Greece), he found Late Miocene mammals that he excavated with the help of the army. In 1940, during World War II, Arambourg was taken prisoner in northeastern France. He took advantage of his forced inactivity to give conferences on paleoanthropology. They became the basis of his book *La Génèse de l'Humanité* (1943), which became very successful, with eight editions up to 1969, and several translations.

Arambourg became interested in paleontology very early, during his college days. He was won over completely in 1909 when he discovered a beautiful Late Miocene fish fauna in his father's vineyard near Oran in Algeria. He studied it and published a series of papers about it from 1921 to 1927. In 1920 he was the first to identify photoluminescent organs in Late Miocene myctophid fishes. Then, he studied various Cretaceous and Cenozoic fishes, from such localities as Sicily (Licata), Spain (Columbares), Iran, Morocco (Djebel Tselfat), Niger, Egypt, and Gabon. One important work is his study of the Maastrichtian-Lutetian vertebrates from the North African phosphates (1936–37, 1950–52), especially the selachians (small sharks) from Morocco. This work allowed him to establish the first biostratigraphical zonation in these marine sediments of strategic economic value. (Such zones pair rock strata and their representative fauna with the time when the sediments were deposited.)

Arambourg was little concerned with amphibians and reptiles. However, he made two important discoveries in these areas: one of the largest-known pterosaurs in Late Cretaceous phosphate deposits in Jordan (1954), and the remarkable Triassic stegocephalian and reptile fauna from Imin n'Tanout, Morocco (1960), which later became the object of 20 years of research by J.M. Dutuit.

From 1929 on, Arambourg focused his work on mammals and hominids. He began with the study and publication (in 1929) of the Late Miocene mammals that he recovered in Salonica during the First World War. Soon after (1931–32, 1934) he reported the discovery of several complete skeletons of Cro-Magnon humans in the Afalou Bou Rhummel site (Upper Paleolithic of Algeria). During this period he also studied various mammals (artiodactyls, such as wild pigs; perissodactyls, such as horses; and carnivores) from Kenya, Angola, Mali, Niger, Egypt, and Libya. In 1932–33 he led an eight-month French exploratory expedition in the Omo Valley of Ethiopia. The results, such as the geology and the discovery of new deinotheres (extinct elephants), were published in various papers (1933–35, 1943, 1947).

In 1949, Arambourg identified at Aïn Hanech (Algeria) calcareous "sphaeroid artefacts" of Villafranchian age that he later (1952) related to the Pebble Culture—the oldest known human industry in North Africa. In 1954 he announced, with R. Hoffstetter, the discovery of the hominid *Atlanthropus mauritanicus* in the Middle Pleistocene of Ternifine (now Tighenif, Algeria), associated with an archaic industry. The excavations at Ternifine yielded important new discoveries. The recovered fauna has been described in many papers and in a final monograph in 1963. In 1962, Arambourg announced E. Ennouchi's discovery of the Jebel Irhoud (Morocco) "Neanderthalian skull," actually a primitive *Homo sapiens*. Three years later, Arambourg reported a classical flake tool–making industry at the site. At the end of his life, Arambourg made another major discovery: the oldest (at that time) australopithecine, *Australopithecus aethiopicus,* from the Early Pleistocene of the Omo Valley, Ethiopia. Arambourg returned to the site with Y. Coppens for three international campaigns in 1967, 1968, and lastly 1969, when he was 84 years old. Arambourg was the forerunner of the successful paleontological researches in the Omo Valley, which continued up to 1976 with nine other international campaigns.

EMMANUEL GHEERBRANT

Biography

Born in Paris, 3 February 1885. Bachelor's degree, Sainte-Croix de Neuilly School, 1903; agricultural engineer, 1908; professor of geology, Institut Agricole d'Algiers, 1920–30; professor of geology, Institut National Agronomique, Paris, 1930–36; professor of paleontology, Muséem National d'Histoire Naturelle de Paris, 1936. Received Fontanes Prize, Académie des Sciences, 1945; received André C. Bonnet Prize, Académie des Sciences, 1955; president, Société Géologique de France, 1950; president, Société Française de Préhistoire, 1956; received Albert Gaudry Prize, Société Géologique de France, 1959; president, 4th Panafrican Congress on Prehistory in Kinshasa, 1959. Discovered Afalou Cro-Magnon skeletons, Late Pleistocene of Algeria, 1928–30; rediscovered (following E. Brumpt's 1902 discovery) Early Pleistocene vertebrates, Omo Valley, Ethiopia, 1932; discovered pithecanthropine *Atlanthropus mauritanicus* associated with an Acheulean industry in Ternifine, Middle Pleistocene of Algeria, 1954–55; discovered Triassic amphibians and reptiles, Imin n'Tanout, Morocco, 1960; 2nd to 4th paleontological expeditions, Omo Valley, discovered Early Pleistocene australopithecine *Australopithecus aethiopicus,* 1967–69. Died in Paris, 19 October 1969.

Major Publications

1927. *Les poissons fossiles d'Oran.* Matériaux pour la Carte Géologique de l'Algérie, 1ère série, Paléontologie, 6. Alger: J. Carbonel.

1943. *La Génèse de l'Humanité.* Que sais-je? Paris: Presses Universitaires de France; 8th ed., 1969.

1943, 1947. Contribution à l'étude géologique et paléontologique du bassin du Lac Rodolphe et de la basse vallée de l'Omo. *Mission Scientifique de l'Omo, Première Partie: Géologie,* I, 2:1–74; *Deuxième Partie: Paléontologie,* I, 3:231–562.

1952. *Les vertébrés fossiles des gisements de phosphates (Maroc, Algérie, Tunisie).* Notes et Mémoire du Service Géologique du Maroc, 92. Paris: Typographie Firmin-Didot.

1963. *Le gisement de Ternifine, I.* Archives de l'Institut de Paléontologie Humaine, mémoire, 32. Paris: Masson.

Further Reading

Coppens, Y. 1979. Histoire des expéditions paléontologiques en Afrique orientale. 10ᵉ anniversaire de la mort de Camille Arambourg. *Trauvaux du Comité Français de la Géologie* 21:1–27.

Courrier, M. 1974. Notice sur la vie et les travaux de Camille Arambourg (1885–1969). *Institut de France, Académie des Sciences* 23:1–32.

Gaudant, J. 1990. Arambourg, Camille. *Dictionary of Scientific Biography.* Vol. 17, Supplement 2, New York: Scribner's.

Lehman, J.-P., B. Geze, L. Balout, and R. Heim. 1965. *Hommage à Camille Arambourg à l'occasion de son 80ᵉ anniversaire. Four speeches and answers by C. Arambourg.* Paris: n.p.

ARCHOSAUROMORPHS

Near the beginning of the Permian, the diapsid reptiles (those with two fenestrations, or openings, toward the rear of the skull) separated into two distinct lineages: the Lepidosauromorpha (comprising lizards, snakes, amphisbaenians, sphenodontians, and some extinct relatives) and the Archosauromorpha. The Archosauromorpha consist of crocodilians, birds, dinosaurs, and all the other diapsids that are more closely related to those groups than to the Lepidosauria (Figure 1). They comprise a diverse assemblage, including some of the smallest and largest of amniotes (vertebrates in which embryos are surrounded by a fluid-filled sac, or amnion),

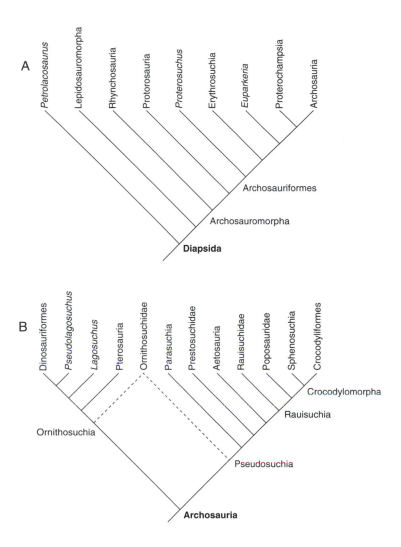

Figure 1. General archosauromorph cladogram. Based in part on Gauthier (1984), Sereno (1991), and parish (1993). *A*, relationships within the Diapsida and Archosauromorpha; *B*, relationships within the crown group Archosauria.

and represented the dominant terrestrial vertebrates for most of the Mesozoic.

The Archosauromorpha in its current sense was first proposed in a doctoral thesis by J.A. Gauthier (1984) and a publication by M.J. Benton (1985). Both authors placed the same taxa within Archosauromorpha, although they disagreed slightly about the relative positions of some constituent taxa.

In addition to crocodilians and dinosaurs (which include birds), the Archosauromorpha contains a variety of other groups: the Rhynchosauria, the Prolacertiformes, the Trilophosauria, the Proterosuchia, the Erythrosuchidae, the Euparkeriidae, the Proterochampsia, and the Archosauria. As currently defined, the Archosauria consists of the last common ancestor of the crocodiles and birds and all of its descendants, including the pterosaurs and all of the dinosaurs. Many of these groups, notably the rhynchosaurs, prolacertiforms, and trilophosaurids, were once believed to have been primitive relatives of the Lepidosauria, the lizard/snake/

sphenodontian clade (a group containing all of a single ancestor's decendants).

The Archosauromorpha can be diagnosed by a number of features, including the following (Benton 1985): tabular bones absent, pineal foramen reduced or absent, no entepicondylar foramen on the humerus, lateral tuber on calcaneum, and complex concave-convex articulation between the two proximal ankle bones, the talus and calcaneus.

The Rhynchosauria were an entirely Triassic group of apparently herbivorous archosauromorphs, with a worldwide distribution. Rhynchosaurs (Figure 2) were squat, medium-sized quadrupeds with distinctive, broad skulls in which the premaxillae (most anterior of the upper jaw bones) lacked marginal teeth, but instead formed a sharp, pointed beak. The medial parts of the maxillae (the main tooth-bearing component of the upper jaw) were expanded as broad tooth plates that contained multiple rows of parallel teeth. Rhynchosaurs had expanded muscular processes on their limbs and expanded

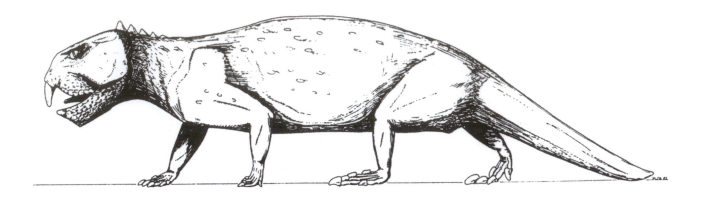

Figure 2. The rhynchosaur *Hyperdapedon.* Illustration by Michael J. Benton. From Benton (1983); used by permission of The University of Chicago Press and Michael J. Benton, © 1983 by the University of Chicago.

fore- and hind feet, suggesting that burrowing might have been an important part of their behavioral repertoire.

The earliest rhynchosaurs, *Mesosuchus* and *Howesia,* are known from the Early Triassic of what is today South Africa. They differed from later rhynchosaurs in that they retained typical marginal dentition (teeth at the edge of the mouth, as in lizards) and had more elongate skulls that more closely resemble those of other archosauromorphs. During the Middle and early Late Triassic, the rhynchosaurs became the most abundant herbivores in most terrestrial ecosystems; they are particularly well represented from India, eastern Africa, and South America. Rhynchosaurs became less common later in the Late Triassic and disappeared entirely by the late Late Triassic (Norian).

The Prolacertiformes were a relatively diverse group of archosauromorphs that had lizardlike bodies and relatively elongate necks. They arose in the Late Permian and persisted until the Early Jurassic. The earliest prolacertiform was *Protorosaurus,* known from the Late Permian of Europe. *Protorosaurus* and several Triassic forms, including *Prolacerta* from the Early Triassic of South Africa and *Malerisaurus* from the Late Triassic of India and Texas, were clearly terrestrial and appear to have been omnivores or carnivores. In the Middle Triassic of Europe, the Tanystropheidae, another family of small to large aquatic prolacertiforms with very long necks, appeared. *Tanystropheus* (Figure 3), known primarily from the marine Middle Triassic of Switzerland, has a neck consisting of 12 elongate vertebrae that is as long as the trunk and tail combined. The skulls of tanystropheids indicate a typical carnivorous habit, so the ecological role of these curious reptiles appears to have been relatively similar to those of the long-necked plesiosaurs. They probably moved their heads in a broad arc for location of prey with only minimal body movement, although the fact that it had relatively few, elongate cervical vertebrae and the presence of long, overlapping sacral ribs appears to have prevented much flexion or torsion within the neck. The latest tanystropheid, *Tanytrachelos,* was a small freshwater form that was locally abundant in many of the Late Triassic–Early Jurassic rift lakes of the Newark Supergroup of the eastern United States.

Another curious group of archosauromorphs were the Trilophosauridae, known from the Late Triassic of North America and Europe. *Trilophosaurus,* from the early Late Triassic of western Texas, is a crocodile-sized, quadrupedal terrestrial herbivore that has long been a puzzle to paleontologists because of its rigid, heavily ossified skull and distinctive teeth, which are transversely broadened, with three mediolaterally aligned cusps. As in rhynchosaurs, the trilophosaurs lacked dentition on the premaxilla, which looks like it anchored a keratinous (horny), turtlelike beak. *Trilophosaurus* was previously united with *Araeoscelis* and marine reptiles such as plesiosaurs, placodonts, and ichthyosaurs within the "Euryapsida," based on the presence of a single temporal opening high on the cheek region. The euryapsid pattern subsequently has been recognized as a modification of the diapsid (two temporal openings) pattern that appears to have occurred several times. In the case of *Trilophosaurus,* the closure of the lower temporal opening probably occurred, along with fusion of the skull bones and development of the transversely broadened cheek teeth, as adaptations for the processing of tough plant material. The archosauromorph affinity of *Trilophosaurus* first was recognized by D. Brinkman (1981), who noticed that the rhynchosaurs, prolacertiforms, trilophosaurs, and archosauriforms shared a unique, distinctive ankle structure, consisting of a double ball-and-socket attachment between talus and calcaneus. The trilophosaur material from the early Late Triassic of Europe is much more fragmentary, based primarily on teeth and jaw fragments.

The remaining archosauromorphs form a group that formerly was designated as the Archosauria but subsequently has been redesignated as the Archosauriformes because Gauthier (1984), followed by most other current systematists, has restricted Archosauria to its crown group, consisting of the last common ancestor of all the living archosaurs (crocodiles and birds) and all the members of the lineage descended from that ancestor. As a result, many taxa that appear in older literature as basal (primitive) archosaurs now are considered to be basal archosauriforms. Derived characters that unite the archosauriforms include the presence of an antorbital fenestra on the side of the face between

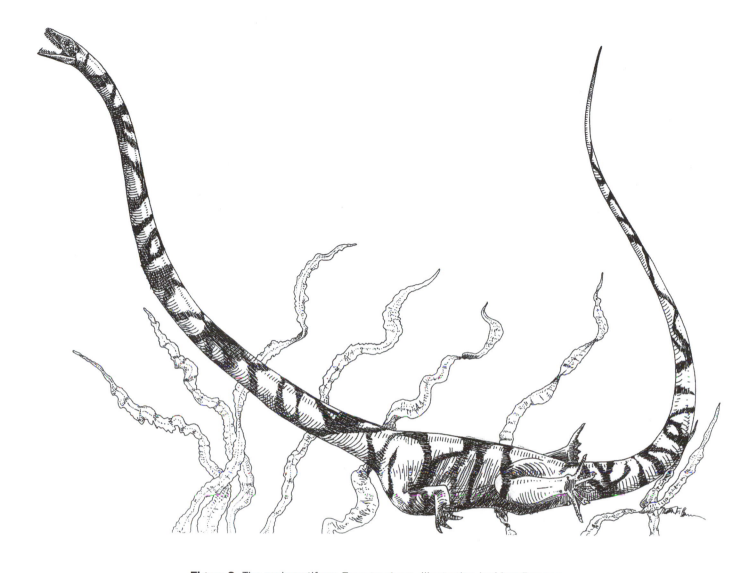

Figure 3. The prolacertiform *Tanystropheus*. Illustration by Matt Bonnan.

the external naris (nasal opening) and orbit (eye socket), a laterosphenoid ossification at the anterior end of the braincase, and an external fenestra on the mandible (jaw).

The most basal group of archosauriforms is the Proterosuchidae, known from the Late Permian through Early Triassic. The Late Permian record of proterosuchids is rather scanty, consisting of a single, fragmentary specimen of *Archosaurus* from Russia and some limb bones and vertebrae of an unnamed proterosuchid from the Kawinga Formation of Tanzania. *Proterosuchus* (Figure 4) is an extremely well known taxon, represented by many skulls and a few skeletons from the early Early Triassic (Scythian) of South Africa and China (Charig and Sues 1976). *Proterosuchus* was an animal very similar in size and probable habits to modern crocodilians: a carnivorous quadruped with a long snout and sprawling limbs that suggest an amphibious habit. Several different genera of proterosuchids have been reported from South Africa and China over the years, but all of the named taxa seem to be simply specimens of *Proterosuchus* differing in size and

in the nature of postmortem distortion of the skull. Two distinct proterosuchids are known from the Early Triassic of Australia, *Kalisuchus* and *Tasmaniasaurus*.

Later in the Early Triassic, a second radiation of archosauromorphs, the Erythrosuchidae, appeared. Unlike the gracile, amphibious proterosuchids, the Erythrosuchidae were large headed, fully terrestrial predators (Figure 5). The erythrosuchids formed a diverse assemblage, with different genera known from South Africa, China, and Russia. Like proterosuchids, they had a sprawling gait, involving long-axis rotation of proximal limb elements (in which the upper arm bone and thigh bone rotate around their axes), although the limbs were splayed out less than in previous diapsids. More problematical erythrosuchid material is known from the late Early Triassic of South America and India, and from the Middle Triassic of North America. *Erythrosuchus,* the largest and one of the best-known erythrosuchids, is represented by one reasonably complete, but disarticulated, skeleton, one complete skull, and several other partial skulls and skeletons, all from the Cape Province region of

South Africa. The latest erythrosuchid, *Shansisuchus,* is known by many disarticulated skeletons from a single, mass-death assemblage from the Middle Triassic of Shansi Province, People's Republic of China. With the rise of the erythrosuchids, the archosauriforms first gained the position of top terrestrial carnivores in Mesozoic ecosystems, a position different members of that lineage continued to occupy until the end of the era.

A relatively rare, but evolutionarily significant, archosauriform is *Euparkeria* (Figure 6), known from a single site from the late Early Triassic of the Cape Province region of South Africa. *Euparkeria* was a small animal that sometimes has been restored as a biped, but seems more likely, based on limb anatomy, to have been predominantly quadrupedal. *Euparkeria* was the first archosauriform to have body armor, in this case, small scutes (bony plates) positioned above the neural spines of the vertebral column of the tail and trunk. It had also lost some cranial features that are primitive for amniotes, including palatal teeth and the pineal foramen (an opening on the top of the skull for the third eye). *Euparkeria* exhibited an almost perfect morphological pattern for the common ancestor of Ornithosuchia (the lineage leading to dinosaurs and birds) and Pseudosuchia (the lineage leading to crocodiles).

Another lineage that diverged from the Archosauriformes just prior to the pseudosuchian/ornithosuchian split was the Proterochampsia, a group of armored quadrupeds known from the Middle and early Late Triassic of South America. The proterochampsids varied widely in size and habits, from the tiny, terrestrial *Tropidosuchus* to the crocodile-sized, aquatic *Proterochampsa.* A small, armored animal from the Late Triassic of North America, *Doswellia* appears to have been a close relative of the proterochampsids.

The crown group Archosauria, comprising the common ancestor to crocodiles and birds and all its descendants, was erected by Gauthier (1984). Although he based his assignment on a number of derived characters, the ones that seem to have remained viable include the absence of palatal teeth and a calcaneal tuberosity (a prominence on the heel bone) directed posterolaterally more than 45 degrees.

Figure 4. The basal archosauriform *Proterosuchus*. Illustration by Matt Bonnan.

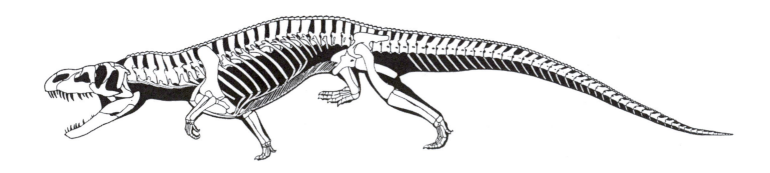

Figure 5. The erythrosuchid *Vjushkovia*. From Parrish (1986). Illustration by Greg Paul.

Figure 6. The basal archosauriform *Euparkeria*. Illustration by Matt Bonnan.

Figure 7. The ornithodiran *Marasuchus*. From Sereno and Arcucci (1994). Illustration by C. Abraczinskas.

As defined by Gauthier (1984), Ornithosuchia consists of all archosaurs more closely related to birds than to crocodilians, and he considered this clade to include *Euparkeria,* Ornithosuchidae, Pterosauria, Lagosuchidae, and Dinosauria. Some debate has emerged about the utility of Gauthier's name, particularly since some subsequent studies (e.g., Sereno 1991, Juul 1994) have suggested that Ornithosuchidae are more closely related to crocodilians than birds, and thus would not be members of the Ornithosuchia.

The family Ornithosuchidae is known from material of three small- to large-sized predators, known from the Upper Triassic of Scotland and South America. The ornithosuchids were unique among archosaurs in having an ankle arrangement that S. Chatterjee (1982) termed crocodile-reverse, wherein a ball on the medial surface of the calcaneus articulated with a socket on the lateral surface of the talus. Gauthier (1984) suggested that this joint was homologous with those in *Euparkeria,* ornithosuchids, *Lagosuchus,* and dinosaurs, and this was one of the characters he used to unite these groups within his Ornithosuchia. Cruickshank and Benton (1985) and Sereno (1991) questioned the homology of the

tarsal structures between *Euparkeria* and the other members of Gauthier's Ornithosuchia. Sereno's (1991) solution to this problem was to move *Euparkeria* out of the Archosauria (a position agreed upon by most scholars today) and to move the Ornithosuchidae into Gauthier's Pseudosuchia, which Sereno redefined and named the Crurotarsi, based on all members of the group having rotary movement of the calcaneus relative to the talus.

Ornithodira was the name given by Gauthier (1984) for a clade comprising pterosaurs, *Lagosuchus, Lagerpeton,* dinosaurs, and birds. Derived characters defining this group include the absence of dermal armor, calcaneal tuber reduced or absent, and an elongate, mediolaterally compressed metatarsus.

Although there has been considerable debate about the position of pterosaurs within the Diapsida, Gauthier (1984), Sereno (1991) and Juul (1994) all support their being the sister group of Dinosauromorpha within the Ornithodira. Dissenting views have this well-established clade of flying reptiles as either Lepidosauromorpha (e.g., Benton 1985) or basal archosauriforms.

Three (or possibly four) unusual small archosaurs from the Chañares Formation of Argentina seem to have been the closest relatives of the dinosaurs. Specimens of these incompletely known, possibly bipedal ornithodirans come from nodules in a sedimentary deposit rich in volcanic ash. The better known of the two genera was initially called *Lagosuchus,* although P.C. Sereno and A.B. Arcucci (1994) suggested that the most complete specimen should be referred to a new genus, *Marasuchus* (Figure 7). Regardless of the name, *Lagosuchus* is a small, long-legged biped that might conceivably have utilized a hopping movement (hence the *lagos*—rabbit—part of the generic name). Based on specializations of the hind limb, pelvis, and ankle, *Lagosuchus* appears to have been very close to the base of the Dinosauria. A relatively similar animal, *Pseudolagosuchus,* was described from the Chañares beds (Arcucci 1987).

A third genus, *Lagerpeton,* was similar in size to *Lagosuchus* and *Pseudolagosuchus* and comes from the same deposits. What distinguishes *Lagerpeton* is the presence of a very reduced ventral part of the pelvis relative to the size of the limbs, and a foot with the lateral digits greatly elongated, as if for grasping. The ecological role of this peculiar animal has been debated, and although the lack of cranial and forelimb material makes such inferences difficult, the elongate digits of the hind foot may indicate a grasping, arboreal (tree-dwelling) habitus. The existence of a monophyletic Dinosauria uniting Saurischia, Ornithischia, and Aves first was proposed by R.T. Bakker and P.M. Galton (1974).

The other lineage of archosaurs, which includes only crocodilians among its extant members, has been given different names (and somewhat different constituent taxa) by different scholars. The name that Gauthier (1984) proposed for archosaurs more closely related to crocodiles than birds was Pseudosuchia, a group that previously had been used by several different authors to define different groups of non-dinosaurian archosaurs. M.J. Benton and J.M. Clark (1988) utilized a new name, Crocodylotarsi, for this same assemblage because of the confusing history of the name prior to Gauthier's designation. Sereno (1991) proposed another name, Crurotarsi, for what in essence is Gauthier's Pseudosuchia. Sereno's use of this name was based on his assertion that a mobile joint between talus and calcaneus was a derived feature for this group. K. Padian and C.L. May (1993) advocated the retention of Pseudosuchia for reasons of priority, but all three names are used, sometimes interchangeably, for the same clade of archosaurs in the current literature. One of the most important features used to unite the Pseudosuchia has been the tarsal arrangement that Chatterjee (1982) dubbed crocodile-normal, with a ball on the talus articulating with a socket on the calcaneus. Sereno (1991) suggested some different interpretations of archosaurian ankles, considering the ornithosuchid (crocodile-reverse) pattern to be a specialization of the crocodile-normal pattern and the tarsal pattern of phytosaurs to be indeterminate in its homology.

The Parasuchia, or phytosaurs, were a group of Late Triassic, large to giant, amphibious predators that were among the most abundant vertebrates of their age. Phytosaurs were very crocodilelike in body form and had similar adaptations to an amphibious existence, including a sprawling gait and an elongate skull with a narrow snout and nostrils located on the top of the skull, often within a bony mound just anterior to the orbits (Figure 8). Phytosaurs also resembled crocodilians in that they had a continuous carapace of bony scutes located on both their dorsal and ventral surfaces. Although all phytosaurs had similar basic body forms, there were ecological distinctions in that some species, like *Rutiodon tenuis,* had very narrow snouts and relatively conical posterior teeth that, based on modern analogs, probably indicate a diet of fish, whereas others, like *Nicrosaurus kappfi,* had broad, expanded snouts and wedgelike posterior teeth that suggest that *Nicrosaurus* may have fed on larger prey items.

A great number of large to gigantic terrestrial pseudosuchian predators are known from the Middle and Late Triassic. Unfortunately, the fossil remains of most of these animals are fragmentary, and their relationships remain a matter of debate. J.M. Parrish (1993) suggested that two distinct groups of large-headed terrestrial carnivores existed within the Pseudosuchia. One group, the Prestosuchidae, consists of some of the least derived (specialized) of pseudosuchians, whereas the other, the Rauisuchia, are much more closely related to crocodilians. Prestosuchids were large to giant quadrupeds with sturdy skulls and relatively stout limbs. One of the best known prestosuchians is *Ticinosuchus,* known from a nearly complete skeleton from the marine rocks of Middle Triassic age from Monte San Giorgio, Switzerland. How this clearly terrestrial animal ended up in a marine deposit remains a mystery. *Prestosuchus* itself comes from the Upper Triassic Santa Maria Formation of southern Brazil. Originally described based on a partial, crocodile-sized skeleton found by F.F. von Huene's expeditions in the 1930s, this material subsequently has been augmented by a beautiful 1.5-meter skull and associated vertebral column described by Mario Barberena in the 1970s. The prestosuchids were also armored, but the plates were restricted to two narrow rows located along the dorsal midline of the body.

The Aetosauria were a relatively diverse group of Late Triassic herbivores and omnivores, ranging in size from the foot-long *Aetosaurus* to crocodile-sized forms like *Desmatosuchus.* Aetosaurs had highly modified skulls, with a short snout flattened at the tip as if for rooting (Figure 9). Except in the most basal forms, which had small, recurved teeth, aetosaurs had blunt, conelike teeth at the rear of the jaws and an edentulous (toothless) anterior end of the jaw that appears to have housed a keratinous (horny) beak. Another distinctive feature of aetosaurs was the structure of its body, which was encased in a turtle-like carapace made up of pairs of mediolaterally expanded paramedian plates that adjoin over the vertebral column and a series of lateral plates that, in taxa like *Desmatosuchus,* were expanded into large spikes in the shoulder region. The combination of relatively broad, clawed forefeet and hind feet, and stout limb bones that had prominent muscular processes, suggests that aetosaurs may have had a burrowing habitat. A piece of indirect evidence supporting this is the mass death assemblage of 24 individuals of *Aetosaurus ferratus* from Heslach, Germany, which appears to represent the collapse of an underground burrow (Fraas 1877). One of the latest aetosaurs, *Typothorax coccinarum,* had a very broad body that, with its extensive bony carapace, made it resemble an aetosaurian version of a turtle.

Two groups of carnivorous archosaurs, the Rauisuchidae and Poposauridae, form a lineage within the Pseudosuchia with the crocodilians and their close relatives. The Rauisuchidae are a group of Middle to Late Triassic quadrupedal archosaurs that are

Figure 8. The phytosaur *Nicrosaurus*. Illustration by Matt Bonnan.

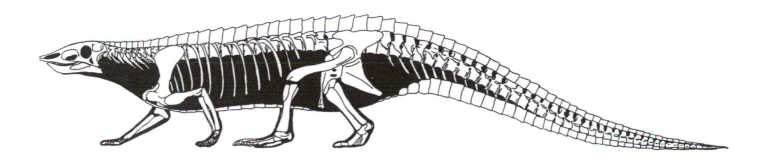

Figure 9. The aetosaur *Stagonolepis*. From Parrish (1986). Illustration by J. Michael Parrish.

known mostly from relatively fragmentary remains. In addition to crocodile-sized forms such as *Rauisuchus* (from the early Late Triassic of Brazil), this group includes giant carnivores such as *Fasolasuchus,* from the latest Triassic of Argentina, and *Lotosaurus,* a crocodile-sized, beaked herbivore or invertebrate eater from the Middle Triassic of southern China. Although members of this group superficially resemble prestosuchids, they have a suite of derived characters in the limbs and skull that establish their closer relationship with the poposaurs and crocodylomorphs.

The Poposauridae are another relatively obscure family that initially was erected on the basis of a poorly known taxon, *Poposaurus,* from the early Late Triassic of Wyoming (Mehl 1915). Among the most distinctive features of this animal were the presence of a prominent buttress on the ilium bone just above the ace-

tabulum (hipsocket) and the development of a large bony foot on the distal end of the pubis. More poposaur material subsequently has come to light from England, Argentina, and North America, and some material from the Late Triassic of Germany that was first identified as phytosaurian by Meyer (1861) also was shown to belong to this family. What seemed to be the best known poposaur, *Postosuchus* (Figure 10), was described from the Late Triassic of Texas by Chatterjee (1985), although R.A. Long and P.A. Murry (1995) suggest that *Postosuchus* is really a rauisuchid.

Within the Crocodylomorpha, a series of changes occurred in the skull, forelimb, hind limb, and pelvis that are retained in extant crocodilians. In the skull, the quadrate bone slants forward and has very extensive sutures with the braincase and bones of the cheek and skull roof. Another significant cranial change involves

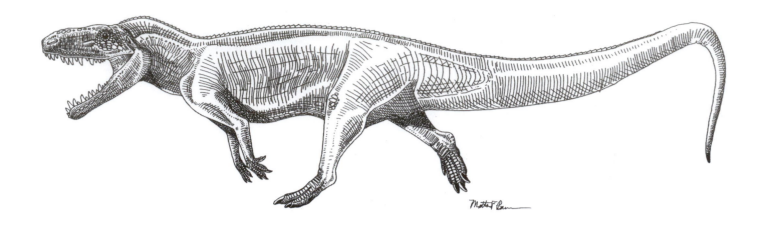

Figure 10. The poposaurid *Postosuchus*. Illustration by Matt Bonnan.

the development of pneumatization (air spaces) of the braincase and quadrates (which form part of the jaw joint). Some of these changes, such as the pneumatized braincase, are seen in the poposaurs as well. Others, particularly the reorientation and fusion of the quadrate bone and the elongation of the coracoid (the ventral of the two bones of the shoulder girdle), are shared by the Crocodyliformes (true crocodilians) and the Sphenosuchia, a group of Upper Triassic–Jurassic forms that, along with the Crocodyliformes, comprise the Crocodylomorpha. Sphenosuchians were small- to medium-sized terrestrial, quadrupedal predators with elongate limbs. Many different genera are known, including *Hesperosuchus* from the Late Triassic of North America, *Sphenosuchus* from the Early Jurassic of South America, and the relatively tiny *Terrestrisuchus* from the Upper Triassic of Great Britain.

For the most part, the archosauromorphs of the Permian and Triassic had global distributions, as they lived during the time of Pangaea, a supercontinent that included most of the present-day land masses. Thus, the geographical ranges of taxa of a particular age seems to be dictated more by the present-day distribution of well-exposed continental rocks of that age (and the relative amount of time invested in their exploration) than on any discrete biogeographic patterns. Environments of this interval were relatively warm and marked by extreme seasonality, particularly during the Triassic.

The non-dinosaurian archosauromorphs reached their greatest diversity in the Late Triassic, with most of their diversity during that time coming from relatively abrupt radiations of pseudosuchian groups, particularly phytosaurs and aetosaurs. Their major terrestrial contemporaries were a diverse assemblage of synapsids (mammal-like reptiles and mammals), which generally decreased in abundance and diversity as the archosauromorph lineage diversified. The paleoecological roles of the basal archosauromorphs have been a subject of debate for some time, with the principal point of dispute being the relative importance of ecological competition and chance in the extinction of these groups and the appearance and rapid spread of the dinosaurs. A.J. Charig

(1972) argued effectively for the competition model, suggesting that most of the early archosauriforms were intermediate in their locomotor capabilities between sprawling tetrapods and the fully erect dinosaurs and birds. Several subsequent studies (e.g., Parrish 1986) suggest that most archosaurs exhibited a fully erect gait rather than the semi-improved gait proposed by Charig. In the early 1980s, Benton (e.g., 1983) argued strongly that the extinctions of basal archosaurs and other Triassic tetrapods had taken place prior to, and independent of, the radiation of the dinosaurs.

Non-dinosaurian archosauromorphs have been collected since the mid–1800s but have rarely been a focus of sustained collection and research. One of the most active workers in the group was F.F. von Huene, who collected and described Triassic archosauromorphs from Germany, South Africa, Russia, and North and South America. His collecting trips to the Santa Maria Formation of Brazil in the 1930s uncovered many important South American Triassic taxa, including good material of the rhynchosaur *Scaphonyx* and the pseudosuchians *Prestosuchus* and *Rauisuchus*.

In North America, Edwin Colbert worked on Triassic archosaurs as early as the 1940s, uncovering important new material of sphenosuchians and phytosaurs from the Upper Triassic Chinle Formation of the southwest and the Newark supergroup of the east coast. Charles Camp made extensive collections from the Chinle Formation of Arizona and New Mexico that subsequently were studied by R.A. Long, P.A. Murry, K. Padian, and others. Other extensive collections are known from the Early Triassic of South Africa, China, and Russia; the Middle Triassic of Tanzania, Britain, and South America; and the Late Triassic of Britain, Morocco, India, Greenland, Texas, and Wyoming. Other scholars that have been particularly active in describing archosauromorphs include M.J. Benton, A.D. Walker, and S. Chatterjee.

J. MICHAEL PARRISH

See also Birds; Crocodylomorphs; Dinosaurs; Pterosaurs

Works Cited

Arcucci, A.B. 1987. Un nuevo Lagosuchidae (Thecodontia-Pseudosuchia) de la fauna de los Chañares (edad reptil Chañarense, Triiásico Medio), La Rioja, Argentina. *Ameghiana* 24:89–94.

Bakker, R.T., and P.M. Galton. 1974. Dinosaurian monophyly and a new class of vertebrates. *Nature* 248:162–72.

Barberena, M.C. 1978. A huge thecodont skull from the Triassic of Brazil. *Pesquisas* 9:63–75.

Benton, M.J. 1983. Dinosaur success in the Triassic: A noncompetitive ecological model. *Quarterly Review of Biology* 58:29–55.

———. 1985. Classification and phylogeny of the diapsid reptiles. *Zoological Journal of the Linnean Society* 84:97–164.

Benton, M.J., and J.M. Clark. 1988. Archosaur phylogeny and the relationships of the Crocodylia. *In* M.J. Benton (ed.), *Phylogeny and Classification of Amniotes*. Systematics Association Special Volume 35A. Oxford: Clarendon Press; New York: Oxford University Press.

Brinkman, D. 1981. The origin of the crocodiloid tarsi and the interrelationships of thecodontian archosaurs. *Breviora* 464:1–22.

Charig, A.J. 1972. The evolution of the archosaur pelvis and hindlimb: An explanation in functional terms. *In* K.A. Joysey and T.S. Kemp (eds.), *Studies in Vertebrate Evolution*. Edinburgh: Oliver and Boyd; New York: Winchester.

Charig, A.J., and H.D. Sues. 1976. Proterosuchia. *Handbuch der Paläoherbetologie* 13:11–39.

Chatterjee, S. 1982. Phylogeny and classification of the thecodontian reptiles. *Nature* 295:317–20.

———. 1985. *Postosuchus,* a new thecodontian reptile from the Triassic of Texas and the origin of tyrannosaurs. *Philosophical Transactions of the Royal Society of London,* Ser. B, 309:395–460.

Cruickshank, A.R.I., and M.J. Benton. 1985. Archosaur ankles and the relationships of the thecodontian and dinosaurian reptiles. *Nature* 317:715–17.

Fraas, O. 1877. *Aetosaurus ferratus* Fraas, die gepanzerte Vogel-Echse aus dem Stubensandstein bei Stuttgart. *Württembergisches Naturwissenschaften Journal* 33:1–21.

Gauthier, J.A. 1984. A cladistic analysis of the higher systematic categories of the Diapsida. Ph.D. dissertation, University of California, Berkeley.

Huene, F.F. von. 1935–42. *Die fossilen Reptilien des südamerikanischen Gondwanalandes.* Munich: Beck.

Juul, L. 1994. The phylogeny of basal archosaurs. *Paleontologica Africana* 31:1–38.

Long, R.A., and P.A. Murry. 1995. Late Triassic (Carnian and Norian) tetrapods from the southwestern United States. *New Mexico Museum of Natural History and Science Bulletin* 4:254.

Mehl, M.G. 1915. *Poposaurus gracilis,* a new reptile from the Triassic of Wyoming. *Journal of Geology* 23:516–22.

Meyer, H.V. 1861. Reptilien aus dem Stubensandstein des Oberen Keupers. *Palaeontographica* 7:253–346.

Padian, K. and C.L. May. 1993. The earliest dinosaurs. *New Mexico Museum of Natural History and Science Bulletin* 3:379–82.

Parrish, J.M. 1986. Locomotor evolution in the hindlimb and pelvis of the Thecodontia (Reptilia: Archosauria). *Hunteria* 1(2):1–35.

———. 1992. Phylogeny of the Erythrosuchidae. *Journal of Vertebrate Paleontology* 12:93–102.

———. 1993. Phylogeny of the Crocodylotarsi and a consideration of archosaurian and crurotarsan monophyly. *Journal of Vertebrate Paleontology* 13:287–308.

Sereno, P.C. 1991. Basal archosaurs: Phylogenetic relationships and functional implications. *Society of Vertebrate Paleontology Memoir 2, Journal of Vertebrate Paleontology* 11 (supplement to no. 4): 1–53.

Sereno, P.C., and A.B. Arcucci. 1994. Dinosaurian precursors from the Middle Triassic of Argentina: *Marasuchus lilloensis,* gen. nov. *Journal of Vertebrate Paleontology* 14:53–73.

Further Reading

Benton, M.J. 1983. The Triassic reptile *Hyperdapedon* from Elgin: Functional morphology and relationships. *Philosophical Transactions of the Royal Society of London,* Ser. B, 302:6205–717.

Ewer, R.F. 1965. The anatomy of the thecodont reptile *Euparkeria capensis* Broom. *Philosophical Transactions of the Royal Society of London,* Ser. B, 248:379–435.

Gauthier, J.A. 1986. Saurischian monophyly and the origin of birds. *Memoirs of the California Academy of Sciences* 8:155.

Krebs, B. (ed.). 1976. *Handbuch der Paläoherbetologie.* Vol. 13. *Thecodontia.* Stuttgart: Fischer-Verlag.

Padian, K. (ed.). 1986. *The Beginning of the Age of Dinosaurs.* Cambridge and New York: Cambridge University Press.

Sill, W.D. 1974. The anatomy of *Saurosuchus galilei* and the relationships of the rauisuchid thecodonts. *Bulletin of the Museum of Comparative Zoology* 146:317–362.

Walker, A.D. 1961. Triassic reptiles from the Elgin area: *Stagonolepis, Dasygnathus,* and their allies. *Philosophical Transactions of the Royal Society of London,* Ser. B, 244:103–204.

———. 1964. Triassic reptiles from the Elgin Area: *Ornithosuchus* and the origin of carnosaurs. *Philosophical Transactions of the Royal Society of London,* Ser. B, 248:53–134.

ARTHROPODS: OVERVIEW

The Arthropoda are a huge phylum, tremendously successful and diverse throughout the fossil record, up to the present day. Three times as many living arthropod species have been described as all other animal groups together. Like annelids (segmented worms), the arthropods are composed of many segments (metameres) (Figure 1). Both groups have a similarly organized nervous system, with the brain situated dorsally, and a double ventral nerve cord joining ganglia (clusters of nerve cell bodies) in each segment. Many arthropod groups have independently reduced the number of body segments by fusing them (a tendency taken to extremes in ostracods, or seed shrimps, and mites, for example). Segments often are grouped into units (tagmata), each with a specialized function (e.g., sensory systems, feeding, locomotion, or housing the viscera). Many arthropod higher taxa have characteristic patterns of tagmosis, a feature that is important in classification. In many respects, arthropods represent the acme of protostome evolution. (Pro-

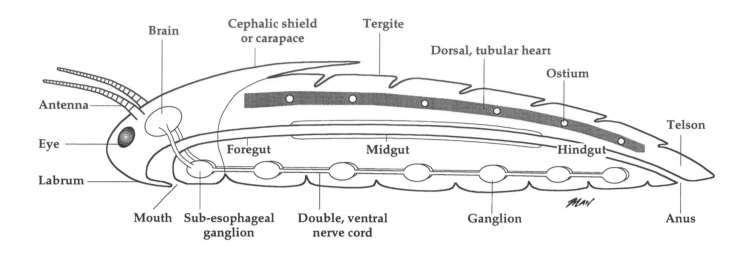

Figure 1. Schematic diagram of a generalized arthropod. Sagittal section showing the relationships of some important organ systems.

tostomes are animals in which mouth and anus develop from the same embryonic opening.) Many of the arthropods' organ systems and behavior patterns are extremely advanced.

Major Arthropod Groups

There are three major living arthropod groups: the uniramians (insects and myriapods—i.e., centipedes, millipedes), the crustaceans (e.g., shrimps, barnacles, woodlice), and the chelicerates (e.g., spiders, scorpions, horseshoe crabs). Uniramians are terrestrial, crustaceans are mostly aquatic, and chelicerates are predominantly terrestrial, although they have a rich marine heritage (Selden 1993). Another familiar group, the marine trilobites, became extinct by the end of the Permian. These four groups (often treated as classes in the literature) are distinguished by the number and form of the appendages that make up the anteriormost tagma, the "head" (Figure 2). Crustaceans, for example, have two pairs of antennae (usually sensory), one pair of mandibles (for chewing food), and two pairs of maxillae, or upper jaws (which assist the mandibles in directing and processing the food). The head segments all are derived from leg-bearing somites that have been incorporated from the trunk. In many primitive arthropods, the appendages at the rear of the head differ little from the trunk limbs that follow. There is much debate among biologists about whether similarly positioned appendages in different taxa are truly homologous. For example, some researchers believe that primitive chelicerates possessed a pair of antennae in front of the chelicerae. Other important anatomical features of the four major groups are summarized in Table 1.

All extant arthropods and most fossils can be readily classified as chelicerates, crustaceans, uniramians, or trilobites. From the turn of the century, an increasing number of fossils were discovered that could not be accommodated in this scheme. These now are classified as "miscellaneous arthropods." While neotologists have concentrated on unraveling how the three living groups and the trilobites are related to each other, paleobiologists have used the additional data from these unaligned fossils to derive a more inclusive classification. This section considers only the four, familiar classes.

Exoskeleton

The bodies of arthropods, unlike annelids, are covered in contiguous plates of cuticle (sclerites), which form the exoskeleton. Cuticle is composed of fibres of chitin in a tanned (sclerotized) protein matrix, producing a light, very strong and partially flexible natural ply. In some groups (e.g., crabs, shrimps, trilobites), the cuticle is mineralized with calcium carbonate, increasing its weight but offering greater strength and protection (Roer and Dillaman 1984). The plates on adjacent segments are joined by means of much thinner membranes (arthrodia), permitting articulation (jointed movement). An external skeleton offers considerable biomechanical advantages for animals up to a few centimeters long. However, such a skeleton also places severe restrictions on growth patterns. Periodically, most arthropods partially resolubilize (soften) the cuticle, molt the outer layers (ecdysis), inflate the body, then reform a larger exoskeleton.

Appendages

In primitive forms each metamere bears a pair of appendages (legs), covered by a tubular, jointed exoskeleton. In some groups, such as the millipedes and trilobites, all the metameres are very similar ("homonomous"). In other forms (e.g., insects, many crustaceans) successive segments and their appendages are modified for very different functions down the length of the body.

Primitive euarthropods (true arthropods) have limbs that are composed of two branches, or "rami"—they are biramous (Figure 3). The inner branch (endopod) of the trunk appendages

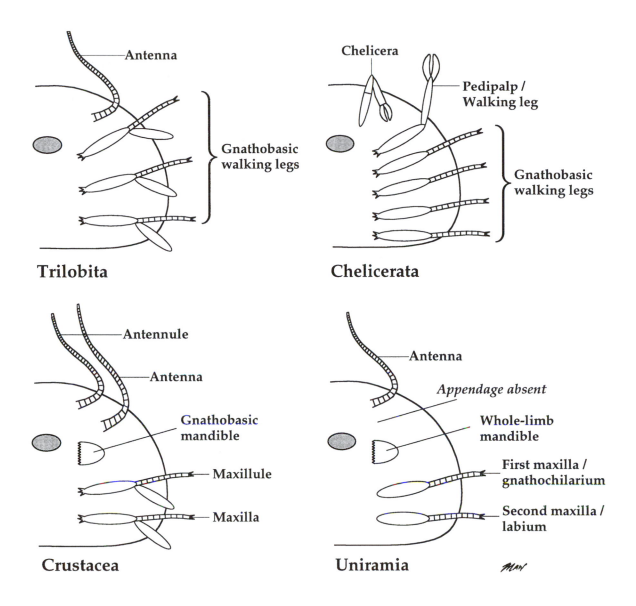

Figure 2. Schematic diagrams of appendage configurations in the heads of the four arthropod "classes."

typically consists of stout segments (podomeres), and is used for walking. The outer branch (exopod) is usually much finer; it often bears gill filaments or is otherwise modified for respiration. The insects and myriapods lack the outer branches of the appendages. Several arthropod groups have secondarily lost one or the other branch from some or all of their limbs (e.g., spiders). The two rami are borne by a "protopod," consisting of a distal "basis" and proximal "coxa," which is attached to the body. In trilobites, the coxa and basis are not separate (i.e., either they are fused or they have never divided). In crustaceans, the protopod may bear additional outgrowths (epipodites), which often have a respiratory function. In many arthropods, the protopod bears spiny outgrowths (endites), which assist in transporting food forward along a central groove to the mouth. These endites may fuse to form heavily sclerotized biting surfaces (gnathobases), which are often most strongly developed in the frontmost

appendages. The mandibles of crustaceans, for example, are massively gnathobasic.

The wings of insects were not derived from walking limbs, and have an independent evolutionary origin. The precise stages in the evolution of flight are still widely debated.

Circulation

Euarthropods (unlike annelids) lack an internally segmented and fluid-filled coelom. As a result, the circulatory system is open (hemocoelic) and composed of a dorsal heart plus a limited number of open-ended vessels. Primitively, the heart is a tubular organ extending the length of the trunk, although it is secondarily restricted to the thorax or part of the abdomen in several groups. Blood is pumped out of the heart anteriorly and posteriorly through a series of vessels (when present) into the hemocoel, where it bathes

Table 1.

Summary of some important anatomical features of the Uniramia, Crustacea, Chelicerata, and Trilobita

Characteristic	Uniramia	Crustacea	Chelicerata	Trilobita
Tagmata	Two (Myriapoda) (head [5 somites] and trunk) or three (Hexapoda) (head [5 somites], thorax [3], and abdomen [11]).	Usually three (head [5 somites] and more or less distinct thorax and abdomen). Trunk undifferentiated in some primitive forms (e.g., remipedes).	Usually two (prosoma [up to 6 somites] and opisthosoma [up to 12]). Opisthosoma may be divided into mesosoma and metasoma.	Three (head [5 or 6 somites], thorax and pygidium).
Cephalic shield or carapace	Absent. Simple head capsule.	Generally present. May be bivalved (e.g., ostracods/phyllocarids), or incorporate trunk tergites (e.g., eumalacostracans).	Carapace-like dorsal shield present in most groups.	Cephalic shield present.
Trunk appendages	All jointed and uniramous.	Primitively jointed and biramous. Secondarily uniramous or phyllopodous in some taxa.	Jointed and secondarily uniramous. Appendages of prosoma endopodal. Appendages of opisthosoma exopodal, when present.s	Jointed and biramous.
Trophic appendages	Mandibles: multiarticulate limbs functioning as whole-limb jaws (biting with their tips). Maxillules may assist in positioning food. Maxillae may be fused to form a labium, or be absent altogether.	Mandibles: multiarticulate limbs functioning as gnathobasic jaws (biting with basal, enditic surfaces). Maxillules and maxillae may assist in positioning and processing food.	Chelicerae jointed and chelate or subchelate; may inject venom into prey. In horseshoe crabs, the pedipalps and first four pairs of walking appendages are strongly gnathobasic, all serving to masticate food. The pedipalps of scorpions are powerfully chelate and grip prey.	Post-antennary cephalic appendages and most trunk limbs bear well-developed endites serving as gnathobases. Food is passed anteriorly along a ventral food groove.
Gas exchange	Aerial gas exchange system composed of tracheae and spiracles.	Aqueous diffusion across branchial surfaces.	Aerial gas exchange system using book lungs, book gills (bellows), or tracheae.	Aqueous diffusion across branchial surfaces.
Excretion	Ectodermally derived Malpighian tubules.	Nephridially derived structures (e.g., antennal glands, maxillary glands).	Coxal glands and/or endodermally derived Malpighian tubules.	?
Eyes	Most with simple ocelli at some stage in the life cycle. Compound eyes common in the Hexapoda.	Simple ocelli and compound eyes occur in most taxa at some stage during the life cycle. Compound eyes are often elevated on stalks.	Simple median eyes, sometimes with high acuity. Primitive compound lateral eyes in horseshoe crabs.	Compound, lateral eyes in many taxa.

the internal organs. It returns via a non-coelomic pericardial sinus and a series of perforations down the length of the heart (ostia).

Gas Exchange

Gas exchange is the process of drawing in oxygen and expelling carbon dioxide. The process is achieved via a variety of surfaces and organs. Some very small crustaceans use just the body surface and thin regions of cuticle (e.g., arthrodial membranes). Most larger crustaceans also have a system of gills. They consist of blood-filled evaginations (outpocketings) of the cuticle that create a large surface area for gas exchange. Gills are delicate and may be internalized for protection, as is the case in crabs. Terrestrial arthropods have overcome the problems of water loss at respiratory surfaces in two main ways. Insects (and to a lesser extent, arachnids) have evolved long, tubular invaginations of the cuticle ("tracheae") that open to the outside via small holes ("spiracles"). Internally, these tubules open directly into the hemocoel or to specific tissues. Arachnids have developed dry, internal gills called book lungs. These are saclike pockets, with thin, extensively folded walls (lamellae). Small muscles help these to function like miniature bellows.

Excretion

The hemocelic circulatory system of arthropods precludes full reliance on a nephridial excretory system such as that possessed by annelids. In annelids, each excretory unit, or nephridium, opens into the fluid-filled coelom by a ciliated funnel, called a nephrosoteme.

Among crustaceans, nepridial remnants persist in association with specific appendages (antennary glands and maxillary glands). Chelicerates have up to four pairs of nephridia, opening at the bases of the walking legs (coxal glands). Terrestrial arthropods have evolved a system of blind-ending, threadlike structures extending from the gut wall into the hemocoel ("Malpighian tubules").

Digestion

The tremendous diversity of arthropod feeding strategies is reflected in the morphology of their guts. At its simplest, the gut is a straight tube that extends from a ventral mouth to a terminal anus. The foregut and hind gut are ectodermally derived, while the midgut is endodermal. The foregut serves to ingest, store, and digest food mechanically, the midgut produces enzymes for chemical digestion, and the hind gut serves primarily to recover water. The midgut often bears a digestive caecum, liver or liver-pancreas.

Eyes

Euarthropods have evolved eyes of several types, varying greatly in complexity. The simplest, "ocelli," use a crude lens to collect light onto one or more light-sensitive cells (photoreceptors). These are sensitive to light intensity but are not capable of forming an image. The single-lens eyes of some spiders contain enough photoreceptors to form a sharp image, and the hunting spiders are able to focus this image to some degree. Many arthropod groups have "compound eyes," composed of many light-gathering units ("ommatidia") (over 10,000 in dragonflies). Each ommatidium comprises a lens and an associated array of photoreceptors ("rhabdome"). In some arthropods, screening pigments prevent light from one ommatidium from falling onto the rhabdome of another, allowing the formation of a mosaic-like image ("apposition eyes"). In other taxa, screening pigments are absent, and visual acuity is sacrificed for light-gathering power ("superposition," or dark-adapted eyes) (Kunze 1979). Some taxa can mobilize screening pigments, switching between apposition and superposition. The eyes of millipedes are composed of from 2 to 80 clustered ocelli that do not form a compound structure. Horseshoe crabs have compound eyes composed of numerous ommatidia, but again these units are not intimately associated. It is possible that compound eyes of the advanced sort found in insects and crustaceans evolved from clusters of discrete ocelli that fused over time. One theory maintains that compound eyes evolved independently in several groups, and the convergence in structural and

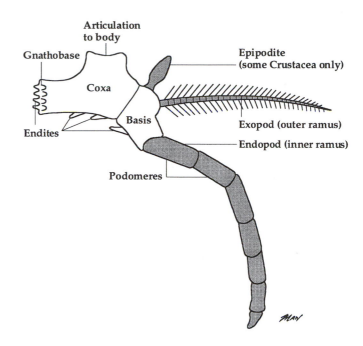

Figure 3. Schematic diagram of a generalized arthropod limb.

optical properties is the result of physical constraints on design. Another theory states that simple compound eyes evolved just once in the ancestral arthropod, and different specializations evolved independently in each arthropod subgroup. These questions have yet to be resolved.

Evolutionary Origins

Biologists are unable to agree whether the arthropods evolved from soft-bodied ancestors (e.g., annelids, molluscs) once ("monophyly"), twice ("diphyly"), or on several occasions ("polyphyly") (Wills et al. 1995). Nowadays, most scholars emphasize the many similarities between the four great groups to argue for a single origin. Others have highlighted supposedly fundamental differences in structures (e.g., compound eyes, jaws) to contend that one group of arthropods could *not* have evolved from another or from some common arthropodan ancestor. The affinities of two other related phyla, the Onychophora and Tardigrada, may shed light on how the full suite of arthropodan characters were acquired. The onychophorans (velvet worms) lack plates of sclerotized cuticle but possess 14–43 pairs of uniramous, fleshy legs ("lobopods") down the length of the body. The tardigrades (water bears) are tiny animals with just four pairs of lobopods, some bearing simple plates of cuticle on the body. Both groups may represent body plans intermediate between the annelids, or annelid-like ancestors, and the arthropods.

Phylogeny

It is still unclear how the four arthropod classes are related to each other. Historically, arthropod scholars have tended to focus on a limited subset of morphological characters or organ systems (e.g.,

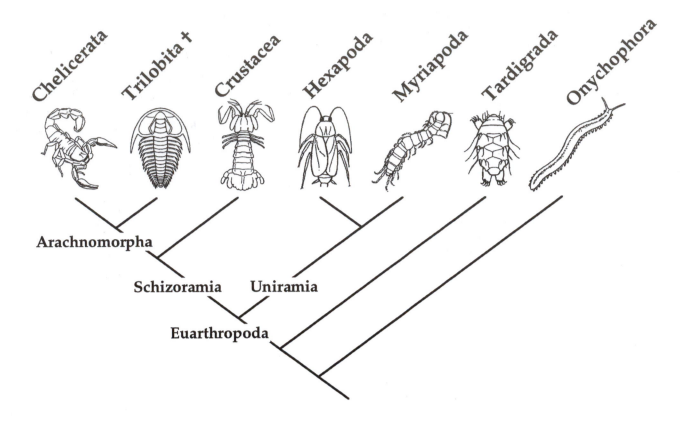

Figure 4. One possible phylogenetic hypothesis for the arthropods and related groups. A host of problematic fossils have not been included in this scheme.

antennae, limbs, tendons) to deduce evolutionary trees (Gupta 1979). Unfortunately, the distributions of these characters often suggest radically different solutions (since characters are incongruent). Recent approaches (e.g., Wheeler et al. 1993; Wills et al. 1995) are attempting to pool all of the data to see which trees require the fewest assumptions overall about character evolution. One simplified hypothesis is shown below (Figure 4), based on our own work. Here, the tardigrades and onychophorans branch off at the bottom of the tree. The basal arthropodan split is between taxa with biramous limbs ("schizoramians") and those with uniramous limbs. The extinct trilobites are seen as the closest relatives of the chelicerates. Equally rigorous studies have produced a variety of other patterns. Most disagreement comes from comparisons between morphological and molecular data. Alternative hypotheses argue, for example, that hexapods and crustaceans are closely related (the Mandibulata), or that the myriapods fall low in the tree (see Figure 1).

The Fossil Record

Most arthropod cuticle lacks any mineral content, so it is prone to decay. The exoskeletons of the vast majority of fossil arthropods are strengthened with calcium carbonate or calcium phosphate (ostracods, decapods, and trilobites). Other taxa are restricted mostly to sites of exceptional preservation (e.g., the Burgess Shale). Many fossils represent "exuviae" (shed skeletons) rather than true body-fossils.

The crustaceans, trilobites, and probably the chelicerates have records extending back to the Cambrian. Myriapods are first recorded from the Late Silurian, while the insects do not appear until the Devonian. Phosphatized tardigrades have recently been recorded from the Upper Cambrian, while the onychophoran lobopods appear to have been a much more diverse clade in the early Cambrian than today.

MATTHEW A. WILLS AND DEREK E.G. BRIGGS

See also Aquatic Invertebrates, Adaptive Strategies of; Arthropods: Miscellaneous Arthropods; Chelicerates; Crustaceans; Defensive Structures: Invertebrates; Eyes: Invertebrates; Feeding Adaptations: Invertebrates; Insects and Other Hexapods; Myriapods; Ornamentation: Invertebrates; Problematic Animals: Phanerozoic Problematica; Trilobites

Works Cited

Gupta, A.P. (ed.). 1979. *Arthropod Phylogeny.* New York: Van Nostrand Reinhold.

Kunze, P. 1979. Apposition and superposition eyes. *In* H. Autrum (ed.), *Comparative Physiology and Evolution of Vision in Invertebrates, A: Invertebrate Photoreceptors. Handbook of Sensory Physiology VII/6A.* Berlin and New York: Springer.

Roer, R., and R. Dillaman. 1984. The structure and calcification of the crustacean cuticle. *American Zoologist* 24:893–909.

Selden, P. 1993. Arthropoda (Aglaspidida, Pycnogonida and Chelicerata). *In* M.J. Benton (ed.), *The Fossil Record 2.* London and New York: Chapman and Hall.

Wheeler, Q.D., P. Cartwright, and C.Y. Hayashi. 1993. Arthropod phylogeny: A combined approach. *Cladistics* 9:1–39.

Wills, M.A., D.E.G. Briggs, R.A. Fortey, and M. Wilkinson. 1995. The

significance of fossils in understanding arthropod evolution. *Verhandlungen der Deutschen Zoologischen Gesellschaft* 57:13–33.

Further Reading

Brusca, R.C., and G.J. Brusca. 1990. *Invertebrates.* Sunderland, Massachusetts: Sinauer.

Gupta, A.P. (ed.). 1979. *Arthropod Phylogeny.* New York: Van Nostrand Reinhold.

Manton, S.M. 1977. *The Arthropoda: Habits, Functional Morphology and Evolution.* Oxford: Clarendon.

ARTHROPODS: MISCELLANEOUS ARTHROPODS

The vast majority of fossil arthropods can be assigned confidently to one of the four great classes: Crustacea, Uniramia, Chelicerata, and the extinct Trilobita. However, some of the oldest fossils have unfamiliar combinations of characters or possess unique features that frustrate their classification. Such taxa are said to be "problematic." Anomalies often arise because of the number or morphology of appendages in the cephalon, or head. Other strange features include the manner in which the segments of the trunk are divided into functional units (tagmata).

The greatest diversity of "problematica" occurs in Cambrian rock strata, shortly after the apparently explosive radiation of multicelled (metazoan) phyla in the fossil record. A small number of sites have proven exceptionally rich in problematic arthropods. The Middle Cambrian Burgess Shale (British Columbia) was the first to be discovered and remains the most extensively studied. Similar, although less rich, localities have since been found at Chengjiang in China and Peary Land in Greenland (both Lower Cambrian). Preservation at these sites (which are called "Konservat-Lagerstätten") is exceptional. Soft tissues are fossilized, as are heavily mineralized skeletons. Most problematic arthropods lack mineralized cuticles, so they are only preserved at such sites.

The initial work on the Burgess Shale arthropods was carried out between 1909 and 1913 by its discoverer, Charles Walcott (Gould 1989). He attempted to interpret the arthropods as early or primitive representatives of the major groups already recognized elsewhere in the fossil record. Over the last 80 years or more, Walcott's extensive collections have been augmented with new material from the Burgess Shale and nearby localities. During the 1970s and 1980s painstaking restudy of many of the animals was conducted by Harry Whittington and his student, Derek Briggs, among others. Their efforts produced new reconstructions, including vital details of the appendage morphology. Representative trilobites, crustaceans, and a chelicerate were found, but most Cambrian arthropods could not be "shoehorned" into these taxa. Since then, other workers (e.g., Gould 1989) have argued that many problematic arthropods represent groups of great morphological distinction. This has led to claims that the Burgess Shale

contains 20 or more arthropod classes, rather than the 4 recognized previously. Recent work has sought to apply the techniques of cladistic analysis to all arthropods, both living and fossil. Studies by the authors (e.g., Wills et al. 1994) have recognized a relatively small number of major groupings (Figure 1), most containing both Recent and fossil taxa. The formerly problematic fossils from the Burgess Shale and other localities are discussed with reference to this classification.

Arachnomorpha

This large group includes the extinct Trilobita, and the living and fossil chelicerates (e.g., horseshoe crabs). It also includes a large number of Cambrian problematica (Figure 2). In most arachnomorphs the dorsal surface of the animal is divided into three sections (trilobed) by a pair of longitudinal furrows or depressions. The furrows define a median (central) region that is flanked on each side by a lateral lobe. Normally, the lateral lobes (pleurae) overlap down the trunk. The front edge of the cephalic (head) shield is often reflexed (curled) under the head to form a "doublure." The appendages on the trunk are biramous (two-branched) and typically have spiny endopods (the inner branch of the limb) and filamentous exopods (outer branch of the limb), and their bases are armed with chewing gnathobases. The anus is located in the last trunk somite (or ventrally in the pygidium, in the case of trilobites). Extending posteriorly, beyond the last trunk somite, is the post-segmental "telson," which is typically developed wither as an elongate spine or as a paddlelike tail.

Sanctacaris

Sanctacaris, a relatively large arachnomorph from the Mount Stephen Formation (near Walcott's quarry), was a formidable predator (Briggs and Collins 1988). The first five of its six cephalic appendages were biramous and grouped into a forward-pointing basket for grasping prey. All but the last of the 11 trunk somites bore biramous appendages, with broad, flat, outer rami. The tail was flattened. The division of the body into functional units ("tag-

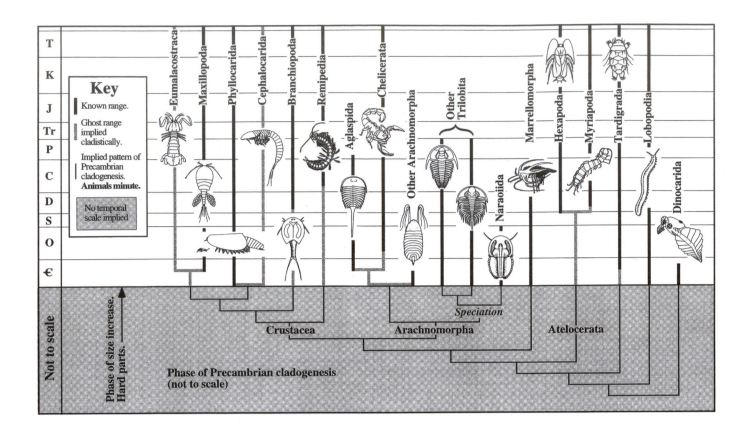

Figure 1. A simplified phylogenetic tree of the arthropods and related groups (including fossil and Recent groups). The Lobopodia includes the Onychophora. The simultaneous appearance of many derived groups at the base of the Cambrian implies an earlier history. The trilobites are already differentiated into several groups when they first appear in the fossil record. Abbreviations in the left-hand column refer to geological periods (Cambrian, Ordovician, Silurian, etc.).

mosis") is similar to that in chelicerates, but *Sanctacaris* does not appear to have been a close relative.

Yohoia

First described by Walcott, this slender arthropod had a cephalon of 4 somites and a trunk of 13 (Whittington 1974). Like *Santacaris,* the rear portion of the animal was developed into a flattened, paddlelike tail. The first appendages ("Great Appendages") were robust and projected forward for catching prey. Each of these appendages was composed of two large, elongate podomeres (leg segments) plus a group of four articulated (mobile) terminal spines. The trunk appendages lacked inner rami, but the outer rami were similar to those of *Sanctacaris.*

Alalcomenaeus

The body of this Cambrian arthropod was divided into a head bearing four pairs of appendages, a trunk of 12 somites, and a horizontal rear plate that was flat, broad, and oval-shaped (Whittington 1981). All of the trunk divisions, with the exception of the last, bore biramous appendages. The forward-most cephalic

appendages ("Great Appendages") were uniramous. Three relatively massive proximal podomeres bore a distal group of spines and extended into a long flagellum. The remaining head appendages were similar to those of the trunk.

Habelia

The high, domed, tubercle-studded cephalon of *Habelia* was followed by a trunk of 12 arched somites, and a posterior, serrated, and jointed spine (Whittington 1981). The head bore a pair of small uniramous antennae, followed by two additional pairs of biramous appendages. The first six trunk limbs were biramous (with a stout inner walking branch and a flattened outer one), while the remainder apparently lacked endopods.

Leanchoilia

One of the larger and more obviously bizarre Burgess arthropods, *Leanchoilia,* bore a huge pair of "Great Appendages" that could be held out in front of the animal or swiveled back along the body while swimming (Bruton and Whittington 1983). These limbs were composed of four massive basal joints, followed by another two that had long, slender, barlike extensions that terminated in long, whiplike flagellae. The last joint was a tapering shaft, terminating in three claws, plus an annulated flagellum. The remaining two cephalic appendages were similar to those of the trunk. These were biramous, with a stout, terminally clawed, walking branch and a large, flaplike exopod, both directed ventrally below the animal. The front of the cephalic shield bore a distinctive, reflexed snout. Posteriorly, there was a stout, triangular telson with articulating spines along the margin.

Sarotrocercus

This tiny, dorsoventrally flattened Burgess arthropod lacked walking branches on the trunk appendages and probably swam on its back using the broad, flaplike exopods (Whittington 1981). A short, broad cephalon bore two pairs of appendages, the first composed of seven stout podomeres with small distal claws, the second similar to those of the trunk. Huge, almost spherical eyes borne on stalks protruded from under the front edge of the carapace. The trunk was composed of ten somites. The first nine each bore a pair of appendages, and the tenth was tubular. A long, thin, terminal extension bore a cluster of splayed spines at its tip.

Sidneyia

Named after Walcott's son Sidney, *Sidneyia* was a large, robustly built Burgess form (Bruton 1981). Uniquely, the cephalon appears to have borne just a single pair of appendages: long filiform (filament-like) antennae. A massive ventral doublure extended farther back under the animal than the broad cephalic shield. The antennae and a pair of stalked eyes emerged from notches on either side of the shield. The walking legs bore huge spines and massive gnathobases. The first four pairs were uniramous, while the following five pairs also bore filamentous gill branches. The abdomen consisted of three ringlike segments, the first two lacking appendages, the last with flattened, paddle-like limbs. These last limbs (uropods) formed a fanlike tail in conjunction with the flattened, terminal telson (much as in modern lobsters).

Cheloniellon

Cheloniellon was described by Broili (1932) from the Devonian Hunsrück Slate in Germany (Stürmer and Bergström 1978). This relatively large, dorsoventrally flattened arthropod shares several features with the chelicerates, and also shows some important differences. The first appendages were long, filiform antennae, rather than chelicerae. The remaining five pairs of cephalic limbs were uniramous, massively gnathobasic, and crowded toward the mouth (reminiscent of horseshoe crabs). A trunk of nine somites bore eight pairs of biramous limbs, with a pair of long, filamentous cerci arising from the last somite. Like the chelicerates, the eyes were borne dorsally on the cephalon. *Cheloniellon* is related to the living chelicerates, and falls into the wider concept of Arachnomorpha.

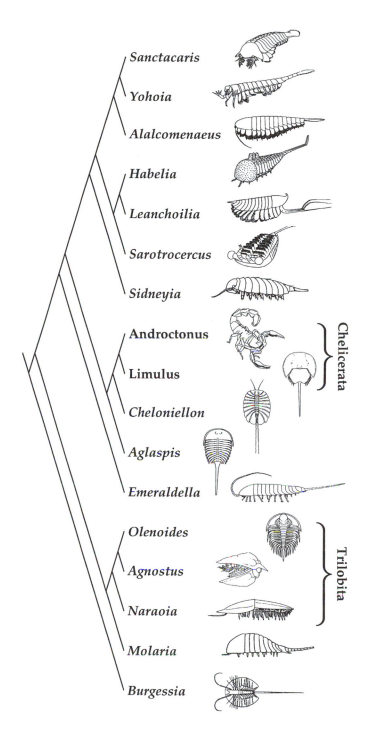

Figure 2. A phylogenetic tree of some arachnomorph taxa. Italics indicate fossils; roman, extant taxa.

Aglaspida

The Aglaspida share with the chelicerates a trunk composed of 11 somites. They also bear an elongate terminal spine, similar to that of the modern horseshoe crabs (Xiphosura). For a long time, scholars assumed that the Aglaspida possessed six pairs of appendages in the head (a chelicerate character); accordingly they were included in the Xiphosura. However, detailed examination of an exceptionally preserved specimen of *Aglaspis spinifer* from the Upper Cambrian St. Lawrence Formation in Wisconsin (Briggs et al. 1979) revealed four (or possibly five) pairs of uniramous cephalic limbs, the first of which were *not* chelicerae. The dorsal aspect of the aglaspid body superficially resembles that of olenellid trilobites, another group to which they have been allied. A consideration of all characters taken together suggests that the Aglaspida, like *Cheloniellon,* are close relatives of the chelicerates. Their fossil record extends from the Cambrian to the Lower Permian.

Emeraldella

Emeraldella was a relatively abundant Burgess arthropod, somewhat tear-shaped in dorsal outline (Bruton and Whittington 1983). The cephalon incorporated six pairs of appendages (similar in number to chelicerates), and was followed by a trunk of 13 somites. The first cephalic limbs were long, filiform antennae, the second uniramous and gnathobasic. The remaining 15 pairs of appendages were biramous and gnathobasic. Terminally, there were two somites covered by nearly cylindrical tergites, plus a long, styliform terminal extension. The anus was covered by a prominent plate fringed with spines.

Molaria

Molaria, another Burgess form, was almost semicircular in cross section. The head bore small antennae, followed by three pairs of gnathobasic, biramous, walking legs (Whittington 1981). These were similar to the eight trunk appendages, each located beneath short, broad tergites. The anus was located ventrally in the last trunk somite, which lacked appendages. There was a long, many-segmented post-anal extension. The segmentation of the cephalon, and the form of the appendages, suggest this animal was a relative of the trilobites. However, the absence of a pygidium (tail section) or trilobation of the dorsal cuticle and the presence of the jointed tail mean it cannot be included in this taxon.

Burgessia

Burgessia was a small, weakly sclerotized (thin-shelled) arthropod, covered by an almost circular, undivided cephalic shield. A pair of large, uniramous, filiform, jointed antennae (almost as long as the carapace) was followed by three pairs of walking limbs with threadlike outer rami. The succeeding seven trunk somites each bore biramous limbs composed of an inner ambulatory endopod, and flattened, unsegmented exopod. The eighth appendages were little more than uniramous, sickle-shaped spikes, curving posteriorly. Posterior to these was an almost cylindrical ninth somite (devoid of appendages), followed by a prominent but slender terminal spine. *Burgessia* has proved one of the more enigmatic Burgess taxa, and among the most difficult to classify (Hughes 1973). It seems most likely that it represents an early offshoot from the rest of the arachnomorph group.

Crustaceans and Crustacean-Like Taxa

The taxa described here are crustaceans or their close relatives, which together form a larger group (Wills et al. 1994). Uncertainty over the placement of particular taxa has usually arisen because the evidence for all their diagnostic characters is equivocal, or because they have additional, unique, or bizarre features.

Canadaspidida (*Canadaspis* and *Perspicaris*)

The morphological similarities of the Burgess genus *Canadaspis* (Figure 3A) to the Malacostraca are compelling (Briggs 1978). The Malacostraca includes such successful modern taxa as shrimp and lobsters. Early workers specifically assigned *Canadaspis* to the Phyllocarida and drew frequent parallels with the living nebaliids. Malacostracan-like similarities include a bivalved carapace with a pronounced anterior adductor muscle, a characteristic five-segment crustacean head, and tagmosis of the trunk into a thorax of eight short, free somites and an abdomen of seven somites plus a telson. However, *Canadaspis* displays an enigmatic mix of supposedly primitive and derived characters (Briggs 1992). The maxillules and maxillae (mouthparts) were little differentiated from the relatively identical trunk appendages. The endopods were composed of numerous podomeres, while the exopods were flaplike and bore several supporting rays.

Perspicaris (Figure 3b), also from the Burgess, had an arrangement of minute antennules and more massive antennae, as did *Canadaspis*. However, the eyes were far more prominent; they projected from a bulblike protuberance on the front of the cephalon (Briggs 1977). The division of the trunk into a thorax of eight appendage-bearing somites and an abdomen of seven somites lacking them, plus a telson, is also comparable. However, the trunk appendages appear to have lacked inner rami, and the telson bore a prominent pair of furcal rami.

Odaraia

The Burgess Shale genus *Odaraia* (Figure 3c) had a bivalved, almost tubular carapace that extended over half of the total length of the body. The trunk was elongate, with between 25 and 50 short, broad somites. The unique telson bore three, large, flat, tapering processes or flukes, two oriented approximately laterally, and the third one dorsally. Walcott considered *Odaraia* to be an unequivocal crustacean, allying it with the phyllocarids. Unfortunately, the cephalon is not particularly well preserved, so classification has relied on the presence or absence of appendages. Antennules and antennae are poorly preserved, but the third cephalic appendage appears to have been a massive gnathobasic mandible. The two front pairs of trunk appendages differ from those following in lacking outer rami, the segmented branches being interpreted as palps (sensory or gustatory structures). Briggs (1981) considered the affinities of *Odaraia* to lie with the modern Branchiopoda, a relationship that has emerged from several cladistic treatments of the morphological data. Other analyses place *Odaraia* close to the phyllocarids, and still others suggest that it may have branched off very close to the base of the crustacean tree.

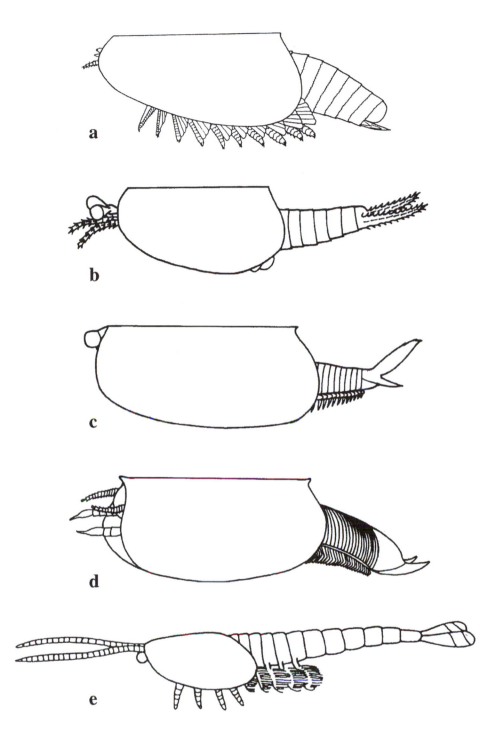

Figure 3. Bivalved, crustacean and crustacean-like arthropods from the Middle Cambrian Burgess Shale. a, Canadaspis perfecta; b, Perspicaris dictynna; c, Odaraia alata; d, Branchiocaris pretiosa; e, Waptia fieldensis.

Branchiocaris

The Burgess Shale *Branchiocaris* (Figure 3d) has proved extremely difficult to classify cladistically (Wills et al. 1995), because it shows affinities with both the crustaceans and the Marrellomorpha (see below). *Branchiocaris* was divided into a simple cephalon bearing two pairs of appendages and a trunk of at least 46 thick, short somites, each bearing a pair of flat, broad

(presumably exopodal) appendages (Briggs 1976). There was also a relatively long telson with a pair of ventral blades. As in the marrellomorphs, the length of the trunk appendages decreased posteriorly. The frontmost appendages were a pair of stout, uniramous antennae, while the second or "principal" appendages were stouter still, and composed of seven or more massive podomeres. The last (or possibly penultimate) podomere was bulbous, and may have been part of a small chela. The carapace was bivalved and hinged along the back, as in many crustaceans.

Waptia

The cephalon of *Waptia* (Figure 3e), a bivalved Burgess form, bore five pairs of appendages and a pair of small eyes borne on stalks. The first appendages were reduced antennules, and the second were much longer, segmented antennae; the detailed morphology of the three posterior pairs of cephalic appendages is unknown. The cephalon was followed by four somites bearing uniramous walking limbs and a further six somites bearing filamentous gill branches. All these appendages lay beneath the carapace and were borne on the thorax. The abdomen was composed of five longer somites, all lacking appendages, plus a telson bearing a divided tail blade with flattened, segmented rami. The affinities of *Waptia* lie close to the phyllocarids.

"Orsten" Taxa

Klaus Müller and Dieter Walossek have described a number of distinctive crustacean genera, exquisitely preserved in phosphatized limestone nodules (orsten) from the Upper Cambrian of Västergötland, Sweden (Müller 1983). Schram (1986) considered it likely that most of these fossils are larvae. Müller and Walossek allied them to several crustacean groups.

Martinssonia (Figure 4a) had a slender body reaching lengths up to 1.5 millimeters in the most advanced instar (juvenile stage) known, which may still have been immature (Müller and Walossek 1986). The cephalon bore five pairs of appendages, which were covered proximally by a modest head shield bearing a rostral projection. The two anterior trunk somites bore limbs, while the remaining five, and the telson, lacked appendages. The first and seventh appendages were uniramous, while the remainder were biramous. The second through fifth appendages bore a stout endopod of five podomeres and a slightly shorter, broader exopod divided into many podomeres with medial, setalike (bristlelike) bars. The telson was large and forked. Müller and Walossek interpreted *Martinssonia* as a stem lineage crustacean, lacking many of the features of the "crown group."

The slender body of *Skara* (Figure 4b) reached lengths of about 1.4 millimeters, and was divided into a cephalon of 5 fused somites covered by a small dorsal shield, and a trunk of 11 somites, the first of which bore appendages. The antennules were unuramous and annulate, while the antennae were biramous, with an exopod of 14 annuli (ring segments) and an endopod of three stout podomeres. The antennae also bore a well-developed comb of protopodal endites. The third appendages (mandibula of Müller 1985) were similar to the antennae, but with less well-developed endites. The fourth, fifth, and sixth appendages were all basically similar, with a slightly curved and flattened exopod bearing marginal setae and an endopod of three podomeres. The remaining trunk somites lacked appendages, save for the terminal, well-developed caudal furca. Müller (1985) speculated on possible affinities of *Skara* with the copepods. Phylogenetic studies by the authors suggest that *Skara* was a close relative of *Martinssonia*, and that both these taxa were probably maxillopods.

The most advanced known developmental stage of *Rehbachiella* is probably preadult (Walossek 1993). The cephalon bore five appendages. The antennules were uniramous and annulate, while the antennae were biramous and gnathobasic. The mandibles were well-developed and probably bore a small biramous palp. The trunk was composed of 13 somites plus an unsegmented abdomen bearing furcal rami. Only the posterior-most thoracic segment lacked appendages of any description. The remaining biramous cephalic and trunk appendages were all constructed similarly, the latter showing a regular decrease in size down the length of the body. The endopods were divided into four podomeres (except in the more posterior limb pairs), while the exopods were all slightly rounded and unsegmented. Walossek (1993) placed *Rehbachiella* in a modified Anostraca (Branchiopoda), while cladistic studies by the authors cast doubt on this.

Bredocaris (Figure 4c) reached lengths of about a millimeter as an adult (Müller and Walossek 1988). An arched carapace covered the cephalon and extended back laterally as far as the anterior thoracic appendages. The antennules were uniramous, while the antennae were biramous with a stout endopod and large protopodal endites. A massive, ventrally dirvected labrum lay in front of the massively-gnathobasic, biramous mandibles. The maxillules bore large medial endites, a stout endopod, and vestigial exopod. The maxillae and seven pairs of thoracic appendages were basically similar although decreasing in size posteriorly, and with less well-developed enditic processes. Each bore an unsegmented exopod and an endopod weakly divided into four segments. The trunk was unsegmented, with a short abdomen bearing a pair of furcae. Müller and Walossek speculated that *Bredocaris* may have been related to the Thecostraca (Maxillopoda). Studies by the authors suggest that it was a close relative of *Rehbachiella*.

Marrellomorpha

Marrella is by far the most abundant arthropod from the Burgess Shale. Dubbed the "Lace Crab" by Walcott, it has proven notoriously difficult to determine its affinities (Whittington 1971). The body was divided into a cephalon bearing two pairs of appendages, a trunk of 24 to 26 somites bearing biramous limbs, and a telson. Viewed from above, the cephalic shield was subquadrangular and bore two pairs of long, stout, dorsoventrally flattened, tapering spines. The first appendages were uniramous antennae, projecting downward and outward from the posterior portion of the ventral cephalon. The second appendages were inserted immediately above and behind the first, and consisted of a massive, long, basal podomere projecting forward and outward, followed by five much shorter podomeres (together about the same length as the first) densely fringed with setae. Behind the cephalic shield, the body, which lacked tergites, was subcircular in cross section, tapering backward. Each somite bore a pair of biramous appendages, which also decreased in size posteriorly. The inner rami of the first eight or nine trunk appendages were relatively long, and functioned as walking legs. The remainder of the appendages curved downward and inward and formed a net (which may have functioned in trapping and filtering food). The outer rami were long and bore fine filaments.

When it was first described, *Marrella* seemed to have no close relatives, either in the living fauna or throughout the fossil record. However, two taxa have since emerged from the Devonian Hunsrück Shale that are almost certainly very close to *Marrella* phylogenetically. The first of these, *Mimetaster,* bears a striking resemblance to *Marrella,* both in general appearance and in many details of morphology (Stürmer and Bergström 1976). The head was composed of a relatively large cephalic shield with a massive labrum, from which arose three pairs of uniramous appendages. The first were filiform and segmented antennae. The second and third pair were massive walking limbs, the former almost disproportionately large (each limb being longer than the entire body). The main, central, oval body of the cephalic shield bore six very long and prominent spines. Each of these spines in turn bore two horizontal rows of smaller, articulated spines. A pair of stalked lateral eyes arose from the dorsal surface of the carapace. The body behind the head was composed of at least 30 somites, decreasing in size and tapering toward the posterior. Each bore a pair of biramous appendages, also decreasing in length posteriorly.

The second, *Vachonisia,* had a massive and entire cephalic shield, covering the whole length of the body (Stürmer and Bergström 1976). Anteriorly, two lateral, winglike lobes projected on either side of a median notch. Posteriorly, the shield was almost rectangular, tapering very slightly, with a V-shaped indentation along the back edge. Ventrally, there was a shelflike ridge around a central, heart-shaped concavity, which sheltered the appendages. The anteriormost appendages were short, uniramous antennae, while the second to fourth pairs were by far the largest and probably used for walking. The second and third walking legs were armed with large endites, directed toward the mouth. Trunk appendages were all of similar appearance, biramous, much smaller than those of the cephalon, lacked gnathobases, and decreased in size down the length of the body. Work by the authors suggests that the Marrellomorphs constitute a sister group to both the arachnomorphs and the crustaceans (Wills et al. 1995).

Euthycarcinoidea

The euthycarcinoids are a group of just eight species in six genera known from the Late Silurian of Western Australia, the Late Carboniferous of France and the United States, and the Middle Triassic of France and eastern Australia. Euthycarcinoids (literally "straight crabs") were originally thought to possess gnathobasic mandibles, biramous trunk appendages, and possibly two pairs of antennae. Therefore, earlier interpretations placed them with the crustaceans, but they have also been regarded as merostome-like animals, partly because they bear a long, slender terminal extension. It was only when Bergström (1980) reexamined material of *Sy-naustrus* and *Kottixerxes* that euthycarcinoid appendages were correctly interpreted as uniramous. There is only one pair of antennae, and the trunk divisions consist of two somites (diplosegments), a feature normally associated with myriapodous uniramians (Diplopoda and Pauropoda). Several work-

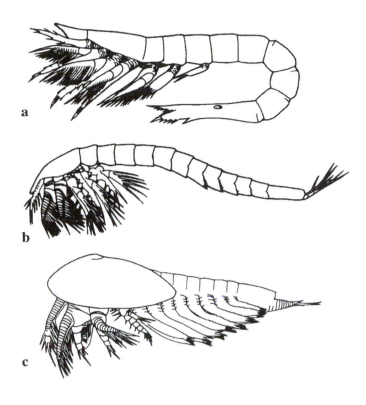

Figure 4. Crustean fossils from the Upper Cambrian "orsten" fana, Västergötland, Sweden. *a, Martinssonia elongata; b, Skara annulata; c, Bredocaris admirabilis.*

ers (e.g., Bergström 1980; Schram and Rolfe 1982; McNamara and Trewin 1993; Wills et al. 1995) have placed the euthycarcinoids in the Uniramia.

Anomalocaridids and *Opabinia*

The story of the discovery and description of the Dinocarida, and the research that ultimately led to their placement in a separate class, is intriguing in its own right. Adequate coverage cannot be given here, but an excellent account is provided by Collins (1996). The sclerotized first cephalic appendages of the giant Cambrian predator *Anomalocaris* were first described from the Mt. Stephen Formation of Mount Field (near the Burgess Quarry), and were originally believed to be the body of a shrimplike animal. A ring of 32 narrow, radiating plates, around what later turned out to be the mouth, was also found isolated and was initially thought to be the body of a jellyfish, *Peytoia.* Whittington and Briggs (1985) discovered the link between these elements, and were the first to describe the rest of the weakly sclerotized body of what turned out to be by far the largest Cambrian predator (some related forms reaching lengths of 2 meters).

The anterior-most appendages of *Anomalocaris* were stout and highly sclerotized. Each was composed of nine or more podomeres and ended in an arrangement of spines. Each podomere itself bore a long spine diverging at right angles from the main axis of the appendage. These appendages could be retracted and curled back under the animal such that their distal tips, and the tips of the long spines, would almost meet at a point just below the grasp of the ventral mouth plates. This apparatus served to grab prey. The remaining three pairs of cephalic appendages were lightly sclerotized, flattened, rounded, fleshy lobes, diverging laterally from the ventral body axis. The trunk appendages were similar, but their ventral lobes were much larger. At the rear of the animal, there was a tail fan composed of three partially overlapping blade pairs, directed dorsolaterally, plus a terminal pair of long, slender cerci. *Anomalocaris* appears to have "flown" underwater using undulating waves of swimming strokes that passed along the limbs. Several other genera of anomalocaridids have since been described from the Burgess Quarry, the Lower Cambrian Chengjiang fauna of Yunnan Province in southern China, and the Lower Cambrian of Poland. Some specimens show evidence of sclerotized, jointed, walking limbs down the trunk.

Opabinia probably has the most bizarre appearance of all Burgess Shale arthropods (Whittington 1975). Only recently has its link with the anomalocaridids been established (Bergström 1986; Collins 1996; Wills et al. 1995). The cuticle, like that of *Anomalocaris,* was not mineralized but still was rigid enough to maintain the shape of the lateral lobes down the body. The body was divided into a head bearing a single pair of fused appendages (functioning as a clawed "proboscis") and a segmented trunk. There were five large compound eyes on the dorsal side of the cephalon, all supported by broad, fleshy stalks. The sclerotized trunk was divided into 15 segments plus a terminal division bearing a three-lobed tail, similar to that of *Anomalocaris.* The dorsoventrally flattened trunk appendages overlapped, the back edge of each overlying the front edge of that following (overlapping in the opposite direction to the limbs of anomalocaridids). All but the first consisted of a lower, smooth lobe of tissue overlaid by a narrower, layered gill.

Collins (1996) united *Opabinia* and the anomalocaridids in their own class, the Dinocarida. Their precise position in the arthropod evolutionary tree is uncertain, but it seems likely that they represent a branch from very near the base. Wills and colleagues (1995) placed them below the Onychophora and Tardigrada (Figure 1). Therefore, many of their arthropod-like characters may have evolved independently.

MATTHEW A. WILLS AND DEREK E.G. BRIGGS

See also Arthropods: Overview

Works Cited

Bergström, J. 1980. Morphology and systematics of early arthropods. *Abhandlungen des Naturwissenschaftlichen Vereins in Hamburg* 23:7–42.

———. 1986. *Opabinia* and *Anomalocaris,* unique Cambrian "arthropods." *Lethaia* 19:241–46.

Briggs, D.E.G. 1976. *The arthropod* Branchiocaris *N. gen., Middle Cambrian, Burgess Shale, British Columbia.* Geological Survey of Canada Bulletin, 264. Ottawa: Canadian Government Printing Bureau.

———. 1977. Bivalved arthropods from the Cambrian Burgess Shale of British Columbia. *Palaeontology* 20:595–621.

———. 1978. The morphology, mode of life, and affinities of *Canadaspis perfecta* (Crustacea: Phyllocarida), Middle Cambrian, Burgess Shale, British Columbia. *Philosophical Transactions of the Royal Society of London,* ser. B, 281:439–87.

———. 1981. The arthropod *Odaraia alata* Walcott, Middle Cambrian, Burgess Shale, British Columbia. *Philosophical Transactions of the Royal Society of London,* ser. B, 291:541–85.

———. 1992. Phylogenetic significance of the Burgess Shale Crustacean *Canadaspis. Acta Zoologica* 73:293–300.

Briggs, D.E.G., D.L. Bruton, and H.B. Whittington. 1979. Appendages of the arthropod *Aglaspis spinifer* (Upper Cambrian, Wisconsin) and their significance. *Paleontology* 22:167–80.

Briggs, D.E.G., and D. Collins. 1988. A Middle Cambrian chelicerate from Mount Stephen, British Columbia. *Palaeontology* 31:779–98.

Bruton, D.L. 1981. The arthropod *Sidneyia inexpectans,* Middle Cambrian Burgess Shale, British Columbia. *Philosophical Transactions of the Royal Society of London,* ser. B, 295:619–56.

Bruton, D.L., and H.B. Whittington. 1983. *Emeraldella* and *Leanchoilia,* two arthropods from the Burgess Shale, Middle Cambrian, British Columbia. *Philosophical Transactions of the Royal Society of London,* ser. B, 300:553–85.

Collins, D. 1996. The "evolution" of *Anomalocaris* and its classification in the Arthropod class Dinocarida (Nov.) and order Radiodonta (Nov.). *Journal of Paleontology* 70:280–93.

Gould, S.J. 1989. *Wonderful Life: The Burgess Shale and the Nature of History.* New York: Norton; London: Hutchinson Radius, 1990.

Hughes, C.P. 1973. Redescription of *Burgessia bella* from the Middle Cambrian Burgess Shale, British Columbia. *Fossils and Strata* 4:415–64.

McNamara, K.J., and N.H. Trewin. 1993. A Euthycarcinoid arthropod from the Silurian of Western Australia. *Palaeontology* 36:319–35.

Müller, K.J. 1983. Crustacea with preserved soft parts from the Upper Cambrian of Sweden. *Lethaia* 16:93–109.

———. 1985. Skaracarida, a new order of Crustacea from the Upper Cambrian of Västergötland, Sweden. *Fossils and Strata* 17:1–65.

Müller, K.J., and D. Walossek. 1986. *Martinssonia elongata.* gen. et sp.n., a crustacean-like euarthropod from the Upper Cambrian "orsten" of Sweden. *Zoologica Scripta* 15:73–92.

———. 1988. External morphology and larval development of the Upper Cambrian maxillopod *Bredocaris admirabilis. Fossils and Strata* 23:1–69.

Schram, F.R. 1986. *Crustacea.* New York: Oxford University Press.

Schram, F.R., and W.D.I. Rolfe. 1982. New Euthycarcinoid arthropods from the Upper Pennsylvanian of France and Illinois. *Journal of Paleontology* 56:1434–450.

Stürmer, W., and J. Bergström. 1976. The arthropods *Mimetaster* and *Vachonisia* from the Devonian Hunsrück Shale. *Paläontologische Zeitschrift* 50:57–81.

———. 1978. The arthropod *Cheloniellon* from the Devonian Hunsrück Shale. *Paläontologische Zeitschrift* 52:78–111.

Walossek, D. 1993. The Upper Cambrian *Rehbachiella* and the phylogeny of the Branchiopoda and Crustacea. *Fossils and Strata* 32:1–202.

Whittington, H.B. 1971. *Redescription of* Marrella Splendens (*Trilobitoidea*) *from the Burgess Shale, Middle Cambrian, British Columbia.* Geological Survey of Canada Bulletin, 209. Ottawa: Canadian Government Printing Bureau.

———. 1974. Yohoia *Walcott and* Plenocaris *N. Gen., Arthropods from the Burgess Shale, Middle Cambrian, British Columbia.* Geological Survey of Canada Bulletin, 231. Ottawa: Canadian Government Printing Bureau.

———. 1975. The enigmatic animal *Opabinia regalis*, Middle Cambrian, Burgess Shale, British Columbia. *Philosophical Transaction of the Royal Society of London,* ser. B, 271:1–43.

———. 1981. Rare arthropods from the Burgess Shale, Middle Cambrian, British Columbia. *Philosophical Transactions of the Royal Society of London,* ser. B, 292:329–57.

Whittington, H.B., and D.E.G. Briggs. 1985. The Largest Cambrian Animal, *Anomalocaris,* Burgess Shale, British Columbia. *Philosophical Transactions of the Royal Society of London,* ser. B, 309:569–609.

Wills, M.A., D.E.G. Briggs, and R.A. Fortey. 1994. Disparity as an evolutionary index: A comparison of Cambrian and Recent arthropods. *Paleobiology* 20:93–130.

Wills, M.A., D.E.G. Briggs, R.A. Fortey, and M. Wilkinson. 1995. The significance of fossils in understanding arthropod evolution. *Verhandlungen der Deutschen Zoologischen Gesellschaft* 57:13–33.

Further Reading

Briggs, D.E.G., D.H. Erwin, and F.J. Collier. 1994. *The Fossils of the Burgess Shale.* Washington, D.C.: Smithsonian Institution Press.

Conway-Morris, S., and H.B. Whittington. 1979. The animals of the Burgess Shale. *Scientific American* 241:122–33.

Gore, R. 1993. The Cambrian period: Explosion of life. *National Geographic* 184:120–36.

Gould, S.J. 1989. *Wonderful Life: The Burgess Shale and the Nature of History.* New York: Norton; London: Hutchinson Radius, 1990.

Ørvig, T. 1967. Phylogeny of tooth tissues: Evolution of some calcified tissues in early vertebrates. *In* A.E.W. Miles (ed.), *Structural Organization of Teeth.* Vol. 1, New York: Academic Press.

Whittington, H.B. 1985. *The Burgess Shale.* New Haven, Connecticut: Yale University Press.

ARTIODACTYLS

Artiodactyls, commonly known as the cloven-hoofed mammals, are an order of ungulates (hoofed mammals), including animals such as pigs (including peccaries), hippos, camelids (camels and llamas), and ruminants (giraffe, deer, antelope, and cattle). They are commonly presented as an evolutionary "success story," not only among ungulates, but also among mammals in general (Figure 1).

Artiodactyls made their first appearance in the fossil record in the early Eocene, some 55 millions of years ago: their evolutionary radiation (spread and diversification) gained speed in the early Miocene (around 20 million years ago). Today, artiodactyls are very diverse, both in numbers of species and numbers of different families, and also in numbers of individuals. Members of this group have also played an important role in human evolution and civilization: most of our domestic animals (not including household pets), which provide our milk, our wool, and most of our meat, are ruminant artiodactyls (Prothero 1994).

Although many texts prominently feature bovids (antelope and cattle) as examples of the success story of ungulate evolution, their present-day diversity is mainly the result of the expansion of savannas in Africa during the Late Cenozoic era, about 1.5 million years ago (Vrba 1985). Meanwhile, other groups of artiodactyls, which were equally diverse in the Miocene but are of limited diversity today, such as camelids, usually are ignored (Prothero 1994).

Characteristics of the Order

There are two main groups of ungulates, artiodactyls and perissodactyls. In contrast to the "odd-toed ungulates," or perissodactyls, artiodactyls are commonly known as "even-toed ungulates," characterized by a foot structure in which the main axis of support passes between the third and fourth digits (Owen 1848). In most artiodactyls (including all of the living ones), the first digit (the thumb or big toe) is missing. Digits three and four form the main support for the limb, while digits two and five (the "side toes") are a little smaller than the central digits (as in pigs), reduced in size (as in deer), or lost entirely (as in camels, giraffe, and antelope). In the camels and the ruminants, the metapodials (hand and foot bones) of digits three and four are elongated and fused together into a "cannon bone," but the toes remain unfused, giving them their characteristic "cloven-hoofed" appearance (Figure 2A).

Artiodactyls can also be characterized by a "double pulley" type of astragalus (talus) bone in the ankle (Schaeffer 1947), where the bone is not only in contact with the shin bone above it (as in humans), but also has a second joint (hence the term "double pulley") with the ankle bone directly beneath it. In most mammals there is just a flat joint surface at this location, with no potential for movement (Figure 2B). Several other rather minor skull and tooth characters also seem to be unique to artiodactyls (Gentry and Hooker 1988; Prothero et al. 1988).

Present-day artiodactyls fall into two broad groupings: The Bunodontia comprise the suiforms (pigs, peccaries, and hippos). Pigs and peccaries are generally omnivorous—they feed on both plants and animals—while hippos evolved a more herbivorous habit independently from other artiodactyls. The Selenodontia comprises the herbivorous camels and ruminants. The suiforms are generally short-legged, with little reduction of the side toes, and with a form of cheek teeth (the molars and premolars)

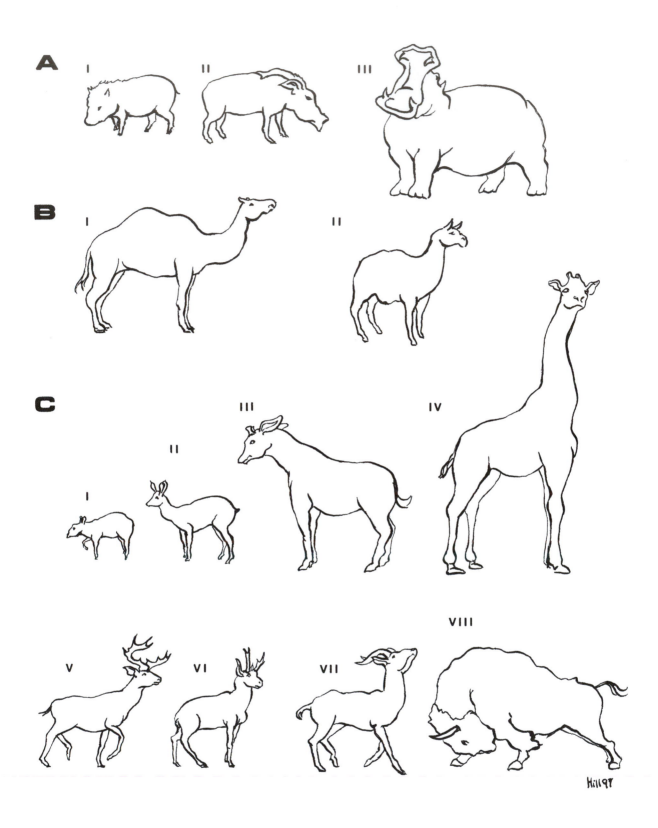

Figure 1. Some representative living artiodactyls. *A*, Suiformes: *I*, Collared peccary, *Tayassu tajacu; II*, Bush pig, *Potamochoerus porcus; III*, Hippopotamus, *Hippopotamus amphibius. B*, Tylopods: *I*, Camel (dromedary), *Camelus dromedarius; II*, Llama, *Lama glama. C*, Ruminants: *I*, Water chevrotain (tragulid), *Hyemoschus aquaticus; II*, Musk deer, *Moschus moschiferus; III*, Okapi, *Okapia johnstoni; IV*, Giraffe, *Giraffa camelopardalis; V*, White-tailed deer, *Odocoileus virginianus; VI*, Pronghorn, *Antilocapra americana; VII*, Kob antelope, *Kobus kob; VIII*, Bison, *Bison bison*. Illustration by Forbes Hill.

termed "bunodont" (low-cusped and bumpy), suitable for crushing such items as stems, roots, and fruit (Figure 2C). (Human cheek teeth are similarly structured.) Camelids and ruminants typically have longer legs, with the side toes reduced or lost; their cheek teeth are "selenodont," made up of sharp ridges that are better designed to shear tough, fibrous plant material such as leaves and grass blades. Many species of camelids and ruminants, especially those that specialize in eating grass, have "hypsodont" cheek teeth. Such teeth have greatly elongated crowns designed to endure a lifetime of abrasive wear. If we humans were to eat nothing but grass, our teeth would be worn to the roots rapidly. However, as the originally exposed surface of the crown of a hypsodont tooth is worn down, more tooth is pushed up from within the jaw. Although such teeth will not last indefinitely (in contrast to the ever-growing cheek teeth of rodents and rabbits), they are certainly an essential modification of the original mammalian tooth design for an animal consuming large quantities of fibrous plant material.

Camelids and ruminants share other similarities besides their herbivorous diets: multiple stomach chambers. Both groups ferment their food in a forechamber of the stomach, adapted to break down the cellulose that comprises the cell walls of plants. The structure of this complex stomach differs in detail between the two groups. In ruminants, there are three chambers in front of the original, or "true," stomach. Camelids have two chambers in front of the original stomach. Nevertheless, the embryological development of the stomach of both groups indicates they share an ancestor with a degree of forestomach enlargement (Langer 1974). Many other mammals also ferment fibrous plant material in this fashion, but most other ungulates (e.g., horses, rhinos, and elephants) and non-ungulates (e.g., rabbits, rodents, and wombats) use a chamber in the large intestine. And while some mammals do have a forestomach site of fermentation (e.g., some monkeys, kangaroos, and even hippos), only camels and ruminants combine this feature with chewing the cud, or "rumination."

Ruminants, especially present-day species, are often characterized by "cranial appendages" above and behind the eyes—that is, horns, antlers, or similar protuberances made from bone. (Contrast this with the horns of living rhino species, horns that are made from keratin.) Although usually only males have such horn-like structures, they may occur in both sexes. In such cases, the female's horns are usually smaller and less robustly constructed. Such adornments are not unique to ruminants. Very ruminant-like horns (including a single horn on the nose) were present in protoceratids, extinct camelid-related artiodactyls. Bony horns were present also in one species of extinct pig, in several species of extinct rhinos, and in several types of extinct rhinolike ungulates. Horns like this also turn up today as occasional "sports" in horses—and even in humans (Janis 1982). Although hornlike structures are typical of ruminants, they do not appear to develop in the same way in different families of horned ruminants. Not only may their form and mode of development differ (Figure 3), but many extinct ruminants lack horns entirely. This is also true of certain living primitive species, such as the Chinese water deer, where the absence of antlers appears to be a primary, or basic, characteristic (Janis 1982).

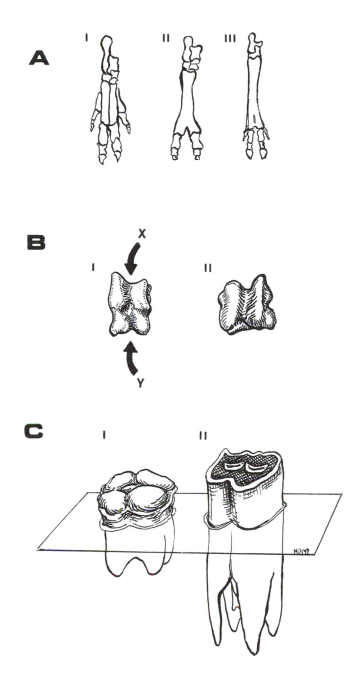

Figure 2. *A,* views of distal hind limbs of various artiodactyls: *I,* pig; *II,* camel; *III,* ruminant (deer). *B,* ungulate tali (astragali): *I,* Artiodactyl: *X* = proximal articulator surface, *Y* = distal articulator surface; *II,* Perissodactyl. *C,* Molar teeth (second left upper molar depicted): *I,* Bunodont, brachydont tooth; *II,* Selenodont, hypsodont tooth. The gum line is illustrated by the plane through the teeth. Illustration by Forbes Hill.

Classification and Description of Living and Fossil Groups

History of Ideas of Artiodactyl Interrelationships

The fundamental division of living artiodactyls into the Bunodontia and the Selenodontia (e.g., Flower 1883; Matthew 1929) is not so clear-cut when one includes fossil groups. Some scholars put cer-

Figure 3. Horn types in ruminant artiodactyls. *A*, Giraffe; *B*, Deer (Cervid); *C*, Pronghorn (Antilocaprid); *D*, Antelope (Bovid). Key to shading on horns: *black*, permanent bone; *single hatching*, deciduous bone; *circles*, permanent keratin; *cross hatching*, deciduous keratin. Illustration by Forbes Hill.

tain fossils, such as the piglike anthracotheres, into a third grouping, Bunoselenodontia (e.g., Zittel 1925). W.D. Matthew (1929) recognized five primary divisions to encompass 17 living and fossil families. G.G. Simpson (1945) reduced this classification to three suborders: (1) Suiformes, including Matthew's Palaeodonta (which includes small, primitive forms and the extinct piglike entelodonts), Hyodonta (pigs, peccaries, and hippos), and Ancodonta (a variety of extinct forms, including the piglike anthracotheres and oreodonts); (2) Tylopoda (camelids and extinct related groups); and (3) Ruminantia (equivalent to Matthew's Pecora). The essence of this classification is retained by most scholars today (e.g., Romer 1966; Carroll 1988). Figure 4 shows a consensus of present-day views about the interrelationships of the major artiodactyl families (except the primitive Eocene groups, which are discussed below). The Ruminantia is monophyletic—it contains all descendants of a single common ancestor—as is an association of Ruminantia and Tylopoda. Both the Tylopoda and Suiformes are probably paraphyletic (i.e., not a unified evolutionary group; for a contrasting position, see Gentry and Hooker 1988).

Primitive Artiodactyla

The three artiodactyl suborders do not usually include the early primitive members lumped together as palaeodonts or dichobunoids, including groups such as the antiacodontids, cebochoerids, choeropotamids, diacodexids, haplobunodontids, helohyids, homacodontids, leptochoerids, and raoellids. (Some groups are sometimes considered to be separate families.) These were small ungulates, known from the Eocene and Oligocene of North Amer-

ica and Eurasia. Most were rabbit-sized, but some were large as pigs, with bunodont or bunoselenodont cheek teeth, suggestive of a fairly omnivorous diet. Recent discoveries of complete skeletons have shown that many of these early artiodactyls were rather long-legged, graceful animals, not the stocky, short-legged pigs that we pictured the "primitive artiodactyls" to be (Rose 1982, 1985).

Dichobunoids are usually portrayed in evolutionary histories as some sort of basal (primitive), "bushy" assembly of animals, broadly related to later, more derived families, rather than as a discrete bunch of closely related species (e.g., Gazin 1955; Romer 1966; Gentry and Hooker 1988; Stucky 1998). Of these groups, the homacodontids appear to be closely related to the Selenodonts; the cebochoerids, choeropotamids, helohyids, and raoellids appear to be related to the Bunodonts, while opinions differ about the placement of the other taxa.

Suiformes

Pigs (suids) and peccaries (tayassuids) have long been recognized as sister (closely related) taxa. Hippos are usually recognized as the closest living relatives to this grouping. In Eurasia and Africa, pigs are known to have existed from the Late Eocene to the present. Their presence in the Americas is due solely to human introduction. Pigs are usually omnivores, but some forms are more herbivorous: the African warthog eats mainly grass, and the Indonesian babirussa (the Celebes pig) is herbivorous and has rather ruminant-like forestomach fermentation. One group of fossil pigs, the Miocene listriodontids, appear to have been specialized leaf-eaters, with teeth like tapirs but with particularly wide snouts,

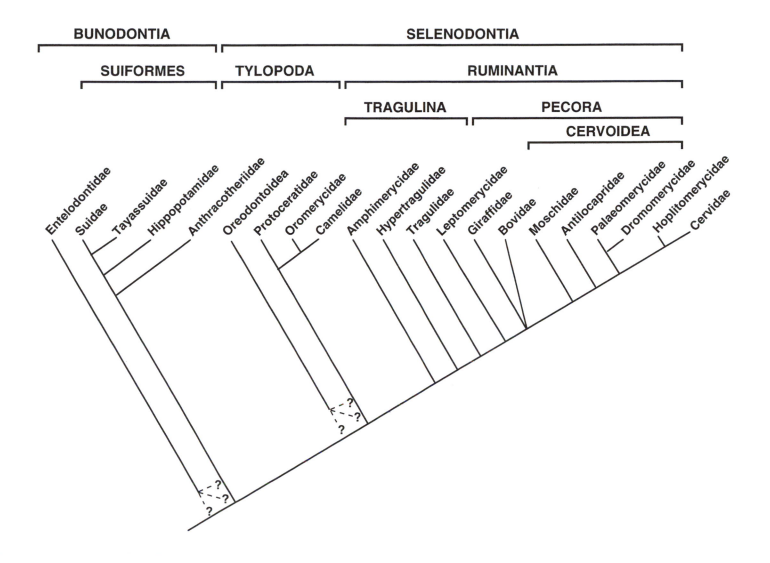

Figure 4. Interrelationships of artiodactyl families (primitive artiodactyls, known as "dichobunoids," omitted).

even wider than those of warthogs. Peccaries, known from the latest Eocene, tend to be more long-legged and more herbivorous than pigs in general; they evolved primarily in North America, with some Old World fossil forms reaching South America in the Pliocene. Hippos first appeared in Africa in the Late Miocene and also were known from Eurasia in Late Miocene to Pleistocene times. Hippos usually are considered to be derived from anthracotheres (see below), but M. Pickford (1983, 1993) maintains that their ancestry lies among the Old World peccaries.

The main fossil families that are included with suiformes living today are the Entelodontidae and the Anthracotheriidae (Figure 5A). Entelodonts, known to have existed in North America and Eurasia from the Late Eocene to Early Miocene, were pig-to-buffalo-sized animals that had piglike bunodont cheek teeth. These animals had enormous heads for their size, and quite derived (specialized) legs that looked more like those of a cow than a pig. Some of the larger forms may have been bearlike

scavengers that ate animal carcasses and cracked their bones (Joeckel 1990).

Anthracotheres, animals usually the size of sheep, are known from the Late Eocene to Early Miocene of North America, and from the Late Eocene to Late Pliocene of the Old World. Their legs were less derived but their cheek teeth were more selenodont, suggesting a more herbivorous diet. Anthracotheres usually are considered as ancestral to hippos (Colbert 1935; Simpson 1945; Romer 1966; Carroll 1988; Gentry and Hooker 1988), but a more recent analysis by D.G. Kron and E. Manning (1998) suggests that anthracotheres are the sister taxon to all living suiformes. The evolutionary position of the entelodonts is much more problematic. Although some scholars believe entelodonts to be closely related to pigs and peccaries (Romer 1966; Gentry and Hooker 1988), others find they are more primitive than any of the other suiformes. This interpretation renders this grouping paraphyletic (Stehlin 1910; Matthew 1929; Kron and Manning 1998).

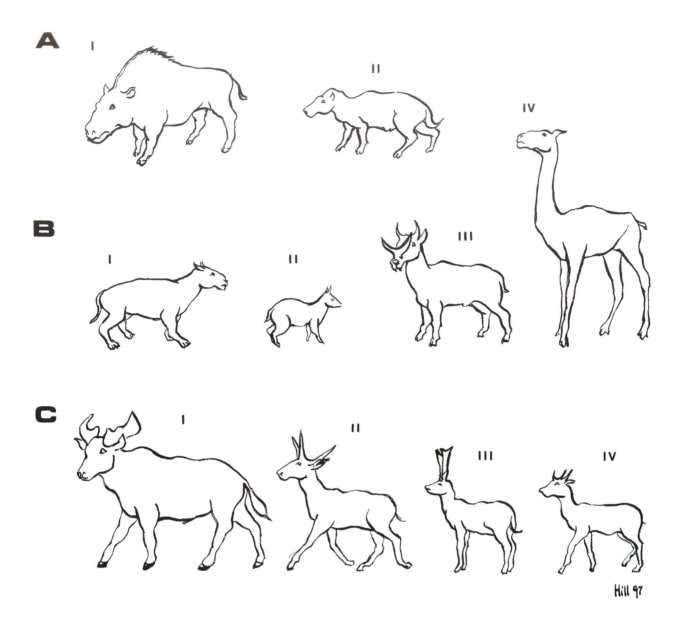

Figure 5. Extinct artiodactyls. *A*, Suiformes: *I, Dinohyus* (entelodont); *II, Bothriodon* (anthracothere). *B*, Tylopods: *I, Merycoidodon* (oreodont); *II, Cainotherium* (cainothere); *III, Syndyoceras* (protoceratid); *IV, Alticamelus* (camelid). *C*, Ruminants: *I, Sivatherium* (sivathere giraffid); *II, Cranioceras* (dromomerycid palaeomerycid); *III, Paracosoryx* (merycodontine antilocaprid); *IV, Hoplitomeryx* (hoplitomerycid). Illustration by Forbes Hill.

Tylopoda

Although W.D. Matthew (1929) constructed the Tylopoda to include only the Camelidae and the extinct Xiphodontidae (his thinking was followed by Colbert 1941; Simpson 1945), later scholars (e.g., Scott 1940; Romer 1966; Carroll 1988) used the term "Tylopoda" to group all selenodont artiodactyls that clearly are not members of the Ruminantia. Other facts confuse the picture even more. Camelids are the only surviving tylopods. The other families are either exclusively Eurasian or exclusively North American, making comparisons difficult. Figure 5B illustrates some extinct tylopods.

North American tylopod families include several extinct groups: oreodonts, oromerycids, protoceratids, and also, perhaps surprisingly, camelids. It is thought that at least some of these groups represent an invasion from an originally Asian stock in the late Eocene. Camelids had a diverse and highly successful radiation in North America: during the Miocene, when much of the Great Plains region was a Serengeti-like savanna environment, the diversity of camelids was similar to the diversity of African antelope today, including small, gazellelike forms and large, longnecked giraffelike forms (Webb 1983). In the Pliocene the ancestors of modern llamas migrated to South America, and the ancestors of humped camels migrated to the Old World. Camelids persisted in North America until the end of the Pleistocene, although their diversity and abundance was reduced when the climate changed and the Miocene savannas gave way to the prairies of the Pliocene and Pleistocene. The camelids met their end in North America in the Late Pleistocene extinctions that also claimed the native mammoths, horses, and sabertooth cats.

Oromerycids were small, gazellelike animals evidently closely related to the camelids (Gentry and Hooker 1988; Prothero 1998) that did not survive the end of the Eocene. Protoceratids were the horned tylopods mentioned earlier, known from the Late Eocene to the earliest Pliocene. Often pictured in popular texts as graceful, deerlike animals, they were actually large-headed with short legs and would have looked more like oversized warthogs! Because of their horns, they originally were classified with ruminants (Colbert 1941; Stirton 1944; Romer 1966), but a more detailed appraisal of their anatomy revealed their camelid affinities (Scott 1940; Patton and Taylor 1973; Webb and Taylor 1980; Gentry and Hooker 1988).

The most problematic group is the oreodonts, dating from the Middle Eocene to Late Miocene. These animals, ranging from rabbit-sized to tapir-sized, combined an odd mixture of primitive and derived artiodactyl features. They had selenodont teeth (although the teeth of some species were rather hypsodont), clearly indicative of a herbivorous diet. However, unlike other selenodont artiodactyls, the oreodonts retained a stubby, short-nosed face, had a skeleton that was even less derived than that of pigs, and had hands and feet that may have retained some grasping ability. (Some early forms had claws and appeared to have tree-climbing abilities; Lander 1998.) Their taxonomic position (relationship to other groups) is still a mystery. Some scholars classify them with the suiformes (e.g., Matthew 1929; Simpson 1945), although the general current consensus would place them as the sister taxon to other selenodont artiodactyls.

Also problematical is the diversity of small- to medium-sized Eocene and Oligocene European selenodont taxa often grouped with the Tylopoda. These include anoplotheres, dacrytheres, and mixtotheres, plus the gracile, camel-like xiphodontids (restricted to the Late Eocene) and the rabbitlike cainotheres (found in the Oligocene and Early Miocene). The decline of these taxa coincides with the appearance in Europe of the early members of the Ruminantia (first known from Asia), so competition with other selenodonts may have possibly played a role in the demise of these tylopods.

Ruminantia

The Ruminantia consists of two major divisions: the paraphyletic, hornless Tragulina, and the more derived, usually horned Pecora (Matthew 1934; Colbert 1941; Simpson 1945; Webb and Taylor 1980; Gentry and Hooker 1988). Figure 5C illustrates a diversity of extinct ruminants. The surviving tragulines are the rabbit-to-dog-sized tragulids (mouse deer or chevrotains), which are found in the tropical forests of Africa and Asia. They have fairly short legs and cheek teeth that are not as highly ridged as those of the pecorans; they eat fruit and soft browse. Tragulines are solitary animals, and the males have large canines used in fights with each other. The fossil families Amphimerycidae, Hypertragulidae, and Leptomerycidae were also small and probably had similar diet and exhibited behavior. They were mainly a Late Eocene radiation, with some forms surviving until the early Miocene. Leptomerycids and hypertragulids lived in both Eurasia and North America, while other tragulines lived only in the Old World.

Pecoran families include the living Bovidae, Cervidae, Giraffidae, Antilocapridae, and Moschidae, along with a number of fossil families, including the Old World Palaeomerycidae. Also included are North American dromomerycids, although some scholars considered this group as a separate family. The gelocids, more derived (although still hornless) ruminants of the Oligocene and Miocene of the Old World, originally were classified with the tragulines but have more recently been shown to be basal members of the Pecora (Webb and Taylor 1980).

Bovids (antelope and cattle), cervids (deer), and giraffids are all found primarily in the Old World, first appearing in the Early Miocene. Bovids attained their maximum diversity in the Plio-Pleistocene savannas of Africa and southern Eurasia. Today they remain the most diverse artiodactyl family, including a number of forms that reached North America in the Pleistocene (e.g., bison, yak, and mountain goat). This group did not reach South America. Many bovids are social, savanna- or prairie-dwelling grazing species that live in mixed-sex herds. Both females and males have horns.

On the other hand, cervids originated and diversified in higher latitudes (they were virtually unknown in Africa) and were more solitary, woodland, browsing animals. The reindeer (caribou) is the only living cervid that lives in mixed-sex herds and has females with antlers. Cervids reached North America in the Pliocene and are quite diverse there today (e.g., the white-tailed deer, moose, and reindeer). In the Pliocene, when the Isthmus of Panama formed, cervids entered South America. Today, they exhibit a diverse tropical and temperate radiation (e.g., the brocket, pudu, and marsh deer).

Most giraffids have been browsers, with low-crowned cheek teeth and at least moderately long necks (although some Miocene European forms may have been grazers) (Solounias, et al. 1988). Until the Pleistocene, giraffids were found in Eurasia as well as Africa, but they never reached the New World. Living giraffids have a very reduced diversity compared with their fossil relatives. This contrasts with bovids and cervids, which are probably as diverse today as they ever were. The only surviving giraffids are the large, high-browsing, savanna-dwelling, social giraffe and the more solitary okapi, which is also high-browsing but is smaller and forest-dwelling. Early Miocene giraffids included forms with branching, deerlike horns, the climatoceratids (Hamilton 1978). Until very recently (Late Pleistocene and possibly even until historic times) (Colbert 1936), a second group developed parallel to "regular" giraffids: the sivatheres of Eurasia and Africa were large (up to bison-sized) and had a hefty build, relatively short legs and neck, and mooselike palmate horns.

Today there is only one living member of the family Antilocapridae: the pronghorn antelope of western North America. Antilocaprids were found only in North America, although they must have had their origins in some Old World stock (Janis and

Manning 1998). In past times antilocaprids were very diverse but were all fairly uniform in design. They spanned the size range of modern gazelles and had long legs (with highly reduced or lost side-toes) and highly hypsodont teeth. However, this morphology (body shape) does not necessarily indicate a grazing habit. The modern pronghorn has a narrow muzzle for selecting a diet of primarily low-lying herbs amid the grass stems of the prairie, although it will eat young, succulent grasses. The pronghorn's hypsodont cheek teeth are probably indicative of wear from grit; fossil antilocaprids probably had a similar way of life.

The antilocaprids make up the Early to Late Miocene merycodontines and the Late Miocene to recent antilocaprines. They reached their peak diversity in the Pliocene. Merycodontines were smaller, with branched horns that were probably initially skin-covered when growing but which later lost their skin, leaving naked bone. These horns are found in the males alone. The merycodontines were probably not as social as the antilocaprines. The latter possessed keratin-covered horns, found in both sexes, and probably lived in mixed-sex herds, similar to the modern pronghorn (Janis and Manning 1998).

Musk deer (moschids) are gazelle-sized, hornless ruminants. They have only recently been recognized as a separate family (Leinders and Heintz 1980; Groves and Grubb 1987), even though J.E. Gray (1921) originally assigned the living Asian *Moschus* its own family status, separate from the true deer. Recently, S.D. Webb and B.E. Taylor (1980) recognized the extinct blastomerycids of the Miocene of North America as related to the Asian musk deer. They also included some deerlike taxa from the Oligocene of Europe in this grouping.

The palaeomerycids (including the North American dromomerycids) were deer-sized, deerlike animals—they had low-crowned cheek teeth and retained their side-toes. The animals were found mainly in the Miocene. Like modern deer, the palaeomerycids were probably fairly solitary browsers in a forest or woodland habitat. They differed from deer in that they had unbranched, skin-covered horns. In addition to the pair over the eyes, some species also had a single, unbranched horn on the back of the head.

Another interesting fossil ruminant is *Hoplitomeryx*, from the late Miocene of Gargano, Italy, an isolated island during that time (Leinders 1983). This animal is so bizarre that it has its own family, Hoplitomerycidae. Its horns looked like those of bovids, but instead of the normal two over the eyes, it had five, arranged around the top of the head like a crown of thorns. Despite the bovidlike nature of the horns, features of the skull and limbs suggest instead a close relationship with cervids (deer).

Most traditional classifications consider cervids as primitive pecorans, due to their low-crowned cheek teeth and their retention of the side toes (e.g., Matthew 1904; Stirton 1944). Bovids and antilocaprids have been united often, based on the derived characters of hypsodont cheek teeth, the loss of the side toes, and some apparent similarities of the horns (Matthew 1904; Simpson 1945; O'Gara and Matson 1975). Giraffes have either been grouped with the cervids (based on their low-crowned cheek teeth) or with bovids (based on their long legs, the loss of the side toes, and some apparent horn similarities) (Thenius 1969; Hamilton 1978; Bubenik 1983; Gentry 1994).

However, features such as hypsodont cheek teeth and the loss of the side toes are probably more closely related to habitat preference than to phylogeny. Moreover, on closer scrutiny the different types of cranial appendages are not very similar (Janis and Scott 1987; Scott and Janis 1993). Considering other derived characters of the limbs and skull unites the antilocaprids and cervids and places the moschids as a sister taxon to that grouping (Leinders and Heintz 1980). The highly specialized giraffids cannot be united with either the cervids or the bovids (Janis and Scott 1987; Scott and Janis 1993). Palaeomerycids have superficially giraffelike horns, so some have allied them with giraffids (Stirton 1944; Ginsburg and Heintz 1966; Qiu et al. 1985). But on other features of the skull, teeth, and limbs, this group appears to be close relatives of cervids (Janis and Scott, 1987; Scott and Janis, 1993).

Evolutionary Patterns

Biogeography: Distribution and Dispersal

Artiodactyls appear simultaneously in the Early Eocene in both North America and Eurasia (Krause and Maas 1990). At that time there was a corridor of land connecting North America and Europe, so many species were found on both continental blocks (Janis 1993). As a result, the actual place of artiodactyl origin is hard to pinpoint, although Asia may be the most likely site (Krause and Maas 1990). However, artiodactyl history has been subdivided rather sharply between Old and New Worlds. (Like the vast majority of placental mammals, artiodactyls never were found in Australia until introduced by humans.) Also, artiodactyls did not arrive in South America until the Pliocene (about five million years ago). At that time, the Isthmus of Panama was formed, creating a savanna corridor for the passage of many mammals (Webb 1991). The artiodactyls found today in South America are a sampling of those that lived in North America in the Pliocene: peccaries, camelids, and cervids. For some reason, antilocaprids did not follow their fellows southward, and bovids arrived in North America too late (during the Pleistocene—about two million years ago) to be able to use the savanna corridor. By that time, it had developed into impassable tropical forest (Webb 1991).

During the Early Cenozoic (about 65 million years ago), the dissimilarity between Old and New World artiodactyls was not so pronounced. In the Eocene, dichobunoids were found on both continents, as were certain traguline ruminants (hypertragulids and leptomerycids). Suiformes (anthracotheres and entelodonts) existed in both regions in the Oligocene and Early Miocene. Tylopods also were found on both continents, but they seem to have belonged to different groups. The North American ones flourished into the later Cenozoic, but the European ones, like many other endemic mammals, were badly hit by the Late Eocene extinctions, when high latitude tropical-like forests turned to temperate woodlands. Most were extinct by the end of the Oligocene.

In the later Cenozoic, during the Miocene, when savanna habitats were spreading across the higher latitudes, the artiodactyl faunas were distinctly separate. Among the suiformes, North America had peccaries, while the Old World had pigs, anthracotheres, and (later) hippos. All Eurasian tylopods were extinct, as were all but a few North American tragulines. The endemic North

American tylopods (camelids, protoceratids, and oreodonts) flourished, at least until the Late Miocene extinctions, when cooling and drying turned the diverse high latitude savannas into less productive plains and prairies. Some Eurasian tragulines survived in the equatorial forests, where the mouse deer are still found.

The major Late Cenozoic radiation of artiodactyls, the ruminants, occurred primarily in the Old World, but it was a strange, separated distribution. Cervids, bovids, giraffids, and palaeomerycids (except for dromomerycids) were unknown in the New World during the Miocene, while antilocaprids and dromomerycids were known only in North America (although they presumably originated in Eurasia). Only the moschids were known on both continents, yet the blastomerycids were a totally separate radiation of moschids from their Old World relatives.

Thus, during the Miocene the savanna woodland environments of North America and the Old World had very different taxonomic composition of artiodactyls, all of which played similar roles in similar ecologies. North America had peccaries for woodland omnivores, dromomerycids and blastomerycids for woodland browsers, and camelids and antilocaprids for savanna grazers, mixed feeders, and high-level browsers. In contrast, the woodlands of the Old World had pigs, deer, and some bovids and giraffids (plus a separate radiation of palaeomerycids and moschids), and on the savanna there were bovids and giraffids (see Janis 1993; Webb 1991).

It was not until the Pliocene, with the loss of the high latitude savanna and the reestablishment of land corridors linking North America to Eurasia across the area now known as the Bering Strait, that extinction and migration changed the character of artiodactyl distribution. In North America, dromomerycids and blastomerycids were extinct by the end of the Miocene, and camelids were extinct by the end of the Pleistocene. (Antilocaprids were nearly so.) Meanwhile, cervids and bovids gained entrance to North America, and camelids made their way to Asia and Africa. The present-day distribution of artiodactyls over the globe is a Plio-Pleistocene phenomenon that took place before human influence and bears little relationship to the group's biogeographic patterns for the greater part of the Cenozoic.

Patterns of Diversification and Competition with Other Ungulates

The present-day radiation of artiodactyls has its roots in the climatic changes of the Miocene. By the end of the Oligocene, early radiations of more primitive forms such as dichobunoids were extinct; others, such as tragulines, were restricted to more tropical latitudes, following the cooling of the high latitudes in the late Eocene. The Early Miocene brought a drying and warming trend to the higher latitudes, turning the temperate woodland into a savanna-woodland mix (Janis 1993). These conditions spurred the radiation of the early pecorans into the various lineages of bovids, cervids, giraffids, and others. Independent evolution of horns or hornlike organs in each family may be explained by the habitat changes that forced each lineage in parallel into a new mode of life that encouraged combat between males of the same species. The changes made animals more dependent on fibrous food, and habitat conditions made male territorial behavior and defense of

females feasible. In North America more rapid habitat changes may have catapulted camelids into more open habitats, which were conducive to mixed-sex herds without the existence of male territoriality, so the group did not pass through a woodland, territorial phase conducive to horn evolution. The more woodland-dwelling protoceratids apparently did radiate in conditions that encouraged horn evolution (Janis 1982).

With regard to the interactions of artiodactyls with other ungulates, ruminants in particular have been portrayed as outcompeting other ungulates, especially perissodactyls, such as horses. There has been a long-held evolutionary truism (from Kowalewsky 1883 to Simpson 1953) that ruminant artiodactyls were competitively superior because their digestive systems, with their multiple-chamber stomachs, were better adapted to digest cellulose. But when the data are examined, patterns of diversification and decline in artiodactyls and perissodactyls do not support a model of competition between the two groups (Cifelli 1982). Ruminants must feed more selectively than hindgut fermenters such as horses. Therefore, the Late Cenozoic success of ruminants may have resulted from climatic and vegetational changes that favored selective feeding over bulk processing (Janis 1989).

Additionally, our view is biased, owing to the fact that bovids are successful today, whereas horses, so successful in the past, are now represented by only a handful of species. It is important to keep in mind that bovids and horses evolved on different continents, bovids in Africa and Eurasia and horses in North America. They were barely in contact with each other until the Pleistocene. Artiodactyls are a highly successful group today, but their evolutionary success must be looked at in the context of the Cenozoic as a whole.

CHRISTINE JANIS

Works Cited

Bubenik, A.B. 1983. Taxonomy of Pecora in relation to morphophysiology of their cranial appendages. *In* R.D. Brown (ed.), *Antler Development in the Cervidae.* Kingsville, Texas: Caesar Kleberg Wildlife Research Institute.

Carroll, R.L. 1988. *Vertebrate Paleontology and Evolution.* New York: Freeman.

Cifelli, R.L. 1982. Patterns of evolution among Artiodactyla and Perissodactyla (Mammalia). *Evolution* 35:433–40.

Colbert, E.H. 1935. Distributional and phylogenetic studies on Indian fossil mammals. IV. The phylogeny of the Indian Suidae and the origin of the Hippopotamidae. *American Museum Novitates* 799:1–24.

——. 1936. Was the extinct giraffe *Sivatherium* known to the ancient Sumerians? *American Anthropologist* 38:605–8.

——. 1941. The osteology and relationships of *Archaeomeryx,* an ancestral ruminant. *American Museum Novitates* 1135:1–24.

Flower, W.H. 1883. On the arrangement of the orders and families of existing Mammalia. *Proceedings of the Zoological Society of London* 1883:178–86.

Gazin, C.L. 1955. A review of the upper Eocene Artiodactyla of North America. *Smithsonian Miscellaneous Collections* 128:1–96.

Gentry, A.W. 1994. The Miocene differentiation Old World Pecora (Mammalia). *Historical Biology* 7:115–58.

Gentry, A.W., and J. Hooker. 1988. The phylogeny of the Artiodactyla. *In* M.J. Benton (ed.), *The Phylogeny and Classification of the Tetrapods.* Vol. 2, *Mammals.* Systematics Association Special Volume, 35B. Oxford: Clarendon; New York: Oxford University Press.

Ginsburg, L., and E. Heintz. 1966. Sur les affinités du genre *Palaeomeryx* (Ruminant du Miocène européen). *Compte Rendu Hebdomadaire des Séances de l'Académie des Sciences Paris* 301:1255–57.

Gray, J.E. 1921. On the natural arrangement of vertebrate animals. *London Medical Repository* 15:296–310.

Groves, C.P., and P. Grubb. 1987. Relationships of living deer. *In* C. Wemmer (ed.), *The Biology and Management of the Cervidae.* Washington, D.C.: Smithsonian Institution Press.

Hamilton, W.R. 1978. Fossil giraffes from the Miocene of Africa, and a revision of the phylogeny of the Giraffoidea. *Philosophical Transactions of the Royal Society (London),* ser. B, 282:165–229.

Janis, C.M. 1982. Evolution of horns in ungulates: Ecology and paleoecology. *Biological Reviews* 57:261–318.

———. 1989. A climatic explanation for patterns of evolutionary diversity in ungulate mammals. *Palaeontology* 32:463–81.

———. 1993. Tertiary mammal evolution in the context of changing climates, vegetation, and tectonic events. *Annual Review of Ecology and Systematics* 24:467–500.

Janis, C.M., and E. Manning. 1998. Antilocapridae. *In* C.M. Janis, K.M. Scott, and L.L. Jacobs (eds.), *The Evolution of Tertiary Mammals of North America.* Cambridge and New York: Cambridge University Press.

Janis, C.M., and K.M. Scott. 1987. The interrelationships of higher ruminant families with special emphasis on the members of the Cervoidea. *American Museum Novitates* 2893:1–85.

Joeckel, R.M. 1990. A functional interpretation of the masticatory system and paleoecology of entelodonts. *Paleobiology* 16:459–482.

Kowalewsky, W. 1883. Monographie der Gattung *Anchitherium* Cov. und Versuch einer natürlichen Klassifikation der fossilen Huftiere. *Palaeontolographica,* new ser. II, 3, 1873–1874:133–285.

Krause, D.W., and M.C. Maas. 1990. The biogeographic origins of the late Paleocene–early Eocene immigrants to the western interior of North America. *Geological Society of America Special Paper* 243:71–105.

Kron, D.G., and E. Manning. 1998. Anthracotheriidae. *In* C.M. Janis, K.M. Scott, and L.L. Jacobs (eds.), *The Evolution of Tertiary Mammals of North America.* Cambridge and New York: Cambridge University Press.

Lander, B. 1998. Oreodontoidea. *In* C.M. Janis, K.M. Scott, and L.L. Jacobs (eds.), *The Evolution of Tertiary Mammals of North America.* Cambridge and New York: Cambridge University Press.

Langer, P. 1974. Stomach evolution in the Artiodactyla. *Mammalia* 38:295–314.

Leinders, J.J.M. 1983. Hoplitomerycidae fam. nov. (Ruminantia, Mammalia), from Neogene fissure fillings in Gargano (Italy). *Scripta Geologica* 70:1–51.

Leinders, J.J.M., and E. Heintz. 1980. The configuration of the lacrimal orifice in pecorans and tragulids (Artiodactyla; Mammalia) and its significance for the distinction between Bovidae and Cervidae. *Beaufortia* 30:155–60.

Matthew, W.D. 1904. A complete skeleton of *Merycodus. Bulletin of the American Museum of Natural History* 20:101–29.

———. 1929. Reclassification of the artiodactyl families. *Bulletin of the Geological Society of America* 40:403–8.

———. 1934. A phylogenetic chart of the Artiodactyla. *Journal of Mammalogy* 15:207–9.

O'Gara, B.W., and G. Matson. 1975. Growth and casting of horns by pronghorns and exfoliation of horns by bovids. *Journal of Mammalogy* 56:829–46.

Owen, R. 1848. Description of teeth and portions of jaws of two extinct Anthracotherioid quadrupeds (*Hyopotamys vectianus* and *Hyop. bovinus*) discovered by the Marchioness of Hastings in the Eocene deposits on the NW. coast of the Isle of Wight: With an attempt to develope Cuvier's idea of the classification of pachyderms by the number of their toes. *Quarterly Journal of the Geological Society of London* 4:103–41.

Patton, T.H., and B.E. Taylor. 1973. The Protoceratinae (Mammalia, Tylopoda, Protoceratidae) and the systematics of the Protoceratidae. *Bulletin of the American Museum of Natural History* 150:347–414.

Pickford, M. 1983. On the origins of the Hippopotamidae together with a description of two new species, a new genus and a new subfamily from the Miocene of Kenya. *Géobios* 16:133–54.

———. 1993. Old World suoid systematics, phylogeny, biogeography and biostratigraphy. *Paleontologia i Evolució* 26–27:237–69.

Prothero, D.R. 1994. Mammal evolution. *In* D.R. Prothero and R.M. Schoch (eds.), *Major Features of Vertebrate Evolution.* Short Courses in Paleontology, No. 7. Knoxville: University of Tennessee and the Paleontological Society.

———. 1998. Oromerycidae. *In* C.M. Janis, K.M. Scott, and L.L. Jacobs (eds.), *The Evolution of Tertiary Mammals of North America.* Cambridge and New York: Cambridge University Press.

Prothero, D.R., E.M. Manning, and M. Fischer. 1988. The phylogeny of the ungulates. *In* M.J. Benton (ed.), *The Phylogeny and Classification of the Tetrapods.* Vol. 2, *Mammals.* Systematics Association Special Volume, 35B. Oxford: Clarendon; New York: Oxford University Press.

Qiu, Z., D. Yan, H. Jia, and B. Sun. 1985. Preliminary observations on the newly found skeleton of a *Palaeomeryx* from Shanwag, Shandong. *Vertebrata Palasiatica* 23:173–95.

Romer, A.S. 1966. *Vertebrate Paleontology.* 3rd. ed., Chicago: University of Chicago Press.

Rose, K.D. 1982. Skeleton of *Diacodexis,* oldest known artiodactyl. *Science* 216:621–23.

———. 1985. Comparative osteology of North American dichobunid artiodactyls. *Journal of Paleontology* 59:1203–26.

Schaeffer, B. 1947. Notes on the origin and function of the artiodactyl tarsus. *American Museum Novitates* 1356:1–24.

Scott, K.M., and C.M. Janis. 1993. Relationships of the Ruminantia (Artiodactyla) and an analysis of the characters used in ruminant taxonomy. *In* F.S. Szalay, M.J. Novacek, and M.C. McKenna (eds.), *Mammal Phylogeny: Placentals.* New York and London: Springer-Verlag.

Scott, W.B. 1940. The mammalian fauna of the White River Oligocene. Part 4, Artiodactyla. *Transactions of the American Philosophical Society* 28:363–746.

Simpson, G.G. 1945. The principles of classification and a classification of the mammals. *Bulletin of the American Museum of Natural History* 85:1–350.

———. 1953. *The Major Features of Evolution.* New York: Columbia University Press.

Solounias, N., M. Teaford, and A. Walker. 1988. Interpreting the diet of extinct ruminants: The case of a non-browsing giraffid. *Paleobiology* 14:287–300.

Stehlin, H.G. 1910. Die Säugetiere des schweizerischen Eozän. *Abhandlungen der Schweizerischen Paläontologischen Gesellschaft, Basel* 36:839–1164.

Stirton, R.A. 1944. Comments on the relationships of the cervoid family Palaeomerycidae. *American Journal of Science* 242:633–55.

Stucky, R. 1998. Primitive artiodactyls. *In* C.M. Janis, K.M. Scott, and L.L. Jacobs (eds.), *The Evolution of Tertiary Mammals of North America.* Cambridge and New York: Cambridge University Press.

Taylor, B.E., and S.D. Webb. 1976. Miocene Leptomerycidae (Artiodactyla, Ruminantia) and their relationships. *American Museum Novitates* 2596:1–22.

Thenius, E. 1969. *Phylogenie der Mammalia.* Berlin: Greyter.

Vrba, E. 1985. African Bovidae: Evolutionary events since the Miocene. *South African Journal of Science* 81:263–66.

Webb, S.D. 1983. The rise and fall of the late Miocene ungulate fauna in North America. *In* M.H. Nitecki (ed.), *Coevolution.* Chicago: University of Chicago Press.

———. 1991. Ecogeography and the Great American Interchange. *Paleobiology* 17:266–80.

Webb, S.D., and B.E. Taylor. 1980. The phylogeny of hornless ruminants and a description of the cranium of *Archaeomeryx. Bulletin of the American Museum of Natural History* 167:117–58.

Zittel, K.A. 1925. *Textbook of Palaeontology.* Vol. 3, *Mammalia.* C.R. Eastman and A.S. Woodward (trans.). London: Macmillan; as *Handbuch der Paläontologie,* Munich: Oldenburg, 1876.

Further Reading

Bubenik, G.A., and A.B. Bubenik (eds.). 1990. *Horns, Pronghorns, and Antlers.* New York and London: Springer-Verlag.

Gentry, A.W., and J. Hooker. 1988. The phylogeny of the Artiodactyla. *In* M.J. Benton (ed.), *The Phylogeny and Classification of the Tetrapods.* Vol. 2, *Mammals.* Systematics Association Special Volume, 35B. Oxford: Clarendon; New York: Oxford University Press.

Janis, C.M. 1982. Evolution of horns in ungulates: Ecology and paleoecology. *Biological Reviews* 57:261–318.

———. 1989. A climatic explanation for patterns of evolutionary diversity in ungulate mammals. *Palaeontology* 32:463–81.

Kingdon, J. 1971. *East African Mammals.* 3 vols. New York and London: Academic Press; rev. ed., Chicago: University of Chicago Press, 1982.

Prothero, D.R. 1994. Mammal Evolution. *In* D.R. Prothero and R.M. Schoch (eds.), *Major Features of Vertebrate Evolution.* Short Courses in Paleontology, 7. Knoxville: University of Tennessee and the Paleontological Society.

Savage, R.G., and M.R. Long. 1986. *Mammal Evolution: An Illustrated Guide.* London: British Museum of Natural History; New York: Facts-on-File.

Scott, K.M., and C.M. Janis. 1993. Relationships of the Ruminantia (Artiodactyla) and an analysis of the characters used in ruminant taxonomy. *In* F.S. Szalay, M.J. Novacek, and M.C. McKenna (eds.), *Mammal Phylogeny: Placentals.* New York and London: Springer-Verlag.

Solounias, N., and B. Dawson-Saunders. 1988. Dietary adaptation and paleoecology of the late Miocene ruminants from Pikermi and Samos in Greece. *Palaeogeography, Palaeoclimatology, Palaeoecology* 65:156–98.

Vrba, E.S. 1992. Mammals as a key to evolutionary theory. *Journal of Mammalogy* 73:1–28.

Webb, S.D. 1983. The rise and fall of the late Miocene ungulate fauna in North America. *In* M.H. Nitecki (ed.), *Coevolution.* Chicago: University of Chicago Press.

ASIA

See China; Indian Subcontinent; Southeast Asia

ATMOSPHERIC ENVIRONMENT

The atmosphere acts mainly as a medium of exchange between Earth's crust and oceans in the cycling of material on geological timescales. Consequently, the composition of the atmosphere has changed dramatically over geological time. The earliest prelife atmosphere (the first several hundred million years of Earth evolution) was devoid of oxygen and, according to computer modeling, possessed extremely elevated carbon dioxide (CO_2) concentrations—up to 20 times those of the present day. Since atmospheric oxygen (O_2) is produced mainly as the result of plant and algal photosynthesis, the evolution of life brought about the oxygenation of the atmosphere between 3,800 and 3,500 million years ago (the dates between which oxygen-producing cyanobacteria and blue-green algae are believed to have evolved).

Over the Phanerozoic (the Paleozoic, Mesozoic, and Cenozoic eras), estimates of the composition of CO_2 and O_2 in Earth's atmosphere have been attained mainly by indirect methods that rely on assumptions made about interactions between the terrestrial biosphere and the atmosphere and/or the ocean and the atmosphere. To date, the methods used to investigate past changes in atmospheric CO_2 include computer modeling of the long-term carbon cycle by assessing changes in the ratio of two forms of carbon in marine sediments and fossil soils and counting the number of pores on the leaves of fossil plants. Despite the fact that these methodologies are different, the general picture each has provided of atmospheric CO_2 fluctuations over the Phanerozoic is consistent. There has been a general trend of declining CO_2 over the Phanerozoic, with elevated periods occurring in the Devonian (490 million years ago), Triassic (251 million years ago), and Jurassic (205 million years ago) and relatively lower concentrations occurring in the Carboniferous (300 million years ago), Permian (290 million years ago), Tertiary (65 to 2 million years ago), and Quaternary (last 2 million years ago). In terms of the geological history of CO_2 changes, the current CO_2 concentration is relatively low, despite the fact that it has risen rapidly over the past 200 years owing to fossil fuel burning and land use change. The general pattern of CO_2 changes over the Phanerozoic is also consistent with the overall climate trends: the glaciations coincide with reduced concentrations of CO_2, and warmer, more equable climates occur during periods of elevated CO_2.

Past concentrations of atmospheric O_2 are estimated through models of the linked carbon and oxygen cycles and by the records of fossil charcoal (which provide an indication of wildfires in the past), enabling upper and lower limits of atmospheric O_2 composition to be proposed. It appears that O_2 levels rose steadily since the evolution of land plants to a peak in the Carboniferous, with estimated upper values 66 percent higher than the current concentration. Following the Carboniferous peak, O_2 concentration is believed to have fallen dramatically into the Triassic and Jurassic, then risen steadily until the Eocene, and fallen again in the remainder of the Tertiary, to the current level of 21 percent by volume. It is speculated that the enormous wing size of Carboniferous insects was possible because of the denser atmosphere that an elevated O_2 environment would have caused and by means of the "vitamin" effect that high O_2 levels would have had on insect growth through enhanced respiration.

Biological, geological, and solar factors have influenced atmospheric composition over geological time. Geological processes such as volcanism, seafloor spreading, and degassing from mid-ocean ridges, result in increased atmospheric CO_2. Chemical weathering of calcium and magnesium silicates (compounds made of silicon and oxygen) and their subsequent deposition as marine carbonates causes a draw-down of CO_2 from the atmosphere. Consequently, the burial of carbon raises atmospheric O_2, and the combustion of organic matter (which requires adequate oxygen) releases CO_2 back into the atmosphere. Similar is the biological process of photosynthesis, essentially the uptake of CO_2 through pores on a plant leaf to produce starches and sugars via a complex biochemical pathway that utilizes solar energy. This process produces O_2 and water as by-products. Therefore, terrestrial and planktonic vegetation draw down atmospheric CO_2 and oxygenate the atmosphere in the process. All of these biological and geo-

logical processes clearly are linked. Likewise, the resultant effect of a change in atmospheric composition on both the terrestrial and aquatic ecosystems is complex with many resultant feedbacks.

Direct evidence of atmospheric composition goes back only as far as the longest ice core record, which spans the last 160,000 years. Ice cores are long tubular core samples taken from glaciers; analysis of layers within the core reveal a variety of data about the environment. Air bubbles incorporated into the ice during ice formation have been analyzed to provide records of CO_2, N_2O (nitrous oxide), and CH_4 (methane), and aerosols (particles) such as volcanic ash and sulfur dioxide. Well-documented CO_2 records across the glacial-interglacial cycles of the Pleistocene correlate well with global air temperatures derived from deuterium isotope (a form of hydrogen weighing twice as much as is normal) data from the same ice cores. These data illustrate on a finer scale the relationship between greenhouse gases (such as CO_2 and methane) and global climate observed in the geological past.

JENNY C. MCELWAIN

See also Global Environment; Ocean Environment; Origin of Life; Paleoclimatology; Terrestrial Environment; Terrestrialization of Animals

Further Reading

Berner, R.A. 1991. A model for atmospheric CO_2 over Phanerozoic time. *American Journal of Science* 291:339–76.

———. 1997. The rise of plants and their effect on weathering and atmospheric CO_2. *Science* 276:544–46.

Chaloner, W.G. 1989. Fossil charcoal as an indicator of palaeoatmospheric oxygen level. *Journal of the Geological Society of London* 146:171–74.

Lovelock, J.E., and M. Whitfield. 1982. Life span of the biosphere. *Nature* 296:561–63.

McElwain, J.C., and W.G. Chaloner. 1995. Stomatal density and index of fossil plants track atmospheric carbon dioxide in the Palaeozoic. *Annals of Botany* 76:389–95.

———. 1996. The fossil cuticle as a skeletal record of environmental change. *Palaios* 11:376–88.

AUSTRALIA: INVERTEBRATE PALEONTOLOGY

The Australian continent can be divided into three cratonic areas (continental blocks): the west, central, and east. The western consists of ancient Archean crust; the central, Proterozoic; and the east, Phanerozoic. Precambrian and Phanerozoic sedimentary basins overlie much of these cratons. The thicknesses of these sediments range from over 15 kilometers in some of the older basins, to a few hundred meters in Cenozoic basins.

The principal Phanerozoic basins on the western craton are the predominantly Paleozoic basins in the north—the Ord, Bonaparte, and Canning—and the Late Paleozoic to Cenozoic

basins in the west—the Carnarvon and Perth. The central craton is largely composed of a number of Paleozoic basins—the Georgina, Amadeus and Officer; the southernmost basin, the Eucla, dates from the Mesozoic and Cenozoic eras. The central part of the eastern craton is covered by what used to be known as the Great Artesian Basin; it now is subdivided into a number of basins: the Warburton, Eromanga, Galilee, Cooper, Adavale, and Surat. These are largely of Mesozoic age. The eastern part of the eastern craton consists of Paleozoic basins, such as the Bowen, Sydney, and Tasmania. In the extreme north is the Cenozoic Carpentaria Basin; in the south the Cenozoic Murray Basin; and the Mesozoic to Cenozoic Otway, Bass and Gippsland Basins.

Australia's Phanerozoic geological history consists of the accretion of younger crust onto the ancient Precambrian cratons in the east, with periodic submersion of the Precambrian cratons by the sea and the establishment of thick sedimentary sequences in a number of structurally downwarped basins. During the Phanerozoic, two supercontinents existed: Gondwana and Laurasia. As part of Gondwana, Australia underwent major latitudinal (north-south) movement, as well as a clockwise rotation. During the Early Paleozoic what is now Australia lay on the northern flank of the great supercontinent of Gondwana. The eastern side of Australia coincided with a convergent margin and underwent a number of periods of orogenesis (mountain-building), leading to the formation of the Tasman Fold Belt System.

During the Paleozoic, Australia moved in a southerly direction, so that by the beginning of the Mesozoic it had attained a high latitudinal, southern polar position. Apart from a counter-clockwise rotation, it remained in this region throughout the Mesozoic. During the Eocene Australia separated from Gondwana and began a northerly migration to its present position. These latitudinal changes, along with the breakup of Gondwana, had a great effect on climate, ocean temperatures, and ocean currents. Those changes had a major impact on the invertebrate fauna, both marine and terrestrial, as reflected in the fossil record.

Australia's invertebrate fossil history is not confined to the Phanerozoic. There is a rich Precambrian fossil record, extending back to the Archean. The 3.5 billion-year-old Warrawoona Group in the Pilbara region of western Australia contains the earliest evidence of life in the form of stromatolites and fossilized microbes, probably cyanobacteria (Schopf 1993). Proterozoic rocks in the Pilbara and in central Australia contain a rich record of stromatolites. These have proved useful for interbasinal biostratigraphical correlation. Some of the earliest evidence of fossilized eukaryotes (cells with a true nucleus) has been found in the eastern Pilbara, in the form of 1.3 billion-year-old rows of circular impressions, interpreted as algae.

The earliest record of metazoans (multicellular animals) is found in the famous "Ediacaran" fauna in the Flinders Range in South Australia. Very Late Proterozoic in age (between 540 and 600 million years old), these very singular fossils have been variously interpreted as direct ancestors of many living groups of organisms, as extinct forms of lichen, or even as a unique group of nonmetazoan organisms known as Vendobionta (Seilacher 1992). Most paleontologists consider that the Ediacaran organisms are related to the major phyla present in the Cambrian. The segmented *Dickinsonia* and *Spriginna* may be related to arthropod or segmented wormlike organisms; the kite-shaped *Parvancorina* may also be an arthropod; *Arkarua* is reminiscent of an echinoderm; *Inaria* is perhaps an actinian coral; *Charniodiscus* is very anthozoan-like; *Charnia* may be a sea-pen or pennatulacean; and *Kimberella* is like a mollusc.

During the Early Cambrian a deep sea lay off what is now eastern Australia. Shallow seas extended across central Australia. Carbonate and detrital sediments were deposited in this shelf region. In the Early Cambrian limestones in South Australia and in western

New South Wales, archeocyathids are common. The limestones contain a rich, "small shelly fauna," including some of the earliest known bivalves, such as *Pojetaia*. The region lay in the *Redlichia* trilobite province, a number of species occurring in the Ord Basin and in the Kanmantoo Fold Belt in South Australia. The Emu Bay Shale on Kangaroo Island contains not only *Redlichia* but also "soft-bodied" animals, including the arthropod *Anomalocaris*. Rich Middle to Late Cambrian limestones are found in northern Queensland and the Northern Territory, with rich trilobite faunas. Among other Cambrian fossils are possible Middle Cambrian corals in western New South Wales, the "eocrinoid" *Cymbionites* in Queensland, and edrioasteroids and carpoids in Tasmania.

During the Ordovician the shelf sea in central Australia widened, producing extensive limestones and shale deposits. These contain a rich trilobite fauna (dominated by asaphids) and nautiloid and gastropodmolluscs, particularly in the Northern Territory and western Queensland. Deeper water deposits in the eastern margin have yielded a rich graptolite fauna (a type of colonial hemichordate), exposed today in parts of Victoria. Unusual arthropods assigned to the family Corcoraniidae also occur here. As the Ordovician progressed the shelf sea contracted eastwards. Middle Ordovician deposits in Tasmania contain the earliest examples of stromatoporoids in the continent. By the Late Ordovician, the craton uplifted, restricting deep water environments in the east.

During the Silurian, thick layers deposited by rivers, lakes, and wind formed on the western margin of the continent. These contain a rich trace fossil fauna, in particular arthropod burrows and trackways. These have been interpreted as among the earliest evidence anywhere in the world for colonization of land by animals (Trewin & McNamara 1995). The only body fossil known from the site is of an unusual arthropod group, the Euthycarcinoida, a group that may be ancestral to insects. In eastern Australia, Silurian deposits occur in Victoria, New South Wales, and in northern Queensland. In the Late Silurian a shallow-water shelly fauna, dominated by brachiopods and trilobites occurs in Victoria. Echinoderms are common locally, including asteroids and mitrates. Early Silurian deposits in Tasmania also have yielded mitrates. In northern Queensland shallow-water limestones of Middle to Late Silurian age are rich in rugose and tabulate corals.

The Devonian is characterized by shallow seas in the northwest and deep marine sedimentation in the east. Most stunning are the development of limestones that would have formed a Devonian Barrier Reef around the Kimberley region of the northwest. These are among the most extensive Paleozoic reef systems in the world. The reef flat facies are typified by bulbous stromatoporoids, corals, algal mats, and oncolites. The reef margin has more stromatolites, the spongelike *Renalcis,* and a wider range of stromatoporoids. Reef slopes have quite different faunas, dominated by ammonoids, trilobites, and crinoids. These show a strong correspondence with Middle to Late Devonian faunas in Europe. The deep water facies are different again, being dominated by pelagic (open-water) forms, including exquisitely preserved fishes, three-dimensionally preserved in limestone nodules, along with "concavicarids," crustaceans, and nautiloids. In eastern Australia, Devonian deposits are confined to eastern Queensland, northeast New South Wales, and Victoria. Rich

Early Devonian silicified trilobite faunas occur in New South Wales. Coral-brachiopod shallow-water marine faunas occur in the Broken Hill region of north Queensland.

During the Early Carboniferous, shallow seas persisted in northwest Australia. But the reefs were replaced by shallow, open seas. Deep seas persisted off the eastern coast. Volcanic activity produced much sediment, which was deposited into the shallow seas. These seas supported a rich marine invertebrate fauna dominated by productid and strophomenid brachiopods, bryozoans, and proetid trilobites. On land, Late Carboniferous insects are known from Tasmania, including an endemic, (locally occurring) order, the Neosecoptera.

By the Early Permian, Australia was in the grip of a major glaciation. Sedimentary basins existed in the Canning and Carnarvon Basins and in the Bowen Basin. In these basins shallow marine faunas are still dominated by brachiopods, but an increasing number of bivalves are present. Crinoids are quite common in Permian deposits in Australia (Webster and Jell 1992). Catillocrinids form the dominant group in eastern Australian deposits.

During the Triassic, seas retracted from most of the continent. Marine sediments occur in the Carnarvon Basin in the west, the only invertebrates of note being ammonoids. Most significant in terms of invertebrate fossils are fossil insects, which occur at a number of sites in southern Queensland, and other invertebrate faunas in freshwater deposits in the Sydney region.

Major transgressions occurred in the Middle Jurassic along the western margin of the continent. Shallow water limestones in the Perth Basin contain a rich invertebrate fauna dominated by molluscs, and are very reminiscent of Tethyan faunas of Europe. Within this fauna is fossilized wood containing the earliest known pholads—wood-boring molluscs. Marine Jurassic faunas do not occur in eastern Australia. However, terrestrial deposits from the Early Jurassic in southern Queensland have yielded the remains of millipedes.

During the Cretaceous, seas flooded much of the continent, such that by mid-Cretaceous times more than half the continent was covered by shallows seas. These waters contained a rich marine fauna dominated by ammonites. Many are of Gondwanan aspect, in particular the rich heteromorph (variably coiled) faunas dominated by ancyloceratids and labeceratids. These are similar to ammonite faunas in southern Africa and Antarctica. During this period the Koonwarra Fossil Bed was deposited under lacustrine (lake system) conditions in southeast Australia. Within this deposit are not only what may be the oldest known flowering plants but also a rich insect fauna (Jell and Roberts 1986). Late Cretaceous faunas occur in the Northern Territory and Western Australia. Santonian chalk deposits in the Perth and Carnarvon Basins in the west contain faunas very similar to coeval deposits in Europe, even down to the same crinoid zone fossils *Marsupites* and *Uintacrinus*. In the Carnarvon Basin occurs the very last Maastrichtian beds with a rich mollusc fauna dominated by ammonites. These contain many species that have a very widespread distribution, many being found throughout Gondwana, while others are cosmopolitan in their distribution.

The first Paleogene deposits are bryozoal calcarenites occurring in the northern Carnarvon Basin. The fauna is dominated by echinoderms, in particular echinoids. These are mainly relict (holdover) Cretaceous elements, in particular holasteroids. The final breakup of Gondwana and the separation of Australia from Antarctica is marked by the appearance of Middle/Late Eocene limestones along the southern coast. The limestones are dominated by echinoids and, to a lesser extent, by molluscs in particular pectinids. Within associated silica-rich beds the first known Cenozoic sphinctozoan sponge has been found. Oligocene faunas are restricted in nature, but unlike other parts of the world, are not too dissimilar from the Eocene faunas.

Miocene marine invertebrate faunas that mark the onset of the Neogene are more widespread along the southern margin in a number of basins, as well as in the Carnarvon Basin in the northwest. While Eocene faunas in the northwest and south are similar, there are differences in the Miocene, with the northern faunas being closer to those of India and Indonesia, rather than containing the higher degree of endemics found in the south. The echinoid and molluscan faunas are of a subtropical nature. However, by the Pliocene there are marked faunal changes associated with the cooling of the Southern Ocean. Echinoid faunas in particular are quite different, resembling those of the region today, while many of the Miocene genera are now found in the subtropics and tropics. Pliocene faunas in the southwest contain one of the richest molluscan faunas in the world.

The changing nature of the Australian marine invertebrate fauna relates to the initial southerly movement and accretion onto Gondwana during the Paleozoic, then to the progressive breakup of Gondwana. As elements of Gondwana broke away, the Australian faunas became progressively more different. As Australia has moved northwards through more than 20 degrees of latitude during the last 40 million years, and the ocean temperatures have cooled, substantial changes occurred to the faunas, reflected in markedly changing fossil faunas through the Cenozoic.

KENNETH J. MCNAMARA

See also Australia: Paleobotany; Australia: Vertebrate Paleontology; Plate Tectonics and Continental Drift

Works Cited and Further Reading

Jell, P.A., and J. Roberts (eds.). 1986. Plants and invertebrates from the Lower Cretaceous Koonwarra Fossil Bed, South Gippsland, Victoria. *Memoirs of the Association of Australasian Palaeontologists* 3:1–205.

Schopf, J.W. 1993. Microfossils of the early Archean Apex Chert: New evidence of the antiquity of life. *Science* 260:640–46.

Seilacher, A. 1992. Vendobionta and Psammocorallia: Lost constructions of Precambrian evolution. *Journal of the Geological Society, London* 149:607–13.

Trewin, N.H., and K.J. McNamara. 1995. Arthropods invade the land: Trace fossils and palaeoenvironments of the Tumblagooda Sandstone (late Silurian?) of Kalbarri, Western Australia. *Transactions of the Royal Society of Edinburgh* 85:177–210.

Webster, G.D., and P.A. Jell. 1992. Permian echinoderms from Western Australia. *Memoirs of the Queensland Museum* 32:311–73.

AUSTRALIA: PALEOBOTANY

Australia is regarded as one of the "megadiverse" continents, and its living flora has evolved under a range of pressures, often in isolation, leading to a unique flora with a very high degree of endemism (restriction to a particular location). Given the unusual character of the Australian flora, it is no surprise that there is an extensive history of paleobotanical research on the continent. Unfortunately, there has been little research on the pre-Cretaceous floras of Australia in the last 20 years, with a few notable exceptions; therefore, the review by R.E. Gould in 1975 is still highly applicable.

However, there has been a recent major upsurge of interest in fossil floras that bear directly on the evolution of the living Australian vegetation, and this is best considered as the time since the arrival of flowering plants in Australia, during the Cretaceous. Over the years since plant fossils first were located and described in Australia, there have been some major shifts in understanding the significance of the fossils, and it is a valuable exercise to trace these changes.

The first major work on Cenozoic plants was undertaken by Baron Constantin von Ettingshausen, who published on the macrofossil flora of the Vegetable Creek tin mines, first in Germany, and later in Australia in an English translation in 1888. Ettingshausen never visited Australia and had an imperfect grasp of the living Australian flora. Nevertheless, he was a great paleobotanist, and by the standards of the time he produced an excellent publication and put Australian Cenozoic paleobotany on the map. However, Ettingshausen had a view of the world that certainly seems to have biased his identifications. In his "cosmopolitan theory," Ettingshausen envisaged a more or less uniform worldwide flora in the Tertiary, which only became regionalized in relatively recent times. At Vegetable Creek he identified not only endemic Australian genera, but also many that now are restricted to the Northern Hemisphere. He identified similar mixes of genera in Cenozoic floras from Europe.

The first Australian actively to question Ettingshausen's cosmopolitan theory was Henry Deane, an engineer who worked on the fledgling railway system in Australia in the decades leading to the turn of the century and in the process discovered many plant fossil deposits in newly exposed cuttings. In his presidential address to the Linnean Society of New South Wales in 1896, Deane stated that Ettingshausen "has expressed views as to the origin of the vegetation in Australia, and of the rest of the world, which appear to be entirely erroneous." While Deane's attack on Ettingshausen was both courageous and correct, unfortunately he went on to produce a series of papers of such poor taxonomic quality that the eminent North American paleobotanist Edmund Berry was moved to write that early in the twentieth century "there have been more worthless articles written about the Cretaceous and Tertiary floras of Australia than any other equal area of the earth's surface." However, the early work on Cenozoic fossils in Australia had a much more subtle damaging effect, since the reception of the research in the decades around the start of the

twentieth century was so poor that, with a few minor exceptions, the whole field of research disappeared until the 1950s. Furthermore, a mind-set developed in researchers of the living flora that the fossil record was completely unreliable. That view persists in some quarters even today.

While Ettingshausen and Deane were developing their views, students of living plants were developing their own theories of the origin of the Australian flora. Joseph Hooker, in his monumental work on the flora of Tasmania in 1860, developed the hypothesis that the Australian flora consisted of three "elements." Hooker believed that past land bridges between Australia and land to the north and south, along with major climatic differences from the present, allowed these elements to enter Australia in the distant past. This developed into the "invasion theory," which reached its culmination in the major review paper by Nancy T. Burbidge in 1960. Curiously, paleobotanists seem to have avoided the debate about the invasion theory more or less completely, although this is at least partly explained by the meagre paleobotanical research until the 1950s.

The turning point in Australian Cenozoic paleobotany was owing to the efforts of a single person, Isabel Cookson. Cookson combined research on fossil pollen and spores (paleopalynology) with research on plant macrofossils, a rarity at any time and almost unheard of today. She almost single-handedly brought Australian paleobotany from a point of virtual nonexistence into the forefront of botanical research. Most of her research was published in the 1950s and early 1960s, but it holds up very well to modern scrutiny, unlike most of the research that preceded her. Cookson effectively began the discipline of paleopalynology in Australia, and this field was kept alive by major oil exploration programs into the 1980s. Cookson also trained several students in paleobotany, and their influence on the current generation has been very significant. The major shift in interpretation of the plant fossil record came with the general acceptance of continental drift and the underlying principle of plate tectonics. Australian paleobotany was particularly influenced by this, since Australia has been such a dynamic continent over the past 60 million years or so, moving through tens of degrees of latitude and therefore markedly altering in climate and geographical proximity to other landmasses.

Australia, along with South America, was one of the last landmasses to separate from Antarctica, and as recently as 40 million years ago was still in close proximity along a broad front, preventing the formation of major oceanic circulation between the two continents. Because of this, the major circulation patterns of oceanic water were along latitudinal gradients, that is, the water circulated from equatorial latitudes to very high latitudes and back again. This, in turn, meant that vast quantities of water were warmed by the equatorial sun and then circulated to very high latitudes. The presence of this warm oceanic water at high latitudes meant that the temperature gradient from the equator to the pole was nowhere as steep as it is today, and even though Australia was much further south than it currently is, southern Australia in particular was probably warmer than it is at present. The relatively warm oceans also meant that there was a large amount of water in the atmosphere, and humidity and rainfall were high and more or less constant throughout the year.

The major factors that altered this climatic regime were the physical separation of both Australia and South America from Antarctica, allowing commencement of the Circumantarctic current that has such a strong influence on global climate today. This event is marked by a global cooling, since water was no longer circulating over such a wide latitudinal range in the Southern Hemisphere and the water in the Circumantarctic current rapidly cooled. Eventually, the ice cap began to form over the South Pole, and as this grew even less radiation could be absorbed, with the result that temperatures fell even further, so that the equator-pole temperature gradient continued to increase. While this was occurring, Australia was moving northward toward the equator, but despite this, over the ensuing tens of millions of years until the present, southern Australia has tended to cool down, or, at the very least, experience a cooler winter. During this period of time rainfall patterns also changed, and Australia dried out and rainfall became more seasonal. As a result of this, the vast rain forests that covered Australia when it was part of the supercontinent Gondwana broke up and simplified, leading eventually to the current pattern of rain forest remnants, mostly along the east coast of the continent.

Other environmental pressures also have had an important role to play in the evolution of the Australian flora during this time. Australia is noted for its extremely poor soils, which are especially depleted in phosphorus and nitrogen, and this has led to a classic sclerophyllous response (thickening and hardening of foliage) from the vegetation over much of the continent. It is clear from the fossil record that this is an ancient phenomenon, dating back at least 55 million years, to the earliest record of plants that can be allied directly to the living flora. The response to the drying climate clearly postdates this, probably beginning about 35 to 40 million years ago.

Closely tied to the low-nutrient soils and the drying climate is an increased role for fire in the environment. Fire is a major factor in much of Australian vegetation today, and this probably is owing largely to the presence of humans on the landmass and the consequent increase in ignition sources. However, there is clear fossil evidence that fire has had an increasing role in the vegetation since at least the Oligocene, approximately 30 to 35 million years ago, with

a rapid rise less than 200,000 years ago associated with a major increase in dominance of the vegetation by *Eucalyptus* species, perhaps as a result of the arrival of Aborigines and their use of fire to manage the vegetation. These are the major trends in the vegetation, but the fossil record has only really been used to interpret them since the late 1970s. Since that time enough data has accumulated to allow a shift in emphasis from the collection of data for industrial purposes or occasionally for narrowly defined scientific purposes to the point where it can be used in a synthetic way both to test broad-scale hypotheses regarding the origin and evolution of the flora and to allow the formulation of new hypotheses for future testing.

A review of the fossil record in 1994 compiled most available data into a single source, but already much new data has come to light and it clearly will be difficult to present a summary in a single place again owing to the vast amount of material accumulating. There are still some obvious weaknesses in the Australian fossil record. The most obvious of these is the intense concentration of data in the southeastern corner of the continent, where much of the population is centered and much of the early exploration work occurred. The history of most of the rest of the continent is only poorly understood, although at present specific projects are targeting this deficiency. There is also a bias toward information pertinent to rain forest evolution—partly a reflection of the need for water in the process of fossilization—so that the history of drier vegetation types is much more poorly documented.

ROBERT S. HILL

See also Australia: Invertebrate Paleontology; Australia: Vertebrate Paleontology

Works Cited and Further Reading

Burbidge, N.T. 1960. The phytogeography of the Australian region. *Australian Journal of Botany* 8:75–211.
Deane, H. 1896. President's address. *Proceedings of the Linnean Society of New South Wales* 10:619–67.
Ettingshausen, C. von. 1888. Contributions to the Tertiary flora of Australia. *Memoirs of the Geological Survey of New South Wales* 2:1–189.
Gould, R.E. 1975. The succession of Australian pre-Tertiary megafossil floras. *Botanical Review* 41:453–83.
Hill, R.S. (ed.). 1994. *History of the Australian Vegetation: Cretaceous to Recent*. Cambridge and New York: Cambridge University Press.

AUSTRALIA: VERTEBRATE PALEONTOLOGY

Like Caesar's Gaul, the history of vertebrate paleontology in Australia may be divided into three parts. From small beginnings, the science grew steadily in the latter two-thirds of the nineteenth century. At the beginning of the twentieth century, activity dropped sharply and remained that way for half a century. Then, between

1950 and 1990, many vertebrate paleontologists became active in Australia, and the field grew at a steep rate. What was done in this science in Australia—and when—was shaped profoundly both by the logistical realities of a vast continent with a low population far from its European roots and by the geological nature of the country.

The Setting

For the most part, Australian vertebrate paleontological research has been financed by universities, geological surveys, and museums of the country and thus was governmental in nature. Private philanthropy played an uneven, but at times vital, role in financing Australian-based vertebrate paleontological research, particularly the collecting phase. Governmental funding began as part of the broader program to document the nature of the country scientifically. In a nation of vast distances and small population, physically remote from its European origins, available funding for scientific research of all kinds has always been modest in proportion to the total area of the continent. The role of transport and communication in shaping Australian society, particularly their high cost and time required, generally has been addressed cogently by G. Blainey in his appropriately titled book, *The Tyranny of Distance* (1966). Both the great distance of Australia from Europe and the lack of cheap internal transportation in a land of few major rivers profoundly affected the country's development.

In paleontology, animals are organized in groups of decreasing diversity. The categories, from most comprehensive to most specific, are kingdom, phylum, class, order, family, genus, and species. Distribution maps of Australian vertebrate localities grouped by class show a remarkably similar pattern (Figure 1). The principal concentration of sites tends to be in the southeast, with somewhat fewer running parallel to the east coast all the way to the northeast corner of the continent. Still fewer are found in western Queensland and New South Wales. Two other areas of relative abundance are north of Adelaide, South Australia, and southwestern Western Australia, in the vicinity of Perth.

This pattern reflects both the geology of the continent and its population density. Historically, the first sites found were close to major population centers. Only later, as Europeans explored the entire country and constructed a network of stock tracks and later roads, were vertebrate fossils collected in the interior with increasing frequency. Even with such infrastructural support, most work has been done on specimens found in areas with higher population densities, closer to major population centers. Since those areas are better known, reports of the fossils were more frequently forthcoming from the general public and people engaged in professional activities, such as mining geologists. Equally as important, the logistics of collecting in such areas were less complicated and, consequently, less costly.

Figure 2 is a histogram showing the numbers of identified vertebrate genera for the different geological periods in Australia. The width of the columns are proportional to the duration of the period, and the area is proportional to the number of genera (singular, genus) known. As can be seen from the heights of the various columns, the abundance of vertebrate fossils is quite uneven, the most dating from the Tertiary and Devonian. This reflects the relative abundance of fossils and area of outcrop of rocks that date from the different geological ages.

Table 2 gives a decade-by-decade record of the number of publications on the various vertebrate groups, and Figure 3 portrays this same information graphically. Mammals and fishes are by far the most widely studied. On closer inspection of the literature, the Quaternary mammals and mid-Paleozoic (particularly Devonian) fish are by far the most abundant fossils available and, hence, the most studied. Marine mammals are, by contrast, a group for which the potential has yet to be realized (Figure 4). Half the southern coastline of Australia is composed of Cenozoic marine sediments that could yield such fossils. However, to date there has never been an Australian specialist devoted to this area. Less than twenty papers have been published on Australian Cenozoic marine mammals since the first appeared in 1877.

Wellington Caves and the Beginnings of Australian Vertebrate Paleontology, 1831–99

For more than two decades after settlement in 1788, the English settlement at Sydney Cove was confined to the area between the sea and the Blue Mountains. Shortly after a route across them was found in 1813, exploration of the country to the west began in earnest. Soon thereafter, a settlement was established at Wellington.

On a visit to the area in 1831, Major Thomas Mitchell, Surveyor-General of New South Wales, was taken to caves near Wellington, where he collected fossil remains of Pleistocene mammals and birds. These were forwarded to Europe, particularly to England, where they aroused intense interest.

Charles Darwin, for example, was influenced by this material when he formulated his "Law of the Succession of Types" in 1839, discussing it again twenty years later in the chapter, "On the Geological Succession of Organic Beings," in *The Origin of the Species*. What Darwin found significant was that the fossils, "were closely allied to the living marsupials on that continent." He saw this as strong support for his idea that new species arose by evolving from preexisting ones, his "descent with modification," as opposed to the alternative view that species were created anew. If they were, there was no reason why a similarity should exist between the Pleistocene mammals and modern ones.

The specimens from Wellington Caves were the first Australian fossil vertebrates ever described. The description was written by Sir Richard Owen, then of the Royal College of Surgeons, London. This was to be a common pattern in the nineteenth century. Australian fossils were sent overseas, most often to England, to be described scientifically and housed permanently in collections there. As a result, it was often necessary for Australians to travel halfway around the world in order to study Australian vertebrate paleontological topics. (To the credit of the foreign institutions, every courtesy to facilitate access to the relevant specimens generally has been extended to Australian research scientists.)

In 1838, Owen described and figured the holotype (the specimen that would represent its unique group) of *Diprotodon australis,* the first Australian vertebrate fossil to receive a name. The specimen consisted of a battered partial row of upper teeth—in hindsight, hardly an auspicious beginning. Over the next forty years, Owen continued to receive fossil bones of *Diprotodon* as well as other extinct Australian mammals and birds, primarily ones that dated from the Pleistocene. In 1877, he was able to illustrate a composite skeleton of *Diprotodon;* he was missing only the feet, a fact he got around by cleverly hiding them behind low plant growth.

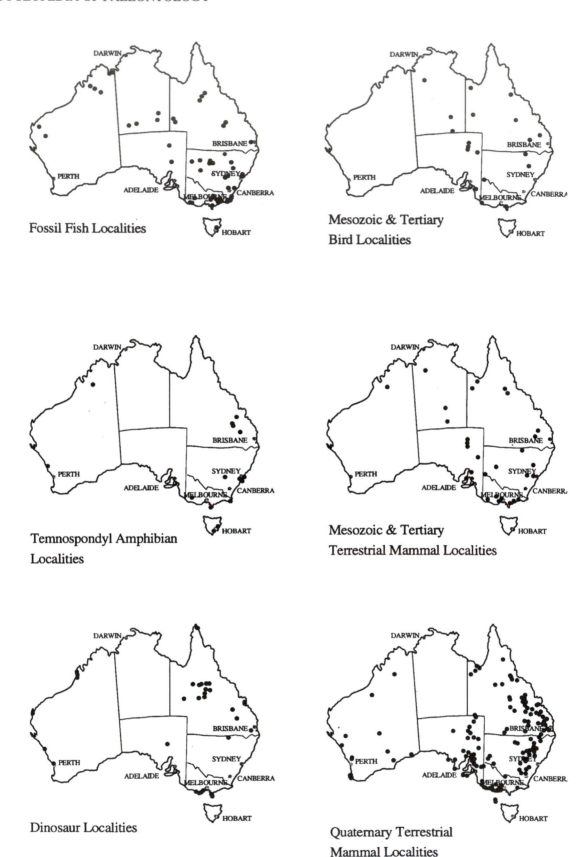

Figure 1. Distribution map of Australian vertebrate fossil sites for various groups. Note the concentration of sites along the Dividing Range, which parallels the east coast, and the paucity of sites in the western half of the continent. Data for dinosaur localities is from Rich (1996); for all the other groups from Vickers-Rich et al. (1991).

Table 1.

Named Vertebrate Genera in the Ordovician-Tertiary Australian Fossil Record*

Geological Period	Ord	Sil	Dev	Car	Per	Tri	Jur	K	T
Duration (millions of years)	71.0	30.5	46.2	72.5	45.0	37.0	62.4	80.6	63.4
Class									
Pteraspidomorphi	2.0	—	4.0	—	—	—	—	—	—
Placodermi	—	—	45.0	—	—	—	—	—	—
Elasmobranchii	—	—	7.0	13.0	4.0	1.0	—	17.0	23.0
Teleostomi	—	3.0	32.0	11.0	6.0	33.0	5.0	21.0	43.0
Amphibia	—	—	1.0	—	1.0	15.0	2.0	—	8.0
Amniota, Class Uncertain	—	—	—	—	2.0	—	—	—	—
Anaspida	—	—	—	—	—	—	—	3.0	4.0
Diapsida	—	—	—	—	—	4.0	1.0	14.0	15.0
Mammalia	—	—	—	—	—	—	—	1.0	132.0
Aves	—	—	—	—	—	—	—	1.0	24.0
Total Genera	2.0	3.0	89.0	24.0	13.0	55.0	8.0	57.0	249.0

*Only named genera and those identified as "new genus" are included. Genera published subsequent to 1991 not included. If genus or age queried in compilation, included in that age.

Data from Vickers-Rich et al. (1991).

The feet would not be found until 1892, a year after Owen's death. That same year, the presence of *Diprotodon* on the floor of the dry Lake Callabonna was reported to the South Australian Museum. Beginning in the following January, at the height of summer and during an intense drought, a South Australian Museum field party struggled with the tough clay of the lake floor for eleven months to excavate *Diprotodon* and other mammals as well, together with the large, flightless bird *Genyornis*. This work occurred during a severe economic depression and was only possible through the financing by Sir Thomas Elder, a South Australian pastoralist. Without that private support, the South Australian Museum, an arm of the colonial government, could never have mounted the expedition. Over a span of 20 years after that expedition, the director of the South Australian Museum, E.C. Stirling, and his assistant, A.H.C. Zietz (who prepared the fossils), jointly published a series of monographs on the various animals from Lake Callabonna, together with an introductory volume covering the history of the work there and the geology of the area.

Although Owen had died by the time of the Lake Callabonna discovery, and thus could take no part in it, earlier he had done much to encourage the progress of Australian vertebrate paleontology. He was far from just a passive recipient of the generosity of his Australian colleagues. In the 1870s a letter from Owen

to the New South Wales government was instrumental in funding renewed work at Wellington Caves by Gerard Kreft of the Australian Museum and Alexander Thompson of the University of Sydney. Although Wellington Caves material continued to reach Owen as late as the 1880s, a significant part of it was described later by two Sydney-based scholars during the last decades of the nineteenth century: E.P. Ramsey published a paper in 1886, and W.S. Dun followed suit in 1893 and 1894. This shift in scholarship reflected the gradual transition toward the time when more Australian vertebrate paleontological research was done by Australians and was published in Australian journals.

During the period prior to 1900, following in the tradition set by Major Thomas Mitchell at the Wellington Caves, Australian explorers often forwarded specimens they had encountered on their journeys to vertebrate paleontologists. Some of these explorers included the Polish Count Strzelecki and the American James Dwight Dana, both of whom found fossil fishes in the 1840s; the former made his discoveries near Booral, New South Wales, the latter in a coal mine at Newcastle, New South Wales. Similarly, L. Leichardt in 1844 and Stutchbury a decade later recovered fossil vertebrates from the Darling Downs of Queensland. Still later, and further afield, William Hann recovered the first Cretaceous marine reptiles from central Queensland in the 1870s.

Figure 2. Number of named vertebrate genera in the Ordovician-Tertiary Australian fossil record. Column widths are proportional to the duration of geological periods; column areas are proportional to the number of genera. Key: *O*, Ordovician, 2 genera; *S*, Silurian, 3 genera; *D*, Devonian, 89 genera; *C*, Carboniferous, 24 genera; *P*, Permian, 13 genera; *Tr*, Triassic, 55 genera; *J*, Jurassic, 8 genera; *K*, Cretaceous, 57 genera; *T*, Tertiary, 249 genera. Data is broken down into finer taxonomic units in Table 1. From Rich and Young (1996); data from Vickers-Rich et al. (1991).

War, Depression, and War, 1900–49

In the first decade after 1899, there was a marked drop in the number of publications dealing with Australian vertebrate paleontology (Figure 3 and Table 2). Two factors appear to explain this.

First, there was a turnover of generations. By 1900 many of the most prolific workers of the previous three decades had died,

others were nearing the end of their careers or their research interests had changed. Charles de Vis, who published 24 papers in the 1880s and 1890s on fossil mammals, would publish only two more, one in 1900 and another in 1907; he published the latter at the age of 78. Robert Etheridge Jr., who published eight papers on the same subject, as well as three on fish and one on turtles, between 1878 and 1897, would publish only one more on mammals in 1918 and two more on fish in 1905 and 1906, his interests having turned more to anthropology.

The second factor was the lingering effects of the devastating Australian Depression of the early 1890s. Towards the end of de Vis' career at the Queensland Museum and Frederick McCoy's as director of the National Museum of Victoria, funds were no longer available to hire collectors or purchase collections. Then came two World Wars and the Great Depression. The adverse effects of the malaise of these events persisted for more than 50 years. Not until the 1960s, for example, would the Queensland Museum be able to mount collecting trips for fossil vertebrates. In the meantime, de Vis' successor as director at the Queensland Museum, Herbert Longman, made what progress he could between 1916 and 1945 by studying specimens donated by the public or collected by State personnel and those of private geological organizations.

The one decade between 1900 and 1949 where the level of Australian vertebrate paleontological activity was comparable to that of the last three of the nineteenth century was the 1920s. During the Depression that followed, that level of activity was not sustained, but still the bulk of the work carried out by individuals who studied fossil vertebrates from one or a few sites not far from where they were based. This approach characterized much of the research from 1900 to 1949, when exploration and development of new localities was at nadir.

Prominent among those whose scientific careers followed this pattern were H.H. Scott, who first published a number of papers on the Pleistocene fauna from King Island, Tasmania, and later, together with C.E. Lord, on fauna from Mowbray Swamp, Tasmania. L. Glauert investigated Pleistocene caves of southwestern Western Australia, particularly Mammoth Cave; R.T. Wade studied Triassic and Jurassic freshwater fish from the Sydney region; and C. Anderson continued work on the Pleistocene faunas from Wellington Caves. E. Sherborne Hills ranged somewhat more widely afield, publishing principally on mid-Paleozoic fish from a number of sites in eastern Australia. He was also the only one of these scholars to continue into the 1950s, publishing as late as 1957. In every case where scholars put their effort principally into collecting and analyzing fossils from one or a few sites, the operating costs were relatively low, and there was a high likelihood that the projects would produce scientifically useful results. This was a thoroughly realistic approach during times when financial resources were limited.

This is not to say the vertebrate paleontologists at this time lacked imagination and resourcefulness. Between 1934 and 1946, for example, L.C. Ball published the first papers on Australian dinosaur footprints. He encountered these specimens while working underground in Queensland coal mines where he found them on the tunnel roofs.

Table 2.

Number of Publications on Australian Vertebrate Paleontological Topics, by Decades

	Mammals	Birds	Reptiles	Amphibians	Fish	Total
1830s	4	—	—	—	—	4
1840s	11	—	—	—	2	13
1850s	3	—	—	—	—	3
1860s	16	1	—	—	1	18
1870s	36	3	—	—	2	41
1880s	42	5	6	1	2	56
1890s	41	1	3	—	13	58
1900s	17	5	1	—	11	34
1910s	25	4	1	—	11	41
1920s	39	2	3	—	7	51
1930s	9	2	5	—	11	27
1940s	10	—	2	—	12	24
1950s	24	6	2	1	8	41
1960s	81	9	9	4	10	113
1970s	128	16	8	13	26	191
1980s	166	30	37	17	98	348
Total	652	94	77	36	214	1,063
1990s	78	—	—	—	—	—

*For mammals, the figure for the 1990s is halfway through 1997; i.e., three-quarters of the decade 1990–99. If that rate holds for the entire decade, 123 publications can be expected.

Source: Vickers-Rich et al. (1991).

Early in this century, B.A. Bensley published two seminal works on the origin and evolution of Australian marsupials. A few years later, in 1906, British scholar A. Smith-Woodward published the first valid record of an Australian dinosaur. Subsequently, he published a few additional papers on various vertebrate groups from eastern Australia, ranging in age from Permian to Cenozoic; one appeared as late as 1941. These contributions were almost the sole work by non-Australian vertebrate paleontologists on Australian material between 1900 and 1949, markedly less than before or since.

A Second Golden Age, 1950–90

After half a century of low productivity in Australian vertebrate paleontology, a second phase of heightened activity began in the 1950s (Figure 3 and Table 2). A convergence of circumstances brought this about.

Internal communications and transportation improved. As late as the 1950s, long distance overland cattle drives were still common. In that decade, for example, a herd of cattle was walked from the Northern Territory to New South Wales, a journey that lasted 49 weeks (Vince Kiernan, former drover, personal communication to T. Rich, 2 July 1997). During the following decade, beef roads were constructed in many parts of Australia so that cattle could be transported quickly by truck. Such road construction made internal transport quicker, more reliable, and less expensive.

In the post–World War II era, there was an optimism about science. Scientific activity was seen as something that should be encouraged. As a consequence, governmental funding of scientific research increased significantly across all disciplines, including vertebrate paleontology.

In the four decades after World War II, the Bureau of Mineral Resources systematically produced geological maps of the entire

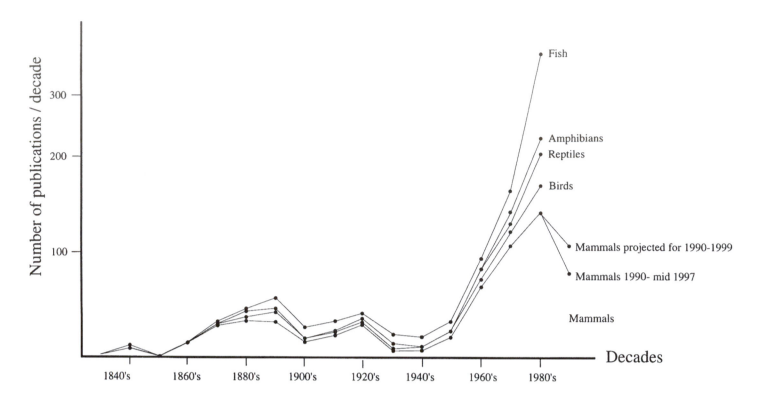

Figure 3. Publications by decade in the different subdisciplines of Australian vertebrate paleontology. Data are tabulated in Table 2. Except for the mammals between 1990 and mid-1997, the data are from Vickers-Rich et al. (1991).

continent at a scale of 1:250,000 or better. In addition, private mining companies were carrying out extensive exploratory projects in many remote areas. As a result, additional vertebrate paleontological sites were discovered. Most lay in the interior of Australia, an area with a poor vertebrate fossil record up until that time.

In the 1950s and early 1960s, three major collaborative efforts between foreign institutions and Australian ones did much to set the pattern for Australian vertebrate paleontological research for the remainder of the century. In 1953, Ruben Arthur Stirton of the University of California, Berkeley, and his student Richard H. Tedford came to Australia as Fulbright scholars, with the express purpose of finding Tertiary terrestrial mammals, which up until then were known from only a handful of specimens. Working in close conjunction with the South Australian Museum, and following suggestions of Sir Douglas Mawson, the noted Antarctic explorer and Professor of Geology at the University of Adelaide, the two Californians searched for Late Cenozoic mammals in the area east of Lake Eyre. On Cooper Creek Stirton and Tedford discovered Quaternary mammal and bird sites originally found by J.W. Gregory and his students from the University of Melbourne at the beginning of the century. The two men also eventually discovered Pliocene terrestrial mammal and bird sites at Lake Palankarinna.

In the following decade, under Stirton's direction, further work at Lake Palankarinna yielded Mid-Tertiary mammals and birds as well as Pliocene ones. North of Cooper Creek, additional sites were found in playa (desert basin) lakes there. This suite of sites provided the first extensive insight into the evolution of terrestrial mam-

mals and birds during the Mid- to Late Tertiary in Australia. At the time of Stirton's death in 1966, as a result of little more than a decade's work, it was clear that the basic differentiation of most Australian terrestrial mammalian groups had been completed (i.e., they had reached the form still seen today) by the Mid-Tertiary, when the record began. The exceptions to this were the macropodoids (kangaroos and potoroos) and diprotodontoids (e.g., phalangers, opossum rats), which showed major changes during the time span of the known record. Thus, it was apparent that to document the basic differentiation of most Australian terrestrial mammals by fossils, sites that dated back to the Cenozoic needed to be discovered. Finding such sites became the objective of many of the paleomammalogists who subsequently worked in Australia.

In 1967, a posthumous paper by Stirton, together with Tedford and a subsequent student, Michael O. Woodburne, outlined the biostratigraphic framework for all the Tertiary terrestrial mammal sites then known in Australia. (In biostratigraphy, rock strata are dated on the basis of the biological materials they contain.) They included not only the sites east of Lake Eyre but also Alcoota, which had been found subsequently in the Northern Territory, as well as sites that long had been known in Queensland, Victoria, and Tasmania. Many had come to light as a consequence of Stirton's program to visit all the major Australian museums as well as Commonwealth and State geological surveys.

Since 1967, work on Tertiary terrestrial mammals has concentrated on exploiting the sites first known to Stirton, as well as those discovered in the 1970s east of Lake Frome, South Australia,

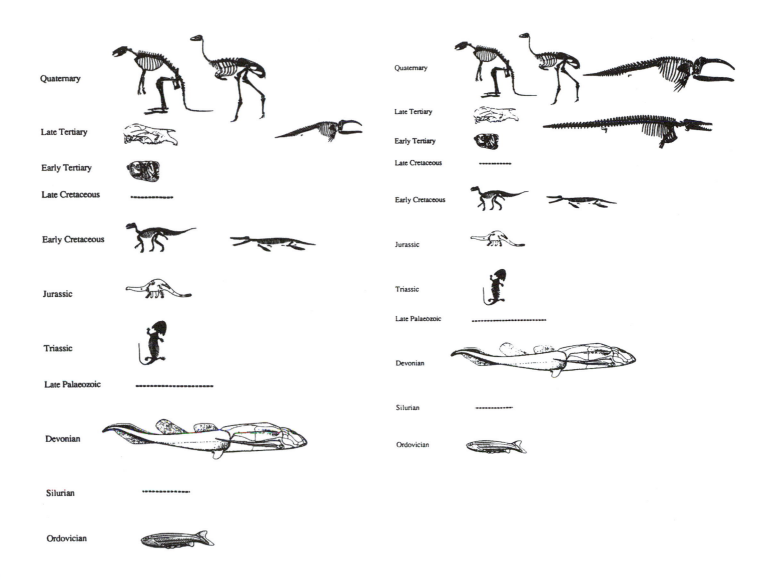

Figure 4. Relative abundance of various fossil vertebrate groups in Australia, indicated approximately by the size of the different symbols. *Left hand column,* estimate based on present record; *right hand column,* author's opinion as to potential relative record.

Bluff Downs near Charters Towers, Queensland, and at Bullock Creek in the Northern Territory. Prominent among the scholars on these localities were Neville Pledge, Woodburne, and Judd Case (Lake Palankarinna), Michael Plane and later Peter Murray, Dirk Megirian, Patricia Vickers-Rich, and Thomas Rich (Bullock Creek), Brian Mackness, Mary Wade and Mike Archer (Bluff Downs), and Tedford, and later Vickers-Rich, Timothy Flannery, Archer, and Rich (east of Lake Frome). As a student of Stirton's, Woodburne carried out the first excavations at Alcoota in the early 1960s. Beginning in the 1980s, Murray, Megirian, and Rod Wells initiated a long-term program of work there.

By far the most work on Tertiary mammals subsequent to 1967 has been carried out at Riversleigh Station, northwestern Queensland. Fossil mammals first were recovered from this area in 1901, and Tedford visited the site briefly in 1963. However, it was not until 1976, the time of the first visit by Archer, that a sustained effort began there. In the subsequent two decades, literally thousands of specimens of Mid- to Late Cenozoic fossil vertebrates have been recovered from numerous sites. Preserved in limestone, the fossils consist of exquisitely preserved individual bones and teeth, complementing both in quality of preservation and sheer quantity the contemporaneous associated and occasionally articulated (preserved with joints and body shape intact) skeletal material from east of Lakes Eyre and Frome in South Australia.

Although known since the early twentieth century to have fossils, the Tingamarra region, near the town of Murgon in southeastern Australia, was not explored until the 1980s, when terrestrial mammals first were recovered there. Since then, this area has yielded an assemblage of about 100 isolated mammal teeth and jaw fragments, including one tooth interpreted as coming from a placental mammal from the Eocene. If it is a placental, it upsets the long-held view that members of this group did not reach Australia until the Late Cenozoic.

In 1985, a jaw of a toothed monotreme (egg-laying mammal, e.g., duck-billed platypus) was recognized in a collection of fossils from the opal field at Lightning Ridge, New South Wales. This was the first Mesozoic mammal from Australia. Subsequently, about a dozen more specimens have been found. Two come from Victoria; all the rest are also from Lightning Ridge. All except one clearly are monotremes.

Since the 1950s, the study of Quaternary terrestrial mammal faunas continued to be divided between open sites and cave sites. Investigations were carried out at classic localities of the nineteenth century, such as the Darling Downs of Queensland (principally by J.T. Woods, followed by Alan Bartholomai) and Wellington Caves in New South Wales (by R.A.L. Osborne, Lynn Dawson, and Mike Augee). In addition, numerous new sites were developed. Among the many of these was Devil's Lair, worked by Duncan Meeriless and his colleagues; Madura Caves, excavated by William Turnbull and Ernest Lundelius; and Naracoorte Caves, worked by Wells and his colleagues. The first two sites are in Western Australia, the last in South Australia. Other scholars devoted themselves to investigating several different Quaternary sites. Prominent among these were Tedford, Jeanette Hope, Murray, Jack Mahoney, Ride, Archer, Wade, and Alex Baynes.

This body of work basically had three objectives. The first was to continue investigating the Quaternary but at a finer resolution, documenting the history of the terrestrial (land-based) vertebrate fauna, particularly as it responded to the ever-increasing aridity of the continent during the Late Cenozoic. The second was to document the fauna that existed on the continent at the time of first human contact, 40,000 or more years ago, as well as that which was present at the beginning of European settlement in 1788. The third, closely related to the second, was the attempt to determine whether the demise of the late Quaternary large mammals and birds ("the Megafauna") was owing to climatic change and/or to the effects of either hunting and/or habitat alteration after the human arrival (Flannery 1994).

On one of Stirton's visits to the Western Australian Museum, he learned from the director, W. David L. Ride, of the discovery of temnospondyl amphibians (precursors of today's frogs and salamanders) from the Triassic Blina Shale in the Kimberley region of northeastern Western Australia. Stirton passed on that information to his Berkeley colleague, Charles L. Camp. Working jointly with staff from the Western Australian Museum, Camp and his student John Cosgriff first collected specimens from there in 1960. Cosgriff would return to Australia several times over the next two decades to both collect and study previously collected Triassic temnospondyls, not only in Western Australia but in Tasmania and New South Wales as well.

Returning from study in Britain in 1969, Anne Warren of LaTrobe University, Melbourne, and her students have continued the work on Triassic temnospondyls, concentrating primarily in Queensland. Warren also has described what at the time were the youngest temnospondyls anywhere in the world, first in the Early Jurassic of Queensland and then in the Early Cretaceous of Victoria. Recently, she described the first Carboniferous amphibian material from Australia.

The third expedition to greatly influence the subsequent course of Australian vertebrate paleontology was that of the Western Australian Museum and Natural History Museum (London) to the Late Devonian locality at Gogo. Only 150 kilometers east of the Triassic temnospondyl site in the Blina Shale, Gogo Station also is located in the remote Kimberley District of northeastern Western Australia. If one site can be said to be the most important fossil vertebrate locality in Australia, Gogo is it. This is because of the unique nature of fossil preservation there. At other sites, mid-Paleozoic fish are preserved, for the most part, as flattened, virtually two-dimensional fossils. At Gogo, by contrast, the remains are completely uncrushed. By careful use of acetic acid to prepare these three-dimensional specimens from the enclosing limestone, details of the skeleton can be determined readily, details that all too often are obscured completely in flattened specimens. Such exquisite preservation has led to solutions of questions on fundamental phylogenetic problems in paleoichthyology (study of ancient fishes) that applied worldwide.

Despite the outstanding preservation of Gogo material, and despite the existence of Gogo specimens in collections in the 1940s, it took Ride, as director of the Western Australian Museum, more than five years to find a paleoichthyologist who would investigate the Gogo area. Finally, in 1963, a joint field party from the Western Australian Museum and the Natural History Museum (London) carried out the first major collecting trip there. Since then, more than half the papers published on Australian fossil fishes have been devoted to Gogo specimens. Prominent among the Australian scholars investigating this material were Ken Campbell, R.E. Barwick, Gavin Young, and John Long. The British workers on these specimens include K. Dennis-Bryan, Brian Gardiner, Roger Miles, Harry Toombs, and Errol White.

Most other Australian paleoichthyological investigations since the 1950s have been devoted to mid-Paleozoic specimens. Particularly of note here are the several joint studies by Cambell and Barwick on lungfishes, principally from New South Wales. Notable fish studies of other periods were of Ordovician and Cretaceous specimens. From the Stairways Sandstone of the Northern Territory have come two genera of heterostracan agnathans (jawless fishes), described by Alexander Ritchie and J. Gilbert-Tomlinson. The better preserved of these, *Arandaspis*, is one of the earliest fishes known from a skeleton rather than as merely disarticulated (broken up, scattered) fragments. A freshwater fish fauna was described by Michael Waldman from the Koonwarra site of Early Cretaceous age in Victoria. Subsequently, the plants and invertebrates from there were described in detail, making the Koonwarra assemblage one of the most thoroughly studied of any Australian fossil vertebrate locality to date.

Susan Turner has pursued a vigorous study of Paleozoic microvertebrates, particularly thelodonts (scaly, jawless fishes), in order to use them as biostratigraphic tools. Systematic investigations of Mesozoic and Cenozoic lungfishes and Cenozoic sharks have been carried out by Anne Kemp and Noel Kemp (no relation), respectively.

After Longman's work in the 1920s through 1940s (except for one 1967 paper by Edwin H. Colbert and Duncan Merrilees noting the presence of dinosaur footprints, or "trackways," near Broome, Western Australia), little was done on Cretaceous tetrapods (animals that move on four legs) until the 1970s. In that decade, Wade, R. Anthony Thulborn, and Ralph E. Molnar became active in Queensland; and Vickers-Rich and Rich did work in Victoria. In the following decade, Paul Willis also worked in Queensland. As well as studying osteological (bone-based) material, Thulborn and Wade and later Timothy Hamley also investigated dinosaur trackways. It has proven to be a highly fruitful approach. Not only have these scholars supplemented the meager Cretaceous record of Australia dinosaurs, but they also have documented the presence of a diverse Jurassic dinosaurian fauna. Other than footprints, Jurassic dinosaurs from Australia are known, but only on the basis of a single partial skeleton. In the Triassic, footprints are the sole basis for knowledge of Australian dinosaurs. The work of Vickers-Rich and Rich in Victoria was part of a program to both document the area's Early Cretaceous vertebrate fauna and determine its biotic and physical setting. Interest in these latter aspects was spurred on by knowledge that the area was located within the Antarctic Circle during that period.

One of the shifts that took place after 1950 was an expansion of the scope of Australian vertebrate paleontological investigations. In addition to systematic and biogeographic analyses (which, however, still remained central), there was a greater emphasis on other aspects such as paleoecology and functional anatomy.

The Way Ahead

The history of vertebrate paleontology in Australia is a reflection of the general progress of science in the country, which in turn is correlated highly with the state of science in Western Europe, particularly Great Britain, and North America. When pure science flourished in those other areas, such as the four decades after World War II, it flourished in Australia as well. At the present time, economic rationalist policy has affected the pursuit of Australian vertebrate paleontology adversely, as it has elsewhere. At this writing (1997), only two persons under the age of 40 are employed permanently as vertebrate paleontologists and one of them is 39. Twenty years ago, about half were younger than that. In addition, in the past ten years, no vacated positions in paleontology have been filled, although two new ones have been created. This reflects the fact that, with the exception of the Queensland Museum, there is no Australian institutional tradition for maintaining an ongoing commitment to vertebrate paleontological research. Rather, vertebrate paleontologists, in general, continue to obtain positions in a geology or biology department and practice the science from there during their careers. When such individuals leave or retire, there is no attempt to maintain a position in vertebrate paleontology, so the position closes behind them.

Indications are that the spectacular growth in vertebrate paleontology through the decades of the 1960s to 1980s (indicated in Figure 3 and Table 2) will not be maintained in the 1990s. Whether the future will see levels of research activity characteristic of those halcyon decades or see them decline to a level comparable to that of the first decade of the twentieth century is yet to be seen. The decline already hinted at in the preliminary publication figures for the 1990s is likely to portend a continuing downward trend because there is no deep, ongoing Australian institutional commitment to intellectual pursuits and because the community of vertebrate paleontologists is aging. Exactly why this lack of intellectual commitment should be so is not altogether clear, but it is nothing new in Australia. McGuire (1939) described a similar phenomenon nearly sixty years ago.

THOMAS H. RICH

See also Australia: Invertebrate Paleontology; Australia: Paleobotany; Plate Tectonics and Continental Drift

Works Cited

Blainey, G. 1966. *The Tyranny of Distance: How Distance Shaped Australia's History.* Melbourne: Macmillan and Sun Books; New York: St. Martin's Press; London: Macmillan, 1980.
Flannery, T.F. 1994. *The Future Eaters.* Chatswood, New South Wales: Reed; New York: Braziller.
McGuire, P. 1939. *Australia: Her Heritage, Her Future.* New York: Stokes; as *Australian Journey,* London: Heinemann, 1939.
Rich, T.H. 1996. What next in Australian dinosaur research? *The Dinosaur Report* 7–9.
Rich, T.H., and G.C. Young. 1996. Vertebrate biogeographic evidence for connections of the East and Southeast Asian blocks with Gondwana. *Australian Journal of Earth Sciences* 43 (6):625–34.
Vickers-Rich, P., J.M. Monaghan, R.F. Baird, and T.H. Rich (eds.). 1991. *Vertebrate Paleontology of Australasia.* Melbourne: Pioneer Design Studio, with the Monash University Publications Committee.

Further Reading

Archer, M., and S. Hand. 1984. Background to the search for Australia's oldest mammals. *In* M. Archer and G. Clayton (eds.), *Vertebrate Zoogeography and Evolution in Australasia: Animals in Space and Time.* Carlisle, Washington: Hesperian.
Mahoney, J.A., and W.D.L. Ride. 1975. Index to the genera and species of fossil Mammalia described from Australia and New Guinea between 1838 and 1968 (including citations of type species and primary type specimens). *Western Australia Museum Special Publications* 6:1–249.
Mather, P., et al. 1986. A time for a museum: The history of the Queensland Museum 1862–1986. *Memoirs of the Queensland Museum* 24:1–365.
Rich, P.V., G.F. van Tets, and F. Knight (eds.). 1985. *Kadimakara: The History of Australia's Backboned Animals.* Lilydale, Victoria: Pioneer Design Studio; 2nd ed., Princeton, New Jersey: Princeton University Press, 1990.
Vickers-Rich, P., J.M. Monaghan, R.F. Baird, and T.H. Rich (eds.). 1991. *Vertebrate Paleontology of Australasia.* Melbourne: Pioneer Design Studio, with the Monash University Publications Committee.
Vickers-Rich, P., and T.H. Rich. 1991. *Wildlife of Gondwana.* Balgowlah, New South Wales: Reed; 2nd ed., Chatswood, New South Wales: Reed, 1993.

AUTOTROPHS
See Skeletized Microorganisms: Algae

AVES
See Bird

BATS

The order Chiroptera (bats) is one of the most widespread, diverse, and highly specialized mammalian orders. It is also the only group of mammals to have evolved powered flight. The bats are divided into two suborders, the Megachiroptera (Old World fruit bats) and the Microchiroptera (echolocating bats). The Megachiroptera consists of a single family, the Pteropodidae, with 42 genera (large groupings; singular, genus) that encompass 166 species. They range from Africa to the tropical parts of Asia, through the Indo-Malayan region to Australia, and east to the Cook Islands. The Microchiroptera is composed of 17 large families, which are subdivided into 135 genera that encompass 830 species. This order has a worldwide distribution, with the exception of Antarctica and some of the more remote ocean islands (Table 1).

The oldest pteropodid is *Archaeopteropus transiens* from the lower Oligocene of Italy. The oldest known microchiropteran is *Icaronycteris index* from the lower Eocene of Europe and North America. Although there are many excellently preserved bat fossils, they provide little information about the origins of bats because the known fossils are already completely evolved megachiropterans or microchiropterans.

Bats are an incredibly diverse group of mammals, so much so that it is impossible to describe adequately that diversity here. The megachiropterans (weighing approximately 20 to 1,500 grams) are generally larger than microchiropterans (approximately 1.5 to 150 grams), although there is a large degree of overlap between the two groups. The megachiropterans feed on fruit, flowers, nectar, and pollen. As shown in Table 1, the microchiropterans also feed on these items, as well as on blood, insects, frogs, lizards, fish, small mammals (including other bats), and even scorpions (Altringham 1996; Hill and Smith 1984).

The morphology (form and structure) of the teeth in the two suborders reflects this dietary diversity. Microbats show a wide diversity in dental morphology. Even so, this diversity is based on the teeth of an "insectivorous" ancestor characterized by large W-shaped shearing crests (ridges) on the molars. Megabats, however, tend to have rounded, bulbous molar teeth with little topographical relief. Bats are generally nocturnal, but the microbats are the only ones with well-developed echolocation abilities. The megabats generally navigate using sight and smell. They may travel long distances between food sources, but some microbats, on the other hand, migrate hundreds of kilometers between foraging sites and hibernation sites.

The most striking feature of any bat is the degree to which the skeleton has become modified for flight. The wing is supported by the forelimb and hand (Figure 1). The form and structure of the arm and hand have become greatly modified, to the point where the fingers can be spread through 180 degrees. The forearm is much longer than the upper arm, and the collarbone is also longer than that of most other mammals. These features result in a wide wingspan. The forelimb bones of bats are lighter and more slender than in most other mammals and are specialized to withstand the forces placed on them during flight. The shoulders of bats, especially microbats, are also highly specialized for flight, and these specializations also may reflect the particular flight mode of a species. Bats with long thin wings usually are found flying in the open air and may migrate long distances. Conversely, bats with shorter and broader wings often are found flying within the forest canopy, where maneuverability is more important. Like birds, many bats have a "keeled" (ridged) breastbone for the attachment of strong flight muscles, although this character is particularly variable among different types of bats.

The hind limbs of bats are also highly specialized and the thigh bones have rotated to the side so that the legs protrude to the side. During flight this arrangement helps to support the tail membrane in an advantageous position. It also gives many bats a "spiderlike" appearance when walking because the legs appear to be attached "backwards."

Because flight takes a lot of energy, bats also have highly specialized body functions. A bat's heart is more than three times larger than that of other mammals of similar size. It also beats very fast during flight, faster than other mammals' hearts beat when running. To further aid in oxygen transport, some bats have relatively more red blood cells than nonflying mammals. Also, bat flight muscles have an increased blood supply, more mitochondria

Table 1: Diversity in Bats

	Current Geographic Distribution	Diet	Temporal Distribution*	Earliest Fossil*	Site
Megachiroptera					
Pteropodidae	Old World tropics	Fruit, flowers, nectar, pollen	Lower Oligocene to Recent	*Archaeopteropus*	Italy
Microchiroptera					
Rhinopomatidae	North Africa to Southeast Asia	Insects	Extant		
Craseonycteridae	Thailand	Insects	Extant		
Emballonuridae	Old and New World Tropics	Insects	Lower Eocene to Recent	*Eppsinycteris*	England
Rhinolophidae	Britain and Africa to SE Asia, Japan and Australia	Insects	Upper Eocene to Recent	*Rhinolophus*	France
Hipposideridae	Old World tropics and subtropics	Insects	Middle Eocene to Recent	*Hipposideros*	Europe
Nycteridae	Africa to Near East, and Southeast Asia, Java, Sumatra, Borneo, Bali, and Kangean Islands	Insects, scorpions, frogs, birds, bats, and other small vertebrates	?Upper Oligocene to Recent	?Nycteridae	France
Megadermatidae	Old World tropics	Insects, fish, frogs, reptiles, birds, bats, rodents, and large invertebrates	Upper Eocene to Recent	*Necromantis*	France
Mystacinidae	New Zealand	Insects, fruit, nectar, pollen, carrion	Extant		
Noctilionidae	New World tropics	Insects, fish, crustaceans	Upper Pleistocene to Recent	*Noctilio*	West Indies
Mormoopidae	New World tropics	Insects	Lower Pleistocene to Recent	*Pteronotus*	Central America
Phyllostomidae	New World tropics	Insects, fruit, nectar, pollen, small vertebrates, and blood	Middle Miocene to Recent	*Notonycteris*	Columbia
Vespertilionidae	Worldwide except Arctic, Antarctic, and some Pacific islands	Insects, fish, small vertebrates	Middle Eocene to Recent	*Stehlinia*	Switzerland

Table 1: Diversity in Bats (Continued)

	Current Geographic Distribution	Diet	Temporal Distribution*	Earliest Fossil*	Site
Natalidae	New World tropics	Insects	Lower Eocene to Recent	*Honrovits*	United States (Wyoming)
Furipteridae	New World tropics	Insects	Extant		
Thyropteridae	New World tropics	Insects	Extant		
Myzopodidae	Madagascar	Insects	Lower Pleistocene to Recent	*Myzopoda*	Africa
Molossidae	Old and New World tropics and temperate regions	Insects	Middle Eocene to Recent	*Wellia*	Canada
Fossil Families					
Philisidae			Upper Eocene	*Philisis*	Egypt
Icaronycteridae			Upper Paleocene to middle Eocene	*Icaronycteris*	Europe and North America
Palaeochiropterygidae			Upper Paleocene to middle Eocene	*Archaeonycteris &* *Palaeochiropteryx*	Europe

* Data on fossil taxa and distributions were taken from Stucky and McKenna (1993), with the following exceptions: Rhinolophidae (Savage and Russell 1983), Emballonuridae (Hooker 1996), and Natalidae (Beard et al. 1992).

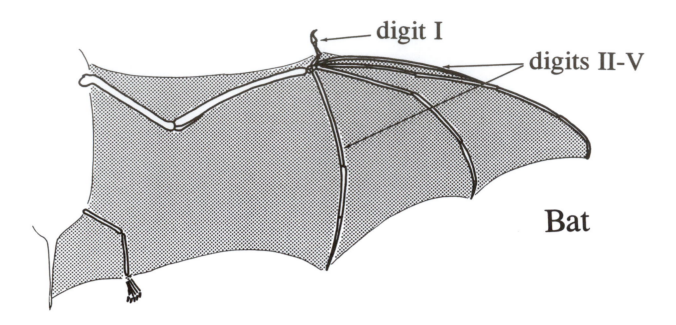

Figure 1. Wing structure in bats. The wing membrane consists of a stippled spread controlled by the fore and hind limbs and the tail. Illustration by S. Christopher Bennett.

(energy-producing structures in cells), and more myoglobin (proteins in muscle cells that transport oxygen from blood to mitochondria). These factors facilitate oxygen transfer, necessary for efficient functioning of the flight muscles.

Echolocation is the means by which microchiropterans orient to their surroundings and capture prey. They emit high-frequency sound pulses (inaudible to the human ear) and listen to the echoes of these pulses as the sound waves bounce off objects. Although echolocation generally is considered to be a characteristic of microbats, some megabats also echolocate (e.g., *Rousettus* uses echolocation to navigate within cave roost sites, producing sound pulses by clicking the tongue). Some insectivorans, birds, cetaceans, and possibly some marsupials and rodents also use echolocation.

Microchiropterans produce sound pulses in the larynx ("voice box"), which is enlarged greatly compared to other mammals. Echolocation call structure varies widely between families of microbats and often is correlated with habitat structure, foraging needs, or other specific requirements. Opinions vary on the degree to which echolocation was developed in the earliest microbats. However, the morphology of the inner ear of these fossils strongly suggests that some degree of echolocation was present in the earliest known microbats, *Icaronycteris* and *Palaeochiropteryx*.

One of the most striking features of many microchiropterans is the great degree of facial ornamentation, in the form of "noseleaves." Such ornamentation may act to focus the sound pulses that these bats emit during echolocation. The external ears (the pinnae) of microbats often are large and complex. A tragus (a projection within the pinna) contributes to the acute sense of hearing and may be adapted for enhanced direction-finding ability. The inner ear of

microchiropterans also is highly specialized for echolocation. The eardrum is small and thin, and the three inner ear bones are very light. This allows the high-frequency echolocation pulses to be more efficiently passed to the inner ear. The bat's inner ear has more complete spiral turns than that of other mammals, and the diameter of the base of the spiral canal is also greater. All of these characters are adaptations to hearing high-frequency sounds.

The evolution of powered flight is a topic that has received much attention for both birds and bats. Most bat researchers would prefer a scenario where bats began living in trees, then glided from branches, and finally evolved flight. This contrasts with the theory popular among many dinosaur and bird experts, in which land-based animals began to evolve flight by hopping from place to place. The key element in the attainment of powered flight is producing enough thrust (the power to move forward) to overcome the effects of drag (air friction that hinders forward movement). The portion of the wing that stretches between the bat's body and the fifth finger produces most of the lift that the bat needs. The portion of the wing made up of the hand produces thrust both during the wing's downstroke and upstroke. In some microbats this part of the wing also has a role in capturing insects.

The Megachiroptera and Microchiroptera traditionally have been considered each other's closest relatives. However, it has been proposed (Pettigrew et al. 1989) that megachiropterans are related to primates more closely than they are to microchiropterans. This hypothesis is based largely on characters of the visual pathways of the brain, which megabats shared with primates and colugos (so-called flying lemurs). This interpretation requires megabats and microbats to have evolved from separate ancestors and requires powered flight and wings to have evolved independently in each lineage. The independent origin of the megachiroptera and microchiroptera, although still supported by some researchers, subsequently has been rejected in numerous studies of morphological and molecular evidence.

An older hypothesis, dating from 1811, proposes that bats and colugos actually belong together in a single group, the Volitantia, because they are related to each other more closely than either is to any other mammalian group. Furthermore, given the extent of their gliding membrane, colugos often have been proposed as a reasonable analogue (model) for a bat ancestor at a preflight stage of evolution. Bats and colugos do share a large number of anatomical similarities, but it is sometimes difficult to determine which characters indicate close evolutionary relatedness and which indicate independent adaptations to a common lifestyle, for example, flight. Such characters include the presence of a flight membrane between the fingers and a gracile postcranial (body) skeleton with greatly elongate limbs. Also, both colugos and bats have a locking mechanism in the tendons of their feet that permits them to hang suspended for long periods of time with little muscular effort. There are also numerous skull and tooth similarities between bats and colugos (Racey and Swift 1995). Given all of these similarities, it is easy to see why early scholars believed bats and colugos to be closely related. This hypothesis still has more support than that of the independent origin of bats.

BRIAN J. STAFFORD AND ERIC J. SARGIS

See also Aerial Locomotion; Dermopterans

Works Cited

Altringham, J.D. 1996. *Bats: Biology and Behavior.* New York and Oxford: Oxford University Press.

Beard, K.C., B. Sige, and L. Krishtalka. 1992. A primitive vespertilionoid bat from the early Eocene of central Wyoming. *Comptes rendus de l'Académie des Sciences* 314:735–41.

Hill, J.E., and J.D. Smith. 1984. *Bats: A Natural History.* London: British Museum of Natural History; Austin, Texas: University of Texas Press.

Hooker, J.J. 1996. A primitive emballonurid bat (Chiroptera, Mammalia) from the earliest Eocene of England. *Palaeovertebrata* 25:287–300.

Pettigrew, J.D., B.G.M. Jamieson, S.K. Robson, L.S. Hall, K.I. McAnally, and H.M. Cooper. 1989. Phylogenetic relations between microbats, megabats and primates (Mammalia: Chiroptera and Primates). *Philosophical Transactions of the Royal Society of London* 325:489–559.

Racey, P.A., and S.M. Swift (eds.). 1995. *Ecology, Evolution, and Behavior of Bats.* Symposia of the Zoological Society of London, 67. Oxford: Clarendon; New York: Oxford University Press.

Savage, D.E., and D.E. Russell. 1983. *Mammalian Paleofaunas of the World.* Reading, Massachusetts: Addison Wesley.

Stucky, R.K., and M.C. McKenna. 1993. Mammalia. *In* M.J. Benton (ed.), *The Fossil Record.* Vol. 2, London and New York: Chapman and Hall.

Further Reading

Wilson, D.E. 1997. *Bats in Question: The Smithsonian Answer Book.* Washington, D.C.: Smithsonian Institution Press.

Wimsatt, W.A. (ed.). 1970. *Biology of Bats.* New York: Academic Press.

BIOMASS AND PRODUCTIVITY ESTIMATES

When paleoecologists seek to understand terrestrial vegetation, one of the parameters they try to assess is biomass, the total estimated abundance or mass of all plants or of particular plant taxa. Such estimates are useful in determining patterns of plant diversity and dominance.

Various biases can distort attempts at biomass estimation. These include (1) uneven patterns of production and shedding of leaves and reproductive organs; (2) unequal rates of decay of dispersed plant parts both prior to and after burial; (3) different transport potentials of isolated plant parts (e.g., a trunk will not travel very far after death whereas a leaf may settle a great distance away); and (4) mixture of spatially and ecologically distinct vegetation types. The study of the processes that precede and lead to fossilization is called taphonomy. Burnham and colleagues (1992) describe the relationship of taphonomic studies to the investigation of fossil plant assemblages.

Most paleoecological studies of plant fossils have focused on compression-impression assemblages, two-dimensional fossils preserved within shales or sandstones. Compression-impression assemblages generally preserve leaves and reproductive organs, although stem remains are common at some sites and in rocks of certain geological ages. Petrified three-dimensional fossils also have been studied quantitatively.

Quantitative estimates of biomass focus on assemblages from deposits where water or other forces have not been involved in transporting plant parts, minimizing the mixing of plants from different sources. Examples include deposits from small lakes, abandoned channels, buried floodplain surfaces, or lagoons. Sampling is generally restricted to a rock unit that represents one kind of depositional environment, even if that environment may have accumulated sediment over a number of years. Often it is possible to make a series of samples in a deposit along specific bedding surfaces to obtain a very detailed picture of the changes in the flora over time. Generally, however, fossils are sampled from the deposit as a whole, without regard to position within the rock unit, to provide an average picture of the source vegetation over the time during which sediment accumulated. In these cases, the fossil assemblage is described as "time averaged."

In most instances, an area varying from a minimum 0.5 meters to a maximum of 3 meters on a side is excavated and treated as a sampling "site," although much larger areas may be sampled. Taphonomic studies indicate that sites of small area draw their samples from less than 1 hectare of surrounding forest. When split open, compression-impression fossils often appear on both sides of the fractured surface. To be sure that data are not doubled, in all instances described below, only one surface of a "part-counterpart" combination is analyzed.

Compressions and Impressions

The estimate method is the simplest means of sampling an assemblage and permits plant taxa to be ordered semiquantitatively. Following the Braun-Blanquet technique, relative abundance of fossil taxa in an assemblage are estimated as "abundant," "common," "rare," or "present" (Spicer 1988). Successful application requires experience, but, because the categories are broad, precision can be high.

The quadrat method, developed by H.W. Pfefferkorn and colleagues (1975), is a way to determine rapidly a numerical assessment of relative abundance. Each hand specimen from an excavation is treated as a "quadrat." Species occurring on each quadrat are noted. Abundances are represented as frequencies: one calculates the percent of the total number of quadrats sampled in which a species occurred. Consequently, abundances are independent, at least hypothetically; all species could be represented on 100 percent of the quadrats. Quadrat methods do have disadvantages. They tend to underestimate the abundances of the most common taxa and overestimate the abundances of the rarest. Nonetheless, the results provide a numerical basis for ranking the abundances of species.

Count methods are more labor intensive than estimates or quadrat analysis but provide interval scale quantitative data (Wing and DiMichele 1996). All individual plant parts are counted and attributed to specific taxa. Then relative species abundances can be ranked as percentages of the total specimen count. This method works best when the entire assemblage consists of similar-sized leaves, a situation most likely to be encountered with assemblages dominated by angiosperms (flowering plants). The count method can greatly under- or overestimate abundance when the assemblage consists of species that produce identifiable parts of different sizes, such as leaves mixed with pinnules or large stem fragments.

Several methods have been developed to provide quantitative estimates of biomass while avoiding the pitfalls of counting methods. All are labor intensive and generally require exposure of bedding surfaces. Point counting was employed by A.C. Scott (1978), who used a one square meter piece of plexiglass with 100 holes drilled randomly in the surface. Placed on the exposed bedding surface, all plant parts under holes were identified, providing a quantitative estimate of species abundances. W. Lamboy and A. Lesnikowska (1988) also employed point counting but made their estimates in the laboratory. A square-meter sample area was filled with specimens; meter rulers were placed at right angles along each side to act as x and y axes; random x-y coordinates were generated for 100 points; plant parts were identified and tallied. S.L. Wing and colleagues (1995) employed a line-intercept method to analyze floodplain vegetation buried in place by volcanic ash. They strung frames at 2 centimeter intervals with parallel lines, further

marked off in 2 centimeter intervals. A frame was placed over excavated blocks of rock, and the number of 2-centimeter intervals intercepted by each identifiable plant fossil was recorded. The line intercept method is a sensitive measure of the bedding surface area covered by a fossil and is thus an excellent tool for estimating original plant photosynthetic surface. Some scholars have placed clear acetate sheets on bedding surfaces and traced the outlines of identifiable fossils; the outlines are then digitized to produce exact measures of surface cover.

Petrifactions

The most common petrified plant deposits analyzed quantitatively are "coal-ball" deposits from Carboniferous age coal beds. Coal balls are concretions, generally of calcium carbonate, that three-dimensionally preserve the original peat stages of the coal, formed from the litter of the peat-swamp forest. Coal balls must be sliced into thin sections, or acetate "peels" must be prepared to expose the petrified plant parts (Phillips et al. 1976). The thin section or acetate peel is attached to a clear acetate grid ruled in square centimeters. For each square centimeter of peel surface, the plant part, its organ affinity, and aspects of its preservation state are recorded. Results can be tabulated by taxa and by organ type. Methods for collecting and quantifying coal-ball samples were developed by T.L. Phillips and colleagues (1977).

WILLIAM A. DiMICHELE AND SCOTT L. WING

See also Population Dynamics; Trophic Groups and Levels

Works Cited

Burnham, R.J., S.L. Wing, and G.G. Parker. 1992. The reflection of deciduous forest communities in leaf litter: Implications for autochthonous litter assemblages from the fossil record. *Paleobiology* 18:30–49.

Lamboy, W., and A. Lesnikowska. 1988. Some statistical methods useful in the analysis of plant paleoecological data. *Palaios* 3:86–94.

Pfefferkorn, H.W., H. Mustafa, and H. Hass. 1975. Quantitative Charakterisierung Oberkarboner Abdruckfloren. *Neues Jahrbuch für Geologie und Paläontologie Abhandlungen* 150:253–69.

Phillips, T.L., M.H. Avcin, and D. Berggren. 1976. *Fossil Peat of the Illinois Basin*. Illinois State Geological Survey, Educational Series, 11. Urbana: Illinois State Geological Survey.

Phillips, T.L., A.B. Kunz, and D.J. Mickish. 1977. Paleobotany of permineralized peat (coalballs) from the Herrin Coal Member of the Illinois basin. *In* D.H. Given and A.D. Cohen (eds.), *Interdisciplinary Studies of Peat and Coal Origins*. Geological Society of America Microform Publication, 7. Boulder, Colorado: Geological Society of America.

Scott, A.C. 1978. Sedimentological and ecological control of Westphalian B plant assemblages from West Yorkshire. *Proceedings of the Yorkshire Geological Society* 41:461–508.

Spicer, R.A. 1988. Quantitative sampling of plant megafossil assemblages. *In* W.A. DiMichele and S.L. Wing (eds.), *Methods and Applications of Plant Paleoecology*. Paleontological Society Special Publication. Knoxville: University of Tennessee-Knoxville.

Wing, S.L., L.J. Hickey, and C.C. Swisher. 1995. Implications of an exceptional fossil flora for Late Cretaceous vegetation. *Nature* 363:342–45.

Wing, S.L., and W.A. DiMichele. 1996. Conflict between local and global changes in plant diversity through geological time. *Palaios* 10:551–64.

BIOMECHANICS

Engineering mechanics deals with movements and forces, structures and mechanisms. Biomechanics is the application of these same elements to organisms, treating plants, animals, and people as problems in engineering. In biomechanical studies of living animals, we analyze film of their movements, measure the forces they exert, and perform a wide variety of experiments. Such methods are not generally available for research on extinct organisms, but biomechanics is nevertheless very useful in paleontology (Alexander 1989a, 1989b; Rayner and Wootton 1991). The following examples illustrate the diversity of paleontological biomechanics.

A Rhipidistian Skull Mechanism

The rhipidistians are the extinct fishes from which the amphibians evolved. We will look at the distinctive structure of a rhipidistian skull and see how it probably functioned in feeding (Thomson 1967). First, we need to know that most modern fishes feed by sucking in food, which they do largely by widening the mouth cavity, and that most modern fishes tilt their snouts up as they open their mouths to feed.

A fish skull consists of a cranium, which encloses the brain, with attachments such as the jaws and the side walls of the mouth cavity. Rhipidistians are peculiar because they had a hinge joint halfway along the cranium (Figure 1B). The side walls of the mouth cavity (the palatoquadrate bones, Figure 1A) were connected to the front half of the cranium by hinge joints with horizontal axes (as indicated by a broken line in Figure 1A). Behind them were the hyomandibular bones, connected to the rear part of the cranium by steeply-sloping hinges. Let us think how the skull would have moved, looking at it as an engineer would examine a mechanism.

When a rhipidistian fed, it presumably enlarged the mouth cavity to suck food in by swinging the palatoquadrate and hyomandibular bones laterally (out to the side). As the lower ends of the hyomandibulars swung outwards they must also have swung forwards, because of the sloping hinges. This would have pushed the palatoquadrates forward and made the front half of the cranium tilt up. Thus, as the mouth cavity was widened to suck food in, the snout would have tilted up automatically.

Jaws of a Synapsid Reptile

A strange transformation occurred as synapsid reptiles evolved to become mammals. Reptiles have many bones in the lower jaw (Figure 2A) but mammals have just one, the dentary bone (Figure 2C). Two of the bones lost from the jaw became incorporated into the mammalian ear, as one of the ear ossicles and the tympanic bulla (bone that holds the eardrum). The old joint between jaw and skull was lost, and a new one formed.

At an intermediate stage, in advanced synapsid reptiles, the original jaw joint was still functional, but the bones forming it were slender and weak (Figure 2B). As the jaw became weaker, the jaw muscles seem to have become much stronger, as evidenced by enlarged areas of muscle attachment on the skull and dentary bone. How could a weak joint be compatible with strong muscles?

A likely explanation emerged when scholars considered the arrangement of jaw muscles (Crompton 1963). The structure of the skull shows that the jaw muscles were arranged much more like those of mammals than of modern reptiles. There are temporalis muscles that pulled upward and backward on the dentary (lower jaw) (arrow *t*, Figure 2B), and masseter and pterygoid muscles that

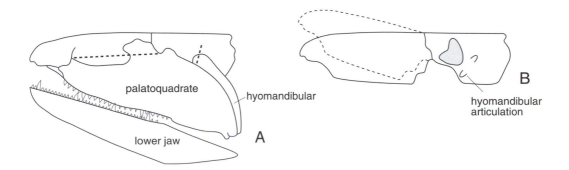

Figure 1. Diagrams of the jaw mechanism of a rhipidistian fish. *A*, broken lines showing the axes of hinge joints; *B*, broken line showing the movement of the joint in the cranium. Redrawn by Catherine P. Sexton after Alexander (1990).

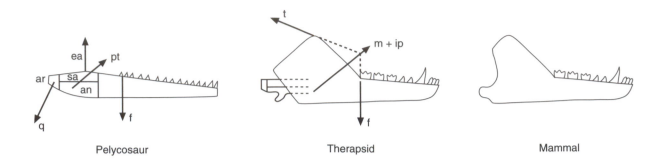

Figure 2. Diagrams of the lower jaws. Arrows represent forces, as described in the text. *A*, a typical reptile; *B*, a synapsid reptile; *C*, a mammal. Abbreviations: *ar*, *sa*, and *an*, bones lost from the jaw as the mammals evolved. Redrawn by Catherine P. Sexton after Alexander (1990).

pulled upward and forward (arrow *m* + *ip*). Imagine a synapsid biting hard with its back teeth, so that the food exerts a vertical force *f* on the jaw. By themselves, the forces *t* and *m* + *ip* could have balanced *f*, without the need for any force in the jaw joint. In contrast, the force *f* on the jaw of a more primitive reptile (Figure 2A) cannot be balanced by the muscle forces *ea* and *pt* alone, because the result of these two forces could not be in line with *f*. An additional force *q* must have acted at the jaw joint. Because the jaw muscles had become stronger in advanced mammal-like reptiles (Figure 2B), their new mammal-like arrangement may have made a strong jaw joint unnecessary.

Plant Stems

Plant stems and tree trunks are always in danger of being bent and broken by the weight of the plant or by wind forces. In the course of evolution, tall plants have acquired the strength to stand upright in several different ways (Mosbrugger 1990). Modern trees owe their strength to wood, which occupies most of the cross section of the trunk. On the outside is just a thin layer of bark and a slender pith may lie in the center. In gymnosperms (seed-bearing plants), the wood consists of tracheids, which serve both as strengthening fibres and as conduits for sap flow; in angiosperms (flowering plants), strengthening fibres and conducting vessels (vessels for conducting water and plant products) are distinct cell types, but in both cases the wood serves both functions.

Palaeozoic lycopods such as *Lepidodendron* (which grew to heights of 40 meters or more) were quite differently constructed. Strength was supplied by a thick outer layer (periderm) composed of fibres with no conducting function. Conduction was performed by relatively weak tracheids in an inner cylinder of wood. When placed around the outside of a trunk, strengthening tissue is most effective against forces tending to bend the trunk. The periderm thickness is typically 20 percent or less of trunk diameter, but this was enough to make the stem almost as strong when bending as if it were solid periderm. The centrally-placed tracheids contributed hardly anything to strength.

Dinosaur Speeds

Fossil footprints have been found of dinosaurs of all sizes, from ones as small as chickens to sauropods six times as heavy as a large elephant. In the course of time, the mud or sand in which the prints were formed has become compacted to become rock, preserving the impressions. By measuring the spacing of the prints, scholars have been able to estimate the speeds at which the dinosaurs were moving (Alexander 1989b).

The principle is simple, but there is a complication. A human takes short strides when walking slowly, longer strides when walking fast, and even longer strides when running. In other words, the faster we go, the longer our strides, and the same is true of animals. The complication is that stride length depends on the size of the animal as well as on its speed. When a dog and a horse are running side by side at the same speed, the dog takes shorter strides, but more of them.

The fossil footprints show that dinosaurs walked and ran like mammals, placing their feet under the body, not far out to the side, as in modern reptiles. For this reason, researchers made comparisons with mammals rather than with modern reptiles as the basis for estimates of dinosaur speeds. The method depends on the concept of "dynamic similarity," which is perhaps most easily explained in terms of motion picture films. Suppose you had films of similarly shaped animals of different sizes (possibly a cat and a tiger) who were walking or running. If you projected the films side by side and ran the projectors at different speeds, you could make the two animals seem to take the same number of strides per second. Also, by positioning the projectors at different distances from the screen you could adjust the sizes of the images to make the cat and tiger appear equal in size. If these adjustments made the movements of the two images identical, you could safely infer that the movements of the real animals were dynamically similar. More generally, dynamically similar movements can be made identical by uniform changes of the scales of length, time, and force. (Heavy tigers exert larger forces on the ground than light cats.)

Gravitational forces (the animal's weight) are obviously important in walking and running. A basic physical principle tells us that if gravity is important, dynamic similarity is possible only if

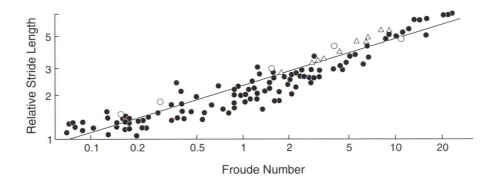

Figure 3. A graph of relative stride length against Froude number. Three groups represented by several points for a range of Froude numbers. Symbols: *triangles,* kangaroos; *hollow circles,* humans; *filled circles,* other mammals; *line,* an equation used for estimating dinosaur speeds from stride lengths. Redrawn by Catherine P. Sexton after Alexander (1989a).

the animals being compared are moving with equal Froude numbers—that is, with equal values of (speed)^2 ÷ (gravitational acceleration × leg length). Animals of different sizes moving in dynamically similar fashion will have equal values of (stride length ÷ leg length), so they must also have equal Froude numbers. For example, if a tiger with legs four times as long as a cat is moving in dynamically similar fashion to the cat, its strides must be four times as long as the cat's and it must be travelling with twice the speed (2^2 = 4).

Cats are not quite the same shape as tigers, and other mammals are more different. Nevertheless, a rule relating relative stride length (stride length ÷ leg length) to Froude number has been shown to work well for mammals ranging from cats to elephants, even bipeds such as humans and kangaroos (Figure 3). It seems reasonable to assume that the same relationship will hold for dinosaurs.

To make the calculations, first the dinosaur's stride length must be measured from the fossil track, and its leg length estimated from the size of the individual footprints. Relative stride length is calculated, and the line in Figure 3 is used to find the corresponding Froude number. Using leg length again, speed is calculated from the Froude number.

All footprints of large dinosaurs investigated in this way show slow speeds, around one meter per second (a slow human walking speed) for sauropods, and two meters per second (a fast human walk) for large theropods. However, a few trackways of smaller dinosaurs seem to show speeds matching a human sprint. Also, calculations based on the thicknesses of their leg bones suggest that large dinosaurs were capable of faster running than the footprints show. For example, the large sauropod *Apatosaurus* had leg bones that seem strong enough for it to have moved with as much agility as a modern elephant. Maximum speeds were probably used only rarely, making it unlikely that they would appear in the relatively few tracks that have been found.

Cephalaspids Swimming

Cephalaspids (Figure 4), fish from the Late Silurian (approximately 415 million years ago), evolved in the sea, then moved into freshwater bodies of water. This ancient fish had a head enclosed in a thick shield of cartilage, with a thin outer covering of bone. The rest of the body was covered by thick bony scales. Cartilage and bone are both denser than water, with specific gravities of about 1.1 and 2.0 respectively, and there is no reason to believe that this early fish had a gas bladder or any other kind of organ to promote buoyancy. Since a cephalaspid must have been considerably denser than the water in which it swam, it must have depended on hydrodynamic lift forces to keep it from sinking to the bottom. (Similarly, aeroplanes are kept airborne by aerodynamic lift.)

S.J. Bunker and K.E. Machin (1991) set out to discover how a cephalaspid got the necessary lift. They used a double-size model of a 38 centimeter cephalaspid. Their goal was to discover the forces that would have acted on the fish when it swam at various speeds, with its body tilted at various angles to the direction of swimming, and with its pectoral flippers held in various positions. The obvious method would have been to hold the model in a stream of water flowing at a likely swimming speed and measure the forces on the model. Instead, Bunker and Machin found it more convenient to make their measurements in a wind tunnel (a standard piece of equipment in aerodynamics laboratories), in which air instead of water flowed past the model.

The pattern of air flow around an object in a wind tunnel is the same as the pattern of water flow around that object in a stream, provided the two flows have equal values of a number called the Reynolds number. This number has the same significance for movements in which viscosity is important as Froude numbers have where gravity is important. For flows around an object in air and in water to have the same pattern, the air must flow 15 times as fast as the water (at 20 degrees centigrade). The forces on a body moving through water at speed v are not the same as the forces in an air flow of speed $15v$ but can be calculated from them.

Most of the measurements were made at an air speed corresponding to a (probably realistic) swimming speed of 1 meter per second. It was found that when the fish was precisely hori-

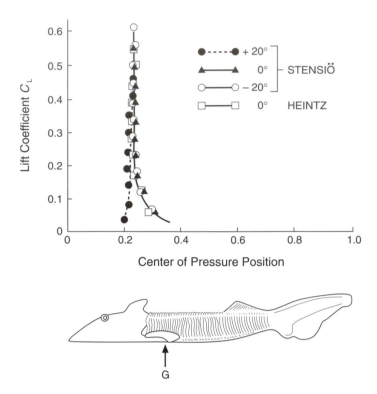

Figure 4. Graph of lift obtainable in a cephalaspid model. Tests of the body tilted at various angles of attack to form different center of pressure positions. Symbols: G, center of mass; miscellaneous symbols, different flipper angles and alternative restorations of the tail by Stensiö and Heintz. Redrawn by Catherine P. Sexton after Bunker and Machin (1991).

zontal, facing into a horizontal current, very little lift acted on it. This implies that in a current the fish could have rested on the bottom, with little danger of being lifted and dislodged by the flow. When the body was tilted head-up, upward lift acted on it. This was estimated to be enough to keep a swimming cephalaspid off the bottom, at any swimming speed over about 0.3 meters per second. (Higher speeds require less tilting of the body.)

Figure 4 shows that regardless of the angle at which the flippers were held and which of two alternative restorations of the tail was used, the center of pressure (the point at which the lift can be considered to act) was always about one quarter of body length back from the snout. This is a little forward of the estimated position of the center of mass of the fish, which was approximately at the center of buoyancy (the geometric center of the body). Therefore, the lift on the body cannot have been the only upward force on the fish; if it were, it would have made the fish tilt progressively more nose-up as it swam. To balance the forces, the beating of the tail must have supplied a little upward lift behind the center of mass. The similarly-shaped tails of sharks have just that effect. It was concluded that cephalaspid swimming worked like shark swimming, with this difference: Sharks get most of their lift from their wing-like pectoral fins, but cephalaspids got most of theirs from the body.

Soaring *Pteranodon*

The giant pterosaur *Pteranodon* had a wing span of seven meters, twice the span of the largest modern albatross. Although not the largest pterosaur known, *Pteranodon* is the largest for which we have sufficiently complete remains to make reasonably confident estimates of flight performance. Although the wings were so long, the body was small and so lightly built that the animal's mass is estimated to have been only 15 to 17 kilograms. (For comparison, the largest vultures, albatrosses, and swans all weigh about 10 kilograms.)

Most of today's very large birds flap their wings very little, keeping airborne by soaring in rising air. Vultures and pelicans gain height by circling in thermals (warm air that is rising over ground heated by the sun). Many other large birds depend on slope soaring, using wind that is deflected upward when it blows against a hillside or a large wave; condors soar over hillsides, and albatrosses soar along waves. Thermal soarers need to be able to glide in tight circles in order to stay within a narrow thermal as they rise. That means they must be able to glide well at low speeds. In contrast, slope soarers need to be able to glide fast, to avoid being blown downwind. Different requirements call for different wing designs, and studies of the two styles form the basis of attempts to discover the flying habits of *Pteranodon* (Brower 1983; Padian 1985).

Gliding performance both of animals and of aircraft depends largely on two quantities, "wing loading" and "aspect ratio." Wing loading is wing area divided by body weight. Low wing loading (relatively large wing area) makes slow gliding possible, as in thermal soaring; high wing loading is better for the fast gliding often needed in slope soaring. Larger birds tend to have higher wing loadings, because a bird twice as long as another but with exactly the same shape has eight (2^3) times the weight but only four (2^2) times the wing area. However, if birds of equal weight are compared, slope soarers generally have wing loadings about twice those of thermal soarers. Estimates of the wing loading of *Pteranodon* are very low for an animal of its size, lower than would be expected even for a thermal soarer.

Aspect ratio is wing span divided by the mean chord of the wing, the distance from the front to the rear edge. This means that high aspect ratio wings are long and narrow, while low aspect ratio wings are short and broad. As a general rule, the higher the aspect ratio the better the gliding performance. Albatrosses have high aspect ratios of 15 to 20; vultures and other birds that soar in thermals over land have lower aspect ratios, typically around 7. A possible explanation is that high aspect ratio wings that had a large enough area to give low wing loading would be enormously long and would be unwieldy for taking off from the ground or from trees. *Pteranodon* seems to have had a high aspect ratio.

Thus *Pteranodon* seems to have had low wing loading like a vulture, but high aspect ratio like an albatross, a combination that gives exceedingly long wings. The only modern birds with wings like this are frigate birds, which have the unusual habit of soaring in thermals over the sea. *Pteranodon* may have had the same habit. However, thermals occur over the sea only in the semitropical Trade Wind zone. *Pteranodon* has been found further north than the likely extent of Trade Winds in its time. Its way of life remains uncertain.

Conclusion

Biomechanics has been used in many other studies of fossil animals and plants, but the examples here are enough to illustrate its value. They have used branches of engineering mechanics ranging from statics to aerodynamics. They also have shown that quite simple applications of mechanics can be illuminating. But it seems sensible to end this article with a warning. Mechanics is a powerful tool, but it is also a demanding discipline. Its concepts are as precisely defined and its use of mathematics as rigorous as in other branches of physics. Mechanics gives precise technical meanings to words (such as "power") that have much broader meanings in everyday use. Many biologists have made superb use of mechanics, but others have gone badly wrong by trying to use concepts they did not fully understand.

R. McNEILL ALEXANDER

See also Functional Morphology

Works Cited

Alexander, R.McN. 1989a. Mechanics of fossil vertebrates. *Journal of the Geological Society* 146:41–52.

——. 1989b. *Dynamics of Dinosaurs and Other Extinct Giants*. New York: Columbia University Press.

——. 1990. *Animals.* Cambridge and New York: Cambridge University Press.

Brower, J.C. 1983. The aerodynamics of *Pteranodon* and *Nyctosaurus. Journal of Vertebrate Palaeontology* 3:84–124.

Bunker, S.J., and K.E. Machin. 1991. The hydrodynamics of cephalaspids. In J.M.V. Rayner and R.J. Wootton (eds.), *Biomechanics in Evolution.* Cambridge and New York: Cambridge University Press.

Crompton, A.W. 1963. On the lower jaw of *Diarthrognathus* and the origin of the mammalian lower jaw. *Proceedings of the Zoological Society of London* 140:697–753.

Mosbrugger, V. 1990. *The Tree Habit in Land Plants.* Berlin and New York: Springer-Verlag.

Padian, K. 1985. The origin and aerodynamics of flight in extinct vertebrates. *Palaeontology* 28:413–33.

Rayner, J.M.V., and R.J. Wootton. 1991. *Biomechanics in Evolution.* Cambridge and New York: Cambridge University Press.

Thomson, K.S. 1967. Mechanism of intracranial kinetics in fossil rhipidistian fishes (Crossopterygii) and their relatives. *Journal of the Linnean Society (Zoology)* 46:223–53.

BIRD, ROLAND THAXTER

American, 1899–1978

Roland Thaxter Bird (known to his colleagues as R.T.) was a collector of vertebrate fossils, particularly dinosaurs and their footprints, for the American Museum of Natural History, New York, during the 1930s and early 1940s. (His brother Junius became a South American archaeologist at the same institution.)

Their father Henry Bird was a successful businessman and amateur entomologist in Rye, New York. Roland's mother Harriet tragically died of tuberculosis when Roland was 15. R.T. had a bout with rheumatic fever and was sent to live on a farm in the Catskills instead of completing his education. He became interested in cattle and invested in the Florida land rush, but he lost his assets in the 1929 stock market crash.

Bird then traveled the American West doing odd jobs, riding a motorcycle he called his "Harley-and-houselet," because he had equipped its sidecar to open into a tent. In Arizona in 1932 he found a jaw of a new fossil amphibian. It went to Barnum Brown at the American Museum of Natural History in New York, who named it *Stanocephalus birdi* after its finder. When Brown later met Bird, he hired him as a field assistant and technician. Starting in 1934 Bird worked for Brown at the famous Howe quarry, Wyoming, where he made the often-reproduced drawing of more than 3,000 bones in situ (in place in the ground) he drew while hanging in a barrel high in the air to get the proper perspective.

Bird led field crews across the west during the 1930s, collecting bones and studying footprints, sometimes with the assistance of Works Progress Administration (WPA) crews. Among major footprint sites worked by Bird were Dinosaur Canyon, Arizona; Mayan

Ranch and Paluxy River (Dinosaur State Park) in Texas; and Purgatoire River, Colorado. Some of the most remarkable collections were made from Red Mountain and other mines in Colorado, where dinosaur footprints were found in the roofs of coal seams.

Bird's emphasis was generally on accessible sites from which display-quality materials could be obtained, but he pioneered the interpretation of trackways to show behavior patterns. At the Paluxy site sauropod tracks were associated with carnosaur tracks in a way that Bird interpreted as the record of an actual attack, although this view is not now generally accepted. He found the first documented sauropod tracks (resolving the long-standing controversy on their posture) and suggested that forefoot impressions at the Mayan Ranch site showed brontosaurs swimming.

During World War II he was assigned to mineral prospecting, but his health deteriorated, perhaps a recurrence of rheumatic fever from his youth. In 1946 Bird married Hazel Russell and retired to Florida in poor health, which prevented him from completing scientific reports of some of his major tracksites. In the early 1950s he returned to New York to assist E.H. Colbert in installing Paluxy River footprints in one of the most splendid dinosaur exhibits at the American Museum.

Slim, wiry, and mustached, Bird was always happiest in the field. Although Bird's professional career was short, his best-known sites have been of great importance and have since been studied intensively. He is commemorated fittingly in the name of the ichnogenus *Brontopodus birdi*. Although his pioneering interpretations did not always survive later scrutiny, they were groundbreaking in his time. "We recognize Bird as one of the originators of the herding hypothesis [of dinosaur behavior] and as the first paleontologist to present largely convincing evidence" (Farlow and Lockley 1989).

Bird was a fine photographer, and many of his pictures have been reproduced widely. Photos of other tracksite finds have led to many being rediscovered and documented. Although he was a reluctant writer, he authored a number of vivid articles, and his posthumous book *Bones for Barnum Brown* is one of the most attractive published accounts of dinosaur fieldwork. He is remembered personally for his "unassuming professional modesty and generosity of spirit . . . in refreshing contrast to the self-serving antics of those who are unwilling to let their discoveries speak for themselves" (Farlow and Lockley 1989).

DAVID A.E. SPALDING

Work Cited

Farlow, J.O., and M.G. Lockley. 1989. Roland T. Bird, Dinosaur tracker: An appreciation. *In* D.D. Gillette and M.G. Lockley (eds.), *Dinosaur Tracks and Traces*. Cambridge and New York: Cambridge University Press.

Biography

Born in Rye, New York, 29 December 1899. Education to ninth grade; later courses with J.W. Gregory in New York. Joined staff of American Museum of Natural History, New York, 1934, where he worked as an assistant to Barnum Brown until World War II. Notable as a collector and student of dinosaurs, particularly for his pioneering work on collecting and interpreting their footprints. Died 24 January 1978, while residing in Homestead, Florida.

Major Publications

1939. Thunder in his footsteps. *Natural History* 43:254–61.
1941. A dinosaur walks into the museum. *Natural History* 47:75–81.
1944. Did *Brontosaurus* ever walk on land? *Natural History* 53:61–67.
1953. To capture a dinosaur isn't easy. *Natural History* 62:104–10.
1954. We captured a "live" Brontosaur. *National Geographic Magazine* 105:707–22.
1985. *Bones for Barnum Brown: Adventures of a Dinosaur Hunter.* Fort Worth: Texas Christian University Press.

Further Reading

Colbert, E.H. 1961. *Dinosaurs: Their Discovery and Their World.* New York: Dutton; London: Hutchinson, 1962.
———. 1978. Roland T. Bird, 1899–1978. *News Bulletin, Society of Vertebrate Paleontology* 114:43–44.
———. 1989. *Digging into the Past: An Autobiography.* New York: Dembner.
Farlow, J.O., and M.G. Lockley. 1989. Roland T. Bird, dinosaur tracker: An appreciation. *In* D.D. Gillette and M.G. Lockley (eds.), *Dinosaur Tracks and Traces.* Cambridge and New York: Cambridge University Press.
Jacobs, L.L. 1995. *Lone Star Dinosaurs.* College Station: Texas A and M University Press.
Lockley, M.G. 1987. Dinosaur trackways and their importance in paleontological reconstruction. *In* S.M. Czerkas and E.C. Olson (eds.), *Dinosaurs Past and Present.* Los Angeles: University of Washington Press.
———. 1991. *Tracking Dinosaur: A New Look at an Ancient World.* Cambridge and New York: Cambridge University Press.
Lockley, M.G., and A.P. Hunt. 1995. *Dinosaur Tracks and Other Fossil Footprints of the Western United States.* New York: Columbia University Press.

BIRDS

Avian paleontology long has been regarded as a poor sister to other disciplines of vertebrate paleontology, often owing to the erroneous belief that birds have a poor fossil record. However, P.G. Davis and D.E.G. Briggs (1995, 1998) showed that the preservation of avian fossil remains was dependent on a concept called "taphonomic windows." (Taphonomy is the study of the events between death and fossilization.) A taphonomic window is a particular environment and set of conditions that are the best for preserving different fossils. In the case of birds, the taphonomic windows that are "open"—are most conducive to fossilization—are lacustrine (lake) and marine environments. Unfortunately, these environments contain a low diversity of birds. Therefore, the problem isn't that birds do not preserve well; it is that birds stand a good chance of being preserved in only a select few environments. This leaves researchers with an impoverished and unrepresentative sampling of taxa.

Before going any further it must be made clear that the study of fossil birds depends upon a detailed knowledge of the separate bones of the skeleton from a vast number of orders, families, genera, and species (for example there are just over 9,000 living species of

birds—all of which have a unique skeletal morphology). Although modern ornithologists use various characters of the skull, plumage, and behavior to classify birds, these categories are all unsuitable to the paleoornithologist. Therefore, the paleoornithologist has to develop a system of taxonomy (classification) based purely on the characters of robust skeletal elements. An excellent reference source for the study of topographical avian anatomy is Baumel (1979).

Systematics

As shown in Table 1, there are 45 extinct and extant orders of birds. The table is intended as a guide for the reader with regards to the rest of this article. For a more detailed synopsis and discussion of avian systematics, see Sibley and Alquist (1990) and Bock (1994).

Mesozoic Birds

Over the last 20 years, knowledge of the diversity and evolution of Mesozoic (245 to 65 million years ago) birds has increased dramatically. Before the start of the 1980s, the information available regarding this group of vertebrates was limited to three taxa, the famous *Archaeopteryx* (Upper Jurassic of Germany) and *Ichthyornis* and *Hesperornis* (Cretaceous of North America). All were described during the last half of the nineteenth century. This section provides a brief overview of the more recent discoveries of fossil birds of the Mesozoic era and describes how they have contributed to our knowledge of birds' evolution and radiation.

The current state of knowledge about the evolution of Mesozoic birds is summarized in the cladogram (diagram of evolutionary relationships) presented in Figure 1. Space constraints make it impossible to deal with every taxon or even with every group of birds known from the Mesozoic. Consequently, this discussion is biased toward some of the more recently discovered and controversial taxa.

Birds: The Living Descendants of the Dinosaurs?

In recent years, the idea that birds are the living descendants, or the crown group, of the dinosaurs has become both established and widely accepted. This theory owes much to the work of John Ostrom of Yale University during the 1960s and 1970s. He was the first to document the many anatomical similarities between theropod dinosaurs, such as *Deinonychus*, and the early birds, such as *Archaeopteryx*. In many features of the skeleton, but especially in the forelimbs, *Archaeopteryx* and *Deinonychus* are identical; the only obvious difference is the presence of feathers on the first bird.

It is worth noting that although the theropod origin of birds remains strongly supported by the known evidence, a few scholars still regard either basal archosaurs (e.g., Tarsitano and Hecht 1980), crocodylomorphs (e.g., Martin 1991), or a variety of other diapsid reptiles (e.g., Feduccia and Wild 1993) as more likely candidates for the ancestors of birds. The problem with these latter arguments is that they rest mainly on a few discordancies between theropod and avian morphology. The vast number of shared-derived features (unique similarities) that united theropods and birds are blithely dismissed as convergent evolution. New discoveries, such as the small compsognathid *Sinosauropteryx* (Chen et al. 1998), which apparently had featherlike structures along its tail and back, may yet serve to strengthen the theropod/bird argument in the future.

The Earliest Birds: *Archaeopteryx* and *Protoavis*

The fossil remains of *Archaeopteryx* from the Jurassic lithographic limestones of Solnhofen, Bavaria, Germany, are considered by most paleontologists to represent the first true bird. To date, eight specimens of *Archaeopteryx* have been described, all from the same deposits in Germany. The first, an isolated impression of a single feather, was described by the paleontologist Hermann von Meyer in 1861, who later reported on the first skeleton. This largely complete specimen now is known as the London Specimen, since it was sold to the British Museum of Natural History in 1863.

Von Meyer was the first to note a curious mosaic of features in the skeleton of *Archaeopteryx*, features that show it to be an intermediate stage between reptiles and birds. Some characteristics—in particular, an elongate bony tail, the presence of teeth,

Class Aves	
Subclass Archaeornithes	*Subclass Neornithes*
Order Archaeropterygiformes	O. Lithornithiformes
O. Alvarezsauriformes	O. Struthioniformes
O. Iberomesornithiformes	O. Remiornithiformes
O. Enantiornithiformes	O. Casuariiformes
O. Hesperornithiformes	O. Dinornithiformes
O. Ichthyornithiformes	O. Apterygiformes
O. Patagopteryiformes	O. Sphenisciformes
O. Ambiortiformes	O. Gaviiformes
	O. Podicipendiformes
	O. Procellariiformes
	O. Pelecaniformes
	O. Ardeiformes
	O. Ciconiiformes
	O. Cathartiformes
	O. Accipitriformes
	O. Anseriformes
	O. Galliformes
	O. Gruiformes
	O. Gastornithiformes
	O. Phoenicopteriformes
	O. Charadriiformes
	O. Columbiformes
	O. Psittaciformes
	O. Musophagiformes
	O. Cuculiformes
	O. Strigiformes
	O. Caprimulgiformes
	O. Apodiformes
	O. Trochiliformes
	O. Sandcoleiformes
	O. Coliiformes
	O. Trogoniformes
	O. Coraciiformes
	O. Bucerotiformes
	O. Piciformes
	O. Passeriformes

Figure 1. Cladogram summarizing the current consensus on the evolution of birds in the Mesozoic.

and claws on the wings—suggest a relationship with reptiles. Other features, such as feathers and a retroverted (backward-pointing) pubis, link *Archaeopteryx* to birds. Currently, most scholars consider the first seven specimens to be variations of a single species, *Archaeopteryx lithographica* (Latin, "feathered wing from the lithographic limestone"). The skeletal specimens vary greatly in size, so that they may represent different developmental stages (Davis 1996). The seventh specimen, described in 1993 by Peter Wellnhofer, shows two features not seen in any of the others: an ossified sternum (breastbone) and interdental plates on the lower jaw. Because of the distinctions, Wellnhofer (1993) classified his find as an adult of a second species, *Archaeopteryx bavarica*.

In recent years, the position of *Archaeopteryx* as the earliest bird has been put in doubt with the discovery and description of specimens of the pheasant-sized *Protoavis texensis* from Upper Triassic sediments of the Dockum Group, Texas (Chatterjee 1987, 1991, 1995). *Protoavis* is represented by two incomplete individual skeletons and a total of 31 isolated postcranial elements. Together, the pieces account for almost every skeletal element. A number of features, most strikingly in the skull, forelimbs, hips, and shoulder girdle suggest that *Protoavis* is a true bird (Chatterjee 1997). If correctly identified as such, *Protoavis* predates *Archaeopteryx* by at least 75 million years, and would imply that the origin of birds can be dated back at least to the Late Triassic. In addition, some of the features of the *Protoavis* skeleton suggest that it was a relatively advanced flying bird, even by Mesozoic standards, implying that by the Jurassic, *Archaeopteryx* was already a living fossil. If so, *Archaeopteryx* should be placed on a separate evolutionary line from modern birds.

Perhaps not surprisingly, some scholars have expressed doubts regarding the validity of this putative Triassic bird, most centering around the fact that the skeletal material appears too "fragmentary and disarticulated" and may, therefore, be subject to different interpretations (e.g., Ostrom 1991, 1996). P.J. Currie and X.-J. Zhao (1993) have stated that "although *Protoavis* does have characteristics suggesting avian affinities, most of these are also found in theropods." Some more technical problems associated with classifying *Protoavis* as a Mesozoic bird have been outlined by G.J. Dyke and J. Thorley (1998). At present, the evidence supporting *Protoavis* as a Triassic bird appears to be insufficient and needs clarification, to the point that paleontologists such as J.H. Ostrom (1991, 1996) are left with a "deep sense of unease and disbelief about the claim."

Enigmatic Alvarezsaurs

Some of the most exciting fossil finds in recent years have been the members of the so-called Alvarezsauridae, a group named by F.E. Novas in 1996. The first reported member of this group was the small, flightless taxon *Mononykus,* from the Late Cretaceous of the Gobi Desert in central Asia (Perle et al. 1993, 1994). Other members of this group include the Patagonian genus *Alvarezsaurus,* first described as a small, non-avian theropod dinosaur by J.F. Bonaparte (1991), and its relative *Patagonykus* (Novas 1997).

This small group of Late Cretaceous forms has attracted a great deal of debate over whether or not they should be considered birds. Several scholars have placed the group within Aves, in a position roughly intermediate between *Archaeopteryx* and the Enantior-

nithes (e.g., Perle et al. 1993, 1994; Chiappe 1996a; 1996b; Chiappe et al. 1996). These scholars claim that alvarezsaurs exhibit a number of derived (specialized) features that are seen only in birds more derived than *Archaeopteryx,* especially with regard to the skull (Chiappe 1995). From what is known of the forelimbs of the alvarezsaurs, it seems these structures are almost vestigial. This observation has led to much of the criticism about the assignment of these taxa as birds, set forth most notably by A. Feduccia (1994), L.D. Martin and C. Rinaldi (1994), and Z. Zhou (1995). Indeed, Wellnhofer (1994) has noted that "it is difficult to imagine how a primitive bird wing, such as that of *Archaeopteryx,* could evolve into a forelimb like that of *Mononykus.*" However, no single feature can remove this group from the avian fold. To do so would negate the many shared-derived features linking birds and alvarezsaurs and would imply a massive degree of convergent evolution. Thus, if alvarezsaurs are to be considered as birds, then their inclusion implies that they lost their ability to fly very early within the group's history.

The Unknown Radiation of the Enantiornithines

Although representatives of the Enantiornithines, a peculiar group of Mesozoic flying birds, were found and described in the scientific literature of over a century ago, enantiornithines remained misidentified as non-avian theropod dinosaurs (e.g., *Ornithomimus*) or were included within modern groups (e.g., *Gobipteryx*) (Elzanowski 1977). The first person to recognize the true nature of this group was Cyril Walker of the Natural History Museum in London. In 1981, he described enantiornithines on the basis of an assortment of bones from the Late Cretaceous Lecho Formation of Argentina. Later, Luis Chiappe of the American Museum in New York fully diagnosed the group on the basis of characters relating to the fusion of the tarsometatarsus (part of the "leg") and articulation of the scapula and coracoid (main elements of the shoulder girdle) (Chiappe 1996b). The arrangement of both these skeletal complexes is the reverse of that seen in all other birds, hence the literal meaning of enantiornithines: the reverse, or opposite, birds. Currently, over 15 distinct species of enantiornithines are known, and the group is thought to have had an almost global distribution throughout the Cretaceous. Material has been found in deposits in South America (e.g., Walker 1981; Chiappe 1991a, 1991b, 1993), North America (e.g., Martin 1983; Varricchio and Chiappe 1995), Asia (e.g., Davis 1997; Nessov and Borkin 1983; Nessov 1984; Nessov and Jarkov 1989), and Australia (e.g., Molnar 1986).

As noted by L.M. Chiappe (1995), almost all of the recorded enantiornithine occurrences have been in nonmarine strata (rock layers). Most likely, such a marked bias in the enantiornithine fossil record suggests that these birds were primarily terrestrial in habit and may have dominated terrestrial avifaunas in the latter half of the Mesozoic.

The evolutionary relationship of the Enantiornithes to other Mesozoic birds is currently a much-debated area of avian paleontology. Scholars have considered the group as closely related to *Archaeopteryx* (e.g., Martin 1983, 1991), as a member of the Ornithurae (modern birds) (e.g., Cracraft 1986), or as an intermediate form between the two (e.g., Chiappe and Calvo 1994). Based on the information available at present, this latter view is preferred (see Figure 1).

Modern Birds of the Cretaceous

When compared to the vast diversity of birds now known from the Mesozoic, the amount of fossil material that can be confidently assigned to a modern group is surprisingly small. However, there is compelling evidence for the existence of several lineages of modern birds, or Neornithines (Figure 1), by the end of the Cretaceous. Taxa supposedly related to the extant orders Procellariiformes (sea birds, e.g., albatross) (e.g., Olson and Parris 1987), Gaviiformes (diving birds, e.g., loons) (Olson 1992), and Charadriiformes (shore birds, e.g., gulls) (e.g., Olson and Parris 1987) have been described from rocks of the correct age. Although knowledge of the diversity of Neornithines during the Mesozoic is incomplete, currently accepted hypotheses regarding the interrelationships of modern birds suggest that other orders existed during this period, perhaps even extant families.

Birds and the KT Extinction

It was long thought that birds were a success story when it came to surviving the Cretaceous extinction event (the "K-T" extinction), which seems to have caused the demise of so many other organisms. However, as our knowledge of the Mesozoic bird fossil record has become more complete in the last 20 years, it has become apparent that the birds suffered heavily at the end of the Cretaceous. Comparing bird families before and after the event, it appears that it caused the extinction of 90 percent of bird families. However, the demise of so many bird families, along with the pterosaurs, the other aerial archosaurs of the Mesozoic, at this time may have promoted the radiation of the neornithine birds during the beginnings of the Tertiary period.

PAUL G. DAVIS AND GARETH J. DYKE

See also Aerial Locomotion; Respiration; Thermoregulation; Theropods

Works Cited

Baumel, J.J. (ed.). 1979. *Nomina Anatomica Avium.* London and New York: Academic Press.

Bock, W.J. 1994. History and nomenclature of avian family-group names. *Bulletin of the American Museum of Natural History* 222:1–281.

Bonaparte, J.F. 1991. Los vertebrados fosiles de la Formación Río Colorado de la cuidad de Neuquen y cercanías. Cretaceo superior, Argentina. *Revista del Museo Argentino de Ciencias Naturales "Bernardino Rivadavia," e Instituto Nacional de Investigación de las Ciencias Naturales Paleontología* 4:17–123.

Chatterjee, S. 1987. Skull of *Protoavis* and early evolution of birds. *Journal of Vertebrate Paleontology* 7, supplement:14A.

———. 1991. Cranial anatomy and relationships of a new Triassic bird from Texas. *Philosophical Transactions of the Royal Society, London,* ser. B, 332:277–346.

———. 1995. The Triassic bird *Protoavis. Archaeopteryx* 13:15–31.

———. 1997. *The Rise of Birds: 225 Million Years of Evolution.* Baltimore, Maryland, and London: Johns Hopkins University Press.

Chen, P., Z. Dong, and S. Zhen. 1998. An exceptionally well-preserved theropod dinosaur from the Yixian Formation of China. *Nature* 391:147–52.

Chiappe, L.M. 1991a. Cretaceous birds of Latin America. *Cretaceous Research* 12:55–63.

———. 1991b. Cretaceous avian remains from Patagonia shed new light on the early radiation of birds. *Alcheringa* 15:333–38.

———. 1993. Enantiornithine (Aves) tarsometatarsi from the Cretaceous Lecho Formation of Northwestern Argentina. *American Museum Novitates* 3083:1–27.

———. 1995. The first 85 million years of avian evolution. *Nature* 378:349–55.

———. 1996a. Early avian evolution in the southern hemisphere: The fossil record of birds in the Mesozoic of Gondwana. *Memoirs of the Queensland Museum* 39:533–54.

———. 1996b. Late Cretaceous birds of southern South America: Anatomy and systematics of Enantiornithines and *Patagopteryx defarrariisi. Muncher Geowissenschaftlichen Abhandlungen* 30:203–44.

Chiappe, L.M., and J.O. Calvo. 1994. *Neuquenornis volans,* a new Late Cretaceous bird (Enantiornithes: Avisauridae) from Patagonia, Argentina. *Journal of Vertebrate Paleontology* 14:230–46.

Chiappe, L.M., M.A. Norell, and J.M. Clark. 1996. Phylogenetic position of *Mononykus* (Aves: Alvarezsauridae) from the Late Cretaceous of the Gobi Desert. *Memoirs of the Queensland Museum* 39:557–82.

———. 1997. *Mononykus* and birds: Methods and evidence. *The Auk* 114:300–2.

Cracraft, J. 1986. The origin and early diversification of birds. *Paleobiology* 12:383–99.

Currie, P.J., and X.-J. Zhao. 1993. A new troodontid (Dinosauria, Theropoda) braincase from the Dinosaur Park Formation (Campanian) of Alberta. *Canadian Journal of Earth Science* 30:2231–47.

Davis, P.G. 1996. The taphonomy of *Archaeopteryx lithographica. Bulletin of the National Science Museum Series C (Geology and Palaeontology)* 22 (3–4):91–106.

———. 1997. An enantiornithine bird from the Lower Cretaceous of Japan. *Abstracts of the 146th Meeting of the Palaeontological Society of Japan (Kyoto 30th Jan.–1st Feb. 1997)*:56.

Davis, P.G., and D.E.G. Briggs. 1995. The fossilization of feathers. *Geology* 23 (9):783–86.

———. 1998. The impact of decay and disarticulation on the preservation of fossil birds. *Palaios* 13 (1):3–13.

Dyke, G.J., and J. Thorley. 1998. Reduced cladistic consensus methods and the avian affinities of *Protoavis* and *Avimimus. Archaeopteryx.*

Elzanowski, A. 1977. Skulls of *Gobipteryx* (Aves) from the Upper Cretaceous of Mongolia. *Paleontologica Polonica* 37:153–65.

Feduccia, A. 1994. The great dinosaur debate. *Living Bird* 13 (4):28–33.

Feduccia, A., and R. Wild. 1993. Birdlike characters in the Triassic archosaur *Megalancosaurus. Naturwissenschaften* 80:564–66.

Hou, L., L.D. Martin, Z. Zhou, and A. Feduccia. 1996. Early adaptive radiation of birds: Evidence from fossils from Northeastern China. *Science* 274:1164–67.

Jurcsak, T., and E. Kessler. 1987. Evolutia avifauna pe territoriul Romaniei: II, Morfologia speciilor fosile [Evolution of the avifauna in the territory of Romania: II, Morphology of the fossil species]. *Nymphaea* 17:581–609.

Martin, L.D. 1983. The origin and early radiation of birds. *In* A. Brush and G. Clark (eds.), *Perspectives in Ornithology.* Cambridge and New York: Cambridge University Press.

————. 1991. Mesozoic birds and the origin of birds. *In* H.-P. Schultze and L. Trueb (eds.), *Origins of the Higher Groups of Tetrapods*, pp. 485–540. Ithaca, New York: Comstock.

Martin, L.D., and C. Rinaldi. 1994. How to tell a bird from a dinosaur. *Maps Digest* 17 (4):190–96.

Meyer, H. von. 1861a. Vogel-Federn und Palpipes priscus von Solnhofen. *Neues Jahrbuch für Mineralogie Geologie und Paleontologie* 1861:561.

————. 1861b. *Archaeopteryx lithographica* (Vogel-Feder) und *Pterodactylus* von Solnhofen. *Neues Jahrbuch für Mineralogie Geologie und Paleontologie* 1861:678–79.

Molnar, R.E. 1986. An enantiornithine bird from the Lower Cretaceous of Queensland, Australia. *Nature* 322:736–38.

Nessov, L.A. 1984. [Upper Cretaceous pterosaurs and birds from Central Asia]. *Paleontological Journal* 1984:47–57. [In Russian]

Nessov, L.A., and L.J. Borkin. 1983. [New records of bird bones from the Cretaceous of Mongolia and Soviet Middle Asia]. *USSR Academy of Sciences, Proceedings of the Zoological Insitute* 116:108–10. [In Russian]

Nessov, L.A., and A.A. Jarkov. 1989. [New Cretaceous Paleogene birds of the USSR and some remarks on the origin and evolution of the class Aves]. *Proceedings of the Zoological Institute of Lenigrad* 197:78–97. [In Russian]

Novas, F.E. 1996. Alvarezsauridae, Cretaceous basal birds from Patagonia and Mongolia. *Memoirs of the Queensland Museum* 39:675–702.

————. 1997. Anatomy of *Patagonykus puertai* (Theropoda, Avialae, Alvarezsauridae) from the Late Cretaceous of Patagonia. *Journal of Vertebrate Paleontology* 17:137–66.

Olson, S.L. 1992. *Neogaeornis wetzeli* Lambrecht, a Cretaceous loon from Chile (Aves: Gaviidae). *Journal of Vertebrate Paleontology* 12:122–24.

Olson, S.L., and D.C. Parris. 1987. The Cretaceous birds of New Jersey. *Smithsonian Contributions to Paleobiology* 63:1–22.

Ostrom, J.H. 1991. Paleontology: The bird in the bush. *Nature* 353:212.

————. 1996. The questionable validity of *Protoavis*. *Archaeopteryx* 14:39–42.

Perle, A., L.M. Chiappe, B. Rinchen, J.M. Clark, and M.A. Norell, 1994. Skeletal morphology of *Mononykus olecranus* (Theropoda: Avialae) from the Late Cretaceous of Mongolia. *American Museum Novitates* 3105.

Perle, A., M.A. Norell, L.M. Chiappe, and J.M. Clark. 1993. Flightless bird from the Cretaceous of Mongolia. *Nature* 362:623–26.

Sibley, C.G., and J.E. Ahlquist. 1990. *Phylogeny and Classification of Birds*. New Haven, Connecticut: Yale University Press.

Tarsitano, S.F., and M. Hecht. 1980. A reconsideration of the reptilian relationships of *Archaeopteryx*. *Zoological Journal of the Linnean Society* 69:149–82.

Varricchio, D.J., and L.M. Chiappe. 1995. A new enantiornithine bird from the Upper Cretaceous Two Medicine Formation of Montana. *Journal of Vertebrate Paleontology* 15:201–4.

Walker, C.A. 1981. New subclass of birds from the Cretaceous of South America. *Nature* 292:51–53.

Wellnhofer, P. 1993. Das siebte Exemplar von *Archaeopteryx* aus den Solnhofer Schichten [The seventh specimen of *Archaeopteryx* from the Solnofen limestone]. *Archaeopteryx* 11:1–47.

————. 1994. New data on the origin and early evolution of birds. *Comptes Rendus de l'Académie des Sciences,* Paris, ser. 2, 319 (3):299–308.

Zhou, Z. 1995. Is *Mononykus* a bird? *The Auk* 112:958–63.

Further Reading

Chatterjee, S. 1997. *The Rise of Birds: 225 Million Years of Evolution*. Baltimore, Maryland, and London: Johns Hopkins University Press.

Chiappe, L.M. 1995. The first 85 million years of avian evolution. *Nature* 378:349–55.

Dingus, L., and T. Rowe. 1998. *The Mistaken Extinction: Dinosaur Extinction and the Origin of Birds*. New York: Freeman.

Feduccia, A. 1996. *The Origin and Evolution of Birds*. New Haven, Connecticut: Yale University Press.

Olson, S.L. 1985. The fossil record of birds. *In* D.S. Farner, J.R. King, and K.C. Parkes (eds.), *Avian Biology*, vol. 8. Orlando, Florida: Academic Press.

BIVALVES

Clams, mussels, oysters, and scallops are familiar members of the class Bivalvia, an ancient group of molluscs traceable to the initial radiation of animals with skeletons, in the earliest Cambrian (Runnegar and Pojeta 1992). The bivalve body (Figure 1) is enclosed in a calcareous (calcium mineral) shell (Figure 2) that is split into two separate units, each being a "valve" (hence the name "bivalve"). The valves are hinged along one edge by a flexible ligament. A muscular foot enables most bivalves to burrow into the substrate (usually sand or mud) to avoid potential predators. While cephalopod molluscs (octopus, squid) have enhanced the head, bivalves show the opposite extreme, the head being reduced to little more than a mouth (decephalization).

Such a body plan would seem to offer few avenues for evolutionary novelty. Indeed, the repeated origins in separate bivalve lineages of many key adaptations including siphons, byssal attachment, and ligament nymphae reflect inherent limitations of the bivalve body plan. Yet, the bivalves exhibit a remarkable variety of forms and habits through geologic time. Their powerful digging foot enabled habitation of shifting sands and muds where they are often the most common and, perhaps, successful invertebrate megafauna. The fast-burrowing Donacidae, for example, are among the few large invertebrates to have ever colonized the harsh environments of surf-pounded beaches, where they occur in densities of thousands per square meter. Their efficient foot enables them to reburrow only seconds after being washed out by waves. Some groups, such as the ancient rudists (Figure 3) and the living watering pots (Clavagellidae), have conelike or tubelike skeletons, giving them an appearance far different from the earliest bivalves. Notwithstanding setbacks in diversity during times of mass extinctions, the bivalves show a steady increase in the number of families

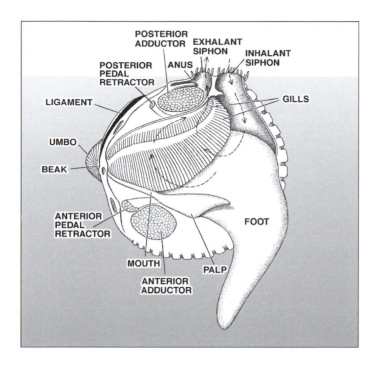

Figure 1. Anatomy of a cockle (Family Cardiidae) in life position in the substrate. Gills (ctenidia) cover the visceral mass. Symbols: *dashed arrows,* feeding currents for suspension feeding. Modified from Barnes (1980).

since the Ordovician (Bambach 1985) and probably have not yet reached their evolutionary acme.

Today, bivalves inhabit nearly every aqueous environment, from the tropics to the poles, from freshwater lakes and rivers, to estuaries, intertidal mudflats, marine shelves, and ocean trenches. Even sulphide-spewing, hot-vent environments at ridges that straddle the spreading seafloor are replete with pale, melon-sized clams (Vesicomyidae) and mussels (Mytilidae), their gills stuffed with symbiotic sulfur-oxidizing bacteria. Unlike the gastropods, however, bivalves have not colonized terrestrial environments, although some pea clams (Pisidiidae) reportedly inhabit damp leaf-litter on forest floors. Among the most abundant megafossils in the geologic record, especially in post-Paleozoic rocks, bivalves are valuable tools for biostratigraphy, for interpreting ancient depositional environments, and for the study of form, function, and patterns of diversity through geologic time.

The Bivalve Body

Vital organs of bivalves, including the digestive system and main parts of the circulatory and nervous systems, are concentrated dorsally (toward the top) in a complex visceral mass below the umbones, the most convex part of the shell. Most bivalves possess a powerful foot that extends ventrally (downward) or anteriorly (forward) from the visceral mass. Ciliated (covered with microscopic hairs) platelike gills on either side of the visceral mass and foot are important for generating currents into and out of the shell, for respi-

ration, and in most bivalves (Autobranchia), are the principal food-gathering organs. The shell is secreted by an underlying sheet of tissue, the mantle, that extends continuously over the dorsal side of the animal (the mantle ishmus) where it secretes the ligament.

In many lineages of bivalves, opposing free edges of the mantle have become fused to various degrees for separating inhalant and exhalant water flow. In burrowers, this adaptation minimizes sediment entering the shell during burrowing and controls the jetting of water to soften sediment in advance of the shell. Most significantly, the fused mantle may be extended as siphons, enabling the animal to burrow deeply while still maintaining contact through the siphon with water above the substrate.

The Bivalve Shell

To the paleontologist, the most distinctive feature of bivalves is the complete separation of the shell into two valves, which begins at the onset of calcification of the larval shell. This is an important distinction because members of the related extinct mollusc class Rostroconchia (Cambrian-Permian) resemble bivalves in shell outline and even possess a pseudobivalved shell as adults. However, the larval shell in rostroconchs is univalved (single), resembling a tiny Chinese hat, and the adult shell shows one or more shell layers extending continuously across the dorsal margin of the shell and connecting the valves (Runnegar and Pojeta 1974).

The bivalve shell is composed of calcium carbonate with a thin protective proteinaceous covering, the "periostracum," only rarely preserved in fossils. The calcified part of the shell may be composed of both aragonite and calcite, although some are wholly aragonite. When present, calcite layers are generally outermost. Oyster shells are predominately calcite but a layer of aragonite (the myostracum) is secreted where muscles attach, as in other bivalves.

Bivalve shells demonstrate a variety of microstructures with different mechanical properties that are important for classification (Carter 1990). For example, pearl oysters (Pteriidae) and their Paleozoic relatives, the Pterineidae (Figure 3), show a tough inner shell layer composed of thin sheets of aragonitic mother-of-pearl (nacreous structure) and an outer prismatic calcite layer extending peripherally beyond the nacreous layer (especially in the less convex right valve). The naceous layer's highly flexible properties ensure a gasketlike seal when the valves are pulled shut (Carter and Tevesz 1978). Some rarer forms of calcium carbonate are known in bivalves. One of these, vaterite, is laid down by the mantle as shell damage is repaired.

During growth, the mantle adds new shell material over the inner surface of the shell and concentrically at the edge of the valves (accretionary growth). Exterior growth lines thus record former positions of the growing shell margin, providing a record of any changes in shell shape during life that might indicate a change in habit.

Diverse ornament occurs on the shell exterior of bivalves, including spines, ridges, ribs, folds, and sulci. Typically arranged in patterns radiating from a central elevation, the umbo (radial) (Figure 3), or paralleling the growing shell margin (comarginal), but occasionally discordant, ornament functions in varied and complex ways: Strengthening the shell and deterring predators cer-

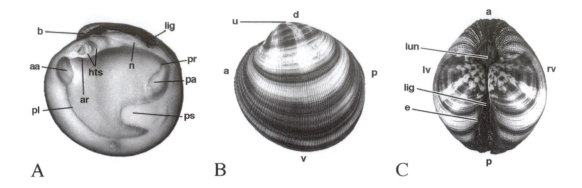

Figure 2. Features of the bivalve shell as exemplified by the heteroconch, *Periglypta puerpera* (Linné), Recent, Philippines. *A*, right valve, internal. *B*, left valve, external; note concentric and radial color bands (rarely preserved in fossils), concentric growth lines, and fine radial ribs. *C*, dorsal view. Abbreviations: *a*, anterior; *aa*, anterior adductor muscle scar; *ar*, anterior pedal retractor muscle scar; *b*, beak; *d*, dorsal; *e*, escutcheon; *hts*, hinge teeth and sockets; *lig*, ligament; *lun*, lunule; *lv*, left valve; *n*, nymph; *p*, posterior; *pa*, posterior adductor muscle scar; *pl*, pallial line; *pr*, posterior pedal retractor muscle scar; *ps*, pallial sinus; *rv*, right valve; *u*, umbo; *v*, ventral.

tainly seem among the most important. Even in burrowing, some kinds of ornament play a role. For example, concentric ribs, asymmetric in cross section, function like a ratchet during burrowing, the ribs preventing the shell from slipping back as the foot probes the substrate (common in early Anomalodesmata).

Not all features of the shell exterior require functional interpretation—some are simply inevitable results of accretionary growth. For example, shallow radial troughs (sulci) may simply reflect a slight retraction of the mantle anteriorly or ventrally where byssal threads exit the shell, the disruption of the mantle being perpetuated through growth as a radial depression. Even prominent external shell features such as the lunule and escutcheon (Figure 2) simply represent growth tracks of the anterior and posterior ends of the hinge plate (a calcareous plate below the beak bearing the dentition and ligament) (Figure 2) (Carter 1967). Impressions on the internal shell surface reflect many features of the soft parts, including attachment scars of the adductor muscles (adductor scars), foot (pedal retractor scars), and mantle muscles (pallial line), enabling paleontologists to reconstruct aspects of the soft anatomy in extinct species.

Ligament

The ligament of bivalves functions like a spring. Adductor muscles (usually two) pull the valves shut, straining the ligament along the dorsal margin. When the adductors relax, deformational energy stored in the ligament opens the shell. Hinge teeth and sockets, if present, help keep the valves in alignment.

The ligament is a layered structure constructed of an organic lamellar component (elastic to tension) and an aragonitic fibrous component (elastic to compression). Attached along the dorsal shell margin, posterior (behind) the beak (opisthodetic; Figure 2) in the most primitive bivalves (Waller 1998), the ligament was altered in many later bivalve lineages, occurring, for example, on both sides of the beak in some (amphidetic), and in others, wholly or partly in a

depression (resilifer) below the beak. Mechanical efficiency is enhanced in some opisthodetic ligaments by a nymph, an elongate ridge of shell (Figure 2) which sharply arches the ligament into a powerful "C-spring." Such variations, together with changes in the arrangement of the fibrous and lamellar components, provide key information for unravelling bivalve phylogeny (Waller 1990).

Reproduction and Dispersal

Bivalves demonstrate diverse reproductive strategies, but most have separate sexes (dioecious) and release gametes that are fertilized in the mantle cavity or in the open sea. While some species show direct development without a planktonic larval stage, most have a free-swimming larva that may drift in ocean currents up to several months (usually two to three weeks) feeding on plankton (Kauffman 1975). A long-lived planktonic larva is of key importance in the dispersal of most modern marine bivalve species and may account for the widespread, even global distribution, of many fossil species, making them valuable for intra- and intercontinental biostratigraphic correlations (dating rock strata by the distinctive fossils found within them) (Kauffman 1975).

Upon settling, the planktonic larva undergoes structural changes (metamorphosis) for adult life. Often differing in shape and ornament from the adult shell (dissoconch), the tiny larval shell (prodissoconch) is visible at the first-formed part of the shell in Recent and well-preserved fossil bivalves (the beak) (Figure 2). For stability, most bivalve larvae (except Palaeotaxodonta) attach to the substrate by byssal threads secreted from a gland in the foot. Usually abandoned with growth, some bivalves retain byssal attachment into adult stages for stability on or within the substrate.

Feeding, Symbioses, and Bivalve Giants

A radula, the rasplike feeding apparatus found in the other living molluscan classes, is absent in the Bivalvia. Instead, most bivalves

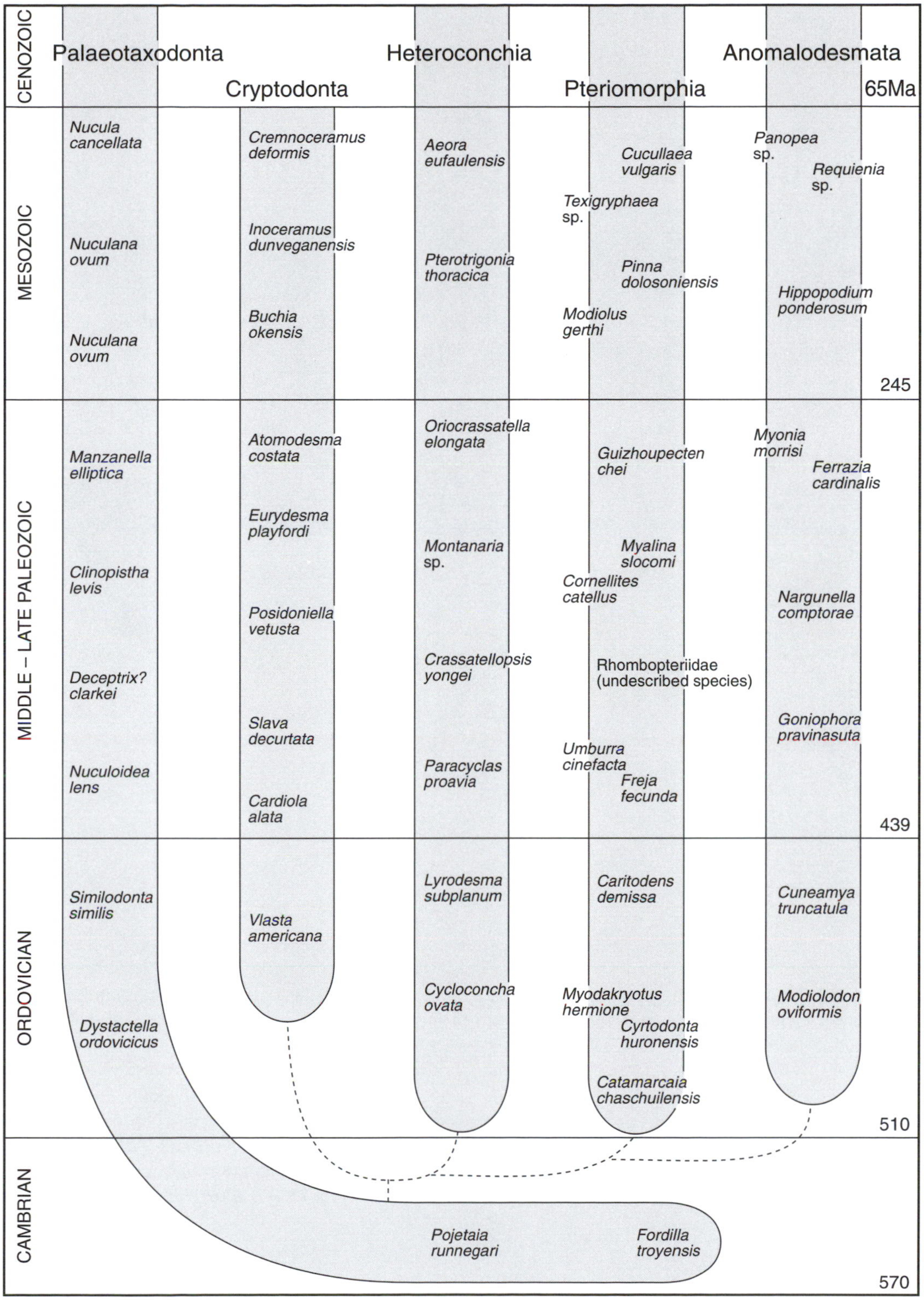

Figure 3. Some bivalves of the Paleozoic and Mesozoic eras arranged in their subclasses. The positions in geologic time shown for individual taxa are approximate.

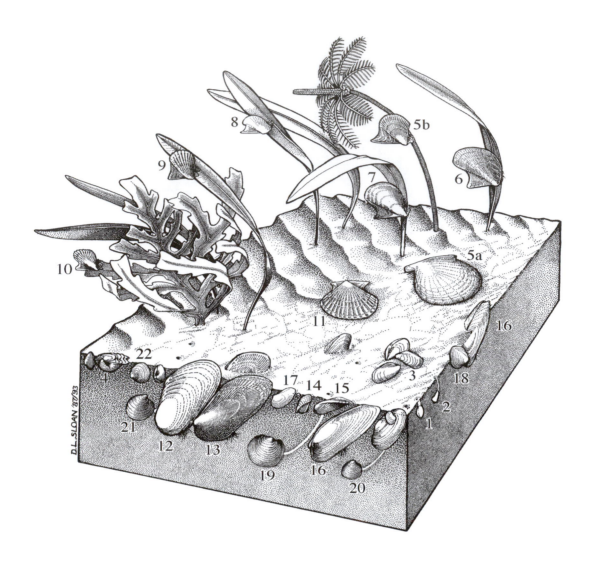

Figure 4. Life habits of bivalves as exemplified by species in the Lower Devonian Taemas Formation of New South Wales, Australia. *1, 2,* infaunal, siphonate, labial palp deposit-feeding burrowers; *3–22,* non-siphonate suspension feeders; *3,* epibyssate; *4,* non-byssate recliner; *5a, 11,* epibyssate recliner; *5b–10,* epibyssate, attached to flexible organisms; *12–16,* endobyssate shallow burrowers; *17, 18, 22,* infaunal shallow burrowers; *19–21,* deep infaunal burrowers with anterior inhalant mucus tube and probably with sulphide-oxidizing symbiotic bacteria. Key to taxa: *1, Polidevcia* cf. *insolita; 2, Nuculites* sp.; *3, Mytilarca bloomfieldensis; 4,* Rhombopteriidae, undescribed species; *5, Limoptera murrumbidgeensis* (*a,* adult; *b,* juvenile); *6, Tolmaia erugisulca; 7, Actinopteria* cf. *murrindalensis; 8, Cornellites talenti; 9, Cornellites campbelli; 10, Cornellites catellus; 11, Pseudaviculopecten etheridgei; 12, Phorinoplax striata; 13, Nargunella comptorae; 14, Goniophora duplisulca; 15, Goniophora pravinasuta; 16, Sanguinolites? phlyctaenatus; 17, Schizodus truemani; 18, Eoschizodus taemasensis; 19, Paracyclas proavia; 20, Paracyclas rugosa; 21, Paracyclas alleni* Johnston; *22, Crassatellopsis lenticularis.* Modified from Johnston (1993), courtesy of John Laurie, Editor, Memoirs of the Association of Australasian Palaeontologists.

(Autobranchia) are filtration feeders, pumping water in and out of the shell through ciliary action and capturing suspended food particles on large efficient gills. Food is passed onto large liplike structures (labial palps) for sorting and manipulation before entering the mouth (Figure 1). In contrast, living nuculoids (subclass Paleotaxodonta) are deposit feeders that plow through sediment, groping for organic detritus (waste material and remains of dead) with tentacle-like extensions of the palps called proboscides. Deposit feeding seems to have characterized the first bivalves although they probably lacked proboscides (Waller 1998). Instead, the foot may have been an important food gathering organ, since it appears to function this way in almost all juvenile bivalves, and even in the adult stages of many small species of otherwise suspension-feeding bivalves (Reid et al. 1992). Surprisingly, carnivorous habits have evolved in certain anomalodesmatans (e.g., family Cuspidariidae) and in the glass scallops (family Propeamussidae); these bivalves inhabit the deep sea where suspended food particles are scarce (Morton 1996).

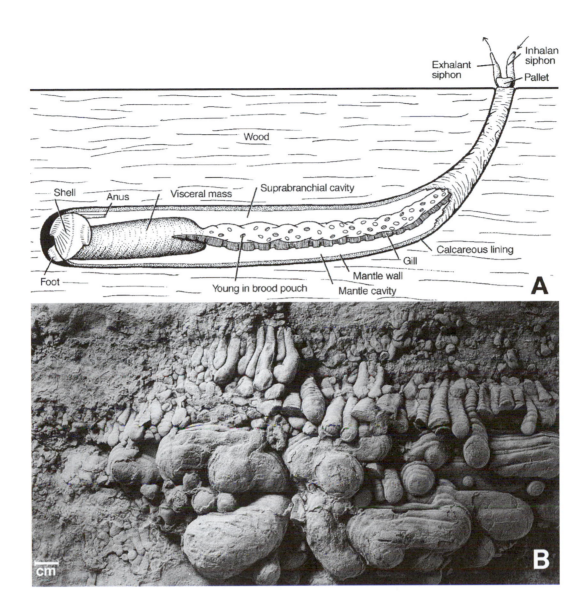

Figure 5. Life mode and trace fossils of wood-boring bivalves. *A*, life position and anatomy of the modern "ship worm" (actually a bivalve), Family Teredinidae; *B*, trace fossils (ichnogenus *Teredolites*) of boring bivalves in Upper Cretaceous wood (Bad Heart Formation, Alberta). The wood has mostly eroded away revealing the sediment-filled borings. *A*, from Barnes (1980); *B*, photo by C.J. Collom.

While inhalant and exhalant flow is restricted to the posterior margin in many, mostly siphonate bivalves (Figure 1), an anterior inhalant current occurs in primitive members of most lineages and probably characterized the earliest bivalves (Morton 1996). This is particularly evident in the burrowing lucinoid bivalves, which construct a prominent, anterior, mucus-lined, inhalant tube connected to the substrate surface (Figure 4).

Since the early 1980s, zoologists have recognized that members of several living bivalve families depend partly or entirely on nutrients manufactured by symbiotic sulphide-oxidizing bacteria within their tissues, to the extent that some living solemyid bivalves with these bacteria lack a gut altogether (Reid 1990). Such bivalves inhabit environments rich in hydrogen sulphide but with at least some oxygen available, as for example around submarine vents (Vesicomyidae, Mytilidae), sea grass beds (Lucinidae), fjords

(Thyasiridae), and even sewage outfalls (Solemyidae) (Cobabe 1991). By contrast, the celebrated giant clam *Tridacna* (which inhabits modern coral reefs) and some members (*Fragum* and *Corculum*) of the related family Cardiidae, host photosymbiotic algae *(zooxanthellae)* that supply nutrients (mainly glucose) (Fankboner and Reid 1990), as in reef-building corals.

The recognition and evolutionary significance of these "endosymbioses" among fossil bivalves are now being explored by paleontologists (Seilacher 1990). Chemosymbiosis was evidently a key innovation in the subclass Cryptodonta, enabling their colonization of low-oxygen/sulphide-rich basinal environments through much of Phanerozoic time (Johnston and Collom 1998). Likewise, photosymbiosis probably had an important role in the success of the reef-building rudists in the Late Mesozoic (Seilacher 1990).

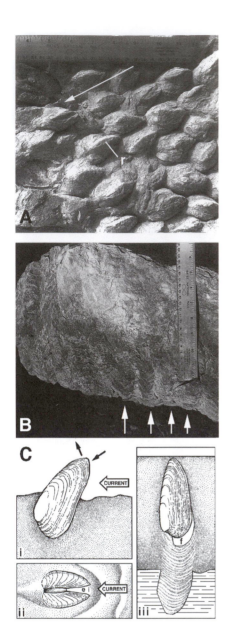

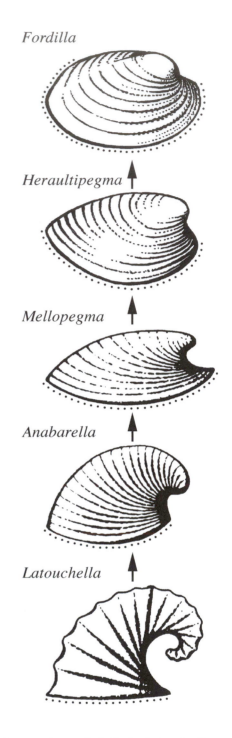

Figure 6. Life mode and behavior of non-marine Upper Cretaceous unionoid bivalves (Dinosaur Provincial Park, Alberta, Canada) inferred from trace fossils. *A,* sole face of fluvial sandstone bed with abundant dwelling traces (domichnia) in convex relief. These trace fossils (ichnogenus *Lockeia,* also known as *Pelecypodichnus*) were produced by the river-dwelling unionoid bivalve *Fusconaia? danae.* Symbol: *r,* ridge on long axis of *Lockeia* produced by downward thrusting of the bivalve foot; *arrow,* inferred paleocurrent direction—the trace fossils show that the bivalves tended to face into the current as do modern unionoid bivalves. *B,* side view of the same sandstone bed. Covered quickly by sand, perhaps after a local flood, the bivalves burrowed upward and backward producing escape structures (fugichnia) in the overlying sediment. Each escape structure arises from an individual *Lockeia* (arrows). Note meniscate laminae within each escape trace. *C,* inferred life mode of *F.? danae* in, *i,* lateral and *ii,* plane view. Symbols: *black arrows,* inhalant and exhalant flow; *iii, F.? danae* escaping upward through overlying sediment. Key: *f,* foot.

Figure 7. Proposed morphological stages in the evolution of bivalves from a monoplacophoran ancestor as represented by Cambrian fossils. The growing margin (i.e., the aperture, signalled by *dotted line*) became increasingly curved (in lateral view) and longer, and the shell became laterally compressed. Like other rostroconchs, *Heraultipegma* shows only partial subdivision of the shell into separate valves, and the larval shell is univalved. In bivalves, the adult and larval shell are split completely into two valves. *Latouchella, Anabarella,* and *Mellopegma* are monoplacophorans; *Heraultipegma* is a rostroconch; *Fordilla* is a bivalve. Based on Runnegar and Pojeta (1974), but see Peel (1991) for alternate interpretation, and Runnegar (1996) for reply.

It seems no coincidence that endosymbioses are known or suspected in the largest known bivalves, including the living giant clam, *Tridacna gigas* (length 1.7 meters), the inoceramid cryptodont *Platyceramus platinus* (1.5 meters), and the hornlike rudist, *Titanosarcolites giganteus* (less than two meters), the latter two being of Late Cretaceous age (Johnston and Collom 1998). While it is tempting to suggest a causal relationship between endosymbiosis and large size, most bivalves containing endosymbionts are not particularly large. Perhaps the most that can be said is that endosymbiosis in bivalves does not necessarily lead to gigantism, but bivalves are unlikely to become giants without it.

Life Habits

Studies of modern bivalves show that morphologic features of the shell are reliable indicators of life habits (Stanley 1970). Paleontologists, therefore, are able to reconstruct habits of extinct bivalves with a level of confidence hardly possible for most fossil groups. Rapid burrowers, for example, show streamlined shells. In deep burrowers, siphons may be so large that they cannot be fully withdrawn into the shell and a permanent gape is developed at the shell posterior. Even without a gape, the presence of siphons in fossil species may be detected by an embayment of the pallial line (the pallial sinus) (Figure 2). Shallow burrowers employing a byssus for stability and living partly buried in the substrate are "endobyssate," a life mode common in the Middle Paleozoic (Figure 4). Byssal attachment enabled many species to exploit life above the substrate—these are "epibyssate" (Figure 4). A notch, sinus, or sulcus normally forms at the shell edge where the byssus exits the shell, and such features are easily recognized in fossils. Bivalves habitually lying on one side (pleurothetic) often show an inequivalved shell, that is, one valve is more convex than the other (Figure 4). Unattached pleurothetic bivalves are "recliners" (Figure 4), a habit rare among modern bivalves (e.g., the window pane shell, *Placuna*), but characteristic of some major fossil groups such as the gryphaeid oysters of the Mesozoic. First appearing in the Silurian, scallops may attach or recline, and some can swim for short distances by clapping their valves. Bivalves that are cementers (e.g., true oysters and rudists) and those that are borers into hard substrates such as rock, coral, and wood (e.g., pholads, teredinids) are often preserved in life position. Both burrowing and boring bivalves produce distinctive trace fossils that supply direct evidence of behavior of fossil bivalves (Figures 5, 6).

A. Seilacher (1990) suggested that photosymbiosis might be inferred in fossil bivalves from special alterations of the shell, such as flanges for extruding the mantle into sunlight (*Tridacna*, some rudists), or, if light was received through the shell, from a dishlike shape, shell-thinning, and microstructural changes for light transmission (*Corculum*, some rudists). However, shell morphology offers few clues to the presence of symbiont bacteria in fossil bivalves (Allison et al. 1995); such inferences must rely principally on geologic setting and phylogenetic relationships with living bivalves that possess chemosymbionts. Studies of isotopes in fossil shells offer some promise for detecting chemosymbiosis (Cobabe 1991) but are not without difficulties (Allison et al. 1995).

Origin and Evolution

Fordilla and *Pojetaia* of Early Cambrian age are the earliest known bivalves. Both are very small (usually one to two millimeters, not exceeding five millimeters) but their shells show the essential features of the class (Runnegar and Pojeta 1992). With laterally compressed shells suited for plowing through the surface layers of the substrate, these bivalves were probably deposit feeders (Waller 1998).

Like the other mollusc classes, the Bivalves were long thought to have evolved from a monoplacophoran-like ancestor, but the transitional stages remained conjectural owing to the lack of direct evidence from the fossil record (Stasek 1972). However, the discovery of a remarkable variety of Early and Middle Cambrian molluscs preserved mostly as phosphatic molds and silica-replaced replicas (Runnegar and Jell 1976) enabled B. Runnegar and J. Pojeta (1974) to propose a series of morphologic stages linking early monoplacophorans and the first bivalves (Figure 5). Important changes included lateral compression of the shell, increased length and curvature of the aperture (growing shell margin), and, ultimately, complete separation of the larval and adult shell into opposing valves.

Following the Early Cambrian origin of the class, the evolutionary history of bivalves is characterized by two major adaptive radiations. The first occurred in the Ordovician, by the middle of which all the subclasses were established (Pojeta 1978). The divergence of the subclasses may have occurred earlier, during Late Cambrian time, but undoubted bivalves of that age remain undiscovered. Bivalves were restricted primarily to inner shelf environments in the Early and Middle Paleozoic (Sepkoski and Miller 1985) but, at least by the Silurian, the cryptodonts (almost hingeless clams) were important exceptions, inhabiting low-oxygen environments of the outer shelf and slope. A second radiation occurred during the Mesozoic, especially the Jurassic, when siphonate bivalves (mostly heteroconchs) greatly diversified, today comprising 85 to 90 percent of species of suspension-feeding marine species (Stanley 1977).

Diversity and Classification

Runnegar and Pojeta (1974) grouped the class Bivalvia (or Pelecypoda according to some authors) with the classes Rostroconchia and Scaphopoda (tusk shells) in the molluscan subphylum Diasoma. However, T.R. Waller (1998) showed that the scaphopods are related more closely to cephalopods and gastropods, so he removed them from the subphylum.

Next to the gastropods, bivalves are the most diverse molluscs, with an estimated 6,000 to 15,000 living species; about 42,000 fossil species are known (Pojeta 1987). While the number of superfamilies of bivalves would probably generate little debate among paleontologists and neontologists, there is little consensus as to their higher classification—subclasses in some recent classifications vary from two (Waller 1998) to seven (Pojeta 1978). These uncertainties stem at least partly from the limited Cambrian and Early Ordovician record of bivalves, a time of the most fundamental diversification of the class. Certainly, a two-fold division of the Bivalvia is reasonable on the basis of gill structure and other characters. One group (the Protobranchia) comprised of the subclass Palaeotaxodonta, shows protobranch gills, and a second, the Auto-

Table 1.

A classification of the Class Bivalvia.
(Familiar names of some members comprising the orders
are given in parentheses.)

Subclass Palaeotaxodonta
Order Nuculoida (nut clams)
?Order Solemyoida (awning clams)

Subclass Cryptodonta
Order Praecardioida (cardiolids, buchiids, inoceramids)

Subclass Heteroconchia
Order Actinodontoida (babinkids, montanariids, cycloconchids)
Order Trigonioida (brooch clams)
Order Unionoida (freshwater mussels)
Order Veneroida (lucinids, cockles, razor clams, venus clams)

Subclass Pteriomorphia
Order Mytiloida (true mussels)
Order Arcoida (arks)
Order Limoida (file clams)
Order Pterioida (pen shells, pearl oysters)
Order Pectinoida (scallops)
Order Ostreoida (rhombopteriids, pseudomonotids, true oysters)

Subclass Anomalodesmata
Order Modiomorphoida (modiomorphids, modiolodontids)
Order Hippuritoida (rudists)
Order Pholadomyoida (pholadomyids, watering pots, cuspidariids)
Order Myoida (myids, geoducks, pholads)

brachia, has filibranch gills (or eulamellibranch derivatives). Notwithstanding this dichotomy, five subclasses are recognized here (Table 1; Figure 3). The Cryptodonta are the only extinct subclass of bivalves, disappearing in the end-Cretaceous mass extinction. However, the classification of the extant order Solemyoida is uncertain. Some authors include it in the Palaeotaxodonta (Pojeta 1978), but it may belong in the Cryptodonta (Newell 1942) and, if so, all subclasses would have living representatives. Members of the Cryptodonta, such as the inoceramids and buchiids (Figure 3), are traditionally classified in the subclass Pteriomorphia, but a recent study shows they were derived from Paleozoic praecardioid cryptodonts (Johnston and Collom 1998).

PAUL A. JOHNSTON

Works Cited

Aberhan, M. 1994. Early Jurassic Bivalvia of northern Chile. Part 1, Subclasses Palaeotaxodonta, Pteriomorphia, and Isofilibranchia. *Beringeria* 13:1–115.

Allison, P.A., P.B. Wignall, and C.E. Brett. 1995. Palaeo-oxygenation: Effects and recognition. *In* D.W.J. Bosence and P.A. Allison (eds.), *Marine Palaeoenvironmental Analysis from Fossils*. Geological Society Special Publication 83. Boulder, Colorado: Geological Society of America; Lawrence: University of Kansas.

Bambach, R.K. 1985. Classes and adaptive variety: The ecology of diversification in marine faunas through the Phanerozoic. *In* J.W. Valentine (ed.), *Phanerozoic Diversity Patterns: Profiles in Macroevolution*. San Francisco, California: American Association for the Advancement of Sciences; Princeton: Princeton University Press.

Barnes, R.D. 1980. *Invertebrate Zoology*. 4th ed. Philadelphia: Holt, Rinehart and Winston.

Carter, J.G. 1990. Evolutionary significance of shell microstructure in the Palaeotaxodonta, Pteriomorphia and Isofilibranchia (Bivalvia: Molluska). *In* J.G. Carter (ed.) *Skeletal Biomineralization: Patterns, Processes and Evolutionary Trends*. Vol. 1. New York: Van Nostrand.

Carter, J.G., and M.J.S. Tevesz. 1978. The shell structure of *Ptychodesma* (Cyrtodontidae; Bivalvia) and its bearing on the evolution of the Pteriomorphia. *Philosophical Transactions of the Royal Society of London*, ser. B, 284:367–74.

Carter, R.M. 1967. On the nature and definition of the lunule, escutcheon and corcelet in the Bivalvia. *Proceedings of the Malacological Society of London* 37:243–63.

Cobabe, E. 1991. Lucinid bivalve evolution and the detection of chemosymbiosis in the fossil record. Ph.D. diss., Harvard University.

Fankboner, P.V., and R.G.B. Reid. 1990. Nutrition in giant clams (Tridacnidae). *In* B. Morton (ed.), *The Bivalvia—Proceedings of a Memorial Symposium in Honour of Sir Charles Maurice Yonge (1899–1986) at the IXth International Malacological Congress, 1986, Edinburgh, Scotland, U.K.* Hong Kong: Hong Kong University Press.

Johnston, P.A. 1993. Lower Devonian Pelecypoda from southeastern Australia. *Memoirs of the Association of Australasian Paleontologists* 14:1–134.

Johnston, P.A., and C.J. Collom. 1998. The bivalve heresies—Inoceramidae are Cryptodonta, not Pteriomorphia. *In* P.A. Johnston and J.W. Haggart (eds.), *Bivalves: An Eon of Evolution—Paleobiological Studies Honoring Norman D. Newell.* Calgary: University of Calgary Press.

Kauffman, E.G. 1975. Dispersal and biostratigraphic potential of Cretaceous benthonic Bivalvia in the Western Interior. *Geological Association of Canada, Special Paper* 13:163–94.

Kauffman, E.G., and B. Runnegar. 1975. *Atomodesma* (Bivalvia), and Permian species of the United States. *Journal of Paleontology* 49 (1):23–51.

Kríz, J. 1979. Silurian Cardiolidae (Bivalvia). *Sborník Geologickych, Paleontologie* 22:1–160.

———. 1985. Silurian Slavidae (Bivalvia). *Sborník Geologickych, Paleontologie* 27:47–111.

Liljedahl, L. 1984. Silurian silicified bivalves from Gotland. *Sveriges Geologiska Undersökning,* ser. C, 804:1–82.

Moore, R.C. (ed.). 1966. *Treatise on Invertebrate Paleontology.* Part N, *Molluska 6, Bivalvia.* Boulder, Colorado: Geological Society of America; Lawrence: University of Kansas.

Morton, B. 1996. The evolutionary history of the Bivalvia. *In* J. Taylor (ed.), *Origin and Evolutionary Radiation of the Molluska.* Oxford and New York: Oxford University Press.

Newell, N.D. 1942. Late Paleozoic pelecypods: Mytilacea. *State Geological Survey of Kansas* 10 (2):1–115.

Newell, N.D., and D.W. Boyd. 1985. Permian scallops of the Pectinacean Family Streblochondriidae. *American Museum Novitates* 2831:1–13.

Peel, J.S. 1991. Functional morphology of the Class Helcionelloida and the early evolution of the Molluska. *In* A. Simonetta and S. Conway Morris (eds.), *The Early Evolution of Metazoa and Significance of Problematic Taxa.* Cambridge and New York: Cambridge University Press.

Pojeta Jr., J. 1978. The origin and early taxonomic diversification of pelecypods. *Philosophical Transactions of the Royal Society of London,* ser. B, 284:225–46.

———. 1987. Class Pelecypoda. *In* R.S. Boardman, A.H. Cheetham, and A.J. Rowell (eds.), *Fossil Invertebrates.* Palo Alto, California: Blackwell Scientific Publications.

———. 1988. The origin and Paleozoic diversification of solemyoid pelecypods. *New Mexico Bureau of Mines and Mineral Resources Memoir* 44:201–71.

Pojeta Jr., J., and B. Runnegar. 1985. The early evolution of diasome mollusks. *In* K.M. Wilbur (eds.), *The Molluska.* Vol. 10, *Evolution.* Orlando, Florida: Academic Press.

Reid, R.G. 1990. Evolutionary implications of sulphide-oxidizing symbioses in bivalves. *In* B. Morton (ed.), *The Bivalvia Proceedings of a Memorial Symposium in Honour of Sir Charles Maurice Yonge (1899–1986) at the IXth International Malacological Congress, 1986, Edinburgh, Scotland, U.K.* Hong Kong, Hong Kong University Press.

Reid, R.G.B., R.F. McMahon, D.O. Foighil, and R. Finnigan. 1992. Anterior inhalant currents and pedal feeding in bivalves. *The Veliger* 35:93–104.

Runnegar, B. 1974. Evolutionary history of the bivalve subclass Anomalodesmata. *Journal of Paleontology* 48:904–39.

———. 1996. Early evolution of the Molluska: The fossil record. *In* J. Taylor (ed.) *Origin and Evolutionary Radiation of the Molluska.* Oxford and New York: Oxford University Press.

Runnegar, B., and P.A. Jell. 1976. Australian Middle Cambrian mollusks and their bearing on early molluskan evolution. *Alcheringa* 1:109–38.

Runnegar, B., and J. Pojeta Jr. 1974. Molluskan phylogeny: The paleontological viewpoint. *Science* 186:311–17.

———. 1992. The earliest bivalves and their Ordovician descendants. *American Malacological Bulletin* 9:117–22.

Sánchez, T.M., and C. Babin. 1993. Un insolite mollusque bivalve, *Catamarcaia* n.g., de l'Arenig (Ordovicien inférieur) d'Argentine. *Comptes Rendus de l'Académie des Sciences,* Paris, 316 (2):265–71.

Sepkoski Jr., J.J., and A.I. Miller. 1985. Evolutionary faunas and the distribution of Paleozoic marine communities in space and time. *In* J.W. Valentine (ed.), *Phanerozoic Diversity Patterns: Profiles in Macroevolution.* San Francisco, California: American Association for the Advancement of Science; Princeton: Princeton University Press.

Seilacher, A. 1990. Aberrations in bivalve evolution related to photo- and chemosymbiosis. *Historical Biology* 3:289–11.

Speden, I.G. 1970. The type Fox Hills Formation, Cretaceous (Maestrichtian), South Dakota. Part 2, Systematics of the Bivalvia. *Peabody Museum of Natural History Bulletin* 33:1–222.

Stanley, S.M. 1970. *Relation of Shell Form to Life Habits of the Bivalvia (Molluska).* Geological Society of America Memoir 125. Boulder, Colorado: Geological Society of America; Lawrence: University of Kansas.

———. 1977. Trends, rates, and patterns of evolution in the Bivalvia. *In* A. Hallam (ed.), *Patterns of Evolution.* Amsterdam and New York: Elsevier.

Stasek, C.R. 1972. The molluskan framework. *In* M. Florkin and B.T. Scheer (eds.), *Chemical Zoology.* Vol. 7, *Mollusca.* New York: Academic Press.

Wade, B. 1926. The fauna of the Ripley Formation on Coon Creek, Tennessee. *United States Geological Survey, Professional Paper* 137:1–72.

Waller, T.R. 1990. The evolution of ligament systems in the Bivalvia. *In* B. Morton (ed.), *The Bivalvia Proceedings of a Memorial Symposium in Honour of Sir Charles Maurice Yonge (1899–1986) at the IXth International Malacological Congress, 1986, Edinburgh, Scotland, U.K.* Hong Kong: Hong Kong University Press.

Waller, T.R. 1998. Origin of the class Bivalvia and a phylogeny of major groups. *In* P.A. Johnston and J.W. Haggart (eds.), *Bivalves: An Eon of Evolution—Paleobiological Studies Honoring Norman D. Newell.* Calgary: University of Calgary Press.

Zakharov, V.A. 1981. Buchiidae and biostratigraphy of the boreal Upper Jurassic and Neocomian. *Trudy Institut Geologii i Geofiziki* (Moscow, Nauka) 458:1–270.

Further Reading

Moore, R.C. (ed.). 1966. *Treatise on Invertebrate Paleontology.* Part N, *Molluska 6, Bivalvia.* Boulder, Colorado: Geological Society of America; Lawrence: University of Kansas.

Pojeta Jr., J. 1987. Class Pelecypoda. *In* R.S. Boardman, A.H. Cheetham, and A.J. Rowell (eds.), *Fossil Invertebrates.* Palo Alto, California: Blackwell Scientific.

Runnegar, B., and J. Pojeta Jr. 1974. Molluskan phylogeny: The paleontological viewpoint. *Science* 186:311–17.

Stanley, S.M. 1970. *Relation of Shell Form to Life Habits of the Bivalvia (Molluska).* Geological Society of America Memoir 125. Boulder, Colorado: Geological Society of America; Lawrence: University of Kansas.

Waller, T.R. 1998. Origin of the class Bivalvia and a phylogeny of major groups. *In* P.A. Johnston and J.W. Haggart (eds.), *Bivalves: An Eon of Evolution—Paleobiological Studies Honoring Norman D. Newell.* Calgary: University of Calgary Press.

BOULE, MARCELLIN

French, 1861–1942

Marcellin Boule played a prominent role in the development of paleoanthropology in France at a crucial period when the very existence of fossil humans was being vindicated and an increasing number of sites were being discovered and excavated. He was among the first to publish paleoanthropological works that were a synthesis of archeology, geology, and zoology and served as the founder and editor of two journals and director of the only paleo-anthropological institute of the time.

Marcellin Boule was born on 1 January 1861 in Montsalvy, Cantal, France. In 1884 Boule earned his master of science in both the natural and physical sciences from the Faculty of Sciences of Toulouse. That same year, Boule described a prehistoric flint mine. In 1887 Boule received his teaching certificate from the Museum of Natural History in Paris, but upon the museum's insistence, Boule turned to geological research instead of teaching. Boule initially expressed an interest in stratigraphy and petrography, but given his close associations with Albert Gaudry and Louis Lartet, Boule shifted his interest toward paleontology, the field to which he would make his most significant contributions.

Boule's research included stratigraphic investigations of newly discovered Mousterian rock shelters and the publishing, with Émile Cartailhac, of a monograph on the Grotte de Reilhac. This publication mapped the gradual transition from the Paleolithic to the Neolithic, and in doing so undermined the classical theory that these two epochs were marked by a clear separation. The importance of Boule's early works is that they utilized an interdisciplinary approach to collect and interpret data. In these works, Boule incorporated aspects of stratigraphic geology, paleontology, and archeology to offer a complete view of prehistoric humans. During this time Boule also cofounded *L'anthropologie* in 1890 and served as its editor from 1893 to 1940.

Following a brief teaching job at Clermont-Ferrand, Boule returned to Paris in 1890 and received his Ph.D. in the natural sciences in 1892. That year Boule turned down a professorship at Montpellier in favor of a position as preparer in the paleontological laboratory of the Museum of Natural History. After serving as Gaudry's assistant, Boule followed Gaudry as professor of paleontology at the Museum of Natural History, a position held from 1902 to 1936. While serving as professor, Boule continued his novel method of paleoanthropological research. Between 1911 and 1913, Boule published a three-part monograph, "L'homme fossile de la Chapelle-aux-Saints," in which he provided a detailed description and reconstruction of the most anatomical complete specimen of the Neanderthals known. This research supported Boule's claim that Neanderthals were a distinct, more primitive species than that of modern humans.

In 1914 Albert I of Monaco founded the Institute for Human Paleontology in Paris and chose Boule as director. Boule also founded the journal *Archives de paléontologie humaine* and served as its catalyst for research.

In 1921, following two decades of research, *Les hommes fossiles: Éléments de paléontologie humaine* was published. In this benchmark work, Boule applied geological, paleontological, and zoological methods of analysis to trace the evolution of both humans and their environment. Such research conveyed Boule's belief that human evolution was not the consequence of mere anatomical changes, but was an ongoing process in which anatomical changes were the result of humans adapting to the changing environment. Marcellin Boule died on 4 July 1942 in Montsalvy, Cantal, France.

EDOUARD L. BONÉ AND BRIAN CALLENDER

Biography

Born in Montsalvy, Cantal, France, 1 January 1861. Received M.S. in natural and physical sciences, Faculty of Sciences of Toulouse, 1884; teaching certificate, Museum of Natural History, Paris, 1887; Ph.D. in natural sciences, Museum of Natural History, Paris, 1892. Appointed preparer, paleontological laboratory, Museum of Natural History, Paris, 1892; professor of paleontology, Museum of Natural History, Paris, 1902–36; director, Institute for Human Paleontology, 1914. Founder (1890) and editor (1893–1940), *L'Anthropologie*. Among the first to produce paleoanthropological research utilizing geology, archaeology, and paleontology. Died in Montsalvy, Cantal, France, 4 July 1942.

Major Publications

1888–89. Essai de paléontologie stratigraphique de l'homme. *Revue d'anthropologie*.

1906–10. *Les grottes de Grimaldi: Géologie et paléontologie*. Monaco: Imprimerie de Monaco.

1911–13. L'homme fossile de la Chapelle-aux-Saints. *Annales de paléontologie* 6–8; Paris: Masson, 1913.

1921. *Les hommes fossiles: Éléments de paléontologie humaine*. Paris: Masson; as *Fossil Men: A Textbook of Human Paleontology*, H.V. Vallois, coauthor; New York: Dryden Press, 1957; London: Thames and Hudson, 1957.

Further Reading

1937. Jubilé de M. Marcellin Boule. *L'anthropologie* 47:583–648.

Vallois, H.V. 1946. Marcellin Boule. *L'anthropologie* 50:203–10.

BRACHIOPODS

The Brachiopoda is a phylum of marine organisms that cover their soft bodies with shells made up of two parts or "valves." The valves are quite different from each other, one on top, the other below it, unlike bivalves where the valves are similar and side by side. Brachiopods are "lophophorates." This means they have an internal organ called a "lophophore" covered in cilia (hairlike structures), a structure that is used for food gathering and respiration. Brachiopods are solitary and do not form colonies, although they may be found in clusters, clinging to one another. They inhabit continental shelves and the upper part of the continental slope. The majority appear to be "fixosessile," that is, fixed to the substrate (sediment, rock, or rock wall). "Plenipedunculate" species have an unbranched stalk, known as a "pedicle," which attaches to the seafloor or some object upon it. "Rhizopedunculate" species have a pedicle that is divided into rootlets or papillae (blunt projections) and attaches to material in the sediment, like algal holdfasts. Other species may encrust or cement themselves to some object via the umbral region of the shell (posterior apex of the bottom valve). The "liberosessile" species are "ambitopic" or free-lying, and may use spines, the pedicle, or their flattened shape to help prevent them from being "knocked about" by currents. The "infaunal" lingulids are burrowing brachiopods. The extinct Productids were "quasi-infaunal" (half in and half out of the sediment), using spines to assist in their support.

Source of the Name

The name Brachiopoda was devised by French biologist and philosopher Georges Cuvier (1769–1832), at a time when the lophophore was regarded as a molluscan foot ("pod"), which evolved into an arm ("brachium"). The common name "lamp shell" was derived from the appearance of the shell of terebratulids when laid on their dorsal (back) valve. They resemble an old-fashioned oil lamp.

Brachiopod Appearance

For simplicity, brachiopods can be divided into two main groups: the "articulates," which use teeth and muscles to assist in opening the shell, and the "non-articulates," which use only muscles. Correct classification of brachiopods is outlined later. Figure 1 illustrates internal and external features of brachiopods.

External Features of Articulated Brachiopods

In articulate brachiopods the "umbo" (pointed end), or beak, is posterior and the commissure (margin) with the widest gape is anterior. The valves pivot posteriorly. In articulate strophic shells the pivot is a straight "hinge line" created by the union of the brachial valve (dorsal) and pedicle valve (ventral) (Figure 1D2, 1D3). At the point of union there may be one or two interareas (the brachial interarea and the pedicle interarea) between the valves. The brachial interarea may contain a triangular notch known as a "notothyrium." The pedicle interarea has a similar triangular gap known as a "delthyrium." It is through the gap between the two valves that the pedicle (Figure 1A) emerges, when present. In some species the gap completely closes during ontogeny (growth). Non-strophic shells have a curved cardinal margin, and the hinge line is tangential to this. The delthyrium may develop two lateral "deltidal plates," which grow inwards to produce a hole, the "foramen," through which the pedicle emerges (Figure 1B2). Details of the pattern produced by the deltidal plates and the degree of posterior movement of the foramen during ontogeny are useful in classification.

The umbo of the pedicle valve is usually protuberant and may be straight or curved towards the brachial valve. "Beak ridges," which may be sharp or rounded, often are present. The two valves may be both convex (biconvex condition), or one convex (usually the pedicle valve) and the other concave (concavo-convex condition). The surface may be smooth or ribbed. The ribs may begin at the umbo or anterior to it. Sometimes the ribs bifurcate (split in two) as they are produced during ontogeny. As the animal grows, new material is added to the shell to form "growth lines." Growth lines may be indistinct, distinct, or prominent. When they meet ribs, a "rugose" (rough) pattern is produced. Strong ribbing often leads to crenulations (zigzag pattern) on the anterior commissure, which may extend to the lateral margins. Also, the valves of some species include spines. They may be solid or hollow, cylindrical or elongate triangular projections.

A "sulcus," or depression, may develop in either one or both valves. Sometimes there is an alternate keel, or fold, to the sulcus. This causes various alterations to the form of the anterior commissure, each of which is given a descriptive name.

"Punctae," or elongated cavities in the shell, created during growth, may be observed as a series of "holes," although these spaces do not penetrate to the surface (Figure 1A12). The density and shape of punctae can be used in classification, since only certain orders develop the cavities.

Adaptive Features of Brachiopods

Special features on the exterior of brachiopods probably had specific functions. To interpret the possible function, scholars make "educated guesses" based upon similar structures in living species. Spines were (and still are) most likely used for protection against predators, anchorage in mud and shifting sediments (e.g., productids), and/or extending the sensitivity range of the sensory setae. The "zigzag" commissure would be useful to sieve food particles from sediment, increase the surface area of sensitivity, and/or assist in the prevention of predation and parasitism, especially where spines were attached to the edges. The sulcus on the anterior commissure probably helps to separate inhaled and exhaled currents, so that food and wastes do not mix.

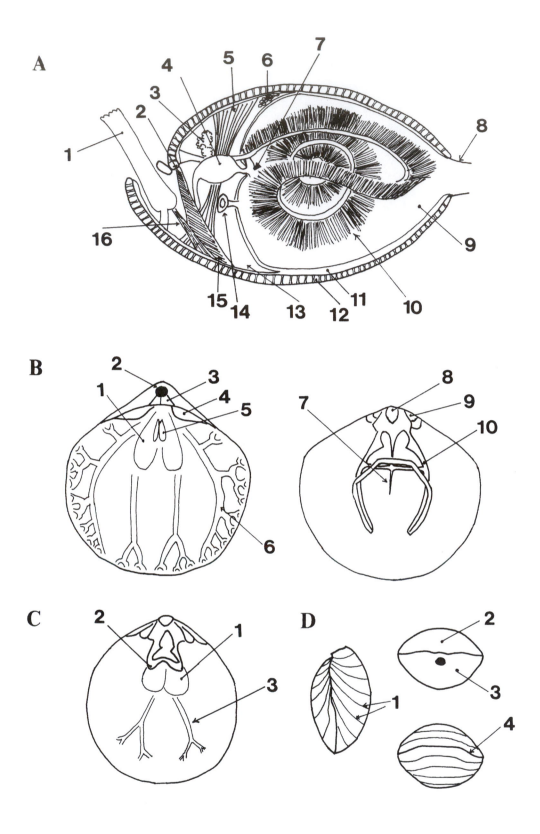

Figure 1. Brachiopod features: *A: 1,* pedicle; *2,* cardinal process; *3,* diverticula; *4,* stomach; *5,* adductor muscles; *6,* gonads; *7,* mouth; *8,* setae; *9,* mantle cavity; *10,* ciliated lophophore; *11,* mantle epithelium; *12,* shell with punctae; *13,* body cavity; *14,* nephridium; *15,* diductor muscle; *16,* pedicle adjustor muscle. *B: 1,* diductor muscle scars; *2,* foramen; *3,* delthyrium with deltidal plates; *4,* hinge teeth; *5,* adductor muscle scars; *6,* pallial markings or mantle canals; *7,* median septum; *8,* cardinal process; *9,* sockets; *10,* long brachidium. *C: 1,* muscle scars; *2,* short brachidium; *3,* mantle canals. *D: 1,* growth lines; *2,* brachial, or dorsal, valve; *3,* pedicle, or ventral, valve; *4,* anterior commissure, or margin. Drawn by Robert S. Craig.

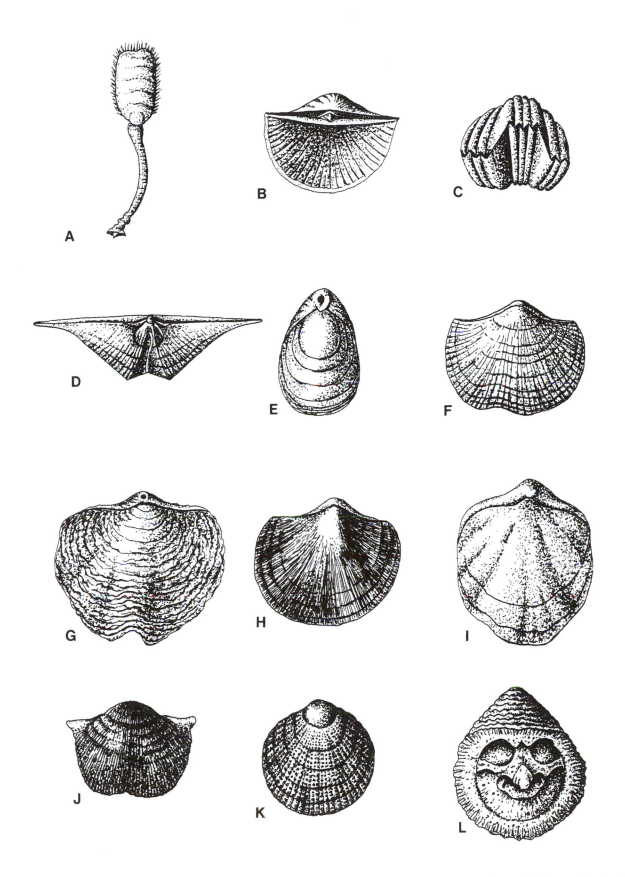

Figure 2. Types of brachiopods. *A,* lingulid; *B,* strophomenid; *C,* rhynchonellid; *D,* spiriferid; *E,* terebratulid; *F,* atrypid; *G,* athyrid; *H,* orthid; *I,* pentamerid; *J,* productid; *K,* tremerallid; *L,* cranid. Drawn by Robert S. Craig.

Internal Features of Articulated Brachiopods

Living brachiopod species have a series of muscles that are used to open and close the valves and adjust the valves about the pedicle. These muscles leave scars in the valves, which may be seen in fossil specimens. "Adductor muscles" close the valves and are attached to each valve in front of the hinge line (Figure 1A5). Two scars are found on each valve. "Diductor muscles" open the shell (Figure 1A15). They run from the cardinal process near the umbo of the brachial valve to the floor of the pedicle valve, again leaving scars. Adjustor muscles for the pedicle (when present) are attached to the pedicle valve and the cardinal process and also leave one or more scars. The pattern of such scars are shown in Figures 1B5 and 1B1.

There are usually a pair of hinge teeth in the pedicle valve which articulate with sockets in the brachial valve. Some strophomenids lost these teeth and instead had a series of small projections, or "denticles" along the hinge line. The shape, position, size, and development of ancillary structures such as "dental plates," which extend to the valve floor, are important morphological features used in classification. Similarly, in the brachial valve, the features associated with the sockets are used in classification. At the posterior end of the brachial valve the cardinal process (Figures 1A2, 1B8), used for muscle attachment, may have a variety of structural features, again used in classification.

All the major organs are contained in the posterior section of the shell, known as the "body cavity." A "mantle" of epithelial tissue lines the floor of the anterior section of the valves. This separates from the floor and forms the anterior body cavity, which encloses the muscles, reproductive, excretory, and digestive organs. Fossil specimens may show signs of "mantle canals," which are projections along the valve floors sometimes called "pallial markings" (Figure 1B6).

In the mantle cavity, anterior to the body wall, is found the lophophore, or "arm-foot," from which the brachiopod acquired its name. This structure is used for respiration and filter feeding (straining food particles from water). The lophophore may be supported by calcite extensions from the valve floor (strophomenids), brachiophores (extensions from the cardinal area; rhynchonellids), or a complex brachidium. This may be arranged spirally, as in atrypids and spiriferids, or in the form of a short or long loop, as in terebratulids. These structures are important in classification. Within the shell, on the body wall, mantle and the lophophore can sometimes be found small irregular bodies of calcite called "spicules."

External Features of Non-Articulated Brachiopods

The Lingulata (Figure 2A) consist of shells composed of chitin (a tough fibrous polysaccharide) and calcium phosphate. The lingulates have elongate oval shells with growth lines. Obolids are suboval to round shells with the interarea separated into two parts (propareas) by a triangular "pedicle groove." Acrotretides may be circular with conical pedicle valves, while dicinids have flat shells that are round or oval. The non-articulates are composed of calcium carbonate. Cranids (or "face shells," so-called because of the facelike markings produced by the internal features) have a flat ventral valve and a conical dorsal valve (Figure 2L). The valves contain punctae but no pedicle, and the shell is cemented to the substrate. Craniopsids are "impunctate" (no punctae). Tremerellacids are large, thick, biconvex shells (Figure 2K). The pedicle valve has a large pseudointerarea.

Internal Features of Non-Articulated Brachiopods

Because there are no teeth or a hinge line, the non-articulates rely entirely on their diductor and adductor musculature to open and close the valves. "Oblique" muscles enable the valves to move from side to side. Muscle platforms or depressions may exist in some species. The lophophore is not supported. A median septum can be located on the brachial valve of some species.

Soft Parts of Brachiopods

The brachiopod mantle consists of thin tissues lining the inner surface of each valve. It is divided into the outer layer, which adheres to the shell, and the inner layer, which lines the cavity. The mantle grows with the shell, and the mantle (epithelium) secretes the shell material, primarily at the anterior and lateral edges. This layer also lays down a "secondary shell" along the inner surface, thus thickening sections of shell already produced.

In articulates the pedicle develops from the larval segment that attaches to the substrate. It grows into a tough, solid cylindrical structure consisting of a core of connective tissue surrounded by epithelial tissue and thick cuticle. The pedicle may have a solid end or be divided into papillae or rootlets.

Non-articulate brachiopods that develop a pedicle do so from the posterior edge of the ventral mantle. The pedicle shares its structure with the mantle from which it forms. The pedicle is a hollow cylinder; muscles either within it or attached to the walls are used to move it. The surface of the lophophore, the primary organ for collecting food, is covered in hairlike cilia. Two long arms, or brachia, extend into the mantle cavity and may be folded, looped, or wound in a spiral. Also, brachia may be either unsupported or suspended by supports. The lophophore divides the mantle cavity into inhalant and exhalant chambers. Water is filtered as it is pumped from one chamber to the other. Two lines of closely spaced filaments, covered in cilia, act like the teeth of a comb, filtering out food material. The cilia's whiplike action propels food-containing material to a food groove. From here the material is moved to the mouth. Food is extracted in the digestive tract, and waste is returned via the same system (when no anus is present). The waste is removed by the exhalant current. Three types of lophophore may develop, but these are not seen in fossil specimens.

Digestion and Waste Removal

Food, consisting of plankton, bacteria, and dissolved organic molecules, is collected by the lophophore and passed into the mouth and then to the gut by wavelike peristaltic contractions. The gut is made up of an esophagus, a stomach, a "liver" (diverticulum), and intestine (Figure 1). One or two digestive glands usually are present. Some systems end with an anus, while others have a blind gut.

Depending on the system, fecal pellets either are excreted via the anus in non-articulates or transported backward and voided by the mouth (James et al. 1992). Excretion is accomplished via a trumpet-like tube called the "metanephridium." In rhynchonellids, two such organs exist; all other orders possess only one. The waste is voided into the mantle cavity.

Circulatory System and Respiration

Like many other invertebrates, brachiopods have an open circulatory system. A contractile sack, or "heart," helps pump circulatory fluid, which "bathes" all the organs. Nutrients and oxygen are exchanged for wastes, which are voided. Brachiopods exchange gases by way of the lophophore, the mantle canals, and possibly the cecum found within the punctae. The gases are carried in the circulatory fluid.

Sensory Systems

In brachiopods, nerves run from the edge of the valve to a central ganglion (nerve cell cluster) around the mouth (the "circumesophageal ring") and also directly to muscles. Ganglia are situated along nerve pathways to assist in the transfer of messages. Besides controlling muscles and feeding, brachiopods receive information about their surroundings via setae (bristles), spines at the shell's edge, the lophophore, and mantle canals. No evidence is available to support the hypothesis that the cecum is involved in sensory reception. Brachiopods appear to have some chemosensitivity, possibly via the lophophore and setae. It is believed that external anterior spines may extend the area of sensitivity, thus functioning as an early warning device.

Reproduction

The reproductive system is made up of a pair of "gonads" (little more than aggregates of germ cells), which are often brightly colored (yellow, orange, or red). Germ cells develop ventrally and dorsally from cells lining the body (celom). Gonads may be tied to the body wall. In some species there are "brood pouches" which allow larvae to go through some development within the mantle cavity before being expelled. Sexes are separate in the majority of species; three species are known to be "hermaphroditic," that is, having both sexes in the same organism. The female lays upwards of 180,000 eggs. After release of eggs and sperm, fertilization may occur either in the water or in the mantle cavity. The latter is certainly true for those species that have brood pouches. The larvae are free-swimming and may remain so from a few hours or days (articulates) up to several weeks (nonarticulates). The larva moves about, selecting an appropriate structure in the sediment to which it will attach. A larva's survival is enhanced once it attaches to a surface. The primary attachment is not cemented, so the larva can be removed by currents without damage to the pedicle bud. Firm attachment occurs within a short period. The larvae prefer gravel over sand. They use pebbles, boulders, and shells most commonly, and larvae often become secure in depressions or in gaps in rock walls.

Environments

All ancient seas appear to have had populations of brachiopods, including inland seas ("epicontinental" seas) as well as the major oceans that existed at various times. In the Southern Hemisphere extant (living) species exist in waters around southern Australia, both north and south islands of New Zealand, southeastern and southwestern Africa, the west and east coasts of South America, and around Antarctica. Northern Hemisphere brachiopods occur on both sides of the North Atlantic, the Arctic, the Caribbean and West Indies, the western coasts of the United States, the Mediterranean Sea, and the waters around Japan.

Environmental Conditions

Brachiopods are sessile (stationary) and may lie upon, burrow within, or be attached to the substrate. Lingulids are capable of burrowing into the substrate, using the pedicle to attach themselves, and leave part of their shell exposed at the burrow mouth to extract food. Attached brachiopods may use the pedicle as a holdfast or may be cemented by their shell to the substrate. The craniforms are particularly adept at cementing themselves to the substrate. Many articulate brachiopods have lost their pedicle during evolution to become "free-lying." The shell may sit on the surface sediment or use spines to prop it upright in soft sediments. Scholars have suggested that all Cenozoic brachiopods used their pedicle only for attachment. Work by Richardson (1981) and her coworkers in New Zealand have found that pedicles from species with a small foramina can be used as a type of "pogo stick," as a means of moving away from predators or enveloping sediments. Richardson has suggested that thickening in the rear section of the shell assists the free-lying brachiopod in righting itself in strong currents.

Attached brachiopods may use rock walls, the shells of other organisms, or isolated rocks as a substrate. In all of these situations, they may live in loose communities with juveniles attached to adults. Brachiopods are marine organisms, with only lingulids able to live in transitional marine conditions, in which salt- and freshwater mix. The flexibility of linguids, together with their ability to burrow, has provided them with a niche (lifestyle) that they have been able to exploit relatively unchanged for nearly 500 million years.

Environments that have a high level of suspended sediment in turbulent currents are not conducive to brachiopods, probably because of their filter-feeding lifestyle. The phylum appears to be reasonably tolerant of depth variations, ranging from 5 to 2000 meters in one species (McCammon 1973). This same species can survive in water temperature of between 8 and 12 degrees centigrade. Work in New Zealand has found that, for 12 of the 30 species recorded, brachiopods range from 8 to greater than 21 degrees centigrade and from less than 10 to over 1000 meters (Lee 1991). M.W. Foster (1989) records brachiopods surviving winter water temperatures as low as −2 degrees centigrade in Antarctica. The range of substrates on which the brachiopods can be found includes biogenic sediments, terrigenous material (material washed out from the land), gravels, sand, and volcaniclastic deposits, especially volcanic pebbles.

Brachiopods are often found in settings that include other filter feeders including bivalves (e.g., clams), bryozoans ("moss animals"), and sessile worms. The suggestion that bivalves outcompeted brachiopods certainly is not supported in these associations. However, bivalves are far more common in a greater variety of habitats. Brachiopods are often encrusted by other organisms, including corals, worms, bryozoans, and cnidarians (corals, sea anemones). Often, marks (trace fossils) of these organisms can be found on the valves, including pedicle attachment sites of the pedicles of other brachiopods. The primary predators of brachiopods appear to be gastropods, and boreholes cut by these predators have been found in fossil specimens. Birds, fishes, parasitic worms, and asteroids (starfishes) are also likely predators (as well as humans from Australia and Japan on lingulids). Commensalism (shared livelihood) has also been detected (Feldmann et al. 1996).

Precise age of brachiopods is difficult to gauge. Growth lines are laid down according to seasonal and environmental changes, so these lines are not clear indicators of actual age. Most research has centered on "growth rates," suggesting an average age of 8 years and a maximum of 15 years; some workers suggest some species are over 40 years old. The chance of survival of brachiopods seems to increase with increased size. Growth rates indicated by growth lines appear to support this, with greater distances between the lines in the posterior part of the shell.

Evolutionary History

Brachiopods appeared in the Early Cambrian. These first brachiopods were moderate in size, had a complex structure, and were diverse: Five orders of non-articulates and one order of articulate are present. This suggests a previous history that so far is unavailable in the rock record. S. Conway Morris and J.S. Peel (1995) have found articulated halkieriids in Lower Cambrian rocks from Greenland and suggest this group may have played a significant part in brachiopod evolution. During the Late Cambrian brachiopod radiation accelerated, with phosphatic lingulids being the most common. One group, the obolellids, developed calcareous shells. The first true articulates, some with rudimentary articulation, also developed. By the end of the Cambrian, orthids and pentamerids were to be found living in marine shelf environments.

The second phase of the evolutionary radiation occurred during the Ordovician, as brachiopods became more diverse and abundant. Two more groups of non-articulates developed calcareous shells. Orthids diversified to include both punctate and inpunctate varieties. Strophomenids arose from the latter, while non-strophic rhynchonellids evolved from the pentamerids during this time. The rhynchonellids gave rise to a spiralled lophophorate group, the atripids, in the Late Ordovician. Of the six orders of articulate brachiopods, five were present by the end of the Ordovician.

Through the Silurian and Devonian, brachiopod diversification continued, and by the end of the Silurian terebratulids had appeared, probably evolved from the rhynchonellids. The end of the Devonian saw the demise of some orders of non-articulates, while pentamerids, strophomenids, and terebratulids suffered major extinctions. Rhynchonellids, spiriferids (which had evolved from

the strophomenids during the Early Silurian), and the remaining orders of non-articulates—including lingulids, acrotretids, discinids, and cranids—were not affected by the extinction events. Along with the strophomenids and terebratulids that had survived, they expanded their numbers until the end of the Permian. Later Paleozoic productids, a suborder of strophomenids, expanded into a new niche due to their quasi-infaunal habit.

The great Permian extinction event left only the non-articulate orders, some rhynchonellids, spiriferids, and the terebratulids to continue into the Mesozoic. Only rhynchonellids and terebratulids, as well as the same four orders of non-articulates, survived at the end of the Jurassic. By the Cretaceous-Tertiary (KT) extinction event, terebratulids had taken over the majority of articulate brachiopod niches. Although some diversification occurred after the KT event, brachiopods no longer held such a prominent place in the fossil record. Recent brachiopod records are patchy, most likely due to their localities (cool, deep water), poor collection, and lack of economic importance.

Classification and Identifying Features

The classification of brachiopods is under constant review. Researchers have used a number of parameters to establish a classification system. These include: (a) shell composition, (b) articulation, and (c) dentition. The features that scholars use to assist in naming and describing a brachiopod are as follows:

- shell shape, composition, and size
- surface features, such as ribs, sulci and folds, punctae, and growth lines
- beak or umbo characteristics
- delthyrium features, such as deltidal plates and foramen shape, size, and position
- teeth and associated structures
- muscle scars (both valves)
- mantle canals (pallial sinuses) (both valves)
- sockets and associated plates
- median septum
- cardinal process
- brachidium or brachiophores

Today, scholars are incorporating biochemical analysis in classification. Areas under present investigation include amino acid analysis (Walton et al. 1993), immunological response of intracrystalline proteinaceous macromolecules (Endo et al. 1994) and arrangement of mantle cavities (Wright 1994). Conclusions from Cohen and Gawthrop's recent work (1996) on brachiopod molecular phylogeny using small subunit ribosomal RNA sequences, contradicts those of Popov et al. (1993) and Endo et al. (1994). A clear picture is still to be found.

When attempting to classify a particular specimen the features outlined previously must be considered. Often, due to the nature of the sediments in which fossil brachiopods are found, the internal structures are surrounded by a hard matrix. It is then necessary to grind (serial section) the specimen and record each milli-

Table 1

Group	Time Range	General Characteristics
LINGULIFORMEA Brachiopods with organophosphatic inarticulate shells		
Lingulida	Early Cambrian to Recent	Small to large gently biconvex shell. Large pedicle.
Acrotretida	Early Cambrian to Recent	Small subcircular shells.
Discinida	Middle Ordovician to Recent	Flat, round or oval shells.
Siphonotredida	Late Cambrian to Middle Ordovician	Similar to Acrotredida, except for shell structure and ontogeny.
Paterinida	Early Cambrian to Middle Ordovician	Small biconvex shells. Pedicle sometimes present.
CRANIIFORMEA Brachiopods without articulation and calcareous shells		
Craniida	Middle Ordovician to Recent	Small, punctate with flat ventral and conical dorsal shells. Muscle scars and median septum give the impression of a face.
Craniopsida	Middle Ordovician to Middle Carboniferous	Similar to Craniida but impunctate shells.
Trimerellida	Middle Ordovician to Late Silurian	Large biconvex shells. Muscle platforms with central buttress often creating two paired chambers.
RHYNCHONELLIFORMEA Brachiopods with calcareous valves hinged by teeth and sockets		
Strophic Brachiopods Those with a straight or nearly straight hinge line or cardinal margin		
Orthids	Early Cambrian to Permian (or Early Triassic)	Small, semicircular, biconvex, densely ribbed shells. Open delthyrium and lack calcified brachidium.
Strophomenids	Ordovician to Permian	Large, "butterfly" shaped, concavo-convex shells. No pedicle opening, resting on pedicle valve often with spines (Productids) and lacking calcified brachidium.
Spiriferids	Ordovician to Permian. (Some authors include Thecideina in this order and thus extend its range to Recent times. Others (Cohen and Gawthrop 1996) may place Thecideina with the short looped Terebratulids.)	Small to large, biconvex, strongly ribbed, "butterfly" shells with hinge or cardinal margin widest part. Open delthyrium and a spiral calcified brachidium.
Astrophic or Non-Strophic Brachiopods Shells with a curved hinge line or cardinal margin		
Pentamerids	Cambrian to Devonian	Large, biconvex bulbous shells. No pedicle opening and lophophore supported by projections from cardinal area and valve floor.
Rhynchonellids	Ordovician to Recent	Small to medium biconvex "wrinkled" shells with a deep depression or sulcus. A pedicle foramen present and simple crural support for lophophore.
Terebratulids	Silurian to Recent	Small to large biconvex, smooth or ribbed "lamp" shells. Pedicle foramen with deltidal plates and a short or long looped brachidium.

meter using either wax, diagrammatic, or photographic format, so that these hidden structures can be determined. It is possible that during fossilization the internal features are destroyed.

Even after considering these difficulties, another problem may manifest itself. Brachiopods are "homomorphic"—their external features can appear to be very similar within genera and even within orders. On the other hand, individuals of a single species may show a wide range of variation, owing to geographical distribution, habitat selection, depth selection, temperature selection, and distortion due to placement between substrate components in early ontogeny. Work done by several researchers has shown that variations in morphology for the same species can exist even within a single population living under similar environmental conditions (Neall 1972; Foster 1989). These facts make identification extremely difficult. As a result, several specimens from the same species and even genera may have been given different names by different researchers.

In 1995, 4827 genera and subgenera of brachiopods had been described. Table 1 presents a classification based on Williams and colleagues (1996). Although incomplete, this scheme gives the major groups of extant and extinct brachiopods. (See Williams et al. for a more comprehensive classification.)

Brachiopods in Paleontology

Brachiopods are quite useful in the analysis of paleoenvironments because they were numerous, found in a great variety of shallow marine environments, and because they still have living species on which to base their ecology. Brachiopods can assist in determining ancient salinity levels, water temperature ranges, turbidity, speed, direction, and sediment content of currents and depth-related zonation. Brachiopods are also quite useful in mapping ancient shore lines. These animals have limited stratigraphical value as identification is hindered by homomorphy and, more importantly, many are long lived species, ranging over many geological time units.

Brachiopod Research

The history of brachiopod research extends to the sixteenth century, when the first drawings of the organisms were prepared. Originally, brachiopods were grouped with other bivalved shelled organisms. The first illustration of the internal structure was prepared by Pallas in 1776. The first brachiopod genus—*Terebratula*—was described by Muller. It was Cuvier who proposed the name "Brachiopoda," believing the lophophore was similar in function to the molluscan foot. Such important palaeontological names such as J. Lamarck, R. Owen, T.E. Huxley, Hancock, and Blockmann contributed to the knowledge of brachiopods in terms of functional morphology and anatomy. In 1891 Beecher synthesized a classification for the phylum Brachiopoda. Primary workers in the classification of brachiopods were J.E. Gray, E.E. Deslongchamps, William King, and C.T. Menke. More recently the works of H.M. Muir-Wood, M.J.S. Rudwick, A. Williams, and G.A. Cooper (who has named over 400 genera) are to be noted.

ROBERT SAMUEL CRAIG

See also Aquatic Invertebrates, Adaptive Strategies of; Feeding Adaptations: Invertebrates; Ornamentation: Invertebrates; Superphyla

Works Cited

Cohen, B.L., and A.B. Gawthrop. 1996. Brachiopod molecular phylogeny. *In* P. Cooper and J. Jisuo (ed.), *Brachiopods*. Proceedings of the Third International Brachiopod Congress, Sudbury, Ontario. Rotterdam and Brookfield, Vermont: Balkema.

Conway Morris, S., and J.S. Peel. 1995. Articulate Halkieriids from the Lower Cambrian of north Greenland and their role in early protosome evolution. *Philosophical Transactions of the Royal Society of London,* ser. B, 347:305–58.

Endo, K., G.B. Curry, R. Quinn, M.J. Collins, G. Muyzer, and P. Westbroek. 1994. Re-interpretation of Terebratulide phylogeny based on immunological data. *Palaeontology* 37 (2):349–73.

Feldmann, R.M., D.I. MacKinnon, K. Endo, and L. Chirino-Galvez. 1996. *Pinotheras laguei* Sakai (Decapod: Pinnotheridae), a tiny crab commensal within the brachiopod *Laqueus rubellus* (Sowerby) (Terebratulida: Laqueus). *Journal of Paleontology* 70 (2):303–11.

Foster, M.W. 1989. Brachiopods from the extreme South Pacific and adjacent water. *Journal of Paleontology* 63 (3):268–301.

James, M.A., A.D. Ansell, G.B. Curry, L.S. Peck, and M.C. Rhodes. 1992. Biology of living brachiopods. *Advances in Marine Biology* 28:175–387.

Lee, D.E. 1991. Aspects of the ecology and distribution of the living Brachiopoda of New Zealand. *In* D.I. MacKinnon, D.E. Lee, and J.D. Campbell (eds.), *Brachiopods through Time*. Proceedings of the 2nd International Brachiopod Congress, University of Otago Dunedin, New Zealand. Rotterdam and Brookfield, Vermont: Balkema.

McCammon, H.M. 1973. The ecology of *Magellania venosa,* an articulate brachiopod. *Journal of Paleontology* 47 (2):266–78.

Neall, V.E. 1972. Systematics of the endemic New Zealand brachiopod Neothyris. *Journal of the Royal Society of New Zealand* 2 (2):229–47.

Popov, L.E., M.G. Bassett, L.E. Holmer, and J. Laurie. 1993. Phylogenetic analysis of higher taxa of Brachiopoda. *Lethaia* 26:1–5.

Richardson, J.R. 1981. Brachiopods and pedicles. *Paleobiology* 7 (1):87–95.

Walton, D., M. Cusack, and G.B. Curry. 1993. Implications of the amino acid composition of Recent New Zealand brachiopods. *Palaeontology* 36 (4):883–96.

Williams, A., S.J. Carlson, C.H.C. Brunton, L.E. Holmer, and L.E. Popov. 1996. A supra-ordinal classification of the Brachiopoda. *Philosophical Transactions of the Royal Society London,* ser. B, 351:1171–93.

Wright, A.D. 1994. Mantle canals on brachiopod interareas and their significance in brachiopod classification. *Lethaia* 27:223–26.

Further Reading

Black, R.M. 1970. *The Elements of Palaeontology.* Cambridge: Cambridge University Press; 2nd ed., Cambridge and New York: Cambridge University Press, 1988.

Boardman, R.S., A.H. Cheetham, and A.J. Rowell (eds.). 1987. *Fossil Invertebrates.* Palo Alto, California: Blackwell Scientific.

Clarkson, E.N.K. 1979. *Invertebrate Palaeontology and Evolution.* Boston and London: Allen and Unwin; 3rd ed., London and New York: Chapman and Hall, 1993.

Doyle, P. 1996. *Understanding Fossils: An Introduction to Invertebrate Palaeontology.* Chichester and New York: Wiley and Sons.

Moore, R.C. (ed.). 1965. *Treatise on Invertebrate Paleontology.* Part H, *Brachiopoda.* 2 vols., Boulder, Colorado: Geological Society of America; Lawrence, Kansas: University of Kansas Press.

Rudwick, M.J.S. 1970. *Living and Fossil Brachiopods.* London: Hutchinson University Library.

Thomson, J.A. 1927. *Brachiopod Morphology and Genera (Recent and Tertiary).* New Zealand Board of Science and Art, Manual 7. Wellington, New Zealand: Dominion Museum.

BRAIN AND CRANIAL NERVES

The vertebrate central nervous system is one of the most complex and diverse organ systems in the animal kingdom. Through cranial and spinal nerves, the brain and spinal cord collect information from the environment and from the organism's inner workings. Appropriate adjustments and reactions to these stimuli are carried out through motor pathways and nerves. In this light, it is obvious that the diversity of brains is as great, if not greater, than the diversity of lifestyles, habitats, and behaviors of vertebrates. Yet this diversity is constrained within a common architectural plan (Figure 1) that originated with the origin of craniates (vertebrates with a braincase) (Northcutt 1995; Nieuwenhuys et al. 1997). There is tremendous variation in brain size (Figure 2) and different portions of the brain have atrophied or become highly developed in different groups of animals. Even whole new senses and structures have evolved. Nonetheless, all brains can be related to this common architecture. The evolutionary history of all of these variations can be traced in the fossil record and by comparative studies with living forms. In addition, specializations in behavior often are reflected in the gross morphology of brains, allowing us to use paleoneurological evidence to speculate on the biology and behavior of extinct animals.

Although nervous systems are composed of very soft tissues, fossilization of the bony braincase can provide a great deal of information about the brain. If a fossilized skull contains a soft matrix that can be chemically removed, the skull then can serve as a mold. A material such as latex may be used to create a replica of the inner surfaces of the endocranial cavity. In other cases, the matrix contained within the skull may be quite hard; if the bones weather away naturally, this leaves a "fossil brain." Such specimens are, of course, quite rare, but have been discovered from several extinct groups (Moodie 1915). More often, fossilized matrix within the endocranial space is exposed manually, by dissecting or chemically removing the overlying fossilized bone.

Another method of retrieving information about the braincase has been used most extensively by the "Swedish school" of paleontologists, beginning with Erik Stensiö. Stensiö and his students pioneered the use of specialized geological sectioning techniques. Scholars carefully grind down fossil skulls several microns to a few millimeters at a time. After each section has been planed away, the profiles of the internal spaces are photographed, drawn and reconstructed as a wax or styrofoam plate. Grinding through the entire skull and assembling the plates results in a three-dimensional wax or styrofoam model of the internal cavities of the braincase, including the channels that housed nerves and blood vessels. Such three-dimensional reconstructions of internal cavities may provide more information about the extinct creature than the actual fossil. Modern technologies also provide new, nondestructive, techniques to provide similar insights into the braincases of rare fossils (Rowe 1996). Like wax models, computer models can be rotated, sliced open, and viewed from multiple perspectives. Computer-assisted tomography (CAT scans) should become an important research tool in paleoneurology.

In some taxa, the brain fills the endocranial space almost completely. In such groups, like many ray-finned fishes, mammals, birds, and pterosaurs, an endocranial cast very closely resembles the brain. In other groups, like jawless fishes, cartilaginous fishes, placoderms, lobe-finned fishes, amphibians, and reptiles, the endocranial volume is generally much greater than that of the brain. In these groups, the brain is surrounded by expanded meningeal tissues (membranes) and blood sinuses. A cast of the endocranial space therefore only vaguely resembles the brain. In such taxa, great care must be taken in reconstructing brain morphology from endocasts. Information about overall brain size can only be estimated crudely. Even relative measures of the size of various brain regions must be viewed skeptically, since different regions may have different relationships with supporting tissues and the endocranium. In the worst cases, where the endocranial volume is much greater than brain volume possibly could have been, the endocranial cast provides an upper limit on the size of a brain reconstruction and may give some bare suggestions regarding the presence or absence of specific brain regions (Figure 3).

In these cases, scholars can reconstruct the brain only with reference to a related living species. For example, P. Whiting and L.B. Halstead Tarlo (1965) deliberately modeled their reconstruction of heterostracan brains after the brain of a living lamprey. In such a case, one must be careful not to conclude that therefore lampreys are related to heterostracans or that lamprey brains retain a primitive organization. The limited information provided by some endocasts is a tempting invitation to circular reasoning, and students should be aware of relying on living forms in paleoneurological reconstructions. H.J. Jerison (1973) has argued this point forcefully and clearly showed that, for instance, the endocast of *Kujdanowiaspis*, a Devonian placoderm, could just as easily have contained a teleost-like brain as a sharklike brain. Given current opinion on placoderm relationships, a sharklike brain is probably more likely but not by any means certain. Further, a sharklike reconstruction of a placoderm brain never should be used as evidence for shark affinities of placoderms or of the primitive nature of shark brains.

Comparisons of living vertebrate brains allow us to draw several conclusions regarding the primitive characteristics of the brain and the evolutionary transitions associated with the origins of various vertebrate groups. All vertebrate embryos go through a similar process of neural development, resulting in a tubular brain divided into three vesicles. The embryonic tissues adjacent to the future neural tube, the presumptive neural crest and neurogenic placodes, also develop into neural structures, including cranial and spinal nerves, the sense organs of the inner ear and lateral line system (which senses water pressure), the olfactory organ, and the pituitary gland, along with many other tissues of the head and trunk.

The caudal-most (rearmost) brain vesicle (called the "rhombencephalon," owing to its shape when viewed from the top) develops into the medulla oblongata and the cerebellum. The

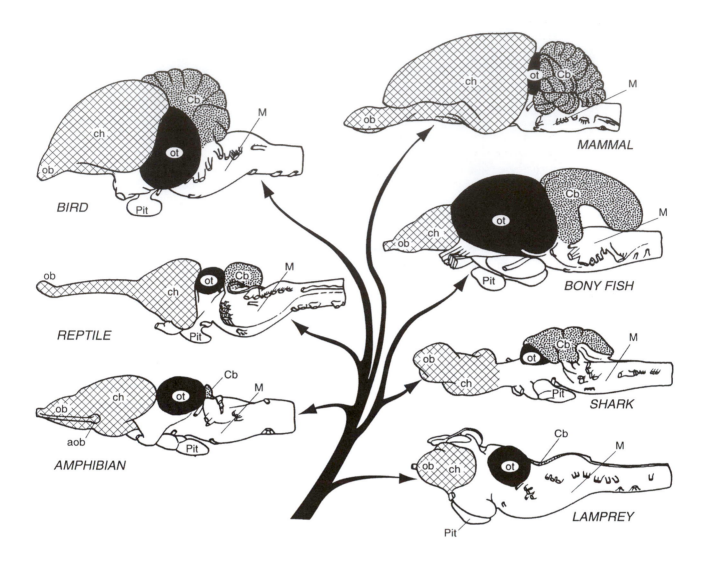

Figure 1. Lateral views of the brains of a number of extant species. While living animals display a tremendous diversity of brain size and shape, this diversity may be reduced to a common architectural plan. All vertebrates have a brain divisible into an olfactory bulb and cerebral hemispheres, a diencephalon (generally not visible in lateral view), a mesencephalon with a dorsal optic tectum, a cerebellum, and a hind brain, or medulla oblongata. A pituitary is also common to all vertebrates. Most tetrapods also have an accessory olfactory system, whose sensory neurons enter the brain in the accessory olfactory bulb. Many vertebrates also have either a pineal or parapineal organ, or both. Key: *ob,* olfactory bulb; *ch (cross-hatched),* cerebral hemispheres; *ot (black),* dorsal optic tectum; *Cb (stippled),* cerebellum; *M,* medulla oblongata (hind brain); *Pit,* pituitary; *aob,* accessory olfactory bulb; *P,* a pineal or parapineal organ, or both.

medulla is the source and the target of all the cranial nerves (except for the terminal, olfactory, optic, oculomotor, and trochlear nerves). The floor of the medulla contains the primary motor centers that control the branchiomeric musculature (muscles that control the gills) and other autonomic and voluntary motor systems of the head. Some basic integrative and reflex neural circuits also are contained within the floor of the medulla. Neurons in the motor regions project out of the brain through the motor cranial nerves. The roof of the medulla is composed of a number of columns, which are the principal targets of the cranial nerves that carry the general and special senses of the head and body (excluding vision and olfaction). These senses include the mechanorecep-

tive and electroreceptive lateral line systems (which detect mechanical or electrical stimuli), the gustatory system (taste), and more general sensations of pain, touch, stretch, temperature, and proprioception (position in space). In specialized species, particular regions of the roof of the medulla may be hypertrophied due to greater development of one or another set of sensory organs and cranial nerves. For example, extant teleost fishes with highly developed gustatory systems have both large numbers of taste buds and a massive development of the facial, glossopharyngeal, and vagal nerves. The medullary targets of these nerves are also greatly expanded, forming large facial and/or vagal lobes that are clearly visible in the gross morphology of the brain. Such local enlarge-

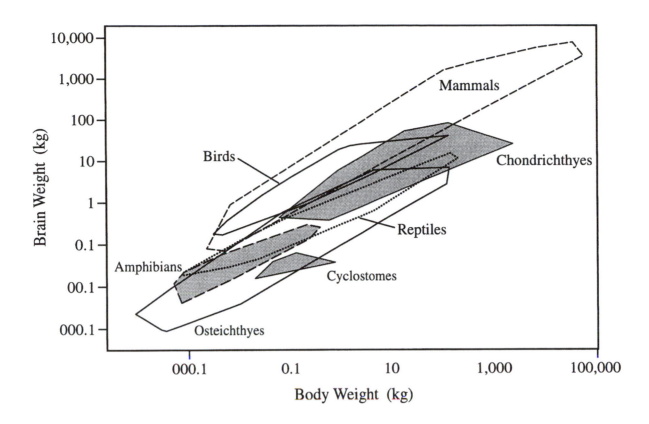

Figure 2. Minimum convex polygons for the brain weight of the main vertebrate groups, plotted against body weight in a double logarithmic graph. These polygons encompass all data points in each group. While there is tremendous variation in brain size, nearly all vertebrates have a similar relationship between brain and body weight. Birds and mammals have larger brains for their body size than do other reptiles and fishes, but the distribution of all the major groups have some degree of overlap. Redrawn from van Dongen (1997).

ments of specific functional regions potentially could be observable in fossil endocasts and may improve our interpretation of the biology of extinct species.

A great enlargement of the lip of the rhombencephalon, the cerebellum, is present in all gnathostomes (jawed vertebrates). The functions of the cerebellum still are somewhat unclear, but they include sensory motor integration, coordination of fine motor control, and the learning and execution of repetitive motor tasks. Despite a remarkably conservative internal circuitry, the size and shape of the cerebellum is greatly variable. It is relatively simple in most cartilaginous fishes, amphibians, bony fishes, and reptiles. Within each of these groups, as in birds and mammals, the cerebellum has increased in size several times in independent lineages. This is taken to the most extreme case in mormyrid teleosts, where the cerebellum is massive and covers nearly all of hind, mid-, and forebrain regions. The functional implications of these multiple and independent evolutionary increases in cerebellar size are unclear, but may they be related to greater integration of increased sensory inputs from the lateral-line system and other sensory modalities.

The cerebellum appears to have a slightly more recent origin than the other brain regions. Among the living jawless fishes, hagfishes have no trace of a cerebellum, and lampreys have the barest

rudiments of a cerebellar crest to the lip of the rhombencephalic vesicle. A true cerebellum appears to have originated sometime near the origin of gnathostomes. Unfortunately, the fossil evidence is not detailed sufficiently to allow us to determine if any other jawless fish possessed a cerebellum. Stensiö (1963) postulated that osteostracans had a rather large cerebellum, but the evidence is not conclusive (see Figure 3 and legend).

The mesencephalon or midbrain lies rostral to (in front of) the rhombencephalon. The midbrain roof is divided into a rostral, primarily visual region, called the "optic tectum," and a more caudal auditory region, the "torus semicircularis." In most vertebrates, the rostral visual center is much larger and dominates the dorsal (top) aspect of the midbrain. While the optic tectum also receives multisensory information, its size is tightly correlated to the importance of vision. In mammals, the midbrain roof is composed of two distinct pairs of hillocks (colliculi): a rostral or superior colliculus and a smaller caudal or inferior colliculus. These hillocks are homologous to the optic tectum and torus semicircularis, respectively. The floor or tegmentum of the midbrain contains the motor neurons whose axons make up the oculomotor and trochlear nerves. These nerves control eye movements, and the midbrain tegmentum also provides important sensory motor integration needed for both vol-

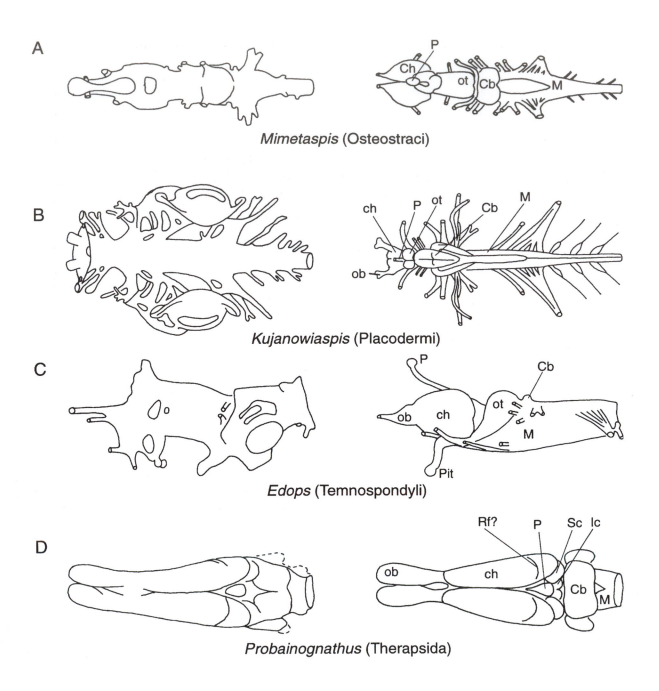

Mimetaspis (Osteostraci)

Kujanowiaspis (Placodermi)

Edops (Temnospondyli)

Probainognathus (Therapsida)

Figure 3. Endocasts *(left)* and reconstructed brains *(right)* of extinct taxa. *A,* dorsal views of an osteostracan endocast and brain. A caudal swelling may represent the cerebellum, but living lampreys have a large expansion of the tela choroidea (a non-neural supportive tissue) in the same position. *B,* dorsal views of a placoderm endocast and brain. This endocast preserves very little information about the brain, and Stensiö openly based his reconstruction on the brains of living elasmobranchs. *C,* lateral views of a temnospondyl amphibian endocast and brain. Note the expanded pituitary that may be related to the large body size of these Carboniferous amphibians. Other than this feature, however, little else can be unambiguously inferred from the endocast. Romer and Edinger's reconstruction is clearly based on living amphibians like *Rana* (frogs). *D,* dorsal views of a cynodont therapsid endocast *(left)* and brain *(right)*. Note that Quiroga's reconstruction of a rhinal fissure is based on a shallow depression in the endocast. The medial swellings that Quiroga included in his reconstruction are interpreted here as the inferior colliculus, but are not clearly visible in his illustrations of the actual endocast. Alternatively, the depression in the endocast may represent the caudal pole of the cerebral hemispheres. Caudal to that would be the superior colliculus; the swelling that Quiroga interprets as the superior colliculus would then be the inferior colliculus. Clearly, even brainlike endocasts pose problems of interpretation. Key: *Cb,* cerebellum; *ch,* cerebral hemispheres; *Ic,* inferior colliculus; *M,* medulla oblongata; *ob,* olfactory bulb; *ot,* optic tectum; *P,* pineal; *Pit,* pituitary; *Rf?,* rhinal fissure; *Sc,* superior colliculus. Source: *A, B,* reconstructed by Stensiö (1963); *C,* reconstructed by Romer and Edinger (1942); *D,* reconstructed by Quiroga (1980).

untary and involuntary movements of the eyes and for maintaining a steady gaze. These oculomotor integrations are crucial for visual perception of both stationary and moving objects. The midbrain tegmentum also contains important motor nuclei that control locomotion.

Proceeding rostrally, the next subdivision of the brain is the diencephalon, or "between brain." The diencephalon is divisible into three zones, the epithalamus, the thalamus, and the hypothalamus. Dorsally, the epithalamus is composed of the pineal and parapineal organs ("third eyes") and a set of nuclei called the "habenular complex." The pineal eyes, when present, are photoreceptive organs intimately involved in circadian rhythms and neuroendocrine regulation. The presence or absence of some form of epithalamic photoreceptive organs (pineal and/or parapineal) is generally recorded in fossil skulls as one or two "pineal foramina," or a thinning in the overlying bone.

The habenula receives information from multiple forebrain targets and may integrate olfactory and nonolfactory senses and provide inputs to other diencephalic regions and portions of the midbrain floor and hind brain. The thalamus is primarily a relay zone for sensory information from the hind brain and spinal cord; this information is relayed to forebrain centers that integrate the information. Conversely, motor commands from higher forebrain centers are conveyed to the thalamus and then projected to hind brain or spinal motor centers. Some integrative and feedback circuitry is present within the thalamus, but in large measure, different sensory modalities remain unmingled in the thalamus.

The hypothalamus is perhaps the most fascinating brain region. It coordinates many biologically crucial behaviors, including species-specific behaviors (those unique to the species), reproduction, courtship, and feeding, as well as coordinating many other complex behavioral systems. The hypothalamus receives a wide variety of sensory information and has an intimate relationship with the pituitary, providing neural control of most endocrine functions. The pituitary body itself is generally encased in bone (the "fossa hypophyseos" or "sella turcica"), and estimation of its size in fossils is often possible. There appears to be a strong correlation between the size of the fossa hypophyseos and gigantism (regulation of body growth is one of the pituitary's functions), most obviously seen in dinosaurs and in large early amphibians (Edinger 1942). However, G. Säve-Söderbergh (1952) demonstrated that the size and shape of the fossa hypophyseos also is influenced by the origin and position of certain extraocular muscles. Extrapolations of pituitary size may be more complicated than T. Edinger assumed.

The rostral-most region of the brain (the "telencephalon" or "endbrain") forms the cerebral hemispheres, part of the preoptic region of the hypothalamus, and the olfactory bulbs. Like the remainder of the hypothalamus, the preoptic region is involved in sensory integration with neuroendocrine regulation and exerts some direct control of pituitary function. The region may be particularly important as a regulator of circadian rhythms in animals that lack pineal or parapineal organs. The cerebral hemispheres are perhaps the most variable regions of the brains of vertebrates. In most vertebrates their function is dominated by olfaction. Classically, it was thought that olfaction was the sole primitive function of the cerebrum, but this belief is no longer tenable. Much of the roof ("pallium") does receive olfactory information, but other inputs are also important for some pallial regions, and multimodal sensory integration is probably a primitive function of much of the pallium. The functions of the pallium are perhaps the most obscure of any region in most vertebrates, but it is clear that the pallium is involved in multisensory integration, associative functions, memory, and other higher brain functions. The subpallium, or floor of the telencephalon, functions in voluntary motor actions, and also transmits olfactory and other information to hypothalamic and limbic (neuroendocrine) centers.

Most spectacularly, part the nonolfactory pallium of mammals forms a massive cortical sheet, which is often thrown into folds called "gyri" (separated by sulci). The visible surface of most mammalian brains is nearly completely covered by this so-called "neocortex." The origins of the great expanse of cortex are still obscure (Northcutt and Kaas 1995), but this unique structure is most likely related to the dorsal pallial regions of other amniotes. The massive development of neocortex and its subsequent evolution is an extremely important phenomenon in mammalian evolution and has provided some of the most dramatic results in paleoneurology (Figure 4). The dorsal neocortex is separated from the more lateral cortices by a deep sulcus, the "rhinal fissure." In many endocasts, this fissure is visible, and the relative amount of neocortex can be measured (Jerison 1990).

Finally, rostral to the cerebral hemispheres, the olfactory bulbs are the primary target of the olfactory sensory neurons. Olfactory information is relayed and processed in the bulbs and projects through the olfactory peduncles to the rest of the brain (primarily to the cerebral hemispheres and hypothalamus). The size of the olfactory peduncles and bulbs are a good estimator of the importance of olfaction for particular vertebrate groups. In addition, most tetrapods (limbed vertebrates) also possess a second "olfactory" system, the accessory olfactory system (also called the "vomeronasal system" or "Jacobson's organ" in some living reptiles). This diverticulum of the olfactory organ has unique receptor cell types that project to a separate portion of the forebrain (the accessory olfactory bulb). Olfactory and vomeronasal information is segregated into distinct pathways throughout the brain and probably serve different functions related to distinct classes of odorants. The presence or absence and the relative size of an accessory olfactory system is potentially recoverable from fossil material, including endocasts of both the cranial cavity and the cavities that contain the olfactory organs.

The evidence of paleoneurology is so vast (Edinger 1975), it is impossible to provide a detailed summary in this essay. Endocasts and brain reconstructions have been described in all groups, with varying degrees of success. Jawless fishes, placoderms, elasmobranchs (e.g., sharks, rays), crossopterygians (coelocanths), dipnoans (lungfishes), and early amphibians all have large endocranial spaces relative to their brains. Accordingly, endocasts from these groups do not allow us to infer brain morphology reliably in great detail. Most published reconstructions suggest that the brains of these animals were similar to those of their living relatives. In all cases, the endocasts are consistent with such interpretations, but it is clear in many cases that a wide range of brain shapes and sizes could also fit in the same braincase (Jerison 1973).

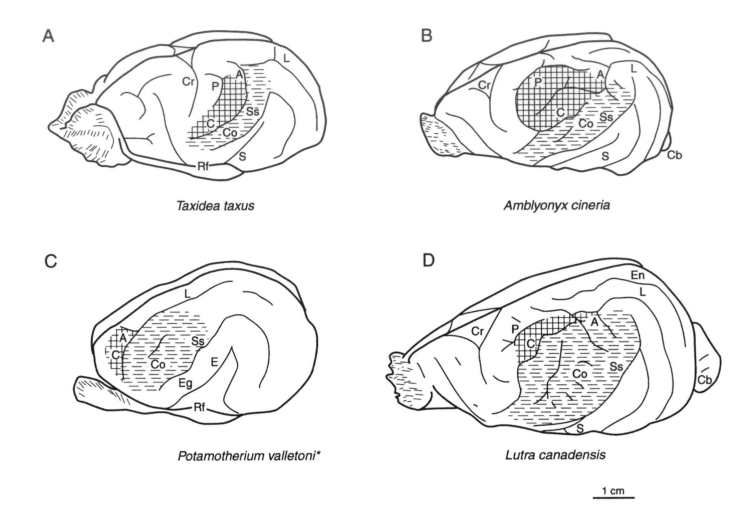

Figure 4. An example of mammalian paleoneurology. A left lateral view of four carnivore brains. *A*, a badger, *Taxidea taxus*, illustrates typical modern carnivore brains; *B*, an oriental small-clawed otter, *Amblyonyx cineria*; *C*, *Potamotherium valletoni*, a specialized Pleistocene otter (now extinct); *D*, *Lutra canadensis*, a river otter. All otters have reduced visual systems and very sensitive somatosensory systems. In living otters, increased somatosensory acuity is generally focused in either the hands (as seen in most small-clawed otters), or in the face and sensory vibrissae (as seen in most fish-eating, or river otters). Behaviorally, fish-eating otters depend on their vibrissae to detect fishes, while small-clawed or clawless otters use their hands to forage for small crustaceans or molluscs on and in the substrate. Electrophysiological mapping studies on many living carnivores have demonstrated that the area of cortical representation for a given sensory modality is proportionate to the acuity of that sense. In somatosensory cortex, the area representing each body region is also proportionate to the sensitivity of that region (Johnson 1990). In otters, increased sensory acuity is reflected in an increased area of cortex devoted to the representation of either the face (coronal gyrus, indicated by *horizontal lines*) or the hands (area between the postcruciate sulcus and the coronal sulcus, indicated by *cross hatching*). This can clearly be seen by comparing *B* and *D*, especially relative to *A*. While primitive in many respects (small size, small area of neocortex, and relatively higher position of the rhinal fissure), the brain of *P. valletoni* already shows enlargement of these putative somatosensory cortical areas. Further, it is clear that this species had a greater representation of the face and probably was similar to living river otters in its feeding strategy. Abbreviations: *A*, ansate sulcus; *C*, coronal sulcus; *Cb*, cerebellum; *Co*, coronal gyrus; *Cr*, cruciate sulcus; *E*, anterior ectosylvian sulcus; *Eg*, anterior ectosylvian gyrus; *En*, entolateral sulcus; *L*, lateral sulcus; *P*, postcruciate sulcus; *S*, sylvian sulcus; *Ss*, suprasylvian sulcus; *Rf*, rhinal fissure. After Radinsky (1968a).

In most actinopterygian lineages (ray-finned fish), including the paleoniscids, the endocranium provides a fairly good representation of the brain. Endocasts of these fossils are quite brainlike and relatively easy to interpret. The brains of these fishes closely resemble the brains of unspecialized modern actinopterygians. A moderately developed cerebellum was already present, and a large optic tectum is present in paleoniscids and ganoids. A small telencephalon seems to characterize these early fishes, and multiple increases in the size of the cerebellum appear to have occurred within later groups, such as the palaeoniscids, saurichthyids, holosteans, and teleosts (Stensiö 1963).

A huge number of dinosaur endocasts have been found and described (Hopson 1979). Like their living relatives, crocodilians, these endocasts do not provide a very detailed impression of the brain. Much has been written about the supposed stupidity of dinosaurs and their diminutive brain, but this clearly was a belief Edinger felt should be eradicated (Edinger 1975). As more data on brain size accumulates, it is clear that dinosaurs were within the range of the brain-body ratio seen in living reptiles (Jerison 1973; Hopson 1977). Quite a bit of variation in brain size was present across dinosaur lineages, however, which may have been related to differences in locomotor efficiency, social structure, and other ecological factors (Hopson 1977).

A small number of endocasts of Mesozoic marine reptiles have been described. Despite the neural specialization that must have accompanied the evolution of fully aquatic lifestyles, there has been little attention paid to these endocasts, and little has been published on the brains of either plesiosaurs, ichthyosaurs, or mosasaurs.

Endocasts have been described from several groups of mammal-like reptiles. These endocasts are quite brainlike and allow fairly detailed reconstructions of their brains. The most detailed endocasts and brain reconstructions are from therapsids. Their brains were apparently somewhat intermediate between a generalized tetrapod brain and a primitive mammalian brain. J.C. Quiroga (1980) claimed that a shallow depression on the endocast of *Probainognathus,* a mid-Triassic therapsid, represents the rhinal fissure, indicating an early development of mammalian neocortex. However, this same structure was interpreted as a blood vessel by Z. Kielan-Jaworoska (1986), and the presence of neocortex in mammal-like reptiles is dubious. The transitional stages in the origins of true mammalian brains remain obscure. Increases in forebrain size seem to characterize successive synapsid radiations, but evidence of neocortex is not seen outside of true mammalian fossils from the Late Jurassic (Jerison 1990; Rowe 1996). Continued increases in brain size also appear to characterize both Tertiary mammalian groups like the Multituberculata and more recent groups.

Within more recent mammalian groups, paleoneurological evidence is extensive and detailed. Mammalian endocasts present clear indications of underlying brain structure. In small mammals, these endocasts can be very detailed. In some cases, individual gyri, whose functions in living mammals are known, can be observed in endocasts, and their evolutionary history has been reconstructed (Figure 4). Repeated increases in brain size, neocortical area, and complex gyral patterns have evolved independently multiple times in several modern mammalian orders (Radinsky 1968a, 1968b, 1969, 1971, 1973).

Endocasts of birds also provide detailed information about their brains. The brains of early birds, such as *Archaeopteryx,* have long been described as more reptilian than birdlike (Edinger 1942). However, Jerison (1973) reinterpreted the orientation of the most detailed specimen and concluded that the brain of *Archaeopteryx* was both much larger and more birdlike than previously believed. According to this reconstruction, the brain of *Archaeopteryx* is intermediate in size between that of dinosaurs and modern birds, but is more birdlike than reptilian in shape. The literature on the brains of later fossil birds is spotty, but it is clear that increases in brain size began as early as the latest Cretaceous and continued through the Cenozoic. Brains comparable in size to those of modern birds may have occurred as early as the Eocene and clearly had reached modern proportions by the end of the Tertiary period.

The other group of reptiles to take flight during the Mesozoic, pterosaurs, also underwent some major evolutionary changes in brain morphology. Like those of birds, pterosaur endocasts are fairly brainlike and provide detailed information about brain size and morphology. Unlike birds, pterosaur brains did not undergo large increases in overall size; instead, they were probably within the size range of other reptile groups (Hopson 1977). Some obvious changes in proportions are seen, however, and it has been remarked that pterosaur brains are more birdlike than reptilian. Pterosaurs had large eyes and correspondingly large optic tecta. As in birds, the cerebellum is relatively large and complex, and although the olfactory system appears to have been reduced, the forebrain is relatively large. These parallel evolutionary changes indicate that selection for improved vision and motor control characterized both bird and pterosaur lineages as their ancestors took to the air.

Most of our understanding of brain function comes from comparative studies of living animals. Functional analyses and physiological and cellular descriptions of behavior can come only from the study of living animals. However, fossils provide a chronological framework to evolutionary schemes and may provide evidence of evolutionary trends. Fossil animals often display combinations of characters found in no living taxa, thus providing essential tests of putative correlations deduced from living forms. The fossil evidence on the evolution of the brain is much more extensive than commonly realized. Evidence of brain structure is present in fossils from every vertebrate class. This wealth of information still presents a mostly unutilized resource.

CHRISTOPHER B. BRAUN AND R. GLENN NORTHCUTT

See also Craniates; Eyes; Hearing and Positional Sense; Lateral Line System; Odor and Pheromone Receptors; Sensory Capsules

Works Cited

Dongen, P.A.M. van. 1997. Brain size in vertebrates. *In* R. Nieuwenhuys, A.J. ten Donkelaar, and C. Nicholson (eds.), *The Central Nervous System of Vertebrates.* Berlin and New York: Springer-Verlag.

Edinger, T. 1942. The pituitary body in giant animals fossil and living: A survey and a suggestion. *Quarterly Review of Biology* 17:31–45.

———. 1975. Paleoneurology 1804–1966. An annotated bibliography. *Advances in Anatomy, Embryology and Cell Biology* 49.

Hopson, J.A. 1977. Relative brain size and behavior in archosaurian reptiles. *Annual Review of Ecology and Systematics* 8:429–48.

———. 1979. Paleoneurology. *In* C. Gans, R.G. Northcutt, and P. Ulinski (eds.), *Biology of the Reptilia.* Vol. 9. London and New York: Academic Press.

Jerison, H.J. 1973. *Evolution of the Brain and Intelligence.* New York: Academic Press.

———. 1990. Fossil evidence on the evolution of the neocortex. *In* E. Jones and A. Peters (eds.), *Cerebral Cortex.* Vol. 8A, *Comparative Structure and Evolution of Cerebral Cortex, Part 1.* New York: Plenum.

Johnson, J.I. 1990. Comparative development of somatic sensory cortex. *In* E.G. Jones and A. Peters (eds.), *Cerebral Cortex.* Vol. 8B, *Comparative Structure and Evolution of Cerebral Cortex, Part 2.* New York: Plenum.

Kielan-Jaworoska, Z. 1986. Brain evolution in Mesozoic mammals. *In* J.A. Lillegraven (ed.), *G.G. Simpson Memorial Volume: Contributions to Geology.* University of Wyoming Special Paper 3. Laramie: University of Wyoming Press.

Moodie, R.L. 1915. A new fish brain from the coal measures of Kansas, with a review of other fossil brains. *Journal of Comparative Neurology* 25:135–81.

Nieuwenhuys, R., A.J. ten Donkelaar, and C. Nicholson (eds.). 1977. *The Central Nervous System of Vertebrates.* Berlin and New York: Springer-Verlag.

Northcutt, R.G. 1995. The forebrain of gnathostomes: In search of a morphotype. *Brain Behavior and Evolution* 46:275–316.

Northcutt, R.G., and Kaas, J.H. 1995. The emergence and evolution of mammalian neocortex. *Trends in Neuroscience* 18:373–79.

Quiroga, J.C. 1980. The brain of the mammal-like reptile *Probainognathus jenseni* (Therapsida, Cynodontia): A correlative paleo-neurological approach to the neocortex at the reptile mammal transition. *Journal für Hirnforschung* 21:299–336.

Radinsky, L.B. 1968a. Evolution of somatic sensory specialization in otter brains. *Journal of Comparative Neurology* 134:495–506.

———. 1968b. A new approach to mammalian cranial analysis, illustrated by examples of prosimian primates. *Journal of Morphology* 124:167–80.

———. 1969. Outlines of canid and felid brain evolution. *Annals of the New York Academy of Sciences* 167:277–88.

———. 1971. An example of parallelism in carnivore brain evolution. *Evolution* 25:518–22.

———. 1973. Evolution of the canid brain. *Brain Behavior and Evolution* 7:169–202.

Romer, A.S., and T. Edinger. 1942. Endocranial casts and brains of living and fossil amphibia. *Journal of Comparative Neurology* 77:355–89.

Rowe, T. 1996. Coevolution of the mammalian middle ear and neocortex. *Science* 273:651–54.

Säve-Söderbergh, G. 1952. On the fossa hypophyseos and the attachment of the retractor bulbi group in Sphenodon, Varanus, and Lacerta. *Arkiv für Zoologi* 38:1–24.

Stensiö, E. 1963. The brain and the cranial nerves in fossil, lower craniate vertebrates. *Skrifter Utgitt av Det Norske Videnskaps-Akademi I Oslo 1. Matematisk Naturviden Skapelig Klasse,* new ser., 13:1–120.

Whiting, P., and L.B. Halstead Tarlo. 1965. The brain of Heterostraci (Agnatha). *Nature* 207:829–31.

Further Reading

Allman, J. 1990. Evolution of neocortex. *In* E.G. Jones and A. Peters (eds.), *Cerebral Cortex.* Vol. 8A, *Comparative Structure and Evolution of Cerebral Cortex, Part 1.* New York: Plenum.

Edinger, T. 1949. Paleoneurology versus comparative brain anatomy. *Confinia Neurologica* 2:5–24.

Finger, T.E. 1997. Feeding patterns and brain evolution in ostariophysean fishes. *Acta Physiologica Scandanavia,* supplement, 161:59–66.

Finlay, B.L., and R.B. Darlington. 1995. Linked regularities in the development and evolution of mammalian brains. *Science* 268:1578–84.

Janvier, P. 1996. *Early Vertebrates.* Oxford: Oxford University Press.

Jerison, H.J. 1960. Quantitative analysis of evolution of the brain in mammals. *Science* 133:1012–14.

———. 1970. Brain evolution: New light on old principles. *Science* 170:1224–25.

Welker, W. 1990. Why does cerebral cortex fissure and fold? A review of determinants of gyri and sulci. *In* E.G. Jones and A. Peters (eds.), *Cerebral Cortex.* Vol. 8B, *Comparative Structure and Evolution of Cerebral Cortex, Part 2.* New York: Plenum.

Wullimann, M.F. 1997. Major patterns of visual brain organization in teleosts and their relation to prehistoric events and the paleontological record. *Paleobiology* 23:101–14.

BREUIL, HENRI ÉDOUARD PROSPER

French, 1877–1961

Henri Breuil, known as "the Abbé Breuil," was a pioneer in the field of prehistoric archaeology, having contributed renowned interpretations of paleolithic industries and analysis of prehistoric cave paintings in Western Europe, China, and South Africa.

Breuil was born in Mortain, Manche, France on 28 February 1877. Following his education at the Sorbonne, Breuil entered the Seminary of Saint Sulpice in 1897 and was ordained an abbé three years later (1900). Cultivating a childhood interest in the natural sciences, in particular geology and human paleontology, Breuil developed an interest in Paleolithic art, the field to which he would make his greatest contributions. This interest lead Breuil to southern France, northern Spain, China, and South Africa to conduct original research on cave art.

Breuil's first fieldwork was conducted with the help of French prehistorian and archaeologist Émile Cartailhac, who was a professor at Toulouse. In 1901 Breuil attended the field meetings in Dordogne and participated in the discovery and reconnoitering of Les Combarelles and Font de Gaume. Breuil also was present at La Mouthe when the authenticity of Paleolithic cave art was accepted, and furthermore, he participated in the discovery of Tuc d'Audoubert in 1912 and Les Trois-Frères in 1916. In 1940 he was the first archaeologist to examine Lascaux, and following World War II Breuil spent six years traveling through southern Rhodesia (today called Zimbabwe), South Africa, and South-West Africa (Namibia), examining thousands of rock shelters, copying the art, and helping establish a typology of the Stellenbosch lithic industries. Later in his career Breuil developed an interest in the megalith monuments in France and Spain and became involved in controversies surrounding the interpretation of cave paintings in South Africa (the White Lady of Brandberg, 1955) and France (Rouffignac, 1956).

Breuil made two major contributions to the archaeological study of cave art. Given the extent of his travels and devotion to prehistory, Breuil meticulously recorded and analyzed Paleolithic cave art and subsequently developed the archetypical methods of analysis. Breuil also contributed a new classification of Paleolithic industries. Presented at the Geneva Congress of Prehistoric and

Prohistoric Sciences in 1912, Breuil's classic paper *Les subdivisions du paléolithique supérieur et leur signification* reclassified the existing Paleolithic industries and demonstrated that these cultural divisions were contemporaneous traditions rather than successive epochs.

During his scientific career, Breuil wrote over 600 publication, served at several institutions, and received numerous awards and honors for his contributions to archaeology. He died on 14 August 1961 in L'Isleadam, Seine-et-Oise, France.

EDOUARD L. BONÉ AND BRIAN CALLENDER

Biography

Born Mortain, Manche, 28 February 1877. Ordained abbé, Seminary Saint Sulpice, Paris, 1900. Lecturer of prehistory and ethnography, University of Fribourg, 1905–10; professor of prehistoric ethnography, Institut de Paléontologie Humaine, Paris, 1910–29; professor of prehistory, Collège de France, 1919–47; elected member, Institut de France, 1938. Gold medalist, American Academy of Science and Society of Antiquaries of London; recipient of Huxley Memorial Medal and Prestwich Medal for Geology; received honorary degrees from Cambridge, Cape Town, Edinburgh, Fribourg, Lisbon, and Oxford. Traveled extensively through Western Europe, China, and Africa; participated in the discovery and analysis of numerous Paleolithic cave sights; reclassified Paleolithic industries. Died in L'Isleadam, Seine-et-Oise, 14 August 1961.

Major Publications

1906. With E. Cartailhac. *La caverne d'Altamira, à Santillane près Santander (Espagne)*. Monaco: Monaco.
1910. With L. Capitan and D. Peyrony. *La caverne de Font-de-Gaume aux Eyzies (Dordogne)*. Monaco: Chêne.
1912. *Les subdivisions du paléolithique supérieur et leur signification*. Lagny:

Seine-et-Marne; 2nd ed., 1937.
1924. With L. Capitan and D. Peyrony. *Les Combarelles aux Eyzies (Dordogne)*. 2 vols. Paris: Masson.
1929. With M.C. Burkitt and M. Pollock. *Rock Paintings of Southern Andalusia: A Description of a Neolithic and Copper Age Art Group*. Oxford: Clarendon.
1933–35. *Les peintures rupestres schématiques de la péninsule ibérique*. 4 vols. Lagny: Grevin.
1949. *Beyond the Bounds of History: Scenes from the Old Stone Age*. London: Gawthorn.
1951. With R. Lantier. *Les hommes de la pierre ancienne paléolithique et mésolithique*. Paris: Payot.
1952. *Quatre cents siècles d'art pariétal: Les cavernes ornées de l'âge du renne*. Montignac, Dordogne: Centre d'études et de documentation préhistorique.
1954. *Les roches peintes du Tassili-n-Ajjer*. Paris: Arts et Métiers graphiques.
1955. *The White Lady of Brandberg*. London: Trianon.
1957. *The Rock Paintings of Southern Africa*. 6 vols. London: Abbé Breuil Publications; Paris: Trianon.

Further Reading

Brodrick, A.H. 1963. *The Abbé Henri Breuil, Prehistorian*. London: Hutchinson; as *Father of Prehistory: The Abbé Henri Breuil: His Life and Times,* New York: Morrow.
Leroi-Gourhan, A. 1967. *Treasures of Prehistoric Art*. New York: Abrams; as *The Art of Prehistoric Man in Western Europe,* London: Thames and Hudson; translation of *Préhistoire de l'art occidental,* Paris: Mazenod, 1965.
Perelló, E.R. (ed.) 1964. *Miscelánea en homenaje al abate Henri Breuil, 1877–1961*. 2 vols. Barcelona: Instituto de Prehistoria y Arqueología.
1957. *Hommage à l'abbé Henri Breuil*. Annales de paléontologie humaine.

BRONGNIART, ALEXANDRE

French, 1770–1847

Alexandre Brongniart was born on 5 February 1770 in Paris, France. After having been trained at the School of Mines, Brongniart served in the army as an engineer before being appointed director of the Sèvres porcelain factory, a position he held until his death. In 1797 he was appointed professor of natural history at the École Centrale des Quatre Nations in Paris. Three years later he published *Essai d'une classification naturelle des reptiles* (Essay on the Classification of Reptiles). In this work, Brongniart divided the Reptilia into four orders: Chelonia, Sauria, Ophidia, and Batrachia (now a separate class, the Amphibia).

Brongniart traveled extensively throughout western Europe, trying to establish stratigraphic correlations between areas ranging from Sweden to Italy. Working in collaboration with Georges Cuvier, Brongniart jointly published his most significant work in 1811. In *Essai sur la géographiae minéralogique des environs de Paris avec une carte géognostique et des coupes de terrain* (Essay on the Mineralogical Geography of the Environs of

Paris, with a Geological Map and Profiles of the Terrain), Brongniart and Cuvier examined the stratigraphy of the Paris basin and incorporated a novel method of strata identification. Prior to this work, geologists commonly relied on the characteristics of the rocks to identify strata, but Brongniart and Cuvier identified strata according to their fossil content. By investigating strata and their fossil content, they also showed the sequence of evolutionary change among the fossils, in particular those of molluscs. By considering paleontological, anatomical, zoological, and mineralogical observations when identifying strata, Brongniart was among the first geologists to stress the primacy of fossil evidence over that of lithology in determining the age of a particular formation. He was also the first to describe and arrange the geological formations of the Tertiary period in chronological order. In this work, Cuvier and Brongniart also concluded that the Paris formations formed under alternating freshwater and saltwater conditions. This discovery helped solve the problem of how freshwater and seawater strata could alternate, a discovery that led to Cuvier's theory of catastrophism and Darwin's theory of evolution.

In 1815 Brongniart became a member of the Académie de Sciences. In 1818 he was appointed professor of mineralogy at the Muséum d'Histoire Naturelle in Paris, and four years later he was appointed chair of that same department. That same year, Brongniart published the first full-length report on the trilobites.

However, geology and paleontology were not Brongniart's only lifetime interests. After taking over the Sèvres factory in 1800, Brongniart revived the business by developing wider ranges of colors for porcelain, thus improving the art of enameling. Under his directorship, the Sèvres factory became one of the leading porcelain factories in Europe. Alexandre Brongniart died on 7 October 1847 in Paris, France.

EDOUARD L. BONÉ AND BRIAN CALLENDER

Biography

Born in Paris, 5 February 1770. Earned degree in mining engineering, 1794. Professor, Société Gymnastique, 1787–94; appointed ingénieur des mines, French army, 1794; appointed professor of natural history, École Centrale des Quatre Nations, Paris, 1797; appointed ingénieur en chef des mines, French army, 1818; appointed professor of mineralogy, Muséum d'Histoire Naturelle, Paris, 1818; chair of mineralogy, Muséum d'Histoire Naturelle, Paris, 1822–47. Elected member, French Académie de Sciences, 1815. Among the first geologists to stress the

importance of fossils in strata identification. Died in Paris, France, 7 October 1847.

Major Publications

1800. Essai d'une classification naturelle des reptiles. *Bulletin de la Société Phili-mathématique* 2:81–91.
1811. With G. Cuvier. *Essai sur la géographie minéralogique des environs de Paris avec une carte géognostique et des coupes de terrain.* Paris: Baudouin.
1821. Sur les caractères zoologiques des formations. *Annales des Mines* 6:537–72; Paris: Imprimerie de Madame Huzard, 1821.
1822. *Histoire naturelle des crustacés fossiles, sous les rapports zoologiques et géologiques.* Paris and Strasbourg: Levrault.
1823. *Mémoire sur les terrains de sédiment supérieurs.* Paris and Strasbourg: Levrault.
1827. *Classification et caractères minéralogiques des roches homogènes et hétérogènes.* Paris and Strasbourg: Levrault.
1829. *Tableau des terrains qui composent l'écorce du globe: ou, Essai sur la structure de la partie connue de la terre.* Paris and Strasbourg: Levrault.
1844. *Traité des arts céramiques; ou, Des parteries, considérées dans leur histoire, leur pratique et leur théorie.* Paris: Béchet jeune.

Further Reading

de Launay, L. 1940. *Une grande famille de savants: Les Brongniart.* Paris: Rapilly.

BROOM, ROBERT

South African, 1866–1951

Robert Broom was born on 30 November 1866 in Paisley, Scotland, and went on to earn acclaim as a physician, paleontologist, anthropologist, and even for a short while as mayor of the town of Douglas in South Africa. Broom "'wanted to know' more intensely than any one else I have ever met," said one of his biographers (Watson 1952). He had an extraordinary memory, impressive visual powers, and displayed a keen attention to detail, all of which aided his work on morphology and the origins of humans.

His enthusiasm for natural science can be attributed to a number of role models in addition to his father. At the age of six, Broom was sent to live with his grandmother in Millport, as he was a sickly child. There he met an old army officer named John Leavach, who gave Broom his first microscope and taught him about marine life. Later, Broom's family introduced him to Peter Cameron, who further excited Broom's interest in such subjects. At ten, Broom began formal schooling at Hutcheson's Grammar School in Glasgow, and in 1883 he worked in the laboratory of Professor J. Ferguson. Broom learned a great deal about the structure of plants by attending F.O. Bower's lectures, and from John Cleland he learned much about comparative anatomy.

In 1887 Broom earned his B.Sc., and in 1889, his M.B. and C.M. Three years later he went to Australia, hoping to examine

marsupials and monotremes. He married Mary Braid Braille there and practiced medicine for four years in Queensland and New South Wales, during which time he also wrote many papers that the Linnean Society of New South Wales greeted with excitement, including an important paper on the Organ of Jacobson (vomeronasal organ) in the Monotremata.

After receiving his M.D. in 1895, Broom determined to go to South Africa to study Karroo fossil reptiles in the hopes that this study would yield information about the origin of mammals. He again set up a medical practice, this time in Little Namaqualand in 1897. In this year he published a paper that was one of the first to use fossils to solve a morphological question concerning living animals; he also drew attention to the septo-maxilla of the armadillo, now recognized as a part of nearly every tetrapod skull. He also discussed fetal marsupial anatomy, laying the groundwork for future discoveries of bone homologies in reptiles, birds, and mammals. Broom later made his way to Pearston, where he put together important collections of Karroo fossils. In 1903 he became a poorly paid but brilliant professor of zoology and geology in Stellenbosch, where he taught popular classes for seven years. During this time he visited many museums throughout the world, and he wrote a significant paper on the Permian vertebrates of Texas, a paper that "revolutionized our knowledge of their structure and relationships, and laid the foundation on which reptilian classification has since been based" (Watson 1952).

With the help of Rev. J.H. Whaits, Broom built an enormous collection of Karroo fossils. He sold this collection to the American Museum of Natural History in New York in 1913. After World War I, Broom returned to South Africa to practice in the Transvaal, where his interest turned to anthropology. He later wrote a book on South African mammal-like reptiles, funded by the Carnegie Trust. He traveled about South Africa and visited England in 1931 as a South African delegate to the British Association's centenary meeting. At the age of 68, Broom became the curator of fossil vertebrates and anthropology in the Transvaal Museum, where he described 26 new genera and 46 new species of fossil reptiles.

Soon after, Broom decided to direct his efforts toward the search for an adult specimen of the "Taung ape" (*Australopithecus africanus*) and other Pleistocene mammals. In 1936 he participated in the discovery of an hominid skull related to the Taung. Broom continued his research at the Sterfontein caves for many years; in 1938 he discovered the Krondraai skull approximately two miles away. He also benefited from studying the fossil collection of S.H. Rubidge of Graaf Reinet. Broom continued his research depite quarrels with the Historical Monuments Commission, which preferred that the caves remain undisturbed.

Broom did not find Darwin's concept of natural selection sufficient to explain evolution, and he set forth some of his own ideas in his 1933 book *The Coming of Man: Was It Accident or Design?* and his article "Evolution: Is There Intelligence Behind It?" He admired the work of Richard Owen, and the respect was mutual: in 1890, Owen is said to have written to Broom, "I cannot help forseeing that you will leave—life and health being spared—a lasting name in the promotion of our common science" (Findlay 1972). Broom continued his brisk pace of travels and lectures into his eighties. Following a brief illness, he wrote *Finding the Missing Link,* a book about his work in the caves, as well as a book on *Plesianthropus* finds (*Plesianthropus* is now recognized as *A. africanus*). He died on 6 April 1951 and is buried in Pretoria.

JULIE ENGLANDER

Works Cited

Findlay, G.H. 1972. *Dr. Robert Broom, F.R.S., Paleontologist and Physician, 1866–1951: A Biography, Appreciation, and Bibliography.* Cape Town: Balkema.

Watson, D.M.S. 1952. Robert Broom, 1866–1951. *Obituary Notices of Fellows of the Royal Society* 8:37–70.

Biography

Born in Paisley, Scotland, 30 November 1866. Received B.Sc. (1887), M.B. and C.M. (1889), M.D. (1895), and D.Sc. (1905), University of Glasgow. Began medical practice, first in Glasgow, then in various towns of Australia and finally South Africa, 1889 (partially retired after 1928); professor of zoology and geology, Victoria College, Stellenbosch, South Africa, 1903–9; palaeontologist and curator of fossil vertebrates and anthropology, Transvaal Museum, Pretoria, 1934–51; part-time lecturer in anatomy and zoology, Universities of the Witwatersrand and Pretoria, 1940–45. Became corresponding member, Linnean Society of London, 1897; corresponding member, Zoological Society of London, 1901; Croonian Lecturer, Royal Society, London, 1913; received Hon. D.Sc., University of South Africa, 1913; fellow, Royal Society, London, 1920; Hon. D.Sc., University of Cape Town, 1924; received Royal Medal, Royal Society, London, 1928; Hon. D.Sc., University of the Witwatersrand, 1934; Hon. D.Sc., Columbia University, 1937; honorary fellow, Royal Society of Edinburgh, 1947; Hon. D.Sc., University of Stellenbosch, 1946; honorary fellow, Royal Society of South Africa, 1946; received Elliot Medal, National Academy of Science, Washington, D.C., 1946; Wollaston Medal, Geological Society of London, 1949. Collected and described many new taxa of Karoo tetrapods; described the first adult Australopithecine skull; made outstanding contributions to the study of South Africa's hominids and their associated faunas; published some 280 studies. Died in Pretoria, 6 April 1951.

Major Publications

1895. On the organ of Jacobson in Monotremata. *Journal of Anatomy, London* 30:70–80.

1896. Report on a bone breccia deposit near Wombeyan Caves in N.S.W., with descriptions of some new species of marsupials. *Proceedings of the Linnean Society of New South Wales* 21:48–61.

1899a. On the development and morphology of the marsupial shoulder girdle. *Transactions of the Royal Society of Edinburgh* 39:749–70.

1899b. On two new species of dicynodonts. *Annals of the South African Museum* 1:452–56.

1903a. On the skull of a true lizard (*Paliguana whitei*) from Triassic beds of South Africa. *Records of the Albany Museum* 1:1–3.

1903b. On the classification of the theriodonts and their allies. *Report of the South African Association for the Advancement of Science* 1903:286–94.

1905. On the use of the term Anomodontia. *Records of the Albany Museum* 1:266–69.

1910a. A comparison of the Permian reptiles of North America with those of South Africa. *Bulletin of the American Museum of Natural History* 28:197–234.

1910b. On *Tritylodon* and on the relationships of the Multituberculata. *Proceedings of the Zoological Society of London* 760–68.

1911. On the structure of the skull in cynodont reptiles. *Proceedings of the Zoological Society of London* 893–925.

1913. On the Gorgonopsia, a suborder of the mammal-like reptiles. *Proceedings of the Zoological Society of London* 225–30.

1914a. On the structure and affinities of the Multituberculata. *Bulletin of the American Museum of Natural History* 33:115–34.

1914b. On the origin of mammals (Croonian Lecture). *Philosophical Transactions of the Royal Society of London,* ser. B., 206:1–48.

1915. Catalogue of types and figured specimens of fossil vertebrates in the American Museum of Natural History. Part 2, Permian, Triassic, and Jurassic reptiles of South Africa. *Bulletin of the American Museum of Natural History* 25:105–64.

1930. The structure of the mammal-like reptiles of the suborder Gorgonopsia. *Philosophical Transactions of the Royal Society of London,* ser. B., 218:345–71.

1932. *The Mammal-like Reptiles of South Africa, and the Origin of Mammals.* London: Witherby.

1933a. *The Coming of Man: Was It Accident or Design?* London: Witherby.

1933b. Evolution: Is there intelligence behind it? *South African Journal of Science* 30:1–19.

1937. The Sterkfontein ape. *Nature* (London) 139:326.

1946. With G.W.H. Schepers. *The South African Fossil Ape-men: The Australopithecinae.* Part 1, *The Occurrence and General Structure of the South African Ape-men.* Transvaal Museum Memoirs, 2. Pretoria: Transvaal Museum.

1947. Discovery of a new skull of the South African ape-man, *Plesianthropus. Nature* (London) 159:672.

1948. A contribution to our knowledge of the vertebrates of the Karroo beds of South Africa. *Transactions of the Royal Society of Edinburgh* 61:577–629.

1949a. With J.T. Robinson. A new mandible of the ape-man *Plesianthropus transvaalensis. American Journal of Physical Anthropology* 7:123–27.

1949b. With J.T. Robinson and G.W.H. Schepers. *Sterkfontein Ape-man, Plesianthropus.* Transvaal Museum Memoirs, 4. Pretoria: Transvaal Museum.

1950. *Finding the Missing Link.* London: Watts; 2nd ed., London: Watts, 1951; Westport, Connecticut: Greenwood, 1975.

1952. With J.T. Robinson. *Swartkrans Ape-man Paranthropus Crassidens.* Transvaal Museum Memoirs, 6. Pretoria: Transvaal Museum.

Further Reading

Findlay, G.H. 1972. *Dr. Robert Broom, F.R.S., Paleontologist and Physician, 1866–1951: A Biography, Appreciation, and Bibliography.* Cape Town: Balkema.

Watson, D.M.S. 1952. Robert Broom, 1866–1951. *Obituary Notices of Fellows of the Royal Society* 8:37–70.

Wells, L.H. 1967. Robert Broom memorial lecture: One hundred years: Robert Broom, 30 November 1866–6 April 1951. *South African Journal of Science* 63:357–66.

BROWN, BARNUM

American, 1873–1963

Barnum Brown was born near Carbondale, Kansas, in 1873, and his interest in fossils was aroused by work in his father's coal mine. He studied at the University of Kansas under Samuel Wendell Williston, and there he became friends with Elmer Riggs (another noted fossil collector, mainly associated with the Field Museum in Chicago). Brown joined Williston collecting vertebrate fossils during vacations. In the field he met a party from New York's American Museum of Natural History, and he joined the field party and staff in 1896. Although he took courses at Columbia University, he did not complete his bachelor's degree until 1907, and he never completed a postgraduate degree, although he was awarded an honorary doctorate by Lehigh University in 1934.

At the museum Brown's collecting ability was highly regarded by Henry Fairfield Osborn, who said he "must be able to smell fossils." In a 66-year association with the museum, Brown rose to be curator of vertebrate paleontology (1927–42), then continued as curator emeritus until his death. He also consulted extensively for oil companies and worked during both world wars on military invasion routes and strategic supplies.

Although part of the largest fossil hunting team of his time, Brown was a loner who never participated in such major projects as the Gobi expeditions (although he did describe some *Protoceratops* material). Roy Chapman Andrews remembered that he would "disappear from the Museum . . . and none of the staff knew where he had gone. . . . invariably his whereabouts were disclosed by a veritable avalanche of fossils descending in carload lots upon the museum" (Brown 1950).

Brown's fieldwork took him to many parts of the world, in search particularly of Tertiary mammals and Mesozoic reptiles. In North America he worked in many western U.S. states and spent several seasons in Alberta, Canada. He collected in Latin America in Cuba, Mexico, Patagonia, and Guatemala. In the Eastern Hemisphere he worked in Ethiopia (then Abyssinia), India, Pakistan, Burma, and Greece. Among many major sites, he is noted for work on the Howe Quarry in Wyoming and Red Deer River in Alberta. His assistants included other noted dinosaur collectors such as Roland Bird and George Sternberg, mammal specialist G.G. Simpson, and his eventual successor, Edwin H. Colbert.

Brown collected extensively from the Upper Cenozoic mammal faunas from the Siwalik Hills in the Himalayas. His dinosaur discoveries included *Tyrannosaurus rex,* several smaller theropods, and numerous hadrosaurs and ceratopsians. Some were described by Osborn, but many by Brown himself, sometimes with associates such as W.D. Matthew and E.M. Schlaikjer. Brown published around 100 papers, mainly technical, but including a few popular accounts of his discoveries. He also was responsible for major exhibits, such as the dinosaur hall in the American Museum and the dinosaur exhibit at the 1964 New York World's Fair (sponsored by Sinclair Oil, who had funded some of Brown's fieldwork). At his death on 5 February 1963, he left a considerable written legacy, but his own projected memoirs were never completed—a gap only partly filled by three entertaining books written by his second wife, Lilian Brown, about her travels with him.

Brown collected far more material than he could describe, providing raw materials for the careers of several of his successors. Despite his rural Kansas background, Brown used to dress "like an eastern dude" in a raccoon coat. He did his best to take care of local politics (although he was quite prepared to ignore local feelings and smuggle fossils out if he had to). He also was expert at milking the most publicity from his more important finds, for which he was admired by some of his associates but intensely disliked by others. He has been well described by James Farlow as "one of the last and greatest of the old time dinosaur hunters," and by Peter Dodson as "a great scholar of dinosaurs."

DAVID A.E. SPALDING

Works Cited

Brown, L. 1950. *I Married a Dinosaur.* New York: Dodd, Mead; London: Harrap, 1951.

Dodson, P. 1996. *The Horned Dinosaurs.* Princeton, New Jersey: Princeton University Press.

Farlow, J. 1985. Introduction to R.T. Bird's *Bones for Barnum Brown: Adventures of a Dinosaur Hunter.* Forth Worth: Texas Christian University Press.

Biography

Born near Carbondale, Kansas, 12 February 1873. Began college studies at University of Kansas; received B.A., Columbia University, 1907; received honorary D.Sc., Lehigh University, 1934. Joined staff (1896), became curator of vertebrate paleontology (1927–42), curator emeritus (1942–63), American Museum of Natural History, New York. Major collector and researcher on fossil vertebrates, particularly dinosaurs and Tertiary mammals, in North America, Europe, India, and South America; discoverer of *Tyrannosaurus rex* and many other dinosaurs. Died in New York, 5 February 1963.

Major Publications

1912. A crested dinosaur from the Edmonton Cretaceous. *Transactions of the Zoological Society of London* 11:77–105.

1913. A new Trachodont Dinosaur, *Hypacrosaurus,* from the Edmonton Cretaceous of Alberta. *American Museum of Natural History Bulletin* 32:395–406.

1914a. *Anchiceratops,* a new genus of horned dinosaurs from the Edmonton Cretaceous, with discussion of the ceratopsian crest and the brain casts of *Anchiceratops* and *Trachodon. American Museum of Natural History Bulletin* 33:539–48.

1914b. *Corythosaurus casuarius,* a new crested dinosaur from the Belly River Cretaceous, with provisional classification of the family Trachodontidae. *American Museum of Natural History Bulletin* 33:559–65.

1914c. *Leptoceratops,* a new genus of Ceratopsidae from the Edmonton Cretaceous of Alberta. *American Museum of Natural History Bulletin* 33:567–80.

1916. A new crested trachodont dinosaur, *Prosaurolophus maximus. American Museum of Natural History Bulletin* 35:701–8.

1940. With E.M. Schlaikjer. The structure and relationships of Protoceratops. *Annals of the New York Academy of Science* 40 (3):133–266.

Further Reading

Bird, R.T. 1985. *Bones for Barnum Brown: Adventures of a Dinosaur Hunter.* Fort Worth: Texas Christian University Press.

Brown, F.R. 1987. *Let's Call Him Barnum.* New York: Vantage.

Brown, L. 1950. *I Married a Dinosaur.* New York: Dodd, Mead; London: Harrap, 1951.

———. 1951. *Cleopatra Slept Here.* New York: Dodd, Mead.

———. 1956. *Bring 'em Back Petrified.* New York: Dodd, Mead; London: Adventurer's Club, 1958.

Colbert, E.H. 1968. *Men and Dinosaurs: The Search in Field and Laboratory.* New York: Dutton; London: Evans.

———. 1989. *Digging into the Past: An Autobiography.* New York: Dembner.

Dodson, P. 1996. *The Horned Dinosaurs.* Princeton, New Jersey: Princeton University Press.

Horner, J.R., and D. Lessem. 1993. *The Complete T. Rex.* New York: Simon and Schuster; London: Souvenir.

Lewis, G.E. 1964. Memorial to Barnum Brown (1873–1963). *Geological Survey of America Bulletin* 75:19–28.

Spalding, D. 1993. *Dinosaur Hunters, 150 Years of Extraordinary Discoveries.* Rocklin, California: Prima Books.

BRYOPHYTES

Simple, small, green land plants in which the haploid generation (haploid cells contain only one member of each chromosome pair, and thus have half the normal number of chromosomes) is dominant are called bryophytes. These embryo-producing plants are distinctive in having a free-living, dominant gametophyte (sexual) phase, and a smaller, attached, diploid sporophyte phase that depends on the gametophyte for its food. They have been called the amphibians of the plant world because water is essential for their sexual reproduction and survival. Currently three major lineages are recognized: liverworts or hepatics, mosses (musci), and hornworts (anthocerotophytes). These are basal members of the embryophytes, in other words, the land plant clade (a group containing all descendants of a common ancestor). Hepatics diverge first from the green plant lineage, then probably hornworts, and then mosses, followed by vascular plants such as ferns and seed plants (Figure 1; Mishler and Churchill 1985; Mishler et al., 1992). Characters that distinguish bryophytes from algae include the presence of multicellular reproductive organs (sporangia, antheridia, archegonia) surrounded by a sterile jacket layer of cells and by the occurrence of embryos. Their haploid-dominant life cycle, the presence of unbranched sporophytes, a lack of strongly lignified, patterned conducting cells, and comparatively less differentiated cells and tissues are characters distinguishing bryophytes from vascular plants.

There are about 900 genera and 25,000 species of living bryophytes, classified in three divisions and several orders (Figure 2). Although the fossil record is less diverse, several hundred extinct species have been named. Living bryophytes can be found in most environments, but especially in cool, moist conditions, and on all continents, including the shoreline of Antarctica. They cannot live

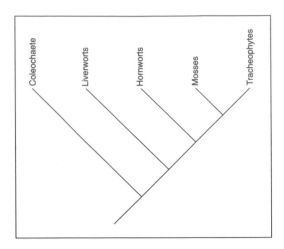

Figure 1. Proposed relationships of the bryophytes. After Mishler et al., 1985.

Figure 2. Major groups of bryophytes.
HEPATOPHYTA
Hepaticopsida
Sphaerocarpales
Metzgeriales
Marchantiales
Jungermanniales
Haplomitriales
Monocleales
Takakiales (this may be a moss)
ANTHOCEROTOPHYTA
Anthocerotales
BRYOPHYTA (MUSCI)
Sphagnopsida
Protosphagnales
Sphagnales
Andreaopsida
Andraeales
Bryopsida
Archidiales
Fissidentales
Pottiales
Funariales
Schistostegales
Eubryales
Isobryales
Grimmiales
Hypnobryales
Buxbaumiales
Tetraphidales
Polytrichales
Dawsoniales

in saltwater. Some possibly key features that have resulted in their wide distribution in various environments are (1) the ability to shut down their metabolism in adverse conditions such as drought or extreme temperatures and then rejuvenate once conditions improve; (2) the tendency to grow in cushions or clumps; (3) the ability to propagate vegetatively via fragmentation (through which a piece of a plant grows into a complete new plant) or gemmae (through which small masses of cells that separate from the parent plant grow into whole new plants); and (4) the ability to colonize barren areas such as exposed rock or where there is little soil or to live in trees. This group of plants often is ignored in considerations of both extant and extinct vegetation, but research shows that they are important components of many ecosystems, either as pioneers, soil binders, understory plants (those beneath the taller trees), or epiphytes (plants that grow on other plants). They are potential environmental indicators, and they may be very relevant to the origin of land plants (Graham 1993; 1996).

General Features of Bryophytes

Fossilized bryophytes sometimes are hard to recognize and in some instances have been described mistakenly as algae or vascular plants. Conversely, other fossils described as bryophytic have been reinterpreted as algae or vascular plants. Thus, it is important to know something about the basic features of bryophytes when trying to recognize fossil ones.

Life History

In all three lineages, haploid plants are the dominant, free-living and photosynthetic structures. They produce gametangia: either the egg-containing archegonium or sperm-producing antheridium. Sperm are released and swim on a film of water to the egg, producing a zygote. This will divide and grow into the diploid embryo, which in turn develops into the spore-producing structure, called a sporophyte. The sporophyte consists of a foot region that attaches to the haploid plant, an unbranched stalk (seta), and a sporangium (capsule). Meiosis in the latter results in the production of haploid spores that are shed and germinate in suitable environments, usually into a threadlike structure called a protonema. This will develop into the next generation haploid plant. Only a very few fossil bryophytes are found with intact reproductive structures.

Whole plants or fragments of thallus (simple plant body), stem, and leaves frequently are the basis for description of fossil taxa.

Morphology

Growth forms vary (Figure 3). The plants are usually only a few centimeters tall, with rare maximum size of about 50 centimeters, and are either thallose (without distinct stem-leaf construction) or leafy. In liverworts, the plants may be thallose, consisting of a dorsiventral pad or ribbon of tissue sometimes with lateral lobes. Numerous flaps, called ventral scales, and hairlike rhizoids extend from the ventral surface. These provide a large surface area over which water moves via capillary action on and into the plant. The rhizoids also attach the plant to the soil. Simple holes or openings lined with specialized groups of cells (air pores), are present on the upper cutinized thallus surface and aid in gas exchange. Reproductive structures are located on or partially embedded in either the upper or lower thallus surface or occur on stalked umbrella-like structures, as in *Marchantia*. Other hepatics, termed "leafy," consist of a stem on which are borne tiered rows of leaves, one row usually smaller than the other (ventrally located, called amphigastria). Gametangia and subsequent sporophytes arise at the tips of the stem-leaf structures or laterally along the stems and are surrounded by several layers of leafy structures or hairs. Many hepatic sporophyte capsules produce both spores and hygroscopic elongated cells called elators that swell or shrink and aid in liberating the spores.

Hornworts are dorsiventral and thalloid (resembling a simple plant body not differentiated into root, stem, or leaves), with a cylindrical, partially photosynthetic, sporophyte that can continue growing over a long period of time from a basal region of dividing cells. Spores and structures referred to as pseudoelators are thus produced over many weeks. The sporophyte capsule splits longitudinally to shed the spores.

Mosses are composed of stems and helically (spirally) arranged leaves, many of the latter showing a distinct midrib and outgrowths of cells on the upper surfaces. Leaves vary in lobing, margin features, and type of hairs. Rhizoids are located in basal (lower) regions of stems, and water movement is largely along the outside of the plant via capillary action. Gametangia are produced at the tips of stems. Moss capsules produce spores only. The subterminal region of the capsule becomes modified into a specialized spore-dispersal structure composed of toothlike flaps called a peristome topped by a lid, or operculum, which breaks open to release spores. Modified archegonial tissue called a calyptra covers the capsule, directing its development. Gas exchange structures, (stomata), occur on sporophyte capsules but usually are not present on gametophytes. They generally differ in construction from vascular plant stomata.

Internal Structures

Bryophytes exhibit differing degrees of complexity in stem/leaf/sporangium organization. Thalli or stems are composed either of all one type of cell or two or more zones of relatively undifferentiated cells (photosynthetic, storage, supporting). Several moss and a few hepatic gametophytes and sporophytes have centrally located cells differentiated for food-conduction (leptoids) or water movement (hydroids). Some researchers regard these as homologous (with a common ancestry) to the phloem and xylem of vascular plants, while others argue that they are simply analogous structures (of unrelated ancestry but with similar function). Studies have shown that most water uptake occurs by surface capillarity, not via the conducting cells.

Thus, the cells and tissues in a bryophyte likely to resist destruction during incorporation of fossils into sediments and their alteration into rocks are epidermal cells covered by a thin cuticle, spores with resistant sporopollenin walls, and other cells for which tests have shown the presence of some type of resistant compound (many similar to phenolics such as lignin). Some of the latter are sporangial wall cells of some liverworts and mosses, elators (elongate filaments in the capsule), and some moss rhizoids (Kroken et al. 1996). These may contribute to the sparse fossil record of bryophytes, especially in older sediment, but it has been noted that lack of preservation is probably more a result of the absence of appropriate depositional environments. Desirable conditions for fossilization of these delicate plants include rapid burial without much turbulence in fine-grained sediment (siltstones, shales) with little compaction or alteration and in the absence of oxygen. Preservation in volcanic ash or in amber (fossilized resin) has resulted in many excellent specimens in younger strata.

Studies of Fossil Bryophytes

Fossil bryophytes first were described by paleobotanists about 150 years ago, at which time several very well preserved forms were documented. Form genera for those not assignable to known families or genera first were established by Adolphe Brongniart (1849, 1915) and revised by later researchers, especially J. Walton (1925, 1928). Other early workers include H.R. Goeppert and R. Caspary. As an example of early work, Goeppert (1853, 1856) described several bryophytes preserved in Baltic amber. These three-dimensionally preserved remains were restudied by Caspary (1906) and some were recognized as tree epiphytes. Recently, R. Grolle (1980a, b; 1981 a, b) described additional types, and it has been determined that the amber-producing plants were part of a subalpine community.

M.F. Neuberg (1960) described several very well preserved mosses from the Permian of the Kuznetsk Basin in what was then the Soviet Union, which showed modern features and vastly expanded our knowledge of diversity of Paleozoic types. V.A. Krassilov (1970, 1973) published on Jurassic bryophytes from the former Soviet Union, again adding new taxa, some with characters not identical to modern types. T.M. Harris (1939) provided the definitive analysis of a Triassic hepatic, *Naiadita*, for which some reproductive structures and some unusual features are known, tentatively allying it to the Sphaerocarpales. Several large bryophyte floras are known from the Tertiary, one of the more extensive coming from the Miocene or early Pliocene of the Canadian Arctic Archipelago (Kuc 1972; Kuc and Hills 1971) and showing a mixture of arctic and temperate taxa. Reviews by Jovet-Ast (1967), Lacey (1969), Krassilov and Schuster (1984), and Miller (1984) reference additional studies.

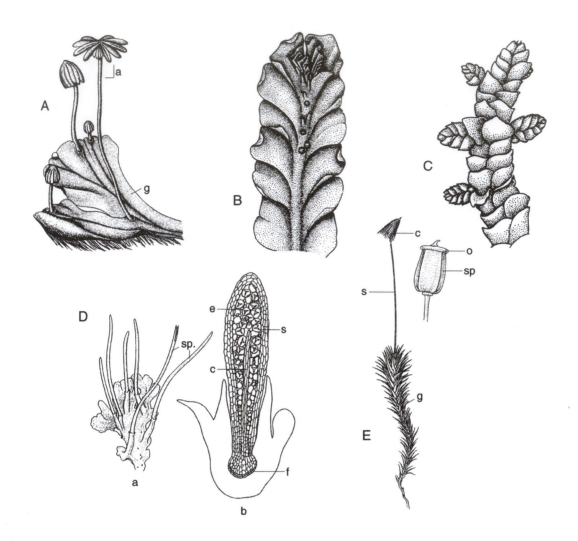

Figure 3. Representative extant (living) bryophytes. *A*, gametophyte *(g)* and gametangium-bearing *(a)* structures of the thalloid liverwort *Marchantia polymorpha*; *B*, *Fossombronia*, a liverwort showing a transitional state between being thalloid and leafy; *C*, the general habit of a leafy liverwort *(Porella)*; *D*, thallus and developing sporangia of the hornwort *Anthoceros*, with the sporangia split from their tip backwards; to the right is a detailed drawing of a longitudinal section of the sporophyte, with the foot *(f)*, the spore-producing region *(s)*, the centrally located sterile columella *(c)*, and the elators, specialized cells that help disperse the spores; *E*, gametophyte and attached sporophyte of the moss *Polytrichum* and a detailed drawing to the right of the sporophyte capsule. The leafy gametophyte *(g)* is at the base; *s*, seta; *c*, caluptra; *o*, operculum (the tip end of the capsule that detaches to release spores). *A–C* from Stewart and Rothwell (1993), reprinted with the permission of Cambridge University Press. *D, E*, from Kenrick and Crane (1997), used by permission of the publisher, the Smithsonian Institution Press, Washington, D.C., copyright © 1997.

First Occurrences

Most bryologists and paleobotanists accept that the earliest occurrence of undoubted liverworts is from the base of the Upper Devonian period, although some recent studies suggest a possible earlier occurrence. Mosses appear in the fossil record probably in the Carboniferous and are varied and modern in appearance by the Permian. Anthocerotes apparently are unknown until the Cretaceous, and early records are based on the occurrence of dispersed spores that are morphologically similar to extant forms (Jarzen 1979). Modern genera of these groups first appear at the end of the Tertiary or in the early Quaternary. Starting with the Carboniferous, at least one record of a bryophyte is known from every continent for most periods of time, with the most information being from

the paleocontinent Laurussia plus the former Soviet Union. Differences in diversity may reflect intensity of fossil research in any given area. Many more records of bryophytes are known from Tertiary and Quaternary deposits than from older sediments and are most abundant from Great Britain.

Hepatics

The earliest undoubted hepatic is called *Pallaviciniites devonicus* from the Upper Devonian of New York State (Hueber 1961; Schuster 1966), so named because it strongly resembles present-day *Pallavicinia* (Metzgeriales), but it is related to the Jungermanniales by Krassilov and Schuster (1984). The plant consists of a dichoto-

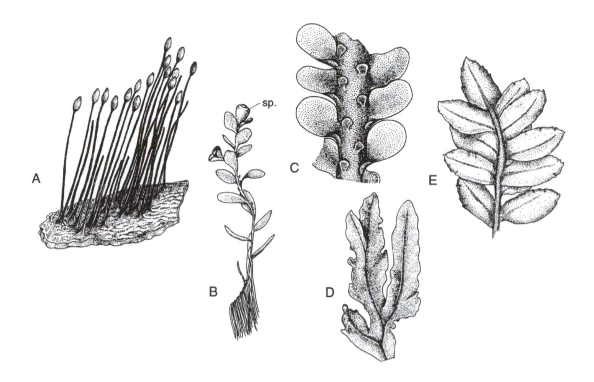

Figure 4. Selected fossil bryophytes. *A*, reconstruction of the enigmatic *Sporogonites exuberans* from the Lower Devonian; *B*, habit drawing of the Triassic liverwort *Naiadita lanceolata* Harris; *C*, ventral view showing dimorphic leaves of the Upper Carboniferous liverwort *Hepaticites kidstoni*; *D*, branching thallus of the Upper Carboniferous liverwort *Thallites willsii*; *E.*, fragment of stem and leaves of the Eocene moss *Aulocomnium heterostichoides*. *A*, from Andrews (1960), reproduced by permission of the *Palaeobotanist*; *B–D*, from Stewart and Rothwell (1993), reprinted with the permission of Cambridge University Press; *E*, drawing by Susan Lerner from photo in Janssens et al. (1979), with permission of the National Research Council of Canada.

mizing ribbonlike thallus with a central thick (axial) structure and lateral wings with serrate edges (Figure 4). Rhizoids are borne on axial regions lacking wings. No reproductive structures were found. Other thalloid hepatics have been described from the Carboniferous, allied to the Metzgeriales, and called *Treubites*, *Metzgeriothallus*, or *Blasiites* (Krassilov and Schuster 1984). Forms whose affinity to modern orders is unclear are referred to *Hepaticites*. Many show a central axial region on which occur lobes or discrete leaves.

Numerous species, some with ventral scales and rhizoids and dorsal pores, allied to Jungermanniales, Marchantiales, Sphaerocarpales, and Metzgeriales, are known from the Mesozoic, suggesting rapid diversification after the Carboniferous. A rich assemblage from the early Jurassic coal mines of Sweden record marchantialean forms and some that appear related to *Riccia* (Lundblad 1954). A more completely known hepatic from the Cretaceous of Montana, *Diettertia*, has bifid leaves borne along the stems (Brown and Robison 1974; Schuster and Janssens 1989) and although first considered a moss, now is allied to the Jungermanniales. Most early Tertiary taxa still differ from modern taxa and are referred to *Jungermannites*, *Plagiochilites*, *Marchantites*, and *Ricciopsis*. A few species from the late Tertiary and most Quaternary forms are referred to modern genera. Especially well preserved remains have been obtained from the Middle Tertiary Baltic amber and some lignites.

Problematic Taxa

Single elongate-oval sporangia terminating unbranched stems that apparently lack vascular tissue are known from the Early Devonian and are called *Sporogonites* (Halle 1916, 1936). Permineralized remains showed a possible central region of sterile cells in the sporangia similar to a columella, surrounded by small spores, as occurs in some bryophytes. This, plus unbranched stems and the absence of vascular tissue, resulted in *Sporogonites* being allied to bryophytes. A distinct columella has not been substantiated, however, and it could equally represent a primitive vascular plant (Hoeg 1967). H.N. Andrews's (1960) report that several of these stalked sporangia emanate from a basal thalloid region, represented by amorphous carbon, also supported its being bryophytic. In many texts it is placed in its own family in the hepatics, but definitive evidence still is lacking.

A second possible bryophyte from Upper Silurian and initial Devonian strata, *Tortilicaulis*, first was described as a sporangium terminating an unbranched stalk that twisted in a manner also seen in some extant mosses (Edwards 1979). Later described specimens have sporangia terminating branched stems (Fanning et al. 1992; Edwards et al. 1994), and thus its affinity now is uncertain. Some other early Devonian plants have been implicated as possible bryophytes or intermediate between bryophytes and tracheophytes (vascular plants) because they lack conducting cells entirely (basal region of *Horneophyton*), or have conducting cells whose walls are not differentially thickened as in tracheophytes (*Aglaophyton;* Edwards 1986). Additionally, the sporangia of *Horneophyton* exhibit tissue that could be considered a columella, as occurs in some mosses and hornworts. However, these plants have branched sporophytes and other features differing from known bryophytes and currently are believed to form separate lineages in the land plant group (Kenrick and Crane 1996).

A pre-Devonian occurrence of bryophytes is again considered possible. Spore tetrads found dispersed in Ordovician and Silurian rocks are compared to sphaerocarpalean spores on the basis of remaining in a permanent tetrad and on the distinctive lamellar layering of walls in some of them (Gray 1985; Taylor 1995). Further supporting this is a study in which sporangial wall, spore, rhizoid, and elator remnants obtained by acetolyzing (cooking in acids) living moss and liverwort sporophytes and gametophytes are compared favorably to fragments of cuticles and tubes found dispersed in rocks from the late Ordovician to the early Devonian (Kroken et al. 1996). D. Edwards and colleagues (1995) described a minute, simple plant from the earliest Devonian with features they interpreted as hepatic-related, such as spore tetrads, possible elator-like and rhizoidal structures, and remnants of oil-body cells. If these findings are further corroborated, an earlier first appearance of bryophytes, and particularly hepatics, will be established.

Mosses

Mosses first appear in the Early Carboniferous, based on *Muscites plumosus* (Thomas 1972), followed by *Muscites polytrichaceous* from the Late Carboniferous of France (Renault and Zeiller 1888). The well-preserved mosses described by M.F. Neuberg (1960) from the Upper Permian Kuznetsk Basin of the former Soviet Union are referable to the true mosses (Bryales) and a distinct group, the Protosphagnales. This and later studies suggest that the Angara region (mostly what was formerly the western Soviet Union) in the Late Paleozoic had an abundant moss component in its vegetation. A permineralized moss of possible Bryalean affinity, *Merceria,* is described from the Permian of Antarctica (Smoot and Taylor 1986), in which thin leaves with midribs are arranged spirally on a stem.

While no mosses are known from the early Triassic, sparse records from Late Triassic through the Cretaceous are largely from the western United States, Europe, the former Soviet Union, and Asia. Mosses are very well known from Tertiary and Quaternary deposits, again especially from North America, Europe, and the former Soviet Union. A well-preserved assemblage from a Tertiary lignite at Lake Hazen, Ellesmere Island, and from several sites in Poland have been used to determine floristic change to the present. Modern genera are recognized in the Tertiary, as for example the well-preserved *Aulacomnium heterostichoides* (Janssens et al. 1979) from the Eocene of British Columbia. From the middle Tertiary on, modern species are recognized, suggesting great longevity for many living species of mosses. North temperate floras indicate that species composition, habitats, and vegetation types of the middle-late Tertiary are similar to those found today. Some species ranges have changed, however; for example, moss species found only in the Mediterranean region today were located north and west of their present range in the Tertiary. For other species, ranges have been compressed to the east, so they are now found only in parts of Asia (Miller 1984). Some connections between Europe and North America can be deduced using fossils. *Sphagnum* initially was found only in fossil deposits in North America, and it was unclear if it was present also in Europe; recent finds in parts of the former Soviet Union and Poland show it was a common element in European Tertiary floras. Other bryophytes have indicated location of tundra vegetation or boreal forests in the Late Tertiary.

Bryophytes (mostly mosses), barely altered from their original form, obtained from Quaternary interglacial (between periods of glaciation) and late glacial (after the last major glaciation about 16,000 to 10,000 years ago) deposits from North America and Europe have been used to understand possible location and migration of these plants as the climate fluctuated (Miller 1976, 1984). During the late glacial many species remained adjacent to the glacier margin, not migrating to a more southerly refuge, and many alpine or high-latitude species occurred south of their present range. Changes after the last glaciation to the present show how the landscape, and plants that inhabited it, altered from tundra to boreal and then temperate forest as the climate changed. Immediately after glaciation, moss floras are rich in calcium-rich rock-loving species; as trees invade, numbers of these types decrease. Similarly, the number and types of wetland areas (bogs and fens) decrease as one approaches the present. Lastly, bryophytes obtained from archaeological deposits, or mammoth and mastodon remains, provide evidence of surrounding vegetation. A mammoth skeleton found in Germany was interpreted as having been trapped in a wet depression with fen vegetation based on the associated moss assemblage. Bryophytes also have been found in their stomachs (Miller 1984).

Summary

The fossil record from the Paleozoic to the present provides intriguing insights into the past history of bryophytes. However, thus far fossils do not answer fundamental questions about moss or hepatic precursors, which group of mosses or hepatics are the more primitive, and how they should be classified. Instead, shortly after the first occurrence of each type, great diversity of form is found. The anthocerote record is extremely sparse. Information about these plants has been useful in reconstructing vegetation associations and paleoenvironment, especially for the Tertiary to present. Knowing more about bryophyte morphology and being aware that bryophytes can be fossilized, coupled with modifications of sampling and improved preparation techniques, should result in expanding knowledge about the past history and evolutionary patterns of these fascinating plants.

PATRICIA G. GENSEL

Works Cited

Andrews, H.N. 1960. Notes on Belgian specimens of *Sporogonites.* *Palaeobotanist* 7:85–89.

Brongniart, A. 1849. Vegetabilia, Plantae. *In Dictionnaire Universel d'Histoire Naturelle.* Vol. 13, Paris: Renard.

———. 1915. *Histoire des végétaux fossiles; ou recherches botaniques et géologiques sur les végétaux renfermés dans les diverses couches du globe.* Vol. 1, Berlin: Junk.

Brown, J.T., and C.R. Robinson. 1974. *Diettertia montanensis* gen. et sp. nov., a fossil moss from the Lower Cretaceous Kootenai Formation of Montana. *Botanical Gazette* 135:170–73.

Caspary, R. 1906. *Die Flora des Bernsteins und anderer fossiler Harze des Ostpreussischen Tertiärs.* Berlin: Königlich Preussissche Geologische Landesanstalt.

Edwards, D. 1979. A Late Silurian flora from the Lower Old Red Sandstone of southwest Dyfed. *Palaeontology* 22:23–52.

Edwards, D., J.G. Duckett, and J.B. Richardson. 1995. Hepatic characters in the earliest land plants. *Nature* 374:635–36.

Edwards, D., U. Fanning, and J.B. Richardson. 1994. Lower Devonian coalified sporangia from Shropshire: *Salopella* Edwards and Richardson and *Tortilicaulis* Edwards. *Botanical Journal of the Linnean Society* 116:89–110.

Edwards, D.S. 1986. *Aglaophyton major,* a non-vascular land-plant from the Devonian Rhynie Chert. *Botanical Journal of the Linnean Society* 93:173–204.

Fanning, U., D. Edwards, and J.B. Richardson. 1992. A diverse assemblage of early land plants from the Lower Devonian of the Welsh Borderland. *Botanical Journal of the Linnean Society* 109:161–88.

Goeppert, H.R. 1853. *Über die Bernsteinflora.* Berlin: Königlich Preussische Akademie der Wissenschaften.

———. 1856. Uebersicht der bis jetzt bekannten in und mit dem Bernstein vorkommenden vegetabilischen Reste. *In* G.C. Berendt (ed.) *Die im Bernstein befindlichen organischen Reste der Vorwelt.* 2 vols., Berlin: Nicolaische Buchhandlung.

Graham, L.E. 1993. *Origin of Land Plants.* New York: Wiley.

———. 1996. Green algae to land plants: An evolutionary transition. *Journal of Plant Research* 109:241–51.

Gray, J. 1985. The microfossil record of early land plants: Advances in understanding of early terrestrialization, 1970–1984. *Philosophical Transactions of the Royal Society of London,* ser. B, 309:167–95.

Grolle, R. 1980a. Lebermoose im Bernstein 1. *Feddes Rep.* 91:183–90.

———. 1980b. Lebermoose im Bernstein 2. *Feddes Rep.* 91:401–7.

———. 1981a. *Nipponolejeunia* fossil in Europa. *Journal of Hattori Botanical Laboratory* 50:143–57.

———. 1981b. Was ist *Lejeunea schumannii* Caspary aus dem baltischen Bernstein? *Occasional Papers Farlow Herb. Harvard University* 16:101–10.

Halle, T.G. 1916. A fossil sporogonium from the Lower Devonian of Röragen in Norway. *Botanisk Notiser* 1916:79–81.

———. 1936. Notes on the Devonian genus *Sporogonites. Svensk Botanisk Tidskrift* 30:613–23.

Harris, T.M. 1939. *Naiadita,* a fossil bryophyte with reproductive organs. *Annals of Bryology* 12:57–70.

Hoeg, O.A. 1967. Psilophyta. *In* E. Boureau (ed.), *Traité de Paléobotanique.* Vol. 2, *Bryophyta, Psilophyta, Lycophyta.* Paris: Masson et Cie.

Hueber, F.M. 1961. *Hepaticites devonicus,* a new fossil liverwort from the Devonian of New York. *Annals of the Missouri Botanical Garden* 48:125–29.

Janssens, J.A.P., D.G. Horton, and J.F. Basinger. 1979. *Aulacomnium heterostichoides,* sp. nov.: An Eocene moss from central British Columbia. *Canadian Journal of Botany* 57:2150–61.

Jarzen, D.M. 1979. Spore morphology of some Anthocerotaceae and the occurrence of *Phaeoceros* spores in the Cretaceous of North America. *Pollen et Spores* 21:211–31.

Jovet-Ast, S. 1967. Bryophyta. *In* E. Boureau (ed.), *Traité de Paléobotanique.* Vol. 2, *Bryophyta, Psilophyta, Lycophyta.* Paris: Masson et Cie.

Kenrick, P., and P.R. Crane. 1996. *The Origin and Early Diversification of Land Plants: A Cladistic Study.* Washington, D.C.: Smithsonian Press.

Krassilov, V.A. 1970. Leafy hepatics from the Jurassic of the Bureja Basin. *Paleontological Journal* 3:131–42.

———. 1973. Mesozoic bryophytes form the Bureja Basin, far east of the USSR. *Palaeontographica* 143B:95–105.

Krassilov, V.A., and R.M. Schuster. 1984. Paleozoic and Mesozoic fossils. *In* R.M. Schuster (ed.), *New Manual of Bryology.* Vol. 2, Nichinan: Hattori Botanical Laboratory.

Kroken, S.B., L.E. Graham, and M.E. Cook. 1996. Occurrence and evolutionary significance of resistant cell walls in charophytes and bryophytes. *American Journal of Botany* 83:1241–54.

Kuc, M. 1972. *Fossil Flora of the Beaufort Formation, Mieghen Island, NWT-Canada.* N.p. 8 Era Canadian-Polish Research Institute.

Kuc, M., and L.V. Hills. 1971. Fossil mosses, Beaufort Formation (Tertiary), northwestern Banks Island, western Canada Arctic. *Canadian Journal of Botany* 49:1089–94.

Lacey, W.S. 1969. Fossil bryophytes. *Biological Reviews* 44:169–205.

Lundblad, B. 1954. Contributions to the geological history of the Hepaticae: Fossil Marchantiales from the Rhaetic-Liassic coal mines of Skromberga (Prov. of Scania), Sweden. *Svensk. Botanisker Tidskrift* 48:381–417.

Miller, N.G. 1976. Quaternary fossil bryophytes in North America: A synopsis of the record and some phytogeographic implications. *Journal Hattori Botanical Laboratory* 41:73–85.

———. 1984. Tertiary and Quaternary fossils. *In* R.M. Schuster (ed.), *New Manual of Bryology.* Vol. 2, Japan: Hattori Botanical Laboratory.

Mishler, B.D., and S.P. Churchill. 1985. Transition to a land flora: Phylogenetic relationships of the green algae and bryophytes. *Cladistics* 1(4):305–28.

Mishler, B.D., P.H. Thrall, J.S. Hopple Jr., E. Deluna, and R. Vilgalys. 1992. A molecular approach to the phylogeny of bryophytes: Cladistic analyses of chloroplast encoded 16S and 23S ribosomal RNA genes. *Bryologist* 95:172–80.

Neuberg, M.F. 1960. Leafy mosses from the Permian deposits of Anagaraland. Trudy Ecological Institute Akademia Nauk. *SSSR* 19:1–104.

Renault, B., and R. Zeiller. 1888. *Flore fossile.* Études sur les terrains houillers de Commentry, Livre deuxième. Paris: Théolier et Cie.

Schuster, R.M. 1966. *The Hepaticae and Anthocerotae of North America East of the Hundredth Meridian.* Vol. 1, New York: Columbia University Press.

Schuster, R.M., and J.A. Janssens. 1989. On *Diettertia,* an isolated Mesozoic member of the Jungermanniales. *Review of Palaeobotany and Palynology* 57:277–87.

Smoot, E.L., and T.N. Taylor. 1986. Structurally preserved plants from the Permian of Antarctica, 2, A Permian moss from the Transantarctic Mountains. *American Journal of Botany* 73:1683–91.

Stewart, W.N., and G.W. Rothwell. 1993. *Paleobotany and the Evolution of Plants.* Cambridge and New York: Cambridge University Press.

Taylor, W.A. 1995. Spores in earliest land plants. *Nature* 373:391–92.

Thomas, B.A. 1972. A probable moss from the Lower Carboniferous of the Forest of Dean, Goucestershire. *Annals of Botany* 36:155–61.

Walton, J. 1925. Carboniferous Bryophyta, 1, Hepaticae. *Annals of Botany* 39:563–72.
———. 1928. Carboniferous Bryophyta, 2, Hepaticae and Musci. *Annals of Botany* 42:707–16.

Further Reading
Bold, H.C., C.J. Alexopoulos, and T. Delevoryas. 1957. *Morphology of Plants*. New York: Harper; 5th ed., as *Morphology of Plants and*

Fungi, New York and London: Harper.
Chandra, S. 1995. Bryophytic remains from the Early Permian sediments of India. *Palaeobotanist* 43(2):16–48.
Oostendorp, C. 1987. *The Bryophytes of the Palaeozoic and the Mesozoic*. Bryophytorum Bibliotheca, 34. Berlin: Cramer.
Schuster, R.M. (ed.). 1984. *New Manual of Bryology*. Vols. 1 and 2, Japan: Hattori Botanical Laboratory.
Taylor, T.N., and E.L. Taylor. 1993. *The Biology and Evolution of Fossil Plants*. Englewood Cliffs, New Jersey: Prentice Hall.

BRYOZOANS

Calcium-carbonate (calcareous) branches, fronds, masses, and crusts of small to moderate size (under one meter maximum), with surfaces covered by many tiny pin-prick-sized holes: these are the fossilized remains of bryozoans, aquatic invertebrate animals whose minute, polyplike individuals (zooids) build a hardened exoskeletal collective framework (colony or zoarium). Bryozoans comprise a major "phylum" (a major division of organisms), the Bryozoa (or Polyzoa of older literature), popularly "moss-animals" or "seamats"; over 1600 genera have been described to date, with an estimated 20,000 species, extending from early in the Ordovician until the present. About a quarter are still living.

Morphology and Biology

Each bryozoan zooid, less than one millimeter long and wide, is enclosed within a hardened exoskeletal case ("zooecium," plural zooecia) and is attached permanently to it. The zooecium contains a U-shaped digestive tract (Figure 1), beginning with an external circle of tentacles (lophophore) surrounding a mouth, descending into the zooecium, and curving back up and out to exit at an anus. Muscle strands strung across the liquid-filled internal space (zooecial cavity) allow the tentacles to be pulled down (retracted) into the zooecium for protection. Other muscles attached to flexible parts of the body wall (zooecial wall), squeeze upon the body liquid, and so push out (extend or protrude) the tentacles for feeding. (This process is somewhat like squeezing water from one end to the other in a water balloon. As water is forced into an area, the area stiffens and extends outward.)

The tentacles then are held outstretched, collectively like a bell or cup. Minute hairlike cilia covering the tentacles' surfaces beat rhythmically in unison, and setting up weak currents in their immediate vicinity, so that algal cells and organic detritus (debris from dead animals and plants) floating suspended in the water are carried into the open mouth and ingested.

After death and fossilization, only the zooecium remains. The zooecial cavity appears empty or is filled with sediment or cement; in addition, in some species, calcareous partitions of various shapes and size cross the zooecial cavity. The opening through which the tentacles are extended and retracted (zooecial aperture or orifice) is evident. The zooecial walls exhibit various microstructures and strengthening rods (acanthostyles, acanthorods, or acanthopores).

Most walls consist of calcite. Usually this material is in the form of low-magnesium calcite, resulting in well-preserved microstructures like laminations, but occasionally it is high-magnesium calcite, which results in microstructures that are obscured by minutely granular recrystallization. In a few species, the walls include aragonite, which either is preserved as coarse recrystallization to calcite or is leached away to leave empty spaces within the fossilized wall.

Within many colonies, most of the zooecia are as described above, fully developed as feeding zooids (autozooids), but interspersed among them are smaller zooecia of different shapes ("polymorphs" or heterozooids). Bryozoan zooecia are bundled together into colonies of greatly varied form (Figure 2). The external surfaces of many larger colonies exhibit small bumps (monticules) or distinct spots (maculae) composed of zooecia or polymorphs of unusual sizes.

Growth within a colony proceeds by asexual budding of new zooids from adjacent preexisting ones (Figure 3). (Budding involves the creation of small outgrowths that contain the body layers and an extension of the gastrointestinal cavity. Once all body systems are duplicated, the bud pinches off and becomes an independent zooid. No sexual interchange is involved.) Such growth sets up clearly visible directions within the colony—"distal" being the direction in which new growth is going, and "proximal" being toward the initially formed part of the colony. Certain zooids are hermaphroditic, producing both male and female sexual reproductive cells (gametes), some of which are shed into the surrounding water, are recaptured, unite, and develop into minute larvae. These swim away, settle down onto the bottom, and metamorphose into a polyplike zooid, which then proceeds to bud off new zooids asexually to establish a new colony.

Taxonomy and Stratigraphy

A number of groups are recognized among bryozoans (Table 1; Figures 4–8), some are soft-bodied and thus are essentially unknown as fossils, and others are well-calcified and hence have an excellent fossil record (Taylor 1993). Classification systems have followed a number of approaches—conventional, phenetic, and cladistic (Bassler 1953; Ryland 1970, 1982; Nielsen 1982; Boardman et al. 1983; Cuffey 1973; Cuffey and Blake 1991; Anstey and Pachut 1995). Certain groups have alternate synonyms or subdivi-

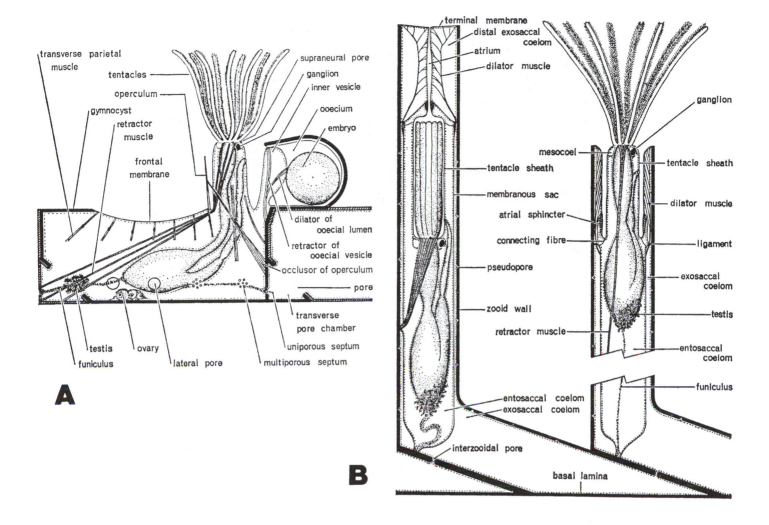

Figure 1. Bryozoan zooids, showing soft parts and zooecia. *A,* boxlike anascan cheilostome with tentacles extended; *B,* tubular cycloostome with tentacles; *(left)* retracted; *(rght)* extended. Modified from Ryland (1970).

sions that appear often enough in the literature that they are mentioned here for the reader's reference but, due to space limitations, not discussed in detail.

To study and identify bryozoans, scholars examine both external and internal characters; the latter requires preparation of cross sections (thin sections of wafer-thin slices cut from the specimen, and peel-sections, or replicas made of acetate materials, created as impressions of acid-etched surfaces cut into the specimen). To standardize comparisons, such sections always are oriented very specifically in terms of the animal's body: Longitudinal sections are cut parallel to the long axis of a branch and contain the central axis, tangential sections are shaved from the side of the branch just below its external surface, and traverse sections are cut perpendicularly across the long axis of a branch.

Subphyla

Soft-part characters separate bryozoans into two subphyla of greatly unequal sizes: entoprocts and ectroprocts. The anus of an entoproct opens inside its circle of tentacles; an ectoproct's anus opens outside or below the zooid's tentacles. During embryonic development the zooids of ectoprocts and entoprocts follow quite different pathways with respect to body cavity formation. Entoprocts have soft membranous body walls, whereas most ectoprocts exhibit some hardening there, ranging from weakly chitinized (impregnated with fibrous, hard starch) to heavily calcified zooecial walls.

The Ectoprocta include virtually all the known Bryozoa (over 1600 genera). In sharp contrast, the Entoprocta (Figure 4) include only about 10 genera, all so similar that they are classified in only one class (Calyssozoa, or Kamptozoa) with one order (Pedicellinida), including both solitary zooid species (suborder Loxosomatina) and encrusting stolon colonies (suborder Pedicellinina). Most are marine, but one is a freshwater group.

The earliest ectoprocts occur at several horizons within the Lower Ordovician. One polyp found in Cambrian deposits in the Burgess Shale of Canada may be a solitary entoproct, but zooids from the European Jurassic are the oldest definite entoprocts.

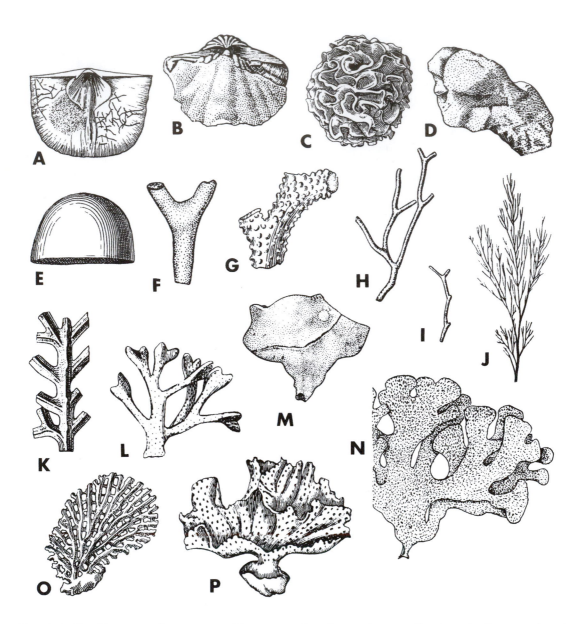

Figure 2. Brachiopod shells with commonly encountered bryozoan colony forms. *A,* encrusting threads; *B,* encrusting sheet; *C,* lettuce-like erect sheets (foliaceous); *D,* irregular (nodular) mass; *E,* hemispherical dome; *F,* cylindrical (ramose) branches, robust thick with smooth surface; *G,* with monticules; *H,* delicate slender; *I, J,* upright tuft of extremely thin branches; flat branches, as ribbonlike fragment; *K,* entire colony; *L,* upright flat fronds, rigid calcareous; *M,* flexible chitinous; *N,* erect lattice or meshwork fronds; *O,* Paleozoic fenestrate; *P,* Cenozoic cheilostome. Scale: all ×1, except *O* (scale, ×5). Modified from: *N,* Hyman (1959); all others, Bassler (1953) *Treatise on Invertebrate Paleontology,* courtesy of and © 1953 The Geological Society of America and The University of Kansas Press.

Systematic placement of the entoprocts is controversial. Some scholars classify them with Byrozoans, viewing the group as surviving remnants of a very early stage in the phylum's evolution. Others consider them an independent phylum far off the lineage leading to the other bryozoans.

Classes

The Ectoprocta are subdivided into two large classes and one small one. The Phylactolaemata (Figure 4) contain roughly 10 genera only, all classified within one order (Plumatellida). It contains

both inconspicuous chitinous-walled encrusting networks (suborder Plumatellina) and large gelatinous masses (Pectinatellina). Their zooids are distinctive because the tentacles are arranged in a U-shaped arrangement. Moreover, these animals live exclusively in freshwater environments, and produce oval, hard-shelled, chitinous resting bodies (statoblasts) capable of resisting harsh environmental conditions, such as winters and droughts. Statoblasts, long known from postglacial lake deposits in the American Midwest, recently have been found in Jurassic shales in Asia.

The Gymnolaemata (or Pyxibryozoa or Eurystomata) and Stenolaemata (or Tubulobryozoa) each houses approximately half

Table 1. Classification and Stratigraphic Ranges of Phylum Bryozoa, Middle Cambrian?, Lower Ordovician–

Subphylum/Class/Order/Suborder	Range through Time, from Earliest to Latest
Subphylum Entoprocta	Middle Cambrian?, Upper Jurassic–Recent
Subphylum Ectoprocta	Lower Ordovician–Recent
Class Phylactolaemata	Middle Jurassic–Recent
Class Gymnolaemata	Lower Ordovician–Recent
Order Ctenostomida	Lower Ordovician–Recent
Suborder Stoloniferina	Lower Ordovician–Recent
Suborder Carnosina	Pennsylvanian?, Middle Triassic–Recent
Order Cheilostomida	Upper Jurassic–Recent
Suborder Anascina	Upper Jurassic–Recent
Suborder Cribrimorphina	Middle Cretaceous–Recent
Suborder Ascophorina	Upper Cretaceous–Recent
Class Stenolaemata	Lower Ordovician–Recent
Order Cyclostomida	Lower Ordovician–Recent
Order Cystoporida	Lower Ordovician–Upper Triassic
Suborder Ceramoporina	Lower Ordovician–Lower Devonian
Suborder Fistuliporina	Lower Ordovician–Upper Triassic
Order Repostomida	Lower Ordovician–Upper Triassic
Suborder Esthonioporina	Lower Ordovician–Middle Devonian
Suborder Amplexoporina	Lower Ordovician–Upper Triassic
Suborder Halloporina	Lower Ordovician–Upper Triassic
Order Cryptostomida	Lower Ordovician–Upper Triassic
Suborder Rhabdomesina	Lower Ordovician–Upper Triassic
Suborder Ptilodictyina	Lower Ordovician–Upper Permian
Suborder Fenestrina	Lower Ordovician–Upper Permian

the known Bryozoa. Both range from early in the Ordovician until today, but stenolaemates heavily dominate Paleozoic faunas, while gymnolaemates are predominant during the post-Paleozoic. Both have tentacles arranged in a circular pattern. Neither produces resistant resting bodies.

The zooecia of gymnolaemates are boxlike, with more or less equidimensional chambers. In extreme cases, the zooecia are nicely cubical or rectangular, but in other cases they may be more cylindrical, ovoid, or even irregular. Generally, the internal cavity is empty, without calcareous cross-partitions. The walls range from thin and chitinous to thick and calcareous. Most are calcitic, but some include aragonite. These bryozoans are mostly marine (saltwater-based), but some species range into brackish (mixture of salt and fresh water) estuaries as well.

Stenolaemates are distinguished by tubelike zooecia. The chambers are noticeably longer than they are wide, varying from very elongate to quite short. (Long-tubed forms—cyclostomes, cystoporates, and trepostomes—may be grouped as a subclass Leptaulata, while short-tubed ones—cryptostomes—comprise a subclass Curtaulata.) The internal cavity varies from empty to crossed by many transverse partitions, such as diaphragms, cystiphragms, and hemisepta. The walls are calcitic and vary greatly in thickness.

Stenolaemates are normal-marine, ranging very seldom into water where salinity is reduced.

Ctenostomida

When its tentacles are retracted, the soft body wall of the upper opening (orifice) of a ctenostome zooid closes by folding into a pleated collar. The body walls are flexible and chitinous, the zooids vary from cylindrical to flat (Figure 4), and the colonies include no brood chambers (chambers where gametes undergo fertilization and larvae develop).

Some ctenostomes, the Stoloniferina, consist of zooids separated by thinner tubes (stolons); their colonies can be threadlike networks that either form a crust upon a hard substrate (surface) or bore down into calcareous shells; some can form bushy branching tufts that stand upright above the bottom. The approximately 30 genera occur in marine or brackish waters. Boring traces (holes and scars) go all the way back to the beginning of the bryozoan fossil record.

Other ctenostomes, the Carnosina, lack stolons, and new zooids are budded off directly from previously formed zooids. Colony forms include encrusting networks up on substrate surfaces,

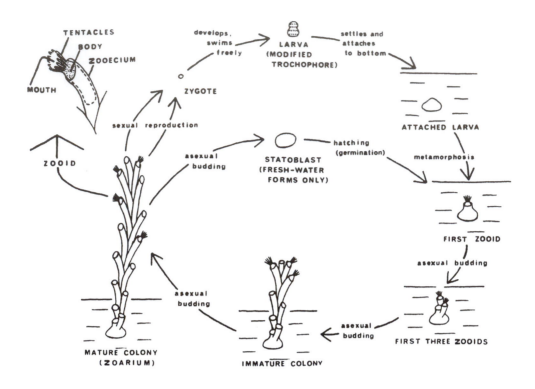

Figure 3. Bryozoan life cycle. From Cuffey (1970), courtesy of *Earth and Mineral Sciences.*

and erect, fleshy, fingerlike branches. In addition to marine and brackish environments, a very few of the 20 genera are found in fresh water. The impression (a fossilized outline) of a possible fleshy colony recently has been retrieved from deposits from the Pennsylvanian system of Appalachia, but the earliest certain carnosan is a bioimmuration (a natural, three-dimensional mold formed in the bottom surface of a subsequent encrustation) from the European Triassic.

Cheilostomida

Zooecia in this order (Figure 5) are variably boxlike, frequently arranged in side-by-side rows that reflect their budding sequence. Some walls are thin chitinous membranes, while others are thick and calcareous. Colonies vary widely in form; most noticeable are thin, encrusting, unilaminar (single-layered) sheets; thicker multilayered masses; cylindrical to flattened erect branches; flexible fronds and tufts; and unattached (free-living) small domes. The zooecial aperture is closed by a hinged chitinous lid ("operculum"). In many species interspersed among the fully developed, feeding zooids are smaller polymorphs, projecting above the zooecial apertures, particularly mousetraplike avicularia, whiplike vibracula, and rootlike rhizoids, and also hollow bulbs (ovicells, or ooecia—brooding chambers to protect embryonic larvae). Most cheilostomes are marine, some brackish.

The colony's upper surface, highest above the substrate, is known as the "frontal surface"; the appearance of the zooecial walls there, adjacent to the apertures, serves to separate cheilostomes into

three suborders. When fossilized, the Anascina, almost 400 genera, have frontal walls with an opening (opesium) much larger than the aperture would be (in life, the frontal wall is membranous, uncalcified, and thus mostly is not preserved). The Cribrimorphina, over 150 genera, display grill-like frontal walls formed by overarching riblike calcareous spines growing over from the lateral (side) edges of the zooecium and fusing in its mid-line. The Ascophorina, with more than 400 genera described so far, possess shieldlike, rigid, fully calcified frontal walls. The first two suborders protrude their tentacles or lophophore by muscles pulling down on the membranous frontal wall and thereby squeezing the liquid body contents out through the aperture; the third performs the same hydrostatic function by expanding a flexible internal sac (ascus or conpensatrix) located just below that rigid frontal wall. These frontal wall types represent both a morphological and chronological progression of increasing calcification with time (Table 1).

Cyclostomida

Colonies of Cyclostomida (also known as the Tubuliporata or Stenostomata) tend to be small and delicately built; members consist of long tubular zooecia, with diameters noticeably smaller than in other stenolaemates and, in most, fused together with the adjacent zooecia (Figure 6). The zooecial walls are thin throughout their length, with finely granular or finely laminated (layered) microstructure, and are interrupted by small pores (interzooecial or communication pores). In many species, similar-looking pores (pseudopores) through the side walls of the exterior are filled with

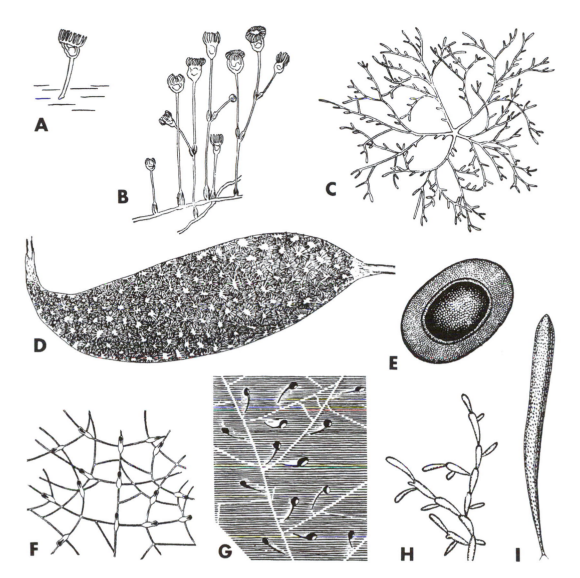

Figure 4. Inconspicuous bryozoans. Entoprocts: *A,* solitary loxosomatid (scale, ×9); *B,* colonial pedicellinid (scale, ×20). Phylactolae-mates: *C,* colonies (chitinous plumatellid encrusting threads; scale, ×2); *D,* gelatinous pectinatellid mass (scale, ×0.5); *E,* statoblast (scale, ×25). Ctenostomes: *F,* stoloniferans (encrusting thread network; scale, ×25); *G,* stoloniferans (boring below shell surface; scale, ×25); *H,* carnosans (encrusting threads; scale, ×10); *I,* carnosans (upright fleshy colony; scale, ×1). From: *A,* redrawn after Hyman (1951); *B,* modified from Hyman (1951); *C, D, E, H,* modified from Hyman (1959); *F, G, I,* modified from Bassler (1953), *Treatise on Invertebrate Paleontology,* courtesy of and © 1953 The Geological Society of America and The University of Kansas Press.

soft tissue cells during life. Zooecial cavities are most often empty, although in a few species they may be crossed by occasional partitions (diaphragms). In some colonies a few zooecia can grow into enlarged hollow chambers (gonozooecia or ovicells), which serve as sheltering brood chambers for developing larvae. About 250 genera are known thus far.

Cyclostomes are the only living survivors from the horde of stenolaemates that dominated Paleozoic bryozoan faunas and, therefore, have been viewed as scientifically interesting as analogs (representatives) for better understanding those many extinct forms. The earliest cyclostomes (in the Ordovician) were small encrusting threads consisting of a chain of pear-shaped zooecia (paleotubuliporids); later ones were thin, encrusting tubes (hederellids). Post-

Paleozoic cyclostomes developed both thin, simply constructed zooecial walls (termed "single" or "fixed" walls) and also thick, complexly built walls (labeled "double" or "free" walls). The form that the colony takes permits recognition of tubuliporids (rigid branches) and crisiids (flexibly jointed tufts) among single-walled cyclostomes, and among double-walled forms cerioporids (or heteroporids; masses and robust branches), lichenoporids (small disks), and hornerids (delicate branches and lattices). These last three resemble unrelated Paleozoic bryozoan groups (e.g., trepostomes, fistuliporoids, and fenestrates) so much that some scholars have raised the possibility that these forms might be relict ("leftovers" from very archaic forms) survivors, rather than independent groups that evolved in similar ways toward similar colony forms.

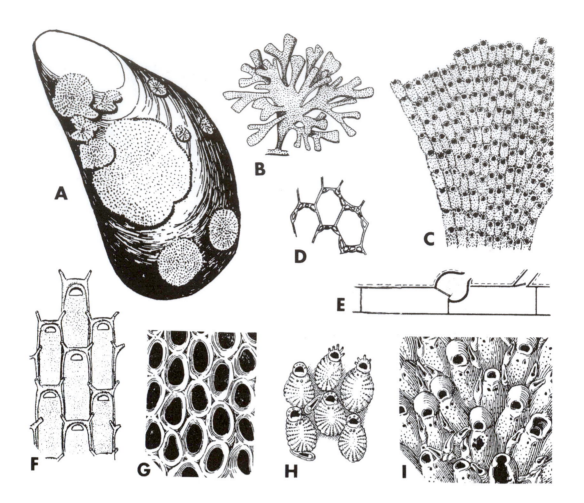

Figure 5. Cheilostome bryozoans. (Scale of colonies, ×1; sections as indicated.) *A*, encrusting sheets on pelecypod shell; *B*, erect flat branches; *C*, upper (frontal) surface (scale, ×8) of encrusting sheet. Sections: *D*, tangential (scale, ×20); *E*, longitudinal (scale, ×25). Frontal walls: *F*, anascans with soft membranous frontal wall (containing, in life, small aperture and operculum; scale, ×35); *G*, anascans with soft membranous frontal wall decayed away to leave large open opesium after death (scale, ×25); *H*, cribrimorph (scale, ×25); *I*, ascophoran with bulbous ovicells (scale, ×25). Modified from: *A, C, F*, Hyman (1959); all others, Bassler (1953), from *Treatise on Invertebrate Paleontology,* courtesy of and © 1953 The Geological Society of America and The University of Kansas Press.

Cystoporida

Zooecia in this order form short to long tubes, many thin-walled throughout their length (Figure 7). In many, zooecia are separated by different types of hollow structures, which enabled scholars to divide cystoporids into two suborders. Colonies vary from encrusting sheets and nodular masses to robust and delicate branches. Zooecial cavities in many are empty, in many others are crossed by a few transverse diaphragms. In most, zooecial apertures are protected partially by a hoodlike or raised-rim extension (lunarium) of one side of the zooecial wall.

The suborder Ceramoporina includes around 30 genera typified by long, thin, empty tubes (exilapores) between and parallel to the adjacent zooecia. Wall microstructure is laminated, and the zooecial walls in most are interrupted by communication pores. The Fistuliporina, roughly 70 genera, are characterized by small bubblelike chambers (cystopores) forming a foamlike tissue that separates adjacent zooecia, whose walls are continuously solid and tend toward a finely granular microstructure.

Trepostomida

Zooecia of trepostomids (Figure 7) are long slender tubes, bundled together in relatively large, cylindrical branches, upright fronds, hemispherical domes, nodular masses, and even encrusting sheets. In colony centers, the thin walls of adjacent zooecia are fused together. Toward colony exteriors, the walls thicken markedly, small tubes (exilapores or mesopores, which are thin tubes crossed by closely spaced diaphragms) may intervene between adjacent zooecia. Also, many transverse partitions—straight and planar (diaphragms), or curved back like bubbles (cystiphragms)—cross the zooecial cavity. Wall microstructure is laminated conspicuously. The walls in many species contain thin, strengthening calcite rods (acanthopores, acanthorods, or acanthostyles), which appear on the zooecial surface as low spines, and in tangential sections as small round blebs along the walls.

For many years, zooecial-wall microstructure was thought to permit scholars to subdivide trepostomes into two suborders (amalgamates and integrates) (Bassler 1953), but that classification has

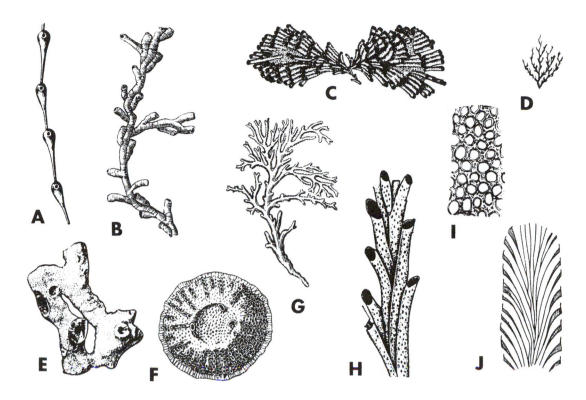

Figure 6. Cyclostome bryozoans. *A–G,* colonies. *A,* encrusting threads (paleotubuliporid; scale, ×25); *B,* encrusting threads (hederellid; scale, ×4); *C,* prostrate or low-lying branches (tubuliporid; scale, ×11); *D,* delicate tuft (crisiid; scale, ×1); *E,* thick branches (cerioporid; scale, ×1); *F,* encrusting disk (lichenoporid; scale, ×10); *G,* delicate branches (hornerid; scale, ×1). *H,* surface with pseudopores in zooecial walls (scale, ×25). *I, J,* sections (scale, ×10): *I,* tangential; *J,* longitudinal. Modified from: *C, H,* Hyman (1959); all others, Bassler (1953), from *Treatise on Invertebrate Paleontology,* courtesy of and © 1953 The Geological Society of America and The University of Kansas Press.

not held up under more extensive studies (Boardman et al. 1983). Recently, small tubular polymorphs and patterns of division of the colony into regions have suggested three suborders (Astrova 1978; Anstey and Wilson 1996): Esthonioporina (no mesopores nor exilapores, no axial, or immature, zone), Amplexoporina (a few exilapores, empty open tubes), and Halloporina (many mesopores). The latter two also exhibit differentiation into inner axial and outer peripheral regions (endozones and exozones, or immature and mature zones, respectively). Approximately 10, 60, and 40 genera, respectively, have been classified in these three suborders.

Cryptostomida

Members of Cryptostomida (Figure 8) consist of short zooecial tubes grouped into small, delicately built colonies, often with zooecial apertures arranged in regular geometric patterns on the colony surface. Zooecial walls are well-laminated, thin in the colony center (endozone), and abruptly becoming quite thick in its outer parts (exozone). Many species in each suborder have zooecial cavities that are empty except for a single cross-partition which goes only partway across the tube well below the colony surface (hemiseptum).

The Ptilodictyina, the 40 genera of the bifoliates, are recognizable by flat thin branches constructed in two-part fashion from a central flat sheet (mesotheca or median lamina); the short zooecia arise in opposite directions on each side of the sheet. Some colonies' zooecial cavities contain a few diaphragms, as well as hemisepta. In certain forms zooecial walls in tangential sections contain small dark spots (acanthostyles). Some specialists separate late Paleozoic bifoliates out as a separate suborder, the timanodictyids.

The Rhabdomesina (sometimes termed rhomboporoids) include approximately 40 genera characterized by slender cylindrical branches. Within each branch zooecia radiate outward in all directions from the center line, or axis. Zooecial cavities in many species include a few complete cross-partitions (diaphragms) instead of a hemiseptum or in addition to one. Zooecial walls in tangential sections contain many large and small spots (acanthostyles or acanthopores). Some rhabdomesids closely resemble the most slender branching trepostomes, although thin-sections will show the diagnostic differences in internal structures.

The Fenestrina (roughly 70 genera) are lattice, meshwork, or reticulate (fenestrate) fronds, that originally stood erect above the bottom but generally preserved as fallen, broken fragments. Each frond consists of a single planar layer of zooecia, all opening outward on the same side (the frontal or obverse side; the other, which has no apertures, is termed the reverse or back side). Outside the zooecial cavity, the frontal wall, and especially the reverse

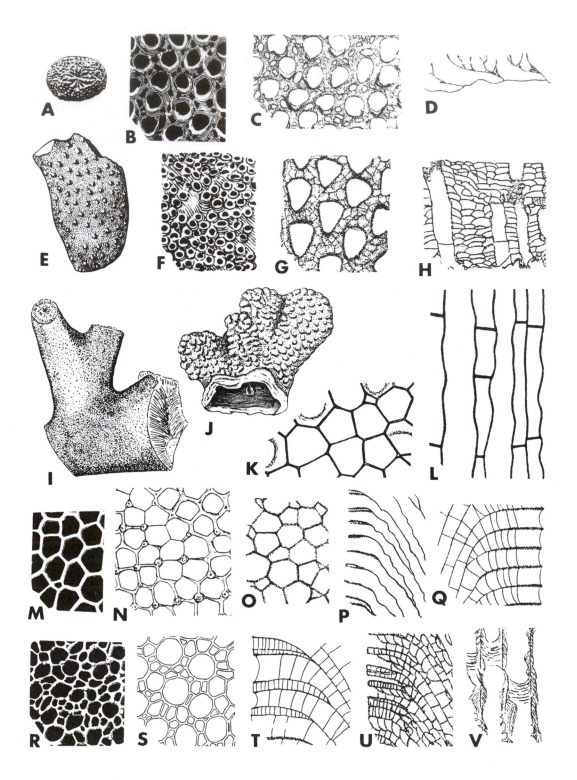

Figure 7. Cystoporate and trepostome bryozoans. (Scale of all thin sections, ×20.) Ceramoporoids: *A,* globular mass (scale, ×2); *B,* surface (scale, ×20). Sections with exilapores and lunaria: *C,* tangential; *D,* longitudinal. Fistuliporoids: *E,* massive colony (scale, ×1); *F,* surface (scale, ×7). Sections with cystopores: *G,* tangential; *H,* longitudinal. Trepostome colonies: *I,* robust branch (scale, ×2); *J,* upright frond (scale, ×1). Esthonioporoids: sections lacking small polymorphs: *K,* tangential, *L,* longitudinal. Amplexoporoids: *M,* surface (scale, ×20); *N,* tangential sections with acanthopores; *O,* exilapores; *P,* longitudinal sections with exilapores; *Q,* diaphragms. Halloporoids: *R,* surface (scale, ×20); *S,* tangential section with mesopores; *T,* longitudinal sections with mesopores and diaphragms; *U,* with mesopores, diaphragms, and cystiphragms. Trepostome wall microstructure: *V,* laminations in longitudinal section. Modified from: *I,* Hyman (1959); all others, Bassler (1953), from *Treatise on Invertebrate Paleontology,* courtesy of and © 1953 The Geological Society of America and The University of Kansas Press.

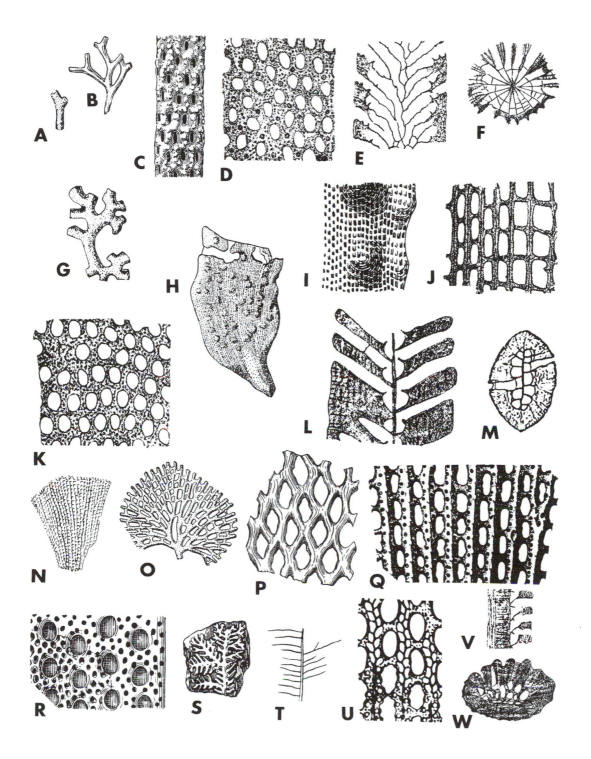

Figure 8. Cryptostome bryozoans (Scale of all colonies ×1; sections ×20, except where otherwise indicated). Rhabdomesids (rhomboporoids): *A, B,* delicate branching colonies; *C,* surface (scale, ×20). Sections: *D,* tangential, with large and small acanthopores; *E,* longitudinal; *F,* transverse. Ptilodictyoids (bifoliates): *G,* narrow flat branches; *H,* broad flat frond; *I,* surface (scale, ×5). Sections: *J, K,* tangential, *L,* longitudinal, *M,* transverse. Fenestrates: *N,* fenestellid, *O,* polyporid. Surfaces (scale, ×10): *P,* reverse (phylloporinid); *Q,* front (fenestellid); *R,* polyporid. Pinnate colonies, *S,* acanthoclad; *T,* pennireteporid. Sections: *U,* tangential (scale, ×10); *V,* longitudinal (scale, ×20); *W,* transverse (scale, ×13). Modified from: *M, U,* Astrova (1960); *Q,* Hyman (1959); all others, Bassler (1953), from *Treatise on Invertebrate Paleontology,* courtesy of and © 1953 The Geological Society of America and The University of Kansas Press.

wall, can become extremely thick and would strengthen the upright frond greatly. Colony forms vary enough to be the basis for several named subgroups. Most conspicuous in sedimentary rocks are fenestrate (lattice or meshwork) colonies, with anastamosing branches (ones that form networks) (phylloporinids), or with branches linked by perpendicular cross-bars (dissepiments). Linked branches either are narrow (two rows of zooecia: fenestellids) or wide (three to five rows of zooecia: polyporids). Pinnate colonies at first glance seem to be just a single broken fenestrate branch, but actually consist of, again, a wide (acanthoclads) or a narrow (penniretegorids) central branch.

Many recent papers involving cryptostomes split the fenestrates out as a separate order, and some also separate out the rhabdomesids. Thus, exactly what the cryptostomes include has come to vary tremendously, enough so that this taxonomic name may have to be abandoned because it has become so ambiguous.

Evolution and Biogeography

Morphologic characters and stratigraphic distributions (position in rock strata) underpin any understanding of bryozoan evolution. However, scholars disagree to such an extent that the following discussion should be taken as tentative.

Bryozoan origins appear to be related most closely to those of the phoronid worms (Larwood and Taylor 1979). These animals also are characterized by a lophophore, as are brachiopods.

In the course of bryozoan evolution, the evolutionary role of entoprocts has provoked continuing disagreement. Early in the Paleozoic, perhaps already in the Mid-Cambrian, solitary entoprocts were in place. One can speculate that eventually such forms simply remained connected after budding to produce colonial entoprocts. This adaptation would have been associated with a shift in embryonic development to become stoloniferous ctenostomes. These forms in turn shortened and lost the stolons to generate carnose ctenostomes, and finally hardened and calcified their zooecial walls to produce the simplest cyclostomes by sometime during the Early Ordovician.

After that, the many Paleozoic suborders of stenolaemates all appeared in the few million years before the end of that era. Each group could be viewed as a simple cyclostome strengthened by different structural strategy, utilizing the various internal cross-partitions, wall structures, small polymorphs, and colony forms, singly or in combination. Thus, these all could be independent derivations unrelated to one another except by their simple-cyclostome common ancestor. Or, alternatively, future studies may be able to detect steps by which several of these suborders might have evolved one into another. Once established, all of the cystoporate, trepostome, and cryptostome suborders continued through much or all of the Paleozoic. Trepostomes dominated early Paleozoic faunas, then gave way to cryptostomes as the fenestrates especially came to great abundance during Mississippian into Permian times.

All these suborders were hit hard by the great extinction at the end of the Paleozoic, but only two became completely extinct then, while four survived (Table 1). After the end-Permian mass extinction severely decimated the Paleozoic stenolae-

mates, a few relicts straggled on through till the end of the Triassic before finally succumbing. Meanwhile, a few cyclostomes and carnose ctenostomes continued on as minor components of early Mesozoic marine faunas. In the Jurassic and Cretaceous, cyclostomes diversified and flourished. At the same time, carnosans—by calcifying their zooecial walls again in much the same way as previously done back in the Ordovician—apparently gave rise to anascan cheilostomes by late in the Jurassic. Soon thereafter, during the Cretaceous, first the cribrimorphs and then the ascophorans appeared and began to diversify. As the cheilostomes expanded (continuing until today), the cyclostomes declined to their present-day diminished ecological importance.

Sometime during the early Mesozoic (possibly much earlier), phylactolaemates evolved, possibly from ctenostome ancestors, which would have been around since the early Ordovician. Some scholars have interpreted phylactolaemate characters as indicating very ancient origin and long separate evolution; others suggest much more recent derivation from carnose ctenostomes that moved into fresh waters.

Finally, both the early Ordovician stenolaemate radiation (diversification and geographical spread) and the Cretaceous cheilostome radiation have an intriguing biogeographic aspect. Although data is still in the early stage, the former may have begun in China, then spread across Russia and the Baltic, before appearing abundantly in North America early in the Middle Ordovician. The latter was underway with numerous representatives in Europe, and few in North America until the Paleocene, when bryozoans became abundant on both sides of the Atlantic.

Paleoecology and Sedimentology

Most bryozoans are normal-marine (they can tolerate wide ranges of salinity), some range into brackish coastal waters, and a few occur inland in fresh water. Bryozoans range through all climatic or temperature regimes, from tropical to polar, although individual species have much more restricted tolerances. Bryozoans also range from shorelines out into deep ocean basins (to more than 5000 meters at least), although they are most numerous and speciose (show the greatest variety of species) on continental shelves and epeiric seas (0 to 200 meter depths).

A principal environmental requirement for bryozoans is hard or firm substrates (the surfaces upon which they live)—shells, algal fronds, rocks, or hard bottoms—on which to encrust. Thus, competition for substrate space is a sizable concern in bryozoans' lives. Such substrates contribute to the kinds of rock deposits in which fossil bryozoans are found most frequently: biofragmental limestones, shaly limestones, calcareous shales, and shelly sands and clays.

Bryozoans make important contributions to the sediments of their environments to both bioclastic skeletal sediments and to reefs and bioherms (fossilized reefs consisting of shell accumulations). In a few of the latter, the bryozoans function as the principal frame-builders erecting the mound (Cuffey 1985); in many others, they encrust within the reef structure as accessories to the dominant corals, stromatoporoids, and algae.

Sites and Students

In North America, bryozoan fragments can be found wherever rocks of suitable ages are exposed. Particularly rich regions include Cincinnati (Upper Ordovician trepostomes), the midcontinent (Late Paleozoic fenestrates and rhabdomesids), and the Atlantic and Gulf coastal plains (Cenozoic cheilostomes). The illustrations in H.W. Shimer and R.R. Shrock (1944) and I. Thompson (1982) will help much in identifying specimens collected.

The earliest known recognition of any bryozoan dates from A.D. 1558, but these animals were confused with marine plants until the early 1800s. A few scientists studied them over the following hundred-plus years. Then, in the 1960s, a number of students focused their attention on these fossils, and since then bryozoan investigations have undergone a renaissance. A review of the contents of the proceedings volumes produced by the International Bryozoology Association (Annoscia 1968; Gordon, Smith, and Grant-Mackie 1996; several volumes between) over the last 30 years indicates both active researchers and current interests concerning this phylum.

ROGER J. CUFFEY AND JOHN E. UTGAARD

See also Aquatic Invertebrates, Adaptive Strategies of

Works Cited

Annoscia, E. (ed.). 1968. Proceedings of the First International Conference on Bryozoa. *Atti della Società Italiana di Scienze Naturali e del Museo Civico di Storia Naturale di Milano* 108:1–377.

Anstey, R.L., and J.F. Pachut. 1995. Phylogeny, diversity history, and speciation in Paleozoic bryozoans. *In* D.H. Erwin and R.L. Anstey (eds.), *New Approaches to Speciation in the Fossil Record*. New York: Columbia University Press.

Anstey, R.L., and M.A. Wilson. 1996. Phylum Bryozoa. *Ohio Geological Survey Bulletin* 70:196–209.

Astrova, G.G. (ed.). 1960. Bryozoa. Indian National Scientific Documentation Centre (trans.). *In* Y.A. Orlov, et al. (eds.), *Fundamentals of Paleontology*. Moscow: Akademiya Nauk S.S.S.R.

———. 1978. *History of Development, Systematics and Phylogeny of Bryozoans: Order Trepostomata*, D.A. Brown (trans.). Moscow: Akademiya Nauk S.S.S.R.

Bassler, R.S. 1953. Bryozoa. *In* R.C. Moore (ed.), *Treatise on Invertebrate Paleontology*. Part G, *Bryozoa*. Boulder, Colorado: Geological Society of America; Lawrence: University of Kansas Press.

Boardman, R.S., et al. 1983. Bryozoa, revised. *In* R.A. Robison (ed.), *Treatise on Invertebrate Paleontology*. Part G, *Bryozoa*. Boulder, Colorado: Geological Society of America; Lawrence: University of Kansas Press.

Cuffey, R.J. 1970. Bryozoan-environment interrelationships: An overview of Bryozoan paleoecology and ecology. *Pennsylvania State University Earth and Mineral Sciences Bulletin* 39 (6):41–48.

———. 1973. An improved classification, based upon numerical-taxonomic analyses, for the higher taxa of entoproct and ectoproct bryozoans. *In* G.P. Larwood (ed.), *Living and Fossil Bryozoa*. London: Academic Press.

———. 1985. Expanded reef-rock textural classification and the geologic history of bryozoan reefs. *Geology* 13:307–10.

Cuffey R.J., and D.B. Blake. 1991. Cladistic analysis of the phylum Bryozoa. *In* F.P. Bigey (ed.), *Bryozoaires Actuels et Fossiles: Bryozoa Living and Fossil*. Nantes: Société des Sciences Naturelles de l'Ouest de la France.

Dutro, J.T., and R.S. Boardman (eds.). 1981. Lophophorates: Notes from a short course. *University of Tennessee Studies in Geology* 5:1–251.

Gordon, D.P., A.M. Smith, and J.A. Grant-Mackie (eds.). 1996. *Bryozoans in Space and Time*. Wellington, New Zealand: National Institute of Water and Atmospheric Research.

Hyman, L.H. 1951. *The Invertebrates*. Vol. 3, *The Pseudocoelomate Bilateria: Phylum Entoprocta*. New York: McGraw Hill.

———. 1959. *The Invertebrates*. Vol. 5, *The Lophophorate Coelomates: Phylum Ectoprocta*. New York: McGraw Hill.

Larwood, G.P., and P.D. Taylor. 1979. Early structural and ecological diversification in the Bryozoa. *In* M.R. House (ed.), *The Origin of Major Invertebrate Groups*. Systematics Association Special Volume 12. London and New York: Academic Press.

McKinney, F.K., and J.B.C. Jackson. 1989. *Bryozoan Evolution*. Boston: Unwin Hyman.

Nielsen, C. 1982. Entoprocta. *In* S.P. Parker (ed.), *Synopsis and Classification of Living Organisms*. Vol. 2. New York: McGraw Hill.

Ryland, J.S. 1970. *Bryozoans*. London: Hutchinson University Library.

———. 1982. Bryozoa. *In* S.P. Parker (ed.), *Synopsis and Classification of Living Organisms*. Vol. 2. New York: McGraw Hill.

Shimer, H.W., and R.R. Shrock. 1944. *Index Fossils of North America*. Cambridge, Massachusetts: MIT Press; London: Chapman and Hall.

Smith, A.M. 1995. Palaeoenvironmental interpretation using bryozoans: A review. *In* D.W.J. Bosence and P.A. Allison (eds.), *Marine Palaeoenvironmental Analysis from Fossils*. London: Geological Society.

Taylor, P.D. 1993. Bryozoa. *In* M.J. Benton (ed.), *The Fossil Record 2*. London and New York: Chapman and Hall.

Thompson, I. 1982. *The Audubon Society Field Guide to North American Fossils*. New York: Knopf.

Woollacott, R.M., and R.L. Zimmer (eds.). 1977. *Biology of Bryozoans*. New York: Academic Press.

Further Reading

Anstey, R.L., and J.F. Pachut. 1995. Phylogeny, diversity history, and speciation in Paleozoic bryozoans. *In* D.H. Erwin and R.L. Anstey (eds.), *New Approaches to Speciation in the Fossil Record*. New York: Columbia University Press.

Astrova, G.G. (ed.). 1960. Bryozoa. Indian National Scientific Documentation Centre (trans.). *In* Y.A. Orlov, et al. (eds.), *Fundementals of Paleontology*. Moscow: Akademiya Nauk S.S.S.R.

———. 1978. *History of Development, Systematics and Phylogeny of Bryozoans: Order Trepostomata*, D.A. Brown (trans.). Trudy: Akademiya Nauk S.S.S.R.

Boardman, R.S., et al. 1983. Bryozoa, revised. *In* R.A. Robison (ed.), *Treatise on Invertebrate Paleontology*. Part G, *Bryozoa*. Vol. 1. Boulder, Colorado: Geological Society of America; Lawrence: University of Kansas Press.

Cuffey, R.J. 1973. An improved classification, based upon numerical-taxonomic analyses, for the higher taxa of entoproct and ectoproct bryozoans. *In* G.P. Larwood (ed.), *Living and Fossil Bryozoa*. London: Academic Press.

Cuffey, R.J., and D.B. Blake. 1991. Cladistic analysis of the phylum Bryozoa. *In* Bigey F.P. (ed.), *Bryozoaires Actuels et Fossiles: Bryozoa*

Living and Fossil. Nantes: Société des Sciences Naturelles de l'Ouest de la France.

Gordon, D.P., A.M. Smith, and J.A. Grant-Mackie (eds.). 1996. *Bryozoans in Space and Time.* Wellington, New Zealand: National Institute of Water and Atmospheric Research.

Hyman, L.H. 1951. *The Invertebrates.* Vol. 3, *The Pseudocoelomate Bilateria: Phylum Entoprocta.* New York: McGraw Hill.

———. 1959. *The Invertebrates.* Vol. 5, *The Lophophorate Coelomates: Phylum Ectoprocta.* New York: McGraw Hill.

Larwood, G.P., and P.D. Taylor. 1979. Early structural and ecological diversification in the Bryozoa. *In* M.R. House (ed.), *The Origin of Major Invertebrate Groups.* Systematics Association Special Volume 12. London and New York: Academic Press.

McKinney, F.K., and J.B.C. Jackson. 1989. *Bryozoan Evolution.* Boston: Unwin Hyman; 2nd ed., Chicago: University of Chicago Press, 1991.

Nielsen, C. 1982. Entoprocta. *In* S.P Parker (ed.), *Synopsis and Classification of Living Organisms.* Vol. 2. New York: McGraw Hill.

Ryland, J.S. 1970. *Bryozoans.* London: Hutchinson University Library.

———. 1982. Bryozoa. *In* S.P. Parker (ed.), *Synopsis and Classification of Living Organisms.* Vol. 2. New York: McGraw Hill.

Shimer, H.W., and R.R. Shrock. 1944. *Index Fossils of North America.* Cambridge, Massachusetts: MIT Press; London: Chapman and Hall.

Smith, A.M. 1995. Palaeoenvironmental interpretation using bryozoans: A review. *In* D.W.J. Bosence and P.A. Allison (eds.), *Marine Palaeoenvironmental Analysis from Fossils.* London: Geological Society.

Taylor, P.D. 1993. Bryozoa. *In* M.J. Benton (ed.), *The Fossil Record 2.* New York and London: Chapman and Hall.

Thompson, I. 1982. *The Audubon Society Field Guide to North American Fossils.* New York: Knopf.

Woollacott, R.M., and R.L. Zimmer (eds.). 1977. *Biology of Bryozoans.* New York: Academic Press.

BUCKLAND, WILLIAM

English, 1784–1856

William Buckland was the son of a Devonshire clergyman. He became interested in natural history, including fossils, as a child. During his studies at Corpus Christi College, Oxford, his interest continued as he collected fossils in the company of his friend, William John Broderip. After taking holy orders in 1809, he became reader in mineralogy at Oxford University in 1813. His lectures, which embraced geology, paleontology, and mineralogy, attracted large audiences. In 1819 he became the first Reader in geology at Oxford University. In the course of many field excursions across Britain and continental Europe during the 1820s, Buckland brought together a large collection of geological and paleontological specimens, which he eventually presented to the university. In 1845 he became dean of Westminster.

Buckland's scientific activity is largely linked to the so-called Diluvial interpretation of Pleistocene events. The Diluvial interpretation stated that the Biblical Deluge (Noah's Flood) had acted as a type of giant tidal wave, sweeping exotic fossils into Europe. The theory was eventually replaced by the Ice Age theory partially due to Buckland's work. Buckland's interest in such topics was kindled by the discovery of abundant fossil teeth and bones in a cave at Kirkdale, Yorkshire, in 1821. He was urged by Georges Cuvier to collect as many specimens as possible from the cave. The fossil remains from Kirkdale Cave belonged to hyenas, elephants, rhinoceroses, hippopotami, horses, oxen, deer, bears, foxes, rodents, and birds. Some of these animals belonged to extinct species; others had living representatives only in tropical countries. Buckland's interpretation of this assemblage was that Kirkdale Cave had once been a hyena den. Tooth marks on broken bones and coprolites (fossilized excrement) found in the cave supported this interpretation, which excited considerable interest in scientific circles. An important aspect of Buckland's interpretation was that the bones had accumulated over a long time span through the activities of hyenas, instead of rapid formation by a cataclysmal event such as a deluge, as had been widely accepted by eighteenth century geologists. Despite its

title, *Reliquiae Diluvianae* (1823), Buckland's work on cave faunas undermined the classical diluvialist theory. For although Buckland accepted that the biblical Deluge had taken place, he did not think it was responsible for the accumulations of fossil bones found in caves all over Europe. Rather, he believed that the remains of exotic animals were antediluvian—they had once lived in Europe, like the hyenas from Kirkland Cave, and that bones had accumulated in caves as the result of slow processes, such as the actions of predators and scavengers. He did accept the action of the Deluge however, to explain the origin of superficial deposits that covered vast areas of Europe. In the 1830s, Swiss naturalists such as Louis Agassiz proposed the Ice Age theory, accrediting the phenomena usually ascribed to the Deluge to widespread glaciation. Buckland quickly converted to this new interpretation and soon discovered signs of glacial action in many parts of Britain.

Buckland also was interested in fossils much older than his Pleistocene hyenas. A rich source of such fossils was the deposit that made up the underground quarries at Stonesfield, near Oxford, where Jurassic rocks were exploited for slate roofing tiles. Among the specimens Buckland obtained from the quarrymen were bones, including a jaw of a large reptile, which he described in 1824 as *Megalosaurus.* (The specific name, *M. bucklandi,* later was proposed in his honor.) *Megalosaurus* turned out to be a theropod dinosaur (a flesh-eating, bipedal dinosaur); therefore Buckland is generally hailed as being the first to have given a scientific name to a dinosaur. Other important fossils that Buckland reported from Stonesfield were tiny mammal jaws, originally found by his friend Broderip. With Cuvier's help, Buckland identified these jaws as belonging to a marsupial. The idea that mammals had been present during the so-called Age of Reptiles was difficult for many paleontologists to accept. Instead, they held a "progressionist" view of Earth history. This view stressed the presence of one group of animals at a time, in an order that moved from less complex animals to more complex ones, ending with the "rule" of humans. Thus, the Stonesfield mammals caused a long-enduring controversy.

Buckland's paleontological research covered a great diversity of topics, including fossil footprints. In 1827, when footprints were found in Triassic sandstone near Dumfries, Scotland, Buckland carried out an experiment in which he induced his pet tortoise to walk on wet flour. To Buckland's delight, the footprints left by the tortoise were similar to the fossil ones.

Buckland was considered as one of the foremost British paleontologists of his time, and fossils were sent to him from many places. In 1829, Buckland described the first British pterosaur, later to be called *Dimorphodon* by R. Owen, found in the Lias deposit of Lyme Regis by Mary Anning. He published one of the first works about the vertebrate paleontology of Asia in 1828, describing fossil reptiles and mammals found along the Irrawaddy River by the British mission under John Crawfurd, sent to the Burmese capital at Ava in 1826–27. He also published on fossil mammals from the Siwaliks Hills deposit in India.

Buckland also was a popularizer of geology and paleontology, not only through his well-received lectures, but also through publications aimed at a fairly large readership. His *Geology and Mineralogy Considered with Reference to Natural Theology* (1836), published as one of the treatises commissioned by the Earl of Bridgewater to demonstrate the "Power, Wisdom, and Goodness of God as manifested in the Creation," was a great success and went through several editions.

Buckland was one of the leading figures in British geology and paleontology in the first decades of the nineteenth century. At this time, these sciences were both taking on a modern aspect and attracting the attention of a large public, mainly because they revealed a hitherto unsuspected history of life on Earth. Buckland clearly had a considerable influence on both developments.

ERIC BUFFETAUT

Biography

Born in Axminster, Dorset, 12 March 1784. Received B.A., Corpus Christi College, Oxford University, 1804; took holy orders, Anglican Church, 1809. Became Reader in mineralogy, Oxford University, 1813; fellow (1813) and later president (1824–25, 1840–41), Geological Society of London; fellow (1818) and later council member (1827–49), Royal Society, reader in geology, Oxford University, 1819; awarded Copley Medal of the Royal Society, 1822; appointed canon, Christ Church College, Oxford University, 1825; president and host, British Association for the

Advancement of Science, 1832; member, French Académie des Sciences, 1839; dean, Westminster, 1845–56; awarded Wollaston Medal of the Geological Society of London, 1848. Explored Kirkdale Cave, Yorkshire, 1821; described *Megalosaurus,* 1824; described *Pterodactylus (*today called *Dimorphodon) macronyx,* 1829. Died in Islip, 14 August 1856.

Major Publications

1823. *Reliquiae Diluvianae; or, Observations on the Organic Remains Contained in Caves, Fissures, and Diluvial Gravel, and on other Geological Phenomena, Attesting the Action of an Universal Deluge.* London: Murray.

1824. Notice on the *Megalosaurus,* or great fossil lizard of Stonesfield. *Transactions of the Geological Society of London* 2(1):390–96.

1828a. Geological account of a series of animal and vegetable remains and of rocks, collected by J. Crawfurd on a voyage up the Irawaddy to Ava, in 1826 and 1827. *Transactions of the Geological Society of London* 2(2):377–92.

1828b. Note sur des traces de tortues observées dans le grès rouge. *Annales des Sciences Naturelles* 13:85–86.

1829. On the discovery of a new species of pterodactyle in the Lias at Lyme Regis. *Transactions of the Geological Society of London* 2(3):217–22.

1836. *Geology and Mineralogy Considered with Reference to Natural Theology.* 2 vols. London: Pickering; Philadelphia: Carey, Lea and Blanchard, 1837; 4th ed., Francis T. Buckland (ed.), London: Bell and Daldy, 1869.

Further Reading

Buckland, F.T. 1858. Memoir of the Very Rev. William Buckland, D.D., F.R.S., Dean of Westminster. *In Geology and Mineralogy Considered with Reference to Natural Theology.* London and New York: Routledge.

Buffetaut, E. 1987. *A Short History of Vertebrate Paleontology.* London and Wolfboro, New Hampshire: Croom Helm.

Cannon, W.F. 1970. Buckland, William. *In* C.C. Gillispie (ed.), *Dictionary of Scientific Biography.* Vol. 2, New York: Scribner's.

Colbert, E.H. 1968. *Men and Dinosaurs.* New York: Dutton; London: Evans; 2nd ed., *The Great Dinosaur Hunters and Their Discoveries,* New York: Dover, 1984.

Rupke, N.A. 1983. *The Great Chain of History: William Buckland and the English School of Geology, 1814–1849.* Oxford: Clarendon; New York: Oxford University Press.

Sarjeant, W.A.S. 1974. A history and bibliography of the study of fossil vertebrate footprints in the British Isles. *Palaeogeography, Palaeoclimatology, Palaeoecology* 16(4):265–378.

BUFFON, GEORGES-LOUIS LECLERC, COMTE DE

French, 1707–88

The naturalist, Georges-Louis Leclerc, Comte de Buffon, was the oldest of five children born to a bourgeois family from Dijon, in the heart of Burgundy. Educated by the Jesuits, Buffon demonstrated an early aptitude for mathematics and, indeed, it was his study of probability theory that was chiefly responsible for his admission to the Royal Academy (Académie Royale des Sciences) in 1734. As a young man, Buffon moved to Paris, where he divided his time between the study of mathematics (he translated Newton's works from English into French), research in botany and forestry, and managing his own financial affairs. With respect to the last, he displayed strong personal aptitudes. At the time of his death, Buffon was a very wealthy man.

Buffon was a typical polymorph of the eighteenth century whose interests encompassed many fields. By the end of the 1730s, he turned his attention to chemistry and biology, as well as to microscopic research on animal reproduction. This work culminated in his appointment as *intendant* of the Jardin du Roi in July 1739. Thereafter, Buffon established a pattern of working in Paris through the winter and living in Montbard during the summer to administer his estates, as well as to continue his own writings.

At the time of his death, Buffon was famous throughout Europe and America, enjoying a membership in every significant scientific society. Louis XV granted him the title Comte de Buffon. The only cloud on Buffon's otherwise bright horizon was his only child; a spendthrift son who was, in fact, to end his life on the guillotine during the French Reign of Terror.

Buffon's works appear in two main series, *Mémoires,* presented to The Académie des Sciences, and the *Histoire naturelle,* an ongoing collection that numbered some 36 volumes at the time of his death. Buffon was a philosopher as well as a scientist. With good reason, he regarded himself as a disciple of John Locke, upholding the British philosopher's emphasis on empirical experience. Buffon, therefore, stood in opposition to all forms of idealism and, hence, countered the conclusions of such prominent thinkers as Plato and Leibniz. Denying also the significance of teleology (a belief in purely mechanical determinism in natural processes), Buffon refused to accept the notion of God's miraculous intervention in nature. He maintained that all events must be explained through the fundamental laws of nature. Unfortunately, because Buffon's theories countered the position of the all-powerful Catholic Church, his views are not always presented as clearly as they could have been. This problem is compounded by Buffon's periodic tendency to change his thinking during his long career.

Thinking that the study of the Earth must proceed the study of animals and plants, in 1749 Buffon produced the *Histoire et théorie de la terre* (published in 1792). This work, composed in the so-called Neptunian style, argues that the essential nature of the Earth—in particular, rock sedimentation—is a function of the sea's former submersion of the present continents. Buffon regarded marine fossils that are found on dry land as clear proof of the submersion. He denied the existence of past cataclysmic events and refused to accept the Biblical flood as a potentially significant geological phenomenon. Hence, in a sense, Buffon was a forerunner of Lyellian "uniformitarianism" (a belief espoused by the British geologist, Charles Lyell, in the gradual, limitless effects of natural forces in the formation of the Earth, as opposed to the Bible's account of creation). Buffon speculated that the Earth was created as a result of natural forces. He hypothesized that a comet struck the sun, which led to a subsequent spilling of liquids and gases into space. These in turn diffused and condensed into the spheres that constitute the planets of our solar system. Buffon should be praised for attempting a cosmology based on Newtonian mechanics; however, even during his lifetime (by 1770), owing to calculations by the Swiss mathematician Leonhard Euler, it became clear that there were difficulties with the hypothesis. Nevertheless, Buffon stubbornly refused to abandon his beliefs. In fact, it is possible to find the ideas of the mid–eighteenth century reappearing even in his final writings.

Although these later writings contain the same general cosmic scheme, Buffon added considerable detail to them about the supposed formation of the Earth. Apparently, the Earth (torn from the sun) began its existence in a very heated state. As it cooled, the water vapors surrounding it began to condense. The condensation eventually gave rise to marine life, while at the same time, sedimentary rocks began to be formed beneath the waves. Buffon hypothesized that the water burst through Earth's thin shell and rushed down into huge subterranean caverns, causing the sea level to decline significantly. This gave rise to bare land, surrounded by water, finally making it possible for animal life to appear. Human beings apparently arrived at the very end of this long process. Incidentally, at one point Buffon speculated that the process may have taken as long as 3 million years. However, by the time he published, Buffon had reduced the Earth's hypothetical time span to a mere 75,000 years, perhaps owing to theological pressure. It is worth noting that this hypothesis was at least an order of magnitude larger than the traditional, biblically based estimate of 6,000 years old. Buffon explicitly stated that "the more we extend time, the closer we shall be to the truth."

Buffon presented his thinking about the organic world against his cosmological and geological background. This first appears in a short treatise titled *Histoire des animaux,* in the second volume of the *Histoire naturelle,* although many of these ideas are elaborated upon in later volumes, particularly in *Discourse sur la nature des animaux* (*Histoire naturelle* IV, 1753) and in other subsequent volumes. The key question was that of reproduction, which Buffon perceived as being the essence of living matter. He rejected the commonly accepted position on reproduction, namely that embryos are preformed from the first instances of life. For Buffon, this would have required ultimately some form of miracle, an act that he hotly contested in his expressed opposition to special interventions by the Deity. Hence, in search of an adequate answer about reproduction, Buffon turned toward some form of epigenetic theory, claiming that organisms are created out of living matter by a kind of imprinting from their parents. Thus, on the one hand, Buffon believed that organisms have a kind of interior pattern or mold *(moule interieure),* while, on the other hand, he believed that living matter cannot be formed out of inorganic matter. He therefore postulated the existence of some kinds of "organic molecules," which coexisted from the beginning with inorganic molecules. In a sense, Buffon's thinking was a strange combination of a kind of Newtonian mechanism and something akin to vitalism (believing that there is a kind of vital force that distinguishes the living, the quick, from the dead).

As a follower of Locke, Buffon was inclined toward nominalism in classification. He rejected any kind of essentialist view of taxonomic units and positioned himself strongly against other systematists of his day, particularly Carolus Linnaeus, the Swedish taxonomist. Buffon accepted the notion of species, but only in the sense that organisms are descended from other organisms, and thus constitute a species through their genealogical relationships. However, Buffon regarded all taxa (groups; singular, taxon) at higher category levels, like families, as no more than fictions.

The obvious question then becomes: Where did Buffon stand on ideas of transformation or evolution? The answer is mixed. On the one hand, as a mechanist, Buffon believed that life originated from a kind of spontaneous generation out of organic molecules, brought about by the actions of heat, light, and other natural processes. He also believed that once the original forms appeared, in some sense they destroyed the conditions for any further generation of life. Therefore, one should not expect to find spontaneous generation occurring today. As soon as life was formed, he envisioned a kind of struggle for existence and natural selection, anticipating Charles Darwin. The nonviable life-forms disappeared quickly, after which there was basic stability. Indeed, given Buffon's views about the internal mold, it follows almost philosophically, rather than scientifically, that he had to turn against the theory of evolution. At the most basic level, such a process of transformation is simply incompatible with Buffonian thoughts on reproduction.

Nevertheless, Buffon acknowledged that there was considerable scope within the overall scheme for some sort of change, primarily of a degeneration that he saw over time. He believed that the growing number of fossils being discovered in Europe and North America at the time point to extinct organisms unlike any living today. Since they often seem to be variations of those in existence today—one sees many examples of fossil forms with much smaller living representatives—it appears that in some way or ways, the environment affects the nature of organisms. In many respects, Buffon was a forerunner to Jean-Baptiste-Pierre Lamarck in his belief that the environment affects characteristics that can be changed during a lifetime; then those changes could be transmitted to future generations. However, Buffon noted that this can happen only within fixed limits. Essentially, Buffon regarded these changes as more in the nature of degeneration, as opposed to any positive, progressivist way moving up to organisms of different or higher form. In this respect, he was in no sense a forerunner to the end-of-the-century evolutionists such as the Englishman Erasmus Darwin (grandfather of Charles Darwin) and the Frenchman Lamarck.

As a man of the Enlightenment, Buffon naturally was interested in our own species. He wrote on the topic explicitly in his *Histoire naturelle de l'homme*, published in 1749 (*Histoire naturelle*, volume 2). In many respects, Buffon saw humans as being part of the animal world. In other crucial respects, however, he viewed humans as absolutely superior to all other organisms. As a Lockian, Buffon naturally placed particular emphasis on language. He argued that reason is possible only through language, and that from language stems the social life that is so distinctive of humans. In terms of human origins, Buffon clearly regarded humans as no different than the rest of nature—humankind was created naturally. There are speculations in Buffon's writings that the earliest humans must have been black in order to withstand the Earth's high temperatures of its earlier state. Apparently, human intelligence allowed for the ability to adapt to different climates and to advance in a way barred to other organisms.

Buffon's ideas fell into disfavor by the beginning of the nineteenth century, particularly under the influence of the age's powerful French scientists, notably Georges Cuvier. Buffon's writings were considered the epitome of the discursive style of the nonprofessional scientist. There was undoubtedly some truth in this. Buffon's frequent writings bear little resemblance to the systematic study of later anatomists and fellow workers. Nevertheless, Buffon's works are remarkable for the extent to which they provide an overall picture of the world of nature. Moreover, his great influence on subsequent thinkers, particularly on men such as the evolutionist Lamarck—who received much encouragement and support when young by Buffon—cannot be overestimated. Buffon's importance must be noted, even in areas such as paleontology, if only for his being the thinker who demonstrated that the world of fossils must be integrated into our thinking about all organisms and not simply put to the side. Buffon truly was one of the past's great naturalists.

MICHAEL RUSE

Biography

Born in Montbard, 7 September 1707. Received primary education at the Collège de Godrans de Jésuits, Dijon, 1717–23; studied law, Dijon, 1723–26; studied mathematics, botany, and chemistry, Collège de l'Oratoire, Angers, 1728–30. Admitted as member (1734) and elected permanent treasurer (1744), Académie Royale des Sciences; appointed *interdant,* Jardin du Roi, 1739; elected member, Royal Society of London, 1739; admitted to Académie Française, 1753; made count, 1772. Best known for multivolume *Histoire naturelle* (1749–1804), which set forth a natural, nontheological explanation for the development of life on Earth. Died in Paris, 16 April 1788.

Major Publications

1749–1804. *Histoire naturelle, générale et particulière, avec la description du cabinet du roi.* 44 vols. [vols. 37–44 edited by the Count de Lacèdépe]. Paris: Imprimerie Royale.
[1753.] *Discours sur le style.* Paris: Belin, 1866.
1884–85. J.L. Lanessan (ed.). *Oeuvres complètes de Buffon.* 14 vols. Paris: Pilon.

Further Reading

Gayon, J. (ed.). 1992. *Buffon 88.* Paris: Vrin.
Lyon, J., and P. Sloan. 1981. *From Natural History to the History of Nature: Readings from Buffon and His Critics.* Notre Dame, Indiana: University of Notre Dame Press.
Roger, J. 1971. *La Science de la vie dans la Pensée Française du XVIIIe Siècle.* Paris: Arman Colin.
———.1989. *Buffon: Un philosophe au jardin du roi.* Paris: Fayard.
Ruse, M. 1966. *Monad to Man: The Concept of Progress in Evolutionary Biology.* Cambridge, Massachusetts: Harvard University Press.

BURROWING ADAPTATIONS IN VERTEBRATES

Many kinds of vertebrates are proficient diggers. There are several reasons why animals dig. One very important reason for digging is to obtain or store food; another is to seek shelter. Burrows provide a safe place to nest or lay eggs, to escape from predators, or to aestivate (become dormant in summer) or hibernate (become dormant in winter). Animals that are particularly adapted for digging are usually referred to as "fossorial," whereas species that live and forage entirely or primarily underground are called "subterranean." Some zoologists restrict the term "fossorial" to subterranean animals, and apply the designation "semifossorial" to those that either grub for food or seek shelter in burrows but are less committed to the subterranean realm for foraging and other activities. The first, more inclusive definition will be used here.

Many species have evolved anatomical specializations— sometimes quite elaborate ones—associated with burrowing behavior. However, except for the more committed fossorial forms, it is not always easy to distinguish anatomically between diggers and nondiggers. For example, dogs are adept diggers, but they have no obvious fossorial modifications. To infer with confidence that certain extinct vertebrates are fossorial, therefore, requires evidence of anatomical specialization for digging. (Rarely, association with burrows of their own construction can be used.) Here we will focus on some of the more specialized extant (present-day) and extinct diggers.

Although vertebrates dig in a variety of ways, certain common requirements have resulted in widespread acquisition of similar features through convergent and parallel evolution (Hildebrand 1974; Rose and Emry 1993). Thus we can group fossorial vertebrates according to body plan and mode of digging. Similar functional morphology (form and structure) has arisen repeatedly, sometimes in animals that are related only very remotely. For example, many fossorial and subterranean tetrapods (terrestrial vertebrates) have become very elongate and have lost one or both pairs of limbs. Examples are snakes, amphisbaenians (legless, burrowing, tropical reptiles with a head and tail that look similar), and caecilians (legless, tropical amphibians). Although not all legless tetrapods are fossorial, limblessness probably evolved in association with burrowing. It streamlines the body for "swimming" through soft sediment and allows passage through smaller tunnels without appreciably reducing body volume. The head in limbless animals has become specialized for burrowing. Many other fossorial tetrapods, however, evolved specialized limbs for digging; some of them also use their head or the incisor teeth (e.g., some frogs, tortoises, and a wide variety of mammals).

Most terrestrial tetrapods use one or more of the following methods of digging (Dubost 1968; Hildebrand 1974, 1985): (1) soil-crawling (used by limbless and nearly limbless diggers), (2) scratch-digging (widespread mode of digging, in which the forelimbs are the principal tools), (3) chisel-tooth digging (seen in rodents, which use their evergrowing incisors to burrow), (4) head-lift digging (active use of the head to excavate tunnels and to compact loose sediment), and (5) humeral-rotation digging (in which the digging stroke results primarily from rotation of the humerus, the long bone of the forelimb, between the elbow and the shoulder, as in talpid moles and probably monotremes).

Characteristics of Fossorial Vertebrates

Present-day diggers have particular specializations evident in the skeleton (Dubost 1968; Hildebrand 1974, 1985; Coombs 1983). When these features occur in fossils we can confidently infer that the extinct animal was fossorial.

The skull (Figure 1) is typically compact, dense, and often flattened and wedge-shaped, especially in head-lift diggers (e.g., amphisbaenians and caecilians). It may be pointed, rounded, or shovel-like in front (sometimes covered with a tough pad), and broad in back to provide attachment sites for strong neck muscles to raise the head (e.g., golden moles, mole-rats). The eyes, external ears, and external auditory canal (ear canal) often are reduced or vestigial (present but nonfunctional). Many subterranean vertebrates are specialized for low-frequency hearing.

Chisel-tooth diggers have continuously-growing incisors, as do all rodents, but to compensate for increased wear these teeth grow much faster than the incisors of nondigging rodents. There is a tendency for chisel-tooth diggers to have more inclined (proödont) incisors, together with robust, flaring cheek bones, which reflect especially well-developed jaw musculature (Agrawal 1967). In some limbed diggers (e.g., moles, marsupial moles, some armadillos), several neck vertebrae are fused, which adds stability to the vertebral column. In others (e.g., armadillos, geomyid rodents, aardvarks), vertebrae next to the sacrum are incorporated into it, and the bony pelvis is expanded.

In edentate mammals (order Xenarthra: armadillos, anteaters, and sloths), extra joints between the lumbar vertebrae also are believed to be a fossorial adaptation that stiffens the spine (Gaudin and Biewener 1992). Diggers usually have a short tail, except in species that use it for support when digging or for nonfossorial purposes (for instance, the prehensile tail of some pangolins, which these scaly anteaters may manipulate, much like a "fifth hand").

The limbs of fossorial vertebrates, particularly the front legs of scratch-diggers, are often highly modified from the generalized condition (Figure 2). They tend to be short and robust, the distal segments shortest except for the terminal phalanges. In order to maximize power (in-force) and leverage of digging musculature, the muscles of the shoulder, elbow, wrist, and digits are enlarged and attach to prominent crests and processes that are displaced away from the joints they move. Thus the scapula usually has a high spine and extended acromion process, overhanging the humeral head, and may have an expanded posterior angle. The deltopectoral crest on the humerus tends to be very prominent and elongate, and there is often a distinct teres tubercle. These scapular and humeral features are associated with muscles that move the arm at the shoulder joint. The distal end of the

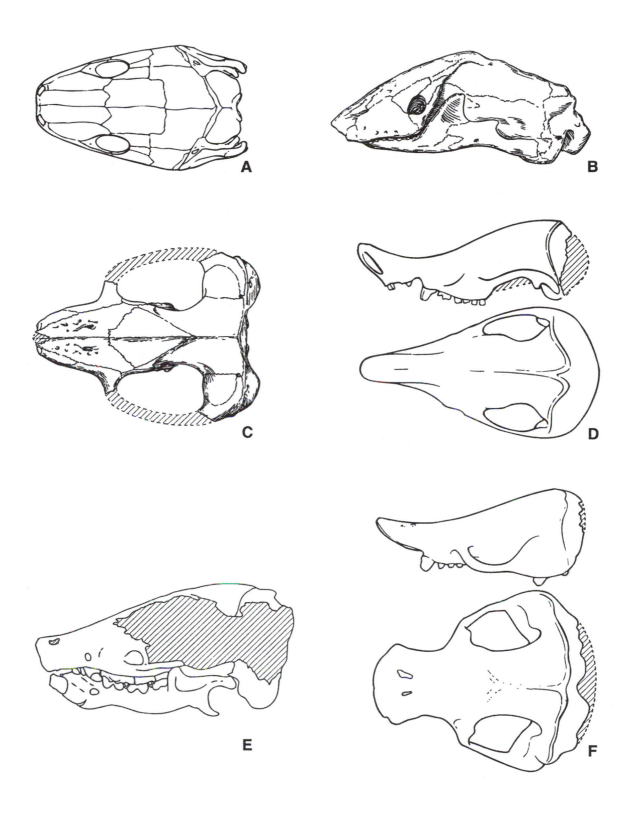

Figure 1. Skulls of some extinct fossorial vertebrates (not to scale). *A,* caecilian *Eocaecilia; B,* amphisbaenian *Spathorhynchus; C,* multituberculate *Lambdopsalis; D,* marsupial *Necrolestes; E,* insectivoran *Mesoscalops; F,* palaeanodont *Xenocranium.* After: *A,* Jenkins and Walsh (1993); *B,* Berman (1977); *C,* Miao (1988); *D,* Rose and Emry (1983); *E,* Barnosky (1981); *F,* Rose and Emry (1983).

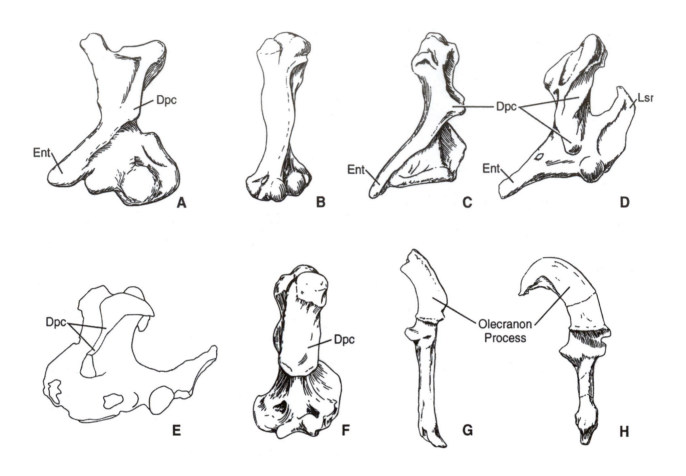

Figure 2. Left forelimb bones of some extinct fossorial vertebrates (not to scale). *A,* dicynodont *Cistecephalus,* humerus; *B, Lambdop-salis* humerus; *C, G, Necrolestes,* humerus and ulna; *E,* insectivore *Mesoscalops,* humerus; *D, H,* palaeanodont *Epoicotherium,* humerus and ulna; *F,* mammal *Ernanodon,* humerus. Abbreviations: *Dpc,* deltopectoral crest; *Ent,* entepicondyle; *Lsr,* lateral supra-condylar ridge. After: A, Cluver (1978); B, Kielan-Jaworowska and Qi (1990); C, D, G, H, Rose and Emry (1983); E, Barnosky (1981); F, Ding (1987).

humerus is always broad, the medial side with a large or elongate projection (entepicondyle) where strong wrist and finger flexor muscles originate, and the lateral side with an expanded flange (lateral supracondylar ridge) for attachment of the wrist and finger extensors. The olecranon process of the ulna is usually very long and may be medially inflected. This enhances the leverage of muscles attaching here that extend the forearm and flex the fingers. The hand is often short and broad, with occasional fusion of elements. Some diggers have broad, spatulate claws (e.g., talpid moles, gopher tortoises, echidna), but most have large, sharp claws, the central ones often much larger than those of the lateral digits and sometimes as long as the forearm. Supporting these claws are distinctive long, curved, mediolaterally compressed terminal phalanges (MacLeod and Rose 1993). The hind limbs are often modified to kick back loose earth.

A Survey of Some Fossorial Vertebrates

Fossorial animals have evolved in nearly all classes of vertebrates, even fishes, such as eels and lungfishes. Lungfishes construct burrows in which they aestivate during periods of drought. Fossil burrows, some containing lungfish skeletons, are known from Devonian-Permian rocks (Romer and Olson 1954; Carroll 1965).

Amphibians

Among living amphibians, most caecilians and some frogs and salamanders are fossorial. Reduction or loss of limbs in burrowing amphibians (as in legless reptiles) is accompanied by an elongation of the body. Caecilians usually have about 100 vertebrae, but some species have more than twice that number. Most caecilians are fossorial; all extant species are entirely limbless, lacking even vestiges of the limb girdles (Edwards 1985). Associated with their burrowing habits, these amphibians have small eye sockets and solidly constructed skulls, with a reduced number of bones owing to fusion or loss (Taylor 1969). The oldest caecilian, *Eocaecilia* from the Early Jurassic of Arizona, was elongate but retained small front limbs and small hind limbs, unlike any living caecilian. Like modern fossorial caecilians, however, it had a dense skull roof and braincase (Figure 1A), and robust jaws (Jenkins and Walsh 1993), suggesting that even then caecilians were fossorial.

Many frogs and toads (anurans) dig for shelter using the hind feet, which are equipped with a claw-like horny tubercle (Emerson 1976; Hildebrand 1974, 1985). The hind limb bones in fossorial frogs and toads tend to be shortened, especially the tibiofibula (the bone between the knee and the ankle). Eocene spadefoot toads (Pelobatidae), known from complete skeletons from Messel, Germany, may have been fossorial, like their extant relatives (Wuttke 1992) but there is little direct evidence of fossorial habits in fossil anurans.

Microsaurs were a diverse group of Late Paleozoic lepospondyls (insect-eating amphibians), some of which were probably the first amphibian burrowers (Carroll 1968; Carroll and Gaskill 1978). Most microsaurs were moderately elongate (but less so than caecilians), and all retained limbs, although often small ones. Permian *Pantylus* had a broad-backed triangular-shaped skull with a flattened, dense roof. The limbs were short and robust, and bony plates armored the belly. All of these features suggest burrowing habits. The most specialized microsaur burrowers (Ostodolepidae) were elongate with short, robust limbs and a short tail, resembling a gila monster. The microsaur *Pelodosotis,* from the Permian of Texas, had a broad-backed skull and a pointed snout extending beyond the tooth-row, as seen in amphisbaenians and some specialized mammalian diggers. It probably used both its head and its forelimbs to dig burrows.

Reptiles

A diversity of extant lizards, snakes, and tortoises are burrowers, and a number of fossil reptiles have definite burrowing adaptations. Among various legless lizards, amphisbaenians are the most obviously adapted for fossorial life (Gans 1974). Like caecilians, they are elongate, and most are limbless (the extant genus *Bipes,* however, retains robust forelimbs used in digging). Amphisbaenian skulls vary from rounded to wedge-shaped to shovel-snouted, but all are densely ossified and used for burrowing (Figure 1B). The snout commonly overhangs the lower jaw. Several families of amphisbaenians are known from fossils of Cenozoic age. A number of other lizard families also have become elongate and limbless, or nearly so. Among the fossils are legless anguids (similar to the extant fossorial glass lizard) from the middle Eocene of Germany (Keller and Schaal 1992).

The Jurassic diapsid (early reptile) *Tamaulipasaurus* may have been the ecological equivalent of amphisbaenians in the Mesozoic, although its precise relationship among diapsids is uncertain. *Tamaulipasaurus* had a compact skull with some fused bones, broad head, and ears adapted for low-frequency hearing (Clark and Hernandez 1994). The close resemblance of its skull to those of extant amphisbaenians indicates that *Tamaulipasaurus* also used its head to excavate tunnels.

Gopher tortoises, known at least as far back as the Eocene, show particular fossorial modifications; modern ones are known to excavate burrows. The most derived (specialized) species have an enlarged inner ear modified for low-frequency hearing, specialized neck vertebrae, and a short, broad hand with large, spatulate claws (Bramble 1982).

Therapsids

No doubt the best examples of digging animals among these "mammal-like reptiles" are dicynodonts. Many different dicynodonts probably grubbed for food, but some small Permian cistecephalids (underground dwellers) and related forms were decidedly burrowers (Cox 1972; Cluver 1978; King 1990). Examples are *Cistecephalus* (Figure 3A) and *Kawingasaurus.* Their fossorial features include a dense, broad-backed, triangular skull with attachment sites for large neck muscles. Dicynodonts also had a robust humerus with well-developed muscle-attachment sites (Figure 2A); short, stout bones in the forearm with a long olecranon process; and a short, broad hand with fused phalanges and long, sharp claws. Curled skeletons of the dicynodont *Diictodon* were found at the bottom of spiral-shaped burrows in the Permian Karoo Formation of South Africa (Smith 1987). Gouges nearby suggest that *Diictodon* dug with its claws and perhaps also its horny, turtlelike beak.

The robust forelimbs of tritylodontids, another mammal-like group, suggest that these herbivores also were diggers (Sues 1984). Relatively little is known of fossorial behavior in cynodonts, the group most closely related to mammals.

Mammals

A wide diversity of present-day mammals exhibit fossorial behavior, including monotremes, wombats, marsupial moles, bandicoots, talpid moles, golden moles, badgers, aardvarks, pangolins, armadillos, anteaters, mole rats, kangaroo rats, gophers, and various squirrels (see Voorhies 1975 for an excellent summary). Fossil relatives of these, when known, often had fossorial characteristics as well (e.g., fossil aardvarks, pangolins, and armadillos). Some larger clawed mammals use their forelimbs more to tear at such things as bark, roots, or termite nests than to dig (Coombs 1983). It is impossible to discuss all digging mammals here, but several extinct fossorial mammals deserve special mention because of their unusual modifications.

One of the most ancient and long-lived mammalian groups, multituberculates (small, rodentlike animals), were not typically diggers. However, Eocene *Lambdopsalis* from China had numerous fossorial features, including a robust humerus, fused neck vertebrae, ears adapted for low-frequency hearing, and a broad-backed, flat skull (Figures 1C, 2B). *Lambdopsalis* may have used both its forelimbs and head to burrow (Miao 1988; Kielan-Jaworowska and Qi 1990).

Oligocene-Miocene proscalopid moles were exceptionally specialized for burrowing. Once thought to belong to the same

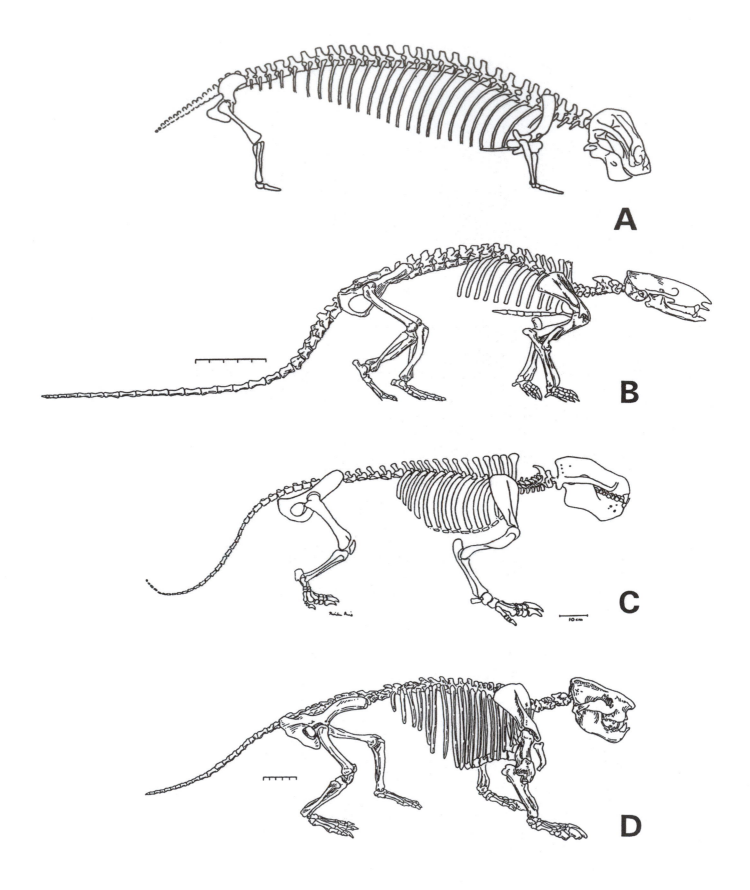

Figure 3. Skeletons of some extinct fossorial vertebrates (not to scale). *A, Cistecephalus; B,* the palaeanodont *Metacheiromys; C,* the taeniodont *Stylinodon; D, Ernanodon.* After: *A,* Cluver (1978); *B,* Simpson (1931); *C,* Schoch (1986); *D,* Ding (1987).

family as present-day moles, these ancient moles are now considered distinct because their forelimb anatomy indicates that they employed a unique digging stroke unlike that of either moles or typical scratch-diggers (Barnosky 1981). The spine of the scapula (shoulder blade) of proscalopids is exceptionally high, the acromion process very long, and the humerus remarkably short, robust, and distally expanded (Figure 2D). The skull, like that of golden moles, was broad and deep in back and had a short, slightly upturned snout, suggesting the presence of a tough nosepad (Figure 1E). Fused neck vertebrae are further evidence that the head was used for digging.

Also displaying remarkable convergence to present-day golden moles is the mouse-sized marsupial *Necrolestes* from the Miocene of Argentina. It had a pointed, upturned snout overhanging the lower jaw; a short, stout humerus; and a very long olecranon process that was inclined toward the body (Figures 1D, 2C) (Patterson 1958; Rose and Emry 1983). These adaptations suggest both scratch-digging and head-lift digging.

Palaeanodonts, early Tertiary probable relatives of modern pangolins, had some of the most extraordinary fossorial modifications of any mammal (Figure 3B) (Simpson 1931; Rose and Emry 1983; Rose et al. 1992). The scapula in these mouse- to armadillo-sized diggers had a very high spine with an enormous bony process overhanging the shoulder joint. The forelimbs were short and very robust, and the foreclaws were long and sharp. The humerus of most palaeanodonts had a very prominent, extensive area for chest and shoulder muscles. In the most specialized species several neck vertebrae were fused, and the humerus was as wide as it was long (Figure 1E). The elbow section of the forearm was as long as the rest of the forearm—longer than in any other mammal. The hand bones were short and compact, except for an enlarged third finger. The finger flexors had enhanced leverage by attachment to a large bone in the wrist, as also seen in armadillos, pangolins, and marsupial moles. Besides these traits, the palaeanodont *Xenocranium* (Figure 1F) had vestigial eyes, an ear specialized for low-frequency hearing, and an upturned, spoon-shaped snout used for head-lift digging.

The early Tertiary taeniodonts, now extinct, were opossum- to bear-sized animals. Some of these mammals evolved bizarre specializations (Figure 3C). They had ponderous front legs, short hand elements, and large, curved claws. Their huge canine teeth were evergrowing and had enamel only in front, thereby resembling giant rodent incisors. Taeniodonts probably used their massive forelimbs and canines to grub for roots and tubers and could dig as well as aardvarks (Schoch 1986).

Two unique extinct mammals of uncertain relationships were among the most derived diggers ever. *Ernanodon,* a Paleocene mammal from China, was about the size of a wolverine but had much shorter and heavier limbs (Figure 3D). Its scapular spine and acromion had very large, bony muscle-attachment sites, and the humerus was exceptionally robust (Figure 2F). The short, broad hands bore large terminal phalanges similar to those of aardvarks. Thus, *Ernanodon* was probably a powerful scratch-digger (Ding 1987). *Plesiorycteropus,* from the Quaternary of Madagascar, was an armadillo-like animal once thought to be an extinct aardvark. It had robust forelimbs, the humerus with an area for extensive chest and shoulder muscles, and the stout ulna having a long olecranon process. The sacrum, situated between the pelvic bones, was extended, and the pelvis reinforced. Because of its unusual suite of features, *Plesiorycteropus* recently was assigned to a new order of mammals (MacPhee 1994).

Finally, we turn to the rodents, several lineages of which independently evolved fossorial habits during the Cenozoic. Of particular note are the marmot-sized mylagaulids, Miocene relatives of the mountain beavers. Mylagaulids had short, flat, broad-backed skulls and powerful forelimbs with large, curved claws (Fagan 1960), suggesting that they used both scratch-digging and head-lift digging. On the snout of *Epigaulus* was a pair of pointed horns, which also may have been used for digging. Slightly smaller was the Miocene beaver *Palaeocastor,* which constructed seven-foot long spiral-shaped burrows known as *Daemonelix,* or "the devil's corkscrew" (Martin and Bennett 1977). It had a broad, flat skull with inclined incisors, but its skeleton was only moderately fossorial, and the claws were unremarkable. Nonetheless, the presence of skeletons, as well as extensive tooth and claw gouges in the burrows, leave little doubt that *Palaeocastor* was the architect of these burrows.

KENNETH D. ROSE

See also Glires; Insectivorans; Lepidosauromorphs; Paleanodonts; Terrestrial Locomotion in Vertebrates; Xenarthrans

Works Cited

Agrawal, V.C. 1967. Skull adaptations in fossorial rodents. *Mammalia* 31:300–12.

Barnosky, A.D. 1981. A skeleton of Mesoscalops (Mammalia, Insectivora) from the Miocene Deep River Formation, Montana, and a review of the proscalopid moles: Evolutionary, functional, and stratigraphic relationships. *Journal of Vertebrate Paleontology* 1:285–339.

Berman, D.S. 1977. *Spathorhynchus natronicus,* a new species of rhineurid amphisbaenian (Reptilia) from the early Oligocene of Wyoming. *Journal of Paleontology* 51:986–91.

Bramble, D.M. 1982. Scaptochelys: Generic revision and evolution of gopher tortoises. *Copeia* 1982 (4):852–67.

Carroll, R.L. 1965. Lungfish burrows from the Michigan coal basin. *Science* 148:963–64.

———. 1968. The postcranial skeleton of the Permian microsaur Pantylus. *Canadian Journal of Zoology* 46:1175–92.

Carroll, R.L., and P. Gaskill. 1978. *The Order Microsauria.* Memoirs of the American Philosophical Society, 126. Philadelphia: American Philosophical Society.

Clark, J.M., and R. Hernandez. 1994. A new burrowing diapsid from the Jurassic La Boca Formation of Tamaulipas, Mexico. *Journal of Vertebrate Paleontology* 14 (2):180–95.

Cluver, M.A. 1978. The skeleton of the mammal-like reptile Cistecephalus with evidence for a fossorial mode of life. *Annals of the South African Museum* 76:213–46.

Coombs, M.C. 1983. Large mammalian clawed herbivores: A comparative study. *Transactions of the American Philosophical Society* 73 (7):1–96.

Cox, C.B. 1972. A new digging dicynodont from the Upper Permian of Tanzania. *In* K.A. Joysey and T.S. Kemp (eds.), *Studies in Vertebrate Evolution*. New York: Winchester; Edinburgh: Oliver and Boyd.

Ding, S. 1987. A Paleocene edentate from Nanxiong Basin, Guangdong. *Palaeontologia Sinica 173*, new ser. C, 24:1–118.

Dubost, G. 1968. Les mammifères souterrains. *Revue d'Écologie et de Biologie du Sol* 5 (1–2):135–97.

Edwards, J.L. 1985. Terrestrial locomotion without appendages. *In* M. Hildebrand, D.M. Bramble, K.F. Liem, and D.B. Wake (eds.), *Functional Vertebrate Morphology*. Cambridge, Massachusetts: Belknap Press of Harvard University.

Emerson, S.B. 1976. Burrowing in frogs. *Journal of Morphology* 149:437–58.

Fagan, S.R. 1960. Osteology of Mylagaulus laevis, a fossorial rodent from the upper Miocene of Colorado. *University of Kansas Paleontological Contributions, 26, Vertebrata* 9:1–32.

Gans, C. 1974. Analysis by comparison: Burrowing in amphisbaenians. *In* C. Gans (ed.), *Biomechanics: An Approach to Vertebrate Biology*. Philadelphia: Lippincott.

Gaudin, T.J., and A.A. Biewener. 1992. The functional morphology of xenarthrous vertebrae in the armadillo Dasypus novemcinctus (Mammalia, Xenarthra). *Journal of Morphology* 214:63–81.

Hildebrand, M. 1974. Digging and locomotion without appendages. *In* M. Hildebrand (ed.), *Analysis of Vertebrate Structure*. New York: Wiley.

———. 1985. Digging of quadrupeds. *In* M. Hildebrand, D.M. Bramble, K.F. Liem, and D.B. Wake (eds.), *Functional Vertebrate Morphology*. Cambridge, Massachusetts: Belknap Press of Harvard University.

Jenkins Jr., F.A., and D.M. Walsh. 1993. An Early Jurassic caecilian with limbs. *Nature* 365:246–50.

Keller, T., and S. Schaal. 1992. Lizards: Reptiles en route to success. *In* S. Schaal and W. Ziegler (eds.), *Messel: An Insight into the History of Life and of the Earth*. Oxford: Clarendon Press; New York: Oxford University Press; as *Messel: Ein Schaufenster in die Geschichte der Erde und des Lebens*. Frankfurt: Krämer, 1988.

Kielan-Jaworowska, Z., and Qi T. 1990. Fossorial adaptations of a taeniolabidoid multituberculate mammal from the Eocene of China. *Vertebrata PalAsiatica* 28 (2):81–94.

King, G. 1990. The Dicynodonts. *A Study in Palaeobiology*. London and New York: Chapman and Hall.

MacLeod, N., and K.D. Rose. 1993. Inferring locomotor behavior in Paleogene mammals via eigenshape analysis. *American Journal of Science* 293-A:300–55.

MacPhee, R.D.E. 1994. *Morphology, Adaptations, and Relationships of Plesiorycteropus, and a Diagnosis of a New Order of Eutherian Mammals*. Bulletin of the American Museum of Natural History, 220. New York: American Museum of Natural History.

Martin, L.D., and D.K. Bennett. 1977. The burrows of the Miocene beaver Palaeocastor, western Nebraska, U.S.A. *Palaeogeography, Palaeoclimatology, Palaeoecology* 22:173–93.

Miao, D. 1988. *Skull Morphology* of Lambdopsalis *bulla (Mammalia, Multituberculata) and Its Implications to Mammalian Evolution*. Contributions to Geology, University of Wyoming, Special Paper 4. Laramie: Department of Geology and Geophysics, University of Wyoming.

Patterson, B. 1958. Affinities of the Patagonian fossil mammal Necrolestes. *Breviora* 94:1–14.

Romer, A.S., and E.C. Olson. 1954. Aestivation in a Permian lungfish. *Breviora* 30:1–8.

Rose, K.D., and R.J. Emry. 1983. Extraordinary fossorial adaptations in the Oligocene palaeanodonts Epoicotherium and Xenocranium (Mammalia). *Journal of Morphology* 175:33–56.

———. 1993. Relationships of Xenarthra, Pholidota, and fossil "edentates": The morphological evidence. *In* F.S. Szalay, M.J. Novacek, and M.C. McKenna (eds.), *Mammal Phylogeny. Placentals*. London and New York: Springer Verlag.

Rose, K.D., R.J. Emry, and P.D. Gingerich. 1992. Skeleton of Alocodontulum atopum, an early Eocene epoicotheriid (Mammalia, Palaeanodonta) from the Bighorn Basin, Wyoming. *Contributions from the Museum of Paleontology, University of Michigan* 28 (10):221–45.

Schoch, R.M. 1986. *Systematics, Functional Morphology and Macroevolution of the Extinct Mammalian Order Taeniodonta*. Bulletin of the Peabody Museum of Natural History, Yale University, 42. New Haven, Connecticut: Peabody Museum of Natural History.

Simpson, G.G. 1931. *Metacheiromys* and the Edentata. *Bulletin of the American Museum of Natural History* 59:295–381.

Smith, R.M.H. 1987. Helical burrow casts of therapsid origin from the Beaufort Group (Permian) of South Africa. *Palaeogeography, Palaeoclimatology, Palaeoecology* 60:155–70.

Sues, H.-D. 1984. Inferences concerning feeding and locomotion in the Tritylodontidae (Synapsida). *Third Symposium on Mesozoic Terrestrial Ecosystems*: 231–36.

Taylor, E.H. 1969. Skulls of Gymnophiona and their significance in the taxonomy of the group. *University of Kansas Science Bulletin* 48 (15):585–687.

Voorhies, M.R. 1975. Vertebrate borrows. *In* R.W. Frey (ed.), *The Study of Trace Fossils*. Berlin and New York: Springer-Verlag.

Wuttke, M. 1992. Amphibia at Lake Messel: Salamanders, toads, and frogs. *In* S. Schaal and W. Ziegler (eds.), *Messel: An Insight into the History of Life and of the Earth*. Oxford: Clarendon Press; New York: Oxford University Press; as *Messel: Ein Schaufenster in die Geschichte der Erde und des Lebens*. Frankfurt: Krämer, 1988.

Further Reading

Dubost, G. 1968. Les mammifères souterrains. *Revue d'Écologie et de Biologie du Sol* 5 (1–2):135–97.

Gans, C. 1974. Analysis by comparison: Burrowing in amphisbaenians. *In* C. Gans (ed.), *Biomechanics: An Approach to Vertebrate Biology*. Philadelphia: Lippincott.

Hildebrand, M. 1974. Digging and locomotion without appendages. *In* M. Hildebrand (ed.), *Analysis of Vertebrate Structure*. New York: Wiley; 4th ed., 1995.

———. 1985. Digging of quadrupeds. *In* M. Hildebrand, D.M. Bramble, K.F. Liem, and D.B. Wake (eds.), *Functional Vertebrate Morphology*. Cambridge, Massachusetts: Belknap Press of Harvard University.

King, G. 1990. The Dicynodonts. *A Study in Palaeobiology*. London and New York: Chapman and Hall.

Nevo, E. 1979. Adaptive convergence and divergence of subterranean mammals. *Annual Review of Ecology and Systematics* 10:269–308.

Nevo, E., and O.A. Reig (eds.) 1990. *Evolution of Subterranean Mammals at the Organismal and Molecular Levels*. Progress in Clinical and Biological Research, 335. New York: Wiley-Liss.

Yalden, D.W. 1966. The anatomy of mole locomotion. *Journal of Zoology London* 149:55–64.

C

CANADA AND ALASKA

Numerous fossils have been uncovered in Canada and Alaska, even though this region was one of the last to be explored on the North American continent. The fossils found here bear witness to most of the events of the Earth's history. Finds include some of the earliest known fossils, more than 2.5 billion years old, and many others from the Cambrian "experiment" in morphological design, through the rise and fall of the dinosaurs and their biotas (ecological environments), up to the development of the modern ecosystems. The origin of life, plant evolution, the extinction of the dinosaurs (as well as their biology and behavior), and mammalian evolution are currently popular subjects of discussions based quite frequently on the fossils from within these political boundaries.

The first collectors of fossils in Canada were not academics from universities, museums, or from any geological or exploratory surveys. Rather, the aboriginal peoples were the first collectors of paleontological resources. As one historian noted, "the first collector was [perhaps] a woman, for Blackfoot legend tells of the wife of a hunter as the gatherer of fossils" (Russell 1988). She gave these objects, called *iniskim,* to her husband to increase his power over the buffalo. *Iniskim* were kept in medicine pouches and were believed to improve the hunter's chances against the buffalo. Some medicine pouches examined included fossils of Cretaceous ammonites and Paleozoic corals. Obviously, the native peoples revered some extinct life-forms—but not all. One nineteenth-century explorer to western Canada, Henry Hind, wanted to follow up a report of a possible mammoth discovery. His native guides refused to follow him to the site, saying that the fossils were the bones of the great spirit, *Manitou.* Since the aboriginal peoples lack a written history, some of their interpretations of fossils were recorded by the explorers to the area (Tokaryk 1997; Spalding 1988).

Most of the exploration in Canada was conducted in the course of surveys to assess the country's natural resources. The Geological Survey of Canada, established in 1841, and the first under the direction of Sir William Logan, was the first organization to make this assessment. According to F.J. Alcock (1948), the Survey's early history, "although primarily geological, was in reality a natural history one" as the Survey systematically accessed new territories where everything recorded was valuable, if not new. As the Survey grew, many spin-off branches were created. One of

these, now called the Canadian Museum of Nature in Ottawa, was the repository of much of the Survey's collection, and its staff continues to do research in the noneconomic areas of paleontology.

Between 1842 and 1870 the Survey was restricted to the territories in what is today the provinces of Quebec and Ontario. In 1870, with the expansion of Canada, activities came to include most of the Atlantic provinces to the east as well as the vast territories to the west and north. A brief ballooning of staff and field explorations accompanied the territorial expansion. While the fossils were used to develop geological charts and maps, and to aid in the identification and exploitation of economic resources, this work did little for the betterment of basic science. For example, although the first dinosaur bone was found in Western Canada in 1874, it was more than 25 years before any serious attempt was made to examine these deposits and their contents. (In 1845, the first reported dinosaur bone found in Canada, *Bathygnathus,* was recorded from Prince Edward Island. The find, however, turned out not to be a dinosaur, but a Pelycosaur, a mammal-like reptile.)

Although the Survey was the only organization funded by the Canadian government to eventually become interested in fossil resources, others also recognized their potential. The Smithsonian Institute obtained many collections from fur traders through its relationship with the large commercial firm, the Hudson's Bay Company, which had outposts throughout much of what is now Canada. Although the collecting was primarily ornithological, anthropological, and mammalogical, these unlikely collectors recovered some fossils and sent them to Washington, D.C., between 1859 and 1868 (Lindsay 1993). (Unfortunately, even now there has been no general assessment as to what these fossils actually were.) In 1797, less successful attempts were made to find commercially useful fossils, such as mammoth tusks, by fur trader and geographer David Thompson: "From the very numerous remains in Siberia and parts of Europe of the Elephant, Rhinoceros, and other large animals . . . I was led to expect to find remains of those animals in the great plains . . . but all my steady researches, and all my enquiries led to nothing" (quoted in Spalding 1988).

The Smithsonian's major contribution to Canadian paleontology came from its secretary (equivalent to director) Charles Walcott in 1909. That year, Walcott and his family discovered the remains of softbodied organisms in the strata of black shale on Mount Wapta in British Columbia. Over the subsequent years ending in 1917, Walcott and his crew collected nearly 80,000 specimens and carted them out by the train-car load. This Cambrian Burgess Shale fauna, which was probably trapped by rapid burial, is quite unique because it represents, according to Stephen J. Gould (1989), an experiment in evolutionary design. The fossils include annelid (segmented worms) and other worms, transitional forms between annelids and arthropods, jellyfish, sea urchins, and many other invertebrates and their precursors, as well as several types that defy current classifications. *Wiwaxia,* for example, has been described in general appearance as "a small plated pineapple with spines." Subsequent collecting efforts by the Royal Ontario Museum (Toronto) have added to the fauna, which now includes nearly 120 species of animal and algal plants from a crucial time in our planet's history. Yoho National Park contains most of the Burgess Shale sites, including the location of Walcott's discovery.

John William Dawson is one Canadian contributor of some note. He was educated at Edinburgh, and in the late nineteenth century fought hard for the establishment of a substantial museum at McGill University in Montreal. In 1882 his dream was realized with the opening of the Peter Redpath Museum. Visitors there learned about fossils from the resources that Dawson purchased or acquired through trade (Dawson gathered, through his own efforts, comparatively little of the collection on display). Dawson, however, and not the museum, was the force that drew much of the public's and scientific community's attention. He was hailed as "the second nominee for the title of creationist extraordinaire" of North America, next to famed Harvard zoologist Louis Agassiz. His popular books describe his frustration with the Darwinian model of evolution and his belief in a more theologically based interpretation of nature. The Dawson legacy continued with his son, George, who, as a member of Her Majesty's North American Boundary Commission expedition, contributed to the economic assessment of many of the sediments he observed during his travels. The young Dawson was also fortunate to find the first dinosaur bone in Western Canada.

Much of Canadian paleontology in the early twentieth century, especially that of vertebrate paleontology, was initiated or performed by American scientists. A rancher from Alberta contacted the American Museum of Natural History in New York regarding large dinosaur-like bones near his property. In 1909 Barnum Brown, an employee of the New York museum and discoverer of *Tyrannosaurus rex* (among other major finds), crossed the border from Montana to Alberta to examine these deposits near what is now the town of Drumheller. Brown was impressed with these late Cretaceous deposits and secured an assignment the following year for a full field season in the long valley. Since it was cut by the Red Deer River, a river system that crosses much of southern Alberta, Brown traveled there by using a method of transport similar to that used in previous expeditions—a raft. It can be said that the "great Canadian dinosaur rush" was triggered by Brown's activities.

Within a few years Brown had collected several hadrosaur, ceratopsian, and ankylosaur skeletons, many of them new to science, and the Canadian government began to take some notice. The "political backdrop of U.S. territorial expansion and Canadian nationalistic wariness of this expansion" was a real issue at the

time (Drake 1980). The Canadians thought that it would not be appropriate to ban Brown from collecting on Canadian soil (although as early as 1913, there were attempts to pass legislation protecting these resources), so the Survey hired the famed American dinosaur hunting family, the Sternbergs, to collect for Canada. Working only miles apart at times, both the Brown and Sternberg expeditions amicably recovered train-car loads of fossils. Their relationship stands in stark contrast to the vehement competition (often called a war) between two collectors, E.D. Cope and O.C. Marsh, in the American Western Territories.

Brown, however, was soon distracted by other regions of the globe, collecting fossil footprints, mammals, and dinosaurs, many new to science. Charles H. Sternberg, the father of the dinosaur hunting family, also left the Alberta badlands after a few field seasons, but his son, Charles M. Sternberg, stayed on with the Survey and then with the national museum, concentrating much of his efforts on Albertan dinosaurs. The other Sternberg brothers also made their marks; George returned to Kansas to collect for others, and Levi remained in Canada at the Royal Ontario Museum. The area where Sternberg and Brown spent most of their time is now called Dinosaur Provincial Park and has been designated a World Heritage Site. The park contains 36 species of dinosaurs and 84 species of other vertebrates. The abundance of late Cretaceous deposits in Alberta has led to the building of one of the largest museums dedicated to paleontology, the Royal Tyrrell Museum, in Drumheller. This institution has continued the activities of earlier investigators and has discovered many new sites and species. One of these is the Late Cretaceous dinosaur nesting grounds in southern Alberta.

The Royal Ontario Museum also participated in the "Dinosaur Rush." This institution, which grew out of the University of Toronto and was somewhat like a provincial museum, was not restricted by political boundaries. This larger mandate allowed director William Parks to amass a number of dinosaur and other reptile skeletons from Alberta between 1918 and 1935. Parks is interesting in that he was intellectually somewhat peripatetic. His expertise was not dinosaurs, nor economic geology, but the primitive Paleozoic life of Ontario. But, like other scientists in the latter nineteenth century, "his involvement in [more] economic geology was more a matter of necessity," supplementing his meager wage at the University of Toronto. (It is also worth noting that the young, brash Thomas Huxley, later to become a renowned evolutionary biologist, applied for a position at the University of Toronto long before Parks joined the staff. In retrospect, it is unfortunate that the university offered the position to someone other than Huxley.)

The Royal Ontario Museum also contributed to the development of the rich Tertiary biotas in southern Saskatchewan. The last glaciation removed much of the Paleocene to Miocene beds in Canada—glaciers can act just like bulldozers—so only a few pockets of strata from these ages can be found. The rich pocket found in southern Saskatchewan was known as early as the 1880s, but it was Loris Russell, who worked mostly with the Royal Ontario Museum, who first exploited it. The faunas, and in some cases floras, found in this region document the transformation from swamp environments after the dinosaur era to the more open grasslands of the Eocene to Miocene epochs. Subsequent work, conducted primarily by the Royal Saskatchewan Museum in Regina, has augmented Russell's research, mostly on the paleomammal faunas, throughout this section of geological time. The Saskatchewan pocket is one of the most well-established, northern Tertiary faunal sections in North America (Storer and Bryant 1997). Eocene freshwater deposits from British Columbia, containing a rich sample of fish and insects, complement our present-day knowledge of Tertiary biotas.

Some of the work on the more eastern paleobiotas also deserve attention. As in the west, much of the early survey work was economically based, yet a few visionaries regarded the rocks differently. George Frederic Matthew was one of the major contributors to paleontology from the Atlantic provinces. A self-taught geologist from New Brunswick who published over 200 papers in his lifetime, Matthew described some 350 species of fossils from the Cambrian to the Jurassic. Much of his information was used by several notable scientists, such as the Dawsons (both father and son), Charles Walcott, and Sir Arthur Smith-Woodward, a paleontologist with London's British Museum (Natural History). With these prominent men recognizing Matthew's talents (if not his drive), his importance should not decrease with time because of his lack of a formal education (two universities would later honor him with degrees). Matthew provided not only valuable information on the paleontological resources of the east coast; he also fostered an environment where intellectual curiosity was encouraged. His son, William Diller Matthew, was one of the beneficiaries of this academic climate. William Matthew thereafter became a "father of mammalian paleontology" at the American Museum of Natural History in New York, under the direction of Henry Fairfield Osborn. (The Atlantic province of Nova Scotia also boasts extremely rich Jurassic fauna and flora, including trackways of diverse early reptiles and dinosaurs.)

Studies and advances in paleontology in Canada underwent a long dry spell during both world wars and the "dirty thirties," a time when much of western Canada almost literally dried up. Most of Canada had been mapped by this point, and with few resources for new explorations, universities and the emerging provincial museums concentrated on managing fossil resources. The provincial museums became guardians of local resources as province after province enacted legislation to protect its fossil resources. Generally, it can be said that most, if not all, fossils became the property of a particular province; in other words, they belong to the people. Unfortunately, not all provincial museums maintain an active vertebrate paleontological program (nor, for that matter, do most of the major universities). Exceptions of course are the Royal Ontario Museum, Royal Saskatchewan Museum, Royal Tyrrell Museum, McGill University, and the universities of Saskatchewan (Saskatoon), Toronto, and Alberta (Edmonton). Economic paleontology, however, is pursued by almost all major universities.

The North

Access to northern latitudes has historically been limited. The cold, unforgiving environment and terrain allow only brief periods that are suitable for paleontological investigation. Despite diversification in transportation over the past century, the cost factor remains prohibitive for most investigators. Nonetheless, Devonian fish faunas are currently being found in the Canadian Arctic, Late Cretaceous marine faunas are known from the Northwest Territories, and,

most spectacularly, an Eocene unfossilized forest was recovered under the auspices of a multi-institutional expedition in the Arctic. Despite current conceptions of these northern regions, the climate apparently was very different million of years ago.

In 1961 R.L. Liscomb worked for the Shell Oil Company near the Colville River in the North Slope of Alaska. He retrieved several dinosaur bones of Late Cretaceous age from along the river, probably of a hadrosaur. Even though the original material was not exceptionally complete, it raised some critical questions. Paleontologists were aware of apparently close relationships between the Asian Cretaceous fauna and that of North America; however, no one had been able to find evidence of a dispersal route between the two continents. The discovery of dinosaurs in Alaska was one of the first physical indications of such a route, yet it raised another, more important question: "Regardless of the dispersal route, the presence of hadrosaurs on the North Slope of Alaska demonstrates the ability of those animals to disperse into far northern latitudes" (Davies 1987). In the 1980s this issue was addressed by fieldwork by University of California researchers, who revisited Liscomb's site. The team's collection of additional fossils and reexamination of the data suggest this region was in a high paleolatitude subject to long periods of solar isolation, which would have affected the forests of conifers and broad leaf trees. In turn, either the dinosaurs migrated from place to place, and the North Slope was just one of their stops, or they experienced a period of reduced activity in the coldest months (temperatures average between 10 to 12 degrees Celsius in the warm months, 2 to 4 degrees Celsius in the cold months). Some scientists believe that the dinosaurs were year-round residents, based on the presence of juveniles. The fossils and their location have some bearing on the issue of how dinosaurs regulate their body temperature, but much more evidence is required to come to any conclusions. Another broader issue is at stake:

> Current hypotheses suggesting an extraterrestrial cause of the extinction of dinosaurs, such as an asteroid's impact . . . invoke lethal effects that include a period of darkness lasting a few weeks or months and a great decrease in ambient temperature. If the North Slope dinosaurs were not migratory, their occurrence in high northern, Late Cretaceous latitudes provides direct evidence of the ability to cope with cold air temperatures. Thus, some of the proposed effects [of catastrophic causes] may not have been the direct cause of the demise of the dinosaurs. (Brouwers et al. 1987)

Alaska may be better known historically for its Ice Age fauna. One of the earliest records of fossil hunting in this state dates to approximately 1816 and was associated with the trade in mammoth tusks that was so popular in the nineteenth century. During the early part of the twentieth century, gold mining operations brought many immigrants to this remote land in search of a better financial future. In their endeavors to remove the accumulated silt from the ice, they used large water "guns," or "monitors." In the process of thawing these Pleistocene ice sheets, several animal carcasses were uncovered. R.D. Guthrie (1990) lists prehistoric bison, mammoth, stag-moose, helmeted musk-ox, and other mammals, all partially or completely preserved with their soft tissues—in other words, they were partially "mummified." "Mammoths were a little known curiosity" to the early miners who were not "acquainted with the issues that made this material valuable" (Guthrie 1990). If the mummies were not destroyed by the hydraulic process, the accompanying sediment, critical for understanding the nature of the deposit and any possible associated organisms, was often eradicated. One rare exception occurred in 1979. A gold miner not only discovered a mummy frozen in the muck, but he left it in place until scientists from the University of Alaska could excavate it. The mummy turned out to be that of an almost complete carcass of an extinct bison, more than 30,000 years old.

A Rare Diversity of Life

Bearing in mind that there is nearly 2.5 billion years of the history of life exposed in the combined bedrock of one of the largest countries in the world—Canada—and the largest state of another—Alaska, they continue to contribute answers to many of the questions posed by scientists. The access to this information—finding, collecting, and interpreting—is limited only by the desire and ability of the investigator.

This cursory overview of some of the major paleontological contributions from Canada and Alaska (as well as the people who have worked on these biotas) provides a basis for further investigations. Paleontological activities are increasing through national, provincial (and state), and regional institutions; yet, as in many other countries, the funding is not always stable. However, it is virtually impossible to resist the opportunity to explore the history of this planet contained within these borders. As Charles H. Sternberg stated in 1917, after his exploits in Canada: "I have seen my choicest treasures . . . leave my hands for ever, to add to the glories of museums I shall in all probability never see. When the opportunity came, however . . . to crown my last days with a monument . . . in that growing Dominion of the North that promises to be one of the great countries in the boundless Western Hemisphere, it seemed to me like a call from heaven" (Sternberg 1990).

TIM T. TOKARYK

Works Cited

Alcock, F.J. 1948. A century in the history of the Geological Survey of Canada. *National Museum of Canada Special Contribution* 47–1.

Brouwers, E.M., W.A. Clemens, R.A. Spicer, T.A. Ager, L.D. Carter, and W.V. Sliter. 1987. Dinosaurs on the North Slope, Alaska: High latitude Latest Cretaceous environments. *Science* 237:1608–10.

Davies, K.L. 1987. Duck-bill dinosaurs (Hadrosauridae, Ornithischia) from the North Slope of Alaska. *Journal of Paleontology* 61:198–200.

Drake, E.T. 1980. Dinosaurs and international relations 1910–17. *Journal of Geological Education* 28:193–98.

Gould, S.J. 1989. *Wonderful Life: The Burgess Shale and the Nature of History.* New York: Norton; London: Hutchinson Radius.

Guthrie, R.D. 1990. *Frozen Fauna of the Mammoth Steppe.* Chicago: University of Chicago Press.

Lindsay, D. 1993. *Science in the Subarctic.* Washington, D.C.: Smithsonian.

Miller, R.G., and D.N. Buhay. 1990. *Life and Letters of George Frederic Matthew, Paleontologist and Geologist.* The New Brunswick Museum Publications in Natural Science, 8. New Brunswick: New Brunswick Museum.

Russell, L.S. 1988. The first fossil hunters. *Alberta* 1:11–16.

Spalding, D.A.E. 1988. The early history of dinosaur discovery in Alberta and Canada. *Alberta* 1:17–26.

———. 1993. *Dinosaur Hunters.* Rocklin, California: Prima.

Sternberg, C.H. 1990. *Hunting Dinosaurs in the Badlands of the Red Deer River, Alberta, Canada.* 4th ed., Edmonton: NeWest.

Storer, J.E., and H.N. Bryant. 1997. Tertiary mammal faunas of the Cypress Hills Formation, southwestern Saskatchewan. *In* L. McKenzie McAnally (ed.), *Canadian Paleontology Conference, Field Trip Guidebook* 6. St. John's, Newfoundland: Geological Association of Canada.

Tokaryk, T.T. 1997. Facing the past: A cursory review of paleontology in southern Saskatchewan. *In* L. McKenzie McAnally (ed.), *Canadian Paleontology Conference, Field Trip Guidebook* 6. St. John's, Newfoundland: Geological Association of Canada.

Zaslow, M. 1975. *Reading the Rocks.* Toronto: Macmillan.

Further Reading

Gould, S.J. 1989. *Wonderful Life: The Burgess Shale and the Nature of History.* New York: Norton; London: Hutchinson Radius.

Guthrie, R.D. 1990. *Frozen Fauna of the Mammoth Steppe.* Chicago: University of Chicago Press.

Lindsay, D. 1993. *Science in the Subarctic.* Washington, D.C.: Smithsonian.

Spalding, D.A.E. 1988. The early history of dinosaur discovery in Alberta and Canada. *Alberta* 1:17–26.

———. 1993. *Dinosaur Hunters.* Rocklin, California: Prima.

Sternberg, C.H. 1917. *Hunting Dinosaurs in the Badlands of the Red Deer River, Alberta, Canada.* Lawrence, Kansas: Sternberg; 4th ed., Edmonton, Alberta: Nu West, 1990.

Zaslow, M. 1975. *Reading the Rocks.* Toronto: Macmillan.

CARNIVORANS

The order Carnivora includes a wide diversity of mammalian vertebrates united by features inherited from a common ancestor. Not all members of this order are carnivorous; therefore, membership in this order reflects a shared evolutionary history, not a shared dietary adaptation. On the other hand, not all carnivorous organisms belong to this order. Members of this order, therefore, are referred to as "carnivorans," while "carnivores" are all organisms that include a significant amount of meat in their diet.

There are many examples of noncarnivorous carnivorans. In an unusual evolutionary step for a carnivoran, the aardwolf *(Proteles)* subsists on a diet of termites and has cheek teeth that are nearly vestigial (structures that have lost their original function and now have diminished size). Sea otters *(Enhydra)* dine primarily on marine invertebrates (e.g., sea urchins and molluscs), unlike their piscivorous (fish-eating) otter relatives. Other examples include pandas *(Ailuropoda)*, which feed primarily on bamboo, omnivorous raccoons *(Procyon)* and skunks *(Mephitis)*, and kinkajous *(Potos)*, which eat fruit (frugivorous) and insects (insectivorous). However, with few exceptions (e.g., the exclusively carnivorous felids and a few others), most carnivorans have varying ratios of animal and plant components in their diets.

Despite dietary differences, carnivorans share several synapomorphies (shared derived, or specialized, evolutionary features) that distinguish them from other orders. One such characteristic is the modification of the upper fourth premolar (P^4) and lower first molar (m_1) into bladelike teeth called "carnassials." During chewing, the carnassials move past each another, slicing through flesh with a scissorlike motion. The back portion of m_1 also has a crushing function as it contacts the upper first molar (M^1). The carnassials of noncarnivorous carnivorans are modified to suit their diet, but still differ in size and function from other teeth.

The rest of the carnivoran teeth can be highly variable. In general, the small incisors and large canines are pointed and used to grasp and penetrate prey, respectively. The premolars and molars are adapted for food processing—crushing and grinding. Highly carnivorous species often increase the slicing function of their premolars and carnassials. Although some carnivorans have lost the molars behind the carnassials, omnivorous species have increased their crushing capabilities. The canines also vary in morphology (shape and structure). The largest occur in the saber-toothed nimravids and machairodontine felids.

Other synapomorphies of extant (living today) carnivorans include changes in the carotid circulation and possession of an ossified (bony) auditory bulla (covering of the middle ear) consisting of three components (Hunt 1974). Among extant carnivorans, only palm civets *(Nandinia)* have a cartilaginous bulla, although the bulla also has three parts. The carnivorans' enlarged bulla may enhance auditory sensitivity.

The postcranial (body) skeleton of most carnivorans is relatively generalized, reflecting the diversity of behavior within each species. These animals may stalk, ambush, or pursue prey. They may transport food to another location, such as a tree, or may bury it. Carnivorans, therefore, may engage in sprinting, long-distance running, climbing, leaping, digging, or swimming. Some carnivorans use only their mouth to contact prey (e.g., canids and hyaenids), while others also use their forelimbs (e.g., felids). When grappling with prey, some groups (e.g., some felids and mustelids) use their hind limbs to eviscerate prey. Although no single species engages in all of these behaviors, all carnivorans have a postcranial skeleton that reflects the multiple demands of finding, capturing, killing, transporting, and eating prey.

One characteristic that varies among carnivorans is the length of the limbs relative to body size. Cursorial animals (those adapted for running), such as cheetahs *(Acinonyx)*, tend to have the relatively longest limbs. Elongating the limbs, and the distal elements (the elements farthest from the body) in particular, allows the animal to run more rapidly by increasing its stride length. Ambulatory species—those that move primarily by walking—such as bears (e.g., *Ursus*), have relatively shorter limbs.

The tail also varies in length and morphology. Small arboreal (tree-dwelling) animals, such as coatis *(Nasua)*, use their long tails for balance while running or leaping between branches. Tails also may be used during swimming (e.g., otters) or as a rudder to facilitate turning while running (e.g., cheetahs). Shorter tails may be used for communication (e.g., lynxes). Among nondomestic terrestrial carnivorans, only giant pandas *(Ailuropoda)* and nonsocial bears have vestigial tails.

Carnivorans also differ in foot posture and the amount of the foot that contacts the ground. Cursorial carnivorans tend to be more digitigrade, which means that their digits (toes) are the only portion of the foot in contact with the ground. Digitigrady is one way to elongate the limb without increasing the length of any of its elements. Ambulatory carnivorans tend to be more plantigrade, which means that the entire foot is placed more or less flat on the ground. A plantigrade foot is very stable, allowing the efficient transmission of forces generated by a heavy animal. Carnivorans vary in their degree of digitigrady or plantigrady, and identification of this characteristic in fossil species can be difficult.

One characteristic that all extant carnivorans share is the fusion of the bones of the forepaw (manus)—the scaphoid, lunate, and centrale bones—into one bone, the scapholunar. This fusion may help stabilize the wrist joint. Differences in scapholunar fusion in feliforms and caniforms have led some to suggest that this character evolved independently in the two carnivoran suborders and is not a carnivoran synapomorphy (Flynn and Galiano 1982). Similar structures have developed in members of other mammalian orders.

Claws were retained from the common carnivoran ancestor and play an important role in food acquisition and locomotion. Even the clawless otter *(Aonyx)* retains vestigial claws on some toes. Some carnivorans, such as felids, viverrids, and extinct members of other families, have retractile claws. This means that the animal holds the terminal phalanges backwards against the middle phalanges when it is at rest. Retracting the claws maintains their sharpness by keeping them from contacting the ground during locomotion. Although sharp claws are a crucial component in the ability of felids to capture prey, cheetahs *(Acinonyx)* are often said to have nonretractile claws. In 1916, Pocock demonstrated that the fleshy claw sheath common to felids is reduced in cheetahs such that the claws are visible, even when retracted. Similarities in the digits of all carnivorans has led some scholars to suggest that retractile claws may have evolved early on in carnivorans and were later lost in some families (Flynn et al. 1988).

Taxonomy

There are at least 10 extant families of carnivorans: Canidae, Otariidae, Phocidae, Ursidae, Procyonidae, Mustelidae, Viverridae, Herpestidae, Hyaenidae, and Felidae. Although the evolutionary relationships between these families are debated, most researchers place them into two larger groupings, the Feliformia and the Caniformia. This division was first recognized by Georges Cuvier in 1800 and later was formalized by Kretzoi in 1945.

Among the extant families, feliforms include herpestids, viverrids, hyaenids, and felids, which are placed in the superfamily Feloidea. These extant families long have been thought to share a common ancestor, although the relationships among the families themselves have been debated (Wozencraft 1989; Flynn 1996). Feloids lack third molars and the M2 is reduced.

Caniforms are divided into two superfamilies: the Canoidea (canids) and the Arctoidea (otariids, phocids, ursids, procyonids, and mustelids). The canoids retain many primitive craniodental features including an m3 and a long snout; they share derived features of the ear and blood supply of the brain. Arctoids share derived features of the ear and lack an intestinal cecum.

The Fossil Record

The Carnivora includes many extinct taxa (groups; singular, taxon). One group of extinct mammals, the Creodonta, was included in the order Carnivora owing to the presence of carnassials (e.g., Simpson 1945). However, the teeth that form the carnassials in creodonts are different (M1/m2 or M2/m3) than those that form carnivoran carnassials. In addition, creodonts have creases in the claw bones and separate scaphoid and lunate bones. Because of these differences, creodonts are now placed in their own order and are considered to be the closest relatives of the Carnivora.

R. Savage has placed both creodonts and carnivorans within the superorder Ferae (1977). The name "Ferae" was created by Linnaeus for his order that included most carnivorous mammals. The name "Carnivora" was proposed by Bowdich in 1821, for a more limited set of mammals. The tiny insectivorous *Cimolestes* from the Late Cretaceous may be ancestral to both creodonts and carnivorans.

The following is an introduction to the carnivoran families and some of their fossil members. Families are organized roughly by their phylogenetic relationships.

The "Miacoidea"

"Miacoids" are a group of Early Cenozoic mammals that lack the features defining the order Carnivora in the strictest sense (e.g., ossified auditory bulla, fused scapholunar bone) but are considered ancestral to carnivorans. The possession of an enlarged, bladelike P4 and m1 has been a primary feature that links miacoids to carnivorans. In 1880, Edward Cope originally placed the miacoids in the Creodonta while at the same time recognizing their relationship to carnivorans. Miacoids later were removed from the Creodonta, but their relationships to modern carnivorans and to each other are still unresolved.

Miacoids have been split into two families (Viverravidae and Miacidae), which probably do not share a common ancestor (Flynn 1996). Some scholars refer to the miacoids as the Miacidae, reducing families to subfamilies.

The Viverravidae are found in the Early Paleocene through the Oligocene. Viverravids were small, viverrid-like creatures adapted for insectivory or moderate carnivory. (Extant viverrids include civets and mongooses.) They lack third molars and have been suggested to be ancestral to feliforms (Flynn and Galiano 1982). Feliforms and viverravids, however, may have lost their third molars independently (Gingerich 1983).

Miacids are found throughout the Eocene and long have been considered the ancestors of caniforms. They retain their third molars, but their teeth have less slicing ability than viverravid teeth. The limbs of miacids were short, the trunk and tail long, and the feet plantigrade. Based on their size and morphology, miacids were probably arboreal omnivore/insectivores. The species *Miacis,* in particular, has been suggested as the ancestor of the Canidae, based on the tendency to elongate the carnassials and reduce the M3 (Matthew 1930; Wang and Tedford 1994). Others have suggested that the miacids are the sister taxon (the closest relative) to a group formed by the Viverravidae and Carnivora (Wyss and Flynn 1993).

The small, arboreal miacoids coexisted with other groups of carnivorous mammals: the cat- or viverrid-like oxyaenids (Order Creodonta), the early pursuit-predator hyaenodontids (Order Creodonta), and mesonychids (Order Condylarthra). Members of these groups were often much larger than the miacoids and probably filled some of the niches inhabited today by carnivorans. At the end of the Eocene, these families became extinct in North America. (Hyaenodontids, however, survived much later in Eurasia and Africa.) L. Radinsky (1982) has suggested that miacoids then underwent an evolutionary radiation in North America, filling these empty niches with modern carnivoran families, including the extinct nimravids (the earliest cats) and amphicyonids (an animal that may be related to bears or dogs).

The Nimravidae

The Nimravidae are an extinct group of catlike carnivorans named by Cope. They often are referred to as "paleofelids," owing to their short skulls and slicing carnassials. Although originally hypothesized to be ancestral to felids (Matthew 1910), nimravids have been suggested to be most closely related to (i.e., share a common ancestor with) felids, feliforms, caniforms, or all other Carnivora.

Nimravids have relatively elongate, compressed upper saber-tooth canines that are larger than those of extant felines but smaller than those of true saber-toothed felines. In the extreme forms, the canines are very flat, curved blades. Nimravids have a reduced number of premolars and molars and bladelike carnassials. The claws are retractile.

The Nimravidae includes two subfamilies: the Nimravinae and Barbourofelinae (Schultz et al. 1970; Bryant 1991). Nimravines are found in the Eocene and Oligocene of North America and Eurasia and are characterized by skull features that are unique among carnivorans. This subfamily has relatively shorter canines and longer limbs than the barbourofelines. Barbourofelines are known from the Miocene of Eurasia, North America, and Africa. Although these species vary in size, some of the skulls were approximately the same size as those of lions (Schultz et al. 1970). The upper canines were relatively long and narrow, and the lower jaw had a large flange that protected the portion of the canine that protruded below the jaw when the mouth was closed. The limbs were short and robust, and the forelimbs very powerful, as in the dirk-toothed machairodontine felids (Martin 1980).

The Felidae

The Felidae, or true cats, are short-faced predators with enlarged canines and carnassials. These animals are exclusively carnivorous; their shortened intestinal tract cannot process vegetation. The teeth behind the carnassials are lost or reduced to such a degree that they lose their crushing function. Felid claws are retractile, and the "wrists" of most felids retain great rotation to help them grasp or grapple with prey.

Felids first appear in the Oligocene of Eurasia and coexist with the nimravids through the Middle Miocene. During the Miocene, felids migrated into North America and Africa, and modern genera appear in Eurasia. Biochemical studies suggest that the common ancestor of extant felids existed approximately 10 million years ago (Wayne et al. 1989). Both large and small felids reached South America during the Late Pliocene, although today that region has only two large felids, pumas (Felis concolor) and jaguars (Panthera onca).

The first cats were relatively small and adapted for forested habitats. In comparison to modern felids, early cats had shorter limbs and slightly longer backs. These cats differentiated into the two subfamilies: the Felinae (conical-toothed felids) and Machairodontinae (saber-toothed felids).

The Felinae vary greatly in body size and prey preference. Most felines are solitary, with the prominent exception of lions (Panthera leo). Felines differ from machairodontines in a variety of features. For example, the cone-shaped upper and lower canines of felines are relatively equal in size. Even in clouded leopards (Neofelis), which have relatively large canines for a feline, both the upper and lower canines are enlarged.

In contrast, machairodontines have enlarged, flattened upper canines, reduced lower canines, and enlarged upper incisors. This extinct subfamily lived in Eurasia, Africa, and North America from the Miocene through the Pleistocene and in South America during the Plio-Pleistocene. In fact, machairodontines lived as recently as 10,000 years ago in the Americas. Although reputed to prefer relatively large prey, saber-toothed species varied in body size and behavioral adaptations, and so the size of their preferred prey probably varied as well.

Some saber-toothed felids are referred to as "dirk-toothed," owing to their long, narrow upper canines. This dental adaptation is often associated with short, robust limbs that probably indicate an adaptation for ambush predation. One example of a dirk-tooth is Smilodon, well-known from the many specimens found at the La Brea Tar Pits in California. Smilodon is the only saber-toothed carnivoran that migrated into South America, replacing the marsupial saber-tooth Thylacosmilus that was present earlier, during the Miocene.

Other species of machairodontines had relatively shorter, broad canines and are called "scimitar-toothed" cats. These felids tend to have relatively long limbs and may have been better adapted for running than the dirk-toothed cats (Martin 1980). Scimitar-toothed cats are often found with the remains of proboscideans (early elephant-like herbivores). For example, at Friesenhahn Cave in Texas, Homotherium skeletons are found with a large number of juvenile mammoths that some scholars suggested were these cats' preferred prey (Rawn-Schatzinger 1992).

Studies of the killing behavior of saber-toothed cats often have focused on Smilodon. A 1941 study by G. Simpson suggested that the sabers were used to make deep punctures in prey, while others suggested that the sabers were used to make shallow wounds. Shallow wounds decrease the chance of hitting bone and breaking a canine. The bite may have been placed on the ventrum (front) of the throat (Emerson and Radinsky 1980) or the abdomen (Akersten 1985). However, the anatomical features of saber-toothed carnivorans are quite diverse, so all species do not share the same killing behavior or ecology.

During the time that machairodontines were the dominant felids, felines remained relatively small. This changed with the appearance of the large, roaring felines (Panthera) in Eurasia and Africa during the Pliocene and later in the Americas. These large felines and machairodontines coexisted for a time until the final disappearance of the machairodontines. The large felines may have survived because their behavior was more generalized and they were better able to adapt to changes in habitat, prey density, and prey diversity (Lewis 1997).

The Hyaenidae

The Hyaenidae probably originated 25 million years ago, based on paleontological and biochemical data, and reached maximum taxonomic diversity in the Late Miocene (Werdelin and Solounias 1991). Fossil representatives of this family are found in Eurasia, Africa, and North America. Early hyaenids were viverrid-like and differed greatly from modern species. Four species exist today: spotted hyenas (Crocuta), striped hyenas (Hyaena), brown hyenas (Parahyaena), and the insectivorous aardwolves (Proteles). The first three species scavenge for carrion in addition to functioning as predators or omnivores. Although many carnivorans are part-time scavengers, no living carnivoran lives exclusively by scavenging carrion.

One feature that all hyaenids, except Proteles, share is an m1 placed closer to the jaw joint in comparison to most other carnivorans (Werdelin 1986). This placement allows the use of greater muscle force at the premolars for bone cracking. Bone cracking involves opening bones by bringing the cusps (points) of the upper and lower teeth into contact. This differs from bone crushing, a method used by large canids, where the bones are ground between flattened teeth (Werdelin 1989). Extant hyaenids, except for aardwolves, crack bones. Nonbonecracking extinct forms, such as Chasmaporthetes, also have this placement of m1.

Chasmaporthetes was the only hyaenid to enter North America and also is known from Eurasia and Africa. In 1921, Hay named this genus and recognized its hyaenid affinities solely from lower jaw fragments without teeth. The orientation and increased slicing area of the carnassials suggest a greater adaptation toward flesh eating (Kurtén and Werdelin 1988). The limbs of the Eurasian specimens are gracile and relatively long, suggesting cursorial adaptations.

The morphology of other extinct hyaenids suggests that they were hyperrobust forms of spotted hyenas. For example, *Pachycrocuta* from the Eurasian and African Plio-Pleistocene has extremely robust, bone-cracking teeth. This genus includes the largest hyaenid, *P. brevirostris,* which was close in size to modern lions. The large body size and proportions of these forms suggest ecological and behavioral differences from modern species (Turner and Antón 1995).

The Viverridae and Herpestidae

Although previously grouped together, herpestids (mongooses) and viverrids (civets and genets) are now thought to be distinct feloid families (Wozencraft 1989). The relationships of these families to other feloids and to each other are unresolved.

Viverrids are a diverse arboreal radiation similar to the earliest carnivorans. Viverrids are relatively small, with short limbs and long tails. The feet may be plantigrade or digitigrade, and the claws are semiretractile. Although many viverrids are strictly carnivorous, others are frugivorous, insectivorous, or omnivorous. Viverrids are known only from Eurasia and Africa, and the first viverrids are found in the Miocene of both continents.

Herpestids frequent the ground more than viverrids and tend to be more carnivorous. Some herpestid species are known to kill even venomous snakes. The ancient Egyptians domesticated the Egyptian mongoose *(Herpestes ichneumon)* for this ability; mongooses, along with domesticated cats, often were mummified by the Egyptians after death (Clutton-Brock 1996). Herpestids are known from the Oligocene to the present in Africa and Eurasia.

The Percrocutidae

The Percrocutidae are an extinct family of Eurasian carnivorans similar to hyaenids in their bone-cracking abilities but different from them in dental features. Percrocutids were considered to be hyaenids until the discovery that their deciduous dentition (teeth that go through one replacement during the life span) resembled that of viverrids more than hyaenids (Schmidt-Kittler 1976). As a result, percrocutids were placed in their own family (Werdelin and Solounias 1991). Over time, percrocutids increased in size and bone-cracking abilities. In essence, hyaenids have converged on percrocutids, since hyaenid bone cracking originated later in time. Although percrocutids and hyaenids coexisted during the Miocene, it is unclear how their ecological niches differed. No postcrania have yet been attributed to a percrocutid species. When found, these skeletal structures may hold the key to understanding the behavior and ecology of these animals.

The Canidae

The Canidae—the group that includes today's dogs, wolves, foxes, coyotes, and jackals—can be broken into three subfamilies: two extinct (Hesperocyoninae and Borophaginae) and one that includes both extant and fossil taxa (Caninae). Although many canids are omnivorous, hypercarnivory (a diet almost entirely of vertebrate flesh) has evolved more than once (Van Valkenburgh 1991).

The hesperocyonines are the earliest canids and are found in North America. *Hesperocyon,* an early form, may be intermediate in form between the arboreal plantigrady of the miacoids and the cursorial digitigrady of later canids (Wang 1993). Later forms were more digitigrade but did not have the slender, elongate limbs found in canines. The hesperocyonines first appear in the Late Eocene and were the dominant small- to medium-sized predators until they were replaced in the Middle Miocene by the borophagine canids.

Borophagines were the dominant canids in North America from the Miocene through the Pliocene. Although found with savanna-dwelling animals, borophagines were not as well-adapted for running as modern canids. This group ranges in body size from fox-sized to lion-sized species and varies greatly in postcranial adaptations (Munthe 1989). Borophagines, however, exhibit dental features that suggest hyaenid-like bone-cracking abilities. In borophagines, the fourth premolars were used for bone cracking, rather than the third premolars used by hyaenids. Both the dentition and postcrania of at least one species, *Osteoborus,* suggest that this species relied more on scavenging than modern hyaenids do (Munthe 1989; Werdelin 1989).

The Caninae replaced the borophagines during the Pliocene, although they originated during the Late Oligocene. Extant canines include foxes and wolves (Tedford et al. 1995). The Canini, for the most part, are swift runners and obtain prey primarily through oral contact with prey. Those species that routinely capture large prey are characterized by larger canines and incisors, broader snouts, and reduced dental grinding areas (Van Valkenburgh and Koepfli 1993). Many Canini today engage in pack hunting and are highly social, such as African hunting dogs *(Lycaon pictus)* and wolves *(Canis lupus).* The foxes are more omnivorous and smaller-bodied.

The Caninae radiated into South America when falling sea levels produced the Panamanian Land Bridge during the Late Pliocene and Early Pleistocene. Disappearance of the large South American herbivores may be responsible for the extinction of the largest South American canids, such as dire wolves *(Canis dirus)* at the end of the Pleistocene (Berta 1987).

The Amphicyonidae

The Amphicyonidae are an extinct family of arctoid carnivores that lived during the Late Eocene through the Miocene of Eurasia and North America and in the African Miocene. Often referred to as "bear-dogs," this family originally was considered to be a part of the Canidae. Amphicyonids are medium- to large-bodied active predators (including bone-crackers and hypercarnivores) and omnivores (Viranta 1996). Some amphicyonids could climb trees, much like bears, while others may have been digitigrade and more cursorial. Some species may have used dens to raise their young.

S. Olsen (1960) suggested that amphicyonids should be considered a subfamily within the Ursidae (bears) based on ursidlike postcranial features. Ursids and amphicyonids also share cranial features. These characteristics suggest either that ursids and amphicyonids are sister taxa or that amphicyonid morphology represents the primitive arctoid condition retained in ursids and lost in other arctoids (Flynn et al. 1988).

The Ursidae

Ursids are currently found in Eurasia and the Americas and include bears and giant pandas. Despite a vast array of dietary and locomotor adaptations, this group is linked by quadrate upper molars and the retention of the primitive arctoid cranial morphology (Hunt 1996).

Ursids have been split into several subfamilies including the Amphicynodontinae, Hemicyoninae, Ursinae, and Agriotheriinae, although the Agriotheriines often are merged with the Ursinae (Hunt 1996). Amphicynodonts are small ursids found from the Late Eocene through the Early Miocene of Eurasia and North America; this group most likely includes the ancestors of later ursids.

Hemicyonines were medium- to large-bodied ursids originally grouped within the Canidae (Simpson 1945). Their snouts were long and narrow, and, unlike modern bears, their teeth retained some shearing ability. Many hemicyonine species were cursorial, evidenced by their elongate, digitigrade feet. Hemicyonines lived throughout the Oligocene and Miocene in North America and Eurasia.

Hemicyonines were not the only ursids to have developed cursorial adaptations. The large agriotheriines, which existed during the Miocene of Eurasia, North America, and Africa, also had long limbs with elongate feet. Their snouts were short and broad. Through time, they developed slicing carnassials and, behind them, molars with both shearing and crushing capabilities. These features suggest both predatory and scavenging behavior. North American species lived in open grassland and savanna environments, alongside large canids and saber-toothed felids.

Ursines differ from earlier ursids in that their teeth are adapted for crushing, not slicing. A Plio-Pleistocene radiation from Eurasia and the Americas, the ursines include all living bears except giant pandas. Two genera, the extinct *Arctodus* and extant *Tremarctos* (spectacled bear), migrated into South America about 2 million years ago. Both genera often are placed in a separate family or subfamily, as they are morphologically distinct from extant ursines. This distinction is supported by molecular data (Wayne et al. 1989).

The evolutionary relationship of giant pandas *(Ailuropoda)* and red pandas *(Ailurus)* to bears also is debated. Molecular evidence suggests that giant pandas last shared a common ancestor with extant ursines 18 to 25 million years ago (Wayne et al. 1989). Miocene fossils of "protopandas" from Asia support this division (Hunt 1996). Giant pandas have elaborately cusped teeth adapted for breaking down bamboo. The radial sesamoid of the forepaw—a small bone on the inside of the wrist—normally tiny, has been elaborated into a thumblike structure used to grip bamboo stems. D. Davis (1964), however, in a thorough study of giant panda anatomy, determined that the giant panda was simply a very specialized bear. Similarities between the giant and red pandas may be owing to their shared vegetarian diets rather than shared ancestry; molecular evidence suggests that red pandas are primitive procyonids (Wayne et al. 1989).

The "Pinnipedia"

"Pinnipedia" is a term used for the marine carnivorans (seals, sea lions, and walruses). There are at least two families: Phocidae (seals) and Otariidae (sea lions and walruses), although some scholars have placed walruses in their own family, the Odobenidae. Pinnipeds share a variety of features related to their marine habitat and are much larger than land carnivores (90 to 3,600 kilograms). The large size of marine mammals, along with layers of blubber, protects them from the cold. The body is torpedo-shaped to reduce drag while swimming. The thumb is the longest of the five digits, helping to form the enlarged, webbed foreflipper. The hind flippers are webbed, as well. The fish-based diet of pinnipeds is reflected in their large canines and simple, conical cheek teeth. No teeth are modified as carnassials.

One of the greatest controversies in carnivoran evolution is the relationship of the pinnipeds to other carnivorans. G. Simpson (1945) placed marine and terrestrial carnivorans into separate suborders: the Pinnipedia and Fissipedia, respectively. Although these terms may be used informally today, pinnipeds are considered to be more closely related to arctoids than to other carnivorans. The relationships between individual pinniped families and arctoids are unclear. Some suggest that the two pinniped families have separate origins, based on biogeographic and fossil evidence (Tedford 1976; Repenning et al. 1979). This hypothesis states that phocids are closely related to mustelids (e.g., weasels), and that otariids (including walruses) are closely related to ursids. Other researchers suggest that the pinniped families share a common origin, based on both molecular and morphological research (Wyss 1987; Flynn 1988). These researchers believe that the shared features of pinnipeds are too similar, despite their behavioral differences, to have evolved independently.

The Procyonidae and Mustelidae

The Procyonidae and Mustelidae are currently thought to be sister taxa. Mustelids are a primarily carnivorous radiation that includes weasels, skunks, and otters. Arctoid carnivorans, therefore, have evolved aquatic adaptations at least twice (pinnipeds and otters). Today, both terrestrial and aquatic mustelids are relatively small, with short faces and limbs. Although the feet may be plantigrade or digitigrade, the claws are never fully retractile. Mustelids are known from North America and Eurasia since the Late Eocene, but these animals did not reach Africa until the Miocene and South America until the Pliocene. Some North American forms reached the size of a puma. One genus, *Enhydriodon*, includes the largest known otter, a species with limbs that were leopard-length.

Procyonids are found in the Americas and include raccoons *(Procyon)* and ringtails *(Bassariscus)*. These species are predominantly omnivorous, nocturnal, and are excellent climbers. The feet are usually plantigrade and the limbs often relatively long. The forepaw is often quite dexterous and used to manipulate food; the teeth are well adapted for crushing. One species, the arboreal kinkajou *(Potos)* has a prehensile tail (a tail that is manipulable, functioning like a "fifth hand"). Coatis *(Nasua)* are unusual—they are arboreal, yet highly social animals. Red pandas *(Ailurus)* are often included in this group, despite similarities to giant pandas (see above). Procyonids probably originated in Eurasia during the Oligocene. By the Miocene they had migrated to North America. Members of this family were the first placental carnivores to reach South America (approximately 7 million years ago), although modern genera arrived later.

Biogeographic and Behavioral Summary of Carnivoran Evolution

The first carnivorans are found in the Early Tertiary of North America and Eurasia. These early carnivorans were viverrid-like and arboreal. From this ancestral condition, today's dietary and locomotor behaviors evolved many times in different families. Prey-grappling, ambush predators first appear during the Oligocene. Saber-toothed carnivorans evolve during the Oligocene (nimravids) and the Miocene (machairodonts). During the Early Miocene, when tropical savanna areas increased, pursuit predation and digging adaptations became more common (Martin 1989). Hypercarnivory, omnivory, bone-cracking behavior, and aquatic adaptations also have evolved several times in carnivorans.

Carnivorans did not reach Africa or South America until the Miocene. Until the Early Miocene, Africa was inhabited by hyaenodontids, which continued to coexist there with amphicyonids, viverrids, herpestids, felids, hyaenids, and nimravids until the Middle Miocene. By the Late Miocene and Pliocene, ursids, canids, and mustelids also had arrived in Africa. By the Late Pleistocene only the modern species were left.

South America was populated by marsupial carnivores (Borhyaenidae) from the Paleocene to the Pliocene. The first true carnivorans to appear were the procyonids during the Late Miocene. Felids and dholelike and foxlike canids appeared later, in the Late Pliocene, followed by wolflike canids in the Middle Pleistocene. Australia was inhabited by marsupial carnivores (Dasyuridae), the largest of which are now extinct. Today, the dominant carnivorans in Australia are canids introduced by humans 12 to 5 thousand years ago (dingos) and during the last century (foxes, feral dogs) (Clutton-Brock 1996).

Modern species of carnivorans, therefore, represent a fraction of the taxonomic and behavioral diversity seen in earlier times. Some extant families reached the zenith of their diversity during the Miocene, while other families did not survive past this time period. Modern carnivoran diversity has been affected dramatically by environmental changes and human behavior (e.g., hunting for meat, fur, pleasure, or eradication as "vermin"; introduction of domestic competitors and diseases; eradication of prey species; and habitat destruction). Many species are on the verge of extinction, and without intervention may be known in the future only from the fossil record.

MARGARET E. LEWIS

Works Cited

Akersten, W. 1985. Canine function in *Smilodon* (Mammalia; Felidae; Machairodontinae). *Contributions to Science, Natural History Museum of Los Angeles County* 356:1–22.

Berta, A. 1987. Origin, diversification, and zoogeography of the South American Canidae. *In* B. Patterson and R. Timms (eds.), *Studies in Neotropical Mammalogy: Essays in Honor of Philip Herskhovitz.* Fieldiana Zoology, new ser., 39. Chicago: Field Museum of Natural History.

Bryant, H. 1991. Phylogenetic relationships and systematics of the Nimravidae (Carnivora). *Journal of Mammalogy* 72:56–78.

Clutton-Brock, J. 1996. Competitors, companions, status symbols, or pests: A review of human associations with other carnivores. *In* J. Gittleman (ed.), *Carnivore Behavior, Ecology, and Evolution.* Vol. 2, Ithaca, New York, and London: Cornell University Press.

Davis, D. 1964. The giant panda: A morphological study of evolutionary mechanisms. *Fieldiana Zoology Memoirs* 3:1–339.

Emerson, S.B., and L. Radinsky. 1980. Functional analysis of sabertooth cranial morphology. *Paleobiology* 6:295–312.

Flynn, J. 1988. Phylogeny: Ancestry of sea mammals. *Nature* 334:383–84.

———. 1996. Carnivoran phylogeny and rates of evolution: Morphological, taxic, and molecular. *In* J.L. Gittleman (ed.), *Carnivore Behavior, Ecology, and Evolution.* Vol. 2, Ithaca, New York, and London: Cornell University Press.

Flynn, J., and H. Galiano. 1982. Phylogeny of early Tertiary Carnivora, with a description of a new species of *Protictis* from the middle Eocene of northwestern Wyoming. *American Museum Novitates* 2725:1–64.

Flynn, J., N. Neff, and R. Tedford. 1988. Phylogeny of the Carnivora. *In* M. Benton (ed.), *The Phylogeny and Classification of the Tetrapods.* Vol. 2, *Mammals.* The Systematics Association Special Volume Number 35B. Oxford: Clarendon; New York: Oxford University Press.

Gingerich, P. 1983. Systematics of early Eocene Miacidae (Mammalia, Carnivora) in the Clark's Fork Basin, Wyoming. *University of Michigan, Contributions from the Museum of Paleontology* 26:197–225.

Hunt Jr., R. 1974. The auditory bulla in Carnivora: An anatomical basis for reappraisal of carnivore evolution. *Journal of Morphology* 143:21–76.

———. 1996. Biogeography of the Order Carnivora. *In* J.L. Gittleman (ed.), *Carnivore Behavior, Ecology, and Evolution.* Vol. 2, Ithaca, New York, and London: Cornell University Press.

Kurtén, B., and L. Werdelin. 1988. A review of the genus *Chasmaporthetes* Hay, 1921 (Carnivora, Hyaenidae). *Journal of Vertebrate Paleontology* 8:46–66.

Lewis, M.E. 1997. Carnivoran paleoguilds of Africa: Implications for hominid food procurement strategies. *Journal of Human Evolution* 32:257–88.

Martin, L. 1980. Functional morphology and the evolution of cats. *Transactions of the Nebraska Academy of Sciences* 8:141–54.

———. 1989. Fossil history of the terrestrial Carnivora. *In* J. Gittleman (ed.), *Carnivore Behavior, Ecology, and Evolution.* Vol. 1, Ithaca, New York, and London: Cornell University Press.

Matthew, W. 1910. The phylogeny of the Felidae. *Bulletin of the American Museum of Natural History* 28:289–316.

———. 1930. The phylogeny of dogs. *Journal of Mammalogy* 11:117–38.

Munthe, K. 1989. The skeleton of the Borophaginae (Carnivora, Canidae), morphology and function. *University of California Publications in Geological Sciences* 133:1–115.

Olsen, S. 1960. The fossil carnivore *Amphicyon longiramus* from the Thomas Farm Miocene. Part 2, Postcranial skeleton. *Bulletin of the Museum of Comparative Zoology* 123:1–45.

Radinsky, L. 1982. Evolution of skull shape in carnivores. Part 3, The origin and early radiation of the modern carnivore families. *Paleobiology* 8:177–95.

Rawn-Schatzinger, V. 1992. The scimitar cat *Homotherium serum* Cope: Osteology, functional morphology, and predatory behavior. *Illinois State Museum Reports of Investigations* 47:1–80.

Repenning, C., C. Ray, and D. Grigorescu. 1979. Pinniped biogeography. *In* J. Gray and A. Boucot (eds.), *Historical Biogeography, Plate Tectonics, and the Changing Environment*. Corvallis: Oregon State University Press.

Savage, R. 1977. Evolution in carnivorous mammals. *Palaeontology* 20:237–71.

Schmidt-Kittler, N. 1976. Raubtiere aus dem Jungtertiär Kleinasiens. *Palaeontographica,* Abt. A, 155:1–131.

Schultz, C., M. Schultz, and L. Martin. 1970. A new tribe of saber-toothed cats (Barbourofelini) from the Pliocene of North America. *Bulletin of the University of Nebraska State Museum* 9 (1):1–31.

Simpson, G. 1945. The principles of classification and a classification of mammals. *Bulletin of the American Museum of Natural History* 85:1–350.

Tedford, R. 1976. Relationship of pinnipeds to other carnivores (Mammalia). *Systematic Zoology* 25:363–74.

Tedford, R.H., B.E. Taylor, and X. Wang. 1995. Phylogeny of the Caninae (Carnivora: Canidae): The living taxa. *American Museum Novitates* 3146:1–37.

Turner, A., and M. Antón. 1995. The giant hyaena, *Pachycrocuta brevirostris,* (Mammalia, Carnivora, Hyaenidae). *Géobios* 29:455–68.

Van Valkenburgh, B. 1991. Iterative evolution of hypercarnivory in canids (Mammalia: Carnivora): Evolutionary interactions among sympatric predators. *Paleobiology* 17:340–62.

Van Valkenburgh, B., and K. Koepfli. 1993. Cranial and dental adaptations to predation in canids. *In* N. Dunstone and M. Gorman (eds.), *Mammals as Predators*. Symposium of the Zoological Society of London, 65. Oxford: Clarendon; New York: Oxford University Press.

Viranta, S. 1996. European Miocene Amphicyonidae—taxonomy, systematics and ecology. *Acta Zoologica Fennica* 204:1–61.

Wang, X. 1993. Transformation from plantigrady to digitigrady: Functional morphology of locomotion in *Hesperocyon* (Canidae: Carnivora). *American Museum Novitates* 3069:1–23.

Wang, X., and R.H. Tedford. 1994. Basicranial anatomy and phylogeny of primitive canids and closely related miacids (Carnivora: Mammalia). *American Museum Novitates* 3092:1–34.

Wayne, R., R. Benveniste, D. Janczewski, and S. O'Brien. 1989. Molecular and biochemical evolution of the Carnivora. *In* J. Gittleman (ed.), *Carnivore Behavior, Ecology, and Evolution.* Vol. 1, Ithaca, New York, and London: Cornell University Press.

Werdelin, L. 1986. Comparison of skull shape in marsupial and placental carnivores. *Australian Journal of Zoology* 34:109–18.

———. 1989. Constraint and adaptation in the bone-cracking canid *Osteoborus* (Mammalia: Canidae). *Paleobiology* 15:387–401.

Werdelin, L., and N. Solounias. 1991. The Hyaenidae: Taxonomy, systematics and evolution. *Fossils and Strata* 30:1–104.

Wozencraft, W. 1989. The phylogeny of the recent Carnivora. *In* J. Gittleman (ed.), *Carnivore Behavior, Ecology, and Evolution.* Vol. 1, Ithaca, New York, and London: Cornell University Press.

Wyss, A. 1987. The walrus auditory region and the monophyly of pinnipeds. *American Museum Novitates* 2871:1–31.

Wyss, A., and J. Flynn. 1993. A phylogenetic analysis and definition of the Carnivora. *In* F. Szalay, M. Novacek, and M. McKenna (eds.), *Mammal Phylogeny: Placentals*. London and New York: Springer-Verlag.

Further Reading

Bryant, H., and C. Churcher. 1987. All sabertoothed carnivores aren't sharks. *Nature* 325:488.

Ewer, R. 1973. *The Carnivores*. New York: Cornell University Press; London: Weidenfeld and Nicolson.

Gittleman, J. 1989–96. *Carnivore Behavior, Ecology, and Evolution.* 2 vols. Ithaca, New York, and London: Cornell University Press.

Kitchener, A. 1991. *The Natural History of the Wild Cats*. Ithaca, New York: Cornell University Press.

Kruuk, H. 1972. *The Spotted Hyena: A Study of Predation and Social Behavior.* Chicago: University of Chicago Press.

Kurtén, B. 1971. *The Age of Mammals*. London: Weidenfeld and Nicholson; New York: Columbia University Press, 1972.

———. 1976. *The Cave Bear Story: Life and Death of a Vanished Animal.* New York and Chichester: Columbia University Press.

Kurtén, B., and E. Anderson. 1980. *Pleistocene Mammals of North America*. New York: Columbia University Press.

Macdonald, D. 1993. *The Velvet Claw*. London: BBC Books; New York: Parkwest.

Marean, C., and C. Ehrhardt. 1995. Paleoanthropological and paleoecological implications of the taphonomy of a sabertooth's den. *Journal of Human Evolution* 29:515–47.

Mech, L.D. 1981. *The Wolf: The Ecology and Behavior of an Endangered Species.* Minneapolis: University of Minnesota Press.

Neff, N. 1986. *The Big Cats: The Paintings of Guy Coheleach.* New York: Abradale.

Schaller, G. 1972. *The Serengeti Lion*. Chicago: University of Chicago Press.

Sheldon, J. 1992. *Wild Dogs: The Natural History of the Nondomestic Canidae*. San Diego: Academic Press.

Turner, A. 1997. *The Big Cats and Their Fossil Relatives: An Illustrated Guide to Their Evolution and Natural History*. New York: Columbia University Press.

CENTRAL AMERICA

See Mexico and Central America

CEPHALOCHORDATES

Cephalochordates, more commonly called lancelets (singular is lancelet or amphioxus), are one of the three groups of chordates, the others being the urochordates and the vertebrates. Approximately 29 morphologically distinct species of cephalochordates are known and are grouped into two genera (Poss and Boschung 1996). They are found worldwide from temperate to tropical oceans, and in Asia they constitute an important food source. Cephalochordates are primarily sedentary infaunal filter feeders—they burrow in sandy near-shore areas and poke their head out to feed. They can, however, vacate their burrows and swim, either head-first or tail-first with equal ease, using lateral undulations of the body.

Amphioxus is an excellent example of the typical chordate body plan, whose body can be divided into three regions: the head, the trunk, and the tail (Figures 1A, 1B). Typical chordate features are as follows: The notochord, unlike in other chordates, extends to the rostral (anterior) tip of the animal (i.e., rostral to the brain, hence the name "cephalochordate") and is thought to assist the animal in burrowing. Dorsal to the notochord is the nerve cord, which, as in vertebrates, sends segmental sensory neurons to a variety of target tissues. At the anterior end of the nerve cord is the cerebral vesicle, which shows some interesting similarities to the vertebrate brain (see below). Lateral to the notochord are the V-shaped myomeres, which are segmental blocks of muscles used for swimming. Ventral to the notochord in the trunk region are over 180 pairs of gill slits used during feeding (see below). Another chordate structure used for feeding is the endostyle, a mucus-secreting organ thought to be the homologue (i.e., corresponding organ) of the vertebrate thyroid gland. Finally, posterior and dorsal to the anus is the tail.

The mouth of amphioxus is surrounded by the oral cirri, fingerlike projections that serve to prevent the entry of large particles and give the animal sensory information regarding water quality.

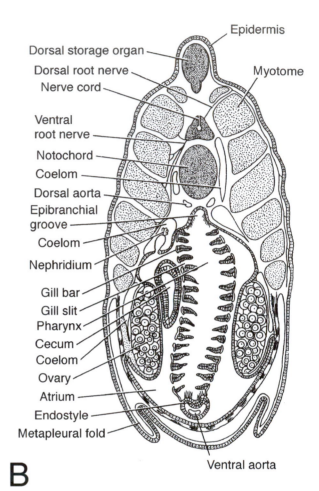

B

Figure 1B. Cross section through the pharynx. Modified from Brusca and Brusca (1990).

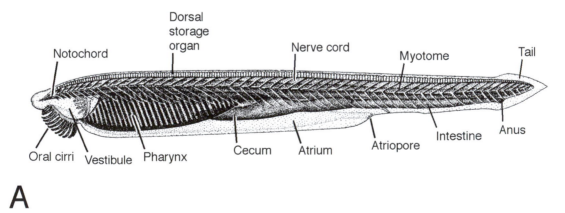

A

Figure 1A. The anatomy of amphioxus. General anatomy of amphioxus (*Branchiostoma lanceolatum*) as seen from the left side of the animal. Modified from Nielsen (1995) by permission of Oxford University Press.

The vestibule receives particles and water from the mouth, which then enter the pharynx. Here, one group of cilia on the gill slits drives the water out of the pharynx and into the atrium; it then exits the animal via the atriopore. The endostyle, a ventral strip of tissue in the pharynx, secretes mucus that envelops the food particles. Another group of cilia on the gill slits drive the food-laden mucus to the dorsal epipharyngeal groove, which gathers the mucus net and transports it posteriorly to the intestine. At the junction of the pharynx with the intestine there is a ventral outpocketing, the hepatic cecum. This digestive gland secretes enzymes into the intestine and is the site of intracellular digestion and food storage. Undigested particles are transported posteriorly and eliminated via the anus.

The anatomy of the circulatory system is well-developed and is an interesting mix of vertebrate and invertebrate characteristics. Gas exchange occurs adjacent to the gills, and the oxygenated blood is collected by two arteries that travel posteriorly and unite to form the dorsal aorta. The blood flows through capillary beds throughout the body and returns to the gills via either the cardinal veins or the hepatic portal vein. Unlike vertebrates, there is no central heart (although certain vessels are strongly contractile). Filtration kidneys (i.e., nephridia) are present in the branchial (gill) region of the body adjacent to the dorsal aortae.

Cephalochordates are dioecious (i.e., they are separated into male and female animals), and the gonads are pronounced along the ventro/lateral region of the animal. When ripe, the gametes rupture from the gonads and exit from the atriopore. Fertilization is external and development follows a pattern typical of deuterostome (e.g., creatures whose mouths and anuses developed from separate embryonic openings). The development of the larva shows some striking asymmetries once thought to be of great phylogenetic significance, but that now appear to be adaptations for larval feeding (Presley et al. 1996). For example, the larval mouth is located on the left side of the animal, the first gill openings are on the right. As the animal matures, the larval mouth becomes the velum, the first gill slits move to the left and another set develops on the right, and the oral hood develops enclosing the vestibule and forming the adult mouth and cirri.

Both morphological and molecular studies indicate that cephalochordates are the sister group of the vertebrates (e.g., Peterson 1995; Wada and Satoh 1994; Figure 2). This lends particular importance to the study of amphioxus in order to better understand the origin of the vertebrates. Remarkable studies using the expression patterns of genes involved in the development of many animals including both amphioxus and vertebrates, combined with elegant microscopical analyses, has shown that, for example, amphioxus has an extensive region of its anterior neural tube that appears to be homologous with much of the vertebrate brain. In fact, the cerebral vesicle of amphioxus appears to be the homologue of the vertebrate diencephalon, or second brain region (Williams and Holland 1996). Genetic studies on amphioxus also have shed light on the molecular evolutionary events underlying the origin of the vertebrates (Holland et al. 1994). It appears that early vertebrates underwent extensive gene duplication events, events that did not happen before amphioxus split off the vertebrate line. Such studies are revolutionizing our understanding of not only the anatomy and development of amphioxus but the origin of the vertebrates as well.

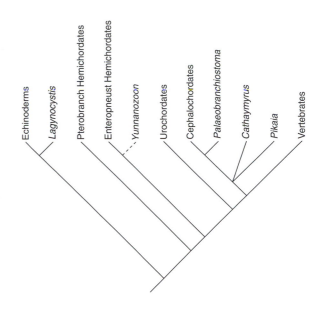

Figure 2. Phylogenetic relationships among deuterostomes based on both morphological and molecular studies. Also shown are the tentative taxonomic assignments of the fossil genera discussed in the text—the dashed line indicates that the enteropneust assignment of *Yunnanozoan* is very contentious.

The oldest described cephalochordate, *Cathaymyrus diadexus*, is from the now famous Lower Cambrian Chengjiang Lagerstätte of China (Shu et al. 1996a). Of considerable interest is that the notochord appears to terminate well before the head region (as is the case for *Pikaia*, see below), suggesting that the rostral extent of the notochord in recent cephalochordates is a derived feature that evolved within the cephalochordate lineage. The other described cephalochordate is *Palaeobranchiostoma hamatotergum* from the Early Permian of South Africa (Oelofsen and Loock 1981). As in modern lancelets, its notochord extends to the rostral tip of the animal, but one prominent difference between the two is the large fins with curved barbs on the dorsal fin of *Palaeobranchiostoma*. *Pikaia gracilens* from the Middle Cambrian Burgess Shale Lagerstätte of British Columbia was announced by S. Conway Morris (1979) to be a fossil cephalochordate. First described as a polychaete worm by Charles Walcott, discoverer of the Burgess Shale, *Pikaia's* repeated myomeres, its notochord, and its lack of a distinct head region clearly show that it is a cephalochordate. As in *Cathaymyrus*, the notochord is confined to the posterior two-thirds of the animal. Two other fossils have been described as cephalochordates: *Yunnanozoon lividum*, also from the Chengjiang fauna, was described by Chen et al. (1995) as a cephalochordate, but reexamination by Shu et al. (1996b) suggests that, instead, its affinities lie within the hemichordates, specifically enteropneusts. Jefferies (1973) described the "calcichordate" *Lagynocystis pyramidalis* as a primitive cephalochordate. Like other calcichordates it has an echinoderm-like skeleton, but it is reconstructed with chordate structures (e.g., notochord). A test of the calcichordate theory of Jefferies suggests that all calcichordates in general, and *Lagynocystis* in particular, are not chordates but echinoderms (Peterson 1995).

KEVIN J. PETERSON

Works Cited

Brusca, R.C., and G.J. Brusca. 1990. *Invertebrates.* Sunderland, Massachusetts: Sinauer.
Chen, J.-Y., J. Dzik, G.D. Edgecombe, L. Ramsköld, and G.-Q. Zhou. 1995. A possible Early Cambrian chordate. *Nature* 377:720–22.
Conway Morris, S. 1979. The animals of the Burgess Shale. *Scientific American* 241:122–33.
Holland, P.W.H., J. Garcia-Fernàndez, N.A. Williams, and A. Sidow. 1994. Gene duplications and the origins of vertebrate development. *In* M. Akam, P. Holland, P. Ingham, and G. Wray (eds.), *The Evolution of Developmental Regulatory Mechanisms.* Cambridge: Company of Biologists.
Jefferies, R.P.S. 1973. The Ordovician fossil *Lagynocystis pyramidalis* (Barrande) and the ancestry of *Amphioxus. Philosophical Transactions of the Royal Society of London,* ser. B, Biological Sciences, 265:406–69.
Nielsen, C. 1995. *Animal Evolution: Interrelationships of the Living Phyla.* Oxford and New York: Oxford University Press.
Oelofsen, B.W., and J.C. Loock. 1981. A fossil cephalochordate from the Early Permian Whitehill Formation of South Africa. *South African Journal of Science* 77:178–80.
Peterson, K.J. 1995. A phylogenetic test of the calcichordate scenario. *Lethaia* 28:25–38.

Poss, S.G., and H.T. Boschung. 1996. Lancelets (Cephalochordata: Branchiostomatidae): How many species are valid? *Israel Journal of Zoology* 42:S13–S66.
Presley, R., T.J. Horder, and J. Slipka. 1996. Lancelet development as evidence of ancestral chordate structure. *Israel Journal of Zoology* 42:S97–S116.
Shu, D.-G., S. Conway Morris, and X.-L. Zhang. 1996a. A *Pikaia*-like chordate from the Lower Cambrian of China. *Nature* 384:157–58.
Shu, D., X. Zhang, and L. Chen. 1996b. Reinterpretation of *Yunnanozoon* as the earliest known hemichordate. *Nature* 380:428–30.
Wada, H., and N. Satoh. 1994. Details of the evolutionary history from invertebrates to vertebrates, as deduced from the sequences of 18S rDNA. *Proceedings of the National Academy of Sciences, USA* 91:1801–4.
Williams, N.A., and P.W.H. Holland. 1996. Old head on young shoulders. *Nature* 383:490.

Further Reading

Barnes, R.D. 1963. *Invertebrate Zoology.* Philadelphia: Saunders; 6th ed., by E.E. Rupert and R.D. Barnes, 1994.
Barrington, E.J.W. 1965. *The Biology of Hemichordata and Protochordata.* Edinburgh and London: Oliver and Boyd; San Francisco: Freeman.
Holland, P.W.H., and J. Garcia-Fernàndez. 1996. *Hox* genes and chordate evolution. *Developmental Biology* 173:382–95.
Jefferies, R.P.S. 1986. *The Ancestry of the Vertebrates.* Cambridge and New York: Cambridge University Press.
Lacalli, T.C., N.D. Holland, and J.E. West. 1994. Landmarks in the anterior central nervous system of amphioxus larvae. *Philosophical Transactions of the Royal Society of London,* ser. B, Biological Sciences 344:165–85.

CEPHALOPODS

The cephalopods are the most specialized, highly evolved group of molluscs (Barnes 1980). They are free-swimming and univalved (with a single shell), with the anterior (front) end of the foot developed as a series of tentacles that surround the head. The head and brain are well-developed, as are a pair of highly evolved eyes that show many similarities to those of vertebrates. Locomotion is by a form of "jet-propulsion," with water being expelled out of the mantle cavity and through a funnel called the "hyponome." Modern cephalopods are carnivores, including the largest living invertebrates, the giant squids, which are up to at least 16 meters long (Barnes 1980).

Our knowledge of fossil cephalopods is based mainly upon forms that had an external shell that contained a number of gas-filled flotation chambers and an anterior body cavity. The early evolution of a buoyant, chambered shell enabled the nektic (free-swimming) cephalopods to exploit food resources unavailable to other benthic (bottom-dwelling) mollusc taxa (Clarkson 1993). A modern survivor of this form of cephalopod is the nautiloid *Nautilus.* Other modern coleoids (e.g., squids, octopus, cuttlefish) retain an internal shell, such as *Spirula* (coiled) and the cut-tlefish *Sepia* (flattened). The octopus has completely lost all remnants of a shell.

Subclass Nautiloidea

Nautiloid fossils are found in rock strata from the Upper Cambrian to Recent. The shells of both nautiloids and ammonoids (an extinct sister taxon) are composed of aragonite (a form of calcium carbonate) and are therefore commonly replaced by calcite or are in fossil specimens, leaving an internal mold. The shell is external (at least in extant, or living, species), and the animal inhabits the body cavity at the broad end (which is the youngest). The opening of the body cavity is called the "aperture." As the animal grows, it seals off successive body cavities by depositing a series of walls, called "septa" (singular, septum) (Figure 1A). This process seals off old body cavities to form enclosed chambers, or "camerae." In nautiloids the septa always have a concave surface towards the body cavity. The chambers are filled with gas at a pressure of less than one atmosphere and give the animal buoyancy. Chambers are connected to each other and the body cavity by a tube called the

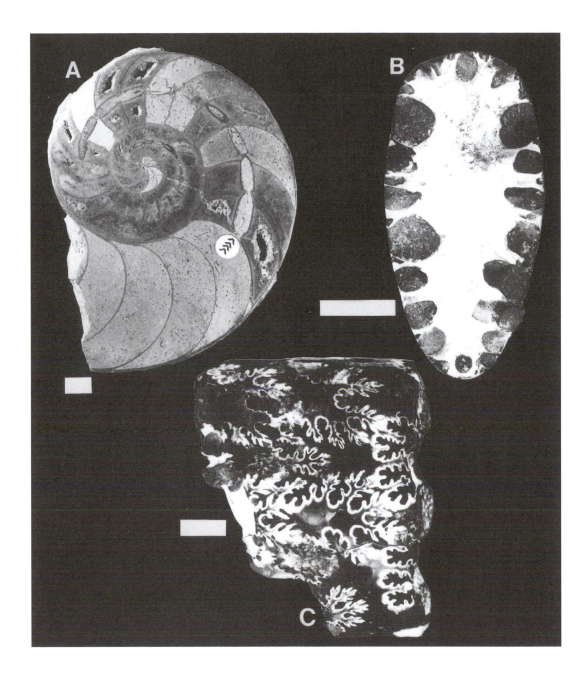

Figure 1. Views of a nautiloid. *A,* indeterminate nautiloid (Mesozoic of Europe), varnished section cut through a planispiral conch close to the plane of coiling; *light-colored chambers,* filled with sediment; *dark colored chambers,* filled with cement; *arrow,* central siphuncle cut in representative chambers; note that the concave-forward orientation of the septa and the absence of the body chamber (here not preserved but originally positioned lower left); *adjacent to arrow,* septal necks support the siphuncle and are oriented away from the aperture. *B, C,* fragments of internal molds of the heteromorph ammonoid *Baculites compressus* (Upper Cretaceous, Pierre Shale, South Dakota, United States) in which, after one or two coiled whorls, the *Baculites'* shell becomes straight or slightly curved. *B,* rear face of a septum, looking toward the front; *bottom,* the ventral position of the siphuncle; *around circumference,* complex foldings of the septum surface. *C,* side view (front left) showing the complexity of the ammonitic suture. Scale bars represent 10 millimeters. *A,* author's collection; *B, C,* University of the West Indies Geology Museum.

"siphuncle." The siphuncle is a strand of body tissue with a good blood supply that extends from the visceral mass back to the larval shell (protoconch) (Barnes 1980). The siphuncle is a conduit for adding fluid to the chambers or removing it from them, thus altering the animal's buoyancy and enabling the nautiloid to move up or down in the water column. Changing the amount of fluid is,

however, a slow process. In each septum a small tube is directed away from the body cavity, called the "septal neck," which supports the siphuncle. The contact between the outer edge of a septum and the inside of a shell is called the "suture line"; suture lines are seen easily in the commonly encountered internal fossilized molds. In nautiloids the suture is always simple.

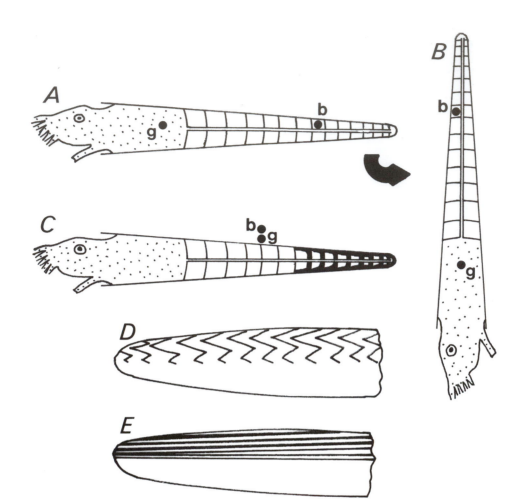

Figure 2. Swimming and camouflage in early orthoconic nautiloids. *A–C,* inferred swimming orientations (drawn in partial section to show positions of the chambers and siphuncle). In the absence of any counterbalance to the weight of the body *(A),* the center of buoyancy *(b)* is strongly displaced from the center of gravity *(g),* resulting in a vertical swimming orientation owing to the natural tendency for the center of buoyancy to lie above the center of gravity. *C,* with the development of cameral deposits *(black)* lining the walls of chambers posteriorly (closer to the back of the animal) and ventrally (belly-ward), *g* is moved back and positioned ventrally of *b,* which has migrated forward to permit a stable, horizontal swimming posture. *D, E,* two Paleozoic orthocones with camouflage color patterns developed on the dorsal *(upper)* surface only. *A, B,* simplified after Flower (1957); *D, E,* after Ager (1963); see also Teichert (1964).

The earliest nautiloid shells were conical, either straight (orthocone) or curved (cyrtocone) and either elongate (longicone) or short and swollen (brevicone). Planispirally coiled nautiloids (those that form a flat spiral) evolved from these uncoiled ancestors (Figure 1A). The uncoiled forms had an obstacle to overcome before they could adopt a horizontal swimming orientation. The heavy body tended to sink, so the shell, which functioned as an elongate flotation organ, pointed toward the surface (Figure 2A, B). This suggests that under normal circumstances the earliest nautiloids were oriented vertically, the animal presumably living by scavenging on the sea floor. By the Early Ordovician, various adaptations for counterbalancing the body's weight had evolved (Holland 1987). One adaption was precipitating calcium mineral deposits in the chambers farthest from the head, to compensate for the weight of the body. This permitted the nautiloid to swim hori-

zontally. These "counterbalance weights" are called cameral deposits (Figure 2C). For increased stability, cameral deposits were concentrated in the more distal chambers and were commonly developed asymmetrically, with thicker deposits on the ventral side of the shell. Strangely, cameral deposits are also rarely found in certain planispirally coiled nautiloids (Teichert 1964). Coiling itself is thought to be sufficient to maintain a horizontal orientation.

Modern *Nautilus* has a shell, or conch, that is external to the body (ectocochlear). However, x-ray photographs of exceptional fossil specimens in which soft tissues are preserved, from the Early Devonian Hunsrückschiefer deposits of Germany, have shown that nautiloids at this time also included species in which the shell was completely internal to the soft tissues of the body (endocochlear) (Stürmer 1970). In these endocochlear forms, soft tissues include fins along the sides.

Figure 3. Four ammonoids *(A–D)* and a coleoid *(E)*. *A, B,* internal molds, displaying their ammonitic sutures. *A,* the goniatite *Goniatites choctawensis* (Mississippian Lower Carboniferous, United States); suture lines have a distinctly zigzag fold, and shell itself is considerably less complex than a Mesozoic ammonoid (see Figures 1C, 3B); *lower right,* preserved ribbed shell; note the preserved infill of the body chamber anterior to the last suture line (at about "3 o'clock"); aperture position would have been at about "7 o'clock," conferring a presumably stable swimming arrangement. *B, Beudanticeras beudanti,* a typical coiled, Mesozoic ammonoid with a highly complex suture (Lower Cretaceous, Gault Clay, Folkestone, Kent, England). *C, Dactylioceras commune* (Lower Jurassic, Yorkshire, England); body chamber would have completed one more whorl, making it unstable when actively swimming. *D, Acanthoscaphites nodosus* (Upper Cretaceous, Pierre Shale, South Dakota, United States); a tight (more involute) coil in which successive whorls partially wrap around preceding whorls. *E,* the belemnite *Acrocoelites* (Jurassic, United Kingdom), side view; note the faint and shallow lateral groove close to the apex of the calicitic guard—unlike ammonite shells, the guards of belemnites are distinctly unsculptured. Scale bars represent 10 millimeters; all specimens whitened with ammonium chloride sublimate. *A,* University of the West Indies Geology Museum 36; *B,* University of the West Indies Geology Museum 585; *C,* author's collection; *D,* University of the West Indies Geology Museum 674; *E,* University of the West Indies Geology Museum 636a.

Orthocones lacked complex shell sculpturing, but exceptionally preserved Paleozoic specimens retain complex color patterns on half the shell only (Figure 2D, E). This coloration has been interpreted as serving as camouflage. The stripes would break up the outline of the shell when a predator looked down; if the predator were looking up from below, the shell would appear plain colored (Kobluk and Mapes 1989). Similar color patterns are known in some modern fish. Such markings would be apparent only if they were external; this is regarded as good evidence that in such taxa the conch was ectocochlear. Additional evidence is given by cells encrusted with oriented patterns of epizoans that attached themselves to the nautiloids during life (Baird et al. 1989). Such an association could not have occurred if the conch were internal. Modern *Nautilus* is known to be encrusted during life by a diversity of epizoans (Landman et al. 1987).

Modern *Nautilus* has many suckerless tentacles and two pairs of gills (unlike the single pair typical of coleoids). Analysis of the stable swimming orientation of living *Nautilus,* with its center of gravity situated beneath the center of buoyancy, enabled researchers to determine the probable swimming orientations of the extinct ammonites.

Subclass Ammonoidea

Superficially, ammonoids are similar in appearance to coiled nautiloids. The ammonoids first appeared in the Devonian and became extinct at the end of the Cretaceous. Mesozoic ammonoids are called "ammonites," a term that presumably originated in the eighteenth century, when all planispirally coiled forms were included in the genus *Ammonites* (Donovan 1994). Ammonoids generally have a coiled shell reminiscent of that of nautiloids, but some Mesozoic species became somewhat uncoiled (heteromorphic). Table 1 outlines the differences in morphology between ammonoids and nautiloids.

The complexity of the ammonite suture probably was related to shell strength and hence potential diving ability (Clarkson 1993). Devonian and Carboniferous ammonoids had a distinctive zigzag suture (Figure 3A), but by the Mesozoic the suture had become highly complex (Figures 1C, 3B). A strongly corrugated suture would provide more support than a simple suture. Such strength may have been of particular importance in ammonoids, because they had a relatively thinner shell than nautiloids (Table 1). Without strengthening, the thin shell would have limited diving capability since it would tend to collapse under pressure. Shell shape also played a role. A strongly rounded shell is better adapted to withstand higher pressures; therefore, an animal with a rounded shell could dive deeper than animals with a flattened conch. However, more flattened conchs are better adapted for rapid locomotion (presumably living in a higher-energy environment) than thicker conchs (suited to a low-energy environment), even within one species (Jacobs et al. 1994).

There are alternative explanations for the complexity of the ammonite suture. It may have been related to muscular attachment of the body to the septum in successive body chambers (Henderson 1984). Muscles attach more securely to a complex,

Table 1.	
Diagnostic differences between nautiloids and ammonoids.	
NAUTILOIDS (Figure 1A)	*AMMONOIDS*
Septa concave forward	Septa convex forward (Figure 1B)
Siphuncle central	Siphuncle ventral (Figure 1B) (dorsal in one Devonian group)
Septal necks point away from the aperture	Septal necks point toward the aperture
Simple suture	Complex suture (Figures 1C, 3A, 3B)
Weak sculpture	Strong sculpture (Figure 3C, 3D)
Thick shell wall	Thinner shell wall

rather than a smooth, surface, so the animal would be less likely to be torn loose from the shell by a predator. Both explanations are plausible and both may be true.

Wing-shaped structures called "aptychi" are interpreted as part of the lower jaw apparatus of ammonoids and nautiloids. In ammonoids, aptychi could act also as an operculum (aperture cover) if the cephalopod withdrew inside the shell (Lehmann and Kulicki 1990). Unlike the argonitic conch, aptychi are calcitic, giving them a higher potential for preservation. Although aptychi are commonly found separated from the conch, rare specimens are preserved inside the body chamber, sometimes even in association with the radula (rasping mouthparts) (Tanabe and Mapes 1995).

Unlike the generally smooth conchs of nautiloids, the external sculpture of ammonoids takes the form of growth lines, ribs (Figure 3A, C, D), and features of the venter (that is, the "edge" of the coil) such as keels and grooves. As planispiral ammonoids and nautiloids coil, the new shell whorl more or less encloses the previous whorls. Conchs in which each successive whorl entirely conceals earlier ones are termed "involute" (Figure 3A); those in which all previous whorls are still visible are called "evolute" (Figure 3C).

The heteromorphic ammonites include aberrant forms that are uncoiled to a greater or lesser degree (Figure 1C), including many bizarre forms. Heteromorphs are known best from the Cretaceous but also occur in the Triassic and Jurassic (Clarkson 1993). Although formerly regarded as bizarre evolutionary experiments that indicated some sort of genetic deterioration, a recent functional analysis of heteromorph swimming orientations has shown that they represent adaptations for maintaining a particular stable attitude when the animal moves through the water (Trueman 1941). This attitude that may change during ontogeny, presumably in response to the changing ecology of the species during various phases of the life cycle (Okamoto 1988).

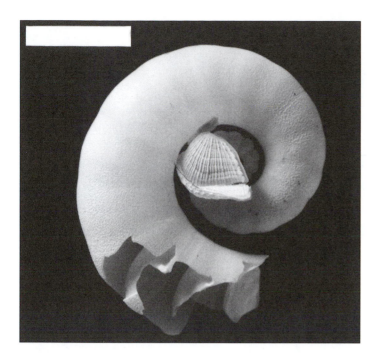

Figure 4. Shell of the Recent coleoid *Spirula spirula* (Linné) encrusted by the goose barnacle *Lepas anatifera* Linné. Encrustation of the shell of *S. spirula* must have occurred postmortem, as the shell is internal in life. This suggests that fossil cephalopods with external shells, such as nautiloids and ammonoids, that preserve encrusters could have been infested either pre- or postmortem, as shells often must have continued to float following death. Scale bar represents 5 millimeters. After Donovan (1989).

Examination of growth series and populations of ammonites from fossilized sea beds has shown that in many cases what researchers once believed to be separate species are actually the female and male of the same species (sexual dimorphism). One type of shell, the macroconch, is always much larger than the other, the microconch. The macroconch generally grew one additional complete shell whorl compared to the smaller microconch. In some species the microconch modified its aperture by growing either a single ventral process called a "rostrum" or two lateral processes called "lappets." Scholars theorize that these structures served to steady the animal during copulation. This suggests that the microconch is male. Growth lines indicate that lappets and rostra were only developed by the microconch during the terminal stage of growth, that is, they were not present before the shell reached (sexual) maturity.

Ammonoids are particularly valuable tools in biostratigraphy. These animals evolved rapidly, were widely distributed, are locally common, and are morphologically distinct (Clarkson 1993). Taxa that are useful in defining rock units (and time intervals) include the carboniferous goniatites, with their distinctive suture (Figure 3A) and the Mesozoic ammonites. The ammonoids reached their acme in the Mesozoic, and an "average" ammonite biozone had a duration of less than one million years.

Subclass Coleoidea

The Subclass Coleoidea includes all extant cephalopods—except for the *Nautilus*—such as squids, octopuses, cuttlefishes, and argonauts. The coleoid shell either is internal, such as in extant *Spirula spirula* (Linné) (Figure 4) or has been lost completely, as in octopuses. Squids still have a weak non-mineralized shell called a "pen." Although rare fossils of soft-bodied coleoids are known (Stürmer 1985), their ancient record is based mainly upon the elongate, cigar-shaped, hard parts of Mesozoic squidlike organisms called "belemnites." The earliest belemnites are from Carboniferous (or possibly Devonian) times, but they are most abundant in many Jurassic and Cretaceous deposits.

The belemnite shell consists of three parts (Clarkson 1993). The guard (Figure 3E) is a large, tapering, bulletlike structure at the rear of the animal. It is composed of radiating calcite crystals; at the front end is a conical indentation called the "alveolus cavity." The guard presumably functioned as a counterbalance weight of some kind (similar to cameral deposits) to enable a horizontal swimming attitude. It is the guard that is commonly preserved. Inside the alveolus cavity is the "phragmocone." It is an aragonitic, septate structure with a ventral siphuncle. Extending anteriorly from the dorsal margin of the guard is a tonguelike structure called the pro-ostracum. Its function is unclear. Rare fossils that show belemnite soft tissues indicate that these animals had eight arms, each bearing hooks.

Diversity, Evolution, and Evolutionary Relationships

The nautiloids' most probable ancestor is a septate monoplacophoran mollusc (Yochelson et al. 1973). Nautiloids showed periods of rapid speciation during the Late Cambrian and the Ordovician, their peak of diversity (Holland 1987). The Early Cambrian nautiloids were small, averaging five to six centimeters with a maximum of about ten centimeters. They had smooth, cyrtoconic conchs with closely spaced septa and chambers devoid of cameral deposits. In contrast, some Ordovician orthocones and cyrtocones reached gigantic proportions—exceptional shells reached a total length approaching 9 meters (Holland 1987). Straight, curved, and coiled nautiloids date from the Paleozoic. Only planispirally coiled forms of the order Nautilida survived into the Mesozoic and Cenozoic.

Ammonoids evolved in the Early Devonian, apparently from the bactritoids, a group of nautiloid-like orthocones. Although not coiled, the bactritoids were otherwise strongly ammonoid-like, with a marginal siphuncle, no cameral deposits, and a bulb-shaped protoconch (Clarkson 1993). The ammonoids show a "boom or bust" pattern of evolution throughout their time range. Characteristically, only one or a few lineages survive major extinction events, and then these survivors undergo major radiations. This pattern was repeated from the Devonian to the Cretaceous, but the group apparently failed to survive mass extinction at the end of the Cretaceous. However, a new theory by Lewy (1996) has proposed that the extant argonauts, in which the mature female secretes an egg chamber with a shape similar to an ammonite shell, may be "nude ammonites" that survived to the present.

Belemnite guards apart, coleoids have a poor fossil record. Like the ammonoids, the coleoids first appeared in the Early Devonian, presumably having evolved from an endocochlear nautiloid ancestor. The earliest squid is Early Devonian, octopods date from the Mesozoic, and the ammonite-like egg cases of argonauts date from the Oligocene and later (Holland 1988). Although generally considered to have become extinct at the same time as the ammonoids, there have been reports of belemnites found in Paleogene deposits.

STEPHEN K. DONOVAN

Works Cited

Ager, D.V. 1963. *Principles of Paleoecology.* New York: McGraw-Hill.

Baird, G.C., C.E. Brett, and R.C. Frey. 1989. "Hitchhiking" epizoans on orthoconic nautiloids: Preliminary review of the evidence and its implications. *Senckenbergiana Lethaea* 69:439–65.

Barnes, R.D. 1980. *Invertebrate Zoology.* 4th ed., Philadelphia: Saunders.

Chen, J., and C. Teichert. 1983. Cambrian cephalopods. *Geology* 11:647–50.

Clarkson, E.N.K. 1993. *Invertebrate Palaeontology and Evolution.* 3rd ed., London and New York: Chapman and Hall.

Donovan, S.K. 1989. Taphonomic significance of the encrustation of the dead shell of Recent *Spirula spirula* (Linné) (Cephalopoda: Coleoidea) by *Lepas anatifera* Linné (Cirripedia: Thoracia). *Journal of Paleontology* 63:698–702.

———. 1994. History of classification of Mesozoic ammonites. *Journal of the Geological Society, London* 151:1035–40.

Flower, R.H. 1957. Nautiloids of the Paleozoic. *In* H.S. Ladd (ed.), *Treatise on Marine Ecology and Paleoecology.* Vol. 2, *Paleoecology.* Geological Society of America Memoir, 67. New York: Geological Society of America.

Henderson, R.A. 1984. A muscle attachment proposal for septal function in Mesozoic ammonites. *Palaeontology* 27:461–86.

Holland, C.H. 1987. The nautiloid cephalopods: A strange success. *Journal of the Geological Society, London* 144:1–15.

———. 1988. The paper nautilus. *New Mexico Bureau of Mines and Mineral Resources Memoir* 44:109–14.

Jacobs, D.K., N.H. Landman, and J.A. Chamberlain. 1994. Ammonite shell shape covaries with facies and hydrodynamics: Iterative evolution as a response to changes in basinal environment. *Geology* 22:905–8.

Kobluk, D.R., and R.H. Mapes. 1989. The fossil record, function, and possible origins of shell color patterns in Paleozoic marine invertebrates. *Palaios* 4:63–85.

Landman, N.H., W.B. Saunders, J.E. Winston, and P.J. Harries. 1987. Incidence and kinds of epizoans on the shells of live Nautilus. *In* W.B. Saunders and N.H. Landman (eds.), *Nautilus.* New York: Plenum.

Lehmann, U., and C. Kulicki. 1990. Double function of aptychi (Ammonoidea) as jaw elements and opercula. *Lethaia* 23:325–31.

Lewy, Z. 1996. Octopods: Nude ammonoids that survived the Cretaceous-Tertiary boundary mass extinction. *Geology* 24:627–30.

Okamoto, T. 1988. Changes in life orientation during the ontogeny of some heteromorph ammonoids. *Palaeontology* 31:281–94.

Stürmer, W. 1970. Soft parts of cephalopods and trilobites: Some surprising results of X-ray examinations of Devonian slates. *Science* 170:1300–2.

———. 1985. A small coleoid cephalopod with soft parts from the Lower Devonian discovered using radiography. *Nature* 318:53.

Tanabe, K., and R.H. Mapes. 1995. Jaws and radula of the Carboniferous ammonoid Cravenoceras. *Journal of Paleontology* 69:703–7.

Teichert, C. 1964. Morphology of hard parts. *In* R.C. Moore (ed.), *Treatise on Invertebrate Paleontology.* Part K, *Mollusca.* Boulder, Colorado: Geological Society of America; Lawrence, Kansas: University of Kansas Press.

Trueman, A.E. 1941. The ammonite body-chamber, with special reference to the buoyancy and mode of life of the living ammonite. *Quarterly Journal of the Geological Society, London* 96:339–83.

Yochelson, E.L., R.H. Flower, and G.F. Webers. 1973. The bearing of the new later Cambrian monoplacophoran genus Knightoconus upon the origin of the *Cephalopoda. Lethaia* 6:275–310.

Further Reading

House, M.R., and J.R. Senior (eds.). 1980. *The Ammonoidea: The Evolution, Classification, Mode of Life and Geological Usefulness of a Major Fossil Group.* Systematics Association Special Volume, 18. New York and London: Academic Press.

Kennedy, W.J., and W.A. Cobban. 1976. *Aspects of Ammonite Biology, Biogeography and Biostratigraphy.* Special Papers in Palaeontology, 17. London: Paleontological Association.

Larson, N.L., S.D. Jorgensen, R.A. Farrar, and P.L. Larson. 1997. *Ammonites and Other Cephalopods of the Pierre Seaway: An Identification Guide.* Tucson, Arizona: Geoscience; Missoula, Montana: Mountain.

Moore, R.C. (ed.). 1957. *Treatise on Invertebrate Paleontology.* Part L, *Mollusca 4: Cephalopoda—Ammonoidea.* Boulder, Colorado: Geological Society of America; Lawrence, Kansas: University of Kansas Press.

———. 1964. *Treatise on Invertebrate Paleontology.* Part K, *Mollusca 3: Cephalopoda—General Features—Endoceratoidea—Actinoceratoidea—Nautiloidea—Bactritoidea.* Boulder, Colorado: Geological Society of America; Lawrence, Kansas: University of Kansas Press.

CERATOPSIANS

The Ceratopsia are a diverse clade of ornithischian (bird-hipped) dinosaurs that include both bipedal and quadrupedal animals and range in size from a large turkey to a small elephant. (A "clade" is a group of organisms descended from a common ancestor.) Ceratopsians first appear in the Early Cretaceous and continued to the very end of the Age of Dinosaurs. Members of this group have been found throughout much of North America and Asia, but so far they appear to be absent in Europe and the Southern Hemisphere. Although this amazing group of herbivores often is called the "horned dinosaurs," this nickname is a bit of a misnomer. While many ceratopsians displayed a dizzying array of head ornamentation, other ceratopsians lacked both horns and the large, bony neck frill that characterized larger members of the group.

Ceratopsians can be broken down into three basic groups: *Psittacosaurus,* a collection of taxa called protoceratopsians, and a group of large taxa (groups; singular, taxon) called the Ceratopsidae. Nonetheless, despite the great range in size, ornamentation, and stance among ceratopsians, all members possess certain unique characteristics found in no other dinosaur group. These characteristics include a narrow, parrotlike beak (with its upper portion formed by a unique bone called a "rostral"), a deep face, and cheeks that flare out to the side.

Psittacosaurus

This small ceratopsian, sometimes called the "parrot-beaked dinosaur," was less than six feet in total length. *Psittacosaurus* is well represented in the fossil record, and entire skulls and skeletons of this dinosaur have been found in Lower Cretaceous sediments in Mongolia and China. The skull of *Psittacosaurus* has the requisite rostral bone forming the upper part of its toothless beak, a deep face with high set nostrils, and the flared cheeks of all ceratopsians but lacks any development of horns. It does, however, have a very short neck frill (or shield) that is more like a short shelf extending off the back of its skull. *Psittacosaurus* probably walked and ran upright on its hind legs (its front legs were a little over half as long as its hind legs).

The dozens of *Psittacosaurus* specimens that have been found include animals of all ages, from babies to full grown adults. Juvenile *Psittacosaurus* specimens are among the tiniest dinosaurs ever found, some skulls being no larger than the size of a quarter (an adult skull is about the size of a large grapefruit).

In two specimens of *Psittacosaurus,* large accumulations of gastroliths, or "stomach stones," were found preserved within their ribcages. Although many dinosaurs have been hypothesized to have had gastroliths, *Psittacosaurus* is one of very few dinosaurs that exhibit the proof. *Psittacosaurus* likely swallowed small stones, which then were retained in their stomach to help pulverize plant material for easier and more efficient digestion. This unusual system is called a "gastric mill." Although gastric mills may seem rather fantastic, some modern crocodilians and birds also employ this manner of digestion (crocodilians and birds are the closest living relatives of dinosaurs).

Protoceratopsians

The protoceratopsians are a varied group of small to moderate-sized ceratopsians that include both bipedal and quadrupedal forms, and some that may have walked on both two and four legs. Protoceratopsians, found in both North America (United States and Canada) and Asia (China and Mongolia), come from Lower to Upper Cretaceous sediments. Known protoceratopsian taxa include *Bagaceratops, Breviceratops, Chaoyangosaurus, Leptoceratops, Microceratops, Montanoceratops, Protoceratops,* and *Udanoceratops.*

The amount of skull ornamentation varies greatly among protoceratopsians. Some taxa, such as *Leptoceratops,* have very short neck frills and lack horns, while others, such as *Protoceratops,* have large, expansive neck frills but small bumps over the nose and eyes instead of horns.

When the characteristics of these protoceratopsian taxa are examined, they appear to form a graded series between *Psittacosaurus* and the Ceratopsidae. Moving up the grade, protoceratopsians tend to increase in size, switch from bipedal to quadrupedal locomotion, increase the size of the neck shield from a short shelf to a long and expansive frill, and begin to ornament their skulls with paired horns over the eyes and a single horn over the nose. For instance, the most primitive of the protoceratopsians, *Chaoyangosaurus,* looks very much like *Psittacosaurus,* while one of the most advanced protoceratopsians, *Montanoceratops,* looks more like a small ceratopsid.

Most protoceratopsians are rare, and only a few specimens of each have been found. For instance, *Montanoceratops* is known from only two partial skeletons. Fortunately, this is not the case for all protoceratopsians. More than 100 skulls and skeletons of *Protoceratops,* ranging from small babies to large adults, have been found in the Gobi Desert of Mongolia and China over the past 70 years. The adult body size is about that of a large collie dog. This wonderful series of skeletons of all ages, called an "ontogenetic series," shows two things: that the horny protuberances and large frill only appear when the animal became a "teenager," and that once these ornamentations begin to appear, they do so in two different styles. These two styles have been interpreted as differentiations between male and female animals.

An analogy to this interpretation is to think of the changes deer undergo as they mature. All fawns look alike, whether they are male or female, just as all small *Protoceratops* specimens look alike. Then, as fawns begin to reach sexual maturity, the males sprout antlers and grow larger, while the females stay smaller and never grow antlers. In *Protoceratops,* both sexes appear to have grown large frills, but one sex grew larger and developed larger protuberances over the nose and eyes. Some scholars believe this larger form represents the male, although this cannot be confirmed.

For many years, large, oblong fossil eggs found in the Gobi Desert were attributed to *Protoceratops*. Bones of a small predator were sometimes found with the eggs. This predator was thought to be preying on the *Protoceratops* eggs, and was named *Oviraptor*, or "egg thief." Recently, however, some of these "*Protoceratops*" eggs were discovered with intact fossil embryos—embryos not of *Protoceratops*, but of *Oviraptor*. *Oviraptor* was not the egg thief after all, but the egg layer. *Protoceratops* eggs remain unknown.

Ceratopsids

The large, quadrupedal, tanklike ceratopsids are what most people think of when they hear the term "horned dinosaurs." Unlike the other groups of ceratopsians, ceratopsids are found only in Late Cretaceous age sediments in Canada and the United States. Some ceratopsids are among the very last of the dinosaurs, and the remains of *Triceratops* can be found right up to the Cretaceous-Tertiary boundary (the rock layer that marks the transition between the two periods) in Montana. While some ceratopsids were about the size of a cow, others reached the size of a small elephant.

Ceratopsids can be divided into two groups: the Chasmosaurinae and the Centrosaurinae. Chasmosaurines include *Chasmosaurus, Pentaceratops, Arrhinoceratops, Anchiceratops, Torosaurus, Diceratops,* and *Triceratops*. Centrosaurines are comprised of *Achelousaurus, Centrosaurus, Einiosaurus, Pachyrhinosaurus,* and *Styracosaurus*. All ceratopsids have large, expansive neck frills and some development of horns over the eyes (called "orbital" or "brow" horns) and nose, although exactly how these ornaments are formed differ between the two groups. For instance, chasmosaurines tend to have small nasal horns, large orbital horns, and complex bones in the nasal opening. Centrosaurines tend toward large nasal horns, short orbital horns, and simple nasal openings. Some unusual centrosaurines *(Pachyrhinosaurus, Achelousaurus)* replace their horns with thick, gnarly, "pachyostotic" bone. Another centrosaurine, *Centrosaurus,* develops curved hooks and banana-shaped growths on the back margin of their frill. The centrosaurines *Styracosaurus, Einiosaurus,* and *Achelousaurus* grow long, pointed spikes from the back of their frill.

Other centrosaurines have been named, including *Avaceratops, Brachyceratops,* and *Monoclonius*. However, these taxa all represent juvenile or subadult animals, and some questions exist over whether or not they are valid taxa. Many juvenile-through-adult centrosaurines have been found that seem to exhibit similar growth patterns to those of *Protoceratops*. In other words, juvenile centrosaurines all seem to look very much alike. It is only when they reach adulthood and start to develop their horns and spikes that they become more differentiated. Time, and more specimens, will allow us to test the hypothesis that *Avaceratops, Brachyceratops,* and *Monoclonius* are unique taxa.

There has been much speculation over the use of the horns and frills of ceratopsians, particularly among the large ceratopsids. For a long time, it was hypothesized that the large frill protected the animal's neck from the killing bite of a predator, while the long, spikelike horns were used as defensive weapons. (Picture *Triceratops* defending itself against the large carnivore *Tyrannosaurus*.) However, studies of modern horned herbivores, such as sheep, cows, and goats, show a different activity pattern. Although these animals will use their horns for defense, they primarily use them as display features among themselves to fight for mates, territory, and food resources. (Imagine a large *Triceratops* fighting not with *Tyrannosaurus,* but with another *Triceratops* for dominance over a territory.) In fact, specimens of some ceratopsids have what appear to be healed puncture wounds on their faces and frill, which may attest to fights between ceratopsids, rather than with predators.

Beside the highly developed orbital and nose horns, ceratopsids have a number of other features that are not found in other ceratopsians. These features include cheek teeth with two roots (rather than one), unique changes in the pelvic bones, and tightly packed cheek teeth that form a dental battery. This dental battery is made up of dozens of teeth packed closely together to form a single, continuous surface. These surfaces are nearly vertical so that as the jaws closed, the upper and lower teeth sheared past each other like a scissors. This made a very effective bite for slicing off and chopping up vegetation. The big, barrel-shaped ribcage of ceratopsids also attests to their vegetarian habits, providing plenty of gut space for fermenting and digesting the vegetation, similar to the structure of the modern cow.

CATHERINE A. FORSTER

See also Ornamentation: Vertebrates; Teeth: Evolution of Complex Teeth

Further Reading

Dodson, P. 1996. *The Horned Dinosaurs*. Princeton, New Jersey: Princeton University Press.
———. 1997. Neoceratopsia. *In* P.J. Currie and K. Padian (eds.), *Encyclopedia of Dinosaurs*. San Diego, California: Academic Press.
Dodson, P., and P.J. Currie. 1990. Neoceratopsia. *In* D.B. Weishampel, P. Dodson, and H. Osmolska (eds.), *The Dinosauria*. Berkeley: University of California Press.
Forster, C.A., and P.C. Sereno. 1997. Marginocephalians. *In* J.O. Farlow and M.K. Brett-Surman (eds.), *The Complete Dinosaur*. Bloomington: Indiana University Press.

CETACEANS

See Whales

CHELICERATES

Second only to the insects and their kin in diversity, the Chelicerata are both an ancient and highly successful class of arthropods. Their fossil record shows both a long evolutionary history and a great diversity of form, especially in regard to their colonization of the land.

Morphology

When only living forms are considered, chelicerates are easy to define. Chelicerates have a body divided into two major divisions, the prosoma and opisthosoma. The prosoma is covered by a dorsal shield, or carapace. While there is evidence that chelicerates evolved from an ancestor with biramous (double-branched) appendages, virtually all living chelicerates have uniramous (single-branched) appendages. Six pairs are found on the prosoma, surrounding the mouth; there are never antennae. The first pair are feeding appendages, usually clawed, known as chelicerae. The chelicerae may be used to crush and tear prey, or may be modified into fangs (as in the true spiders) or piercing organs (as in ticks and many mites). The second pair of appendages, the pedipalps, may be leglike, enlarged and clawed (as in scorpions), or used as sexual organs (as in the true spiders) (Figures 1, 2).

In aquatic chelicerates, the opisthosoma bears platelike appendages instead of walking legs. These fit together like pages in a book to form a book gill (Figure 2). Many land-living forms have internal chambers that hold similar page-like breathing organs; these book lungs open to the outside through small holes or slits, called spiracles. There is some debate over whether the book lung and the book gill are homologous (derived from the same structure in a common ancestor). Other land chelicerates breathe through a system of tracheae, or internal tubes, a feature also found in the insects and representing convergent evolution.

This neat picture becomes muddled when the early fossil record is taken into account. In the Cambrian period, the marine biota included many arthropods that do not fit precisely into any living group. Best known from the famous Burgess Shale, in the Middle Cambrian rocks of British Columbia (Briggs et al. 1994), such "weird wonder" arthropods are also known from Lower Cambrian sites in China and Poland and Middle Cambrian sites in Utah, to name a few. The Burgess Shale arthropod *Sanctacaris uncata* has been described as the first chelicerate, with six pairs of walking legs on the prosoma (Briggs and Collins 1988; Figure 3). It lacks claws, however, and its identity as a true chelicerate has been questioned (e.g., Delle Cave and Simonetta 1991). Nevertheless, *Sanctacaris* and some other Cambrian arthropods do seem to be closer to chelicerates than to any other major group, although they lack features of living chelicerates or have features not found in living chelicerates. These are provisionally classed in a loosely defined grouping, informally called the "Arachnomorpha." Cambrian "arachnomorphs" include *Sidneyia, Sanctacaris, Burgessia,* and *Yohoia* from the Burgess Shale, and *Fuxianhuia* from China, to name just a few (Wills et al. 1994; Waggoner 1996; Figures 3, 4, 5).

The eighteenth-century systematist Carolus Linnaeus grouped the chelicerates in the class Insecta, together with practically all other wingless arthropods. Some biologists were still classifying arachnids with the insects well into the nineteenth century (e.g., Packard 1869). Jean-Baptiste de Monet de Lamarck, in 1801, was the first to define the arachnids as a class separate from the insects, although he originally placed all other wingless arthropods into his "Arachnidae." Later biologists altered and redefined Lamarck's class many times over the next century; the Chelicerata finally was established in 1901. Most biologists now place the chelicerates closest to the trilobites out of all major arthropod groups (Wills et al. 1994; Waggoner 1996; Figure 6).

Major Groups of Chelicerates

Xiphosurans

The four living species of horseshoe crab are the only living members of a very ancient order of chelicerates, the Xiphosura. The common name "horseshoe crab" is misleading: These animals once were classified with the true crabs, but in 1881 the English zoologist E. Ray Lankester showed conclusively that horseshoe crabs were more closely related to arachnids than to crustaceans (Lankester 1881).

The group gets the name Xiphosura (Greek, "sword-tail") from the long, pointed telson, a specialized terminal segment of the body. The prosoma is covered by a large, semicircular carapace, on which there are both compound eyes on the sides and simple eyes on the midline (although some fossil forms were blind). The opisthosoma also is covered by a single shield in living horseshoe crabs, but some fossil forms had a segmented opisthosoma; most of these are classified in the suborder Synziphosurina (Figure 6).

Today, one horseshoe crab species (*Limulus polyphemus;* Figures 1, 2) lives along the Atlantic coast of North America, from Maine to the eastern Gulf of Mexico and the Yucatán Peninsula. The other three species overlap from southern Japan, along the coast of southeast Asia as far west as India, and eastward to the Philippines, Malaysia, and much of Indonesia (Sekiguchi 1988). Living xiphosurans are found in coastal environments at depths of several tens of meters. Most are fully marine, but a few populations have adapted to brackish water. They feed on small invertebrates such as mollusks and segmented worms, although algae also may be eaten occasionally (Shuster 1982). At mating time, which in temperate waters falls in the summer, horseshoe crabs swarm on sandy beaches near the high-tide line, laying clusters of eggs in the sand. The eggs hatch out free-swimming "trilobite larvae," which as their name suggests superficially resemble trilobites. While no horseshoe crab species is officially endangered yet, habitat destruction, disease, and commercial harvesting for bait, fertilizer, and biomedical use have caused concern for the future of these animals.

Xiphosurans are classic "living fossils"; the group goes back at least to the Ordovician, and some possible Cambrian representatives have been described. Some early xiphosurans resemble eurypterids

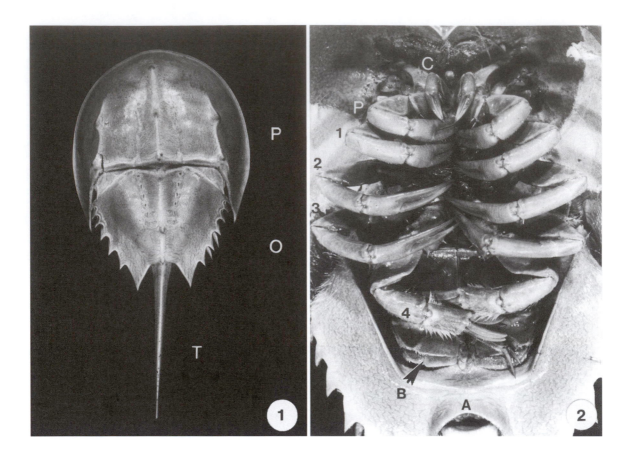

Figure 1. Dorsal view of the American horseshoe crab, *Limulus polyphemus*, showing typical chelicerate features. *O*, opisthosoma; *P*, prosoma; *T*, telson. **Figure 2.** Close-up ventral view of the horseshoe crab. *A*, anus; *B*, book gills; *C*, chelicera; *P*, pedipalps.

(see below) in some respects, and the two probably had a common ancestor in the Cambrian. Essentially modern forms were present by the Pennsylvanian (Bergström 1975; Figure 8). The group was once more diverse, and it inhabited brackish and fresh waters as well as the oceans. At least some Paleozoic horseshoe crabs may have spent some time out of the water (Fisher 1979).

Eurypterids

The extinct eurypterids bear the common name "sea scorpions," which is partly misleading: most eurypterids lived in brackish or fresh water, and some have walked on land, at least for short periods (Størmer et al. 1955; Shear 1990). Eurypterids first appeared in the Early Ordovician. Most numerous and diverse in the Silurian and Devonian, they survived into the Early Permian; over 60 genera are known (Tollerton 1989; Figure 9). They included the largest arthropod of all time, a species of *Pterygotus* that reached three meters in length. Like xiphosurans, eurypterids originally were classified as crustaceans.

Also like xiphosurans, eurypterids bore both compound and simple eyes. The long opisthosoma bore 12 segments plus a telson, which could be long and slender or flat and paddlelike in different species. The opisthosoma was divided into a wider preabdomen of seven segments and a narrower postabdomen. Very typical of euryp-

terids is a paddlelike sixth appendage used in swimming, from which the group was named (Greek, "broad-wing"). Some eurypterids were excellent swimmers; the giant *Pterygotus,* for example, was probably a swimming form, with its large paddlelike sixth appendage, tail fin–like telson, and streamlined body. *Pterygotus* and other eurypterids with large claws were able to seize and crush large prey with hard skeletons—possibly including armored fish. Many eurypterids, however, had much smaller claws (Figure 10), and probably preyed on small invertebrates, such as their living kin the horseshoe crabs.

Arachnids

All living chelicerates, except for the horseshoe crabs, are members of the Arachnida. This is a highly diverse group, with roughly 70,000 living species known. Unfortunately, fossil arachnids are generally rare, and there are many large gaps in our knowledge of the group; few arachnids have been found from the entire Mesozoic, for instance. We do know that arachnids were among the first land animals. The later Paleozoic saw both the origin of most modern arachnid groups and the rise and fall of several short-lived, unusual arachnid groups.

Arachnids bear only simple eyes, with the exception of many early scorpions, which had compound eyes like their eurypterid kin. The earliest arachnids were aquatic, but members of the

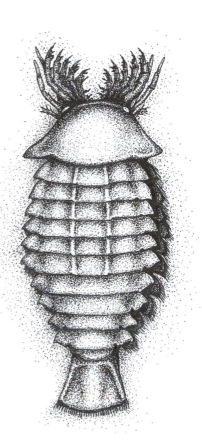
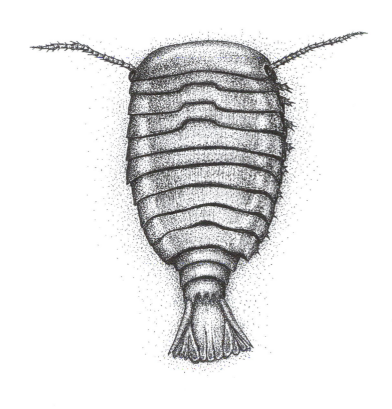

Figure 3. (Left) The earliest probable chelicerate currently known, *Sanctacaris uncata*. Middle Cambrian; Burgess Shale, British Columbia. Illustration by Lonny Stark. **Figure 4.** (Right) An "arachnomorph," *Sidneyia inexpectans*. Middle Cambrian; Burgess Shale, British Columbia. Illustration by Lonny Stark.

group made the transition to land very early. Today, with the exception of a number of mites and a very few others that have returned to the water, all arachnids live on land. Virtually all arachnids feed on liquids, whether they prey on other animals or suck blood or plant juices: predatory arachnids generally tear their prey up, secrete digestive enzymes directly onto their prey, and feed on the liquefied tissues.

Scorpions. True scorpions (Scorpiones) almost certainly are descended from a eurypterid ancestor or else share a close common ancestor with the eurypterids. It is possible that they had a separate evolutionary origin from the rest of the arachnids (Delle Cave and Simonetta 1991); if so, they will have to be classified outside the Arachnida. About 1,500 scorpion species exist today. Like eurypterids, scorpions have an opisthosoma divided into two parts: a thick mesosoma of seven segments and a slender, elongated metasoma, or tail, with five segments. Like eurypterids, scorpions have a telson; unlike eurypterids, the telson is tipped with a poisonous sting, or aculeus. On the underside of a scorpion, just behind the legs, is a pair of comb-shaped organs, or pectines, which are thought to sense vibration and ground texture and help the scorpion locate its prey. Scorpions are unique among arachnids in giving birth to live young, which actually are nourished during development within

the mother's body. After giving birth, the mother carries the young scorpions on her back at least until their first molt, and in some species the offspring live in the mother's burrow for several months.

Found on all continents except Antarctica, scorpions are most diverse in desert areas and are not found above about 50 to 55 degrees north or south latitude. The southern third of Baja California is the world's richest region in scorpion species, and the Mojave and Sonora Deserts are also rich in scorpions. Scorpions are able to tolerate desert environments in part because of their burrowing habit, watertight cuticle, low metabolic rate, and nocturnal habits. Scorpions also are found in forests and grasslands, and a few even are found in the marine intertidal zone (Polis 1990).

Scorpions first appeared in the Middle Silurian, about 450 million years ago. Almost all Paleozoic scorpion species were aquatic, breathing with gills inside specialized gill chambers on the opisthosoma. These aquatic scorpions included some giants: the Devonian species *Praearcturus gigas* and *Brontoscorpio anglicus* approached one meter in length. Until recently, only two Paleozoic scorpions with book lungs were known, both from the Carboniferous (Kjellesvig-Waering 1986). Very recently, however, remains of a Lower Devonian scorpion with well-preserved book lungs have been found in Canada, suggesting that land scorpions

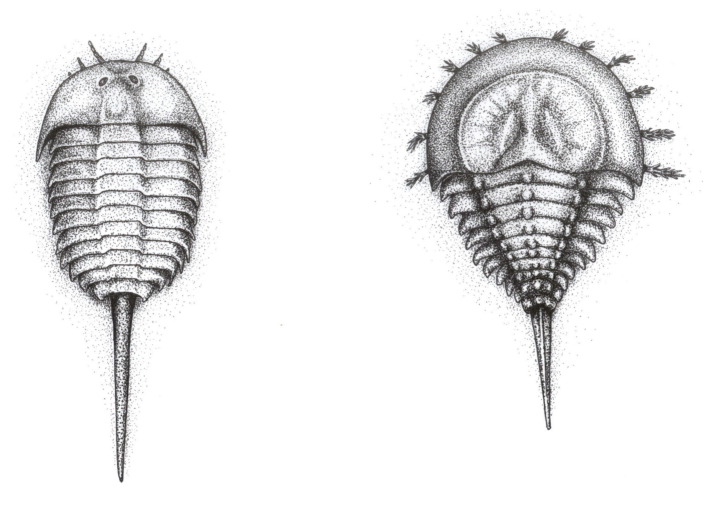

Figure 5. (Left) An aglaspid, *Aglaspis spinifer.* Upper Cambrian; Richland County, Wisconsin. Illustration by Lonny Stark. **Figure 6.** (Right) A synziphosuran, *Weinbergina opitzi,* unusual in having six appendage pairs on the prosoma in addition to the chelicerae. Lower Devonian; Hunsrückscheifer, Germany. Illustration by Lonny Stark.

are older than was thought (Shear et al. 1996). Aquatic scorpions survived at least into the Jurassic (Kjellesvig-Waering 1986), while rare Cenozoic fossil scorpions are known from amber (Figure 17) and from sediments.

Spiders and spider-like fossils. True spiders (Aranei) are the most diverse arachnid group, with about 34,000 living species. The chelicerae of true spiders are modified into fangs and equipped with poison glands. (Relatively few spiders are dangerous to humans. Only two North American species, the black widow and the brown recluse spider, are known to have caused human fatalities.) The second pair of appendages, the pedipalps, are used to handle prey; male spiders have highly modified pedipalps that they use to transfer sperm into the female. The prosoma and opisthosoma are joined by a slender pedicel, or "wasp waist." The earliest fossil spiders had a segmented opisthosoma, but this segmentation is absent in all living spiders except for a few primitive East Asian species. All spiders can produce silk from specialized glands and extrude it through appendages known as

spinnerets, although not all spin webs. Spider silk is a remarkable material: composed of proteins called fibroins, a strand of spider silk is stronger for its cross-sectional area than rubber or cellulose and is about half as strong as steel. An orb-weaving spider may produce as many as eight different kinds of silk, each produced from a different type of gland and having a different function (Foelix 1996).

The oldest known true spiders are Middle Devonian (Shear 1990), and a number of spider fossils are known from the Carboniferous. A small but growing number of fossil spiders have turned up in Mesozoic rocks (Eskov 1987; Selden 1990). Notable examples include a small tarantula-like spider from the Middle Triassic of France (Selden and Gall 1992) and Jurassic and Cretaceous relatives of living web-spinning spiders (Eskov 1987; Selden 1990). One Lower Cretaceous spider from northern Spain bore three claws on its feet, characteristic of modern spiders that walk on webs (Selden 1990). This is direct evidence for web-weaving, although the behavior is probably much older

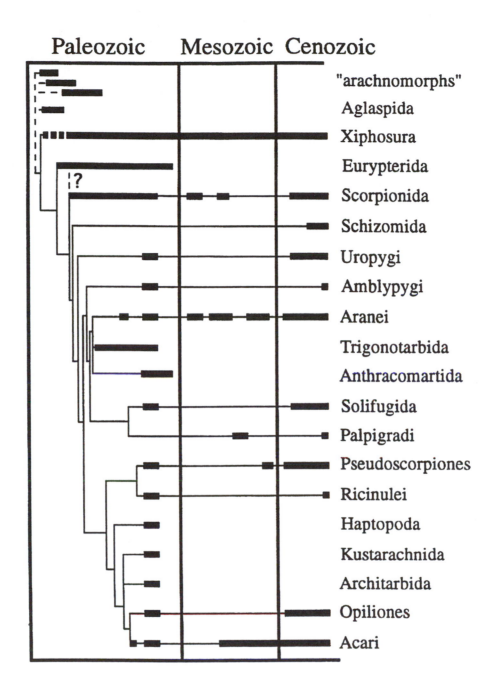

Paleozoic   Mesozoic Cenozoic

"arachnomorphs"

Aglaspida

Xiphosura

Eurypterida

Scorpionida

Schizomida

Uropygi

Amblypygi

Araneí

Trigonotarbida

Anthracomartida

Solifugida

Palpigradi

Pseudoscorpiones

Ricinulei

Haptopoda

Kustarachnida

Architarbida

Opiliones

Acari

Figure 7. Possible evolutionary tree of the chelicerates, with their temporal ranges superimposed. Dashed lines indicate questionable relationships and ranges. Based on the work of Beall and and Labandeira (1990).

(Shear and Kukalová-Peck 1990). Again, Cenozoic spiders have been documented both from amber (Figure 12) and sedimentary rock (Figure 13).

Other spiderlike arthropods, now extinct, lived on land in the Late Paleozoic. These have been divided into the Trigonotarbida and the Anthracomartida (Størmer et al. 1955), but the two groups are not greatly different and eventually may be classified

together (Shear and Kukalová-Peck 1990). Both groups were armored with a thick, sometimes spiny exoskeleton, lacked silk glands, and had a wide joint between prosoma and opisthosoma, instead of the narrow "wasp waist" typical of true spiders (Figure 19). Currently, the oldest land arachnid known is a Late Silurian trigonotarbid (Jeram et al. 1990). Trigonotarbids and anthracomartids often are considered close relatives of the spiders (e.g.,

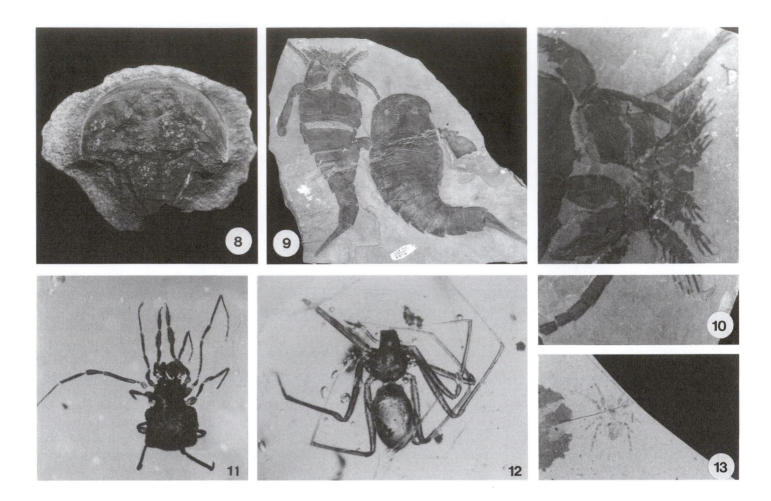

Figure 8. Xiphosuran, *Palaeolimulus* sp. Upper Pensylvanian; Mazon Creek region, Illinois. University of California Museum of Paleontology Collection, locality D-2260. **Figure 9.** Two eurypterids, *Eurypterus lacustris*. Silurian; Erie County, New York. University of California Museum of Paleontology Invertebrate Type Collection, Specimen 31472. **Figure 10.** Close-up of the underside of the head of *Eurypteris lacustris*. The chelicerae on this species are very small and not easily seen, but appendages two through six are visible. **Figure 11.** Harvestman, *Kinnula* sp. (Opiliones: Phalangodidae), preserved in amber. Oligocene; Dominican Republic. Courtesy of George O. Poinar Jr. Collection of Dominican Amber, Oregon State University. **Figure 12.** Spider, species unidentified, preserved in amber. Oligocene; Dominican Republic. Courtesy of George O. Poinar Jr. Collection of Dominican Amber, Oregon State University. **Figure 13.** Spider, species unidentified, preserved in thinly bedded sediments. Miocene; Humbolt County, Nevada. University of California Museum of Paleontology Collection.

Beall and Labandeira 1990). Shear (1990), however, suggested that trigonotarbids were close to the common ancestry of all land arachnids except scorpions.

Mites and ticks. Mites and ticks (Acari) encompass the greatest lifestyle diversity of any arachnid group. Some species of Acari are economically important pests, such as the "red spider" mites and blister mites that attack fruit crops. Others are parasites on animals: ticks, scabies mites, mange mites, and chiggers. These not only cause discomfort, they may spread bacterial diseases; ticks, for instance, are notorious as carriers of Lyme disease, Rocky Mountain spotted fever, and other human diseases. Most mites, however, are harmless, free-living forms; in fact, some mites are beneficial by preying on harmful mites or insects. Free-living mites include predators, scavengers, and feeders on bacteria, algae, plants, and fungi (Krantz 1978). Mites may be extremely abundant in soils, on plants and in plant litter, on mosses and lichens, and in fresh water. There

are even over 600 species of mites in the oceans, found from the intertidal zone to deep-sea trenches (Bartsch 1988).

About 30,000 living mite species are known, but this is probably only a small fraction of the true number. Mites have lost the sharp distinction between prosoma and opisthosoma, and the body is known as the idiosoma. A specialized projection from the head end of the mite, the gnathosoma, bears the chelicerae and pedipalps, which may be highly modified for the mite's diet. As a consequence of the evolution of small size, many mites have lost typical arachnid characters such as eyes, the heart, the respiratory system, and sometimes one or more pairs of legs (Krantz 1978).

Mites have the honor of being among the earliest land animals surviving today: the Early Devonian Rhynie Chert from Scotland contains fossil mites, together with the earliest known insect relatives and vascular plants (Shear 1990; Bernini 1991). These early mites probably were all feeders on plant litter and rot-

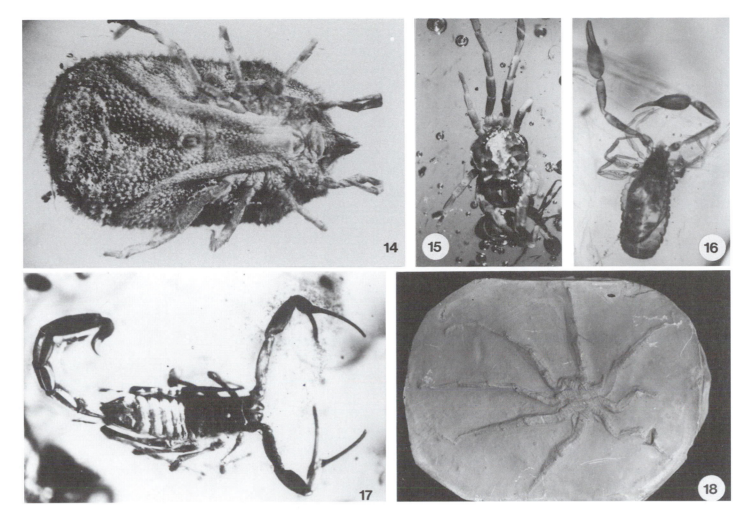

Figure 14. Soft tick, *Ornithodorus antiquus* (Acari: Argasidae), preserved in amber. Oligocene; Dominican Republic. Courtesy of George O. Poinar Jr. Collection of Dominican Amber, Oregon State University. **Figure 15.** Velvet mite (Acari: Trombidiformes) preserved in amber. Oligocene; Dominican Republic. Courtesy of George O. Poinar Jr. Collection of Dominican Amber, Oregon State University. **Figure 16.** Pseudoscorpion, species unidentified, preserved in amber. Oligocene; Dominican Republic. Courtesy of George O. Poinar Jr. Collection of Dominican Amber, Oregon State University. **Figure 17.** Scorpion (Scorpiones: Buthidae) preserved in amber. Oligocene; Dominican Republic. Courtesy of George O. Poinar Jr. Collection of Dominican Amber, Oregon State University. **Figure 18.** Pycnogonid, *Palaeopantopus maucheri*. The head end is at the top. Lower Devonian; Hunsrückscheifer, Germany. Cast in University of California Museum of Paleontology Collection; original in Bavarian State Collection, Munich, WS-2812.

ting wood (Shear and Kukalová-Peck 1990). Because of their small size, however, the Acari are rare in the rock record; most fossils have been found in Cenozoic amber (Figures 14, 15).

Other arachnids. Other living arachnids include harvestmen, daddy-longlegs, or grandfather-greybeards (Opiliones; Figure 11); false scorpions or moss scorpions (Pseudoscorpiones; Figure 16); wind scorpions or sun scorpions (Solifugida or Solpugida); tailed whip-scorpions or vinegaroons (Uropygi); tailless whip-scorpions (Amblypygi); tick spiders (Ricinulei); schizomids (Schizomida); and palpigrades or microwhip-scorpions (Palpigradi). All are extremely rare in the fossil record. Most are small and live in environments where they almost never would fossilize. Wind scorpions and whip-scorpions live today in deserts, while palpigrades, schizomids, tick spiders, pseudoscorpions and harvestmen are most common in humid environments, such as moss, leaf litter, decaying wood, moist soil, and caves. However, scattered represen-

tatives of most of these classes have been found in Pennsylvanian or even earlier deposits (Figure 7).

Finally, the remaining Paleozoic arachnid taxa include the extinct Architarbida (or Phalangiotarbida), Haptopoda, and Kustarachnida. Kustarachnids (Figure 20) and haptopods (Figure 22), known from three and one Pennsylvanian species respectively, may be close kin to the Opiliones, if not Opiliones themselves (Shear and Kukalová-Peck 1990) but are still not well known. The 15 or so species of architarbids (Figure 21), also Pennsylvanian, are more difficult to interpret: B.S. Beall and C.C. Labandeira (1990) place them close to the Opiliones and Acari.

Problematic Groups

Sea spiders (Pycnogonida) are bizarre arthropods indeed. Often grouped with the Chelicerata, sea spiders lack many chelicerate

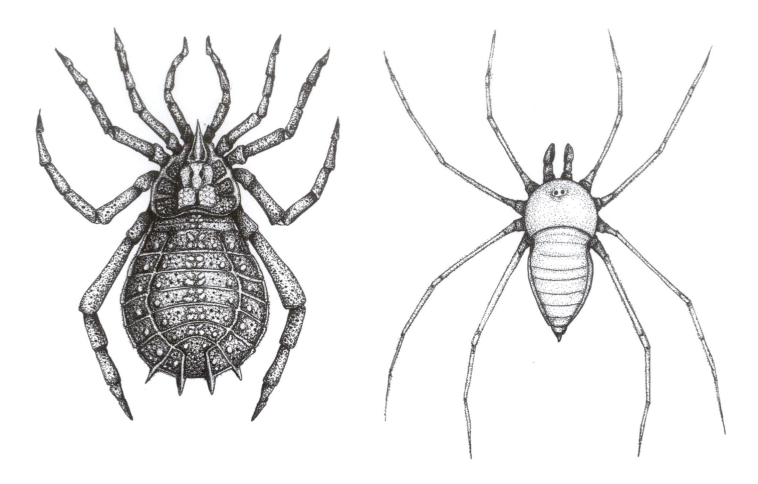

Figure 19. (Left) A trigonotarbid, *Eophrynus prestvicii*. Upper Carboniferous; Dudley, England. Illustration by Lonny Stark. **Figure 20.** (Right) A kustarachnid, *Kustarachne extincta*. Pennsylvanian; Mazon Creek, Illinois. Actual leg length is not certain. Illustration by Lonny Stark.

traits and may represent a separate offshoot of the arthropods. Living sea spiders (about 500 to 1,000 known species) feed on detritus or on soft-bodied invertebrates through a sucking proboscis that may be longer than the animal's body. The abdomen is reduced to a tubercle, the body is short and thin, and tubelike extensions of the gut protrude far into the extremely long walking legs (usually four pairs). Near the proboscis there are typically three more pairs of appendages: a pair of chelicerae, a pair of palps, and a pair of ovigers, long appendages that the male uses to carry masses of eggs until hatching. Some pycnogonids lack chelicerae, palps, or both. Pycnogonids are found in all seas, but are remarkably diverse in the polar oceans (King 1973). Living pycnogonids are usually small and delicate (although a few forms reach a leg span of 40 centimeters) and would not be expected to fossilize readily. Only three certain fossil pycnogonids are known, all from the famous Hunsrück Slate of the Devonian of southern Germany (Bergström et al. 1980; Figure 18).

Aglaspids (Aglaspida) are a somewhat obscure group of Cambrian and Ordovician fossils. Looking something like trilobites, aglaspids lacked the facial sutures and trilobation of trilobites, and most bore a long, pointed telson. Unlike all other chelicerates, their exoskeleton was mineralized with calcium phosphate (Figure 3).

Their place in evolution is not well understood, largely because only one specimen has been found with its appendages preserved. Traditionally, aglaspids have been classified as chelicerates within, or close to, the Xiphosura. Restudy of the only aglaspid specimen with appendages suggests that aglaspids are probably not chelicerates: the specimen had four or at most five pairs of appendages on the prosoma, not six, and there is no evidence for chelicerae (Briggs et al. 1979). Still, aglaspids probably belong somewhere among the "arachnomorphs," although whether they are closer to the trilobites or to the true chelicerates is not certain.

Ecology

Most chelicerates are predators, and judging from the fossil record, the group always has been predatory. Living horseshoe crabs feed on smaller invertebrates, and fossil xiphosurans and eurypterids probably did the same. The first land arachnids probably preyed on small insects and other arthropods, which in turn fed on early land plants or their litter. Trigonotarbids had weak chelicerae and may have scavenged, or taken only small, soft-bodied prey (Shear and Kukalová-Peck 1990). By the Pennsylvanian, arachnids had become taxonomically diverse and probably had developed a vari-

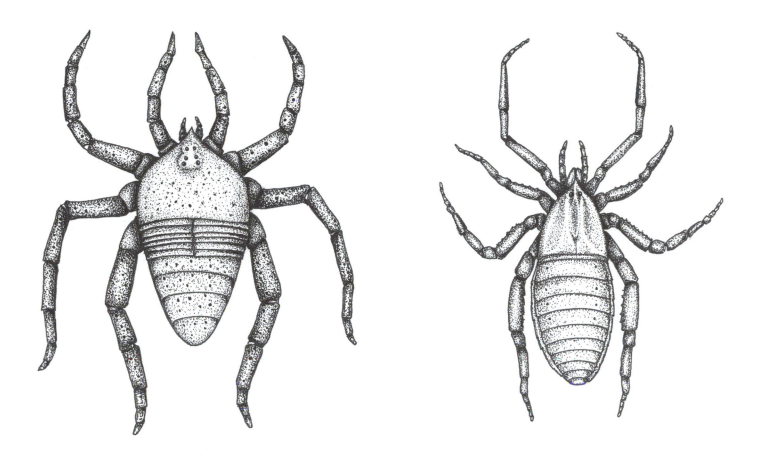

Figure 21. (Left) An architarbid, *Orthotarbus robustus*. Pennsylvanian; Mazon Creek, Illinois. Illustration by Lonny Stark. **Figure 22.** (Right) The only known haptopodid, *Plesiosiro madeleyi*. Upper Carboniferous; Coseley, England. Illustration by Lonny Stark.

ety of lifestyles and feeding strategies, although the general lack of fossils in key environments such as deserts makes it difficult to reconstruct arachnid paleoecology completely (Figure 23).

Most arachnids today prey on insects or other arthropods, although a few large spiders, scorpions, and solifugids have been known to capture and eat fish, tadpoles, reptiles, or even small mammals. Many arachnids are masters of the "sit and wait" feeding strategy. Web-building spiders are the most obvious examples of "sit and wait" predators, but burrowing spiders, as well as most scorpions, also depend on waiting for prey to come close before pouncing. Other arachnids, like jumping spiders, a few scorpions, and solifugids, are more active hunters that stalk or even chase down prey. The ability to poison prey is found in several groups, notably scorpions and spiders. Note that although scorpion stings and some spider bites can be painful, very few species can even potentially kill humans, and even "deadly" species are not often lethal (Polis 1990; Foelix 1996). Some arachnids have evolved rather more peaceful lifestyles: many harvestmen scavenge dead animal and plant matter, and many mite species are scavengers, parasites, or plant or microbe feeders.

One problem with life on land is the problem of mating where eggs and sperm can no longer be shed into the water. Most arachnids have solved this problem by evolving indirect sperm transfer. Most male arachnids produce special sperm-containing packets called *spermatophores*. In scorpions, pseudoscorpions, and tailed and tailless whip-scorpions, the male deposits a spermatophore on the ground and then maneuvers the female over it so that it contacts her genital opening. Tick spiders and sun spiders insert spermatophores directly into the female genital opening. True spiders lack spermatophores; the male simply fills hollow structures on his highly modified pedipalps from a sperm droplet and inserts them into the female. Only harvestmen and some mites have penises. Arachnid mating behavior is often quite complex, with elaborate "courtship rituals" that include the exchange of visual, touch, and odor signals. These rituals often involve the male coaxing, maneuvering, or forcing the female into position so that the spermatophore contacts her genital opening, or so that the male can reach her genital opening. They may also involve pacifying the female so that she does not attack and eat the male—at least not before mating.

Fossil Localities

The earliest "arachnomorphs" appear in Cambrian rocks. *Sanctacaris* and other possible chelicerate relatives appear in the famous Burgess Shale of the Middle Cambrian of the Canadian Rocky

Figure 23. Reconstruction of a Pennsylvanian swamp with a diverse chelicerate fauna. The foreground shows two xiphosurans, *Euproops danae.* Within a decayed hollow trunk of the sphenophyte tree *Calamites,* a scorpion *(Eoctonus miniatus)* preys on a dipluran insect *(Testajapyx thomasi)* while the primitive true spider *Arthrolycosa antiqua* looks on. The architarbid *Architarbus rotundatus* is to the left, in the foliage of the sphenophyte *Annularia;* the trigonotarbid *Pleophrynus ensifer* is seen to the right, on the trunk of a lycopod tree. Illustration by Lonny Stark.

Mountains (Briggs et al. 1994). Various "arachnomorph" lineages outside of the major chelicerate groups survived into the Devonian. Although aglaspids and aglaspid-like arthropods range from the Lower Cambrian to the Upper Ordovician, Middle and Upper Cambrian localities in Wisconsin have yielded the most important fossils. Possible xiphosurans also are known from the Cambrian (Bergström 1975).

After the Cambrian, both marine and land chelicerates were most common and diverse in North America and Europe, which were near the equator for much of the Paleozoic. This may mean that early chelicerates preferred warm climates, but better exploration of other continents may yield more fossils and overturn this hypothesis (Bernini 1991). Late Silurian limestones of central New York contain spectacular eurypterids; in fact, eurypterids are the official state fossil of New York (Fisher 1984). Mid-Paleozoic strata in the midwestern United States, Britain, and northern and eastern Europe also contain well-preserved eurypterids. Some of these same rocks contain fossil trails that can be matched with known eurypterid fossils, allowing us to reconstruct in great detail how these animals moved and lived (e.g., Hanken and Størmer 1975). The marine Hunsrückscheifer, or Hunsrück Slate, of the Devonian of Germany has produced the only fossil pycnogonids (Bergström et al. 1980) and exquisitely preserved xiphosurans and scorpions.

Arachnids are fairly scarce as fossils, and unless the preservation is outstanding, fossil arachnids may be difficult to identify. Aquatic scorpions first appear in the mid-Silurian but had made the transition to land at least by the Early Devonian (Shear et al. 1996). The oldest land arachnid currently known, however, is a single Late Silurian trigonotarbid from Ludford Lane, England, 414 million years old (Jeram et al. 1990). Slightly younger are the mites and trigonotarbid from the Lower Devonian Rhynie Chert, near Aberdeen, Scotland, and the eurypterids, scorpions, and trigonotarbids from a Lower Devonian locality at Alken-an-der-Mosel, Germany. A Middle Devonian site near Gilboa, New York, has yielded abundant mites, the oldest known spiders and pseudoscorpions, some true scorpions and trigonotarbids, and possibly other arachnids as well (Shear et al. 1984; Shear 1990). Later Paleozoic arachnids are best known from the Late Pennsylvanian Mazon Creek fauna of central Illinois, which also has yielded fine xiphosurans and eurypterids (Figure 23). Sites of about the same age in the coal measures of northern England, in France, and in Eastern Europe have also produced noteworthy land arachnid fossils. Mesozoic chelicerates are rare, but the number of finds is growing. A Triassic site at Bromsgrove, England, has yielded fragmentary but very well preserved scorpion remains (Wills 1947). A few spiders, scorpions, and other arachnids are known from Mesozoic rocks (e.g., Kjellesvig-Waering 1986; Eskov 1987; Gall 1990; Selden 1990; Selden and Gall 1992). Spiders, mites, and other arachnids have been found in Cretaceous amber, but most have not yet been described (Schawaller 1991; Poinar 1992).

The Cenozoic fossil record of arachnids is much more complete, largely owing to the spectacular fossil arachnids found in Cenozoic amber. The Oligocene amber from the Dominican Republic has yielded more than 100 species of spider. Baltic amber has yielded over 300 species of spider, most of which are related to living spiders in tropical habitats (Poinar 1992; Foelix 1996).

Amber from these and other sites also has yielded mites, scorpions, and other arachnids. Outside of amber, Cenozoic arachnids sometimes are found in association with fossil insects: for instance, S.H. Scudder (1890) listed over 30 species of spider from the Florissant Shale of Colorado (Oligocene), famous for its diverse fossil insects.

History of Chelicerate Paleontology

Spiders in amber may have been seen in ancient times, but it wasn't until 1819 that the first fossil spider was described by a scientist. The American entomologist A.S. Packard and the British paleontologist H. Woodward did important early work on Paleozoic chelicerates (e.g., Packard 1886; Woodward 1866). Samuel H. Scudder, the entomologist and paleontologist who almost singlehandedly founded paleoentomology in the United States, described many land arachnids in his great monographs (e.g., Scudder 1890). Reginald I. Pocock summarized the Paleozoic fossil arachnids of Britain (Pocock 1911). Ukrainian-born American paleontologist Alexander Petrunkevitch was the greatest single contributor to arachnid paleontology, describing a vast number of fossil spiders and other arachnids (e.g., Petrunkevitch 1942, 1949; Størmer et al. 1955). Both Pocock and Petrunkevitch also carried out important studies on living chelicerates. Erik Kjellesvig-Waering published many papers on eurypterids and fossil arachnids, crowned by his magnificent, posthumously published study of all fossil scorpions (Kjellesvig-Waering 1986). Swedish paleontologist Leif Størmer contributed much to our knowledge of marine chelicerates (e.g., Størmer et al. 1955) in addition to his work on trilobites.

Today, the influx of fossils from the Burgess Shale and elsewhere is providing new insights and new questions about the early evolution of all arthropods. Scientists such as Derek E.G. Briggs, Harry Whittington, Matthew A. Wills, and Simon Conway Morris in the United Kingdom; Alberto Simonetta and L. Delle Cave in Italy; Jan Bergström in Sweden; Desmond Collins in Canada; Richard Robinson in the United States; and Hou Xian-guang in China have described many of these arthropods and attempted to understand their evolutionary relationships. A steady stream of new discoveries of land arthropods is sharpening the picture of the colonization of the land by chelicerates and their later evolutionary history. Many of these finds have been described by William A. Shear in the United States, A.J. Jeram and Paul A. Selden in the United Kingdom, Kirill Eskov in Russia, and their colleagues.

BEN WAGGONER

Works Cited

Bartsch, I. 1988. Halacaroidea. In R.P. Higgins and H. Thiel (eds.), Introduction to the Study of Meiofauna. Washington: Smithsonian Institution Press; rev. ed., 1992.

Beall, B.S., and C.C. Labandeira. 1990. Macroevolutionary patterns of the Chelicerata and Tracheata. In D.G. Mikulic (ed.), Arthropod Paleobiology: Short Courses in Paleontology 3. Knoxville, Tennessee: Paleontological Society.

Bergström, J. 1975. Functional morphology and evolution of xiphosurids. Fossils and Strata 4:291–305.

Bergström, J., W. Stürmer, and G. Winter. 1980. *Palaeoisopus, Palaeopantopus,* and *Palaeothea,* pycnogonid arthropods from the Lower Devonian Hunsrück Slate, West Germany. *Paläontologische Zeitschrift* 54:7–54.

Bernini, F. 1991. Fossil Acarida: Contribution of palaeontological data to acarid evolutionary history. *In* A. M. Simonetta and S. Conway Morris (eds.), *The Early Evolution of Metazoa and the Significance of Problematic Taxa.* Cambridge and New York: Cambridge University Press.

Briggs, D.E.G., D.L. Bruton, and H.B. Whittington. 1979. Appendages of the arthropod *Aglaspis spinifer* (Upper Cambrian, Wisconsin) and their significance. *Palaeontology* 22:167–80.

Briggs, D.E.G., and D. Collins. 1988. A Middle Cambrian chelicerate from Mount Stephen, British Columbia. *Palaeontology* 31 (3):779–98.

Briggs, D.E.G., D.H. Erwin, and F.J. Collier. 1994. *The Fossils of the Burgess Shale.* Washington, D.C., and London: Smithsonian Institution Press.

Delle Cave, L., and A.M. Simonetta. 1991. Early Palaeozoic arthropods and problems of arthropod phylogeny; with some notes on taxa of doubtful affinities. *In* A. M. Simonetta and S. Conway Morris (eds.), *The Early Evolution of Metazoa and the Significance of Problematic Taxa.* Cambridge and New York: Cambridge University Press.

Eskov, K. 1987. A new archaeid spider (Chelicerata: Araneae) from the Jurassic of Kazakhstan, with notes on the so-called "Gondwanan" ranges of recent taxa. *Neues Jahrbuch für Geologie und Paläontologie Abhandlungen* 175:81–106.

Fisher, D.C. 1979. Evidence for subaerial activity of *Euproops danae* (Merostomata, Xiphosurida). *In:* M.H. Nitecki (ed.), *Mazon Creek Fossils.* New York: Academic Press.

Fisher, D.W. 1984. Our new state fossil—the old eurypterid. *The Conservationist* 39 (3):50.

Foelix, R.F. 1996. *Biology of Spiders.* 2nd ed. New York and Oxford: Oxford University Press; 1st ed., Cambridge, Massachusetts: Harvard University Press, 1982; as *Biologie der Spinnen,* Stuttgart: Thieme, 1979.

Gall, J.-C. 1990. Les voiles microbiens. Leur contribution à la fossilisation des organismes au corps mou. *Lethaia* 23:21–28.

Hanken, N.-M., and L. Størmer. 1975. The trail of a large Silurian eurypterid. *Fossils and Strata* 4:255–70.

Hou, X., and J. Bergström. 1991. The anthropods of the Lower Cambrian Chengjiang fauna, with relationships and evolutionary significance. *In* A. M. Simonetta and S. Conway Morris (eds.), *The Early Evolution of Metazoa and the Significance of Problematic Taxa.* Cambridge and New York: Cambridge University Press.

Jeram, A.J., P.A. Selden, and D. Edwards. 1990. Land animals in the Silurian: Arachnids and myriapods from Shropshire, England. *Science* 250:658–61.

King, P.E. 1973. *Pycnogonids.* London: Hutchinson; New York: St. Martin's Press.

Kjellesvig-Waering, E.N. 1986. A restudy of the fossil Scorpionida of the world. *Palaeontographica Americana* 55.

Krantz, G.W. 1978. *A Manual of Acarology.* Corvallis: Oregon State University Book Stores.

Lankester, E.R. 1881. *Limulus* an arachnid. *Quarterly Journal of Microscopic Science* 21:504–8, 609–49.

Packard, A.S. 1869. *Guide to the Study of Insects.* Salem, Massachusetts: Naturalist's Book Agency.

———. 1886. On the Carboniferous xiphosurous fauna of North America. *Memoirs of the National Academy of Sciences* 3 (2):143–57.

Petrunkevitch, A. 1942. A study of amber spiders. *Transactions of the Connecticut Academy of Arts and Sciences* 34:119–464.

———. 1949. A study of Palaeozoic Arachnida. *Transactions of the Connecticut Academy of Arts and Sciences* 37:69–315.

Pocock, R.I. 1911. *A Monograph of the Terrestrial Carboniferous Arachnida of Great Britain.* London: Palaeontographical Society.

Poinar, G.O., Jr. 1992. *Life in Amber.* Palo Alto, California: Stanford University Press.

Polis, G.A. 1990. *The Biology of Scorpions.* Palo Alto, California: Stanford University Press.

Schawaller, W. 1991. The first Mesozoic pseudoscorpions, from Cretaceous Canadian amber. *Palaeontology* 34:971–76.

Scudder, S.H. 1890. *The Fossil Insects of North America.* Vol. 2, *The Tertiary Insects.* New York: Macmillan.

Sekiguchi, K. 1988. *Biology of Horseshoe Crabs.* Tokyo: Science House; as *Kabutogani no Seibutsugaku,* 1984.

Selden, P.A. 1990. Lower Cretaceous spiders from the Sierra de Montsech, north-east Spain. *Palaeontology* 33:257–85.

Selden, P.A., and J.-C. Gall. 1992. A Triassic mygalomorph spider from the northern Vosges, France. *Palaeontology* 35:211–35.

Shear, W.A. 1990. Silurian-Devonian terrestrial arthropods. *In:* D.G. Mikulic (ed.), *Arthropod Paleobiology: Short Courses in Paleontology 3.* Knoxville, Tennessee: Paleontological Society.

Shear, W.A., P.M. Bonamo, J.D. Grierson, W.D.I. Rolfe, E.L. Smith, and R.A. Norton. 1984. Early land animals in North America: Evidence from Devonian age arthropods from Gilboa, New York. *Science* 224:492–94.

Shear, W.A., P.G. Gensel, and A.J. Jeram. 1996. Fossils of large terrestrial arthropods from the Lower Devonian of Canada. *Nature* 384:555–57.

Shear, W.A., and J. Kukalová-Peck. 1990. The ecology of Paleozoic terrestrial arthropods: The fossil evidence. *Canadian Journal of Zoology* 68:1807–34.

Shuster, C.N. 1982. A pictorial review of the natural history and ecology of the horseshoe crab *Limulus polyphemus,* with reference to other Limulidae. *In* J. Bonaventura, C. Bonaventura, and S. Tesh (eds.), *Physiology and Biology of Horseshoe Crabs.* New York: Liss.

Størmer, L.W., A. Petrunkevitch, and J.W. Hedgpeth. 1955. Chelicerata. *Treatise on Invertebrate Paleontology, Pt. P, Arthropoda* 2:1–181.

Tollerton, V.P., Jr. 1989. Morphology, taxonomy, and classification of the Order Eurypterida Burmeister, 1843. *Journal of Paleontology* 63:642–57.

Waggoner, B.M. 1996. Phylogenetic hypotheses of the relationships of arthropods to Precambrian and Cambrian problematic fossil taxa. *Systematic Biology* 45 (2):190–222.

Wills, L.J. 1947. *A Monograph of British Triassic Scorpions.* London: Palaeontographical Society; New York: Johnson.

Wills, M.A., D.E.G. Briggs, and R.A. Fortey. 1994. Disparity as an evolutionary index: A comparison of Cambrian and Recent arthropods. *Paleobiology* 20:93–130.

Woodward, H. 1866. *A Monograph on the British Fossil Crustacea, Belonging to the Order Merostomata.* London: Palaeontographical Society.

Further Reading

Boardman, R.S., A.H. Cheetham, and A.J. Rowell. 1987. *Fossil Invertebrates.* Palo Alto, California: Blackwell.

Cloudsley-Thompson, J.L. 1958. *Spiders, Scorpions, Centipedes and Mites.* Oxford: Pergamon; 2nd ed., 1968.

Foelix, R.F. 1982. *Biology of Spiders.* Cambridge, Massachusetts: Harvard University Press; 2nd ed., New York and Oxford: Oxford University Press, 1996; as *Biologie der Spinnen,* Stuttgart: Thieme, 1979.

Kettle, D.S. 1982. *Medical and Veterinary Entomology.* New York: Wiley; London: Croom Helm, 1984; 2nd ed., Wallingford, Oxfordshire: CAB, 1995.

Kjellesvig-Waering, E.N. 1986. A restudy of the fossil Scorpionida of the world. *Palaeontographica Americana* 55.

King, P.E. 1973. *Pycnogonids.* London.: Hutchinson; New York: St. Martin's Press.

Knutson, R.M. 1992. *Furtive Fauna: A Field Guide to the Creatures Who Live on You.* New York: Penguin.

Krantz, G.W. 1978. *A Manual of Acarology.* Corvallis: Oregon State University Book Stores.

Levi, H.W., and L.R. Levi. 1990. *Spiders and Their Kin.* New York: Golden; rev. ed., 1990.

Poinar, G.O., Jr. 1992. *Life in Amber.* Palo Alto, California: Stanford University Press.

Polis, G.A. 1990. *The Biology of Scorpions.* Palo Alto, California: Stanford University Press.

Savory, T.H. 1935. *Arachnida.* London: Arnold; 2nd ed., London and New York: Academic Press, 1977.

Sekiguchi, K. 1988. *Biology of Horseshoe Crabs.* Tokyo: Science House; as *Kabutogani no Seibutsugaku,* 1984.

Størmer, L.W., A. Petrunkevitch, and J.W. Hedgpeth. 1955. Chelicerata. *Treatise on Invertebrate Paleontology, Pt. P, Arthropoda* 2:1–181.

CHINA

The ancient Chinese recognition of fossil plants and animals can be traced back at least to the third and seventh centuries respectively. Chinese knowledge of petrifaction, geological characters, and the implications of those fossils was recorded in classical literature, sometimes with amazing accuracy and brilliant insights even in light of modern paleontological research. These observations derived from the intuition of the ancient Chinese scholars, whose avid pursuits in poetry and painting were related intimately to observing nature. Thus, for those early paleontological observations and inferences, it does not seem ". . . at all likely that any stimulus was received by the Chinese from the West at the beginning of their best period" (Needham 1959). Paleontological research as an organized scientific enterprise in China is, however, occidentally rooted (rooted in Western culture) and often is coupled with a twist of historical accident.

Scattered literature on Chinese fossils was published in the latter part of the nineteenth century and at the beginning of the twentieth century by Western explorers. Notable among them were F. von Richthofen, B. Willis, and E. Blackwelder. Richthofen and others published the fourth and fifth volumes of the book *China* between 1883 and 1911, which contain several papers on invertebrate fossils from China. However, C.D. Walcott's 1906 monograph, entitled "Cambrian Faunas of China" has generally been regarded as the first major publication on Chinese fossils.

The Beginnings, 1912–20

The Chinese pioneer of paleontological research was V.K. Ting. He was a graduate of the University of Glasgow and the founder and head of the Geological Survey of China in 1912. Parallel to the Survey was the Geological Institute, a training school headed by H.T. Chang. Together with Ting and W.H. Wong, Chang trained the first two dozen students in geology and paleontology in the mid-1910s. Many of these students later became leaders in various geological and paleontological disciplines. Almost all of them conducted paleontological investigations in China, at least at the beginning of their professional careers.

Paleontological research and education took a great leap forward from 1920 onward, with Ting's hiring of a renowned American paleontologist, A.W. Grabau, to join his survey and the Department of Geology at Peking University. Despite his distinguished career, Grabau had been asked to leave Columbia University for indiscretions involving female students. On the recommendation of J.S. Lee and through the introduction of David White, Ting personally invited Grabau to come to China. In the following two and a half decades, Grabau, in his capacity as chief advisor and foremost educator, was instrumental in promoting paleontological research in China. He was awarded the prestigious Hayden Memorial Geological Award by the Philadelphia Academy of Natural Sciences in 1941. The Chinese immortalized him by burying him on the scenic campus of the famous Peking University. The only other American who received such an honor was Edgar Snow, a journalist and personal friend of Mao Tse-tung.

The War Years, 1920–49

From 1920 to 1949, China was almost constantly at war, first among the various warlord factions, then against the Japanese invasion, and finally in a civil war between nationalists and communists. One might assume an aesthetic scientific discipline such as paleontology only flourishes in wealthy countries and then only during peaceful times. Chinese paleontological research, however, laid much of its groundwork amidst the turmoil of these war years.

In 1920 another eminent paleontologist, J.S. Lee, joined the faculty of the Department of Geology at Peking University. Fresh out of graduate school at the University of Birmingham, Lee was destined to become one of the leading figures in the Chinese Earth sciences for the following half a century. In 1928, he founded the Institute of Geology within *Academia Sinica*, and after the communists' victory in 1949, he became the People's Republic's minister of geology until his death in 1971. Establishment of the

Chinese Geological Survey and the Institute of Geology provided employment for professional paleontologists. As a result, geology departments were set up during the 1920s to train professionals in several national universities such as Sun Yat-sen University, Southeast or Central University (now known as Nanking University), and Tsinghua University. That same decade also witnessed the debut of a series of important Chinese geological and paleontological journals such as *Bulletin of the Geological Survey of China* and *Palaeontologia Sinica*. Three publications authored by Chinese paleontologists are deemed pioneering and benchmark contributions; they are T.C. Chow's *The Cretaceous Plant Fossils from Shantung* (1923), Y.C. Sun's *Contributions to the Cambrian Faunas of North China* (1924), and C.C. Young's *Fossile Nagetiere aus Nord-China* (1927).

From 1920 to 1937, paleontological research in China experienced the first burst in progress since its belated but propitious beginning. More than a score of Chinese paleontologists, either western-trained or "home-grown," were fully competent: They were talented, devoted, and extremely active. Despite starting from scratch, in less than two decades these scientists accomplished fieldwork in many Chinese provinces and published on major groups of fossil animals and plants. Notable among these are the following studies by: J.S. Lee and H. Chen on fusulinids; Y.C. Sun and S.C. Hsu on graptolites; Y.C. Sun on trilobites; C.C. Yu, S.S. Yoh, and Y.S. Chi on corals; Y.T. Chao and T.K. Huang on brachiopods; C.C. Tien and T.H. Yin on cephalopods; C. Ping on gastropods and insects; H.C. Sze, T.C. Chow, and C.H. Pan on fossil plants; and C.C. Young on vertebrates. To this list, one must add W.C. Pei's epic discovery of Peking Man in 1929. These studies were published mostly in Chinese journals in English or other European languages. It also should be noted that these paleontological studies led to the establishment of a solid biostratigraphic framework (dating of rock strata by representative fossil groups) for the major chapters of China's Earth history. Amazingly, all was accomplished under extremely difficult circumstances: insufficient funding, poor transportation, and above all, the hostile environment of a war-torn country. Many risked their lives in the field. V.K. Ting died of carbon monoxide poisoning, and Y.T. Chao was killed by bandits in a remote Yunnan province. Chao was a rising star among his peers when he died at the age of 31. The loss was felt so deeply that to this day he is still remembered as one of the most brilliant and devoted paleontologists China ever has had.

The Japanese invasion of the Chinese mainland in 1937 only made difficult working conditions worse for Chinese paleontologists. Most of the scientists retreated into the southwestern and northwestern reaches of the country. Even then, they carried out fieldwork and laboratory research with ever-growing enthusiasm and utter devotion. The Japanese invasion sent many Chinese paleontologists flocking to southwestern China, prompting a paleontological renaissance in that region. Among the significant contributions were C.C. Young's studies of the Lufeng vertebrate fauna, which include such well-known fossils as *Lufengosaurus huenei*, a complete prosauropod dinosaur skeleton, and *Bienotherium*, a mammal-like reptile. Young, a scholar, poet, and socialite, received his doctorate in 1927 from the University of Munich, Germany. He was the founder of the Cenozoic Research Labora-

tory, now known as the Institute of Vertebrate Paleontology and Paleoanthropology (IVPP), *Academia Sinica*.

The war also brought a blessing in disguise to paleontological education at the Department of Geology at Chungking University in Chungking, the wartime capitol. Having been established only a year before the Japanese invasion, the department boasted a distinguished paleontology faculty, including S. Chu, C.C. Yu, and H. Chen. After the war broke out, the department added more distinguished paleontologists to its visiting faculty roster, including J.S. Lee, T.K. Huang, and C.C. Young. The department also attracted the best and brightest high school graduates throughout the nation, among whom were M.C. Chow, H.H. Lee, J.C. Sheng, and later W.T. Chang. All four are now internationally renowned: Chang, a leading trilobite specialist; Lee, the International Paleobotanical Organization's 1996 Birbal Sahni IOP Medal recipient and the foremost Chinese paleobotanist today; Sheng, a prominent micropaleontologist and the Joseph A. Cushman Award winner in 1996; and Chow, a renaissance paleontologist specializing in mammalian fossils and the Society of Vertebrate Paleontology's Romer-Simpson medalist for 1993. The accomplishments of these men are truly remarkable and can only be matched by graduates from the stellar paleontology graduate program at Yale in the late 1960s.

The departments of geology at Peking and Tsinghua universities, which then merged into the Department of Geology, the United University of Southwest China, also related to the southwestern part of the country during the war with the Japanese. Though overshadowed by the UUSC's high-profile departments of mathematics, physics, and humanities, the geology department was an important institution of paleontological training and research. It trained a number of students who later became leaders in the People's Republic's paleontological establishments, such as Y.C. Hao, C.W. Ku, A.Z. Mu, T.S. Liu, and H.C. Wang.

There are several points worth noting in tracing the early history of paleontological research in China. First, it took a relatively short time to develop from its feeble beginning to its full bloom, owing to the tutelage of Grabau, Ting, H.T. Chang, and J.S. Lee. Second, the promoters of Chinese paleontology were a politically well-connected intellectual elite, among whom Ting served as warlord Chuan-fang Sun's chief of staff in Sun's short-lived Shanghai government, and W.H. Wong served as the prime minister of the Chiang Kai-shek's nationalist government. Third, the best science is conducted by the most curious minds with single-mindedness, and the first generation of Chinese paleontologists formed just such a group of extraordinary individuals. Finally, paleontological research was conducted with the full participation and partnership of western colleagues, including Grabau, T.G. Halle, W. Gothan, J.G. Andersson, D. Black, O. Zdansky, and Teilhard de Chardin. The open collaboration with the West came to a sudden halt with the communists' rise to power in 1949. Chinese paleontologists spent the following three decades in virtual isolation from the West, especially the United States.

The People's Republic in Isolation, 1949–76

With the founding of the People's Republic, the mood for building a strong China prevailed throughout the country: A utopian scheme was always enticingly attractive to the Chinese intellectuals. The new government wasted no time in promoting geological investigations in general and mineral explorations in particular. Chinese geologists and paleontologists immediately followed suit. Some of them returned to the motherland to participate in the new socialist reconstruction after their studies in the West. They rolled up their sleeves and launched a full-scale regime of paleontological research that marked the second burst in progress.

Within a few years, reorganized as well as new research institutions sprang up, and paleontological teaching institutions were expanded greatly. Under the prevailing political atmosphere of the time, the paleontological education and research infrastructure was modeled strictly after the Soviet system. The overall frame of the infrastructure still persists in China to this day, even though in recent years many Chinese paleontologists have voiced a desire to overhaul the system. There was (and largely still is) a tripartition of responsibilities among the paleontological establishments. The primary function of the institutes under the Chinese Academy of Sciences *(Academia Sinica)* is pure research. Unlike their western counterparts, the Chinese institutions of higher education did not place much emphasis on original research until recently. Numerous provincial geological survey teams mainly dealt with the practical aspects of paleontology. Although paleontologists number in the thousands, actual researchers only add up to several hundreds. Still, this represents a tremendous increase in the total number of professionals as compared to about thirty nationwide before 1949.

Two institutes in the Chinese Academy of Sciences have been devoted to paleontological research: the Nanjing Institute of Geology and Paleontology (NIGP), and the Institute of Vertebrate Paleontology and Paleoanthropology (IVPP) in Beijing. The NIGP was established in the early 1950s to study invertebrate and plant fossils, and the IVPP was created to concentrate on vertebrate and hominid fossils. Both institutes were headed by two German-trained scientists: H.C. Sze, a renowned paleobotanist, and C.C. Young, a world-class vertebrate paleontologist. Although there have been a few paleontologists scattered in other institutions within the Academy, such as the Institutes of Geology, Botany, Hydrobiology, and Oceanography, by and large the NIGP and IVPP have been *the* paleontological research centers in China for almost half a century.

The paleontological investigations in China between the 1950s and 1970s benefited greatly from comprehensive and systematic geological surveying and mapping. These studies discovered large numbers of fossils and worked out their taxonomic identifications. Thousands of fossil invertebrate species were described; many were new ones. The NIGP expanded to employ a couple of hundred paleontologists and to include experts on virtually every invertebrate and plant fossil group, both macro- and microfossils. Although data accumulation was characteristic of the period, serious taxonomic and morphological papers and monographs were published. In many cases, faunal assemblages and biostratigraphic zones were also established. The NIGP compiled five volumes of *Index Fossils of China* in 1953 and between the early 1960s and the mid-1970s published 17 volumes of monographs under the general title of *All Groups of Fossils of China*. In addition, the NIGP also published a bimonthly, *Acta Palaeontologia Sinica,* several volumes of *Palaeontologia Sinica,* and other irregularly issued monographs. The output was truly impressive, and the general quality of the work was highly acclaimed. Among the most important research completed during this period were the works on Paleozoic trilobites, corals, fusulinids, graptolites, brachiopods, conodonts, cephalopods, Cathaysian flora, Mesozoic bivalves, gastropods, ammonites, conchostracans, Mesozoic and Cenozoic flora, ostracods, charaphytes, spores, and pollen.

At the beginning, the IVPP was known as the Laboratory for Vertebrate Paleontology and Cenozoic Studies, a subsidiary of the NIGP. In 1953, the IVPP became independent and only housed a half dozen scientists. However, it made up with zest for what it lacked in size. Under Young's directorship, the IVPP grew rapidly and gained immediate international recognition. In the early 1950s, Young's political savvy and great showmanship dictated the IVPP's resumption of excavations at Chou-k'ou-t'ien, the famous Peking Man site, and of dinosaur hunting in Shantung's Cretaceous beds. The results were an instant success. More hominid fossils and artifacts were discovered at Chou-k'ou-t'ien, and dinosaur skeletons of *Tsintaosaurus* and *Psittacosaurus* were collected from Shantung. In the meanwhile, Young recruited two recently returned doctorate students from the United States: J.K. Woo, an anatomist and anthropologist trained at Washington University at St. Louis, and M.C. Chow, a paleontologist trained at Lehigh and Princeton universities. This recruitment turned out to be much more important than the fossil discoveries because later, these two men would each attract a cluster of excellent scholars. Young was undoubtedly one of the most celebrated scientific giants in modern Chinese history. He was both patriotic and worldly, strict yet tolerant, passionate but principled, rigorous but flexible, idealistic but practical, and visionary but down-to-earth.

Throughout the 1950s and the early half of the 1960s, the IVPP flourished and its scientific staff increased to over 100. It published three serials, including the quarterly, *Vertebrata PalAsiatica,* and several monographs. The IVPP organized expeditions to many parts of the country and discovered numerous vertebrate fossil localities. Even during the Cultural Revolution (1966–76), the Institute managed to conduct both field and laboratory research, although it was limited severely by the political climate. The accomplishments were, however, astonishing. These include studies on the Devonian fishes, Mesozoic and Cenozoic teleosts, Late Permian and Jurassic lower tetrapods, dinosaurian faunas, Miocene birds, Cenozoic mammals, and hominid fossils and artifacts.

In addition to the NIGP and IVPP, there was the Chinese Academy of Geological Sciences under the auspices of the Ministry of Geology, which ran a strong research program in Precambrian and Paleozoic paleontology. There were also about a dozen universities and geological colleges with paleontology programs, such as Peking University, Nanking University, and geological colleges in Beijing, Chengdu, and Changchun. Although these educational institutions made limited contributions to paleontological research, they were responsible for training thousands of paleontologists to meet the increased demand arising from large scale paleontological investigations being conducted across the country during this time.

It is noteworthy that central planning and isolation from the West are two of the most important characteristics of Chinese paleontological research during this period. Central planning gave a constant impetus to basic research and provided reliable funding for it, as the government saw fit. In the case of Chinese paleontology, the government saw its utility in both theoretical and practical aspects. Theoretically, paleontological research supports the theory of evolution, which conforms to atheistic Marxism adhered to by the Chinese communist government. Paleontology is also a branch of science that is relatively inexpensive to support and, with China's vast land mass and rich fossil resources, is likely to excel. In addition, both J.S. Lee and C.C. Young were politically well-connected. All these factors favored a healthy growth of the discipline even despite repeated political upheavals.

However, isolation from the West was certainly detrimental to the progress of paleontological research during these years. Throughout the 1950s and early 1960s, China sent several dozen students to study paleontology in the former Soviet Union and Eastern Block countries. Many of these students are leading figures in the field today in China, including M.M. Chang, a renowned paleoichthyologist and charismatic academic "ambassador," Z.Q. Qiu, a distinguished paleomammalogist, and P.X. Wang, an outstanding micropaleontologist and oceanographer. There were also frequent scholarly exchanges and joint expeditions, including an ill-fated Sino-Soviet joint expedition between the IVPP and the Paleontological Institute, Moscow, to China's far northwestern provinces. Limited contacts with some European countries, such as Great Britain, France, and Sweden, did exist. But, overall, Chinese colleagues were isolated severely during these years. The fact that they accomplished so much under such circumstances epitomizes the legacy of the first generation of Chinese paleontologists—their devotion to discipline and the groundwork that they laid. However, the isolation soon would end abruptly. Like all great empires in world history, China was waiting for its great emperor to die before drastic changes could take place. In 1976 Mao Tse-tung's death realized just that.

The People's Republic Opens Its Doors, 1976 to the Present

With the death of Mao and the fall of the "Gang of Four" in 1976, China entered a new era that can be best described in famous Dickensian rhetoric as "the season of Light" and "the spring of hope." A new national leader, Deng Xiaoping, immediately emerged and declared that "the spring of science is here!" Since then, for the last two decades the sciences in China in general, and paleontological research in particular, have enjoyed an unprecedented boom. This period represents the third and by far the greatest upsurge in activity for Chinese paleontology.

Deng jump-started the severely bruised education and science programs by improving the social status and livelihood of Chinese educators and scientists and by allowing them to teach and conduct research. Chinese paleontologists were energized quickly. Fieldwork and research activities were restored, and graduate studies and professional societies were resumed. More importantly, under Deng's open-door policy, academic ties with the outside world were reestablished. The resurgence was so swift that by the mid-1980s Chinese paleontologists had become active members in the world paleontological community. As Teichert

and Yin (1981) excitedly reported, Deng's relaxation in policy during that period

triggered a tremendous surge of scientific activities, resulting in a veritable deluge of high quality publications in all branches of paleontology in an ever increasing number of publication outlets. On the systematic side, no field of study was neglected from micropaleontology to invertebrate and vertebrate paleontology and paleobotany. Great strides were made in biostratigraphy and stratigraphic correlation, including what may be the final step toward an understanding of the marine faunal succession at the Permian-Triassic transition. Large areas such as Xizang (Tibet) were opened up to scientific exploration on a large scale for the first time, and other, previously poorly known, parts of the country were extensively investigated.

Such an upbeat assessment was completely warranted, for Teichert himself (then the president of the International Palaeontological Association) led the IPA's first ever delegation to visit China in 1979 and observed it firsthand. The mood among Chinese scholars was overwhelmingly optimistic, the political atmosphere extremely relaxed (at least for a short time), and as a result, research productivity soared. On the other hand, because of their isolation in the past decades and especially because of the disruption in research during the Cultural Revolution, Chinese paleontologists had a lot of catching up to do. The 1970s witnessed an exciting scientific revolution in the earth sciences unfolding in the West—a new paradigm of plate tectonics. At the same time, cladistics, a new school of thought in systematic biology, also began to gain a firm footing, a prelude to its revolutionary takeover in the following two decades. When the Chinese paleontologists were emancipated in the late 1970s from rigid political bondage, an avalanche of literature on plate tectonics and cladistics was waiting for them to consume. For many, the first task was to learn English and other major European languages.

By the early 1980s, open scholarly exchanges between Chinese and western paleontologists already began to bear fruit. Through the exchange of visits, Chinese paleontologists received not only books and reprints, specimen casts, and honorarium-exempted speakers, but also fresh ideas about state-of-the-art in paleontological research. Likewise, western scholars benefited a great deal from access to Chinese fossils, joint expeditions, and cooperative research projects. These exchanges truly have been a two-way street. Again, the NIGP and IVPP have been both the chief benefactors and beneficiaries, due to their international reputation. In the last two decades, they have received hundreds of international visitors and constantly have sent their staff members abroad to attend international conferences, receive further education, display exhibits, or spend sabbatical leaves. The result is the achieved prominence of Chinese paleontology in the world scientific community in recent years.

Beyond the basic descriptive taxonomic work, Chinese paleontologists have paid more attention to a whole array of topics in paleobiology, such as phylogenetics, functional morphology, patterns and processes in evolution, paleoecology and taphonomy, paleobigeography, and major events in the history of life. This increased awareness of international research trends led to the establishment of the Laboratory of Paleobiology and Stratigraphy (LPS) in the 1980s. The LPS is an elite research laboratory affiliated with the NIGP, receiving special funding from the Academy, the Chinese National Science Foundation, and other grant agencies. Under the stewardship of its able director Y.G. Jin, the LPS has become the most prominent paleontological research group, the "dream team," in China. One of the world's leading authorities on brachiopod paleobiology and Permian boundaries himself, Jin has played a pivotal role in the conception, organization, and operation of the LPS during the past decade. He has gathered around him a group of young, energetic, and active researchers such as W.G. Sun (Precambrian paleobiology), J.Y. Rong (brachiopods), X. Chen (graptolites), J.Y. Chen (cephalopods), X.N. Mu (fungi), P.J. Chen (conchostracans), and Q. Yang (molecular paleobiology) among many other upcoming scientists. He has at his disposal a facility with state-of-the-art equipment. Under his able leadership, the LPS has managed to raise sufficient money to fund its ambitious research activities, and its scholars have published some of their research in the most prestigious international scientific journals.

Among many of the NIGP's and LPS' accomplishments in this period, the discovery and studies on the Chengjiang fauna and the "Cambrian explosion" must be highlighted. The Chengjiang fauna is a beautifully preserved, soft-bodied metazoan assemblage (gathering of many species of metozoan, or multicellular, organisms) from the late Early Cambrian strata in Yunnan Province, China. This find dates earlier than the better known Middle Cambrian Burgess Shale fauna from British Columbia, Canada, and reveals a remarkable morphological diversity in early animal body plans. The NIGP and LPS colleagues also have been instrumental in the selections of the internationally accepted boundary stratotype sections, both in China and abroad.

The IVPP continued to enjoy the benefits of a strong leadership during this period. After Young passed away in 1979, Chow took over as the IVPP's director and immediately launched a series of initiatives aimed at bringing the IVPP to world preeminence. With his personal connections in the United States, Chow was able to lead the IVPP's delegation in 1980 to tour all of the major U.S. institutions of vertebrate paleontgy. During that visit, he reestablished many old ties and cultivated new friendships. The visit also paved the way for many leading American vertebrate paleontologists to pay reciprocal visits to the IVPP. Soon there were Chinese visiting scientists or graduate students in virtually every major U.S. vertebrate paleontological institution. The scholarly exchanges were equally active and productive between the IVPP and its counterparts in Europe, Australia, and Japan. At the pinnacle of his achievements and popularity, Chow suddenly stepped down in the mid-1980s and handed the directorship to M.M. Chang, an unusual move at the time and, in retrospect, a wise one. Chang has proved to be the most effective leader in difficult times. Her academic accomplishments, international reputation, toughness and fairness, and above all, charisma, helped her forge relationships in the world scholarly commu-

nity. She cut through a complex web of perplexing politics to safeguard the successful completion of the Sino-Canadian Dinosaur Project (1986–90). She secured the funds to build a magnificent office/collection building for the IVPP at a time when governmental funding for basic research was severely curtailed and when competition for funding was fierce.

Thanks to Chow's and Chang's visionary measures, the IVPP has become one of the most important research centers of vertebrate paleontology and paleoanthropology in the world today. It excels in research areas such as Paleozoic fishes and the origin of tetrapods; Mesozoic and Paleogene mammals; the origin and early diversification of major groups such as rodents, rabbits, elephants, and primates; Neogene mammals and biostratigraphy; Mesozoic non-dinosaurian reptiles (especially the mammal-like reptiles); Mesozoic birds and the origin of birds and flight; and higher primates and hominid fossils. It also boasts a spectacular dinosaur collection.

One of the most important changes during the post-Mao era in Chinese paleontology has been the pluralization of its research infrastructure. For better or for worse, the monopoly enjoyed by the NIGP and IVPP has come to an end. Now the paleontology programs in the universities and colleges, as well as natural history museums, are playing an increasingly important role in original research. Consequently, competition has intensified in recent years for funding, fossil specimens, and opportunities to collaborate with western colleagues. For the paleontologists in the West who wish to work in China or on Chinese fossils, the task of trying to figure out the politics involved often is a Penelope's web. However, one should be well advised but not discouraged.

Epilogue

However inconsequential it may seem, the history of paleontological research in China is an integral part of the grand history of modern China. Perhaps the observation by the celebrated American traveler and writer, Paul Theroux (1988) is worth quoting: "China has suffered more cataclysms than any other country on earth. And yet it endures and even prospers." The same observation can be made about several generations of Chinese paleontologists.

Desui Miao

Works Cited

Needham, J. 1954. *Science and Civilisation in China*. Vol. 3. Cambridge and New York: Cambridge University Press.

Teichert, C., L. Liu, and P.J. Chen (eds.). 1981. *Paleontology in China, 1979*. Geological Society of America Special Paper, 187. Boulder, Colorado: Geological Society of America.

Teichert, C., and Z.X. Yin. 1981. Preface. *In* C. Teichert, L. Liu, and P.J. Chen (eds.), *Paleontology in China, 1979*. Geological Society of America Special Paper, 187. Boulder, Colorado: Geological Society of America.

Theroux, P. 1988. *Riding the Iron Rooster: By Train through China*. New York: Putnam's; London: Hamilton.

Walcott, C.D. 1906. Cambrian faunas of China. *Proceedings of the United States National Museum* 30:563–595.

Further Reading

Chang, H.T. 1936. *A Short History of Development of Geology in China.* Shanghai: Commerce Press. [In Chinese.]

Grady, W. 1993. *The Dinosaur Project: The Story of the Greatest Dinosaur Expedition Ever Mounted.* Toronto: MacFarlane, Walter and Ross; Edmonton: Ex Terra Foundation.

Liu, C.M. 1985. *History of Geology in China.* Taipei: Commerce Press. [In Chinese.]

Teichert, C., L. Liu, and P.J. Chen (eds.). 1981. *Paleontology in China, 1979.* Geological Society of America Special Paper, 187. Boulder, Colorado: Geological Society of America.

Wang, Z.X., and H.L. Wang. 1985. *The Concise History of Geology.* Zhengzhou: Henan Science and Technology Press. [In Chinese.]

Yang, Z.Y., Y.Q. Cheng, and H.Z. Wang. 1986. *The Geology of China.* Oxford Monographs on Geology and Geophysics, No. 3. Oxford: Clarendon; New York: Oxford University Press.

CHIROPTERANS

See Bats

CHONDRICHTHYANS

Ecology

Excluding the jawless cyclostomes (lampreys and hagfishes), which represent the only extant jawless fishes, all fishes today belong to two main groups: the Chondrichthyes (cartilaginous fishes), and the Osteichthyes (bony fishes). Both of these groups have articulated (jointed) jaws and therefore belong to the Gnathostomes (jawed fishes). Nearly all extant chondrichthyans are marine (saltwater) animals, but nonmarine exceptions include a freshwater family of South American rays (Dotamotrygoidae) and, in a loose sense, the bull shark *Carcharinus leucas,* which is essentially a marine species but has also been reported from lakes and rivers. A few fossils forms also lived in freshwater environments, mainly the Paleozoic Xenacanthiformes (sharks that had a continuous fin along the back), but also to a lesser extent the Mesozoic and Early Cenozoic hybodonts. Present-day selachians (sharks, skates, and rays) are present at all latitudes and occur in almost all marine habitats—from coasts to the open ocean and at depths exceeding 2,000 meters. All selachians are carnivorous, although the biggest species, including the giant whale-shark, feed mainly on plankton.

Morphology

Chondrichthyans have a typical vertebrate body structure but differ from Osteichthyes in that their internal skeleton never ossifies (it is made of cartilage, not bone), although it is often strengthened by superficial calcification. Hence, their prismatic calcified cartilage is the main characteristic of the Chondrichthyes. All Paleozoic chondrichthyans, with a few exceptions among the Subterbranchiala, retained a notochord, the axial support that gives the name to the phylum Chordata. Almost all living chondrichthyans replace the notochord with vertebrae composed of cartilage. Among extant taxa, only a few primitive forms retain a notochord; most of these belong to the dogfish family (Squalea). In further contrast to bony fishes, chondrichthyans do not have a swim bladder. Instead, present-day sharks have developed a large oil-filled liver, which helps them to reduce their specific gravity, thus helping to keep sharks from sinking.

Reproduction

All modern chondrichthyans reproduce by internal fertilization, assisted by paired intromittent organs called "claspers." This struc-ture is supported by the skeleton of the pelvic fin and is used to inseminate the female during copulation. Subsequently, sharks usually are either ovoviviparous (eggs incubate internally) or viviparous (young develop within an oviduct). Some species lay a few large, yolky eggs.

Evolutionary History

Extant chondrichthyans are divided into two subclasses: the diverse Elasmobranchii, which includes the sharks, skates, and rays, and the much rarer and poorly known Subterbranchiala, which includes the chimaeras, or ratfishes (Holocephali). The elasmobranchs and the holocephalans diverged early in the history of the chondrichthyans (Gaudin 1991). The most ancient remains attributable to Chondrichthyes are isolated scales from the Early Silurian (430 million years ago) of Canada, Russia, and Central Asia, but their exact relationships within the chondrichthyans remain unknown. Table 1 lists some of the groups within Chondrichthyes, along with information about their morphological characteristics, their stratigraphic range, and their paleoecology.

Elasmobranchii

The most fundamental difference between the elasmobranchs and the subterbranchs lies in the morphology of the gill region (Zangerl 1981). In elasmobranchs the gill region is elongate and spaced well away from the braincase, while in the holocephalans (and bony fishes) the gill region is shorter and close to the braincase. Other morphological characteristics of the skeleton are less clear, particularly in fossil forms, since preservation of the cartilaginous skeleton of chondrichthyans requires exceptional conditions that are rarely found in the fossil record. Fortunately, elasmobranchs produce highly mineralized dermal elements that are readily fossilizable, and their scales (dermal denticles), teeth, and fin spines are commonly found as fossils. A group of Paleozoic sharks called the Lepidomoria produce the simplest type of scales. They consist of a cone of dentine developed over a pulp cavity and are usually capped with a hard, shiny layer of enamel. Scale growth occurs by the progressive addition of layers, a growth pattern called "cyclomorial" (Stensiö 1975) (Figure 1). However, in all modern sharks, as well as some Paleozoic genera, the scales show

Table 1.

Simplified classification of the Chondrichthyes.

Class Chondrichthyes

Subclass Elasmobranchii

  Order Cladoselachiformes*

  Order Coronodontiformes

  Order Symmoriiformes*

  Order Orodontiformes*

  Order Eugeneodontiformes*

  Order Petalodontiformes*

  Order Squatinactiformes

  Order Desmiodontiformes*

  Order Xenacanthiformes

 Cohort Euselachii

  Superfamily Ctenacanthoidea

  Superfamily Hybodontoidea

  Superfamily Protacrodontoidea

 Subcohort Neoselachii

  Division Galea

  Order Heterodontiformes

  Order Orectolobiformes

  Order Lamniformes

  Order Carcharhiniformes

  Division Squalea

  Order Chlamydoselachiformes

  Order Hexanchiformes

  Order Echinorhiniformes

  Order Dalatiiformes

  Order Centrophoriformes

  Order Squaliformes

  Order Squatiniformes

  Order Pristiophoriformes

  Order Rajiformes

Subclass Subterbranchiala

  Order Inioterygiformes

  Order Polysentoriformes

 Superorder Holocephali

  Order Helodontiformes

  Order Bradyodontiformes

  Order Chondrenchelyiformes

  Order Chimaeriformes

Asterisk indicates orders that may or may not belong to the Elasmobranchii. Modified from Capetta (1997); Janvier (1996); and Shirai (1996).

Figure 1. A single lepidomorium and aggregates of two, three, and four lepidomoria (seen from below). Size of each is approximately 450 microns. From Zangerl (1966), courtesy of The Field Museum, Chicago.

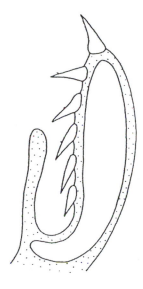

Figure 2. Shark mandible in cross section, showing the replacement of tooth rows. Redrawn by Gilles Cuny after Capetta (1987).

no growth pattern, and their definitive size occurs when they first form. Such scales are called "placoid." They are replaced throughout the life of the animal and, since their shapes vary according to the part of the body they come from, their use in taxonomy is problematic.

Elasmobranch teeth are derived from elaborate scales along the margin of the jaws and are attached by connective tissue only, without a real root anchoring them to the jaws. Furthermore, they are primitively polyphyodont—they are continually replaced throughout life by a complicated process of tooth migration. They are formed on the tongue-side of the jaws, then move upward to the edges (Figure 2). During migration the teeth rotate nearly 180 degrees, which leads to the appearance of replacement tooth rows. Each tooth remains in a functional position for a relatively short period of time—two weeks on average—then is replaced. The teeth usually show a wide range of morphology within one species.

Most elasmobranch sharks also have a spine in front of each of their dorsal fins. These fin spines have two components: the trunk and the mantle (Maisey 1975) (Figure 3). The trunk is a stout component that extends deep into the shark's body, and consists of two concentric layers of dentine. The mantle covers the surface of the trunk, forming an "ornament." In all sharks the mantle consists primarily of dentine; in modern forms the mantle is overlain by a thick layer of enamel.

Because of poor preservation, many chondrichthyan genera are only known from isolated teeth, spines, or scales (particularly in the Paleozoic), and "well-known" genera frequently are represented by very few specimens. Isolated teeth of the oldest, Devonian chondrichthyans are sometimes difficult to recognize, and many teeth once described as chondrichthyan from Lower Devonian sediments appear in fact to belong to an unrelated group, the Acanthodians ("spiny sharks"). The most ancient teeth definitely attributed to elasmobranchs come from Lower Devonian strata of Spain (409 to 386 million years ago), and represent the possible xenacanthiform genus *Leonodus*. Also, *Phoebodus* from the United States and *Mcmurdodus* from Australia and Antarctica are found in the lower-Middle Devonian (385 million years ago). However, these two families are considered to be "advanced sharks," suggesting a much more ancient origin for the elasmobranchs. The elasmobranchs underwent a widespread radiation during the Carboniferous Period (363 to 290 million years ago), but by the end of the Paleozoic Era, most of the genera had become extinct. Following a complete revision of the group by Zangerl (1981), many new orders of elasmobranchs were named, but their precise relationships in evolutionary history remain unclear.

Cladoselachiformes

Members of the order Cladoselachiformes are known from Upper Devonian strata of the United States (377 to 363 million years ago), in particular *Cladoselache* (Figure 4), which is represented by many beautifully preserved skeletons. Hence, *Cladoselache* is the earliest well-known shark genus. Like other primitive sharks, *Cladoselache* has a spindle-shaped body outline, up to two meters in length. [The upper jaw (palatoquadrate) has two connections with the braincase (Figure 5A), a direct one with the postorbital process (just behind the eye) and an indirect one via the hyomandibular (dorsal part of the second gill arch)]. This is termed amphistylic jaw suspension. The teeth are cladodont—they have a single major cusp and smaller side cusps above a broad base. *Cladoselache* has no anal fin and no claspers on the pelvic fins. Externally, the caudal (tail) fin is nearly symmetrical, but internally the notochord bends upward into the dorsal lobe, while the ventral lobe is supported by small cartilaginous rods called "radials." This is the heterocercal condition, which is present in most elasmobranchs (Figure 6A). This crescent-shaped caudal fin indicates a potential for fast swimming, while the narrow, well-articulated base of the pectoral fin allows considerable maneuverability. As in most sharks, the paired fins were used for steering and stabilization. Scales are restricted to the fin margins and to a circle of specialized denticles surrounding the eye.

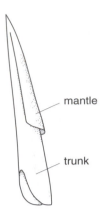

Figure 3. The components of the dorsal fin spine of elasmobranchs. Redrawn by Catherine P. Sexton after Maisey (1975).

Coronodontiformes

This poorly known order is restricted to Upper Devonian (377- to 363-million-years-old) rocks of North America. The jaw suspension is amphistylic, and the caudal fin has a relatively small ventral lobe. Coronodonts have at least one, and possibly two, dorsal fins (preservation of this part of the skeleton is too poor to be certain). There is no anal fin, nor fin spine.

Symmoriiformes

Many virtually complete skeletons of symmoriiforms are found in Upper Devonian to Carboniferous rocks of the United States (377 to 290 million years ago). These sharks appear quite similar to Cladoselachiformes—they also have cladodont teeth, an amphistylic jaw suspension, a crescent-shaped caudal fin, sparse scale covering, and no anal fin (Figure 7A). They differ from coronodonts by the presence of a single spineless dorsal fin situated nearer the tail, and by the structure of the pectoral fins. As in most primitive Paleozoic sharks, the supports for the part of the pectoral fin closest to the body (the "basals") are arranged in a line (Figure 7B). Among the symmoriiforms, however, this axis ends in a free whip of unknown function. Furthermore, the males of the family Stethacanthidae show several different types of courtship structures behind the head, including a brush-shaped device in *Stethacanthus*, and a club-shaped structure in *Falcatus* (Figures 7C, 7D).

Orodontiformes

Orodonts, also known as edestids, are mainly represented by isolated teeth from Upper Devonian to Lower Permian strata in Europe and North America (363 to 269 million years ago). More complete material recently discovered in Carboniferous sediments of North America indicates that these animals were among the largest of all Paleozoic sharks, growing up to four

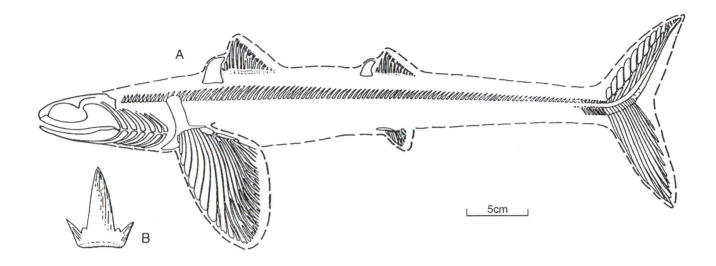

Figure 4. The cladoselachiform *Cladoselache*. *A*, reconstructed complete skeleton, showing paired fins and shoulder girdle; *B*, tooth. From: *A*, Zangerl (1981); *B*, Schaeffer and Williams (1977).

meters in length. The body is elongate with small paired fins but otherwise is quite similar to symmoriids, with a single, spineless dorsal fin and no anal fin (Figure 8). A platform of broad, blunt teeth form what is called a "pavement dentition," which is especially efficient at crushing shellfish. A row of sharper teeth is situated in the midline at the front of the lower jaw (symphyseal teeth).

Eugeneodontiformes

Eugeneodonts are found in Carboniferous to Triassic strata of the northern hemisphere (363 to 208 million years ago). Symphyseal teeth are very large, and replacement teeth often accumulate to form a complex spiral, or tooth whorl (Figure 9B). Each spiral has a series of teeth joined together in such a way that the largest teeth at the top are in use, and new teeth rotate into position when older ones wear away or break. The side teeth form a crushing pavement, functionally comparable with that of modern skates and rays, which indicates a diet mainly composed of hard-shelled invertebrates.

Knowledge of the skeleton of these sharks is limited, as it tends to be weakly calcified, but it was probably quite similar to that of cladoselachians and symmoriiforms. The body is spindle-shaped, with an externally symmetrical caudal fin (Figure 9A). The anal fin is absent and there is only a single, spineless dorsal fin located above the shoulder girdle. The pectoral fin has an elongate axis directed towards the tail, but it is not as long as the whip found in symmoriids. Pelvic fins appear to have been entirely lost, and the palatoquadrate is much reduced or perhaps even absent.

Petalodontiformes

Petalodonts are mainly represented by large isolated teeth (up to 10 centimeters in size), from rocks ranging from Lower Carboniferous to Permian (350 to 245 million years ago), again of the northern hemisphere. They had a mixture of sharp, cutting teeth and blunt, crushing teeth. The best-known genus, *Belantsea* (Figure 10), is comparable to some extant reef fishes, with its high body with compressed sides. Its anterior teeth formed a beaklike cropping mechanism, which may have allowed it to crack shells and graze coral, as do modern-day parrot fish. However, it has only one gill opening, which raises a question about the placement of petalodonts within the Elasmobranchii.

Squatinactiformes

Squatinactiforms are known from the single, very peculiar North American genus *Squatinactis* of the Lower Carboniferous (325 million years ago). It has a skatelike body plan with greatly expanded pectoral fins. It also has cladodont, sharp-cusped teeth. Its long, straight tail has a spine near its end, like that of stingrays. Like petalodonts, the evolutionary affinities of squatinactiforms are unclear.

Desmiodontiformes

Restricted to Lower Carboniferous rocks of the United States (363 to 323 million years ago), desmiodonts are mainly known from isolated teeth of variable morphology. The only known skeleton, that of *Heteropetalus* (Figure 11), has a straight diphycercal tail. It also has an elongate dorsal fin with a weak spine. The palatoquadrate and the braincase are not joined, and, as in present-day neoselachians, the upper jaw is only supported by the hyomandibular. This is termed hyostylic jaw suspension (Figure 5B).

Xenacanthiformes

Xenacanths are known from Lower Devonian to end Triassic freshwater deposits of North and South America, Europe, and China (409 to 208 million years ago). They possess very characteristic "diplodont" teeth, where the lateral cusps tooth are enhanced and the central cusp is reduced or absent (Figure 12B). Jaw suspension is amphistylic (Figure 5A). The dorsal fin is highly derived (specialized) and extends from just behind the head to the level of the caudal fin (Figure 12A). The spine associated with this fin may articulate with either the shoulder girdle or the rear of the skull. In some xenacanths, the tail fin is not heterocercal, but diphycercal (Figure 6C). The pectoral fins display radials both in front and behind the main fin axis, a condition called "archipterygial." This contrasts with most Paleozoic sharks, which only have radials in front of the main pectoral fin axis. In other xenacanths, the radials may be replaced by more flexible rods of collagen, called "ceratotrichia." These peculiar pectoral and caudal fins, together with the presence of two anal fins, allow increased sinusoidal (s-shaped) movements of the body during swimming. Owing to the highly derived structure of the fins, relationships of the xenacanths were problematic for some time, but they now appear to be most closely related to the Euselachii.

Despite a relatively poor fossil record, Paleozoic sharks exhibit a much wider spectrum of adaptations than modern genera. The peak of diversity occurred during the Carboniferous. In addition to filling the niches now occupied by sharks, there were several lineages within the Squatinactiformes that had a similar lifestyle to modern skates and rays. Several groups evolved pavement dentitions (Eugeneodontiformes, Orodontiformes, Petalodontiformes) that have no counterpart among living taxa. The freshwater Xenacanthiformes also represent a unique experiment. Several orders occupied habitats that were taken over after the Triassic by various groups of bony fishes. The evolutionary relationships of these primitive sharks remain poorly known, and it is unclear whether most of these orders (with the exception of the Xenacanthiformes) are "true" Elasmobranchii (Janvier 1996). In fact, orodonts, eugeneodonts, petalodonts, and desmiodontiforms are sometimes considered to be closer to Holocephali than to Elasmobranchii.

Ctenacanthoidea

Although the Ctenacanthoidea are known as "advanced sharks," members of this group represent some of the oldest chondrichthyans ever found, including the genus *Phoebodus* from Lower Middle Devonian rocks of the United States (386 to 381 million years ago). Their range is known to extend up to the end of the Triassic Period (208 million years ago). They have been found only in North America and Europe, where peak diversity was reached during Carboniferous times. They are poorly known, with only a few complete skeletons discovered (Figure 13A), and are represented mainly by isolated cladodont teeth (Figure 13B) and fin spines. The two dorsal fin spines of these sharks have a mantle with an external enameloid substance, similar to that covering the crowns

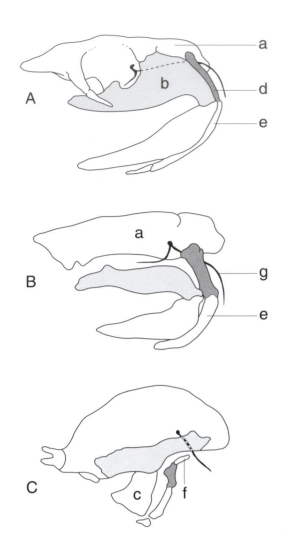

Figure 5. Three types of jaw suspension among Chondrichthyes. *A*, amphistylic; *B*, hyostylic; *C*, holostylic (or autostylic). Key: *a*, braincase; *b*, palatoquadrate; *c*, Meckel's cartilage (lower jaw); *d*, hyomandibular; *e*, ceratohyal; *f*, pharyngohyal; *g*, hyomandibular branch of the facial nerve. Redrawn by Catherine P. Sexton after Arambourg and Bertin (1958).

of the teeth. This feature is not found in the primitive Paleozoic sharks and thus appears to be a derived character.

The distal end of the spine is exposed to the surface and not covered by the skin. The pectoral fins show the first indications of the "tribasal" structure common to present-day sharks. Here, the main basal bone (metapterygium) that supports the radials along the proximal margin of the fin is reinforced by two new basals in front of it called the mesopterygium and propterygium (Figure 14).

Ctenacanths are rather generalized elasmobranchs, with the exception of *Bandringa,* found in both freshwater and marine deposits of Middle Carboniferous age (311 to 303 million years ago) of North America. *Bandringa* has a greatly elongate rostrum (snout), and thus has been placed in a family of its own, the Bandringidae.

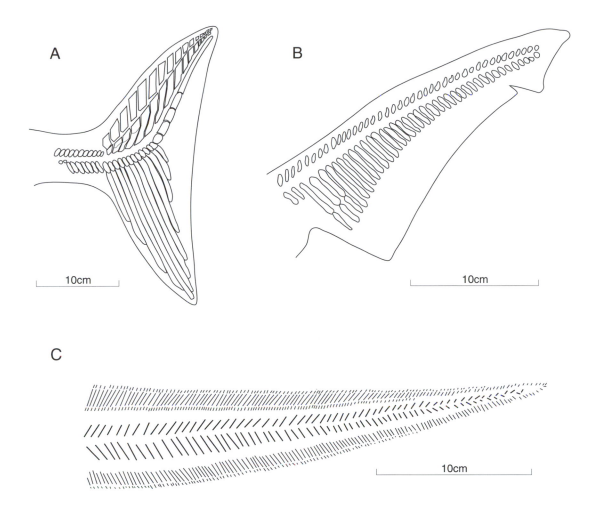

Figure 6. Different types of tail fin among elasmobranchs. *A,* heterocercal (symmetric, crescent-shaped); *B,* asymmetric heterocercal; *C,* diphycercal. Redrawn and modified by Catherine P. Sexton after: *A, B,* Maisey (1982); *C,* Zangerl (1981).

Protacrodontoidea

These poorly known sharks are found in rocks ranging in age from the Upper Devonian of Europe and North America to the Carboniferous of North America (377 to 290 million years ago). The shape of their teeth is similar to that of orodonts, though the internal structure of protacrodont teeth is similar to that of the ctenacanths.

Hybodontoidea

Hybodonts are distributed globally from the Early Carboniferous to the end of the Cretaceous (363 to 65 million years ago), although they may have originated in the Late Devonian, as indicated by some loosely identified fin spines and isolated teeth of possible hybodont affinity. Hybodonts reached maximum diversity during the Mesozoic Era, when they replaced ctenacanths as the dominant predatory sharks. Hybodonts were in turn replaced by the modern neoselachians during the Late Cretaceous (89 to 65 million years ago). Reasonably well known Paleozoic genera occur in Carboniferous rocks, including *Tristychius* and *Onychoselache,* both from Scotland, and *Hamiltonichthys* (Figure 13E) from the United States. In hybodonts the tribasal pattern of the pectoral fins is well established (Figure 14B) and, except in some Paleozoic forms, the radials are replaced distally (toward the fin margin) by ceratotrichia. The caudal fin is heterocercal, with a very small ventral lobe (Figure 6B).

Hybodonts are characterized by having one or two pairs of hook-shaped spines on the head, which appear only to be present in the males. These may have played a specific role in courtship behavior and perhaps also were used in defense (Rieppel 1981). Most hybodonts had a modified amphistylic jaw suspension (Figure 5A), with the joint between the palatoquadrate and the neurocranium closer to the "nose" of the animal than in most other Paleozoic sharks. One genus *(Tribodus)* from the Brazilian Lower Cretaceous (112 to 97 million years ago) has a hyostylic jaw suspension. Most Mesozoic hybodonts have a variety of tooth shapes within the cladodont pattern, indicating that these sharks fed upon a wide range of organisms. Other hybodonts (e.g., acrodontids and ptychodontids) have more specialized, crushing teeth. Today, this kind of dentition is restricted to benthic (bottom-dwelling) sharks, skates, and rays. It is therefore reasonable to suggest that these types of hybodonts also had bottom-dwelling habits.

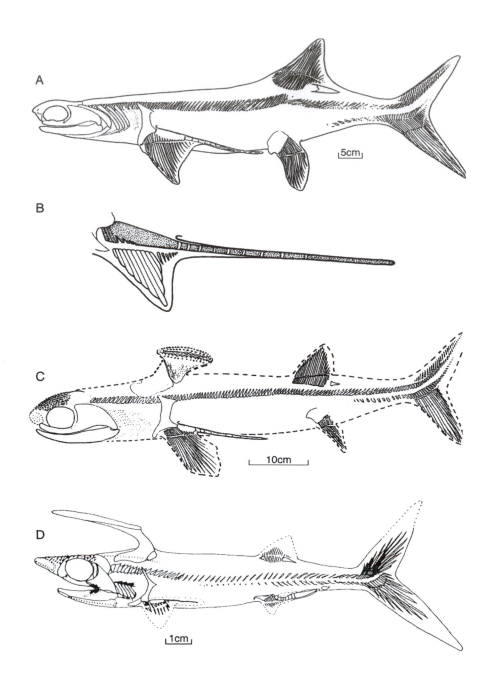

Figure 7. Symmoriiformes. *A, Cobelodus,* reconstructed complete skeleton; *B, Denaea,* pectoral fin skeleton; *C, Stethacanthus,* reconstructed complete skeleton; *D, Falcatus,* reconstructed complete skeleton. From: *A,* Zangerl and Case (1976); *B,* Schaeffer and Williams (1977); *C,* Zangerl (1981); *D,* Lund (1985).

Neoselachii

As previously mentioned, neoselachian sharks, or modern sharks, may date back to the Devonian period (409 to 363 million years ago) as indicated by some isolated teeth from Australia and Antarctica attributed to the genus *Mcmurdodus*. Today, the neosela-

chians are represented by at least 36 families and have the following characteristics. The vertebral centra are strongly calcified to resist the compressional forces associated with swimming. They have more mobile pectoral fins in which the ceratotrichia are the main support elements. They also have reduced fin spines without

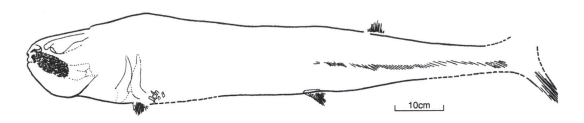

Figure 8. Orodontiformes. *Orodus,* tentative reconstruction. From Zangerl (1981).

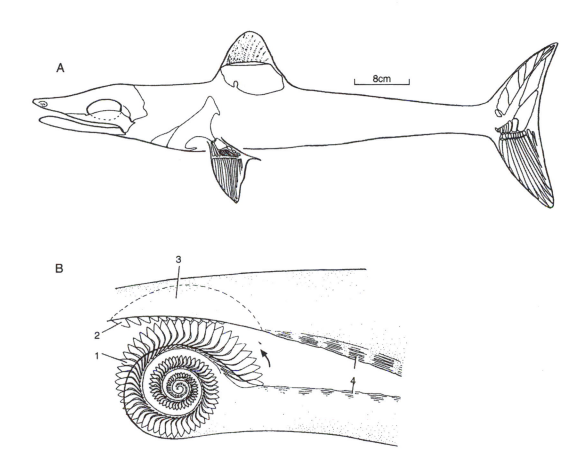

Figure 9. Eugeneodontiformes. *A, Caseodus,* reconstruction; *B, Helicoprion,* attempted reconstruction of symphysial (anterior) region of the lower jaw and snout. *1,* lower symphysial tooth spiral; *2,* upper parasymphysial tooth series; *3,* space between the upper parasymphysial teeth to accommodate the lower symphysial tooth spiral; *4,* lateral teeth. From: *A,* Zangerl (1981); *B,* Janvier (1996), by permission of Oxford University Press.

ornamentation. Consequently, neoselachians swim faster than other elasmobranchs. The jaws have a hyostylic suspension, which gives a wider gape than in Paleozoic sharks. The snout is usually longer than the lower jaw, which means the mouth opens beneath the head rather than at the front. The size of the nasal capsules is increased, providing a better sense of smell. Along with all these improvements in feeding, locomotion, and sensory input, neoselachians have larger brains than their Paleozoic ancestors and other

jawed fishes. In fact, large predatory sharks and advanced rays have a brain weight to body weight ratio that is higher than that of many birds and mammals (Northcutt 1977).

Details of early neoselachian evolution are poorly known. Most of the available fossils are isolated teeth. The teeth of neoselachian sharks are derived in that their enameloid is formed from three distinct layers, while all other elasmobranchs have only one layer (Reif 1973). Since the enameloid tooth structure of *Mcmur-*

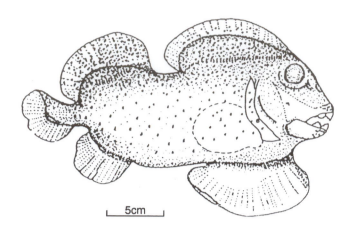

Figure 10. Petalodontiformes. *Belantsea,* life reconstruction. From Benton (1997).

dodus is currently unknown, it is impossible to definitively call it the earliest neoselachian.

The next oldest possible neoselachian teeth belong to *Anachronistes,* found in the Carboniferous of Britain (363 to 290 million years ago) and the Permian of North America (290 to 245 million years ago). However, these teeth lack an enameloid cover, so it is very difficult to confirm their neoselachian affinities. As a result, the earliest unequivocal neoselachian tooth with a triple-layered enameloid is known from the Lower Triassic of Turkey (245 to 241 million years ago). Recently, similar teeth have been reported from Middle Triassic strata of Nevada (241 to 235 million years ago).

The first significant radiation of this group took place during the Late Triassic Period (235 to 208 million years ago), with a total of eight species known in Europe. The primary evidence consists of isolated teeth, fin spines, and vertebrae, causing their exact relationship to extant sharks to be unclear. The most primitive

Jurassic families include the Palaeospinacidae (although these may have evolved as early as the Lower Triassic (240 million years ago) and the Orthacodontidae (known with certainty from the Lower Jurassic, 200 million years ago). Their evolutionary position relative to the two modern divisions, Galea and Squalea, is still unclear.

Galea

Sharks of the Division Galea are active swimmers with fusiform (torpedo-shaped) bodies. They are the dominant marine carnivores in tropical oceans. If we exclude the Palaeospinacidae from this group, the first galeans appear at the top of the Lower Jurassic (204 million years ago). These are primitive members of the Orectolobiformes (a group that today includes the nurse and the whale sharks) and the living genus *Heterodontus* (Figure 15A). The latter is the only neoselachian outside the skates and rays to possess a crushing dentition. As a result, it is put in a group of its own, the Heterodontiformes. The Carcharhiniformes, a group that includes tiger, blue, and hammerhead sharks (Figure 15D), are first reported from the Upper Jurassic (166 million years ago).

The first Lamniformes, a group that includes basking, mako, and great white sharks, as well as the strange megamouth shark, *Megachasma* (Figure 15B), discovered in 1976, are not reported prior to the early Cretaceous (141 million years ago). Carcharhiniforms and lamniforms, which today represent more than 60 percent of the modern species, are characterized by a complete lack of dorsal fin spines. Galean sharks hold several records. The whale shark is regarded as the biggest fish ever known, reaching up to 18 meters in length and weighing up to 41 tons. Similarly, the group boasts the biggest predatory shark, *Carcharocles megalodon* (Figure 15C), which lived during the Miocene and the Pliocene (from 23 to 2 million years ago). This shark attained an estimated length of 13 meters, although it is only known from isolated teeth of up to 168 millimeters in height. By comparison, one of the biggest great white sharks, caught near Cuba in 1940, was "only" 6 meters long and weighed 3,320 kilograms.

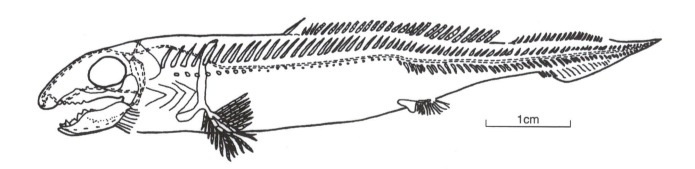

Figure 11. Desmiodontiformes. *Heteropetalus,* reconstructed skeleton. From Zangerl (1981).

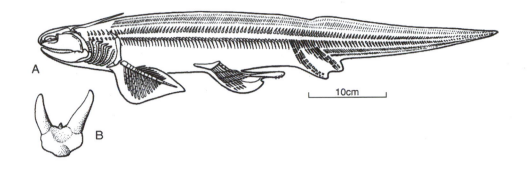

Figure 12. Xenacanthiformes, *Expleuracanthus*. *A,* reconstructed complete skeleton; *B,* tooth. From Schaeffer and Williams (1977).

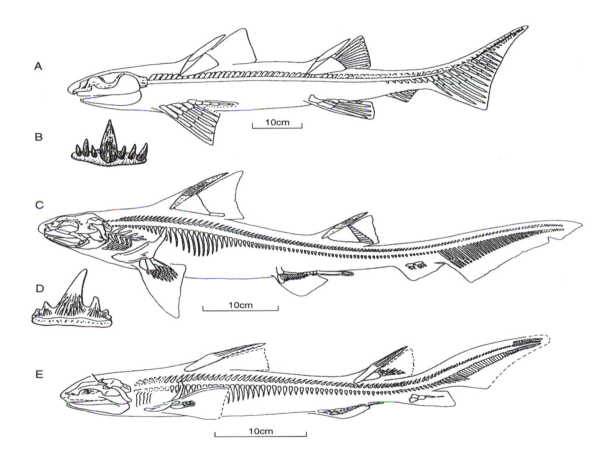

Figure 13. Ctenacanthoidea and Hybodontoidea. *A,* idealized Ctenacanthoidea, reconstructed skeleton; *B, Ctenacanthus,* tooth; *C, Hybodus,* a Mesozoic hybodont, reconstructed complete skeleton; *D, Egertonodus,* a Mesozoic hybodont, tooth; *E, Hamiltonichthys,* another Mesozoic hybodont, reconstructed complete skeleton. From: *A,* Maisey (1975); *B,* Janvier (1996), by permission of Oxford University Press; *C,* Maisey (1989); *D,* Maisey (1983); *E, Hamiltonichthys,* Maisey (1982).

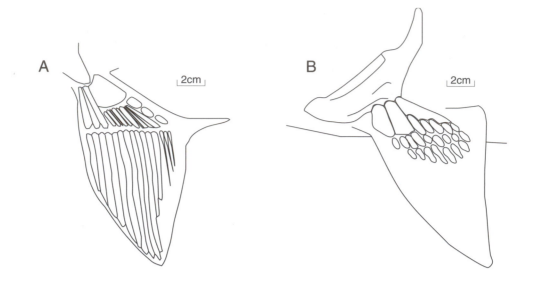

Figure 14. *A*, the primitive basal pattern of the pectoral fin (*Caseodus* sp.); *B*, the tribasal pattern of the advanced elasmobranchs (*Hybodus* sp.). Redrawn and modified by Catherine P. Sexton after: *A*, Zangerl (1981); *B*, Maisey (1982).

Squalea

Squalean sharks appear more primitive in their general anatomy than galeans. The first known neoselachian, *Mcmurdodus* (of the Lower-Middle Devonian) may belong to a squalean order, the Hexanchiformes. However, "true" Hexanchiformes did not appear prior to the early Jurassic (208 million years ago). Squaleans are characterized by the loss of the anterior dorsal fin and both fin spines. The most primitive squalean family appears to be the Chlamydoselachidae, often included with the Hexanchiformes. Since the Chlamydoselachidae has not been recorded before the late Cretaceous (89 million years ago), there appears to be a discrepancy between the phylogenetic position of this group and the fossil record.

The saw sharks (pristiophoriformes) display a very long rostrum armed with a laterally directed toothlike structures. Most of the other squalean sharks, for example *Squalus*, the spiny dogfish (Figure 16A), show some specializations for a bottom-dwelling lifestyle. Full realization of this ecological niche was attained by the Rajiformes (rays), the first of which, *Jurobatos*, dates from the Lower Jurassic of Germany (187 million years ago). Rajiformes have an easily recognizable flattened body shape, rather like a pancake, with the eyes placed on the top of the animal. The vertebrae closest to the head are fused into a "synarcual," similar to that of the unrelated placoderms. The flaplike pectoral fins are greatly enlarged and fused to the head above the gill opening, while the dorsal fins are reduced or absent (Figure 16C). There is no anal fin, and the tail fin is reduced, often to a mere whiplike structure. Indeed, unlike most other sharks, the propulsive fins of the Rajiformes are the pectoral pair, not the caudal fin. The jaws are extremely mobile, with a modified hyostylic suspension, and the teeth often form a crushing pavement, permitting an omnivorous diet (including hard-shelled invertebrates). Among Rajiformes, the Pristidae (sawfish) (Figure 16B) display a rostrum very similar to that of the Pristiophoriformes.

Subterbranchiala

The Subterbranchiala include the Holocephali (ratfish) and similar forms, but the evolutionary relationships of the different members of this subclass are far from fully understood. The earliest record of this subclass comes from the Devonian period. As a result of their short gill region, holocephalans, like bony fishes, have developed a special structure called an operculum to protect the gill openings. Elasmobranchs, by contrast, do not possess an operculum and have as many as seven pairs of separate gill openings. Another feature that distinguishes the subterbranchs from the elasmobranchs is the connection between the upper jaw and the braincase. There is a tendency among subterbranchs toward complete fusion between the palatoquadrate and the braincase, giving rise to a jaw suspension called "holostylic" or "autostylic" (Figure 5C). Furthermore, fin spines of subterbranchs show considerable contrast to those of elasmobranchs and, therefore, are probably not homologous.

Holocephali

The Holocephali are known from the late Devonian (367 million years ago) and encompass four groups: Helodontiformes (Figure 17A), Bradyodontiformes, Chondrenchelyiformes (Figure 17B), and Chimaeriformes (Figure 17C). Only the latter is extant, and it is represented by just five genera. Among the Holocephali, the anterior vertebrae are fused to form a synarcual. A dorsal spine articulates with the synarcual. In some modern forms, this spine is connected to a poison gland. The caudal fin is reduced, and the canals of the sensory-line system are strengthened by small, calcified rings. In addition to having claspers on the pelvic fins, the males have prepelvic claspers (retractable extensions of the pelvic girdle) and an unpaired clasping organ on the top of the head. Paleozoic genera belonging to the Bradyodontiformes and Chondrenchelyiformes have paired frontal claspers with various morphologies. The

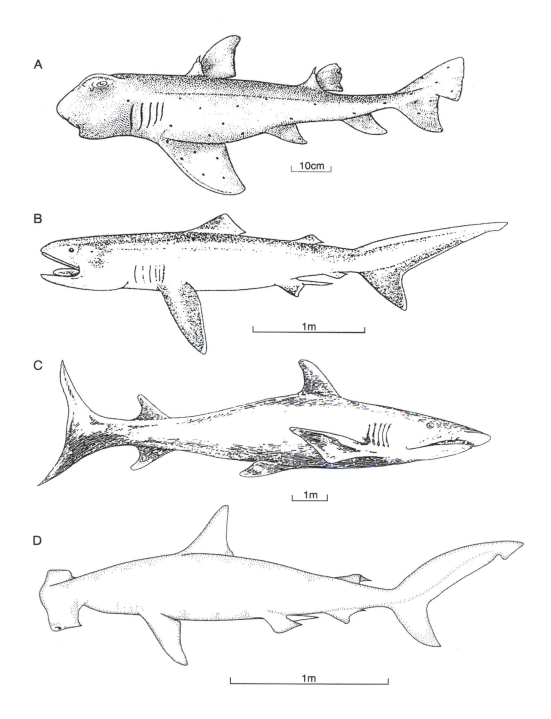

Figure 15. Galea. *A, Heterodontus* (Heterodontiformes, bullhead shark); *B, Megchasma* (Lamniformes, megamouth shark); *C, Carcharocles megalodon* (Lamniformes); *D, Sphyrna* (Carchariniformes, hammerhead shark). From: *A,* Dean (1909); *B,* Compagno (1984), courtesy of the Food and Agriculture Organization of the United Nations; *C,* Bultynck et al. (1992); *D,* redrawn by Catherine P. Sexton after Johnson (1995).

latter, however, have an overall body shape very similar to that of the Xenacanthiformes. In modern Chimaeriformes, the teeth are reduced to two pairs of tooth plates in the upper jaw and one in the lower jaw. These plates are not replaced but grow at the margin. These teeth indicate a diet composed mainly of shelled organisms.

Some Paleozoic Chimaeriformes, however, have a quite different tooth pattern. For example, in addition to more typical tooth plates, the Cochliodontidae possess several small plates in the anterior part of the jaw that resemble shark teeth. The Menaspidae, a possibly unrelated group, show a single functional tooth in each of

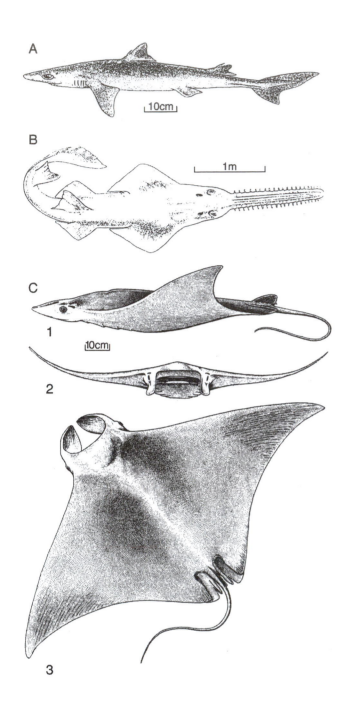

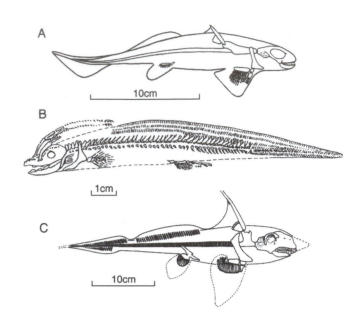

Figure 17. Holocephali. *A,* reconstructed *Helodus* (Helodontiformes); *B,* reconstructed complete skeleton of *Harpagofututor* (Chondrenchelyiformes); *C,* reconstructed *Ischyodus* (Chimaeriformes). From: *A,* Moy-Thomas and Miles (1971); *B,* Lund (1982); *C,* Patterson (1965).

Figure 16. Squalea. *A, Squalus* (Squaliformes); *B, Pristis* (Rajiformes, sawfish); *C, Mobula* (Rajiformes, ray): *1,* lateral view; *2,* front view; *3,* dorsal view. *A,* and *B,* from C. Arambourg and L. Bertin, *Traité de Zoologie,* vol. 13, no. 3, P.P. Grassé (ed.), copyright © Masson, 1958, rights reserved; *C,* from P. Saint-Seine, C. Devillers, and J. Blot, *Traité de Paléontologie,* vol. 4, no. 2, J. Piveteau (ed.), copyright © Masson, 1969, rights reserved.

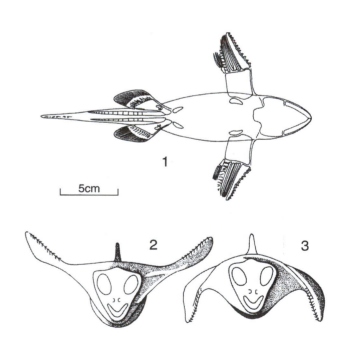

Figure 18. Iniopterygiformes *(Ionopteryx)* showing the assumed swimming position of the pectoral fins. *1,* ventral view; *2, 3,* frontal view. From Zangerl and Case (1973), courtesy of The Field Museum, Chicago.

the upper and lower jaws. Menaspids have a nearly continuous dermal armor that contrasts strongly with the unarmored skin of the Chimaeriformes. On the other hand *Similihariotta,* a chimaera from Carboniferous rocks of the United States, appears extremely similar to present-day species. Indeed, by the Jurassic Period, chimaeras such as *Ischyodus* had developed the same general appearance as the modern representatives.

Bradyodontiformes, which existed between the late Devonian and the end of the Permian (377 to 245 million years ago), also show a unique dentition. The Copodontidae show a dentition quite similar to that of the Cochliodontidae, with several small anterior plates resembling shark teeth. The most primitive dentition is found in the Helodontiformes, known only from freshwater Carboniferous deposits (laid down 363 to 290 million years ago). They had no large tooth plates but instead had smaller elements formed by the partial fusion of flattened, sharklike teeth. Such a diversity of tooth patterns helps us understand how the large tooth plates of extant members of the Chimaeriformes formed from the fusion of separate tooth families throughout the evolution of the Holocephali.

The following orders of Subterbranchiala show no direct affinities with the Holocephali.

Iniopterygiformes

Iniopterygians are known only from the Upper Carboniferous of the United States (310 to 295 million years ago). Their pectoral fins lie in a dorsal position and have additional claspers (Figure 18). They show no fused vertebrae or dorsal fin spine, and the jaw suspension is not consistently holostylic. The tooth pattern is different from the holocephalian pattern, with teeth arranged in a series of tooth whorls or in tooth files similar to those of elasmobranchs.

Polysentoriformes

This group is known only from Middle Carboniferous strata of the United States (311 to 303 million years ago). They have a hyostylic jaw suspension. They also have a continuous dorsal fin that extends from the shoulder region to the dorsal lobe of the tail. Their teeth are unknown.

GILLES CUNY AND GILES SMITH

See also Micropaleontology, Vertebrate; Pharyngeal Arches and Derivatives; Skeleton: Dermal Postcranial Skeleton; Skull; Teeth: Earliest Teeth

Works Cited

Arambourg, C., and L. Bertin. 1958. Classe des Chondrithyens. *In* P.P. Grassé (ed.), *Traité de Zoologie* 13 (3). Paris: Masson.

Benton, M.J. 1997. *Vertebrate Palaeontology.* 2nd ed., London: Chapman and Hall.

Bultynck, P., D. Cahen, A.V. Dhondt, M. Germonpre, J. Godefroid, G. Lenglet, and M. Martin. 1992. *Dinosaurs & Co., Fossiles et Robots.* Brussels: Editions de l'Institut Royal des Sciences Naturelles de Belgique.

Capetta, H. 1987. *Chondrichthyes. 2, Mesozoic and Cenozoic Elasmobranchii.* Handbook of Paleoichthyology, 3B. Stuttgart: Fischer Verlag.

Carroll, R.L. 1988. *Vertebrate Paleontology and Evolution.* New York: Freeman.

Compagno, L.V.J. 1984. *Sharks of the World: An Annotated and Illustrated Catalogue of Shark Species Known to Date.* Rome: United Nations Development Programme.

Dean, B. 1909. *Studies on Fossil Fishes (Sharks, Chimaeroids, and Arthrodires).* Memoirs of the American Museum of Natural History, 9. New York: American Museum of Natural History.

Gaudin, T.J. 1991. A reexamination of elasmobranch monophyly and chondrichthyes phylogeny. *Neues Jahrbuch für Geologie and Paläontologie, Abhandlungen* 182 (2):133–60.

Janvier, J. 1996. *Early Vertebrates.* Oxford Monograph on Geology and Geophysics, 33. Oxford: Clarendon; New York: Oxford University Press.

Johnson, R.H. 1995. *Requins des mers tropicales et tempérées.* Singapore: Les éditions du Pacifique.

Lund, R. 1982. *Harpagofututor volsellorhinus* new genus and species (Chondrichthyes, Chondrenchelyformes) from the Namurian Bear Gulch Limestone, *Chondrenchelys problematica* Traquair (Visean), and their sexual dimorphism. *Journal of Paleontology* 56:938–58.

———. 1985. The morphology of *Falcatus falcatus* (St. John and Worthen), a Mississippian stethacanthid chondrichthyan from the Bear Gulch Limestone of Montana. *Journal of Vertebrate Paleontology* 5:1–19.

Maisey, J.G. 1975. The interrelationships of phalacanthous selachians. *Neues Jahrbuch für Geologie and Paläontologie, Monatshefte* 9:553–67.

———. 1982. The anatomy and interrelationships of Mesozoic hybodont sharks. *American Museum Novitates* 2724:1–48.

———. 1983. Cranial anatomy of *Hybodus basanus* Egerton, from the Lower Cretaceous of England. *American Museum Novitates* 2758:1–64.

———. 1989. *Hamiltonichthys mapesi* g. and sp. nov. (Chondrichthes; Elasmobranchii), from the Upper Pennsylvanian of Kansas. *American Museum Novitates* 2931:1–42.

Moy-Thomas, J.A., and R.S. Miles, 1971. *Palaeozoic Fishes.* 2nd ed., London: Chapman and Hall; Philadelphia: Saunders.

Northcutt, R.G. 1977. Elasmobranch central nervous system organization and its possible evolutionary significance. *American Zoologist* 17:411–29.

Patterson, C. 1965. The phylogeny of the chimaeroids. *Philosophical Transactions of the Royal Society of London,* ser. B, 249: 101–219.

Reif, W.E. 1973. Morphologie und Ultrastruktur des Hai-"Schwelzes." *Zoologica Scripta* 2:231–50.

Rieppel, O. 1981. The hybodontiform sharks from the Middle Triassic of Monte San Giorgio, Switzerland. *Neues Jahrbuch für Geologie and Paläontologie, Abhandlungen* 161 (3):324–53.

Saint-Seine, P. de, C. Devillers, and J. Blot. 1969. Holocéphales et élasmobranches. *In* J. Piveteau (ed.), *Traité de Paléontologie* 4 (2). Paris: Masson.

Schaeffer, B., and M.E. Williams. 1977. Relationships of fossil and living elasmobranchs. *American Zoologist* 17:293–302.

Shirai, S. 1996. Phylogenetic interrelationships of neoselachians (Chondrichthyes: Euselachii). *In* M.L. Stiassny, L.R. Parenti, and G.D. Johnson (eds.), *Interrelationships of Fishes.* San Diego, California: Academic Press.

Stensiö, E.A. 1962. Origine et nature des écailles placoïdes et des dents. *In* J.P. Lehman (ed.), *Problèmes Actuels de Paléontologie: Evolution des Vertébrés.* Paris: Editions du Centre National de la Recherche Scientifique.

Zangerl, R. 1966. A new shark of the family Edestidae. *Ornithoprion hertwigi,* from the Pennsylvanian Mecca and Logan Quarry shales of Indiana. *Fieldiana: Geology* 16:1–43.

———. 1981. *Chondrichthyes.* 1, *Paleozoic Elasmobranchii.* Handbook of Paleoichthyology, 3A. Stuttgart and New York: Fischer Verlag.

Zangerl, R., and G.R. Case. 1973. Iniopterygia, a new order of chondrichthyan fishes from the Pennsylvanian of North America. *Fieldiana, Geology Memoirs* 6: 1–67.

———. 1976. *Cobelodus aculeatus* (Cope), an anacanthous shark from Pennsylvanian black shales of North America. *Palaeontographica* A 154:107–57.

Further Reading

Benton, M.J. 1990. *Vertebrate Palaeontology.* London and New York: Chapman and Hall; 2nd ed., 1997.

Capetta, H. 1987. *Chondrichthyes.* 2, *Mesozoic and Cenozoic Elasmobranchii.* Handbook of Paleoichthyology, 3B. Stuttgart: Fischer Verlag.

Carroll, R.L. 1988. *Vertebrate Paleontology and Evolution.* New York: Freeman.

Long, J.A. 1995. *The Rise of the Fishes.* Baltimore, Maryland: Johns Hopkins University Press.

Stiassny, M.L., L.R. Parenti, and G.D. Johnson. 1996. *Interrelationships of Fishes.* San Diego, California: Academic Press.

CHORDATE AND VERTEBRATE BODY STRUCTURE

The primary characteristics of chordates originated as their Precambrian ancestors adapted to an active life in water. Chordates have an elongate body with distinct head and tail, bilateral (left-and-right-side) symmetry, and dorsoventral (back-to-belly) orientation—all of which favor efficient forward movement.

A large pharynx with lateral openings, pharyngeal slits, which pass from the pharyngeal cavity through the body wall to the outside, forms a food-collector sieve that dominates the front of the body. In early chordates, cilia forced water through the slits and, because water contains oxygen, the slits were ideal sites for the gills that later developed there.

Rows of lateral muscles, the locomotor power train, dominate the rear of the body. Because the muscles are bilaterally symmetrical but contract in alternating waves, they provide balanced power to flex the body laterally. Each muscle unit conveys force along a connective tissue sheet, the myoseptum, through a flexible skeletal rod, the notochord, and on to flip the tail-fin propeller back and forth.

Head sense organs submit information about the approaching world to the nearby brain, which conveys instructions along an unusual dorsal, hollow nerve cord to the locomotor muscles. Chordates apparently early on produced thyroid hormone, which enhances metabolic rate, requires greater energy input, and promotes feeding efficiency. Head-tail polarity, bilateral symmetry, dorsoventral orientation, large head-pharynx, trunk locomotor muscles, and post-anal tail are the essence of fishlike, and therefore chordate, anatomy.

Early Paleozoic vertebrates maintained this body plan, but generally they grew larger and more active, evolved more precise locomotor control, and enhanced their ability to regulate metabolism. Cartilage and bone evolved, which better support a large body than does soft tissue. Neural crest cells, which only vertebrates form along the dorsal crest of the embryonic nervous system, formed pigment cells, endocrine glands, neurons of the anterior brain and peripheral nervous system, and cartilage of the head and pharynx.

The entire nervous system expanded to better process the great load of data from the large, numerous, and complex sensors; to integrate the activities of internal organs; and to coordinate the contraction of muscles. Because nerve cells lengthen with the body, a greater increase in activity became possible with the appearance in jawed vertebrates of the insulative myelin nerve sheath, which accelerated nervous transmission.

Vertebrates have a braincase, or cranium (hence their alternate name, "craniates"). They also evolved vertebrae, which better supported the large body and more powerful locomotor muscles than could the notochord (hence their name "vertebrates").

Prevertebrate chordates relied on cilia to move food-bearing water through the pharyngeal sieve. Early vertebrates evolved powerful muscles to pump water through the filter, and by early Silurian times vertebrates recruited some of those muscles to power predatory jaws. Jaws evolved from skeletal bars of the anterior gill arch, which folded forward and enlarged along the margins of the mouth, where bony scales became teeth. Vertebrate teeth have canals that radiate within a bone matrix and are quite unlike other teeth.

Active vertebrates have a high metabolic rate that requires substantial kidney function to filter water from the blood, which early vertebrates accomplished by evolving special kidney tubules.

Although the basic pattern of blood vessels remained the same as in early chordates, with a dorsal aorta that carried blood to the rear of the body and several major ventral vessels, including the ventral aorta, that carried blood forward, early vertebrates enlarged part of the ventral vessel behind the gills into a muscular heart and evolved capillaries to connect arteries with veins. Capillaries off-load respiratory gases, nutrients, and hormones and on-load wastes, but they also permit the heart to raise and control blood pressure, and they contain blood cells so that they do not get stranded among the body tissues. Veins, which carry blood toward the heart, become a capacious reservoir from which the heart draws as it pumps more blood.

Vertebrates specialize a gut pouch that served in digestion in primitive chordates into two large and highly active digestive glands, the liver, which stores and processes nutrients and wastes, and the pancreas, which produces digestive enzymes.

Jawed vertebrates have paired fins with muscles and bones. During late Silurian or early Devonian times, ancestors of sarcopterygian fishes moved into poorly oxygenated, swampy waters, where they evolved long, lobed fins and the ability to extract oxygen from a bubble of air that they swallowed and held in a pouch, a primitive lung, at the rear of the pharynx. The lobed fins could

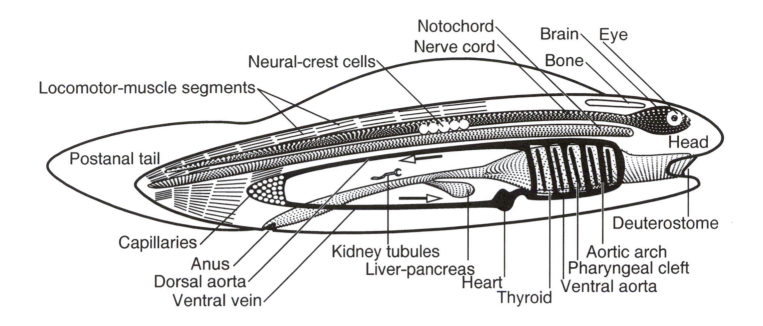

Figure 1. Basic chordate body plan.

push them about in shallow water or onto land. Lungs gave them access to abundant oxygen from their swamp-water habitats. With lungs and lobed fins they could continue living in their swamps, but toward that end they also became better adapted for land life. Some sarcopterygians became amphibians, the first tetrapods.

The underlying structure of tetrapods clearly comes from their fish ancestors. The transition from fish to tetrapod was gradual, but the most obvious change was that of lobed fin to limb. Knee, ankle, elbow, and wrist joints became flexible, so that the limb could push the body up into the air, a nonbuoyant medium. Single fin muscles split into several, which gave greater mobility to the limbs. New sensors, the muscle spindles and joint receptors, made tetrapods sure-footed on land. Vertebrae formed interconnecting struts, the zygapophyses, which kept them from sagging. Whereas in fish the post-temporal bones braced the shoulder against its skull, tetrapods formed a neck that gave the head greater mobility.

Fishes cannot hear well in air, but early tetrapods improved hearing by developing a large eardrum and the stapes, which could translate sound into motion and convey it to the inner ear.

Most amphibians preferred wet areas where their moist and permeable skin could eliminate carbon dioxide, but some adapted well to drier habitats. The changes they began ultimately produced early amniotes, the first reptiles, sometime during early Carboniferous times.

Amniotes adapted well to land. Their epidermis (skin) contains a waterproofing lipid, abundant abrasive-resistant keratin, and much light-shielding pigment. They developed strong expiratory (breathing) muscles that easily eliminate carbon dioxide from the lungs. Their shelled egg and membrane-enclosed embryos are the key to their success on land. Egg shell and shell membranes protect the embryo, and embryonic membranes—chorion, allan-

tois, and amnion—provide the embryo a refuge from the rigors of a dry, hostile world.

Many tetrapods propel themselves by flexing limbs and spine. Frogs, larger reptiles, birds, and mammals relied more on limbs, which promoted changes to shoulder and pelvis.

Mammals evolved from the pelycosaur-therapsid lineage of reptiles during Triassic times. They inherited a suite of characteristics that includes hairs and mammary glands. Most have prolonged internal development. The presence of three ear bones (incus, malleus, stapes), but a single lower jaw bone—the dentary—and a jaw joint only between dentary and squamosal bones distinguish mammals. Birds appeared during the Jurassic, probably from bipedal theropod dinosaurs that evolved wings and feathers, but the structural boundary between birds and dinosaurs is not clear. Scales already may have evolved into feathers in bird ancestors. Modern birds have a more rigid trunk skeleton than early forms.

RONALD G. WOLFF

See also Brain and Cranial Nerves; Chordates; Craniates; Fins and Limbs, Paired; Gnathostomes; Hemichordates; Pharyngeal Arches and Derivatives; Sensory Capsules; Skeleton; Skull; Urochordates

Further Reading
Carroll, R.L. 1988. *Vertebrate Paleontology and Evolution.* New York: Freeman.
Wolff, R.G. 1990. *Functional Chordate Anatomy.* Lexington, Massachusetts: Heath.

CHORDATES

Chordates (phylum Chordata) are multicellular animals that develop a suite of traits including bilateral symmetry; a coelom; radial cleavage; deuterostome; segmental body; notochord; pharyngeal clefts; dorsal, hollow, nerve cord; and, probably, thyroid endocrine cells. Most of these characteristics (explained in detail below) must have evolved during pre-Cambrian times, although the earliest chordates that we know from the fossil record are middle Cambrian (e.g., *Pikaia* from the Burgess Shale). All vertebrates, cephalochordates (e.g., *Branchiostoma*), urochordates (tunicates), and possibly a few more primitive animals are chordates.

With bilateral symmetry (i.e., the right and left sides roughly mirror each other), a trait that they share with many worms, molluscs, arthropods, and echinoderms, chordates have distinct dorsoventral (back/belly) orientation, a head and a tail (body polarity), and efficient forward locomotion. The coelom is a body cavity with an opening to the outside that develops within the mesoderm (middle layers) in the embryo; chordates share the coelom with molluscs, annelid worms, arthropods, and echinoderms. In radial cleavage, cell divisions of the early embryo produce cells that lie one above the other in tiers. The chordate mouth is a "secondary" mouth, or deuterostome, because it comes, not from the blastopore of the embryo (gastrula mouth or protostome), but from elsewhere. Chordates share radial cleavage and deuterostomy only with echinoderms and hemichordates. A segmental body (metamerism) results from the repeating during development of similar body segments (metameres or somites) along the long axis of the body. Chordate metamerism is distinct in muscles, skeleton, nervous system, some blood vessels, and the pharynx; they share metamerism only with annelid worms and arthropods.

A distinctly chordate suite of characteristics—notochord; pharyngeal slits; dorsal, hollow nerve cord; postanal tail; and endocrine thyroid cells—gives them a similar body plan. The notochord is a flexible skeletal rod that develops in all embryos and extends from near the anterior end of the head to near the tip of the tail; it seems to develop fully only in chordates, although a simpler version may occur in closely related forms. Pharyngeal clefts perforate the pharynx in vertebrates, cephalochordates, urochordates, and hemichordates (e.g., pterobranchs) as feeding sieves, although they form gills, important respiratory organs, in vertebrates. A dorsal, hollow, nerve cord develops early in chordates and, especially in vertebrates, expands anteriorly to form a brain; its hollow core contains cerebrospinal fluid that appears critical to the neuronal environment. The thyroid gland develops within the floor of the pharynx; it secretes thyroxine, a regulator of metabolism, into the blood. Although some non-chordates seem to produce thyroxine, they probably secrete it into the gut, rather than into the blood.

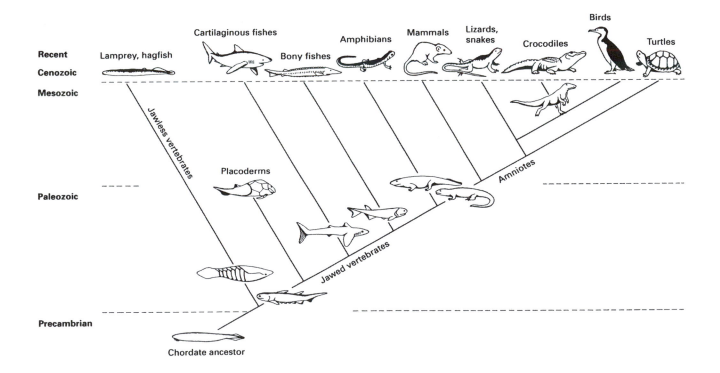

Figure 1. Evolution of the chordates. From Ronald Wolff, *Functional Chordate Anatomy.* Copyright © 1991 by D.C. Heath and Company. Used by permission of Houghton Mifflin Company.

Although their general relationships seems clear from the characteristics that they share, chordate origin itself is obscure. One theory that many paleontologists have accepted without fossil evidence suggests an origin from some sedentary filter-feeding animal, perhaps one similar to modern pterobranch hemichordates, but which maintained juvenile characteristics into adulthood. Another theory, one which infers similarities in soft anatomy, suggests that the extinct Paleozoic mitrates (carpoids or calcichordate echinoderms) might be ancestors of the chordates, but skeletal anatomy shows no similarity. Several theories have placed arthropods as possible ancestors because of similarities in anatomy, histology (minute structures), or biochemistry, yet there remain irreconcilable differences in structure that make this origin seem unlikely. Others have suggested that annelid worms (segmental worms) may be ancestral, but their early development and certain structural features seem too different.

Chordates, exceptional because of the complexity and flexibility of their development and structure, have adapted to a greater variety of habitats than any equivalent group. Although they originated in the earliest Paleozoic as relatively simple aquatic animals, they have radiated into aquatic habitats from ocean depths to raging mountain streams; into terrestrial habitats from water margins to the driest deserts; into temperature regimes from the warmest tropical to the coldest polar zones, both in water and on land. The underlying evolutionary plasticity of their teeth and limbs has allowed them to exploit most foods and to move efficiently and competitively in water, on most terrains, and in the air.

RONALD G. WOLFF

See also Cephalochordates; Chordate and Vertebrate Body Structure; Craniates; Hemichordates; Superphyla; Urochordates

Further Reading

Carroll, R.L. 1988. *Vertebrate Paleontology and Evolution.* New York: Freeman.

Hickman, C.P., and L.S. Roberts. 1995. *Animal Diversity.* Dubuque, Iowa: Brown.

Wolff, R.G. 1990. *Functional Chordate Anatomy.* Lexington, Massachusetts: Heath.

CIRCULATORY PATTERNS

Paleontology generally concerns itself with the the preserved hard parts of extinct organisms. In animals, skeletal structures permit the reconstruction of surrounding soft tissues with greater or lesser degrees of accuracy. On rare occasions soft parts themselves—skin, stomach outlines, heart impressions, muscle fibers—are preserved, as in the famous Solnholfen, Santana, and Messel deposits. However, even in these fossils it is impossible to make out any details of the vascular pattern. Therefore, patterns of veins and arteries can only be reconstructed from evidence provided by the skeleton.

Blood vessels leave behind a network of grooves, canals, and foramina (holes) that betray their former presence. Study of these features often occurs in tandem with the study of nerves, which also can leave similar traces. In fact, nerves and arteries often accompany each other so closely that they use the same apertures and tunnels—a fact that can be both helpful and misleading (if the artery is inconstant) (Conroy and Wible 1978). In similar fashion, some veins and arteries (e.g., those running along the internal surface of the braincase) parallel each other, and establishing which kind of vessel occupied a particular trace can prove to be a difficult exercise (Figure 1).

Although it is an area studied by a small number of specialists, vascular investigations can yield important information. First of all, accurate reconstructions of circulatory patterns can yield a large number of character states that can be used in phylogenetic (evolutionary historical) analysis. For example, in primitive tetrapods the brachial artery and median nerve often pierce the humerus through an *entepicondylar foramen*. This feature, which is lost and regained many times in different lineages, can be useful for linking or separating taxa.

Since the embryology of blood vessels is relatively well understood, study of patterns preserved in extinct animals can open a window onto processes of developmental retardation, acceleration, or alteration. Primitive vascular patterns persisting within highly derived musculoskeletal environments are excellent illustrations of mosaic evolution and developmental uncoupling.

Sometimes changes in vascular supply can be used to support or undermine morphological or functional hypotheses. For example, the reduced number and small size of neurovascular foramina in the face of early primates is thought to imply the loss of tactile vibrissae (whiskers) at the base of the primate radiation (i.e., the earliest common ancestors).

A final reason to study vascular traces is simply to understand ancient anatomies. It is immensely frustrating to look at a fossil riddled with holes and tunnels and not know what they mean. Were these traces occupied by nerves, arteries, veins, or various combinations of the three? Is the pattern truly novel or simply a distorted version of a known primitive pattern? Once these questions are answered, it is then possible to address higher-order questions concerning evolution, development, morphology, and function.

In order to accurately reconstruct the circulatory pattern of an extinct animal, one needs to approach the relevant fossils from a number of different angles. A first step is often the use of modern analogs. If there is a close correspondence between the fossil and living taxa, and if the soft tissue contents of the living form are well known, then it is a simple matter of extrapolating the anatomy of the living form onto the extinct one. The vascular patterns

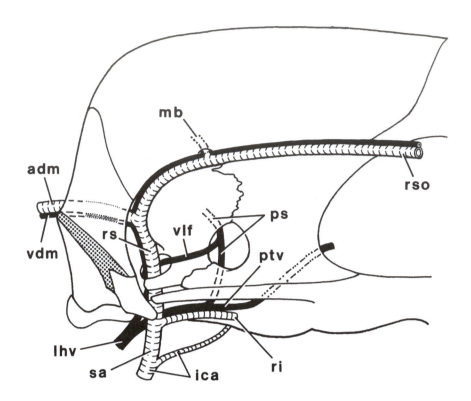

Figure 1. Reconstruction of the cranial vasculature of the primitive cynodont *Thrinaxodon*. Right braincase in lateral view. Dashed segments of arteries and veins are hidden behind bone; stippled segments are intramural; dotted and dashed segments are intracranial. Abbreviations: *adm*, arteria diploëtica magna; *ica*, internal carotid artery; *lhv*, lateral head vein; *mb*, meningeal branch; *ps*, prootic sinus; *ptv*, post-trigeminal vein; *ri*, ramus inferior; *rs*, ramus superior; *rso*, ramus supraorbitalis; *sa*, stapedial artery; *vdm*, vena diploëtica magna; *vlf*, vein in lateral flange vascular groove. From Wible and Hopson 1995.

in the head of extinct Tertiary placental mammals are not that different from living representatives.

The use of transformation series is critically important for bridging the gap between known modern patterns and drastically different extinct ones. J.R. Wible (1989) has shown such an evolutionary progression wherein arteries that ran external to the braincase in advanced therapsids (mammal-like reptiles) gradually sank into the bone (intramural course) and reemerged internally as the meningeal arteries of mammals.

Sometimes embryonic vascular patterns resemble extinct ancestral adult patterns more closely than they do the actual adult form into which the embryo will develop. For example, the embryos of the opposums *Didelphis* and *Monodelphis* retain the tympanic portion of the lateral head vein, an intramural vessel that is lost or highly reduced in the adult stage of modern marsupials. However, this vein is complete and well-developed in Cretaceous marsupials. The embryonic evidence has proven helpful in restoring the vascular pattern of these early marsupials that preserve the canal of the lateral head vein (Wible 1990; Wible and Hopson 1995).

It was thought by some that early placental mammals had two internal carotid arteries, one running within the middle ear

and one medial to the middle ear. Developmental and comparative anatomical evidence convincingly showed that there could only be one (Wible 1986). The medial "arterial groove" of these early mammal skulls eventually was shown to be occupied by a vein. This example illustrates the use of the "exclusionary principle." In other words, for bilateral but otherwise singular structures you can only hypothesize the presence of one per side, even in the face of a multiplicity of traces.

Blood vessels often have characteristic relationships to surrounding bones and muscles, nerves, soft tissue features, and even other blood vessels. All these relationships can be used to narrow the list of possibilities when identifying the occupants of vessel traces in fossil vertebrates.

Studies of vascular patterns in fossil vertebrates (the only class in which such studies can be undertaken) are not evenly distributed across taxa or anatomical regions. Most of the work has been concentrated on the skull, for a number of reasons. Elsewhere in the body, blood vessels mainly weave around the skeletal elements, leaving no trace. It is only in the head that there is considerable penetration of the bone owing to its large size, complex topography, hollow construction, and metabolically active organs and tissues housed within.

Studies of cranial vasculature are best suited to those taxa in which the skull is heavily ossified (e.g., "ostracoderm" fishes, mammals). Animals such as lizards, in which the skull is largely a framework of thin struts, make difficult subjects. Finally, in selecting taxa to study, personal preference of the paleontologist plays a large role. Even though the skulls of caecelians (an order of limbless amphibians) and amphisbaenians (an order of limbless squamates) are heavily constructed (as a burrowing adaptation) nobody is interested in studying the vessel traces that undoubtedly permeate them. Most of the work in recent years has been directed at therapsids (Figure 1), Mesozoic mammals, and Cenozoic mammals, with the latter body of work emphasizing primates, insectivorans, and a number of extinct mammalian orders of small body size (e.g., plesiadapiforms). There is also a significant body of work devoted to the neurovascular anatomy of jawless fishes and gnathostomes, particularly those with heavily ossified, strongly sutured braincases (e.g., osteostracans, galeaspids, placoderms).

Within the skull, some regions are more informative than others and therefore are subject to greater scrutiny. These include the bones that house the inner and middle ears, the side wall of the braincase, the cranial base, and the orbit.

Not all cephalic blood vessels are given equal scrutiny. Those vessels that seldom or never penetrate the skull are, perforce, omitted. Also omitted are vessels that are relatively invariant within and across major taxonomic boundaries, such as the superior sagittal venous sinus. Among mammals and their nearest relatives, the cynodonts, work has focused on several key arteries and arterial systems. These include (1) the stem of the internal carotid artery, with emphasis on its entrance into the skull and its subsequent course through the cranial base (Wible 1986); (2) the stapedial artery, a major branch of the internal carotid artery that supplies much of the face, orbit, and braincase (MacPhee and Cartmill 1986; Wible 1987; Diamond 1991); and (3) the arteria diploëtica magna, a major supply that enters the skull from the rear (Rougier et al. 1992).

Among veins, the orbitotemporal sinus system has proven to be of great interest to students of mammalian evolution. This system includes veins that, at least at some point in development, parallel the branches of the stapedial artery. Many of these veins are reduced to meningeal veins in humans (Diamond 1992). Several other venous sinuses have received attention, such as the prootic sinus, the inferior petrosal sinus, the occipital sinus, and the marginal sinus. The latter two have assumed some importance in discussions of hominid evolution and adaptation (Falk et al. 1995).

Emissary (exit) veins and perforating arteries that pierce the skull as they leave or enter are usually included in any study of cranial vasculature. Dean Falk (1990) believes that the emissary veins of fossil hominids are useful for phylogenetic analysis. Falk also theorizes that their frequency has shifted in response to an enlarging brain and increased heat stress. These arguments are still controversial.

MICHAEL K. DIAMOND

Works Cited

Conroy, G.C., and J.R. Wible. 1978. Middle ear morphology of *Lemur variegatus:* Some implications for primate paleontology. *Folia Primatologica* 29:81–85.

Diamond, M.K. 1991. Homologies of the stapedial artery in humans, with a reconstruction of the primitive stapedial artery configuration of euprimates. *American Journal of Physical Anthropology* 84:433–62.

———. 1992. Homology and evolution of the orbitotemporal venous sinuses of humans. *American Journal of Physical Anthropology* 88:211–44.

Falk, D. 1990. Brain evolution in *Homo:* The "radiator" theory. *Behavioral and Brain Sciences* 13:333–81.

Falk, D., T.B. Gage, B. Dudek, and T.R. Olson. 1995. Did more than one species of hominid coexist before 3.0 Ma? Evidence from blood and teeth. *Journal of Human Evolution* 29:591–600.

MacPhee, R.D.E., and M. Cartmill. 1986. Basicranial structures and primate systematics. In D.R. Swindler and J. Erwin (eds.), *Comparative Primate Biology.* Vol. 1, *Systematics, Evolution, and Anatomy.* New York: Liss.

Rougier, G.W., J.R. Wible, and J.A. Hopson. 1992. Reconstruction of the cranial vessels in the Early Cretaceous mammal *Vincelestes neuquenianus:* Implications for the evolution of the mammalian cranial vascular system. *Journal of Vertebrate Paleontology* 12:188–216.

Wible, J.R. 1986. Transformation in the extracranial course of the internal carotid artery in mammalian phylogeny. *Journal of Vertebrate Paleontology* 6:313–25.

———. 1987. The eutherian stapedial artery: Character analysis and implications for superordinal relationships. *Zoological Journal of the Linnean Society* 91:107–35.

———. 1989. Vessels on the side wall of the braincase in cynodonts and primitive mammals. *In* H. Splechtna and H. Hilgers (eds.), *Trends in Vertebrate Morphology: Proceedings of the 2nd International Symposium on Vertebrate Morphology,* Vienna, 1986. Fortschritte der Zoologie, 35. Stuttgart and New York: Fischer-Verlag.

———. 1990. Petrosals of Late Cretaceous marsupials from North America and a cladistic analysis of petrosal features in therian mammals. *Journal of Vertebrate Paleontology* 10:183–205.

Wible, J.R., and J.A. Hopson. 1993. Basicranial evidence for early mammal phylogeny. *In* F.S. Szalay, M.J. Novacek, and M.C. McKenna (eds.), *Mammal Phylogeny.* Vol. 1, *Mesozoic Differentiation, Multituberculates, Monotremes, Early Therians and Marsupials.* New York and London: Springer-Verlag.

———. 1995. Homologies of the prootic canal in mammals and non-mammalian cynodonts. *Journal of Vertebrate Paleontology* 15:331–56.

Wible, J.R., G.W. Rougier, M.J. Novacek, M.C. McKenna, and D. Dashzeveg. 1995. *A Mammalian Petrosal from the Early Cretaceous of Mongolia: Implications for the Evolution of the Ear Region and Mammaliamorph Interrelationships.* American Museum Novitates, No. 3149. Mew York: American Museum of Natural History.

CLUB MOSSES AND THEIR RELATIVES

Living organisms are endowed with the capacity to adapt to changing environmental conditions. An excellent example of the emergence of a suite of such adaptations is found in the Silurian Period, following the gradual migration of aquatic plants into terrestrial habitats. Thus, as we approach the Devonian Period, many terrestrial plants already possessed a root system for anchorage and absorption of water; an erect shoot, often with green appendages or true leaves for manufacturing carbohydrates; stomata (leaf-openings) for gaseous exchange; and a heterosporous (micro- and megaspores) mode of reproduction. Heterospory eventually was to culminate in the formation of seeds and seedlike structures, characteristic of higher vascular plants.

Biologists often follow different classification systems. For readers' convenience, here we follow the classification system of Thomas and Brack-Hanes (1984; modified by Taylor and Taylor 1993). Under this system the Lycophyta—the club mosses and related forms—is divided into seven orders: Drepanophycales, Protolepidodendrales, Lepidodendrales, Lycopodiales, Selaginellales, Pleuromeiales, and Isoetales.

To understand the vegetative and reproductive biology of fossil lycopods, it is essential to look at the structure and development in their extant (present-day) relatives. In the present-day flora, the club mosses, as the renowned taxonomist Linnaeus called them, have worldwide distribution. However, the two main genera (groupings; singular, genus)—club mosses (with about 400 species) and *Selaginella* (with over 700 species)—are more abundant in tropical and wet temperate regions. The quillworts, comprised of two genera, *Isoetes* and *Stylites,* are found only in areas that are submerged for at least part of the year. *Stylites,* in the present-day flora, is restricted to the Peruvian Andes. Lycopodiales and Selaginellales have many features in common but are quite distinct from the quillworts. Both are herbaceous plants—they form no woody structures, so they are relatively small. Lycopodiales are homosporous plants (all their spores are identical), and they have true roots attached to a horizontal rootlike stem called a "rhizome." In the club mosses the arrangement of the conducting tissues—xylem and phloem—of the stelar structure show considerable variation between species. Selaginellales, on the other hand, are "ligulate"—they bear a leaflike appendage attached to each vegetative leaf and reproductive leaf (sporophyll). Also, Selaginellales are heterosporous. At the end of each branch in *Selaginella* grows a cone-shaped structure called a strobilus, which incorporates two types of sporangia; one type produces male microspores, and the other produces female megaspores. The Isoetales are herbaceous plants with ligulate leaves and a heterosporous reproduction.

Considering the wide distribution of club mosses in the extant flora and their fossil history, one would expect to find convincing evidence for their fossil representatives. However, few fossils described so far belong undoubtedly to this group. One problem associated with lycopodialean fossils is that often they are indistinguishable from those of Lepidodendrales (arborescent, or tree-sized, lycopods). On the other hand, fossils such as

Selaginella fairponti, a herbaceous lycopod of the Carboniferous Period, show close affinities with extant species of *Selaginella* (Schlanker and Leisman 1969). The nature and formation of its root system, however, is similar to that of the lepidodendrids. K.B. Pigg and G.W. Rothwell (1983) described an isoetalean fossil genus *Chaloneria* from the Upper Pennsylvanian strata in North America. Although the unbranched stem produced ligulate leaves, they were not attached to leaf cushions. The base of the plant was cormlike—corms are vertical, thick structures for food storage. Such structures also are found in extant Isoetales. Secondary growth resulted in secondary xylem surrounding the protostele and a distinct periderm layer at the periphery. (Secondary growth occurs when a layer of cells within the vascular tissue remains capable of constantly dividing and producing more layers of cells. These new cells mature into more vascular tissue, referred to as "secondary vascular tissue." Since secondary tissue is formed by a layer of cells, the cells are lined up in rows. Secondary growth allows plants to increase in diameter, as seen in trees, thus supporting higher stems.) Recent reports of *Clevelandodendron ohioensis,* a lycopsid fossil of Isoetalean affinities (Chitaley and Pigg 1996), have extended the fossil record of the quillworts back to the Late Devonian period.

It is believed that the Lower Devonian Zosterophyllum were ancestral to both the herbaceous and arborescent lycopods. Most Devonian lycopods were herbaceous plants. H.N. Andrews, H.P. Banks, and others have discussed Devonian plant fossils in detail, exploring their significance in the origin and evolution of early land plants. Several of the Devonian herbaceous fossils were either true lycopods or their ancestors. These lycopods were able to survive the many catastrophic changes for over 400 million years, maintaining their structural and reproductive integrity to the present day. W.G. Chaloner (1967) discussed the various lycopod fossil genera described by previous workers. The arborescent lycopods, the lepidodendrids (also called the Stigmarian lycopods), dominated the tropical Carboniferous coal swamps but became extinct during the Permian period. Because of their abundance in the Paleozoic floras of the world and, more importantly, owing to their excellent preservation, a volume of literature on fossil lycopods has accumulated over the past several years. Here, we deal only with selected examples of the major groups.

Drepanophycales

The Drepanophycales comprises Silurian and Devonian lycopods. We will consider three genera: *Baragwanathia, Drepanophycus,* and *Asteroxylon.* The best-known fossil in this group is *Baragwanathia longifolia,* described by W.H. Lang and I.C. Cookson (1935), from what is now considered as Late Silurian rock strata from Victoria, Australia. The structure and organization of this plant is similar to modern-day *Huperzia*—erect, dichotomously (split into two smaller branches) branched herbaceous shoots bearing simple leaves. The leaves were much larger than their modern counterparts. Individual sporangia (spore-producing structures), perhaps attached to the leaves, produced only one kind of spore (homosporous). The North American species of *Baragwanathia*, *B. abitibiensis* Hueber, had leaves arranged in a spiral (helical) pattern as well, but no sporangia have been found yet. Another herbaceous Devonian fossil linked to lycopods is *Drepanophycus spinaeformis*, which has a dichotomously branched shoot system arising from an underground rhizome and simple leaves with stomata. However, one of the best-known fossils of this group is *Asteroxylon*. As the name suggests, the xylem in *Asteroxylon* is star shaped. R. Kidston and W.H. Lang (1920) described them as erect plants arising from an underground rhizome and simple leaves borne on aerial shoots.

Protolepidodendrales

Two examples of protolepideodendrids, *Protolepidodendron* and *Leclercqia*, are considered here. Protolepidodendrales also were herbaceous plants or short-statured trees. Leaves of *Protolepidodendron*, helically arranged around the aerial shoots, were branched at their tips. Fertile leaves bore a pair of sporangia. *Leclercqia complexa* is a small herbaceous plant found in many parts of the world. Leaves, also helically arranged on aerial shoots, divided at midpoint. Sporangia are attached on the adaxial (upper) surface of the leaves.

Lepidodendrales (The Arborescent Lycopods)

Lepidodendrids were some of the most elegant trees in the fossil record. Their widespread occurrence accounts for much of the organic matter in the tropical peat-forming swamps that subsequently were transformed into large coal reserves in the Carboniferous strata in Europe and North America. Although coals have been reported from the Precambrian and Devonian periods, they appeared in thin seams only, primarily owing to the lack of adequate organic matter. A.T. Cross and T.L. Phillips (1990) reconstructed the vegetation and paleoecology of various coal-bearing strata in North America. The Devonian-Mississippian transition is marked by the gradual change from herbaceous to arborescent lycopods. T.L. Phillips and W.A. DiMichele (1992) discussed the structure, development, reproduction, and paleoecological significance of arborescent lycopods. Although Mississippian and Pennsylvanian fossils are abundant only in eastern North America, there are sporadic occurrences in Utah and Arizona (Tidwell et al. 1992). Owing to the enormity of fossils and the variety in their preservation, the Carboniferous floras may comprise the best-known fossils ever.

Several form genera (classification system based on physical characteristics) are used to describe different parts of the lepidodendrid tree. For instance, *Lepidodendron* originally was used for the shoot system and *Lepidophyllum* for the leaves. More recently, however, the genus *Lepidodendron* refers to the entire plant (DiMichele and Bateman 1992). Lepidodendrids were tall, bipolar trees (Figure 1), some attaining a height of over 45 meters. It has been suggested that these trees had a short life span (10 to 15 years). Although the tree trunk was unbranched for much of its length, dichotomous branches were produced at both ends; hence, these "trees" are called

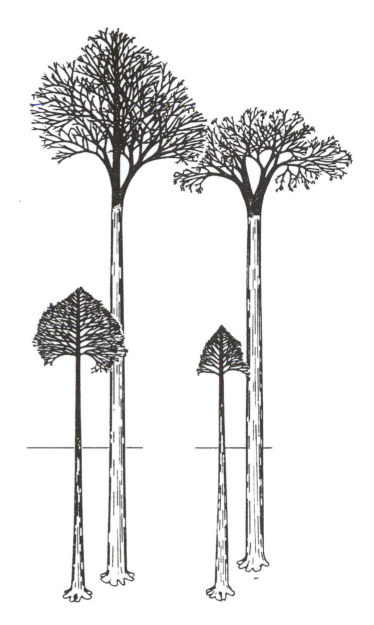

Figure 1. *Lepidodendron* species from Pennsylvania coal swamps, showing size variations and morphology of four species. From DiMichele (1981).

bipolar. Attached to the aerial structures were *Lepidophyllum* leaves, some close to a meter long. The scars of the absciced (dropped) leaves are indicated by "leaf cushions" to which they were originally attached. The nature of the leaf cushions is diagnostic (specific to species), so it has been used to discriminate between different species. The diamond-shaped leaf cushions, with markings of the ligule, are arranged helically on the *Lepidodendron* branches. Also present are markings of the vascular bundles that supplied the leaves and an aerating system called the "parichnos." The presence of functional stomata and the parichnos in the leaf bases has led to the suggestion that parichnos were meant for internal gas exchange for photosynthesis (Phillips and DiMichele 1992).

Permineralized trunks of *Lepidodendron* have been used to study the development of these trees. Eggert (1961) has analyzed lepidodendrid trees at different height levels. Secondary growth of the tree trunk is quite different from that in the seed plants (gymnosperms and angiosperms). Although secondary growth was accomplished through the cambium (similar to higher vascular plants), the cambial layer produced new cells toward the center only. The newly produced cells differentiated (specialized) into secondary xylem. No secondary phloem has been reported. Phillips and DiMichele (1992) suggested that the products of photosynthesis did not move far from the production site in lepidodendrid trees and that growth and maintenance occurred close to photosynthetic sites. Structural support for the tree trunks mainly was provided by the periderm (outer bark).

Lepidophlois, another stem genus, is related closely to *Lepidodendron.* However, there are differences in the shape of the leaf cushions and also in the attachment of the parichnos to the leaf cushions. *Lepidophlois australes* had considerably shorter leaves. *Sigillaria,* another arborescent lycopod, was a shorter tree that produced very few branches.

Stigmaria is the generic name for the dichotomously branched, underground part of the lepidodendrid trees. These were used to anchor the plant to the soil. A stigmarian root system is found in the clay layer below the coal seams, suggesting that this layer represents the original soil in the peat-forming swamps. The primary branches of the stigmarian root system indicate secondary thickening, which resulted in wide rays made of thin-walled cells in the secondary xylem and a complicated network of tissues in the periderm layer. Lateral appendages were helically arranged, but not irregularly, as in most root systems.

The polar branching of the lepidodendrid trees was coordinated with production of reproductive structures. Several genera of fruiting structures (e.g., *Lepidostrobus, Flamingites,* and *Achlamydocarpon*) have been described from Europe and North America. *Lepidostrobus oldhamius* produced *Lycospora* spores, whereas *Flamingites schopfii* produced bisporangiate cones (bearing two types of sporangia), which resembled a *Selaginella*-type strobilus. It is interesting to note that S. Chitaley and D.C. McGregor (1988) reported an Upper Devonian lycopod, *Bisporangiostrobus,* with a *Flamingites*-type cone structure—it bore microsporangia at the top of the strobilus and megasporangia at the base.

Pleuromeiales

Pleuromeiales are arborescent Mesozoic lycopods. They are considered to be related to modern *Isoetes. Pleuromeia,* a Triassic lycopod with worldwide distribution, is a small tree (about two meters tall) with a basal four-lobed anchoring structure to which the roots are attached. Ligulate, elongate leaves are attached in a terminal crown. Absticed leaves are indicated by leaf scars. It has been suggested that *Pleuromeia* was a dioecious plant—one that bore male cones on one plant and female structures on another.

From the preceding, it is clear that the modern-day lycopods have a long and rich history as a dominant group of plants for millions of years. Since their origin during the Silurian, the lycopods diversified into herbaceous and arborescent plants. The

herbaceous habit was more suitable to changing environmental conditions; the arborescent lycopods became extinct after the Permian Period. A significant aspect of the lycopod fossil history is the diversification of herbaceous lycopods through a heterosporous mode of reproduction. These were precursors to higher vascular plants.

E.M.V. NAMBUDIRI

Works Cited

Chaloner, W.G. 1967. Lycophyta. *In* E. Boureau (ed.), *Traité de Paléobotanique.* Vol. 2, Paris: Masson.

Chitaley, S., and D.C. McGregor. 1988. *Bisporangiostrobus harrisii* gen. et sp. nov., an eligulate lycopsid cone with *Duosporites* megaspores and *Geminospora* microspores from the Upper Devonian of Pennsylvania, U.S.A. *Palaeontographica* 210B:127–49.

Chitaley, S., and K.B. Pigg. 1996. *Clevelandodendron ohioensis* gen. et sp. nov., a slender upright Lycopsid from the Late Devonian Cleveland shale of Ohio. *American Journal of Botany* 83:781–89.

Cross, A.T., and T.L. Phillips. 1990. Coal-forming plants through time in North America. *International Journal of Coal Geology* 16:1–46.

DiMichele, W.A. 1981. Arborescent lycopods of Pennsylvanian age coals: Lepidodendron, with description of a new species. *Palaeontographica,* 175B:85–125.

DiMichele, W.A., and R.M. Bateman. 1992. Diaphorodendraceae, fam. nov. (Lycopsida: Carboniferous): Systematics and evolutionary relationships of *Diaphorodendron* and *Synchysidendron,* gen. nov. *American Journal of Botany* 79:605–17.

Eggert, D.A. 1961. The ontogeny of Carboniferous arborescent Lycopsida. *Palaeontographica* 108B:43–97.

Kidston, R., and W.H. Lang. 1920. On Old Red Sandstone plants showing structure from the Rhynie Chert Bed, Aberdeenshire. Part 3, *Asteroxylon mackiei,* K. and L. *Transactions of the Royal Society of Edinburgh* 52:643–80.

Kenrick, P., and P.R. Crane. 1997. *The Origin and Early Diversification of Land Plants.* Washington and London: Smithsonian Institution Press.

Lang, W.H., and I.C. Cookson. 1935. On a flora, including vascular land plants, associated with *Monograptus* in rocks of Silurian age, from Victoria, Australia. *Philosophical Transactions of the Royal Society of London* 224B:421–49.

Phillips, T.L., and W.A. DiMichele. 1992. Comparative ecology and life history biology of arborescent lycopods in Late Carboniferous swamps of Euramerica. *Annals of Missouri Botanic Gardens* 79:560–88.

Pigg, K.B., and G.W. Rothwell. 1983. *Chaloneria* gen. nov., heterosporous lycophytes from the Pennsylvanian of North America. *Botanical Gazette* 144:32–47.

Schlanker, C., and G.A. Leisman. 1969. The herbaceous Carboniferous lycopod *Selaginella fairponti* comb. nov. *Botanical Gazette* 130:35–41.

Taylor, T.N., and E.L. Taylor. 1993. The biology and evolution of fossil plants. Englewood Cliffs, New Jersey: Prentice-Hall.

Thomas, B.A., and S.D. Brack-Hanes. 1984. A new approach to family groupings in the lycophytes. *Taxon* 33:247–55.

Tidwell, W.D., J.R. Jennings, and S.S. Beus. 1992. A Carboniferous flora from the Surprise Canyon Formation in the Grand Canyon, Arizona. *Journal of Paleontology* 66:1013–21.

Further Reading

Andrews, H.N. 1973. Paleobotany. *Annals of Missouri Botanic Gardens* 61:170–72.

Banks, H.P. 1970. Evolution and plants of the past. Belmont, California: Wadsworth; London: MacMillan, 1972.

DiMichele, W.A., and R.M. Bateman. 1992. Diaphorodendraceae, fam. nov. (Lycopsida: Carboniferous): Systematics and evolutionary relationships of *Diaphorodendron* and *Synchysidendron,* gen. nov.

American Journal of Botany 79:605–17.

Stewart, W.N., and G.W. Rothwell. 1983. *Paleobotany and the Evolution of Plants.* Cambridge and New York: Cambridge University Press; 2nd ed., 1993.

White, M.E. 1986. *The Greening of the Gondwana.* French Forest, New South Wales: Reed; as *The Flowering of Gondwana,* Princeton, New Jersey: Princeton University Press, 1990; 2nd ed., Chatswood, New South Wales: Reed, 1994.

COELENTERATES

The Coelenterates (simple marine invertebrates with two cell layers) are divided into two separate phyla, the Cnidaria and the Ctenophora (comb jelly). Whereas the Cnidaria, which includes the corals, sea anemones, hydras, and jellyfishes, are well represented in the fossil record, the ctenophores were virtually nonexistent in the record until relatively recently.

Organization and Classification

Cnidarian organization is very simple: They are composed of essentially a saclike body with a mouth surrounded by tentacles (Figure 1). The "cnidae," from which the name is derived, refer to the stinging cells (nematocysts) which characterize this phylum. They generally are concentrated in the tentacles. The sac wall consists of an ectoderm (outer membrane), a structureless, jellylike middle layer called the "mesogloea," and an "endoderm" (inner membrane), which lines the gastric cavity. The Cnidaria are distinguished by their structure. When the sac rests on the seafloor with the mouth as the uppermost part, it is a "polyp" (Figure 1B), such as an anemone. (If the animal has a similar arrangement and secretes a calcareous skeleton beneath itself, it is a "coral.") When the sac floats in the water and has a body column that terminates with its mouth oriented downward, it is a "medusa," or jellyfish (Figure 1A).

There are three main divisions, or classes, of Cnidaria: the Hydrozoa, Scyphozoa (jellyfishes), and Anthozoa (anemones and corals) (Figure 2). Hydrozoans and scyphozoans may contain either body form, in which case medusae are produced by budding off from the polyp. The medusae, in turn, release male and female gametes, which fuse to form a planula (larva) that settles on the seafloor and metamorphoses into a polyp. Both polyps and medusae are well developed in most hydrozoans, but in the Scyphozoa, the polyp stage is reduced to little more than a factory for producing medusae. In the Anthozoa, the medusa is omitted altogether; the polyps become sexually mature and release gametes. Another important discriminating feature among the three classes is the interior sac (enteron). Hydrozoans lack an enteron. Its nature differs between the Scyphozoa and Anthozoa: Scyphozoans have four radial flanges extending into the interior; the Anthozoans possess more varied and complex internal partitions, called "mesenteries."

The polyp stage may become colonial, or modular, with multiple polyps produced by budding. Polyp colonies are well known among the Anthozoa and Hydrozoa. In the Anthozoa, colonies are simple, with little or no differentiation between the modules; but in the Hydrozoa, various modules may specialize to perform a particular function in the colony, such as feeding or reproduction. In extreme cases, the colony is very elaborate, with different specialized modules of mixed polypoid and medusoid origin that act like the various organs of a more highly evolved animal. These hydrozoan "superindividuals" belong to the "chondrophores" (including the living *Velella,* the "By-the-wind-sailor") and the siphonophores (including the living *Physalia,* the "Portuguese man of war").

Earliest Records and Relationships of the Classes

The Cnidaria have a long geological history, extending back to the Late Precambrian (Nudds and Sepkoski 1993) (Figure 3). The earliest records are questionable (Scrutton 1979), including a Late Precambrian-to-Early Palaeozoic group of medusaeform fossils, the Protomedusae. Most are included in a single genus, *Brooksella,* first recorded from 1.1 to 1.3 billion-year-old rocks in the Grand Canyon Supergroup deposits of Arizona, and extending into the Palaeozoic. These remains are controversial. Although some are quite morphologically (structurally) complex, they have been regarded variously as stellate trace fossils, or as gas evasion artifacts. Their cnidarian affinities have yet to be convincingly demonstrated; therefore, they are omitted from Figure 3.

The earliest clear cnidarians occur in the famous Late Precambrian (Vendian) Ediacaran fauna, first reported from Australia (Sprigg 1947) and now known worldwide. These were all non-mineralized soft-bodied organisms, that, significantly, show no sign of predation. They were preserved as internal and external molds in siltstones and fine sandstones. Some claim that cnidarians compose over 60 percent of this fauna (Glaessner 1984), but there is considerable controversy concerning the affinities of some of these early forms. Representatives of all three main classes have been recorded (Jenkins 1992). The Anthozoa are represented by sea pens (Pennatulacea), some strikingly similar to modern forms, of which *Charniodiscus* is a most convincing representative (Figure 4A). The scyphozoans include various jellyfishes, some of which are attached to the sea bottom by a short stalk. Others are free-swimming, including a morphologically complex form, *Kimberella,* that is similar to a living carybdeidan scyphomedusae. For the

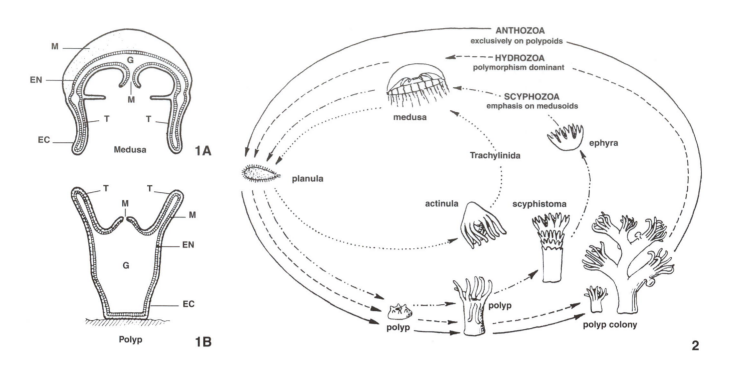

Figure 1. *A,* cross section of a medusa; *B,* cross section of a polyp. Abbreviations: *ec,* ectoderm; *en,* endoderm; *g,* gastric cavity (enteron); *m,* mouth; *me,* mesogloea; *t,* tentacles. Reprinted from Haas and Knorr (1982), THE ILLUSTRATED GUIDE TO MARINE LIFE published by Harold Starke Publishers, Ltd., London, ISBN 0 287 00056 6. **Figure 2.** Life cycle of the three main Cnidarian classes. Note that the Trachylina, regarded as closest to the ancestral cnidarians, are usually classified in the Hydrozoa. From Moore (1956), *Treatise on Invertebrate Paleontology,* courtesy of and © 1956 The Geological Society of America and The University of Kansas Press.

Prec	Palaeozoic						Mesozoic			Cenozoic
Vend	Camb	Ord	Sil	Dev	Carb	Perm	Trias	Jurassic	Cretaceous	Tertiary

Geological ranges table showing:

Trachylinida
medusae of the Hydroida
Chondrophorina
Hydroida — calcified hydroids
Hydrozoa — hydroids
Milleporina
Stylasterina
scyphomedusae
Scyphozoa — scyphopolyps
Conulata
Ceriantipatharia
Alcyonacea
Cenothecalia
Anthozoa — Octocorallia — Gorgonacea
Pennatulacea
corals
Zoantharia — anemones (trace and body fossils)
Hydroconozoa
Ctenophora

(Cnidaria)

Figure 3. Geological ranges of Cnidaria and Ctenophora. In each class, ranges of selected subdivisions are shown; living cnidarians without a fossil record are omitted. Continuous lines do not indicate a continuous fossil record. In most cases the record is very patchy. The fossil record of the Anthozoa Zoantharia is shown in greater detail under Anthozoans. Horizontal scale proportional to geological time. Key: *bold,* Cnidarian classes.

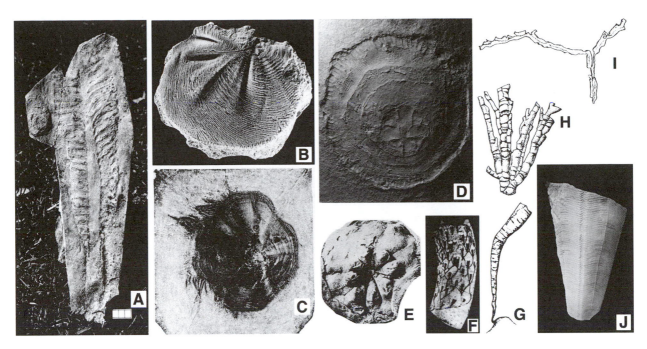

Figure 4. *A, Charniodiscus oppositus,* a Late Precambrian (Ediacaran) sea pen. The arrangement of lateral polyp leaves to the main stalk is extremely similar to that in some living sea pens. Flinders Range, South Australia. Scale, ×0.18. *B, Chondroplon bilobatum,* a Late Precambrian (Ediacaran) chondrophore float. The remainder of the colony, including feeding and reproductive structures, would have hung below the float but are not preserved here. Flinders Range, South Australia. Scale, ×0.2. *C, Conchopeltis alternata,* a possible scyphozoan. The symmetry of the test, of unknown but possible scleroprotein composition, is strictly bilateral rather than quadrilateral. Note the ends of tentacles extending beyond the test in places around its margin. Middle Ordovician, New York. Scale, ×0.5. *D, Rhizostomites admirandus,* a scyphozoan jellyfish. This is a very fine impression of a subumbrella surface preserved in a lithographic limestone. The jellyfish has a cruciform mouth with a clearly preserved outer annulus of concentrically striated muscle. Upper Jurassic, Germany. Scale, ×0.13. *E, Kirklandia texana,* a trachyline hydrozoan jellyfish. Subumbrella surface showing eight stomach pouches. Lower right edge of bell folded back. Lower Cretaceous, Texas. Scale, ×0.4. Reproduced by permission of the Treatise on Invertebrate Paleontology. *F, Protulophila gestroi,* a hydroid colony incorporated into a calcareous worm tube. Here the outer layers of the tube have been eroded to reveal the triangular polyp bases and the basal stoloniferous mat (hydrorhiza) of the colony preserved in pyrite. Lower Cretaceous, Kent, England. Scale, ×2.5. *G, Byronia annulata,* a scyphopolyp. This scleroprotein tube was attached to the seafloor and housed a polyp-like structure from which medusae were budded. Middle Ordovician, Poland. Scale, ×0.25. *H, Pragnellia arborescens,* a gorgonian. This arborescent colony consists of linked calcified segments. Upper Ordovician, Manitoba. Scale, ×0.14. *I, Desmohydra flexuosa,* a benthonic hydroid colony. The scleroprotein periderm has been extracted from a limestone by acid digestion. Ordovician, Poland. Scale, ×36. *J, Paraconularia derwentensis,* a conulariid. The four-sided test of chitinophosphatic composition has strongly marked ribs parallel to the apertural margin. The ribs alternate in the shallow grooves, which run up the test where the four sides meet. Permian, Tasmania. Scale, ×0.3. From: *C, E,* Moore (1956), *Treatise on Invertebrate Paleontology,* courtesy of and © 1956 The Geological Society of America and The University of Kansas Press; *G, H, I,* Scrutton (1979).

hydrozoans, flat, discoidal structures have been interpreted as the floats of chondrophores, of which *Ovatoscutum* and *Chondroplon* (Figure 4B) are examples. There are also many unassigned medusoids. Some specialists regard most of these supposed cnidarians as belonging to the phylum but lacking the distinguishing characteristics of the three main classes (Fedonkin 1992). There are also more formless, saclike structures assigned to the Petalonamae, variously considered a separate, primitive phylum or a discrete class assigned to the Cnidaria. These types became extinct before the beginning of the Cambrian. Some believe that the supposed sea pens should be assigned to this class. There also have been other suggestions for these Ediacaran forms, cnidarians included, that place them in an extinct phylum of tough-skinned, quilted organisms, the Vendozoa (Seilacher 1989), or, surprisingly, that reinterpret the fauna as lichens (Retallack 1994).

Even if these Ediacaran organisms are true cnidarians, they throw little light on the relationships between the three main classes, nor do they hint at the origins of the Cnidaria. The most convincing cnidarians include quite advanced forms, such as anthozoan polyp colonies (the sea pens) and hydrozoan chondrophores. This suggests that there was a significant period of evolution before the appearance of this fauna. There has been much discussion as to which class evolved first and whether the medusa or the polyp was the ancestral form. The most widely accepted view is that a hydrozoan medusa evolved from a simple, planuloid ancestor, termed a "metagastraea," sometime earlier in the Precambrian. Several lines of evidence support the Hydrozoa as the ancestral cnidarian, including the undivided enteron, and their more varied nematocysts, while the Anthozoa are structurally the most complex of the cnidarians. The polyp evolved subsequently as a prolonged, juvenile attached stage from which the medusae budded. Such a scenario points to the actinula larva of the Trachylinida, in which the polyp stage is reduced or absent, as is seen in the ancestral hydrozoan and the most primitive cnidarian (see Figure 2).

Phanerozoic History

After the Precambrian, soft-bodied organisms, including nonmineralized cnidarians, become rare. One explanation is a change in conditions of preservation, especially the evolution of active macrophagus (large-prey) predators and scavengers, the destructive activities of burrowing organisms, and possibly the increasing influence of the meiofauna (microscopic animals), all contributing to the early destruction and breakdown of soft tissue (Fedonkin 1992). However, scattered records of various cnidarians (some of doubtful validity) are known, many of which are associated with well-known lagerstätter (sites where soft-bodied animals are preserved). In addition, there are occasional trace fossils that scholars interpret as having been formed by the activities of burrowing anemones. The difficulties of recognizing unmineralized cnidarians are best illustrated by the reinterpretation of a supposed medusa, *Peytoia nathorsti,* from the Middle Cambrian Burgess Shale of British Columbia. This fossil is now interpreted as the mouth parts of a very large, extinct, and rather bizarre arthropod, *Anomalocaris* (Whittington and Briggs 1985).

Hydrozoa

Of the hydrozoan cnidarians, the living Trachylinida are medusae that live almost exclusively in open oceans and are found more commonly in warmer waters. Despite earlier claims, there are no confirmed pre-Mesozoic examples, notwithstanding the hypothesis that these are the most primitive cnidarians. The first more convincing records come from the Middle and Upper Jurassic of Germany (e.g., *Hydrocraspedota*) and the Lower Cretaceous of Texas *(Kirklandia)* (Figure 4E).

In contrast, the medusae of the Hydroida are most common today in coastal waters, close to the benthonic (bottom dwelling), largely colonial hydroids from which they are budded. They are not, however, known with certainty as fossils since the rare earlier records have been disputed or reassigned. *Crucimedusina* from the Late Carboniferous is among the more convincing. The hydroids themselves, on the other hand, have been described from the Ordovician and Silurian of Scandinavia and from erratic boulders in Poland, probably derived from the same deposits (Figure 4I). Several genera are known, some sufficiently well preserved that the delicate, scleroprotein periderm could be separated from the calcareous matrix (Skevington 1965). Some Cambrian finds have been reassigned to the group called the Graptolithina, with which superficially they easily can be confused. Very few living hydroids inhabit freshwater, but a fossil form, *Drevotella,* has been recorded from freshwater deposits in the Upper Carboniferous Mason Creek deposits of Illinois. In the Mesozoic and Early Tertiary of western Europe and the Middle East, the molds of hydroid colonies have been preserved by overgrowth in the walls of various species and genera of serpulid worms on which they were growing

(Scrutton 1975) (Figure 4F). Over this range, the parts preserved remained so constant in form that they are all referred to as a single species, *Protulophila gestroi,* although it is likely that several different hydroids were involved.

The chondrophores, classified with the Hydroida and the most securely represented hydrozoans in the Late Precambrian faunas, are relatively common as fossils, compared with other noncalcified cnidarians in the Early and Mid-Palaeozoic (Stanley 1986). Most are the remains of the float, which has a stiff, scleroprotein envelope that increases its preservation potential. Species of the Lower Palaeozoic genus *Scenella,* previously considered to be molluscan shells, now are reinterpreted as chondrophores. Reconstructions of the well-preserved remains of *Plectodiscus* from the Lower Devonian Hunsrückschiefer of Germany show it to be remarkably similar to the living *Velella,* complete with sail. Curiously, records of chondrophores are very rare after the Late Carboniferous, with only a single Late Cretaceous record, but this may simply be due to the difficulty of correctly identifying these fossils. The highly evolved pelagic (open-water), polymorphic hydrozoan colonies of the order Siphonophorida appear to have no fossil record.

There is a small number of calcified hydrozoan colonies. Of these, the thin encrusting, horny or calcareous mat of *Hydractinia,* commonly found on gastropod (mollusk) shells today, is referred to the Hydroida and can be traced back to the Eocene, possibly to the Mesozoic. Two other small orders with calcareous basal skeletons are the Milleporina and Stylasterina. Both are recorded from the Late Cretaceous onward, and the Milleporina extend back to the Upper Triassic (if *Heterastridium* is included here). *Millepora* is a prominent component of living reef faunas, particularly in the Caribbean.

Finally, it is worth noting that two major groups of calcified coralline organisms with good fossil records previously were assigned to the Hydrozoa. These are the Stromatoporata and the Chaetetida (although most western paleontologists more commonly classified the latter as tabulate corals). Both now are accepted firmly as the calcareous basal skeletons of various groups of demosponges (Wood 1990), and spicules (spike-shaped skeletal structures) have been described from some, confirming their assignment to the Porifera (sponges).

Scyphozoa

Apart from one controversial group, the fossil record of scyphozoans is sparse. Although several genera of Ediacaran scyphomedusae have been claimed, the majority of these lack convincing features that unequivocally place them in the Scyphozoa. In the Phanerozoic, there are very few records, and even those are doubtful. One exception is be the famous Upper Jurassic Solnhofen Limestone deposit in southern Germany. This deposit contains several genera of convincing scyphomedusae, including a number of detailed impressions of *Rhizostomites admirandus,* which attained a diameter of 0.5 meters (Figure 4D). Scyphopolyps (attached polyps) are also sparse in the fossil record, the most convincing being the narrow, conical structure *Byronia* from the Upper Cambrian of British Columbia and Middle Ordovician of Poland (Figure 4G). *Byronia* is remarkably similar to the living coronatid scyphopolyp *Stephanoscyphus,* both of which possess a scleroprotein tube.

Conulata

Much more common than Scyphozoa are the Conulata. Evidence of these organisms consists of narrow conical tubes made up of a combination of chitin and phosphate, found in deposits from the Lower Ordovician to the Triassic. Representatives may date all the way back to the Lower Cambrian (Figure 4J). Usually, the tubes are square in cross section, and rare examples have internal ribs or projecting septa (incomplete partitions) in multiples of four. Some Conulata exhibit structures for attachment to the bottom, but according to disputed evidence, adult stages may have detached and become drifting or weakly swimming forms. The four-part symmetry has been regarded as reflecting the tetrameral symmetry of the Scyphozoa, but conulatan soft parts are unknown. Some reconstructions show tentacles, but this interpretation is considered speculative; in part, the questions arise from the fact that the reconstruction is based upon the Middle Cambrian *Conchopeltis,* which is not now considered closely related (Oliver 1994). *Conchopeltis* has a very broad conical form with a periderm of scleroprotein, a bilateral, pseudotetrameral symmetry, and abundant tentacular impressions around the margin (Figure 4C). It, and the possibly related Ediacaran *Conomedusites,* are cnidarians of uncertain affinities, but most likely are scyphozoans. Rather than scyphozoans, the Conulata have been considered a completely unrelated phylum (Babcock and Feldmann 1986). The latest work, however, tends to reaffirm scyphozoan affinities (van Iten 1992), and they are considered a distinct class close to the Scyphozoa.

Anthozoa

The class Anthozoa has by far the best fossil record of the Cnidaria through the corals. Corals are treated elsewhere, but it is useful to include a brief discussion of the fossil record of other anthozoans, most of which lack a massive calcareous skeleton. These are solitary polyps, anemones, or polyp colonies: The record of noncalcified forms is extremely rare. Of the three subclasses, the Ceriantipatharia has relatively few living representatives. The antipatharians are polyp colonies with a horny axis, of which only one fossil genus has been claimed from the Miocene. No fossil ceriantharians are known, but these are solitary, burrowing, anemone-like polyps, so they may have left trace fossils, although none so far have been specifically related to this group.

The Octocorallia is a much bigger subclass and includes the sea fans (gorgonians) and sea pens (pennatulaceans). Several genera of Ediacaran pennatulaceans have been claimed, some of which are very convincing. Then a long gap appears in the record with few, dubious assignments followed by scattered, more convincing remains in the Mesozoic. Of these, the first, *Prographularia* from the Triassic of Germany, is noteworthy. Fossil gorgonians are very rare before the Jurassic, with a doubtful Cambrian record. There is more convincing Ordovician material, including *Pragnellia* (Figure 4H) and questionable Permian and Triassic forms. From the Jurassic onward, however, several genera with solid, calcified horny axes are known through scattered fossils. The first alcyonarian spicules have been recorded in the Lower Silurian of Sweden. The cenothecalian octocorals stand out by having a nonspicular, solid calcareous skeleton. The genus *Heliopora,* the blue coral, is known from the Cretaceous onward. *Heliopora* bears some resemblance to the Palaeozoic tabulate coral *Heliolites,* and the stoloniferan octocoral *Tubipora,* the organ-pipe coral, similar to the tabulate coral genus *Syringopora.* Such similarities have led to claims that some tabulate corals, including those mentioned, were octocorals. The similarities are superficial, however, and the tabulate corals, despite some controversy over their relationships, are assigned to the Zoantharia.

The final anthozoan subclass is the Zoantharia, which contains the corals and the true anemones. Fossil anemones are exceptionally rare. The oldest appears to be from the Lower Cambrian of China. *Mackenzia costalis* from the Middle Cambrian Burgess Shale of British Columbia, was originally considered to be a holothurian (sea cucumber). Despite the present consensus that it is an actinian anemone, it is in need of revision. Another example is *Palaeactinia* from the Middle Ordovician of New York, also a questionable actinian. This sparse record is augmented indirectly by trace fossils interpreted as the remains of actinian dwelling burrows. Several ichno genera have been described, including *Intrites,* restricted to the Vendian, and *Bergaueria,* the best-known genus, which has a range from the Vendian to the Middle Ordovician of North America and Europe. Other genera are scattered through the Phanerozoic. *Dolopichnus* has been recorded from the Early Triassic, which is otherwise free of Anthozoan remains.

Hydroconozoa

A small number of solitary, coral-like organisms have been described from the Lower Cambrian of Siberia by K.B. Korde (1963), who referred them to a new class of Cnidaria, the Hydroconozoa. Members are small, conical skeletons with a basal expansion, and some demonstrate vertical and radial canals and radiating plates rather like septa. Their coral-like appearance is probably due to convergence (independent evolution in unrelated groups), although they could be anthozoans and are probably cnidarians. Their original classification is considered the most suitable, pending a thorough reinvestigation of the material.

Ctenophora

The phylum Ctenophora consists of small, pelagic, jellylike blobs (sea gooseberries) and bands (Venus girdle), known as comb jellies. These animals are common in shelf waters today. In particular, they are distinguished by eight shimmering stripes along the body, the effect produced by the rhythmic beating of ciliary bands (the combs) that provide limited locomotion. Their body plan is similar to cnidarians but lack nematocysts. Until a few years ago, fossil ctenophores were unknown. However, Stanley and Stürmer (1983) published a description of a very convincing specimen from the Lower Devonian Hunsrückschiefer deposits in Germany. Shortly afterward, a second ctenophore, belonging to a different genus and species, was described from the same location.

COLIN T. SCRUTTON

See also Anthozoans; Aquatic Invertebrates, Adaptive Strategies of; Problematic Animals; Reefs and Reef-Building Organisms

Works Cited

Babcock, L.E., and R.M. Feldmann. 1986. The phylum Conulariida. *In* A. Hoffman and M.H. Nitecki (eds.), *Problematic Fossil Taxa.* Oxford: Clarendon Press; New York: Oxford University Press.

Fedonkin, M.A. 1992. Vendian faunas and the early evolution of Metazoa. *In* J.H. Lipps and P.W. Signor (eds.), *Origin and Early Evolution of the Metazoa.* New York: Plenum.

Haas, W. de, and F. Knorr. 1982. *The Illustrated Guide to Marine Life.* R.C. Fischer (ed). London: Stark.

Jenkins, R.J.F. 1992. Functional and ecological aspects of Ediacaran assemblages. *In* J.H. Lipps and P.W. Signor (eds.), *Origin and Early Evolution of the Metazoa.* New York: Plenum.

Korde, K.B. 1963. Hydroconozoa—novy klass kishechnopolostnykh zhivotnykh. *Paleontologicheskii Zhurnal* 1963:20–25.

Moore, R.C. (ed.). 1956. *Treatise on Invertebrate Paleontology,* Part F, *Coelenterata.* Boulder, Colorado: Geological Society of America; Lawrence: University of Kansas Press.

Oliver Jr., W.A. 1994. Conchopeltis: Its affinities and significance. *Palaeontographica Americana* 54:141–47.

Retallack, G.J. 1994. Were the Ediacaran fossils lichens? *Paleobiology* 20:523–44.

Scrutton, C.T. 1975. Hydroid-serpulid symbiosis in the Mesozoic and Tertiary. *Palaeontology* 18:255–74.

———. 1979. Early fossil cnidarians. *In* M.R. House (ed.), *The Origin of Major Invertebrate Groups.* Systematics Association Special 12. London and New York: Academic Press.

Seilacher, A. 1989. Vendozoa: Organismic constructions in the Proterozoic biosphere. *Lethaia* 22:229–39.

Skevington, D. 1965. Chitinous hydroids from the Ontikan limestones (Ordovician) of Öland, Sweden. *Geologiska Föreningens i Stockholm Förhandlingar* 87:152–61.

Sprigg, R.C. 1947. Early Cambrian (?) jellyfishes from the Flinders Ranges, South Australia. *Transactions of the Royal Society of South Australia* 71:212–24.

Stanley Jr., G.D. 1986. Chondrophorine hydrozoans as problematic fossils. *In* A. Hoffman and M.H. Nitecki (eds.), *Problematic Fossil Taxa.* Oxford: Clarendon Press; New York: Oxford University Press.

Stanley Jr., G.D., and W. Stürmer. 1983. The first fossil ctenophore from the Lower Devonian of West Germany. *Nature* 303:518–20.

van Iten, H. 1992. Microstructure and growth of the conulariid test: Implications for conulariid affinities. *Palaeontology* 35:359–72.

Whittington, H.B., and D.E.G. Briggs. 1985. The largest Cambrian animal, *Anomalocaris,* Burgess Shale, British Columbia. *Philosophical Transactions of the Royal Society, London,* ser. B, 309:569–618.

Wood, R. 1990. Reef-building sponges. *American Scientist* 78:224–35.

Further Reading

Glaessner, M. 1984. *The Dawn of Animal Life: A Biohistorical Study.* Cambridge and New York: Cambridge University Press.

Haas, W. de, and F. Knorr. 1982. *The Illustrated Guide to Marine Life.* H.J. Fisher (trans.), R.C. Fisher (ed.). London: Starke; as *Was lebt im Meer an Europas Küsten? Mittelmeer, Atlantik, Nordsee, Ostee.* Stuttgart: Kosmos, 1965.

Nudds, J.R., and J.J. Sepkoski Jr. 1993. Coelenterata. *In* M.J. Benton (ed.), *The Fossil Record.* Vol. 2. London and New York: Chapman and Hall.

Oliver Jr., W.A., and A.G. Coates. 1987. Phylum Cnidaria. *In* R.S. Boardman, A.H. Cheetham, and A.J. Rowell (eds.), *Fossil Invertebrates.* Palo Alto, California: Blackwell Scientific.

Scrutton, C.T., and B.R. Rosen. 1985. Cnidaria. *In* J.W. Murray (ed.), *Atlas of Invertebrate Macrofossils.* Harlow: Longman; New York: Wiley.

COEVOLUTIONARY RELATIONSHIPS

Coevolution was first defined by P.R. Ehrlich and P.H. Raven (1964) as the reciprocal and stepwise selective responses between organisms that ecologically are linked closely. Although the term has been defined in many ways in the years since Ehrlich and Raven published their paper, most scholars agree that coevolution involves the evolution of organisms in response to one another. This requires that organisms be in close ecological association; therefore we often exemplify coevolution by examining associations that involve predation and symbioses such as parasitism and mutualism. Consider a parasitic relationship, in which the parasitic organism lives on or in the host organism and gains all of its nourishment and shelter from its host. We easily can invoke coevolution as the driving evolutionary force for these two organisms by assuming that the host is evolving traits to defend itself against the parasite while the parasite is evolving traits to counter the host's defenses. We can just as easily apply this argument to mutualism (in which both organisms benefit from their interaction) or predation.

The difficulty in assessing whether coevolution occurs among interacting organisms is to show that traits evolve *reciprocally* and not just *unilaterally.* Tightly linked relationships such as parasitism and mutualism are not necessarily the result of coevolution but might merely represent "an end point along an adaptive continuum which has been channeled by phyletic constraints" (Steneck 1992). In other words, modern associations or specializations among organisms might seem coevolved, but these organisms might be associated only because of the relationships among their ancestors. Coevolution, therefore, must be considered on two scales. The quotation from R.S. Steneck describes a "macroevolutionary approach," which examines the historical relationships among the interacting organisms and their ancestors. This approach requires knowledge of the interacting species' phylogenetic relationships and the timing of their ancestors' origins and radiations. The alternative "microevolutionary approach" investigates reciprocally evolving individual traits between organisms. This includes understanding genetic changes within a species, changes that evolve in response to another species.

The fossil record can be helpful in providing evidence for understanding the macrocoevolutionary relationships among organisms. It is often difficult to use the fossil record to evaluate the role of coevolution in an association since it is difficult to find a detailed temporal series for one species, much less for two species that interact. For this reason, most evidence for coevolution in the fossil record is inferential. However, scholars can use paleontological evidence to evaluate coevolutionary hypotheses based on the timing and origin of particular species or groups.

Paleontological Evidence and Interpretation

In 1990 A.J. Boucot compiled and interpreted the literature on behavioral and coevolutionary relationships in the fossil record. Among his many examples, Boucot provides evidence of symbiotic barnacles on whales and corals from the Miocene, flealike parasites on decapods (crustaceans) from the Upper Jurassic, parasitic nematodes (worms) in a variety of arthropods (e.g., insects and spiders) from as early as the Eocene, and a variety of plant galls (swollen plant tissue) from the Miocene. Each of these paleontologic associations has a modern counterpart. Since this indicates that these relationships have a long history, Boucot infers that they formed suddenly, with initial rapid coevolution followed by a long period of stasis. Since few of these fossils are represented in more than one time period or stratum, there is no direct evidence that coevolution took place, though some of the examples are compelling.

It is often easier to disprove a hypothesis than to support it. Hypothesizing about coevolution in the fossil record is no exception. Fossils have been used effectively to demonstrate that coevolution could not have occurred. Paleontologic evidence can be useful for suggesting that two species were not associated at key moments when it is presumed that coevolutionary traits evolved. Steneck (1992) provides an excellent example of this, using the fossil record to investigate the modern mutualism between the limpet *Tectura testudinalis* and the coralline alga *Clathromorphum circumscriptum*. Based on algal defenses and limpet life history and grazing behavior, the association between *T. testudinalis* and *C. circumscriptum* is presumed to be a highly coevolved pairwise association. Using the fossil record and phylogenetic relationships of both coralline algae and limpets, Steneck demonstrated that the timing of specific adaptations and coadaptations within the limpet and algae groups was not synchronized—the traits evolved at times too far apart to represent responses to each other. Traits within the coralline algae that are interpreted as herbivore resistant traits, such as sunken reproductive structures, coralline crust, and a thick epithallus (layer of outer cells), appeared during the Late Precambrian, long before the appearance of limpets in the Middle Triassic. When limpets do appear in the fossil record, coralline algae were rare. The ability of limpets to excavate calcium carbonate is essential for them to graze on coralline algae, but is this a coevolved trait? Marks caused by grazing limpets are found on calcium carbonate shells from the Jurassic but are not common on coralline algae until the Cenozoic. Therefore, it is more likely that limpets evolved the ability to excavate calcium carbonate by grazing diatoms (single-celled organisms with calcium-impregnated outer covering) off shells of bivalves and ammonites than from grazing coralline algae. Given the phylogenetic and fossil history of the two species, there is no evidence to suggest that reciprocal adaptations occurred within these groups of limpets and coralline algae.

C.C. Labandeira and T.L. Phillips (1996) discuss paleontological evidence from the Carboniferous that suggests the diversification of holometabolous (completely metamorphosed) insects before the evolution of angiosperms (flowering plants). This is significant, since the prevailing view holds that insects and angiosperms coevolved during the Cenozoic, after angiosperms originated and radiated (diversified and spread geographically). Labandeira and Phillips (1996) found fossils of galls on fronds of a Carboniferous tree fern, *Psaronius*. Several other studies describe evidence of various types of predatory behavior on *Psaronius* fronds, including damage in response to piercing, sucking, and chewing of various insects. Combined, these studies reveal a morphologically and ecologically differentiated insect fauna by the Late Pennsylvanian. The implication is that coevolution among insects and angiosperms did not drive trophic (nutritional) diversification within the insects, since this diversification occurred much earlier than the origin of angiosperms.

MARY F. POTEET

See also Fungi; Insects and Other Hexapods; Lichens; Plants: Overview; Vent and Seep Faunas

Works Cited

Boucot, A.J. 1990. *Evolutionary Paleobiology of Behavior and Coevolution.* Amsterdam and New York: Elsevier.

Ehrlich, P.R., and P.H. Raven. 1964. Butterflies and plants: A study in coevolution. *Evolution* 18:586–608.

Labandeira, C.C., and T.L. Phillips. 1996. A Carboniferous insect gall: Insight into early ecologic history of the Holometabola. *Proceedings of the National Academy of Sciences USA* 93:8470–74.

Steneck, R.S. 1992. Plant-herbivore coevolution: A reappraisal from the marine realm and its fossil record. *In* D.M. John, S.G. Hawkins, and J.H. Price (eds.), *Plant-Animal Interactions in the Marine Benthos.* Oxford: Clarendon; New York: Oxford University Press.

Further Reading

Behrensmeyer, A.K., J.D. Damuth, W.A. DiMichele, R. Potts, H.D. Sues, and S.L. Wing. 1992. *Terrestrial Ecosystems through Time: Evolutionary Paleoecology of Terrestrial Plants and Animals.* Chicago: University of Chicago Press.

Futuyma, D.J., and M. Slatkin. 1983. *Coevolution.* Sunderland, Massachusetts: Sinauer.

Poinar Jr., G.O. 1992. *Life in Amber.* Stanford, California: Stanford University Press.

Thompson, J.N. 1994. *The Coevolutionary Process.* Chicago: University of Chicago Press.

Vermeij, G.J. 1987. *Evolution and Escalation: An Ecological History of Life.* Princeton, New Jersey: Princeton University Press.

COMPARATIVE ANATOMY

Comparative anatomy is the study of similarities and differences in body structure among organisms, usually to understand form, function, variation, and evolutionary relationships. The earliest distinctly comparative studies of anatomy come from Aristotle, the fourth-century B.C. Greek philosopher, although detailed comparative analyses did not become a formal part of anatomy until the nineteenth century, as greater insights about fossils and the acceptance of modern concepts of evolution developed. During that time, the comparative method of anatomy—comparative anatomy—became of critical importance to paleontology. Modern comparative anatomy owes its evolutionary basis to Charles Darwin.

Fossils, many of which are actual body parts, preserve the sole direct record of body structure of past life. Living organisms preserve, through their evolution, an indirect record of body structure. Paleontologists apply, through comparative anatomy, our understanding of living organisms to fossilized body parts and extrapolate ideas on form, function, adaptation, and evolution of past life. Comparative studies of living and fossilized body parts allow paleontologists to verify whether structurally similar parts of different organisms are homologous (i.e., have a common evolutionary origin), or whether they are analogous (evolved independently, but with a similar function). The concepts of homology and analogy, which Richard Owen, paleontologist and contemporary of Darwin, developed, is key to our understanding of phylogenetic relationships and to the reconstruction of phylogenies (evolutionary histories).

Although similarity in structure among organisms may imply homology and, therefore, an evolutionary relationship, some similarities arise when organisms independently adapt to similar conditions, a phenomenon that evolutionary biologists call convergence. Convergent structures are more likely to evolve among genetically similar organisms living in similar environments, which makes the structures appear more likely to be homologous. Homologous structures do, and convergent structures do not, trace back to a common origin. Paleontology is the only direct source of information that can verify homology and convergence.

Because the environments in which ancestors lived influence the anatomy of descendants, comparative anatomy can help us understand the environments to which organisms, through evolution, adapted. Comparative anatomy thus has significance to paleoecological studies.

Some body parts correlate more obviously to external influences and others more to internal influences. Teeth and feet, for examples, are closely tied to diet and locomotion, respectively, which are external influences, whereas liver and kidney are more closely tied to body physiology. Comparative studies help us to understand how body parts integrate with each other and to the outside world.

Thus, the most illuminating use of comparative anatomy comes from the consideration, not of a few body parts, but of entire bodies—their forms, functions, adaptations, and origins.

RONALD G. WOLFF

See also Adaptation; Biomechanics; Homology; Functional Morphology

Further Reading

Carroll, R.L. *Vertebrate Paleontology and Evolution.* New York: Freeman.
Radinsky, L.B. 1987. *The Evolution of Vertebrate Design.* Chicago: University of Chicago Press.
Wolff, R.G. 1990. *Functional Chordate Anatomy.* Lexington, Massachusetts: Heath.

COMPUTER APPLICATIONS IN PALEONTOLOGY

Developing computer-based technologies have promoted many changes in applied and theoretical paleontology. The wide availability of personal computers (microcomputers) now forms the basis for a range of innovative paleontological techniques (Tipper 1991). Microcomputer software is widely available for data analysis, modeling together with simulation, and computer-based reconstructions of sectioned and deformed material. More recently computer-aided learning programs have been generated by microcomputer technologies. Some of these computer-based studies are now explained in student texts (e.g., Benton and Harper 1997).

Microcomputers have catalyzed significant advances in the acquisition and statistical analysis of paleontological data (see Davis 1986 for an explanation of the techniques). Both individuals and communities can be described by precise measurements and parameters, communicated and compared with inferential statistics. Through computer-based image analysis systems, counters, and digital calipers, data may be entered directly into commercial spreadsheets such as Excel and Lotus or into the data capture and retrieval software of more specialized packages. The PALSTAT package (Ryan et al. 1995) was specifically designed to analyze measurements on paleontological material from either samples of individual fossil populations or from samples of paleocommunities.

For a multivariate measurement set, most packages generate a range of univariate statistical descriptors, including a vector of means and variances together with measures of skew and kurtosis. Intervariate relationships may be expressed in variance-covariance or correlation matrices. The dynamics and survivorship of fossil populations are analyzed both statistically and graphically, whereas bivariate analyses based on scattergrams are commonly summarized and compared by the fit on a Reduced Major Axis line to either the raw data or a logarithmic transform where allometric effects are present. Phenetic methods such as Principal Components Analysis and Cluster Analysis, based on the interrogation of similarity matrices, have helped define interspecific variation and compare the shapes of two or more similar fossil population.

Cladistic methods rely on the identification of apomorphic or derived features in related organisms to construct a genealogy or cladogram. Computer packages such as PAUP (Swofford 1993) generate the shortest or most parsimonious trees together with a range of statistical parameters. The shortest tree may not necessarily reflect the most realistic phylogeny. Trees generated by PAUP may be exported to software such as MacClade (Maddison and Maddison 1992), where trees may be manipulated and analyzed statistically.

Paleoecological data derived from paleocommunities and other fossil assemblages may be summarized by diversity, dominance, and evenness indices and the raw data represented by a variety of bar and pie charts (Ryan et al. 1995). Distance and similarity coefficients either in R mode (exploring the relationships between taxa) or Q mode (investigating the relationships between sites) form the basis for further investigation by Cluster Analysis and Principal Components Analysis. Paleocommunities may be defined and compared on the basis of these multivariate analyses.

Biostratigraphic or fossil range data have been plotted and analyzed by a variety of software packages. Graphical correlation, developed to aid oil exploration, is one of the most effective techniques. Two stratigraphic sections are plotted along the x and y axes, respectively; the first and last occurrences of taxa (groups; singular, taxon) in both sections are plotted as x,y coordinates. A regression line fitted to the points define a straight line of stratigraphic correlation, permitting interpolation and thus the accurate correspondence of the entire lengths of each section. GrafCor software (Hood 1995) accepts range data and generates graphical correlations together with associated statistics. Seriation is an ordering technique. Fossil range data measured against a stratigraphic section are rearranged with stratigraphically higher taxa on the left side of the range chart and stratigraphically lower taxa on the right. Computer-based techniques have seriated not only stratigraphic data but also have established gradients within paleobiogeographic and paleoecological data (Ryan et al. 1995).

Large-scale biological change in the fossil record has been investigated through plotting the number of families in a sequence of stratigraphic intervals such as stages or series together with numbers of originations and extinctions in each unit (Benton 1995). Data are stored in Excel or an equivalent spreadsheet and exported to commercial graphics packages for time-series plots.

Biogeographic data based on the spatial distributions of fossil taxa have been analyzed by both phenetic (Ryan et al. 1995) and cladistic methods (Swofford 1993). Phenetic methods, which group together either sites or suites of co-occurring taxa on the basis of distance and similarity matrices, are commonly presented as dendrograms in a cluster analysis. These methods are particularly relevant to dispersal models where the ranges of organisms have expanded from a center of origination. Alternatively, cladistic techniques are more suited to a vicariance model where an initially unified province has since fragmented. These fragments are characterized by new taxa (analogous to apomorphies of organisms) that define the branches and nodes of the tree or cladogram.

Computer models have been widely used to simulate the ontogeny, or growth, of fossil organisms. The development of an individual or a population is generated according to a set of rules; the results can be tested against reality and the efficacy of the model assessed. Models can be deterministic, conforming to fixed parameters, or stochastic (in which the parameter values can be random). Moreover, models also can be dynamic, so that the results of one phase have an effect on the next phase; in contrast, static models lack any feedback mechanisms. The first computer-based models (Raup 1966) were focused on the growth of shelled invertebrates and required lengthy computations on large main-frame computers. Such models involved the generation of a variable logarithmic spiral based on four main parameters; these simulations were deterministic, static, and ideal. Shelled organisms with accretionary exoskeletons may be generated in a variety of shapes; some but not all may be matched with actual brachiopods and molluscs. Raupian models are now available for microcomputers (Swan 1989). Simple deterministic and static models also have been applied to the astogeny (growth) of colonial organisms and the relationship of colony growth of stromatoporoids (spongelike organisms) to sedimentation rates. Computer modeling has also helped understand long-term patterns of biological change through time both in the description and prediction of extinction (Raup 1996) and radiation events and their analysis (Sepkoski 1996).

Reconstructions of fossils such as brachiopods and corals from serial sections have been modeled by a number of computer-based algorithms. CorresGrow, for example, is available to reconstruct a three-dimensional image of range of fossils (Herbert et al. 1995); image rotation in three dimensions is now available. More sophisticated three-dimensional ontogenetic and phylogenetic modeling is now possible, together with more realistic morphometric analysis. In addition, reconstructions of fossils from deformed material can be achieved by a number of graphics packages. Seven previously described, quite different species of trilobite from the Cambrian of Kashmir were shown to represent only one variably deformed morphotype (Hughes and Jell 1992). The containing rocks are now confidently assigned to the Middle Cambrian, and this part of the Himalayas was associated then with India and northern China on the basis of faunal similarity.

Computer Aided Learning (CAL) packages are currently under construction involving both fossil images stored on compact disc and more interactive teaching and assessment exercises using a wide range of labeled and animated specimens.

Recently, the most significance advances have been made in the area of communications. Most professional paleontologists and many amateurs communicate by E-Mail. All manner of data, text, and illustrations now can be moved between sites electronically. Many museums and paleontological institutes have their own web pages often with fossil data, catalogs, photographs of local or spectacular, well-preserved fossils, and reconstructions of ancient environments and their animals and plants. Moreover, some web pages occasionally offer useful computer software. University sites list courses and often course material and relevant bibliographies.

DAVID A.T. HARPER

See also Biomass and Productivity Estimates; Biomechanics; Extinction; Fossil Record; Paleoecology; Radiological Imaging and Associated Techniques; Radiological Imaging and Associated Techniques; Statistical Techniques; Systematics

Works Cited
Benton, M.J. 1995. Diversification and extinction in the history of life. *Science* 268:52–58.
Benton, M.J., and D.A.T Harper. 1997. *Basic Palaeontology*. Essex: Addison, Wesley and Longman, Harlow.
Bruton, D.L., and D.A.T. Harper (eds). 1990. *Microcomputers in Palaeontology*. Contributions from the Palaeontological Museum, University of Oslo. Oslo: University of Oslo.
David, B., and B. Laurin. 1992. *Procrustes, Version 2.0: An Interactive Program for Shape Analyses Using Landmarks*. Dijon: Paléontologie Analytique, Université de Bourgogne.
Davis, J.C. 1986. *Statistics and Data Analysis in Geology*. 2nd ed., New York and Chichester: Wiley.
Harper, D..A.T., and P.D. Ryan. 1990. Towards a statistical system for palaeontologists. *Journal of the Geological Society, London* 147:935–48.
Herbert, M.J., C.B. Jones, and D.S. Tudhope. 1995. Serial section reconstruction of geoscientific data. *The Visual Computer* 11:343–59.
Hood, K.C. 1995. Evaluating the use of average composite sections and derived correlations in the graphic correlation technique. *In* K.O. Mann and H.R. Lane (eds), *Graphic Correlation*. SEPM Society for Sedimentary Geology, Special Publication, 53. SEPM Society for Sedimentary Geology.

Hughes, N.C., and P.A. Jell. 1992. A statistical/computer-graphic method for assessing variation in tectonically deformed fossils and its application to Cambrian trilobites from Kashmir. *Lethaia* 25:317–30.
Maddison, W.P., and D.R. Maddison. 1992. *MacClade: Analysis of Phylogeny and Character Evolution, Version 3*. Sunderland, Massachusetts: Sinauer.
Raup, D. 1966. Geometric analysis of shell coiling: General problems. *Journal of Paleontology* 40:1178–90.
Raup, D.M. 1996. Extinction models. *In* D. Jablonski, D.H. Erwin, and J.H. Lipps (eds.), *Evolutionary Paleobiology*. Chicago: University of Chicago Press.
Ryan, P.D., D.A.T. Harper, and J.S. Whalley. 1995. *The PALSTAT Package, Version 1*. London: Chapman and Hall.
Sepkoski, J.J. 1996. Competition in macroevolution: The double wedge revisited. *In* D. Jablonski, D.H. Erwin, and J.H. Lipps (eds.), *Evolutionary Paleobiology*. Chicago: University of Chicago Press.
Swan, A.R.H. 1990. A computer simulation of evolution by natural selection. *Journal of the Geological Society, London* 147:223–28.
Swofford, D. 1993. *PAUP: Phylogenetic Analysis Using Parsimony, Version 3.1.1*. Washington D.C.: Smithsonian Institution.
Tipper, J.C. 1991. Computer applications in palaeontology: Balance in the late 1980s. *Computers and Geosciences* 17:1091–98.

Further Reading
Benton, M.J., and D.A.T Harper. 1997. *Basic Palaeontology*. Essex: Addison, Wesley and Longman, Harlow.
Bruton, D.L., and D.A.T. Harper (eds). 1990. *Microcomputers in Palaeontology*. Contributions from the Palaeontological Museum, University of Oslo. Oslo: University of Oslo.
Davis, J.C. 1973. *Statistics and Data Analysis in Geology*. New York and Chichester: Wiley; 2nd ed., 1986.
Jablonski, D., D.H. Erwin, and J.H. Lipps (eds.), *Evolutionary Paleobiology*. Chicago: University of Chicago Press.
Tipper, J.C. 1991. Computer applications in palaeontology: Balance in the late 1980s. *Computers and Geosciences* 17:1091–98.

CONDYLARTHS
See Ungulates, Archaic

CONIFEROPHYTES

The Coniferales (which includes the Taxaceae, commonly known as yews) are represented by over 500 living species and rank among one of the world's most successful forest trees. The conifers occupy of a wide range of ecological habitats and are well adapted to most of the world's vegetation zones. Some, such as the Pinaceae (pine family) form extensive, nearly monotypic (single species) stands throughout the boreal (northern coniferous) regions of the Northern Hemisphere, while others, such as the Taxodiaceae (redwood family) are restricted in their distribution and occur in small relict populations (representative species that are "left overs" from a time when they were far more prevalent). The Coniferophyta, which include the extinct representatives of the Cordaitales and

Coniferales (including the Voltziales) have had a long evolutionary history, extending from the Late Paleozoic. The "modern" families appeared and disversified during Mesozoic time.

Cordaitales
The Cordaitales, which are regarded as being the first coniferophytes, are represented by one family, the Cordaitaceae, that first appeared during the Lower Pennsylvanian and flourished until Permian time. Members of this group were distributed worldwide and were prominent constituents of the Late Paleozoic landscape, often forming dense forests. Some species were known to have been

Figure 1. A reconstruction of a shrublike cordaitalean plant that grew on the peat in coal-forming swamps. Redrawn by Narda Quigley from Stewart and Rothwell (1993).

shrublike forms (Figure 1) which grew on the peat of coal-forming swamps, or small mangrovelike trees (Figure 2), which grew in swamps that bordered marine and estuarine habitats. The majority were large trees (Figure 3) (heights of nearly 30 meters) that inhabited the swamps, floodplains, and possibly upland environments.

The arborescent (treelike) forms consisted of a main trunk with crowns of helically arranged strap-shaped leaves that were up to 1 meter long and 15 centimeters wide (Figures 2, 3). While there is no doubt that the Cordaitales are indeed coniferophytes, anatomical features of the wood and basic design of the microsporangiate and megasporangiate cones (seed- and pollen-producing structures) allows scholars to dicriminate between cordaitalean and coniferophyte remains.

A note about nomenclature: For a number of reasons—such as fossilization conditions and destructive activities by other organisms that feed upon dead plant life—paleobotanists often find only parts of a plant—perhaps a stem, a root system, a cone or other reproductive structure. Later, another part of the plant may be discovered. In fact, the entire plant, preserved in such a way that shows how various parts relate to each other, may never be found. As a result, in order to discuss various finds, scholars name each part they have discovered. The results of this practice can be disconcerting for newcomers, since it produces a plant with parts that do not have the same name. This will happen in all discussions in this essay.

The pollen and ovule-bearing organs are both assigned to the genus *Cordaitanthus* (Figures 4, 5). These were borne in the axils of modified leaves called "bracts." These were arranged on fertile shoots, scattered among the leaves. *Cordaitanthus* pollen cones produced a type of pollen known as *Florenites* in microsporangia that grow at the tip of the bract (the distal position). Flattened, bilaterally symmetrical, winged ovules were also borne distally on separate cones (Figure 5). As is the case with most fossilized plant remains, ovules of different preservational types are commonly given different names. Among the Cordaitales, if the actual structure of the ovule is preserved, it is assigned to *Cardiocarpus* or *Mitrospermum;* if the ovule is preserved only as a compression fossil, it is assigned to *Samaropsis.*

Although the generic name *Cordaites* was created to accommodate isolated cordaitalean leaves, the name also has been used to describe anatomically preserved leaves, as well as the entire tree. Continued use of the name *Cordaites* to describe anything other than isolated cordaitalean leaf compressions has unfortunately created a number of nomenclatural problems that still are being dealt with today. Nevertheless, recent research on cordaitalean systematics has facilitated recognition and reconstruction of a number of whole plants. Two of the best known genera include *Cordaixylon* and *Mesoxylon* (Trivett and Rothwell 1991; Trivett 1992).

The origin of the Cordaitales is by no means clearly understood, but there is little doubt that they evolved from a progymnosperm ancestor. However, it is not clear whether they arose from the aneurophytes with a lyginopterid seed fern as an intermediate or directly from the archaeopteridalean line (Stewart and Rothwell 1993).

Figure 2. A reconstruction of a small mangrovelike cordaitalean plant with stilt roots. This plant grew in and around the swamps that bordered marine and estuarine habitats. Redrawn by Narda Quigley from Stewart and Rothwell (1993).

Figure 3. A reconstruction of a large cordaitalean tree. Such trees were nearly 30 meters tall and inhabited the swamps, floodplains, and possibly upland environments. Redrawn by Narda Quigley from Stewart and Rothwell (1993).

"Voltziales"—The Transition Conifers

Clarification of some nomenclatural problems associated with this extinct group of conifers and the discovery of new taxa have allowed recognition of a number of new families, reorganization of some of the existing families, and provided insight into the diversity of the group (see Taylor and Taylor 1993 or Stewart and Rothwell 1993). Consequently, in the most recent system of classification proposed, T.N. Taylor and E.L. Taylor (1993) have eliminated the Voltziales, and all of the families previously assigned to this order now are assigned to the Coniferales. An excellent summary of these new families is provided in Taylor and Taylor (1993).

Although the concept of the Voltziales presently is outdated, what is important to recognize here is that there was a group of distinct conifers that coexisted with the Cordaitales during the Paleozoic and persisted until the Mesozoic. They are characterized

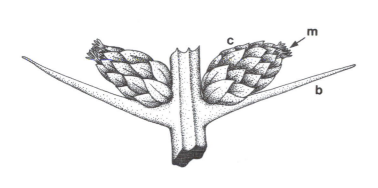

Figure 4. A reconstruction of part of a fertile shoot showing two male *Cordaitanthus* cones bearing terminal microsporangia in the axils of modified leaves called bracts. Key: *c,* cones; *m,* axils of leaves; *b,* bracts. Redrawn by Narda Quigley from Stewart and Rothwell (1993).

Figure 6. A reconstruction of *Lebachia* Florin, a voltzialean conifer previously assigned to the Lebachiaceae, but now assigned to the family Utrechtiaceae. Redrawn by Narda Quigley from Florin (1951).

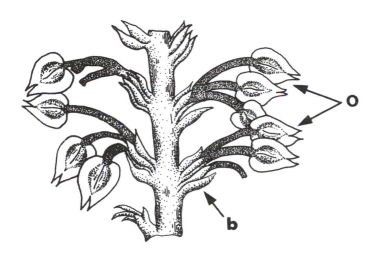

Figure 5. A reconstruction of part of a *Cordaitanthus* compound stobilus showing four seed cones in the axils of bracts. Note that each cone bears a number of flattened, bilaterally symmetrical, winged ovules. Key: *b,* bracts; *o,* ovules. Redrawn by Narda Quigley from Schagel et al. (1984).

by a branching pattern and leaf morphology (Figure 6), that resembles that of the extant *Araucaria heterophylla,* or Norfolk Island pine. More importantly, the intermediate stages in the evolution from the lax (flexible) *Cordaitanthus* cones of the Cordaitales to the highly reduced compound cones seen in modern conifers clearly is seen in the reproductive organs among various taxa within this group.

Florin's (1951) research on conifer reproductive organs has had a significant and long-lasting impact on our interpretation of them and the phylogenetic (evolutionary) relationships that can be derived using them. The cordaitaleans produced *Cordaitanthus*-bearing shoots. They consisted of short, lateral axes, upon which simple microsporangiate or megasporangiate cones were borne in the axils of bracts. Although the morphology (shape and structure) of modern pollen cones has changed since the Late Paleozoic, they still are considered to be simple structures because each cone is borne in the axil of a bract. However, recent evidence indicates that two divergent groups may have existed within the Voltziales, one producing simple cones, the other compound cones (Stewart and Rothwell 1993).

Modern megasporangiate cones, however, are compound structures that have been derived from entire cordaitalean megasporangiate axes. Some of the more significant events in the evolution of the conifer seed cone include the reduction, compression, and fusion of a megasporangiate *Cordaitanthus* cone into a single ovule-bearing scale, a shift from erect to inverted ovules, and the transition from radially to bilaterally symmetrical ovules and seed-cone scales. While it may at first seem unlikely that each ovuliferous scale from a modern conifer cone was derived from an entire cordaitalean cone, a number of intermediate evolutionary steps can be clearly seen in the reproductive organs of some of the extinct Voltzialean conifers.

Living Coniferales

Most conifers are tall, single-trunked or monopodial trees, with *Sequoiadendron giganteum* being the largest in the world. Others are of a much smaller stature and occur as shrubs, while one species of Podocarpaceae, *Parasitaxus ustus,* is known to be parasitic. Branches are borne helically along the trunk or at regular intervals forming whorls. Leaf morphology is variable and includes needle, scale, and broadly flattened types. Most conifers are evergreen, but some, such as *Larix, Pseudolarix, Metasequoia,* and *Taxodium,* are deciduous and lose their leaves in the fall. Morphological features that separate

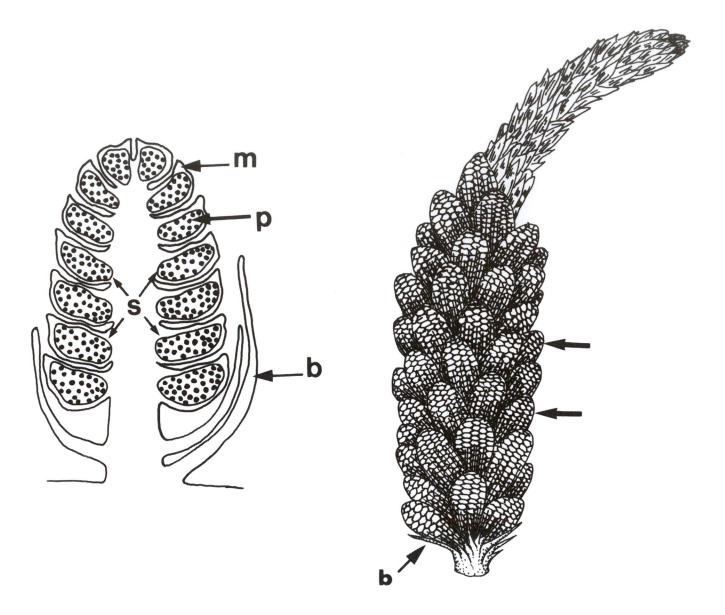

Figure 7. A cross section of a living pollen cone subtended by a bract (b) showing the microsporophylls (m) with pollen (p) in abaxial microsporangia (s). Drawn by Narda Quigley.

Figure 8. A shoot of *Pinus contorta* Douglas, or lodgepole pine, showing numerous pollen cones (arrows) concentrated near the tip of a small branch. Note that each pollen cone is subtended by a bract (b). Redrawn by Narda Quigley from Chamberlain (1966).

the conifers from other gymnosperms (plants with naked seeds, i.e., not enclosed in a fruit) include a relatively small pith relative to the amount of secondary wood, the presence of a primary vascular cylinder and cortex, pycnoxylic wood, simple needle and scalelike leaves, and separate male and female cones. Most genera are monoecious—both male and female cones are produced on the same plant. Others however, are dioecious—they produce male and female cones on separate male and female plants.

The pollen is produced in simple cones that consist of modified leaves called "microsporophylls," which are arranged around a central cone axis. Two to fifteen pollen sacs, each containing pollen grains, are borne on the outer (abaxial) surface of each microsporo-

phyll (Figure 7). Although pollen cones can occur individually on a branch, more commonly they are concentrated in regions near the tips of small branches in the lower part of the tree (Figure 8). Development of the male gametophyte, a process called "microsporogenesis," resembles that seen in the cycads and *Ginkgo*.

The megasporangiate cones consist of a central axis around which fertile and sterile ovuliferous scales are arranged (Figure 9A). The ovuliferous or cone scales are borne in the axils of modified leaves called bracts (Figure 9C). Ovules are borne on the adaxial surface of the fertile cone scales (Figure 9B). Morphologically, the cones and bract-scale complexes vary considerably at the level of family and genus, with species level identification often being achieved by examining features of the seed cones alone.

The origin of the Coniferales continues to remain problematic. Based on reproductive organs, it commonly was believed that they evolved from the Cordaitales via the Voltziales (Florin 1951, 1954). Recent data indicate that the Coniferales and Cordaitales indeed are closely related, but that they evolved as distinct lineages from either an archaeopteridalean progymnosperm (Beck 1981) or a seed fern of the Coniferous period (Rothwell 1982). Although our understanding of the evolutionary relationship between the Cordaitales and Coniferales continues to improve, the evolutionary significance of the extinct Mesozoic families and origin of the modern conifers cannot be answered unequivocally.

Pinaceae (Pine Family)

The Pinaceae includes 10 genera and approximately 215 living species of evergreen and deciduous needle-leaved conifers. The family is the largest, most widely distributed group of conifers in the world, and with the exception of one species of *Pinus*, the group is endemic to the Northern Hemisphere. The Pinaceae occupy a wide range of ecological habitats throughout the boreal, montane, and subalpine forests of North America, Asia, and Europe.

The seed cones are composed of numerous helically arranged ovuliferous scales, each adjacent to and enclosed (subtended) by a bract. The bracts are small and relatively thin compared to the cone scales and are free from scales except near the base. Bract morphology has been shown to be a consistent character within species and appears to be useful in discriminating among other genera of conifers (LePage and Basinger 1995). The ovuliferous scales are flattened, vary in shape and size, and bear two inverted winged seeds on their adaxial surfaces. The pollen cones are composed of numerous helically arranged microsporophylls, each of which bears two microsporangia abaxially.

Compsostrobus noetericus, from the Triassic of North Carolina, is thought to be the earliest representative of the Pinaceae, but its position within the Pinaceae is equivocal. C.N. Miller (1988) indicates that the oldest members of the Pinaceae are Early Cretaceous in age; however, even older *Pseudolarix* remains, from Late Jurassic sediments in the Bureya River Basin of southeastern Russia and the Fuxin Basin of northeastern China, provide the earliest unequivocal evidence for the family (LePage and Basinger 1995). Other genera such as *Pinus, Pityostrobus* (extinct), and *Pseudoaraucaria* (extinct) appear in Europe during the Early Cretaceous and become widely distributed throughout North America and Eurasia by Late Cretaceous time. The remaining genera appear during the Late Cretaceous and Early Tertiary; a time of significant diversification for the family (Miller 1988).

Taxodiaceae (Redwood or Bald Cypress Family)

The Taxodiaceae consists of 10 genera and 15 species with distribution of species occurring in both hemispheres. Species are confined largely to the warm-temperate regions of Asia, North America, and Australia, where precipitation is high and climate is warm, humid, and generally frost free.

Taxodiaceous seed cones are terminal, solitary, commonly small and round, and bear numerous helically arranged bract-scale complexes. Fusion between the bract and scale is extensive among genera, and in some, such as *Athrotaxis, Cunninghamia,* and *Taiwania,* the ovuliferous scale is highly reduced and the bract forms the bulk of the complex. Each complex bears two to nine winged seeds adaxially. The pollen cones are solitary, terminal, or axillary and occur in long racemes or panicles. Pollen cones are composed of numerous microsporophylls bearing two to nine microsporangia abaxially. A number of taxa are deciduous and, with the exception of *Glyptostrobus,* which possesses all three morphotypes, all possess either cryptomeroid and cupressoid or taxodioid and cupressoid leaves.

The fossil record of the Taxodiaceae indicates that representatives of this now highly restricted family once were distributed widely throughout the Northern Hemisphere during the Mesozoic (Florin 1963). Major tectonic and geomorphic changes during the Early and Late Tertiary led to significant climatic changes that resulted in restricted distribution and regional extinction for members of the family (Ferguson 1967).

Cupressaceae (Cedar or Cypress Family)

The Cupressaceae family consists of 22 genera and about 140 species of monoecious or dioecious evergreen trees and shrubs that are distributed worldwide. The leaves are arranged oppositely or whorled, may be scalelike, and are commonly resinous. The pollen cones are small and consist of whorled microsporophylls bearing three to six microsporangia. The seed cones are also small and are composed of a few oppositely arranged, fused, woody to fleshy bract-scale complexes. Each scale bears two to many erect, winged seeds.

Fossil Cupressaceae are known equivocally from the Late Triassic, and fossils assignable to the modern genera first appeared during the Early Cretaceous. Most of the cupressaceous fossils known consist of isolated vegetative fragments that have been assigned to the genus *Cupressinocladus;* however, J. Watson (1982) has demonstrated that most of the fossils assigned to this group actually belong to the Cheirolepidiaceae, an extinct group of conifers. Consequently, the fossil record of this family continues to remain poorly understood.

Podocarpaceae (Podocarpus Family)

The Podocarpaceae consists of about 150 species of trees and shrubs that are now restricted to the Southern Hemisphere. Leaf morphology is variable and includes small scalelike leaves to long strap-shaped leaves that are either positioned on opposite sides or helically arranged. The pollen cones bear bractlike microsporophylls possessing two microsporangia. The seed cone consists of a reduced bract subtending an ovule, which is partly to completely enveloped by a fleshy ovuliferous scale called an "epimatium."

The fossil record indicates that a number of distinct podocarpaceous lineages appeared in Antarctica, Africa, Australia, and New Zealand during the Triassic and Jurassic (Miller 1977). While the ancestry of the Podocarpaceae is far from being understood com-

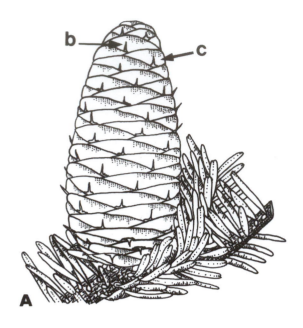

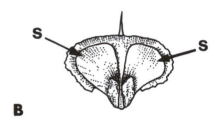

Figure 9. *A,* a mature seed cone of *Abies* Miller, a fir, showing helically arranged cone scales and slightly exserted bracts; *B,* adaxial view of a cone scale showing two winged seeds; *C,* abaxial view of a cone scale showing the bract subtending the cone scale. Key: *c,* cone scales; *b,* bracts; *s,* winged seeds. Redrawn by Narda Quigley from Rushforth (1987).

pletely, scholars have suggested that the group diverged from the Voltziales sometime during the Paleozoic. The Triassic *Rissikia* is of particular interest: its foliage is clearly podocarpaceous, but the seed cones associated with the foliage show affinity with the Voltziales.

Araucariaceae (Monkey-Puzzle Tree Family)

The Araucariaceae are a Southern Hemisphere group of evergreen, dioecious or monoecious trees that include the genera *Agathis,* *Araucaria,* and *Wollemia,* the recently discovered Wollemi pine. The leaves are linear or broad and oppositely to helically arranged. The pollen cones bear helically arranged microsporophylls; each possesses 5 to 20 pendant microsporangia. The bracts and ovuliferous scales are fused. The seed cones are compact and consist of a number of helically arranged cone scales, with each bearing a single recurved ovule. Each cone scale consists of a highly reduced ovuliferous scale that is fused almost completely to the subtending bract. In *Agathis* the ovuliferous scale is reduced to the point that it is more or less absent.

The fossil record of this group indicates the family was distributed widely, including North America, throughout the Mesozoic. While reports of Paleozoic araucarian fossils are equivocal, the family is well-represented in the Late Triassic, with maximum species diversity occurring during the Jurassic (Miller 1977).

Cephalotaxaceae (Plum Yew Family)

The Cephalotaxaceae is represented by the genus *Cephalotaxus,* and includes six species of small dioecious trees and shrubs that are distributed in southeast Asia. The pollen cones are composed of microsporophylls that bear three to eight microsporangia each. The seed cones consist of opposite and decussate bracts that each subtend two erect ovules. At maturity the ovules resemble those of the Taxaceae. Although the fossil record of the family is meager, vegetative remains assigned to the genus *Thomasiocladus* provide evidence that representatives of the family were present by Jurassic times (Miller 1977).

Taxaceae (Yew Family)

The Taxaceae includes six genera and about twenty species. Most are small dioecious evergreen trees and shrubs, but some species of *Taxus* and *Torreya* are arborescent. The leaves are linear, needlelike, and helically arranged. The pollen- and ovule-bearing structures differ significantly from that seen in the conifers (and forms the basis for assignment of the Taxaceae to the Taxales in classification systems where the Taxaceae are considered to be distinct from the conifers). The pollen cones consist of a number of microsporangiophores each bearing two to eight pollen sacs. The megasporangiate structure consists of a fleshy outer covering called an aril which encloses the ovule.

The fossil record of the Taxaceae extends to the Middle Jurassic and indicates that representatives of this group have been distinct from the other modern conifer families for a very long time. However, placing the Taxaceae within the gymnosperms continues to be a problem. R. Florin (1958) suggested that they be assigned to a separate class called the Taxopsida because the terminal ovule in the Taxaceae was not homologous with the laterally derived conifer ovules. Alternatively, T.M. Harris (1976) proposed that the ovuliferous shoots of the taxads could be derived from the fertile lateral shoots of *Utrechtia* (*Walchia,* one of the voltzialean conifers). This could occur through reduction of the shoot axis and sterile scales located above the ovule and shifting the ovule from a lateral to a terminal position. If Harris is correct, then the terminal ovule in the taxads is homologous with the laterally derived ovule of the conifers and assignment to the Coniferales would be justified.

BEN A. LEPAGE

Works Cited

Beck, C.B. 1981. *Archeopteris* and its role in vascular plant evolution. *In* K.J. Niklas (ed.), *Paleobotany, Paleoecology, and Evolution.* Vol. 1. New York: Praeger Scientific.

Chamberlain, C.J. 1935. *Gymnosperms: Structure and Evolution.* Chicago: University of Chicago Press.

Ferguson, D.K. 1967. On the phytogeography of Coniferales in the European Cenozoic. *Palaeogeography, Palaeoclimatology, Palaeoecology* 3:73–110.

Florin, R. 1951. Evolution in cordaites and conifers. *Acta Horti Bergiani* 15:285–388.

———. 1954. The female reproductive organs of conifers and taxads. *Biological Review* 29:367–88.

———. 1958. On Jurassic taxads and conifers from northwestern Europe and eastern Greenland. *Acta Horti Bergiani* 17:257–402.

———. 1963. The distribution of conifer and taxad genera in time and space. *Acta Horti Bergiani* 20:121–312.

Foster, A.S., and E.M. Gifford Jr. 1974. *Comparative Morphology of Vascular Plants.* 2nd ed., San Francisco: Freeman.

Harris, T.M. 1976. The Mesozoic gymnosperms. *Review of Palaeobotany and Palynology* 21:119–34.

LePage, B.A., and J.F. Basinger. 1995. The evolutionary history of the genus *Pseudolarix gordon* (Pinaceae). *International Journal of Plant Sciences* 156:910–50.

Miller Jr., C.N. 1977. Mesozoic conifers. *Botanical Review* 43:217–80.

———. 1988. The origin of modern conifer families. *In* C.B. Beck (ed.), *Origin and Evolution of the Gymnosperms.* New York: Columbia University Press.

Rothwell, G.W. 1982. New interpretations of the earliest conifers. *Review of Palaeobotany and Palynology* 37:7–28.

Rushforth, K.D. 1987. *Conifers.* New York: Facts on File; London: Helm.

Schagel, R.F., R.J. Bandoni, J.R. Maze, G.E. Rouse, W.B. Schofield, and J.R. Stein. 1984. *Plants: An Evolutionary Survey.* Belmont, California: Wadsworth.

Stewart, W.N., and G.W. Rothwell. 1993. *Paleobotany and the Evolution of Plants.* 2nd ed. New York: Cambridge University Press.

Taylor, T.N., and E.L. Taylor. 1993. *The Biology and Evolution of Fossil Plants.* Englewood Cliffs, New Jersey: Prentice-Hall.

Trivett, M.L. 1992. Growth architecture, structure, and relationships of *Cordaixylon iowensis* nov. comb. (Cordaitales). *International Journal of Plant Sciences* 153:273–87.

Trivett, M.L., and G.W. Rothwell. 1991. Diversity among Paleozoic Cordaitales. *Neue Jahrbücher für Geologie und Paläontologie Abhandlungen* 183:289–305.

Watson, J. 1982. The Cheirolepidiaceae: A short review. *In* D.D. Nautiyal (ed.), *Phyta: Studies on Living and Fossil Plants.* Allahabad: Society of Plant Taxonomists.

Further Reading

Chamberlain, C.J. 1966. *Gymnosperms: Structure and Evolution.* New York: Dover.

Foster, A.S., and E.M. Gifford Jr. 1959. *Comparative Morphology of Vascular Plants.* San Francisco: Freeman; 2nd ed., 1974.

Rushforth, K.D. 1987. *Conifers.* New York: Facts on File; London: Helm.

Schagel, R.F., R.J. Bandoni, J.R. Maze, G.E. Rouse, W.B. Schofield, and J.R. Stein. 1984. *Plants: An Evolutionary Survey.* Belmont, California: Wadsworth.

CONTINENTAL DRIFT

See Plate Tectonics and Contintental Drift

COPE, EDWARD DRINKER

American, 1840–97

Edward Drinker Cope was born on 28 July 1840, at the family home in Philadelphia. The Copes had amassed a sizable fortune from the family shipping business.

At an early age Cope showed an intense interest in natural history; when he was eight years old, on a visit to the Philadelphia Academy of Natural Sciences he made a detailed sketch of the skeleton of an ichthyosaur, with accompanying written comments about the sclerotic plates around the eyes. He was educated at home by his father, then at Westtown School, a Quaker institution in the outskirts of the city. But Cope never went on to a university; he was too far advanced in his interests and knowledge of natural history to be confined within a university curriculum. He did have a year of instruction in anatomy from Joseph Leidy, professor in the medical school at the University of Pennsylvania.

By the time Cope had reached his early twenties, he had become an independent scholar, studying and publishing widely on vertebrates, both fossil and recent. He was appointed secretary of the Philadelphia Academy in 1865 and curator in 1873. Since much of his research was carried on independently, he leased two adjacent "town houses" on Pine Street, which served as his office, laboratory, and storage facility. In 1877 he purchased *The American Naturalist,* a scientific journal, to serve in part as a vehicle for his own scientific contributions.

Cope spent prodigious effort and large sums of his own money on his work. Then, in 1871 Cope made his first western field trip, to the Niobrara Cretaceous beds in western Kansas. From then until 1894, Cope traveled widely throughout the continent west of Mississippi, as well as into northern Mexico. These were study and collecting trips, and he usually hired trained collectors to work for and with him. Indeed, he often had several expeditions in the field simultaneously, while he journeyed back and forth to supervise and participate in the work. He also participated closely with some of the government territorial surveys, notably the Hayden and Wheeler surveys in today's Wyoming. Among his assistants were Charles H. Sternberg, Samuel Wendell Williston, and Jacob Wortman, all of whom established outstanding paleontological reputations in their own rights.

Although Cope's field surveys were monumental affairs, they did not hinder his published scientific output. During his lifetime he published more than 1,400 scientific papers and monographs. Although many of his papers were relatively brief, he produced some very large monographs, of which his massive work *The Vertebrata of the Tertiary Formations of the West,* often referred to as "Cope's Bible," is a prime example.

Naturally, much of Cope's published output consists of descriptions of fossils, but he also wrote extensively on theoretical subjects. As a young man, Cope was an avid reader of Darwin and various authors' discussions of the Darwinian concept of organic evolution. But Cope rejected a strict acceptance of Darwin's *Origin of Species.* He favored an interpretation of Lamarck's theory of the transmission of acquired characters—to such a degree that he became known in the scientific world as a neo-Lamarckian. Just how far he carried his line of thought may be debated; it is an example of Cope's original and perhaps unorthodox line of scientific speculation. It is also an example, supplemented by others, that the true worth of a scientist's contributions may be found not so much in his philosophical speculations but in his solid accumulation of facts. Cope had many theoretical ideas about the mechanisms of evolution, but the true value of his prodigious efforts is to be found in his empirical descriptions of the animals that engaged his attention.

It is interesting that this genius of natural history (for he was no less than that) is regarded as a wellspring, or a sort of patron saint, by three disciplines of the field. Among the vertebrate paleontologists, Cope is revered as a giant, the ichthyologists consider Cope as a founding father of their science, and so do the herpetologists. Indeed, the official journal of the American Society of Ichthyologists and Herpetologists is *Copeia,* a quarterly.

Cope's life was not totally quiet, however. He engaged in one of the most bitter fights in the history of paleontology with O.C. Marsh over the priority in discovering U.S. fossil dinosaurs. Ultimately, the feud damaged the reputations of both men. In his later years Cope lived a rather spartan existence, sleeping on a cot in a back room of one of the Pine Street houses. In the 1880s, he had invested what was left of his share of the family fortune in Mexican silver mines. The mines failed to produce the income for which he had hoped. Because of his financial problems, in 1887 Cope was forced to join the faculty of the University of Pennsylvania, where he taught until his death, on 12 April 1897.

Cope had left instructions that, after his death, his remains were to be donated to the Academy of Natural Sciences of Philadelphia. It is said that Cope did this so that his cranium could be compared to that of his rival O.C. Marsh, who did not take up the challenge. (Marsh was buried normally in New Haven, Connecticut.)

EDWIN H. COLBERT

Biography

Born in Philadelphia, Pennsylvania, 28 July 1840. Did not attend university but studied anatomy with Joseph Leidy of the University of Pennsylvania. Elected member (1861), secretary (1865), and curator (1873), Academy of Natural Sciences of Philadelphia; professor of comparative zoology and botany, Haverford College, Pennsylvania, 1964–67; part owner and senior editor of *American Naturalist,* 1878–97; received Gold Medal, Geological Society of London, 1879; named professor of geology and mineralogy (1889–95) and professor of zoology and comparative anatomy (1895–97), University of Pennsylvania; at times associated with the Canadian Geological Survey, Indiana Geological Survey, Texas Geological Survey, and U.S. Geological Survey; member of such scholarly organizations as the National Academy of Sciences and the American Association for the Advancement of Science (president, 1896). Student of fossil vertebrates, recent fishes, amphibians, and reptiles; conducted numerous collecting expeditions, western North America; more than 1,400 publications, describing numerous species and discussing problems of classification and evolution; recognized internationally as the premier authority in his fields. Died in Philadelphia, Pennsylvania, on 12 April 1897.

Major Publications

1869–70. *Synopsis of the Extinct Batrachia: Reptilia and Aves of North America.* Transactions of the American Philosophical Society, 14(2–3). Philadelphia: American Philosophical Society.

1873. *On the Extinct Vertebrata of the Eocene of Wyoming Observed by the Expedition of 1872, with Notes on the Geology.* Sixth Annual Report, U.S. Geological Survey of the Territories, F.V. Hayden, Geologist in Charge. Washington, D.C.: Government Printing Office.

1875a. Relation of man to Tertiary Mammalia. *Penn Monthly,* December.

1875b. *The Vertebrata of the Cretaceous Formations of the West.* Report of the U.S. Geological Survey of the Territories, F. V. Haven, Geologist in Charge. Vol. 2, Washington, D.C.: Government Printing Office.

1881. On the Vertebrata of the Wind River Eocene beds of Wyoming. *Bulletin of the U.S. Geological and Geographical Surveys of the Territories* 6(1):132–202.

1883. *The Vertebrata of the Tertiary Formations of the West.* Report of the U.S. Geological Survey of the Territories, F.V. Haven, Geologist in Charge, Book 1, Washington, D.C.: U.S. Government Printing Office.

1886. *The Origin of the Fittest: Essays on Evolution.* 8 vols. New York: Appleton; London: Macmillan, 1887.

1889. *The Batrachia of North America.* Bulletin of the U.S. National Museum, 34. Washington, D.C.: U.S. Government Printing Office.

1915. With W.D. Matthew. *Hitherto Unpublished Plates of Tertiary Mammalia and Permian Vertebrata.* American Museum of Natural History Monograph Series, 2. New York: American Museum of Natural History.

Further Reading

Colbert, E.H. 1968. *Men and Dinosaurs.* New York: Dutton; London: Evans; 2nd ed., *The Great Dinosaur Hunters and Their Discoveries,* New York: Dover, 1984.

Osborn, H.F. 1931. *Cope: Master Naturalist.* Princeton, New Jersey: Princeton University of Press; London: Milford.

Shor, E.N. 1974. *The Fossil Feud between E.D. Cope and O.C. Marsh.* Hicksville, New York: Exposition.

CRANIAL NERVES
See Brain and Cranial Nerves

CRANIATES

The Craniata, or "craniates," are characterized by the presence of a skull (or cranium, hence their name). This skull consists of a cartilaginous or bony element, the neurocranium, that encloses the brain and sensory capsules, along with a variable number of more ventrally ("belly-side") placed elements, collectively termed the "splanchnocranium." In gilled animals the splanchnocranium consists of branchial, or gill, arches, which support the gills; in jawed cranites, the hyoid and mandibular arch support the jaw (Figure 1C).

There are a number of other craniate characters, essentially in the head; in fossils these can only be inferred. One of them is the neural crest (Figure 2A), a structure that occurs during the development of the embryo. Initially, the fertilized egg develops three distinct layers, the "ectoderm" (outer layer), "mesoderm" (middle), and the "endoderm" (inner). The layers go on to produce specific systems in the body. For example, the ectoderm produces the nervous system, the mesoderm produces muscles, and the endoderm produces the digestive tract. In craniates, the "neural crest" arises as a thickening of the ectoderm. The crest, a special source of embryonic tissue, develops along the margins of the "neural tube," a structure that forms the central nervous system in the embryo. The neural crest then migrates ventrally to give rise to a variety of organs, such as the gill and jaw endoskeleton, pigment cells, nerve ganglia, and "dentinous tissues" in the exoskeleton (elements of the external skeleton, i.e., scales, dermal bones, and teeth). Therefore, if one finds fragments of exoskeleton with dentinous tissues, they provide good evidence that one is dealing with a craniate.

Another important craniate character is the presence of "placodes" (Figures 2B, 2C), a thickening of the embryonic ectoderm that gives rise to part of the sensory capsules (olfactory organs, eye lens, sensory organs of inner ear) and the lateral line system (a sensory system that, in fishes and some amphibians, detects pressure produced by movement through the water). Fragments of exoskeleton with grooves or canals for the sensory line system is thus also good evidence for craniate derivation. Finally, early craniates possess endoskeletal rays (long internal bony structures), at least in the unpaired fins, a character that is also observable in fossils.

The term Craniata sounds less familiar than Vertebrata, or "vertebrate," although scholars have regarded these two names as synonymous for some time. In fact, scientists now prefer to use the name craniates (Figure 4) for all animals that, in classical textbooks, are referred to as vertebrates. The reason for this is that all these animals have a skull, whereas a small number of them have no backbone, or "vertebral column." Among living craniates, hagfishes alone have no backbone proper; their body axis is strengthened only by a cartilaginous rod, the "notochord" (Figure 1A). The other craniates have, in addition to the notochord, a series of skeletal elements called "arcualia," which flank the spinal cord. These elements contribute to the formation of the vertebrae (Figures 1B, 1C, 3). Therefore, the presence of the notochord or arcualia qualifies organisms to be called vertebrates (Løvtrup 1977; Janvier 1981, 1996a).

In most Recent vertebrates, the vertebrae include the arcualia, which lie dorsal (on the "back" side) to the notochord (and also ventral to it in the jawed vertebrates) (Figure 3B), but these are attached to a more massive, axial element, the "centrum," also called the "vertebral body," in a human vertebra, for example. The vertebral centrum arose independently at least seven times in vertebrates: by calcification (embedding of calcium) of the notochord in advanced sharks and rays (Figure 3B), and by ossification (transformation into bone) of the notochordal sheath in bichirs, gars, bowfins, teleosts (bony fishes), some fossil lungfishes, and in tetrapods (four-legged terrestrial animals) and some of their fossil piscine relatives.

Living vertebrates consist of lampreys and all the jawed vertebrates, the latter representing practically the totality of the group. Hagfishes and lampreys share some apparently unique characters, such as horny teeth, a peculiar tonguelike feeding device (often referred to as the "lingual" apparatus) (Figure 1A, 1B), and pouch-shaped gills. As a result, for a long time these two groups were gathered in a group called "cyclostomes" (rounded-mouth), which some still regard as monophyletic (descended from a single common ancestor) (Yalden 1985). In contrast, lampreys share with the jawed vertebrates, or "gnathostomes," about 25 characters that do not occur in hagfishes (or occur in a more primitive state). Some such characters are morphological (relate to form or structure). Examples are the arcualia, radial muscles in unpaired fins, two vertical semicircular canals, eye muscles, innervated heart with closely set atrium and ventricle, true lymphocytes, condensed pancreas, and spleen. Physiological characters include hemoglobins with low O_2 affinity and significant Bohr effect and hyperosmoregulation.

Despite the somewhat similar eel-shaped aspect of both groups, there is now overwhelming evidence that lampreys and hagfishes do not form a monophyletic group and that lampreys are related more closely to the gnathostomes than to hagfishes (Figure 4). Some zoologists, however, still accept the classical idea that hagfishes look primitive because they are "degenerate," a situation that results from their burrowing habits. This is, for example, how these zoologists explain the absence of an eye lens in hagfishes, despite the presence of an optic placode in the embryo.

Gnathostomes are characterized by jaws (*gnathos,* hence their name) but also by numerous other anatomical features, such as medially (centrally) placed gill arches, pelvic fins, horizontal semi-

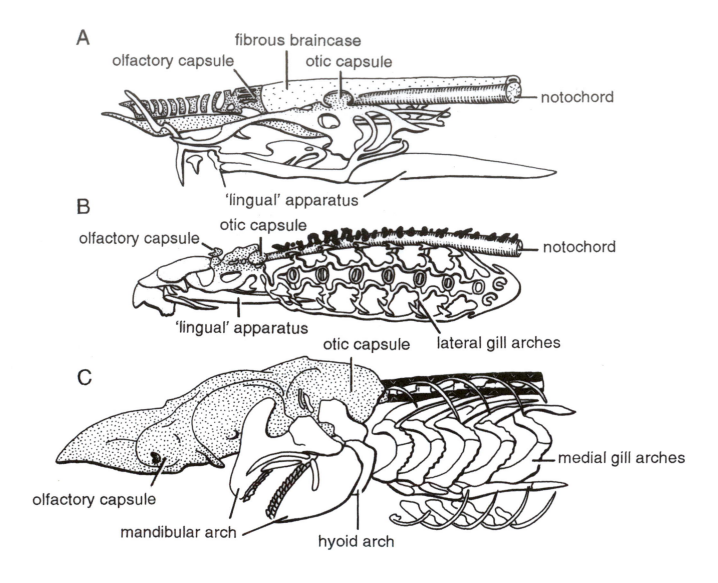

Figure 1. Craniate characters in side views. *A,* hagfish; *B,* lampreys; *C,* gnathostomes. Key: *stippled,* neurocranium; *white,* splanchnocranium; *black,* arcualia of the vertebral column. Modified after Janvier (1996a).

circular canal in ear, nerve fibers covered with a substance called "myelin," and sperms passing through the male urinary system. Among living craniates, only the gnathostomes possess a calcified internal and external skeleton (endo- and exoskeleton, or "dermal skeleton"), in contrast to hagfishes and lampreys, which only have a cartilaginous internal skeleton. However, as we shall see below, several fossil groups of jawless vertebrates possessed a massively calcified and ossified skeleton, both internal and external.

The living gnathostomes include the "chondrichthyans" ("cartilaginous fishes," i.e., sharks, rays, chimeras) (Figure 4) and the "osteichthyans" ("bony fishes," i.e., ray-finned fishes, lobe-finned fishes, and four-legged, terrestrial vertebrates) (Figure 4). Although primitive (archaic) in some respects, living chondrichthyans are highly specialized fishes. Contrary to a common belief (arising in part from the fact that hagfishes and lampreys are carti-

laginous), the cartilaginous internal skeleton of chondrichthyans is not a primitive condition. It is now clear that chondrichthyans once possessed bone in the endoskeleton, and that it has been progressively lost to be replaced by a layer of prismatic calcified cartilage, which today is their main defining character. The fossil, jawless vertebrates that are related most closely to the gnathostomes possess perichondral bone (bone that develops below the outer membrane covering a cartilaginous structure). This characteristic suggested that this was the primitive condition for the gnathostomes; direct evidence came from the discovery of thin patches of perichondral bone overlying the prismatic calcified cartilage in several Recent chondrichthyans (Peignoux-Deville et al. 1982).

Osteichthyans are characterized by "endochondral bone" in their internal skeleton; that is, bone which pervades and progressively replaces the cartilage, within the perichondral bone. Their

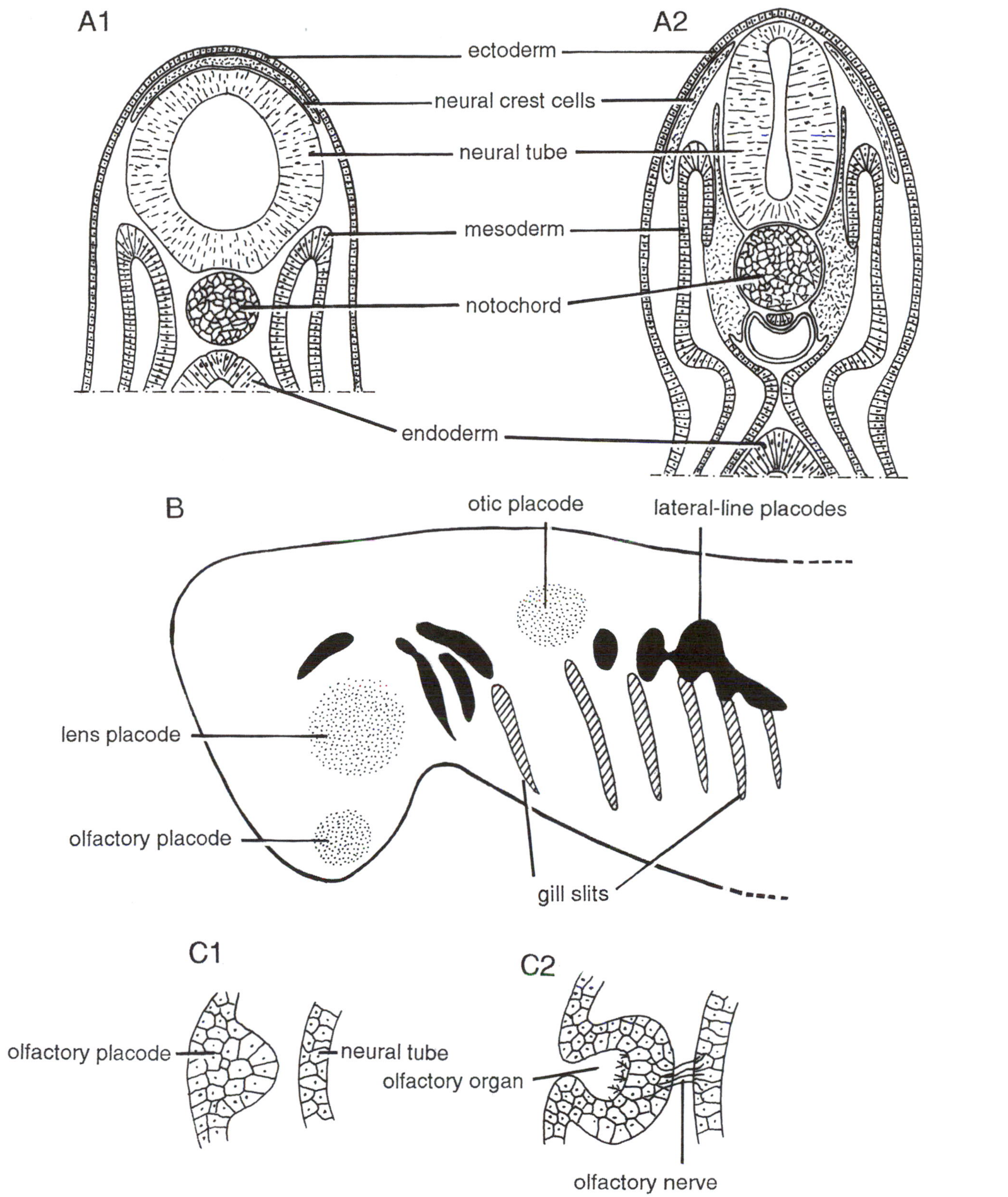

Figure 2. Craniate characters. *A,* transverse sections through a shark embryo at two successive developmental stages, showing the ventral migration of the neural crest tissue; *B,* distribution of the placodes in the head of a shark embryo in lateral view; *C,* transverse section through the olfactory placode of a shark embryo, two successive developmental stages, showing the rise of the olfactory nerve between the placode and the neural tube. Key: *stippled,* olfactory, lens, and otic placodes; *black,* lateral line placodes. From: *A,* after Bjerring (1968); *B* and *C,* after Wake (1979).

A

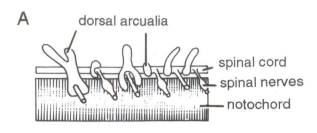

dorsal arcualia

spinal cord
spinal nerves
notochord

B

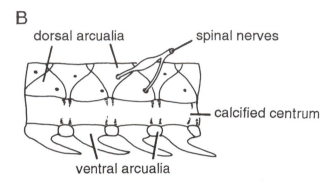

dorsal arcualia   spinal nerves

calcified centrum

ventral arcualia

Figure 3. Vertebrate characters: the arcualia in the vertebral column. *A,* lamprey; *B,* gnathostomes (shark). From: *A,* after Janvier (1996a); *B,* after Goodrich (1909).

external skeleton is made up of large bony plates—in particular an "opercular bone series" that covers the gill slit—and their teeth are attached to the exoskeletal jawbones that line the mouth. The fins of osteichthyans are covered with small, tile-shaped scales called "lepidotrichs."

Among osteichthyans, the "actinopterygians" (ray-finned fishes) (Figure 4) are the largest group of living fishes, including bichirs, sturgeons, paddlefishes, gars, bowfins, and thousands of species of teleosts, such as goldfish, mackerels, pikes, salmons, and herrings. In contrast, the other osteichthyan group, the "sarcopterygians" (Figure 4), comprises only a few living fish species, the coelacanth and five species of lungfishes—but it also includes thousands of species of tetrapods (i.e., the four-legged land vertebrates, including those which have lost their limbs, such as snakes, or returned to an aquatic life, such as whales).

Past Diversity

The present, large-scale diversity pattern of the craniates, characterized by the predominance of actinopterygian fishes in the sea and of tetrapods on land, arose by the Late Palaeozoic or Early Mesozoic, approximately 200 to 250 million years ago. In Early Palaeozoic times (400 to 470 million years ago), for example, the dominant craniate groups, in terms of abundance and diversity, were armored jawless vertebrates, formerly referred to as "ostracoderms" (Figure 4). These animals became extinct by the end of the Devonian period, 370 million years ago.

For a long time, ostracoderms were regarded as remote ancestors to hagfishes and lampreys, which scholars assumed had lost the bony skeleton (Jarvik 1980). The current theory is that in fact ostracoderms are related more closely to the gnathostomes than to lampreys (Gagnier 1993a, 1993b; Forey and Janvier 1993, 1994; Janvier 1996a, 1996b). Some of them, such as osteostracans, share with the gnathostomes an extensively ossified exoskeleton made up of true bone (containing bone cells), a perichondrally ossified endoskeleton (at any rate in the braincase and arcualia), externally open endolymphatic duct, paired fins with musculature and attached to an endoskeletal girdle, and an upwardly tapering ("epicercal") tail (Figure 4). During the Devonian period, the diversity of all ostracoderm groups declined, possibly as a consequence of the rise of the gnathostomes but more likely because of changes in their favorite environments—sandy bays and deltas—until they finally became extinct (Janvier 1985, 1996a).

The three major ostracoderm groups, in terms of diversity and number of species, are the heterostracans ("pteraspids"), galeaspids and osteostracans ("cephalaspids") (Blieck 1984; Wang 1991; Pan 1992; Janvier 1981, 1984). Other, minor groups are the astraspids, eriptychiids, arandaspids, anaspids, and pituriaspids, all represented by only a few species (Elliott 1987; Ørvig 1989; Gagnier 1993a, 1993b; Young 1991; Ritchie 1964; Sansom et al. 1997). Thelodonts are a controversial group. Some regard it as monophyletic and close to the gnathostomes (Turner 1991), whereas others consider it as paraphyletic (having many ancestral lines) and ancestral to most other ostracoderm groups and to the gnathostomes (Janvier 1981, 1996a, 1996b) (Figure 4).

A long-enigmatic group, the conodonts, formerly known from minute, isolated denticles, recently has been included in the craniates by some paleontologists, on the basis of the discovery of articulated (found in an assembled, jointed form) specimens that show an eel-shaped body with chevron-shaped muscle blocks (interrelated groups); large, paired eyes; and a caudal (tail) fin with radials (endoskeletal rays) (Aldridge et al. 1993) (Figure 4). Although conodonts (or, at any rate, true conodonts—the only ones known from articulated specimens) are likely to be craniates or craniate relatives, there are heated controversies about their phylogenetic position (position in evolutionary history) (Pridmore et al. 1996). Some have claimed that the structure of the conodont denticles are very close to that of vertebrate bone, dentine, and enamel (Sansom et al. 1992, 1994; Smith et al. 1996), whereas others reject this interpretation (Schultze 1996). The debate is still going on, but the structure of the conodont denticles admittedly looks at odds with that of classical vertebrate dermal and epidermal tissues, even at the histochemical level (level of minute structures) (Kemp and Nicoll 1996). On the other hand, the body morphology of the two complete forms known to date (the Ordovician *Promissum* and the Carboniferous *Clydagnathus*) is strikingly craniate- and even vertebrate-like (Gabott et al. 1995).

Apart from the controversial conodonts, which appear in the Late Cambrian (about 520 million years ago), the earliest known undisputed craniate remains are from the Early Ordovician (475 million years ago) of Queensland in Australia. They are represented by dermal bone fragments referred to the genus *Poropho-*

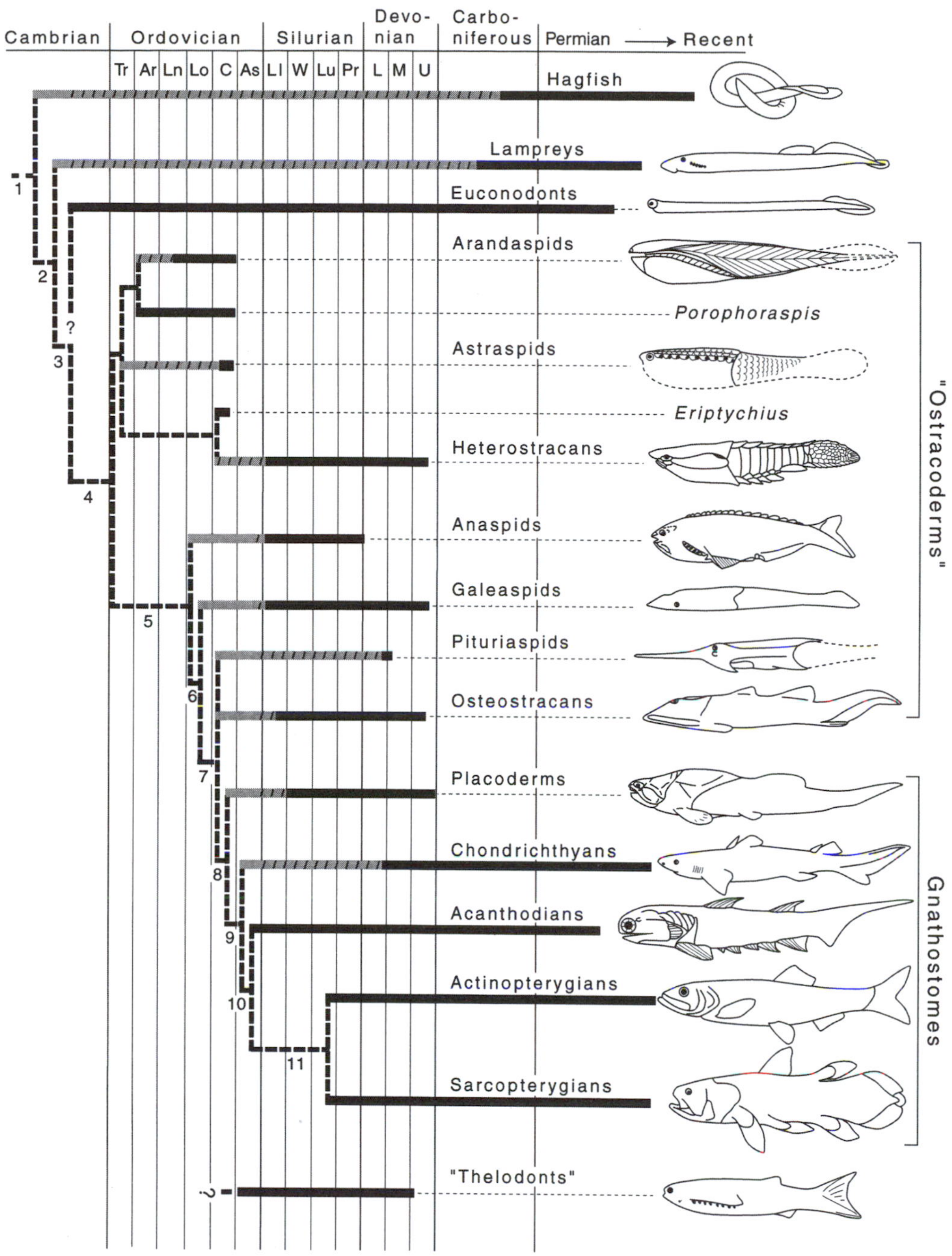

Figure 4. Simplified phylogenetic tree of the Craniata. Key: *black,* actual range of the higher taxa; *gray hatched,* inferred ("ghost") range. Taxa and their major characters: *1,* Craniata (skull, neural crests, placodes, radials in unpaired fins); *2,* Vertebrata (arcualia, extrinsic eye muscles, two vertical semicircular canals, cardiac innervation, atrium and ventricles of heart closely set, cartilaginous braincase surrounding the brain, radial muscles in fins, lateral-line neuromasts, spleen, condensed pancreas, tripartite adenohypophysis, true lymphocytes); *3,* unnamed taxon (? mineralized dermal skeleton in the oral cavity only); *4,* unnamed taxon (mineralized dermal skeleton in the entire body, developed metencephalon); *5,* unnamed taxon (ventrolateral fin folds, anal fin); *6,* unnamed taxon (perichondral calcification or ossification, externally open endolymphatic duct); *7,* unnamed taxon (paired, pectoral fins with musculature inserted onto an endoskeletal girdle, epicercal caudal fin, cellular bone, sclerotic ring); *8,* Gnathostomata (jaws, horizontal semicircular canal, pelvic fins, medial gill arches); *9,* crown-group Gnathostomata (superior oblique muscle in anterior position, dental lamina); *10,* Teleostomi (ventral fissure of braincase, otoliths); *11,* Osteichthyes (endochondral ossification of endoskeleton, teeth borne by dermal bones, lepidotrichiae). The "Thelodonti" are regarded as paraphyletic, so any thelodont species can branch off anywhere between nodes 4 and 8. Abbreviations: geological scale: *Tr,* Tremadoc; *Ar,* Arenig; *Ln,* Llanvirn; *Lo,* Llandeilo; *C,* Caradoc; *As,* Ashgill; *Ll,* Llandovery; *W,* Wenlock; *Lu,* Ludlow; *Pr,* Pridoli; *L,* lower; *M,* middle; *U,* upper.

raspis, which is probably a close relative of arandaspids, a group of ostracoderms closely related to heterostracans (Young 1997) (Figure 4). Some still enigmatic carapace (shell) fragments, made up of calcium phosphate and found in Late Cambrian and Ordovician rocks, have been included in the craniates because of their structure, which somewhat recalls the exoskeleton of arandaspids (Young et al. 1996; Smith et al. 1996), but despite a dentinelike tissue in one of them *(Anatolepis),* this remains debated.

The craniates of the Ordovician period are essentially ostracoderms (i.e., arandaspids, astraspids, eriptychiids, and thelodonts), although there is some evidence for early gnathostomes (possibly sharks and acanthodians scales) as early as mid-Ordovician times (Sansom et al. 1996; Karatayute-Talimaa and Predtechenskyj 1995; Young 1997) (Figure 4). The newly described Ordovician vertebrate *Skiichthys* (Smith and Sansom 1997) is of undecided affinity (relationship), yet it has typical cellular bone, as in osteostracans and most gnathostomes. In the Early Silurian (420 million years ago), all other ostracoderm groups undergo a rapid diversification, which reaches its acme in the Lower Devonian.

The earliest undoubted gnathostomes appear in the Latest Ordovician of Siberia and are acanthodians. In the Silurian, the gnathostomes are already diversified and include essentially acanthodians, placoderms, osteichthyans, and possibly chondrichthyans (Pan and Dineley 1988; Janvier 1996a; Thanh et al. 1997; Karatayute-Talimaa 1995). However, the gnathostomes remain very rare until the Lower Devonian, when all the major, present-day gnathostome groups (i.e., chondrichthyans, actinopterygians, and sarcopterygians) are already represented although are far less diverse than they are nowadays.

In contrast, the highest diversity of the Devonian gnathostomes is found among two extinct groups, the placoderms and acanthodians, which disappeared 365 and 260 million years ago, respectively (Denison 1978a, 1978b). Placoderms possessed a massive bony armor with a neck joint, and in many respects, their internal anatomical structure retains what may have been that of the ancestral gnathostome (Figure 4). For example, they retain the posterior (rear) position of the upper oblique eye muscle, like osteostracans, and their jaw musculature is attached medially on the mandibular arch. Therefore, placoderms are regarded as the sister group (closest relation) of all other fossil and living gnathostomes (Schaeffer 1975; Young 1986). Acanthodians look like spiny sharks (Figure 4), with large bony spines in front of each fin, but they now are regarded as more closely related to osteichthyans than to sharks or placoderms (Miles 1973). It is, however, not ruled out that they are not a natural group and in fact, include relatives of osteichthyans and chondrichthyans respectively.

In Devonian times, piscine sarcopterygians were admittedly more diverse than present-day ones, despite the absence of any tetrapod before the end of this period. There were already coelacanths, a large number of lungfish species, and also four major groups that are now extinct. One of these groups, the onychodontiforms, still is of debated affinities—it may be the most primitive sarcopterygian group. Others (porolepiforms) were relatives of lungfishes, and still others (rhizodontiforms, osteolepiforms, elpistostegalians) were relatives of the tetrapods. Among the latter, the osteolepiforms and elpistostegids (or panderichthyids) possessed

internal "nostrils," or choanae (like tetrapods), and the internal skeleton of their paired fins foreshadows the structure of the tetrapod limbs (Cloutier and Ahlberg 1995; Vorobyeva and Schultze 1991; Schultze 1994).

Fossils and Origins

Although the question of the phylogenetic position of craniates among metazoans (multicellular animals) has long been a matter of debate, there is now a broad consensus that craniates probably are related more closely to the tunicates (sea squirts) and cephalochordates (lancelets) than to any other animal group (Schaeffer 1987; Gee 1996). Together, these three groups are called "chordates," because they share the same type of axial support, the notochord. There is also a consensus over the theory that, among chordates, craniates are related more closely to the cephalochordates than to the tunicates, because both groups share many unique anatomical, developmental, and physiological characters (e.g., the chevron-shaped body muscle blocks), and basically the same structure of the central nervous system. Craniates and cephalochordates are included in a group called myomerozoans, or "euchordates."

There are some theories about the evolutionary processes involved in the rise of craniate characters, such as the skull, the neural crest, and the placodes. One of these theories is that the rise of the craniate head is largely owing to the duplication of a group of genes called the *Hox*-class homeobox gene cluster. In the headless cephalochordates, this cluster controls the development of a large portion of the neural tube. The duplication of this gene cluster is thought to be responsible for the rise of the hindbrain of craniates and for the development of specific morphogenetic processes (Holland and Garcia-Fernandez 1996). Recently, T.C. Lacalli and colleagues (1994) suggested that the median "eye" of cephalochordates is homologous to the more complex, paired eyes of craniates. This may explain why the eyes are so closely set and anteriorly placed in some of the earliest known fossil craniates (e.g., arandaspids and conodonts).

In contrast, fossils are powerless in providing a link between craniates and any noncraniate chordate. Some poorly informative fossils preserved as imprints, such as *Pikaia* and another, unnamed fossil from the Cambrian Burgess Shale, have been regarded variously as either cephalochordates or primitive craniates (Conway-Morris and Whittington 1979; Simonetta and Insom 1993), but with no fossilized structures these samples remain poorly informative. These Burgess Shale fossils actually may turn out to be craniates—possibly relatives of hagfishes and lampreys—since the current craniate phylogeny predicts that the divergence of these two groups respectively is older than the earliest known ostracoderms (the Early Ordovician) (Figure 4).

The most interesting—yet highly controversial—theory about craniate origins is the "calcichordate theory." It assumes that craniates (along with the cephalochordates and tunicates) arose from an ensemble of asymmetrical Paleozoic animals, collectively called "calcichordates" (Jefferies 1986, 1997). In general, these animals are regarded as highly specialized, extinct echinoderms (the group to which sea urchins, sea lilies, and sea cucumbers belong), because their skeleton is made up of typical, echinoderm-like, calcite plates. This theory implies that the bilateral symmetry (mirror-image body plan) of craniates is secondary (developed later) and that all three chordate groups (tunicates, cephalochordates, and craniates) have lost the calcitic skeleton. Admittedly, the group of calcichordates thought to be most closely related to craniates possess a large "head" and a "tail," which recalls the morphology of the earliest known craniates, but what is known of their internal anatomy is largely at odds with currently accepted general craniate anatomy. Whatever its strength, the calcichordate theory remains the only recent, paleontology-based theory about the origin of craniates. Its rejection by a majority of paleontologists is perhaps owing to the fact that it implies too many transformations involving losses of characters and is thus less parsimonious than considering these fossils as echinoderms (Peterson 1995).

In contrast, fossils of duly recognized early craniates, such as the Early Paleozoic ostracoderms, clearly show associations of characters that no longer exist in the living world. Thanks to this property of fossils, they provide a link between such two widely different extant (present-day) groups as the lampreys and gnathostomes. Among living craniates, for example, only the gnathostomes have bone and paired fins, while jawless craniates (hagfishes and lampreys) are naked, cartilaginous, and devoid of paired fins. Ostracoderms show that "jawlessness" can be associated with bone, and, in the case of osteostracans, even paired fins (Figure 4). In this respect, they fill a large morphological gap between lampreys and the gnathostomes (Maisey 1988; Janvier 1996a, 1996b). However, ostracoderms are powerless to explain how the jaws of the gnathostomes arose.

In classical theory jaws are modified gill arches. However, the medially placed gill arches of the gnathostomes have no homologue in fossil and Recent jawless craniates and are regarded as a unique gnathostome character. One theory is that the ancestral craniate possessed both lateral and medial branchial, hyoid, and mandibular arches; the medial ones then were lost in hagfishes and lampreys, except for the mandibular arch (Mallatt 1996). Another theory is that jaws (or part of them) are the homologue (similar structures) of the velum, a special pumping and antireflux organ (a structure that prevent water from moving in the "wrong direction" over the gills) of jawless craniates. This implies the structures have never been true gill arches (Janvier 1996a, 1996b). Whatever the theory, no fossil jawless craniate, even osteostracans (which are thought to be the closest relatives of the gnathostomes), provide any information on how jaws arose. Only the placoderms, which are fossil gnathostomes, display a possibly primitive type of jaw, in which the musculature is medial to the skeletal mandibular arch, and where a dental lamina (a skin fold in which teeth develop) may have been lacking (Young 1986).

Within the gnathostomes, fossils are crucial to understanding the shaping of various groups. "Bradyodonts," an ensemble of Devonian-to-Permian chondrichthyans, provide a link between the supposedly primitive, sharklike aspect of early chondrichthyans and the highly specialized morphology of modern chimeras (Lund 1986). Acanthodians, in turn, provide a basis to reconstruct the most primitive osteichthyan anatomy (Miles 1973). The primitive Devonian lungfish *Diabolepis* has been crucial to elucidating the riddle of lungfish affinities, providing a link between them and a group of fossil sarcopterygians, the porolepiformes (Chang 1995).

Most impressive are the elpistostegid sarcopterygians, which are the most tetrapod-like fishes (Vorobyeva and Schultze 1991). The skull is strikingly similar to that of the earliest tetrapods, such as *Acanthostega,* although elpistostegids still have paired fins with large fin webs. However, the internal skeleton of these fins is almost identical to the limb skeleton of early tetrapods, lacking only digits and phalanges. (Digits are the actual fingers and toes; phalanges are the connecting bones in the hand and foot.) The pattern of interrelationships of the living craniates probably would not be significantly different from the current one if we had no knowledge of the fossil craniates, but the timing and order of the appearance of various anatomical structures, such as dermal bone, paired fins, or limbs, would be unknown.

Environment and Changes in Craniate Diversity through Time

The living craniates are adapted to practically all kinds of environments, including very cold, polar environments that did not exist during most of Earth history. The earliest known craniates lived in shallow, marine (saltwater) environments. In Silurian times some pelagic (open water) fishes appeared, particularly among chondrichthyans and acanthodians. There are debates about the date that fishes conquered freshwater. Some consider that many Devonian fish faunas, commonly found in cross-bedded sandstones, are freshwater and lived in large rivers. Others regard these faunas as marine but subject to important variations of salinity due to sudden flooding. Such events would cause mass mortality of the fishes (Janvier 1985). There is no clear evidence for freshwater craniates before the latest Devonian or the Carboniferous. The groups that became adapted to freshwater essentially were the actinopterygians and the early tetrapods and their closest piscine relatives, but there are also freshwater lungfishes and possibly coelacanths and chondrichthyans.

During the past decade, paleontologists have taken various quantitative approaches to assess fluctuations in biodiversity during the last 500 million years, in terms of rates of the origination of species or groups and of extinction (e.g., Sepkoski 1986). This approach resulted in the discovery of a number of periods of mass extinction involving all kinds of living beings. Notwithstanding the fact that there are vivid debates about whether these mass extinction periods, or crises, are a reality or a consequence of biases in the systems being used (Patterson and Smith 1987), five major events are currently recognized: those at the ends of the Ordovician (420 million years ago), Frasnian (370 million years ago), Permian (245 million years ago), Triassic (208 million years ago), and Cretaceous (65 million years ago). Generally these events are followed by a period of "recovery" for the surviving groups, and often feature major evolutionary radiations (diversification and geographic spread) of new groups, which invade niches left empty by extinct groups.

As for craniates, most of the known Ordovician taxa (major groupings) (except for conodonts, thelodonts, and acanthodians) seem to disappear at the end of this period. The Early Silurian is a period of adaptive radiation for the various ostracoderm groups, in particular heterostracans, osteostracans, and galeaspids. Then, the gnathostomes seem to diversify rapidly in the Late Silurian and Early Devonian. The end-Frasnian mass extinction, in the Late Devonian, has little effect on craniates. The ostracoderms already were declining in the Middle Devonian, and none of them seems to reach the end of the Frasnian (Figure 4). Among the gnathostomes, the placoderms seem to have an impoverished diversity after the end-Frasnian event (Carr 1995), but they disappear only at the end of the Devonian. The extinction of the placoderms and the impoverishment of piscine sarcopterygians resulted in the radiation during the Carboniferous of the actinopterygians and chondrichthyans, which had profound consequences on marine craniate diversity that persist today (Long 1993).

PHILIPPE JANVIER

See also   Gnathostomes; Jawless Fishes

Works Cited

Aldridge, R.J., D.E.G. Briggs, M.P. Smith, E.N.K. Clarkson, and N.D.L. Clark. 1993. The anatomy of conodonts. *Philosophical Transactions of the Royal Society of London*, ser. B, 340:405–21.

Bjerring, H. 1968. The second somite with special reference to the evolution of its myotomic derivatives. *In* T. Ørvig (ed.), *Current Problems of Lower Vertebrate Phylogeny*. New York: Interscience.

Blieck, A. 1984. *Les Hétérostracés Ptéraspidiformes Agnathes du Silurien-Devonien, du continent Nord-Atlantique et des blocs avoisinarts: Révision. Systématique, phylogénie, biostratigraphie, biogéographie.* Cahiers de Paléontologie. Paris: Centre National de la Recherche Scientifique.

Carr, R.K. 1995. Placoderm diversity and evolution. *Bulletin du Muséum National d'Histoire Naturelle, Paris* 17:85–125.

Chang, M.M. 1995. *Diabolepis* and its bearing on the relationships between porolepiforms and dipnoans. *Bulletin du Muséum National d'Histoire Naturelle, Paris* 17:235–68.

Cloutier, R., and P.E. Ahlberg. 1995. Sarcopterygian interrelationships: How far are we from a phylogenetic consensus? *Géobios, Mémoire Special* 19:241–348.

Conway-Morris, S., and T. Whittington. 1979. The animals of the Burgess Shale. *Scientific American* 241:122–31.

Denison, R.H. 1978a. Placodermi. *In* H.-P. Schultze (ed.), *Handbook of Paleoichthyology*. Vol. 2. Stuttgart and New York: Fischer.

———. 1978b. Acanthodii. *In* H.-P. Schultze (ed.), *Handbook of Paleoichthyology*. Vol. 5. Stuttgart and New York: Fischer.

Elliott, D.K. 1987. A reassessment of *Astraspis desiderata,* the oldest North American vertebrate. *Science* 237:190–92.

Forey, P.L., and P. Janvier. 1993. Agnathans and the origin of jawed vertebrates. *Nature* 361:129–34.

———. 1994. Evolution of the early vertebrates. *American Scientist* 82:554–65.

Gabbott, S.E., R.J. Aldridge, and J.N. Theron. 1995. A giant conodont with preserved muscle tissue from the Upper Ordovician of South Africa. *Nature* 374:800–3.

Gagnier, P.Y. 1993a. *Sacabambaspis janvieri,* Vertébré ordovicien de Bolivie. 1, Analyse morphologique. *Annales de Paléontologie* 79:19–57.

———. 1993b. *Sacabambaspis janvieri,* Vertébré ordovicien de Bolivie. 2, Analyse phylogénétique. *Annales de Paléontologie* 79:119–66.

Gee, H. 1996. *Before the Backbone*. London and New York: Chapman and Hall.

Goodrich, E.S. 1909. Vertebrata Craniata. First fascicle: Cyclostomes and fishes. *In* E.R. Lankester (ed.), *A Treatise on Zoology.* Vol. 9. London: Black.

Holland, P.W.H., and J. Garcia-Fernandez. 1996. *Hox* genes and chordate evolution. *Developmental Biology* 173:382–95.

Janvier, P. 1981. The phylogeny of the Craniata, with particular reference to the significance of fossil "agnathans." *Journal of Vertebrate Paleontology* 1:121–59.

———. 1984. The relationships of the Osteostraci and Galeaspida. *Journal of Vertebrate Paleontology* 4:344–58.

———. 1985. Environmental framework of the diversification of the Osteostraci during the Silurian and Devonian. *Philosophical Transactions of the Royal Society of London,* ser. B, 309:259–72.

———. 1996a. *Early Vertebrates*. Oxford: Clarendon; New York: Oxford University Press.

———. 1996b. The dawn of the vertebrates: Characters versus common ascent in the rise of current vertebrate phylogenies. *Palaeontology* 39:259–87.

Jarvik, E. 1980. *Basic Structure and Evolution of Vertebrates*. 2 vols. London and New York: Academic Press.

Jefferies, R.P.S. 1986. *The Ancestry of the Vertebrates*. British Museum (Natural History), London; Cambridge and New York: Cambridge University Press.

———. 1997. A defence of the calcichordates. *Lethaia* 30:1–10.

Karatayute-Talimaa, V. 1995. The Mongolepida: Scale structure and systematic position. *Géobios, Memoire Special* 19:35–37.

Karatayute-Talimaa, V., and N. Predtechenskyj. 1995. The distribution of the vertebrates in the Late Ordovician and Early Silurian paleobasins of the Siberian Platform. *Bulletin du Muséum National d'Histoire Naturelle, Paris* 17:39–55.

Kemp, A., and R.S. Nicoll. 1996. A histochemical analysis of biological residues in conodont elements. *Modern Geology* 20:287–302.

Lacalli, T.C., N.D. Holland, and J.E. West. 1994. Landmarks in the anterior central nervous system of amphioxus larvae. *Philosophical Transactions of the Royal Society of London* 344:165–85.

Long, J.A. 1993. Early-Middle Palaeozoic vertebrate extinction events. *In* J.A. Long (ed.), *Palaeozoic Vertebrate Biostratigraphy and Biogeography*. London: Belhaven; Baltimore, Maryland: Johns Hopkins University Press, 1994.

Løvtrup, S. 1977. *The Phylogeny of Vertebrata*. New York: Wiley.

Lund, R. 1986. The diversity and relationships of the holocephali. *In* T. Uyeno, R. Arai, T. Taniuchi, and K. Matsuura (eds.), *Indo-Pacific Fish Biology*. Tokyo: Ichthyological Society of Japan.

Maisey, J.G. 1988. Phylogeny of early vertebrate skeletal induction and ossification patterns. *Evolutionary Biology* 22:1–36.

Mallatt, J. 1996. Ventilation and the origin of jawed vertebrates: A new mouth. *Zoological Journal of the Linnean Society* 117:329–404.

Miles, R.S. 1973. Relationships of acanthodians. *In* P.H. Greenwood, R.S. Miles, and C. Patterson (eds.), *Interrelationships of Fishes*. Zoological Journal of the Linnean Society, Supplement 1, 53:63–103.

Ørvig, T. 1989. Histologic studies of ostracoderms, placoderms and fossil elasmobranchs. Part 6, Hard tissues of Ordovician vertebrates. *Zoologica Scripta* 18:427–46.

Pan, J. 1992. *New Galeaspids (Agnatha) from the Silurian and Devonian of China*. Beijing: Geological Publishing House.

Pan, J., and D. Dineley. 1988. A review of early (Silurian and Devonian) vertebrate biogeography and biostratigraphy of China. *Proceedings of the Royal Society of London,* ser. B, 35:9–61.

Patterson, C., and A. Smith. 1987. Is the periodicity of extinctions a taxonomic artefact? *Nature* 330:248–52.

Peignoux-Deville, J., F. Lallier, and B. Vidal. 1982. Evidence for the presence of osseous tissue in dogfish vertebrae. *Cell and Tissue Research* 222:605–14.

Peterson, K.J. 1995. A phylogenetic test of the calcichordate scenario. *Lethaia* 28:25–38.

Pridmore, P.A., R.E. Barwick, and R.S. Nicoll. 1996. Soft anatomy and the affinities of conodonts. *Lethaia* 29:317–29.

Ritchie, A. 1964. New light on the morphology of the Norwegian Anaspida. *Skrifter utgitt av det Norske Videnskaps-Akademi, 1, Matematisk-Naturvidenskapslige Klasse* 14:1–35.

Sansom, I.J., M.P. Smith, H.A. Armstrong, and M.M. Smith. 1992. Presence of the earliest vertebrate hard tissues in conodonts. *Science* 256:1308–11.

Sansom, I.J., M.P. Smith, and M.M. Smith. 1994. Dentine in conodonts. *Nature* 368:591.

———. 1996. Scales of thelodont and shark-like fishes from the Ordovician of Colorado. *Nature* 379:628–30.

Sansom, I.J., M.P. Smith, M.M. Smith, and P. Turner. 1997. *Astraspis*—The anatomy and histology of an Ordovician fish. *Palaeontology* 40 (3):625–43.

Schaeffer, B. 1975. Comments on the origin and basic radiation of the gnathostome fishes with particular reference to the feeding mechanism. *In* J.P. Lehman (ed.), *Problèmes actuels de paléontologie: Evolution des vertébrés.* 2 vols. Colloques internationaux du Centre National de la Recherche Scientifique, No. 218. Paris: Centre National de la Recherche Scientifique.

———. 1987. Deuterostome monophyly and phylogeny. *Evolutionary Biology* 21:179–235.

Schultze, H.-P. 1994. Comparison of hypotheses on the relationships of sarcopterygians. *Systematic Biology* 43:155–73.

———. 1996. Conodont histology: An indicator of vertebrate relationships? *Modern Geology* 20:275–85.

Sepkoski, J.J. 1986. Phanerozoic overview of mass extinction. *In* D.M. Raup and D. Jablonski (eds.), *Pattern and Processes in the History of Life.* Berlin and New York: Springer-Verlag.

Simonetta, A.M., and E. Insom. 1993. New animals from the Burgess Shale (Middle Cambrian) and their possible significance for the understanding of the Bilateralia. *Bolletino di Zoologia* 60:97–107.

Smith, M.M., and I.J. Sansom. 1997. Exoskeletal micro-remains of an Ordovician fish from the Harding Sandstone of Colorado. *Palaeontology* 40 (3):645–58.

Smith, M.M., I.J. Sansom, and J.E. Repetski. 1996. Histology of the first fish. *Nature* 381:538.

Smith, M.M., I.J. Sansom, and P. Smith. 1996. "Teeth" before armour: The earliest vertebrate mineralized tissues. *Modern Geology* 20:303–19.

Tong-Dzuy Thanh, Ta Hoa Phuong, A.J. Boucot, D. Goujet, and P. Janvier. 1997. Vertébrés siluriens du Viêt Nam Central. *Comptes Rendus de l'Académie des Sciences, Paris,* ser. IIa, 324:1023–30.

Turner, S. 1991. Monophyly and interrelationships of the Thelodonti. *In* M.M. Chang, Y.H. Liu, and G.R. Zhang (eds.), *Early Vertebrates and Related Problems of Evolutionary Biology.* Beijing: Science Press.

Vorobyeva, E.I., and H.-P. Schultze. 1991. Description and systematics of panderichthyid fishes with comments on their relationship to tetrapods. *In* H.-P. Schultze and L. Trueb (eds.), *Origins of the Higher Groups of Tetrapods: Controversy and Consensus.* Ithaca, New York: Comstock.

Wake, M.H. (ed.). 1979. *Hyman's Comparative Vertebrate Anatomy.* 3rd ed., Chicago: University of Chicago Press.

Wang, N.Z. 1991. Two new Silurian galeaspids (jawless craniates) from Zhejiang province, China, with a discussion of galeaspid-gnathostome relationships. *In* M.M. Chang, Y.H. Liu, and G.R. Zhang (eds.), *Early Vertebrates and Related Problems of Evolutionary Biology.* Beijing: Science Press.

Yalden, D.W. 1985. Feeding mechanisms as evidence for cyclostome monophyly. *Zoological Journal of the Linnean Society* 84:91–300.

Young, G.C. 1986. The relationships of placoderm fishes. *Zoological Journal of the Linnean Society* 88:1–57.

———. 1991. The first armoured agnathan vertebrates from the Devonian of Australia. *In* M.M. Chang, Y.H. Liu, and G.R. Zhang (eds.), *Early Vertebrates and Related Problems of Evolutionary Biology.* Beijing: Science Press.

———. 1997. Ordovician microvertebrate remains from the Amadeus Basin, central Australia. *Journal of Vertebrate Paleontology* 17 (1):1–25.

Young, G.C., V.N. Karatayute-Talimaa, and M.M. Smith. 1996. A possible Late Cambrian vertebrate from Australia. *Nature* 383:810–12.

Further Reading

Gee, H. 1996. *Before the Backbone.* London and New York: Chapman and Hall.

Janvier, P. 1993. Patterns of diversity in the skull of jawless fishes. *In* J. Hanken and B.K. Hall (eds.), *The Skull.* Vol. 2, *Patterns of Structural and Systematic Diversity.* Chicago: University of Chicago Press.

———. 1996. *Early Vertebrates.* Oxford: Clarendon; New York: Oxford University Press.

Jarvik, E. 1980. *Basic Structure and Evolution of Vertebrates.* 2 vols. London and New York: Academic Press.

Long, J.A. (ed.). 1993. *Palaeozoic Vertebrate Biostratigraphy and Biogeography.* London: Belhaven; Baltimore, Maryland: Johns Hopkins University Press.

———. 1995. *The Rise of Fishes.* Sydney: University of New South Wales Press; Baltimore, Maryland: John Hopkins University Press.

Maisey, J.G. 1986. Heads and tails: A chordate phylogeny. *Cladistics* 2:201–56.

Moy-Thomas, J.A. 1939. *Palaeozoic Fishes.* London: Methuen; New York: Chemical Publishing; 2nd ed. extensively revised by R.S. Miles, London: Chapman and Hall, 1971; Philadelphia: Saunders, 1971.

Schultze, H.-P. 1993. Patterns of diversity in the skull of jawed fishes. *In* J. Hanken and B.K. Hall (eds.), *The Skull.* Vol. 2, *Patterns of Structural and Systematic Dversity.* Chicago: University of Chicago Press.

CREODONTS

Creodonts were carnivorous placental mammals who roamed North America, Europe, Asia, and Africa for about 50 million years before becoming extinct less than 10 million years ago. (Placental animals are those in which fertilization takes place internally and development occurs in an organ called the uterus, in which the placenta is attached to the inner wall and to the developing fetus or embryo, thereby providing nourishment to the fetus and discharging wastes. This process contrasts with the other two types of mammals: marsupials, in which females bear immature young that are nourished in a pouch—or marsupium—enclosing nipples on the abdominal wall; and monotremes, in which development takes place externally, in a shell-encased egg.) Scholars know of more than 180 species of creodonts. Some of these, such as *Isohyaenodon matthewi* from the Miocene of Africa (20 million years ago) were small and weasel-like (Savage 1965), while others, such as *Hyaenodon horridus* from the Oligocene of North America (33 to 36 million years ago), resembled large, long-muzzled wolves (Mellett 1977). Most ranged from the size and shape of a mongoose to that of a red fox (Gebo and Rose 1993; Polly 1996). Although they were carnivores, creodonts resembled marsupials more than present-day members of the Order Carnivora. Large creodonts, such as *Hyaenodon,* looked more like the recently extinct Tasmanian wolf, *Thylacinus cynocephalus,* than present-day wolves or coyotes. This is because creodonts and the Tasmanian wolf had relatively longer heads and shorter legs than present-day members of the dog family.

Creodont species were quite varied. Most were carnivorous but, like current carnivorans, had a wide range of diets. The earliest creodonts had teeth like present-day possums and probably ate a variety of meat, insects, and plant material. Later forms, such as *Dipsalidictis* and *Oxyaena,* had powerful jaws and tightly interlocking teeth and were probably powerful carnivores like the wolverine. Some creodonts, such as *Hyaenodon* and *Hyainailouros,* had catlike teeth, while others, such as *Pterodon,* had teeth more like those of the bone-crushing hyenas. There were even a few saber-toothed species, such as *Machaeroides eothen* and *Apataelurus kayi.* Some creodonts, such as *Quercytherium* and *Teratodon,* probably ate molluscs, nuts, or other hard foods. An especially bizarre creodont, *Apterodon,* found in the Eocene and Oligocene of Africa and Europe, had long piercing premolars and strangely specialized molars that were almost completely worn away during the individual's lifetime. This animal may have eaten fish or shellfish.

There were two main groups of creodonts: hyaenodontids and oxyaenids. Oxyaenids were the earliest creodonts and the least diverse, and they remain poorly understood. *Tytthaena parrisi,* the first oxyaenid, lived about 59 million years ago during the mid-Paleocene in Wyoming (Gingerich 1980). The oxyaenids' last survivors, *Prolaena parva* and *Sarkastodon mongoliensis,* lived during the Middle Eocene in what is now China (43 to 47 million years ago). Most of the 29 known species lived in North America during the Late Paleocene and Early Eocene. Some oxyaenids were similar to badgers or wolverines (e.g., *Oxyaena* and *Patriofelis*). Others were larger and resembled bears (e.g., *Sarkastodon mongoliensis*). A few were quite small (e.g., *Tytthaena parrisi*). Although oxyaenids are the oldest known creodonts, they are not the ancestors of hyaenodontids (Van Valen 1966; Polly 1996). This is evident because oxyaenids had only two molars; hyaenodontids, like ancestral placental mammals, had three. The evolutionary loss of this third molar indicates that oxyaenids were a specialized branch of creodonts; however, the fossil record has not yet yielded the secrets of the earliest creodont radiations (diversification and geographical spread).

In contrast to oxyaenids, hyaenodontid creodonts were diverse and widespread during most of the Cenozoic. More than 100 species of hyaenodontids are known. The first good records of hyaenodontids are from the earliest Eocene of North America and Europe, about 55 million years ago. At that time, at least seven species appeared, immigrants from some other region of the world (Gingerich 1989). One recently studied fauna from the Paleocene of China contains a single tooth of what appears to be a hyaenodontid creodont, indicating that the group may have originated in East Asia (Meng et al. 1998). Hyaenodontids reached their greatest diversity during the latest Eocene and earliest Oligocene, when a variety of species were spread over four continents. Many species in Europe and Asia became extinct in the Middle to Late Oligocene, and in North America they disappeared completely at the same time. In Africa, however, hyaenodontids continued to be the dominant mammalian carnivores through most of the Miocene (Savage 1965). And, during most of the Miocene, an extremely large hyaenodontid, *Hyainailouros,* lived both in Europe and south Asia. The very last records of hyaenodontids are the species *Dissopsalis pyroclasticus* from the Late Miocene of Kenya (11 to 19 million years ago) and *D. carnifex* from the Miocene of Pakistan (9 to 16 million years ago).

In size and shape, hyaenodontids were more diverse than oxyaenids. *Megistotherium osteothlastes,* from the Miocene of Libya, was the largest terrestrial mammalian carnivore to ever exist (Savage 1973), while *Isohyaenodon pilgrimi* and *I. matthewi,* from the Miocene of Kenya, were about the size of small weasels (Savage 1965). There were species that lived in trees (e.g., *Prolimnocyon atavus* and *Thinocyon velox*); quick, wolflike species (e.g., various *Hyaenodon* species); ambling, bearlike species (e.g., *Hyainailouros sulzeri* and *Hemipsalodon grandis*); and unusual species that may have been semiaquatic (e.g., *Apterodon macrognathus*).

Creodonts long were thought to be ancestors or closely related to the Order Carnivora (Matthew 1909; Flynn et al. 1988). However, there is little evidence to support this, and it is more likely that the carnivores are more closely related to the lipotyphlan insectivores (insect-eating, molelike mammals) than to the creodonts (Fox and Youzwyshyn 1994; Polly 1996). It is also possible that oxyaenids and hyaenodontids were not related closely to each other. Many of the features they had in common evolved independently in many other groups of mammals; the same could have occurred with oxyaenids and hyaenodontids (Van Valen 1966; Polly 1996). All that scholars can say with certainty about oxyaenids and hyaenodontids is that they were part of the complex and poorly understood early radiation of placental mammals that took place during the Paleocene and Eocene. It also has been hypothesized that the Order Carnivora was biologically better adapted than Creodonta and, therefore, contributed to the extinction of the latter group. This scenario is unlikely because carnivorans evolved before creodonts, and members of the two groups coexisted throughout most of the Cenozoic.

PAUL DAVID POLLY

See also Carnivorans; Feeding Adaptations: Vertebrates; Teeth: Classification of Teeth

Works Cited

Flynn, J.J., N.A. Neff, and R.H. Tedford. 1988. Phylogeny of the Carnivora. In M.J. Benton (ed.), The Phylogeny and Classification of the Tetrapods. Vol. 2, Mammals. Systematics Association Special Volume No. 35B. Oxford: Clarendon; New York: Oxford University Press.

Fox, R.C., and G.P. Youzwyshyn. 1994. New primitive carnivorans (Mammalia) from the Paleocene of western Canada, and their bearing on relationships of the order. Journal of Vertebrate Paleontology 14:382–404.

Gebo, D.L., and K.D. Rose. 1993. Skeletal morphology and locomotor adaptation in Prolimnocyon atavus, an early Eocene hyaenodontid creodont. Journal of Vertebrate Paleontology 13:125–44.

Gingerich, P.D. 1980. Tytthaena parrisi, oldest known Oxyaenid (Mammalia, Creodonta) from the late Paleocene of western North America. Journal of Paleontology 54:570–77.

———. 1989. New earliest Wasatchian mammalian fauna from the Eocene of northwestern Wyoming: Composition and diversity in a rarely sampled high-floodplain assemblage. University of Michigan Papers on Paleontology 28:1–97.

Matthew, W.D. 1909. The Carnivora and Insectivora of the Bridger Basin, Middle Eocene. Memoirs of the American Museum of Natural History 9:289–567.

Mellett, J.S. 1977. Paleobiology of North American Hyaenodon (Mammalia, Creodonta). Contributions to Vertebrate Evolution 1:1–134.

Meng, J., R. Zhai, and A.R. Wyss. 1998. The late Paleocene Bayan Ulan fauna of Inner Mongolia, China. Bulletin of the Carnegie Museum of Natural History 34:148–85.

Polly, P.D. 1996. The skeleton of Gazinocyon vulpeculus n. gen. and comb. (Hyaenodontidae, Creodonta) and the cladistic relationships of Hyaenodontidae (Eutheria, Mammalia). Journal of Vertebrate Paleontology 16:303–19.

Savage, R.J.G. 1965. Fossil mammals of Africa-19: The Miocene Carnivora of East Africa. Bulletin of the British Museum (Natural History) 10:239–316.

———. 1973. Megistotherium, gigantic hyaenodont from Miocene of Gebel Zelten, Libya. Bulletin of the British Museum (Natural History) 22(7):485–511.

Van Valen, L. 1966. Deltatheridia, a new order of mammals. Bulletin of the American Museum of Natural History 132:1–126.

Further Reading

Benton, M.J. 1991. The Rise of the Mammals. New York: Crescent Books.

Carroll, R.L. 1988. Vertebrate Paleontology and Evolution. New York: Freeman.

Denison, R.H. 1938. The broad-skulled Pseudocreodi. Annals of the New York Academy of Sciences 37:163–256.

Gunnell, G.F., and P.D. Gingerich. 1991. Systematics and evolution of late Paleocene and early Eocene Oxyaenidae (Mammalia, Creodonta) in the Clarks Fork Basin, Wyoming. Contributions from the Museum of Paleontology, University of Michigan 28:141–80.

Lange-Bardé, B. 1979. Les créodontes (Mammalia) d'Europe occidentale de l'Éocène supérieur a l'Oligocène supérieur. Mémories du Muséum National d'Histoire Naturelle (N.S.), Série C, Sciences de la Terre, 42:1–249.

Romer, A.S. 1933. Vertebrate Paleontology. Chicago: University of Chicago Press; 3rd ed., 1966.

Savage, R.J.G., and M.R. Long. 1986. Mammal Evolution: An Illustrated Guide. London: British Museum (Natural History); New York: Facts on File.

CROCODYLIANS

Crocodylia includes the last common ancestor of living alligators, crocodiles, and gharials, and all of its descendants. Once this name included a wide variety of extinct crocodylomorphs extending back to the Late Triassic. The current definition, based on work by James Clark (Benton and Clark 1988; see also Norell 1989; Norell et al. 1992), excludes most of these, but stabilizes the definition on a single common ancestor.

Living crocodylians are semiaquatic ambush predators, preferring to hunt in the water but spending time on land to absorb solar energy. They generally will eat whatever they can swallow. Hatchling diets consist largely of small arthropods and fish, whereas larger individuals prefer large fishes, birds, turtles, and mammals. Only two species—the Nile crocodile (Crocodylus niloticus) and the Indopacific saltwater crocodile (Crocodylus porosus)—regularly pursue humans as prey.

Crocodylians are related most closely to birds among living tetrapods (Gauthier et al. 1988). This seems counterintuitive at first, since crocodylians outwardly resemble lizards so much more closely, but in fact, crocodylians and birds share many derived (specialized) features. Members of both groups have a four-chambered heart and muscular diaphragm; both are noted for nest-building behavior and postnatal care of the young; both communicate with an elaborate system of vocalization; and both are capable of some degree of upright posture. In crocodylians, upright posture is expressed in the capacity to rotate the hind limbs under the body during locomotion (Gatesy 1991), a gait called "high walking."

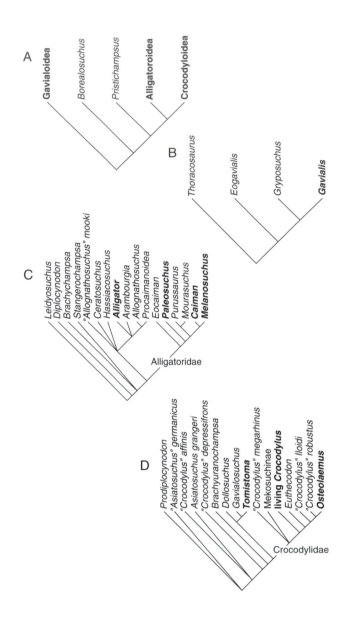

Figure 1. Relationships among fossil and living crocodylians. *A,* broad-scale relationships within Crocodylia based on morphological data; *B,* relationships among gavialoids; *C,* relationships among alligatoroids; *D,* relationships among crocodyloids. Boldface indicates groups with living members. Based on *A,* Brochu (1997b) and Norell (1989); *B, C, D,* Brochu (1997b).

Crocodylians retain many of the features inherited from their earlier crocodylomorph ancestors: They have long wrist elements, the pubis (one of three pelvic bones) is excluded from the hip socket, a complex pneumatic system (a system of air-filled channels and cavities) surrounds the braincase, and a long secondary palate separates the mouth and nasal passages, allowing the animal to eat and breathe at the same time. Unlike most other crocodylomorphs, the crocodylian internal choanae (nasal openings) are completely surrounded by a set of bones called pterygoids. Also, crocodylians have procoelous vertebrae in which the front

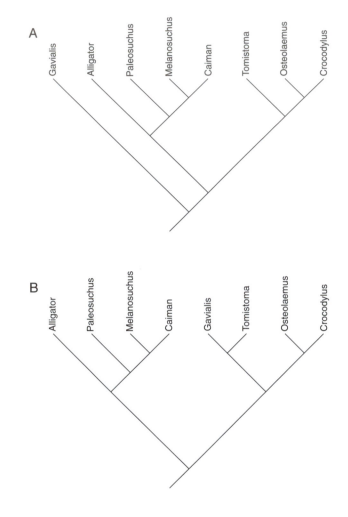

Figure 2. Debated placement of *Gavialis* between *(A)* morphological and *(B)* molecular data sets. Trees are restricted to living genera. From Poe (1997) and Brochu (1997b).

articulating surface is concave and the back is convex. However, since these features are found in some noncrocodylian neosuchians, these two characters are not unique characteristics (synapomorphies) that distinguish crocodylians from all other groups. The morphological differences between crocodylians and noncrocodylian eusuchians are very subtle. They involve the loss of a pit on the medial wall of an opening that is in the upper back section of the head and of a boss (bony knob) at the base of the skull.

Three primary stem-based lineages can be recognized within Crocodylia (Figure 1A): Gavialoidea (the Indian gharial and its relatives; Figure 1B); Alligatoroidea (alligators, caimans, and their allies; Figure 1C); and Crocodyloidea (true crocodiles; Figure 1D). Scholars debate the relationships among these lineages (Figure 2). Morphological evidence (i.e., that based upon shape and structure) indicates a close relationship between Alligatoroidea and Crocodyloidea (Kälin 1931, 1955; Tarsitano et al. 1989; Norell 1989; Brochu 1997b); however, protein distances and DNA sequence data (molecular evidence) support a closer relationship between Gavialoidea and Crocodyloidea (Densmore 1983; Densmore and Owen 1989; Poe 1997; Gatesy and Amato 1992).

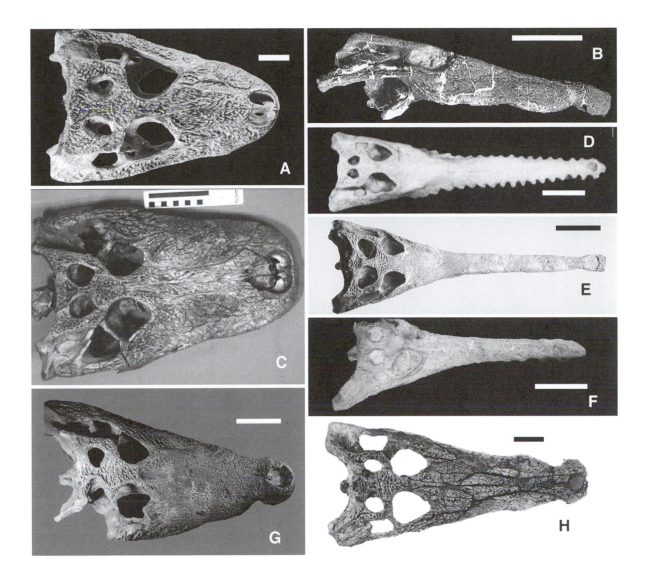

Figure 3. Fossil crocodylians. *A, Alligator mcgrewi* (Miocene, Nebraska), scale bar equals 1 centimeter; *B, Pristichampsus vorax* (Eocene, Wyoming), scale bar equals 10 centimeters; *C, Brachychampsa montana* (Cretaceous, Montana); *D, Euthecodon arambourgii* (Miocene, Libya), scale bar equals 10 centimeters; *E, Thoracosaurus macrorhynchus* (Cretaceous, Sweden), scale bar equals 10 centimeters; *F, Tomistoma cairense* (Eocene, Egypt); *G, Prodiplocynodon langi* (Cretaceous, Colorado), scale bar equals 10 centimeters; *H, Borealosuchus acutidentatus* (Paleocene, Saskatchewan), scale bar equals 5 centimeters. Specimens from: *A*, American Museum of Natural History, New York; *B*, Field Museum of Natural History, Chicago; *C*, University of California Museum of Paleontology, Berkeley; *D*, Museum National d'Histoire Naturelle, Paris; *E*, University of Lund, Sweden; *F*, Staatliches Museum für Naturkunde, Stuttgart, Germany; *G*, American Museum of Natural History, New York; *H*, Canadian Museum of Nature, Ottawa.

Within each, a "node-based crown group" can be recognized on the basis of the last common ancestor of living members; for example, Alligatoroidea includes living *Alligator mississippiensis* and all taxa closer to it than to *Crocodylus* or *Gavialis,* but Alligatoridae includes the last common ancestor of living alligators and caimans and all of its descendants.

If one accepts the phylogeny (evolutionary history) indicated by morphological analyses, Gavialoidea currently is restricted to a single living species, the Indian gharial, *Gavialis gangeticus. Gavialis* is characterized by a long, narrow snout adapted for catching and eating fish. The earliest gavialoid, *Thoracosaurus* (Figure 3E), first appears in the Late Cretaceous of North America (Schwimmer 1986) and Africa (Lavocat 1955). Fossil gavialoids occur in Africa and Eurasia throughout the Tertiary, and an assemblage of derived (specialized) gavialoids in the Late Tertiary of South America, such as *Gryposuchus* (Langston 1965; Langston and Gasparini 1997; Sill 1970; Buffetaut 1982), suggests that these animals dispersed across the Atlantic during or shortly after the Eocene.

Alligatoroidea includes Alligatoridae and several extinct non-alligatorid lineages. These include *Leidyosuchus canadensis* from Alberta (Lambe 1907), the widespread European lineage *Diplocynodon* (e.g., Pomel 1847; Berg 1966; Buscalioni et al. 1992; Norell et al. 1992; Ginsburg and Bulot 1997), *Brachychampsa* from the Cam-

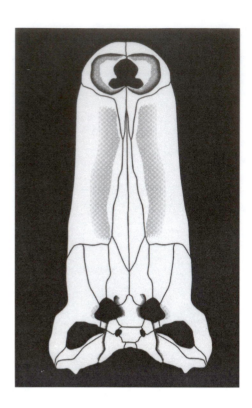

Figure 4. *Mourasuchus.* Based on Price (1959) and Bocquetin (1984).

panian and Maastrichtian of North America (Gilmore 1911; Norell et al. 1992; Williamson 1996) (Figure 3C), and *Stangerochampsa* from Alberta (Wu et al. 1996). All of these (except *Diplocynodon*) are found in the Late Cretaceous; *Diplocynodon* is found first in the Lower Eocene but must extend to the Late Cretaceous, based on the presence of other alligatoroid lineages that far back.

At maturity, most basal alligatorids were relatively small (2 meters total length), had blunt snouts, and bore enlarged, anvil-like back teeth, possibly adapted for crushing hard-shelled prey (Abel 1928; Carpenter and Lindsey 1980) (Figure 3A). One of them—*Ceratosuchus* from the Paleocene of North America—even had horns (Schmidt 1938; Bartels 1984). Although the group probably extends into the Cretaceous, the first alligatorids appear in the Paleocene of North America (Simpson 1930) and Patagonia (Rusconi 1937). This implies a dispersal between then-separated North and South America at or near the boundary between the Cretaceous and Tertiary periods, even though living alligatorids are much less tolerant of seawater than other crocodylians (Taplin and Grigg 1989; Jackson et al. 1996).

The name *"Leidyosuchus"* often is used for several generalized taxa from the Cretaceous through Eocene of North America (e.g., Erickson 1976; Gilmore 1910; Mook 1930; Sternberg 1932), but based on recent phylogenetic analysis, none of these taxa is related closely to *Leidyosuchus canadensis* (Brochu 1997b). Most of them form a group named *Borealosuchus* (Figure 3H), which lies outside the group that includes alligators and crocodiles (Figure 1A).

The oldest known crocodyloid is *Prodiplocynodon langi*, based on a single skull from the Maastrichtian of Wyoming (Mook

1941) (Figure 3G). However, because both Gavialoidea and Alligatoroidea are known from the Late Cretaceous, Crocodyloidea also must extend that far back. Tertiary crocodyloids outwardly resembled modern true crocodiles *(Crocodylus)* and often have been classified within the living genus; this is why several *"Crocodylus"* in Figure 1D are in quotation marks. The oldest known crocodyloids descended from the last common ancestor of living *Crocodylus* are from the Miocene (Brochu in press b).

Crocodylidae includes the last common ancestor of living crocodyloids and all of its descendants. This unequivocally includes modern *Crocodylus* and the African dwarf crocodile, *Osteolaemus tetraspis.* Morphological analyses indicate that the Indonesian false gharial *(Tomistoma schlegelii)* and its fossil relatives (e.g., *Tomistoma cairense*) (Figure 3F) are also crocodylids, but molecular analyses instead regard *Tomistoma* as the closest relative of *Gavialis.* Among fossils, Crocodylidae may include an isolated Australian lineage known as Mekosuchinae, although some analyses place Mekosuchinae outside Crocodylidae (e.g., Salisbury and Willis 1996; Willis et al. 1993).

The long, narrow snout seen in *Gavialis* has appeared independently several times within Crocodylia. Long snouts occur in several living species of *Crocodylus (C. cataphractus, C. intermedius,* and *C. johnstoni),* the extinct African crocodylid *Euthecodon* (Ginsburg and Buffetaut 1978) (Figure 3D), and *Tomistoma* and its relatives. Indeed, this morphology appeared more than once among non-crocodylian crocodylomorphs (thalattosuchians, pholidosaurs, and dyrosaurids).

Some fossil crocodylians are very different from their living relatives. At least two different Tertiary taxa—Pristichampsinae (Langston 1975) (Figure 3B) and the mekosuchine *Quinkana* (e.g., Willis and Mackness 1996)—had deep snouts and blade-shaped, laterally compressed, serrated teeth, much like the non-crocodylian sebecosuchians, and may have been terrestrial predators. One lineage of caimans from the South American Tertiary—*Mourasuchus*—had long, broad snouts and large numbers of very small teeth (Langston 1965; Bocquetin 1984) (Figure 4).

Gigantism has arisen several times within this group. Although the poorly known *Deinosuchus* of the North American Cretaceous often is touted as the "largest crocodile," others—including the Miocene caiman *Purussaurus* and the Miocene gavialoid *Rhamphosuchus*—were at least as large. Current estimates place the maximum length of *Deinosuchus* at approximately 10 to 15 meters in total length.

CHRISTOPHER A. BROCHU

See also Aquatic Locomotion; Aquatic Reptiles

Works Cited

Abel, O. 1928. *Allognathosuchus,* ein an die cheloniphage Nahrungsweise angepaßter Krokodiltypus des nordamerikanischen Eozäns. *Paläontologische Zeitschrift* 9:367–74.

Bartels, W.S. 1984. Osteology and systematic affinities of the horned alligator *Ceratosuchus* (Reptilia, Crocodilia). *Journal of Paleontology* 58:1347–53.

Benton, M.J., and J.M. Clark. 1988. Archosaur phylogeny and the relationships of the Crocodylia. *In* M.J. Benton (ed.), *The Phylogeny and Classification of the Tetrapods.* Vol. 1, Oxford: Clarendon; New York: Oxford University Press.

Berg, D.E. 1966. *Die Krokodile, insbesondere* Asiatosuchus *und aff.* Sebecus?, *aus dem Eozän von Messel bei Darmstadt/Hessen.* Abhandlungen des Hessischen Landesamtes für Bodenforschung, 52. Wiesbaden: n.p.

Bocquentin, J.C. 1984. Un nuevo Nettosuchidae (Crocodylia, Eusuchia) proveniente da la Formación Urumaco (Mioceno Superior), Venezuela. *Ameghiniana* 21:3–8.

Brochu, C.A. 1997a. A review of *"Leidyosuchus"* (Crocodyliformes, Eusuchia) from the Cretaceous through Eocene of North America. *Journal of Vertebrate Paleontology* 17 (4):679–97.

———. 1997b. Fossils, morphology, divergence timing, and the phylogenetic relationships of Gavialis. *Systematic Biology* 46 (3):479–522.

Buffetaut, E. 1982. Systematique, origine et évolution des Gavialidae Sud-Américains. *Géobios, Mémoire Special* 6:127–40.

Buscalioni, A., J.L. Sanz, and M.L. Casanovas. 1992. A new species of the eusuchian crocodile *Diplocynodon* from the Eocene of Spain. *Neues Jahrbuch für Geologie und Paläontologie, Abhandlungen* 187 (1):1–29.

Carpenter, K., and D. Lindsey. 1980. The dentary of *Brachychampsa montana* Gilmore (Alligatorinae; Crocodylidae), a Late Cretaceous turtle-eating alligator. *Journal of Paleontology* 54:1213–17.

Densmore, L.D. 1983. Biochemical and immunological systematics of the order Crocodilia. *In* M.K. Hecht, B. Wallace, and G.H. Prance (eds.), *Evolutionary Biology.* Vol. 16, New York: Plenum Press.

Densmore, L.D., and R.D. Owen. 1989. Molecular systematics of the order Crocodilia. *American Zoologist* 29:831–41.

Erickson, B.R. 1976. Osteology of the early Eusuchian crocodile *Leidyosuchus formidabilis,* sp. nov. *Monographs of the Science Museum of Minnesota (Paleontology)* 2:1–61.

Gatesy, J., and G.D. Amato. 1992. Sequence similarity of 12S ribosomal segment of mitochondrial DNAs of gharial and false gharial. *Copeia* 1992 (1):241–44.

Gatesy, S.M. 1991. Hind limb movements of the American alligator *(Alligator mississippiensis)* and postural grades. *Journal of Zoology* 224:577–88.

Gauthier, J., A.G. Kluge, and T. Rowe. 1988. Amniote phylogeny and the importance of fossils. *Cladistics* 4:105–209.

Gilmore, C.W. 1910. *Leidyosuchus sternbergii,* a new species of crocodile from the Cretaceous Beds of Wyoming. *Proceedings of the United States National Museum* 38:485–502.

———. 1911. A new fossil alligator from the Hell Creek beds of Montana. *Proceedings of the United States National Museum* 41:297–302.

Ginsburg, L., and E. Buffetaut. 1978. *Euthecodon arambourgii* n. sp., et l'évolution du genre *Euthecodon,* crocodilien du Néogène d'Afrique. *Géologie Méditerranéen* 5:291–302.

Ginsburg, L., and C. Bulot. 1997. Les *Diplocynodon* (Reptilia, Crocodylia) de l'Orléanien (Miocène inférieur à moyen) de France. *Geodiversitas* 19 (1):107–28.

Jackson, K., D.G. Butler, and D.R. Brooks. 1996. Habitat and phylogeny influence salinity discrimination in crocodilians: Implications for osmoregulatory physiology and historical biogeography. *Biological Journal of the Linnean Society* 58:371–83.

Kälin, J.A. 1931. Über die Stellung der Gavialiden im System der Crocodilia. *Revue Suisse de Zoologie* 38 (19):379–88.

———. 1955. Zur Stammesgeschichte der Crocodilia. *Revue Suisse de Zoologie* 62:347–56.

Lambe, L.M. 1907. On a new crocodilian genus and species from the Judith River Formation of Alberta. *Proceedings and Transactions of the Royal Society of Canada* 4:219–44.

Langston, W. 1965. *Fossil Crocodilians from Colombia and the Cenozoic History of the Crocodilia in South America.* University of California Publications in Geological Sciences, 52. Berkeley: University of California Press.

———. 1975. Ziphodont crocodiles: *Pristichampsus vorax* (Troxell), New Combination, from the Eocene of North America. *Fieldiana: Geology* 33 (16):291–314.

Langston, W., and Z. Gasparini. 1997. Crocodilians, *Gryposuchus,* and the South American Gavials. *In* R.F. Kay, R.H. Madden, R.L. Cifelli, and J.J. Flynn (eds.), *Vertebrate Paleontology in the Neotropics: The Miocene Fauna of La Venta, Colombia.* Washington, D.C., and London: Smithsonian Institution Press.

Lavocat, R. 1955. Découverte d'un crocodilien du genre *Thoracosaurus* dans le Crétacé Supérieur d'Afrique. *Bulletin du Muséum National d'Histoire Naturelle,* ser. 2, 27:338–40.

Mook, C.C. 1930. A new species of crocodilian from the Torrejon Beds. *American Museum Novitates* 447:1–11.

———. 1941. A new crocodilian from the Lance Formation. *American Museum Novitates* 1128:1–5.

Norell, M.A. 1989. The higher level relationships of the extant Crocodylia. *Journal of Herpetology* 23:325–35.

Norell, M.A., J.M. Clark, and J.H. Hutchinson. 1992. The Late Cretaceous alligatoroid *Brachychampsa montana* (Crocodylia): New material and putative relationships. *American Museum Novitates* 3116:1–26.

Poe, S. 1997. Data set incongruence and the phylogeny of crocodilians. *Systematic Biology* 45 (4):393–414.

Pomel, A. 1847. Note sur les animaux fossiles découverts dans le département de l'Allier. *Bulletin de la Societé Géologique de France,* ser. 2, 4:378–85.

Price, L.I. 1959. Sôbre o cranio de um grande crocodilídeo extinto do Alto Rio Jurua, Estado do Acre. *Anais da Academia Brasiliera de Ciencias* 36:59–66.

Rusconi, C. 1937. Nuevo aligatorino del Paleoceno Argentino. *Boletin Paleontologico de Buenos Aires* 8:1–5.

Salisbury, S.W., and P.M.A. Willis. 1996. A new crocodylian from the Early Eocene of southeastern Queensland and a preliminary investigation of the phylogenetic relationships of crocodyloids. *Alcheringa* 20:179–227.

Schmidt, K.P. 1938. New crocodilians from the upper Paleocene of western Colorado. *Geological Series of the Field Museum of Natural History* 6 (21):315–21.

Schwimmer, D.R. 1986. Late Cretaceous fossils from the Blufftown Formation (Campanian) in western Georgia. *The Mosasaur* 3:109–23.

Sill, W.D. 1968. Nota preliminar sobre un nuevo gavial del Plioceno de Venezuela y una discusión de los gaviales sudamericanos. *Ameghiniana* 7:151–59.

Simpson, G.G. 1930. *Allognathosuchus mooki,* a new crocodile from the Puerco Formation. *American Museum Novitates* 445:1–16.

Sternberg, C.M. 1932. A new fossil crocodile from Saskatchewan. *Canadian Field-Naturalist* 46:128–33.

Taplin, L.E., and G.C. Grigg. 1989. Historical zoogeography of the eusuchian crocodilians: A physiological perspective. *American Zoologist* 29:885–901.

Tarsitano, S.F., E. Frey, and J. Riess. 1989. The evolution of the Crocodilia: A conflict between morphological and biochemical data. *American Zoologist* 29:843–56.

Williamson, T.E. 1996. *?Brachychampsa sealeyi*, sp. nov. (Crocodylia, Alligatoroidea) from the Upper Cretaceous (lower Campanian) Menefee Formation, northwestern New Mexico. *Journal of Vertebrate Paleontology* 16 (3):421–31.

Willis, P.M.A., and B.S. Mackness. 1996. *Quinkana babarra,* a new species of ziphodont mekosuchine crocodile from the Early Pliocene Bluff Downs Local Fauna, northern Australia with a revision of the genus. *Proceedings of the Linnean Society of New South Wales* 116:143–51.

Willis, P.M.A., R.E. Molnar, and J.D. Scanlon. 1993. An early Eocene crocodilian from Murgon, southeastern Queensland. *Kaupia* 3:27–33.

Wu, X.C., D.B. Brinkman, and A.P. Russell. 1996. A new alligator from the Upper Cretaceous of Canada and the relationships of early eusuchians. *Palaeontology* 39 (2):351–75.

CROCODYLOMORPHS

Crocodylomorpha includes everything conventionally called a "crocodilian" in the older literature (e.g., Steel 1973), including living crocodylians and a wide range of extinct taxa (groups; singular, taxon) (Walker 1970; Benton and Clark 1988; Parrish 1993). Current diversity is low (23 species), and many living species are endangered, but past diversity was much higher. For example, one Late Cretaceous locality from Madagascar indicates the coexistence of at least six crocodylomorph taxa (Buckley and Brochu 1996, 1999). Crocodylomorph fossils have been used extensively in biogeography, paleoclimate reconstruction, and the study of diversity patterns over time (Buffetaut 1981; Hutchinson 1982, 1992; Markwick 1994a, 1994b; Taplin and Grigg 1989; Voorhies 1971; Berg 1965).

Because some fossil crocodylomorph taxa from as far back as the Jurassic are outwardly similar to modern forms, many view this group as "unchanged" over millions of years and a prominent example of a "living fossil" lineage (Buckland 1836; Meyer 1984). In fact, however, crocodylomorphs did not assume the familiar "crocodile shape" until the Jurassic, and even after that period the fossil record reveals numerous fundamental changes in the locomotor system and braincase (Frey 1988; Busbey and Gow 1984; Walker 1990; Tarsitano et al. 1989). Several lineages have diverged from the basic crocodile *gestalt* to do very bizarre things. It is more accurate to liken Crocodylomorpha to a musical canon or fugue—the underlying *bauplane* ("musical phrase") has remained more or less stable throughout, but it has grown more complex during phylogeny (evolutionary history), and every so often a single lineage, like a solo instrument, has flown off on its own.

The crocodylomorph fossil record figured prominently in nineteenth-century anatomical work. For example, Richard Owen (1850) referred to the skull of the living crocodile in his attempt to homologize head segmentation to portions of the vertebral column. Thomas Henry Huxley, an early supporter of Charles Darwin, regarded the known fossil record of Crocodylomorpha as a progression from the primitive "mesosuchians" of the Jurassic and Cretaceous to the more advanced "eusuchians" of the Cenozoic, and T.H. Huxley used this progression as evidence for evolution (1875).

Until recently, Huxley's classification was retained in modified format. Triassic and Early Jurassic taxa with a modest secondary palate (the bone that separates mouth and nasal passages, allowing the animal to eat and breathe at the same time) were classified as "sphenosuchians" and "protosuchians"; those with more elaborate secondary palates, but lacking ball-and-socket joints between the vertebrae, were classified as "mesosuchians"; and members of Eusuchia shared ball-and-socket joints between the vertebrae and complete secondary palates in which the internal choana (nasal opening) is completely surrounded by the pterygoid bones (Figure 1). Recent phylogenetic work has refocused our understanding of the relationships within this group. We no longer recognize "Sphenosuchia" or "Mesosuchia" as valid groups; Crocodylia now is restricted to the group that includes the last common ancestor of living crocodiles, alligators, and gharials and all related extinct descendants; and Crocodylia is nested within a monophyletic (a group embracing all the descendants of a common ancestor) Eusuchia (Figure 1; Benton and Clark 1988).

Crocodylomorpha can currently be diagnosed, in part, on the basis of the following features (Parrish 1993): elongate proximal carpals, or wrist bones (radiale and ulnare); secondary palate comprised of maxilla (major bone of upper jaw) and premaxilla (bone at tip of snout); no more than four phalanges (individual bones) in fourth digit of the foot; and an inturned femoral head (articular knob at top of femur), in which the medial and lateral sides are parallel (Figure 2). Other possible characters are listed by Parrish (1993), Benton and Clark (1988), and Wu and Chatterjee (1993).

The earliest crocodylomorphs were small and very gracile (slender, slight) animals—*Saltaposuchus* (also known as *Terrestrisuchus;* Crush 1984) had limb proportions reminiscent of a gazelle. By lengthening the proximal carpals (wrist bones), they added an extra functional segment to their forelimbs. They were probably more terrestrial than their living relatives.

Crocodylomorphs are also characterized by a complex system of air-filled channels and cavities (pneumatic system) surrounding the braincase and by the beginnings of a bony secondary palate, characters that become elaborated among more derived (specialized) members (Owen 1850; Busbey and Gow 1984; Crompton and Smith 1980; Walker 1990; Witmer 1997; Tarsitano et al. 1989). The function of the pneumatic system remains unclear; in living crocodylomorphs, the secondary palate allows the manipulation of food while breathing and strengthens the snout (Busbey 1995).

The oldest known crocodylomorphs—the "sphenosuchians"—are from the Upper Triassic (Crush 1984; Haughton 1915; Bonaparte 1971). "Sphenosuchia" may form a paraphyletic assemblage (a group with a common ancestor that does not embrace all its descendants) (Figure 1A) (Walker 1970, 1990; Benton and Clark 1988), although X.C. Wu and Chatterjee (1993) have argued for its monophyly.

Figure 1. Phylogenetic relationships among crocodylomorph archosaurs. *A*, basal crocodylomorphs ("sphenosuchians" and "protosuchians"); *B*, basal mesoeucrocodylians ("mesosuchians"); *C*, neosuchians. Taxa with asterisks were more parsimoniously grouped with Thalattosuchia in Clark (1994). Based on: *A*, Benton and Clark (1988), Clark (1994), and Wu and Chatterjee (1933); *B*, Benton and Clark (1988), Gasparini et al. (1991), Buckley and Brochu (in press), Wu et al. (1994b), and Clark (1994); *C*, Benton and Clark (1988), Norell and Clark (1990), Clark and Norell (1992), Wu and Brinkman (1993), and Brochu (1997).

Crocodyliformes is a group that is nested within Crocodylomorpha and that includes "protosuchians," "mesosuchians," and living crocodylians (Figure 1). This group can be diagnosed, in part, by the presence of dermal sculpturing on the surface of some of the skull bones; exclusion of the supraoccipital (bone that partly forms the back of the skull) from the foramen magnum (opening in skull through which spinal cord passes); and a reduction or loss of the antorbital fenestra (skull opening in front of the eye socket) (Clark 1994). Other characters are discussed by M.J. Benton and J.M. Clark (1988) and Wu and colleagues (1994a, 1997).

The interrelationships of the most primitive members of this group—the "protosuchians"—are debated. Analyses by Benton and Clark (1988) and Clark (1994) strongly indicate the paraphyly of "Protosuchia" (Figure 1A), whereas studies by Wu and colleagues (1994a, 1994b, 1997) suggest the monophyly of this assemblage. Little is known about the ecology of protosuchian-grade crocodyliforms; most authors have considered them to be largely terrestrial (land-based), although others (e.g., Buffetaut 1989) have argued for a semiaquatic habit for at least some of them. Nearly all such taxa are known from the Late Triassic or Early Jurassic, with a few occurrences in the Cretaceous of Asia (Osmólska 1972; Wu et al. 1997). Good anatomical descriptions are presented by E.H. Colbert and C.C. Mook (1951), A.B. Busbey and C.E. Gow (1984), D. Nash (1975), K.N. Whetstone and P.J. Whybrow (1983), A.W. Crompton and K.K. Smith (1980), and Wu and colleagues (1994a, 1997).

Nested within Crocodyliformes is Mesoeucrocodylia, a large and diverse group including those taxa conventionally called "mesosuchians" as well as living crocodylians. The relationships within this group are debated, and the reader is encouraged to consult Clark (1994) and Wu and colleagues (1994b) for current discussion on this issue. The tree shown in Figure 1B is derived primarily from Clark (1994), with additional information from Wu and colleagues (1994b) and Buckley and Brochu (1999). Mesoeucrocodylians extend the crocodylomorph secondary palate by shifting the internal choanae between or behind the rearmost bones of the palate (palatine bones), and the pubis (one of the three pelvic bones) does not participate in the hip joint (Clark 1994).

Among the most common fossil mesoeucrocodylians are the thalattosuchians, a group of long-snouted taxa outwardly resembling the living Indian gharial (Figure 3A). The thalattosuchians are known largely from marine deposits and range stratigraphically from the Lower Jurassic to the Lower Cretaceous. Because of their abundance in European marine sediments, they

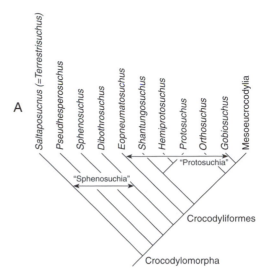

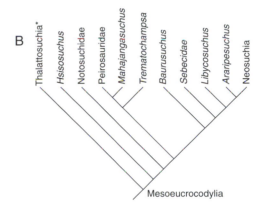

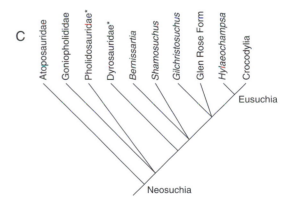

Figure 1

were also among the first fossil vertebrates to receive extensive study (e.g., Geoffroy Saint-Hilaire 1825). Beautifully preserved skeletons of the thalattosuchian *Steneosaurus*, like that shown in Figure 3A, are abundant in the Holzmaden shales (Lower Jurassic) of Germany, and growth series are known for several taxa (Westphal 1962; Duffin 1979; Wenz 1968).

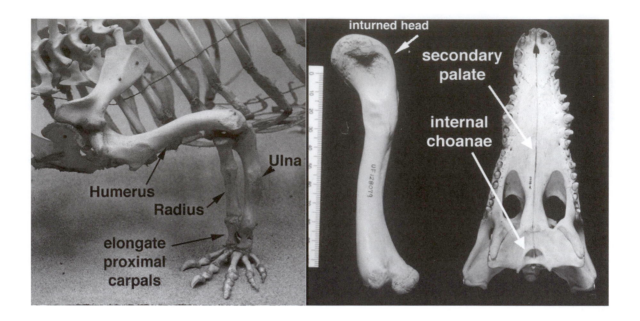

Figure 2. Characters diagnosing Crocodylomorpha. Elongate proximal carpals can be seen on the *Alligator mississippiensis* forelimb on the left; to the right, an *Alligator mississippiensis* right femur shows the inturned femoral head, and the skull of *Crocodylus acutus* demonstrates the secondary palate, which is most elaborately developed in eusuchians. All photos by Christopher A. Brochu.

Numerous morphological features suggest a highly aquatic habit for thalattosuchians. Elongation of the snout, a feature that reoccurs many times throughout Mesoeucrocodylia, is thought to be an adaptation to catching and eating fishes (Langston 1973). The limbs are reduced in length and the bones themselves are curved; in the most derived members, the metriorhynchids, the limb bones are almost platelike and resemble paddles (e.g., Westphal 1962).

The vertical orientation of the zygapophyses (articular projections connecting adjacent vertebrae) is thought to facilitate dorsoventral flexion (an up-and-down motion), much as in modern whales (Hua 1993). Some very derived metriorhynchids show a downward flexure of the tail vertebrae, suggesting a caudal (tail) fin. Swimming mechanics have been analyzed by S. Hua (1994) and J.A. Massare (1988), both of whom agree that thalattosuchians were predators that ambushed their prey rather than pursuing them, a strategy that emphasized tail propulsion. Thalattosuchians are known best from the Jurassic of Europe; Steel (1973) lists several dozen species, most of which are probably not valid. Remains also have been described from the Western Hemisphere (Buffetaut 1979b; Gasparini 1980; Gasparini and Díaz 1977) and Asia (Li 1993). The largest thalattosuchian known is *Machimosaurus*, a blunt-snouted teleosaur from the Late Jurassic of Europe that may have reached 9.5 meters in length (Krebs 1967; Buffetaut 1982b).

Thalattosuchians are the focus of much systematic (field of study concerned with evolutionary relationships) debate. Figure 1B indicates the phylogenetic placement that most scholars generally prefer (e.g., Buffetaut 1982a): basal within Mesoeucrocodylia. However, a recent analysis (Clark 1994) instead supports the monophyly of a group including Thalattosuchia, Dyrosauridae, and Pholidosauridae. Dyrosaurids and Pholidosaurids are lineages of long-snouted taxa similar in general form to thalattosuchians

but usually are regarded as more closely related to living crocodylians (Figure 1C). Clark (1994) suggested that suites of non-independent characters related to snout shape may be responsible for this anomaly—for instance, elongation of the snout might require reorientation of the palatal bones. However, more data are required to resolve this issue.

Several mesoeucrocodylian lineages may have been more terrestrial than living crocodylians. These include the sebecids of the South American Tertiary (Figure 3C), which some scholars think were attempting to fill the terrestrial predator niches left open by the extinction of non-avian dinosaurs at the end of the Mesozoic. Sebecids had deep snouts and bladelike, serrated teeth with compressed sides, much like those of non-avian theropod dinosaurs (Simpson 1932, 1937; Colbert 1946; Busbey 1986; Gasparini et al. 1993). Taxa possibly related to the sebecids are known from Europe (e.g., Berg 1966), and although fragmentary remains from North America once were thought to be sebecid (Langston 1956), they now are known to represent a crocodylian that acquired similar characteristics independently (Langston 1973).

Several other assumably terrestrial mesoeucrocodylians are known from the Cretaceous and Tertiary. Some of these groups—in particular, the trematochampsids of Africa, Madagascar, and possibly South America and Europe—are very poorly known (Buffetaut 1974, 1976; Buffetaut and Taquet 1979). Recent discoveries indicate the presence of small-bodied, robust forms notable for the presence of multicuspate teeth (i.e., having multiple cusps) that resemble mammal molars in the back of the jaw (Clark et al. 1989; Wu et al. 1995; Wu and Sues 1966; Gomani 1997). The jaws of these animals probably were capable of forward-backward occlusion (the way that teeth in upper and lower jaws meet), much like that of extant *Sphenodon* (the tuatara). Wu and col-

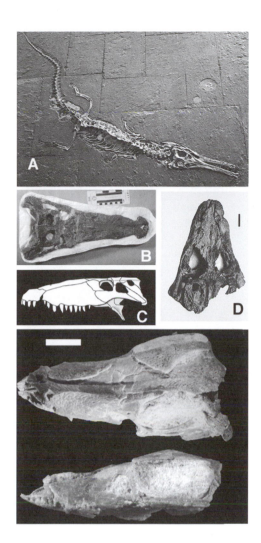

Figure 3. Fossil mesoeucrocodylians. *A, Steneosaurus bollensis,* a thalattosuchian (Jurassic, Germany); *B, Goniopholis stovalli* (Jurassic, Oklahoma); *C, Sebecus; D, Theriosuchus pusillus* (Jurassic, England); *E, Araripesuchus* (Cretaceous, Madagascar). *Scale:* bar equals 1 centimeter. Specimens from: *A,* Staatliches Museum für Naturkunde, Karlsruhe, Germany; *B,* Oklahoma Museum of Natural History, Norman, Oklahoma; *C,* based largely on reconstructions by Colbert (1946); *D,* Natural History Museum, London. Photos and illustration by Christopher A. Brochu.

The more advanced mesoeucrocodylians, the neosuchians (Figure 1C), began to assume a more familiar crocodile-like appearance. These animals first appeared in the Jurassic and include the widespread goniopholidids from the Jurassic and Cretaceous (Figure 3B); the diminutive atoposaurids of the Jurassic (Figure 3D); and *Bernissartia,* known from the Lower Cretaceous of Belgium and Spain (Dollo 1883; Buffetaut 1975; Norell and Clark 1990; Buscalioni and Sanz 1990). Neosuchians probably lived much like living crocodylians, although the structures of their palates and vertebral columns were very different from those of modern taxa. Interrelationships among neosuchians have been discussed by Benton and Clark (1988), Clark and M.A. Norell (1992), and Wu and D.B. Brinkman (1993).

Eusuchia was once diagnosed on the basis of two characters: a "complete" secondary palate, in which the internal choanae are surrounded completely by the pterygoid bones; and procoelous vertebrae with ball-and-socket joints between vertebral centra. In fact, procoelous vertebrae diagnose a more inclusive group than Eusuchia (Benton and Clark 1988; Wu and Brinkman 1993; Brochu 1997) and occur in unrelated crocodyliform groups (Michard et al. 1990). At present, Eusuchia is diagnosed only by the presence of pterygoidal choanae.

The oldest members of the crown group (all living forms and their common ancestor, along with the extinct descendants of that ancestor) Crocodylia appear in the Campanian (Late Cretaceous). Non-crocodylian eusuchians are very rare through the Cretaceous, and clearly the diversity of this group must have been much higher. The oldest and most primitive known eusuchian is *Hylaeochampsa vectiana* from the Lower Cretaceous of the Isle of Wight (Owen 1874; Clark and Norell 1992). The next-oldest records of eusuchians are from the Cenomanian of Egypt (Stromer 1925, 1933). The Cenomanian occurrences include *Stomatosuchus,* a strange animal with a long, broad, oarlike snout and an edentulous (toothless) lower jaw; F. Nopsca (1926) suggested that it bore a pelican-like throat pouch, but because all known material from this animal was lost during the Second World War, not much more can be said about it.

CHRISTOPHER A. BROCHU

See also Crocodylians

leagues (1995) suggested herbivory for a Chinese form *(Chimaerasuchus),* on the basis of cusp (point on a molar) morphology.

These bizarre, robust mesoeucrocodylians suggest some interesting biogeographic patterns. One of the best-known taxa is *Araripesuchus,* found in the Late Cretaceous of Brazil (Price 1959; Hecht 1991), Niger (Buffetaut 1979a, 1981), and Madagascar (Buckley and Brochu 1996) (Figure 3E). Other Cretaceous fossils from Madagascar suggest closer relationships to contemporary mesoeucrocodylians from South America than to African forms, supporting hypotheses that a Late Cretaceous dispersal route existed between South America and Madagascar, independent of mainland Africa (Krause and Grine 1996).

Works Cited

Benton, M.J., and J.M. Clark. 1988. Archosaur phylogeny and the relationships of the Crocodylia. *In* M.J. Benton (ed.), *The Phylogeny and Classification of the Tetrapods.* Vol. 1, Oxford: Clarendon; New York: Oxford University Press.

Berg, D.E. 1965. Krokodile als Klimazeugen. *Geologische Rundschau* 54:328–33.

———. 1966. *Die Krokodile, insbesondere* Asiatosuchus *und aff.* Sebecus?, *aus dem Eozän von Messel bei Darmstadt/Hessen. Abhandlungen des Hessischen Landesamtes für Bodenforschung,* 52. Wiesbaden: n.p.

Bonaparte, J.F. 1971. *Los tetrapodos del sector superior de la Formación Los Colorados, La Rioja, Argentina.* Opera Lilloana, 22. Tucuman: Universidad Nacional de Tucuman.

Brochu, C.A. 1997. Fossils, morphology, divergence timing, and the phylogenetic relationships of Gavialis. *Systematic Biology* 46 (3):479–522.

Buckland, W. 1836. *Geology and Mineralogy Considered with Reference to Natural Theology.* London: Pickering; Philadelphia: Carey, Lea and Blanchard, 1837.

Buckley, G., and C.A. Brochu. 1996. Campanian crocodyliforms from Madagascar and their biogeographic implication. *Journal of Vertebrate Paleontology* 16 (3):24A.

Buckley, G.A., and C.A. Brochu.1999. An enigmatic new crocodile from the Upper Cretaceous of Madagascar. *In* D.M. Unwin (ed.), *Cretaceous Fossil Vertebrates.* Special Papers in Paleontology, 60. London: Palaeontological Association.

Buffetaut, E. 1974. *Trematochampsa taqueti,* un crocodilien nouveau du Senonien inférieur du Niger. *Comptes Rendus Hebdomadaires des Séances de l'Académie des Sciences* ser. D, 279:1749–52.

———. 1975. Sur l'anatomie et la position systématique de *Bernissartia fagesii* Dollo, L. 1883, crocodilien du Wealdien de Bernissart, Belgique. *Bulletin de l'Institut Royal des Sciences Naturelles de Belgique (sci. Terre)* 51:1–20.

———. 1976. Osteologie et affinités de *Trematochampsa taqueti* (Crocodylia, Mesosuchia) du Senonien inférieur d'in Beceten (Republique du Niger). *Géobios, Mémoire Special* 9:143–98.

———. 1979a. An Early Cretaceous terrestrial crocodilian and the opening of the South Atlantic. *Nature* 280:486–87.

———. 1979b. Jurassic marine crocodilians (Mesosuchia: Teleosauridae) from central Oregon: First record in North America. *Journal of Paleontology* 53 (1):210–15.

———. 1981. Die biogeographische Geschichte der Krokodilier, mit Beschreibung einer neuen Art, *Araripesuchus wegeneri. Geologische Rundschau* 70:611–24.

———. 1982a. Le crocodilien *Machimosaurus* von Meyer (Mesosuchia, Teleosauridae) dans le Kimmeridgien de l'Ain. *Bulletin Trimestriel de la Société Géologique de Normandie et Amis du Muséum du Havre* 69:17–27.

———. 1982b. Radiation évolutive, paléoécologie et biogéographie des crocodiliens mésosuchiens. *Mémoires de la Société Géologique de France* 60:1–88.

———. 1989. Evolution. *In* C.A. Ross (ed.), *Crocodiles and Alligators.* New York: Facts on File.

Buffetaut, E., and P. Taquet. 1979. Un nouveau crocodilien mésosuchien dans le Campanien de Madagascar: *Trematochampsa oblita,* n. sp. *Bulletin de la Société Géologique de France* 21:183–88.

Busbey, A.B. 1986. New material of *Sebecus* cf. *huilensis* (Crocodilia: Sebecosuchidae) from the Miocene La Venta Formation of Colombia. *Journal of Vertebrate Paleontology* 6 (1):20–27.

———. 1995. The structural consequences of skull flattening in crocodilians. *In* J.J. Thomason (ed.), *Functional Morphology in Vertebrate Paleontology.* Cambridge and New York: Cambridge University Press.

Busbey, A.B., and C.E. Gow. 1984. A new protosuchian crocodile from the Upper Triassic Elliot formation of South Africa. *Palaeontologica Africana* 25:127–49.

Buscalioni, A., and J.L. Sanz. 1990. The small crocodile *Bernissartia fagesii* from the Lower Cretaceous of Galve (Teruel, Spain). *Bulletin de l'Institut Royal des Sciences Naturelles de Belgique* 60:129–50.

Clark, J.M. 1994. Patterns of evolution in Mesozoic Crocodyliformes. *In* N.C. Fraser and H.-D. Sues (ed.), *In the Shadow of the Dinosaurs.* Cambridge and New York: Cambridge University Press.

Clark, J.M., L.L. Jacobs, and W.R. Downs. 1989. Mammal-like dentition in a Mesozoic crocodylian. *Science* 244:1064–66.

Clark, J.M., and M.A. Norell. 1992. The Early Cretaceous crocodylomorph *Hylaeochampsa vectiana* from the Wealden of the Isle of Wight. *American Museum Novitates* 3032:1–19.

Colbert, E.H. 1946. *Sebecus,* representative of a peculiar suborder of fossil Crocodilia from Patagonia. *Bulletin of the American Museum of Natural History* 87:221–70.

Colbert, E.H., and C.C. Mook. 1951. The ancestral crocodilian *Protosuchus. Bulletin of the American Museum of Natural History* 97:147–82.

Crompton, A.W., and K.K. Smith. 1980. A new genus and species of crocodilian from the Kayenta Formation (Late Triassic?) of northern Arizona. *In* L.L. Jacobs (ed.), *Aspects of Vertebrate History.* Flagstaff, Arizona: Museum of Northern Arizona Press.

Crush, P.J. 1984. A late Upper Triassic sphenosuchid crocodilian from Wales. *Palaeontology* 27 (1):131–57.

Dollo, L. 1883. Première note sur les crocodiliens de Bernissart. *Bulletin de la Musée Royal des Sciences Naturelles de Belgique* 2:309–38.

Duffin, C. 1979. Pelagosaurus (Mesosuchia, Crocodilia) from the English Toarcian (Lower Jurassic). *Neues Jahrbuch für Geologie und Paläontologie, Monatshefte* 8:475–85.

Frey, E. 1988. Das Tragsystem der Krokodile—eine biomechanische und phylogenetische Analyse. *Stuttgarter Beiträge zur Naturkunde,* ser. A, 426:1–60.

Gasparini, Z. 1980. South American Mesozoic crocodiles. *Mesozoic Vertebrate Life* 1:67–72.

Gasparini, Z., L.M. Chiappe, and M. Fernandez. 1991. A new Senonian peirosaurid (Crocodylomorpha) from Argentina and a synopsis of the South American Cretaceous crocodilians. *Journal of Vertebrate Paleontology* 11 (3):316–33.

Gasparini, Z., and G.C. Díaz. 1977. *Metriorhynchus casamiquelai* n. sp. (Crocodilia, Thalattosuchia), a marine crocodile from the Jurassic (Callovian) of Chile, South America. *Neues Jahrbuch für Geologie und Paläontologie, Abhandlungen* 153:341–60.

Gasparini, Z., M. Fernandez, and J. Powell. 1993. New Tertiary sebecosuchians (Crocodylomorpha) from South America: Phylogenetic implications. *Historical Biology* 7 (1):1–19.

Geoffroy Saint-Hilaire, E. 1825. Recherches sur l'organisation des Gavials. *Mémoire. Muséum National d'Histoire Naturelle,* Paris 12:97–155.

Gomani, E. 1997. A crocodyliform from the Early Cretaceous dinosaur beds, northern Malawi. *Journal of Vertebrate Paleontology* 17:280–94.

Haughton, S.H. 1915. Investigations in South African fossil Reptilia and Amphibia. 9, A new thecodont from the Sormberg beds. *Annals of the South African Museum* 12:98–105.

Hecht, M.K. 1991. *Araripesuchus* Price, 1959. *In* J.G. Maisey (ed.), *Santana Fossils: An Illustrated Atlas.* Neptune City, New Jersey: T.F.H. Publications.

Hua, S. 1993. Sur des vertèbres d'un crocodilien marin. *Bulletin Trimestriel de la Société Géologique de Normandie et Amis du Muséum du Havre* 80:45–48.

———. 1994. Hydrodynamique et modalités d'allègement chez *Metriorhynchus superciliosus* (Crocodylia, Thalattosuchia): Implications paléoécologiques. *Neues Jarhbuch für Geologie und Paläontologie, Abhandlungen* 193:1–19.

Hutchinson, J.H. 1982. Turtle, crocodilian, and champsosaur diversity changes in the Cenozoic of the north-central region of western United States. *Palaeogeography, Palaeoclimatology, Palaeoecology* 37:149–64.

———. 1992. Western North American reptile and amphibian record across the Eocene-Oligocene boundary and its climatic implications. *In* D.R. Prothero and W.A. Berggren (ed.), *Eocene-*

Oligocene Climatic and Biotic Evolution. Princeton, New Jersey: Princeton University Press.

Huxley, T.H. 1875. On *Stagonolepis robertsoni,* and on the evolution of the Crocodilia. *Quarterly Journal of the Geological Society* 31:423–38.

Krause, D., and F.E. Grine. 1996. The first multituberculates from Madagascar: Implications for Cretaceous biogeography. *Journal of Vertebrate Paleontology* 16:46A.

Krebs, B. 1967. Der Jura-Krokodilier *Machimosaurus* H. v. Mayer. *Paläontologische Zeitschrift* 41:46–59.

Langston, W. 1956. The Sebecosuchia: Cosmopolitan crocodilians? *American Journal of Science* 254:605–14.

———. 1973. The crocodilian skull in historical perspective. *In* C. Gans and T. Parsons (ed.), *Biology of the Reptilia.* Vol. 4, London and New York: Academic Press.

Li, J. 1993. A new specimen of *Peipehsuchus teleorhinus* from Ziliujing Formation of Daxian, Sichuan. *Vertebrata PalAsiatica* 31:85–94.

Markwick, P.J. 1994a. "Equability" contentinality, and Tertiary "climate": The crocodilian perspective. *Geology* 22:613–16.

———. 1994b. Crocodilian distribution and diversity across the Cretaceous-Tertiary Boundary: Implications for climatically-induced extinction. *Geological Society of America Abstracts with Programs* 26 (7):A-395.

Massare, J.A. 1988. Swimming capabilities of Mesozoic marine reptiles: Implications for method of predation. *Paleobiology* 14:187–205.

Meyer, E.R. 1984. Crocodilians as living fossils. *In* N. Eldredge and S.M. Stanley (eds.), *Living Fossils.* New York: Springer-Verlag.

Michard, J.G., F. de Broin, M. Brunet, and J. Hell. 1990. Le plus ancien crocodilien néosuchien spécialisé à caractères "euschiens" du continent africain (Crétacé inférieur, Camerouh). *Comptes Rendus de l'Académie des Sciences de Paris,* ser. 2, 311:365–70.

Nash, D. 1975. The morphology and relationships of the crocodilian *Orthosuchus stormbergi* from the Upper Triassic of Lesotho. *Annals of the South African Museum* 67:227–329.

Neill, W.T. 1971. *The Last Ruling Reptiles: Alligators, Crocodiles, and Their Kin.* New York: Columbia University Press.

Nopcsa, F. 1926. Neue Beobachtungen an *Stromatosuchus. Zentralblatt für Mineralogie, Geologie und Paläontologie* B:212–15.

Norell, M.A., and J.M. Clark. 1990. A reanalysis of *Bernissartia fagesii,* with comments on its phylogenetic position and its bearing on the origin and diagnosis of Eusuchia. *Bulletin de l'Institut Royal des Sciences Naturelles de Belgique* 60:115–28.

Osmolska, H. 1972. Preliminary note on a crocodilian from the Upper Cretaceous of Mongolia. *Palaeontologia Polonica* 27:43–47.

Owen, R. 1850. *Monograph on the Fossil Reptilia of the London Clay, and of the Bracklesham and Other Tertiary Beds.* Part 2, *Crocodilia (Crocodilus, etc.)* London: Palaeontographical Society.

———. 1874. Monograph on the fossil Reptilia of the Wealden and Purbeck Formations. 6, *Hylaeochampsa. Palaeontographical Society Monographs* 27:1–7.

Parrish, J.M. 1993. Phylogeny of the Crocodylotarsi, with reference to archosaurian and crurotarsan monophyly. *Journal of Vertebrate Paleontology* 13 (3):287–308.

Price, L.I. 1959. Sôbre um crocodilídeo notossúquio do Cretácico Brasileiro. *Boletim Divisao de Geologia e Mineralogia* 188:1–55.

Ross, C.A. (ed.). 1989. *Crocodiles and Alligators.* New York: Facts on File.

Simpson, G.G. 1932. The supposed association of dinosaurs with mammals of Tertiary type in Patagonia. *American Museum Novitates* 556:1–21.

———. 1937. New reptiles from the Eocene of South America. *American Museum Novitates* 927:1–3.

Steel, R. 1964. *Crocodiles.* London: Helm.

———. 1973. *Handbuch der Paleoherpetologie.* Vol. 16, *Crocodylia.* Portland: Fischer-Verlag.

Stromer, E. 1925. Ergebnisse der Forschungsreisen Prof. E. Stromers in den Wüsten Ägyptens. 2, Wirbeltier-Reste der Baharije-Stufe (Unterstes Cenoman). 7, *Stromatosuchus inermis* Stromer, ein schwach bezahnter Krokodilier. *Abhandlungen der Bayerischen Akademie der Wissenschaften, Mathematisch-naturwissenschaftliche Abteilung* 30:1–9.

———. 1933. Ergebnisse der Forschungsreisen Prof. E. Stromers in den Wüsten Ägyptens. 12, Die Procölen Crocodilia. *Abhandlungen der Bayerischen Akademie der Wissenschaften, Mathematisch-naturwissenschaftliche Abteilung,* N.F., 15:1–55.

Taplin, L.E., and G.C. Grigg. 1989. Historical zoogeography of the eusuchian crocodilians: A physiological perspective. *American Zoologist* 29:885–901.

Tarsitano, S.F., E. Frey, and J. Riess. 1989. The evolution of the Crocodilia: A conflict between morphological and biochemical data. *American Zoologist* 29:843–56.

Voorhies, M.R. 1971. Paleoclimatic significance of crocodilian remains from the Ogallala Group (Upper Tertiary) in northeastern Nebraska. *Journal of Paleontology* 45:119–21.

Walker, A.D. 1970. A revision of the Jurassic reptile *Hallopus victor* (Marsh), with remarks on the classification of crocodiles. *Philosophical Transactions of the Royal Society of London,* ser. B, 257:323–72.

———. 1990. A revision of *Sphenosuchus acutus* Haughton, a crocodylomorph reptile from the Elliot Formation (Late Triassic or Early Jurassic) of South Africa. *Philosophical Transactions of the Royal Society of London,* ser. B, 330:1–120.

Webb, G., and C. Manolis. 1993. *Crocodiles of Australia.* French's Forest, New South Wales: Reed.

Wenz, S. 1968. Contribution a l'étude du genre *Metriorhynchus:* Crâne et moulage endocranien de *Metriorhynchus superciliosus. Annales de Paléontologie (Vertébrés)* 54:149–91.

Westphal, F. 1962. Die Krokodilier des deutschen und englischen oberen Lias. *Palaeontographica,* ser. A, 118:23–118.

Whetstone, K.N., and P.J. Wybrow. 1983. A "cursorial" crocodilian from the Triassic of Lesotho (Basutoland), southern Africa. *Occasional Papers of the Museum of Natural History, the University of Kansas* 106:1–37.

Witmer, L.M. 1997. The evolution of the antorbital cavity of archosaurs: A study in soft-tissue reconstruction in the fossil record with an analysis of the function of pneumaticity. *Society of Vertebrate Paleontology Memoir* 3:1–73.

Wu, X.C., and D.B. Brinkman. 1993. A new crocodylomorph of "mesosuchian" grade from the Upper Cretaceous Upper Milk River Formation, southern Alberta. *Journal of Vertebrate Paleontology* 13 (2):153–60.

Wu, X.C., D.B. Brinkman, and J.C. Lu. 1994a. A new species of Shantungosuchus from the Lower Cretaceous of Inner Mongolia (China), with comments of *S. chuhsienensis* Young, 1961 and the phylogenetic position of the genus. *Journal of Vertebrate Paleontology* 14 (2):210–29.

Wu, X.C., and S. Chatterjee. 1993. *Dibothrosuchus elaphros,* a crocodylomorph from the Lower Jurassic of China and the phylogeny of the Sphenosuchia. *Journal of Vertebrate Paleontology* 13 (1):58–89.

Wu, X.C., J.L. Li, and X.N. Ming. 1994b. Phylogenetic relationship of *Hsisosuchus. Vertebrata PalAsiatica* 32:166–80.

Wu, X.C., and H.D. Sues. 1966. Anatomy and phylogenetic relationships of *Chimaerasuchus paradoxus,* an unusual crocodyliform reptile from the Lower Cretaceous of Hubei, China. *Journal of Vertebrate Paleontology* 16:688–702.

Wu, X.C., H.D. Sues, and Z.M. Dong. 1997. *Sichuanosuchus shuhanensis, a new ?Early Cretaceous protosuchian (Archosauria: Crocodyliformes) from Sichuan (China), and the monophyly of Protosuchia. *Journal of Vertebrate Paleontology* 17:89–103.

Wu, X.C., H.D. Sues, and A. Sun. 1995. A plant-eating crocodyliform reptile from the Cretaceous of China. *Nature* 376:678–80.

Further Reading

Neill, W.T. 1971. *The Last Ruling Reptiles: Alligators, Crocodiles, and Their Kin.* New York: Columbia University Press.

Ross, C.A. (ed.). 1989. *Crocodiles and Alligators.* New York: Facts on File.

Steel, R. 1964. *Crocodiles.* London: Helm.

Webb, G., and C. Manolis. 1993. *Crocodiles of Australia.* French's Forest, New South Wales: Reed.

CRUSTACEANS

Evolutionary Relationships

Crustaceans are a group of segmented, jawed arthropods that are found primarily in marine environments. These animals have five pairs of appendages on the head. The first two pairs (the antennae and antennules) consist of single branches (uniramous) and lie to the front (anterior) of the mouth; the last three pairs are to the rear (posterior) of the mouth and usually are used in feeding. Appendages on the trunk of the body usually have two segments (biramous) (i.e., bear both a "leg" and a gill).

The systematics (evolutionary relationships) of the crustaceans is complex and is constantly in a state of change. Although many groups maintain remarkably stable positions as individual taxonomic units, the uncertain relationship among the groups leads to constant discussion, debate, and reorganization of the Crustacea among specialists. W.L. Schmitt (1931) published the most readable general discussion of the crustaceans, which was followed by a very lucid presentation by McLaughlin (1980) and later by a more technical monograph (Schram 1986).

The evolution of the crustaceans is not well known, and some groups might be composed of unrelated taxa that evolved similar morphologies independently. This type of evolution is called polyphyletic. The fossil record of the crustaceans consists of isolated specimens preserved within other faunas as well as a few spectacular "laggerstätten"—prime fossil beds in which are preserved great numbers of specimens, exceptionally complete organisms, or an exceptional diversity of crustaceans. Although hampered by a general lack of fossils, the overall pattern of evolutionary development of crustaceans appears to involve: (1) the development of robust phyllocarid (shrimplike) faunas in the Paleozoic; (2) the evolution of ostracods (bivalved crustaceans) with an adaptive radiation (diversification and geographic spread) in the Cambrian; (3) the evolution of the decapods (shrimp, lobsters, crabs) in the Devonian, followed by several adaptive radiations in the Jurassic, Cretaceous, and Eocene; and (4) evolution of the barnacles in the Carboniferous. Many other diverse types of crustaceans are not represented or are so poorly represented in the fossil record that their patterns of evolution cannot be determined. The classification presented below is amended and emended after McLaughlin (1980). Groups represented by abundant fossils are printed in boldface.

Morphological, Behavioral, and Taxonomic Diversity

The overall body plans of crustaceans are diverse. The group includes many important fossil groups that comprise crabs, lobsters, shrimp, barnacles, ostracods, and many other less well-known groups. The diversity and abundance of crustaceans in easily accessible waters along the coasts of the continents has made them some of the most collected and best understood groups of invertebrates. Their abundance, diversity, and ecologic and commercial importance have led many biologists to spend their lives studying their systematics, ecology, physiology, embryology, and other aspects of their biology.

From a paleontologist's perspective, the crustaceans are an exciting group to study because they are an important, rapidly evolving, extant group of complex organisms and have a modest fossil record. Fossil crustaceans have been described by M.J. Rathbun (1926, 1935), M.F. Glaessner (1929, 1969), H.B. Stenzel (1945), R.C. Moore and L. McCormick (1969), P. Tasch (1973), and D. Guinot (1978).

This group of organisms exhibits a tantalizing spectrum of morphologies including swimming forms (crabs); forms occupying discarded shells of molluscs (hermit crabs); forms tied to fossorial (burrowing) modes of life (ghost shrimp and mantis shrimp); those cemented to hard surfaces and encased in calcified exoskeletons (barnacles); interstitial forms living within or between sand grains on the beach (amphipods); boring forms, which excavate living places in hard rock or in the skeletons of other organisms (acrothoacians); external parasitic forms, which attach to fish or to other crustaceans' gills (isopods); and invasive internal parasites, which grow throughout the tissue of the host and capture the host's reproductive system (rhizocephalians). Some groups are well represented by body fossils (ostracods, cirripeds, some malacostracans), others are represented primarily by trace fossils (bopyrid isopods, acrothoracians, many types of burrowing shrimp), and many remain unrepresented in the fossil record.

Descriptive, Functional, and Evolutionary Morphology

The descriptive morphology of this diverse group will be short and emphasize those organisms that have left a fossil record. The more important groups include the phyllocarids, the cirripeds, the ostracods, and the mantis shrimp, crabs, shrimp, and lobsters.

The phyllocarids, small shrimplike animals with prominent gills, have a relatively sparse fossil record except for abundant local Early Paleozoic records in Middle Silurian of Scotland, Upper Devonian of Germany and Australia, and the Pennsylvanian of Indiana. Some local faunas preserve appendages.

Phylum Crustacea		
Class	**Description**	
Class Cephalocarida	(Recent)	
Class Remipedia		
Class Branchiopoda	(Early Devonian–Recent)	
*Class **Ostracoda***	(Cambrian–Recent) (Bivalved microorganisms; common microfossils)	
Class Mystacocarida	(Recent) (Microscopic interstitial beach dwellers)	
Class Copepoda	(Early Cretaceous? Miocene–Recent) (Fossils known from two localities)	
Class Branchiura	(Recent) (Fish lice)	
*Class **Cirripeda***	(Late Silurian–Recent)	
	Order Acrothoracia	(Devonian–Recent) (Represented by trace fossils)
	Order **Thoracia**	(Late Silurian–Recent) (Barnacles preserved as body fossils)
	Order Ascothoracia	(Cretaceous–Recent)
	Order Rhizocephala	(Recent) (Interesting internal parasitic barnacles)
*Class **Malacostracea***		
Subclass **Phyllocarida**	(Cambrian–Recent) (Includes Burgess Shale genus *Canadaspis*)	
Subclass Hoplocarida	(Carboniferous–Recent) (Burrowing forms known as mantis shrimp)	
Subclass Eumalacostracea	(Devonian–Recent) (The "true" malacostracans)	
Superorder Peracarida	(?Carboniferous/Permian–Recent)	
	Order Isopoda	(Permian–Recent) (Pill bugs, sea roaches, parasitic types)
Superorder Eucarida	(Middle Carboniferous–Recent)	
	Order **Decapoda**	(Permo-Triassic–Recent) (Includes crabs, lobsters, and shrimp)

The cirripeds (barnacles) are a group of attached, generally shell-enclosed crustaceans that usually are cemented to some hard surface, either by a fleshy stalk (lepedomorphs), by having their enclosing calcareous acornlike exoskeleton directly cemented to the substrate (balanomorphs). Some bore into calcareous substrates (acrothoracians), or live as parasites (rhizocephalians). Most cirripeds are strongly attached to counteract the effects of high-energy water conditions, whether it is surf at the beach, a rapidly swimming host (e.g., whales or sea turtles), or flotsam (e.g., logs, bottles, boats).

The exoskeleton of barnacles is typically calcified and consists of a series of overlapping plates from which the animal's legs sweep the water capturing suspended particulates and organisms for food.

The ostracods have paired shells, which typically are calcareous, dorsally hinged carapaces that completely enclose their body. Within the carapace are two pairs of antennae and a series of limbs, all of which are involved in locomotion—swimming, crawling, and climbing. Ostracods include filter feeders, detritus feeders, scavengers, and carnivores. In fossil forms, the carapace is usually

Figure 1. Fossilized decapod crustacean; Cretaceous crab carapace and appendages preserved in a concretionary nodule; *Longusorbis cunniculosus*; GAB Specimen 124, British Columbia.

the only portion preserved, and an intricate classification scheme has been developed to accommodate abundant morphologic forms. Paleontologists usually study ostracods as part of a group of small fossils called "microfossils." Because of their small size and wide ecologic distribution, ostracods are often abundant in microfossil samples collected during drilling of water or oil wells.

Exceptional remains of 25 arthropod taxa, including many crustaceans (predominantly phosphatocopine ostracodes), have been found in a phosphatic laggerstäten preserved in anthraconite ("orsten or sinkstone") lenses in Sweden. Most of the animals are tiny (two millimeters or less), and the phosphate appears to be an overgrowth of chitinous and especially phosphatic body parts that includes internal features seldom preserved in ostracodes.

The malacostracans, possessing 19 body segments, contain a great diversity of taxa exhibiting highly variable body plans and functional morphologies. Included in the malacostracans are the hoplocarids (stomatopods), syncarids from the Mazon Creek area of Illinois and the Southern Hemisphere, isopods, amphipods, and the decapods (crabs, lobsters, and shrimp).

The Superorder Hoplocarida is a relatively homogeneous group that contains the Order Stomatopoda, or the mantis shrimp. This is a group of carnivorous, burrowing, flattened crustaceans with rebent, jackknife, clawlike appendages capable of extremely rapid and debilitating rapacious action (hence the common name "thumb crackers"), and enlarged abdomens. The placement of eyes and antennules on movable "rings" of segments suggests that these are primitive crustaceans, although relatively few have been found in the fossil record.

The Syncarida are small, elongated crustaceans that lack a carapace and have biramous thoracic appendages. These animals flourished in the Late Paleozoic are now restricted to a few genera (e.g., *Anaspides*) in Tasmanian lakes and rivers.

The Isopoda (pill bugs) are poorly represented as body fossils in the fossil record, but their presence is sometimes evidenced by trace fossils preserved on other body fossils. Ectoparasitic bopyrids settle as larvae on the gills of crabs, lobsters, or shrimp. There

they grow and cause an inflation of one gill chamber. Such an obvious asymmetry of the host organism can be preserved in the fossil record.

The Amphipoda are unknown as fossils, but their bioturbation (mixing) of the ocean floor is a significant feature of sediments. When such turbation is found, in a sense, it represents a trace fossil.

The Decapoda (Figure 1), the largest group of fossilized crustaceans, have five pairs of thoracic appendages, a carapace, and an abdomen that is either extended or bent forward beneath the cephalothorax. Decapods (which include crabs, lobsters, and shrimp) are adapted to various modes of life that are reflected in body morphology. Generally speaking, swimming forms are often laterally compressed while benthic forms are often dorsal-ventrally compressed. Burrowing or boring forms are often cylindrical and use their burrows as skeletal elements—the burrow functions as support structure against which the animal braces its legs.

Biology and Behavior

Most crustaceans pass through a naplier larval stage and periodically shed their exoskeleton during a process called "ecdysis," or molting, to allow for body growth. During ecdysis, the organism sheds its exoskeleton, increases in size, and secretes a new exoskeleton. The carapace from each molt is capable of being preserved as a fossil virtually indistinguishable from its living source, which can bias the fossil record by artificially inflating the number of fossils.

Temporal Span

Canadaspis perfecta, a phyllocarid, was cited as the earliest crustacean by D.E.G. Briggs in 1978 and by E.N.A. Clarkson in 1986. It or its related forms rapidly gave rise to numerous lineages of crustaceans. In 1978, Schram, Feldman, and Copeland recognized *Palaeopalaemon newberryi* as the earliest decapod crustacean. It is known from Devonian deposits in Iowa, New York, and Kentucky. Its discovery pushed the origin of decapods back about 100 million additional years. However, not all researchers agree that *Palaeopalaemon* is a decapod. Its unusual array of characters may exclude it from membership in the Decapoda. On the other hand, its extreme age might account for the morphological gap between *Palaeopalaemon* and more conventional decapods.

In 1984 Schram and Mapes described *Imocaris tuberculata*, from the Upper Mississippian of Arkansas. This species is assigned to an extant group of crabs, the Dromiacea. Its discovery pushes the origin of the Dromiacea back from the Early Jurassic to the middle of the Carboniferous (Figure 2).

Triassic

There are a limited number of Triassic exposures. They consist largely of terrestrial rocks with limited marine sedimentary rocks. Few crustacean taxa have been documented from the North American Triassic, including lobsters from the Thaynes Formation near Hot Springs, Idaho, the Upper Triassic of Nevada, the Lower Jurassic of Canada, and a crayfish from the Late Triassic Chinle Formation of the Petrified Forest National Park.

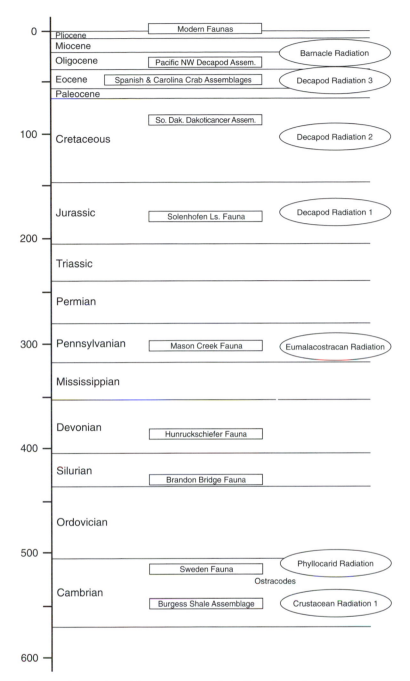

Figure 2. Stratigraphic occurrence of significant crustacean faunas.

Jurassic

Jurassic exposures also are limited. Often they are deeply buried beneath younger sediments. During the Jurassic the North Atlantic Ocean was just beginning to open, while marine deposition was controlled by the distribution of the circumequatorial Tethys Seaway. Jurassic rocks, some of them marine, have not been searched seriously for any decapod faunas they might include. In spite of this, a few decapods already have been described; these have turned up in mapping or paleontological exploration. Herrick and Schram described a marine decapod fauna from the Sun-

dance Formation of Wyoming in 1978, and in 1979 Feldmann described a lobster from the same fauna.

In 1980 Feldmann and McPherson reviewed most of the known Canadian decapods, including two Jurassic lobsters, and in 1988 Feldmann and Copeland described a new erymid lobster from the Lower Jurassic of Southwestern Alberta.

European faunas are much more well-represented, partly because of the world-famous Solnhoffen Limestone of Germany, which has yielded so many finely preserved crustaceans. The sparse Jurassic fauna of the Americas, when compared to the extensive European record, quite obviously is severely understudied, probably because of lack of collecting.

Cretaceous

Cretaceous rocks were deposited largely under marine conditions and carry extensive marine faunas. The decapod record of the Lower Cretaceous of the United Kingdom is diverse; that of the Americas is sparse and restricted to a few specimens. However, in 1986 G.A. Bishop described a diverse decapod fauna consisting of eleven crustacean species from the Lower Albian Glen Rose Limestone of Central Texas. The decapod record of the Late Cretaceous is substantial and constantly increasing in quantity and quality, reflected by numerous papers by several authors. It is these Late Cretaceous faunas that launched decapod paleontology in North America beyond the inventory phase and set the stage for analyses of evolution, biostratigraphy, paleoecology, functional morphology, and taphonomy.

Taphonomy and Fossilization

Recognition of the importance that taphonomy (the study of the preservational aspects of fossils) plays in the preservation of decapod crustaceans was first recognized by the Europeans. Taphonomy of decapods has been directly addressed by only a few works, such as those by Wilhelm Schäfer (1951, 1972); R. Mundlos (1975); and G.A. Bishop (1981, 1986a, 1986b). Bishop (1981) described the taphonomic history of the *Dakoticancer* assemblage from the Late Cretaceous Pierre Shale of South Dakota as leading to apatite-preserved decapod community fractions and presented a holistic review of the taphonomy of North American decapods in a paper generally applicable to decapod taphonomy (1986b). Bishop and Williams (1986) applied those concepts to a lobster assemblage from the Cretaceous Carlile Shale of the Black Hills of South Dakota, presenting a hypothesized worm-decapod short cycle that leads to preservation of apatite-preserved decapod assemblages, a theme documented in a subsequent paper in 1987 that postulated a positive taphonomic feedback cycle that periodically led to preservation of decapod community fractions as apatite-preserved, decapod assemblages.

GALE A. BISHOP

See also Aquatic Invertebrates, Adaptive Strategies of; Defensive Structures: Invertebrates; Eyes: Invertebrates; Feeding Adaptations: Invertebrates; Ornamentation: Invertebrates

Works Cited

Bishop, G.A. 1981. Occurrence and fossilization of the *Dakoticancer* Assemblage, Upper Cretaceous Pierre Shale, South Dakota. *In* J. Gray, A.J. Boncot, and W.B.N. Berry (eds.), *Communities of the Past.* Stroudsburg, Pennsylvania: Hutchinson Ross.

——. 1986a. Occurrence, preservation and biogeography of the Cretaceous crabs of North America. *In* R.H. Gore and K.L. Heck (eds.), *Crustacean Issues 4, Crustacean Biogeography.* Boston and Rotterdam: Balkema.

——. 1986b. Taphonomy of the North American decapods. *Journal of Crustacean Biology* 6 (3):326–55.

Bishop, G.A., and A.B. Williams. 1986. The fossil lobster *Linuparus canadensis*, Carlile Shale (Cretaceous), Black Hills. *National Geographic Research* 2:372–87.

Briggs, D.E.G. 1978. The morphology, mode of life, and affinities of *Canadaspis perfecta* (Crustacea: Phyllocarida), Middle Cambrian, Burgess Shale, British Columbia. *Philosophical Transactions of the Royal Society of London,* ser. B, 281:439–87.

Feldmann, R.M. 1979. *Eryma foersteri,* a new species of lobster (Decapoda) from the Jurassic (Callovian) of North America. *American Museum Novitates* 2668:1–5.

Glaessner, M.F. 1929. *Crustacea Decapoda.* Fossilium Catalogus, 41. Berlin: Junk.

——. 1969. Decapoda. *In* R.C. Moore (ed.), *Treatise of Invertebrate Paleontology.* Part R, *Arthropoda 4, 2.* Boulder, Colorado: Geological Society of America; Lawrence, Kansas: University of Kansas Press.

Gould, S.J. 1989. *Wonderful Life: The Burgess Shale and the Nature of History.* New York: Norton; London: Hutchinson Radius, 1 990.

Guinot, D. 1978. Principles of a new classification of the Crustacea Decopoda Brachyura. *Bulletin Biologique de la France et de la Belgique* 3:211–92.

Herrick, E.M., and F.R. Schram. 1978. Malacostracan crustacean fauna from the Sundance Formation (Jurassic) of Wyoming. *American Museum Novitates* 2652:1–12.

McLaughlin, P.A. 1980. *Comparative Morphology of Recent Crustacea.* San Francisco: Freeman.

Moore, R.C., and L. McCormick. 1969. General Features of Crustacea. *In* R.C. Moore (ed.), *Treatise of Invertebrate Paleontology.* Part R, *Arthropoda 4, 2.* Boulder, Colorado: Geological Society of America; Lawrence, Kansas: University of Kansas Press.

Mundlos, R. 1975. Ökologie, Biostratinomie und Diagenese brachyurer Krebse aus dem Alt-Tertiär von Helmstedt (Niedersachsen, BRD). *Neues Jahrbuch für Geologie und Paläontologie, Abhandlungen* 148 (2):252–71.

Rathbun, M.J. 1926. The fossil stalk-eyed Crustacea of the Pacific Slope of North America. *Bulletin of the United States National Museum* 138:i–viii, 1–155.

——. 1935. *Fossil Crustacea of the Atlantic and Gulf Coastal Plain.* Boulder, Colorado: Geological Society of America; Lawrence: University of Kansas Press.

Schäfer, W. 1951. Fossilisations-Bedingungen brachyurer Krebse. *Abhandlungen der senckenbergischen naturforschenden Gesellschaft* 485:221–38.

——. 1972. *Ecology and Palaeoecology of Marine Environments.* Chicago: University of Chicago Press; Edinburgh: Oliver and Boyd; as *Aktno-Paläontologie nach Studien in der Nordsee,* Frankfurt am Main: Kramer, 1962.

Schmitt, W.L. 1931. *Crustaceans.* Washington, D.C.: Smithsonian Institution Press.

Schram, F.R. 1986. *Crustacea.* New York: Oxford University Press.

Schram, F.R., and R.M. Mapes. 1984. Imocaris tuberculata, n. gen., n. sp. (Crustacea: Decapoda) from the Upper Mississippian Imo Formation, Arkansas. Transactions of the *San Diego Society of Natural History* 20 (11):1–168.

Stenzel, H.B. 1945. Decapod crustaceans from the Cretaceous of Texas. *University of Texas Bureau of Economic Geology* 4401:401–76.

Tasch, P. 1973. *Paleobiology of the Invertebrates*. New York: Wiley.

Further Reading

Gore, R.H., and K.L. Heck (eds.). 1986. *Crustacean Issues 4, Crustacean Biogeography*. Boston and Rotterdam: Balkema.

Gould, S.J. 1989. *Wonderful Life: The Burgess Shale and the Nature of History*. New York: Norton; London: Hutchinson Radius, 1990.

McLaughlin, P.A. 1980. *Comparative Morphology of Recent Crustacea*. San Francisco: Freeman.

Moore, R.C. (ed.). 1969. *Treatise of Invertebrate Paleontology*. Part R,

Arthropoda 4, 2. Boulder, Colorado: Geological Society of America; Lawrence, Kansas: University of Kansas Press.

Schäfer, W. 1972. *Ecology and Palaeoecology of Marine Environments*. Chicago: University of Chicago Press; Edinburgh: Oliver and Boyd; as *Aktuo-Paläontologie nach Studien in der Nordsee*, Frankfurt am Main: Kramer, 1962.

Schmitt, W.L. 1931. *Crustaceans*. Washington, D.C.: Smithsonian Institution.

Schram, F.R. 1986. *Crustacea*. New York: Oxford University Press.

Tasch, P. 1973. *Paleobiology of the Invertebrates*. New York: Wiley; 2nd ed., 1980.

CUVIER, GEORGES

French, 1769–1832

Georges Cuvier, the "father of comparative anatomy," was born 23 August 1769 in Montbéliard, Württemberg, as Léopold-Chrêtien-Frédéric-Dayobort; he took the name Georges following the death of an elder brother of that name. The child of a poor, although bourgeois, Lutheran family from a province not annexed by France until 1793, Cuvier had to depend on his own talents to find his way. He was sent to school in Germany with the intention that he would become a civil servant for the rulers of his province. However, as no opportunity presented itself, Cuvier left for France proper and the tutorship of the children of a noble (also Protestant) family. He remained with the family throughout the worst excesses of the Terror away from Paris in Normandy.

Ambitious from the start, Cuvier moved to Paris as soon as he could and became affiliated with the *Museum d'Histoire Naturelle* stationed in the *Jardin des Plantes*. For a short time, he roomed with the man who later was to become his bitter rival, the equally young anatomist Geoffroy Saint-Hilaire. Cuvier's rise was quick. In 1795, at the age of 26, he became a member of the Académie des Sciences through his labors and his networking. In 1800 he began to teach at the College de France, and in 1803 he became the permanent secretary of the Physical Sciences division of the Académie. Under Napoléon, Cuvier became a Chevalier in 1811, and he continued to flourish under the Restoration after 1815. In 1818 Cuvier joined the Académic Française. He became a baron in 1819, a grand officier of the Legion of Honor in 1824, and a peer of France in 1831.

As a Protestant, Cuvier had to move carefully in an increasingly conservative, Catholic environment. He cleverly used his liabilities to serve the state in the realm of non-Catholic education. Fond of status, Cuvier expected deference from his inferiors, just as he displayed to his superiors. He was responsible for designing the quasi-military uniforms worn by the members of the institute, causing the British geologist Charles Lyell to remark that a meeting of the group resembled nothing so much as a gathering of well-behaved butlers. Although Cuvier was successful in the external world, his personal happiness was greatly marred by the deaths of all four of his children. While there is no reason to doubt that Cuvier upheld the tenets of the Protestant faith, it is likely that toward the end of his life, his sorrow led him to doubt the beneficence of the Deity.

Cuvier published much in his lifetime. His major works in zoology include: *Tableau élémentaire de l'histoire naturelle des animaux* (1797); *Leçons d'anatomie comparée,* written in collaboration with C. Duméril and G. Duverney (1805); and *Le régne animal* (with a section on insects by Pierre Latreille) (1817). In addition, Cuvier published a major work on paleontology, *Recherches sur les ossemens fossiles des quadrupè* (1812). The text's introduction, or *Discours préliminaire,* was printed separately under the title of *Discours sur les révolutions de la surface du globe*. At the end of his life, Cuvier was entrenched in a massive work on fish, *Histoire des poissons*. The first volume appeared in 1828, and the ninth had just been published at the time of his death in 1832. The scholar Achille Valenciennes took over the task; the series ended in 1849 with the twenty-second volume.

More than any other biologist of the modern period, Cuvier was committed to a teleological perspective. His questions always focused on the function or the ends of organisms and their parts. Aristotle, in whose works Cuvier immersed himself, particularly during his time in Normandy, was undoubtedly the greatest influence on the biologist. However, it was highly likely that Cuvier's German education also bore some influence. The hand of the German philosopher Immanuel Kant certainly can be recognized behind much that Cuvier wrote. Cuvier was notorious for his claim to be able to construct an organism from a single part—given a tooth, he demonstrated that it was possible to determine whether or not the animal was carnivorous or herbivorous. If, for example, it was a carnivore, then the organism would require other carnivore-like characteristics. It would need claws, for instance, rather than hooves, agility, as opposed to stealth. Cuvier articulated the need for the anatomist to explain in terms of final causes, or what he called, the "conditions of existence":

> Natural history nevertheless has a rational principle that is exclusive to it and which it employs with great advantage on many occasions; it is the *conditions of existence* or, popularly, *final causes.* As nothing may exist which does not include the conditions which made its existence possible, the different parts of each creature must be coordinated in such a way as to make possible the whole organism, not only in itself but in its relationship to whose which surround it, and the analysis of these condi-

tions often leads to general laws as well founded as those of calculation or experiment. (in Coleman 1964)

How was this principle to be used as a means of understanding and, in particular, of systematizing the living world? Subsequent to the conditions of existence, Cuvier thought there was a secondary principle, which he called the "subordination of parts." When once, as it were, one has a basic idea of the organism, then only certain options are open. For example, when considering a carnivore, herbivorous options are eliminated. Within the carnivore domain, however, a variety of options remain. As these are specified, fewer and fewer alternatives remain, until finally, only the organism in question is practicable.

> For a good classification . . . we employ an assiduous comparison of creatures directed by the principle of the *subordination of characters,* which itself derives from the conditions of existence. The parts of an animal possessing a mutual fitness, there are some traits of them which exclude others and there are some which require others; when we know such and such traits of an animal we may calculate those which are coexistent with them and those which are incompatible; the parts, properties or consistent traits which have the greatest number of these incompatible or coexistent relations with other animals, in other words, which exercise the most marked influence on the creature, we call *caractères importants, caractères dominateurs;* the others are the *caractères subordonès,* and there are thus different degrees of them. (in Coleman 1964)

With these principles in hand, Cuvier turned to the animal world and argued famously for the division of the animal kingdom into four major groups, or *Embranchments*. These groups or classes are the vertebrates and three groups of invertebrates: molluscs, articulata, and radiata. About these groupings, Cuvier wrote:

> In considering the animal kingdom from this point of view and being concerned with only the animals themselves, and not with their size, usefulness, our knowledge of them, great or small, or any other accessory circumstances, I have found that there exist four principal forms, four general plans, upon which all of the animals seem to have been modeled and whose lesser division, no matter what names naturalists have dignified them with, are only modifications superficially founded on development or on the addition of certain parts, but which in no way change the essence of the plan. (in Coleman 1964)

It is hardly an exaggeration to say that the major task of comparative anatomy in the nineteenth century was the refining and, where need be, the refuting of Cuvier's divisions. Many a reputation was founded on demonstrating that the great anatomist's system needed revision.

Cuvier's excursions into paleontology and geology were no less influential, although many of his ideas concerning the latter were simply modified hypotheses from the eighteenth century. It is interesting to note that Cuvier was one of the first to interpret the fossil record in a progressive fashion. He recognized that the most primitive forms are found in the lowest rock strata in the fossil record and, consequently, are the oldest, whereas the more sophisticated and familiar forms are highest in the record, and, consequently, the youngest. Cuvier explained this phenomenon in terms of a series of great upheavals, or what his English translators termed, "catastrophes." He maintained that organisms were wiped periodically from the Earth by floods and fires and other natural factors, allowing for an invasion or proliferation of new forms. Cuvier probably did not believe that there was a reinvention of organisms after each catastrophe, but rather that life-forms migrated from other points on the globe. As a sophisticated French thinker, Cuvier would not tolerate theological incursions into his science. However, glimpses of his Protestant reading of the Bible can be occasionally discerned. Indeed, he seems to have used the Bible as a pertinent document about the past. Cuvier identifies Noah's Flood as the last cataclysm.

Although a progressionist, Cuvier should never be thought of as a quasi-evolutionist. Perhaps religion was a factor in his opposition to evolution, a doctrine then being promulgated by his colleague at the Muséum, the invertebrate specialist Jean Baptiste de Lamarck. But, it certainly was not religion that formed Cuvier's arguments against evolution. On the empirical level, Cuvier provided much that called the doctrine into question, most notably the gaps in the fossil record and the famous mummified specimens Napoléon's conquering army brought back from Egypt. Because the birds and other organisms from the time of the Pharaohs were identical to those living today, Cuvier believed that he had definitive proof against organic change over time. Lamarck, to the contrary, argued that such evidence simply demonstrated that change takes place over a longer period of time.

Cuvier's philosophy of zoology was even more powerful than his empirical arguments. His conditions-of-existence thesis rendered evolution an impossibility. If organisms change from one form to another, then at some point in the process of change it is necessary to come out of teleological or adaptive focus. An organism half the way down the path of evolution is neither fish nor fowl. According to Cuvier's line of reasoning, this was an impossibility. All organisms must fit neatly into their categories and there can be no transitional forms. This is a logical, not simply an empirical claim.

Sociological and political factors certainly influenced Cuvier in his opposition to evolutionism. In the years after the French Revolution, this doctrine was held to be radical and was associated with those antiauthoritarians who were committed to progressivist and secular doctrines of change. Cuvier, the consummate civil servant, abominated all such beliefs. He regarded them as responsible for those terrible events that had rocked France at the end of the eighteenth century. Hence, he was determined above all else to oppose the scientific flagship of such beliefs and argued vehemently against evolution. On the other hand, there was also a personal motive in his demonstrations. As a Protestant living in a conservative France, it was necessary for Cuvier to portray himself as purer than the pure. He used his opposition to evolutionism to convince his political masters of his orthodoxy and utility.

Cuvier linked other quasi-scientific approaches to nature with the theory of evolution. That branch of German morphology that stresses homology (fundamental similarities based on common descent) over function, *Naturphilosophie,* was particularly objectionable. Cuvier was first exposed to these ideas as a student in Germany, and he continued to oppose them throughout his life. There is little doubt that in some sense he saw *Naturphilosophie* as being pantheistic. This doctrine, which readily lends itself to a theological interpretation, stresses the unity of organisms as a function of transcendent ideas (perhaps of a Platonic form). Furthermore, *Naturphilosophie* emphasize ideal forms, or archetypes, and recognizes homologies between organisms as opposed to the importance of the role of adaptation and function. The entire theory represents the antithesis of Cuvier's philosophy of nature; hence, he remained an ardent opponent to this school of thought.

This opposition generated vehement conflicts with Geoffroy Saint-Hilaire, a proponent of a homegrown form of *Naturphilosophie.* (Georges Buffon was probably the greater influence, owing to his full awareness of the similarities between very different forms of animals.) Through the second decade of the nineteenth century, Geoffroy pursued with increasing success his anatomical investigations of the isomorphisms, or homologies, that exist between different parts of different animals. His triumph was his demonstration of the homological nature of the vertebrate ear. By the 1820s Geoffroy was ready to extend his investigations and hypotheses, even arguing in favor of links between vertebrates and invertebrates. At this point, Geoffroy began to underpin his arguments with evolutionary ideas, no doubt stemming from Geoffroy's long friendship with Lamarck. Cuvier was directly challenged, not just in his philosophy, but in his classification of organisms into absolutely nonoverlapping *embranchements.* Toward the end of his life, Cuvier became embroiled in a very public and notorious debate with Geoffroy over the existence of analogies between organisms of different kinds. History has typically regarded this division as one related to the theory of evolution. The rift, however, runs considerably deeper, separating two completely different perspectives regarding the organic world.

Cuvier was one of the greatest scientists in the history of biology, despite his position on the wrong side of the most important debate of all. His renown can be explained best by one of those brilliant paradoxes for which French intellectuals are noted. The late Michel Foucault (1970) argued that Cuvier influenced the history of evolutionism more than the evolutionist Lamarck. In this evaluation, Foucault noted that it was Cuvier particularly who emphasized the teleological nature of the organic world. Charles Darwin elaborated on this point in his theory of natural selection, to explain the adaptiveness of organisms. Like all paradoxes, this one is an exaggeration. Lamarck's place in the history of evolutionism remains undiminished—certainly, he was influential in Darwin becoming an evolutionist. However, Foucault correctly draws attention to Cuvier for revolutionizing modern thinking about the nature of organisms and the connections between them. Although he may not have been able to provide an underlying the-

oretical interpretation of the organic world, Cuvier certainly prepared the way for those who would do so later in the century.

MICHAEL RUSE

Works Cited

Coleman, W. 1964. *Georges Cuvier Zoologist: A Study in the History of Evolution Theory.* Cambridge, Massachusetts: Harvard University Press.

Foucault, M. 1970. *The Order of Things: An Archaeology of the Human Sciences.* New York: Pantheon; London: Tavistock Publications; as *Les Mots et les choses: Une archeologie des sciences humaines,* Paris: Gallimard, 1966.

Biography

Born in Montbéliard, Württemberg, 23 August 1769. Studied comparative anatomy, Académie Caroline (Karlsschule), Stuttgart, 1784–88. Worked as a tutor, Caen, 1788–95; began work as an assistant, Muséum d'Histoire Naturelle, 1795; appointed chair of general natural history, Collège de France, 1800; became professor of comparative anatomy, Muséum d'Histoire Naturelle, 1802; elected to council of state, 1813; named vice president, Ministry of the Interior, 1817. Elected member (1795) and permanent secretary (1803), Académie des Sciences; granted title *chevalier,* 1811; elected member, Académie Française, 1818; created a baron, 1819; made grand officer, Légion d'Honneur, 1824; made a peer of France, 1831; nominated as minister of the interior, 1832. Died in Paris, 13 May 1832.

Major Publications

1797. *Tableau élémentaire de l'histoire naturelle des animaux.* Paris: Baudoin.

1800–5. With A.M.C. Duméril and G.L. Duverney. *Leçons d'anatomie comparée.* Paris: Baudoin.

1810. *Rapport historique sur les progrès des sciences naturelles depuis 1789, et sur leur état actuel.* Paris: Imprimerie Impériale.

1812. *Recherches sur les ossements fossiles des quadrupèdes.* Paris: Déterville. [The first chapter, Discours préliminaire, was published independently in 1825 as *Discours sur les révolutions de la surface du globe,* Paris: Dufour and d'Ocagne.]

1817a. With P. Latreille. *Le règne animal distribué d'après son organisation, pour servir de base à l'histoire naturelle des animaux et d'introduction à l'anatomie comparée.* 4 vols. Paris: Déterville; 2nd ed., in 5 vols., 1829–30.

1817b. *Mémoires pour servir à l'histoire et à l'anatomie des mollusques.* Paris: Déterville.

1828–31. *Histoire naturelle des poissons, ouvrage contenant plus de cinq mille espèces de ces animaux, décrites d'ápres nature.* Vols. 1–9, Paris, Levrault. [Vols. 10–22 edited by M.A. Valenciennes, 1832–49.]

Further Reading

Coleman, W. 1964. *Georges Cuvier Zoologist: A Study in the History of Evolution Theory.* Cambridge, Massachusetts: Harvard University Press.

Foucault, M. 1970. *The Order of Things: An Archaeology of the Human Sciences.* New York: Pantheon; London: Tavistock Publications; as

Les Mots et les choses: Une archéologie des sciences humaines, Paris: Gallimard, 1966.

Outram, D. 1984. *Georges Cuvier: Vocation, Science and Authority in Post-Revolutionary France.* Manchester and Dover, New Hampshire: Manchester University Press.

Ruse, M. 1979. *The Darwinian Revolution: Science Red in Tooth and Claw.* Chicago: University of Chicago Press.

———. 1996. *Monad to Man: The Concept of Progress in Evolutionary Biology.* Cambridge, Massachusetts: Harvard University Press.

CYCADS

Cycadophytes encompass both the order Cycadales, which includes fossil and recent species, and Cycadeoidales (Bennetti-tales), which includes only extinct species. Cycadales and Cycadeoi-dales were among the dominate plants of the Mid-Mesozoic.

The order Cycadales includes nine recent genera, all found in the tropics and subtropics, often in areas that are arid and well-drained. The nine genera are: *Bowenia, Lepidozamia,* and *Macrozamia* from Australia; *Ceratozamia* and *Dioon* from Mexico; *Cycas* from Australia, China, the East Indies, India, and southern Japan; *Encephalartos* from central and southern Africa; *Microcycas* from western Cuba; *Stangeria* from southern Africa; and *Zamia* from Florida, the West Indies, Mexico, Central America, northern South America, and from the Andes Mountains south to Chile. Characters that help identify a cycad leaf include a central stalk that is never forked and veins that are pinnate (branch from a central midrib) and nearly parallel.

Cycads generally look similar to palms and tree ferns. The stem can range from short and bulbous to tall and columnar. The size ranges from 10 centimeters to 18 meters, although the average is about two meters. A reconstruction of *Cycas revolutas* is featured in Figure 1. The evergreen leaves are large, tough, and bear leaflets, or pinnae, along each side of a central axis. They also can be spiny or bipinnate, having primary and secondary divisions of the pinnae. The traces of the leaf bases in the stem are unique among the gymnosperms (the vascular plants that produce naked seeds, such as conifers). All recent cycads that have been investigated carefully are dioecious, which means that each plant is either a male that produces the "microspores," or a female that bears the "megaspores." (These structures form one of the major cycles of plant growth, the gametophyte stage.)

Cycads and cycadeoids are similar in their vegetative parts but differ very much in their reproductive structures, even though both have monocolpate pollen (with a single germinal furrow or "colpa"). To determine if a leaf is from a cycad or a cycadeoid, botanists must study the stomata (small openings for gases to pass through the outermost layer of a leaf). In cycads the mother cell of the stoma (the original cell that gave rise to the other cells) divides into two guard cells; this is called the "haplocheilic type" (simple-lipped, Figure 2). In cycadeoids, the mother cell of the stoma divides into three cells. This is called the "syndetocheilic type" (compound-lipped, Figure 3).

The earliest evidence of Cycadales is the genus *Spermopteris* from the Upper Carboniferous rock strata of Kansas (Figure 4). When the leaf carries the ovary that later develops into a seed, it is called the "ovulate phase." In *Spermopteris* the seeds were situated along the margins of the leaf, one row on each side. The sterile leaves (those with no reproductive function) are called *Taeniopteris;* these are common in the Upper Paleozoic. *Archaeocycas* (Figure 5) and *Phasmatocycas* (Figure 6) are from the Lower Permian of Kansas. *Archaeocycas* had an ovule-bearing leaf with cycadlike characters. *Phasmatocycas* was an entire leaf with two rows of ovules attached to the lower surface (Figure 7). Other fossils from the Permian, Triassic, and Jurassic periods show characteristics identical to those of recent cycads. A common cycad leaf from the Jurassic is *Nilssonia comptus* (Figure 8).

The order Cycadeoidales (also called Bennettitales) appeared in the Triassic period and became extinct by the end of the Cretaceous period. The earliest suggestion of cycadeoids is found in some Carboniferous seed ferns that have syndetocheilic stomata. However, cycadeoids did not become common until the Triassic, and by the Late Cretaceous cycadeoids were living on most continents. Common cycadeoid leaf fossils are *Anomozamites* (Figure 9). Figure 10 shows an example of an *Anomozamites minor* leaf impression. Other common forms are *Nilssoniopteris* (Figures 11, 12), *Otozamites, Pterophyllum* (Figure 13), *Ptilophyllum,* and *Zamites.*

Cycadeoidales includes two families—the Williamsoniaceae and the Cycadeoidaceae. Williamsoniaceae is characterized by long slender stems with few branches. The best known is *Williamsonia sewardiana* from the Jurassic of India. It was a small tree, approximately two meters tall. Near the top of the trunk were pinnate leaves of the *Ptilophyllum* type (leaflets alternated on either side of the midrib instead of occurring in pairs). Cycadeoidaceae species are characterized by massive trunks with a crown of leaves of the *Ptilophyllum* type; a very popular reconstruction is *Cycadeoidea* sp. (Figure 14). The genera *Williamsoniella* and *Cycadeoidea* can be distinguished from cycads by their bisporangiate cones, which means that both seed- and pollen-producing organs are in the same closed cone. *Cycadeoidea* cones had very short branches that never extended above the surface of the trunk.

The genus *Wielandiella* appeared in Late Triassic times in Sweden. Its stem is thin (1.5 centimeters in diameter) and divides into two "branches," one of which terminated in a cone. The leaves are approximately eight centimeters long and are of the *Anomozamites* type (Figures 9, 10). The center of the cone holds seed-producing organs; this area is surrounded by a ring of pollen-producing organs. *Williamsoniella,* from the Jurassic deposits of Yorkshire, was a shrubby plant that had leaves of the *Nilssoniopteris* type (Figures 11, 12). The isolated stem is called *Bucklandia indica,* and the fronds are of the cycadeoid type *Ptilophyllum cutchense.* Unattached pollen-producing organs of cycadeoids are iden-

Figure 1. Recent *Cycas revolutas* from Naples, Italy. Illustration by Brenda Middagh.

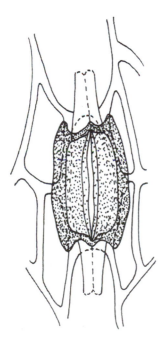

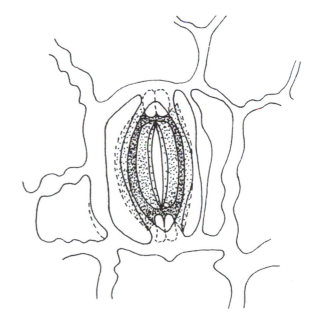

Figure 2. Haplocheilie stoma of *Microcycas* sp. Redrawn by Brenda Middagh from Florin (1933).

Figure 3. *Pseudocycas* sp. syndetochelic stomata. Redrawn by Brenda Middagh from Florin (1933).

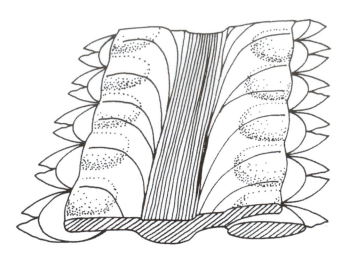

Figure 4. *Spermopteris coriaceae*. Redrawn by Brenda Middagh from Cridland and Morris (1960).

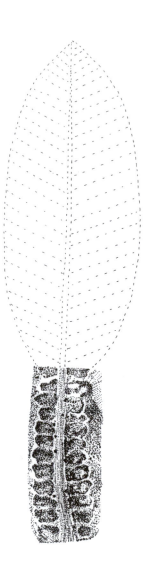

Figure 6. *Phasmatocycas* sp. Permian. Redrawn by Brenda Middagh from Mamay (1976).

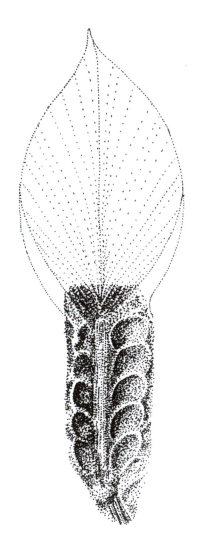

Figure 5. *Archaeocycas* sp. Permian. Redrawn by Brenda Middagh from Mamay (1976).

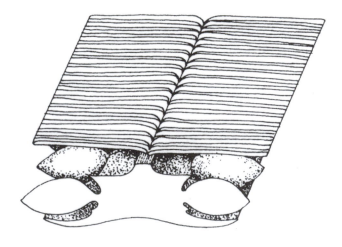

Figure 7. *Phasmatocycas* showing details of sporophyll and attached ovules. Redrawn by Brenda Middagh from Crane (1988) with permission.

Figure 8. *Nilssonia comptus* from Yorkshire in the collection of University of Copenhagen. Scale, one centimeter. Photograph by Rasmus B. Koppehus, from the collection at the University in Copenhagen, Denmark.

Figure 10. *Anomozamites minor.* Scale, one centimeter. Photograph by Rasmus B. Koppehus, from the collection at the University in Copenhagen, Denmark.

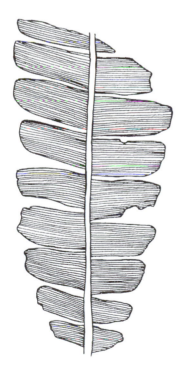

Figure 9. *Anomozamites* sp. Jurassic. Redrawn by Brenda Middagh from Harris (1932).

Figure 11. *Nilssoniopteris major* Jurassic. Redrawn by Brenda Middagh from Harris (1969).

Figure 12. *Nilssoniopteris major* from Yorkshire, UK. Scale, one centimeter. Photograph by Rasmus B. Koppehus, from the collection at the University in Copenhagen, Denmark.

tified as *Weltrichia;* they are found in the Jurassic beds of England and India but are rare.

Cycadeoids self-pollinated, but some *Cycadeoidea* cones show evidence of insect borings, which suggests that insects might have had an influence on pollination. It has been suggested that self-pollination was an important factor in the extinction of the cycadeoids. Without the genetic "mixing" that results from cross-fertilization, cycads were less able to evolve and adapt in response to environmental changes (Taylor and Taylor 1993).

Fossil cycadeoid trunks have been found in North America, Europe, and Asia. The first described fossilized cycadophyte trunk came from the Isle of Portland in the United Kingdom. William Buckland, English naturalist of the early nineteenth century, established the Cycadeoideae in 1813, with two species of Cycadeoidea, noting their similarity to living *Cycas* and *Zamia.* The richest place for cycadeoids in North America was discovered in the Black Hills of South Dakota (Andrews 1980) and was made know by G. R. Wieland (1906, 1916) in the two volumes of his *American Fossil Cycads,* which hold much information on recent cycads and fossil cycadeoids.

The origins of Cycadales and Cycadeoidales still are not solved, but cladistic analyses (based upon unique shared traits) support a hypothesis that Cycadales originated from the seed fern order Medullosales of the Paleozoic (Crane 1985). The pollen

Figure 13. *Pterophyllum* sp. from Lünz, Ostria. Scale, one centimeter. Photograph by Rasmus B. Koppehus, from the collection at the University in Copenhagen, Denmark.

organs of the Cycadeoidea have been compared to seed ferns (Pteridospermales). This group once was thought to be the link between ferns and cycads, although scholars now believe that the two groups evolved independently. It has also been suggested that Cycadeoidea are related closely to angiosperms (flowering plants) (Doyle and Donohue 1986).

It has been mentioned that a cycad is a "living fossil," just like *Ginkgo biloba.* Both of these plants have existed, virtually unchanged, since they arose in the Mesozoic. Looking at them is like looking at the ancient past.

EVA BUNDGAARD KOPPELHUS

See also Ginkgos; Gymnosperms; Seed Ferns

Works Cited

Andrews, H.N. 1980. *The Fossil Hunters: In Search of Ancient Plants.* Ithaca, New York, and London: Cornell University Press.

Figure 14. *Cycadeoidea* sp. reconstruction of plant from the Cretaceous. Redrawn by Brenda Middagh from Delevoryas (1971).

Crane, P.D. 1985. Phylogenetic analysis of seed plants and the origin of angiosperms. *Annals Missouri Botanical Garden* 72:716–93.

———. 1988. Major clades of relationships in the "higher" gymnosperms. *In* C.B. Beck (ed.), *Origin and Evolution of Angiosperms.* New York: Columbia University Press.

Cridland, A.A., and J.E. Morris. 1960. Spermopteris, a new genus of pteridosperms from the Upper Pennsylvanian series of Kansas. *American Journal of Botany* 47:855–59.

Devevoryas, T. 1971. Biotic provinces and the Jurassic–Cretaceous flora transition. *Proceedings of the North American Paleontological Convention,* Part L, 1660–74.

Doyle, J.A., and M.J. Donohue. 1986. Seed plant phylogeny and the origin of angiosperms: An experimental cladistic approach. *Botanical Review* 52:321–431.

Florin, R. 1933. Studien uber die Cycadales des Mesozzoikums. Kungl. *Svenska Vetenskapsakademiens Handlinger* 3(12): 1–134.

Foster, A.S., and E.M. Gifford Jr. 1974. *Comparative Morphology of Vascular Plants.* 2nd ed., San Francisco: Freeman.

Harris, T.M. 1932. The fossil flora of Scoresby Sound East Greenland. *Meddelelser om Grønland* 85:1–133.

———. 1969. *The Yorkshire Jurassic Flora III. Bennettitales.* London: British Museum (Natural History).

Mamay, S.H. 1976. *Paleozoic Origin of the Cycads.* U.S. Geological Survey Professional Paper, 934. Washington, D.C.: U.S. Government Printing Office.

Stewart, W.N., and G.W. Rothwell. 1993. *Paleobotany and the Evolution of Plants.* 2nd ed., Cambridge and New York: Cambridge University Press.

Taylor, N.T., and E.L. Taylor. 1993. *The Biology and Evolution of Fossil Plants.* Englewood Cliffs, New Jersey: Prentice-Hall.

Tidwell, D.W. 1975. *Common Fossil Plants of Western North America.* Provo, Utah: Brigham Young University Press.

Wieland, G.R. 1906. *American Fossil Cycads.* Carnegie Institution of Washington Publication 34. Washington, D.C.: Carnegie Institution of Washington.

———. 1916. *American Fossil Cycads*. Vol. 2, *Taxonomy*. Washington, D.C.: Carnegie Institution of Washington.

Further Reading

Andrews, H.N. 1980. *The Fossil Hunters: In Search of Ancient Plants*. Ithaca, New York, and London: Cornell University Press.

Foster, A.S., and E.M. Gifford Jr. 1959. *Comparative Morphology of Vascular Plants*. San Francisco: Freeman; 2nd ed., 1974.

Stewart, W.N. 1983. *Paleobotany and the Evolution of Plants*. Cambridge and New York: Cambridge University Press; 2nd ed., with G.W. Rothwell, 1993.

Taylor, N.T., and E.L. Taylor. 1993. *The Biology and Evolution of Fossil Plants*. Englewood Cliffs, New Jersey: Prentice-Hall.

Tidwell, D.W. 1975. *Common Fossil Plants of Western North America*. Provo, Utah: Brigham Young University Press; 2nd ed., Washington, D.C.: Smithsonian, 1998.

Wieland, G.R. 1906. *American Fossil Cycads*. Carnegie Institution of Washington Publication 34. Washington, D.C.: Carnegie Institution of Washington.

———. 1916. *American Fossil Cycads*. Vol. 2, *Taxonomy*. Washington, D.C.: Carnegie Institution of Washington.

D

DART, RAYMOND ARTHUR

Australian/South African, 1893–1988

Raymond Arthur Dart always will be remembered for his recognition of *Australopithecus africanus,* the first Plio-Pleistocene hominid to be discovered in Africa. The chain of events began with a holotype—a single specimen upon which the description of a new species is based. The specimen, now known to represent *A. africanus,* was recovered from Buxton Limeworks, near the Tswana town of Taung ("the place of the lion"), north of Kimberley, South Africa, early in November 1924. Previously, the deposit had yielded cercopithecid fossils, mainly of *Parapapio.* The skull of what came to be called "the Taung child" was brought to Dart at the Department of Anatomy, University of the Witwatersrand, Johannesburg, on 28 November 1924. His account of the fossil appeared in *Nature* on 7 February 1925. He regarded it as a "man-ape," because the skull showed departures from the morphology (shape and structure) of present-day African great apes, *Pan* and *Gorilla.* Dart recognized these departures as humanlike, derived (specialized) characters, such as evidence that the head had been poised on a nearly upright spinal column and the presence of relatively small canine teeth. On the other hand, the endocranial capacity—the size of the inside of the skull, an indicator for brain size—was small, as in *Pan* and *Gorilla.* When Dart made a cast of the inside of the skull, he thought he could detect on the cast the impression of the "lunate sulcus" at the back as in humans, unlike in apes, where it is more toward the front. Later studies failed to confirm this claim.

Because of the skull's unique characteristics, Dart erected a new genus and species to accommodate the Taung skull, but its features, he believed, excluded the genus from both of the recognized hominoid families at the time, Hominidae and Pongidae. He proposed a new family Homo-simiadae ("man-apes"). This proposal gained no support. If there were a case for a new family, the correct term would be Australopithecidae, and Dart later adopted it (1929). Most scholars of the day believed the Taung skull belonged to an unusual ape. However, W.J. Sollas (1926) at Oxford University, from a study of median sagittal craniograms (skull sutures, or places where bones join), concluded that Taung was closer to the human form. He even said that he might have called it "Homunculus." In 1933 Robert Broom was the first to make a firm claim that *Australopithecus* belonged in the hominid family (as then recognized), but it was not until the 1950s that the hominid status of *Australopithecus* became accepted generally.

Australopithecus and Dart's claims for its status are an example of what Stent (1972) called a "premature discovery," that is, the logic of Dart's interpretation of the Taung skull could not be explained in the context of the generally accepted knowledge of the day. Among the tenets of the prevailing paradigm (system of beliefs) in 1925 were these: (1) humans had evolved in Asia, not Africa; (2) claims from Africa were suspect (owing to a European bias against Africa) (Bowler 1992); (3) the brain must have enlarged early in hominid evolution, not later; (4) Piltdown, a specimen discovered in Piltdown, England, in 1908, with its apelike jaw and its modern human brain, showed the pathway of hominid evolution—in comparison, Taung had no bearing on hominid phylogeny (genetic history); (5) specific traits that were distinctive to particular species could be discerned unequivocally only after puberty (Taung was a child); (6) the dating of an ancestor should fall in the early Pleistocene, which made Taung too recent. These tenets had to be addressed, revised, and replaced before the paradigm proposed by Dart could be substituted (Tobias 1996).

Such changes take time. The turning point followed the discovery of many australopithecine fossils during African expeditions at Sterkfontein, Kromdraai, Makapansgat, and Swartkrans; the appearance of Broom's monographs on the australopithecines; the morphological studies of Wilfrid LeGros Clark; the provision of data on the variability of extant apes by S. Zuckerman, E. Ashton, and others; and the exposure of the fact that the Piltdown fossil was actually a forgery in 1953 and 1955. Dart lived long enough to witness the turning of the tide and to see his discovery rated as one of the 20 most important scientific discoveries that molded human thought in the twentieth century (*Science* 1984).

Two historical aspects of the discovery may be highlighted. In *The Descent of Man* (1871), Charles Darwin held that Africa had been the home of the human family. Dart (1925) claimed triumphantly that the Taung discovery vindicated the Darwinian prophecy, and Elliot Smith hailed it as "the first definite confirmation of the opinion expressed by Darwin." In July 1925 the Scopes trial took place in Dayton, Tennessee, when the schoolmaster John Thomas Scopes was found guilty of teaching evolution in a Dayton high school. Against this background, R. Broom (1925) declared, "if the discovery [of Taung] results in the universal acceptance of the belief in man's evolution from the lower forms, the discovery of *Australopithecus* may have nearly as great an influence on human progress as the publication of Darwin's *Origin of Species.*"

For a few decades after the Taung controversy, Dart played little further part in palaeoanthropology. Then, after World War II he reentered the field as a result of discoveries made by a party of students at Makapansgat, north of Johannesburg. The area's limeworks were rich in fossil bones. From 1947 onward, australopithecine fossils were found there by James Kitching and Alun Hughes. Dart described what he called a new species of *Australopithecus*, namely *A. prometheus* (later classified as *A. Africanus transvaalensis*). Dart's study of thousands of broken bones of antelopes from the Makapansgat Formation led him to a revolutionary idea. He proposed that before the Stone Age there had been a Bone Age, one in which *Australopithecus* had used bones, teeth, and horns of prey animals as implements. This novel concept, Dart's (1957) "Osteodontokeratic Culture," aroused much interest but largely was rejected as evidence accumulated that big cats, hyenas, and porcupines were probably the bone-breakers and accumulators (Brain 1981). There was, however, a remarkable spin-off. When Dart proposed his theory in 1955, little was known of how other animals—or elements of the environment, such as sun and water—altered bones after death. To test Dart's hypothesis, scholars had to create new studies, and a new discipline came into being, taphonomy (*taphos,* Greek, a grave), which is the study of fossilization. Dart's ideas were a major catalyst in the development of this field. Thus, it may be claimed that Dart triggered a revolution in knowledge about humankind's place in nature and precipitated the foundation of a new scientific discipline.

PHILLIP V. TOBIAS

Works Cited

Bowler, P. 1992. Commentary on Piltdown: The case against Keith. *Current Anthropology* 33:260–61.

Brain, C.K. 1981. *The Hunters or the Hunted? An Introduction to African Cave Taphonomy.* Chicago and London: University of Chicago Press.

Broom, R. 1925. On the newly discovered South African man-ape. *Natural History* 25:409–18.

———. 1933. *The Coming of Man: Was it Accident or Design?* London: Witherby.

Darwin, C. 1871. *The Descent of Man.* London: Murray; New York: Appleton.

Sollas, W.J. 1926. A sagittal section of the skull of *Australopithecus africanus. Quarterly Journal of the Geological Society of London* 82:1–11.

Stent, G. 1972. Prematurity and uniqueness in scientific discovery. *Scientific American* 227:84–93.

Tobias, P.V. 1996. Premature discoveries in science with especial reference to *Australopithecus* and *Homo habilis. Proceedings of the American Philosophical Society* 140:49–64.

Biography

Born in Toowong, Brisbane, Australia, 4 February 1893. Received B.Sc., University of Queensland, 1913; M.Sc., University of Queensland, 1915; M.B., Ch.M., University of Sydney, 1917; M.D., University of Sydney, 1927. Senior demonstrator in anatomy (1919–20, 1921–22), lecturer in histology (1921–22), University College, London; fellow, Rockefeller Foundation, 1920–21; head, Department of Anatomy (1923–58), dean, Faculty of Medicine (1925–43), and emeritus professor (1958–88), University of the Witwatersrand, Johannesburg; United Steelworkers of America Professor of Anthropology, Avery Postgraduate Institute, Institute for the Achievement of Human Potential, Philadelphia, 1966–86. Recipient, Senior Captain Scott Memorial Medal, South African Biological Society, 1955; Viking Fund Medal and Award for Physical Anthropology, Wenner-Gren Foundation of New York, 1958. Member of such scholarly and professional organizations as the Royal Society of South Africa; South African Archaeological Society; South African Association for the Advancement of Science; South African Museums Association; and South African Society for Physiotherapy. Recognized and named *Australopithecus africanus,* 1925; *Australopithecus prometheus (A. africanus transvaalensis),* 1947. Died in Sandton, Johannesburg, South Africa, 22 November 1988.

Major Publications

1925. *Australopithecus africanus:* The man-ape of South Africa. *Nature* 115:195–99.

1929a. Mammoths and other fossil elephants of the Vaal and Limpopo watersheds. *South African Journal of Science* 26:698–731.

1929b. Notes on the Taung skull. *South African Journal of Science* 26:648–58.

1948. Promethean *Australopithecus* from Makapansgat valley. *Nature* 162:375–76.

1949. Innominate fragments of *Australopithecus prometheus. American Journal of Physical Anthropology* 7:301–34.

1954. *Africa's Place in the Human Story.* Johannesburg: South African Broadcast Corporation.

1955. Cultural status of the South African man-apes. *Annual Report of the Board of Regents of the Smithsonian Institution* 317–38.

1956a. The myth of bone-accumulating hyena. *American Anthropologist* 58:40–62.

1956b. The relationships of brain size and brain pattern to human status. *South African Journal of Medical Sciences* 21:23–45.

1957. *The Osteodontokeratic Culture of Australopithecus Prometheus.* Transvaal Museum Memoirs, 10. Pretoria: Transvaal Museum.

1959. With D. Craig. *Adventures with the Missing Link.* New York: Harper; London: Hamilton; 3rd. ed., Philadelphia: Better Baby, 1982.

1961. The Makapansgat pink breccia australopithecine skull. *American Journal of Physical Anthropology* 20:110–26.

1963. The carnivorous propensity of baboons. *Tenth Symposium of Zoological Society of London* 10:46–56.

1964. The ecology of the South African man-apes. *In* D.H.S. Davis (ed.), *Ecological Studies in Southern Africa.* The Hague: Junk.

1968. *Beyond Antiquity: A Series of Radio Lectures on the Origin of Man.* Johannesburg: South African Broadcast Corporation.

Further Reading

Broom, R. 1950. *Finding the Missing Link.* London: Watts.

Tobias, P.V. 1984. *Dart, Taung and the "Missing Link."* Johannesburg: Witwatersrand University Press.

Wheelhouse, R. 1983. *Raymond Arthur Dart: A Pictorial Profile, Professor Dart's Discovery of the "Missing Link."* Sydney: Transpareon.

DARWIN, CHARLES ROBERT

English, 1809–82

Charles Robert Darwin was born 9 February 1809 in Shrewsbury, England. His paternal grandfather was Erasmus Darwin, the eighteenth-century physician and evolutionist. His maternal grandfather was Josiah Wedgwood, the industrialist responsible for the development of the pottery trade in England. His father, Robert Darwin, was a respected physician in the English Midlands who apparently amassed a fortune through money lending.

Charles Darwin was educated first at Shrewsbury school, one of the great so-called public schools (in reality, private schools) of England. He then attended the medical program at Edinburgh University for two years before realizing that he did not want to become a physician. In 1827 Darwin went to Cambridge University to complete a Bachelor of Arts degree; he intended to become an Anglican clergyman. In 1831, he accepted the position of captain's companion on board the British Warship H.M.S. *Beagle,* which was about to depart on an exploratory trip around South America. The *Beagle* voyage lasted approximately five years, returning to England in 1836. After his return, Darwin worked first in Cambridge, then in London. After marrying his first cousin, Emma Wedgwood, he left London and settled in the village of Downe in Kent, where he and his wife lived for the rest of their lives, raising the large family typical of Victorians.

Racked with an unknown illness after his return to England, Darwin became a semirecluse. Fortunately, the family's great wealth relieved any pressing material needs so that he could devote all his energies to his scientific endeavors. Recognized as a great scientist even during his lifetime, Darwin received many honors, culminating in his burial at Westminster Abbey beside the great Sir Isaac Newton.

Although Darwin's education was not formally scientific in any sense, from childhood on he exhibited a keen interest in science. Later, while at Edinburgh, he socialized with natural historians and first was exposed to Jean-Baptiste de Lamarck's theory that organisms evolve through the inheritance of acquired characters. (This theory posits that the behavior of an animal affects its physical makeup; the animal then passes on the change to its offspring.) At Cambridge, Darwin joined the scientific society, and for a full three years he attended lectures given by the noted professor of botany, John Henslow. Toward the end of his studies at Cambridge, Darwin became captivated by the geologist Adam Sedgwick and accompanied him to Wales for an intensive course in practical geology before embarking on the *Beagle* voyage. The geologist Charles Lyell however, was to become the most significant scientific influence in Darwin's life.

Darwin first encountered Lyell through his writings, long before meeting him in person. Darwin read the first volume of Lyell's *Principles of Geology* (1830) and had the second and third volumes (published in 1832 and 1833, respectively) sent to him while on his voyage. Almost immediately, Darwin became a resolute Lyellian and worked diligently to find evidence supporting "uniformitarianism" (Lyell's theory on the history of the Earth—it replaces the Biblical story of creation with one of natural factors

working over a period of time.) In so doing, Darwin disregarded Sedgwick's teachings of "catastrophism" (it promotes a series of revolutions, or catastrophes, as the primary factor in the history of the Earth). Not only did he reject Sedgwick's concept of major upheavals, Darwin maintained that the Earth exists in a kind of steady state, subject to only minor fluctuations. He therefore denied that the Earth is headed in a specific direction, irreversibly from hot to cold, for instance. In an effort to substantiate his beliefs, Darwin sought evidence for changes in the past that could be explained by causes operating today. He strove to interpret geological events in terms of Lyell's "theory of climate," a theory in which climate changes on the Earth are seen to be a function of naturally occurring rises and falls of the land. The new land-water distributions then create significant variations in temperature, rainfall, and other climatic factors. This Lyellian approach led Darwin almost immediately to his famed theory concerning coral reefs. He argued that the existence of such reefs are the result of the gradual sinking of the islands around which the reefs occur. The coral, a living organism that thrives near the surface of the sea, continues to grow upward as the land sinks. Darwin was later to devote an entire book to this topic.

In South America, Darwin continued his geological investigations. He was much impressed by fossil remains of animals significantly larger than any living examples. At the same time, Darwin began to focus his attention on biogeography, the study of animal and plant distributions as indicators of past areas of relative rise and decline. With this background, Darwin was prepared to appreciate the peculiar distributions of the birds and reptiles on the Galápagos Islands in the Pacific, a place that the *Beagle* visited late in 1835. While the giant tortoise and birds (primarily mockingbirds, but also those that are now known as "Darwin's finches") are very similar from island to island, they are not quite identical. At this point, however, while on the voyage, Darwin was not yet an evolutionist. Some months after his return to England in early 1837, the ornithologist John Gould assured Darwin that the specimens he had collected on the islands were of different species. Reasoning that the only natural process that could explain these and other phenomena was evolution, Darwin slipped quietly and easily over the divide.

It was not until late 1838 that Darwin hit upon the mechanism for which he is best known: natural selection as an outcome of the struggle for existence. Darwin arrived at this theory after his extensive study of animal and plant breeding practices as conducted for hundreds of years by farmers and growers. When a farmer chose the animals that he wished to breed, he was looking for certain valuable characteristics—perhaps milk production in a dairy herd, for instance. The cow and bull with the best history were the animals that were "most fit" for reproduction, and the process of selection was "artificial selection." In "natural selection," the bull that was most fit would be the one that could maintain control over a herd of cows and be strong enough to fight off other bulls.

Darwin's reading of a conservative sociopolitical tract by the

Reverend Thomas Robert Malthus, *An Essay on the Principle of Population*—a work in which the struggle for existence is described graphically—led Darwin to apply the struggle to nature. He adapted Malthus' doctrine by arguing that the ongoing process of evolutionary change was caused by the struggle for existence and the natural equivalent of artificial selection.

Darwin's theory was more than just a mechanism for change, however. In his acceptance of the natural theology of the day, gleaned primarily from Archdeacon William Paley's *Natural Theology,* Darwin was convinced that the most important aspect of organic nature is its design and order. He recognized that organisms are not just randomly thrown together; instead, they are sophisticated entities with "adaptations" that enable them to function, survive, and reproduce. Natural selection precisely addressed this issue and provided the mechanism to explain sophisticated organic features such as the hand and the eye. When Darwin became an evolutionist, he did not uphold his theory as a challenge to God's existence. Instead, he believed that God works at a distance through unbreakable law. Later in life, however, the problem of evil inclined him more toward agnosticism.

Darwin generally remained silent about his evolutionary ideas, although in 1842 he briefly committed them to paper, and in 1844 he expanded them into a 230-page unpublished essay. Publicly, he wrote extensively on geological matters, drawing both on his observations and the theories from his work during the *Beagle* voyage, and also expanding his Lyellian ideas developed through his ensuing work in Britain. Noteworthy among these writings was a paper he published in the *Transactions of the London Royal Society* on the "parallel roads of Glen Roy," a valley in the north of Scotland. Darwin argued that the parallel tracks around the sides of the valley are marks of a retreating sea's shorelines. In fact, this explanation was entirely mistaken. The Swiss ichthyologist (specialist in fishes) Louis Agassiz was to show shortly thereafter that the tracks are a function of lake water that had been dammed up in the valley by glaciers. Although Darwin always regarded his own explanation as a dreadful error, it was, in fact, very much in line with his Lyellian perspective and his successful explanation for the formation of coral reefs. In Scotland, as in the South Seas, Darwin was looking for evidence of land rise and fall.

By the early 1840s, Darwin's interests turned more to general biological questions, particularly with regard to evolution, despite his reputation as a geologist. For eight years, he devoted himself to a massive taxonomic study of barnacles, paying some attention to the fossil forms, but concentrating more on the systematic study of the living organism. In the mid-1850s, Darwin focused directly on writing his theory of evolution through natural selection. At the end of 1859, he published his revolutionary work, *On the Origin of Species by Means of Natural Selection.* This work, which Darwin described as "one long argument," attempts to demonstrate how the widest range of biological phenomena can be explained by the evolutionary hypothesis. The issues of instinct, biogeography—as would be expected given its crucial role in Darwin's route to discovery—embryology, classification, and morphology figure prominently in his demonstration. His theories of adaptation and the role of natural selection are significant features in the *Origin,* in keeping with his earlier beliefs.

Naturally, the geological record received detailed attention. Part of Darwin's task in the *Origin* was to demonstrate that the record does not speak against evolution. He was, therefore, much concerned with issues such as gaps in the record, trying to account for them as functions of incomplete fossilization and other natural inadequacies. At the same time, he used the record to illustrate that the general progression seen in life from the earliest periods (as far as Darwin was concerned this was the Cambrian period, from 540 to 515 million years ago) up to the present, is explained best through an evolutionary mechanism rather than as a miraculous function of Divine intervention. It is interesting to note that in later editions of the *Origin,* he proffered a kind of forerunner to what biologists today call an "arms race," as a mechanism to explain life's upward development. Darwin supposed that organisms compete—predator and prey, for instance—with comparative improvement of adaptations. The predator becomes faster, and so does the prey, resulting in progress. Darwin explicitly declared that ultimately this kind of progress will lead to absolute improvements (in his opinion), such as intelligence.

Darwin continued to work hard for the rest of his life; however, paleontological questions became less a part of his occupation. He focused, rather, on such issues as the evolutionary adaptation of plants and the effect of earthworms on the development of soil. However, Darwin did devote some considerable attention to the evolution of humans, both in his major work, *The Descent of Man* (1871), and in what was essentially a supplementary volume, *The Expression of the Emotions in Men and in Animals* (1872). In *The Descent of Man,* in particular, Darwin makes some reference to past human history. There is a brief mention of recently discovered Neanderthal remains. More broadly, Darwin discusses and endorses an African origin for humans. But obviously, given the lack of solid evidence at the time, he could do no more than loosely speculate. As was fashionable at the time, Darwin's thinking was set firmly in a progressivist framework, not only with respect to life in general, but also for humans in particular. He believed that human evolution is an upward rise, from primitive brains to the modern mind of humans, and indeed, with Europeans and upperclass Englishmen at the top of the scale.

By the time he published the *Descent,* Darwin was losing touch with many significant developments in modern biology, and he was certainly not as involved in advances and trends as were some of his younger followers, namely the British biologist Thomas Henry Huxley. When Darwin speculated on the nature of heredity, for instance, he had to be given a quick briefing in cell theory. (His speculations eventually led to his theory of "pangenesis," which assumes that little gemmules—hypothetical living units bearing heredity attributes—are given off all over the body and collected in the sex cells.)

In subjects such as paleontology and morphology, Darwin's emphasis on adaptationism was distinctly out of favor because the new generation of researchers focused on Germanic ideas about common structure ("homology"). Although posterity favored Darwin, his theory of adaptation was extremely controversial in his own time, even among his closest friends and supporters. In the *Descent,* for example, it would be misleading to leave the impression that the origin of humans was Darwin's main concern. At least as much, indeed more, attention was paid to concerns such as the evolution and function of morality, as well as the ways in which sexual preferences can affect evolution. (The *Descent* contains a major discussion on a secondary mechanism, sexual selection.) With respect to today's interest in the genetic role in social behavior ("sociobiology"), much of Darwin's work has a very contemporary flavor.

The *Descent,* in fact, points to a wider matter of importance. Somewhat paradoxically, given his early attention to geology, paleontology figures in Darwin's work as only one part—admittedly a large part—of the overall picture. For paleontologists, as for all other evolutionists, however, ultimately it was Darwin who set the agenda and defined the framework. For this reason, he must always be regarded as one of the greatest influences on contemporary thinking about the history of the organic world. Darwin may have said comparatively little about the paths of evolution, but he established the general structure of evolutionary theory. From today's perspective, he discovered and championed the chief mechanism that makes everything in life both possible and actual.

MICHAEL RUSE

Biography

Born in Shrewsbury, 9 February 1809. Studied medicine, Edinburgh University, 1825–27; received B.A. in divinity, Christ Church College, Cambridge University, 1831. Accompanied geological expedition to north Wales, 1831; naturalist aboard H.M.S. *Beagle,* 1831–36. Made a fellow (1836), served on governing council (1837–51), and served as secretary (1838–41), Geological Society of London; elected to the Athenaeum, 1838; elected to the Royal Society of London, 1839; awarded Wollaston Medal, Geological Society of London, 1859; was a member of 57 leading foreign learned societies. Initially known for geological work; best known today for his theory of natural selection as an explanation of evolution, first advanced with the 1859 publication of *On the Origin of Species by Means of Natural Selection.* Died in Downe, Kent, 19 April 1882.

Major Publications

1839. *Journal of Researches into the Geology and Natural History of the Various Countries Visited by H.M.S.* Beagle, *under the Command of Captain FitzRoy, R.N., from 1832 to 1836.* London: Colburn; 2nd ed., London: Murray, 1845; New York: Appleton, 1845; 3rd ed., London: Murray, 1852; New York: Appleton, 1871.

1842. *The Structure and Distribution of Coral Reefs; Being the First Part of the Geology of the Voyage of the* Beagle, *under the Command of Captain FitzRoy, R.N., during the Years 1832 to 1836.* London: Smith, Elder; 3rd ed., London: Smith, Elder, 1889; New York: Appleton, 1889.

1844. *Geological Observations on the Volcanic Islands, Visited during the Voyage of H.M.S.* Beagle, *Together with Some Brief Notices on the Geology of Australia and the Cape of Good Hope; Being the Second Part of the Geology of the Voyage of the* Beagle, *under the Command of Captain FitzRoy, R.N., during the Years 1832 to 1836.* London: Smith, Elder; 3rd ed., London: Smith, Elder, 1891; New York: Appleton, 1891.

1846. *Geological Observations on South America; Being the Third Part of the Geology of the Voyage of the* Beagle, *under the Command of Captain FitzRoy, R.N., during the Years 1832 to 1836.* London: Smith, Elder.

1859. *On the Origin of Species by Means of Natural Selection; or, The Preservation of Favoured Races in the Struggle for Life.* London: Murray; New York: Appleton, 1860; 6th ed., with additions and corrections to 6th ed. of 1872, London: Murray, 1876; New York: Appleton, 1886.

1862. *On the Various Contrivances by Which British and Foreign Orchids Are Fertilised by Insects, and on the Good Effects of Intercrossing.* London: Murray; 2nd ed., London: Murray, 1877; New York: Appleton, 1877.

1868. *The Variation of Animals and Plants under Domestication.* London: Murray; New York: Orange and Judd; 2nd ed., London: Murray, 1875; New York: Appleton, 1876.

1871. *The Descent of Man and Selection in Relation to Sex.* 2 vols. London: Murray; New York: Appleton; 2nd ed., London: Murray, 1874; New York: Appleton, 1874.

1872. *The Expression of the Emotions in Man and Animals.* London: Murray; New York: Appleton, 1873.

1875. *Insectivorous Plants.* London: Murray; New York: Appleton.

1876. *The Effects of Cross and Self Fertilisation in the Vegetable Kingdom.* London: Murray; New York: Appleton, 1877; 2nd ed., London: Murray, 1878.

1877. *The Different Forms of Flowers on Plants of the Same Species.* London: Murray; New York: Appleton, 1880; 2nd ed., London: Murray, 1880; New York: Appleton, 1884.

1880. With F. Darwin. *The Power of Movement in Plants.* London: Murray; New York: Appleton, 1881.

1881. *The Formation of Vegetable Mould through the Action of Worms, with Observations on Their Habits.* London: Murray; New York: Appleton, 1882.

1892. F. Darwin (ed.). *Charles Darwin: His Life Told in an Autobiographical Chapter, and in a Selected Series of Published Letters, Edited by His Son Francis Darwin.* London: Murray; New York: Appleton; 2nd ed., London: Murray, 1908; as *The Autobiography of Charles Darwin, 1809–1882, with Original Omissions Restore,* Nora Barlow (ed.), London: Collins, 1958; New York: Harcourt Brace, 1958.

Further Reading

Bowler, P.J. 1990. *Darwin: The Man and His Influence.* Cambridge and New York: Cambridge University Press.

Browne, J. 1995. *Charles Darwin: Voyaging. Volume 1 of a Biography.* New York: Knopf; London: Cape.

Burkhardt, F., and S. Smith (eds.). 1985–. *The Correspondence of Charles Darwin.* 10 vols. to date, Cambridge and New York: Cambridge University Press.

Desmond, A., and J. Moore. 1991. *Darwin: The Life of a Tormented Evolutionist.* New York: Viking Penguin; London: Michael Joseph.

Moore, J. 1995. *The Darwinian Legend.* London: Hodder.

Rudwick, M.J.S. 1974. Darwin and Glen Roy: A great "failure" in scientific method? *Studies in the History and Philosophy of Science* 5:97–185.

Ruse, M. 1979. *The Darwinian Revolution: Science Read in Tooth and Claw.* Chicago: University of Chicago Press.

———. 1996. *Monad to Man: The Concept of Progress in Evolutionary Biology.* Cambridge, Massachusetts: Harvard University Press.

DATING METHODS

Determining the numerical age in thousands or millions of years of rocks, fossils, and other geological features is essential to interpreting Earth history. There are several common ways of doing this.

Radiometric Techniques

Radioactive decay of an unstable element (usually called an "isotope") begins when it becomes part of a mineral (crystallization) in a rock. The decay occurs at a geometric rate—that is, over a given time interval the proportion of atoms that decay to the number that remain stays the same, no matter how long the decay process continues. When half of the atoms decay, we refer to this as one half-life. If we know the rate of decay and how much decay has taken place, then we can estimate how long the decay has been going on, in other words, the age of the mineral.

To determine this information, we need to know the "parent" isotope and the "daughter" isotope. The unstable element in the decay process is called the parent isotope, and it changes to become a more stable isotope called the daughter. (The daughter isotope may also be radioactive.) In determining rock ages, the most common parent isotope studied is radioactive potassium (K^{40}), which decays to its daughter, the noble gas argon (Ar^{40}). One half-life in the K/Ar parent-daughter system is 1.25 billion years. Uranium-lead (U-Pb) and rubidium-strontium (Rb-Sr) are other parent-daughter isotope pairs widely used to determine the ages of rocks.

Carbon 14 (C^{14}) is the unstable form of carbon produced in the upper atmosphere and then absorbed by living plants and animals. After an organism dies, the C^{14} in its body begins to decay to nitrogen 14 (N^{14}), a process with a very short half-life: 5,730 years. Because of its short half-life, C^{14} dating generally is used only for objects no older than about 40,000 years. Organic matter older than that has so little C^{14} remaining that it is virtually impossible to detect. Therefore, C^{14} dating is applied almost exclusively to archeological problems, those that deal with human activities.

Using radioactive decay to determine the ages of rocks or fossils relies on a closed system to achieve accuracy. The parent isotope in the specimen must be only what was in the mineral when it crystallized originally, and the daughter isotope present must only be the product of radioactive decay of the parent. If any parent or daughter isotopes are incorporated in the specimen or removed from it, their proportions will not provide an accurate estimate of how much time has passed since the mineral crystallized originally. Breakdown of this closed system is the most obvious potential source of error in radiometric dating. Indeed, many minerals with radioactive elements have not remained stable enough to maintain the closed parent-daughter system, so they cannot give accurate age estimates. Furthermore, relatively few rocks—almost exclusively those of igneous (volcanic) origin—contain enough radioactive material to be dated.

Radiation Damage Phenomena

Radioactive decay also can damage or alter minerals. If the rate and amount of this damage can be determined, then the duration of the process can be estimated. Three common methods are used to do this.

Electron Spin Resonance

Electron spin resonance measures the absorption of microwave radiation by unpaired electrons—that is, those having very little stability—in radiation-damaged minerals and glasses when they are exposed to a powerful magnetic field. The results provide estimates of the amount of damage to the electrons, a type of damage that occurs at a known rate in some settings.

Thermoluminescence

Radiation damage displaces electrons from a parent atom, and the displaced electrons become trapped in the atom's crystal lattice. When the mineral is heated, the electrons return to their stable configuration, releasing excess energy as light, or luminescence. To estimate the amount of original radiation damage, the luminescence is measured on a glow curve. This technique is used mostly in archeology on glasses, ceramics, bone, and flints.

Fission Tracks

During radioactive decay, the fission fragments leave a trail of damage called "fission tracks" in a mineral or volcanic glass. The longer the decay, the greater the density of tracks, so counting tracks can give an estimate of the duration of decay. Tracks, however, are very sensitive to temperature changes. If the rock is heated, tracks fade and disappear (heal), so determining the number of fission tracks usually can only give the age of a mineral since the most recent thermal event. That event may have occurred much later than the time when the rock was formed.

Paleomagnetic Stratigraphy

Over the history of the Earth, the magnetic poles have switched, or flipped. In recent years, geologists have made a concentrated effort to decipher the history of the Earth's magnetic field. To do this, geologists have determined the magnetic polarities of rocks from the seafloor. These were formed by lavas, and the numerical ages of some have been calculated. As a result, we now know with fair accuracy the Earth's magnetic polarity history back to the Middle Jurassic. Referred to as the "geomagnetic polarity timescale," it provides a globally consistent pattern of normal and reverse polarity intervals that can be used to estimate the ages of rocks and the events they record.

The first step in age estimation is determining the magnetic polarity history of a succession (layers, or strata) of rocks. The alignments of the rock layers reveal their piece of geomagnetic polarity history, which then can be matched (correlated) to the matching section of the geomagnetic polarity timescale. In such correlation, geologists look for a signature—a distinctive pattern of magnetic polarity reversals—to establish a match.

Unfortunately, not all local successions nor all portions of the geomagnetic polarity timescale contain distinctive signatures. Then geologists use an alternative technique to get a general idea of the age of the local rock succession—either an index fossil or a numerical age—to help narrow down the possible correlation of magnetic reversal histories. This means that in most cases magnetic-polarity-based correlations are not an independent means of correlation—they are used together with other dating techniques.

Biostratigraphy

Identifying and differentiating layers of sedimentary rock based on their fossil content is called "biostratigraphy." Strata with distinctive fossil content are biostratigraphic zones, and these zones provide a basis for correlation, establishing the equivalence of rock layers in age and/or stratigraphic position. An "index fossil" is one that can be used to identify and determine the relative age of the layer in which the fossil is found. Index fossils represent plants or animals that lived only during a relatively short interval of geological time.

Biostratigraphic correlation and the use of index fossils do not establish numerical ages. The techniques only determine relative ages and are the basic foundation on which the relative geological timescale was constructed. Biostratigraphic correlation of rocks for which numerical ages have been calculated integrates the numerical timescale with the relative timescale.

Astronomical Cycles

Some sedimentary rocks and fossil bones and shells preserve a record of solar and other astronomical cycles. Diurnal (day-night), lunar (moon-based), annual, sunspot, and Milankovitch cycles produce regular, periodic changes in sediment deposition or of chemical precipitation in bones or shells. Typically, these changes appear as alternating layers of organic and inorganic material.

Milankovitch cycles are three cycles in which the relationship between the sun and the Earth vary—the distance between the Earth and sun, tilt of the Earth's axis, and shape of Earth's orbit—and produce variation in cycles that occur, respectively, about every 20,000, 41,000, and 100,000 years. Cyclical layers of sediment at least as old as Triassic are thought to record Milankovitch cycles. If the cycle can be identified, then it should be possible to measure time by counting the layers that represent the response. For example, "varves" are alternating lake sediment layers of finer and coarser silt or clay—one pair is assumed to equal one year. Therefore, a set of pairs indicates the duration of a stack of lake sediments.

Dendrochronology is a special form of dating based on how trees grow in response to astronomical cycles. Many trees form new rows of wood cells annually, creating distinctive rings. The width of a ring increases and decreases with the seasons and rainfall, producing a distinctive pattern. The tree ring record of bristlecone pines (*Pinus longaeva*), for example, is known back approximately 6,000 years.

Other Physical Processes

Any physical process that has a known, constant rate can be used to estimate the age of a rock or geological feature. Rates of erosion and weathering sometimes are known and, therefore, can be so used. Particularly useful in some climates is to measure the degree of varnish, or the thickness of mineral coatings such as calcite, on rocks. If the rate of polishing or accumulation is known, geologists can estimate how long the process has proceeded.

The rate at which sediment accumulates was one of the first methods used to estimate the Earth's age. If one knows an average rate of sedimentation (usually expressed in millimeters per year), then one can use the thickness of sediments (factoring out compaction) to estimate the duration of sedimentation. The most serious drawback of this method is that sedimentation is rarely continuous or constant. Because the sedimentary record is full of gaps, age estimates based on sediment thickness are often inaccurate.

Other Biological Processes

Biological processes with fixed rates also may be used to determine the age of a rock or fossil. For example, "lichenology" is the determination of rock age by the density of lichen growth. Another technique, used primarily in analyzing bones in archaeological settings, is "amino acid racemization," which measures the degree of chemical change of amino acids to a racemic acid. Given the short span of most biological processes, which are usually on the order of hundreds or at most thousands of years, these dating techniques are only useful for the youngest geological phenomena.

SPENCER G. LUCAS

See also Fossil Record; Geological Timescale; Paleomagnetism; Sedimentology; Stable Isotope Analysis; Trace Element Analysis

Further Reading

Eicher, D.L. 1968. *Geologic Time*. Englewood Cliffs, New Jersey: Prentice-Hall; 2nd ed., 1976.
Faul, H. 1966. *Ages of Rocks, Planets, and Stars*. New York: McGraw-Hill.
Lemon, R.R. 1990. *Principles of Stratigraphy*. Columbus, Ohio: Merrill.
Tarling, D.H. 1983. *Paleomagnetism*. London and New York: Chapman and Hall.

DAWSON, JOHN WILLIAM

Canadian, 1820–99

John William Dawson was born on 13 October 1820 at Pictou, Nova Scotia, son of immigrants from Scotland. The young Dawson was exposed to the intellectual world through his father's work (he was a bookseller) and began collecting plant fossils at the age of 10, assembling a large collection by the time he was 20. In 1841 he met and impressed the English geologists William Logan, who became the first director of the Geological Survey of Canada, and Charles Lyell, who toured geological sites with him and helped Dawson to make an impact on geology in Britain.

Dawson studied intermittently at the University of Edinburgh. In 1850 he became the first superintendent of education for Nova Scotia and used the travel opportunities to complete his book *Acadian Geology*, which appeared in the first of its four editions in 1855. He also did some consulting for mining interests.

In 1855 he became principal of the then-fledgling McGill University, Montreal, and remained in this position for almost 40 years, becoming a dominating figure in Canadian science and education. Throughout this period he was also a professor in the natural sciences, continued research particularly in paleontology, and began a series of best-selling books on the natural sciences.

As a paleontologist he produced 198 papers, of which 109 were on the plants of the Paleozoic. He was the first North American paleontologist to use thin sections to study minute anatomy, but he was without the benefit of other modern techniques. He described 125 species, including Devonian floras that were then the oldest known land plants. This work was not taken seriously in Great Britain (where the Royal Society—which had invited him to give the 1870 Bakerian lecture—refused to publish his report), but he was vindicated when other plant material of that age was described from the Scottish Rhynie Chert in 1917.

Dawson found and published extensively on other terrestrial life of the Paleozoic, including insects and vertebrates. Perhaps his richest site was at Joggins, Nova Scotia, from which he described amphibians and discovered what was then the oldest reptile, described by Richard Owen as *Dendrerpeton*.

Dawson is strongly associated with the controversial supposed pre-Cambrian fossil *Eozoon*. He maintained its organic origin, initially with much support from fellow scientists, and later almost alone. He was involved in other controversies, usually on what is historically seen as the "wrong side." Thus he supported the floating iceberg origin of Pleistocene deposits and opposed Darwin's evolutionary views vigorously to the end of his life.

In addition to his scientific papers, Dawson wrote several books, which were generally popular. For instance, *The Story of the Earth and Man* (which first appeared in 1873) went through thirteen editions. In his books he successfully presented his scientific discoveries to a popular audience. A staunch Presbyterian, Dawson also explored the relations between science and Christian belief, a field of enormous interest to the reading public as the implications of evolution worked through the natural sciences.

Dawson was a very popular lecturer and also founder of the Redpath Museum at McGill. Among the Dawson's family of four boys and two girls was George Mercer Dawson (1849–1901), an important pioneer geologist. J.W. Dawson described many of the Cretaceous plants collected by his son in western Canada.

When Dawson died on 19 November 1899, he was perhaps the last major scientist in North America who did not accept Darwin's evolutionary views. He thus had become increasingly irrelevant to younger scientists, who did not always appreciate his very real and important contributions to paleontology and to scientific and popular education.

DAVID A.E. SPALDING

Biography

Born in Pictou, Nova Scotia, 13 October 1820. Received M.A. (1856), LL.D. (1884), University of Edinburgh. Superintendent of education, Nova Scotia (1850–53); principal, McGill University, Montreal (1855–93). Elected fellow, Geological Society of London, 1854; fellow, Royal Society (London), 1862; president, American Association for the Advancement of Science (1882–83); first president, Royal Society of Canada, 1882; fellow (1886) and president (1893), Geological Society of America; president, British Association for the Advancement of Science, 1886; member, Academy of Arts and Sciences (Boston); member, American Philosophical Society (Philadelphia). Awarded Lyell Gold Medal, Geological Society of London, 1881; knighted by Queen Victoria, 1884. In his time famous as educator, naturalist, paleontologist, and popular writer on the natural sciences; conducted notable researches on Paleozoic plants and terrestrial life, controversial research on supposed pre-Cambrian fossil *Eozoon;* associate of Charles Lyell and William Logan, and father of geologist George Mercer Dawson; perhaps the last major scientist in North America who did not accept Darwin's evolutionary views. Died 19 November 1899.

Major Publications

1855. *Acadian Geology: An Account of the Geological Structure and Mineral Resources of Nova Scotia and Neighboring Provinces of British America.* Edinburgh and London: Oliver and Boyd; 4th ed., as *The Geology of Nova Scotia, New Brunswick, and Prince Edward Islands*, London: Macmillan, 1891.

1859. On fossil plants from the Devonian rocks of Canada. *Quarterly Journal of the Geological Society of London* 15:477–88.

1860. On a terrestrial mollusk, a Chilognathous myriapod, and some new species of reptiles from the coal formation of Nova Scotia. *Quarterly Journal of the Geological Society of London* 16:268–77.

1862. Flora of the Devonian period in north-eastern America. *Quarterly Journal of the Geological Society of London* 18:296–330.

1863a. *Air Breathers of the Coal Period.* Montreal: Dawson; London and New York: Bailliere.

1863b. Further observations on the Devonian plants of Maine, Gaspe, and New York. *Quarterly Journal of the Geological Society of London* 19:458–69.

1871. The fossil plants of the Devonian and Upper Silurian formations of Canada. *Geological Survey of Canada,* 1–92. Montreal: Dawson.

1873. *The Story of the Earth and Man.* London, Hodder and Stoughton; New York: Harper; 13th ed., 1903.

1877. *The Origin of the World, According to Revelation and Science.* Montreal: Dawson; London: Hodder and Stoughton; New York: Harper; 6th ed., London: Hodder and Stoughton, 1893.

1888. *The Geological History of Plants.* London: Kegan Paul, Trench; New York: Appleton.

1893. On the correlation of early Cretaceous floras in Canada and the United States and on some new plants of this period. *Royal Society of Canada, Proceedings and Transactions for 1892* 10 (Sec. 4):79–93.

1901. R. Dawson (ed.). *Fifty Years of Work in Canada: Scientific and Educational.* London and Edinburgh: Ballantyne, Hanson.

Further Reading

Adams, F.D. 1900. Memoir of Sir J. William Dawson. *Bulletin of the Geological Society of America* 11:550–80.

Andrews, H.N. 1980. *The Fossil Hunters: In Search of Ancient Plants.* Ithaca, New York, and London: Cornell University Press.

Berger, C. 1983. *Science, God and Nature in Victorian Canada.* Toronto and Buffalo, New York: University of Toronto Press.

Clark, T.H. 1972. Sir John William Dawson (1820–1899), paleontologist. *Geological Association of Canada Proceedings* 24 (2):1–4.

Hook, E.L. 1990. *Sir William Dawson and Henry Marshall Tory. The Achievements and Ideological Attitudes of Two Great Canadian Educators.* Ottawa: Carleton University.

Merrill, G.P. 1906. The Eozoon question. *In* G.P. Merrill, *Contributions to the History of American Geology.* U.S. National Museum Annual Report for 1904. Washington, D.C.: U.S. Government Printing Office.

O'Brien, C.F. 1971. *Sir William Dawson, A Life in Science and Religion.* Memoirs of the American Philosophical Society, 84. Philadelphia: American Philosophical Society.

Sheets-Pyenson, S. 1996. *John William Dawson: Faith, Hope and Science.* Montreal and Buffalo, New York: McGill-Queens University Press.

———. 1988. *Cathedrals of Science: The Development of Colonial Natural History Museums during the Late Nineteenth Century.* Kingston, Ontario: McGill-Queens University Press.

Spalding, D. 1995. Bathygnathus, Canada's First "Dinosaur." *In* W.A.S. Sarjeant (ed.), *Vertebrate Fossils and the Evolution of Scientific Concepts.* Amsterdam: Gordon and Breach.

Zeller, S. 1987. *Inventing Canada. Early Victorian Science and the Idea of a Transcontinental Nation.* Toronto and Buffalo, New York: University of Toronto Press.

DEFENSIVE STRUCTURES: INVERTEBRATES

Defensive structures are those that protect an animal's soft tissue from damage by a hostile environment, typically from predators but also from such physical factors as water currents and wave action. Thus, the limpet resists being dislodged by the sea and by predators by virtue of its low conical profile and because the thickened margin of its shell fits precisely into a depression that the animal etches into the rock (the "home scar") and to which the animal returns at low tide.

Swarming is the most common defense among planktic (drifting) organisms. This behavior may account for dense bedding plane accumulations of single graptolite species (graptolites are colonial hemichordates) (Underwood 1993). Individual graptolite zooids inhabited a chamber (theca) whose aperture was sometimes protected by spines. Other graptolite species had thecae that were bent, hooked, lobate, or which developed shinglelike lappets. All these morphologies limited access to the zooid by potential predators.

Among nektic organisms—those that live in open waters—rapid locomotion through the water is an important defense mechanism. This is illustrated best in the invertebrates by the cephalopods (e.g., squid, octopuses, cuttlefish). Appearing in the Late Cambrian, the straight-coned nautiloids possessed a chambered shell that not only protected the animal in the body chamber but also facilitated vertical movement in the water column by pressure regulation in the remaining chambers. By Mesozoic times, the wide diversity of shell form in the Ordovician had been replaced entirely by the coiled form. The coiled conch also characterized the ammonites, a related group of extinct cephalopods. These animals were the numerically dominant, externally shelled group of the Mesozoic. The internally shelled and presumably faster-moving belemnites also flourished in the later Mesozoic. The successful cephalopods of the Cenozoic have been those that lack an external shell or possess much-reduced internal shells, such as the fast-moving squid and cuttlefish. Only the relatively slow-moving *Nautilus* relies on an external conch for its defense. The shell-less octopus is a benthic form (one that lives on the sea bottom) that relies on cunning rather than speed and, like many benthic groups, uses camouflage as a defense.

Within both the vagrant and sessile benthos (free-moving and fixed animals of the seafloor, respectively), armor in the form of a shell covering, variously enhanced by protruberances such as spines, bony knobs, and ridges, characterizes many groups. Gastropods (e.g., snails) possess coiled shells, commonly with thick walls to protect them against boring predators (largely other snails). Gastropods also often have spines and tubercles, which provide additional strength—and provide an awkward mouthful for any shell-crushing predator. The coiled form enables the animal to withdraw into the conch and makes it difficult for a predator to extract it. Additional defense may be provided by the modification of the aperture by folds and flanges and by reducing the apertural size. Turreted shells provide successful defense against shell-peeling crabs, but the high spire is vulnerable to shell crushers (Vermeij 1987). Strongly sculptured shell surfaces on gastropods and other shells are utilized by calcareous algae, sponges, bryozoa, and other epibionts (animals that live on the surface of another animal) and provide camouflage for their slow-moving hosts. Many gastropods possess opercula (lids over the aperture), some of which are calcareous and are therefore preservable in the fossil record. Gastropods with opercula first appeared in the Ordovician (Yochelson 1979). Among other mollusc classes, the rudist bivalves are notable for having evolved a loft valve with an operculum. Opercula evolved independently in several other phyla including the hyoliths, the goniophyllid corals, and the richthofeniid brachiopods, the last with an opercular dorsal valve.

Discarded gastropod shells are used for protection by various animal groups—the best known being that of the hermit crabs, which are found from Jurassic time onward (Glaessner 1969). However, G.T. Vermeij (1987) points out that examples of heavily encrusted shells, the pattern of which suggests occupation by conchioles, are known from Late Ordovician time; a notable example is bryozoan-encrusted *Lophospira* (McNamara 1978).

Spines are uncommon in bivalve molluscs; best known are those of the spiny oyster *Spondylus*. In extant forms the defensive function of the spines appears to be that they attract epibionts, which then provide camouflage (Feifarek 1987). In bivalves, defensive structures are basically those that prevent predators from prying the valves apart. Crenulated margins ensure a tight seal in some forms, while others, such as the pteriomorphs, have a retractable mantle that can suffer peripheral damage without the seal being broken. Gapers, such as the clam *Mya,* rely on deep burrows for defense. Spines are relatively more common in brachiopods, where they serve many purposes (Wright and Nõlvak 1997). One defensive role is to protect the mantle edges that seal the shell. The mantle edges may also be protected by a lamellose shell morphology and by frills.

Many echinoderms depend on defensive spines to supplement the primary internal protective skeleton of porous calcareous plates. Spines are known from Early Ordovician asterozoans, and from the earliest echinoid *Bothriocidaris,* in which protective spines are sited adjacent to the tube feet (Paul 1977). The spiny echinoids outlived other thick-plated thecate stocks, such as the cystoids and blastoids, into the Mesozoic. The Jurassic saw the development of burrowing echinoids, which utilized the protection of the sediment instead of an armored test. In these animals, the endoskeleton became thin and delicate, along with shorter and thinner spines that served nonprotective functions. However, echinoids living on open hard surfaces developed rigid tests and strong flexible spines. The plates of the test were joined with an advanced peg-and-socket articulation that was coming to typify most Cenozoic warm water forms (Smith 1984).

The body segments of arthropods are protected by exoskeletal sclerites, which may be supplemented by spines. The latter may have functions other than defense. The spines of the trilobite *Agnostus* have been shown by K.J. Müller and D. Walossek (1987) to have a balancing function—they are situated at each corner of the conch when cephalon (head shield) and pygidium (tail shield) are folded into the slightly gaping feeding position. Although not unique to the group, the ability to roll up is a common means of defense in arthropods and characterizes many trilobite families (Bergström 1973). In addition to the enrolled fossils themselves,

various morphological indicators, such as vincular furrows, provide evidence for the close fit of enrolled forms.

Morphological defenses indicate only part of the defensive capability of an animal; behavioral and physiological defenses, such as the stinging cells of cnidarians, ink in cephalopods, and various poisonous and noxious secretions in diverse groups are part of the armory. However, none of these commonly leaves a trace on a fossil. Defense always must be a compromise between an effective armor, to protect the animal from the external environment, and the need to maintain contact with that environment for respiration and nourishment.

ANTHONY D. WRIGHT

See also Aquatic Invertebrates, Adaptive Strategies of; Exoskeletal Design; Feeding Adaptations: Invertebrates; Predation; Skeletized Microorganisms; Skeletized Organisms and Tissues: Invertebrates

Works Cited

Bergström, J. 1973. Organization, life, and systematics of trilobites. *Fossils and Strata* 2:1–69.

Feifarek, B.P. 1987. Spines and epibionts as antipredator defenses in the thorny oyster *Spondylus americanus* Hermann. *Journal of Experimental Marine Biology and Ecology* 105:39–56.

Glaessner, M.F. 1969. Decapoda. *In* R.C. Moore (ed.), *Treatise on Invertebrate Paleontology.* Part R, Arthropoda 4 (2). Boulder, Colorado, and Lawrence, Kansas: Geological Society of America and University of Kansas.

McNamara, K.J. 1978. Symbiosis between gastropods and bryozoans in the late Ordovician of Cumbria, England. *Lethaia* 11:25–40.

Müller, K.J., and D. Walossek. 1987. Morphology, ontogeny and life habits of *Agnostus pisiformis* from the Upper Cambrian of Sweden. *Fossils and Strata* 19:1–56.

Paul, C.R.C. 1977. Evolution of primitive echinoderms. *In* A. Hallam (ed.), *Patterns of Evolution as Illustrated by the Fossil Record.* Amsterdam and New York: Elsevier.

Smith, A.B. 1984. *Echinoid Palaeobiology.* London and Boston: Allen and Unwin.

Underwood, C.J. 1993. The position of graptolites within Lower Paleozoic planktic ecosystems. *Lethaia* 26:189–202.

Vermeij, G.T. 1987. *Evolution and Escalation: An Ecological History of Life.* Princeton, New Jersey: Princeton University Press.

Wright, A.D., and J. Nõlvak. 1997. Functional significance of the spines of the Ordovician lingulate brachiopod *Acanthambonia. Palaeontology* 40:113–19.

Yochelson, E.L. 1979. Gastropod opercula as objects for paleobiogeographic study. *In* J. Gray and A.J. Boucot (eds.), *Historical Biogeography, Plate Tectonics, and the Changing Environment.* Corvallis: Oregon State University Press.

Further Reading

Boucot, A.J. 1990. *Evolutionary Paleobiology of Behaviour and Coevolution.* Amsterdam and New York: Elsevier.

Vermeij, G.T. 1987. *Evolution and Escalation: An Ecological History of Life.* Princeton, New Jersey: Princeton University Press.

DEFENSIVE STRUCTURES: PLANTS

The evidence from extant (present-day) and fossil plants for interactions between plants and microorganisms and between plants and herbivores provides impressive information on the evolution of defense systems in plants. As primary producers, plants are at the base of the food chain. Therefore, mechanisms for protection from being consumed to extinction must have evolved early on. Unable to run from attackers or hide from them, plants must depend on their ability to adapt to their environment and to evolve efficient defense systems. In the interactions between plants and other organisms, response mechanisms also have evolved for distinguishing parasites (organisms that live off plants) from mutualists (organisms that coexist with plants).

Fungi-Plant Interactions: Saprotrophism, Parasitism, Mutualism

Fungi are heterotrophs (they cannot manufacture their own food, as plants do), so they depend on other organisms or upon their remains for subsistence. Saprotrophic fungi and bacteria (those that feed on dead organic matter) are the most important extant (present-day) decomposers of organic material, recycling the available nutrients in the ecosystem. The exact time of the evolution of "saprotrophism" has been relatively difficult to establish because paleobotanists, focused on collecting structurally perfect specimens, have disregarded fossils that show signs of decomposition. Fungal fossils have been found from the Precambrian, but their identification is not clear cut. However, clearly identified fungal fossils are known from Silurian formations. Saprotrophic activity of fungi on vascular plants was detected first in the flora from the Upper Devonian, but these interactions may extend back to the Silurian. In tracheids (water-conducting tubes) of *Callixylon,* a progymnosperm, numerous erosion troughs, or scars, were present; these probably were caused by the hyphae (long filaments) of fungi (Taylor and Osborne 1996). These erosions are similar to those produced by extant wood-decaying basidiomycetes (a type of fungi), where fungal enzymes remove a substance called "lignin" from the secondary walls.

How widespread wood-rotting fungi were at that time has not been determined. According to one hypothesis about the evolution of lignin, a complex aromatic compound that is a prominent cell-wall component essential for mechanical support and water transport in terrestrial plants, such fungi would have been limited. This hypothesis suggests that the evolution of lignin may have hindered the decay of the Carboniferous coal-swamp flora, thus allowing the massive accumulation of organic carbon as coal. In the early land plants (many found in Rhynie chert deposits in Scotland), lignin was prominent only in the vascular elements. Lignin's evolution may have been driven initially by the selective advantage it provided in defending against parasitic fungi and bacteria. The presence of lignin in the extant green alga *Coleochaete,* a presumed close relative of land plants, supports this hypothesis. However, the dispersal of spores from elevated positions on elongate, lignin-strengthened axes (stems) over wider ranges may have exerted greater selective pressure, since it provided for increased

fitness. The complexity of the genetic control of lignin biosynthesis supports the assumption that multiple factors favored the evolution of lignin (Ralph et al. 1997). Nonetheless, lignin was probably a plant defense against a wood-rotting fungus.

In the fossil record, it is difficult to distinguish parasitic associations from mutualistic associations. The gametophytes (the stage of the plant life cycle that produces male and female gametes) of extant *Lycopodium* (clubmoss, Lycopsida), which usually do not produce chlorophyll, contain mycorrhizal fungi, forming a mutualistic association—the fungus supplies the plant with mineral nutrients necessary for growth and development, and the gametophyte supplies the fungus with food and amino acids, the building blocks of proteins. Unfortunately, free-living fossil gametophytes of Lycopsida have not been identified. In fact, very few gametophytes from the Paleozoic have been preserved, while the arborescent sporophytes (tree-like, spore-producing generations) are abundant in the Carboniferous fossil record. In the tissues of the dichotomously branched (divided into equal sections) bases on which the massive lycopod trunks grew, spores resembling those of modern mycorrhizal fungi have been found. Arbuscules, identical to those in extant arbuscular mycorrhizae, have been identified in *Aglaophyton major,* a lower Devonian land plant (Remy et al. 1994). The presence of hyphae, chlamydospores, and arbuscules in Rhynie chert plants has led to the hypothesis that mycorrhizal fungi were instrumental in enabling plants to become terrestrial. However, it cannot be excluded that at least some of these fungi were actually saprotrophs or even pathogens, nor do these interactions explain the origin of mutualism. While bacteria associated with wood rot have not been identified in these fossil woods, some fossil bacteria infecting the wall layers of pollen grains from the Carboniferous have been identified.

Defenses against Pathogens
Structural Defenses

Since the fossil record provides only static pictures, distinguishing between saprotrophic and parasitic fungal activity can be difficult. However, comparing the characteristic structural responses of extant plant cells with those in fossils enables scholars to determine the difference between fossil pathogen attacks and saprotrophic effects. Among the structural responses to pathogens are characteristic changes in cell walls, especially wall thickenings. Carboniferous specimens of a gymnospermous cone (*Lasiostrobus polysacci*) infected with fungi unambiguously show cell wall appositions (the addition of one layer after another) (Stubblefield et al. 1984). Synthesizing callose (a carbohydrate deposit), cellulose, or lignin, which resulted in cell wall thickening, was a response to infections and produced both structural and chemical barriers.

In a somewhat similar vein, sporopollenin, the highly persistent outer layer of spores, may have evolved to protect this precious and vulnerable reproductive structure against microorganisms and environmental factors. It is, however, an essential structure that was not induced originally by infection or environmental stress. The hypersensitive reaction—in which host cells surrounding the invading pathogen undergo apoptosis (programmed cell death), effectively isolating the pathogen from its energy source—has not been demonstrated unambiguously in fossils, although it has been commonly observed in modern plants.

Chemical Defenses

Chemical defense systems against invading pathogens are highly diverse and common in extant plants—and probably are more efficient than physical barriers or morphological modifications (changes in shape and structure). The modern arsenal ranges from small molecules that combat infection to large protein molecules that have evolved in response to pathogens, including lethal enzyme cocktails (Stacy et al. 1996). Evidence for chemical defenses cannot be detected in fossil plants, even though it is very probable that these systems evolved early on. However, evidence for one specific chemical defense system is preserved in, for instance, *Callixylon newberryi* from the Upper Devonian, as well as in Upper Pennsylvanian *Lasiostrobus* (Stubblefield et al. 1984). These specimens, infected with wood-decaying fungi, contain large globules of resinous material. Scholars can analyze the resin because it is preserved as amber. Large amounts of resin in fossil trees may have functioned in preventing invasion by pathogens or discouraging grazing and browsing animals. Resin ducts are common in many extant conifers and sometimes are induced by stress and injury. Mucilaginous material in Cycadophyta may serve similar functions.

Plant-Animal Interactions

Unambiguous proof of plant-herbivore interaction comes from insect "coprolites," fossilized fecal material containing undigested remains of plant tissues and spores. These have been found in the Lower Devonian and also may have been present in the Silurian. They were certainly abundant in the Carboniferous.

Bite marks, such as those found on *Glossopteris* leaves from the Permian, on angiosperm leaves from the Eocene, or with leaf miner activity in Tertiary leaves, constitute the "smoking gun" for the presence of phytophagous (plant-eating) animals. While few such "damaged" fossil specimens have been studied so far, they exist in fossil collections and represent a challenge to find further evidence for herbivory. The inspected specimens show relatively more herbivore damage on young than on older leaves, the same as happens in extant plants. With age, increases in fibrous tissues, epicuticular (outermost) waxes, and secondary substances such as tannin and phenolics render the leaves less palatable. Phytophagous habits obviously have changed little over time.

Plant-animal interactions probably started in watery habitats, where algae provided food for protozoans and invertebrates. Many modern marine algae contain an enzyme that is active only upon cell damage, such as that inflicted by a herbivorous protozoan. The enzyme converts a normally produced substrate into a nonpalatable or even poisonous substance (Wolfe et al. 1997). No fossil evidence for algal defense mechanisms is available.

The occurrence of periderm (cork cell layer) in limited amounts in Rhynie chert plants, where herbivory of terrestrial arthropods is well documented, has been interpreted as evidence of wound repair. In response to the herbivore attacks, plants evolved a variety of other defense strategies as well. The defense response of plants led to the selection for animal mechanisms to defeat the plant defense. This kind of one-upmanship is characteristic for herbivore-plant interactions, as well as for pathogen-host plant interactions, and continues today. For a while, the defense system of the plant is ahead; then, changes in the pathogen or herbivore occur through natural selection and result in a mechanism to defeat the defenses. This kind of coevolution is accelerated and, therefore, particularly obvious in the selection of pesticide-resistant species and pathovars (a variety of pathogenic microorganisms of a species) that have given rise to antibiotic-resistant pathogenic bacteria. Every time a pesticide or antibiotic is applied, only the resistant strains can survive. The manifold pesticide-resistant or antibiotic-resistant strains of bacteria and fungi bear clear testimony to these interactions.

In contrast to the continuous coevolution of hosts and pathogens stand the evolutionary holdovers from previous interactions. Certain plants in the Central American lowland forests served as food sources for Pleistocene vertebrates, for example. Today, these plants continue to form spines, even though the browsing herbivores are long extinct (Janzen and Martin 1982).

Defenses against Herbivores
Structural Defenses

Since plant fossils are usually found broken apart rather than whole and intact, browsing damage (damage to branches and leaves) from large animals, such as phytophagous dinosaurs, is not identified easily. The structure of plants is modular, and often repeats again and again those sections that produce new vegetative groups. This repetition may have evolved in response to herbivore pressure. For example, if tissue that produces a new shoot is removed, the plant is stimulated to produce more buds elsewhere. The growth response to herbivory is different from the structural features that afford plants protection from herbivores, including the formation of trichomes (hairs), thorns, and spines. Trichomes function not only as structural barriers against certain arthropods (e.g., insects), their terminal cells often accumulate chemicals that may constitute even stronger repellents than the physical impediment. Adopting the ultimate defense, some extant plants, such as *Drosera* or *Dionaea,* lure and digest the perpetrator. Their glandular hairs secrete sticky material to trap insects and enzymes to digest them.

Reproductive structures of plants usually contain high concentrations of proteins, carbohydrates, or lipids, making them a prime target for herbivory. Protecting them from being eaten is obviously of great importance to plants. Structural adaptations to protect spores, sporangia, and seeds are manifold. The sclerenchyma (lignified tissues) that surround the pollen organ in the seed fern *Medullosa* is an effective defense against plant-feeding insects. Cup-shaped structures surrounding the ovules may have provided a selective advantage to early seed plants. A thickened integument is an important structural feature that protects seeds from litter-dwelling arthropods, as is the formation of the ornamented, thickened walls of spores.

The evolution of an elongating plant axis, which raised reproductive structures above the litter zone, may have been driven by the selective advantage of being able to disperse wind-driven spores over a wide area. In the process, the longer axes also placed these fruiting structures out of reach of litter-dwelling animals. Although the evolution of winged insects during the Upper Devonian occurred shortly after the first arborescent (treelike) plants appeared in the fossil record, it is likely that the two events were not connected. Nonetheless, wings gave the flying insects access to important food sources.

Chemical Defenses

The fossil evidence for chemical defense systems, while not as dramatic as for morphological defenses, can be inferred from extant plants. Here, the defense arsenal ranges from the large array of secondary products of metabolism, including bitter-tasting substances and toxins, to complex proteins, including enzyme inhibitors (Stacy et al. 1996). While such compounds are not preserved in fossils and, at least currently, are out of reach of chemical analysis, inorganic crystals are often present, some of which indicate chemical defenses. Silica crystals in *Equisetum* and many grasses render these plants less digestible. The basic component of plant cell walls—cellulose—also must be considered a chemical defense, since most animals cannot digest it unless their gut contains specialized microorganisms that can do so. Lignin decreases the digestibility of cell walls even further. The cuticle—a hallmark of land plants—and epicuticular waxes, all well-preserved in fossils, present chemical and structural defenses against herbivores as well as pathogens. The secretion and accumulation of resins—as evidenced from the secretory canals of certain Carboniferous seed ferns, Cordaites, and most extant conifers—indicate their importance in the defense strategies of plants.

Protection from Environmental Stress, Especially Water Loss

In most environments, water is the growth-limiting factor; consequently, many different water-conserving structures and mechanisms have evolved in plants. The cuticle, a waxy coating on stems and leaves, is an adaptation to life on land that reduces water loss. It also serves as a structural defense and certainly hinders the growth of other organisms that grow on stem and leaf surfaces (epiphytes), which is common in algal communities. Sunken stomata, prevalent in extant plants of arid climates, protect plants against water loss, serving the same function in fossil plants. Specialized stems or leaves may minimize plant surface areas, and they evolved independently in different groups. Stem succulence (broad stems that hold water reserves), reduces surface area; these structures evolved independently in euphorbs and *Stapelia* in the Eastern Hemisphere and in cacti in the Western Hemisphere. Both fleshy stems and leaves, serving as water storage organs, are common in environments in which water stress occurs. Fossils with succulent tissues have been found as well.

If sufficient water is available to maintain water flow in a plant, leaves can be protected from heat by evaporative cooling. Thick boundary layers also insulate the leaves from the surrounding hot air. A different strategy is adopted by the "pubescence" of leaves and stems, a protective mechanism that traps a layer of air as insulation for the leaf and stem. Dense coverage of leaf surfaces, especially with colorless trichomes that reflect infrared light effectively, shields the leaf from heat damage. Fossils possessing trichomes are abundant since the Paleozoic.

The role of hormones in regulating environmental stress, a field of great current research interest, is not preserved in the fossil record. Undoubtedly such mechanisms existed in plants known to us only as fossils.

Many of the adaptations that protect plants from the uncertainties of the environment also protect them from herbivores and pathogens. The selective advantages of these features reinforced their retention, sometimes beyond the existence of the initial danger, at other times changing rapidly with the changing environment.

MANFRED RUDDAT

See also Plants: Adaptive Strategies; Plants: Mechanical Plant Design; Plants: Vegetative Features

Works Cited and Further Reading

Janzen, D.H., and P.S. Martin. 1982. Neotropical anachronisms: The fruits the gomophotheres ate. *Science* 215:19–27.

Ralph, J., J.J. MacKay, R.D. Hatfield, D.M. O'Malley, R.W. Whetten, and R.R. Sederoff. 1997. Abnormal lignin in a loblolly pine mutant. *Science* 277:235–39.

Remy, W., T.N. Taylor, H. Hass, and H. Kerp. 1994. Four hundred-million-old vesicular arbuscular mycorrhizae. *Proceedings of the National Academy Sciences USA* 91:118541–43.

Stacy, G., B. Mullin, and P.M. Gresshoff (eds.). 1996. *Biology of Plant-Microbe Interactions: Proceedings of the 8th International Symposium, Molecular Plant-Microbe Interactions, Knoxville, Tennessee, July 14–19, 1996*. St. Paul, Minnesota: International Society for Molecular Plant-Microbe Interactions.

Stubblefield S.P., T.N. Taylor, C.E. Miller, and G.T. Cole. 1984. Studies of Paleozoic fungi. Part 3, Fungal parasitism in a Pennsylvanian gymnosperm. *American Journal of Botany* 71:1275–82.

Taylor, T.N., and J.M. Osborn. 1996. The importance of fungi in shaping the paleoecosystem. *Review of Paleobotany and Palynology* 90:249–62.

Wolfe, G.V., M. Steinke, and G.O. Kirst. 1997. Grazing-activated chemical defense in a unicellular marine alga. *Nature* 3878:894–97.

DEFLANDRE, GEORGES VICTOR

French, 1897–1973

Georges Deflandre was born in the small town of Dizy-Magenta in the Champagne-Ardenne, France, on 18 March 1897. His paternal grandfather was a distinguished organist and composer, his maternal grandfather was an inventor of some distinction, and his father, a railway operative, was a competent artist. Deflandre thus was exposed to an array of abilities that were to prove valuable in his professional life. His father's early death, however, forced him into a series of unfulfilling short-term jobs—in the railways and as a school teacher—until he was called for service in World War I. He became a sublieutenant of infantry, earning the Croix de Guerre. When wounded and taken prisoner in June 1918, he used his time to master the German language.

Following release and repatriation, Deflandre returned to teaching school. However, he was becoming fascinated with microscopy, so in his spare time, he took up the study of protistology (the biology of unicellular organisms, such as algae, yeasts, and protozoans). This work came to the attention of the cryptogamic botanist L. Mangin, a specialist in plants that develop from spores. Mangin allowed Deflandre to continue his studies at the Muséum d'Histoire Naturelle in Paris. Deflandre's thesis on the freshwater microscopic plants of the Paris region and Haute-Savoie was so outstanding that, without having obtained any lesser degrees, he was awarded a doctorate by the University of Paris in 1926.

Deflandre's research horizons expanded steadily. Soon they included a variety of marine algae and microscopic animals. The animals were aquatic single-celled organisms called protozoans, which were characterized by a fully formed nucleus. Many of these animals incorporated minerals from the water around them to create distinctive shells and moved either by means of a flagellum (a long, hairlike projection that whips back and forth to propel the organism) or of cilia (fine, hairlike projections that move in waves to propel the organism). Still others were amoeboid—they moved by extending a portion of the cell body and "pulling" themselves along.

Deflandre first studied amoeboid protozoans, such as the camoebians and heliozoans, and a variety of marine algae. Then he began examining organic remains that he found when he sieved dissolved ancient sediments. At first he concentrated on siliceous protozoans (organisms that incorporated silicon), such as radiolarians, diatoms, silicoflagellates, and tintinnids. Soon afterward, Deflandre made major discoveries. While studying a New Zealand deposit formed mainly of diatom shells, he found two new aquatic siliceous organisms: an algae called archaeomonads (1932) and the first siliceous dinoflagellates (minute marine plants, many of which are phosphorescent) (1933). Later, he would also discover the first dinoflagellates that incorporated calcium in their shells (calcareous) (1947).

Deflandre also had begun examining calcarous microfossils. He conducted major studies of coccoliths (minute calcarous plates that form the armor of the walls of certain algae) and discovered discoasters (fossil star-shaped plates with an apparently similar function). His fascination with microfossils continued to widen; soon it embraced plant phytoliths (small crystals found in grasses

that probably function to deter grass-eating animals), the skeletal plates found in tunicates (marine animals with a saclike body enclosed in a structure that resembles a tunic), the jaw structures of segmented worms, and a variety of other microfossils whose affinity he could not determine.

In approximately 1932 Deflandre also began using the microscope to study thin flakes of Cretaceous flint, some from nodules collected from chalk quarries in the Paris region, others found on the paths or in the flower beds of the Jardin des Plantes. In these he observed the preserved remains of dinoflagellates with organic walls and the spiny microfossils that the German microscopist Otto Wetzel had just named "hystrichospheres." Using simple chemical and mechanical techniques, Deflandre extracted similar microfossils from Jurassic, Silurian, and Carboniferous sediments. These fossil dinoflagellates now have been shown to represent not the mobile, functioning (motile) stage in the life cycle but resting or reproducing cysts. Many of Wetzel's "hystrichospheres" are now known to be dinoflagellate cysts; the remaining problematic forms are now called "acritarchs."

Deflandre's first postdoctoral years were difficult financially. When the Centre de la Recherche Scientifique was established in 1932, Deflandre was appointed "chargé de recherches" and, in 1936, "maître de recherches." When the Ecole Pratique des Hautes Etudes was established in 1943, with quarters in the Jardin des Plantes, Deflandre became the first director of its Laboratoire de Micropaléontologie. One early employee was Marthe Emilie Françoise Rigaud, who was to become a distinguished researcher on the microscopic remains of echinoderms (marine animals with a spiny skeleton and radial body), especially holothurians (sea cucumbers). She and Deflandre were married in 1941. She worked with him on the many microfossil catalogues and literature reviews that were the laboratory's prime product—in particular the *Fichier micropaléontologique,* originally published as a card file and later as a series of volumes. After Deflandre's death, Marthe Deflandre-Rigaud succeeded him as director.

In addition to his numerous research papers, Deflandre was author of popular works: *Microscopie pratique* (1930, 1948), *Les flagellés fossiles* (1936), and *La vie créatrice des roches* (1941). He also made major contributions to the *Traité de Zoologie* (1952) and its companion *Traité de Paléontologie* (1952). He inspired a number of students, notably Lionel Valensi, whose studies of flint demonstrated how to use microfossils to determine the sources of Palaeolithic artifacts, and Jean Deunff, who became a major researcher on the Paleozoic microfossils of Brittany. A collaboration with the Australian paleobotanist Isabel C. Cookson inaugurated studies of the fossil Mesozoic plankton (microscopic animals or plants found floating in water) of Australia and Papua.

In his later years, Deflandre and his wife worked in Paris only during the winter; the rest of the year was spent in southeastern France at their "summer laboratory" at Forcalquier, in Provence-Alpes-Côte d'Azur. Deflandre died in Paris on 17 June 1973.

Georges Deflandre's work has had a profound effect upon geology. His major early studies of microfossil groups—in particular, the dinoflagellates, radiolarians, and coccoliths—now have profound importance in stratigraphical correlation. That is, he determined the age of "signature microorganisms"—certain varieties of organisms that lived during a certain geological period. Therefore, if a certain rock strata contained a particular microorganism, explorers could infer the strata's age and composition. This work proved invaluable to people who were exploring for petroleum. In a sense, this is paradoxical—Deflandre was wholly uninterested in biostratigraphy; his interest was always in the past and present life found in fresh and marine waters. Deflandre's precise identification and naming of organisms, his high-quality illustrations, and his important compilations of data formed an ideal basis for erecting charts that correlated types of organisms and the age and structure of particular rock strata. These correlations have proved very valuable to our understanding of the Earth's structure, both regional and global.

WILLIAM A.S. SARJEANT

Biography

Born in Dizy-Magenta, France, 18 March 1897. Docteur de l'Université de Paris, 1926. Became chargé de recherches (1932) and later maître de recherches (1936), Centre de la Recherche Scientifique, Paris; appointed directeur, Laboratoire de Paléontologie, Ecole Pratique des Hautes Etudes, Paris, 1943; microscopist, algologist, and micropaleontologist. Discovered new groups or types of microfossils (archaeomonads, calcareous and siliceous dinoflagellates); contributed substantially to knowledge of other forms (radiolarians, coccoliths, chitinozoans, and related problematic forms). Died in Paris, 17 June 1973.

Major Publications

1930. *Microscopie pratique. Le microscope et ses applications. La faune et la flore microscopique des eaux. Les microfossiles.* Encyclopédie pratique du naturaliste 25. Paris: Lechevalier; new ed. 1948.

1936–37. Microfossiles des silex crétacés. *Annales Paléontologie* 25:151–91; 26:51–103.

1936. *Les flagellés fossiles. Aperçu biologique et paléontologique. Rôle géologique.* Actualités Scientifiques et Industrielles 335. Paris: Hermann.

1941 *La vie créatrice des roches. Le rôle bâtisseur des êtres microscopiques et la genèse des houilles et des pétroles.* Paris: Presses Universitaires de France, 7th ed., 1967.

1949. *Titres et travaux scientifiques de Georges Deflandre.* Laboratoire de Micropaléontologie, école Pratique des Hautes études.

1951. Recherches sur les ébriédiens. Paléobiologie. évolution. Systématique. *Bulletin Biologique de la France et de la Belgique* 65:1–84.

1952a. Protistes. Généralités. Sous-embranchement des flagellés. Groupes Incertae Sedis. *In* J. Piveteau (ed.), *Traité de Paléontologie*, 1. Paris: Masson.

1952b. Dinoflagellés fossiles. *In* P.P. Grassé (ed.), *Traité de Zoologie*, 1. Paris: Masson.

Further Reading

Monod, T. 1973. Notice nécrologique sur Georges Deflandre. *Académie des Sciences, Paris, Comptes-rendus* 277:85–94.

Noel, D. 1975. Georges Deflandre 18 mars 1897–17 juin 1973. *Bulletin de la Société Géologique de France* 17:13–24.

Sarjeant, W.A.S. 1973. Two great palynologists: Gunnar Erdtman and Georges Deflandre. *Microscopy* 32(3):319–31.

———. 1991. Sclerites, spicules and systematics: The researches of Marthe Deflandre-Rigaud (1902–1987). *Micropaleontology* 37(2):191–95.

DENISON, ROBERT HOWLAND

American, 1911–85

Robert H. Denison began as a paleomammalogist, collecting Tertiary mammals and writing a Ph.D. thesis on the broad-skulled Pseudocreodi (primitive carnivores), for which he was awarded a Cressy Morrison Prize in Natural Science in 1937 by the New York Academy of Sciences; he published the work in 1958. A student of William K. Gregory, Denison received a broad anatomical education and dissected and described parts of a whale shark held in the collections of the American Museum of Natural History at that time (1937). That project was his first detailed research of fish.

At the Dartmouth College Museum, Denison was in charge of the Patten collections of Silurian agnathans from Saaremaa (Ösel), Estonia, and of Devonian fishes from the Miguasha region of Quebec, Canada. He described lungs and spiral intestine in the antiarch *Bothriolepis* from Miguasha (1941), a much cited and disputed interpretation. On the osteostracan *Tremataspis* from Saaremaa, he demonstrated a close connection between the lateral line system and the pore-canal system (1947), which was not generally accepted until twenty years later. His collecting and research in later years focused on North American Paleozoic agnathans, or jawless fishes (Osteostraci and Heterostraci) and on fishes—mainly placoderms—of North America. The latter were primitive jawed fish with heavily armored heads and trunks. Beginning with detailed descriptions of morphology (form) and histology (microscopic anatomy) of these groups, he progressed to a survey and classification of the agnathans (Osteostraci, 1951; Cuanthaspididae, 1964; Pteraspididae, 1967, 1970) and placoderms (1975, 1978, 1983). His classification of Osteostraci was accepted by L.B. Halstead (1982) and opposed by P. Janvier (1985); his classification of syanthaspids is still accepted, but that of the pteraspids is in the process of being overturned. Denison's phylogenetic concepts corresponded with those of A.S. Romer and G.G. Simpson. He was not an advocate of the new cladistic approach (W. Hennig's phylogenetic approach), although he employed it in the handbook on placoderms (1978). Earlier (1975), he had published a traditional bushy-branching arrangement of placoderm groups, and he returned to that style in 1983. In 1985 he published an analysis of the only known complete ptyctodont placoderm of North America.

Of general interest was Denison's paper on the paleoenvironment of early vertebrates. He confirmed that vertebrates originated in marine waters, as W. Gross had stated first in 1950. At this time, this position was highly disputed among Anglo-American scientists. He described the earliest lungfish with denticles (instead of dental or tooth plates) from the Lower Devonian of Wyoming (1968a, 1968b). He compiled his broad knowledge of placoderms and acanthodians in two volumes of the *Handbook of Paleoichthyology* (1978, 1979). Throughout his life Denison accumulated a solid body of scientific work on Paleozoic agnathans and fishes and a well-organized fossil fish collection in the Field Museum of Natural History of Chicago, Illinois.

HANS-PETER SCHULTZE

Works Cited

Halstead, L.B. 1982. Evolutionary trends and the phylogeny of the Agnatha. *In* K.A. Joysey and A.E. Friday (eds.), *Problems of Phylogenetic Reconstruction*. New York and London: Academic Press.

Janvier, P. 1985. *Les Céphalaspides du Spitsberg. Anatomie, phylogénie et systématique des Ostéostracés siluro-dévoniens. Révision des Ostéostracés de la Formation de Wood Bay (Dévonien inférieur du Spitsberg)*. Cahiers de Paléontologie. Paris: Centre National de la Recherche Scientifique.

Biography

Born in Somerville, Massachusetts, 9 November 1911. Received A.B., Harvard College, Cambridge, Massachusetts, 1933; M.A., Columbia University, 1934; Ph.D., Columbia University, 1938. Recipient, Cressy Morrison Prize, New York Academy of Science, 1937; assistant curator for zoology, Dartmouth College Museum, Dartmouth, New Hampshire, 1937–47; instructor in zoology (1938–43) and assistant professor (1943–47), Dartmouth College, Dartmouth, New Hampshire; paleontologist, University of California African Expedition, 1947–48; curator for fossil fishes (1948–70) and research associate (1971–85), Field Museum of Natural History, Chicago; Guggenheim fellow, 1953–54; secretary (1959–60) and president (1962–63), Society of Vertebrate Paleontology; member, Paleontological Society. Collected Tertiary mammals in Wyoming, Montana, Nebraska, and South Dakota, 1931, 1932, 1934, 1938, and in Egypt and Kenya 1947–48; later collected Silurian and Devonian fishes in New Brunswick, Nova Scotia, Quebec, Alberta, British Columbia, Arizona, Utah, Idaho, Colorado, Wyoming, Michigan, Ohio, Pennsylvania, New Jersey, New York, Norway, and Great Britain, 1939, 1949, 1950–54, 1956, 1957, 1959–61, 1963–65. Died in Lincoln, Massachusetts, 7 September 1985.

Major Publications

1937. Anatomy of the head and pelvic fin of the whale shark *Rhineodon*. *Bulletin of the American Museum of Natural History* 78:477–515.
1938. The broad-skulled Pseudocreodi. *Annals of the New York Academy of Sciences* 37:163–256.
1941. The soft anatomy of *Bothriolepis*. *Journal of Paleontology* 15:553–61.

1947. The exoskeleton of *Tremataspis*. *American Journal of Science* 245:337–65.
1951a. Evolution and classification of the Osteostraci. *Fieldiana: Geology* 11 (3–4):155–96.
1951b. The exoskeleton of early Osteostraci. *Fieldiana: Geology* 11 (5):197–218.
1952. Early Devonian fishes from Utah. Part 1, Osteostraci. *Fieldiana: Geology* 11 (6):263–87.
1953. Early Devonian fishes from Utah. Part 2, Heterostraci. *Fieldiana: Geology* 11 (7):291–355.
1956. A review of the habitat of the earliest vertebrates. *Fieldiana: Geology* 11 (8):359–457.
1958. Early Devonian fishes from Utah. Part 3, Anthrodira. *Fieldiana: Geology* 11 (9):461–551.
1963. New Silurian Heterostraci from Southeastern Yukon. *Fieldiana: Geology* 14 (7):105–41.
1964. The Cyathaspididae, a family of Silurian and Devonian jawless vertebrates. *Fieldiana: Geology* 13 (5):307–473.
1966. *Cardipeltis*. An Early Devonian agnathan of the order Heterostraci. *Fieldiana: Geology* 16 (4):89–116.
1967a. A new *Protaspis* from the Devonian of Utah, with notes on the classification of Pteraspididae. *Journal of the Linnean Society (Zoology)* 47:31–37.
1967b. Ordovician vertebrates from Western United States. *Fieldiana: Geology* 16 (5):131–92.
1968a. Early Devonian lungfishes from Wyoming, Utah, and Idaho. *Fieldiana: Geology* 17 (4):353–413.
1968b. The evolutionary significance of the earliest known lungfish, *Uranolophus*. *In* T. Ørvig (ed.), *Current Problems of Lower Vertebrate Phylogeny, Nobel Symposium*. Stockholm: Almqvist and Wiksell; New York and London: Interscience.
1969. New Pennsylvanian lungfishes from Illinois. *Fieldiana: Geology* 12:193–211.
1970. Revised classification of Pteraspididae with description of new forms from Wyoming. *Fieldiana: Geology* 20 (1):1–41.
1974. The structure and evolution of teeth in lungfishes. *Fieldiana: Geology* 33 (3):31–58.
1975. Evolution and classification of placoderm fishes. *Breviora* 432:1–24.
1978. Placodermi. *In* H.-P. Schultze (ed.), *Handbook of Paleoichthyology*, vol. 2. Stuttgart and New York: Fisher Verlag.
1979. Acanthodii. *In* H.-P. Schultze (ed.), *Handbook of Paleoichthyology*, vol. 2. Stuttgart and New York: Fisher Verlag.
1983. Further consideration of the phylogeny and classification of the order Arthrodira (Pisces: Placodermi). *Journal of Vertebrate Paleontology* 4:396–412.
1985. A new ptyctodont placoderm, *Ptyctodopsis*, from the Middle Devonian of Iowa. *Journal of Paleontology* 59:511–22.

Further Reading

Gross, W. 1950. *Die paläontologische and stratigraphische Bedeutung der Wirbeltierfaunen des Old Reds und der marinen altpaläozoischen Schichten*. Abhandlungen der Deutschen Akademie der Wissenschaften zu Berlin, mathematisch-naturwissenschaftliche Klasse. Berlin, Germany: Akademie-Verlag.
Schultze, H.-P., and R. Zangerl. 1986. Robert H. Denison, 1911–1985. *Society of Vertebrate Paleontology, News Bulletin* 136:59–61.
Zangerl, R. 1986. Robert H. Denison, 1911–1985. *Field Museum of Natural History Bulletin* 57 (4):19.

DERMOPTERANS

The living colugos are large gliding mammals that inhabit the region that includes Indonesia and Malaysia. The name "flying lemur" often is used for these animals, which is very confusing because they are not lemurs and they do not fly. These enigmatic animals belong to their own order, the Dermoptera, but they represent only one of the several groups of mammals in which gliding has evolved. The other living gliders are the flying squirrels (Pteromyinae), scaly-tailed flying squirrels (Anomalurinae), and three different kinds of gliding marsupials (*Acrobates, Petaurus,* and *Petauroides*). The bats also may have evolved gliding independently of other mammals.

In the fossil record, at least one species of primitive rodent (Eomyidae) and one species of dormouse (Gliridae) now are known to have been gliders. In colugos the gliding membrane (the patagium) completely encloses the animal and is the most extensive of any gliding or flying mammal. The postcranial (body) skeleton also is highly specialized. The limbs are very long and thin, as are the fingers, to support the gliding membrane. The hand provides a movable wing tip that may act to reduce induced drag (friction caused by air flow), increase stability against rolling, or enhance other aspects of control and maneuverability.

The skull and teeth of the colugos are very striking (Figure 1). The cranium is very broad and flat. The braincase is small, and the skull has extensive bony structures that serve as attachments for the muscles of mastication. The molar teeth retain a basically tribosphenic plan (triangular tooth structure) but have greatly enhanced shearing edges in order to deal with the colugos' folivorous (foliage-based) diet. The lower incisors are the most specialized of all. Each tooth is formed of multiple small tines. These teeth meet with a toothless space between the reduced upper second incisors (the upper first incisor has been lost). This arrangement, called a "tooth comb," is not unlike that seen in ruminants such as deer and camels, but there has been some debate over the function of the dermopteran tooth comb. There is some evidence that it is used in grooming, but almost none that it is used in feeding.

The Dermoptera comprise a single family, Cynocephalidae, containing two extant (living) species: *Cynocephalus volans* and *Galeopterus variegatus.* The Philippine colugo *(C. volans)* inhabits the southern Philippine islands, while the Sundaic colugo *(G. variegatus)* inhabits the Indonesian islands of the Sunda shelf and the southern portion of the Southeast Asian mainland. The distribution of the two genera agrees with the biogeographical fault line described by Huxley's Line and coincides with deep water channels between Borneo and the Philippine Islands. During periods of glaciation, the level of the oceans would have fallen, exposing the Sunda shelf and connecting the islands that we see today with the Southeast Asian mainland. This "land bridge" would have permitted contact between populations of Sundaic colugos, but the deep water still would have remained between Borneo and the Philippines, maintaining a barrier between the two genera, even during periods of intense glaciation.

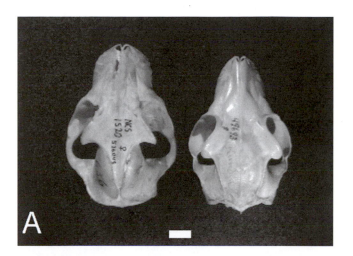
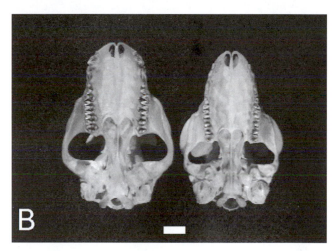
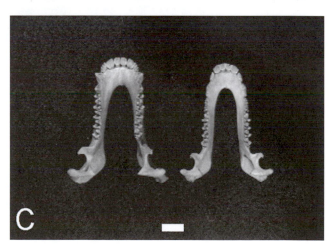

Figure 1. The Philippine colugo *Cynocephalus volans* (USNM 536049, left), and the Sundaic colugo *Galeopterus variagatus* (USNM 49693, right). *A,* dorsal view of the cranium; *B,* ventral view of the cranium; *C,* dorsal view of the mandible. Scale bars equal 1 millimeter.

Biology and Behavior

E.W. Wischusen's (1990) study of Philippine colugos on Mindanao represents the only scientific study of these animals' biology and behavior, although there are abundant anecdotal reports of colugos. Wischusen found that Philippine colugos are nocturnal animals that live in trees, feeding on leaves. They have rapid rates of digestion and rely on immature leaves for the majority of their diet. Solitary animals, they inhabit home ranges of about 10 hectares and travel about 1,400 meters nightly. Gliding is the most common method of travel, but within trees the most common mode of locomotion is done by hanging by four hands (quadrumanous suspension). Glides of over 100 meters have been reported. During the day, colugos spend their time in tree cavities, in dense tangles of foliage, or in hanging slothlike from more exposed branches. Their coloration effectively mimics the pattern of lichens on tree bark and serves as excellent camouflage. Mating behavior seldom has been observed, and gestation is reported as being anywhere from 60 to 150 days. Females appear to become pregnant before weaning previous offspring, and infants are present throughout most of the year. There have been no scientific studies of the Sundaic colugos.

Evolutionary Relationships

Colugos long have been viewed as the closest relatives of the bats (*Volitantia illiger*), a theory supported by a large body of anatomical and molecular evidence. Colugos also have been seen as a "living fossil" (a form that is evolutionarily conserved, i.e., has changed little from an ancient ancestor) that may represent a preflapping stage in the evolution of bats. These views have been based largely on the postcranial similarities between colugos and bats that give the colugos a very batlike appearance. For example, the fact that the patagium (part of the wing) in the colugos encloses the hand often has been seen as an intermediate stage in the acquisition of powered flight in bats. However, there is no fossil evidence supporting this hypothesis, and the postcranial similarities between dermopterans and bats could be convergent (i.e., similar selective forces acting on gliding and flying animals may produce similar body structures), although this seems unlikely.

Although there are no undisputed fossil dermopterans, several groups of fossil mammals have been proposed. *Dermotherium major* from the Upper Eocene of Thailand is the best candidate for inclusion in the Dermoptera (Ducrocq et al. 1992). The material is fragmentary (a piece of the left jaw with two broken molars) but seems to be similar to *G. variegatus*, although much larger. The Plagiomenidae also have been considered to be dermopterans, although many authors feel that the anatomy of the skull and teeth of this group is too specialized to indicate dermopteran ties. However, K.D. Rose and E.L. Simons (1977) have shown similarities in the wear facets (worn-down areas on teeth that show how they rub against each other) of colugo and plagiomenid teeth, indicating that the masticatory systems in these groups have similar functions. The colugos also have been linked to the Paromomyidae (i.e., archaic primates), based on similarities in the structure of the wrist, digital (finger and toe) proportions, and cranial anatomy (Beard 1993; Kay et al. 1992). However, J.A. Runestad and C.B. Ruff (1995) have analyzed cross sections of limb bones of living gliders and shown they are very different from those of the archaic primates. Alternately, F.S. Szalay and S.G. Lucas (1993) provide detailed data from the elbow region that links the Mixodectidae to the Dermoptera (supported by Gunnell 1989), and links the Dermoptera to the Megachiroptera. Should any of these groups prove to be dermopterans, it would extend the time span of the Dermoptera back into the Paleocene and extend their geographic range into North America and Europe. However, until more complete fossil evidence is uncovered, it is best to consider dermopterans as an order found only in the Indomalayan subregion, with their first appearance in the Upper Eocene.

BRIAN J. STAFFORD

See also Aerial Locomotion; Bats

Wogrks Cited and Further Reading

Beard, K.C. 1993. Phylogenetic systematics of the Primatomorpha, with special reference to the Dermoptera. *In* F.S. Szalay et al. (eds.), *Mammal Phylogeny.* Vol. 2, *Placentals.* Berlin and New York: Springer-Verlag.

Ducrocq, S., E. Buffetaut, H. Buffetaut-Tong, J.J. Jaeger, Y. Jongkanjanasoontorn, and V. Suteethorn. 1992. First fossil flying lemur: A dermopteran from the late Eocene of Thailand. *Palaeontology* 35:373–80.

Gunnell, G.F. 1989. *Evolutionary History of Microsyopoidea (Mammalia, Primates) and the Relationship between Plesiadapiformes and Primates.* University of Michigan Papers on Paleontology, 27. Ann Arbor: Museum of Paleontology, University of Michigan.

Kay, R.F., J.G.M. Thewissen, and A.D. Yoder. 1992. Cranial anatomy of *Ignacius graybullianus* and the affinities of the Plesiadapiformes. *American Journal of Physical Anthropology* 89:447–98.

Rose, K.D., and E.L. Simons. 1977. Dental function in the Plagiomenidae: Origin and relationships of the mammalian order Dermoptera. *Contributions from the Museum of Paleontology* 24:221–36.

Runestad, J.A., and C.B. Ruff. 1995. Structural adaptations for gliding in mammals with implications for locomotor behavior in paromomyids. *American Journal of Physical Anthropology* 98:101–20.

Szalay, F.S., and S.G. Lucas. 1993. Cranioskeletal morphology of Archontans, and the diagnoses of Chiroptera, Volitantia, and Archonta. *In* R.D.E. MacPhee (ed.), *Primates and Their Relatives in Phylogenetic Perspective.* New York: Plenum.

Wischusen, E.W. 1990. The foraging ecology and natural history of the Philippine flying lemur (*Cynocephalus volans*). Ph.D. dis., Cornell University.

DIAPSIDS

See Sauropsids

DIET

The chances of any individual organism being preserved as a fossil are very small, and the possibility that paleontologists can learn the specific dietary preferences of a fossil organism may seem even more remote. This is probably true of the majority of extinct organisms, although there may be enough evidence to determine general feeding patterns or preferences. But there are also cases where the evidence is so strong that the food items of an organism can be identified with a high degree of confidence. For the purposes of this essay, I will consider the evidence as being of three different types: fossil evidence of eating, fossil evidence of being eaten, and geochemical evidence of diet.

Evidence of Eating

The most reliable evidence for dietary preferences takes the form of food preserved in the process of being eaten. This category includes some of the most remarkable and unlikely fossils, such as the specimen of *Holdenius* (a placoderm fish from the Devonian of Ohio) that was killed by trying to eat a ctenacanth shark. As *Holdenius* bit down, the rigid spine on the shark's dorsal fin pierced the upper palate and punctured the braincase of the placoderm, probably killing it instantly (according to written communications of W.J. Hlavin in Boucot 1990). Other cases of fossil predatory fish that preserve their prey items within the digestive tract are too numerous to list here, but M.E. Williams (1990) and G. Viohl (1990) include many excellent examples. Other well-known examples from among vertebrates include ichthyosaurs and plesiosaurs with masses of squid hooklets or belemnite rostra preserved in their stomachs (Keller 1976). There are also a number of fossils that preserve invertebrates caught in the act of feeding, such as starfish feeding on gastropods (Blake and Zinmeister 1979) and bivalves (Blake and Guensberg 1994), a squid with a fish in its grasp (Boucot 1990), spiders caught in amber with their prey (Wunderlich 1986), and insects with digestive tracts full of pollen (Scott and Taylor 1983). Stomach contents in the form of gastroliths, gizzard stones, or stomach stones also provide indirect evidence of diet. These are consumed by some extant animals, particularly birds, to assist with the internal breakdown or "milling" of food. They also are known from the extinct giant flightless bird, the Moa, and a number of extinct reptiles, although their role in the latter may have been as ballast rather than digestive (Boucot 1990).

A second, and only slightly less reliable, indicator of eating patterns comes from fossils that preserve consumers in intimate association with their food. Perhaps the most dramatic example is the dinosaur specimen from Mongolia that preserves together a "raptor" and a ceratopsian, apparently locked in mortal combat. However, the possibility that such rare specimens preserve chance associations of individuals never can be discounted completely, and inferences of predatory activity may not be correct. A similar interpretation was given to another Mongolian dinosaur specimen preserving an *Oviraptor* apparently overwhelmed by sand and pre-

served in the act of eating the eggs of another species (Osborn 1924). Only recently have the eggs been identified as belonging to *Oviraptor*, and rather than nest-robbing, such specimens preserve a unique snapshot of dinosaur brooding behavior (Norell et al. 1995). Nevertheless, this type of evidence can provide reliable indications of dietary preferences, for example, insect larvae feeding inside a plant stem (Jarzembowski 1980), nematodes preserved in amber along with their fungal food material (Poinar 1977), and parasites preserved attached to their host (Boucot 1990; Conway Morris 1990). A specimen preserving a tooth of a *Squalicorax* shark embedded in a hadrosaur bone (Schwimmer et al. 1997) provides an interesting example; because *Squalicorax* sharks and hadrosaurs did not live in the same environments this is almost certainly a case of scavenging of a hadrosaur carcass by the shark, and not predation (Schwimmer et al. 1997).

Teeth can provide important clues regarding dietary preferences and feeding. Tooth shape gives some indication of possible foodstuffs that an extinct animal could have eaten, but more reliable information comes from analysis of tooth wear. During feeding, teeth may come into contact with each other, with food, or with abrasive particles taken into the mouth along with food (such as sand grains on foliage or bone chips in meat). This contact produces wear that accumulates over the life of the animal, or, in animals that shed and replace their teeth, the life of the tooth. Dietary inferences can be made from gross wear patterns, such as whether an animal preferred abrasive or nonabrasive food, but more detailed conclusions can be reached if the microscopic features developed within wear facets are analyzed. These microscopic features, known as microwear, are distinctive polished, scratched, or pitted textures produced in vivo by the action of abrasives in food and by the compressive and shearing forces that act on enamel during feeding (Teaford 1988a). These textures reflect the mechanics of food breakdown, the relative motion of teeth, and the nature of food consumed; microwear analysis thus represents a powerful and direct tool for investigating feeding in extinct animals. Its application to fossils is complicated by the possibility of postmortem abrasion, but in studies of mammal teeth, this can be excluded because in vivo wear forms only as distinctive facets at specific locations on functional surfaces (Teaford 1988b), and teeth that exhibit wear on nonfunctional surfaces can be excluded from analysis. Microwear techniques can reveal subtle difference in diet, and N. Solounias and L.-A.C. Hayek (1993), for example, were able to differentiate Miocene browsing herbivores from those that fed by both grazing and browsing. Primates have been a particular focus of study, primarily in order to understand the dietary preferences of early hominids (e.g., Ungar and Grine 1991). Analyses of microwear are restricted almost exclusively to mammals, but recent work has demonstrated its potential for understanding feeding in other groups of extinct animals (Purnell 1995).

Direct evidence of the relationship between consumer and consumed is extremely rare in the fossil record, and most interpretations of what an extinct organism ate or could have eaten come from studies of gross morphology and anatomy. The degree of precision with which specific dietary preferences can be inferred is generally limited, but analysis can yield useful and reliable information. In most cases this approach can be considered as analysis of functional morphology, often relying heavily on comparisons between the structures used by a fossil organism to feed and those of a living organism, ideally a close relative. This approach is very widespread, and it is only possible to give a few examples here. Vertebrates provide a good illustration of how the nature of the evidence changes as the phylogenetic relationship between modern analogues and fossil organisms becomes increasingly remote with increasing time. Among living mammals, tooth and skull morphology often is correlated closely with diet; members of the cat family, for example, have sharp, pointed, and bladelike teeth adapted for piercing and slicing, typical of carnivores, whereas the molar teeth of herbivorous mammals, such as ungulates, are flattened and ridged to maximize chewing and grinding efficiency. Fossil representatives of these groups exhibit similar tooth morphology, and researchers can infer generally similar dietary preferences. Investigating vertebrates whose living relatives are less closely related to fossil taxa present more problems. Interpretations of herbivory derived from simple morphological and functional comparisons with living animals would not result in reliable interpretations of diet in dinosaurs, for example. More sophisticated analyses of skull kinematics (e.g., Weishampel 1984) and tooth wear patterns can, however, produce sound results.

The morphology of invertebrates also can provide evidence from which dietary preferences can be interpreted, again with variable degrees of precision and confidence. The possession of supports for a lophophore (filter-feeding apparatus) provides good evidence that, like their living relatives, extinct brachiopods were suspension feeders (e.g., Rowell and Grant 1987). Their food must have been microscopic plankton, but more precise statements regarding dietary preferences are not possible. Arthropods also provide some good examples, such as biting and piercing mouthparts in ticks and mosquitoes preserved in amber (e.g., Lane and Poinar 1986), and spinnerets and web spinning in spiders (e.g., Selden 1989).

Evidence of Being Eaten

The fossil record contains considerable evidence of things being eaten, such as bite marks, grazing traces, and coprolites (fossil feces). These fossils provide unequivocal evidence of organisms and substrates that were food, but identifying what was eating or trying to eat them is often very difficult or impossible. This is probably true of most grazing trace fossils and coprolites, but there are exceptions. Striking examples of tooth marks in the shells of Pennsylvanian nautiloids and ammonoids, and Cretaceous ammonites have been identified as the result of attacks by sharks (Mapes and Hansen 1984) and mosasaurs (Kauffman 1990). Prominent parallel scratches on bones of a variety of Late Cretaceous vertebrates have been interpreted as evidence of scavenging by *Squalicorax* sharks (Schwimmer et al. 1997). Similarly, characteristic radiating patterns of scratches on mollusc shells as old as the Trias-

sic can be identified as traces of feeding activity of echinoids (Bromley 1975; Fürsich and Wendt 1977). A.J. Boucot (1990) gives many more examples.

Coprolites are notoriously difficult to relate back to their creator. Many lack any morphological characteristic that could be of use, but coprolites with spiral structure and well-preserved internal features have been interpreted as the gut fills of sharks (Williams 1972), with the spiral valve in the shark's intestine producing the spiral structure in the fossil. These indicate that the sharks in question were "subsisting primarily on palaeoniscoids, with lungfish as a secondary source of food" (Williams 1972). Regurgitated pellets produced by hunting birds also have been recognized in the fossil record, and it may be possible to differentiate owl pellets from those produced by diurnal (daytime) raptors (Walton 1990). Recently reported coprolites of Silurian and Devonian age from the Welsh borderland provide interesting information regarding ancient diets. The identity of the producer is unknown, but the coprolites are full of terrestrial plant spores, and they represent the first evidence of herbivory in land animals (Edwards et al. 1995). Tertiary dung beetle balls and nests (Retallack 1990), although not strictly coprolites, represent perhaps one of the most unlikely examples of fossil evidence for dietary preferences.

Stable Isotopes and Trace Elements as Evidence

Recent decades have seen a great deal of work using stable isotopes of elements such as carbon, nitrogen, and oxygen as indicators of an organism's diet or its relative position on a trophic ladder (food chain). Such work is based primarily on two factors observed in modern ecosystems: first, that the isotopic composition of an organism's tissues is influenced by the isotopic composition of the food and fluids it consumes, and second, that in animals occupying progressively higher trophic levels, the heavier isotopes of carbon and nitrogen (^{13}C, ^{15}N) tend to become increasingly enriched relative to ^{12}C and ^{14}N. This increase is generally small, only a few parts per thousand, but it is enough to be detected and to be useful in determining the relative positions of organisms within a food web. It also is possible sometimes to discriminate between terrestrial browsers and grazers because the photosynthetic pathways of grasses adapted for warm or dry habitats produce different levels of ^{13}C fractionation than the photosynthetic pathways of trees, most herbs and shrubs, and grasses adapted for cool or wet habitats. These differences are reflected in the isotopic composition of the tissues of the consumers. Marine and terrestrial food sources also can be differentiated isotopically.

Application of these techniques to extinct animals is limited by the factors controlling the preservation of an organism's tissues and their isotopic composition. Work has focused on decay-resistant organic molecules such as collagen recovered from bones and teeth, and it has been possible, for example, to determine from carbon isotopes that mammoths and mastodons from the late Pleistocene of the east coast of what is today the United States differed in what they ate. The mammoths ate significant amounts of dry/warm adapted grasses, whereas mastodons did not (Krueger 1991). Comparisons of nitrogen isotopes between Neanderthals and known herbivores and carnivores have been taken to indicate that Neanderthals were primarily carnivorous (Bocherens et al. 1991). For more examples see Koch et al. (1994).

The difficulty in analyzing the isotopic signatures of fossils is that, in geological terms, organic molecules break down very rapidly; even collagen rarely survives beyond 100,000 years (Koch et al. 1994). It can be extremely difficult, even in relatively young fossils, to determine whether extracted organic material is made up of digested products, remnants of original collagen or other molecules, or contaminants from the surrounding matrix (i.e., rock in which the fossil is embedded), or a combination. Thus isotopic studies of diet based on organic residues extracted from fossils may not be reliable. However, analysis of high-molecular-weight organic extracts from Cretaceous vertebrate fossils has yielded carbon and nitrogen stable isotope ratios that are consistent with previous interpretations of the trophic position of the animals investigated (Ostrom et al. 1993).

Biogenic minerals such as the calcium phosphate of bones and teeth or the calcium carbonate of eggshells or invertebrate skeletons are more stable over geological time scales. It is possible to look at their carbon and oxygen isotopic composition, but the applications for dietary analysis of fossils seem rather limited (see Koch et al. 1994). Trace elements, however, may be of some use. A. Sillen and J.A. Lee-Thorp (1994), for example, used strontium/calcium ratios to determine that fossil leopards preyed primarily upon baboons, with hyraxes as a secondary dietary component.

MARK A. PURNELL

See also Feeding Adaptations; Gastroliths; Teeth; Trace Fossils

Works Cited

Blake, D.B., and T.E. Guensburg. 1994. Predation by the Ordovician asteroid *Promopalaeaster* on a Pelecypod. *Lethaia* 27:235–39.

Blake, D.B., and W.J. Zinmeister. 1979. Two early Cenozoic sea stars (Class Asteroidea) from Seymour Island, Antarctic Peninsula. *Journal of Paleontology* 53:1145–54.

Bocherens, H., M. Fizet, A. Mariotti, B. Langebadre, B. Vandermeersch, J.P. Borel, and G. Bellon. 1991. Isotopic biogeochemistry (^{13}C, ^{15}N) of fossil vertebrate collagen: Application to the study of a past food web including Neanderthal man. *Journal of Human Evolution* 20:481–92.

Boucot, A.J. (ed.). 1990. *Evolutionary Paleobiology of Behavior and Coevolution.* Amsterdam and New York: Elsevier.

Bromley, R.G. 1975. Comparative analysis of fossil and recent echinoid bioerosion. *Palaeontology* 18:725–39.

Conway Morris, S. 1990. Parasitism. *In* D.E.G. Briggs and P.R. Crowther (eds.), *Palaeobiology: A Synthesis.* Oxford and Boston: Blackwell Scientific.

Edwards, D., P.A. Selden, J.B. Richardson, and L. Axe. 1995. Coprolites as evidence for plant-animal interaction in Siluro-Devonian terrestrial ecosystems. *Nature* 377:329–31.

Fürsich, F.T., and J. Wendt. 1977. Biostratinomy and palaeoecology of the Cassian Formation (Triassic) of the Southern Alps. *Palaeogeography, Palaeoclimatology, Palaeoecology* 22:257–323.

Jarzembowski, E.A. 1980. Fossil insects from the Bembridge Marls, Palaeogene of the Isle of Wight, southern England. *Bulletin of the British Museum (Natural History), Geology* 33:237–93.

Kauffman, E.G. 1990. Mosasaur predation on ammonites during the Cretaceous: An evolutionary history. *In* A.J. Boucot (ed.), *Evolutionary Paleobiology of Behavior and Coevolution.* Amsterdam and New York: Elsevier.

Keller, T. 1976. Magen- und Darminhalte von Ichthyosaurien des süddeutschen Posidonienschiefers. *Neues Jahrbuch für Geologie und Paläontologie, Monatshefte* 5:266–83.

Koch, P.L., M.L. Fogel, and N. Tuross. 1994. Tracing the diet of fossil animals using stable isotopes. *In* K. Lajtha and R.H. Micheneer (eds.), *Stable Isotopes in Ecology and Environmental Science.* Oxford and Boston: Blackwell Scientific.

Krueger, H.W. 1991. Exchange of carbon with biological apatite. *Journal of Archaeological Science* 18:355–61.

Lane, R.S., and G.O.J. Poinar. 1986. First fossil tick (Acari: Ixodidae) in New World amber. *International Journal of Acarology* 12:75–78.

Mapes, R.H., and M.C. Hansen. 1984. Pennsylvanian shark-cephalopod predation: A case study. *Lethaia* 17:175–83.

Norell, M.A., J.M. Clark, L.M. Chiappe, and D. Dashzeveg. 1995. A nesting dinosaur. *Nature* 378:774–76.

Osborn, H.F. 1924. Three new therapods, protoceratops zone, central Mongolia. *American Museum Novitates* 144:1–12.

Ostrom, P.H., S.A. Macko, M.H. Engel, and D.A. Russell. 1993. Assessment of trophic structure of Cretaceous communities based on stable nitrogen isotope analyses. *Geology* 21:491–94.

Poinar, G.O. 1977. Fossil nematodes from Mexican amber. *Nematoligica* 23:232–38.

Purnell, M.A. 1995. Microwear on conodont elements and macrophagy in the first vertebrates. *Nature* 374:798–800.

Retallack, G. 1990. The work of dung beetles and its fossil record. *In* A.J. Boucot (ed.), *Evolutionary Paleobiology of Behavior and Coevolution.* Amsterdam and New York: Elsevier.

Rowell, A.J., and R.E. Grant. 1987. Phylum Brachiopoda. *In* R.S. Boardman, A.H. Cheetham, and A.J. Rowell (eds.), *Fossil Invertebrates*, Palo Alto, California: Blackwell Scientific.

Schwimmer, D.R., J.D. Stewart, and G.D. Williams. 1997. Scavenging by sharks of the genus *Squalicorax* in the Late Cretaceous of North America. *Palaios* 12:71–83.

Scott, A.C., and T.N. Taylor. 1983. Plant-animal interactions during the Upper Carboniferous. *Botanical Reviews* 49:259–307.

Selden, P.A. 1989. Orb-web weaving spiders in the early Cretaceous. *Nature* 340:711–13.

Sillen, A., and J.A. Lee-Thorp. 1994. Trace-element and isotopic aspects of predator-prey relationships in terrestrial foodwebs. *Palaeogeography, Palaeoclimatology, Palaeoecology* 107:243–55.

Solounias, N., and L.-A.C. Hayek. 1993. New methods of tooth microwear analysis and application to dietary determination of two extinct antelopes. *Journal of Zoology* 229:421–45.

Teaford, M.F. 1988a. A review of dental microwear and diet in modern mammals. *Scanning Microscopy* 2:1149–66.

——. 1988b. Scanning electron microscope diagnosis of wear patterns versus artifacts on fossil teeth. *Scanning Microscopy* 2:1167–75.

Ungar, P.S., and F.E. Grine. 1991. Incisor size and wear in *Australopithecus africanus* and *Paranthropus robustus. Journal of Human Evolution* 20:313–40.

Viohl, G. 1990. Piscivorous fishes of the Solnhofen Lithographic Limestone. *In* A.J. Boucot (ed.), *Evolutionary Paleobiology of Behavior and Coevolution.* Amsterdam and New York: Elsevier.

Walton, A.H. 1990. Owl pellets and the fossil record. *In* A.J. Boucot (ed.), *Evolutionary Paleobiology of Behavior and Coevolution*. Amsterdam and New York: Elsevier.

Weishampel, D.B. 1984. Evolution of jaw mechanisms in ornithopod dinosaurs. *Advances in Anatomy, Embryology and Cell Biology* 87:1–110.

Williams, M.E. 1972. The origin of "spiral coprolites." *University of Kansas Paleontological Contributions* 59:1–19.

———. 1990. Feeding behavior in Cleveland Shale sharks. *In* A.J. Boucot (ed.), *Evolutionary Paleobiology of Behavior and Coevolution.*

Amsterdam and New York: Elsevier.

Wunderlich, J. 1986. *Fossil Spinnen in Bernstein und ihre heute lebenden Verwandten: Spinnenfauna gestern und heute*. Wiesbaden: Bauer bei Quelle und Meyer.

Further Reading

Boucot, A.J. (ed.). 1990. *Evolutionary Paleobiology of Behavior and Coevolution*. Amsterdam and New York: Elsevier.

DINOSAURS

Dinosaurs are a group of terrestrial vertebrates, now believed to include living and extinct birds (Class Aves), as well as a host of non-avian (i.e., nonbird), earthbound animals that lived from about 230 million years ago until 65 million years ago. Fundamentally, dinosaurs were and are land-dwelling creatures. There are no known marine dinosaurs, and the only dinosaurs that flew are birds; even in these creatures, however, basic terrestrial adaptations inherited from nonflying dinosaurian ancestors remain. Within the terrestrial realm, dinosaurs inhabited a virtually unlimited range of environments: dinosaurs have been found on all continents and in a variety of settings, from swamps to deserts, and from cold environments to hot ones. Dinosaurs always have been significant components of the faunas in which they lived. Birds currently constitute a major proportion of the Earth's vertebrate diversity, and during most of the Mesozoic Era, non-avian dinosaurs were the most abundant terrestrial vertebrates.

The first-recorded western discovery of dinosaurs were the teeth of the dinosaur *Iguanodon,* found by Mary Mantell in 1822 and described in print by her husband Gideon two years later. The name "Dinosauria" was not applied to the group until 1841, however, when the English anatomist Sir Richard Owen coined the term to encompass the partial remains of three large, extinct reptiles known at the time: *Iguanodon, Megalosaurus,* and *Hylaeosaurus.* Through the work of the English natural historian Harry Sealy, the name soon came to be considered simply a common name for two major, disparate groups of somewhat distantly related reptiles: Ornithischia (bird-hipped) and Saurischia (lizard-hipped). This view held sway for over 150 years. During that time, some of the great dinosaur collections of all time were made. In the 1870s to 1890s, E.D. Cope (Philadelphia Academy of Sciences) and O.C. Marsh (Yale University) ignited an acrimonious, productive, and now-legendary rivalry, scouting the western United States for dinosaur fossils. The early part of the twentieth century also increased dinosaur collections significantly: C.H. and C.M. Sternberg (father and son) collected rich Cretaceous dinosaur faunas along the Red Deer River of Alberta (Canada), and W. Janensch led a series of astounding expeditions to the Late Jurassic Tendaguru beds of Tanzania. The 1920s brought R.C. Andrews's daring expeditions to the Gobi Desert of Mongolia and northern China, and a fabulous bounty of

dinosaur fossils and eggs. This region was further collected by Z. Kielan-Jaworoska and her Polish colleagues in the 1960s and early 1970s. In addition to these large, impressive multiyear expeditions, people kept returning to famous and not-so-famous dinosaur localities and finding new material. P. Dodson estimates that new dinosaur species currently are named at a rate of one every seven weeks.

In the 1970s and early 1980s, paleontologists such as R.T. Bakker, P.M. Galton, J.H. Ostrom, and J.A. Gauthier concluded that, as originally implied by Owen, all dinosaurs are more closely related to each other than they are to anything else. Ostrom and Gauthier identified a host of distinguishing features that unite Dinosauria, including most notably a pelvis and rear limb design that only allows movement forward and backward in the plane of the body. Rotational and sideways motion (such as one sees, for example, at the human ankle) are minimized. The unique suite of characters that make up the pelvis and rear limb design generally are interpreted as providing efficient locomotion on land. Ornithischia and Saurischia are now considered to be subgroups within Dinosauria.

Saurischians and ornithischians have features that members of each group uniquely bear: among the many characters that all ornithischians have in common is the presence of a new, unique bone, the *predentary,* which is present at the front of the lower jaws. All saurischians, too, bear a series of unique features, including an opening beneath the nostril area, the *subnarial foramen,* and an elongation of the rearward neck vertebrae, contributing to a tendency for long necks seen in many saurischians.

Even in Owen's time the place of dinosaurs among other vertebrates was reasonably well understood. Dinosaurs are members of the larger group Archosauria ("ruling reptiles"), a highly diverse, mainly extinct assemblage of reptiles whose only living members are crocodiles and birds. The nearest living common ancestors of dinosaurs (including birds) are, therefore, crocodiles.

The origin of dinosaurs remains somewhat shrouded in the mists of time. They clearly came from basal (primitive) archosaurian stock, and based upon the most primitive members of the group, the earliest dinosaur must have been a small, bipedal carnivorous saurischian, with well-developed hind legs and cursorial (running) adaptations. An animal that bears many of the features that must have characterized the first dinosaur is a small Triassic

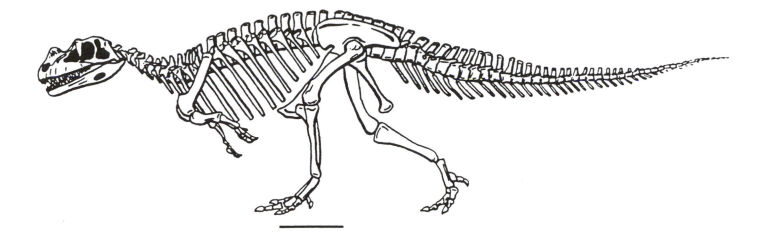

Figure 1. The large-bodied theropod *Ceratosaurus,* from the Late Jurassic of North America. Scale = 50 cm. From Fastovsky and Weishampel (1996), reprinted with the permission of Cambridge University Press.

archosaur from Argentina, *Lagosuchus. Lagosuchus,* however, does not have the characteristic ankle of a dinosaur (part of the suite of hind limb features that guide the leg in its single plane of motion), and thus cannot be considered a dinosaur. Ornithischia rapidly radiated from saurischian stock, and within less than 3 million years of the oldest dinosaur, *Eoraptor,* the earliest ornithischians first appear in the fossil record.

Dinosaurs generally are divided into seven distinctive groups. Saurischia includes Theropoda and Sauropodomorpha, while Ornithischia includes Ornithopoda, Stegosauria, Ceratopsia, Ankylosauria, and Pachycephalosauria. Theropods, sauropodomorphs, and ornithopods are known from the Late Triassic; stegosaurs first appeared in mid-Jurassic times; and the other three groups are largely Cretaceous forms, with probable antecedents in the Late Jurassic. Stegosaurs and ankylosaurs are united within the group Thyreophora on the basis of their possession of dermal armor (extensive plates of bone embedded in the skin). Ceratopsians and pachycephalosaurs are linked together in the group Marginocephalia, based upon the shared possession of a shelf of bone at the back of the head. All dinosaurs were herbivores except for theropods.

Theropods

Non-avian dinosaurs explored a variety of adaptations and behaviors. The carnivorous theropods built their adaptations on a basic bipedal body plan. Their mouths were equipped with laterally compressed, recurved, and serrated teeth used for slicing flesh, and their bones were hollow, with a tendency to develop openings in the cranium. Although the mouths were not designed for chewing, the slicing action of the teeth undoubtedly was augmented by well-developed claws on both the hands and feet. In general, theropods evolved—and reevolved—two major body types. The first is a large-bodied form, exemplified by such creatures as *Tyran-*

nosaurus. The other is a smaller type, exemplified by a diversity of forms such as *Compsognathus,* and *Deinonychus.*

Large-bodied theropods are informally called "carnosaurs" (Figure 1). These organisms had large heads, a tendency to evolve tiny arms, and a tendency to reduce the number of fingers in the hand (as few as two—digits I and II—on the largest and most recent exemplars). Most were built quite stoutly and in many cases were equipped with bulbous teeth, although considerable variation exists within carnosaurs, depending upon the genus being studied. These adaptations have suggested scavenging to some paleontologists. To others, the robust teeth are simply a by-product of growing to a large size. Their immense size—up to 15 meters—and unique adaptations render them somewhat enigmatic, because no living analog exists with which they can be compared.

Small-bodied theropods (Figure 2) came in a variety of sizes and shapes, but virtually all had relatively small skulls filled with sharp theropod teeth, long necks, long legs, long, well-developed arms with three fingers (digits I, II, and III) on the hand, and well-developed claws on both hands and feet. Most small-bodied theropods were gracile organisms (i.e., lightly built). The hands were equipped with partially opposable thumbs, suggesting grasping. In many instances, this group reveals large braincases, implying avian levels of intelligence and concomitant motor skills. A number of large-brained theropods are equipped with rigid tails that must have served as counterbalancing mechanisms to the long arms and grasping hands. Virtually all aspects of these animals suggest cursorial (running) adaptations and a fierce predatory existence. Their small size relative to that of potential prey has suggested to some paleontologists that these animals could have hunted in packs.

A number of Cretaceous-aged theropods had no teeth at all. These include the highly gracile ornithomimids (ostrich mimics) and a variety of enigmatic forms such as *Oviraptor* (egg-stealer),

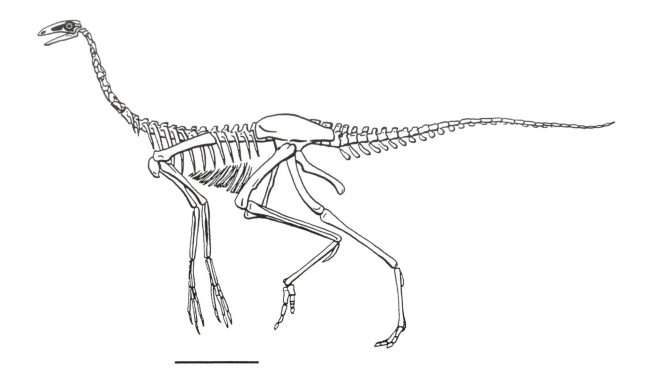

Figure 2. The ornithomimid *Dromiceiomimus,* from the Late Cretaceous of North America. Scale = 50 cm. From Fastovsky and Weishampel (1996), reprinted with the permission of Cambridge University Press.

whose body found lying across across eggs in Mongolia originally suggested theft (hence the name) to R.C. Andrews, its discoverer, but suggests maternity to M.A. Norell and colleagues, who found *Oviraptor* babies inside the eggs. Whether these creatures were even carnivorous remains unknown.

Perhaps the most significant dinosaur ever discovered is the Late Jurassic feathered theropod, *Archaeopteryx,* found in the Bavarian quarry of Solnhofen. While feather impressions clearly indicate that it is a bird, J.H. Ostrom's 1979 treatise on its morphology convincingly demonstrated that in most respects it is a typical theropod. It is through *Archaeopteryx* that Ostrom (and later, Gauthier) were able to establish the fundamentally dinosaurian nature of birds.

Decidedly unbirdlike were the sauropodomorphs. This group of fully land-dwelling dinosaurs includes the prosauropods and the sauropods, the latter epitomized by "brontosaurus." Prosauropods are primitive saurischians, rarely occurring in rocks younger than Middle Jurassic in age. They had a global distribution but are known best from sites in Europe, eastern North America, and South Africa. These dinosaurs were almost certainly herbivorous, but little is known of their behavior. Among the most famous genera are *Plateosaurus* and *Anchisaurus.*

Sauropods

Sauropods are far better known (Figure 3). They were fully quadrupedal and had long necks, tiny heads, long tails, and great size. The largest sauropods were longer than 40 meters, and are the largest (both by estimated weight and by length) land animals ever to have existed. Although typical of the Late Jurassic in North America, they were important global faunal members through the Middle Jurassic–Cretaceous interval. Their skeletons show startling adaptations to great size on land, such as pillarlike legs for support and a girderlike arrangement of the bones in the neck and tail for both strength and lightness.

Sauropods as a group tended to have reduced dentitions and nostrils that showed an evolutionary predilection for migrating to the top of the skull, suggesting to paleontologists that a trunk or muscular upper lip may have been present. The sauropod mouth was not well developed for chewing; in one group, exemplified by *Diplodocus,* the teeth are restricted to pencil-like sticks only at the front of the jaw. The mouth and skull have thus been interpreted as vegetation-cropping organs. The animals must have relied upon a muscular gizzard and stomach bacteria for masticating food. Indeed, there is some evidence for this, as gastroliths (stomach stones for crushing vegetation) have been found along with sauropod skeletons. Beautifully preserved trackways of walking sauropods show rows of footprints and no tail marks; sauropods must have traveled in herds and must have carried their long tails in the air while they did so.

Ornithischians

Ornithischians present a range of divergent morphologies and herbivorous adaptations. Ornithopods were forms that moved back

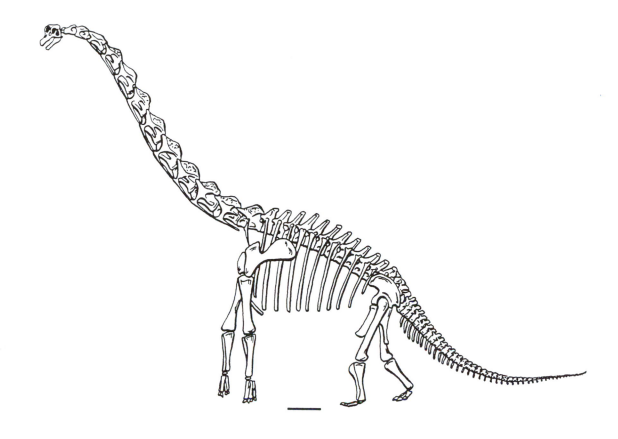

Figure 3. The sauropod *Brachiosaurus,* from the Late Jurassic of North America and Tanzania. Scale = 1 m. From Fastovsky and Weishampel (1996), reprinted with the permission of Cambridge University Press.

and forth between bipedality and quadrupedality, with hooves on certain digits of the front and all digits of the back legs (Figure 4). A variety of large and small ornithopods existed globally from the Early Jurassic until the end of the Cretaceous. During this time they became among the most common and diverse of all dinosaurs and were found in virtually every dinosaur-bearing environment. The most famous ornithopods are the duck-billed dinosaurs (hadrosaurs), a group of animals common in terrestrial deposits from the Cretaceous of North America and Asia.

Among the most striking features of all ornithopods are their chewing adaptations. Mammals are unique among living vertebrates as chewing organisms. Quite independently, however, both ornithopods and ceratopsians invented chewing by developing strong muscles, jaw bone modifications, a mass of constantly replacing shearing teeth, and muscular cheeks. A beak at the end of the snout cropped off vegetation, which was then ground by the shearing masses of teeth in the mouth, before being digested. In the case of hadrosaurs such as *Anatosaurus* and *Saurolophus,* the adaptation is especially striking, since the skulls were kinetic: certain bones of the skull moved to enhance the shearing action as the animal chewed.

Ornithopods are also the group of dinosaurs in which maternal care was first hypothesized. J.L. Horner's late-1970s and early-1980s discoveries of groups of nests, babies, and adult hadro-saurs *(Maiasaura)* in Montana suggested to him that adults were caring for the young. Although the idea of maternal care has been criticized, few would disagree that the find at least gives clear evidence of social behavior in ornithopods.

Finally, many North American hadrosaurs developed complicated and extensive head structures, with convoluted tubes and cavities connecting from the nose to the throat. Based on the 1980s studies of D.B. Weishampel, these great hollow tubes and cavities are now believed to have served as resonating chambers. His suggestion was that these dinosaurs communicated by sound, an idea that is not implausible when it is considered that the closest living relatives of these dinosaurs are birds, for whom sound is an important means of communication and expression.

The other abundant group of herbivorous ornithischians are the ceratopsians (Figure 5). These great frill-bearing, horned quadrupedal herbivores were restricted to the Cretaceous of Asia and North America. Ornithopod ancestry is clearly suggested by the most primitive member of the group, *Psittacosaurus,* a small Asian biped with a tiny frill, no horns, but a rostral bone—a bone on the snout that is unique to ceratopsians. The other Asian forms (e.g., *Bagaceratops, Protoceratops*) remain relatively small, although the typical quadrupedal stance is achieved in these dinosaurs. Eggs and nests of babies are known from *Protoceratops,* an animal that seems to have lived in an arid, sand dune environment.

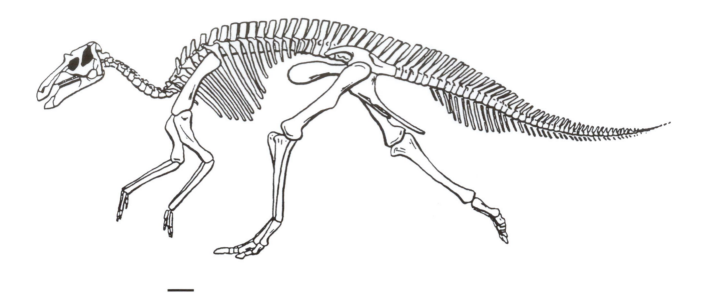

Figure 4. Skeleton of the duck-billed ornithopod *Maiasaura,* from the Late Cretaceous of North America. Scale = 50 cm. From Fastovsky and Weishampel (1996), reprinted with the permission of Cambridge University Press.

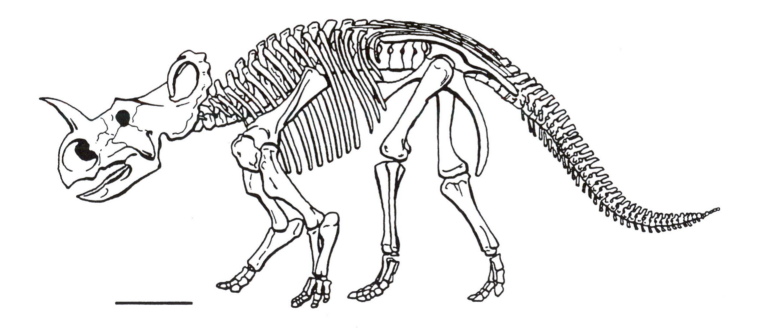

Figure 5. The Late Cretaceous ceratopsian *Centrosaurus,* from North America. Scale = 50 cm. From Fastovsky and Weishampel (1996), reprinted with the permission of Cambridge University Press.

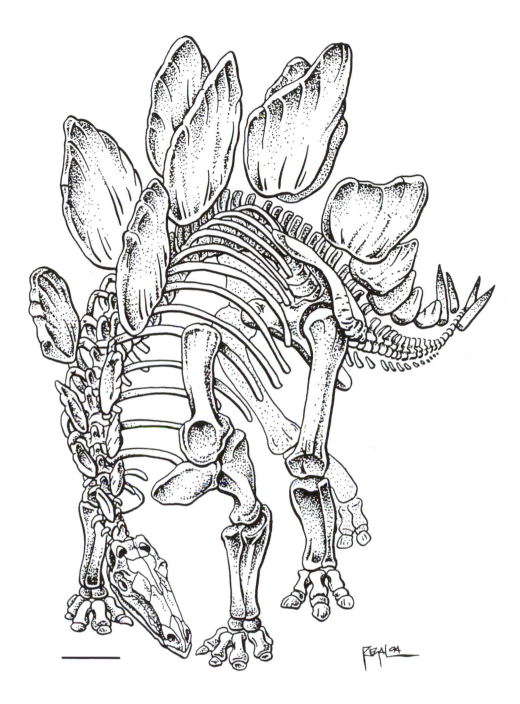

Figure 6. The Late Jurassic stegosaur *Stegosaurus,* from North America. Scale = 50 cm. From Fastovsky and Weishampel (1996), reprinted with the permission of Cambridge University Press.

The North American forms (such as *Triceratops, Torosaurus,* and *Pachyrhinosaurus*) tended to be large (four to five meters; excepting a few small forms, such as *Leptoceratops*), quadrupedal, beaked, frilled herbivores with a tendency toward horns. The horns—originally considered to be defensive in nature—are now thought to pertain to intraspecific competition, as well as perhaps to defense. The well-developed frills have been loosely interpreted as defensive; however, many of them have great open spaces and may instead have been used for muscle attachment for the great chewing muscles that

characterized these dinosaurs. Recently, it was hypothesized that the frill also was used as a temperature regulation mechanism.

Like their fellow ornithischians the ornithopods, there is considerable evidence that North American ceratopsians roamed across the ancient flood plains of great river systems in large herds. Astounding numbers of their fossils are found in the Great Plains region of North America in rocks from the last 15 million years of the Cretaceous. Indeed, the youngest non-avian dinosaur ever found is a ceratopsian *(Triceratops).*

Figure 7. The Late Cretaceous ankylosaur *Ankylosaurus,* from North America. Scale = 50 cm. From Fastovsky and Weishampel (1996), reprinted with the permission of Cambridge University Press.

The other three great groups of ornithischians dinosaurs—stegosaurs, ankylosaurs, and pachycephalosaurs—are much rarer and more poorly known than ceratopsians and ornithopods. Stegosaurs (Figure 6) were a dominantly Jurassic form, occurred globally, and were epitomized by, of course, *Stegosaurus.* These large-sized dinosaurs had—it has been determined after considerable controversy—two rows of alternating plates running down the back of the animal. The plates are highly vascularized, leading paleontologist J. Farlow and colleagues to conclude that the blood within them could be cooled and warmed. Unambiguously defensive are large spines projecting laterally from the tails of stegosaurs. Stegosaur skulls are small, with tiny teeth, and a beak (and no teeth) at the front of the snout. Presumably vegetation was cropped and then sent posteriorly for digestion. Fossils are not common, and little is known of stegosaur behavior beyond that which can be learned from their anatomy.

Ankylosaurs are the great armored dinosaurs of the Mesozoic (Figure 7). Although largely Cretaceous in age, at least one Jurassic form exists. They are currently known from Europe, Asia, Australia, and North America and are exemplified by a host of genera such as *Hylaeosaurus, Pinacosaurus, Minmi,* and *Ankylosau-*

rus. Ankylosaurs were apparently defensive in all respects: great, armored, quadrupedal fortresses. The skulls developed extensive dermal armor that obscured the typical openings that characterize dinosaurs; even the eyelids had dermal armor. The dorsal surface of the body developed a large, flexible, armoring of small pieces of bone embedded in the skin, so the resultant dermal armor was much like a coat of chain mail. In certain instances, great spikes adorned the flexible carapace (back shell). Some—but not all—ankylosaurs developed large bony clubs and hatchets on their tails. Ankylosaurs must have been extraordinarily heavy. Although the fossils are quite rare, an assemblage of juveniles is known from Mongolia, suggesting that maternal care and/or social behavior in this group is a possibility.

Pachycephalosaurs were highly specialized, bipedal dinosaurs with domed skulls (Figure 8). Like ornithomimids, hadrosaurs, and ceratopsians, they were Cretaceous in age and restricted to Asia and North America. They varied in size from about two meters *(Stygimoloch)* to as large as eight meters *(Pachycephalosaurus).* The domes were masses of solid bone, with the region of maximum strength occurring at the top of the skull. Behind the skull, the neck vertebrae bore interlocking tongue-and-groove

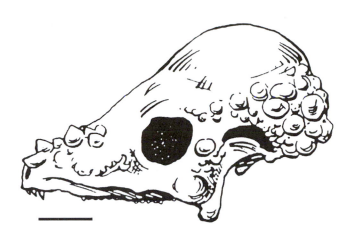

Figure 8. The skull of *Pachycephalosaurus,* from the Late Cretaceous of North America. Scale = 25 cm. From Fastovsky and Weishampel (1996), reprinted with the permission of Cambridge University Press.

structures, making them strong and rigid. All in all, the design of the skull and neck have suggested to scholars that the animals butted with their heads. The rarity of these animals, however, renders what is known of them quite limited.

Metabolism

Although Sir Richard Owen originally envisioned dinosaurs as maintaining endothermic ("warm-blooded" mammalian-type) metabolic rates, the "reptilian" bones of dinosaurs convinced scholars around the turn of the century that non-avian dinosaur metabolisms had to be ectothermic, that is, "cold-blooded," similar to that of a crocodile or lizard. This viewpoint was maintained until the early 1970s, when J.H. Ostrom and R.T. Bakker began to reinterpret the skeletons of extinct dinosaurs as endotherms. Controversy ensued, and approaches to the interpretation of dinosaur metabolism have become increasingly sophisticated in the intervening years. A variety of lines of evidence now suggests that different dinosaurs may have maintained different metabolisms. For example, sauropods may have been mass homeotherms, relying upon low surface-to-volume ratios to maintain constant temperatures, while small, agile, brainy theropods may have been endothermic somewhat in the manner of modern humans and birds. More ambiguous are medium-sized (five- to eight-meter) non-avian dinosaurs such as hadrosaurs and ornithomimids, whose style of endothermy may have been somewhat between that of modern ectotherms and modern endotherms. The details of such a metabolism, however, remain unspecified.

Extinction

The disappearance of non-avian dinosaurs remains one of the great mysteries of natural history. In their 160 million years on earth, dinosaur species turned over at a relatively rapid rate; species longevities were 1 to 2 million years. Thus, Late Cretaceous faunas, for example, consisted of very different dinosaurs from faunas of the mid-Cretaceous. However, according to the work of P. Dodson (1996), dinosaurs were never more diverse than during the last 10 million years of the Cretaceous. So, did their demise occur instantaneously, at the end of that 10 million years, or did it occur slowly, through as much as 10 million years?

Opinion is very much divided as regards the final extinction of non-avian dinosaurs. Based upon the rather limited database available (from the western interior of North America), the diversity of non-avian dinosaurs appears to have been unchanged until the moment that the extinction occurred; it appears geologically instantaneous. The fossil record, however, does not have the detail to make the statement that the extinction was ecologically instantaneous.

Causative agents are not easy to obtain. A substantial marine regression (withdrawal of oceans from the continents) occurred at the end of the Cretaceous, which has been implicated in the extinction by J.D. Archibald (1996). However, dinosaurs survived many regressions previously in their history, and this one does not appear terribly different from previous ones. Likewise, climate has been suggested as a potential cause of the extinction. In this case, independent work based upon marine organisms does not indicate a serious climatic shift across the boundary. Moreover, the gradual extinction that is suggested by a regression and by climatic change does not match the instantaneous disappearance undergone by non-avian dinosaurs. Although volcanos also have been implicated in the non-avian dinosaur extinction, highly explosive volcanism seems not to have been present at this time.

For the present, the consensus within the geological community is that the extinction was caused by the impact of an asteroid with the earth. The fact of an end-of-Cretaceous impact is well-documented globally, through the presence of iridium, shock-metamorphosed quartz, microtektites, and, most recently, the crater itself (in the Yucatan Peninsula of Mexico). It has been estimated that such an impact would have had many deleterious effects on the environment, the most egregious of which would have been the blocking of sunlight for several months. The relationship between the known fact of the impact and the extinction of non-avian dinosaurs is the coincidence in time of the two events. The extinction was geologically instantaneous, a result predicted from and concordant with extinction by asteroid impact. For these reasons, the asteroid impact is today the favored candidate for the cause of the extinction of non-avian dinosaurs.

DAVID E. FASTOVSKY

See also Saurischians; Ornithischians

Further Reading

Archibald, J.D. 1996. *Dinosaur Extinction and the End of an Era: What the Fossils Say.* New York: Columbia University Press.
Bakker, R.T. 1986. *The Dinosaur Heresies.* New York: Morrow; London: Penguin, 1988.

Benton, M.J. 1990. *Sur les Traces des Dinosaures*. Laval, Québec: Intrinsèque.

Dodson, P. 1996. *The Horned Dinosaurs*. Princeton, New Jersey: Princeton University Press.

Fastovsky, D.E., and D.B. Weishampel. 1996. *The Evolution and Extinction of the Dinosaurs*. Cambridge and New York: Cambridge University Press.

Horner, J.R., and J. Gorman. 1988. *Digging Dinosaurs*. New York: Workman.

Jacobs, L. 1993. *Quest for the African Dinosaurs*. New York: Villard.

Lessem, D. 1992. *Kings of Creation*. New York: Simon and Schuster.

Lucas, S.G. 1994. *Dinosaurs: The Textbook*. Dubuque, Iowa: Brown; 2nd ed., 1997.

McGowan, C. 1991. *Dinosaurs, Spitfires, and Sea Dragons*. Cambridge,

Massachusetts: Harvard University Press; London: Harvard University Press, 1992.

Norman, D. 1985. *The Illustrated Encyclopedia of Dinosaurs*. New York: Crescent; London: Salamander.

Rosenberg, G.D., and D.L. Wolberg (eds.). 1994. *Dino Fest*. The Paleontological Society Special Publication, 7. Knoxville, Tennessee: Paleontological Society.

Wilford, J.N. 1985. *The Riddle of the Dinosaur*. New York: Knopf; London: Faber, 1986.

Weishampel, D.B. 1991. *Plant-Eating Dinosaurs*. New York: Franklin Watts.

Weishampel, D.B., P. Dodson, and H. Osmólska, (eds.). 1990. *The Dinosauria*. Berkeley: University of California Press.

DIVERSITY

Biological diversity consists of the number and variety of different kinds of life. Therefore, assessing diversity should take both "number" and "variety" into account. Nevertheless, studies of diversity in the fossil record have tended to summarize diversity as "species richness" (the number of species—for instance, types of lions, or leopards) or richness in higher groups (the number of types of species of, for instance, large cats). Studies of diversity in paleontological settings have concentrated on two topics: (1) reconstructing trends in richness over time and (2) understanding the elements—both biological and nonbiological—that control the evolution of new species (speciation) and the extinction of existing species (Figure 1).

"Variety" among species refers to the degree to which species are functionally or ecologically different from each other. Such differences are difficult to determine; to do so, scholars reconstruct the ecology of extinct organisms and quantify their morphology. For instance, one can assess the amount of variety within a community by inferring relative abundance—that is, if a community is dominated by one species, or by only a few, the community is considered less varied (e.g., Rose 1981). Scholars also can assess variety among communities, habitats, or regions according to the composition of its animal life (fauna) (Sepkoski 1988).

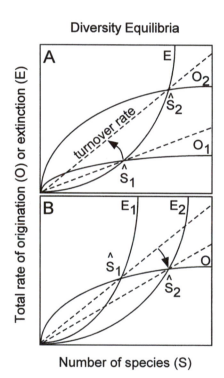

Diversity Equilibria

Figure 1. Variation in total rates of origination and extinction at continental scales. With increasing diversity, originations are assumed to decelerate, and extinctions to accelerate. Equilibrium is attained when originations match extinctions. The slope of the dotted line represents the rate of species turnover, which is inversely proportional to the average age of species. *A*, increased origination (*S2* vs. *S1*) results in higher equilibria and a higher turnover rate; *B*, reduced extinction (*E2* vs. *E1*) results in higher equilibria and a lower turnover rate. When rates of origination and extinction vary at the same rate (not shown), the dominant effect on turnover is that of extinction. Abbreviations: *S*, species; *O*, originations; *E*, extinctions. Redrawn from Ricklefs and Schluter (1993).

Problems in Assessing Diversity in the Fossil Record

The fossil record provides us with a biased estimate of past diversity. Because of the fossilization process, organisms and the habitats from all time periods have not been preserved equally well. Moreover, diversity appears high during times represented by a large amount of preserved sedimentary rock, because the more rock there is, the more fossils will likely be recovered (Raup 1976). The number of species known from a time interval can vary for a number of other reasons as well, from how interested paleontologists are in that period to how large the sample size gleaned from that time period is.

Diversity methods can also skew results. A technique called "time-averaging," or pooling species that lived at different times into the same sample, can make the amount of diversity appear to be quite high, while at the same time obscuring any short-term fluctuations in diversity that may have taken place during the time period (Kidwell and Flessa 1995). Because extinction and origination rates can vary with the amount of time over which they are measured (Foote 1994), scholars often compare rates calculated only over equal time intervals (Alroy 1996).

Taxonomic richness has been estimated at different levels in the taxonomic hierarchy (from most inclusive to most specific—phylum, class, order, family, genus, species), depending on the data available and the question under investigation. A few studies counted species, but most count higher taxa (above the level of species) when species are unavailable or unreliable. Higher taxa and their appearances also have been used as stand-ins for the evolution of novel adaptations. One common view is that the number of phyla, classes, and orders reflect biological variety, whereas the number of families and genera reflect species richness (Foote 1996). Accordingly, many databases on global diversity have been tabulated for families, the highest taxonomic level believed to reflect species dynamics.

Rise in Richness and Diversity Equilibria

The fossil record of the richness of life is best documented for families of marine animals (Figure 2). The basic history of their diversification is as follows:

1. rapid diversification in the Late Precambrian through Early Cambrian;
2. less rapid diversification in the Ordovician;
3. near steady-state in the number of families in the Paleozoic though the next 200 million years;
4. sharp drop in number of families in the mass extinction at the end of the Permian;
5. slow diversification from the Early Triassic to the present, interrupted by another mass extinction at the end of the Cretaceous.

This pattern is evident in several taxonomic databases (Sepkoski et al. 1981). Updated data at the family level show evidence that family diversification slowed in the Late Cenozoic, perhaps as a result of Quaternary extinctions (Sepkoski 1993). The history of marine life at the level of genera is remarkably similar but with larger fluctuations (Sepkoski 1997). In sum, richness has increased, erratically rather than steadily, with a long period of oscillation about a steady-state, times of diversification, and a couple of major setbacks.

Increasing richness may not need an explanation if diversification has proceeded unconstrained. Exponential, or unconstrained, growth is expected when rates of origination and extinction vary randomly with respect to diversity (Stanley 1979). It is only possible to deviate from exponential growth when these rates are

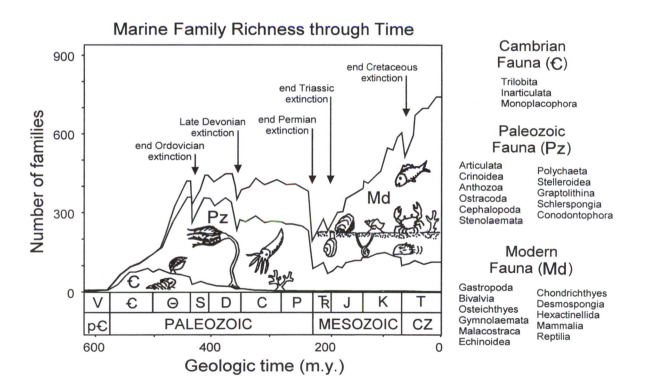

Figure 2. Marine family richness through time. Distances between curves represent family richness of each evolutionary fauna, listed on right. Cartoons illustrate representative life-forms for each evolutionary fauna and, more roughly, ecological tiering. Redrawn from Sepkoski (1992a) and Kidwell and Brenchley (1996).

"diversity-dependent": that is, if diversity rises, originations slow down, extinctions accelerate, or both (Figure 1). Some scholars claim that total family richness (marine plus terrestrial) has increased exponentially through time (Benton 1995). Rather than an exponential curve, the total family richness curve is approximated by a fit of several logistic curves with rates of diversification that decrease as diversity increases, suggesting that real turnover rates may be diversity dependent (Courtiliot and Gaudemer 1996).

Further evidence comes from direct measurement. Total origination rates first slow down and then decline as diversity increases in Paleozoic marine orders and families (Sepkoski 1978, 1979). Also, per-taxon origination rates decline as diversity increases in species of Miocene horses (Maurer 1989) and Cenozoic mammals (Alroy 1996). Extinction rates, however, exhibit little diversity dependence, suggesting either that equilibria are maintained by constraints on origination or that extinction effects are cryptic.

Using statistical analysis, it has been possible to divide the fossil record of marine animals into three representative groupings of "evolutionary faunas"—Cambrian, Paleozoic, and Modern—each of which shares similar diversification rates and time periods (Sepkoski 1991, 1992b) (Figure 2). Each evolutionary fauna has had lower rates of extinction and turnover than its predecessor (Valentine et al. 1991). And, when statistically modeled, each evolutionary fauna appears to approach a higher "carrying capacity" in number of species (Sepkoski 1996). This follows the model in Figure 1B, which predicts that when extinction intensity declines, equilibrium diversity should be higher and the rate of turnover should be lower. That is what has occurred among marine animals (Valentine et al. 1991). Distinct evolutionary floras also occur among terrestrial plants, but these evolutionary groups do not follow the same pattern: each flora has had higher rates of extinction and turnover than its predecessor, not lower as in marine animals (Valentine et al. 1991). Evolutionary faunas of terrestrial vertebrates have not yet produced clear trends (Valentine et al. 1991).

Finally, increases in diversity have been accompanied by greater use of space and resources—and greater subdivision of them. Increased richness of shallow marine fauna seems to be accommodated primarily by increasing the number of guilds (groups with a similar way of life) and secondarily by increasing the number of species within guilds (Bambach 1983). Use of vertical space also has increased through time (Figure 2). The Cambrian evolutionary fauna used mainly the first few centimeters above the sea bottom; the Paleozoic evolutionary fauna became more "epifaunal," expanding into space above the sea bottom; and the Modern evolutionary fauna became more "infaunal," living more often below the seafloor, with burrowing adaptations (Ausich and Bottjer 1991).

The succession of marine evolutionary faunas has had a geographic component: each fauna has appeared first near shore and later expanded into offshore habitats, replacing the fauna already living there (Sepkoski 1991). Over the entire history of marine animals, increasing richness has been attributed to increasing provinciality—the degree to which fauna are limited to given regions of the oceans, so large regions of the oceans differ in faunal composition (Valentine and Moores 1970). In the Paleozoic, however, when diversity is broken down into within-habitat and between-habitat components, increased richness seems to be a result of greater packing of species within habitats and the appearance of new habitats, such as reefs, not of increasing provinciality (Sepkoski 1988). Among terrestrial plants, each evolutionary flora has been associated with reproductive innovations that may have allowed invasion of new habitats (Valentine et al. 1991). Increased richness of terrestrial vertebrates seems to have been accomplished primarily by adding new guilds, secondarily by specialization within guilds, and only lastly by provinciality (Benton 1991).

The Cambrian Explosion

Life has existed for at least 3,500 million years, but complex multicellular animals, or "metazoans," are known only from the last 550 million years. The relatively sudden appearance of modern metazoans in the Cambrian suggests that either these animals differentiated rapidly or they had a long Precambrian history without leaving fossils (perhaps because early metazoans were small or lacked durable skeletons). Some evidence on age comes from "molecular clocks," an analysis of changes in RNA or DNA that are believed by some to occur at predictable intervals of time and in predictable order. Although molecular clocks estimate that metazoan lineages diverged deep in the Precambrian, early separation would not eliminate the possibility of a later origin of the features that actually characterize the separate groups (Wray et al. 1996). New geologic dates, however, restrict most first appearances of modern metazoans to the first 8 million years of the Cambrian, suggesting relatively rapid changes in the composition and ecology of marine life-forms at that time (Grotzinger et al. 1995).

The magnitude of this "Cambrian explosion" of animal life has been inferred from taxonomic structure (Valentine 1969; Erwin et al. 1987). Virtually all phyla (large, inclusive groups) had appeared by the end of Cambrian, but the number of species has continued to increase through time (Valentine 1969). This pattern is expected because phyla are higher taxa of organisms that diverged earlier than the lower taxa included within them. To an extent, phyla represent separate "body plans"—such as arthropods (crustaceans), annelids (segmented worms), mollusks (clams), and chordates (animals with backbones). Therefore, early appearance of phyla suggests early occurrence of large morphological changes. There are two hypotheses to account for the observation that no new phyla (body plans) have evolved since the Cambrian. The "ecospace hypothesis" states that a more crowded world makes large evolutionary changes less likely; the genome hypothesis states that genetic and developmental programs for constructing body plans are now less flexible (Valentine 1995).

Although Cambrian communities probably did not include as many guilds as Recent communities (Bambach 1983), scholars have suggested that Cambrian metazoans had a disparity (a range in anatomical design) that approached or exceeded that of the Recent fauna (Gould 1991). Attempts to quantify disparity in all metazoans are hampered by the difficulty of comparing organisms with few features in common. Instead, disparity within arthropods (the phylum that includes crustaceans, insects, and spiders) has been used as an approximation for disparity among all metazoans. Arthropod disparity in the Cambrian seems to have been at least as great as in the Recent (Wills et al. 1994). That means that if this disparity were attained within 8 million years at the base of the Cambrian (Grotzinger et al. 1995), there probably was rapid morphological evolution. Although the "Cambrian explosion" may have occurred relatively rapidly, the increase in organismal "complexity"—measured as the number of different types of cells found in an organism—may have increased more slowly through time (Valentine et al. 1994).

Mass Extinction and Diversity

Extinction is the fate of every species, but at certain times extinction has been particularly intense (Figure 2). These "mass extinctions" are defined as times when extinction intensity was elevated above "background" levels, affecting many taxonomic groups in many different habitats (Jablonski 1986). Although this definition implies a distinction between background and mass extinction patterns, extinctions probably have a continuous range of intensities and frequencies (Raup 1996). Mass extinctions seem to diminish the world's diversity of life-forms to the extent that it sometimes takes millions of years for recovery, perhaps because it takes that much time for new adaptations to evolve. For example, each mass extinction has decimated the dominant reef-building organisms (e.g., an extinct group of Cretaceous bivalves) and been followed by lengthy intervals in which reefs do not exist until the next group of reef builders appears (Copper 1988).

Mass extinctions are thought to have greatly influenced the composition of the biosphere, causing some previously extinction-resistant taxa to disappear and allowing other taxa to diversify in their place, with the diversification of mammals after the end-Cretaceous dinosaur extinction as an often-cited example (Jablonski 1991; Benton 1996; Raup 1996). Computer models of biotic replacements typically find, however, that extinctions influence the timing, but not necessarily the final outcome, of replacements (Sepkoski 1996). Even competitive replacements may occur only as fast as incumbent species go extinct (Rosenzweig and McCord 1991).

A few studies have investigated what factors influence the probability of survival during times of background and mass extinction, including diversity within a taxonomic group. Although during times of background extinction, species-rich genera have higher survivorship than species-poor genera, species richness does not generally improve genetic survivorship during mass extinction events (Jablonski 1991). Species-rich taxa may be at risk during mass extinction if they are characterized by high turnover, that is, if they couple high origination and extinction rates. Such groups may possess organismal or population-level traits that foster both speciation and extinction. For example, some molluscs are not dependent on plankton for food during the free-swimming larval stage. This promotes limited larval dispersal, isolation, and (probably) speciation, but it may put isolated populations at risk because of their restricted geographic ranges and low environmental tolerances (Jablonski and Flessa 1986).

Spindle Diagrams

A time-honored way of dissecting trends in diversity is through diversity profiles, or "spindle diagrams," in which the richness of a taxon or other group is plotted through time (Figure 3). Spindle diagrams can be used to trace the diversification history of ecologically similar species and to determine the effects of introduced newcomers or novel adaptations (Gould et al. 1987; Hunter and Jernvall 1995; Uhen 1996).

Diversity profiles often are tapered at both ends, resembling a spindle. The spindle is tapered at the bottom because taxa arise from a single ancestral species. It is tapered at the top because taxa go extinct when their last included species go extinct (although the latter might be truncated by a mass extinction). The overall shape of a diversity profile is described by its "center of gravity" (Gould et al. 1987). "Bottom-heavy" taxa attain most of their diversity early in their history, whereas "top-heavy" taxa attain most of their diversity later. Bottom-heavy taxa may be more prevalent during early phases of diversification, for example, after mass extinctions (Gould et al. 1987). It is commonly thought that paraphyletic taxa (taxonomic groups containing an ancestor and some, but not all descendants of that ancestor) may appear "bottom-heavy" if late-arising descendants are excluded from their diversity profiles (Smith 1994). Among computer-simulated taxa and extinct mammalian families, however, early-arising and paraphyletic taxa are slightly biased towards top-heaviness (Uhen 1996).

Diversification within Higher Taxa

Species are not evenly distributed across taxonomic groups. Diversification within taxa should be promoted by factors that foster species richness in communities, such as area, intermediate levels of productivity and disturbance, and the variety of habitats that exist in the area where the community is found (Cracraft 1985).

Diversity is also influenced by the ecological concept called "trophic level." Trophic levels refer to successive steps in a

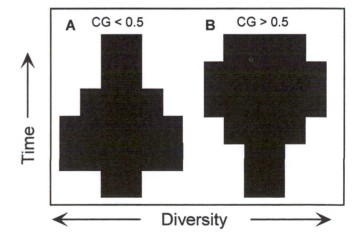

Figure 3. Idealized spindle diagrams. *A*, bottom-heavy taxon; *B*, top-heavy taxon. *CG* equals center of gravity, or the relative position in time of a taxon's mean diversity. Redrawn from Gould et al. (1987).

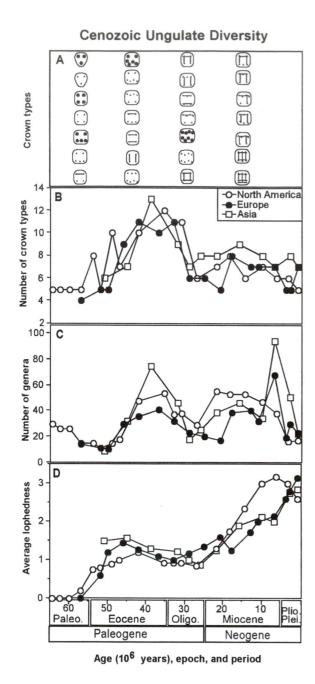

Figure 4. Cenozoic ungulate diversity on the northern continents. *A,* cartoons representing the types of crowns found in the upper molars present in artiodactyl (cloven-hoofed mammals), perissodactyl (horses and related groups), and condylarth ungulates (archaic herbivores); *B,* richness in crown types; *C,* richness in number of genera; *D,* average lophedness (a tooth characteristic consisting of a number of ridges; it is used to measure herbivory), calculated as average number of lophs per crown type. In the Paleogene, richness in crown types tracks richness in genera; rise in richness in genera during the Neogene occurs among fewer crown types and is accompanied by a rise in the general level of herbivory. Redrawn from Jernvall et al. (1996).

food chain. The organisms in each level are characterized by generalized terms. The first level includes producers—plants and other organisms that acquire energy for nutrition and growth primarily from the sun; the second trophic level includes herbivores (plant-eaters), which acquire energy by consuming producers (e.g., grass, seaweeds, algae); the third trophic level includes carnivores) (meat-eaters), which consume herbivores (e.g., praying mantis, foxes, birds of prey) to acquire energy. Higher trophic levels include higher carnivores (e.g., large predators such as sharks, lions, bears, humans), those that consume smaller carnivores. At each level, energy becomes a more limiting resource; the number of animals that can be supported by the amount of available energy (food) decreases with higher trophic levels. As a result, trophic level usually is related inversely to diversity—there will be more herbivores (e.g., rabbits) in a community than carnivores (e.g., foxes or coyotes) because less energy is available at higher trophic levels than at lower ones. Nevertheless, in terms of today's species richness, herbivorous insects probably outnumber plants.

Some higher level taxa fall into more than one trophic level—bears, for instance, eat fish, small mammals, and berries and other vegetation. Others are more specialized. Specialization is often thought to foster diversity, either because specialists subdivide resources more finely than generalists (Benton 1991) or because specialists are forced to evolve when their resources disappear (Vrba 1987). However, insofar as specialization sometimes imposes low population size, specialists also may be at high risk of extinction (Levinton 1979). Body size often is considered to limit species richness because many groups, for example Recent North American birds and mammals, include many small-bodied species but few large ones (Brown 1995). Among Late Cretaceous marine clams, however, size had no influence on survivorship during either background or mass extinction (Jablonski 1996).

"Key innovations" sometimes are invoked to explain patterns of species richness (Benton 1991). These traits may allow a species to colonize previously unoccupied habitats, to adopt new ways of life, or perform some function more efficiently, so that other tasks can be performed at a reduced cost (Rosenzweig and McCord 1991). Explanations that involve key innovations are difficult to test; at a minimum, scholars need multiple examples and a biological connection between the innovation and diversity. For example, in mammals the hypocone (an upper molar tooth cusp) evolved independently at least 20 times and seems to be a prerequisite for specialized herbivory (Hunter and Jernvall 1995). In this case, the biological connection with diversity is trophic level: mammals with hypocones are more likely to evolve plant-eating adaptations than those without hypocones, and taxa of herbivores usually are more species-rich than related taxa of carnivores.

Morphological Diversity

In recent years, new methods have arisen that measure morphological diversity separately from counts of taxa, providing a way to estimate the "variety" component of diversity. These methods have been applied to study "ecomorphology" (the relationship between the morphology of organisms and their ecological role), disparity, and phylogenetic (genealogical) separation. Ecomorphological studies reconstruct guilds of extinct organisms, then follow trends in the number and composition of guilds through time. For example, guild structure among Cenozoic carnivorous mammals has remained relatively stable over time, despite considerable taxonomic turnover within guilds (Van Valkenburgh 1995). "Disparity studies" quantify patterns of morphological differences among samples but do not always associate particular traits with particular functions (Roy and Foote 1997). Studies of "phylogenetic separation" also quantify morphological differences but do so along evolutionary lineages, or segments of a phylogenetic tree (Wagner 1997). Phylogenetic separation may be better for estimating the amount or rate of morphological change than for measuring direct morphological diversity (Roy and Foote 1997). In these studies, scholars commonly create an abstract "morphospace," which they define by morphological variables, and quantify "diversity" as the volume or the average distance between samples in this morphospace (Roy and Foote 1997). Some morphospaces are empirically derived, defined by the morphology of real specimens; others are theoretical, including all possible forms (Foote 1995). For example, out of a possible 790 mammalian tooth crown types, only 34 occur in the Recent fauna (Jernvall 1995) and 28 (Figure 4) occur in a subset of fossil ungulates (hoofed mammals) (Jernvall et al. 1996).

Recent applications have used morphological data to address several long-standing issues, including that of Cambrian versus Recent metazoan disparity. The occurrence of large morphological change early in the history of groups, hypothesized originally from the early appearance of higher taxa, was verified in some groups of organisms, while other groups (such as trilobites) attained peak morphological diversity later in their history (Foote 1996). Morphospaces are also used to infer whether extinction has been selective with respect to morphology. Among the trilobites, high disparity in the face of dwindling numbers of taxa suggests random extinction, whereas certain classes of trilobites simultaneous decline in both taxonomic richness and disparity implies emptying regions of morphospace (Foote 1993).

It is sometimes possible to relate trends in morphological diversity to ecological factors. Among Cenozoic ungulates, for example, early diversification in the Paleogene occurred among species with diverse forms of teeth and diets, whereas later diversification, in the Neogene, occurred only among species with teeth adapted to high-fiber herbivorous diets (Jernvall et al. 1996). In sum, taxa and morphology provide different perspectives, and often different pictures, of diversification because they measure different components of diversity: the number and variety, respectively, of forms of life.

JOHN P. HUNTER

See also Adaptation; Coevolutionary Relationships; Evolutionary Novelty; Evolutionary Trends; Extinction; Faunal Change and Turnover; Paleobiogeography; Selection; Speciation and Morphological Change; Systematics; Variation

Works Cited

Alroy, J. 1996. Constant extinction, constrained diversification, and uncoordinated stasis in North American mammals. *Palaeogeography, Palaeoclimatology, Palaeoecology* 127:285–311.

Ausich, W.I., and D.J. Bottjer. 1991. History of tiering among suspension feeders in the benthic marine ecosystem. *Journal of Geological Education* 39:313–18.

Bambach, R.K. 1983. Ecospace utilization and guilds in marine communities through the Phanerozoic. *In* M.J.S. Tevesz and P.L. McCall (eds.), *Biotic Interactions in Recent and Fossil Benthic Communities.* New York: Plenum.

Benton, M.J. 1991. Why is life so diverse? *In* E.C. Dudley (ed.), *The Unity of Evolutionary Biology: Proceedings of the Fourth International Congress of Systematic and Evolutionary Biology.* 2 vols. Portland Oregon: Dioscorides.

———. 1995. Diversification and extinction in the history of life. *Science* 268:52–58.

———. 1996. On the nonprevalence of competitive replacement in the evolution of tetrapods. *In* D. Jablonski, D.H. Erwin, and J.H. Lipps (eds.), *Evolutionary Paleobiology: In Honor of James W. Valentine.* Chicago: Chicago University Press.

Brown, J.H. 1995. *Macroecology.* Chicago: University of Chicago Press.

Copper, P. 1988. Ecological succession in Phanerozoic reef development: Is it real? *Palaios* 3:136–52.

Courtillot, V., and Y. Gaudemer. 1996. Effects of mass extinctions on biodiversity. *Nature* 381:146–48.

Cracraft, J. 1985. Biological diversification and its causes. *Annals of the Missouri Botanical Garden* 72:794–822.

Erwin, D.H., J.W. Valentine, and J.J. Sepkoski Jr. 1987. A comparative study of diversification events: the early Paleozoic versus the Mesozoic. *Evolution* 41:1177–86.

Foote, M. 1993. Discordance and concordance between morphological and taxonomic diversity. *Paleobiology* 19:185–204.

———. 1994. Temporal variation in extinction risk and temporal scaling of extinction metrics. *Paleobiology* 20:424–44.

———. 1995. Morphological diversification of Paleozoic crinoids. *Paleobiology* 21:273–99.

———. 1996. Models of morphological diversification. *In* D. Jablonski, D.H. Erwin, and J.H. Lipps (eds.), *Evolutionary Paleobiology: In Honor of James W. Valentine.* Chicago: University of Chicago Press.

Gould, S.J. 1991. The disparity of the Burgess Shale arthropod fauna and the limits of cladistic analysis: Why we must strive to quantify morphospace. *Paleobiology* 17:411–23.

Gould, S.J., N.L. Gilinski, and R.Z. German. 1987. Asymmetry of lineages and the direction of evolutionary time. *Science* 236:1437–41.

Grotzinger, J.P., A. Bowring, B. Saylor, and A.J. Kauffman. 1995. New biostratigraphic and geochronological constraints on early animal evolution. *Science* 270:598–604.

Hunter, J.P., and J. Jernvall. 1995. The hypocone as a key innovation in mammalian evolution. *Proceedings of the National Academy of Sciences, USA* 92:10718–10722.

Jablonski, D. 1986. Evolutionary consequences of mass extinctions. *In* D.M. Raup and D. Jablonski (eds.), *Patterns and Processes in the History of Life.* Berlin and New York: Springer-Verlag.

———. 1991. Extinctions: A paleontological perspective. *Science* 253:754–57.

———. 1996. Body size and macroevolution. *In* D. Jablonski, D.H. Erwin, and J.H. Lipps (eds.), *Evolutionary Paleobiology: In Honor of James W. Valentine.* Chicago: Chicago University Press.

Jablonski, D., and K.W. Flessa. 1986. The taxonomic structure of shallow-water marine faunas: implications for Phanerozoic extinctions. *Malacologia* 27:43–66.

Jernvall, J. 1995. Mammalian molar cusp patterns: Developmental mechanisms of diversity. *Acta Zoologica Fennica* 198:1–61.

Jernvall, J., J.P. Hunter, and M. Fortelius. 1996. Molar tooth diversity, disparity, and ecology in Cenozoic ungulate radiations. *Science* 274:1489–92.

Kidwell, S.M., and P.J. Brenchley. 1996. Evolution of the fossil record: Thickness trends in marine skeletal accumulations and their implications. *In* D. Jablonski, D.H. Erwin, and J.H. Lipps (eds.), *Evolutionary Paleobiology: In Honor of James W. Valentine*. Chicago: Chicago University Press.

Kidwell, S.M., and K.W. Flessa. 1995. The quality of the fossil record: Populations, species, and communities. *Annual Review of Ecology and Systematics* 26:269–99.

Levinton, J.S. 1979. A theory of diversity equilibrium and morphological evolution. *Science* 204:335–36.

Maurer, B.A. 1989. Diversity-dependent species dynamics: Incorporating the effects of population-level processes on species dynamics. *Paleobiology* 15:133–46.

Raup, D.M. 1976. Species diversity in the Phanerozoic: An interpretation. *Paleobiology* 2:289–97.

———. 1996. Extinction models. *In* D. Jablonski, D.H. Erwin, and J.H. Lipps (eds.), *Evolutionary Paleobiology: In Honor of James W. Valentine*. Chicago: Chicago University Press.

Ricklefs, R.E., and D. Schluter. 1993. Species diversity: Regional and historical influences. *In* R.E. Ricklefs and D. Schluter (eds.), *Species Diversity in Ecological Communities: Historical and Geographic Perspectives*. Chicago: University of Chicago Press.

Rose, K.D. 1981. Composition and species diversity in Paleocene and Eocene mammal assemblages: An empirical study. *Journal of Vertebrate Paleontology* 1:367–88.

Rosenzweig, M.L., and R.D. McCord. 1991. Incumbent replacement: Evidence for long-term evolutionary progress. *Paleobiology* 17:202–13.

Roy, K., and M. Foote. 1997. Morphological approaches to measuring biodiversity. *Trends in Ecology and Evolution* 12:277–81.

Sepkoski Jr., J.J. 1978. A kinetic model of Phanerozoic taxonomic diversity. 1, Analysis of marine orders. *Paleobiology* 4:223–51.

———. 1979. A kinetic model of Phanerozoic taxonomic diversity. 2, Early Phanerozoic families and multiple equilibria. *Paleobiology* 5:222–51.

———. 1981. A factor analytic description of the Phanerozoic marine fossil record. *Paleobiology* 7:36–53.

———. 1988. Alpha, beta, or gamma: Where does all the diversity go? *Paleobiology* 14:221–34.

———. 1991. A model of onshore-offshore change in faunal diversity. *Paleobiology* 17:58–77.

———. 1992a. Phylogenetic and ecologic patterns in the Phanerozoic history of marine biodiversity. *In* N. Eldredge (ed.), *Systematics, Ecology, and the Biodiversity Crisis*. New York: Columbia University Press.

———. 1992b. Proterozoic-Early Cambrian diversification of metazoans and metaphytes. *In* J.W. Schopf and C. Klein (eds.), *The Proterozoic Biosphere*. Cambridge and New York: Cambridge University Press.

———. 1993. Ten years in the library: New data confirm paleontological patterns. *Paleobiology* 19:43–51.

———. 1996. Competition in macroevolution: The double wedge revisited. *In* D. Jablonski, D.H. Erwin, and J.H. Lipps (eds.),

Evolutionary Paleobiology: In Honor of James W. Valentine. Chicago: Chicago University Press.

———. 1997. Biodiversity: Past, present, and future. *Journal of Paleontology* 71:533–39.

Sepkoski Jr., J.J., R.K. Bambach, D.M. Raup, and J.W. Valentine. 1981. Phanerozoic marine diversity and the fossil record. *Nature* 293:435–37.

Smith, A.B. 1994. *Systematics and the Fossil Record: Documenting Evolutionary Patterns*. Oxford and Cambridge, Massachusetts: Blackwell Scientific.

Stanley, S.M. 1979. *Macroevolution: Pattern and Process*. San Francisco: Freeman.

Uhen, M.D. 1996. An evaluation of clade-shape statistics using simulations and extinct families of mammals. *Paleobiology* 22:8–22.

Valentine, J.W. 1969. Patterns of taxonomic and ecological structure of the shelf benthos during Phanerozoic time. *Palaeontology* 12:684–709.

———. 1995. Why no new phyla after the Cambrian? Genome and ecospace hypotheses revisited. *Palaios* 10:190–94.

Valentine, J.W., and E.M. Moores. 1970. Plate-tectonic regulation of faunal diversity and sea level: A model. *Nature* 228:657–59.

Valentine, J.W., B.H. Tiffney, and J.J. Sepkoski Jr. 1991. Evolutionary dynamics of plants and animals: A comparative approach. *Palaios* 6:81–88.

Valentine, J.W., A.G. Collins, and C.P. Meyer. 1994. Morphological complexity increase in metazoans. *Paleobiology* 20:131–42.

Van Valkenburgh, B. 1995. Tracking ecology over geological time: Evolution within guilds of vertebrates. *Trends in Ecology and Evolution* 10:71–76.

Vrba, E.S. 1987. Ecology in relation to speciation rates: Some case histories of Miocene-Recent mammal clades. *Evolutionary Ecology* 1:283–300.

Wagner, P.J. 1997. Patterns of morphological diversification among the Rostroconcha. *Paleobiology* 23:115–50.

Wills, M.A., D.E.G. Briggs, and R.A. Fortey. 1994. Disparity as an evolutionary index: A comparison of Cambrian and Recent arthropods. *Paleobiology* 20:93–130.

Wray, G.A., J.S. Levinton, and L.H. Shapiro. 1996. Molecular evidence for a deep Precambrian divergence among metazoan phyla. *Science* 274:568–73.

Further Reading

Briggs, D.E.G., D.H. Erwin, and F.J. Collier. 1994. *The Fossils of the Burgess Shale*. Washington, D.C.: Smithsonian Institution.

Conway Morris, S. 1993. The fossil record and the early evolution of the Metazoa. *Nature* 361:219–25.

Erwin, D., J. Valentine, and D. Jablonski. 1997. The origin of animal body plans. *American Scientist* 85 March–April:126–37.

Gould, S.J. 1989. *Wonderful Life: The Burgess Shale and the Nature of History*. New York: Norton; London: Hutchinson Radius, 1990.

Hoffman, A. 1989. *Arguments on Evolution: A Paleontologist's Perspective*. New York: Oxford University Press.

Huston, M.H. 1994. *Biological Diversity: The Coexistence of Species on Changing Landscapes*. Cambridge and New York: Cambridge University Press.

Jablonski, D. 1995. Extinctions in the fossil record. *In* J.H. Lawton and R.M. May (eds.), *Extinction Rates*. Oxford and New York: Oxford University Press.

Levinton, J.S. 1988. *Genetics, Paleontology, and Macroevolution.* Cambridge and New York: Cambridge University Press.

Magurran, A.E. 1988. *Ecological Diversity and its Measurement.* Princeton: Princeton University Press; London: Chapman and Hall; 2nd ed., London: Chapman and Hall, 1991.

McMenamin, M.A.S., and D.L.S. McMenamin. 1990. *The Emergence of Animals: The Cambrian Breakthrough.* New York: Columbia University Press.

Ricklefs, R.E., and D. Schluter. 1993. *Species Diversity in Ecological Communities: Historical and Geographical Perspectives.* Chicago: University of Chicago Press.

Rosenzweig, M.L. 1995. *Species Diversity in Space and Time.* Cambridge and New York: Cambridge University Press.

Sepkoski Jr., J.J. 1991. Diversity in the Phanerozoic oceans: A partisan review. *In* E.C. Dudley (ed.), *The Unity of Evolutionary Biology: Proceedings of the Fourth International Congress of Systematic and Evolutionary Biology.* Portland, Oregon: Dioscorides.

Signor III, P.W. 1990. The geologic history of diversity. *Annual Review of Ecology and Systematics* 21:509–39.

———. 1994. Biodiversity in geological time. *American Zoologist* 34:23–32.

Valentine, J.W. 1992. The macroevolution of phyla. *In* J.H. Lipps and P.W. Signor (eds.), *Origin and Early Evolution of the Metazoa.* New York and London: Plenum.

Valentine, J.W., S.M. Awramik, P.W. Signor III, and P.M. Sadler. 1991. The biological explosion at the Precambrian-Cambrian boundary. *Evolutionary Biology* 25:279–356.

DOLLO, LOUIS ANTOINE MARIE JOSEPH

French/Belgian, 1857–1931

Louis Dollo was born on 7 December 1857 in Lille, France. While Dollo was a man of varied interests, the bulk of his scientific work and his greatest contributions were made in the field of paleontology. Yet, it was not always Dollo's subject matter that made his work significant; rather, it was the methodology of his ethological analysis, in which he explained the historical development of and reasons for a particular organism's adaptation. He died on 19 April 1931 in Brussels, leaving behind a body of work whose most important contributions still stand as paramount examples of paleobiological research.

As a student Dollo studied at the University of Lille and received a degree in civil and mining engineering in 1877. As a student, Dollo was influenced by the geologist Jules Gosselet and the zoologist Alfred Giard. In 1879 Dollo moved to Brussels, Belgium, where he briefly worked as an engineer for a gas company. However, three years later, in 1882, Dollo followed his interest in paleontology and was appointed the junior naturalist at the Royal Museum of Natural History in Brussels. Then, in 1891, he was appointed curator of the vertebrate section, a post that he kept almost to the end of his life. In 1909 Dollo was appointed extraordinary professor at Brussels University, where he taught paleontology and animal geography.

As curator of vertebrates, Dollo developed a particular interest in the problems of adaptation and ethology. Through the ethological study of fossils, Dollo investigated the history of adaptation. By focusing not only on functional significance but on historical development as well, Dollo was able to explain the reasons for a particular organism's adaptation. This type of methodological and theoretical research enriched Darwinian transformism through Dollo's famous biological law on the "irreversibility of evolution." Formulated around 1890, Dollo's Law states that evolution is not reversible; those structures or functions lost in the course of evolution will not reappear in a given line of organisms.

Dollo applied his methodology to a variety of subjects, but he concentrated his research and publications on fossil reptiles. In a series of brief articles, Dollo analyzed the reasons for the adaptation of certain fossil reptiles, in particular iguanodonts, to their conditions of existence. In another study, he looked at the ethological attributes of *Triceratops* and *Stegasaurus* and determined, unexpectedly, that these quadrupedal animals had functionally bipedal ancestors. Dollo's study of fossil sea turtles and mosasaurians followed the complex path of these organisms' historical development from land forms to sea forms. In one of his most significant works, the conclusions of which are still valid, Dollo examined the evolutionary characteristics of the lungfish. Dollo applied a similar method of observation and ethological analysis to rhynchocephalians, crocodiles, and ichthyosaurs.

However, Dollo's work encompassed more than fossil reptiles. He also applied his method of ethological research to such invertebrates as cephalopod molluscs and arthropods. Dollo also employed this method of analysis on the appendages of extant marsupials to establish their origin.

For his work Dollo was recognized as a member of the Royal Academy of Belgium and a corresponding member of many foreign academies. In 1884 he received the Kuhlmann Prize, followed by the Lyell Medal in 1889 and the Murchison Medal in 1912.

EDOUARD L. BONÉ AND BRIAN CALLENDER

Biography

Born in Lille, France, 7 December 1857. Received degree in civil and mining engineering, University of Lille, 1877. Appointed junior naturalist, Royal Museum of Natural History in Brussels, 1882; appointed curator of vertebrates, Royal Museum of Natural History in Brussels, 1891; became extraordinary professor, Brussels University, 1909. Member, Royal Academy of Belgium; received Kuhlmann Prize, 1884; Lyell Medal, 1889; Murchison Medal, 1912. Developed methodological and theoretical analysis that examined the ethological and historical development of an organism and how it relates to adaptation. Died in Brussels, 19 April 1931.

Major Publications

1893. Les lois de l'évolution. *Bulletin de la Société Belge de Géologie, de Paléontologie et d'Hydrologie* 7:164–66.

1895. Sur la phylogénie des dipneustes. *Bulletin de la Société Belge de Géologie, de Paléontologie et d'Hydrologie* 9:79–128.

1899. Les ancêtres des marsupiaux étaient-ils arboricoles? *In* A. Giard (ed.), *Miscellanées biologiques dédiées au Prof. A. Giard à l'occasion du XXVᵉ anniversaire de la fondation de la station zoologique de Wimereux, 1874–1899.* Paris: n.p.

1903. Sur l'évolution des chéloniens marins (considérations bionomiques et phylogéniques). *Bulletin de l'Académie Royale de Belgique, Classe des Sciences* 8:801–30.

1909. La paléontologie éthologique. *Bulletin de la Société Belge de Géologie, de Paléontologie et d'Hydrologie* 23:377–421; Brussels: Hayez, 1910.

Further Reading

Abel, O. 1931. Louis Dollo. 7 December 1857–19 April 1931. Ein Rückblick und Abschied. *Palaeobiologica* 4:321–44.

Brien, P. 1951. Notice sur Louis Dollo. *Annuaire de l'Académie Royale de Belgique: Notices biographiques* 69–138.

Jackson, R.T. 1936. Louis Dollo. *Proceedings of the American Academy of Arts and Sciences* 70:527–28.

Van Straelen, V. 1933. Louis Dollo (1857–1931). *Bulletin du Musée d'Histoire Naturelle de Belgique* 9:1–6.

DUBOIS, MARIE EUGÈNE FRANÇOIS THOMAS

Dutch, 1858–1940

Marie Eugène François Thomas Dubois—anthropologist, anatomist, paleontologist, and geologist—was born in Eijsden, Netherlands, 28 January 1858. Eugène Dubois is best known for his discovery of *Pithecanthropus erectus* (now *Homo erectus*), the supposed "missing link" between the apes and humankind (1891–93).

Dubois was educated as a physician and anatomist at Amsterdam University (1877–84), where he began his career as an assistant to the anatomist Max Fürbringer (1881–87). Later, in 1899, he became professor of crystallography, mineralogy, geology, and paleontology at Amsterdam University. Between 1887 and 1899, Dubois followed his predilection for paleoanthropological research (the study of ancient humans). He left his job in Amsterdam and embarked upon a search for hominid fossils in what he believed to have been the cradle of mankind, the Netherlands East Indies. From 1888 until 1895 he worked as a health officer in the Dutch colonial army, first in Sumatra, then in Java. At first, he searched for hominid fossils in his spare time. On the strength of his discoveries, in 1889 the colonial government appointed Dubois to the office of Director of Education, Religion, and Industry, enabling him to dedicate himself full-time to his excavations. He discovered the famous remains of *Pithecanthropus* (a skullcap, a thigh bone, and a few molars) and a wealth of other vertebrate fossils near the village of Trinil, Java, in the years 1891–93. These remains provided Dubois with what he interpreted as convincing evidence for humankind's descent from more primitive primates. He considered *Pithecanthropus* to represent the missing link—the *only* missing link—between the apes and the human species.

For several years after his return to Europe, Dubois spent all his energy trying to convince the world of the importance of his finds. Although researchers came to no consensus of opinion on the exact nature of the fossils, most agreed that *Pithecanthropus* represented a link in the chain that connects modern humans to their more primitive ancestors. Thus, Dubois' fossils were the first hominid remains ever to be accepted as material proof for human evolution. Dubois' fossils also induced researchers to accept an evolutionary interpretation of the Neanderthal remains, which had been discovered in 1856 but had been ascribed previously to a primitive but fully human race. In this way, Dubois' pioneering efforts helped to give shape to the rising science of paleoanthropology.

After 1900 Dubois withdrew from the debate on *Pithecanthropus* and devoted himself to various anatomical, paleontological, and geological studies. Among the most important of these was an investigation of vertebrate cephalization (i.e., the mathematical relationship between brain size and body size), including the hominids. Dubois' results have been severely criticized, yet from a historical perspective they represent a pioneering attempt to understand allometric relations. His cephalization studies convinced him that vertebrate evolution had proceeded in jumps. The distance between the apes and humans, he believed, had been covered in two jumps: one from the apes to *Pithecanthropus,* and one from *Pithecanthropus* to *Homo.* Since Dubois clung to this theory until his death, it is understandable that he never accepted the new *Pithecanthropus* finds that were made in Java in the 1930s. Their discoverer, G.H.R. von Koenigswald, concluded from his investigation of the new evidence that *Pithecanthropus* had been much closer to *Homo sapiens* than Dubois was prepared to allow on the basis of his cephalization studies. However, von Koenigswald's conclusions were generally accepted, and Dubois died a bitter man.

BERT THEUNISSEN

Biography

Born in Eijsden, Netherlands, 28 January 1858. Received M.D., Amsterdam University, 1884; honorary Ph.D. in botany and zoology, Amsterdam University, 1896. Assistant to Max Fürbringer, Amsterdam University, 1881–87; appointed lecturer in anatomy, Amsterdam University, 1886; professor extraordinary in crystallography, mineralogy, geology, and paleontology, Amsterdam University, 1899–1928; curator, Teylers Museum of Haarlem, 1897–1940. Excavated to establish human origins in the Netherlands East Indies (Sumatra, Java); discovered *Pithecanthropus* (now *Homo erectus*) near Trinil, Java (1891–93);

essays defending *Pithecanthropus* fostered its acceptance as the first hominid fossil and as proof of human evolution, as well as essays establishing an evolutionary role for Neanderthals (1856); pioneered in use of allometrics to study vertebrate (especially hominid) cephalization. Died in Haelen, Netherlands, 16 December 1940.

Major Publications

1889. Over de wenschelijkheid van een onderzoek naar de diluviale fauna van Ned. Indië, in het bijzonder van Sumatra. *Natuurkundig Tijdschrift voor Nederlandsch-Indië* 48:148–65.

1893. Die Klimate der geologischen Vergangenheit und ihre Beziehung zur Entwicklungsgeschichte des Sonne. Nijmegen, Leipzig: Thieme und Spohr.

1894. *Pithecanthropus erectus, eine menschenähnliche Übergangsform aus Java*. Batavia, Java: Landesdruckerei; New York: Stechert (Hafner), 1915.

1921. The proto-Australian fossil man of Wadjak, Java. *Proceedings of the Section of Sciences of the Koninklijke Akademie van Wetenschappen* (henceforth *Proceedings*) 23:1013–51.

1924. On the principal characters of the cranium and the brain, the mandible and the teeth of *Pithecanthropus erectus*. *Proceedings of the Section of Sciences of the Koninklijke Akademie van Wetenschappen* 27:265–78, 459–64.

1926. On the principal characters of the femur of *Pithecanthropus erectus*. *Proceedings of the Section of Sciences of the Koninklijke Akademie van Wetenschappen* 29:730–43.

1930. Die phylogenetische Grosshirnzunahme autonome Vervollkommnung der animalen Funktionen. *Biologia Generalis* 6:247–92.

1932. The distinct organization of *Pithecanthropus* of which the femur bears evidence, now confirmed from other individuals of the described species. *Proceedings of the Section of Sciences of the Koninklijke Akademie van Wetenschappen* 35:716–22.

1935. On the gibbon-like appearance of *Pithecanthropus erectus*. *Proceedings of the Section of Sciences of the Koninklijke Akademie van Wetenschappen* 38:578–85.

1940. The fossil human remains discovered in Java by Dr. G.H.R. von Koenigswald and attributed by him to *Pithecanthropus erectus*, in reality remains of *Homo wadjakensis* (syn. *Homo soloensis*). *Proceedings of the Section of Sciences of the Koninklijke Akademie van Wetenschappen* 43:494–96, 842–51, 1268–75.

Further Reading

Brongersma, L.D. 1941. De verzameling van Indische fossielen (Collectie Dubois). *De Indische Gids* 63:97–116.

Theunissen, B. 1988. *Eugène Dubois and the Ape-Man from Java: The History of the First Missing Link and Its Discoverer*. Boston and London: Kluwer Academic Publishers; as *Eugène Dubois en de aapmens van Java: Een bijdrage tot de geschiedenis van de paleoantropologie*, Amsterdam, Netherlands: Rodopi, 1985.

DWARFISM
See Phyletic Dwarfism and Gigantism

E

ECHINODERMS

The Echinodermata is a phylum that comprises a wide range of groups that have been classified into more than 20 different classes by some authorities. Only five of these classes are still living. Three features characterize the phylum: (1) possession by adults of a five-fold symmetry (although the larvae have bilateral symmetry); superimposed upon (2) a hydrostatic system known as the "water vascular system"; (3) a calcium carbonate skeleton comprising a series of individual plates made up of a mesh-work structure known as "stereom."

Echinoderms are morphologically very diverse, from mobile groups with an external skeleton (e.g., echinoids or sea urchins); to mobile forms with reduced, internal skeletons (e.g., holothuroids or sea cucumbers); to sessile, fixed forms with an external skeleton (e.g., crinoids or sea lilies) (Figure 1). Echinoderms have a long fossil history, extending back to the Early Cambrian, with possible ancestors in the Late Proterozoic. However, due to the nature of their exoskeleton (skeleton outside the body), which consists of individual plates, many groups after death readily disarticulate (break apart). As a consequence, these groups have poor fossil records, despite having been common elements of the marine invertebrate fauna. Such groups include the Asteroidea (starfish), Ophiuroidea (brittlestars), and Holothuroidea. Today, echinoderms are widespread in marine habitats, where they range from the intertidal zone (shoreline region affected by tides) to abyssal depths.

Most classifications divide the Echinodermata into at least 20 different classes. For example J. Sprinkle (1980) has five subphyla: the Crinozoa, Blastozoa, Asterozoa, Homalozoa and Echinozoa. Into these he places 20 classes (see Table 1). A.B. Smith (1984), however, adopts a more cladistic approach, with fewer classes, arguing that what have been regarded as classes are not necessarily all of the same hierarchical status (Table 2). Sprinkle's Crinozoa comprises mainly the Crinoidea; the Blastozoa, blastoids and blastoidlike groups; Asterozoa, the asteroids (starfish) and ophiuroids; Homalozoa, the early Paleozoic groups formally called "carpoids"; and Echinozoa, echinoids, holothuroids, and a number of rare Paleozoic forms like edrioasteroids. For discussion of the merits of these opposing classifications, the reader is directed to Smith (1984); for a discussion of their evolutionary relationships, see Paul and Smith (1988).

Evolutionary History

The earliest possible echinoderms are the Late Proterozoic Ediacaran *Tribrachidium* and *Arkarna*. However, there has been much debate over whether the superficial similarity between Ediacaran fossils and later phyla represents true phylogenetic (historical, evolutionary) relationships or not. Three groups of echinoderms—the eocrinoids, helicoplacoids, and edrioasteroids—have been recorded from the Early Cambrian and probably represent the earliest unequivocal echinoderms in the fossil record. These forms are limited in their diversity and their geographic and stratigraphic ranges. By the Middle Cambrian the crinoids, cyclocystoids, ctenocystoids, stylophorans, homosteleans, and homoiosteleans had appeared. All except the crinoids were geologically short-lived, being essentially Early Paleozoic in age. These echinoderms were mainly suspension feeders, which feed upon particles suspended in water, or detritus feeders, which feed upon the remains of dead animals and plants.

A second, much more significant radiation (diversification and geographic spread) took place in the Early and Middle Ordovician. Diversity levels of both genera and species increased markedly at this time. The most common echinoderms were suspension-feeding stemmed crinoids, which were elevated above the seafloor by a stalk and held in place by a specialized structure called a "holdfast." Of the four remaining living groups, asteroids and ophiuroids first appeared in the Early Ordovician, echinoids and holothuroids in the Middle Ordovician. However, all were of relatively low diversity during the Paleozoic. Greatest echinoderm diversity occurred in the Middle Ordovician, when 17 different major groups were present. Their diversity decreased throughout the Paleozoic. Those that became extinct were mainly small, probably highly specialized groups. At the generic and specific levels diversity remained high throughout the Paleozoic, reaching their

Table 1

Classification of Echinodermata According to Sprinkle (1980).

Subphylum Crinozoa
    Class Crinoidea   M. Cambrian, E. Ordovician–Recent
    Class Paracrinoidea   E. Ordovician–E.Silurian

Subphylum Blastozoa
    Class Blastoidea   M. Ordovician?, M. Silurian–L. Permian
    Class Rhombifera   E. Ordovician–L. Devonian
    Class Diploporita   E. Ordovician–E. Devonian
    Class Eocrinoidea   E. Cambrian–L. Silurian
    Class Parablastoidea   E.–M. Ordovician

Subphylum Asterozoa
    Class Asteroidea   E. Ordovician–Recent
    Class Ophiuroidea   E. Ordovician–Recent

Subphylum Homalozoa
    Class Stylophora   M. Cambrian–M. Devonian
    Class Homoiostelea   M. Cambrian–E. Devonian
    Class Homostelea   M. Cambrian
    Class Ctenocystoidea   M. Cambrian

Subphylum Echinozoa
    Class Echinoidea   L. Ordovician–Recent
    Class Holothuroidea   M. Cambrian?, M. Ordovician–Recent
    Class Edrioasteroidea   E. Cambrian–L. Carboniferous
    Class Ophiocistioidea   E. Ordovician–E. Carboniferous
    Class Helicoplacoidea   E. Cambrian
    Class Cyclocystoidea   M. Ordovician–M. Devonian
    Class Edrioblastoidea   M. Ordovician

Table 2

Phylogenetic Classification of Echinodermata According to Smith (1984).

Phylum Echinodermata
    plesion (Family) Helicoplacidae
    Subphylum Pelmatozoa
        plesion (Superclass) Cystoidea
        Class Crinoidea
            plesion (Genus) *Echmatocrinus*
            plesion (Subclass) Camerata
            plesion (Subclass) Flexibilia
            Subclass Articulata
    Subphylum Eleutherozoa
        plesion (Genus) *Stromatocystites*
        plesion (Class) Edrioasteroidea
        Superclass Asterozoa
            Class Asteroidea
        Superclass Cryptosyringida
            Subsuperclass Ophiuroidea
            Subsuperclass Echinozoa
                Class Echinodea
                Class Holothuroidea

maximum during the Carboniferous, when crinoids, blastoids, and echinoids were widespread. Consequently, those groups occur very commonly in the Paleozoic fossil record, particularly crinoids.

The Permo-Triassic mass extinction event severely affected suspension-feeding stemmed echinoderms. Blastoids became extinct, while crinoid diversity was reduced to a single genus. The only groups to survive were those that are living today. During the Mesozoic and Early Cenozoic, echinoids increased greatly in diversity and became the dominant echinoderm group. Asteroids, ophiuroids, and holothuroids are more diverse today than at any time in the past.

Echinoderm Morphology and Anatomy

The plates that form the unique skeletal structure in echinoderms are secreted by the animal as a single crystal of calcium carbonate. This may, however, contain up to 15 percent magnesium carbonate. Plates are secreted within the mesoderm (an internal layer of cells), and the honeycomb-like stereom is permeated by soft tissue. This enables the plates to grow, be repaired or resorbed, a process in which plates are "dissolved" and the materials are absorbed into the body. Resorption usually is a part of the growth process, so materials are recycled into a newer, larger skeleton. New plates may be added throughout life and rate of production will vary between species. Generally, the rate of plate growth is greatest early in development, diminishing as the organism increases in size. In some groups, such as echinoids and crinoids, the plates form a rigid box around the animal. Many different types of stereom can form and may be restricted to certain parts of the skeleton.

The water vascular system consists of a series of pipes and pressure chambers running through the body of the echinoderm (the "coelom"). In echinoderms with an exoskeleton, the external manifestation of the water vascular system is the tube feet that emerge through the skeleton through pores or slits over large areas of the animal's body. The tube feet, small fingerlike structures, are used variously for locomotion, food acquisition, respiration, chemical sensing, light sensing, and, in infaunal (burrowing) echinoids, funnel building. The external opening of the water vascular system is a porous plate called the "madreporite." Its sievelike structure keeps unwanted objects from entering the water vascular system. A tube called the "stone canal" extends from the madreporite to a "ring canal" that surrounds the mouth.

Five radial canals extend outward from the ring canal along the feeding arms, or just beneath the surface of the body. The rows of plates beneath which they run are known as "ambulacra." Intervening areas are called "interambulacra." Short lateral canals extend from the radial canals, leading to small, muscular swellings (ampullae) that in turn lead into the tube feet. Constrictions of the ampullae squeeze water into the tube feet, which extend by the outward pressure of the water (hydrostatic pressure). In some echinoderms the radial canals and ampullae are set within the skeleton. In others, canals are outside and ampullae inside; ampullae are lacking in crinoids. Tube feet may be terminated by suckers. These allow attachment to objects or to the substrate. (The substrate is the surface on which an animal lives, e.g., ocean bottom; coral reef.) Some may be terminated by fine papillae that secrete mucus.

The circulatory system is poorly developed in echinoderms, comprising a series of ring canals that surround the mouth and anus. Nutrients and waste products also move through the coelom. Gas exchange occurs via tube feet and coelom extensions. The ner-

vous system is complex. Sensory cells cover the tube feet and respond to tactile stimuli, the chemical environment, and radiation.

Crinoidea (Sea Lilies)

The Crinoidea is the only group of echinoderms in which the mouth is directed upward (Figure 1d). Likewise, the anus is directed upwards. Crinoids are radially symmetrical. They may be free-living (comatulids) or attached to the substrate by a jointed column. This column may or may not bear cirri (flexible structures at the base of the column that enable movement), and its base swells into a holdfast. Living, stalked crinoids are the isocrinids, cyrtocrionids, and bourgueticrinids. They are members of the subclass Articulata. This group encompasses all post-Triassic crinoids. Three other extinct subclasses, comprising predominantly stalked forms, occur in the Paleozoic, during which time they were the dominant group of echinoderms. About 750 Paleozoic genera are known. Living genera number 165.

The main body of the crinoid, located at the top of the column, consists of a plated cup, or "calyx." From this, five arms or "brachia" extend. These may be simple or may be branched. A ventral covering called the "tegmen" protects the viscera. Free-living forms have a dorsal plate, called the "centrodorsal," which may bear cirri used for grasping the substrate. The calyx comprises a number of plates. Apart from in the earliest genus, the "calyx plates" are arranged in regular circlets of five each. These alternate with "radial plates." Some forms have a third row called "infrabasals." This arrangement may be modified in a number of ways. Plates above the radials may not form arms but may be incorporated into the calyx, increasing its size. Plates that form the arms are known as "brachial plates." When incorporated into the calyx, intervening plates are known as "interbrachials." In some genera basal and infrabasal plates may fuse so that only three are present in a row.

The brachial plates in the arm are cylindrical or wedge-shaped. Arms may be unbranched or branched. They may be short, consisting of as few as 10 brachials, or long, with hundreds of them. Small-side extensions called "pinnules" may occur on the arms. Both arms and pinnules have tiny tube feet. Ambulacral grooves have small cover plates that protect the tube feet, opening when the crinoid is feeding, closing when it is not. Ambulacral grooves are lined with cilia (small, hairlike structures that move in waves), which transport food down the arms and pinnules to the mouth. Gonads are borne by lower pinnules.

The stem attaches to a hard substrate via a branched rootlike system. Others possess an anchoring structure for attachment. Early forms, including the earliest crinoid *Echmatocrinus*, from the Middle Cambrian Burgess Shale, possess a holdfast that consists of a number of small plates. This primitive form also has a calyx made up of a more irregular arrangement of plates than found in later forms. The first groups to appear in the Early Ordovician were the inadunates and camerates. The third Paleozoic group, the flexibles, evolved in the Middle Ordovician. Early inadunates had a small conical calyx, and many had long, simple arms, which usually lacked pinnules. Early camerates had a large conical calyx, with many brachial plates fixed to it. Arms were long and often bore pinnules. The first flexibles were similar to the inadunates, but with loosely connected plates in the calyx. Some of the inadunates evolved a bilaterally symmetrical calyx and lived in a recumbent (prone) position on the seafloor. During the Late Paleozoic many inadunates had a bowl-shaped calyx and long, branched arms, while flexibles reduced the size of their calyx. Similarly, camerates evolved a calyx with fewer plates.

These three groups almost became extinct at the end of the Permian. The single surviving inadunate genus gave rise, scholars believe, to the articulates that first appeared in the Early Triassic. This group diversified during the Mesozoic. Many had very reduced cups and elongate arms. Cretaceous forms, such as *Marsupites* and *Uintacrinus* were very widespread and are useful zone fossils (fossils that indicate the age of the rock in which they are found). Cretaceous crinoids had long been thought to have been floating forms, but more recently scholars have suggested that they lived on the seafloor (Milsom et al. 1994). Although 650 species are living today, their remains are not particularly common in the Cenozoic. Many living species lack stems and are either active swimmers or crawlers. Predation pressure may have favored the selection of such forms over fixed crinoids. Those with stems are more common in deep water environments, where predation pressure is likely to be lower.

Blastoidea

Blastoids are members of a major group of echinoderms, the Blastozoa. Regarded by some workers as a subphylum, the blastozoans consisted of stemmed, compact-bodied echinoderms with respiratory structures that pass though the plates. Their water vascular system was reduced, and they may have lacked tube feet. They were quite common during the Paleozoic and consisted of four groups: Blastoidea, Rhombifera, Diploporita, and Eocrinoidea.

Blastoids ranged from the Middle Silurian to the Late Permian (with a possible presence in the Middle Ordovician). They were the largest group of blastozoans. The swollen body, or "theca," is globular to conical, with series of roughly pentameral plates (arranged on five sides symmetrically). From the basal plates extends a columnar stem. Each of the radial plates above the basals supports an ambulacrum in a large, central sinus (cavity). Between the ambulacra are five radial plates that encircle a centrally positioned mouth. Well-developed respiratory structures called "hydrospires" are present, extending from the radials and deltoids into the coelomic cavity beneath the ambulacrum. These may be open or closed—if closed, they occur as folds beneath the ambulacra, opening into large holes called "spiracles." These surround the mouth, alongside which is the anus. Like crinoids, blastoids were high-level suspension feeders.

During the Silurian and Devonian, blastoids replaced the echinoid group, the rhombiferans. Blastoids differ in having fewer thecal plates, more distinct five-fold symmetry, more complex respiratory folds and ambulacra. Many thecal shapes evolved in blastoids, and ambulacra varied greatly in length. Silurian and many Devonian forms possessed a conical theca and short ambulacra. By the Middle Devonian, forms with a more globular thecal shape and longer ambulacra had evolved. These expanded greatly in diversity in the Early Carboniferous. However, both long and short ambulacra forms persisted until the group became extinct at the end of the Permian.

Rhombifera

The Rhombifera were medium-sized blastozoans that lived from the Early Ordovician to the Late Devonian. They are characterized by having respiratory "rhombs" that cover two adjoining plates. These rhombs were slitlike shapes shared between a pair of plates. Rhombiferans possessed either a globular, elongate, or flattened theca, with many plates organized into four or five circlets. Food-gathering arms extended from the top of the theca. Rhombiferans attached to the substrate via a stem composed of columnar discs. Often the stem was swollen near its connection with the theca. Overlapping discs allowed flexibility between the stem and theca. It is possible that such forms were active swimmers.

Rhombiferans had a worldwide distribution in the early Paleozoic, being most common in the Late Ordovician and Silurian. Early rhombiferans in the Ordovician had a globular to elongate theca, short ambulacra and many rhombs. A greater diversity of shapes evolved in later forms, ambulacra becoming longer and the number of rhombs reducing to just three, in fixed positions. Rhombiferans competed with, and were eventually replaced by, blastoids during the Devonian. Both occupied a similar suspension-feeding niche.

Diploporita

The Diploporita were a blastozoan group that had a rounded to elongate theca. The plates are regular and pentameral in some forms but irregular in others. Small armlike appendages attached on the dorsal surface around the mouth. Some diplophorans have a stem; in others it is missing. The most diagnostic feature is a set of paired pores, called "diplopores." These pass through most thecal plates. Around the diplopore there is a raised rim, which may have housed a globular structure used for respiration. Diploporans ranged from the Early Ordovician to Early Devonian. Feeding appendages are poorly known. The brachioles are smaller than in crinoids.

Eocrinoidea

The Eocrinoidea were the earliest brachiole-bearing echinoderms. The theca may be irregular or composed of an organized arrangement of plates. Two to five ambulacra bear long brachioles. Early forms possessed a holdfast, often consisting of many plates. Later forms evolved a stem with columnals. Respiration was via pores situated at the junction between plates.

These are amongst the earliest known echinoderms, and ranged from the Early Cambrian to Late Silurian. In all likelihood, eocrinoids were ancestral to all later blastozoans. They evolved a columnar stem independent of, and earlier than, the crinoids. Thecal plates were poorly organized in the Early and Middle Cambrian forms. In later ones organization was better, and some thin plates lacked pores. Eocrinoids were amongst the first high-level

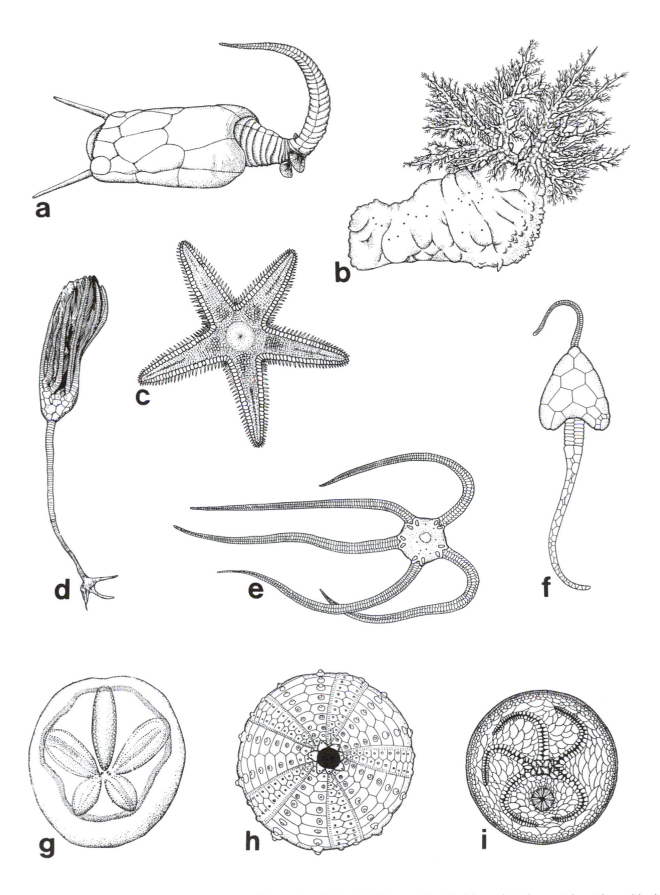

Figure 1. Echinoderms. *a,* stylophoran; *b,* holothuroid; *c,* asteroid; *d,* crinoid; *e,* ophiuroid; *f,* homoiostelean; *g,* irregular echinoid; *h,* regular echinoid; *i,* edrioasteroid.

suspension feeders, although some are likely to have lived reclining on the seafloor.

Asteroidea (Sea Stars)

The pentagonal to star-shaped body of the Asteroidea bears 5 to 25 arms, which may be very short (Figure 1c). These arms contain extensions of the coelom. The theca, or "test," comprises many small plates. The mouth is centrally placed on the lower surface. The gut is short and straight with an anus on the upper surface. On the lower surface of the arms, an ambulacra groove bears an open radial water vessel and many large tube feet. The coelomic cavity extends into the arms, including both gonads and part of the digestive system. The plates of asteroids are connected by connective tissue, which gives the body much flexibility. However, this structure also results in rapid disarticulation after death, making complete specimens a rarity in the fossil record. Today, some asteroids are detritus or suspension feeders, but many are carnivorous predators, a feeding strategy that may have evolved very early in their evolutionary history. Carnivorous asteroids prey on other echinoderms, molluscs, barnacles, and corals. Some species today live infaunally (buried in sediment). In reproduction, gametes are released into the water, where fertilization takes place at random, or fertilization occurs internally and eggs are retained until hatching.

Asteroids range from the Early Ordovician to the present day. Living asteroids occur most commonly in shallow-water marine environments. Sometimes included within the Asteroidea are the somasteroids, an Early Paleozoic group that appears to have been intermediate between the asteroids and ophiuroids. Asteroids do not occur commonly in Paleozoic deposits, becoming much more widespread in the Mesozoic and Cenozoic. More than 300 genera and 1800 species are known today (Rowe and Gates 1995).

Ophiuroidea (Brittle Stars)

The Ophiuroidea is characterized by a central disc 10 to 100 millimeters wide, from which radiate five long, thin, flexible arms (Figure 1e). The disc is composed of many small plates arranged with pentameral symmetry. The mouth is centrally positioned on the ventral surface. The gut is large and fills most of the inside of the central disc. It is blind and has no anus. Waste products are regurgitated through the mouth. Ophiuroids differ from asteroids in that the coelomic cavity and stomach are restricted to the disc. On the underside of each arm is an open radial water vessel from which emerge many small tube feet. These are used for feeding, locomotion, and respiration. The arms articulate (move) by means of an axial row of large plates called "vertebrae." Surrounded by small plates and spines, the vertebrae allow rapid, flexible movement, making ophiuroids the most mobile of echinoderms. Pouchlike structures called "genital bursae" are situated alongside the undersurface of the arms beneath the disc. These are thought to function in both reproduction and respiration. Many species give birth to live young; others brood their young. Sexual dimorphism (physical differences based on sex) is not uncommon, the much smaller males living on the ventral surface of the female's

disc. All are principally detritus or suspension feeders. A few are carnivorous. Some live infaunally or ectocommensally (on the surface of other organisms).

Ophiuroids range from the Early Ordovician to the present day. Unlike asteroids, ophiuroids are common in deep water. They were uncommon during the Paleozoic but suffered little from the Permo-Triassic mass extinction event. They became a little more common in the Mesozoic and Cenozoic, becoming an important part of today's marine invertebrate fauna; nearly 250 genera and 2000 species having been described (Rowe and Gates 1995).

Holothuroidea (Sea Cucumbers)

Holothuroidea are distinctive echinoderms (Figure 1b). They possess an elongate, flexible body. The internal skeleton is poorly developed, consisting of minute sclerites (bony fragments), rather than plates. Individuals may contain up to 20 million sclerites, varying from wheel or hook to anchor-shapes. In this respect holothuroids are paedomorphic (juvenilized) echinoderms (i.e., animals whose physical structure at maturity resembles the juvenile stage of related groups). The sclerites represent very early development of a skeleton that has not progressed beyond an early embryonic state. Here, the five-fold symmetry found in all echinoderms is represented externally by the rows of tube feet that extend from one end of the body. Small numbers of plates surround the mouth, supporting specialized feeding tube feet. Holothuroids feed by picking up detritus from the seafloor by means of mucus secreted by the tube feet. The tube feet then pass this into the mouth. The gut has one loop and extends to an anus situated at the opposite end of the body from the mouth. Internally, near the anal opening, is a cloaca, within which are respiratory trees. Holothurians pump water through their anus, and bathe these respiratory trees. Along the outside of the body are rows of tube feet used for locomotion. While most holothuroids today are benthic (live on the seafloor), some are swimmers. In contrast, a few that have some external plates attach to hard substrates, in a similar fashion to the edrioasteroids.

Sclerites that resemble those of modern holothuroids have been found in rocks as far back as the Middle Cambrian. Their abundance increased through the Paleozoic, and they continued through the Mesozoic and Cenozoic. Complete holothuroids are very rare, but specimens have been found in the Devonian, Carboniferous, and Jurassic.

Stylophora

The Stylophora is one member of an extinct group of unusual echinoderms, the Homalozoa (formerly known as carpoids). Homalozoans' shapes range from asymmetrical to bilaterally symmetrical, with a flattened theca and a single armlike appendage, the "aulacophore."

Stylophorans range from the Middle Cambrian to Middle Devonian. The theca bears an outer margin of large plates with the rest covered by many small, thin plates. Markedly asymmetric forms are known as "cornutes," bilaterally symmetric forms as "mitrates." Some forms also have spinose (spiny) margins. A large aulacophore attaches to one end of the theca. Close to the theca this structure is large, hollow, and consists of ringlets made up of four plates. The portion farthest from the theca has a pronounced food groove protected by overlapping cover plates. The mouth is situated at the base of the aulacophore. The anus is situated at the opposite end of the theca. Adjacent to the mouth are a series of elongate pores presumed to have served a respiratory function.

Stylophorans may have been suspension-feeding benthic echinoderms, the aulacophore having been held up into the water column. Alternatively they could have been detritus feeders. The aulacophore may have been used for locomotion. Some paleontologists have argued that stylophorans were ancestral to chordates (Jeffries 1986). Proponents of this idea use the term "calcichordates," arguing that the aulacophore was a "tail" and that certain internal structures in the theca are similar to structures present in early vertebrates. Most researchers do not accept this view, arguing that stylophorans have a typical echinoderm plate structure of single-crystal calcite, have a water vascular system, and that many of the characteristics of the aulacophore are very similar to ambulacra in other echinoderm groups (Parsley 1988).

Homoiostelea

The Homoiostelea is a small group of extinct homalozoans that range from the Middle Cambrian to Early Devonian. The theca is flattened and asymmetric to bilaterally symmetrical (Figure 1f). The homoiosteleans are unique in that they have a small aulacophore at one end and a larger, tail-like appendage at the other. The mouth is thought to have been positioned at the junction of the aulacophore with the theca, the anus at the corner of the theca at the opposing end. The presence of an enlarged region in the tail, close to the theca, suggests the presence of strong musculature, which probably enabled the animal to "swim."

Edrioasteroidea

The Edrioasteroidea range from the Early Cambrian to the Late Carboniferous and occurred mainly in North America and Europe. They are characterized by their discoidal, flattened shape, with a rounded upper surface and a flat to concave lower surface (Figure 1i). The lower surface formed an attachment site to a hard substrate, either hard ground or living or dead organisms present on the seafloor. The mouth is on the upper surface and is covered by a number of protective plates. The anus is also on the upper surface, situated closer to the margin. Radiating out from the centrally positioned mouth are five straight or curving ambulacra. The rest of the theca is covered by large numbers of disc-shaped interambulacral plates. Minute plates cover the margin. Close to the mouth lies a slitlike hydropore in the same interambulacrum as the anus.

Although not common in the fossil record, when edrioasteroids do occur they are found in very large numbers—up to many thousands on single bedding surfaces. It is thought that edrioasteroids were low-level suspension feeders, utilizing tube feet or open ambulacral grooves. The presence of pores in the ambulacra is evidence for the presence of a water vascular system.

Echinoidea (Sea Urchins and Sand Dollars)

The Echinoidea is characterized by its rigid theca, or "test." It comprises a series of interlocking plates that radiate in rows from the apex to the mouth on the ventral surface. In living echinoids the plates form five alternating double columns of ambulacra and interambulacra. Ambulacral plates possess pore pairs, through which tube feet extend. Echinoids possess a closed ambulacrum; the radial water vessels and other radial structures are internal to the skeleton. Regular echinoids have a radial, pentameral symmetry, whereas irregular echinoids have bilateral symmetry (Figures 1g, 1h).

In echinoids each plate bears tubercles that support either movable spines or very small, pincerlike structures called "pedicellariae." In regular echinoids spines are usually large and few in number, but they are much greater in number and far smaller in irregular echinoids. Regular echinoids have radial symmetry, irregular echinoids bilateral symmetry. In regulars the mouth is central on the lower surface, the anus central on the upper surface. In irregulars the mouth is on the lower surface, but is often not central. The anus is on the posterior (rear) or lower surfaces.

The apical system is on the upper surface, consisting of a ring of five genital plates alternating with five ocular plates. All, or some, of the genital plates are pierced by pores (gonopores), through which gametes are released. The ocular plates are terminal ambulacral plates and have tiny pores through which projects the end of the radial water vessel. In regular echinoids the apical system encircles the "periproct," which consists of a series of flexible plates through which the anus passes. In irregular echinoids the periproct is situated outside the apical system in a posterior position.

The mouth is situated on the oral surface, inside the test. In many echinoid orders, inside the mouth is a dental apparatus called the "lantern." It consists of five teeth that are moved by muscles attached to internal processes set inside and surrounding the mouth. In orders where the lantern is absent, there is a completely different style of feeding, deposit-feeding, rather than grazing. This is further reflected in habitats: Regular echinoids are epifaunal (living on the surface of the sediment); most irregulars are infaunal.

Tube feet in echinoids serve various functions, including respiratory, sensory, feeding, and funnel construction. Echinoids also move by using a combination of spines and tube feet. For those echinoids that are epibenthic (principally regular ones), tube feet play an important role in locomotion. Endobenthic echinoids, principally the irregulars, use spines for locomotion and for digging into the sediment.

Regular echinoids "graze" on algae using the lantern. Early Jurassic irregular echinoids, such as pygasteroids and holectypoids, retained the lantern throughout life. However, in some later groups the lantern was lost or retained only in juveniles. Many irregular echinoids have lost the lantern entirely and have evolved alternate feeding methods. Their evolution in the Jurassic saw a major shift in feeding habits, from large seaweeds to single-celled algae. In spatangoids (heart urchins), profound modifications of spines, tube feet, and body shape have occurred to assist with feeding. The tube feet used in feeding are highly modified, bearing a disc covered by papillae (tiny protrusions) and are situated in a specialized structure around the mouth.

Both direct and indirect development occurs in echinoids. Direct developers either brood their young directly on the surface of the test, nestled between spines, or in depressed regions of the tests, known as "marsupia."

Echinoids are marine benthic organisms. Regular echinoids mainly inhabit rocky or hard bottoms, although some do live on the sediment. Irregular echinoids can burrow, often quite deeply, in sediments ranging from coarse gravels to very fine muds. For these animals, the ability to inhabit such a muddy sediment requires on the oral surface modified spines, for digging, as well as "fascioles," organs that secrete mucus to cover the entire test. Deeper burrowing spatangoids, particularly those inhabiting fine-grained sediments, have evolved a more wedge-shaped test, with a high posterior end and deep paired petals, to facilitate water flow over the respiratory tube feet.

Clypeasteroids (sand dollars) shallow burrow more shallowly than spatangoids. Although usually inhabiting relatively sheltered environments, some clypeasteroids can survive in regimes of relatively high hydrodynamic activity, such as the surf areas near the shore. Clypeasteroids feed by picking up individual grains of sand or diatoms with tube feet coated with mucus, like spatangoids. However, it is not just the tube feet around the mouth that participate in feeding. Individual tube feet pass the grains to adjoining tube feet, until the food grains reach the food grooves on the oral surface, down which they are transported as aggregated mucus cords to the mouth (Telford et al. 1985).

Living echinoids are attacked by a wide variety of predators, including other echinoids, asteroids, fishes, gastropods, crustaceans, birds, sea otters, and Arctic foxes—as well as humans. Of these, only gastropods (e.g., clams and snails), which cut or drill holes in the test, leave a recognizable trace in the fossil tests. Echinoids, including burrowing irregular echinoids, are known to suffer quite high levels of predation from the gastropod family Cassidae. Many of the morphological features possessed by echinoids, and the evolutionary trends in echinoids over the last 150 million years, have been driven by predation pressure (McNamara 1994).

Paleozoic echinoids are rare. The first echinoids evolved in the Late Ordovician (Kier 1965). Ordovician and Silurian species were small, with few plates. Later Paleozoic forms were larger, with many ambulacral and interambulacral columns. The earliest cidaroid, the only group of echinoids to survive the Permo-Triassic mass extinction, evolved in the Early Carboniferous. These echinoids had just two columns of plates in each ambulacrum. By the Permian all had only two columns in the interambulacrum.

Echinoids are far more common in Mesozoic and Cenozoic deposits. This is in part due to the evolution of burrowing echinoids, which inhabited the sediment, increasing their chance of preservation. During the Early Jurassic irregular echinoids evolved. Major morphological changes occurred. The periproct moved posteriorly out of the apical system, the test elongated, spines increased in number and reduced in size, ambulacral pores on the upper surface became petaloid, teeth were lost, and the mouth moved anteriorly. These changes enabled the echinoids to burrow in the sediment. Evolutionary trends in spatangoids include petals becoming more sunken, the development of an an anterior notch, a decrease in plate thickness, an increase in the number and type of fascioles, enlargement of plastron on lower surface, and increased differentiation of tube feet and spines. These all relate to moving into areas with finer grained sediments. The last, major evolutionary event was the evolution of the clypeasteroids in the Early Cenozoic. The first forms were tiny, the size and shape of a grain of rice. From these evolved a wide range of larger, flattened forms, common in shallow water environments today.

KENNETH J. McNAMARA

See also Aquatic Invertebrates, Adaptive Strategies of; Birds; Chordates; Feeding Adaptations: Invertebrates; Skeletized Organisms and the Evolution of Skeletized Tissues; Skeleton: Dermal Postcranial Skeleton

Works Cited

Jefferies, R.P.S. 1986. *The Ancestry of the Vertebrates.* Cambridge and New York: Cambridge University Press.

Kier, P.M. 1965. Evolutionary trends in Paleozoic echinoids. *Journal of Paleontology* 39:436–65.

———. 1974. Evolutionary trends and their functional significance in the post-Paleozoic echinoids. *Paleontological Society Memoir* 5:1–95.

McNamara, K.J. 1994. The significance of gastropod predation to patterns of evolution and extinction in Australian Tertiary echinoids. *In* B. David, A. Guille, J.-P. Féral, and M. Roux (eds.), *Echinoderms through Time.* Rotterdam and Brookfield, Vermont: Balkema.

Milsom, C.V., M.J. Simms, and A.S. Gale. 1994. Phylogeny and palaeobiology of *Marsupites* and *Uintacrinus. Palaeontology* 37:595–607.

Parsley, R.L. 1988. Feeding and respiratory strategies in Stylophora. *In* C.R.C. Paul and A.B. Smith (eds.), *Echinoderm Phylogeny and Evolutionary Biology.* Oxford: Clarendon; New York: Oxford University Press.

Paul, C.R.C., and A.B. Smith (eds.). 1988. *Echinoderm Phylogeny and Evolutionary Biology.* Oxford: Clarendon; New York: Oxford University Press.

Rowe, F.W.E., and J. Gates. 1995. Echinodermata. *In* A. Wells (ed.), *Zoological Catalogue of Australia Series.* Vol. 33. Canberra: CSIRO Australia.

Smith, A.B. 1984. Classification of the Echinodermata. *Palaeontology* 27:431–59.

Sprinkle, J. 1980. Origin of blastoids: New look at an old problem. *Geological Society of America Abstract Program* 12 (7):528.

Telford, M., R. Mooi, and O. Ellers. 1985. A new model of podial feeding in the sand dollar *Mellita quinquiesperforata* (Leske): The sieve hypothesis challenged. *Biological Bulletin* 169:431–48.

Further Reading

David, B., A. Guille, J.-P. Féral, and M. Roux (eds.). 1994. *Echinoderms through Time.* Rotterdam and Brookfield, Vermont: Balkema.

Jefferies, R.P.S. 1986. *The Ancestry of the Vertebrates.* Cambridge and New York: Cambridge University Press.

Paul, C.R.C., and A.B. Smith (eds.). 1988. *Echinoderm Phylogeny and Evolutionary Biology.* Oxford: Clarendon; New York: Oxford University Press.

EDENTATES

See Xenarthrans

EDIACARAN BIOTA

"Ediacaran Biota" is a noncommittal term for an association of soft-bodied organisms that inhabited shallow sea bottoms during the 50 million years between the last Precambrian glaciation and the Cambrian evolutionary explosion. In contrast to later fossils in Conservation Lagerstätten (e.g., Burgess or Solnhofen types), these fossils are preserved not in fine-grained black shales or micritic limestones, but as delicate impressions in rather coarse sands and silts. Therefore, initially they were connected to beach sands, in which soft-bodied organisms such as jellyfish are stranded and leave preservable imprints as they dry out. Today, we think that these deposits were formed under water, below the level of daily wave action. In the Precambrian, sediment mixing by burrowing animals was virtually absent, so microbial mats formed, gluing the upper millimeters of these sediments into a leathery seal that was resistant to moderate levels of erosion. Such sediments are called "matgrounds." Sediments that are mixed by animals are called "mixgrounds." The presence of such mats can be inferred from sediment structures that are typical for Precambrian rocks but later became restricted to hostile environments where, once again, no mixing by animals took place. We mention this because in Precambrian oceans biomats were not only the chief sites of primary production (production of organic substances through photosynthesis); they also played a major role in the biology and preservation of associated larger organisms.

Affiliation of Ediacaran Fossils

A first critical issue is the nature of the Ediacaran organisms. By their sizes (up to one meter) and distinct shapes, they certainly look like higher plants or animals. Therefore, it is not surprising that for a

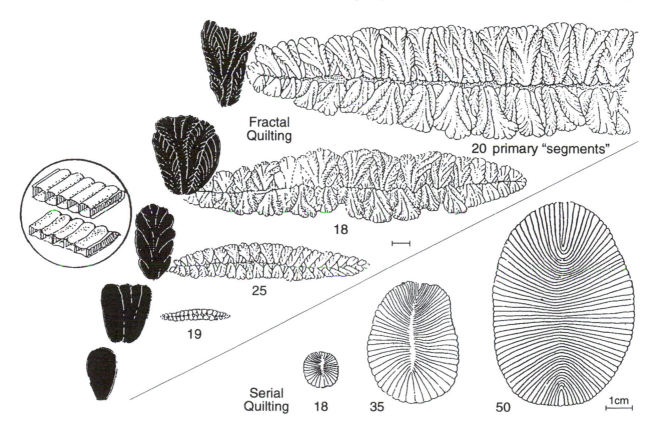

Figure 1. Vendobiontan allometric compartmentalization. Serial or fractal quilting of an elastic cuticle allowed vendobionts to maximize stiffness and body surface. At the same time it compartmentalized the living content. Since compartmentalization increased allometrically during growth, one might conclude that this content was not multicellular, but plasmodial. Modified from Seilacher (1992).

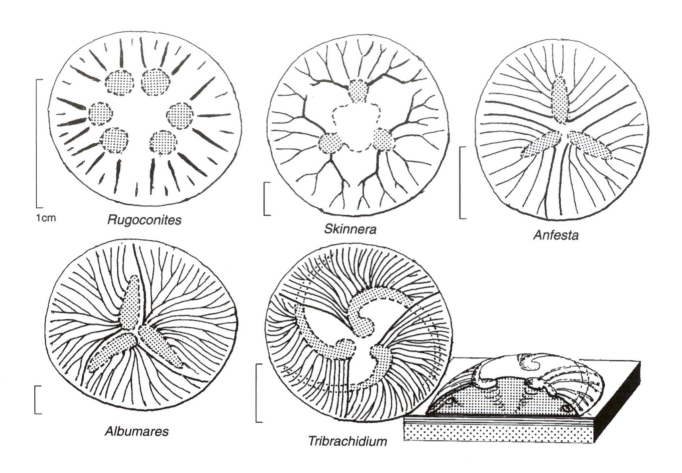

1cm

Rugoconites

Skinnera

Anfesta

Albumares

Tribrachidium

Figure 2. Trilobozoan mat encrusters. Since these organisms are always found with their convex sides up, one can conclude that they were attached to a resistant microbial mat. A sponge relationship is suggested by narrow (inhaling) canals in the periphery and wider (exhaling) ones in the center. After casts provided by Jim Gehling and photos in Fedonkin (1990).

long time they were thought to be the soft-bodied ancestors of later animal phyla (Glaessner 1984). This concept somewhat softened the "Cambrian Explosion," the term for the seemingly sudden appearance of metazoan phyla at the beginning of the following period.

Vendobionta

Upon closer inspection, however, the similarities between Ediacaran fossils and modern animals become less convincing. The "jellyfishes" probably could not swim. The "seapens" could not act as filter fans because their branches were fused into leaflike structures. We also cannot distinguish organs, such as a mouth or appendages. On the other hand, forms that have very different appearances share a similar construction: they are foliate (leaf-shaped) and subdivided by regularly spaced quiltings. Having a tight skin over a hydrostatic fluid content, this design of the organisms increased their rigidity as well as surface area. Thus, it is reasonable to assume that these organisms interacted with their environment directly through their body surface. This would make them analogous to plants, with the option to take up energy either in the form of light (photosymbiosis), methane or H_2S (chemosymbiosis), or as dissolved organic substances.

For these and other reasons, the Vendobionta hypothesis (Seilacher 1992) claims that the majority of large Late Precambrian (Vendian) organisms represent a failed evolutionary experiment—giant plasmoidal (fluid-filled) organisms (Figure 1) not ancestral to today's plants and animals. In a way, the Ediacaran biota could constitute a kingdom of their own. As a result, any similarities to extant organisms are due mainly to similar modes of self-organizational pattern formation, not phylogenetic (natural evolutionary) relationship. Apart from some questionable survivors (Conway Morris 1993), the Vendobionta became extinct in the Cambrian Revolution.

Spongelike Animals

For another group of Ediacaran organisms, the *Trilobozoa* (Fedonkin 1990) (Figure 2), metazoan relationships are more likely. They are always shaped like a round disk, with the domed upper surface bearing the impressions of canal systems with a triradiate symmetry (symmetry built upon three rays). Since there is always a clear distinction between narrow canals in the periphery and three or six large ones for exhalation near the elevated center, we may be dealing with a kind of early sponge that

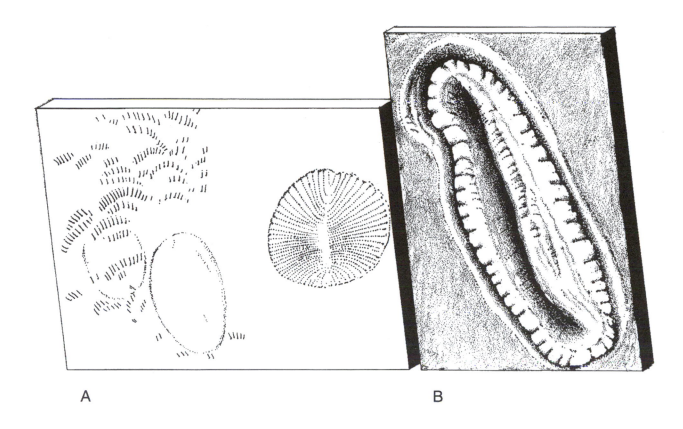

A   B

Figure 3. Ediacaran mat scratchers. Two independent lines of evidence indicate soft-bodied molluscs. *A,* fan-like arrays of scratches from Australia suggest paired radula teeth strong enough to carve into a biomat that did not yield under the weight of the bulky producer. A nearby large vendobiont *(Dickinsonia)* was left unharmed. Elliptical impressions in the scratched area fit the outline of the hypothesized producer. *B, Kimberella* differs from other Ediacaran impressions by its strong and variously deformed relief. The lobed elliptical area is interpreted as a molluscan foot, whose center became deeply impressed by compaction after the guts had decomposed. The smooth margin resembles a mantle fold. As shown by the deformation on the left side, the corresponding shell was as yet conmineralized and perhaps segmented. Yet in the presence of a leathering biomat, the foot could press it so tightly to the substrate that no sediment could enter the mantle cavity during the fatal depositional event. After slides courtesy of Jim Gehling and M. Fedonkin.

probably had a basal (primitive) sand skeleton. One such disk-shaped fossil (*Palaeophragmodictya;* Gehling and Rigby 1996) shows another typical sponge feature: the rectangular grit of minute spicules. If, as is likely, the spicules were originally composed of silica, this would be the earliest case of the mineralization of a biological structure.

Mollusca

The only Ediacaran body fossil strongly indicating the presence of triploblastic (three-layered) animals is *Kimberella* (Figure 3), whose reconstruction from White Sea material (Fedonkin and Waggoner 1996) shows a large, limpet-like animal. This interpretation is supported by a completely different kind of evidence from Australia: faint scratches on bedding planes—originally thought to be caused by trilobites or other arthropods—are markings from the radula (strip of skin imbedded with minute teeth for scraping algae from rocky surfaces) of a large mollusc. This means that tanned proteins—the material from which mol-

luscs make their hard, radular teeth—had been developed by Vendian times.

Shelly Tubes

The Cambrian Explosion is often referred to as a "skeletonization event," a time when animals began using minerals to form skeletons. This is true mainly for calcareous skeletons, whose abundance made them major rock constituents. Yet there is a small Vendian fossil, *Cloudina* (Figure 4), which heralded this historic innovation. *Cloudina's* conical shell is difficult to affiliate with modern animal phyla. This is because it did not grow by adding materials at the edges but by stacking calcareous molts, forming a single composite shell.

Worm Burrows

Almost by definition, taxonomic uncertainly also applies to the "worm burrows" found on Vendian bedding planes. However,

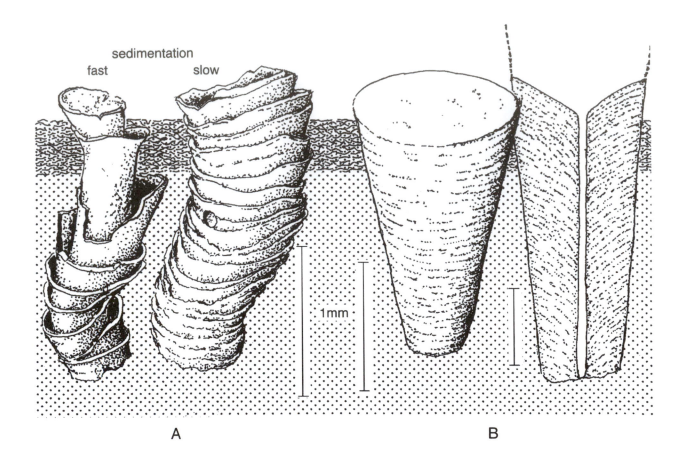

Figure 4. Mat stickers. Although their taxonomic affiliations remain problematic, *Cloudina* (*A*, with a calcareous shell) and *Volborthella* (*B*, with an agglutinated ballast inside an organic shell) can be identified as "sediment stickers"—except that they are too small to be stabilized by loose sediment. Their strategy worked, however, if they grew within a sticky biomat. After Bengtson (1994) and Nyers (1985).

these fossils reflect the activity of peristalsis, an activity that is largely restricted to triploblastic animals with a coelom (internal body cavity).

Ecologic Guilds

Irrespective of their taxonomic position, Ediacaran organisms also can be classified into "ecologic guilds" by means of functional morphology and preservation criteria. As it turns out, most of these guilds are poorly represented in Phanerozoic and recent biota. This is because they are related to matgrounds, which became drastically reduced when soft bottoms turned into mixgrounds after the Cambrian Revolution (Seilacher and Pflüger 1994) (Figure 5).

Mat Encrusters

As we can see from their behavior in a turbidity current (stalked forms being felled, reclining ones not transported and not aligned), bottom-dwelling Vendobionta were glued to the substrate (Figure 6). Equally, the Trilobozoa (Figure 2) are never turned over or even

inclined. Rather, they resemble rock-attached barnacles—including torsion during growth, which in the barnacle is seen only in the plate at the bottom of the animal. This lifestyle would have been impossible on the surface of loose sands, silts, and muds, unless the surface were bound into a leathery microbial mat.

Mat Stickers

Cloudina (like other Precambrian tube fossils and the similar Early Cambrian *Volborthella*) (Figure 4) would be morphologically classified as a "sediment sticker." In this lifestyle, the shell anchors the immobile animal by growing up with sedimentation and at the same time expanding into an inverted cone. However, in contrast to typical sediment stickers (rugose corals, brachiopods, and rudist bivalves), the millimeter-sized *Cloudina* (Figure 4) appears too small to become effectively anchored, even in the most quiet waters—unless it was glued into the substrate by a sticky biomat. Representations of this lifestyle in extreme environments, where matgrounds persisted into later times (*Saccocoma* and other Jurassic microcrinoids), support this picture.

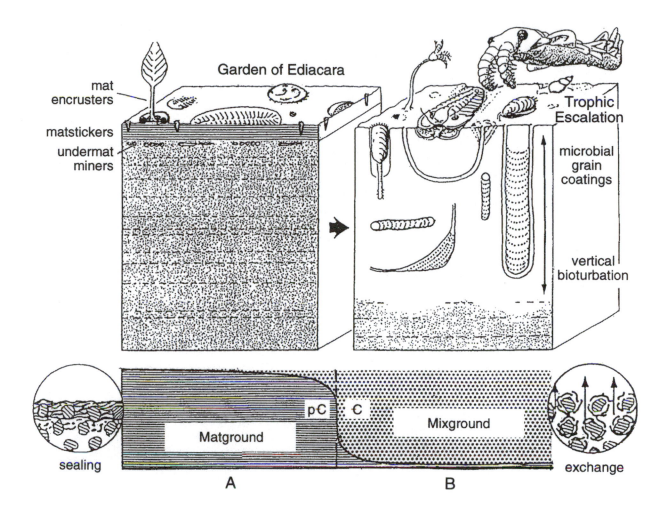

Figure 5. The agronomic revolution. *A,* Precambrian benthic life centered around ubiquitous biomats that sealed the surfaces of otherwise loose sediments. Since megascopic predators and scavengers were also absent, large and differentiated vendobionts and other strange organisms could evolve in the favorable climate of the terminal Proterozoic. *B,* this situation changed completely in the early Cambrian, when many of the newly established animal groups became infaunal in response to increasing predator pressure. The transition of oceanic bottoms from a matground to a bioturbational mixground state may be compared to the impact that human agriculture had on terrestrial ecosystems. Modified from Seilacher and Pflüger (1994).

Undermat Miners

It has long been noted that Precambrian trace fossils (any fossil that records the presence of an animal—e.g., burrows) follow bedding planes rather than penetrate into the sediment. Nevertheless, these traces are burrows, not trails, made where the sediment and the water meet. The paradox resolves if we assume that the trace makers mined the zone of decaying materials underneath living mats. While they did this in a rather random fashion 1.1 billion years ago (Seilacher et al. 1998), by Vendian times some of these undermat miners had evolved sophisticated search programs (e.g., meandering and systematic branching); the same behaviors can be seen in relic matground environments of the Cambrian (Figure 7). This means that wormlike coelomates are probably a very ancient stock that remained confined to a furtive existence before their rise

to dominance and new basic designs in the Cambrian evolutionary explosion.

Mat Scratchers

While undertrack miners appear to have been decomposers, radular scratch marks *(Radulichnus)* (Figure 3) signal the first step to plant-eating life. Because of their shape and pattern, there is no doubt that the scratches were made from above the sediment. Nevertheless, they did not become wiped out as the heavy animal that made them bulldozed over them. Also, the muscular foot of *Kimberella* (the possible maker of the radular marks) is always fully exposed, as if it had been clinging to the surface of the underlying bed. This again implies that the sand was bound

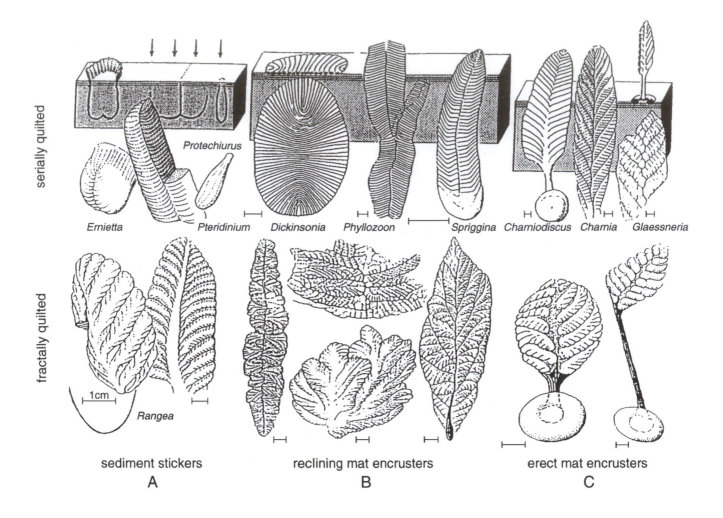

Figure 6. Vendobiontan lifestyles; unnamed forms from Newfoundland. Vendobionts are here interpreted as immobile photo- or chemosymbiotic organisms. They were originally glued to leathery biomats by their lower surfaces *(A)*, but some of them *(B)* lived immersed in the sediment, while others *(C)* managed to elevate their fronds above the ground. Modified from Seilacher (1992).

into a resistant biomat. Yet, these early consumers did not disrupt the peace of the "Garden of Ediacara": the large, armorless Vendobionta around them remained unharmed (Figure 3). Nor were the mollusc grazers common enough to alter the mat-ground state of the sediment.

Thus, the Ediacaran biota represent not simply a prelude to the Phanerozoic, but a world of its own. The lack of predators and the presence of a favorable climate allowed soft-bodied organisms to develop large sizes and strange designs. The ubiquity of leathery biomats also favored lifestyles that were impossible in the mixground state of later sea bottoms. Therefore, the Cambrian Revolution marks the extinction (or near extinction) not only of evolutionary lineages, but also of ecologic guilds that had dominated the Precambrian world. Evolutionary blooming, mass extinction, and recovery were also involved in later historic revolutions in biology; but only the Precambrian/Cambrian transition resembled the mass extinction of our time, in which the

disappearance of species is combined with a basic shift in global ecology.

ADOLF SEILACHER

See also Problematic Animals

Works Cited

Bengtson, S. 1994. The advent of animal skeletons. *In* S. Bengtson (ed.), *Early Life on Earth*. Nobel Symposium, 84. New York: Columbia University Press.

Conway Morris, S. 1993. Ediacaran-like fossils in Cambrian Burgess Shale-type faunas of North America. *Palaeontology* 36:593–635.

Fedonkin, M.A. 1990. Systematic description of Vendian Metazoa. *In* B.S. Sokolov and A.B. Ivanovskij (eds.), *The Vendian System: Paleontology*. Berlin and New York: Springer-Verlag.

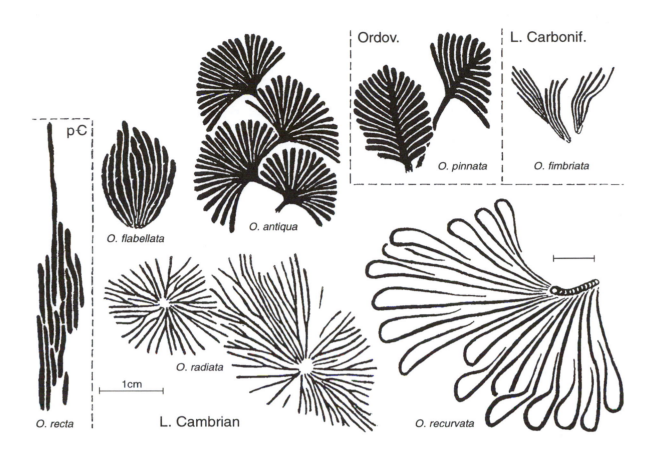

Figure 7. Undermat miners. The trace fossil *Oldhamia* reflects an ancient lifestyle: small animals mining the decomposing zone below active biomats. The earliest representative (*O. recta*) was found in North Carolina together with the vendobiont *Pteridinium* (Figure 6). In contrast to most other Ediacaran organisms, the unknown makers of these burrows lived in deep- sea habitats, where the Cambrian Agronomic Revolution (Figure 5) arrived with some delay. This allowed them to evolve a variety of improved search programs during the first stage of the Cambrian (examples from Puncoviscana Fm, Argentina). Later forms are rare and come from particular deep-sea environments in Europe. Courtesy of Adolf Seilacher.

Fedonkin, M.A., and B.M. Waggoner. 1996. The Vendian fossil *Kimberella:* The oldest mollusk known. *Geological Society of America Abstract with Program* 28, A53.

Gehling, J.G., and J.K. Rigby. 1996. Long expected sponges from the neoproterozoic Ediacara fauna of South Australia. *Journal of Paleontology* 70:185–95.

Glaessner, M.F. 1984. *The Dawn of Animal Life: A Biohistorical Study.* Cambridge and New York: Cambridge University Press.

Nyers, A. 1985. The genus *Volborthella* from the autochthonous beds of the Vassbo area (L. Cambrian; NW Dalarna, Sweden). *Neues Jahrbuch* Heft 3.

Seilacher, A. 1992. Vendobionta and Psammocorallia: Lost constructions of Precambrian evolution. *Journal of the Geological Society* (London) 149:609–13.

Seilacher, A., P. Bose, and F. Plüger. 1998. Triploblastic animals more than 1 billion years ago: Trace fossil evidence from India. *Science* 282 (5386):36–75.

Seilacher, A., and F. Pflüger. 1994. From biomats to benthic agriculture: A biohistoric revolution. *In* W. Krumbein, D.M. Paterson, and L.J. Stal (eds.), *Biostabilization of Sediments*. Oldenburg: Bibliotheks- und Informationssystem der Univ. Oldenburg.

EGG, AMNIOTE

The evolution of the amniote egg defines the evolutionary change from amphibians to reptiles. Most amphibians live in moist habitats. In order to survive, their anamniotic (one lacking amniote structures) eggs must be laid directly in water or moisture rich environments. A thickened jelly layer surrounds the developing larvae with no outer fibrous membrane or shell layer. This arrangement limits the size of the egg, provides no protection from desiccation (drying out) or structural stress, and limits respiratory exchange. The developing amphibians hatch in a larval state, then continue metamorphosis until they attain adult form. In contrast, reptiles, which evolved from amphibians, adapted to terrestrial environments. Their success on land was due in large part to reproductive changes involving the development of the amniote egg.

The amniote egg consists of an outer shell layer and inner membranes that are not part of the embryo (extraembryonic membrane). The extraembryonic membranes are the chorion, allantois, amnion, and yolk sac (Figure 1). The wall of the vascular (involved with blood vessels) allantois joins the outermost membrane, the chorion, where gaseous exchange takes place. Oxygen rich air is brought in and noxious gases such as carbon dioxide, the byproducts of metabolic and respiratory processes of the developing embryo, are expelled (Rhan et al. 1979). The fluid-filled amnion surrounds the embryo, cushioning and protecting it while providing a watery environment for development. The highly vascularized yolk sac allows for transport of nutrients from the yolk to the developing embryo (Elinson 1989).

Due to a lengthy incubation period, amniotes are well developed when they hatch, appearing much like small adults. This is possible because the amniote egg is larger, accommodating this increase in hatchling size. The self-contained nature of the amniote egg gives it another advantage—it can be laid in diverse terrestrial habitats rather than being restricted to aquatic habitats for its survival.

All tetrapods (four-legged animals) other than amphibians are amniotes. Recent taxa (groups; singular, taxon) that lay amniotic eggs are birds (aves) and reptiles (reptilia), including lizards and snakes (squamata), turtles (chelonia), and crocodilians (crocodylia). Of these groups, most are oviparous—this group lays eggs that require a lengthy incubation for full development of the young prior to hatching. All placental mammals and a few species of snakes and lizards are viviparous—they give live birth and the embryos fully develop within the mother.

There are three types of amniote eggshells: soft, flexible, and rigid. Within these types, there are many variations of the eggshell structure (Mikhailov 1991). Soft shells are laid by snakes and lizards, flexible shells are laid by sea turtles and snapping turtles, and rigid-shelled eggs are laid by land tortoises, crocodiles, some geckos, birds, and dinosaurs (Hirsch 1994). The eggshell is composed of organic membranes and crystalline calcite or aragonite. The eggshell is composed of closely abutting or interlocking individual shell units (Figure 2). Formation of the shell layer begins in the oviduct. Calcite crystals initiate the growth of individual shell units. All growth is in an outward, vertical direction. The structural specifics of eggshell growth are determined by constraints of phylogeny (evolutionary history) and physiology.

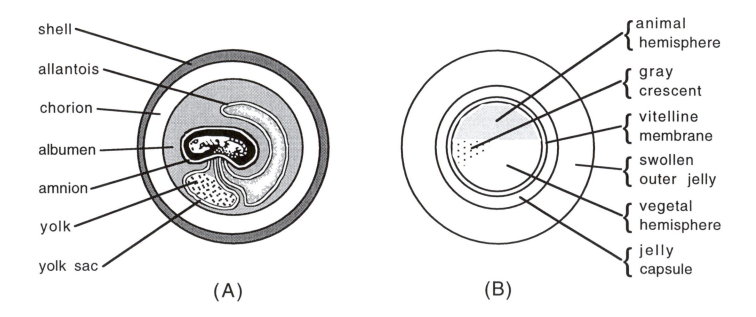

(A)   (B)

Figure 1. Structure features of (A) the amniote egg and (B) the anamniote egg.

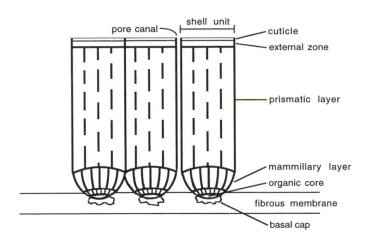

Figure 2. Radial view of an avian eggshell. Eggshell is composed of individual shell units adjoining one another. *Top,* outer surface of egg; *bottom,* inner surface.

Eggshell features include the following: size and shape of the egg; thickness of the eggshell; sculpturing of the shell's outer surface; the type, positioning, and frequency of pore canals; the arrangement of shell units; and the composition of the shell's micro- and ultrastructure. These features vary in accordance with the biologic necessities of the egg-layer. The ability to lay an egg well suited for survival in the animal's nesting environment is an absolute necessity for the success and continuity of the species. Eggs laid in arid environments must be able to withstand heat and dryness, whereas eggs laid in humid environments must be protected from excess moisture and able to meet the needs of increased gas exchange.

Among modern taxa, the microstructure of the rigid eggshell is diagnostic (evidence for) of the identity of the egg-layer. Birds lay eggs with a microstructure different from that of turtles, which in turn are different from that of crocodiles. Therefore, a taxonomic stability of eggshell microstructure exists. This continuity of eggshell structural types among taxa extends to the interpretation and diagnosis of fossil eggs and egg-layers. Only eggs with a thick, well-formed, calcareous eggshell have a good

chance of being preserved as fossils. The eggshell's crystalline calcite structure is retained after it is replaced by minerals during the fossilization process. The inner organic extraembryonic membranes readily decay, and so they have little chance of being preserved. If the bones of the developing embryo have grown to an advanced stage and are well developed, they too may be preserved, although such finds are rare. The type of eggs known from the fossil record are the rigid-shelled eggs of avian, crocodilian, chelonian, geckoid, and dinosaurian origin. Though dinosaurs have no modern corollary, their eggshell structures are unique and diverse, with one structural type similar to that of ratite birds. Numerous dinosaur eggs are known from Jurassic and Cretaceous deposits worldwide.

EMILY S. BRAY

See also Reproductive Strategies: Vertebrates

Works Cited

Elinson, R.P. 1989. Egg evolution. *In* D.B. Wake and G. Roth (eds.), *Complex Organismal Functions: Integration and Evolution in Vertebrates.* Chichester and New York: Wiley.

Hirsch, K.F. 1994. The fossil record of vertebrate eggs. *In* S.K. Donovan (ed.), *The Palaeobiology of Trace Fossils.* Chichester: Wiley; Baltimore, Maryland: Johns Hopkins University Press.

Mikhailov, K.E. 1991. Classification of fossil eggshells of amniote vertebrates. *Acta Palaeontologica Polonica* 36:193–238.

Rahn, H., A. Ar, and C.V. Paganelli. 1979. How bird eggs breathe. *Scientific American* 240 (2):38–47.

Further Reading

Carpenter, K., K.F. Hirsch, and J.R. Horner (eds.). 1994. *Dinosaur Eggs and Babies.* Cambridge and New York: Cambridge University Press.

Deeming, D.C., and M.W.J. Ferguson (eds.). 1991. *Egg Incubation: Its Effects on Embryonic Development in Birds and Reptiles.* Cambridge and New York: Cambridge University Press.

Sumida, S.S., and K.L.M. Martin (eds.). 1997. *Amniote Origins Completing the Transition to Land.* San Diego: Academic Press.

EHRENBERG, CHRISTIAN GOTTFRIED

German, 1795–1876

Christian Ehrenberg was born on 19 April 1795 in Delitzsch, Electorate of Saxony (later part of Germany). After briefly studying medicine in Leipzig, he moved in 1817 to the University of Berlin in what was then the Kingdom of Prussia, earning his degree in 1818 with a thesis describing 250 species of fungi (including 62 new species) from the Berlin region. He made original observations on the process of reproduction in fungi and was first to observe cryptogamous reproduction (reproduction and development from spores) in molds, helping to refute con-

temporary misconceptions that lower organisms came into being spontaneously.

Ehrenberg's work on fungi gained him a temporary botanical appointment at the University of Königsberg (now Kaliningrad, Russia). When it ended in 1820, he and his friend Wilhelm F. Hemprich attached themselves as naturalists to an archeological expedition to Egypt—one that was poorly organized and quickly disintegrated. Undaunted, Ehrenberg and Hemprich stayed on in Egypt, traveling down the Nile Valley into Nubia, then to the

Sinai Peninsula. After their early collections had been taken to Alexandria for shipment back to Prussia, they traveled in Syria and Lebanon, then sailed down the Red Sea, visiting the Dahlak Archipelago and Farasan Islands and landing at Djedda in Arabia to make a hurried journey to Mecca. A visit to Massawa (now Eritrea) followed, but then Hemprich succumbed to typhus.

Greatly saddened by his friend's death, Ehrenberg traveled back (by ship, camel, and river boat) to Alexandria, and then homeward. Upon arriving in Trieste (now Italy) in December 1825, Ehrenberg was quarantined for a prolonged period before being allowed to return to Berlin.

The collections that Ehrenberg and Hemprich accumulated were vast—around 34,000 zoological and 46,000 botanical specimens, samples of 300 rock types, plus archeological and ethnographic material and many geological maps and sketches. Altogether, there were 114 crates. The condition of some was poor, and the volume so huge that it was disheartening; Ehrenberg was never to describe the material properly, and his account of his travels was never completed. He did, however, do studies of lasting importance of Red Sea corals and medusae (free-swimming jellyfish).

In 1827 Ehrenberg was appointed assistant professor at the University of Berlin, but he was soon again on the move. In 1830, along with the mineralogist Gustav Rose, Ehrenberg joined an expedition to Russia led by Alexander von Humboldt. The group traveled to Nizhni Novgorod, up the Volga to Kazan and Ekaterinenburg, then to the northern Urals and western Altai, returning in 1831 via Astrakhan and down the Volga to the Caspian Sea.

For all Ehrenberg's travels, it was through his microscopical studies that he was to earn lasting renown. During his travels he had examined microorganisms in many different waters: the River Spree in Prussia, the Mediterranean, the Nile, the Red and Caspian Seas, and the rivers of Russia and Sudan. He perceived the essential unity of these microscopic life-forms, observing that their morphology (shape and structure) was much more complex than had been recognized before—that, indeed, these "single cells" performed all the functions of higher organisms: movement, feeding, excretion, reproduction. These ideas were embodied in his monograph *Die Infusionsthierchen als Volkommene Organismen* (1838c).

Subsequently, Ehrenberg carried his ideas too far, endeavoring to demonstrate that these organisms possessed a complete set of digestive and nervous organs, proclaiming the essential unity of the Infusoria with higher organisms. These misconceptions were facilitated by his refusal to use higher microscopical magnifications in his studies; they also hindered his acceptance of Darwinian evolutionary concepts. Nevertheless, Ehrenberg's classification of the Infusoria represented a great step forward in biology.

Ehrenberg's work in micropaleontology was of profound importance. During studies of chalks and limestones from Egypt, Syria, Sicily, and Pomerania (Germany), he gave the first descriptions of coccoliths, the minute platelets that armor the walls of certain green algae. Moreover, he showed that these microfossils, along with a group of microorganisms called foraminifera, could be so immensely abundant as to actually form rock strata, a startling concept at that time.

Examining transparent flakes of Jurassic and Cretaceous chert and flint, Ehrenberg recognized the fossil remains of dinoflagellates (single-celled organisms that move via flagella—long, whiplike structures). He also found spiny bodies that he supposed to be Desmids or "xanthidia"; both are now known to represent hard-shelled resting or reproductive cysts of dinoflagellates. (Only later do these organisms reach the functioning "motile" stage in the life cycle.) However, while looking at the silicon residues of Tertiary marine sediments, Ehrenberg also first reported stellate plates that made up the internal skeletons of what were truly motile dinoflagellates. Indeed, it was Ehrenberg who began the study of fossil dinoflagellates. Today, knowledge of these organisms is so extensive that the presence of a particular group in a rock helps scholars to date the strata accurately.

Ehrenberg was the first to describe many other microfossil groups and species: diatoms, radiolaria, foraminifera, ostracodes, and spores. He was the first to recognize plant phytoliths (small fossilized plant remains), and to study the dissemination of microorganisms by water and wind. He examined and discussed edible earths, both from the scientific and ethnographic viewpoints. He explained the origin of dust storms and colored rains in southern Europe through strong winds from the Sahara and showed that phosphorescence, red tides in the seas, and red snows in high mountains alike resulted from concentrations of microorganisms.

Beyond doubt, Ehrenberg was the foremost microscopist and micropaleontologist of his time. He was a good correspondent and made friends readily; Joseph Hooker, Charles Darwin, Edward Forbes, James D. Dana, Edward Hitchcock, and Benjamin Silliman were among those who sent him specimens for study. Although he never created a scientific school, Ehrenberg's visits served to inaugurate research in many European countries. For example, Ehrenberg's visit to England in 1838 greatly stimulated the studies of Henry H. White and other important microscopists.

Ehrenberg was elected vice chancellor of the University of Berlin in 1853, also serving four terms as dean of its medical faculty. He received many honors, most notably the first Leeuwenhoek Memorial Medal of the Amsterdam Academy of Sciences. Deteriorating eyesight inhibited, but never prevented, his microscopical researches. They continued until his death in Berlin on 27 June 1876.

WILLIAM A.S. SARJEANT

Biography

Born in Delitzsch, Saxony (now Germany), 19 April 1795. Received M.D., University of Berlin 1818. Appointed assistant professor, University of Berlin, 1827; appointed professor of Medicine, University of Berlin, 1839; recipient Pour le mérite, 1842; dean, University of Berlin Medical Faculty, 1848, 1853, 1860, 1863; elected vice chancellor, University of Berlin, 1853; rector, University of Berlin, 1855–56; member, Leopoldina, Berlin Academy of Science; member, Royal Society (London); received Leeuwenhoek Medal, 1875. Traveled extensively in Egypt and adjacent countries, 1821–25, and in Russia 1830–31, collecting many zoological, botanical, and geological specimens and examining aquatic microorganisms; made major contributions to micropaleontology, reporting the first coccoliths, opal-phytoliths, and fossil dinoflagellates; reported many hundreds of new species; established that whole rock strata could be formed by microorganisms; established the first sound classification of the "Infusoria." Died in Berlin 27 June 1876.

Major Publications

1828. *Reisen in Aegypten, Libyen, Nubien und Dongola.* Berlin: Mittler.

1838a. Über die Bildung der Kreidefelsen und der Kreide mergels durch unsichtbare Organismen. *Abhandlungen der Königlich Preussischen Akademie der Wissenschaften* 25:59–108.

1838b. Über das Massenverhältnis der jetzt labenden Kiesel—Infusorien und über ein neues Infusoriun—Conglomerat als Polierschiefer von Justraka in Ungarn. *Abhandlungen der Königlich Preussischen Akademie der Wissenschaften* 25:109–35.

1838c. *Die Infusionsthierchen als vollkommene Organismen. Ein Blick in das tiefere organische Leben der Natur.* Leipzig: Voss.

1843. Über die Verbreitung des jetzt wirkenden kleinsten organischen Lebens in Asien, Australien und Afrika und über die vorherrschenden thalamischen Thiere. *Verhandlung der Königlich Preussischen Akademie der Wissenschaften* 100–6.

1854. *Mikrogeologie: Das Erden und Felsen schaffende Wirken des unsichtbar kleinen selbständigen Lebens auf der Erde.* Leipzig: Voss.

1875. Die Sicherung der Objektivität der selbständigen mikroskopischen Lebensformen und ihrer Organisation durch eine zweckmässige Aufbewahrung. *Monatsberichte der Königlich Preussischen Akademie der Wissenschaften* 71–81.

Further Reading

Humboldt, A. von. 1826. *Bericht über die naturhistorischen Reisen der Herren Ehrenberg und Hemprich durch Ägypten, Dongola, Syrien, Arabien und den östlichen Abfall des Habessinischen Hochlandes, in den Jahren 1820–1825.* Berlin: Gedruckt in der Druckerei der K. Akademie der Wissenschaften.

Jahn, I. 1971. Ehrenberg, Christian Gottfried. *In* C.C. Gillispie (ed.), *Dictionary of Scientific Biography.* New York: Scribner's.

Koehler, O. 1943. Christian Gottfried Ehrenberg, 1795–1876. *In* H. Gehrig (ed.), *Schulpforte und das deutsche Geistesleben.* Darmstadt: Buske.

Sarjeant, W.A.S. 1978. Hundredth year memoriam. Christian Gottfried Ehrenberg 1795–1876. *Palynology* 2:209–11.

———. 1991. Henry Hopley White (1790–1877) and the early researches on Chalk "Xanthidia" (marine palynomorphs) by Clapham microscopists. *Journal of Micropaleontology* 10:83–93.

EISENACK, ALFRED

German, 1891–1982

In the lives of most scientists, the early years of research usually are the most productive ones; scientists' productivity declines sharply, often ceasing altogether, after they have attained their sixtieth year. Alfred Eisenack was exceptional in that his hardihood enabled him not only to survive to that age but also to be most productive during the last 30 years of his long life.

Alfred Eisenack was born on 13 May 1891 in Altfelde, West Prussia, Germany. In childhood he developed an interest in natural history that never diminished. After initial studies at the University of Jena, he moved to Albertus Magnus University, Königsberg, East Prussia. There he began a thesis on the stratigraphy (the study of rock strata, their formation, and the fossils they contain) of the Late Jurassic sediments of northern Italy. It was never completed. With the outbreak of the First World War, he volunteered for army service. During the battle of Lodz in August 1914, he was wounded, taken prisoner by the Russians, and was sent to a prison camp in Chita, Siberia, close to the Mongolian border.

His imprisonment was prolonged—six years—but it was not altogether a barren time. Eisenack was quite well treated; he was allowed to work as a chemist in Chita and sent to a spa when his health broke down. He was even able to learn further geology from a fellow prisoner and a professor at Chita Academy. However, he was not released until 1920, to travel homeward via Vladivostok.

Eisenack recommended his geological studies in Königsberg but, following his marriage in 1922 to Helene Schulze, increasingly difficult economic circumstances caused him to abandon them. Instead he took the state examinations and became a schoolteacher in Königsberg. Geology became only a part-time occupation. In particular, he interested himself in two fields. One

was investigation of the life histories of the Paleozoic colonial organisms called graptolites, extinct single-celled organisms that formed colonies during the Lower Paleozoic era. The other was the origin of the glacial drift deposits of the Baltic region.

In the course of these investigations, Eisenack dissolved some limestone boulders in hydrochloric acid and examined the residues under the microscope. Not only did he find fossils of familiar single-celled organisms—graptolite fragments, ostracodes, and what he believed to be foraminifera—but also microfossils hitherto unknown to him. Jurassic and Eocene limestone boulders yielded not only dinoflagellates (organisms that moved through water via long, whiplike structures that moved back and forth), but also the spiny microfossils that, at that time, Otto Wetzel was naming "hystrichospheres" (spiny spheres). When Eisenack subjected Ordovician and Silurian limestone blocks to acid treatment, they yielded both spiny bodies and simple spheres without spines. Considering the former to be "hystrichospheres," Eisenack named the latter "leiospheres," or smooth spheres. Eisenack's first publication on these discoveries (1931) earned him a university degree at last.

Two other groups that Eisenack encountered in Early Paleozoic limestones were entirely new to science—microscopic flask-shaped bodies, sometimes with spines or other ornaments, which he named "Chitinozoa," and a group of generally elongate, solid, and brittle structures that he named "melanosclerites." His thesis on the latter gained him recognition as a university lecturer and an appointment in the University of Königsberg (1941).

Unfortunately for Eisenack, Germany was by then embroiled in World War II—a conflict in whose outcome he had so little confidence that, before the war began, he and his wife sent off his type specimens (examples on which he based his new species) and some other possessions for safekeeping in Switzerland. It was well that they did so. When the Russians captured Königsberg in 1945, the Eisenacks' home was destroyed. Since Eisenack held a military rank, albeit only in the air-raid precautions service, he was again taken prisoner and sent to Siberia.

This second captivity was much harsher, and it endured for four years. Ultimately his age and declining health caused him to be released. In late December 1949, to his joy, he was reunited with his wife, who had fled from Königsberg (by then Kaliningrad, Russia) to Thuringia. They were permitted to cross the border into Württemberg, West Germany, where, after a brief hospitalization, Eisenack faced the need to seek employment anew at age 60. After working a while as a teacher in Reutlingen, he obtained his *Venia legendi* in geology (1951) and from that time served as adjunct professor at the University of Tübingen until he retired in 1957.

Eisenack's geological researches were wide-ranging, including renewed studies of graptolites, investigations into the processes of fossilization, mineralogical investigations and, in particular, palynological researches (study of fossilized pollen and spores). By then the "hystrichospheres" were known to be dinoflagellate cysts (a stage at which spores are enclosed in a mineral hard casing). The "leiospheres," along with the spiny bodies Eisenack had discovered in Early Paleozoic limestones, had been named "acritarchs." Eisenack studied assemblages of these microfossils from middle Cretaceous and Eocene deposits of Germany, as well as undertaking renewed work on the Paleozoic microfossils of the Baltic region. Officially or unofficially, Eisenack also supervised researches by a number of students—Serge von Cube, Gerhard Alberti, Hans Gocht, Johann Agelopoulos, Ellen Gerlach, and Karl Klement—upon dinoflagellates and acritarchs from Germany and other parts of eastern Europe. When the Australian palynologist Isabel C. Cookson quarreled irrevocably with her initial French collaborator, Georges Deflandre, it was with Eisenack that she continued her studies of Mesozoic and Tertiary marine palynofloras from Australia and Papua. The last results of their joint researches were published posthumously through the efforts of Hans Gocht, Eisenack's most faithful and productive student and collaborator.

Eisenack's own studies were always done on material he had prepared himself—a process that involved crushing, chemical preparation, picking individual specimens from wet mounts by pipette, mounting on slides, drawing, and photography. He employed an old Leitz monocular microscope and a box camera made from a biscuit tin, exposing glass negatives until their unavailability forced him to use film. With this unsophisticated equipment, his results remain impressive.

Another major achievement was his inauguration of the *Katalog der fossilen Dinoflagellaten, Hystrichosphären und verwandten Fossilien (Catalog of Fossil Dinoflagellates, Hystriochospheres and Kindred Fossils)*, a compilation work whose first volume appeared in 1973 and that continues to be published, long after his death.

The death of Helene Eisenack on 7 May 1975 was a blow from which Alfred could not recover. Even so, he continued his researches, not only in palynology but also of fossil annelids (segmented worms) and pseudofossils, the sources of minute glass spheres in sediments, and the origins of riebeckite porphyry boulders in the North German Drift. He died just one month short of his ninety-first birthday, on 19 April 1982.

WILLIAM A.S. SARJEANT

Biography

Born in Altfelde, West Prussia, 13 May 1891. Studied at the Universities of Jena and Königsberg, ultimately graduating 1931; appointed faculty member, university of Königsberg, 1941; *Venia legendi,* University of Tübingen, 1951; adjunct professor, University of Tübingen, 1951–57. Studies included graptolites and pseudofossils; concentrated on marine organic-walled microfossils, in particular dinoflagellates and acritarchs; discovered and named the chitinozoans and melanosclerites. Died in Reutlingen, Baden-Württenberg, 19 April 1982.

Major Publications

1931–37. Neue Mikrofossilien des Baltischen Silurs. *Paläontologisches Zeitschrift* 13:74–118; 14:257–77; 16:52–76; 19:217–42.

1942. Die Melanoskleritoiden, eine neue Gruppe silurischer Mikrofossilien aus dem Unterstamm des Nesseltiere. *Paläontologische Zeitschrift* 23:157–80.

1961. Eininge Erörterungen über fossile Dinoflagellaten nebst Übersicht über die zur Zeit bekannten Gattungen. *Neues Jahrbuch für Geologie und Paläontologie, Abhandlungen* 112:281–324.

1963. Hystrichosphären. *Biological Reviews of the Cambridge Philosophical Society* 38:107–39.

1968. Über Chitinozoen des baltischen Gebietes. *Palaeontographica,* Ser. A, 131:137–98.

Further Reading

Gocht, H., and W.A.S. Sarjeant. 1983. Pathfinder in palynology: Alfred Eisenack (1891–1982). *Micropaleontology* 29:470–77; supplementary note, *Micropaleontology* 30:223.

Sarjeant, W.A.S. 1980. *Geologists and the History of Geology: An International Bibliography from the Origins to 1978.* 5 vols. London: Macmillan; New York: Arno; with *Supplement 1979–1994 and Additions,* 2 vols., Malabar, Florida: Krieger, 1987; *Supplement 2: 1985–93 and Additions,* 3 vols., 1996.

———. 1985. Alfred Eisenack (1891–1982) and his contribution to palynology. *Review of Palaeobotany and Palynology* 45:3–15.

———. 1992. Microfossils other than pollen and spores in palynological preparations. *In* S. Nilsson and J. Praglowski (eds.), *Erdtman's Handbook of Palynology.* Copenhagen: Munksgaard.

ELECTRORECEPTORS

See Lateral Line System

ENAMEL MICROSTRUCTURE

Tooth enamel is the hardest tissue in the animal body, containing up to 96 percent hydroxyapatite (dahllite) and only a few percent of organic matter, such as proteins. The apatite forms microscopic crystal needles of several micrometers in length, the so-called crystallites. In mammalian enamel, these crystallites are not irregularly distributed as in many non-mammalian vertebrates, but arranged in higher units, the enamel prisms (P) and the interprismatic matrix (IPM; Figure 1). The enamel prisms (henceforth, simply called prisms) are bundles of parallel-oriented crystallites of only 3 to 5 microns in diameter, but up to several millimeters in length depending on the enamel thickness. The prisms originate at the enamel-dentin junction (EDJ) and run through the entire enamel thickness to the outer enamel surface. Near the outer enamel surface, prisms fade or are confluent with the crystallites of the IPM forming the prismless external layer (PLEX) a few microns thick.

The IPM is the second construction element of the enamel, filling the space between the prisms. In the IPM, crystallites are oriented parallel to each other but are not bundled into prisms. The crystallites of the IPM may run parallel to or at acute or right angles to the long axis of the prisms (Figure 1).

Enamel prisms and IPM are produced by the ameloblasts (enamel forming cells). During amelogenesis (enamel formation), the ameloblasts migrate starting from the basal membrane located at what is later the EDJ to the outer surface; en route, the ameloblasts leave the enamel prisms as traces behind them. This is easily demonstrated by squeezing a tube of toothpaste: the extruding toothpaste corresponds to the prism and the tube to the ameloblast. The prism is formed by the Tomes's process at the rear end of the ameloblast, which also controls the shape of the prism cross section (Moss-Salentijn et al. 1997).

The formation of enamel is not continuous but periodical; this periodicity of enamel growth produces growth lines, microscopically visible on the enamel surface and in polished sections, the so-called striae of Retzius. Due to its hardness and high resistance against recrystallization, fossil and modern enamel is likewise appropriate for microstructure investigation.

Crystallites

Compared to the very short hydroxyapatite crystallites in bone tissue, the crystallites in tooth enamel are extremely long. Comparative studies in amphibians, reptiles, and Mesozoic mammals have shown that in the primitive condition for amniotes, crystallites run nearly parallel to each other from the EDJ to the outer surface. Columnar enamel crystallites form clearly demarcated columnar structures separated by discontinuities in crystallite orientation (Sander 1997). A subtype of this enamel type with small columnar units (5 to 10 microns in diameter) is the synapsid columnar enamel that is found, for example, in the Lower Jurassic mammal *Morganucodon* (Wood and Stern 1997). These columnar units have been called "pseudoprisms" by some authors; it should be emphasized, however, that they are not homologous to the true prisms

that are formed individually by a single ameloblast. Besides the polygonal cross section of the columnar units and their larger diameter, the lack of IPM between the columnar units is another important difference from true prisms. In primitive prismatic enamel, the prisms are always embedded in thick IPM. In all of these aprismatic structures, a true prism sheath is missing. There exists a confusing and partially inconsistent terminology ("pseudoprismatic," "preprismatic," "prismatic without prism sheath") in the literature, reflecting the uncertainty in this field (Sander 1997).

Aprismatic enamel is not restricted to Mesozoic mammals. In bats, for example, a thick layer of aprismatic enamel covers the prismatic enamel; it is called "postprismatic" by some authors to distinguish it from primitive aprismatic enamel. Other groups where the external enamel layer often is aprismatic are carnivores, ungulates (hoofed mammals), and rodents. In prismatic enamel, orientation of crystallites within the prisms can be used to distinguish between different prism types. Orientation of crystallites within the IPM of different enamel types also varies in characteristic ways.

Prisms

Typical for true prisms is the presence of a rounded, open or closed prism sheath forming a plane of discontinuity in crystallite orientation and separating the prisms from the IPM. In the evolutionary history of mammals, prisms originated at least twice, possibly several times independently (Wood and Stern 1997). The earliest occurrence of prisms in therian mammals (placentals, marsupials, and relatives) was observed in dryolestids (also known as eupantotheres), relatives of modern mammals, from the Upper Jurassic of Portugal (Figure 2). Somewhat later, in the upper Lower Cretaceous, prisms appear independently in multituberculates, an extinct lineage of early mammals which is not closely related to dryolestids, metatherians, or eutherians (placentals).

For quantitative and qualitative analyses of prism shape, typically cross sections perpendicular to the long axis are used; density of prism arrangement and shape of prism cross sections preferably are also studied. Different prism types have been defined based on the shape of the prisms in cross section (Boyde 1965). In Boyde's "type A" ("cetacean type" after Shobusawa 1952), the cross section of the prisms is rounded and they are widely spaced, embedded in IPM. If the prisms are more closely packed, their cross-sectional shape becomes hexagonally rounded (Shobusawa's "carnivore type"; Figure 3). Prisms may be arranged in incipient rows that are developed more clearly in ungulates (Boyde's "type B," Shobusawa's "ungulate type"). IPM forms plate-like structures ("interrow sheets") between the prism rows, and crystallites of the IPM run approximately perpendicular to the prisms. Some primates and proboscideans (such as elephants) have strongly derived prism types with keyhole-shaped cross sections. Prisms are very densely packed, and IPM is very sparse or missing (Shobusawa's "primate type", Boyde's "type C"; Figure 4). Not a prism type but an enamel type is the "rodent type," after Shobusawa, and called "type D" by Boyde, which occurs only

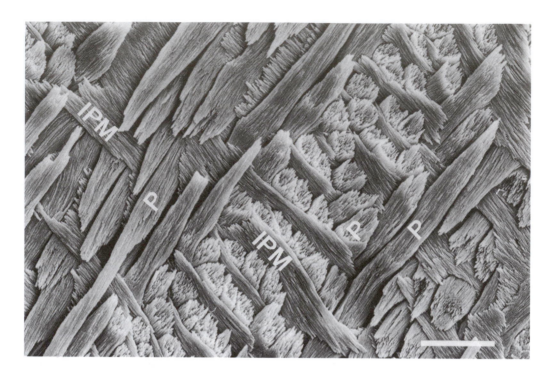

Figure 1. Mammalian enamel consists of prisms *(P)* and interprismatic matrix *(IPM)*. In the example figured, IPM forms plates between the prism rows. Crystallites within prisms and IPM are clearly visible, and IPM-crystallites run at right angles to the prism long axes. *Kannabateomys amblyonyx* (Rodentia, Caviomorpha), longitudinal section of lower incisor; tip of the incisor is oriented to the top, enamel-dentin junction *(EDJ)* to the left side. Scale bar equals 10 microns (μm).

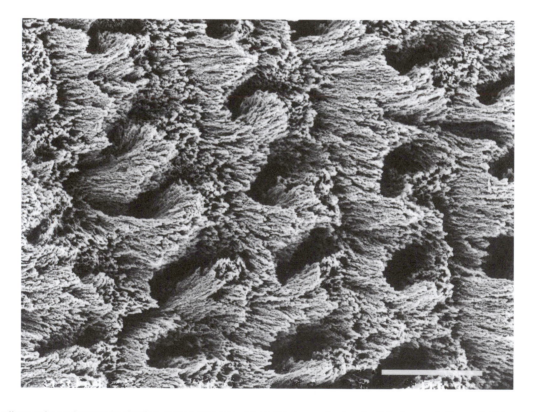

Figure 2. The earliest prisms known in therian mammals occur in Late Jurassic dryolestids (eupantotheres). Prisms have incomplete prism sheaths and are widely spaced, embedded in thick IPM. Some prisms are completely etched away by preparation and in these cases are visible only as holes. Dryolestidae, gen. et. sp. indet., lower molar; Late Jurassic of Guimarota coal mine near Leiria, Portugal. Scale bar equals 5 μm.

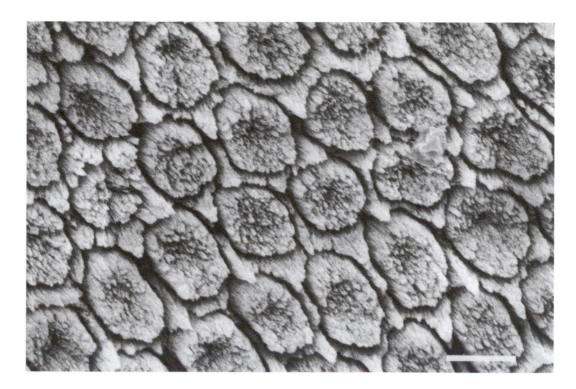

Figure 3. Densely packed prisms have roundel hexagonal cross sections. Since this prism type often is found in carnivores, it has been called "carnivore type." IPM fills the space between the prisms, and crystallite orientation of the IPM is parallel to the prism long axes. *Ursus spelaeus* (cave bear), molar, Pleistocene. Scale bar equals 5 μm.

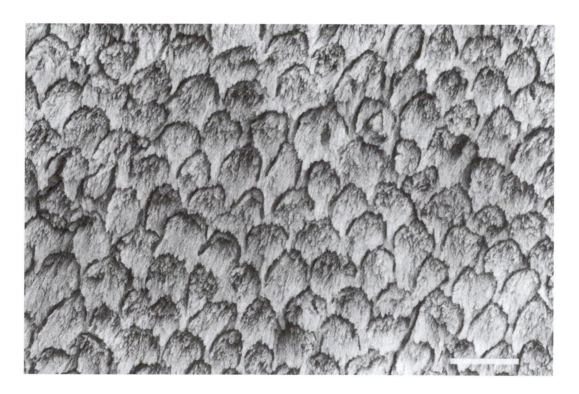

Figure 4. Very densely packed, nearly without IPM between them, are prisms in the keyhole pattern type. This prism type characterizes, among others, primates, proboscideans (elephants and extinct relatives), and sea cows. *Trichechus manatus* (Caribbean manatee), molar. Scale bar equals 10 μm.

in uniserial Hunter-Schreger bands (HSB, see below). This is not a separate prism type, however, and the structure can be understood only in the arrangement in uniserial HSB. With the refinement of investigation techniques and the increasing number of studied taxa, it has become obvious that Boyde's system is oversimplified and does not account for the diversity and complexity of existing structures. The phylogenetic sequence of prism types (A-B-C-D) implied by Boyde is not the case. Within the same tooth, different prism types may occur, and single prisms may even change their cross-sectional shape on their way from the EDJ to the outer surface. For a three-dimensional understanding of the structures involved, the enamel must be studied comprehensively.

In some mammals, such as marsupials and multituberculates, tubelike canaliculi (minute canals) run through the enamel. These are called tubules and are regarded as a primitive mammalian character retained in lipotyphlans (true insectivorans, such as moles and shrews), chiropterans (bats), and primates.

Enamel Types

Enamel types are units of enamel in which the prisms have similar orientations (Koenigswald and Clemens 1992). To understand the enamel in three dimensions, an enamel sample has to be sectioned in three different planes (longitudinal, transverse, and tangential). The enamel of a tooth can consist of only one enamel type, or two or three enamel types can be present in a specific three-dimensional order (a schmelzmuster). In order to analyze and describe the three-dimensional orientation of prisms, the enamel dentine junction (EDJ) serves as a practical reference plane. Despite great variability in tooth morphology, the number of enamel types is limited; so far four basic types have been recognized: radial enamel, tangential enamel, Hunter-Schreger bands, and irregular decussation.

Radial Enamel

In radial enamel, the long axes of the prisms are oriented radially from the EDJ. Usually, they are somewhat inclined toward the occlusal surface (the grinding or biting surface), and the angle of inclination can vary through the length of the prism. Radial enamel is a primitive enamel type for therian mammals and is found in insectivorans and marsupials, for example. Radial enamel may fill the whole enamel thickness or just a layer in a more complex schmelzmuster as in rodent incisors. Orientation of IPM crystallites relative to prism long axes may vary from parallel to an angle of about 90 degrees and is useful for the distinction of subtypes of radial enamel. Highly angled IPM anastomoses (connects in a networklike fashion) between the prisms.

Modified Radial Enamel

Radial enamel is a derived enamel type in which the "plywood effect" is achieved by alternating layers of prisms and IPM. A highly derived enamel type is the modified radial enamel with thick plates of IPM between the prism rows. Because it is often found in the high-crowned molars of ungulates, it has been called "ungulate enamel." IPM plates may reach the thickness of a prism

diameter and do not anastomose (Figure 5). This enamel type, in high-crowned molars of herbivores, often forms the innermost enamel layer adjacent to the EDJ and is an adaptation to the high radial tensile stresses that occur particularly in this region (Pfretzschner 1994).

Tangential Enamel

In tangential enamel the prisms remain parallel, but their outward course from the EDJ is laterally deflected from a simple radial orientation. Prism decussation (crossing to form an "X") does not occur, and the inclination of prisms is generally low (below 20 degrees). In most cases, the IPM runs at a right angle to the prism direction. Tangential enamel frequently occurs adjacent to a layer of radial enamel (Figure 6).

Hunter-Schreger Bands (HSB)

HSB are a highly derived enamel type and are found mainly in placental mammals, but occur also in some marsupials such as the wombat, for example. HSB are most clearly visible in longitudinal sections and are characterized by a regular decussation of prisms (Koenigswald and Clemens 1992). Within the bands, prisms run parallel but decussate in adjacent bands at a high angle (about 90 degrees). HSB usually are oriented horizontally in the tooth but rise somewhat apically (toward the tip of apex); the angle between an HSB and a horizontal plane perpendicular to the EDJ indicates the inclination. En route from the EDJ to the outer enamel surface, one prism may pass through several HSB because prisms are inclined slightly more steeply than HSB. At the border between two HSB, prisms are forced to change their direction about 90 degrees; this switching of prisms is visible in the transition zones in longitudinal sections (Figure 7). In general, HSB are 10 to 15 prisms thick; in rodent incisors, HSB are thinner, and thickness may even be reduced to a single prism (uniserial HSB) (Martin 1997). IPM may run parallel to the prisms (primitive) or at acute or even right angles (derived) to the prism long axes, forming plates between the prism rows (interrow sheets). In most cases, HSB are oriented horizontally and are visible most clearly in longitudinal sections. Biomechanically, HSB are believed to act as strengthening devices and crack-propagation inhibitors (Pfretzschner 1994).

Vertical HSB

Besides the normal horizontal arrangement, HSB may be oriented vertically in the tooth. These vertical HSB occur in the molars of some large herbivores such as rhinoceroses and a few extinct South American ungulates (e.g., *Astrapotherium* and *Pyrotherium*), and in the incisors of a few rodents. Vertical HSB probably are derived from horizontal HSB by a garlandlike bending-upward as has been described in tapirs and the extinct chalicotheres (Koenigswald and Clemens 1992). In the occlusal surface of a rhinoceros molar, vertical HSB are visible under low magnification by a pocket lens with lateral illumination as alternating dark and bright bands. Vertical HSB are a special adaptation to tensile stresses vertical to the EDJ (Pfretzschner 1994).

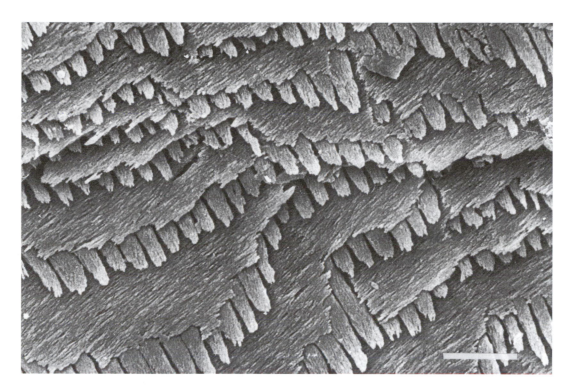

Figure 5. Modified radial enamel in longitudinal section. Between the rows of parallel arranged prisms are thick plates of IPM that do not anastomose. Crystallite orientation within the IPM is at a right angle to the prism long axes. *Phacochoerus* sp. indet. (warthog), molar. Scale bar equals 10 μm.

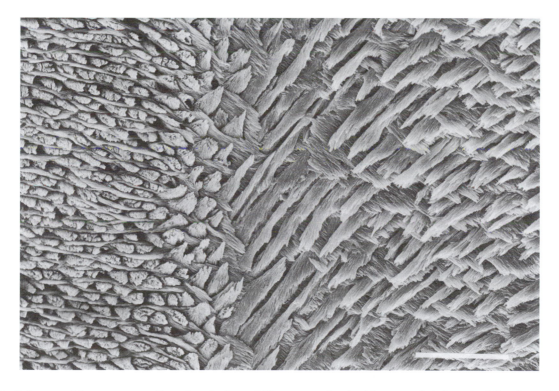

Figure 6. Tangential enamel in a cross section of an incisor of *Macropus rufus* (red kangaroo); left part of the figure formed by radial enamel. As in radial enamel, in tangential enamel no prism decussation occurs. The main difference between radial and tangential enamel is the orientation of prisms and IPM relative to the occlusal surface of the tooth. In radial enamel, prisms and IPM are somewhat rising apically, while in tangential enamel, prisms and IPM are oriented approximately parallel to the occlusal surface. In the example figured, tangential enamel arises from radial enamel by a 90 degree turn of prisms and IPM. Scale bar equals 20 μm.

Figure 7. Hunter-Schreger bands (HSB) in a longitudinal section of an incisor of *Kannabateomys amblyonyx;* tip of the incisor is oriented to the top, EDJ to the left. HSB originate at the EDJ and rise somewhat apically. Between adjacent HSB, switching of prisms from one band to another is visible in the transition zones where prisms are sectioned more or less longitudinally. At the right side a thin layer of radial enamel is visible. Scale bar equals 10 µm.

Irregular Decussation

This enamel type consists of bundles of enamel that have irregular patterns of decussation. These patterns evolved independently from HSB of different thicknesses. From uniseral HSB originated the "less-ordered lamellar enamel" found in members of the rodent subfamily Lemminae (e.g., lemmings). In proboscideans, thick bundles of prisms are interwoven; this subtype of irregular enamel is called 3-D enamel.

Schmelzmuster

Only in few cases is the enamel of a tooth formed by a single enamel type. Normally two or more enamel types are present and are arranged in a characteristic way. This three-dimensional arrangement of enamel types has been named with the German term "schmelzmuster" which means enamel pattern (Koenigswald and Clemens 1992). Since this phrase is commonly used to describe the distribution of enamel bands on occlusal surfaces of hypsodont (high-crowned) teeth and to avoid confusion, schmelzmuster is retained. The schmelzmuster may vary in different teeth (incisors, molars, etc.) of the same dentition, but is constant in one tooth category of the same species. This makes the schmelzmuster a reliable tool for systematic and phylogenetic analysis. Particularly well studied examples are the evergrowing rootless incisors of rodents, in which the schmelzmuster evolves independently from the molars.

Enamel Microstructure and Phylogeny

In contrast to bone tissue, which is continuously remodeled in the living organism by osteoclasts and osteoblasts (cells associated with bone dissolution and formation, respectively), the tooth enamel is not changed after its formation. Accordingly, the schmelzmuster formed by the ameloblasts reflects the information fixed in the genes without considerable epigenetic alteration (i.e., alteration to a previously established genetic plan). Therefore, enamel microstructure is a potential powerful tool for phylogenetic questions (Koenigswald et al. 1993). As in other characters, in enamel microstructure a distinction must be made between convergent characters (similar forms that arise independently) owing to biomechanical constraints (i.e., the same form evolves twice because the teeth are subject to similar environmental stresses) and characters inherited from a common ancestor. A typical example for a convergent structure is the layer of modified radial enamel at the EDJ that occurs in the high-crowned molars of large herbivores belonging to different orders. However, within restricted taxonomic groups (e.g., Rodentia), enamel microstructure can yield valuable information for the reconstruction of phylogeny (Martin 1993, 1997). On the other hand, it is hardly possible to determine single species by enamel microstructure, since only four enamel types with a few subtypes exist. On the level of genera and families the schmelzmuster distribution within the whole dentition is useful, while the schmelzmuster of single tooth categories (e.g., rodent incisors) yields valuable information for the level of families to orders.

THOMAS MARTIN

Works Cited and Further Reading

Boyde, A. 1965. The structure of developing mammalian dental enamel. *In* M.V. Stack and R.W. Fearnhead (eds.), *Tooth Enamel.* Bristol: Wright.

Koenigswald, W. von, and W.A. Clemens. 1992. Levels of complexity in the microstructure of mammalian enamel and their application in studies of systematics. *Scanning Microscopy* 6:195–218.

Koenigswald, W. von, T. Martin, and H.U. Pfretzschner. 1993. Phylogenetic interpretation of enamel structures in mammalian teeth—possibilities and problems. *In* F.S. Szalay, M.J. Novacek, and M.C. McKenna (eds.), *Mammal Phylogeny.* New York and London: Springer-Verlag.

Martin, T. 1993. Early rodent incisor enamel evolution: Phylogenetic implications. *Journal of Mammalian Evolution* 1:227–54.

———. 1997. Incisor enamel microstructure and systematics in rodents. *In* W. von Koenigswald and P.M. Sander (eds.), *Tooth Enamel Microstructure.* Rotterdam: Balkema.

Moss-Salentijn, L., M.L. Moss, and M.S. Yuan. 1997. The ontogeny of mammalian enamel. *In* W. von Koenigswald and P.M. Sander (eds.), *Tooth Enamel Microstructure.* Rotterdam: Balkema.

Pfretzschner, H.U. 1994. Biomechanik der Schmelzmikrostruktur in den Backenzähnen von Großsäugern. *Palaeontographica*, ser. A, 234:1–88.

Sander, P.M. 1997. Non-mammalian synapsid enamel and the origin of mammalian enamel prisms: The bottom-up perspective. *In* W. von Koenigswald and P.M. Sander (eds.), *Tooth Enamel Microstructure.* Rotterdam: Balkema.

Shobusawa, M. 1952. Vergleichende Untersuchungen über die Form der Schmelzprismen der Säugetiere. *Okajimas Folia Anatomica Japonica* 24:371–92.

Wood, C.B., and D.N. Stern. 1997. The earliest prisms in mammalian and reptilian enamel. *In* W. von Koenigswald and P.M. Sander (eds.), *Tooth Enamel Microstructure.* Rotterdam: Balkema.

ERDTMAN, OTTO GUNNAR ELIAS

Swedish, 1897–1975

Gunnar Erdtman was born at Hjorted, in the Swedish province of Småland, on 28 November 1897. His father was a distinguished impressionist painter, a talent inherited by Gunnar who, in later life, was to have some of his watercolors exhibited in Stockholm. Gunnar had also a strong interest in music, being a keen concert-goer and an able flutist. However, these were lesser concerns; it was nature, and especially plants, that interested him the most.

When Erdtman began to study botany at Stockholms Hög-skola (now the University of Stockholm), by chance, two of his teachers had a particular interest in pollen and spores. Gustav Lagerheim had investigated pollen as a means of determining the plants that had formed Swedish and Danish peats, while Ernst Jakob Lennart von Post had shown that the fluctuating percentages of arboreal pollen (that from trees) not only identified climatic changes very accurately, but even identified particular layers in Quaternary sediments (i.e., the presence of such pollen enabled paleontologists to determine the age of a rock stratum). As a consequence, von Post, who was then employed by the Swedish Geological Survey, was able to construct a stratigraphical sequence of Swedish peats and even to establish the date of the retreat of the Pleistocene ice sheets. In 1918 when von Post was commissioned to make a quantitative and qualitative survey of Sweden's peat resources, he chose Gunnar Erdtman as his assistant. Four years later (1922), Erdtman presented the first thesis ever to be based on pollen analysis, gaining his doctorate at the unusually early age of 24.

Upon completing his doctorate, Erdtman traveled to Great Britain for the first time. The samples he collected in Scotland and its islands demonstrated the possibility of the international correlation of rock strata by pollen analysis. His work aroused interest throughout Europe and was soon followed up in several other countries.

Unfortunately, von Post and Erdtman both had strong personalities; they had clashed to so great a degree that they never again worked together. Moreover, when von Post was appointed to a professorship in the Stockholm Högskola, he saw to it that Erdtman was excluded from its laboratories. The consequence was a time of prolonged difficulty for Erdtman. There were a series of short-term teaching appointments and a year in Canada on a Rockefeller Scholarship. In 1930 he accepted a school teaching appointment on the Swedish island of Visby, remaining there for five years.

However, his interest in palynology did not diminish during those years of "exile," even though he had to purchase his own equipment and gained no professional credit from his publications. In 1927 he published a first bibliography of palynological literature (i.e., writings on pollen and spores, living or fossil). Supplements were to follow annually for 30 years. In association with his brother Holger, he developed the technique of acetolysis, a process that concentrated pollen grains from deposits rich in cellulosic plant debris. That technique is still in use today.

In 1935 Erdtman moved to another school appointment in Västeras, much closer to Stockholm. His research continued steadily, being reported each year in further short papers. In 1943 he published his first book, the classic *Introduction to Pollen Analy-*

sis. A year later he secured a position in Stockholm, at a modern school in the new suburb of Bromma. There, at last, his work gained official recognition; he was allowed to establish a small pollen-analytical laboratory and permitted free time to develop his research.

From that point on, his eminence grew apace. Financing from the Swedish National Research Council enabled him to set up a more spacious laboratory at Lilla Frescati in the suburb of Solna (1948). This soon became a gathering place for palynologists from all over the world.

A variety of new techniques were developed during the next few years. In particular, electron and ultraviolet microscopy permitted studies of the structure of the layers in the walls of pollen, work reported in a massive study of *Pollen Morphology and Plant Taxonomy* (the first volume appeared in 1952). Erdtman inaugurated the international journal *Grana Palynologica* (now *Grana*) with a series of reprints, but the journal soon featured original papers, many written by himself and his coworkers. Among the latter was an American, John R. Rowley, who was eventually to succeed him as director of the laboratory, following Erdtman's retirement in 1969.

Although *Grana Palynologica* at times reported researches on microfossils from more ancient strata, Erdtman's prime interest was always in the Quaternary—in the pollen and spores of recent and present times. He produced another major textbook, *Handbook of Palynology* in 1969, and it was of such lasting importance that it has been reprinted, in a revised edition, as recently as 1992. The aim of his latter years was to produce a *World Pollen and Spore Flora,* a project that had only begun when Erdtman died on 18 February 1975.

By the time of his death, Gunnar Erdtman had earned many honors, among them a titular professorship, awarded by the Swedish National Research Council (1955), a doctorate *honoris causa* of the University of Munich, Germany (1964), and the inauguration by Indian palynologists of the Gunnar Erdtman International Medal for Palynology (1973). He had traveled very widely, gaining such a measure of international renown and authority that he was known as "the Pope of Palynology." Much of our present knowledge, not only of the detailed structure of pollen and spores and their relation to Quaternary climatic changes, but also of European prehistory and the significance of these structures, is founded upon Erdtman's research.

WILLIAM A.S. SARJEANT

Biography

Born in Hjorted, Småland, 28 November 1897. Ph.D., Stockholms Högskola, 1922; titular professorship, Swedish National Research Council, 1955; doctorate *honoris causa,* University of Munich, 1964. Held teaching appointments in Visby (starting 1930), Västeras (starting 1935), and Bromma (starting 1944), then inaugurated the Palynological Laboratory, Stockholm-Solna, 1948–69. Contributed to the development of palynological techniques, the microstructures of pollen grains, and the interpretation of Quaternary floras, environments, and biostratigraphy. Died in Stockholm, 18 February 1975.

Major Publications

1943. *An Introduction to Pollen Analysis.* Waltham, Massachusetts: Chronica Bottanica; 2nd ed., 1954.

1952. *Pollen Morphology and Plant Taxonomy.* 4 vols. Stockholm and Waltham, Massachusetts: Almqvist and Wiksell.

1967. Glimpses of palynology 1916–1966. *Review of Palaeobotany and Palynology* 1:23–29.

1969. *Handbook of Palynology. Morphology—Taxonomy—Ecology: An Introduction to the Study of Pollen Grains and Spores.* Copenhagen: Munksgaard; New York: Hafner; 2nd ed., S. Nilsson and J. Praglowski (eds.), *Erdtman's Handbook of Palynology.* Copenhagen: Munksgaard, 1992.

Further Reading

Faegri, K. 1973. In memoriam O. Gunnar, E. Erdtman 1897–1973. *Pollen et Spores* 15:5–12.

Sarjeant, W.A.S. 1973. Two great palynologists: Gunnar Erdtman and Georges Deflandre. *Microscopy* 32(8):319–31.

———. 1980. *Geologists and the History of Geology: An International Bibliography from the Origins to 1978.* 5 vols., London: Macmillan; New York: Arno; with *Supplement 1979–1994 and Additions,* 2 vols., Malabar, Florida: Krieger, 1987.

EUROPE: EASTERN EUROPE

Three major factors determine the development of a natural science such as paleontology: the personality of the researchers, their findings, and their working conditions as fostered by the institutions that mold and shape them. On account of this last element, eastern Europe has seen development in the science of paleontology from the combined efforts of scholars in Poland, former Czechoslovakia, Romania, Hungary, and a considerable part of the Balkans.

During the fifty years after World War II, research conditions were similarly advantageous in these countries. Prior to this period, from the eighteenth through the mid-twentieth centuries, the eastern European states were subject to frequent border changes. In order to best understand the nature of a paleontologist's scientific thought, the researcher must be understood within the context of his or her nationality as opposed to the political status of the area where he or she worked.

The Origin of Paleontological Research in Eastern Europe

This development of paleontology in eastern Europe followed the same pattern as that of other countries. First, researchers characterized fossils and tried to catalogue their occurrence. This stage occurred sporadically, depending on scientific personalities and working conditions. Next, researchers strove to define the stratigraphic range of fossil findings, using this information to determine the age of rock formations. Finally, they attempted to reconstruct the development of various systematic groups and their mutual correlation and dependencies. The level of achievement reached in these last two stages was dependent on the researchers and their relation with the world scientific community.

Fossil organisms have attracted attention since the dawn of human history. In eastern Europe, archaeological sites reveal an ancient interest in fossil specimens. The early Neolithic graves at Zlota on the middle Vistula River (near Krakow) have yielded numerous shells of Miocene snails. A differentiated collection of this fauna has been found on the border of the Holy Cross Mountains. In the Middle Ages, the bones of "Diluvial" mammals aroused interest. These were believed to be the remnants of legendary giants that had lived before the Biblical flood. In the Royal Cathedral of Krakow, a skull of a Diluvial rhinoceros and bones of a mammoth remain preserved in their artificial resting place.

In the mid-eighteenth century, scientific interest in paleontology began in most of eastern Europe as in western Europe. In those territories that remained under Turkish Ottoman rule—Albania, Romania, Bulgaria, and a part of what would become Yugoslavia—the science of paleontology did not begin until the mid-nineteenth century. The exception is in the portion of the Balkans situated within the borders of the Austro-Hungarian Empire. In this region, Baltazar Hacquet can be viewed as the forerunner of paleontology with the first published observations of fossil forms in his four-volume work, *Oryctographia Carniola* (1778–89).

In Poland, Jan Jaskiewicz was the first natural history professor at Krakow University. In 1787, he wrote: "Petrifications . . . attending to which . . . are both abundant and extraordinary here." Despite Poland's loss of independence, partitioning among its neighbors, and the cataclysm of the Napoleonic Wars, work progressed in paleontology. Much is owed to Stanislaw Staszic, the "father of Polish geology," who included figures of fossilized plants and animals in his work *O ziemiorodztwie Karpatów* (1815; published 1955). Later, Norbert Alfons Kumelski published the first paleontological handbook, *Rys systematyczny nauki o skamienialosciach czyli petrefaktologii* (1826). Staszic recruited a geologist of Saxon origin, Jerzy Bogumil Pusch, to become a professor at the Polish Mining Academy, the first Polish institution of its kind, located in Kielce. Pusch presented more than 200 fossils of flora and fauna from Poland in his *Polens Paleontologie* (1837).

Similarly, Bohemian interest in paleontology began when Franciscus Zeno, a Jesuit, described fossil trilobites from Prague in his work, *Neue physicalische Belustigungen* (1770). Zeno rejected the idea that these forms were simply caprices of nature. Czech interest in the natural sciences took a leap forward in 1818 when Earl Kaspar Stemberk established the National Museum in Prague. Stemberk was a significant advocate of phytopaleontology (botani-

cal paleontology), owing in large part to his *Versuch einer geognostisch-botanischen Darstellung der flora der Vorvelt.*

The Nineteenth Century

Work in Bohemia continued with a detailed monograph on Early Paleozoic fauna by a French scientist, Joachim Barrande. Beginning in 1852, Barrande published 22 volumes of a work, *Systeme Silurien du centre de la Boheme.* He included 1160 tables with 3560 fossil species, all of which he attributed to the Silurian period. Barrande died before completing his studies. He bequeathed his entire collection, library, and funds for continuing his work to the National Museum in Prague. In his honor, the Paleozoic sediments in central Bohemia have been named Barrandien, and the Paleozoic fauna section of the museum bears his name as well. Barrande maintained scientific contacts with, among others, Dionis Stur, the "father of Slovakian geology." Stur is most noted for his studies of Silurian and Carboniferous flora and fauna of Bohemia, Moravia, and Silesia, as published in his classic works, *Carbon-Flora der Schatzlaer Schichten* (1885) and *Die Culm-Flora* (1875–87).

Geologists from Poland, Czechoslovakia, Hungary, and Romania have all examined the Carpathian Mountains, the chain of mountains situated on the border of these countries. Frequently, this research brought scientists of different disciplines and nationalities together. Ludwik Zejszner, a professor at Krakow University, conducted research on Mesozoic fossils in the Polish and Slovakian portions of the Carpathian Mountains. He published a paper in Prague on Jurassic brachiopods from Inwald in the Polish Carpathian Mountains and wrote numerous regional monographs. In 1845, he began editing *Paleontologia Polska* (1846) at his own expense. Owing to his lack of funds, he never completed this publication.

Other early paleontologists from eastern Europe also published their works in the scientific centers of western Europe and Russia. Between 1832 and 1843, Wojciech Zborzewski, a teacher at the Polish college at Krzemieniec and Edward Eichwald, a former professor at the Polish University of Vilnius, published the first micropaleontological observations in Moscow. Works by Polish, Czech, and Slovakian paleontologists also began to come out of Germany and Austria in the first half of the nineteenth century. Most of these publications were sponsored by university agencies or scientific societies, although some paleontologists, such as Joachim Barrande and to some extent Ludwik Zejsner, carried out research at their own expense.

At the end of the nineteenth century and until World War I, activity in paleontological research greatly accelerated in eastern Europe. New institutions were born in Poland, Czechoslovakia, and Hungary, while the output of published reports increased. Work in the Balkans was at first conducted by foreign scientists, but local researchers emerged as well. Three professors from Prague University, Ottomar Novak, Jaroslav Perner, and Filip Pocta, continued Barrande's research in Bohemia on Early Paleozoic fauna. Antonin Fric described the land fauna of the Permian in Moravia, while Vaclav Capek studied Diluvial bird fauna. Ferdynand Stoliczka, a paleontologist with the Geological Survey of India, examined local Cretaceous fauna until his death in India.

During this pre-war period, Polish paleontological research was conducted primarily in Galicia: at the universities in Krakow and Lvov, as well as at the Dzieduszycki Museum in Lvov and the Academy of Sciences in Krakow. Among the Dzieduszycki Museum's publications, W. Friedberg published the first part of a monograph, *Mieczaki miocenskie Ziem Polskich* (1911–28).

Józef Siemiradzki, a professor of paleontology at Lvov University, published his research concentrating mainly on Jurassic fauna in Krakow and Germany. The Academy of Skills in Krakow published numerous paleontological works by A. Alth, W. Friedberg, J. Nowak, W. Teisseyre, S. Zareczny, and other authors, all concentrating on various groups of fossil fauna of Poland. Wladyslaw Szajnocha, one of the founders of the Geological Department at Krakow University (1886), described the plentiful assemblage of Middle Jurassic fauna from Balin near Krakow. Austrian paleontologists, including M. Neumayr and G. Laube, also studied this material.

Marian Raciborski, a botanist, pioneered the study of Paleozoic and Mesozoic floras with his monographs. These and other inquiries into fossil faunas provided a better understanding of the organisms' environment and allowed for the completion of stratigraphic schemes.

In 1894, Józef Grzybowski, a young paleontologist from Krakow, laid the foundations for a new branch of paleontological research—applied micropaleontology. In the second half of the nineteenth century, the increased demand for oil called for devising a method for identifying monotonous flysch deposits (thick series of sandstone interbedded with conglomerates), which are almost completely devoid of fossils. Gryzbowski examined many rock-oil profiles from drillings in the Carpathian Mountains. He paid careful attention to the foraminifers (microscopic marine organisms that lived in calcium-based shells), creating sets of these organisms that are still used today to identify horizons (major stratigraphic boundaries) in the Carpathian Mountains. This method remains commonly accepted in oil geology. Gryzbowski is also credited with founding the Paleontology Department at Krakow University in 1912. A number of his students—F. Bieda, M. Dylazanka, and later, W. Zelechowski, S. Geroch, S. Liszka, and others—continued micropaleontological research in Krakow and Warsaw. August Emanuel Reuss initiated this field in Bohemia and Slovakia, where it continues to develop until today. Czech micropaleontological research, conducted by A. Rzechak, R.J. Schubert, W.J. Prochazka, F. Pocta, M. Vasicek, and many others, includes foraminifers, ostracods (tiny freshwater crustaceans), and other groups of microfossils.

During this pre-War period, conditions for carrying out paleontological research in the Polish territory that fell to the Russian Empire were less advantageous; however, many works were published. One such publisher was in Warsaw at a scientific institution, The Mianowski Memorial Fund. In the small village of Pulawy, called Nowa Alexsandria at that time, Nikolaj Krisztafowicz, a librarian at the Academy of Agriculture, edited the bulletin *Jezegodnik po Geologii Rosii.*

Several Polish scientists exiled to Siberia for their involvement in independence movements collected geological and paleontological specimens and made observations while there. The biggest achievements in this field are attributed to Benedykt Dybowski, Aleksander Czekanowski, and Jan Czerski.

At the same time, local representatives of the geological sciences already were working in the other eastern European countries. In Bulgaria, Georgi Zlatarski researched the stratigraphy of the Mesozoic and the Tertiary. In Hungary, Franz Nopcsa conducted research on dinosaur remains and made significant contributions in the field of paleobiology. By the end of his life, Nopcsa had become the director of the Hungarian Geological Institute. Spiridion Brusina, a founder of the Academy of Sciences Museum in Zagreb, researched molluscs of the Tertiary in the territory of Yugoslavia.

The Interwar Period

Geological surveys emerged from the eastern European countries that regained their independence after World War I: in 1919 for Poland and Czechoslovakia and in 1930 for Yugoslavia. In the formerly created countries—Hungary and Romania—geological surveys had been largely developed by 1869 and 1906, respectively.

New geological societies appeared in Poland (1921), Czechoslovakia (1923), Bulgaria (1925), and Romania (1930). The Hungarian Geological Survey, in existence since 1850, extended its activity to the current borders of the state. These institutions organized or facilitated research in both the geological and paleontological sciences, then published their findings. University departments, academies of sciences and similar institutions, and natural science museums continued to conduct paleontological research. Several natural science museums possessing fossil collections had been established earlier: the National Museum in Prague (1818), the Natural History Museum in Bucharest (1834), a museum in Zagreb (1866), and the Mineralogical and Paleontological Department of the National Museum of Budapest (1870).

In the first 20 years of Poland's independence after World War I, the Museum of Earth was established, joining Poland's other museums in Krakow, Warsaw, and Lvov that had been founded in the eighteenth and nineteenth centuries. The first Museum of the Earth was established in 1938 by Roman Kozlowski, an eminent paleontologist, and others with the suggestion of Stanislaw Malkowski, a petrographer with broad interests. The museum assembled collections, organized exhibitions, initiated scientific research, edited reports, and propagated knowledge of the earth sciences. The museum also promoted the protection of geological monuments in their natural environments. After World War II, the museum developed an even broader range of activity.

In 1929, Eugenjusz Panow, a researcher at the Physiographic Museum of the Polish Academy of Skills, unearthed a unique Diluvial woolly rhinoceros *(Coelodonta antiquitatis blum)* in a mineral wax mine. Some of the specimen's soft parts and contents of the digestive system were preserved. In 1930, this fossil became the subject of a hallmark monograph. The Polish Academy of Skills followed up with subsequent publications on Diluvial flora and fauna in a library edition, *Starunia.* Between 1934 and 1953, 30 publications came out under this title.

Kozlowski was also a founder of the Warsaw Paleontological School. He authored a monograph *Les Brachiopodes du Carbonifere*

Superieure de Bolivie (1914), which was edited in Paris. Thereafter, Kozlowski concentrated his studies on Paleozoic brachiopods. In 1929, he published the first volume of a journal entitled *Paleontologia Polonica* that is still published today. At the Krakow Mining Academy, Jan Jarosz continued describing brachiopods of the Lower Carboniferous of Poland, while Jan Zerndt began research on sporogenesis (spore formation) and the use of the megaspore (an asexual spore that produces gametophytes) to determine the stratigraphy of the Carboniferous. Zerndt continued his work at the Geological Department of Jagiellonian University. The results of his research are contained in his two-volume work, *Les Megaspores du Bassin Houilier Polonais* (1934). These volumes and a few other publications became a basis for the palynological (fossil pollen) method of stratigraphy. In these same years following the war, at the reborn Vilnius University Roman Kongiel published several works on Cretaceous echinoderms (starfishes, sea cucumbers, and similar forms).

During the interwar period, Czech researchers were productive in Prague, Bratislava, and Brno. Bedrich Boucek revised the Czech Paleozoic *Conularia* (organisms with tapering shells), Maria Kettnerowa researched corals of the Paleozoic, and Jaroslaw Perner, a professor of paleontology at the University of Prague since 1927, continued Barrande's research into Paleozoic fauna in Bohemia. Filip Pocta described rudistans (a class of bivalves) and sponges, and Anton Rzehok studied foraminifers. In Hungary, Ferenc Nopesca and Gyule Rakusz published "Die oberkarbonischen Fossilien von Dobsina und Nagyvisnyo" (1932). In Budapest, a paleontological symposium was held in 1928. For this, Andreas Kubacska prepared a publication, *Die Grundlagen der Literatur über Ungarns Vertebraten-Paleontololgie,* in which he compared 150 publications from the years 1668 to 1847.

During this same period paleontological research in Romania and Bulgaria focused primarily on fossil faunas of the local Mesozoic and Tertiary formations. In Yugoslavia, paleontology was concentrated in three centers: Croatia, Serbia, and Ljubljana. In Croatia, Dragutin Gorjanowic-Krumberger uncovered a famous Diluvial human habitat at Krapina and described these finds in affiliation with the Academy of Sciences Museum in Zagreb. In Serbia, Belgrade was the center of research where Jovan Zujovic and Vladimir Petkovic laid the foundations for the stratigraphy and fossil faunas of this region. Also in Belgrade, Vasilije Simic published his monograph *Gornji Perm u Zapadnoj Srbiji* (1933), the first volume of *Memoires du service geologique du Royaume de Yougoslavia.* In Ljubljana, which was firmly tied to Austrian scientific developments, researchers continued studies of the fossil faunas of the Carnian Alps. In 1933, Ivan Rakovec was appointed assistant professor there, and in 1939, he became full professor as well as custodian of the geological department of the Ljubljana Museum. Rakovec dealt mainly with Diluvial fauna. He was an educator of the postwar generation of Slovenian paleontologists.

World War II and the Post-War Years

The outbreak of World War II prevented further developments in paleontological research in Eastern Europe. Many scientists were murdered by the Nazis. Jan Nowak, J. Grzybowski's successor at the Paleontology Department in Krakow, died a few days after leaving the concentration camp where he had been imprisoned together with all the other educators from Krakow's schools of higher learning. At the close of the war, Jan Zerndt, one of the imprisoned professors, was forced to change his nationality and died subsequently in unaccountable circumstances. Jaroslaw Sulc, a researcher of the Lower Paleozoic microfossils of Bohemia, was executed in prison.

After 1945 when the eastern European countries, Germany-Saxony, and Prussia came under the Soviet Union's dominion, science was subject to the Communist Party's dictates. Those scientists who opposed the party were either put to death or deprived of work opportunities. Aleksander Kelus, one of Poland's first paleontologists to analyze the inner structure of fossil organisms and a researcher of Devonian brachiopods and corals, died in a Warsaw prison. Ferdinand Prantl, the founder of the Czech paleontological school, custodian of Barrandeum, and a conspicuous advocate of science, died shortly after being released from prison.

The sums of money the Communist governments spent on paleontological research and other earth sciences in eastern Europe, as well as in Soviet Russia, were significant for practical reasons: The outcome of research for mining and other purposes yielded prestige in the international scientific community. Therefore, the expenditures invested in institutions, research expeditions, and an increasing number of publications were relatively large. Eastern European governments, however, suppressed independent research organizations. Often they were included in academies of sciences, which customarily owned paleontological agencies. These agencies coordinated geological surveys and other research conducted by the academies. A highly hierarchized system of dependencies arose among scientists. The personality of the highest grade of scientists was extremely important. Despite the authorities' intentions, pressure from the greater scientific community could not be avoided. For example, paleontological papers and abstracts generally were published in English, French, or German; they were rarely printed in Russian.

The development of the science of paleontology in Poland after 1945 was shaped mainly by Roman Kozlowski. He was a proponent of understanding structure, development, and the systematic correlation between ancient organisms, and to a lesser extent, of determining these factors' relevance to stratigraphy. Marian Ksiazkiewicz, founder of the Polish geological school and professor at Krakow University, paid particular attention in his study of sedimentary rocks and formations to the interrelationship between organisms, as well as to traces of their life and conditions of sedimentation. Further contributions came from the Polish Academy of Sciences, working in conjunction with other institutions to organize expeditions to Spitsbergen (northern Norway), Cuba, and Antartica. Zofia Kielan-Jaworowska led a project that produced interesting results on the dinosaur and early mammal remains in Mongolia. The Academy of Sciences and the Geological Survey edited paleontological works. More than 50 volumes of monographs were published as part of the series, *Paleontologia Polonica,* including: nine parts of the *Results of the Polish-Mongolian Paleontological Expeditions,* the first parts of *Paleontological Spitsbergen Studies,* and *Paleontological Results of the Polish Antarctic Expeditions.* The monographs also included *Travaux de la Musée de la Terra,* edited by the Museum of the Earth, as well as works by the State Geological Institute. There were several publications in the fields of paleozoology and paleobotany: the journal *Acta Paleontologica Polonica* (published since 1956), *Annales Societatis Geologorum Poloniae,* and others.

Between 1945 and 1990, approximately 150 Polish paleontologists and geologists published their scientific works in the fields of paleobiology, paleozoology, paleobotany, palynology, and other areas of research dealing with fossil organisms. In *Les Graptolithes et quelques nouveaux groupes d'animaux du Tremadoc de la Pologne,* Kozlowski's analysis of well-preserved graptolites yielded a revision of their systematic relationships. Henryk Makowski deliberated on the sexual dimorphism of ammonites (coiled cephalopods) in *La faune calovienne de Luków en Pologne* (1952). In her *Pachyphillinae et Phillipsastraea du Frasnien de Pologne* (1953), Maria Rozkowska pioneered Polish paleontological research into corals from the Paleozoic and the Mesozoic. The Museum of the Earth initiated paleobotanical works in its research center with the publication of *The Fossil Flora of Turów near Bogatynia* (1959), edited by Hanna Czeczot. Marian Ksiazkiewicz's *Trace Fossils in the Flysch of the Carpathians* (1977) was a fundamental monograph on ichnology (fossilized footprints) from the Carpathian Mountains. Polish paleontology's long period of development justified the need for elaborating on its history. Franciszek Bieda, a researcher in nummulites (tiny organisms that incorporate lime in their protective shells), first chronicled this history in 1948. In 1976, *Zarys dziejów paleontologii w Krakowie* offered an extensive investigation of this subject.

Paleontologists from eastern and western Europe, as well as from non-European countries, traveled to the scientific centers in Warsaw and Krakow to improve their paleontological, stratigraphic, and sedimentological research methods. Likewise, Polish paleontologists traveled to the United States, western Europe, and Russia to further their skills and to conduct research.

After the war, the large, established geological museums and science institutes in the German Democratic Republic lacked scientific researchers. Despite the hard economic (and physical) conditions, the museums in Berlin that housed original collections, such as *Archaeopteryx simensi* Dames, underwent restoration. About 7,000 original specimens from the Paleontological Museum were saved. During these years, the Geological Science Society of the German Democratic Republic was formed, serving as a forum for the exchange of opinions and promotion of its activities and as a link to the world of science. The society organized several international seminars as well. Much of the society's work can be attributed to its president, Robert Daber, a paleobotanist and director of the Paleontological Museum in Berlin. Two departments within the society, paleozoology and paleobotany, edited a bulletin, *Palaontologische Abhandlungen.*

In Czechoslovakia, the same research centers developed as during the interwar period. Progress within the science of paleontology, however, was checked by repeated political oppression, and especially by the imprisonment and death of Ferdynand Prantl. Josef Augusta, a Prague University professor, collaborated with Z. Burian, a painter, to publish several albums illustrating ancient life of the Cambrian to the Quaternary. These albums were published numer-

ous times in many different countries. At the same time, a number of Czech paleontological institutions published scientific works. From 1963 onward, the Geological Survey edited a bulletin, *Sbornik Geologickych Ved, Paleontologie.* Several monographs also appeared, such as *The Upper Devonian and the Lower Carboniferous Trilobites of the Moravian Karst* (1966) by Ivo Chlupac. In a library edition of *Paleontographica Bohemica,* the Academy of Sciences published monographs including *Tertiary Frogs from Central Europe* (1972) by Zdenek V. Špinar. Interest in fossil microorganisms had a long tradition in Czechoslovakia, culminating in Vaclav Pokorny's handbook *Zaklady zoologicke mikropaleontologie (Principles of Zoological Micropaleontology),* published in 1954 and subsequently translated and edited in Germany and England.

After World War II, paleontological research in Hungary was concentrated primarily in two centers: the Geological Institute and in the Nature Department of the National Museum of Budapest. The museum possesses a large collection of fossils from Hungary and abroad. Although it was seriously damaged during the Soviet Union's invasion in 1956, it was restored quickly with aid from foreign scientific institutions. The museum's combined geological and paleontological department is one of the best in eastern Europe and is noteworthy for its Paleozoic Bukk Mountains and Tertiary collections.

Both scientific centers are responsible for publications. The Geological Institute edits *Geologica Hungarica Series palaeontologica,* a journal of paleontological essays by Hungarian and foreign scientists. The National Museum publishes the work of its associates in two series. The first, *Annales historico naturales Musei Nationalis Hungarie,* has been in existence since 1908. The paleontology section in this series focuses on the museum collections from Hungary and other countries, covers relevant museum activities, and prints associates' publications. The second series, *Fragmenta mineralogica et palaeontologica,* covers scientific news in English and German. As of 1996, eighteen issues had been released since the first issue in 1970.

In Romania, Bulgaria, and Yugoslavia, post-war conditions were more adverse, affecting the development of paleontological research. The more extensive Romanian works were published abroad, including *Les Decapodes du Tithonique Inferior de Wozniki* (1966), by Dan Patrolius, and *Les Scleractiniaires du Jurassique Superieru de la Dobrogea Centrale Roumania* (1976), by Aurelia Barbulescu and Ewa Roniewicz; both volumes were published in Poland. Several studies of Tertiary fauna conducted by young Romanian paleontologists were developed further in Leningrad. During these same years, many Bulgarian scientists received an education in fossil organisms, leading to the first research in this field. Young geologists from Vietnam, Algiers, and Cuba also contributed to this area. Wasil Tsankov was professor of paleontology in Sofia since 1948. Until 1975, paleontological research was published in the *Bulletin of the Geological Institute*'s Paleontological Series. Later, the Academy of Sciences took over the bulletin and changed the name to *Paleontology, Stratigraphy, and Lithology.* The fifty volumes of this series were devoted primarily to descriptions of local fossil groups. In 1968, *Monograph on the Bathonian Ammonite Genus Siemiradskia,* by July Stephanov, was published posthumously.

In Yugoslavia, after the war paleontology mainly developed in the part of the country called Slovenia. The Academia Scientiarum et Artium Sloveniae edited paleontological works in a series of approximately 12 monographs called *Rozprawe, Classe Natural History*. Katica Drobne and Rajko Pavlovec published descriptions of foraminifers, Dragica Turnsek described Cretaceous corals, and Anton Ramovs described the Paleozoic fauna of the Carnian Alps. In Zagreb, Croatia, the Societe Geologique Croate and the Geological Survey edited *Geoloski Viesnik* with news of fossil faunas. Professor Vanda Kochansky-Devide addressed the general subject of evolution in his *Makroevolutionstheorien und ihre Cytogenetische Grundlagen* (1985). In Belgrade, Serbia, the Serbian Academy of Sciences published paleontological news in its bulletin, *Glas, Classe des Sciences Naturelles et Mathemathiques*.

Eastern European paleontological research has contributed to the science most notably in its elaboration of regional fossil groups and of stratigraphic horizons. Additionally, important monographs and paleobiological, paleoecological, and evolutionary studies have come out of Poland, Czechoslovakia, and Hungary. Despite difficult conditions, paleontologists from these countries have attempted to maintain contact with the world scientific community and to make a significant contribution to it.

STANISLAW CZARNIECKI

See also Europe: Western Europe; Russia and the former Soviet Union

Works Cited

Barbulescu, A., and E. Roniewicz. 1976. *Les Sclératiniraies du Jurassique Supérieur de la Dobrogea Centrale Roumaine*. Paleontologia Polonica. 34. Warsaw: Panstwowe Wydawnictwo Naukowe.

Barrande, J. 1852–1902. *Système Silurien du centre de la Bohême, Bd. I-VIII*. Prague, Paris: l'Auteur.

Chulupac, I. 1966. *The Upper Devonian and Lower Carboniferous Trilobites of Moravian Karst*. Sbor. Geol Ved., Vol. 7. n.p.

Czeczot, H. (ed). 1959, 1961. Flora kopalna Turowa kolo Bogatyni [The fossil flora of Turow near Bogatynia]. *Prace Muzeum Ziemi* 3/4:117, 128

Friedberg, W. 1911–28. *Mieczaki mioceňskie Ziem Polskich/Mollusca Miocaenica Poloniae. 1, Gastropoda*. Lwow: Nakladem Muzeum Imienia Dzieduszyckich we Lwowie.

———. 1934, 1936. *Mieczaki mioceňskie Ziem Polskich/Mollusca Miocaenica Poloniae. 2, Lamellibranchiata*. Krakow: Wydano z Zasilku Funduszukultury Narodowej.

Hacquet, B. 1778–89. *Oryctographia Carniolica oder Physikalische Erdbeschreibung des Herzogtums Krain, Istrien und zum Theil der benachbarten Lander*. Vols. 1–4. Leipzig: n.p.

Kochansky-Devide, V. 1985. *Makroevolutionstheorien und ihre Cytogenetische Grundlagen*. Zagreb: Jugoslavenska akademija znanosti i umjet nosti.

Kozlowski, R. 1914. Les Brachiopodes du Carbonif ère supérieur de Bolivie, avec une notice geologique par A. Dereins. *Annales Paléont* 9:100.

———. 1929. Les Brachiopodes du Gothlandiens de la Podolie Polonaise. *Palaeontologia Polonica* 1:247.

———. 1948. Les Graptolithes et quelques nouveaux groupes d'animaux du Tremadoc de Pologne. *Palaeontologia Polonica* 3:247.

Ksiazkiewicz, M. 1977. Trace fossils in the Flysch of the Polish Carpathians. *Palaeontologia Polonica* 36:208.

Kubacska, A. 1928. *Die Grundlagen der Literatur uber Ungarns Vertebraten-Palaeontologie*. Budapest: n.p.

Kumelski, N. 1826. *Rys systematyczny nauki o skamienialosciach czyli petrefaktologii [A Systematic Outline of Petrefactology]*. Vilnius: n.p.

Makowski, H. 1952. La Faune callovienne de Luków en Pologne. *Palaeontologia Polonica* 4:64.

Patrolius, D. 1956. Decapoda dolnego tytonu z Woznik (Polskie Karpaty Zachodnie) [Les Décapodes du Tithonique inférieur de Wozniki (Carpates Polonaises Occidentales)]. *Annales Societatis Geologorum Poloniae* 36:495–517.

Pokorny, V. 1954. *Zaklady zoologicke mikropaleontologie*. Prague: Nakl. Ceskoslovenske akademie ved.

Pusch, G.G. 1837. *Polens Paläontologie oder Abbildung und Beschreibung der vorzüglichsten und noch unbeschriebenen Petrefakten aus den Gibirgsformationen in Polen Volhynien und den Karpathen*. Stuttgart: E. Schweizerbart's Verlagshandlung.

Rozkowska, M. 1953. Pachyphyllinae et Phillipsastraea du Frasnien de Pologne. *Palaeontologia Polonica* 5:86.

Rakusz, G., and F. Nopesca. 1932. *Die oberkarbonischen Fossilien von Dobsina und Nagyvisnyo*. Geologica Hungarica Series Palaeontologica, 8. Budapest: n.p.

Simic, V. 1933. *Gornji Perm u Zapadnoj Srbiji (Das Oberperm in Westserbien)*. Belgrad: n.p.

Špinar, Z.V. 1972. *Tertiary Frogs from Central Europe*. The Hague: Junk.

Staszic, S. 1955. *O ziemiorodztwie Karpatów i innych gór i równin Polski [Geology of Carpathians and Other Mountains and Plains of Poland]*. Warsaw: Wydawn. Geologiczne.

Stephanov, J. 1968. *Monograph on the Bathonian Ammonite Gunus Siemiradzkia Hyatt 1900*. Sophia: n.p.

Stur, D. 1875–87. *Die Clum-Flora: Beitrage zur Kenntniss der Flora der Vorwelt*. Vol. 1. Vienna: Fischer.

———. 1885. *Die Carbon-Flora der Schatzlarer Schichten*. Abhandlungen der Kaiserlich-Königlichen Geologischen Reichsanstalt 11(1). Vienna: A. Holder.

Zejszner, L. 1946. *Paleontologia polska: Opis zoologiczny, i geologiczny wszystkich zwierzat i roslin skamienialych polskich do poznania warstw ziemi sluzacy wraz z wizerunkami swzystkich gatunków rysowanymi z natury. [Polish Paleontology: Zoological, Botanical and Geological Description of All Polish Petrified Animals and Plants, Serving the Knowledge of Earth Layers, Accompanied by Pictures of All Species]*. Warsaw: n.p.

Zeno, F. 1770. *Neue physikalische Belustigungen*. Prague: n.p.

Zerndt, J. 1934, 1937. *Les Mégaspores du Bassin Houiller Polonais*. Vols. 1–2. Krakow: Nakl. Polskiej Akademji Umiejetnosci.

Further Reading

Bieda, F. 1948. *Historia paleontologii w Polsce*. Nakl: Polskiej Akademji Umiejetnosci.

———. 1976. *Zarys dziejów paleontologii w Krakowie*. Krakow: Zakland Narodowy im Ossolinskich.

Czarniecki, S. 1964. *Zarys historii geologii na Uniwersytecie Jagiellonskim [An Outline of the History of Geology in the Jagiellonian University in the Years 1782–1962]*. Krakow: Wydawnictwa jubileuszowe.

———. 1993. Grzybowski and his school: The beginnings of applied micropalaeontology in Poland at the turn of the 19th and 20th centuries. *In* M.A. Kaminski, S. Geroch, D.G. Kaminski, *The Origins of Applied Micropalaeontology: The School of Józef Grzybowski*. Oxford: Alden.

Geczy, B. 1994. *Brief History of the Hungarian Palaeontology*. Budapest: n.p.

Kettner, R. 1931. *O vyvoji geologie v Cechach, Vyvoj Ceske Prirodovedy 1869–1929*. Prague: n.p.

Kubucska, A. *Die Grundlagen der Literatur über Ungarns Vertebraten-Palaeontologie*. Budapest: n.p.

EUROPE: WESTERN EUROPE

For the purposes of this article, western Europe is defined as that part of the ancient Pangaean supercontinent that today comprises the British Isles and Ireland, the Benelux countries (Belgium, the Netherlands, and Luxembourg), Germany, Austria, Switzerland, France, Italy, Spain, and Portugal, as well as their marine environments.

Western Europe has undergone many profound changes since Cambrian times: completely new oceans appeared (e.g., the Tethys, which stood between northern Laurasia and southern Gondwana, and which today persists as the Mediterranean Sea), innumerable rises and falls of sea level took place, and continents continually migrated, rotated, collided, and pulled apart.

A good example of this constant change in the relationship of land to sea through geologic time is provided by Germany, which today occupies a central and rather substantial part of western Europe. In Devonian times it was largely covered by the sea. Large parts of it emerged later in the Carboniferous period. Carboniferous Germany was covered by dense forests that would ultimately be transformed into thick coal deposits. During the Permian and Triassic periods, Germany was covered alternately by dunes of red desert sands and a shallow sea. During the Jurassic, Cretaceous, and Early Tertiary periods, much of Germany was a seafloor. The water eventually receded to expose the present landscape. Similar stories could be told about the rest of western Europe.

The original eastern part of Laurasia (Angara, the future Eurasia) did not fully separate from the western part (Laurentia, the future North America) until the Eocene. Geological upheavals related to this fissioning create unusual discontinuities in the European geological record. For example, a Late Pliocene warm weather terrestrial fauna located in the Dutch Tegelen region lies just a few miles from a Late Cretaceous deposit in Belgium (Maastricht) that contains the remains of the large mosasaur *Mosasaurus*.

This article will treat successively, (1) the history of paleontology in Europe, (2) its geological history, (3) major fossil localities, (4) important taxa, (5) paleoanthroplogy, and (6) major museums and collections.

The Origin of Paleontology: The Role of Western Europe

In some sense, Bernard Palissy of France (1510–90) might be considered a forerunner to later paleontologists. Later scholars, such as Niels Steensen of Denmark (1638–1737) and Robert Hooke of England (1635–1703) expressed some precocious thoughts on fossils, and important collections of fossils (recovered from such localities as Monte Bolca in Italy and the German Muschelkalk) were accumulated by amateur naturalists. However, no real scientific development took place until the work of Georges Buffon (1707–88) and Georges Cuvier (1769–1832). The question of "lost species" was specifically addressed by Buffon in *Les époques de la nature* (1778), and Cuvier in *Les révolutions du globe* (1825). Both Buffon and Cuvier were instrumental in establishing the science of comparative anatomy, an essential prerequisite for interpreting traces of past life.

The realization that species succeeded each other in time was hampered by the absence of any real stratigraphy. The very first steps in recording a European stratigraphic history were taken by Giraud Soulavie (*Histoire naturelle de la France*, 1780), William Smith (*Tabular View of the Order of Strata, 1799),* and Edward Lhuyd.

A full appreciation of life's history was did not take place until Charles Lyell (*Principles of Geology*, 1830–33) presented evidence for the great age of the Earth and until an evolutionary perspective on life was adopted. Jean Baptiste Lamarck (*Philosophie zoologique,* 1809) provided a (now discredited) mechanism for evolutionary change that was subsequently replaced by the far more convincing paradigm introduced by Charles Darwin (*On the Origin of Species,* 1859). Other pioneers of the nineteenth century who were instrumental in the birth of paleontology included A. Brogniart, A. D'Orbigny, and A. Gaudry of France; J. Lindley, J. Hutton, D.H. Scott, A. Sedgwick, E.T. Newton, and R.I. Murchison of Great Britain; and H.R. Goeppert of Germany.

Western European Paleontology and Stratigraphy

The importance of western Europe in establishing a global geological sequence cannot be overstated. European localities gave us the names for such geological periods as the Cambrian, Ordovician, Silurian, Devonian, and Jurassic.

Paleozoic Era (540–240 Million Years Ago)

The Paleozoic era saw the rise of all modern animal phyla and an equal number of extinct ones. Many kinds of land plants appeared, beginning in the Silurian.

In Great Britain, Cambrian limestones and shales are well exposed in the Northwest Highlands of Scotland, the Midlands, Warwickshire, and South Wales. Trilobites (*Paradoxides, Olenellus*), brachiopods (*Linguella*), and graptolites (*Dictyonema, Monograptus*) can be found here.

Ordovician faunas were collected as early as the eighteenth century in the Wenlock limestone of North Wales, the Lake District of England, and the Southern Uplands of Scotland. Brachiopods, trilobites, corals, bryozoans, echinoderms and other invertebrate phyla from this region resemble contemporaneous forms from the so-called Bohemian fauna of Slovakia. There was probably a sea connecting the two regions during this period.

Heavily armored jawless fishes ("ostracoderms") appear in Europe at the end of the Silurian and the beginning of the Devonian. They have been valuable in correlating rocks in Europe, Greenland, and North America.

The Devonian Old Red Sandstone is well represented in Scotland and Wales. It has yielded such jawless fishes as the osteostracan *Cephalaspis* and the heterostracan *Pteraspis*. Associated with these vertebrates are the horny brachiopod *Lingula*, a large bivalve, *Archanodon,* and numerous arthropods including the eurypterid *Pterygotus*. During the time that the Old Red Sandstone was deposited, southwest England, including Devonshire, was covered by a sea that extended eastward into Belguim, northern France, and Germany. A wide variety of animals lived in this sea including corals *(Heliolites)*, brachiopods *(Stringocephalus)*, goniatite ammonoids, trilobites, and fishes. Thick limestone deposits formed from the calcareous skeletons of corals are today thrust up to mountainous heights in the Eifel area of Germany, the Dolomites in the Southern Alps, and the Belgian Ardennes.

The Carboniferous System, consisting mainly of interbedded limestone and coal, is broadly represented over western Europe. In several places it reaches a thickness of several thousand feet. Representative taxa include brachiopods, corals, cephalopod molluscs, bryozoans, crinoids, fishes *(Psammodus, Helodus),* and amphibians *(Megalocephalus).* Stratigraphically useful microfossils include algae, foraminiferans, ostracods, and conodonts. The Lower Carboniferous (Waulsortian) Black Marble of Dinant, Belgium, is a marine deposit that contains exceptionally well-preserved examples of fish *(Benedenius, Denea, Sphenacanthus,* and the famous *Cratoselache),* nine genera of sea urchins (some of which are the largest in the world), the surprising medusa *Medusina boulengeri,* dendroid graptolites, and productid brachiopods, whose shells are ornamented with long spines. Quite a few holotypes from this deposit are housed at the Maredsous Abbey, Namur Province, Belgium.

A prolonged period of arid or semiarid conditions began after the Carboniferous, and prevailed throughout the Permian and part of the subsequent Triassic Period.

Mesozoic Era (240–65 Million Years Ago)

The lower boundary of the Mesozoic era has been precisely defined in western Europe on the basis of an abupt faunal transition (Permo–Triassic Boundary) and by the orogenic transition of the hercynian alpine cycle. Temperate and even glacial conditions are associated with the beginning of this era.

Among coelenterates (e.g., corals, jellyfishes), the Hexacorallia gradually replace the tetracoralia and tabulata. Among ammonoids (a group of cephalopod molluscs), goniatites replace ceratites. Among tetrapods, the stegocephalia and theromorphs become extinct during the Triassic.

The upper limit of the Mesozic occurs at the Cretaceous–Tertiary boundary, where a mass extinction claims the belemnite cephalopods, rugose corals, and, of course, the dinosaurs.

The three main periods of the Mesozoic were first recognized in western Europe. The Triassic (240–200 million years ago) occurs in a succession of characteristic formations in Central Germany, including the Buntsandstein (up to 800 meters thick), the Muschelkalk, and the Keuper (Alberi 1834). The Jurassic (200–140 million years ago) was modelled on the Swiss canton Jura (von Humboldt 1795). The Cretaceous (140–65 million years ago) is marked by thick chalk formations throughout southern Great Britain, northern France and Belgium (Omalius d'Halloy 1822).

Triassic Period. The Triassic Period in Europe is a time of emerging lands and desertlike conditions. Europe looked like a huge red immensity (New Red Sandstone). Continetal faunas are best represented in western Germany (Scwabe and Franconie), eastern France (Vosges and Lorraine, "poudingue de Saint-Odile"), and Great Britain. Triassic tetrapods include the archosauromorph *Tanystropheus,* marine reptiles such as plesiosaurs, the footprints of *Cheirotherium,* and *Anchisaurus* (a primitive dinosaur).

Jurassic Period. The Jurassic is characterized by specific geological zones delineated on the basis of ammonite fossils (33 zones were defined by A. Oppel in 1856 and appear still to be valid). The microfauna of the time included microscopic animals with calcareous-impregnated shells (radiolaria and foraminifera). Marine environments were populated by various shelled invertebrates, such as a variety of clams and brachiopods. Perfectly preserved fishes *(Amia, Lepidosteus, Hybodus)* have been discovered in the lithographic chalk of Cérin (France), the Oxford and Kimmeridge clay (Great Britain), and Solenhofen (Bavaria, Germany). Bone beds rich in terrestrial vertebrates are found in Hettangian layers (Luxembourg) and the Purbeck beds (Great Britain), including primitive mammals (including multituberculates). Huge reptiles lived during this period (the fishlike *Ichthyosaurus,* the giant flying *Pterosaurus,* and *Stegosaurus*). It saw the rise of pterosaurs, *Archaeopteryx* (a primitive bird with characters that link reptiles and birds, five specimens of which have been recovered since 1861), and the first teleosts (higher ray-finned fishes).

Other important localities include: Paris Basin, Burgundy, and the estuary of the Seine River (Calvados France); Portland, Bridgeport, and Charmouth (Dorset), Somerset, in Great Britain; Monte-Domaro (North Italy); Aalen and Boll (Württemberg), Holzmaden, Solenhofen, and Eichstätt (Bavaria).

Cretaceous Period. The Cretaceous period follows the Jurassic times. The warm climate is conducive to the proliferation of life and proliferation of the gymnosperms and the ammonoids. The marine Jurassic transgression continued and the emerged lands shrank. This period sees the rise of angiosperms (flowering plants); animals include belemnites, ammonites, teleosts, and ornithopods (e.g., *Iguanodon* of the Weald clay, in the Isle of Wight and Bernissart, Belgium). Important formations include: Hastings Beds, Weald Clay, "craies de Ciply," Spiennes, "tuffeau de Maastricht" in the Netherlands and Belgium. However, a widespread reduction in reptiles took place at the end of the period, while marsupials and placental mammals began to increase as significant parts of the world fauna.

Cenozoic (65–2 million years ago)

The Cenozoic era, commonly called the "Age of Mammals," is divided into two unequal periods: the long Tertiary (approximately 65 million years ago) and the shorter Quaternary (1.6 million years ago). During the Early Tertiary period, the climate in Europe was tropical. In the vicinity of Frankfurt/Main, remains from the Lower Miocene epoch have been found of cinnamon trees and palm leaves. Silicified tree trunks have been discovered at Chemnitz (eastern Germany). Generally speaking, animals and plants prefigured the present biological diversity. From the very beginning of the era, all the major, modern groups were represented with the exception of the monocotyledon plants (e.g., grasses), which first appeared during the Oligocene period. The Cenozoic is a particularly important era for the development of the mammalian fauna, during which the living species achieved their present distribution. Toward the end of the Tertiary, temperatures decreased. Plants from this period still grow in Europe, as is beautifully demonstrated in the Pliocene "glass herbarium" in Frankfurt-Niederrad, although most of the Tertiary plants died during the ice ages of the Pleistocene.

There are numerous fossil sites in western Europe. Some of them were discovered and exploited very early in the history of paleontology, before parallel and sometimes richer assemblages were identified on other continents. Western European sites, therefore, figure prominently in the development of paleontology as a science. Some of the sites are even regarded, worldwide, as "classical," and they contributed substantially to establishing the general scheme for both stratigraphy and taxonomy on a planetary scale. The basis for understanding the evolution of numerous biological groups owes much to these early studies in western Europe. Thus, the present division of the Tertiary era has been proposed based upon the changing percentage of modern species of marine molluscs: Paleocene, Eocene, Oligocene, Miocene, Pliocene. This chronostratigraphy has become more or less universally accepted.

Among the many important Cenozoic sites, several in particular should be mentioned: From the Paleocene, one should note the marine Thanet Beds and the continental sites in Cernay, Berru (Reims, France); Walbeck (Germany); and Hainin (Belgium). From the Eocene, one should note the marine site of the Paris Basin with its various exceptionally exposed layers (from Yprésien to Bartonien), as well as the following continental sites: London clay, "Conglomérat de Meudon" (Paris), Cuise, Argenton sur Creuse, Issel, Lissieu, Lautrec, Quercy, Euzet-les-Bains (Gard) (France); Croydon and Bracklesham (Great Britain); Egerkingen (Switzerland); Erquelinnes, Vinalmont, Dormaal (Belgium); Messel, Helmstedt, Heidenheim, Frohnstetten, and Mehringen (Germany); and Lerida and Huesca, Douro (Salamanca), and Ebra (Sampedor) Basin, Oviedo (Spain). From the Oligocene, one should note the marine site of the Paris basin and the continental sites at Quercy, Ronzon (Velay), Thorigny (Seine et Marne), Lobsann, Alsace (France); Hampstead (Isle of Wight); Bernloch, Doberg, Ehingen, Gussenstadt, Neustadt, Oerlinger Tal (Germany); and Tarrega, Calaf, Mallorca, Cetina de Aragon (Spain). From the Miocene, one should note the continental sites at "Sables de l'Orléanais," Léognan (Gers), La Romieu (Agen), Rhône Valley, Sansan, La Grive Saint-Alban (Isère), Saint-

Gaudens (Haute-Garonne), "sables de Montpellier" (Hérault), Mont-Lubéron (France); Monte Bamboli (Tuscany, Italy); Elm, Schnaitheim, Attenfeld, Diessen, Freising, Günzburg, Hohenhöwen, Bermersheim, Ebingen, Salmendingen, Trochtelfingen (Germany); and Vallès Penedès (Cataluna), Tage and Douro Basin (Valladolid, Palencia, Saldana), Alfacar (Granada), Arenas del Rey (Spain). From the Pliocene, one should note the marine Belgian Campine and the continental sites at Saint-Vallier, Senèze (France); Herbolzheim (Germany); and Alcoy (Valencia) (Spain).

Quaternary or Pleistocene. The fossiliferous deposits of the Pleistocene are of both marine and nonmarine origin. The fauna consists largely of still living species. In Great Britain, Red Crag and Norwich Crag have yielded a large number of molluscs (bivalves and gastropods), as well as a great variety of mammals.

Taxonomy

It is impossible within the limits of this article to propose even a brief or succinct view of the specific contributions made by the fossil plant and invertebrate kingdoms of western Europe through the span of a half billion years, from the Cambrian to the Quaternary. Most phyla have yielded important useful documentation, much of it original, despite their early contribution to the structure of stratigraphic paleontology. It is also apparent that in western Europe, as elsewhere in the world (yet more so because of this region's pioneers), invertebrate studies have blazed the trail for further development of paleontological science. The foraminifera, conodonts, trilobites, brachiopods, cephalopods, crinoids, and graptolites are especially significant in order to understand the history of life and the influence on sedimentation by the many sea transgressions.

For similar reasons, five classes of primitive vertebrates (the "fishes") will not be dealt with explicitly in this article. Without entering into details, it is worth noting that important and precious fossil documents have been recovered from well-known and famous sites: Agnatha (ostracoderms, like *Drepanaspis,* from Bundenbach, German Lower Devonian), which became extinct in the Devonian, placoderms (such as *Pterichthyodes* or *Bothriolepis,* from the Scottish Devonian), acanthodians (Lower Silurian to Permian), chondrichthyans (such as *Xenacanthus,* Upper Devonian to Triassic), and ostecthyans (such as *Mene,* Eocene, Monte Bolca, Verona, Italy).

Amphibians. The very first amphibian to be discovered has an unusual history. In 1726, J.J. Scheuchzer uncovered a strange creature in the Upper Miocene layers close to Oedingen (Switzerland), which he incorrectly identified as a "human witness of the biblical flood." Subsequently, he named his find Homo diluvii testis, when in truth it was simply a huge salamander, and not even a primitive one. Although the amphibian class exhibits a rather limited diversity in the modern fauna, it played a very important role at the end of the Paleozoic and beginning of the Mesozoic. It first appeared in the Upper Devonian and developed in the Lower Carboniferous (350 million years ago).

One of the first European representatives of the amphibians is a stegocephalian. It was discovered by G.F. Jäger in 1824 in the Lettenkohle of Württemberg (Germany). Many more amphibian specimens were recovered from different sites all over western

Europe: They belong to four different subclasses and demonstrate an imperfect adaptation to terrestrial life. The rather primitive stegocephalians (e.g., *Actinodon*) became extinct in the Lias. They were followed at the beginning of the Triassic era by more advanced forms: stereospondyls (with 20 different genera, including *Mastodonsaurus, Plagiosaurus, Trematosaurus*), temnospondyls, embolomeres, and lepospondyls. The genera often are very similar to those identified in North America, thus providing more evidence for the contiguity of the two continental masses, which remained closely connected until the end of Mesozoic times.

Among the main western European Carboniferous sites, one should note in particular the following: in Scotland, Upper Visean, with *Megalocephalus*; in Great Britain, the coal-measures of Lancashire and Northumberland, with *Eugyrinus* and *Anthracosaurus*; in Ireland, Jarrow near Kilkenny, with *Ichthyerpeton*; in Bohemia, the Nyran site, contemporary with Linton in the United States, and the Boskovice site with *Memonomenos*. Of the Permian sites, one should note the following: in France, Autun Basin with *Actinodon* and *Branchiosaurus*; in Germany, Saarland, Palatinat, Thuringe, and Niederhässic (Dresde); in Great Britain, Kenilworth with *Dasyceps*.

Those scientific leaders who should be included among the many other western European paleontologist-pioneers who investigated amphibians are: H. Burmeister, F. Fraas, A. Fritsch, A. Gaudry, H.B. Geinitz, G.F. Jaeger, R. Lydekker, F.R. Parrington, J. Piveteau, F. von Huene, and D.M.S. Watson.

Reptiles. The main characteristic of the reptiles is its shelled egg. It is this structure that enabled these animals to live completely free of any aquatic environment. The shell (a leathery structure, not the hard shell of birds) prevents the egg from drying out, so it can be laid out of the water. Within the shell is a system of membranes and a yolk. The membrane called the "amnion" functions as a "lung," allowing gases to move in and out of the egg. The yolk is a food supply, and it is connected to the embryo by a series of vessels. This ready food supply enables the new reptile to hatch at a more advanced stage than occurs with amphibians and other earlier animals. Called the "amniotic egg," this structure is the result of a long series of transformations initiated in Devonian times, as various adaptations to life out of water.

The very first reptiles were described in the early eighteenth century by the German J.J. Baier in his *Oryctografia Norica*, but they were considered to be vertebrates linked to some kind of fish. Soon after this publication, other specimens were recovered from the Thuringe Permian *(Protorosaurus)*, in the Lias formations of Great Britain (by E. Home in 1814), and in Boll and Holzmaden formations (Germany), by A. König and G.F. Jaeger.

Primitive reptiles, such as the Cotylosauria, are not represented in western Europe. Sauropterygia, developed from these tetrapod reptiles, returned to a marine life or to a lacustrine (freshwater lake) environment. These long-necked aquatic reptiles swam mainly by paddling with their finlike legs. They are well known in Triassic or Liassic formations of Germany (Württemberg, Silesia, Muschelkalk of Rüdersdorf, and Laineck, Bayreuth), France (Lorraine), Italy (Tessino), Great Britain, with several genera, including *Nothosaurus, Simosaurus, Plesiosaurus,* and *Eretimosaurus*. *Cryptoclides* comes from the Upper Jurassic period of England.

Ichthyopterygia, with their dolphin-shaped bodies and long snouts, were even better adapted to marine life. They are numerous in the marine sediments from Mid-Triassic to Upper Cretaceous, with genera like *Ichthyopterygius, Ichthyosaurus, Stenopterygius,* and *Eurypterygius* present. Locations of finds include: in Germany (Holzmaden), Switzerland, Italian Tessino (Monte San Giorgio), France (Curcy, Normandy, and Saint Colombe, Yonne), Great Britain (Oxford), Belgium, and Luxembourg. Ichthyosaurs have a very short neck and a torpedo-shaped body, indicative of a strong swimmer. The caudal (tail) fin provided the propulsion; the arms and legs were transformed into fins.

The first placodont *(Placodus),* a primitive marine reptile, was described in 1833 by L. Agassiz from Laineck, Bavaria. More placodonts have been recovered from parallel Triassic layers at Steinfurt (Heidelberg), Tübingen, and more recently in the Monte San Giorgio. These animals have been studied thoroughly by the Swiss Bernard Peyer.

Chelonia (early turtles) have been known since Permian times. They belong to 23 various families. The most ancient known specimen is *Archaeochelys* (Permian, St. Affrique, France). The German Keuper has yielded exceptionally rich remains, especially Halberstadt and Württemberg. Numerous specimens have been described all through the French Tertiary: from Paleocene (Cernay) and Eocene (La Débruge), to Miocene (Sansan), up to the Pliocene of the Roussillon, which constitutes a particularly beautiful example of polyphyly (developed from more than one ancestral type) for the genus *Clemmys*. *Trionyx* demonstrates an exceptional development in Tertiary layers of the Venice Basin.

Thecodontia, a land-based group, had a rather short existence. They are limited to the Triassic; however, they demonstrate a remarkable diversity, explosive evolution, and adaptive radiation, which explains their position at the origin of all the archosauria (Crocodilians, Dinosaurs, Petrosauria) and even birds. Their best representatives are probably *Aëtosaurus* (Württemberg), *Stagonolepis* (Bayreuth), and *Ornithosuchus* (Elgin Sandstone, Scotland).

Among the Squamata, the Mosasauridae represent an aquatic form possibly related to monitor lizards and are a very well-diversified family, appearing throughout the world's oceans, from Upper Cénomanien up to the Danien in North and South American layers, in New Zealand, Timor, and Russia. *Mosasaurus* became famous in the nineteenth century because of G. Cuvier's classical memoir about "the big animal from Maestricht." It is rather analogous to *Tylosaurus* (from the North American Cretaceous). There is reasonable evidence to support the theory that this marine reptile swam upstream to reproduce in fresh waters. *Platecarpus* and *Plioplatecarpus* were found in Upper Cretaceous layers in France and Belgium.

The first dinosaurs were described in 1824 by F.T. Buckland (Mid-Jurassic of Oxford) and in 1825 by G.A. Mantell (Lower Cretaceous of southern England). This group is well represented in western Europe from approximately 140 million years ago. The two orders, Saurischia and Ornithischia, are distinguished on the basis of the structure of the pelvic bones. Both groups appear in the Lower Triassic (Muschelkalk), are abundant in the Keuper, and are beautifully represented in the Upper Triassic of Württemberg. The continental Lias is poorly represented. Diversification of the dinosaurs was still occurring from the Mid-Jurassic through the Upper Cretaceous. They became extinct rather suddenly: No specimen has ever been found above the Danian era. More than 40 western European fossil sites are known to have yielded dinosaur specimens.

Among the Saurischia, the most significant European genera are *Palaeosaurus* and *Teratosaurus* (Upper Triassic of Great Britain and Württemberg), *Compsognathus* (Upper Jura of Bavaria, France, and Belgium), *Magnosaurus* (British Lias), and *Megalosaurus* (Dogger, from Oxford, Caen, Germany, Portugal). *Plateosaurus* was probably the largest Triassic form (8 meters long and 5.5 meters high). It once lived in arid regions or in lagoons throughout Europe. It has been uncovered in marls at Halberstadt (German Thuringe) and Württemberg, and at Poligny (French Jura). *Bothriospondylus* (from British Mid- to Upper Jura) was a still larger form (15 to 20 meters long). Other important genera include *Pelosaurus* (Upper Jura to Lower Cretaceous from England, Portugal, Boulonais), *Brachiasaurus* and *Brontosaurus* (Portugal), and *Titanosaurus* (Lower Cretaceous from Isle of Wight, southern France).

The Ornithischia have been recovered mostly from the Cretaceous period. Among other genera, *Ignanodon* should be mentioned, the first specimens of which were recovered from the Wealdian clay of Great Britain (Isle of Wight and Tilgate). Other specimens were found in Germany, France, and Portugal. The most spectacular discovery was made at Bernissart (Belgium), where 29 specimens were excavated, twenty of them almost complete. They have been reassembled and are on exhibition at the Royal Institute of Natural History, Brussels. *Camptosaurus*, *Orthomerus* (family Hadrosauridae), and *Omosaurus* (family Stegosauridae) are other important western European genera, exhibiting close affinities with North American genera.

Pterosauria (Lower Lias–Upper Cretaceous) were first recognized in 1801 by Cuvier in a fossil specimen uncovered in Italy by Collini. The flying reptile was named *Pterodactylus longirostris* because of its wing supported by one long finger. More fossils were found in the Lower Lias (Lime Regis) of Great Britain (*Dimorphodon*), of Holzmaden (*Campylognathus*), and in the Upper Jura of Württemberg (*Dorygnathus, Rhamphorynchus*). Indeed, pterosaurs, or flying reptiles, achieved their acme during Jurassic times. The best-known genus in western Europe remains *Pterodactylus* with 23 different species. Exceptionally well-preserved specimens have been found in the very fine-grained limestone of Bavaria and Württemberg (Germany), in the Oxfordian–Wealdian layers of Great Britain, as well as in Cerin (French Jurassic).

Reptile fossil footprints are particularly abundant: *Brontozoum*, tridactyl imprints are found in South Wales; in continental western Europe, *Cheirotherium* is rather common. In Upper Jurassic of Portugal, at Cape Mondego, 70 spectacular footprints have been exposed, most likely made by a carnivorous theropod identified as *Megalosaurus*. In the Hastings (southern England) Wealdian Sandstone, one can observe some 60 footprints of *Iguanodon*.

Birds. The conquest of the air was initiated by insects during the Paleozoic era. It was pursued further during the Mesozoic by some reptiles, reaching its full and successful development since the Upper Jurassic by the Bird class. Their reptilian ancestor must lie among the Triassic reptiles: in western Europe, *Pseudosuchus, Ornitosuchus* (from Scotland), and *Aëtosaurus* (from Württemberg), all closely related to the South African genus *Euparkeria*. Bird bones are particularly fragile because they are hollow. This characteristic plus the birds' special mode of life makes fossilization rare and difficult. The best conditions for bird preservation are provided by lacustrine or marine formations, or by filling deposits in caves. In 1782, the first solid indication of paleornithology was proposed by a French naturalist, Lamanon, who recognized bird prints in the plasterstone of Montmartre (Paris). A more spectacular find was made in 1861 by H. von Meyer in Upper Jurassic layers of Bavaria, with the discovery of *Archaeopteryx*. Various specimens have been recovered from Solenhofen and Eichstätt (Germany); St. Gérand-le-Puy (Allier, France), a find complete with fossilized feathers and eggs; and Lerida (Spain). The various paleontologists involved in the early study of *Archaeopteryx* include H. Woodward, T.H. Huxley, R. Owen, J. Evans, Sir Gavin de Beer, A. Smith-Woodward, and T. Edinger.

Mammals. Western Europe has played a prominent role in shaping mammalian paleontology. Hundreds of fossil sites have been excavated throughout the Cenozoic sequence, from Paleocene to Villafranchian and Pleistocene times. With approximately 100 sites, concentrated mainly in Württemberg, Bavaria and around Frankfurt/Main, Germany, made a major contribution to the history of this class of vertebrates. With approximately 50 sites, France functioned very early on as a pioneer in the field, with Cuvier's spectacular collection from the Paris basin ("gypse de Montmartre") and in the Quercy area. In Spain, four basins—Ebro, Tage, Douro, and Vallès-Penedès—were particularly important for understanding mammal migrations. The United Kingdom, from Scotland in the north to the Isle of Wight in the south, also made a quite specific contribution.

The mammalian structure probably appeared among the therapsid reptiles at the end of the Triassic period. (The very first mammal to be identified as such, *Amphilestes,* was discovered as early as 1704 in the Mid-Jurassic Purbeck Beds of Stonesfield, Great Britain; in 1828, T.L. Phillips recognized the fossil as a *Triconodon.*) Nonetheless, throughout the Mesozoic (millions of years) primitive mammals were dominated by dinosaurs reptiles (whose diversity allowed them to occupy practically all ecological niches) and were confined to restricted areas. During this period, mammals showed very limited evolutionary capacities. With the beginning of the Cenozoic, however, mammals manifested a sudden and remarkable expansion.

Multituberculates (subclass Allotheria), including *Plagiaulax* (British Purbeckian), and *Neoplagiaulax* (Cernay, France), occupied the western European Paleocene, and were later replaced by rodents in the same ecological niche. This pattern is evidenced in Europe as well as in America.

The lower Theria (marsupial and placental mammals) are well represented in Great Britain by Pantotheria (*Spalacotherium,* from the Upper Jurassic of Wales, and *Amphitherium* from the Purbeck Beds of Stonesfield); in France and Belgium by Metatheria or Marsupials (Didelphidae *Didelphis* and *Peratherium*) from the Paleocene to the Oligocene (at Cernay, Montmartre, La Débruge, Quercy, Ronzon, La Limagne, Dormaal).

The Eutheria (placentals), which appear at the upper limit of the Mesozoic era, underwent a spectacular radiative diversification throughout the Cenozoic, constituting the most dominant element of the faunal assemblage. Primitive carnivores (Creodonta) include: *Arctocyon* (Upper Paleocene of La Fère), *Palaeonictis* and *Paroxyaena* (Lower Eocene of Quercy and Dormaal), *Quercytherium* (Upper Eocene of Euzet les Bains), *Proviverra* and *Propterodon* (Eocene of Egerkingen, Switzerland and Dormaal, Belgium).

Larger-brained fissipeds (carnivorans with separate toes, such as bears, badgers, and dogs) appear in the Lower strata of Quercy (Oligocene) with *Cynodictis;* the genus *Canis* appears in the Pontian and has been identified in the French Roussillon, in the Villafranchian at Val d'Arno (Italy), and at Mosbach and Mauer (Germany). *Alopeocyon* has been recovered from La Grive Saint-Alban, Sansan, and Göriach; *Pachycynodon,* from Quercy; *Hemicyon* from Sansan, Pontlevoy, Vallès-Penedès, Göriach, and Wintershof-West; *Vulpes* and *Ursus* occupy the middle latitudes during the European Late Pleistocene glaciations.

Mustelidae (weasels, martens, skunks, badgers) are represented by *Plesiogale* (Upper Oligocene–Lower Miocene), *Martes, Plesictis;* Viverridae (in the warm areas of western Europe) by *Stenoplesictis, Palaeoprionodon,* and *Herpestes* (Quercy Oligocene). Hyaenidae appear in the Late Oligocene, Vindobonian (Middle Miocene), or Pontian with *Nimravus* and *Eusmilus* (Quercy), *Crocuta, Ictitherium,* and *Euryboas* (at Perrier, Saint-Vallier, Senèze, Sainzelles, Mont Léberon, Val d'Arno, Villaroya); Felidae is represented by *Felis* (at La Grive), *Lynx, Machairodus* (at Eppelsheim), *Homotherium, Acinonyx,* and *Felis* (in the Villafranchian).

Pinnipedia (e.g., sealions, seals, and walruses), which are probably descendants from some undifferentiated canoid type, became adapted to marine life. They are represented in the western European Pliocene with *Trichicodon* and *Alachterium.* Phocidae (true seals), which were studied by van Beneden, are particularly abundant in Belgium with *Phoca* (from the Anversian or Middle Miocene on) and other genera *(Phocanella, Pristiphoca).*

The order of artiodactyls (hoofed, even-toed animals), is characterized by various adaptations for running—mainly modification of limbs, especially of the foot bones. The first artiodactyls (*Diacodexis* and *Protodichobune,* followed by *Metriotherium, Mixtotherium, Cebochoerus*) probably migrated through Morocco and Spain from central Africa. Fossils of these animals are found in the Upper Eocene formations of France (Quercy), Belgium, and Switzerland (Egerkingen).

Suidae (pigs) developed from an Asian origin during the Oligocene–Miocene period: they are present at St.-Gérand-le-Puy *(Palaeochoerus),* in the Vienna Basin Miocene (*Listriodon* and *Hyotherium*), and at the Italian Pontian of Monte Bamboli *(Sus).*

The group Bunoselenodontia (early ruminants) is particularly well represented in the Eocene–Oligocene formations throughout western Europe; featured are *Xiphodon, Haplomeryx, Dichobune, Amphimeryx, Dacrytherium, Tapirulus, Anoplotherium, Elomeryx, Anthracotherium,* and *Cainotherium.* Oreodonta were found at Eppelsheim (Pontian) with the genus *Dorcatherium.*

The infraorder Pecora was first identified with *Procervulus* (at Pont-Levoy, Loir et Cher, in the Orléans sands). It developed along three lines during the Late Oligocene–Miocene: (a) Cervoidea

(deer), such as *Lagomeryx, Amphitragulus, Dremotherium, Dicrocerus, Cervocerus, Procervus, Cervus, Rangifer, Palaeomeryx,* and *Megaceros;* (b) Giraffoidea (giraffes), especially in Spain with *Triceromeryx* (Upper Burdigalian of Manzanarès) and *Decennatherium* (Pontian of Guadalajara); (c) Bovoidea (ruminants with permanent hollow frontal horns), including: *Eotragus, Parabos* (in Montpellier and Perpignan), *Leptobos* (Senèze), *Bos* (Paris), *Myotragus* (Baleares Islands), *Megalovis,* prospered during Mio-Pliocene times before migrating to other continents during the Villafranchian.

Condylarthra (archaic ungulates) flourished in the Paleoce–Eocene and were especially abundant in North America and more so in South America, yet were relatively scarce in Europe: four genera should be mentioned: *Phenacodus, Pleuraspidotherium, Tricuspiodon* (at Cernay and Dormaal, Thanetian), and *Palaeotherium.*

Western European Proboscidea (elephants and their relatives) can be organized into three superfamilies: (a) Mastodontoidea were represented largely throughout the ancient world since the Mid-Miocene, with *Trilophodon* (Vindobonian, in Sansan and Simorre, France; Pontian in Eppelsheim), *Serridentinus* (France and Portugal), and *Tetralophodon* (Eppelsheim). *Anancus* can be found between 38 and 58 degrees north, from Great Britain and Portugal to Greece, especially in the Lower Pliocene Crag, and in the French and German Villafranchian; (b) *Deinotherium* (a large proboscidean that was incorrectly identified as a giant tapir by Cuvier, later as a hippo by Kaup, or as a rhino by Mayer, and finally as a sirenian by H.M. de Blainville) has been excavated from a number of Mio-Pliocene sites, including Schwabe (Eppelsheim) and Bavaria, Abstdorf (Moravia), Franzensbad (Bohemia), and Cantal department (France); (c) Elephantoidea extensively occupied western Europe from Villafranchian times all through the Pleistocene, from south England to the Iberic Peninsula, Italy, France, Germany, and the Danube Basin. Five different species have been established: *Elephas planifrons, meridionalis, trogontherii, primigenius* (some 20,000 specimens have been excavated), and *antiquus.* The most significant sites are in Great Britain (Upnor, Cromer Forest bed), France (Hte Loirein Solilhac, Chagny, Senèze, Lyon, Somme, and Seine terraces), Italy (San Pablo, Asti, Viterbe, Val d'Arno), and Germany (Mosbach, Sussenborn—second interglacial, Rixdorf, Weimar—third interglacial, Steinheim). An unusual dwarf form even was found on the Mediterranean islands (Malta, Sicily).

Fossil dugongs and seacows (Sirenia), characterized by their bulky body and adaptation to marine life, have been identified: *Halitherium* (Lower Oligocene–Lower Miocene) in the Mainz Basin (Germany), and *Halianassa* (Miocene), particularly abundant in the Loire estuary (France).

The order Perissodactyl (hoofed mammals distinguished by an odd number of toes) is represented by four superfamilies in the western European fossil fauna. (a) Equoidea: *Hyracotherium* is probably the most ancient genus (Lower Eocene) and gives evidence (also with *Coryphodon* and *Pachyaena*) for frequent migrations between North America and Europe during that time. Other genera have been identified through the Eocene epoch: *Palaeotherium* (Egerkingen, Vitry, Vaucluse), *Plagiolophus, Pachynolophus, Lophiotherium, Propalaeotherium, Anchilophus.* Mammal exchanges with North America resumed in the Lower Oligocene. *Anchitherium,* however, found its route to Europe only in the Miocene, 30 million years later. *Hipparion* (Pontian to Villafranchian) occurs frequently in western European forest facies, as in Villaroya (Spain) and Montpellier (south France); *Equus* (Villafranchian to Recent). (b) Chalicotheroidea (Oligocene–Pleistocene) occupy these same forest facies. The most important sites include: Sansan, La Grive St. Alban, Eppelsheim (Pontian), Neudorf March, and Nikolsburg (Moravia). (c) Rhinocerotoidea probably originated in Asia and after important migrations, invaded Europe in the Early Oligocene from North America. *Dicerorhinus* (Eppelsheim) demonstrates a remarkable stratigraphic series from Mid-Oligocene to Pleistocene and continues to be evident in Mid-Paleolithic times, but with only one species as it approaches extinction. *Aceratherium, Diceratherium, Brachypotherium, Chilotherium, Diceros,* and *Hispanotherium* are all limited to Pontian; *Coelodonta* survived into the Pleistocene (Abbeville, France). (d) Tapiroidea are present with three main genera: *Lophiodon* (Robiac and Minervois) and *Chasmotherium* in Mid-Eocene, replaced by *Tapirus* (Miocene–Pleistocene).

Pholidota (anteaters and pangolins) are found in Oligocene–Miocene period with *Necromanis* and *Leptomanis* (Quercy, France and Wintershof-West, Solenhofen, Bavaria).

Rodent genera constitute almost 10 percent of the total number of fossil mammals. Due to their rapid rate of evolution, their universal distribution, and their small size, they have proven to play an essential role in micropaleontology as stratigraphical indicators. The most ancient western European representatives are found in the Paleocene epoch, but the roots of the various families (Castoridae, Hystricidae, Dinomyidae, Sciuridae, Gliridae, and the ubiquitous Muridae) reach back to the Mesozoic era.

Insectivora are known from 125 various fossil genera. They belong mostly to the Soricidae (shrew) and Talpidae (mole) families and are present since the Eocene or possibly the Paleocene with *Adapisorex* (Cernay), *Saturninia* (Vaucluse), *Amphidozotherium,* and *Heterohyus* (Quercy). Oligocene formations have yielded *Geotrypus, Paratalpa,* and *Mygatalpa* (Auvergne), and *Palaeoerinaceus* and *Dimylechinus* (Allier).

Chiroptera (bats) occupied western Europe from late Eocene (Bartonian) times. They were studied best in the Quercy series of France or Soleure (or Solothurn, Switzerland). The most frequent representatives include *Palaeophyllophora, Pseudorhinolophus, Necromantis, Vespertiliavus,* and *Rhinolophus.*

Nonhuman Primates. Fossil primates have been recovered from more than 25 sites, ranging from Paleocene (Thanetian-Sparnacian) up to the Plio-Pleistocene limit (Villafranchian), that are located in France (Quercy, Sansan, Cernay, Montpellier, Saint-Gaudens), Germany (Eppelsheim, Württemberg), Switzerland (Egerkingen, Solothurn), Italy (Val d'Arno, Casino), Spain (Seo de Urgel, Vallès Penedès), Great Britain, the Netherlands (Tegelen), and Belgium (Dormaal). The fossil primate fauna available represents some 22 genera, belonging to the suborder of Prosimii, the Cercopithecidae, and the Pongids. The first discovery to be explicitly recognized—a *Pliopithecus*—was made in 1834 by E. Lartet in Sansan (Gers, France), only one year after the first identified fossil primate was recovered from the Siwaliks (India).

In the Late Paleocene–Early Eocene, the Prosimii—Lemurids, and Necrolemurids—occupied the large boreal continent (western Europe and North America), with identical or parallel genera recognized from east to west. The most ancient and likely ancestor of the group is *Teilhardina* (Dormaal, Belgian Sparnacian), later *Adapis* (very similar to the American *Notharctus*) and *Necrolemur*. After the European continental plate was isolated (Mid-Eocene), they developed their own process of evolution in the same physical and biological environment during the Late Eocene. *Adapis, Pseudoloris, Microchoerus, Caenopithecus,* and *Alsaticopithecus* are among the most important representatives. Anthropoids appeared in the Miocene of western and central Europe, with the cercopithecoids *Austriacopithecus* and *Semnopithecus,* and in the Pliocene, with *Mesopithecus* (Pontian) and *Dolichopithecus* (Early Pliocene-Villafranchian). *Pliopithecus* is a primitive catarrhine anthropoid that was first discovered in Sansan (France) and later at localities in France, Germany, and Austria. A related genus, *Epipliopithecus,* was described by Hurzeler from Neudorf (Slovakia).

Platyrrhini are a very special group of primates limited to South America, and thus are not found in western European layers. Among Catarrhini, Cercopithecids (Old World monkeys) are represented in western Europe with one single genus, *Macacus,* recognized in quite a number of Pliocene formations: Tegelen (Limburg, Netherlands), Val d'Arno (north Italy), Senèze (France), and quite a few pisolithic sites in Württemberg (Germany) associated with pongids and other mammals of the Pontian fauna of Eppelsheim.

Fossil pongids were discovered in western Europe from the Early Miocene (Burdigalian) up to the end of the Pliocene (Villafranchian). In Burdigalian times, indeed, the mammalian fauna was profoundly renewed, with the appearance of the first mastodons and cervids. The most ancient pongid to be present in this new assemblage is *Oreopithecus* (recovered by J. Hürzeler in 1957 from Monte Bamboli, near Grosseto in Tuscany, Italy; and more recently from Sardinia Island). *Dryopithecus,* exhibits a rather broad chronological and geographical extension: It has been discovered from the Upper Vindobonian to the Pontian, in Spain (Seo de Urgel), France (St. Gaudens, La Grive Saint-Alban), and Germany (Melchingen, Salmendingen, Trochtelfingen, Rhine Valley). It is remarkable that this genus was first described from the Siwaliks (India), thus providing further evidence for the subtropical climate of western Europe during this Mio-Pliocene period. *Hispanopithecus* (Vallès Penedès, Spanish Miocene), and *Paidopithex* (Eppelsheim, Upper Miocene) are two other more specialized pongid genera that probably adapted to particular environments.

Human Paleontology. The search for human origins and evolution has become a special and important chapter of paleontology. The term "Human Paleontology" was coined in 1853 by M. de Serres. Western Europe has played a very special role in this field for two main reasons: as early as 1829 the western European subcontinent yielded the very first human fossil remains *(Homo neanderthalensis).* After the publication of Charles Darwin's *Descent of Man* (1871), European scholars developed a special interest in human ancestry and established a tradition of scientific research in this area. Even after the discovery of more ancient stages of human evolution outside of Europe (Java, China, south and east Africa), European scholars remain active in the field, either initiating research or participating in expeditions launched by American, African, or Asiatic colleagues in remote sites.

The pioneers in this field are many: E. Dubois (discovery of *Pithecanthropus erectus* in 1891), J.K. Fuhlrott, B. de Perthes, P.C. Schmerling, E. Lartet, M. Boule, G.R. von Koenigswald (Trinil and Sangiran, Modjokerto, Java), J.L. Quatrefages de Bréau, L.L. de Mortillet, P. Teilhard de Chardin, and O. Zdansky (Zhoukoudian 1921–23), C. Arambourg (Ternifine, Algeria), J. Piveteau, A.T. Marston (Swanscombe), F. Weidenreich, H. Weinert, W.E. LeGros Clark, J. Kälin, J.R. Napier *(Homo habilis),* K. Oakley (who revealed the Piltdown-fraud made with *Eoanthropus dawsoni*), D. Garrod, and A.C. Blanc. More recently, L.S.B. and M. Leakey, Y. Coppens, J. Chaline (in Tanzania), B. Vandermeersch (in Palestine), and H. and M.A. de Lumley (Tautavel, southern France).

Human fossil remains earlier than *H. erectus* have not been recovered in western Europe. However, humans appeared as early as 1.3–1 million years ago at Chilac (Massif Central), Terra Amata (Nice, France), and Cullar de Baza (Granada, Spain), based on finds of very crudely manufactured tools. More abundant and convincing remains, dating to approximately 800,000 years ago, have been unearthed in France (Le Vallonnet, Roque-Brune) and Italy.

Dating between 780,000 and 200,000 years ago, the most ancient human fossil remains from western Europe (aff. *H. erectus*) are Atapuerca (near Burgos, Spain), Mauer (Germany), Vergranne (Jura), Boxgrave (southern England), Vertesszöllos (Hungary), Tautavel (south France), Swanscombe (Great Britain), and Steinheim (Germany).

Homo (sapiens) neanderthalensis (from approximately 100,000 years ago) has been found at quite a number of sites: in Germany (Ehringsdorf, Neandertal), Belgium (Spy, Engis, Sclayn, and Dinant), France (La Chapelle-aux-Saints, Le Moustier), Spain (Gibraltar), and Italy (Saccopastore, Monte Circeo).

The most noteworthy discoveries of *Homo sapiens sapiens,* that include their prehistoric environment (Upper Paleolithic tools, rock paintings, sculptures) were made in Les Eyzies, Dordogne (Cro Magnon), Grimaldi, Chancelade, Rouffignac, Lascaux (France), Willendorf (Germany), Altamira, and a few other places in Cantabric Spain. All date between 18,000 to 40,000 years old. The western European scholars involved in their discovery or study include D. Peyrony, L. Capitan, Henri Martin, H. Breuil, and A. Leroi Gourhan.

Fossil Collections in Western European Institutions

Institutes and museums throughout the world have accumulated precious documentation of paleontology from western Europe. Large collections of autochthonous fossils from western European sites, as well as fossil remains from elsewhere in the world, have been assembled by European expeditions and described by European scholars. The primary collections are housed in the British Museum of Natural History (London), the Muséum National d'Histoire Naturelle (Paris), the Museum für Naturkunde an der Humboldt-Universität (Berlin), and the Naturhistorisches Museum Senckenberg (Frankfurt). Smaller but more specific collections of local fauna can be found at a large number of smaller institutions, including the exceptional Solenhofener Plattenkalke fossils (Jura) in Eichstätt (Germany), the spectacular *Iguanodon* fauna (Wealdian) in Brussels, the Saint-Vallier faunal assemblage in Lyons, the Monte Bolca fishes in Monte Bolca (Verona, Italy), and the Monte San Giorgio fishes in Zürich. A unique collection of exceptionally well-preserved fossils recovered from the Lower Carboniferous is housed at the Centre Grégoire Fournier, in the Benedictine Abbey of Maredsous (Belgium).

EDOUARD L. BONÉ

Further Reading

Adam, K.D. 1975. *Die mittelpleistozäne Säugetier-Fauna aus dem Heppenloch bei Gutenberg.* Abhandlungen zur Karst und Hohlenkunde, D, 1. Württenberg: Blauberen.

Andrews, C.W. 1910. *Descriptive Catalogue of the Marine Reptiles of the Oxford Clay: Based on the Leeds Collection in the British Museum (Natural History).* Vol. 1. London: British Museum (Natural History).

Borradaile, L.A., L.E.S. Eastham, F.A. Potts, and J.T. Saunders. 1932. *The Invertebrates.* New York: Macmillan; Cambridge: Cambridge University Press; 4th ed., Cambridge: Cambridge University Press, 1961.

Buffetaut, E. 1987. *A Short History of Vertebrate Paleontology.* London and Wolfeboro, New Hampshire: Croom Helm.

Conway-Morris, S. 1979. The Burgess Shale (Middle Cambrian) fauna. *Annual Review of Ecology and Systematics* 10:327–49.

Denison, R.H. 1956. A review of the habitat of the earliest vertebrates. *Fieldiana, Geology* 11:359–457.

———. 1975. Evolution and classification of placoderm fishes. *Breviora* 432:1–24.

Desmond, A. 1982. *Archetypes and Ancestors: Palaeontology in Victorian London, 1850–1875.* London: Blond and Briggs; Chicago: University of Chicago Press, 1984.

Galton, P.M. 1974. The ornithiscian dinosaur *Hypsilophodon* from the Wealden of the Isle of Wight. *Bulletin of the British Museum (Natural History), Geology* 25:1–152.

Gingerich, P.D. 1977. New species of Eocene primates and the phylogeny of European Adapidae. *Folia Primatologica* 28:60–80.

Jaekel, O. 1915–16. Die Wirbeltierfunde aus dem Keuper von Halberstadt. *Palaeontologische Zeitschrift* 2:88–214.

Jarvik, E. 1980. *Basic Structure and Evolution of Vertebrates.* Vols. 1 and 2. London and New York: Academic Press.

Jones, S., R. Martin, and D. Pilbeam (eds.). 1992. *The Cambridge Encyclopedia of Human Evolution.* Cambridge and New York: Cambridge University Press.

Kuhn-Schnyder, E. 1974. Die Triasfauna der Tessiner Kalkalpen. *Neujahrsblatt der Naturforschenden Gesellschaft Schaffhausen Zuerich* 176:1–119.

Kurtén, B. 1968. *Pleistocene Mammals of Europe.* London: Weidenfeld and Nicholson; Chicago: Aldine.

Lillegraven, J.A., Z. Kielan-Jaworowska, and W.A. Clemens (eds.). 1979. *Mesozoic Mammals: The First Two-thirds of Mammalian History.* Berkeley: University of California Press.

Macdonald, D.W. 1984. *The Encyclopedia of Mammals.* London: Allen and Unwin; New York: Facts on File.

McGowan, C. 1983. *The Successful Dragons: A Natural History of Extinct Reptiles.* Toronto and Sarasota: Samuel Stevens; 2nd ed., as

Dinosaurs, Spitfires, and Sea Dragons, Cambridge, Massachusetts, and London: Harvard University Press, 1991.

Moy-Thomas, J.A. 1939. *Palaeozoic Fishes.* London: Methuen; New York: Chemical; 2nd ed., with R.S. Miles, London: Chapman and Hall, 1971; Philadelphia: Saunders, 1971.

Ostrom, J.H. 1985. The meaning of *Archaeopteryx.* In M.K. Hecht, J.H. Ostrom, G. Viohl, and P. Wellnhofer (eds.), *The Beginnings of Birds.* Willibaldsburg, Eichstätt: Freunde des Jura-Museums Eichstätt.

Padian, K. (ed.). 1986. *The Beginning of the Age of Dinosaurs: Faunal Changes across the Triassic-Jurassic Boundary.* Cambridge and New York: Cambridge University Press.

Patterson, C. 1964. A review of Mesozoic acanthopterygian fishes, with special reference to those of the English chalk. *Philosophical Transactions of the Royal Society, London,* ser. B, 247:213–482.

Peyer, B. 1950. *Geschichte der Tierwelt.* Zurich: Büchergilde Gutenberg.

Sigogneau-Russell, D. 1979. Les champosaures Européens: Mise au point sur le Champosaure d'Erquelinnes (Landénien Inférieur, Belgique). *Annales de Paléontologie Vertébré* 65:93–154.

Sudre, J. 1978. *Les Artiodactyles de l'Eocene Moyen et Supérieur d'Europe occidentale (systématique et évolution).* Mémoires et travaux de l'Institut de Montpellier, 7. Montpellier: Institut de Montpellier.

Turner, C., and R.G. West. 1968. The subdivision and zonation of interglacial periods. *Eiszeitalter und Gegenwart* 19:93–101.

von Hune, F. 1926. The carnivorous Saurischia in the Jura and Cretaceous formations principally in Europe. *Revista Museo de La Plata* 29:35–167.

von Meyer, H. 1845–60. *Zur Fauna der Vorwelt.* Vol. 2, *Die Saurier des Muschelkalkes, mit Ruecksicht auf die Saurier aus buntem Sandstein und Keuper.* Frankfurt am Main: Schmerber.

Walker, A.D. 1968. *Protosuchus, Proterochampsa,* and the origin of phytosaurs and crocodiles. *Geological Magazine* 105:1–14.

EVOLUTIONARY NOVELTY

Oftentimes, a group of animals will evolve a new feature that appears to have a dramatic effect on its evolution. Take, for example, limbs. Fishes have fins, all other vertebrates have limbs. Limbs first appear in the Devonian (about 370 million years ago) and are associated with the invasion of land by amphibians. Limbs are often called "evolutionary novelties" because they were a newly evolved structure that enabled their possessor to invade new environments. Novelties also can be associated with large increases in the diversity of the groups that possess them. The 3.5-billion-year history of life on Earth has seen the origin of many important evolutionary novelties. Examples include the origin of cellular organelles in the Precambrian, the origin of heads in the Cambrian, and of feathers in the Jurassic.

How do novelties arise in evolution? One metaphor that is of great help in understanding the evolution of novelty is François Jacob's notion of "tinkering" (Jacob 1977). Evolution, according to Jacob, does not act like an engineer. An engineer typically works according to a preconceived plan that is specifically designed for its current use. Videotape, for example, was not derived from celluloid film. In evolution, on the other hand, new features are not produced from scratch. Evolution is like a tinkerer. New features arise from the modification of existing ones: bird feathers are modified scales, and tetrapod limbs are modified fins. Therefore, the name "novelty" is a bit of a misnomer. Novelties are not altogether new; they arise by changing existing features of organisms. This notion of tinkering implies that an understanding of evolutionary history is important if we are to understand the mechanisms by which novelties evolve.

Understanding how novelties arise in evolution often involves understanding how they arise in embryological development (Raff 1996). In reality, it is not structures themselves that are modified during evolution; it is the genetic and developmental processes forming them that have actually changed. As a consequence of this, one important form of "tinkering" is to change the way that organisms develop. Each organism inherits genes that specify the recipe to build its body. These genes are activated at different times and different places as the animal develops from an embryo to an adult. The body plan of an organism arises through a complex interaction of numerous genes that are active in different places within the embryo. Any small change in these genes can lead to a change in the structure of the organism. So-called homeotic mutants are examples of how extensive this change can be (Raff 1996). Homeotic mutations are simple genetic shifts that cause a change in the position where structures develop. In one famous homeotic mutation of the fruit fly *Drosophila,* legs develop where antennae usually form. This is a particularly dramatic example of how a single genetic shift can yield a novelty in the organism's body plan. Not all genetic shifts are this major; some can cause minor changes in the way that organisms develop.

One historically important view of the evolution of novelty was that of recapitulation (Gould 1977). Many classical comparative anatomists subscribed to the notion that organisms progress through their evolutionary history during normal development. Mammals, for instance, will go through a stage in their early development in which they resemble fishes in possessing gill slits and other primitive features. This notion of recapitulation was later contradicted when comparative and experimental embryologists found instances in which evolution did not happen in this fashion. One key example is the case of a creature that evolves to look like the juvenile of its ancestor. Typically, larval salamanders have a host of aquatic features such as external gills and fleshy tails. These features are lost when the larva metamorphoses into a more terrestrial adult. Some species of salamanders are fully aquatic as adults, however. These adults resemble the juveniles of other salamanders in that they retain fleshy tails and external gills, among other features. This is a case in which a novel way of life evolved by the truncation of normal development.

The salamander example reveals one of the most fundamental ways in which new features arise: novelties often emerge by a change in the timing of developmental events. This process, known as heterochrony, has been invoked to explain the evolution of novel structures, behaviors, growth strategies, and biochemical processes (McKinney and McNamara 1991). Broadly speaking, there are two major results of heterochrony. The first of these results is descendants that look like juveniles or larval stages of their ancestors. The other major result is descendants that possess features that are exaggerated versions of those seen in ancestors. The former result is known as pedomorphosis; the latter, peramorphosis. Pedomorphosis can be produced by a truncation or slowing of normal development. In a hypothetical example of truncation, an ancestor that normally undergoes five stages of development (A-B-C-D-E) produces an offspring that undergoes only three stages (A-B-C). The adult of this creature will remain at stage C and will look like an intermediate stage of its ancestor. This same result could be obtained if the descendant evolved at a slower developmental rate. If the developmental rate was sufficiently lowered, then the descendant species might be smaller or look more juvenile than its ancestor. One famous (if controversial) example is human evolution. Adult humans and adult chimpanzees do not look much alike: brain and body weight ratios, proportions of the body, and the shape of the face are markedly different. These differences are minimized when humans are compared with juvenile chimpanzees. These similarities, coupled with the fact that humans have a greatly extended childhood, have suggested to some scholars that pedomorphosis is an important part of human evolution (Gould 1977). This conclusion is controversial because human growth and development is not only slower than that of chimpanzees, it appears to be extended in places as well (McKinney and McNamara 1991).

Peramorphosis can be viewed as the opposite of pedomorphosis. In this case evolution proceeds by an extension or acceleration of normal development. One result of these shifts is that the descendant will possess features that are exaggerated or larger than those seen in its ancestor. Interestingly, if peramorphosis has happened in a lineage, one might be able to detect a pattern of evolution that looks much like the recapitulation that classical biologists described.

Heterochrony often produces one of the most important types of "tinkering" observed in the fossil record: changes in body size. Changes in the size of organisms can produce a variety of correlated effects that have important influences on their functional anatomy and ecology. The relationship between a property of an organism and its size is known as allometry. Many features of organisms are either directly or indirectly related to size: the shape of the skeleton, the heart rate, life span, and home range are but a few examples (Calder 1984). Novel designs in evolution are often produced by shifts in the proportion and size of structures. Galileo Galilei was one of the first to observe that many novel designs are associated with a shift in size. The upper leg bone (femur) of an elephant looks little like that of a mouse. An elephant's femur is oval in cross section and is broad and flat, while that of a mouse is rounded and more elongate. This comparison suggests that as terrestrial animals increase in mass, their bones must change in shape to meet the constraints imposed by gravitational forces. A mouse cannot be scaled up to the same size as an elephant—its legs would break if the femur did not change in shape. These changes in size

and proportion can be produced developmentally either by peramorphosis or by pedomorphosis.

Evolutionary novelties often appear to arise by a shift in the function of an existing feature, rather than by shift in size, proportion, or development. Charles Darwin described this phenomenon as "preadaptation." The shift in the function of a feature can open whole new pathways of evolution (Bock 1959). Fingers appear to be an example of a structure in which a change in function was at least as important as a change in development or proportion during its evolution. Fingers typically are associated with life on land; primitive amphibians use fingers for support as they walk on land. Some of the earliest-known amphibians have fingers, but they appear to be fully aquatic. Likewise, one extinct group of fishes has fingerlike structures in its fin paddle. These discoveries suggest that fingers (or fingerlike structures) originally evolved in aquatic animals. The major step in the early evolution of fingers was a functional shift from being used to propel an animal in water to being used to help walk on land. Functional shifts like this one can set the stage for whole new pathways of change and are often used to explain major shifts in evolution.

Shifts in function are not limited to structural evolution: similar concepts can be applied to evolutionary changes at the genetic level. Molecular biologists recently have made some surprising discoveries about the genetic basis of evolutionary change (Raff 1996). Vastly different anatomical structures in different creatures often employ similar genes during development. The genetic signals that are involved in the development of the wing of a fly are exceedingly similar to those involved in the formation of the leg of a mouse. Furthermore, many of these genetic signals are not limited to these organs: they appear to be involved in the formation of other aspects of the body plan as well. This observation implies that one of the major process in the evolution of novelty is the evolutionary cooption (or recruitment) of existing genes to make new structures. The genes involved in wing or leg development originally evolved to make other structures. It appears likely, therefore, that tinkering at the genetic level ultimately produced many of the structures that living organisms have evolved over the past 600 million years.

NEIL H. SHUBIN

See also Adaptation; Allometry; Growth, Development, and Evolution; Growth, Postembryonic; Heterochrony; Homology; Molecular Paleontology; Speciation and Morphological Change

Works Cited
Bock, W.J. 1959. Preadaptation and multiple evolutionary pathways. *Evolution* 13:194–211.
Calder, W.A. 1984. *Size, Function, and Life History.* Cambridge, Massachusetts: Harvard University Press; London: Dover, 1996.
Gould, S.J. 1977. *Ontogeny and Phylogeny.* Cambridge, Massachusetts: Harvard University Press.
Jacob, F. 1977. Evolution and tinkering. *Science* 196:1161–66.
McKinney, M.L., and K.J. McNamara. 1991. *Heterochrony: The Evolution of Ontogeny.* New York: Plenum.

Raff, R. 1996. *The Shape of Life*. Chicago: University of Chicago Press.

Further Reading

Calder, W.A. 1984. *Size, Function, and Life History*. Cambridge, Massachusetts: Harvard University Press; London: Dover, 1996.

Gould, S.J. 1977. *Ontogeny and Phylogeny*. Cambridge, Massachusetts: Harvard University Press.

Jacob, F. 1977. Evolution and tinkering. *Science* 196:1161–66.

McKinney, M.L., and K.J. McNamara. 1991. *Heterochrony: The Evolution of Ontogeny*. New York: Plenum.

Raff, R. 1996. *The Shape of Life*. Chicago: University of Chicago Press.

EVOLUTIONARY THEORY

For many people, the terms "evolution," "theory of evolution," and "evolutionary theory" are synonymous and interchangeable. They are not, and the distinction is a profound one.

Evolution—the idea that organisms change through time, with ancestral species giving rise to descendent species, and with all life arising from a common origin—is an established fact that is the foundation of all modern biology. Evolution is as well corroborated as the idea that the earth orbits the sun, matter is composed of atoms, or that germs can cause disease. The "theory of evolution" is at least as secure as the theory of a heliocentric solar system, atomic theory, or germ theory.

The concept of evolution predates the nineteenth-century writings of Charles Darwin and was not particularly controversial prior to Darwin's time. What Darwin did was to introduce a soulless mechanism—natural selection—that explained evolution and the origin of species. Natural selection is a theory, a *model* that explains the *fact* of evolution. When people talk about the "theory of evolution," they often are really talking about the "theory of evolution by natural selection." By conflating a theory of evolution (natural selection) with the fact of evolution (organic change through time), the public is led to believe that evolution is "just a theory" and that it is controversial and unproven. Nothing could be farther from the truth.

A theory itself is not a lesser order of truth. Theories do not grow up and become "laws." A law is simply a formal statement about the nature of the universe and reality (e.g., the law of gravity). A theory is an explanatory model (e.g., gravitational theory) that is invoked to explain a law or other observed fact. Some models are admittedly rather hypothetical, such as the idea that hominids evolved bipedal locomotion to exploit an expanding savanna habitat. Other models, such as natural selection, are highly corroborated through strong circumstantial evidence and through the observations and results of natural and artificial experiments.

Evolutionary theory is that body of information that seeks to explain the fact of evolution in all its complexity. Natural selection occupies only a small (albeit important) corner of evolutionary theory.

There are numerous other theories of *selection,* some of which are extensions of natural selection and others which are quite independent. *Natural selection* mainly concerns the differential reproductive success of superior individuals in competition for scarce resources. A related theory, *sexual selection,* seeks to explain many features and behaviors as ones that arise simply through competition for mates (e.g., long tail feathers in some male birds). Features that arise through sexual selection can reduce overall fitness (it is harder to fly with long tail feathers) but paradoxically increase reproductive fitness. Another related theory, *kin selection,* explains altruistic behavior (such as a bee eater bird helping to provision his younger siblings) as a means of propagating one's genes through helping close relatives (who share a good many genes with their benefactor). *Neutral theories of selection* (genetic drift, founder effect, evolutionary bottlenecks) posit that selection can at times be quite random, with profound consequences for future generations. Various theories of selection are invoked at, and only at, particular hierarchical levels. There are theories of selection that operate on the genetic and cellular level and that seek, among other things, to explain why 97 percent of human DNA is noncoding "junk." Other theories operate at the level of the individual (natural and sexual selection), the group or population (group selection), and the species (species selection). Theories operating above and below the level of the individual are more controversial and harder to prove or invalidate.

Evolutionary theory concerns much more than selection. Whether they are paleontologists or neontologists (that is, biologists concerned with extinct or with living organisms, respectively), evolutionary biologists have much more on their mind.

When a fossil is found, a paleontologist must be able to identify it in order to make proper comparisons. This may be easy or difficult, depending on how complete the specimen is and how easily diagnosed it is. For example, many theropod furculae (wishbones) look very much like gastralia (belly ribs). Once the fossil is identified there there are many kinds of analyses that can be applied to it in order to extract useful information.

Homology

For appropriate comparisons to be made with other organisms, a fossilized element must be accurately homologized with elements of other organisms. *Homology* is a concept that is crucial to most analyses of evolutionary relationships and for tracing morphological transformations: it is the search for true correspondence between structures or features. How one defines a "true" correspondence is something of a muddle. Similarity, owing to inheritance from a common ancestor, is currently the most popular basis for declaring homology between two structures or features. However, there are several other definitions that may be used (Roth 1988). There are many tests for homology (e.g., detailed structural correspondence, similar topological relationships, morphocline analysis, similar developmental patterns) none of which is foolproof and none of which can be applied in all situations. Much argument in paleontology revolves around questions of homology. Continuing an example introduced above, most paleontologists agree that the furcula of birds is homologous with the left and right clavicles of other tetrapods. However, a minority camp argues that the furcula is a neomorph (newly evolved structure) that is not homologous with the clavicle. The opposite of homology is *homoplasy* (false resemblance). This can arise through convergence, parallelism, and evolutionary reversal. For example, the marmosets of South America are the only primates to have claws (a primitive mammalian feature). Comparisons with living and fossil primates (all of whom have nails) demonstrate that the presence of claws in these monkeys is an evolutionary reversal. Thus, by the criterion of common ancestry, the claws of marmosets cannot be homologous with the claws of primitive placental mammals (even though they are structurally indistinguishable).

Variation

If all features of an organism were characteristic and invariant, there would be no problem in assigning an element to a species or in telling one species from another. However, such a world exists only in the imagination, for all organisms vary and without *variation* there would be no evolution. Both *phenotypic* variation (variation in morphology, behavior, physiology, etc.) and *genotypic* variation (variation in the genetic code) are fundamental aspects of biology and are inextricably linked with each other (in a roundabout way), but only phenotypic variation can be recognized in the fossil record (since DNA can last only a short time after burial and only in exceptional circumstances). Without understanding the extent and limits of variation it is all too easy to split one species into several or to lump several species into one.

Normal variation (the scatter about the mean) is probably the most prevalent type of variation, but others need to be taken into account. Temporal variation is the variation that occurs through time, and this can be considerable in a continually evolving lineage. Age-related variation relates, of course, to the differences between adults and juveniles. *Polymorphism* is the existence of multiple types within a population (e.g., white tigers versus orange tigers). *Polytypism* is the existence of separate populations with different characteristics (in other words, subspecies). Other types of variation are highly patterned and reflect an organism's behavior and habits. The most important of these is variation due to sexual dimorphism: differences between males and females in size and morphology. Other kinds of variation seen in living populations—multiple reproductive morphs, multiple trophic morphs, environmentally determined morphs—are unlikely to be recognized in a fossil context. There always will be controversies about whether a new and unusual specimen represents a new species or is merely a juvenile, a hitherto unrepresented sex, a temporal variant, a mere subspecies, or just a statistical outlier. However, simply asking such questions is a vast improvement over outdated typological thinking in which the first, or type specimen, was the only true reference point.

Variation can inform one about the evolutionary process. Increases in variation can mark the transition from one species to another in a gradually evolving lineage, as has been documented in fossil horses (MacFadden 1992). Increased variation can indicate a loosening of selection, perhaps related to decreased importance of a structure.

Identifying, homologizing, describing, and assigning a fossil is only the beginning of an evolutionary analysis. Most investigators want to know how the fossil worked. This is the realm of *functional morphology* and *biomechanics*. Functional morphologists seek to infer the meaning behind morphology. For example, an animal with an elongate hind limb in which the distal elements are disproportionately lengthened and which shows a reduction in the number of toes along with fusion of ankle bones and metatarsals (instep bones) can be indicative of a running or hopping mode of locomotion. This is an example of a "form-function" correlation. Frequently, modern analogues are used to reduce the number of multiple working hypotheses. Features (or creatures) without modern analogues, such as the clawed, gorilla-like herbivore *Chalicotherium* (a relative of the horse) are so strange as to confound attempts to reconstruct its habits. Specialists in biomechanics take an engineering approach to morphology, reconstructing forces, stresses, strains, masses, and movements of ancient bodies and body parts. Biomechanical analysis reveals that *Tyrannosaurus* was nowhere near as fleet-footed as the one depicted in the movie *Jurassic Park* (Farlow et al. 1995).

Adaptation

Functional analysis may or may not lead to a hypothesis regarding the adaptive significance of a feature. *Adaptation* is often very easy to speculate about and very difficult to prove. First of all, many features are nonadaptive (Gould and Lewontin 1979). Some features apparently arise for no reason at all. This may apply to the fused frontal bones of tarsiers and anthropoids (the "higher" primates). All other primates retain the separate left and right frontal bones of primitive placental mammals. A minority of humans do have separate left and right frontal bones and they function normally. Other nonadaptive features may develop as an architectural necessity arising from adaptive changes going on elsewhere. For example, the central hollow axis of a gastropod shell (used as a brood chamber in some species) is a necessary byproduct of torsion (Gould 1996). Still other nonadaptive features may just be the result of genetic "piggybacking" (e.g., the enlargement of a sesamoid bone in the panda's foot being a nonadaptive effect of adaptive pleiotropic enlargement of a sesamoid bone in the panda's hand to create a new "thumb") (Gould 1980).

A feature may have arisen purely through sexual selection, and its function may be simply to attract members of the opposite sex and/or ward off rivals of the same sex. Other features may simply be recognition devices that allow individuals to identify *conspecifics* (members of the same species). Many features have multiple adaptive roles. The "sails" that extend from the dorsal midline of some pelycosaurs, theropods, sauropods, and ornithopods may have been used for both display and thermoregulation.

Current adaptation may not reflect initial adaptation, and therefore a feature may have arisen for other than obvious reasons. To cite a somewhat overworked example, the feathers of birds initially arose not for flight, but probably for insulation. Rudimentary and vestigial structures, such as the tiny hind limbs of the archaeocete whale *Basilosaurus,* would certainly either have lost all function or would have been used very differently from their fully developed antecedents.

At the opposite extreme, features may not easily betray their immediate use because they are slow or unable to shake off signs of their previous use. Optimal design is often hindered because a structure designed for one role is not easily or quickly commandeered for a different role ("heritage versus habitus"). The aardwolf, a hyaenid that specializes in eating termites and insect larvae, still has the skull of a carnivore, albeit one with unusually weak teeth. If it were known only from fossils, one would never guess its preferred food. Historical constraint is a pervasive theme throughout life's history, for evolution can only work with what is available, with only the occasional neomorph or evolutionary reversal for assistance.

Adaptation is best demonstrated by repeated events of convergent evolution that create analogous or homoplastic morphologies. Long, toothless or nearly toothless snouts and powerful front limbs armed with long claws are a sure sign of a specialized diet of ants and termites. This suite of features has arisen in spiny anteaters (echidnas), numbats (marsupial anteaters), New World anteaters, giant armadillos, pangolins, and aardvarks. One must, however, use this line of reasoning cautiously. Similar lifestyles can be achieved through very different means (e.g. flamingos, and the pterosaur *Pterodaustro* both filter(ed) plankton but use very different oral apparatuses), and similar morphologies need not always imply similar habits (e.g., the horny beaks of leatherback turtles chomp jellyfish while the horny beaks of hadrosaurs cropped vegetation).

Novelty

While the study of adaptation to some extent addresses the question of how new features arise, there is much more to this central issue of evolutionary theory. There are many roads to *novelty,* and these are well documented in the fossil record.

One such route already discussed is *exaptation,* the recruitment of an old structure or feature to take on a new function (Gould and Vrba 1982). This is probably the most common route taken in the history of life. For example, the first anal fin ray of poeceliids (live-bearers that include guppies) is modified to form an intromittent organ for internal fertilization. Any structure is a potential candidate for modification, whether it is initially adaptive or nonadaptive.

Serially repeating and segmental structures (also known as serially homologous structures) are prime candidates for recruitment. The built-in redundancy of a repeated series of identical or near-identical elements invites some to be modified while retaining the original function of the remainder. The example cited above serves to illustrate; the remaining anal fin rays of poeceliids still serve in their original role as fin supports.

Redundancy of any kind serves as the raw material for evolutionary modification. In advanced cynodonts (the group of mammal-like reptiles closest to mammals) a new jaw joint (the dentary-squamosal) developed alongside the old jaw joint (quadrate-articular). Both functioned side-by-side for a time. Eventually, however, in at least three mammalian lineages, the old jaw joint became miniaturized, detached itself from the lower jaw, and took on an exclusively acoustic function as ear ossicles. The dentary squamosal joint then became the only jaw joint of mammals (Gould 1996).

In rare instances, new features can arise from nowhere—*de novo evolution.* The dorsal fins of ichthyosaurs and whales have no precursors. The pteroid bone of pterosaurs and the calcar of bats, structures that support the wing membrane, are also brand new structures.

When new features and structures arise, how do they fit in to maintain a functioning organism? In some cases, a good deal of modification is necessary in surrounding areas to maintain an integrated whole. The massive bony shells of armadillos, glyptodonts, turtles, and some placodonts do not rest on primitively constructed spines, ribs, and limb girdles. These have been extensively modified to support, and to allow the animal to function beneath, the protective "roof." In other cases, profound changes can occur without affecting anything nearby. This results in *mosaic evolution,* in which parts of an animal evolve at different rates. The highly modified and expanded teeth of the docodont mammal *Haldanodon* are implanted in what is otherwise a very conservative skull (Lillegraven and Krusat 1991). The radically modified hind limbs of the first hominids were surmounted by a basically chimplike head.

Some investigators try to ferret out the proximate mechanisms behind morphological changes seen in the fossil record. These investigations focus on genetic, developmental, and ontogenetic (growth) explanations for alterations in morphology. Tremendous progress has been made in the past two decades identifying those regulatory genes and gene products that are critical for determining spatial patterning and cell differentiation. Genes that determine head from tail, belly from back, left from right, and proximal from distal have been identified and experimentally manipulated. Alterations in developmental timing (heterochrony) and sequence have been implicated in many major structural alterations. Juvenilization (pedomorphosis) and hypermaturation (peramorphosis) have affected many taxa and lineages, causing significant changes in adult morphology (Kluge 1988). Deletions, insertions, and inversions of developmental steps also have been important (as in the insertion of elaborate larval stages in the development of advanced insects). The extension or truncation of postnatal growth trajectories (allometry) are simple means by which to alter size, proportions, and surface characteristics. Theoretically, these developmental changes can be a response to natural selection or they can occur spontaneously and be a driving force for evolutionary change. As an example, the earliest and most primitive coelacanth fish, *Miguashaia,* has a second dorsal fin that is soft and supported by numerous rays. All later coelacanths have a fleshy lobe-shaped second dorsal fin that is a near duplicate of its lobe-shaped paired fins. Evidently a "homeotic" mutation occurred that extended the domain of a regulatory gene from the paired fins to the second dorsal fin. Here genetics seems to have driven evolution instead of the other way around.

Speciation

Morphological change is closely tied to speciation. When two animal populations have diverged sufficiently in morphology, physiology, or behavior, this is inevitably accompanied by reproductive isolation—and that, in a nutshell, is what defines a species. Evolutionary biologists are concerned with many aspects of speciation.

How rapidly does speciation occur? There is no general response to this question because speciation rates vary enormously. Speciation can be very rapid during adaptive radiations following a mass extinction or after invasion of an unoccupied habitat. In a mere 12,000 years, a single ancestral cichlid fish species that invaded newly formed Lake Victoria diversified into approximately 300 different species of widely different habits including scale biters, eye biters, mud suckers, algae scrapers, and rapacious pursuit predators.

Although it is still controversial, it seems likely that radical morphological change can take place in a single generation. We know from the fossil record that primitive sharks all had five gill openings. Two modern sharks, *Hexanchus* (the six-gilled shark) and *Chlamydoselachus* (the seven-gilled or frilled shark) have added additional openings along with accompanying skeletal supports, muscles, nerves, and blood vessels. There is no way to gradually evolve additional gills—a sudden mutation must have added an additional element or two to a serially repetitive sequence. While the first individual could not have been reproductively isolated, its distinguishing characteristic could have quickly spread through a small local population, leading to eventual reproductive isolation. The history of life is littered with structures that are "either/or" propositions that would necessarily have to have evolved in instantaneous fashion (e.g., the predentary bone of ornithischian dinosaurs).

Rates of change—fast or slow—can be smooth or can be jumpy; in other words, *tempo* can vary. Gradualism—steady change through time—has been documented in several lineages of Eocene mammals from Wyoming. Punctuated equilibrium—rapid change followed by long periods of stasis—has been inferred for some hominids such as *Australopithecus afarensis*. An intermediate pattern, punctuated gradualism—periods of slow evolution interspersed with spasms of rapid change—is also a possibility, although it is more difficult to document.

Speciation gets even more complex when one incorporates considerations of *pattern.* A single species may transform into a daughter species in what is called anagenetic or straight-line evolution. In this case one arbitrarily selects a point where one species ends (a pseudo-extinction) and the other begins. An ancestral species may split into two daughter species in what is known as a cladogenetic event. Finally, an ancestral species can "bud off" one or more daughter species but continue to persist unchanged. During an adaptive radiation, speciation is so rapid (geologically speaking) and resolution so concomitantly poor that all you can reconstruct is a spray of daughter species arising from some unknown ancestor. Any evolving lineage is likely to be complex, bushy, and characterized by varying rates, tempos, and patterns at different times and different places.

Analysis of speciation extends to ultimate causes. What is the driving force behind speciation events? Many factors are held responsible for speciation—geographic isolation, rebound from mass extinctions, invasion of new habitats, climate change, new food resources, fragmentation of ecosystems—to name a few. However, pinpointing the cause or causes is often difficult or impossible for long extinct lineages and ecosystems.

Extinction and Survival

Speciation has its antithesis: *extinction.* Although it involves death, this is a very lively area of study for evolutionary biologists. It has long been recognized that there are two major types of extinction: mass extinction and normal, or background, extinction. During normal times species appear and blink out at relatively steady and equable rates leading to a stable level of diversity. Causative agents for background extinction could include competition from other species, climate change, and vegetation change. During mass extinctions, which occur at intervals of tens of millions of years, many lineages disappear, and global diversity crashes. The cataclysms that underlie mass extinction have been a highly publicized subject of investigation. Meteor impacts, massive releases of carbon dioxide from the ocean bed, vulcanism, rises and drops in continental elevation and sea level, continental collisions and fissioning, climatic change, and numerous other agents have been held partly or wholly responsible for any number of these global catastrophes.

If background and mass extinction have causative factors, then so must survival. What enables some species and lineages to survive while others perish? While this is an even more difficult question to investigate, it seems that it helps to be (1) small, (2) generalized in diet and habit, and (3) widely distributed. Dumb luck, however, might be the overriding factor in mass extinctions. Some species and lineages seem to be remarkably long-lived. One family of diapsid reptiles, the choristoderes, extend from the Permian to the Eocene, and in the process it weathered two major mass extinctions and several minor ones. One modern genus of ray-finned fishes, *Amia,* has survived unchanged for 80 million years. Are these taxa special in some way or are they just lucky? After all, if (as has been argued) chance of extinction follows a bell-shaped curve, then some taxa are going to occupy the tail end of the distribution.

Diversity, Disparity, and Evolutionary Trends

Extinction and origination rates are not uniform through time or among taxa. As a result, global *diversity,* morphological diversity, and taxonomic diversity vary widely but with detectable patterns. For example, when a major adaptive threshold has been reached, there often follows a major period of experimentation and an adaptive radiation characterized by maximum *disparity.* Disparity is an assessment of the number of radically different body plans present. The earliest tetrapods and the earliest mammals were very disparate internally, even though, externally, they would have looked like overgrown salamanders and rats, respectively. During the Cambrian (540–515 million years ago) all 35 modern animal phyla and probably a like number of extinct phyla originated in a burst of creativity. Within each phylum diversity was low, but disparity (as measured by the number of unique body plans) was never greater. After the initial period of experimentation, the number of body plans is whittled down to a few surviving lineages, each of which then diversifies to fill the available ecospace (Gould 1989).

Taxonomic diversity can be low throughout a lineage's existence (e.g., aardvarks). It can be high early on and then decrease (e.g., perissodactyls or odd-toed ungulates), or it can be low at first and then increase (e.g., teleosts or higher bony fishes). These patterns are often depicted in "spindle diagrams" plotting diversity against time.

Morphological diversity, which is only indirectly related to taxonomic diversity, can be assessed in many ways. One might assess morphological diversity on the basis of the total number of locomotor adaptations, dietary adaptations, niches occupied, body size range, or any other criterion chosen. One might base one's assessment on how many adaptive zones are occupied or how finely each adaptive zone is partitioned.

Initial disparity that is subsequently whittled down with the surviving lineages diversifying is an example of an *evolutionary trend*. Other trends have come under scrutiny in recent years and have either been supported, modified, or falsified. Cope's Law states that average body size in a lineage increases over time (for a number of presumed adaptive reasons). This has recently been shown not to be true for molluscs (Jablonski 1997). It most likely holds true for dinosaurs, however. Similarly, it has been suggested that the earliest members of all major lineages are small. This certainly seems to be true for basal mammals, primates, and birds, to name a few. It does not seem to hold true for basal tetrapods, amniotes, and turtles. Other trends would seem to be (1) the development of a "head" region in metazoan phyla (multicellular animals); (2) the elaboration and differentiation of mouth parts, limbs, and gills in many metazoan phyla; (3) the differentiation and specialization of body segments in segmented metazoans; and (4) the simplification of the skull in numerous tetrapod lineages. It remains to be seen how "robust" each of these observations will turn out to be.

Systematics

A major focus of evolutionary studies is *systematics,* or how animals are related to each other. A subspecialty is taxonomy, which concerns the naming of taxa and their placement in the proper hierarchical level. There have been many schools of systematics, but today the field is dominated by cladistics (Charig 1982). Cladistics seeks to group taxa on the basis of shared-derived character states. For example, mice, platypuses, and humans are united by the possession of hair and mammary glands, shared-derived character states of mammals. We also all possess five-digit hands and feet. This character state does not unite us, however, because it evolved much earlier, in early tetrapods. Five-fingered extremities are simply shared-primitive character states and are not informative.

Cladistics differs from older traditional methods (called evolutionary systematics), in a number of ways. A cladistic analysis seeks to construct a cladogram, which is simply a nested set of ever more closely related taxa. It seeks only to identify "sister taxa." Tra-

ditional methods construct phylogenetic trees, which are explicit statements specifying direct ancestors and direct descendents. While seemingly more detailed, a phylogenetic tree is much more difficult to prove.

Most cladists eschew the time element in their analysis. Because of the patchiness of the fossil record it is quite possible to find a primitive form higher in the stratigraphic record than a more derived relative. Traditional methods use time as one means of establishing a phylogeny.

Cladistics does not recognize "key adaptations" as a basis for classification. Therefore, birds, with their many derived character states (feathers, endothermy) do not constitute a separate class (as traditional methods call for) but are merely a subset of coelurosaurian theropods.

Cladistics identifies and names only *monophyletic groups* (clades). A monophyletic group is an ancestor or ancestral lineage and *all* its descendants. "Birds" is a monophyletic group but "reptiles" is not. This is because some reptiles are more closely related to mammals than to other reptiles and because the traditional use of the term "reptiles" does not include birds. The term "amniote" has replaced "reptile" in cladistic parlance because the ancestral amniote gave rise to all "reptiles," birds, and mammals, constituting a monophyletic group. Traditional methods recognize both monophyletic groups and *paraphyletic groups* (grades). Paraphyletic groups, such as "reptiles," represent a level of organization and constitute a group held together by shared primitive character states and the absence of derived character states—exactly the opposite of cladistic methods.

Cladistic taxonomy strives to precisely reflect cladistic relationships. Traditional taxonomy strives for stability, even if this does not precisely reflect phylogeny. Cladistic taxonomy tends to be unstable, inconsistent, and almost impossible for a nonspecialist to comprehend. The same taxon, for example "mammals," will be used differently by different workers depending on where they determine the cutoff for mammals is. One also finds different names applied to the same monophyletic group. Cladistic taxonomy is unstable because cladograms are unstable. A few recoded character states is often enough to shuffle the taxa on a cladogram, rendering old names obsolete and requiring the old names to be redefined or new names to be imposed. It quickly becomes impossible to follow the changing labels.

Cladistics is a powerful tool that has introduced rigor and repeatability into what was once a subjective exercise. It has cleared up many formerly muddy phylogenetic questions. Nevertheless, it is not a panacea. Often human error creeps into an analysis due to bias in character selection and subjectivity in coding character states. It is often difficult to establish "character polarity," that is, to distinguish between primitive and derived character states. Rampant convergence, parallelism, and evolutionary reversal often bedevils attempts to establish homology between character states, which is necessary for accurate analysis. Finally, cladistics performs very poorly in certain situations. It does not do well in analyzing closely related taxa or taxa with a continuous fossil record (another method called stratophenetics is useful in the latter instance). In such cases the difference between two species is often a statistical one (e.g., different means in overlapping frequency distributions).

Cladistic analysis depends on abrupt breaks between character states. It cannot handle, or handles poorly, variable characters that might express several character states for a single species.

Paradoxically, cladistics works best between distantly related taxa or when the fossil record is poor or patchy with large gaps between related taxa. The patchiness of the fossil record imposes gaps that are necessary to create the abrupt breaks between character states that facilitate an analysis.

MICHAEL K. DIAMOND

See also Adaptation; Allometry; Coevolutionary Relationships; Diversity; Evolutionary Novelty; Evolutionary Trends; Extinction; Faunal Change and Turnover; Growth, Development, and Evolution; Heterochrony; Homology; Paleobiogeography; Selection; Speciation and Morphological Change; Systematics; Variation

Works Cited

Charig, A.J. 1982. Systematics in biology: A fundamental comparison of some major schools of thought. *In* K.A. Joysey and A.E. Friday (eds.), *Problems of Phylogenetic Reconstruction.* London and New York: Academic Press.

Farlow, J.O., M.B. Smith, and J.M. Robinson. 1995. Body mass, bone "strength indicator," and cursorial potential of *Tyrannosaurus rex. Journal of Vertebrate Paleontology* 15:713–25.

Gould, S.J. 1980. *The Panda's Thumb: More Reflections in Natural History.* New York: Norton; Harmondsworth: Penguin, 1983.

Gould, S.J. 1989. *Wonderful Life: The Burgess Shale and the Nature of History.* New York: Norton; London: Hutchinson Radius, 1990.

Gould, S.J. 1996. Creating the creators. *Discover* 17 (10):42–54.

Gould, S.J., and R.C. Lewontin. 1979. The spandrels of San Marco and the Panglossian paradigm: A critique of the adaptationist programme. *Proceedings of the Royal Society of London,* ser. B, 205:581–98.

Gould, S.J., and E. Vrba. 1982. Exaptation: A missing term in the science of form. *Paleobiology* 8:4–15.

Jablonski, D. 1997. Body-size evolution in Cretaceous molluscs and the status of Cope's rule. *Nature* 385:250–52.

Kluge, A.G. 1988. The characterization of ontogeny. In C.J. Humphries (ed.), *Ontogeny and Systematics.* New York: Columbia University Press; London: British Museum (Natural History).

Lillegraven, J.A., and G. Krusat. 1991. Cranio-mandibular anatomy of *Haldanodon exspectatus* (Docodonta; Mammalia) from the Late Jurassic of Portugal and its implications to the evolution of mammalian characters. *Contributions to Geology, University of Wyoming* 28:39–138.

MacFadden, B. 1992. *Fossil Horses: Systematics, Paleobiology, and Evolution of the Family Equidae.* Cambridge and New York: Cambridge University Press.

Roth, V.L. 1988. The biological basis of homology. *In* C.J. Humphries (ed.), *Ontogeny and Systematics.* New York: Columbia University Press; London: British Museum (Natural History).

Further Reading

Benton, M.J. 1990. *Vertebrate Paleontology.* London and Cambridge, Massachusetts: Unwin Hyman; 2nd ed., New York: Chapman and Hall, 1997.

Carroll, R.L. 1997. *Patterns and Processes of Vertebrate Evolution.* Cambridge: Cambridge University Press.

Futuyma, D.J. 1979. *Evolutionary Biology.* Sunderland, Massachusetts: Sinauer; 3rd ed., 1998.

Jablonski, D., D.H. Erwin, and J.H. Lipps (eds.). 1996. *Evolutionary Paleobiology.* Chicago: University of Chicago Press.

EVOLUTIONARY TRENDS

The fossil record reveals a broad range of patterns, many of which have been called evolutionary trends. A trend is defined as a pattern of directional change over time. The phrase "evolutionary trend" describes a situation in which some trait of a lineage, species, or clade tends to change in a particular direction over geologic time as the result of evolutionary processes (a clade is the group including all descendants of a common ancestor). Commonly cited examples of evolutionary trends include increases in body size and complexity of metazoans (multicellular animals) over their history. While a trend is often easy to identify, the processes generating it are not always so evident.

Occasionally, patterns arise in the fossil record that are not truly evolutionary trends. For example, there are three-parted medusoids (a stage in the life cycle of jellyfishes) known from the Vendian, four-parted medusoids known from the Ordovician, and some five-parted medusoids known today. While this is an interesting pattern, it cannot be accurately described as a trend. Jellyfishes do not fossilize well; this sampling bias denies us adequate information to know that this pattern resulted from an evolutionary process. Occasionally, other patterns do not meet the criteria of an evolutionary trend, but are identified as such in the paleontological literature. Therefore, they deserve brief mention. The acquisition of a series of characters along a branch of a phylogenetic tree (i.e., diagram of ancestor-descendant relationships) and the patterns of parallel and convergent evolution (e.g., the multiple evolution of flightlessness in insular species of beetles or the numerous times that eyes, jaws, and gills have evolved) are often termed trends. These are meaningful patterns, but they do not illustrate the key factor of sustained directional change through time.

In order to clarify the discussion of evolutionary trends, we can distinguish between two broad categories. The single most important distinction is the *phylogenetic breadth* over which the trend is observed. A directional change in some measurable character can occur within a single evolving lineage (anagenetic) or within a clade (cladogenetic). Cladogenetic trends can be broken down further into passive (those that are driven by increases of variance) and active (those that result from sorting mechanisms).

Anagenetic Trends

Sustained directional change of a feature along an unbranching lineage constitutes an anagenetic trend. Figure 1 shows body size through time for two closely related lineages, A and B. Lineage A displays an increasing trend while Lineage B exhibits stasis.

Anagenetic trends are caused by the action of an evolutionary process on a heritable character. The well-studied case of "industrial melanism" in the peppered moth, *Biston betularia,* is an example of an anagenetic trend in gene frequency. Increased industrialization, and with it pollution that blackened the tree bark on which moths land, generated selective pressures against light-colored moths; predators could see light-colored moths more easily against the dark bark. This brought about a directional change in the frequency of the gene controlling moth coloration, resulting in a populational shift from light to dark. As a counter example, consider increasing human height in industrial countries over the past 200 years. Dietary changes would appear to be a better explanation for this shift than evolutionary processes such as natural selection, genetic drift, or gene flow.

Shifting our focus to the fossil record, anagenetic trends are not commonly preserved. However, there are some nice examples

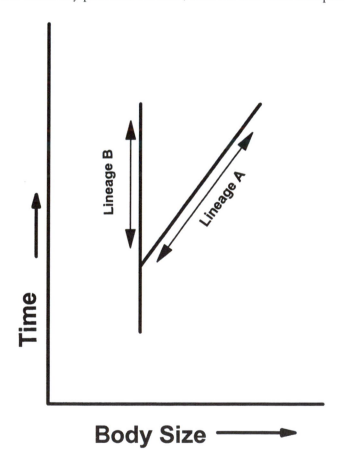

Figure 1.

that do show sustained directional change in unbranching lineages. B. Malmgren and J.P. Kennett (1981) studied fossils of planktonic foraminifera that had accumulated on the deep sea floor over an 8-million-year period. With excellent time resolution, they were able to trace a single unbranching lineage, *Globorotalia,* through five different named forms. They found that some characters (e.g., mean number of chambers) showed an anagenetic trend. R.P. Sheldon (1987) documented anagenetic trends of increasing pygidial rib number during a 3-million-year interval in eight separate lineages of benthic trilobites. These two studies were both based on uncharacteristically well preserved records and a large sample size. Although a number of examples of anagenetic trends are found in the fossil record, their relative rarity illustrates what may be a general pattern of evolution: anagenetic trends usually occur over relatively short periods of geological time. This observation is central to the theory of punctuated equilibrium.

Cladogenetic Trends

Cladogenetic trends are larger scale and more complex phenomena than anagenetic trends. When a clade is considered as a whole over geologic time, trends in clade-level characters may be observed. A clade-level character is any aspect of a clade that can be measured (e.g., the minimum, mean, or maximum of a trait such as body size or complexity). Two types of cladogenetic trends exist, passive and active (*sensu* Wagner 1996). *Passive* trends are those that directly result from changes in variance of the character being considered, and thus, the initial morphologies are maintained. *Active* cladogenetic trends are derived from a variety of sorting mechanisms, and initial morphologies tend to be replaced by subsequent morphologies.

Passive trends were characterized by S.M. Stanley (1973) in his reassessment of Cope's Rule, which states that body size increases over time. Stanley reasoned that a diversifying clade can only increase in body size since there is a minimum size below which it would be impossible to evolve. As illustrated in Figure 2, the diversification (or branching) leads to an increase in variance of the distribution of body sizes. By itself, diversification would not lead to any change in the mean body size of the clade. It is the instance of an ancestor arising near the lower boundary that causes the distribution, and therefore the mean, to be skewed upward over time. S.J. Gould (1988) has argued that passive trends are predominant in the history of life. And indeed, good examples of passive trends abound. J.T. Bonner (1965) showed that living organisms as a whole have increased in maximum body size, J.W. Valentine and colleagues (1994) documented an increasing trend in maximum metazoan complexity, and S.J. Gould (1988) provided evidence for an increase in both mean and maximum body size of planktonic foraminifera from the Cretaceous to the Tertiary. In each case, the original condition is maintained throughout the life of the clade.

Active trends are generated by one or more various sorting mechanisms such as differential rates of speciation, differential rates of extinction, or morphological constraints. Continuing with the example of body size, these three mechanisms are illustrated in Figures 3, 4, and 5. Figure 3 shows how differential spe-

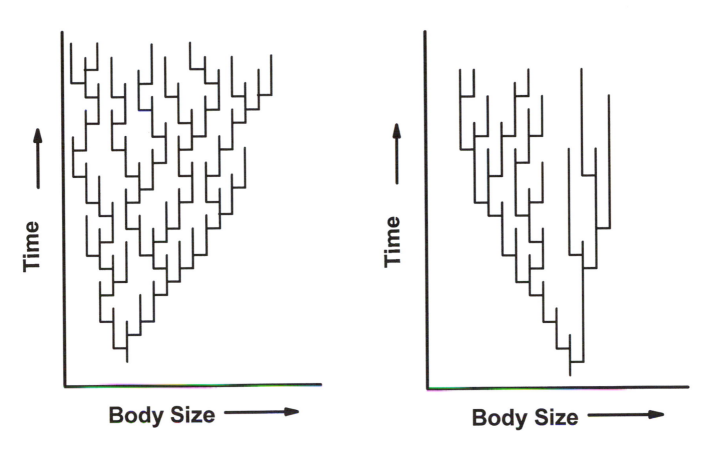

Figure 2.

Figure 3.

ciation rates result in a cladogenetic trend. Lineages with smaller body size speciate much more rapidly than large-bodied lineages, resulting in a trend toward smaller average body size. Compare this with differential extinction rates as illustrated in Figure 4. Lineages with smaller body size are preferentially eliminated relative to large-bodied lineages during an extinction event (dotted line). This results in a cladogenetic trend toward increased average body size of the clade. Another sorting mechanism that controls the expression of morphologies in various parts of the clade is morphological constraint. Figure 5 presents an example in which both small- and large-bodied forms are constrained to produce even larger bodied forms, causing a cladogenetic trend toward greater body size.

An example from P.J. Wagner (1996) will help to clarify the interplay among these three mechanisms. His investigation of the shell morphology of Paleozoic gastropods was framed in an explicit phylogenetic context, allowing him to pose and test hypotheses concerning the causes of observed trends. He sought to understand which mechanisms were responsible for an increase in spire height. He found that morphological constraint among high-spired species limited the generation of descendant species with lower spires. Interestingly, differential extinction, during one period of faunal turnover in the Middle Ordovician, also played a key role in the upward trend in spire height. No support was found for the hypothesis that differential speciation contributed to this trend.

A Note on Progressive Evolutionary Trends

At first glance, the existence of evolutionary trends may imply that progress is part of the history of life. Progress in organismal evolution would mean that organisms have become better with time. As there is no going back in time, the question is largely unanswerable. Yet, it remains a popular idea. The fossil record provides evidence that is interpreted both to support and refute the hypothesis of progress. S.D. Cairns (1987) proposed that hydrozoans of the family Stylasteridae have undergone gradual progressive evolution toward optimal feeding efficiency and enhanced polyp protection throughout the Cenozoic. Another suite of examples of sustained, progressive trends toward improved design in bryozoans was offered by F.K. McKinney and J.B.C. Jackson (1989) in their discussion of bryozan growth forms. In contrast, P.T. Crimes and M.A. Fedonkin (1994) found no evidence for a trend toward optimal foraging strategy in the record of trace fossils throughout the Phanerozoic. Gould (1985) took a theoretical approach to the question and concluded that evolutionary progress has yet to be demonstrated. In this view, the effects of natural selection within a population cannot be extrapolated to explain long-term evolutionary patterns. Consider a popular example of progressive evolution, the development of the large human brain. The human brain is useful to us in our daily lives and has most likely been the subject of selective pressures toward greater capacity. However, the human

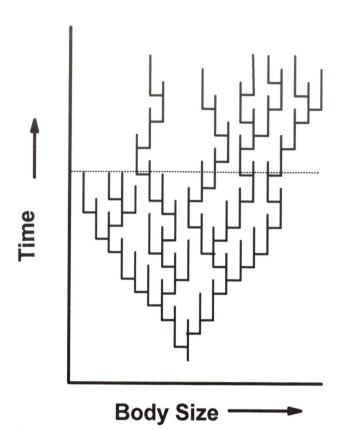

Figure 4.

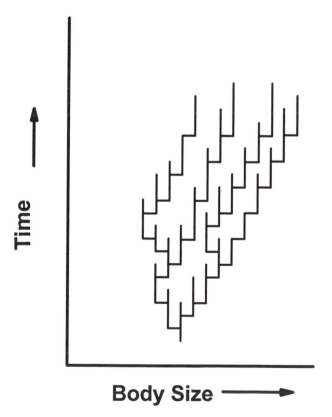

Figure 5.

brain may not make our species any less likely to become extinct or more likely to speciate than other species with smaller brains, or no brains at all. Whether one is inclined to argue for or against the existence of progressive evolutionary trends, one should be aware that an assessment of progress requires a value judgment and is thus extremely difficult to apply without bias. In evaluating the human brain, it may be especially important to consider the source.

ALLEN G. COLLINS

See also Adaptation; Allometry; Coevolutionary Relationships; Diversity; Evolutionary Novelty; Extinction; Faunal Change and Turnover; Growth, Development, and Evolution; Heterochrony; Homology; Paleobiogeography; Selection; Speciation and Morphological Change; Systematics; Variation

Works Cited

Bonner, J.T. 1965. *Size and Cycle: An Essay on the Structure of Biology.* Princeton: New Jersey: Princeton University Press.

Cairns, S.D. 1987. Evolutionary trends in the Stylasteridae (Cnidaria, Hydrozoa). *In* J. Bouillon, F. Boero, F. Cicocgna, and P.F.S. Cornelius (eds.), *Modern Trends in the Systematics, Ecology, and Evolution of Hydroids and Hydromedusae.* Oxford: Clarendon Press; New York: Oxford University Press.

Crimes, P.T., and M.A. Fedonkin. 1994. Evolution and dispersal of deep-sea trace. *Palaios* 9:74–83.

Gould, S.J. 1985. The paradox of the first tier: An agenda for paleobiology. *Paleobiology* 11:2–12.

———. 1988. Trends as changes in variance, a new slant on progress and directionality in evolution. *Journal of Paleontology* 62:319–29.

Malmgren, B.A., and J.P. Kennett. 1981. Phyletic gradualism in a late Cenozoic planktonic foraminiferal lineage; DSDP Site 284, southwest Pacific. *Paleobiology* 7:230–40.

McKinney, F.K., and J.B.C. Jackson. 1989. *Bryozoan Evolution.* Boston: Unwin and Hyman; London: University of Chicago Press, 1991.

Sheldon, P.R. 1987. Parallel gradualistic evolution of Ordovician trilobites. *Nature* 330:561–63.

Stanley, S.M. 1973. An explanation for Cope's Rule. *Evolution* 27:1–26.

Valentine, J.W., A.G. Collins, and C.P. Meyer. 1994. Morphological complexity increase in metazoans. *Paleobiology* 20:131–42.

Wagner, P.J. 1996. Contrasting the underlying patterns of active trends in morphologic evolution. *Evolution* 50:990–1007.

Further Reading

Gould, S.J. 1988. Trends as changes in variance, a new slant on progress and directionality in evolution. *Journal of Paleontology* 62:319–29.

McKinney, F.K., and J.B.C. Jackson. 1989. *Bryozoan Evolution.* Boston: Unwin and Hyman; London: University of Chicago Press, 1991.

McNamara, K.J. (ed.). 1990. *Evolutionary Trends.* Tucson: University of Arizona Press; London: Belhaven.

Nitecki, M.H. (ed.). 1988. *Evolutionary Progress.* Chicago: University of Chicago Press.

Wagner, P.J. 1996. Contrasting the underlying patterns of active trends in morphologic evolution. *Evolution* 50:990–1007.

EXOSKELETAL DESIGN

A majority of extant marine invertebrates lack hard preservable skeletons; the ability to secrete skeletal material developed about 550 million years ago, prior to which only soft-bodied creatures (which arguably can be regarded as invertebrates) constituted the late Precambrian Ediacara fauna (Glaessner and Wade 1966; Seilacher 1985). Animals with mineralized skeletons of calcium carbonate, calcium phosphate, or silica are the most readily preserved. Nonmineralized skeletons, composed simply of organic material such as chitin, are only preserved under exceptional preservational conditions such as in the Burgess Shale of Canada (Whittington 1980).

Exoskeletons are designed to protect the animal from external physical and biological forces, to provide attachment surfaces for muscles, and to retain the shape of the individual animal. Additionally, the shell of some brachiopods has minute, tissue-containing perforations (puncta) that hold up to 50 percent of the animal's soft tissue (Peck 1992). This arrangement frees space in the mantle cavity for the feeding organ.

A fundamental pattern in metazoans (multicellular animals) is the development of either solitary or modular (colonial) organization, both of which are seen in some of the first animals to secrete calcareous skeletons, the Cambrian archaeocyathids. The modular forms of this group are now regarded as aspiculate calcareous sponges. These colonies were the first reef builders, producing small reef mounds (bioherms) on hard substrates with massive branching and encrusting growths that could spread across large areas. The basic archaeocyathid structure is a two-walled inverted cone. Water was drawn in at the sides; it passed through the tissue sandwiched between the inner and outer walls and finally expelled in an upward direction by means of passive flow. As with corals, the living tissue was restricted to the upper parts of the skeleton (Wood et al. 1992).

Other sponges have a spicular skeleton, although in one type, the stromatoporoids, the spicules are largely fused into laminae (layers). Spicules may be composed of organic collagen-like protein, silica, or calcium carbonate and form internal skeletons, providing a varying degree of rigidity to the animal's basically sack-like form. As in the archaeocyathids, more typical sponges take in water at the sides, but the water is actively expelled upward through a central opening called an osculum.

Although the brachiopods are solitary, other lophophorates (animals with feeding arms) are colonial. One important lophophorate phylum is the Bryozoa. These colonial animals affix themselves to hard substrates or the shells of other animals. Some are encrusters while other "creeping" forms stay low to the surface. Some erect forms assume a simple twiglike shape, while other colonies grow in a complex fashion to form leafy, bushy, netlike, and screw-shaped skeletons. Some, such as the trepostomes, were massive. Individual bryozoan animals are called "zooids." They may inhabit boxlike calcareous "zooecia" arranged along the colony's branches. Stoloniferous bryozoans, in which the zooecia are connected to a common tube, or stolon, do not usually have a calcareous skeleton.

Graptoloids were colonial hemichordates that were abundant during the Paleozoic. While most species were bottom-dwelling, bushy forms, the less diverse pelagic (open water) species were humerically dominant and are stratigraphically more important. Graptoloid colonies ("rhabdosomes") show a complex geometrical symmetry. Many appear to have propelled themselves vertically through the water column by slowly gyrating. Other colonies may have drifted passively. In some taxa, descent through the water column was slowed by disc-shaped skeletal extensions or by weblike sheets of thin periderm. Slow descent is thought to have enhanced feeding efficiency in these filter feeders.

Most colonial corals belong to the rugose, tabulate, and scleractinian subclasses. Morphology varies from massive to lacy. Solitary forms are typically horn-shaped, but some were discoidal or cylindrical. Rugose corals of the family Goniophyllidae were pyramidal or slipper-shaped, and the individual corallites (polyp chambers) were covered by a lid, or operculum.

This design of a "cone with a lid" is also found in hyoliths, rudist bivalves, and gemmellaroiid brachiopods; the first is free-swimming, but the other groups have specialized adaptations to reef-type environments. The basic design of a bivalve mollusc is of two equal valves that form mirror images and are hinged along the dorsal margin (the back edge of the shell); a brachiopod, however, consists of two differently shaped valves, commonly hinged at the posterior (rear of the shell) and with the plane of symmetry perpendicular to the place where the two valves join.

Among the molluscs that form only one shell (univalved) the most important fossil groups display a coiled conch. The gastropods have a basic helicoidal form, while coiled nautiloids and most ammonoids were planispiral. The heteromorph ammonoids of the Cretaceous assumed widely varying shapes; some of these species may have been pelagic, but most are thought to have been nektobenthic (near-bottom). The behavior of ammonoids has often been compared to that of the extant *Nautilus,* which practices slow vertical ascents and descents. Some ammonoids with heavily ornamented, ponderous shells were probably slow-moving bottom huggers, but other kinds, such as the streamlined "oxycones," were much swifter.

The echinoderms, with their five-rayed symmetry, possess skeletons of porous calcite plates with tube feet connected to the unique water vascular system. The sessile pelmatozoans include cystoids, blastoids, and the extant crinoids (feather stars, sealilies). The basic design is a theca containing the main soft parts, which is attached to the seabed by a stem and holdfast. Sessile crinoids, with arms extending upward, were abundant in the past, but today mobile feather stars have become important in shallow seas. The eleutherozoans, which includes starfishes and brittle stars, are all mobile and all have five long, thin, flexible arms. The design of echinoids varies from the globular, strongly spined tests of sea urchins to the burrowing, bilaterally symmetrical and delicately spined heart urchins and flat sand dollars.

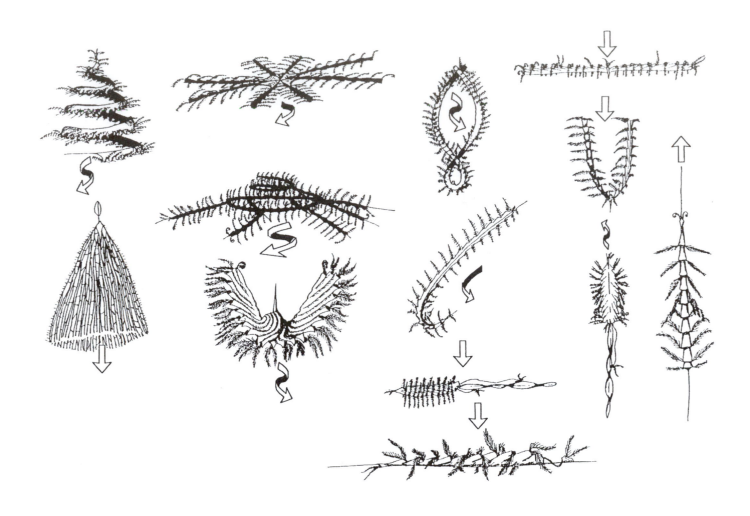

Figure 1. Graptolite architectures related to vertical feeding descents through the water column. *Arrows* indicate either spiral or linear motion. From Underwood (1993), by permission of Scandinavian University Press.

Arthropods can only grow in size by molting their exoskeletons. Until the new exoskeleton hardens, the animal is vulnerable. Arthropods are primitively segmented, and each segment bears a pair of appendages. This segmentation is apparent in trilobites, despite some fusion in the cephalon (head shield) and pygidium (tail shield). Stocks like the smooth illaenids are segmented only at the thorax. Crabs have lost segmentation in their carapace (shells) but, like trilobites, possess a preservable skeleton. The many arthropod groups that possess only a lightly hardened organic cuticle are rarely preserved as fossils; the Burgess Shale and the earlier Cambrian Chengjiang faunas show a diversity of arthropods, from trilobites (both with and without mineralized exoskeletons), crustaceans, and forms with unusual body plans that now are grouped with onychophores *(Aysheaia),* armored lobopods *(Hallucigenia),* and stem group arthropods *(Opabinia, Anomalocaris)* (Budd 1996).

The last three are transitional groups that are closely related to extant arthropods. The onychophores combine arthropod features with those of annelids (segmented worms). Worms lack exoskeletons, but some annelids do construct dwelling tubes from carbonate (serpulids) or cemented sand grains (sabellids).

ANTHONY D. WRIGHT

See also Aquatic Invertebrates, Adaptive Strategies of; Defensive Structures: Invertebrates; Feeding Adaptations: Invertebrates; Ornamentation: Invertebrates; Skeletized Organisms and Tissues: Invertebrates

Works Cited

Budd, G.E. 1996. The morphology of *Opabinia regalis* and the reconstruction of the arthropod stem-group. *Lethaia* 29:1–14.

Bulman, O.M.B. 1970. Graptolithina, with sections on Enteropneusta and Pterobranchia. *In* C. Teichert (ed.), *Treatise on Invertebrate Paleontology.* Part 5, *Graptolithina, with Sections of Enteropneusta.* 2nd ed., Boulder, Colorado, and Lawrence, Kansas: Geological Society of America and University of Kansas.

Glaessner, M.F., and M. Wade. 1966. The late Precambrian fossils from Ediacara, South Australia. *Palaeontology* 9:599–628.

Kirk, N.H. 1969. Some thoughts on the ecology, mode of life and evolution of the Graptolithina. *Proceedings of the Geological Society of London* 1659:273–92.

Peck, L.S. 1992. Body volumes and internal space constraints in articulate brachiopods. *Lethaia* 25:383–90.

Seilacher, A. 1985. Discussion of Precambrian Metazoans. *Philosophical Transactions of the Royal Society of London* B311:47–48.

Underwood, C.J. 1993. The position of graptolites within Lower Palaeozoic planktic ecosystems. *Lethaia* 26:189–202.

Whittington, H.B. 1980. The significance of the fauna of the Burgess Shale, Middle Cambrian, British Columbia. *Proceedings of the Geologists' Association* 91:127–48.

Wood, R., A. Zhuralev, and F. Debrenne. 1992. Functional biology and ecology of the Archaeocyatha. *Palaios* 7:131–56.

Further Reading

Glaessner, M.F. 1984. *The Dawn of Animal Life: A Biohistorical Study.* Cambridge and New York: Cambridge University Press.

Gould, S.J. 1989. *Wonderful Life: The Burgess Shale and the Nature of History.* New York: Norton; London: Hutchinson Radius, 1990.

Murray, J. (ed.). 1985. *Atlas of Invertebrate Macrofossils.* Harlow: Longman, for the Palaeontological Association; New York: Wiley.

EXTINCTION

Extinction is the ending of a biological lineage or groups of lineages making up a species. Successful reproduction and survival of young to sexual maturity ends, population size falls to zero, and a species disappears. If this species is the only member of a genus or a higher taxonomic group—a family, order, or class—its passing could cause one or more of the higher taxonomic categories to be lost.

Since the earliest days of scientific study of geology and the fossil record, scientists recognized that the evolution of Earth's continents and ocean basins and the life-forms in them did not follow paths of constant change. Abrupt changes in fauna (animal life) and flora (plant life) documented in the fossil record served as convenient places to draw boundaries between units of the geological timescale. Thus, the loss of dinosaurs (other than birds) from the terrestrial record, the disappearance of some conspicuous groups of marine invertebrates including the ammonites (relatives of the modern chambered nautilus, a fist-sized, coiled-shelled animal), and a major regression of the world's oceans provided practical criteria for drawing a boundary to mark the end of the Cretaceous and the beginning of the Tertiary.

Scholars' early attempts to delineate the geological timescale prompted vigorous debates concerning the reality of extinction of species. Did the disappearance of organisms from the then-known fossil record actually document the extinction of species? Were the species of dinosaurs found in the Mesozoic strata of Europe, well-known to early natural scientists, still flourishing in some other area of the Earth? Could their apparent loss simply reflect changes in their geographic ranges, restricting the species to unsampled areas? The question of the reality of the extinction of species was addressed late in the eighteenth century when Georges Cuvier, a leading French scientist, demonstrated that the bones of Ice Age (Pleistocene) mammoths found in western Europe represented an extinct lineage closely related to but distinct from those of the living African and Indian elephants. By that time, scientists had reached many remote areas of the world, and the probability that mammoths or other large animals known only from the fossil record still survived in some remote region was greatly reduced. Natural history surveys of the nineteenth century and related studies confirmed the reality of extinctions of lineages of prehistoric animals and plants.

Currently, it is estimated that more than 99.9 percent of all species that ever lived on Earth are now extinct (Raup 1991). This statistic, based on counts and estimates of the diversity of biota (all living things) throughout Earth history, does not distinguish between two types of extinction phenomena: lineage extinctions and pseudoextinctions. "Lineage extinctions" are extinctions of biological lineages; they occur at different times and at varying frequencies and continue to be a major process contributing to the evolution of Earth's biota. For example, the fossil record of organisms that lived near the end of the Cretaceous Period (70 million years ago) tells of rich marine faunas (animals) in which ammonites were abundant. On land in western North America, great herds of duck-billed dinosaurs *(Edmontosaurs)* and the rhinolike *Triceratops* provided food for *Tyrannosaurus rex* and other carnivorous or scavenging dinosaurs. About 65 million years ago, the ammonites, as well as *Edmontosaurus, Triceratops, Tyrannosaurus,* and other lineages of dinosaurs (except for birds), died out and left no direct descendants. All are examples of lineage extinctions.

The second type of extinction is "pseudoextinction," the loss of a distantly related group that is ancestral to a later species. Consider the very well documented history of the horse family, the Equidae (MacFadden 1992). This is one of the most frequently cited examples of the evolution of a major group of vertebrates. Its oldest known member, the *Hyracotherium* (sometimes called *Eohippus,* or "dawn horse"), was a diminutive, multitoed inhabitant of tropical forests almost 60 million years ago. *Hyracotherium* included the common ancestor of the members of all the species referred to as *Hyracotherium.* It also included the common ancestor of *Orohippus,* the next member of the equid family tree. In the jargon of modern classification techniques, *Hyracotherium* is a "paraphyletic genus"—it includes its common ancestor, the "founder," and some (but not all) of the common ancestor's descendants.

Orohippus is followed by such genera as *Miohippus, Merychippus,* and *Dinohippus,* ultimately leading to today's genus, *Equus,* which includes modern horses, zebras, asses, and closely related species. Each of these genera are distinguished by various morphological characters. The fossil record of the lineage clearly documents increase in body size, loss of toes, and other significant morphological changes. Like *Hyracotherium,* each of these are a paraphyletic genera. And, except for *Equus,* all are now extinct.

But how real are these extinctions? They did not mark the end of the equid lineage. As the animals evolved, they changed enough to become new species, as determined by taxonomy, the system of recognizing and naming groups of organisms. The line remained intact; the only things that changed were the names. As a result, a loss of paraphyletic groups owing to the forces of evolutionary change within a lineage is termed pseudoextinction.

If both lineage extinctions and pseudoextinctions are considered, as they are in most current analyses, most of the species that once existed on Earth are now extinct. A biologically significant but still unknown statistic is the relative proportions of these two types of extinctions. Currently, paleontologists are debating whether distinguishing between the two would modify their interpretations of the patterns and processes of extinction significantly.

Evaluations of the severity and patterns of extinction cannot be based on direct, uncritical readings of our current knowledge of the fossil record. Many Earth scientists have noted that the rock and fossil records resemble a poor grade of Swiss cheese, with extensive voids and little substance. Sedimentary rock deposits, which contain most of the fossil record, are intermittent, episodic, and are not formed continuously. Additionally, the chances of any particular organism contributing to the fossil record are minuscule. Most organic remains are broken down and recycled through the activities of many carnivores and scavengers, as well as through natural decay. In general, fossilization occurs only when the remains of organisms are removed rapidly from the areas in which they lived and are protected by burial in other environments. In addition, only a small part of fossil-containing strata are exposed at the surface, where they can be sampled by paleontologists. Finally, the history of paleontological research adds another bias and level of uncertainty. The available collections of fossils have been studied at different times with different scientific approaches, and the published records, from which counts of the survival and extinction of groups are compiled, are far from uniform in the way they catalog the past diversity of life. All of this must be considered when analyzing our knowledge of the available fossil record.

Recognizing that the fossil record available during his lifetime provided few glimpses of prehistoric life, Charles Darwin argued that the apparent times of catastrophic extinctions of many lineages were results of the fossil record. The data suffered from shifts in the geographic ranges of species outside sampled areas as well as from the low probabilities of preservation and discovery of the remains of prehistoric life. Therefore, Darwin felt that apparent mass extinctions did not discredit his concept of evolution as a gradual accumulation of changes through the interaction of speciation (developing new species through evolution) and extinction. Today, additional sampling has reduced many of the gaps in the record and now clearly illustrates changes in the tempo of both processes. Recent studies of regional or global mass extinctions suggest that on the geological timescale the loss of many lineages can occur as gradual, stepwise, or sudden catastrophic events. All these patterns may have occurred but to evaluate any particular event, the completeness of the rock and fossil record must be taken into account.

In geological or evolutionary contexts, "completeness" refers to the proportion of an interval of time that is documented in the rock or fossil record. The degree of completeness can influence greatly our perception of a speciation or extinction event. Consider a situation in which a large number of lineages became extinct gradually over an interval of 10 million years, an example of a relatively constant background rate of extinction. If the available fossil record of these events consisted of only two samples, one from the beginning of the interval and the other from its end, it would appear to document a catastrophic extinction event. Adding two or three samples of intermediate age could show what appeared to be a series of stepwise extinctions of small numbers of lineages. Only with the addition of more samples would the true picture of a gradual pattern of extinction emerge. Most likely, major extinction events of gradual, stepwise, or catastrophic patterns have occurred during the history of life on Earth. Therefore, in any attempt to evaluate claims of the occurrence of one pattern or another at a particular time, one must assess the completeness of the rock and fossil record on which the hypothesis is founded.

Since Darwin recognized the importance of the interplay of the origin and extinction of species in controlling the course of evolution, analysis of the patterns and processes of speciation has advanced much more rapidly than the study of these aspects of extinction. Only in recent decades, aided by a greatly increased knowledge of the fossil record, have paleontologists become interested increasingly in analyzing rates and patterns of extinction and tried to understand the processes involved in termination of lineages. In a key, provocative paper, D.M. Raup and J.J. Sepkoski (1982) argued that rates of extinction could be separated into periods of relatively low background rates of extinction that were punctuated by periods of mass extinction events. In these periods many lineages were terminated within a short interval. It must be stressed that the terms "background" and "mass extinction" refer to extremes in a spectrum of variation in rates of extinction and that the establishment of a boundary between the two categories is arbitrary. The initial Raup and Sepkoski analysis was based on compilations of records of extinctions of large groupings of marine invertebrates since the beginning of the Cambrian Period, about 600 million years ago. Temporally, these records of extinctions (including both lineage extinctions and pseudoextinctions) were ordered on a scale of geological stages—the units of this scale being about 6 million years. Subsequent studies were refined to analyze smaller groupings and incorporated records of marine vertebrates.

From these data, Raup (1991) proposed a model, the "kill curve," that describes the observed patterns and provides a basis for considering the causes of extinction. This analysis highlighted the fact that during the last 600 million years of Earth history, the rates of extinction in a majority of the stages were low. Only in a minority of stages was the number of groups becoming extinct greater than usual. Included in these stages are the apparently brief (on a geological timescale), commonly recognized, major mass extinction events that occurred at or near the end of the Ordovician, Devonian, Permian, Triassic, and Cretaceous periods—the so-called Big Five global mass extinctions.

In addition to patterns of extinction, the processes of extinction also have been the objects of considerable current research. Here, it is useful to distinguish between two levels of causes for extinction. "Proximal causal factors" are those that directly affect individual organisms and result in their death. "Distal causal factors" are regional or global events that trigger changes in local physical and biological environments, ultimately affecting individual organisms. For example, the distal factors of today's global warming would include the various sources of atmospheric pollution, while proximal factors would include the impact of local changes in the annual temperature on individuals and the species they represent. Of course, differentiating between distal and proximal factors is not precise.

The concept of the ecological "niche" is extremely important in understanding the proximal causes of extinction. In part, a niche includes a description of the place where a species lives. It also describes all the factors necessary to maintain a species, including temperature, rainfall, food resources, and much more. For each of these factors, there is a range of conditions—a range of tolerance—that is optimum for the members of a species. Within these ranges they flourish and successfully reproduce. Frequently, a species can tolerate either extreme of the optimum range, but at the price, for example, of reduced body size or abundance of individuals. If an essential environmental factor exceeds or falls below the tolerable range, a species will no longer be able to exist in the area.

Consider, however, what happens when just one (or a few) of these essential environmental factors changes and shifts outside the average range of tolerance for a species. Assume, for example, the environment becomes warmer and summer maximum temperatures consistently increase beyond the level of tolerance of most, but not all, members of a species. If tolerance of high environmental temperature during the summer is heritable, then natural selection would select for those individuals able to tolerate the new conditions and select against those that could not. Evolution would take place. Another possibility that might result is that the geographic range of the species would shift and, in this example, move to a cooler climate. If the evolution of a new range of temperature tolerance did not occur, or if the species was unable to shift its geographic range, then the species will become extinct.

Another factor that needs to be kept in mind when studying patterns and processes of extinction are thresholds—the maximum and minimum values of ranges of tolerance. A change in value of one essential environmental factor, bringing it close to a limit of tolerance, might be reflected in reduction of population density or in subtle changes in the species. However, the species would continue to survive. Once the limit of tolerance was exceeded—once the threshold was crossed—all members would die off and the species would be abruptly terminated. To use the example of increasing

aridity, it would not matter whether it was the result of a gradual trend of climatic change or the sudden onset of several years of severe drought. Once the amount of available water dropped below the threshold for a species, it would become extinct. On both biological and, especially, geological timescales, extinction of a species is an abrupt event, but that abruptness does not indicate whether the key environmental change was either sudden or gradual.

Although the concepts of an ecological niche and thresholds are well documented in studies of many modern organisms, such concepts are almost impossible to apply in detail to specific extinct organisms. This leads to unresolved debates such as the ones about the physiology of nonavian dinosaurs—were they hot blooded, cold blooded, or just tepid, having a unique, intermediate metabolic pattern? The so-called living fossils, lineages of great duration that have undergone little evolutionary change in those morphological characters preserved in the fossil record (e.g., horseshoe crabs and cockroaches), also illustrate the problems involved in identifying the exact proximal causes of extinction. The long-term survival of these organisms suggests that they had extraordinarily broad ranges of tolerance for all their essential environmental conditions, but this might not be the case. Quite possibly the keys to the long-term survival of these forms lie in the evolution of their physiology, behavior, and other characters that are not preserved in the fossil record.

Some students of extinction suggest that it is futile to try to identify proximal causal factors of the extinction of prehistoric species, particularly regarding questions about why some species survived and others did not in an extinction event. This is because so many factors are involved in the existence of a species and so few are documented in the fossil record. On the other hand, the principles of the ecological niche and thresholds offer significant guidelines for studying causal factors of extinction. They tell us that the extinction of dinosaurs (other than birds) did not require a cataclysmic environmental change. Their demise could have resulted from exceeding the range of tolerance of only one critical factor shared by these closely related vertebrates. Similarly, the concept of thresholds provides another useful tool. It tells us that although extinction of a species is an abrupt event, the proximal causal factor(s) might have exceeded the species' range of tolerance as a result of either a gradual or a catastrophically abrupt environmental change. Thus, abrupt extinctions are not necessarily evidence of rapid change in the environment.

Nonetheless, analyses of the distal factors of extinctions, particularly mass extinctions, are more tractable and currently are the focus of considerable attention. In part, this stems from the development of the plate tectonic theory. It provides the mechanisms involved in the movements and changes in configurations of continents and ocean basins. Plate tectonics has modified a variety of aspects of the physical environment, contributing to the course of biological evolution. Change in Earth's geography would have immediate and obvious consequences on patterns of oceanic circulation and continental topography, both of which influence many aspects of climate. The warming of the climate in what is today western Europe by the expansion of the North Atlantic and the development of the Gulf Stream, and the rain shadows that developed with the formation of the North American Sierra Nevada are examples of how changes in geography contributed to proximal factors influencing the survival or extinction of species.

Marked changes in sea level are associated with the changes in configurations of continents and ocean basins. Earth history during the last 600 million years records many instances of the spread of shallow seas over large continental areas (transgressions) followed by their withdrawal to basins of much more limited geographic extent (regressions). The effects of the modern El Niño provide a small-scale example of how changes in oceanic circulatory patterns and water temperature in the Pacific can generate extensive climatic changes on the continents forming its margins. The major transgressions and regressions of the past would have had much greater effects on marine circulatory patterns and global climates. A. Hallam (1992) and other scholars have noted that some major extinction events, particularly the Permian and Cretaceous mass extinctions, occurred at the same time as great marine regressions, and such research has stimulated further studies to determine the degree to which regressions were implicated in triggering the proximal causal factors of extinctions of relatively great numbers of lineages of marine and terrestrial organisms.

Changes in configurations of the continents and oceans also affect Earth's biota (life-forms) by modifying the distribution patterns of plants and animals. For example, the rise of the Panamanian Isthmus in the last few million years allowed the interchange of terrestrial organisms that previously had evolved in isolation in either North or South America. This led to a complex evolution of the biotas of the Americas. Both North and South America biotas were enriched by immigrants from the other continent. North America gained the armadillo and the porcupine, while South America gained deer, peccaries (a type of pig), and the ancestors of the llama. At first, the biotas of the Americas appear to have undergone partial mixing with little lineage extinction, suggesting little competition between species. Then, about 11,000 years ago, terrestrial vertebrate animals of both American continents were decimated by extinctions of many species with a large adult body size. The causes of these extinctions are debated, but they probably include both climatic change and human predation.

Some scholars have speculated that other instances of the formation of new land bridges or new connections between ocean basins could have contributed to major extinctions through the introduction of new diseases, competitors, or predators. Although plausible, the possibility that extinctions resulted from the introduction of new diseases is difficult, if not impossible, to test. Also, recent experiments that used disease in attempts to control animal populations frequently have resulted instead either in survival of the lineages through natural selection for nonvirulent strains of the disease or in greater resistance in the susceptible animals. Currently, most scientists argue that interspecific competition is not the major force in the animal replacements that Darwin envisioned. Others suggest that competition plays a significant but smaller-scale role. For example, J.D. Archibald (1996) hypothesized that the demise of many lineages of North American Late Cretaceous marsupials may have been the result of competition with archaic hoofed mammals from Asia. The question of the degree to which competition contributes to extinction remains to be resolved.

Volcanic activity continues to play a significant role in modifying Earth's environments. Similar to extinction phenomena, Earth's volcanic history has been characterized by periods of intense eruptive activity and intervals of relative quiet. Volcanic eruptions produce quantities of particulate matter (e.g., dust), aerosols (very fine particles), and acids. The clouds of particulate matter can block the sun's radiation, decreasing temperatures and later trapping heat and producing a "greenhouse" warming of the climate. Increased amounts of acid rain also usually result from volcanic eruptions. The climatic and environmental effects of recent major volcanic eruptions, such as Tambora in 1816, Krakatau in 1883, and Mt. Pinatubo in 1991, were global in extent. Therefore, periods of greater-than-average volcanism would be expected to be times when extinction was favored through climatic modification. Significantly, both the Permian and Cretaceous mass extinctions occurred during times of exceptional volcanic activity. Recently, attention has focused on the possibility that increased volcanic activity resulted in significant modification of atmospheric composition, particularly changes in the concentrations of oxygen and carbon dioxide. If so, these changes might have had a direct effect on animal and plant metabolism.

Although hypotheses concerning extraterrestrial causes of extinction had existed earlier, the current high level of attention being given to this cause was stimulated by a paper by L.W. Alvarez and colleagues (1980). They argue that a gigantic asteroid hit Earth about 65 million years ago, and they hypothesized that the impact produced a variety of catastrophic changes in marine and terrestrial environments, ultimately causing the extinction of virtually all the dinosaurs, the ammonites, and a variety of other organisms. The distal mechanisms of extinction of this "impact hypothesis" are, in large part, the same as those of intense volcanic activity: the formation of dust clouds that first would produce cooling by blocking solar energy and then cause a greenhouse effect by trapping heat in the atmosphere. There also would be acid rain and extensive wildfires.

The impact hypothesis generated a remarkable amount and diversity of research. The resulting search for craters and other evidence of impacts on Earth's surface overturned the previous view of Earth's history, which stated that, after an initial period of possibly intense bombardment, during the last 600 million years few (if any) large extraterrestrial bodies struck Earth. Now, both terrestrial and lunar explorations have demonstrated that earlier beliefs were mistaken. An increased number of documented impact events during the last 600 million years suggests that impacts were associated with many of the Big Five mass extinctions. There is also a hypothesis that major impacts occurred in a periodic pattern and thus perhaps were controlled by astronomical mechanisms—a "Death Star" that regularly disrupted the motions of asteroids and comets and sent them crashing into Earth.

Currently, the hypothesis of periodicity of impacts is suspect in the eyes of some scholars. Today, strong evidence tells that a major impact occurred in the region of Chicxulub, on what is now the Yucatan Peninsula, at the time of the mass extinctions at the end of the Cretaceous. How and to what degree the effects of this impact contributed to the proximal causal factors of these extinctions are being debated hotly. Finally, it is important to note that the search for craters and other evidence of impacts of extraterrestrial bodies has revealed that some major impacts did not trigger mass extinctions, while the most severe of the mass extinctions, the Permian mass extinction, took place at a time of extraordinary volcanic activity but with no evidence of an impact.

The preceding paragraphs summarize current thought about the principal distal causal factors that, in one combination or another, lie behind the Big Five mass extinctions and lesser extinction events. A summary of the status of one of the extinctions will illustrate the problems involved in discovering the exact causes. Although apparently not as devastating as the mass extinction used to mark the end of the Permian, the mass extinction at the end of the Cretaceous has been studied in more detail. Because explanations involved the hypothesis of an extraordinary catastrophic event, the impact of a gigantic asteroid, and extinction of the many lineages of gigantic dinosaurs, this event commands greater attention in the popular press and scientific journals. It exemplifies the kinds of data that are available, the range of hypotheses that have been proposed, and how they are being tested.

The database for study of the extinction of nonavian dinosaurs and some other groups of terrestrial vertebrates approximately 65 million years ago is geographically and stratigraphically limited and far from complete. Dinosaurs of Late Cretaceous age are found on all continents, but detailed records of the last members of these lineages have been found and studied in only a few areas on the eastern slopes of the Rocky Mountains of North America. The statement that the extinction of dinosaurs was an instantaneous, global event is a hypothesis that has yet to be tested adequately. The record of change in plant life, based on both studies of pollen and leaves, comes from a much wider geographic area. Interestingly, it shows that the extinctions of plants at the end of the Cretaceous were most severe in the Northern Hemisphere, particularly in what are today the western interior of North America and in eastern Asia.

Patterns of survival and extinction of lineages of terrestrial vertebrates at the end of the North American Cretaceous have been analyzed in detail by J.D. Archibald and L.J. Bryant (1990). In contrast to the extinction of all lineages of nonavian dinosaurs, other groups of vertebrates, including placental mammals, frogs, salamanders, turtles, and crocodilians, were affected little or not at all. Statistical analyses suggest this pattern of survival and extinction of terrestrial vertebrates was not a product of chance (Raup 1991). The demise of all the nonavian dinosaurs suggests that they were particularly susceptible to some aspect of the environmental changes of the time. The fact that other lineages survived argues against hypotheses involving a short-term catastrophic environmental change that would have devastated the entire biota.

In contrast to supporters of the impact hypotheses, some scholars argue that the Cretaceous extinctions were the product of several long- and short-term changes in the environment. Among the long-term changes, the major marine regression at that time probably was responsible largely for the general cooling trend of the climate and caused an increased differential between equatorial and polar temperatures. Nonavian dinosaurs had reached their zenith in diversity approximately 10 million years prior to the end of the Cretaceous and, in North America at least,

the last dinosaurian faunas were characterized by decreased taxonomic diversity (Horner and Dobb 1997). This reduced diversity might reflect a reduction of the rate of origin of new species, without a significant increase in the rate of extinction, related to the long-term climatic change or other environmental factors (Padian and Clemens 1985).

As a result of the marine regressions, land bridges formed, and several lineages of Asian terrestrial vertebrates moved into the western interior of North America. This scenario has led some scholars to suggest that interspecific competition or introduction of new diseases played a role in causing the mass extinction. At least two other factors that probably had biological effects must be included in the environmental changes across the Cretaceous-Tertiary boundary. In peninsular India, volcanic eruptions lasting for more than a million years produced the massive Deccan Traps. The debris injected into the atmosphere by these eruptions no doubt had a significant effect on the climate of the latest Cretaceous. Also, the hypothesized impact of an asteriod in Yucatan could have contributed to a very short-term modification of the environment.

As with studies of other mass extinction events, there is no shortage of potential causal factors for the mass extinctions used to mark the Cretaceous-Tertiary boundary. New, pertinent data continue to be the products of active field and laboratory research, and debates on competing hypotheses are commonplace in scientific gatherings and in the literature. The extinction of a species is relatively easy to explain; one essential environmental factor exceeded the species' range of tolerance. Identification of the causal factors of mass extinctions, however, is a much more complex challenge because of the need to weigh the potential contributions of a variety of long- and short-term events of both terrestrial and extraterrestrial origin.

W. A. CLEMENS

See also Adaptation; Coevolutionary Relationships; Diversity; Evolutionary Novelty; Evolutionary Trends; Faunal Change and Turnover; Growth, Development, and Evolution; Paleobiogeography; Selection; Speciation and Morphological Change; Systematics; Variation

Works Cited

Alvarez, L.W., W. Alvarez, F. Asaro, and H.V. Michel. 1980. Extraterrestrial cause for the Cretaceous-Tertiary extinction. *Science* 208:1095–1108.

Archibald, J.D. 1996. *Dinosaur Extinction and the End of an Era: What the Fossils Say.* Critical Moments in Paleobiology and Earth History Series. New York: Columbia University Press.

Archibald, J.D., and L.J. Bryant. 1990. Differential Cretaceous-Tertiary extinctions of non-marine vertebrates: Evidence from northeastern Montana. *In* V. Sharpton and P. Ward (eds.), *Global Catastrophes in Earth History: An Interdisciplinary Conference on Impacts, Volcanism, and Mass Mortality.* Geological Society of America Special Paper 247. Boulder, Colorado: Geological Society of America.

Hallam, A. 1992. *Phanerozoic Sea-Level Changes.* New York: Columbia University Press.

Horner, J.R., and E. Dobb. 1997. *Dinosaur Lives: Unearthing an Evolutionary Saga.* New York: Harper.

MacFadden, B.J. 1992. *Fossil Horses: Systematics, Paleobiology, and Evolution of the Family Equidae.* Cambridge and New York: Cambridge University Press.

Padian, K., and W.A. Clemens. 1985. Terrestrial vertebrate diversity: Episodes and insights. *In* J.W. Valentine (ed.), *Phanerozoic Diversity Patterns: Profiles in Macroevolution.* Princeton, New Jersey: Princeton University Press; San Francisco: Pacific Division, American Association for the Advancement of Science.

Raup, D.M. 1991. *Extinction: Bad Genes or Bad Luck?* New York: Norton.

Raup, D.M., and J.J. Sepkoski. 1982. Mass extinctions in the marine fossil record. *Science* 215:1501–3.

Further Reading

Alvarez, L.W., W. Alvarez, F. Asaro, and H.V. Michel. 1980. Extraterrestrial cause for the Cretaceous-Tertiary extinction. *Science* 208:1095–1108.

Archibald, J.D. 1996. *Dinosaur Extinction and the End of an Era: What the Fossils Say.* Critical Moments in Paleobiology and Earth History Series. New York: Columbia University Press.

Eldredge, N. 1991. *The Miner's Canary: Unraveling the Mysteries of Extinction.* New York: Prentice-Hall; London: Virgin, 1992; 2nd ed., London: Virgin, 1993.

MacLeod, N., and G. Keller (eds.). 1995. *The Cretaceous-Tertiary Mass Extinction: Biotic and Environmental Effects.* New York and London: Norton.

Padian, K., and W.A. Clemens. 1985. Terrestrial vertebrate diversity: Episodes and insights. *In* J.W. Valentine (ed.), *Phanerozoic Diversity Patterns: Profiles in Macroevolution.* Princeton, New Jersey: Princeton University Press; San Francisco: Pacific Division, American Association for the Advancement of Science.

Raup, D.M. 1991. *Extinction: Bad Genes or Bad Luck?* New York: Norton.

Raup, D.M., and J.J. Sepkoski. 1982. Mass extinctions in the marine fossil record. *Science* 215:1501–3.

Ryder, G., D. Fastovsky, and S. Gartner (eds.). 1996. *The Cretaceous-Tertiary Event and Other Catastrophes in Earth History.* Geological Society of America Special Paper, 307. Boulder, Colorado: Geological Society of America.

Sharpton, V., and P. Ward (eds.). 1990. *Global Catastrophes in Earth History: An Interdisciplinary Conference on Impacts, Volcanism, and Mass Mortality.* Geological Society of America Special Paper, 247. Boulder, Colorado: Geological Society of America.

Stanley, S.M. 1987. *Extinction.* Scientific American Library, 20. New York: Scientific American Books.

EYES: INVERTEBRATES

Living marine invertebrates are well equipped with sensors of different kinds for monitoring the environment in which they live, especially visual, chemosensory, tactile, and auditory organs. Of these, most are constructed of soft tissue, and few have much chance of being preserved in the fossil record. There are, however, many instances, chiefly among fossil arthropods, where at least the external part of the sensory equipment was constructed of preservable material, so that, up to a point, its functions can be interpreted.

In all arthropods, the external skeleton, despite its hard, rigid appearance, is highly sensory. On the surface are many kinds of sensillae (such as pressure sensors, current monitors, vibrosensors, and chemosensors) linked to the animal's nervous system by straight tubular or helically coiled canals that run vertically through the exoskeletal cuticle. Fossilized cuticles preserve these well; the canals and surface senillae of fossil crustaceans and insects are broadly similar to those in their living counterparts.

In extinct arthropods many kinds of cuticular sensors may be preserved, although it cannot always be established how these functioned. The most extensively studied of any arthropod sensory organs are the eyes. In trilobites (Lower Cambrian to Upper Permian) these are often superbly well preserved (Clarkson 1979, 1993; Levi-Setti 1993); they are present, although less well known, in some eurypterids (Ordovician to Permian).

The trilobite exoskeleton is constructed of calcite set in an organic base, and not uncommonly the cuticular structures, including sensory organs, may be preserved in fine detail suitable for electron micrographic study. The paired compound eyes of trilobites, laterally placed upon the head, are the most ancient known eyes of any kind, and they are already present in the earliest Cambrian trilobites. In these, the preserved component is an array of calcitic lenses arranged on a curving visual surface. Although nothing is known of the internal structure of these eyes, the lenses are so shaped as to ensure sharp focusing of the light rays, and thus optimization is already present in some Lower Cambrian eodiscid trilobites (Zhang and Clarkson 1990). This suggests that trilobite eyes were quite efficient.

In most trilobites, the eye is holochroal (Figure 1A, 1C), with many small contiguous lenses, and sometimes with accessory sensory pits arranged along the base of the lentiferous surface. The calcite lenses were arranged with their c-axes (the only direction light can travel down a calcite crystal without being refracted) perpendicular to the surface, thus minimizing birefringence (double-refraction). Such eyes probably functioned like the eyes of living marine crustaceans.

In the order Phacopina (Lower Ordovician to Upper Devonian) the eyes are schizochroal (Figure 1B, 1D), with about 60 to 150 separate large, biconvex lenses. There are no direct modern counterparts of these eyes, but the lenses are highly optimized for bringing light to a sharp focus. They are aplanatic doublets in which the upper lens unit of oriented calcite interlocks with a lower bowl-like unit of slightly less refractive index (Clarkson and Levi-Setti 1975). This bowl may in addition enhance the transmissivity of light to the photoreceptors below. Remarkably, the lenses are biologically optimized even during cuticular regenera-

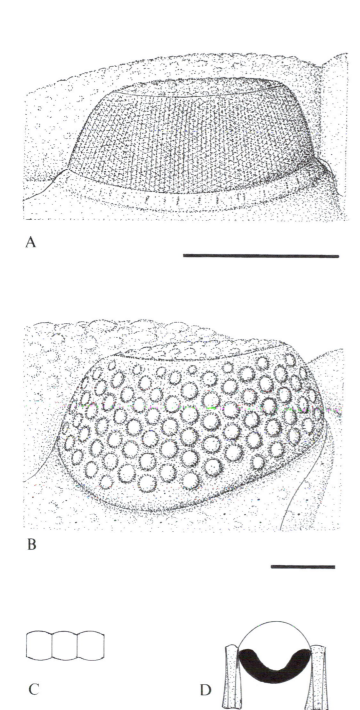

Figure 1. *A,* Holochroal eye (left) of *Paladin eichwaldi shunnerensis,* Middle Carboniferous, Yorkshire, England, showing accessory sensory pits on the eye socle, below the lens surface, and sensory tubercles of the glabella (midline head bulge). *B,* Schizochroal eye (left) of *Phacops rana crassituberculata,* Middle Devonian, Ohio, showing facial suture, large separated lenses, and sensory pits and tubercles on the glabella and other parts of the cuticle. *C,* Section through lenses of *Paladin,* as above. *D,* Section through lens of *Phacops,* as above, showing intralensar bowl. Scale bars: 1 mm.

tion following ecdysis (molting). Since the juvenile form of the adult holochroal eye is effectively a miniature schizochroal eye it is probable that the latter derived from the former by paedomorphosis—the retention of juvenile features into adulthood (Clarkson and Zhang 1991). Schizochroal eyes may well have been adapted for dim light, but precisely how they functioned remains tantalizingly uncertain (Horvath et al. 1997).

In many trilobites the eyes are lost. In the upper Devonian this takes place progressively, in parallel lineages, and is probably a response to the adoption of an endobenthic (subsurface) habit during changing environmental conditions (Feist 1991). In others (e.g., the blind Ordovician Trinucleida) the extraordinary pitted fringe that surrounds the cephalon (head of a tribolite) may be the primary sense organ and was probably vibrosensory or rheotactic (sensitive to fluid movement). In trilobites generally the surface of the exoskeleton is covered with pits, or simple or compound tubercles, connected to canals leading downward through the cuticle. Particular types often are confined to specific areas of the exoskeleton, and there are often dramatic changes in type and form throughout ontogeny—growth and development (Clarkson and Zhang 1991). While these organs were undoubtedly sensory, their specific functions remain unknown. Other sensory organs in trilobites (antennae and anal cerci) are known only from Fossil-Lagerstätten, particularly the Burgess Shale.

E.N.K. CLARKSON

See also Eyes: Vertebrates

Works Cited

Clarkson, E.N.K. 1979. The visual system of trilobites. *Palaeontology* 22:1–22.

———. 1993. *Invertebrate Palaeontology and Evolution.* 3rd ed., London and New York: Chapman and Hall.

Clarkson, E.N.K., and R. Levi-Setti. 1975. Trilobite eyes and the optics of Des Cartes and Huygens. *Nature* 254:663–763.

Clarkson, E.N.K., and Xi-guang Zhang. 1991. Ontogeny of the Carboniferous trilobite *Paladin eichwaldi shunnerensis* (King 1914). *Transactions of the Royal Society of Edinburgh: Earth Sciences* 82:277–95.

Feist, R. 1991. The late Devonian trilobite crises. *Historical Biology* 5:197–214.

Horvath, G., E.N.K. Clarkson, and W. Pix. 1997. Survey of modern counterparts of trilobite eyes: Structural and functional similarities and differences. *Historical Biology* 12:229–64.

Levi-Setti, R. 1993. *Trilobites, a Photographic Atlas.* 2nd ed., Chicago: University of Chicago Press.

Zhang, Xi-guang, and E.N.K. Clarkson. 1990. The eyes of lower Cambrian eodiscid trilobites. *Palaeontology* 33:911–32.

Further Reading

Clarkson, E.N.K. 1979. *Invertebrate Palaeontology and Evolution.* London: Unwin Hyman; 3rd ed., London and New York: Chapman and Hall, 1993.

Levi-Setti, R. 1975. *Trilobites, a Photographic Atlas.* Chicago: University of Chicago Press; 2nd ed., 1993.

EYES: VERTEBRATES

Eyes are structures that appear independently in various forms in diverse groups of animals. There are two main sorts of eyes: the light-sensitive eye spot, which allows the animal to move toward or move away from light; and the image-forming eye, which requires more complex mechanisms. Again, there are two main types of image-forming eyes: those with lenses, as in vertebrates or cephalopods; and compound eyes, as in trilobites or other arthropods. In vertebrates light-sensitive and image-forming eyes are present in the earliest forms.

There also are two types of light-sensitive eyes, eyes in vertebrates, the parietal (also called parapineal eye) eye and the pineal eye, which are independently lost in many lineages. The position of these two eyes often is marked by a median depression (one centered between the right and left side of the head) called the pineal recess, on the inner surface of the skull roof. In some agnathans (jawless fishes), the position of this eye may be indicated by a group of elevated tubercles (bony knobs) on the outer surface of the skull roof. Sometimes there are two side-by-side internal depressions made by the two dorsal median eyes (Gagnier 1995). Larval stages of cephalochordates (close vertebrate relatives) possess a rostral (nasal or beak area) median photoreceptive patch; this has been suggested to be homologous (having a similar origin) with the pineal organ of vertebrates but is now believed to be more likely homologous with the lateral eyes.

In some Ordovician agnathans and some Devonian fishes, the pineal is bigger than the parapineal eye. In sarcopterygians (lobe-finned fishes) and tetrapods, the parietal eye dominates. In many tetrapods (vertebrates that have four legs or two legs and two arms), the pineal organ loses its eye function but the organ persists as a glandular structure, the epiphysis. It appears to have endocrine functions related to its original light-perceiving ability.

The vertebrate's lateral eyes (those on the sides of the head), which are image-forming, sit in a recess or opening in the dermal skull known as the orbit. Behind it is the optic sensory capsule of the underlying endoskeletal (i.e., bone preformed in cartilage) braincase of the endoskeleton (skeleton covered over by a skin). Fossilized sensory capsules appear in the osteichthyans (bony fishes), but in the earlier jawless vertebrates, the capsule is not present. Scholars can detect only impressions left on the dermal (i.e., bone formed directly from undifferentiated cells in a young organism) bone. The orbit had a variety of forms. It could be a simple notch in the dermal head shield or could consist of specialized dermal bones that delimit the eye position. Fossils even reveal the presence of true image-forming eyes: A lens can be established by the presence of ossifications (centers of bone formation), which give information on the position of the muscles that control the eye and thus the presence of a lens. The outermost sheath of the eyeball is the sclera (the "white" of the human eye), which protects the eye from pressure. This stiff structure sometimes is fossilized as a black spot, as in acanthodian fishes (an extinct group of gnathostomes with a poorly ossified internal skeleton). The sclera is sometimes ossified to form a scleral ring. In some agnathan eyes, the conical shape left as molds in the dorsal shield suggests a rudimentary nonmuscularized eye, as seen in the living hagfish. It should be noted that it is not uncommon to have secondary regression in cave or deep-sea fishes. As these vertebrates evolve in a lightless environments, the eyes become less and less functional. Such reduction can eventually lead to eyelessness, as in some burrowing animals.

The size of the eye and orbit informs the paleontologist about the relative importance of that sense. Large eyes are seen in animals that depend on vision for their survival, such as some nocturnal primates or birds of prey. On the other hand, small eyes suggest a behavior based on other senses, such as smell, sound, or touch, as found in bats or moles.

The eye position in most vertebrates is lateral, but there are many variations. In conodonts and anaspids, jawless vertebrates from the Ordovician, the eyes are positioned close together at the rostral tip of the animal, a position that may be primitive for vertebrates. A tendency in many vertebrates is the migration of the eyes to the top of the skull roof. The high position of the eyes permits an overlapping field of vision and possible three-dimensional vision. In fishes this position is highly suggestive of bottom-dwelling animals. Eyes high on a flat skull roof in tetrapods suggest an amphibious way of life. This position allows for placement of the orbits above the water line. Such an adaptation is well known in frogs, crocodiles, and hippopotamuses. It is also true of a special group of fishes from the Devonian, the panderichthyids, which are believed to be the closest relative of tetrapods.

PIERRE-YVES GAGNIER

See aslo Sensory Capsules; Skull

Work Cited

Gagnier, P.-Y. 1995. Ordovician vertebrates and agnathan phylogeny. Proceedings of the Seventh International Symposium on lower vertebrates. *Bulletin du Muséum National d'Histoire Naturelle, Paris,* série 4, section C, 17 (1–4):1–37.

Further Reading

Nilsson, D.E. 1989. Vision optics and evolution. *Bioscience* 93:298–307.

F

FAUNAL AND FLORAL PROVINCES

Prior to 750 million years ago, the terrestrial world probably consisted of one supercontinent, which has been given the name "Rhodinia." By the Early Cambrian, about 550 million years ago, Rhodinia had broken up into several small continents and one large one called "Gondwana." Terrestrial life was still unknown, but marine life had become very diverse. Trilobites were the best-preserved fossils of the Cambrian seas. It was possible to detect two distinct provinces, or ecologically distinct life zones (Fortey and Owens 1990) (Figure 1).

By the Early Ordovician (about 510 million years ago), trilobites, brachiopods, and graptolites were divisible into four continental shelf provinces (Cocks and Fortey 1990) (Figure 2). The pelagic species could be separated according to latitude into tropical and cool water provinces, and the deep water species had cosmopolitan distributions. In the Silurian (439 to 408 million years ago), the northern continents moved closer together, establishing new biogeographic relationships for the marine fauna (Figure 3). The first fossils of terrestrial, vascular plants were discovered in late Silurian deposits.

The first land vertebrates (tetrapods) appeared in the Late Devonian, about 400 million years ago. The tetrapods occupied the equatorial regions of Gondwana and the northern continents. The first seed plants (pteridosperms) appeared, enabling land plants to leave the swamps and invade the higher, drier parts of the Earth. Devonian land plants occurred in three different regions (Raymond 1987) (Figure 4).

In the Carboniferous and Permian Periods (362 to 245 million years ago), the continents continued to move closer together. A series of biogeographic realms and provinces were depicted for the marine fauna (Bambach 1990). The innovation of the amniote egg (an egg enclosed in a protective shell) permitted the land vertebrates to expand into the drier, upland habitats. Terrestrial plants could be separated into three distinct geographic realms (Erwin 1993) (Figure 5).

By the start of the Triassic (245 to 208 million years ago), the terrestrial parts of the Earth were once again gathered into a supercontinent, this time called "Pangaea." At that time, most of the terrestrial flora and fauna was very broadly distributed. But, in the Late Triassic, regional differences began to appear. The reptiles and amphibians were divided in two provinces (Rage 1988) (Figure 6). Land plants were separable into three latitudinal regions.

During the Jurassic (208 to 145 million years ago), the continents once again began to pull apart. It was now possible to recognize four different floral belts (Vakhrameev 1991) (Figure 7). In the Cretaceous (145 to 65 million years ago), the continents were flooded by vast continental seas, and a warm climate prevailed. Angiosperm (flowering) plants had evolved by about 112 million years ago, emerging at low latitudes. By the Late Cretaceous, angiosperms had become the dominant plant group. They may have originated in southeast Asia and dispersed from there (Takhtadzhian 1969) (Figure 8).

A relatively warm global climate prevailed through the Early Eocene until about 50 million years ago. Both Antarctica and the lands surrounding the north pole were occupied by broad-leafed deciduous and evergreen forests. Tropical forests covered most of the lower latitudes. As the continents approached their present positions, ocean currents were altered, and mountain chains were formed. These changes affected the global climate, which began to turn colder. By the Early Oligocene, about 35 million years ago, ice sheets had formed in the Antarctic. The climatic deterioration continued until the beginning of our present series of ice ages in the late Pliocene, about 3 million years ago.

The worldwide climate change, which took place over the past 50 million years, had a profound effect on the evolution and distribution of plants and animals. The ocean surface may now be divided into four major temperature zones, each with its own characteristic life-forms (Figure 9). The same zones are evident on land. Within these zones, and within the various oceans and continents, biogeographers recognize many realms, regions, and provinces (Briggs 1995).

JOHN C. BRIGGS

See also Global Environment; Ocean Environment; Paleobiogeography; Paleoclimatology; Plate Tectonics and Continental Drift; Terrestrial Environment

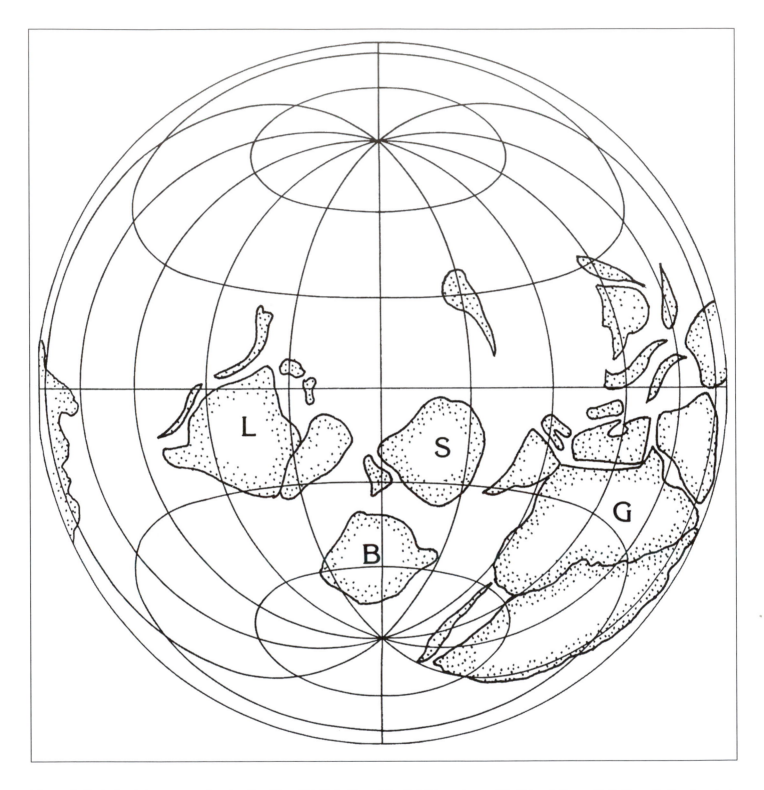

Figure 1. Early Cambrian maps, showing the Olenellid *(B, L, S)* and Redlichiid provinces *(G)*. Abbreviations: *B,* Baltica; *G,* Gondwana; *L,* Laurentia; *S,* Siberia. From Briggs (1995), after Fortey and Owens (1990). Reprinted with kind permission of John C. Briggs and Elsevier Science - NL, Sara Burgerhartstraat 25, 1055 KV Amsterdam, The Netherlands.

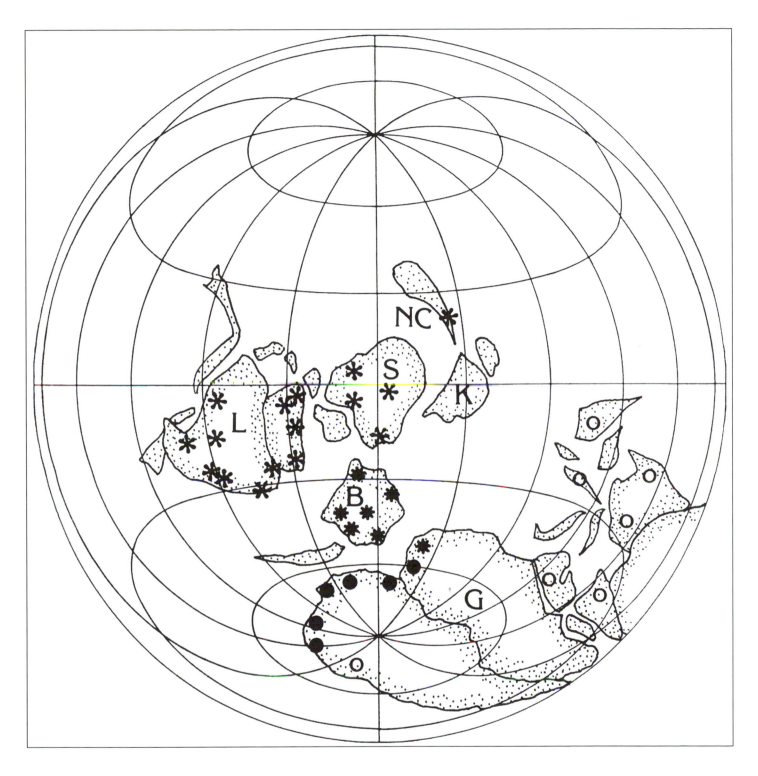

Figure 2. Four Early Ordovician continental shelf assemblages, each indicated by a different symbol. Abbreviations: *B*, Baltica; *G*, Gondwana; *K*, Kazakhstan; *L*, Laurentia; *NC*, South China; *S*, Siberia. From Briggs (1995), after Cocks and Fortey (1990). Reprinted with kind permission of John C. Briggs and Elsevier Science - NL, Sara Burgerhartstraat 25, 1055 KV Amsterdam, The Netherlands.

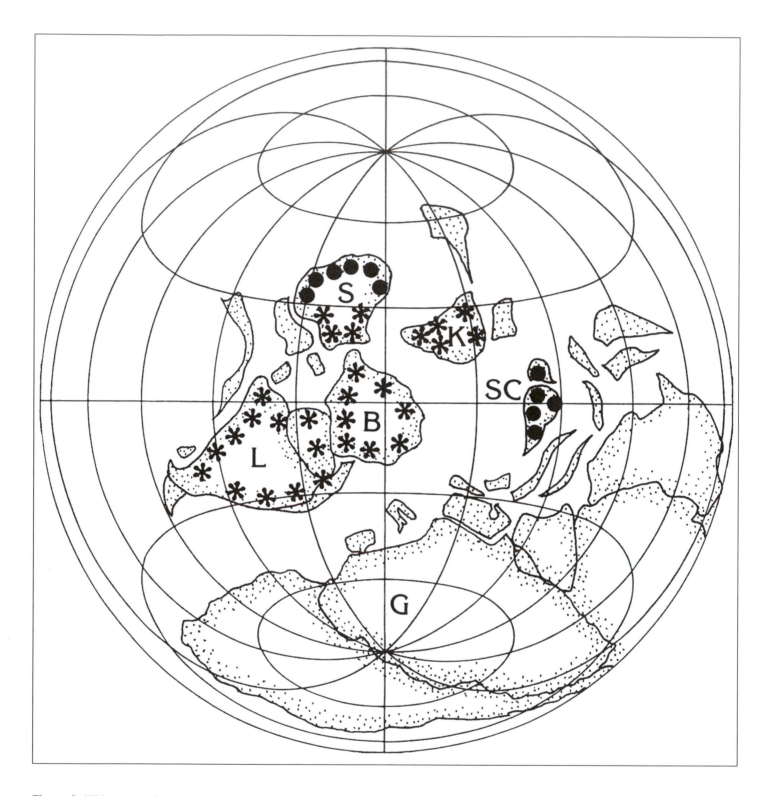

Figure 3. With contact between Laurentia and Baltica; a combined North American–Siberian–Baltic Province became established. The distribution of the Mongolian Province (●) in northern Siberia and south China appears to be incongruous. Abbreviations: *B,* Baltica; *L,* Laurentia; *S,* northern Siberia; *SC,* south China. From Briggs (1995), after Tuckey (1990). Reprinted with kind permission of John C. Briggs and Elsevier Science - NL, Sara Burgerhartstraat 25, 1055 KV Amsterdam, The Netherlands.

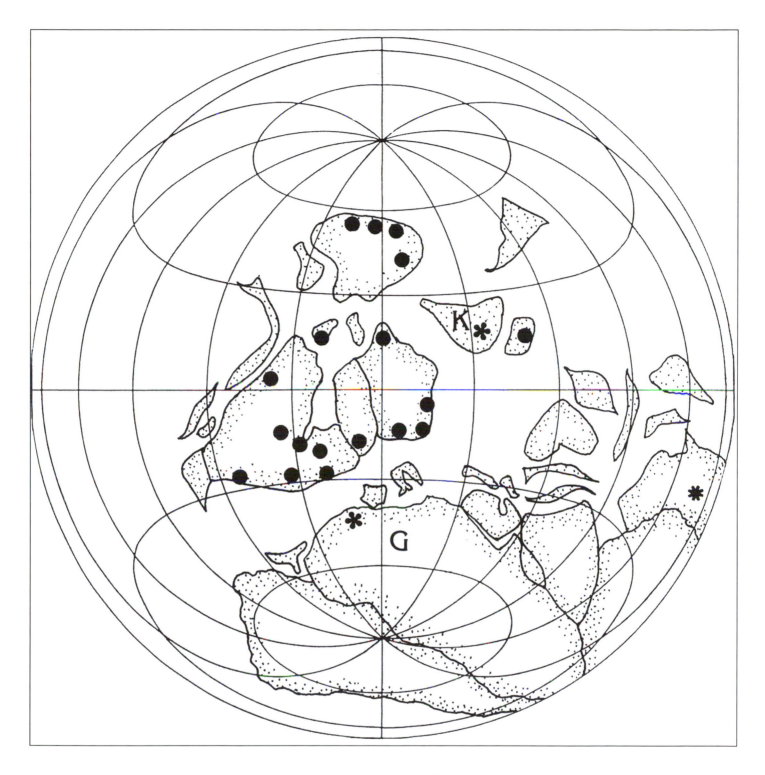

Figure 4. Devonian terrestrial plant assemblages. Relationship between Kazakhstan and Gondwana appears to be incongruous. Abbreviations and Symbols: G, Gondwana; K, Kazakhstan; ●, equatorial-middle latitude unit; ✳, Kazakhstan-north Gondwanan unit; ✻, Australian unit. From Briggs (1995). Reprinted with kind permission of John C. Briggs and Elsevier Science - NL, Sara Burgerhartstraat 25, 1055 KV Amsterdam, The Netherlands.

Figure 5. Permian geographic realms for plant life. Symbols: ≡, north temperate Anagram Realm; |||, tropical Euramerican Realm; ooooo, tropical Cathaysian Realm; .∴∵∴∵., and south temperate Gondwanan Realm. From Briggs (1995), after Erwin (1993). Reprinted with kind permission of John C. Briggs and Elsevier Science - NL, Sara Burgerhartstraat 25, 1055 KV Amsterdam, The Netherlands.

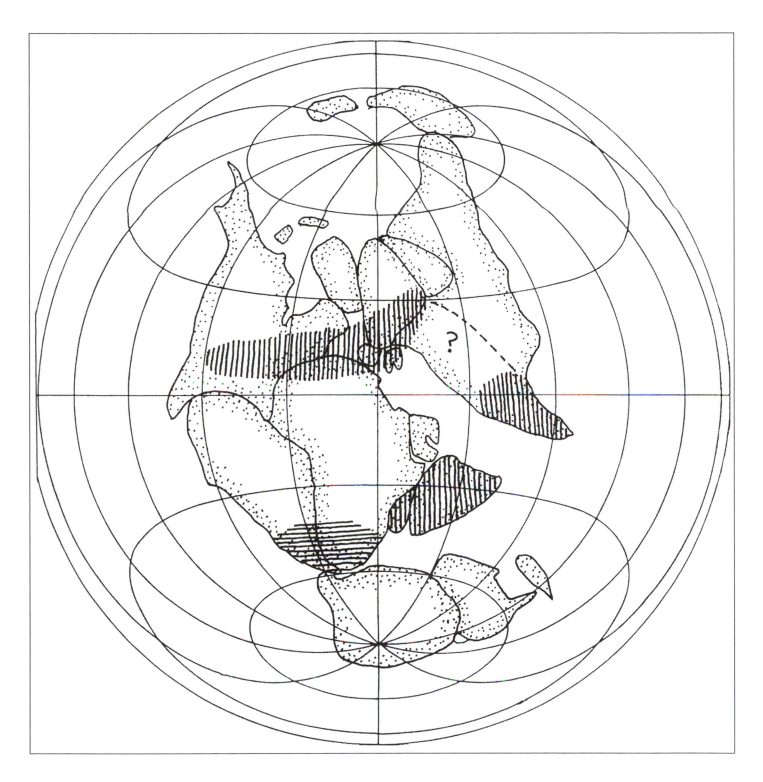

Figure 6. Late Triassic provinces. Symbols: |||, Peri-tethyan Province; ≡, Southern Gondwanan Province. From Briggs (1995), after Rage (1988). Reprinted with kind permission of John C. Briggs and Elsevier Science - NL, Sara Burgerhartstraat 25, 1055 KV Amsterdam, The Netherlands.

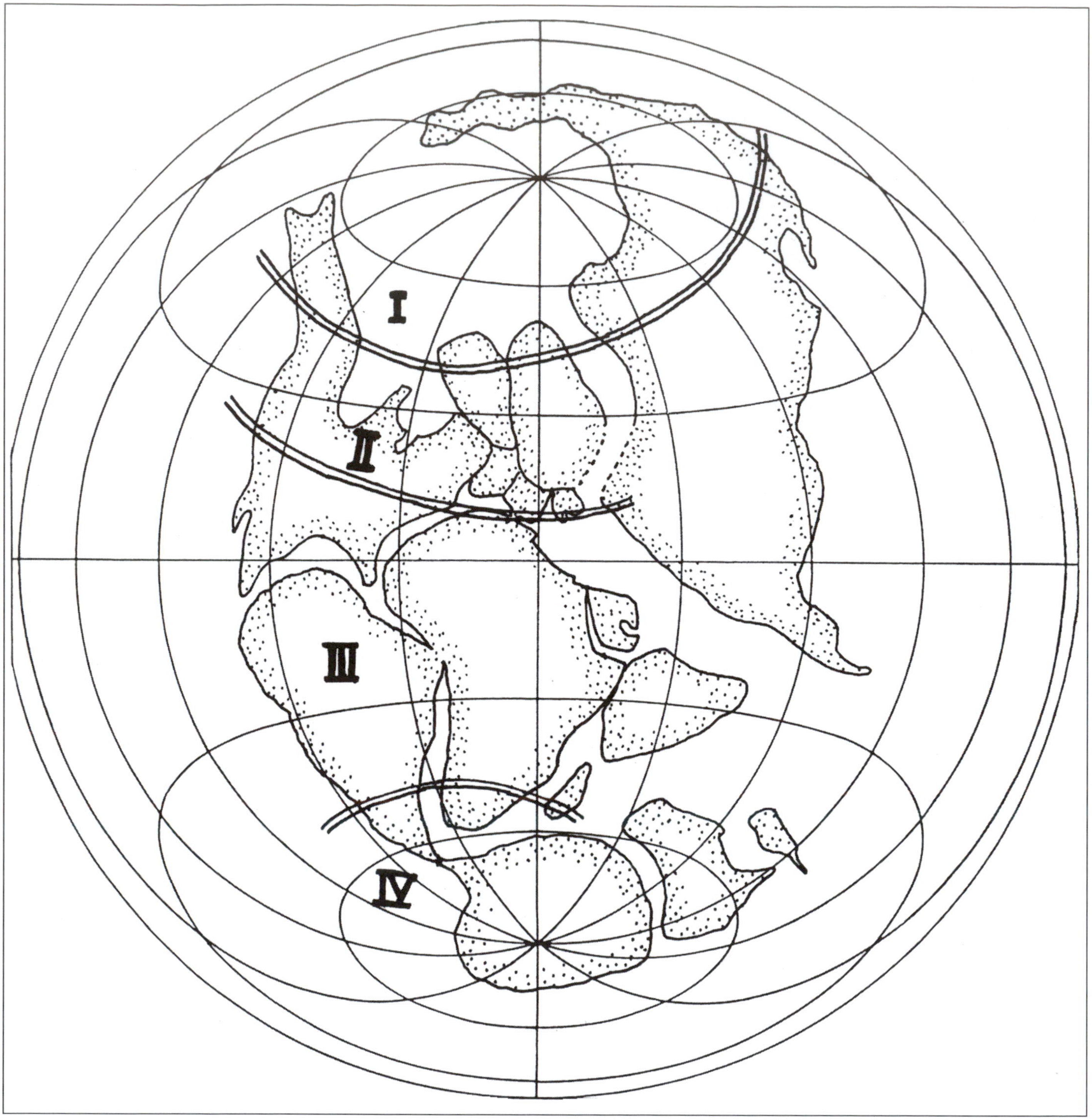

Figure 7. Climatic belts for the late Jurassic. From Briggs (1995), after Vakhrameev (1991). Reprinted with kind permission of John C. Briggs and Elsevier Science - NL, Sara Burgerhartstraat 25, 1055 KV Amsterdam, The Netherlands.

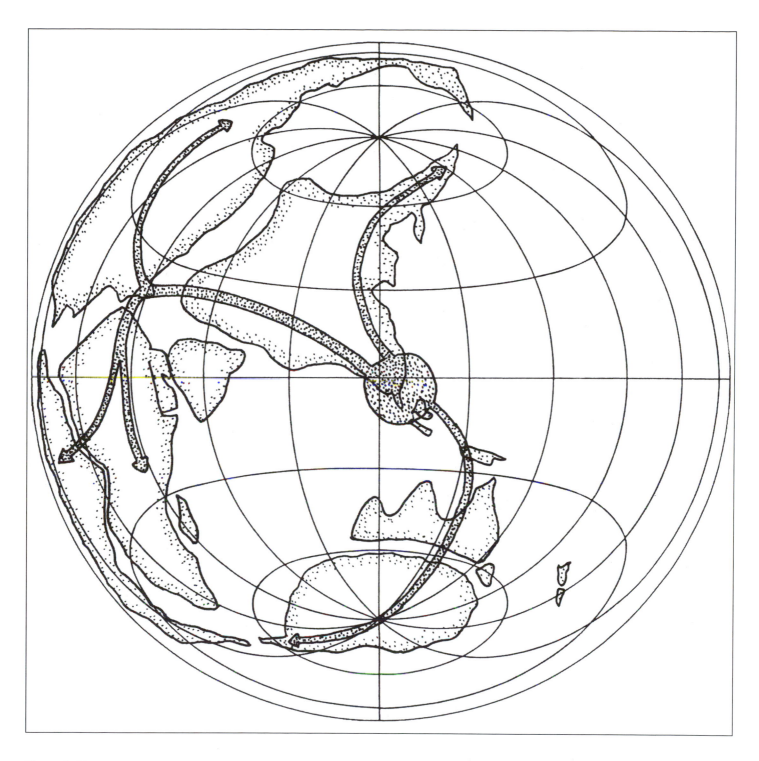

Figure 8. Hypothetical dispersal of primitive angiosperms and other plant life from southeast Asia. From Briggs (1995). Reprinted with kind permission of John C. Briggs and Elsevier Science - NL, Sara Burgerhartstraat 25, 1055 KV Amsterdam, The Netherlands.

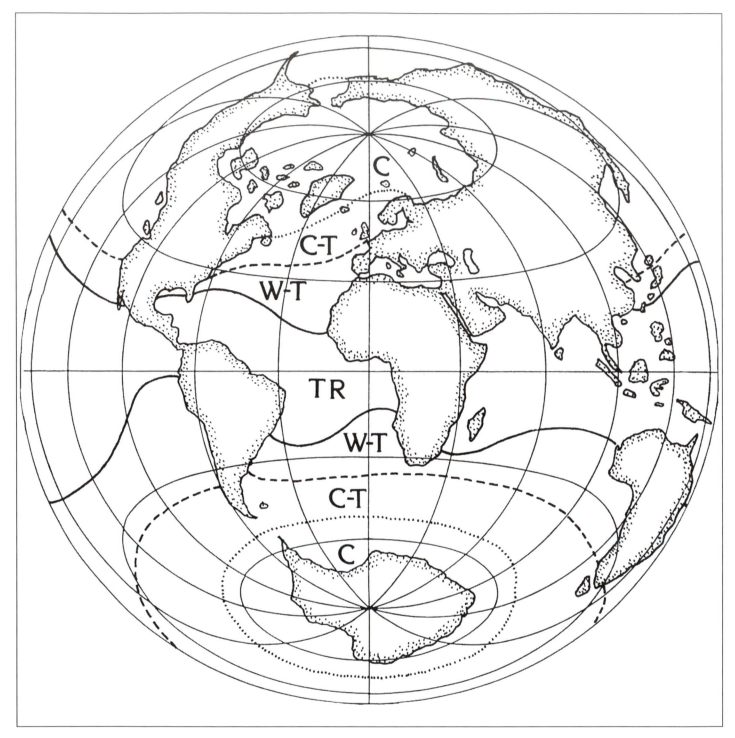

Figure 9. The four major temperature zones of the ocean surface. The Tropical Zone is delimited by the 20 degree centigrade isotherm for the coldest month. It is bordered by a Warm-Temperate Zone, a Cold-Temperate Zone, and a Cold or Polar Zone. Abbreviations: *C*, Cold or Polar Zone; *C-T*, Cold-Temperate Zone; *TR*, Tropical Zone; *W-T*, Warm-Temperate Zone. From Briggs (1995). Reprinted with kind permission of John C. Briggs and Elsevier Science - NL, Sara Burgerhartstraat 25, 1055 KV Amsterdam, The Netherlands.

Works Cited

Bambach, R.K. 1990. Late Paleozoic provinciality in the marine realm. *In* W.S. McKerrow and C.R. Scotese (eds.), *Palaezoic Palaeogeography and Biogeography, Geological Society of London* 12:307–23.

Briggs, J.C. 1995. *Global Biogeography.* Amsterdam and New York: Elsevier.

Cocks, L.R.M., and R.A. Fortey. 1990. Biogeography of Ordovician and Silurian faunas. *In* W.S. McKerrow and C.R. Scotese (eds.), *Palaeozoic Palaeogeography and Biogeography, Geological Society of London* 12:97–104.

Erwin, D.H. 1993. *The Great Paleozoic Crisis.* New York: Columbia University Press.

Fortey, R.A., and R.M. Owens. 1990. Evolutionary radiations in the Trilobite. *In* P.D. Taylor and G.P. Larwood (eds.), *Major Evolutionary Radiations.* Oxford: Clarendon; New York: Oxford University Press.

Rage, J.-C. 1988. Gondwana, Tethys and terrestrial vertebrates during the Mesozoic and Cenozoic. *In* M.G. Audley-Charles and A. Hallam (eds.), *Gondwana and Tethys.* Geological Society Special Paper, 37. Oxford and New York: Oxford University Press.

Raymond, A. 1987. Paleographic distribution of early Devonian plant traits. *Palaios* 2:113–32.

Takhtadzhian, A. 1969. *Flowering Plants: Origin and Dispersal.* Washington, D.C.: Smithsonian Institute Press; Edinburgh: Oliver and Boyd.

Tuckey, M.E. 1990. Distributions and extinctions of Silurian Bryozoa. *In* W.S. McKerrow and C.R. Scotese (eds.), *Palaeozoic Palaeogeography and Biogeography, Geological Society of London* 12:197–206.

Vakhrameev, V.A. 1991. *Jurassic and Cretaceous Floras and Climates of the Earth.* Cambridge and New York: Cambridge University Press.

Further Reading

Briggs, J.C. 1995. *Global Biogeography.* Amsterdam and New York: Elsevier.

Bănărescu, P. 1990–95. *Zoogeography of Fresh Waters.* 3 vols. Wiesbaden: AULA-Verlag.

Hallam, A. 1994. *An Outline of Phanerozoic Biogeography.* Oxford and New York: Oxford University Press.

Takhtadzhian, A. 1986. *Floristic Regions of the World.* Berkeley: University of California Press; as *Floristicheskie oblasti Zemli,* Leningrad: Nauka, Leningrad otd-nie, 1978.

FAUNAL CHANGE AND TURNOVER

Earth's biosphere has undergone pronounced changes in morphologic diversity and abundance throughout the Phanerozoic era (that starting 570 million years ago). Because these faunal turnovers are marked by evolutionary innovation among entire classes of organisms leading to the exploitation of either vacated or newly created ecological niches, understanding them is a core objective of evolutionary paleoecology. Although research over the past 30 years has focused on both the pattern of major faunal turnovers and their possible causes, much work still needs to be done, especially in finding links between patterns and processes of faunal change. This has become a challenging endeavor because faunal turnovers of different magnitudes occur across many temporal scales and undoubtedly resulted from a variety of causes.

Recognizing Faunal Turnover in Geologic History

The basis for identifying patterns of faunal change relies fundamentally upon the paleontological record of both diversity and ecology of organisms across geologic time. Thus, a sound taxonomic framework, an understanding of an organism's ecology, and both stratigraphic and temporal precision are fundamental criteria for recognizing patterns in faunal turnover. Although faunal change can occur on a variety of scales, most studies have concentrated on turnover at or above the paleocommunity. At this level, trends have been identified across episodes of faunal change including species richness, guild utilization, tiering, and onshore-offshore trends in origination and extinction.

At the broadest scale, J.J. Sepkoski (1981, 1984) has recognized three major evolutionary marine faunas in the Phanerozoic (Figure 1). Although there is significant overlap, each evolutionary fauna begins in an adaptive radiation following mass extinction. The Cambrian Fauna, which has its origin in the Vendian-Cambrian radiation, is characterized by sedentary or creeping epifauna (bottom-dwellers) dominated by trilobites, inarticulate brachiopods (marine invertebrates with bivalve shells), and monoplacophorans (a class of molluscs) among other small shelly taxa. Following the Late Cambrian extinctions, the Paleozoic Fauna is dominated by mostly epifaunal suspension-feeding invertebrates including articulate brachiopods, crinoids (stalked echinoderms with long arms for gathering food), corals, stenolaemate bryozoans (a class of small, tufted, branched marine organisms), and cephalopod molluscs. The Modern Fauna has its origin in the aftermath of the greatest of mass extinctions at the end of the Permian and is characterized by bivalve and gastropod molluscs, bony fishes, gymnolaemate bryozoans (one of the three classes of bryozoans), certain crustaceans, and echinoids (e.g., sea urchins and sand dollars) representing an increase in trophic variety ranging from deep infaunal suspension-feeders (deeply planted filter feeders) to active nektonic predators (open water free swimmers).

Global change in Earth's biota can be identified at progressively finer scales, such as ecologic and evolutionary units (EEUs), which are groups of paleocommunities occurring within a major environmental unit (Boucot 1983, 1990). Like the evolutionary faunas, EEUs often begin within adaptive radiations following mass extinctions. Exceptions are known, however, such as between the Lower and Middle Triassic, where the division between EEUs is more the result of a protracted recovery and adaptive radiation than a pronounced extinction event. In these cases where the adjacent EEUs are not bound by extinctions, the taxonomic and guild differences between successive EEUs can nonetheless be sharp.

Process in Faunal Turnover

Among the most important processes leading to faunal turnover are differential extinction and origination rates in response to environmental perturbation or long-term changes. Each major turnover involves a combination of (1) a mass extinction that reduces

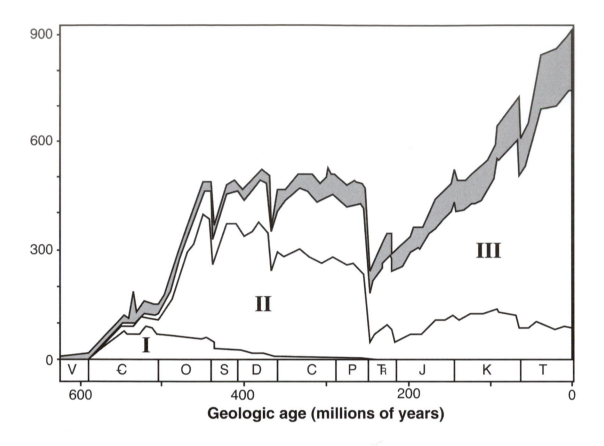

Figure 1. Diversity curves showing the three great evolutionary faunas. *I,* the Cambrian Fauna, *II,* the Paleozoic Fauna, and *III,* the Modern Fauna. After Sepkoski (1990).

diversity and opens ecospace and (2) a period of repopulation of survivors and adaptive radiation. It is these radiations that account for most of the morphological innovation in the form of new higher-level taxa that characterize faunal turnover. While it is clear that the magnitude and mode of extinction and survivorship responsible for faunal turnover is variable with respect to the ecology and geographic distribution of affected organisms, the degree of randomness in survivorship, especially in some of the large biotic crises, is not yet fully understood.

The geographic distribution of organisms can enhance the probability of survivorship during times of mass extinction. Although survivorship rates for marine invertebrates are greater for wide-ranging taxa and those inhabiting lower latitudes, an onshore-offshore environmental gradient has been identified as a major contributing element in faunal turnover (Jablonski and Bottjer 1990; Jablonski 1995; Flessa and Jablonski 1996). This pattern is reflected in the development of the Paleozoic and Modern Faunas, which originated in onshore environments and subsequently spread into offshore settings (Sepkoski and Miller 1985; Bottjer and Jablonski 1988; Miller 1988; Jablonski and Bottjer 1990). While the process is not yet fully understood, it may be that an onshore setting fosters origination (or enhances survivorship during times of extinction) of derived morphotypes (newly derived forms) during faunal turnover.

A second, and more controversial, process of faunal turnover can be found in competitive replacement. The translation of competition theory from modern populations to fossil species is not direct and requires careful analyses of disparate ecologic, geographic, and taxonomic data. Competition, recognized by inverse correlation of a group's diversity (Figure 2), can be invoked only when the "competitors" both have similar modes of life and share the same habitat with a significant overlap in resource needs. The simple "double wedge" pattern of a competitive replacement (Figure 2) is losing favor among some paleontologists (Sepkoski 1996) because it lacks predictive value and does not take into account short-lived perturbations in diversity. Although it often is mentioned in the paleontological literature, few studies have attempted to quantitatively document competitive replacement in the fossil record. A notable exception, but no less controversial, is that of bivalves supplanting brachiopods following the end-Permian mass extinction (Gould and Calloway 1980; Sepkoski 1996).

Conclusions

Major episodes of faunal change provide the turning points in the history of life. Such changes can be attributed to a variety of processes occurring at several rates among different taxonomic and ecologic hierarchies. Over the past 20 years, numerical analyses on

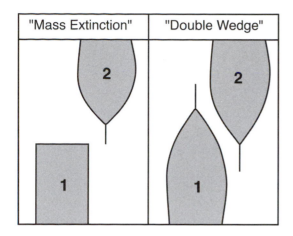

Figure 2. Patterns of faunal turnover as exhibited in spindle diagrams of a taxonomic group's diversity. *Left,* the extinction model where one group radiates following the extinction of another; *right,* the double wedge of competitive replacement where the demise of one group is correlated with the success of another. Abbreviations at bottom of timescale refer to the following geological periods, from left to right: Vendian, Cambrian, Ordovician, Silurian, Devonian, Carboniferous, Permian, Triassic, Jurassic, Cretaceous, Tertiary.

morphologic and ecologic data have identified several different patterns of faunal turnover from the three great evolutionary faunas to the ecologic structure of individual paleocommunities. Although a host of causal factors, many of which are not yet fully understood, may cause the major changes observed in the paleontological record, current research is focusing on differential extinction and origination rates with respect to a variety of abiotic and biotic controls such as an organism's geographic and environmental distribution.

CHRISTOPHER A. MCROBERTS

See also Coevolutionary Relationships; Faunal and Floral Provinces; Mortality and Survivorship; Paleobiogeography; Trophic Groups and Levels; Vent and Seep Faunas

Works Cited

Bottjer, D.J., and D. Jablonski. 1988. Paleoenvironmental patterns in the evolution of post-Paleozoic benthic marine invertebrates. *Palaios* 3:540–60.

Boucot, A.J. 1983. Does evolution take place in an ecological vacuum? 2. *Journal of Paleontology* 57:1–30.

———. 1990. Community evolution: Its evolutionary and biostratigraphic significance. *In* W. Miller (ed.), *Paleocommunity Temporal Dynamics: The Long-term Development of Multispecies Assemblies.* Paleontological Society Special Publication, 5. Knoxville: Department of Geological Sciences, University of Tennessee.

Flessa, K.W., and D. Jablonski. 1996. The geography of evolutionary turnover: A global analysis of extant bivalves. *In* D. Jablonski, D.H. Erwin, and J.H. Lipps (eds.), *Evolutionary Paleobiology.* Chicago: University of Chicago Press.

Gould, S.J., and C.B. Calloway. 1980. Clams and brachiopods: Ships that pass in the night. *Paleobiology* 6:383–96.

Jablonski, D. 1995. Extinctions in the fossil record. *In* J.H. Lawton and R.M. May (eds.), *Extinctions Rates.* Oxford and New York: Oxford University Press.

Jablonski, D., and D.J. Bottjer. 1990. Onshore-offshore trends in marine invertebrate evolution. *In* R.M. Ross and W.D. Allmon (eds.), *Causes of Evolution: A Paleontologic Perspective.* Chicago: University of Chicago Press.

Miller, A. 1988. Spatio-temporal transitions in Paleozoic Bivalvia: An analysis of North American fossil assemblages. *Historical Biology* 1:252–73.

Sepkoski, J.J. 1981. A factor analytic description of the Phanerozoic marine fossil record. *Paleobiology* 7:36–53.

———. 1984. A kinetic model of Phanerozoic taxonomic diversity. 3, Post-Paleozoic families and mass extinctions. *Paleobiology* 10:246–67.

———. 1990. Evolutionary faunas. *In* D.E.G. Briggs and P. Crowther (eds.), *Palaeobiology: A Synthesis.* Oxford and Boston: Blackwell.

———. 1996. Competition in macroevolution: The double wedge revisited. *In* D. Jablonski, D.H. Erwin, and J.H. Lipps (eds.), *Evolutionary Paleobiology.* Chicago: University of Chicago Press.

Sepkoski, J.J., and A.I. Miller. 1985. Evolutionary faunas and the distribution of Paleozoic marine communities in space and time. *In* J.W. Valentine (ed.), *Phanerozoic Diversity Patterns.* Princeton, New Jersey: Princeton University Press, and San Francisco: American Association for the Advancement of Sciences.

Further Reading

Hart, M.B. (ed.). 1996. *Biotic Recovery from Mass Extinction Events.* Geological Society of London Special Publication, 102. London: Geological Society of London.

Donovan, S.K. (ed.). 1989. *Mass Extinctions: Processes and Evidence.* London: Bellhaven, and New York: Columbia University Press.

Jablonski, D., D.H. Erwin, and J.H. Lipps (eds.). 1996. *Evolutionary Paleobiology.* Chicago: University of Chicago Press.

Miller, W., III. (ed.). 1990. *Paleocommunity Temporal Dynamics: The Long-term Development of Multispecies Assemblies.* Paleontological Society Special Publication, 5. Knoxville: Department of Geological Sciences, University of Tennessee.

Valentine, J.W. (ed.). 1985. *Phanerozoic Diversity Patterns.* Princeton, New Jersey: Princeton University Press, and San Francisco: American Association for the Advancement of Science.

FEEDING ADAPTATIONS: INVERTEBRATES

In the living world, four basic problems need to be solved for survival: respiration, feeding, reproduction, and protection. Food is an essential requirement for life, and each invertebrate group has developed a repertoire of feeding mechanisms and strategies that enable them to get the necessary nutrients from the surrounding environment. What an animal eats, where this food source is located relative to the animal's living site, and the abundance of this resource determine the specific adaptations for food acquisition. In the case of ancient invertebrates, multiple and varied structural and behavioral feeding adaptations are recorded by their fossilized hard parts (i.e., exoskeleton) and by the "traces" (e.g., burrows, scars, and boreholes on prey) produced by their feeding activities. Skeletons are a reliable source of functional information; they support and protect the soft parts of the animal and, as such, are coadapted with the soft tissue anatomic features to form a harmoniously integrated body plan. On the other hand, trace fossils record the actual solutions to survival tactics. This information, locked in the fossil record, is the main focus of invertebrate paleoecologists.

Food Source, Mode of Life, and Trophic Type

Marine biologists recognize incredibly diverse and ingenious ways of feeding in invertebrates. These scientists' perspective is, however, quite different from that of an invertebrate paleoecologist (one that studies ancient ecosystems). Biologists are focused largely on particular features such as the size of food particles, but pay little attention to what, where, and how they are eaten (Crame 1990). The paleoecologist simplifies this intricate picture to a few major trophic types and feeding strategies, both of which can be reconstructed from the fossil evidence. "Trophic categories" (also commonly called trophic or feeding types, feeding groups, or feeding habit) can be broadly defined as "groups of organisms that feed, in general, in the same fashion" (Walker and Bambach 1974; Bambach 1983). In other words, a certain source of food is exploited in a similar manner. Table 1 summarizes a classification of feeding types in invertebrates. Although it is based mostly on marine (salt water–based) invertebrates, some examples from the terrestrial (land-based) realm have been included where appropriate.

Trophic types are based on the general type of food, its location (in relation to the interface between water and sediments), and the general feeding mechanism. There are three major feeding categories: suspension feeders, deposit feeders, and carnivores. However, other unconventional categories can be recognized by careful examination of body fossils, trace fossils, and evidence from sedimentary facies (characteristics). An animal's mode of life is related intimately to the feeding type. Three basic modes of life can be recognized (Bambach 1983): "pelagic" (living in open water as minute life-forms such as plankton or nekton), "epifaunal" (living on the surface of the ocean floor), and "infaunal" (living buried in sediments). (Surfaces upon which animals live—

usually called "substrates"—can include a wide variety of things, e.g., the ocean bottom, a coral reef, the shell of a clam.) The epifaunal mode of life is subdivided into "mobile" (e.g., creeping, walking), "attached low" (e.g., cemented, pedunculate, byssate forms that do not extend very far above the substrate), "attached erect" (colonial forms or stalked forms that elevate high into the water column), and "reclining" (animals that simply lie on the substrate). The infaunal mode of life is subdivided into "shallow passive and active forms" (in which the animal inhabits the upper levels of the substrate, and the animal body is in contact with the overlying water) and "deep passive and active forms" (in which the animal is located at some depth below the surface of the substrate, so that the animal maintains contact with the overlying water by pumping water either through the sediment, through a burrow, or through fleshy siphons).

Suspension feeders capture suspended particles from the water column and commonly are sessile forms that do not move around to acquire the necessary nutrients. Filter feeding is one type of suspension feeding in which the animal uses an organic filtration mechanism in food acquisition (e.g., the featherlike fan of a barnacle) (Walker and Bambach 1974). "Epifaunal suspension feeders" are tiered in the water column at various heights to take advantage of different food resources (Figure 1). Low attached (e.g., byssate bivalves, which are fastened down by sticky "threads," and pedunculate articulate, or flexible, brachiopods) and reclining forms (e.g., oysters) are located immediately above the sediment-water interface, and they feed essentially on resuspended material (Figure 1). Attached erect forms (e.g., corals, stalked crinoids) feed at higher levels in the water column, where organic content is low compared with the sediment-water interface, but water circulation (i.e., the volume of water that passes by a given point over time) is better. Peculiar devices and adaptations have been developed to attain the appropriate position in the water column and for trapping particles. For example, some suspension-feeding brittle stars (Ophiuroidea, Echinodermata) can coil their arms and hence are well adapted for clinging on corals and other elevated structures; others, such as the basket star, display delicate branching arms that form a basket that exudes mucus for trapping food and that is directed toward the current (Barnes 1980). Although these feeding adaptations tell us a great deal about an organism's lifestyle, they are preserved in the fossil record in only exceptional conditions.

Deposit feeders ingest organic matter trapped in the substrate and, therefore, commonly need to move around in search of food. Because the surface and uppermost parts of the substrate are richest in nutritious particles, they are heavily populated by deposit feeders (Figure 1). Deposit feeders can be selective (i.e., those who extract from the sediment only the grains rich in nutrients) or nonselective (i.e., those who engulf the sediment uncritically and digest what they can from it). Detritus feeding (feeding upon dead plant and animal matter), browsing, and scavenging organisms are transitional between those that are deposit feeding and those that are carnivorous, and are not

Table 1.

Summary of Feeding Categories Based on Body- and Trace-Fossil Information. Modified from Walker and Bambach (1974).

Feeding Category	Food Resources	General Remarks	Examples
Suspension feeding	Swimming and floating organisms, organic particles in suspension, dissolved and colloidal organic molecules	Major trophic category. Filter feeders included. Suspension feeding animals may either live in the water column or draw water into burrows.	Sponges, cnidarians, brachiopods, bryozoans, bivalves, phoronids, polychaetes, trilobites, crustaceans, aquatic insects, ophiuroids, holothuroids, crinoids
Deposit feeding	Particulate organic detritus and organic-rich grains within the sediment	Major trophic categories. Deposit feeders may swallow sediment in bulk or selectively.	Trilobites, nuculoid bivalves, polychaetes, ophiuroids, echinoids, holothuroids, sipunculids
Detritus feeding	Particulate organic detritus and organic-rich grains at the sedimentwater interface	Transitional to deposit feeding. Detritus feeders exploit the organic-rich sediment-water interface.	Trilobites, tellinid bivalves, nematodes, polychaetes, crustaceans, ophiuroids, echinoids, holothuroids, echiurans
Browsing	Benthic flora and plant material	Transitional to deposit feeding. Scraping algae from the substrate or chewing larger plant particles.	Gastropods, turbellarians, nematodes, polychaetes, oligochaetes, insects, echinoids
Scavenging	Dead, partially decayed organisms	Transitional to carnivores or detritus feeders.	Crustaceans, nemerteans, turbellarians, gastropods, polychaetes, xiphosurids, insects, ophiuroids
Carnivores	Benthic epifaunal and infaunal meio- and macrofauna	Major trophic category. "Active carnivores" capture live prey after active search. "Passive carnivores" wait in a stationary position for the prey.	Gastropods, crustaceans, cnidarians, ctenophores, turbellarians, nemerteans, cephalopods, polychaetes, trilobites, arachnids, onychophorans, myriapods, insects, asteroids
Farming	Cultivated bacteria and fungi	Inferred from biogenic structures (recent and fossil).	?
Trapping	Migrating meio- and microfauna	Transitional to farming. Inferred from biogenic structures (recent and fossil).	Polychaetes
Photosymbiosis	Symbiotic algae and zooxanthellae	Evidence from recent coral reef communities. Highly specialized morphologies. Inferred from the body-fossil record.	Bivalves, corals
Chemosymbiosis	Chemoautotrophic bacteria	Transitional to farming. Recent evidence from hydrothermal vent communities. Inferred from the trace-fossil record.	Bivalves, vestimentiferan worms, gastropods
Parasitism	Fluids and soft tissue	Evidence from recent faunas. Lamentable fossil record.	Trematodes, nematodes, turbellarians, gastropods, polychaetes, crustaceans, insects

always easy to distinguish in the fossil record. Although detritus feeding is not a universally recognized category, it represents an important distinction in community and trace fossil analysis (Bromley 1996). Detritus feeders concentrate on the depositional interface (any surface where deposited materials accumulated), an area rich in organic matter (Bromley 1996). Browsers

are basically herbivores who scrape plant material from the depositional surface or chew or rasp (scrape) larger plants. Browsers commonly eat some superficial detritus too, so this category is actually transitional to detritus feeding. Scavengers feed on large particles of dead animals found at the sediment-water interface. As particle size decreases, this category also grades into detritus

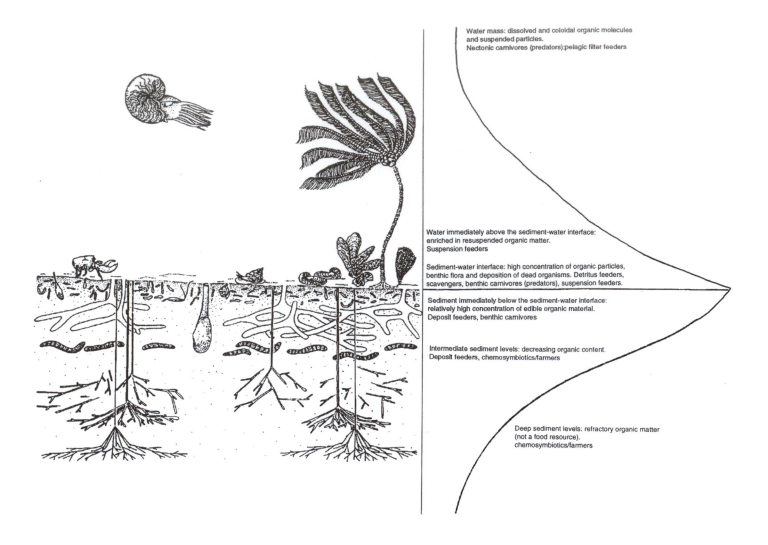

Figure 1. Location of food resources with respect to the sediment-water interface and epifaunal and infaunal tiering structure, as exemplified by body fossils and trace fossils. Curve based on Walker and Bambach (1974)

feeders. On the other hand, some carnivores may eat dead, undecayed animals; therefore scavengers may intergrade with carnivores (Walker and Bambach 1974).

Carnivores feed on living animal matter and represent the highest levels of the food chain. In terms of the trophic chain, they commonly are referred to as "predators." Predators can be passive or active, according to whether they wait in a fixed position for their prey (e.g., tube-worm polychaetes) or they actively pursue their prey (e.g., crustaceans, gastropods, cephalopods).

Trapping, farming (gardening), photosymbiosis, and chemosymbiosis are unconventional feeding categories. "Trapping" comprises the passive capture of migrating meiofauna or other microorganisms within spiral or complex structures. "Farming" is a feeding adaptation that involves culturing suitable bacteria or fungi in order to feed on them (Seilacher 1977). Chemosymbiosis and photosymbiosis are sophisticated feeding adaptations that have been traditionally overlooked. In the fossil record, both have been proposed on the basis of morphological and behavioral adaptations and are well represented in some inver-

tebrate groups, such as bivalves (Seilacher 1990). Photosymbiosis has been recognized in corals and several recent bizarre bivalves (e.g., *Tridacna, Corculum*). In all cases, the symbionts, alga or zooxanthella (a microscopic alga that dwells in animal tissue), are contained within the bivalve's mantle tissue and the gills. The modern bivalve *Corculum* is an epifaunal form that has the overall shape of a disc antenna, which increases considerably the exposed surface. Local areas of the shell display an unusual prismatic structure (resembling small windows) that allows light to penetrate into the interior of the shell. There, alga or zooxanthella use the sunlight to produce nutrients that the bivalve requires. Such dependence can be substantial; zooxanthella supply as much as two-thirds of the nutrients needed by some stony corals.

The "chemosymbiosis" concept involves animal endosymbiosis with chemoautotrophic bacteria. This adaptation has been studied extensively in relation to deep sea vent ecosystems, where chemosymbiotic bacteria allow real oases of life to develop in an otherwise life-depleted setting (Grassle 1985). The sulfuricant bacteria commonly are located in the animal's gills (e.g., the gills of the

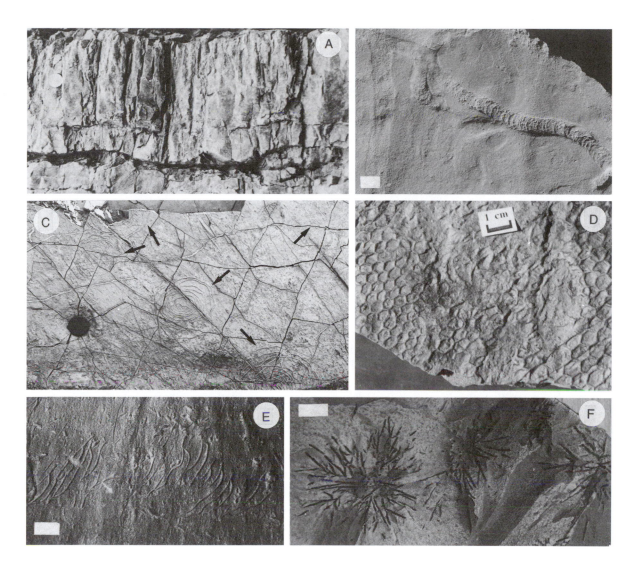

Figure 2. Feeding adaptations based on trace fossils. *A, Skolithos,* a simple, vertical dwelling structure of suspension feeders (Cambrian-Ordovician, Santa Rosita Formation, northwest Argentina); *B, Taenidium,* a meniscate back-filled burrow of deposit feeders (Permian, Patquía Formation, western Argentina); *C, Spirorhaphe* (indicated by arrow), spiral traces interpreted as trapping structures (Eocene, Guarico Formation, northern Venezuela); *D, Paleodictyon,* regular hexagonal networks interpreted as trapping or farming structures (Eocene, Tarcau Sandstone, Eastern Carpathians, Romania); *E, Urohelminthoida,* a meandering trace with a lateral branch on the apex of each undulation; interpreted as a probable farming trace; side branches are thought to provide better aeration to the burrow system (Eocene, Tarcau Sandstone, Eastern Carpathians, Romania); *F, Chondrites,* a branching burrow system interpreted as a chemosymbiotic structure (Tertiary? of Algonia). Scale bar equals one centimeter. Specimens of *Chondrites* housed at the National Museum, Prague.

gigantic mussel *Calyptogena*), where the bacteria are able to oxidize vent-derived hydrogen sulfide (H_2S) in the presence of sufficient oxygen. Chemosymbiosis is also an effective strategy in other environments, such as dysaerobic muds (those with very little oxygen) in stagnant basins, eel grass beds, and mangrove swamps, where oxygen and sulphydric acid are found in close proximity. In these environments, a family of bivalves called amphisiphonate lucinids is known to host chemoautotrophic bacteria in its gills (e.g., *Thyasira, Codakia*). Although extremely rare in the fossil record, "parasitism," or the symbiotic association in which an individual gains nutritional benefit at the expense of another, is a widespread feeding strategy in modern faunas (Conway Morris 1990).

Feeding Adaptations in the Fossil Record

Morphological (body fossils) and/or behavioral evidence (trace fossils) allow scholars to place ancient marine invertebrates into three main feeding types: suspension feeders (including filter feeders), deposit feeders, and carnivores. By comparing fossil structures with similar adaptive morphological structures of recent invertebrates, scholars can infer lifestyle and feeding habits from the stratigraphic record (the fossils contained in rock strata). For instance, invertebrate groups exhibit various anatomical structures for capturing particles suspended in seawater. Some suspension-feeding body plans (e.g., sponges, cnidarians) include chambers or internal cavities lined with tissue. Water is drawn into the cavity, where a variety of projections capture particles: cilia (numerous, small, and hairlike), seta (bristlelike), flagella (less numerous than cilia, long and whiplike), or amoeboid pseudopodia (small tentacle-like structures).

Most suspension-feeder animals construct vertical burrows, such as the ichnogenus (trace fossil) *Skolithos* (Figure 2A). The design of brachiopods, bryozoans (colonial animals), and suspension-feeding bivalves is more complex, with anatomical structures particularly adapted to filter water. The "head," or lophophore, of a brachiopod, for instance, is a circular structure surrounded with ciliated filaments. The filaments perform three interrelated functions, as a pump, a sieve, and a respiratory organ. Although this fleshy structure commonly is not preserved in the fossil record, the brachidium may supply significant information on its morphology and function.

Suspension-feeding bivalves have complex gills, which are used for both respiration and particle collection from the area inside the shell (mantle cavity). In bivalves, shell form and external morphology are strikingly similar among groups that, evolutionarily and genetically, are unrelated. This similarity strongly suggests that these similarities are of major adaptive significance and related mostly to the exploitation of similar ecological niches. Skeletal features—such as general form, shell thickness, interior shell features (e.g., muscle scars), and external shell features (e.g., long spines, prominent ribs that radiate outward, ornamentation) may shed light on the mode of life and feeding type. For example, a set of morphological features such as streamlined shape, deep pallial sinus (a pocket within that houses the siphon when retracted), marginal posterior gape (opening at the rear), and absence of a prominent shell ornamentation are all characteristics of deep-living suspension-feeding bivalves. The presence of a deep pallial sinus is related unequivocally to siphons that exit through the rear of the shell. The posterior gape indicates the existence of a long siphon that cannot be withdrawn entirely into the shell, in which case the animal is confined permanently in a deep burrow safe from the hazards of the shallower burrows. This type of siphon is associated almost invariably with suspension feeders. The relatively thin shell, streamlined shape, and lack of coarse ornamentation tend to reduce resistance from the substrate, so the animal must expend less energy when burrowing (energy cost of penetration). These adaptations also are suggestive of a deep endobenthonic habit.

Based on morphological evidence, such as the absence of mouth parts and chelate appendages (those used to capture prey), trilobites were most likely epifaunal to shallow infaunal deposit feeders, and occasionally also were scavengers and hunters of small soft-bodied animals (Whittington 1992). The so-called "trunk-limb feeding mechanism" involves the rhythmical inward motion of such appendages, which convey the gathered particles to the mouth through a food groove (Clarkson 1993; Levi-Setti 1993). Some features, such as the presence of a spiny surface on these appendages and the backfacing mouth, suggest that larger size particles probably were squeezed and shredded along the groove and subsequently pushed forward to the mouth (Whittington 1992). Although the record of representative forms supports a predominant deposit-feeding habit for benthic trilobites, commonly coupled with horizontal burrowing activity *(Cruziana)*, it also supplies

substantial evidence for the existence of suspension feeders (filter feeders) and predators in the ecosystem. Clusters of trilobite resting traces *(Rusophycus)* that are oriented in specific ways on bedding surfaces may indicate the way that a suspension feeder responded to bottom currents. Some trilobite trace fossils also suggest predatory behavior in capturing prey. S. Jensen (1990) extensively documented the intimate association of trilobite and worm traces and noted that the trilobites consistently positioned themselves so that only the legs of one side were in contact with the worm burrow; this position suggests a capture technique in which the legs of that one side were flexed around the prey.

Passive predation has been developed by some polychaetes (tube worms), sea anemones, and other anemone-like anthozoans (Ceriantharia). Some tube-dwelling worms are typically carnivores; they use the tube as a protective retreat and reach out from the opening to seize passing prey (Barnes 1980). Sea anemones hide in rock crevices or live attached to corals or shells; some forms burrow in sand or mud. All varieties feed on various invertebrates, such as bivalves and crustaceans, swept by currents or waves, and some large species can capture fish. The prey is paralyzed by nematocysts (stinging cells) on tentacles, caught by the tentacles, and carried to the mouth (Barnes 1980). The presence of sea anemone-like animals in paleocommunities can be inferred through the record of biogenic sedimentary structures (those sediment characteristics that have a biological origin) produced by burrower forms. Mucus-lined, plug-shaped burrows—in some cases with an apical disc, a double ring of plates that surrounds the anus—are commonly associated with the ichnogenera (trace fossils) *Bergaueria, Conostichus,* or *Conichnus* and are attributed to the activities of sea anemones. Active predation is the main mode of predation. This method was developed successfully by many invertebrate groups and literally all vertebrate predators.

In terms of biomass (mass of biological material in an environment), carnivores commonly are underrepresented in the fossil record, yet they played a critical role in shaping long-term trends in adaptation (Vermeij 1987). Predation involves several phases (Bishop 1975): search, capture, penetration, ingestion, digestion, and defecation. Direct evidence of predation in the fossil record includes trace fossils that show penetration and ingestion of prey items and digestive contents and fecal products (i.e., coprolites) of predators. The most common predatory trace fossils are bites or crush marks on the prey exoskeleton and circular and parabolic bore holes produced by drilling (Figures 3A, 3B, 3C).

Crustaceans have developed varied techniques to kill their prey, such as peeling (i.e., piece by piece breakage), crushing them between claws, or pounding their prey with expanded segments of their large appendages (Brett 1990). Distinctive scalloped fractures on the outer lips of gastropods produced by peeling crustaceans are known from the Middle Ordovician onward but are relatively more common in the Mesozoic and Tertiary. Drilling is a specialized mode of predation, mostly restricted to marine molluscs (Brett 1990). Circular drilling holes produced by gastropods, commonly called the ichnogenus *Oichnus*, are well represented in the fossil record.

Evidence of predators actually attacking prey is fascinating but extremely rare. An exceptional example is the record of a starfish (Asterozoa) attacking a probable bivalve prey from the Devo-

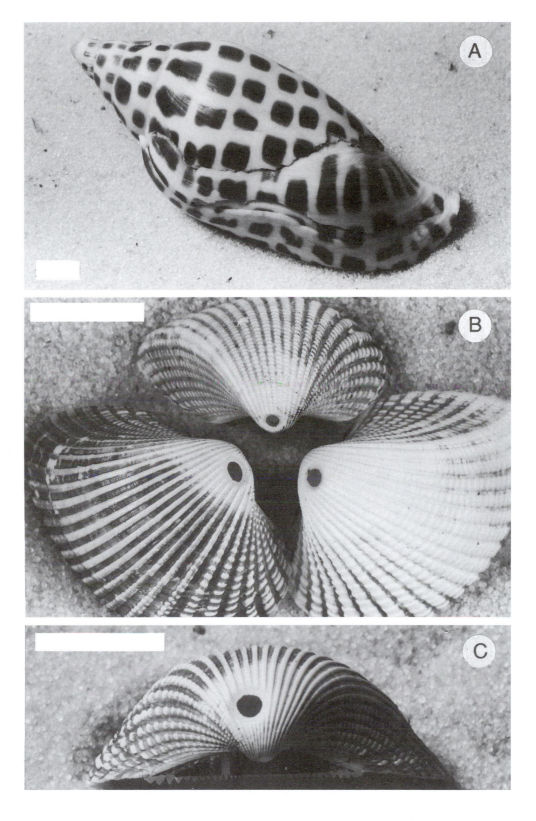

Figure 3. Trace fossil evidence of predation. *A, Scaphella junonia,* showing peel damage and shell repair—the gastropod survived two attacks of a crustacean predator, probably a crab (Sanibel Island); *B,* round holes (ichnogenus *Oichnus*) drilled by naticid gastropods in the bivalve *Noetia ponderosa*—boring is positioned selectively at the umbonal area (Sapelo Island); *C,* close-up of one specimen from *B,* showing details of round hole. Scale bar equals one centimeter. Specimens provided by Sally Walker.

nian of New York (Brett 1990). Ingested prey within gut and gastric contents or fecal products (i.e., coprolites) is also an uncommon source of evidence, mostly found in exceptional preservation of soft tissues (conservation lagerstätten). Remarkable examples are found in the Middle Cambrian deposits of Burgess Shale (Canada). The gut content of the predatory arthropod *Sidneya* is composed of ostracodes, small trilobites, hyolithids, and inarticulate brachiopod fragments, while the guts of the priapulid *Ottoia* contain whole hyolithids and small, inarticulate brachiopods (Conway Morris 1986). Some ammonites (molluscs that lived in coiled shells), found in several Lower Jurassic Lagerstätten in Europe, preserve gastric residues containing foraminifera, ostracods, and jaws of juvenile ammonites (Pollard 1990).

Indirect evidence for predatory behavior can be inferred through morphological comparisons with living carnivores, or can be provided by the organs used for predation, which are commonly heavily calcified or chitinized and therefore are likely to be fossilized. Examples of such preservable tools include the crushing claws of crustaceans, chelicerae of eurypterids, calcified cephalopod beaks, the radula (scraping tongues) of gastropods, and jaws of polychaete worms known as scolecodonts (Brett 1990).

As organisms evolve and adapt, there is a compromise between adaptations for feeding and adaptations for avoiding becoming food (Owen 1980). The search for protection from environmental hazards and potential predators explains why invertebrates adapted successfully to endobenthic life. Most infaunal organisms are deposit feeders that rework the sediment as they search for nutritious particles, in the process producing biogenic structures (Bromley 1996). The endobenthic life also provides protection as a refuge for soft-bodied animals, which have low potential for fossilization but commonly are well represented by their biogenic sedimentary structures. Additionally, many hard-bodied animals tend to economize by reducing their exoskeleton, diminishing their potential to fossilize. However, biogenic structures within the sediment are common in the stratigraphic record, providing evidence of their living sites and feeding habits. In many cases, the morphology and nature of the infill (material that filled in the space, such as a burrow) of these trace fossils unquestionably support a deposit-feeding habit of the tracemaker. For example, an actively infilled burrow (i.e., whose fill has been subject to biological processing as it passed through the animal's gut) commonly displays material that contrasts with the host rock, and in many cases, is pelletized or packed as backfilled material (Figure 2B). In other cases, behavioral analogy with recent forms can provide valuable clues on the feeding habit.

Scholars can infer some strategies of benthic invertebrates, such as farming (gardening) or trapping, from peculiar patterns of biogenic structures constructed in the sediment. (Such structures are grouped into the ethologic category "Agrichnia.") These feeding types have been inferred from complex, regular architectural patterns of biogenic sedimentary structures that are difficult to explain in terms of a deposit-feeding behavior. Complex network designs with secondary undulations, side branching, and anastomoses (networks) commonly are suspected to represent trapping (Figures 2C, 2D) or farming structures (Figure 2E) (Seilacher 1977). Although commonly overlooked, these feeding adaptations

may be the cornerstone of some sophisticated food chains. These types of specialized strategies are developed in response to depleted food conditions and the absence of sunlight, conditions that characterize the plains of the deep abyss. Several criteria are useful in tentatively identifying photosymbiosis in fossil species (Seilacher 1990): overall shape that resembles a disc antenna, local changes in the shell's classical cross-lamellar microstructure or a translucent shell, undulated commissure (wavy edges where the shell halves meet), large size, and affinities with coral reef environments in tropical areas, where clear waters and direct sunlight make conditions optimal for photosynthesis. Based on some of these criteria, possible photosymbiotic candidates in the fossil record are the Jurassic *Opisoma*, the Triassic *Dicerocardium*, and the Cretaceous *Scaphotrigonia* (Seilacher 1990).

Chemosymbiosis is an unusual mode of nutrition that requires physiological adaptations and protection from a surrounding environment that is toxic. The gills of the recent bivalve *Solemya* are packed with bacteria. The animal is so reliant upon the bacteria for nutrients that its gut is very reduced or completely absent (Yonge 1936). However, such modifications in the soft parts are not reflected by the morphology of the shell, which is largely unaffected. Accordingly, indirect evidence, such as trace fossil architecture and facies criteria, may be crucial to recognize chemosymbiotic forms in the fossil record.

Many odd burrows, such as the ichnospecies *Solemyatuba ypsilon* from the Upper Triassic of Germany, have been interpreted as specialized chemosymbiotic designs. *Solemyatuba ypsilon* displays a basic U-shaped design that allows burrow ventilation and a downward blind extension, presumably used for pumping sulphide from the surrounding sediment (Seilacher 1990). Some very well-known trace fossils (e.g., the ichnogenus *Chondrites*), whose branching design cannot be satisfactorily explained as the work of a deposit feeder, may actually represent "sulphide wells" constructed by the activity of a chemosymbiotic wormlike animal (Figure 2F). Moreover, *Chondrites* has been recognized as an indicator of low-oxygen conditions and commonly is associated with dark shales.

Parasitism is common in many habitats and includes representatives of most of the invertebrate phyla. However, its fossil record is extremely poor because of the soft-bodied nature of most parasites; also, they exist in soft tissues that are rarely preserved (Conway Morris 1990). The fossil record of parasitism can be traced to the Cambrian. Some fossil examples include the activity of Mesozoic parasitic isopods in decapods, Paleozoic and Mesozoic parasitic gastropods in echinoderms, and Cenozoic beetles parasitized by nematodes.

Paleoecological analyses of feeding groups, trophic levels, and community trophic structure traditionally have concentrated on the marine realm. The continental realm, however, offers different feeding possibilities and requires quite different adaptations. Terrestrial invertebrates can feed on living and dead plants using multiple strategies, including piercing-and-sucking, chewing, galling, scraping, and boring. These adaptations require appropriate feeding structures and can be traced in the fossil record not only by studying arthropod body fossils but also plant-arthropod interactions (Labandeira 1998). On land, primary decomposers are more important than primary consumers (Owen 1980). In fact, while there are few primary decomposers in marine food chains and webs, primary decomposers are essential elements of terrestrial ecosystems, so much so that this group gives rise to a second food chain. Woody, supporting tissues, which form the bulk of vegetation, only become available as food after death. Analysis of plant-arthropod interactions in the fossil record provides valuable information on the extent and diversity of plant-tissue degradation throughout the Phanerozoic. According to trace fossil evidence, oribatid mites, which are important decomposers today, also were major agents in late Paleozoic decomposer food webs (Labandeira et al. 1997).

M. Gabriela Mángano and Luis A. Buatois

See also Aquatic Invertebrates, Adaptive Strategies of; Feeding Adaptations; Vertebrates; Trophic Groups and Levels; *see also entries on particular invertebrate taxa*

Works Cited

Bambach, R.K. 1983. Ecospace utilization and guilds in marine communities through the Phanerozoic. *In* M.J.S. Tevesz and P.L. McCall (eds.), *Biotic Interactions in Recent and Fossil Benthic Communities.* New York: Plenum.

Barnes, R.D. 1980. *Invertebrate Zoology.* 4th ed., Philadelphia: Saunders.

Bishop, G.A. 1975. Traces of predation. *In* R.W. Frey (ed.), *The Study of Trace Fossils.* New York: Springer.

Brett, C.E. 1990. Predation: Marine. *In* D.E.G. Briggs and P.R. Crowther (eds.), *Palaeobiology, a Synthesis.* Boston and Oxford: Blackwell.

Bromley, R.G. 1996. *Trace Fossils: Biology, Taphonomy and Applications.* 2nd ed., London and New York: Chapman and Hall.

Clarkson, E.N.K. 1993. *Invertebrate Paleontology and Evolution.* 3rd ed., London and New York: Chapman and Hall.

Conway Morris, S. 1986. The community structure of the Middle Cambrian Phyllopod Bed (Burgess Shale). *Palaeontology* 29:423–67.

———. 1990. Parasitism. *In* D.E.G. Briggs and P.R. Crowther (eds.), *Palaeobiology, a Synthesis.* Boston and Oxford: Blackwell.

Crame, J.A. 1990. Trophic structure. *In* D.E.G. Briggs and P.R. Crowther (eds.), *Palaeobiology, a Synthesis.* Boston and Oxford: Blackwell.

Grassle, J.F. 1985. Hydrothermal vent animals: Distribution and biology. *Science* 229:713–17.

Jensen, S. 1990. Predation by early Cambrian trilobites on infaunal worms—evidence from the Swedish Mickwitzia Sandstone. *Lethaia* 23:29–42.

Labandeira, C.C. 1998. Insect diversity in deep time: Implications for the Modern Era. *In* W.W.M. Steiner (ed.), *The Role of Insect Diversity in Agriculture: Ecological, Evolutionary and Practical Considerations.*
Washington, D.C.: U.S. Department of the Interior, Biological Resources Division.

Labandeira, C.C., T.L. Phillips, and R.A. Norton. 1997. Oribatid mites and the decomposition of plant tissues in Paleozoic coal-swamp forests. *Palaios* 12:319–53.

Levi-Setti, R. 1993. *Trilobites.* 2nd ed., Chicago: University of Chicago Press.

Owen, J. 1980. *Feeding Strategy.* Oxford: Oxford University Press; Chicago: University of Chicago Press, 1982.

Pollard, J.E. 1990. Evidence for diet. *In* D.E.G. Briggs and P.R. Crowther (eds.), *Palaeobiology, a Synthesis.* Boston and Oxford: Blackwell.

Seilacher, A. 1977. Pattern analysis of *Paleodictyon* and related trace fossils. *In* T.P. Crimes and J.C. Harper (eds.), *Trace Fossils 2.* Liverpool: Seel House.

———. 1990. Aberrations in bivalve evolution related to photo- and chemiosymbiosis. *Historical Biology* 3:289–311.

Vermeij, G.J. 1987. *Evolution and Escalation.* Princeton, New Jersey: Princeton University Press.

Walker, K.R., and R.K. Bambach. 1974. Feeding by benthic invertebrates: Classification and terminology for paleoecological analysis. *Lethaia* 7:67–78.

Whittington, H.B. 1992. *Trilobites.* Suffolk and Rochester, New York: Boydell.

Yonge, C.M. 1936. Mode of life, feeding, digestion and symbiosis with zooxanthellae in the Tridacnidae. *Great Barrier Reef Expedition, Scientific Reports.* Vol. 1, London: British Museum.

Further Readming

Barnes, R.D. 1963. *Invertebrate Zoology.* Philadelphia: Saunders College Press; 6th ed., Forth Worth: Saunders, 1994.

Bishop, G.A. 1975. Traces of predation. *In* R.W. Frey (ed.), *The Study of Trace Fossils.* New York: Springer.

Bromley, R.G. 1990. *Trace Fossils: Biology, Taphonomy and Applications.* London and Boston: Unwin Hyman; 2nd ed., London and New York: Chapman and Hall, 1996.

Clarkson, E.N.K. 1979. *Invertebrate Paleontology and Evolution.* London and Boston: Allen and Unwin; 3rd ed., London and New York: Chapman and Hall, 1993.

Crimes, T.P., and J.C. Harper (eds.). 1977. *Trace Fossils 2.* Liverpool: Seel House.

Levi-Setti, R. 1975. *Trilobites.* Chicago: University of Chicago Press; 2nd ed., 1993.

Owen, J. 1980. *Feeding Strategy.* Oxford: Oxford University Press; Chicago: University of Chicago Press, 1982.

Vermeij, G.J. 1987. *Evolution and Escalation.* Princeton, New Jersey: Princeton University Press.

Whittington, H.B. 1992. *Trilobites.* Suffolk and Rochester, New York: Boydell.

FEEDING ADAPTATIONS: VERTEBRATES

The ability of an animal to obtain food is paramount to its survival, its reproduction, and ultimately, its contribution to future generations, factors that in turn determine its place in the evolutionary scheme of things. Feeding provides nutrients that all vertebrates need to supply the materials for growth and reproduction and to fuel metabolism. Failure to obtain required nutrients in correct amounts results in starvation or in other serious conditions caused by nutrient deficiency. Malnourished animals may have reduced fertility and an increased risk of death from disease or predation. It is no wonder then, that feeding adaptations are among the most important vertebrate structures.

Vertebrates have a remarkably diverse array of mechanisms for feeding. There is no question that structures associated with feeding adaptations provide a fruitful area for the study of adaptive evolution. But, how do we identify an adaptation? The exact characteristics that a feature must exhibit to qualify as an adaptation remain hotly debated. For our purposes, we define a feeding adaptation as "a genetically determined structure that facilitates the acquisition and/or processing of food."

So, how do scholars identify adaptations in the fossil record? They generally use the comparative method, which derives from the scientific method. First, they observe that a specific structure in a living animals is used for a specific function, which allows scholars to hypothesize a relationship between a structure and its function. If *all* living animals that have a given structure use it in the same way, then scholars can "predict" that fossil animals with that structure also would have used it that way. As with all historical sciences, paleontological applications of functional anatomy depend upon assumptions about uniformity. In this case, the assumption is on "uniformity of use": anatomical features used a certain way today would have functioned the same way in the past.

This approach does have its limitations. For example, many features in the fossil record have no modern counterpart (analog). In such cases, scholars cannot directly infer function from comparison. Did the long canines of Pleistocene saber-toothed cats function to kill prey, or were they used mostly for display during social interactions? Studies of the mechanics of anatomical structures can provide some clues as to what function a trait is best "designed" for, but hypothesized relationships between structure and function must remain speculative for attributes with no modern analogs.

Vertebrate Ancestors

It is difficult to appreciate the remarkable variation in vertebrate feeding structures without first considering what the ancestors of vertebrates may have looked like. Perhaps the best example of a still living but primitive relative of the vertebrates is *Branchiostoma lanceolatum* (formerly *Amphioxus*). *Branchiostoma* is a simple fishlike marine organism, with a basic jawless mouth, a simple tubular throat and digestive system, and numerous pairs of gill slits (sometimes as many as 50). This animal uses a form of filter feeding, a method that was probably typical of ancestral jawless vertebrates and that persists today in the larval stages of some living vertebrates (e.g., the larva of the lamprey). In filter feeding, *Branchiostoma* draws water and organic particles into the mouth and pharynx by the action of cilia (short, continually beating hairlike structures). Then this water is ejected through the gill slits. In the process, food particles become stuck in sticky mucus secreted into the pharynx. Mucus with food particles then flows into the digestive system.

The earliest vertebrates in the fossil record, the ostracoderms, appeared about 520 million years ago. These jawless vertebrates were mostly bottom-feeding detritivores (animals that feed upon dead plant and animal materials), with filtering systems similar to that of *Branchiostoma*. Bordering the mouths of some ostracoderms were bony plates with small denticles (teethlike structures) that may have been used to scrape organic material from surfaces. One group of ostracoderms, the anaspids, had vertical jawless mouths and streamlined body forms, suggesting that these early vertebrates were active swimmers. These anaspids may have been "ram feeders," swimming through the ocean with an open mouth, collecting organic nutrients in pharyngeal mucus, and ejecting filtered water through gill slits.

Today's lampreys and hagfishes (agnathans) are living representatives of ancient jawless vertebrates. These eel-like fishes have cartilaginous skeletons (made of cartilage instead of bone) and lack jaws, scales, and paired fins. The marine lamprey *(Petromyzon)* feeds on living fish by attaching itself to their skin and scales with a suction cup–like mouth. The lamprey bores a hole through the skin of the fish with a remarkable rasplike tongue and drinks the blood and other body fluids. The hagfishes also possess a rasplike tongue, but because they are scavengers, they employ it to burrow into dead fish rather than using it in active predation. However, the larvae of the marine lamprey use filter feeding similar to that of *Branchiostoma*, with the exception that water flow into the mouth is caused by muscular action rather than by the movement of cilia.

Early Jawed Vertebrates

The first jawed fishes, the placoderms (armored fishes) and the acanthodians (spiny fish related to sharks), appeared between 410 and 430 million years ago. The evolution of bony jaws represented a major improvement that allowed a remarkable adaptive radiation (diversification and geographical spread) in feeding structures. In the skulls of ancestral jawless vertebrates, each pair of gills was supported by an arch of cartilage. The hard bony parts of typical vertebrate jaws evolved from an anterior (near the head) set of such arches. It has been suggested that jaws evolved when ostracoderms began to feed on larger particles. Natural selection probably favored the use of an anterior flexible arch, which may have enabled the fish to open the mouth more widely and to manipulate food items. These changes would increase the ability to obtain food. The first teeth (hard, conical structures) appeared along with jaws and probably originated from scales on the skin surface near the mouth.

The evolution of jaws made possible the predominant mode of feeding in fishes today. Nearly all living fishes use "suction feeding." In suction feeding, the closed mouth cavity is expanded, creating negative pressure. When the mouth is opened, water containing prey items is sucked in. When the mouth is again closed, the prey is trapped, and water is forced out of the gill covering, past the gills. Whereas living fish feed in an immense variety of ways—they harvest particles from the water column; capture food at the surface, in standing water, or at the bottom; and scavenge—almost all of these feeding modes share this single feature: ingestion by suction.

The design of a fish's suction feeding mechanism is very well matched to the type of feeding that the fish practices. In any particular suction feeding design, a balance must be achieved between the ability to move large volumes of water, and the ability to transmit force. Because of design constraints—for instance, in the way that muscles are arranged in the jaw—a fish cannot maximize both volume of water moved and force transmitted. For example, some predatory fish have the ability to move much larger volumes of water than fish that scrape algae from surfaces. Sucking large volumes of water is helpful when feeding on fast-swimming prey. Likewise, the ability to generate force would be valuable among fish that crush their food (e.g., those that feed on coral or molluscs). Understanding the mechanical tradeoff between volume and force, along with examination of jaw angle and muscle attachments, has allowed paleontologists to infer that some early bony fish (e.g., primitive rayfins) had a wide gape with a fast but weak bite and that early lungfish (e.g., *Dipterus*) were able to deliver a strong crushing bite. Evolutionary modifications of other structures, such as lips (e.g., a suckerlike mouth for bottom feeding) and the angle of the mouth (e.g., angled up for surface feeding or down for bottom feeding), improve the efficiency of suction feeding for particular feeding modes.

In air, suction feeding cannot produce enough force to overcome the weight of most prey items. So, even though other vertebrates besides fish utilize suction feeding (e.g., many salamanders, some frogs, and some turtles), this mechanism is restricted to aquatic habitats. The gill slits of some aquatic amphibians (especially during metamorphosis) are reduced or absent, so these animals must grasp prey firmly before ejecting ingested water from the mouth. The esophagus can expand to accommodate excess water drawn in from suction until the animal can eject it without risking the loss of the food item. Indeed, the poor performance of suction feeding in air probably necessitated the evolution of new methods to acquire food. Likewise, problems posed by an ever-increasing diversity of plant foods necessitated the evolution of specialized processing adaptations.

Adaptations to Terrestrial Feeding

Prey Capture and Dispatch

For amphibians and reptiles, the most common mode of prey capture is biting and grasping. To successfully bite and grasp prey, the head and jaws must be placed close to the intended food item. This is accomplished by striking either with the entire body (as in most lizards, crocodilians, salamanders, frogs, and toads) or by propelling the head forward (as in snakes and some turtles). Early amphibians (e.g., *Ichthyostega, Euryops, Cacops*) and their fish ancestors (early lobe-finned fishes) had large fanglike teeth attached to their palates and a wide gape (Figure 1). These animals were no doubt predators that struck with their entire body. Based on their jaw articulation (the way in which the lower jaw joins the skull) and muscle attachment points, the animals could probably deliver a very strong bite. The earliest wholly terrestrial amniote animals (e.g., *Hylonomus, Paleothyris*) were small and lizardlike, with relatively small heads (compared to some of the earlier amphibians, such as *Ichthyostega*), and with tooth structures and jaw musculatures similar to those of present-day insectivorous lizards. It may be that the ability to subsist on terrestrial arthropods (such as insects and spiders) was key in the invasion of land.

Other adaptations also contributed to this type of feeding behavior. Many vertebrates utilize a long flexible neck to propel only the head and jaws forward, instead of the whole body (e.g., modern snakes and turtles, fossil snakes and presumptive snake ancestors such as *Pachyrachis* of the Lower Cretaceous). This same adaptation is seen in some of the extinct large marine reptiles (e.g., some of the plesiosaurs and some of the elasmosaurs).

Some predators must subdue prey that is relatively large and capable of inflicting damage in return. In such cases, fantastic mechanisms have evolved for dispatching the prey item. The large sickle-shaped claw of the dinosaur *Deinonychus* is an excellent example (Figure 2). The group of organisms that exhibits the widest diversity in prey dispatch mechanisms may well be the snakes. Many snakes utilize an embellished bite and grasp technique known as "constriction." Once grasped, coils of the snake's body are wrapped around the struggling food item. Breathing and other movements of the prey provide the constrictor with the opportunity to tighten its coils. Rather than being "crushed," as is often believed, the prey is prevented from inhaling by the powerful coils and gradually succumbs to suffocation. After the prey ceases to struggle, the snake releases its death grip and proceeds to swallow, starting from the head. This mode of food dispatch was certainly present in the early snake *Dinilysia*, an Upper Cretaceous member of the Boidae.

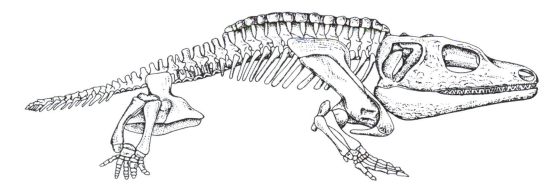

Figure 1. The Permian temnospondyl amphibian *Cacops*. Note the sharp, peglike teeth and large size of the head and gape in comparison to body size. From S.W. Williston, 1910. Cacops, Desmospondylus: New genera of Permia vertebrates. *Bulletin of the Geological Society of America* 21:249–84.

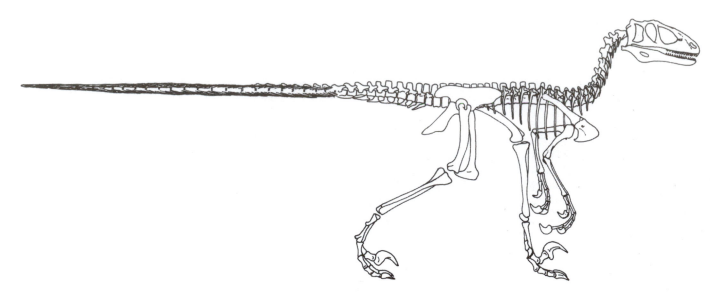

Figure 2. The upper Cretaceous coelurosaur *Deinonychus*. Note the large claws on the hind feet, presumably used to dispatch large active prey. From J.H. Ostorom, 1976, On a new specimen of the Lower Cretaceous theropod dinosaur *Deinonychus antirrhopus*. *Breviora* 439:1–21. Courtesy of the Museum of Comparative Zoology, Harvard University. Copyright © 1976 by the President and Fellows of Harvard College.

Snakes are perhaps best known for being venomous. Although sometimes used in defense, there is little doubt that venom delivery systems evolved to kill or immobilize prey, making it safer and less costly to swallow. Venom delivery systems are composed of a venom-producing gland, ducts to transport the venom from gland to teeth, and modifsied teeth for injection. Such systems have probably evolved independently several times among lizards and snakes. Because much of the morphology (shapes and structures) associated with venom delivery is composed of bony structures, scholars find persistent evidence of venom delivery in the fossil record. Among present-day lizards, only the gila monsters and Mexican beaded lizards possess venom. These animals acquire prey with bite and grasp, and venom seeps down grooves in the teeth during prolonged chewing. Among snakes, there is evidence that venom delivery systems evolved at least three times. Scholars use three distinct patterns of fang morphology to classify fossil snakes (Figure 3A–C).

The first category is rear-fanged snakes *(opisthoglyphous)*, in which a series of two to five enlarged, grooved teeth are located near the back of the jaw (Figure 3A). This pattern is common among some colubrine snakes, including the lyre, the mamba, and the hognosed snakes. The second category is front-fanged snakes *(proteroglyphous)*, in which two small hollow fangs are fixed in the upper jaw at the front of the mouth (Figure 3B). This pattern is typical of the snakes in the family Elapidae, including kraits, cobras, coral snakes, sea snakes, and their allies. The third category is movable-fanged snakes *(solenoglyphous)*. While not in use, the long hollow fangs fold flat against the roof of the mouth. Because of increased fang length, this mechanism is far more efficient at subduing large prey with thick hair or feathers (Figure 3C). Movable fangs are found in snakes of the family Viperidae, including pit vipers and rattlers.

Adaptations to Large Meals

Some predators are well adapted to ingesting very large meals. For example, the early amphibian *Cacops* (Figure 1) had a huge head and gape relative to its body size. Some snakes can swallow meals up to 1.6 times their own body weight. The skull and jaws of the snake are inherently flexible, allowing a large gape. Such a condition is referred to as "kinetic," meaning that the upper jaw and palate can move freely relative to the rest of the skull (e.g., the braincase). A moment's reflection will reveal that the opposite condition is the norm for mammals. Also, unlike the condition seen in many mammals, the upper and lower, right and left tooth rows of the snake can move independently of each other and of the rest of the skull, which allows a large degree of flexibility and a very large gape.

Mammalian Feeding Adaptations

The origin and adaptive radiation of the mammals marks an important milestone in the evolution of terrestrial vertebrate feeding adaptations. With the exception of certain herbivorous (plant-eating) dinosaurs, mammals are unique among vertebrates in their ability to chew the foods they eat prior to swallowing. Indeed, many of the traits that distinguish mammals as a class can be related to this milestone. The morphology of the joint between the lower jaw and the skull, and the differentiation of the teeth and muscles that act to move the lower jaw are important distinguishing features of mammals.

In chewing, the upper and lower teeth come together in a specific manner called "occlusion." This is accomplished by a complex combination of vertical, horizontal, and fore-aft movements of the mammalian mandible, into which the lower teeth attach (Figure 4). Unlike the reptilian lower jaw, the mammalian

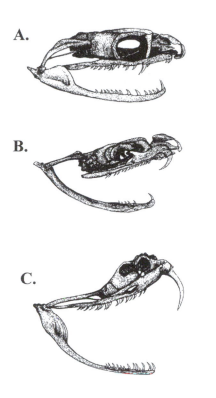

A.

B.

C.

Figure 3. Three forms of venom delivery systems in extant snakes: *A,* opisthoglyphous, or rear-fanged condition; *B,* proteroglyphous, or fixed-front-fanged condition; *C,* solenoglyphous, or movable-front-fanged condition. Modified from Phelps (1981).

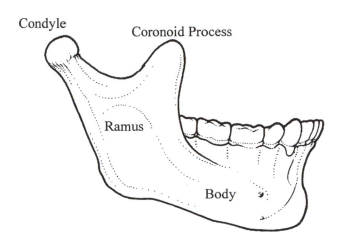

Figure 4. Human dentary bone, or mandible. Modified from Aiello and Dean (1990).

mandible consists of a single bone, the dentary or mandible. It has a horizontal body (into which the teeth attach) and a vertical portion (the ramus), with a posterior (rear) projection called the "condyle" and an anterior projection called the "coronoid process." The condyle attaches to a joint surface on the base of the squamosal bone of the skull. This joint configuration allows the jaw to move not just vertically (as in many vertebrates) but also horizontally to some degree.

The coronoid process rests deep to the flaring zygomatic arch, or cheek bone. In mammals and some of their mammal-like reptile predecessors (e.g., *Cynognathus*), two major jaw muscles (the temporalis and masseter) originate from the side of the skull and zygomatic arch on one hand and are attached to the coronoid process and the ramus of the mandible, respectively. Each muscle is itself differentiated into bundles of fibers that run in different directions, allowing the precise control over jaw movements necessary for occlusion. Because mammals need occlusion during chewing, it is impractical to replace teeth continuously, a situation that occurs in many lower vertebrates, where new ones may erupt at different times. Diphyodonty, in which incisors, canines, and premolars are only replaced once—and molars are not replaced at all—is the alternative condition present in mammals; this situation is unique to them.

But why have mammals evolved the ability to bring their upper and lower teeth into precise occlusion? Vertebrates survived for hundreds of millions of years, through most of the Paleozoic and into the early Triassic, with little more than the ability to open and close their hingelike jaws vertically. This allowed them to capture, contain, and in many cases kill with their pegshaped teeth. So then why do mammals chew? In order to understand this, we need to appreciate that mammals have a higher metabolic rate than do most other vertebrates. This high metabolic rate allows mammals to maintain a high, constant body temperature independent of the temperature of the environment. This condition, called "endothermy," enables them to exist in a greater variety of ecological niches. However, this ability also comes at a price—modern mammals require ten times more food and oxygen than reptiles of comparable size.

Given a high metabolic rate, those animals that could process more or higher quality foods efficiently would be most successful—would be "selected for." Basically, mastication (chewing) results in the mechanical breakdown of foods, which makes for more efficient and complete digestion. Smaller pieces have more surface area exposed to digestive enzymes in the gut. Studies have shown that efficiency of digestion in mammals can be tied to how finely foods are chewed, especially those that are difficult to digest such as the exoskeletons of insects—and the earliest mammals were probably insectivorous. It is also noteworthy that the other endothermic vertebrates, the birds, grind their food by means of a primitive gizzard, which has a lower digestive efficiency than the mammalian system.

Mammalian Dental Adaptations

While early mammals must have had changes in their soft-tissue gut morphology related to increasing digestive efficiency, in the fossil record the most direct evidence of food processing is teeth. Fortunately, they are abundant, providing some important clues to the sorts of foods that extinct vertebrates ate. Why? Because selection favors teeth with a shape well-suited to break down the sorts of foods a mammal prefers to eat.

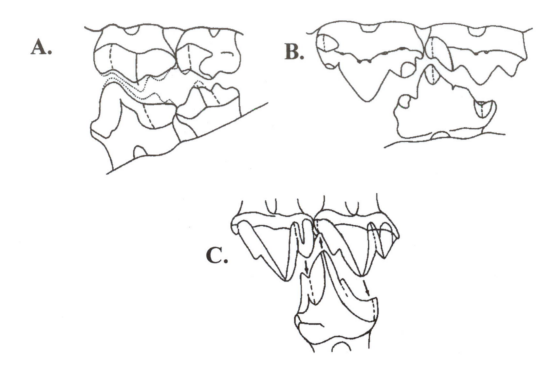

Figure 5. Primitive mammalian molar teeth. *A, Morganucodon; B, Megazostrodon; C, Kuehneotherium.* Symbols: in *C*, arrows indicate direction in which lower molars shear past upper molars. From VERTEBRATE PALEONTOLOGY AND EVOLUTION by Robert L. Carroll, ©1988 by W.W. Freeman and Company, Used with permission.

To break down a food item, teeth must first initiate a crack, then continue it until the item fragments. Hard, brittle foods (e.g., bones or nuts) may require considerable force to initiate a crack, but then they fracture fairly easily. Softer, tougher foods (e.g., meat, leaves) may not need high force to start a fracture but require more work to continue it. Thus, for efficient breakdown different foods require different sorts of teeth. While a scissorlike shearing morphology is well suited to slicing through meat or leaves, a "hammer and anvil" dental anatomy can better pulp fruits or crush hard nuts or bones. Indeed, numerous studies have shown clear relationships between diet and tooth form in living mammals, and paleontologists have used this relationship as a baseline to infer the diets of fossil forms from the shapes of their teeth.

To understand the changes in a structure like a tooth, one must understand its most primitive condition. Evolution dictates that morphology reflects a combination of function and heritage (the ancestral condition). For example, while natural selection will alter teeth to more effectively process preferred food items, tooth shape is modified from a specific ancestral condition, what is called "phylogenetic baggage." Therefore, morphological specializations in an increasingly varied pattern of adaptations can be viewed as elaborations or modifications of an ancestral form. This is certainly true of the evolution of mammalian tooth shapes during the eutherian radiation that followed the extinction of the dinosaurs. (Eutherians are also called "placental" mammals—fertilization takes place internally, and offspring develop in a uterus with a placenta before being born live.)

The molar teeth of primitive eutherian mammals probably resembled those of Jurassic eupantotheres. These mammals had molars with three pointed cusps (Figure 5). These teeth are called "tribosphenic," and can be thought of as opposing reversed triangles, with the lowers fitting between the uppers. Lower molars also had a low heel (talonid) attached to the back end of the triangle. Wear patterns indicate that the crests (ridges between cusps) of opposing upper and lower molars slid past one another like scissor blades as the teeth were drawn into precise occlusion. Such teeth are well-suited to slicing insects. These characteristics, in combination with their small body size, suggests that primitive eutherians were primarily insectivorous.

In subsequent eutherians scholars have viewed the shapes of teeth as elaborations on this basic tribosphenic form. Mass extinctions at the end of the Mesozoic evidently emptied a great variety of environmental niches, reduced the pool of predators, and allowed the proliferation of new adaptive zones for vertebrates through the expansion of flowering plants (angiosperms). Placental mammals responded with an adaptive radiation that has led to their preeminence as land vertebrates, occupying diverse niches throughout much of the Cenozoic. This radiation led to seemingly innumerable new feeding adaptations and to modifications from the primitive eupantothere-like tooth morphology.

To understand feeding adaptations in fossil mammals, we need to be able to relate dental morphology to specific diets in living mammals. Most mammals get their nutrients from plants, animals, or both. "Faunivores" often specialize on either vertebrate or invertebrate prey. In addition, mammals are unusual among the

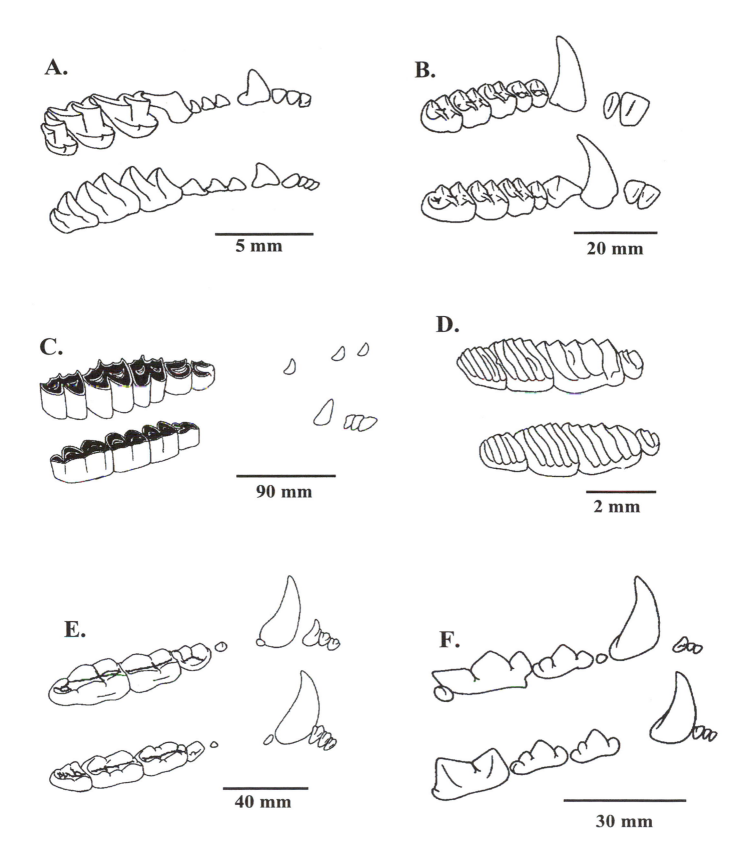

Figure 6. Upper and lower tooth rows (uppers above lowers) for various mammal species. *A, Talpa* (mole); *B, Macaca* (macaque); *C, Acinonyx* (cheetah); *D, Muscardinus* (common dormouse); *E, Ursus* (bear); *F, Camelus* (camel). Variation in tooth morphology reflects differences in diet. Modified from Hillson (1986), with the permission of Cambridge University Press.

vertebrates in that about two-thirds of living and fossil mammalian orders contain herbivorous species. "Herbivores" usually graze on grasses or browse on leaves, flowers, seeds, and fruits. Finally, "omnivores" take a combination of vegetable and animal resources.

Many omnivorous mammals have flat, squarish molars with broad basins (valleys between cusps and ridges) and four or more low, rounded cusps separated by grooves and fissures. These teeth are called "bunodont" and are well suited to crushing and grinding. Bunodont molars are found in a broad range of mammals, including many raccoons, bears, primates, and pigs (Figure 6E). To grind up softer foods (e.g., many fruits), the lower teeth move up and horizontally against the uppers. Hard objects, on the other hand, are crushed with more vertical forces. The degree of cusp relief (general high-low outline of elevation) seems to relate to hardness of preferred items. For example, in primates, hard-object feeders have lower, blunter cusps than soft-fruit eaters.

Herbivory presents a special challenge to mammal teeth. Cellulose is incorporated into the cell walls of plants, but no vertebrate has evolved a digestive enzyme that can break it down. In fact, even with help of microorganisms that live in the gut and chemically digest cellulose, mammals must still use their teeth to break through the cell wall mechanically in order for them to process enough plant material to maintain their high metabolic rates.

Many herbivores have coalesced the individual cusps of bunodont molars together into folds that form low-relief cutting ridges called "lophs." Lophed teeth take many forms. For example, early Tertiary uintatheres (large, rhinoceros-like mammals) and present-day Old World monkeys are bilophodont (Figure 6B)—the two front and two back cusps are combined into two simple lophs. In contrast, many artiodactyls (e.g., camels, ruminants) have selenodont molars (Figure 6C), in which lophs appear as crescent-shaped folds with their long axes running from front to back. Furthermore, elephants and dormouses have occlusal morphologies with multiple lophs that form parallel plates (as many as 30 in the wooly mammoth) running the length of the tooth (Figure 6D). When such teeth are worn, they present sharp ridges of enamel interspersed with softer layers of dentine. This structure very effectively shears plant foods between opposing ridges as the lower molars move back and forth or side to side against the uppers.

Dental specializations in omnivorous and herbivorous mammals are not limited to the molar teeth. Incisors (front teeth) take on a particularly important role in food acquisition and ingestion. For example, primates that feed on gum from trees have long incisors that point outward for gnawing through bark. Primates that habitually eat large fruits (i.e., those that must be broken into smaller chunks before they can be chewed) have broader incisors. Likewise, among ungulates, grazers, whose diet is based on multiple parts of plants, have broader incisors than more selectively feeding browsers, whose diet is restricted to more specialized parts of plants. Finally, rodents and lagomorphs (rabbits, pikas, and hares) have continuously growing front teeth, with enamel limited to specialized outer surfaces and lower incisors that wear across the uppers in such a way that both retain a chisel-like surface for gnawing.

Insectivores do not require the elaborate cheek tooth (molar) specializations seen in many herbivorous mammals. The primitive tribosphenic molar is well-suited to processing insects as it is. First, while insect chitin, the material that constitutes the exoskeleton, is structurally similar to plant cellulose, once the exoskeleton is perforated, little chewing is necessary to release the soft innards. Furthermore, enzymes to digest chitin are found in the digestive tracts of many insectivorous mammals. Indeed some, such as certain anteaters and pangolins, swallow large numbers of small colonial insects whole—they do not even have teeth to chew with. Still, most modern insectivorans and insect-eating bats have molars with a high cusps and sharp intervening crests (Figure 6A). This morphology is particularly effective for consuming insects and other small invertebrates.

The carnivorous mammals must deal with another set of problems. First, they must be able to use their front teeth to obtain, hold, and kill prey that is struggling to escape. Further, they must be able to crush hard, brittle bone and slice through softer, tougher soft tissues. Most early Tertiary creodonts (primitive meat-eaters) and modern carnivorans have modified bladelike cheek teeth called "carnassials" for slicing through meat and skin (Figure 6F). Upper and lower carnassials oppose one another like the blades of a pair of scissors. In front or back of carnassials, many have bunodont cheek teeth with crushing and grinding basins for cracking bone and other hard objects. Interestingly, while primitive aquatic carnivores retain carnassials, more advanced groups, such as seals and sea lions, develop pointed homodont (identically shaped) teeth, which aid in capturing and killing small prey that they consume whole.

As with herbivorous mammals, differences in food procurement and ingestion among carnivorans are reflected in differences in the morphology of the front teeth. For example, dogs have robust incisors for grasping prey (which they kill with quick and shallow ripping bites) and other food items. In contrast, cats have smaller incisors but robust canines, which they use to kill with strong, deep, sustained bites. Of particular interest is the development of an elongated saberlike canine tooth in the felids *Smilodon* and *Homotherium*. Such canines would have been particularly effective for killing large, slow-moving prey.

In sum, then, we can relate aspects of dental morphology to diet in living mammals and gain important clues as to the diets of fossil forms. While feeding adaptations occur in both the skull and body skeleton, as well as in soft-tissue structures that generally do not fossilize, teeth provide the bulk of evidence for diet in extinct mammals—both because they frequently are preserved, and because they are so important in the mechanical breakdown of food prior to digestion.

Life without Teeth: Specializations of the Beak

No modern birds possess teeth, but early birdlike dinosaurs (*Archaeopteryx, Hesperornis, Ichthyornis*) all did. The evolutionary reasons for tooth loss among birds remain obscure but may be related to reduction of mass for flight. In the absence of teeth, the beak itself became the major food-acquiring feature. Among several groups of birds, beak morphology has undergone a stunning adaptive radiation to differing food types or feeding modes. For example, birds that search for insects in foliage tend to have thin, dexterous bills. Nectar feeders exhibit long, thin, and sometimes sharply curved bills. Woodpecker-like birds have stout sharp beaks. Seed eaters tend to have short thick bills capable of generating high crushing force. Extraordinary examples of adaptive radiation in beak morphology are found among the Galapagos finches *(Geospiza)* and the Hawaiian honeycreepers (Family Drepanididae). In the Tertiary fossil record, there are several large flightless birds (e.g., *Phorusrhacus, Diatryma)* whose large skulls and powerful crushing beaks suggest that they may have been formidable predators.

PETER S. UNGAR AND STEVEN BEAUPRE

See also Biomechanics; Diet; Functional Morphology; Teeth*; particular taxa discussed in this essay*

Works Cited

Aiello, L., and C. Dean. 1990. *An Introduction to Human Evolutionary Anatomy.* London and New York: Academic Press.

Carroll, R. 1988. *Vertebrate Paleontology and Evolution.* New York: Freeman.

Hillson, S. 1986. *Teeth.* Cambridge and New York: Cambridge University Press.

Phelps, T. 1981. *Poisonous Snakes.* Poole, Dorset, and New York: Blandford.

Further Reading

Biknevicius, A.R., and B. van Valkenburgh. 1996. Design for killing: Craniodental adaptations of predators. *In* J.L. Gittleman (ed.), *Carnivore Behavior, Ecology and Evolution.* Vol. 2., Ithaca, New York: Cornell University Press; London: Comstock.

Carroll, R. 1988. *Vertebrate Paleontology and Evolution.* New York: Freeman.

Chivers, D.J., B.A. Wood, and A. Billsborough. 1984. *Food Acquisition and Processing in Primates.* New York: Plenum.

Futuyma, D.J. 1979. *Evolutionary Biology.* 2nd ed., Sunderland, Massachusetts: Sinauer, 1986.

Gans, C. 1974. *Biomechanics, an Approach to Vertebrate Biology.* Philadelphia: Lippincott.

Gerking, S.D. 1994. *The Feeding Ecology of Fish.* San Diego, California: Academic Press.

Hillson, S. 1986. *Teeth.* Cambridge and New York: Cambridge University Press.

Janis, C.M., and M. Fortelius. 1988. On the means whereby mammals achieve increased functional durability of their dentitions, with species reference to limiting factors. *Biological Reviews of the Cambridge Philosophical Society* 63:197–230.

Parker, H.W., and A.G.C. Grandison. 1965. *Natural History of Snakes.* London: Trustees of the British Museum (Natural History); 2nd ed. as *Snakes: A Natural History.* Ithaca, New York: Cornell University Press; London: British Museum (Natural History), 1977.

Phelps, T. 1981. *Poisonous Snake.* Poole, Dorset, and New York: Blandford; 2nd ed., London and New York: Blandford.

Radinsky, L.B. 1987. *The Evolution of Vertebrate Design.* Chicago: University of Chicago Press.

Rayner, J.M.V., and R.J. Wootton. 1991. *Biomechanics in Evolution.* Society for Experimental Biology, Seminar Series, 36. Cambridge and New York: Cambridge University Press.

Romer, A.S., and T.S. Parsons. 1949. *The Vertebrate Body.* Philadelphia and London: Saunders; 5th ed., 1977.

Walker, W.F. 1987. *Functional Anatomy of the Vertebrates, an Evolutionary Perspective.* Philadelphia: Saunders; 2nd ed., 1994.

Young, J.Z. 1950. *The Life of Vertebrates.* Oxford: Clarendon Press; New York: Oxford University Press; 3rd ed., 1981.

FERNS AND THEIR RELATIVES

The division Pteridophyta (ferns) often includes a variety of plant groups, many of which have a large leaf (frond) that is the dominant part of the spore-producing (diploid) plant. This spore-producing plant is the sporophyte stage of the life cycle in Figure 1. (In the sporophyte stage, cells have two sets of chromosomes, the diploid condition.) All plants produce spores, which then develop into the haploid stage of the life cycle; that is, cells that have a single set of chromosomes. However, some plants cover their spores with special structures that protect the spore plus the haploid gametophyte stage; a seed is an example of this type of protection. Ferns are seedless vascular plants that disperse by spores, which develop into a free-living gametophyte. Seed plants do not have a free-living gametophyte; the haploid stage develops inside the spore wall.

The general term "fern" still is used for a number of groups that probably are unrelated except that they all descended from a primitive plant group, the trimerophytes, found in the Devonian. Seed plants probably descend from the trimerophytes as well.

Ferns range in size from 2.5 centimeters to 24 meters. They have well-developed root, stem, and leaf systems (Figure 1). Many ferns have rhizomes (underground stems) from which the leaves and roots arise. When ferns form a treelike stem, they produce a mantle of roots around the stem. These roots hold the stem upright. The more roots there are, the larger the "trunk" and the greater the height of the plant. The vascular system, called a "stele," consists of both "xylem" (water-conducting tissue) and "phloem" (food-conducting tissue) in a variety of arrangements. The most common arrangements are the "protostele" (a solid central cylinder of vascular tissue) and "siphonostele" (a hollow cylinder of vascular tissue). When the vascular tissue diverges to the leaf, there is a break in the siphonostele of the stem—a leaf gap. If many leaves are produced in a short distance on the rhizome, the leaf gaps overlap and the vascular tissue appears to be divided into many segments; this arrangement has been called a "dictyostele."

Within the xylem, in particular, the cells may mature in a precise order. If the first-formed cells are on the inside of the tissue, the

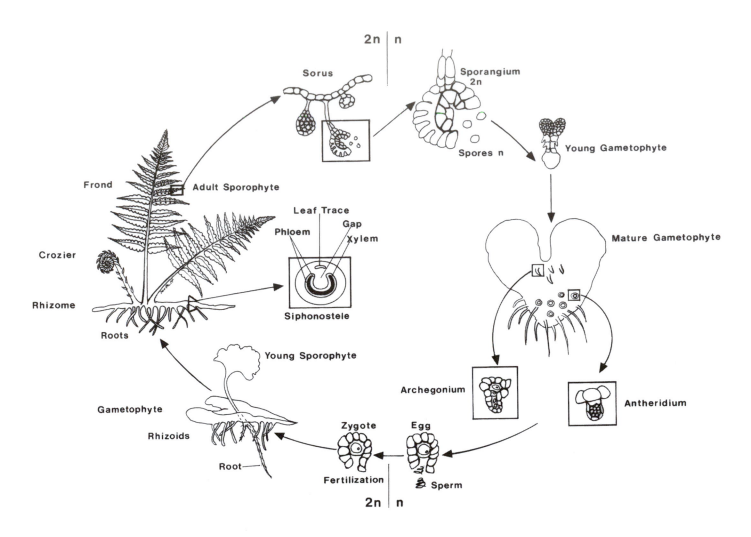

Figure 1. Life cycle of a typical leptosporangiate fern. The diploid stages are on the left (2n) side of the diagram, and the haploid (n) stages are on the right. The only exceptions are at the top, where the spores (n) are indicated in the sporangium (2n) and at the bottom where the zygote and young sporophyte (2n) are shown growing from the gametophyte, with its rhizoids and archegonium (n). A section of a siphonostele is shown to the right of the whole fern sporophyte. Illustration by Ellen Seefelt.

maturation pattern is called "endarch." If the first-formed cells are on the outside of the tissue, maturation is called "exarch." If the first-formed cells are in the middle of the tissue, maturation is called "mesarch." These patterns often are used in fossil material to help distinguish one plant from another or one plant part from another.

The leaves, or fronds, are "megaphylls," large leaves with several-to-many veins. The newly emerging fronds are coiled (circinnate vernation) and are called "croziers" (fiddleheads). Usually the fronds are pinnately compound (resembling feathers) (Figure 1), but some are undivided simple leaves and a few fossil species have leaves that divide from a central point (palmately compound). When the leaves are compound, the leaflets are called "pinnules." In some ferns the fertile leaves are distinct from the sterile leaves, a condition called "dimorphic fronds."

The sporangia (saclike structures that produce spores) are borne on the underside of the leaves, in discrete groups called "sori" (singular sorus), attached at the margins or on the surface. Occasion-

ally, an outgrowth of the leaf covers the sorus; this outgrowth is called an "indusium." Within the sporangia, some cells form spores through meiosis, each cell producing four spores in a tetrahedral shape with either trilete or monolete markings or sutures (Figure 2). Since the spores are covered with a resistant layer (sporopollenin) and often are preserved in the fossil record, the ornamentation of the spores has been important in fern classification. Some of the diversity of this ornamentation is shown in Figure 2.

The ferns are classified into two groups based on the development of the sporangium: eusporangiate and leptosporangiate. The thick-walled eusporangium forms from a series of cells, does not produce an "annulus" (a layer of specialized cells to open the sporangium), and produces thousands of spores from many cells that divide by meiosis. The thin-walled leptosporangium forms from a single cell, has an annulus, and produces generally 16 to 128 spores from only 4 to 32 cells that undergo meiosis. (In meiosis a single diploid cell produces four haploid cells.)

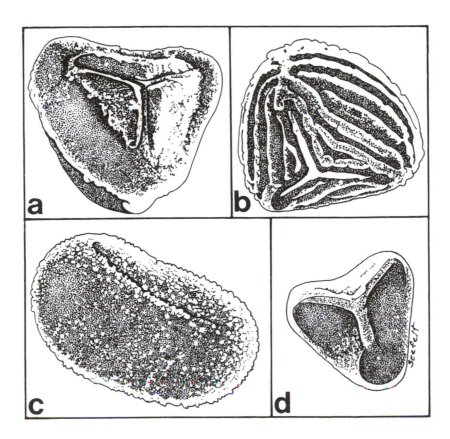

Figure 2. Examples of spore morphology found in the Filicales. *a, Cibotium barometz* (Dicksoniaceae), showing the trilete mark, an equatorial flange, and a granular surface; *b, Mohria caffrorum* (Schizaeaceae), with prominent trilete mark and strong ridges on spore surface; *c, Drynaria fortunei* (Polypodiaceae), with a monolete mark and globules on the surface; *d, Trichipteris stipularis* (Cyatheaceae) young spores with pitted surface and a raised trilete mark. Illustration by Ellen Seefelt, after photographs from Tryon and Lugardon (1991).

Sexual reproduction in ferns occurs in two stages (Figure 1). The sporophyte is the mature diploid plant, which bears the sporangia on its leaves. The sporangia release the haploid spores, which have been formed through meiosis. Spores can be homosporous (one size of spore) or heterosporous (two sizes of spore, the smaller microspore forming the male gametophyte—the haploid, gamete-producing phase of the life cycle—and the larger megaspore forming the female gametophyte). All spores grow into haploid gametophytes that produce the male and female sex cells, the sperm and the egg, through mitosis. Fertilization of the egg by the sperm generally occurs through the sperm swimming to the egg; water is thus required for fertilization. The diploid zygote develops into the sporophyte. Ferns commonly reproduce asexually as well, and either the gametophyte, the sporophyte, or both are capable of asexual reproduction.

The fossilized remains of ferns usually are found as fragments of stems, leaves, sporangia, sori on leaves, and/or spores. To date, there have been no fossilized gametophytes found assignable to the ferns. During the Middle to Upper Devonian, a variety of groups appeared that have been implicated in fern evolution, since they exhibit a trend toward megaphylls, sporangia on the leaves, and more complex vascular systems.

The Cladoxylales often have been regarded as pre-ferns. However, these plants are diverse, and some of them probably are related more closely to other plant groups than to the Pteridophyta. The Cladoxylales first appear in the Lower Devonian, are found mainly in Europe, and disappear in the Lower Carboniferous. These plants were up to 3 meters tall at the maximum. The fertile and sterile appendages are separate and borne spirally on the stem. The vascular system generally consists of several bundles, sometimes with a central pith area. The primary xylem usually contains a hole or a cluster of small, thin-walled cells near the areas where the growth of the xylem first begins (protoxylem)—these areas are called peripheral loops (Figure 3). The eusporangia appear at the tips of the appendages, are long, and probably opened by a slit, as was characteristic of the early trimerophytes. The group's characteristics are rather general and can be interpreted as related to ferns, sphenopsids (horsetails), the trimerophytes (early vascular plants), and even the pteridosperms (seed ferns). It is almost certainly an unnatural group that needs further study. Genera traditionally included in this group—*Cladoxylon, Pseudosporochnus, Calamophyton,* and *Hyenia*—are not defined clearly, and some may, in fact, prove to be identical.

The Iridopteridales, also an early group often implicated in fern evolution, are found from the Middle Devonian to the Upper

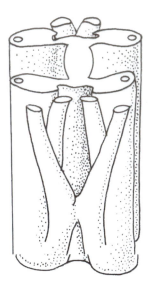

Figure 3. Diagram of a quadriseriate (four-parted) branching pattern based on *Etapteris scottii*. In the center of the diagram, the circles at the edges of the H-shaped petiole trace indicate the position of peripheral loops. The four branches are illustrated around the outside of the petiole. Illustration by Ellen Seefelt, after Phillips (1974).

Devonian. Only fossils of stems and leaf traces are known. The spiral arrangement of the leaf traces arises from the five-lobed protostele of the stem. Phloemlike cells occur outside of the xylem. These plants are known from eastern North America and include five genera (*Arachnoxylon*, *Ibyka*, *Iridopteris*, *Reimannia*, and *Asteropteris*). Also, some scholars have suggested that the Iridopteridales are related to the Sphenopsida (horsetails).

The Rhacophytales are known from well-preserved specimens of the Upper Devonian in Europe and eastern North America. The plants were about 1.5 meters high, with the semi-erect stem bearing crowded fertile and sterile fronds in two rows of paired structures. Complete specimens show that the spirally arranged fronds are placed quite closely around the stem. The fronds are in excess of 30 centimeters. Some are three dimensional (branching in three directions), while others are somewhat flattened (branching in two directions). There are abundant fertile fronds with many terminal, fusiform (spindle-shaped) sporangia. The fronds are borne on branches that divide into two equal parts several times (dichotomizing). This single genus, *Rhacophyton*, is sometimes included in the Zygopteridales, because the two exhibit similar branching patterns (Figure 3) and anatomy (including xylem cells that are arranged in rows).

Owing to the fragmentary nature of plant fossils, it often is difficult to determine relationships among plant specimens. Many Paleozoic fossil plant fragments had features that reminded researchers of ferns, but either were poorly known or did not fit the criteria to be considered true ferns. These previously were placed into a single order called the Coenopteridales. This order currently is being reclassified into the following separate groups in order to recognize more fully the relationships of the individual plants: Rhacophytales, Zygopteridales, Stauropteridales, Anachoropteridales, Botryopteridales, and Filicales. The artificial designation "coenopterids" is used occasionally in a general sense to indicate primitive fernlike plants of the Carboniferous whose affinities are uncertain.

The Stauropteridales were fairly small, bushy plants that lacked true leaves. They exhibited quadriseriate branching (Figure 3), which results in four vertical rows of branches along the main axis of the plant, similar to *Rhacophyton*. Pairs of small, leaf-like appendages were associated with each level of branching. Sporangia were located on the ultimate branches of these plants and opened with a pore that formed on one end of the sporangium. The spores were shed through this pore. Both homosporous and heterosporous species have been described. The vascular cylinder characteristically has four lobes. These plants occurred in Lower to Middle Pennsylvanian of the southeastern United States and in central Europe and currently include three genera: *Stauropteris*, *Rowleya*, and *Gillespiea*.

Zygopteridales includes four genera: *Diplolabis*, *Etapteris*, *Metaclepsydropsis*, and *Zygopteris*. These were also bushy plants with quadriseriate branching. The sporangia were distinctly shaped, elongate and curved like bananas. Each sporangium had a complex wall structure, including an annulus several cells wide. Unlike other ferns, which produce vascular tissue only from growth that occurs at the apex of the plant (primary growth), the Zygopterids exhibit secondary growth in the vascular tissue of the fronds. Secondary growth occurs when a layer of cells within the vascular tissue remains capable of constantly dividing and producing more layers of cells. These new cells mature into additional vascular tissue, referred to as secondary vascular tissue. Since secondary tissue is formed by a layer of cells, the cells are lined up in rows. Secondary growth allows plants to increase in diameter, as seen in trees, thus supporting higher stems. The fronds of the zygopterids had a blade (lamina) and were flattened rather than three-dimensional. The vascular bundle of the petiole (leaf stalk) was in the form of an "H" when seen in cross section and formed peripheral loops (Figure 3). The genera are distinguished by the differences in shape of this vascular cylinder. Some members may have had rhizomes (underground stems) with protosteles. They occur in Middle to Late Pennsylvanian coal deposits from eastern United States and western Europe.

The fossil members (i.e., extinct members) of the Filicales ("true" ferns) listed below have not been proven consistently to have leptosporangia; however, they often are included in the Filicales because of the other characteristics that these ferns share, emphasizing the probable close evolutionary relationship of the groups.

The family Anachoropteridaceae existed in the Middle Pennsylvanian (Carboniferous) and became extinct in the Permian. Specimens, obtained primarily from coal ball deposits (calcium-rich rocks that form among coal deposits) of Illinois and Belgium, are mainly based upon stems and petioles. It may, in fact, be an unnatural group, but it still is useful for those plants that have only these parts preserved. The stem had an exarch protostele with roots and spirally arranged petiole traces on the rhizome. A distinctive C-shape of the petiolar xylem, which curved away from the stem, is characteristic of this group. Also characteristic is axillary branching (branches formed in the angle of the stem and the leaves).

The Botryopteridaceae appeared in the Lower Carboniferous and were extinct by the end of Permian. Specimens have been found in Scotland, France, the United States, and western Germany. These plants are characterized by an Omega-shaped (ω) xylem bundle in the petiole. These rhizomatous ferns exhibited spirally arranged branch complexes or primitive megaphylls. Stems in *Botryopteris* are radially organized and bear spirally arranged petioles. One species, *B. forensis* from the Upper Pennsylvanian, lived on the surface of a tree as an epiphyte (a plant that lives on the surface of another without parasitizing it).

The family Tedeleaceae is found primarily in the central United States in Upper Carboniferous coal balls as reproductive leaves. The stem anatomy consists of a protostele with an outer edge that appears fluted in cross section. Arising from the stem stele in a spiral sequence are frond traces that assume a characteristic H-shaped configuration in the petiole.

The family Sermayaceae is found in the Upper Carboniferous of Europe and North America as well-preserved petrified specimens (those preserved as rock). The main feature of *Sermaya* is the presence of leptosporangia. Sporangia either are sessile (having no stalks) or have stalks and occur in sori on the underside of pinnules. The wall has a distinct oblique (angled) or transverse (crosswise) annulus, with two rows of cells rather than a single row, as found in modern ferns. In *Sermaya* and *Doneggia* the petioles are of the *Anachoropteris* type.

The Psalixochlaenaceae, from the Carboniferous layers of England, were similar in their sporangial structure to the Botryopteridaceae, except the sporangia were arranged in sori, and the sporangia did not mature simultaneously. The stems branched dichotomously or had axillary branching. Some of the species are relatively small, scrambling plants. The stem has a primitive protostele.

The filicalean fossil ferns, closely related to modern forms, are the most diverse fern group as a whole, and modern filicalean ferns are second only to the angiosperms in their diversity. After the first-known occurrence in the Carboniferous, the six families present then disappeared, to be replaced by many families that are still represented in today's flora. During the Carboniferous ferns formed a large part of the flora; however, at the beginning of the Triassic the number of ferns diminished. Most of the ferns at that time can be assigned to modern orders and often even modern families, but others apparently are unrelated to modern forms. By Late Triassic the ferns were more abundant and diverse and were again common components of the vegetation, probably as understory plants (plants whose structures did not reach as high as those that formed the canopy) of the coniferous forests.

The Osmundaceae is one of the most primitive families and sometimes has been considered to be an intermediate group between the eusporangiate and leptosporangiate ferns. The fossil record of this family extends from the Permian, becoming quite diverse in the Mesozoic, but today is represented by only 16 species worldwide. The rhizomes, which are the most commonly preserved parts of this family, are generally a siphonostele with the phloem forming to the outer side of the xylem, and the vascular tissue is interrupted frequently by leaf gaps. The leaves are produced in a tight spiral. The leaf traces are C-shaped and face toward the axis of the plant. Roots form on the rhizome, which is generally erect. Many genera of fossil stems have been described, but the leaves of few genera are known. Only foliage genera *Todites* and some species of *Cladophlebis* have been assigned to this family. One plant from the Early Jurassic, *Raphaelia,* found in Siberia, has both sterile and fertile foliage preserved. The sporangia of the Osmundaceae have an annulus offset to one side, are large, and produce many spores. Generally the leaves are dimorphic, a character that probably appeared by the Middle Jurassic. It has been suggested that characteristics of the stem and the fertile parts implicate the Anachoropteridaceae as ancestors, but no direct link to this Carboniferous family is currently known. Probably, an extinct family, the Guaireaceae, is related closely to the Osmundaceae. It consists only of tree fern stems that have been found from the Permian to the mid-Mesozoic and resembles the Osmundaceae so closely that many originally were described as belonging to it.

The Schizaeaceae, whose origin is Late Triassic or Early Jurassic, is represented by the extant genera *Schizaea, Actinostachys, Anemia, Lygodium,* and *Mohria.* The oldest example is the genus *Norimbergia* from the Upper Triassic of France and Lower Jurassic in Germany. *Anemia* is found in the Cretaceous, when the other modern genera most likely appeared. This family has a characteristic annulus on the sporangium in the form of a ring of cells at the tip. The sporangia are borne singly and usually are naked, except in *Lygodium,* where they are covered by an extension of the lamina. The spores are trilete, except in *Schizaea* and *Actinostachys,* which are monolete. The distinct pattern of ridges on many of the spores (Figure 2b) allow identification of the family in many fossil deposits. It occurs in abundance through the Jurassic and Lower Cretaceous, then shows a decrease in diversity. *Lygodium* continued to have a worldwide distribution through the Tertiary. Today, members of the family are found mainly in tropical and subtropical regions.

The family Matoniaceae appeared in the Late Triassic (genus *Phlebopteris*) and is represented by two genera living today (*Matonia* and *Phanerosorus*) in southeast Asia. In the Mesozoic there were more genera, and the family was more widespread. The fronds in this family have a peltate arrangement of the pinnae—that is, they radiate from the tip of the petiole. Often, the sporangia are arranged in a circle within the sorus, and in more recent genera an "indusium" (a protective outgrowth from the leaf) formed over the sori. An unusual Cretaceous fern, *Weichselia,* probably is related closely to this modern family. Often, this fern is found preserved as charcoal and probably lived in an environment subject to fire.

The family Dipteridaceae is similar to the Matoniaceae in time and space distribution. The two families, along with the Gleicheniaceae, may be related through a common ancestor. The Dipteridaceae also was more diverse in the past but is now represented only by the genus *Dipteris* in southeast Asia. Sporangia are in sori without indusia on the surface of the leaf, and they have an oblique annulus. The family was worldwide during the Late Triassic and Early Jurassic—it was especially prevalent in the northern areas—then began to decrease.

The Gleicheniaceae is another very old family of leptosporangiate ferns, with the first occurrence (genus *Chansitheca* from eastern Asia) found in the Late Carboniferous or Permian. There are about 130 species known today, mainly in tropical regions. The leaf has a characteristic growth pattern in which the frond divides into two portions, then a bud forms in the center of the branched portions until the side shoots are complete. The bud then continues development of the leaf. The sori form a ring of sporangia, there is no indusium, and the annulus is oblique. This family also was important through the Mesozoic and then decreased in abundance with little fossil record through the Tertiary.

The family Dicksoniaceae contains mainly tree ferns. The sorus is at or near the margins and is protected by a bivalved indusium. Some of the indusia are joined at the base. The spores consistently are trilete with variations in contours (Figure 2a). This family appears during the Early Triassic. It was widespread during the Jurassic through the Cretaceous in the northern hemisphere but is rare in the southern hemisphere. It is now confined to tropical regions of the world, since the ferns prefer wet forests or thickets. There are five living genera: *Cibotium, Culcita, Dicksonia, Thyrsopteris,* and *Cystodium.* The subfamily Thyrsopteroidae is abundant from Early Jurassic through the Cretaceous in the Northern Hemisphere and now is confined to the Juan Fernandez Islands off the coast of South America. The subfamily Dicksonioidae became more abundant later in the Jurassic and has about 40 species today. Few fossils are found in the Tertiary.

The Cyatheaceae is a family that occurs widely in the tropics and occasionally in temperate regions. Members of the family prefer wet montane forests, steep slopes, and low elevations. Some genera, however, can grow in more disturbed habitats. Fossil species of the family, most often found as petrified stems, have been described worldwide, especially from the Jurassic and Cretaceous periods. There are few preserved leaf fossils. The family may have been diverse and widespread in the later Mesozoic, especially if the record of fossilized spores is accurate. There is much diversity in form of spores (Figure 2d), and family assignments may not always be accurate. It has been suggested that the family originated in the Southern Hemisphere, but its fossil record is relatively poor.

The Tempskyaceae consists of a single genus, *Tempskya,* known from petrified remains of its stem-trunk in the northern hemisphere during the Cretaceous. In overall habit, the fern resembles a tree fern; however, rather than a single stem, the "trunk" is composed of many stems and branches embedded in a mantle of supportive roots. The C-shaped petiole traces are known, but little of the leaf blade. Scholars suggest that the small leaf blades formed at the top of the "trunk." Relationships between this group and others are currently unknown.

The "Polypodiaceae" is the largest group within the filicalean ferns today. With worldwide distribution, it is divided now into many families, most of which have little or no fossil record. All members of this group have a small leptosporangium containing 64 spores (range of 16 to 128) with a vertical annulus. The spores vary from ellipsoidal with one suture (monolete) (Figure 2c) to more spherical and trilete. There are few fossils known before the Late Cretaceous. Some of the earliest representatives of the leptosporangiate ferns are related to the extant families Dry-

opteridaceae, Dennstaedtiaceae, and Thelypteridaceae. These ferns may have had their origins in the more humid temperate regions during the Cretaceous and became the undergrowth plants that could spread rapidly, especially vegetatively, through expanding rhizomes, for instance. As other families of ferns decreased during the Late Mesozoic and Early Tertiary, these ferns became more abundant.

Among the Filicales there appear to have been three major evolutionary radiations (diversifications and geographic spreadings). The first was in the Carboniferous forests, among the families formerly considered to be coenopterid ferns. The second occurred in the Late Paleozoic and Early Mesozoic, when the primitive families of the Filicales appeared, probably as understory plants in the coniferous forests. The third radiation involved the modern leptosporangiate "polypodiaceous" ferns, which arose after the flowering plants began to dominate the land.

Within the leptosporangiate ferns there are a few heterosporous and almost exclusively aquatic ferns, either placed in a single order as the Hydropteridales or into two orders: the Marsileales and the Salviniales. The two orders were established because the heterosporous ferns appeared to have distinct origins from within the filicalean ferns. Recently, a fossil representative from the Paleocene of British Columbia, *Hydropteris,* has led scholars to reclassify these families as a single order with a single origin. Molecular data have indicated close affinities between these two groups, and the fossil record indicates that the Marsileaceae appeared prior to the Salviniaceae.

The modern representatives of the Marsileaceae are found worldwide in aquatic areas. The leaves of the genus *Marsilea* often float on the water surface and look like large four-leaf clovers. These ferns have a creeping rhizome that grows on the bottom of the pond, and the roots are produced on the stem at the nodes (point of attachment of the leaves). The reproductive structures are modified pinnules, which form a sporocarp, which looks like a seed with a hard outer coating. When the sporocarp is broken in the presence of water, a long gelatinous mass (the sorophore) begins to expand out in a long strand. This strand contains the megasporangia and microsporangia, within which megaspores and microspores form. As the sporangia decay, the spores are released into the water. The gametophytes then form inside the spores. Fertilization occurs in the megaspore, and the sporophyte emerges. The Marsileales appeared in the Early Cretaceous, and megafossils (fossils of the plant itself, rather than its spores) are rare. Most of the fossils are megaspore complexes with microspores entrapped in extensions of the spore wall. Sporocarps also are found, some with associated vegetative structures. One of the Cretaceous megafossils is *Marsilea johnhallii,* found in Kansas. Another sporocarp, *Rodeites,* has been described from the Early Tertiary of India.

The genera *Azolla* and *Salvinia,* which, if the two aquatic groups are kept separate, are in the order Salviniales, are found as megafossils from the Paleocene-Upper Cretaceous boundary. Older fossils that have been associated with the Salviniales include *Azollopsis, Glomerisporites, Ariadnaesporites,* and *Parazolla.* These are all spores (microfossils) with a limited occurrence during the Cretaceous. *Ariadnaesporites* appears to be one of the oldest known genera within the Salviniales, arising in the late Early Cretaceous, but it shows only weak heterospory and is very different from the other genera in this order. Spores from *Parazolla*, *Glomerisporites*, and *Azollopsis* occur in the Late Cretaceous. Megafossils have been described, mainly the leaves and plants of *Azolla* from the Upper Cretaceous and Tertiary and *Salvinia* leaves from the Tertiary. The modern genera become worldwide in the Tertiary, and the older genera disappear.

The last two orders of ferns are both eusporangiate, homosporous ferns that have modern members: Marattiales and Ophioglossales. In each the sporangium is large with many spores and opens along a longitudinal line or apical pore. Because of this similarity, the two groups sometimes have been grouped together, but there is little fossil evidence to support this. One important difference between the two groups is the presence of synangia (groups of sporangia within a common wall), or at least sporangia tightly packed into sori in the Marattiales; the Ophioglossales, on the other hand, have individual sporangia borne on a fertile spike portion of the leaf. The Marattiales exhibit croziers and have canals containing mucilage in the stems, roots, and leaves. The Ophioglossales do not form croziers or canals.

The extant Marattiales are terrestrial ferns found in the tropics, mostly in moist environments. Although the order is worldwide, some genera are found only in the eastern or western hemispheres. They are considered primitive in comparison with other living ferns, and representative members can be traced at least as far back as the Mississippian period. The living members of this order (as well as direct ancestors from the Mesozoic) are placed in the family Marattiaceae, and the arborescent (treelike) members from the Carboniferous and Permian are placed in the Psaroniaceae. Seven extant genera are recognized, based on differences in the sorus: *Angiopteris*, *Marattia*, *Danaea*, *Christensenia*, *Archangiopteris*, *Macroglossum*, and *Protomarattia*.

The Marattiaceae have tough, fleshy stems that function as horizontal, underground rhizomes or upright, short, thick trunks. Like the Ophioglossales, there is basically endarch maturation in the xylem of the Marattiaceae, but in contrast, phloem maturation is also endarch. Typically, the arrangement of vascular tissue begins as a protostele, enlarges to a siphonostele, and eventually becomes a dictyostele. The dictyostele may develop from two to many cylinders (polycyclic) of vascular tissue.

Fronds of the Marattiaceae are large and fleshy. They vary from being once-pinnate to four or five times pinnate and may be up to seven meters long, the longest of any fern. *Danaea* fronds may be dimorphic. In *Christensenia* the fronds are palmate, with a network of veins. A widely recognized characteristic of the Marattiaceae is the presence of large, persistent stipules (paired flaps of additional tissue at the base of leaves) that may be utilized for protection of the young leaves and asexual reproduction. The roots are also fleshy and thick, with many air spaces present.

Sori occur along veins on the lower surface of the leaves. *Marattia*, *Danaea*, and *Christensenia* have synangia, while *Angiopteris* is usually free-sporangiate. The sporangia of *Angiopteris* are arranged in a double row and open by a longitudinal slit. The synangia of *Marattia* also exhibit longitudinal slits but produce monolete spores. Members of the genus *Danaea* have synangia partly submerged in the leaf and covering the lower surface of fronds. They open by terminal pores to release bilateral spores. The sori of all genera are linear except for those of *Christensenia*, which are radially symmetrical.

The slow-growing gametophytes of the Marattiaceae are terrestrial, photosynthetic, bisexual, and grow in association with a fungus. The gametophyte has a conspicuous midrib on the underside and may be elongate or heart-shaped. The antheridia (sperm-producing structures) and archegonia (egg-producing structures) (Figure 1) often are sunken in the surface of the gametophyte.

During the Carboniferous, members of the extinct family Psaroniaceae were tree ferns up to 10 meters tall. They became treelike because they developed a huge mantle of fleshy roots. The Psaroniaceae was a significant group in the Upper Carboniferous flora. Also, scholars have found evidence from the Late Pennsylvanian that *Psaronius* interacted with arthropods. The evidence is in the form of arthropod dung (coprolite) that contains ground vegetative tissue, which was found within the stems of *Psaronius*. *Psaronius* was similar to the extant ferns belonging to this group because of its fleshy trunks, root structure, sori, and large pinnate leaves.

Many types of fertile fronds have been associated with *Psaronius*, indicating diversity of the Marattiales during the Carboniferous. Usually sporangia or synangia were borne in two rows on the lower side of fronds. Species of *Scolecopteris* fronds produced synangia that were were borne on stalks and that split open longitudinally. *Chorionopteris* synangia also were stalked, but they hung near the edges of pinnules. A species of *Acitheca* found in the Middle Pennsylvanian of Oklahoma exhibited circular synangia that had lost their stalks. *Eoangiopteris* had linear, abaxial synangia with fused bases and free ends, approximating extant *Angiopteris*. Other fertile fronds revealed sunken synangia, like those of extant *Danaea*, but without apical pores.

The leaf arrangement of *Psaronius* was helical or whorled, and the fronds were one-to-four times pinnate, the divisions becoming smaller and fused near the end of the frond. Neither stipules nor pulvini (fleshy region at the base of the petiole) have been found in *Psaronius*, which is an important distinction from the living Marattiales. Some *Psaronius* fronds show mucilage canals.

The real stem of *Psaronius* narrowed toward the base; the way that the root mantle expanded from the apex downward gave the tree an overall conical shape. Some evidence suggests that the earliest tree ferns were smaller than those in the Middle Pennsylvanian and had simpler dictyosteles with only one ring of vascular tissue. Otherwise, the vascular pattern is similar to that seen in the living Marattiales: protostele to siphonostele to dictyostele. As the complex dictyostele developed, each new cycle joined the previous one internally, creating a structure that resembled a column of inverted cones. To vascularize a leaf from the stem, a strand of vascular tissue would arise from the center cycle of the dictyostele and subsequently merge and split with the outer cycles, leaving as many leaf traces as there were vascular cycles. Xylem and phloem maturation was endarch, and no secondary vascular tissues were produced. *Psaronius* stems usually had some sclerenchyma (cells with two wall layers), and some had mucilage canals.

The roots of *Psaronius* were the largest of all ferns. These roots originated horizontally and then grew down, developing into a compact zone on the inside and a loose zone peripherally. The compact zone was formed by secondary cortex (bark) from stem and root tissues, which filled and compacted the inner zone of roots. Some sclerenchyma tissue and air spaces occurred in *Psaronius* roots.

An Upper Mississippian, small, siphonostelic species of the Psaroniaceae was discovered in noncoal deposits, suggesting that *Psaronius* established itself first outside peat swamps. The fossil record indicates that Psaroniaceae occurred throughout tropical areas, and that ferns grew opportunistically in areas during the late Paleozoic.

In the tropical wetland mires of the Upper Pennsylvanian, *Psaronius* moved into new areas left by Middle-Late Pennsylvanian plant extinctions, becoming the dominant tree form. In the tropical wetlands, *Psaronius* shared dominance with the gymnosperms, and this association probably lasted into the Permian. *Psaronius* diversified and radiated into these environments because it could take advantage of new, disrupted areas. Spores dispersed rapidly over wide areas, the largely simple tissues grew rapidly, and the ferns could tolerate the low levels of nutrients in the soil.

Fossil evidence for the Marattiaceae is discontinuous. A genus that was a contemporary of *Psaronius,* though not nearly as common, was *Radstockia.* It exhibited elongate synangia very similar to the extant *Marattia. Radstockia* can be dated from the Middle Pennsylvanian and, along with *Qasimia* (Upper Permian), may have given rise to present-day *Danaea, Marattia,* and *Angiopteris. Qasimia* had synangia and spores very similar to modern *Marattia,* except that the synangia of *Qasimia* spanned halfway across the rounded pinnules (modern *Marattia* has tapered pinnules). Other ferns that closely resembled *Marattia* have been discovered in the Permian of China, eastern Russia, and southeast Asia. *Angiopteris blackii,* from Middle Jurassic times, is alleged to be ancestral to the freesporangiate marattialeans (*Angiopteris, Archangiopteris, Macroglossum,* and *Protomarattia*), but no other fossils are known until the Recent. Solid evidence for *Marattia* ancestors exists from the Triassic. Fossils of these plants were found through the Jurassic. Also in Triassic strata, fertile fronds very similar to modern *Danaea* have been found.

The second order of eusporangiate ferns are the Ophioglossales. Ferns of this order are typically perennial, forming one leaf per year. The stem is usually short, upright, and unbranched, exhibits endarch xylem maturation, has no sclerenchyma cells, possesses leaves with stipules, and has thick, radiating roots. Roots of the Ophioglossales form singly, near the base of the leaves, and contain an endophytic fungus (one that lives within a structure of another organism, here the root). Members of this order display a very large spore output, ranging up to 15,000 per sporangium in some species. The order consists of three genera: *Botrychium, Helminthostachys,* and *Ophioglossum.* These genera are defined by the form of the sterile leafblade found on the vegetative segment. In *Botrychium* the blade exhibits dichotomous arrangement of the veins (venation) and may be unbranched or up to four-times pinnate. Leaves of *Helminthostachys* have three parts, with dichotomous venation. *Ophioglossum* has leathery leaves with a network of veins and an undivided lamina, and it is probably more derived.

Until recently there was no fossil record of this family. Then, a *Botrychium* was described from Paleocene in Alberta,

Canada, that closely resembles the modern *B. virginianum* in frond morphology, sporangia characteristics, and spore features. The ancestry of the order remains uncertain. Modern molecular work indicates a relationship for these ferns within the pteridophytes, but the suggestion also has been made for relationships with the progymnosperms (forms that immediately preceded seed-bearing trees).

The eusporangiate ferns were most abundant during the Paleozoic (Marattialeans and prefilicalean types) and are now much less important in the flora. Their importance decreased through the Mesozoic, although it is during this time that the modern genera probably appeared.

The relationships and phylogeny of the ferns have been much discussed and many views have been presented. Several of the references below present alternative hypotheses of fern phylogeny, but the inclusion of the fossil forms in these phylogenies always has been difficult because of the lack of evidence for certain distinctive characters. Many of the phylogenies are based on molecular data only or include only the extant ferns.

JUDITH E. SKOG

See also Gymnosperms; Progymnosperms; Seed Ferns

Works Cited

Phillips, T.L. 1974. Evolution of vegetative morphology in coenopterid ferns. *Annals of the Missouri Botanical Garden* 61:427–61.
Tryon, A.F., and B. Lugardon. 1991. *Spores of the Pteridophyta.* New York: Springer-Verlag.

Further Reading

Camus, J.M., A.C. Jermy, and B.A. Thomas. 1991. *A World of Ferns.* London: Natural History Museum Publications.
Gifford, E.M., and A.S. Foster. 1959. *Comparative Morphology of Vascular Plants.* San Francisco: Freeman; 3rd ed., *Morphology and Evolution of Vascular Plants,* New York: Freeman, 1989.
Hill, C.R., and J.M. Camus. 1986. Evolutionary cladistics of marattialean ferns. *Bulletin of the British Museum of Natural History, Bot.,* 14:219–300.
Kubitzki, K. (ed.). 1990. The families and genera of vascular plants. *In* K.U. Kramer and P.S. Green (eds.), *Pteridophytes and gymnosperms.* Vol. 1, Berlin and New York: Springer-Verlag.
Lovis, J.D. 1977. Evolutionary patterns and processes in ferns. *Advances in Botanical Research* 4:229–415.
Meien, S.V. 1987. *Fundamentals of Palaeobotany.* London and New York: Chapman and Hall.
Phillips, T.L. 1974. Evolution of vegetative morphology in coenopterid ferns. *Annals of the Missouri Botanical Garden* 61:427–61.
Rothwell, G.W., and R.S. Stockey. 1994. The role of *Hydropteris pinnata* gen. et sp., nov. in reconstructing the cladistics of heterosporous ferns. *American Journal of Botany* 81:479–92.
Stewart, W.N., and G.W. Rothwell. 1983. *Paleobotany and the Evolution of Plants.* Cambridge and New York: Cambridge University Press; 2nd ed., 1993.
Taylor, T.N., and E.L. Taylor. 1993. *The Biology and Evolution of Fossil Plants.* Englewood Cliffs, New Jersey: Prentice-Hall.

Tidwell, W.D., and S.R. Ash. 1994. A review of selected Triassic to early Cretaceous ferns. *Journal of Plant Research* 107:417–42.

Tryon, A.F., and B. Lugardon. 1991. *Spores of the Pteridophyta*. New York: Springer-Verlag.

Tryon, R.M., and A.F. Tryon. 1982. *Ferns and Allied Plants with Special Reference to Tropical America*. New York: Springer-Verlag.

Wolf, P.G. (comp.). 1995. Use of molecular data in evolutionary studies of pteridophytes. *American Fern Journal Special Issue* 85:101–428.

FIELD TECHNIQUES

Fossils come in all kinds, shapes, and sizes—from minute, delicate spheres of plant pollen to complete skeletons of gigantic sauropod dinosaurs. Yet all these fossils have one thing in common: paleontologists must search them out and carefully remove them from the ground. This nearly endless variety of fossils requires an enormous array of techniques for their extraction and safe transport back to the lab, and each technique must be matched carefully to the particular fossil and situation. Without these field techniques, no fossil would ever make it back to museums intact.

Finding the Fossil

The first step is to find the fossil. This search takes various forms. For instance, moderate to large fossils are usually found by "prospecting." The paleontologist does this by slowly walking across the fossil-bearing sediments, eyes to the ground, searching for fossils that are weathering out of the ground. Paleontologists never simply start digging, hoping to strike a fossil. In the best scenario, the fossil is just beginning to be exposed at the surface, and most of it still lies, undisturbed and unweathered, below ground. In the worst scenario, a paleontologist finds the fossil after it has been completely exposed and nearly destroyed.

But not all fossils require prospection for each specimen. For instance, the collection of very small fossils (like tiny mammal teeth or fish vertebrae) and pollen is done by locating a fossiliferous layer and "mining" it: collecting large amounts of this sediment, which are then taken to a processing area to extract the fossils.

Uncovering Fossils

Once a fossil is discovered weathering from the ground, the paleontologist carefully exposes its surface. The kind of fossil is ascertained, as is its condition, size, and completeness. Sometimes a paleontologist is rewarded with a beautiful, complete specimen. But as often as not, the find is only partial, poorly preserved, or already too weathered to be collected.

The tools used to excavate fossils vary greatly, depending on the kind of fossil and the properties of the rock that surround it. For instance, excavating a small, delicate mammal jaw from soft rock may require nothing more than a dental pick. Dinosaur bones in hard sandstone may require a large gas-powered jackhammer. Generally, one wants to use the gentlest tool that the rock allows—fossils are fragile and overdoing the excavation can be destructive.

Dental picks, chisels, and ice picks are all frequently used to excavate fossils; shovels, picks, jackhammers, and even heavy machinery help to clear excess sediments around the fossil. Paintbrushes of all sizes are used to gently clean the fossil of debris. The upper surfaces of the bones should just barely be exposed. The paleontologist must be careful not to excavate too much of the fossil in the field—it is always better to uncover most of the fossil in the lab under controlled conditions. Often, when a paleontologist has found a wonderful new fossil and is eager to see what it looks like, it is hard to resist overexposing it. But paleontologists must resist the urge or run the risk of permanently damaging or destroying the specimen.

Consolidating the Fossil

Although it often is said that fossils have "turned to stone," they are actually quite fragile and often fragmented. To keep the pieces together, and to keep the fossil from further damage during excavation, they must be stabilized with some kind of consolidant (glue).

The best field consolidants hold the fossil together well, are easily removed later in the lab, and do no damage. Many years ago, the glue of choice for paleontologists was shellac. But shellac becomes yellow and brittle with age, discoloring the fossil and allowing it to fall apart. Many new, more stable glues are available, many of them polyvinyl or butylvinyl acetates. While some of these glues require acetone or other volatile liquids as their base, other consolidants dissolve in water. This is not only better for the health of the paleontologist, but often more convenient for fieldwork; large volumes of acetone (difficult to find in some areas of the world) need not be carried to distant places.

Consolidants are used sparingly—excess glue glopped onto a fossil in the field will only have to be removed later in the laboratory. Consolidants usually are applied by dribbling the liquid glue onto the fossil from a squirt bottle. Sometimes the glue is applied gently onto the fossil with a soft paintbrush. The glues usually can be mixed to different viscosities—very thick, gummy glue to hold large pieces together, or thin, runny glue for small objects in a hard matrix.

Jacketing and Extracting the Fossil

Once the extent of the fossil is ascertained, the paleontologist begins preparing the fossil for removal. Occasionally, the fossil and the rock around it can be lifted out of the ground without any additional reinforcement. This usually only works for small specimens in hard rock, such as small fishes on slabs of shale. Most large or delicate fossils require reinforcement: a protective shell, or "jacket," to hold it together during removal and transportation. After all the work of finding and uncovering a specimen, paleontologists do not want to risk having the fossil crumble to pieces by pulling it from the ground without protection.

First, a deep trench (reaching below the level of the fossil) is dug around the perimeter of the fossil, leaving just a small rim of rock around the outermost bones. Sometimes the fossil is too big to be taken out in one block. In this case the paleontologist must decide where to divide the large block into smaller blocks, trenching carefully down between bones.

Then comes the dangerous part: undercutting the block. This can be precarious, especially if the rock is soft or tends to break apart easily. The paleontologist digs underneath the perimeter of the block, leaving the fossil supported only by a pedestal of rock at its center. Paleontologists must gauge how much of a pedestal to leave based on the size of the block and the strength of the rock.

The technology and materials used to make field jackets has not changed for more than a century—burlap and plaster were used by F.D. Cope and O.C. Marsh and are still used today. Other, newer materials are available (such as spray foams and fiberglass), but plaster and burlap are cheap and readily available worldwide—and they still do the job. Plaster jackets are also easy to open and remove in the lab.

Once the specimen is trenched and pedestaled, it must be coated with a "separator" to keep the plaster from directly touching the fossil. Plaster sticks to the bone surface and is very difficult to remove. Most commonly the separator is damp toilet paper or paper towel layed over the fossil and tamped down tightly to its surface with a wet paintbrush. Aluminum foil also makes a good separator for small fossils. The paleontologist must then have the jacketing materials ready: water, plaster, mixing bucket, and enough rolled strips of burlap for the job. Each strip of burlap is presoaked in water; the plaster will not stick to dry burlap.

Water is poured into the bucket, and the dry plaster is stirred into the water until it is the desired consistency. If it is too thin, it will be too runny and weak; if too thick, it will harden before the jacket is finished. The strips of damp burlap are soaked in the liquid plaster and rolled onto the block in overlapping layers and alternating directions. They are wrapped around the sides and underneath the perimeter of the block; this is why the fossil is pedestaled. The plaster bandages wrapped under the perimeter of the block keep the fossil from falling out the bottom of the jacket when it is lifted.

The paleontologist must judge from experience the amount of plaster and burlap for each jacket. Too much and the block becomes unnecessarily heavy and difficult to open later. Too little

and the jacket will lack the strength to hold together. Once the jacket has dried to a hard shell, the entire block is quickly turned over, and the exposed rock on the base of the jacket is "topped" with a layer of burlap and plaster. For very large fossils, lengths of wood are incorporated into the jacket as supporting struts. These struts can extend beyond the edge of the block to be used as handles to carry the finished block back to the truck.

For small jackets, preplastered gauze bandages can be used, the same kind that doctors use to set a broken arm or leg. These handy bandages are efficient, easy to use, and light to carry, but they are suitable only for small fossils.

Some tiny fossils are collected in a very different manner—by collecting large volumes of fossiliferous sediments for later processing. For instance, for "microvertebrates" (tiny bits of small animals such as teeth and vertebrae), tons of fossiliferous sediments are collected from a locality and brought back to a processing area. There the sediment is gently run through a fine mesh about the size of a window screen. This can be done dry or wet (washing the sediment through with water). In each case, the very fine dirt particles fall through the screen, leaving behind a "concentrate" of tiny rocks and fossils. Hundreds of small fossils can be collected this way.

Transporting Fossils

Fossils need to be carefully packed for transportation back to the lab from the field. Even jacketed specimens must be packed so they cannot move around; bouncing around the back of a truck can jar and shatter the contents of a jacket. Once in the lab, each fossil is carefully freed of all sediment, repaired, cataloged, studied, and sometimes put on display.

CATHERINE A. FORSTER

See also Paleontology: Overview; Photographic Techniques; Preparation Techniques

Further Reading

Gilette, D.D. 1997. Hunting for dinosaur bones. *In* J.O. Farlow and M.K. Brett-Surman (eds.), *The Complete Dinosaur*. Bloomington: Indiana University Press.
Kummel, B. 1965. *Handbook of Paleontological Techniques*. San Francisco: Freeman.
Leiggi, P., and P. May. 1994. *Vertebrate Paleontological Techniques*. Cambridge and New York: Cambridge University Press.

FINS AND LIMBS, PAIRED

Fingers and toes have long been considered unique features of tetrapods (amphibians, reptiles, mammals, and birds). As a result, limbs often are viewed as the major characteristic that separates tetrapods from virtually all known types of fishes. No other char-

acteristic can claim this distinction. Gills, commonly thought to be present only in fishes, also are found in many amphibians. Likewise, lungs, a characteristic that we think as separating tetrapods from other vertebrates, are seen in some fishes.

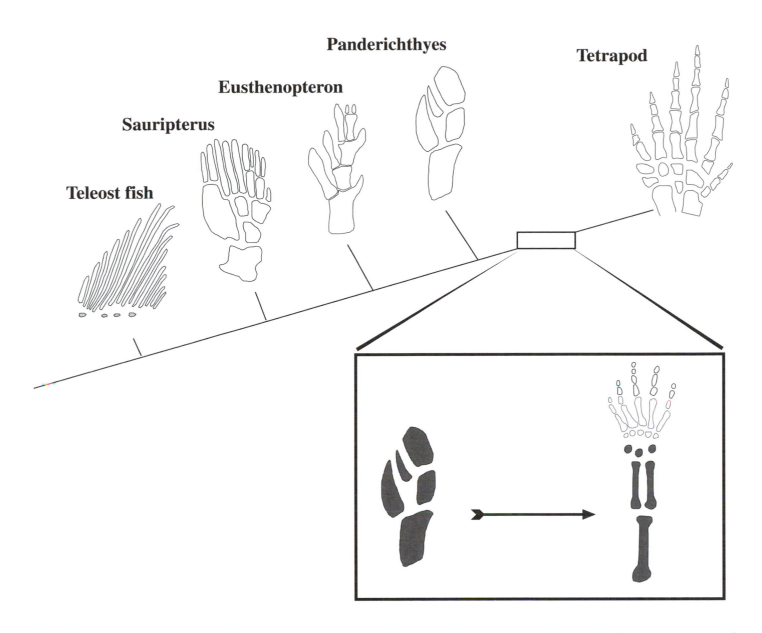

Figure 1. Different types of fins are shown on a branching diagram that depicts their relationship to tetrapod limbs. *Panderichthyes* and *Eusthenopteron* are considered to be close relatives of tetrapods; hence, they are shown on this diagram to branch closer to tetrapods than do either *Sauripterus* or teleost fishes. *Sauripterus* has eight rods that project from the fin, which are exceedingly digitlike. Despite this, recent work suggests that *Sauripterus* might not be closely related to tetrapods. Teleost fishes are an example of a type of bony fish that has an extensive set of fin rays but a small endoskeletal portion of the fin (shaded). The box shows why some authors have hypothesized digits to be evolutionary novelties. No structure in the fin of Panderichthyes corresponds to digits. Most of the similarities in pattern lie in the base of the fin.

Recent discoveries from paleontology and developmental biology have provided new information on how fins transformed over time into limbs. Fingers and toes arose as one group of fishes evolved and adapted to newly emerging freshwater environments that arose in Late Devonian times (about 370 million years ago).

The origin of limbs is a major event in the history of life because it enabled tetrapods to live in a host of new environments. There are numerous examples of this phenomenon. The specialized jumping habits of rabbits, frogs, and kangaroos are largely the result of evolutionary changes to their limbs. Birds, pterosaurs,

and bats all evolved different types of wings that allow different types of gliding and powered flight. Hominids evolved specialized hands that allow for the precise control of fingers. Each of these cases shows how the evolution of limbs is associated with the ability of organisms to exploit their environment in new ways.

There are two major questions that can be asked about the origin of limbs: how they evolved and why they evolved. When we ask how limbs evolved from fish fins, we are concerned with identifying the anatomical, developmental, and genetic changes that enabled the origin of fingers and toes. Why limbs evolved is a more difficult question because it seeks to provide an adaptive explanation for the origin of limbs.

How Limbs Evolved

All tetrapod limbs share a common skeletal design. Bird wings, whale flippers, and human arms all possess a similar arrangement of bones. One set of corresponding arm and leg bones, the humerus and femur, lie within the upper arm and thigh regions, respectively. Two other sets of corresponding bones, the radius/ulna and tibia/fibula, lie within the forearm and foreleg. One can continue these comparisons through the wrist and ankle to the digits. Different types of limbs, whether they be wings, flippers, or hands, evolved by changing the number, size, and shape of bones of this fundamental pattern. Bat wings, for example evolved by expanding the size of all five fingers, whereas the wings of pterosaurs evolved by expanding only a single finger, finger IV.

Most fish fins do not have a skeleton that is similar to tetrapod limbs. Bony fishes (all fishes except sharks and their relatives) have a fin made up of two types of bone: endochondral bone and fin rays. The endochondral bone is originally formed within a cartilage model. This endochondral part of the fin skeleton sits at the fin base and, unlike tetrapods limbs, comprises a small part of the fin. Most of the surface area of the fin is made up of numerous fin rays. These fin rays are elongate spicules that radiate from the endochondral bones of the fin. Tetrapod limbs do not possess these fin rays; the limb skeleton is composed exclusively of endochondral bone. One of the major shifts, then, in the origin of limbs is the expansion of the endochondral component of the skeleton and the loss of the fin rays.

One group of fishes possesses fins that have an endoskeleton that is, in part, similar to that of tetrapod limbs. These fishes, sarcopterygians (or lobe-finned fishes), have a fleshy lobe at the base of the fin. This lobe contains an endoskeleton that is similar to part of the limb of tetrapods, the upper (or proximal) part. The forefin (pectoral) contains a humerus, radius, and ulna. The hind fin (pelvic) contains a femur, tibia, and fibula. Convincing evidence of these structures are seen in the Devonian sarcopterygians *Eusthenopteron* and *Sauripterus*. While the fins of these two fishes do not look similar in shape or size, both possess these sets of endoskeletal bones.

The closest relatives of tetrapods, panderychthid sarcopterygians, have fins that are designed along a simple bifurcate pattern: each segment of the fin contains a short, rectangular bone (basal) and a more elongate bone (radial). In some classical accounts radials have been compared with digits, but there are significant differences. One major difference is that these radials are not jointed like fingers and toes.

Several hypotheses have been proposed to explain the origin of digits. One hypothesis maintains that digits are evolutionary novelties because no known fish fin contains these structures. The origin of tetrapods, then, would be associated with the evolution of a new anatomical structure, one with no antecedents in other creatures. This view has been supported by recent molecular studies of the development of fish fins and tetrapod limbs.

Limb and fin skeletons develop along a standard sequence; elements close to the body appear in earlier developmental stages than do elements at the tips of the appendage. Digits, then, are among the last portions of the limb skeleton to emerge. This same reasoning appears to apply at the genetic and molecular level and may provide insights into the origin of digits. The genetic mechanisms that are thought to control digit formation are active in later stages of development. These observations have led some to suggest that the origin of digits involved the origin of new genetic events that have been added to the end of a primitive developmental sequence.

Other hypotheses seek to find structures in fish fins that could be compared to digits. Some sarcopterygian fins contain elongate rods (radials) that lie at the margins of the fin. Various authors have proposed that some or all of these radials are comparable to digits. Some sarcopterygians have fins that are very similar in pattern to tetrapod limbs. One example of these similarities is seen in the fin of the Devonian fish *Sauripterus*. *Sauripterus* contains a fin with eight jointed radials that point away from the fin. These rods are similar in number and position to the eight fingers seen in some early tetrapods such as *Acanthostega*. It is tempting to compare these radials to the fingers of tetrapods, but there are still many uncertainties about this creature. *Sauripterus* is only known from the fin skeleton; the head has not yet been discovered. Furthermore, some scholars have suggested that *Sauripterus* is not the closest relative of tetrapods, and it might, as a consequence, have evolved these digitlike structures independently from tetrapods.

Why Limbs Evolved

Fingers and toes were long thought to be novelties associated with the invasion of land by tetrapods. This traditional notion has been challenged because the most primitive fossil in which digits are known, *Acanthostega,* is aquatic. *Acanthostega* has a limb that looks very aquatic in its design: the bones are somewhat flattened, and there are eight digits in the expanded paddle region. All early tetrapods have more than five digits in their limbs, though the exact number varies. *Acanthostega* poses a challenge to the traditional view that digits arose to enable animals to walk on land. Either digits arose in an amphibious animal that was primarily aquatic, or digits arose in an as-yet undiscovered land-living animal, and *Acanthostega* is secondarily aquatic (i.e., it evolved from terrestrial ancestors but returned to the water).

Digits need not have arisen to meet the demands of life on land and could have evolved originally in fishes living in aquatic ecosystems. Devonian tetrapods and their relatives are typically found in shallow streams or ponds, many of which are likely to have been choked with plant life. Limbs could have been used in a variety of contexts in these environments. They could have been used for occasional forays onto land. Limbs also could have been used to maneuver through shallow water, either to enable the animal to walk on the bottom or navigate through plant-choked shallows. The origin of limbs reflects a commitment to the use of the appendages in locomotion, a pattern that stands in contrast to many fishes, which use movements of the back and tail to navigate. The specific functions of these early appendages is likely to remain a matter of debate for years to come.

NEIL H. SHUBIN

See also Aquatic Locomotion; Gnathostomes; Skeleton: Axial Skeleton; Skeleton: Dermal Postcranial Skeleton; Terrestrial Locomotion in Vertebrates

Further Reading

Ahlberg, P.E., and A.R. Milner. 1994. The origin and early diversification of tetrapods. *Nature* 368:507–12.
Coates, M.I. 1994. The origin of vertebrate limbs. *Development* (suppl.):169–80.
———. 1995. Fish fins or tetrapod limbs: A simple twist of fate? *Currrent Biology* 5:844–48.
———. 1996. The Devonian tetrapod *Acanthostega gunnari* Jarvik: Postcranial anatomy, basal tetrapod interrelationships and patterns of skeletal evolution. *Transactions of the Royal Society of Edinburgh* 87:363–421.
Jarvik, E. 1996. The Devonian tetrapod *Ichthyostega*. *Fossils and Strata* 40:1–213.
Shubin, N. 1995. The evolution of paired fins and the origin of tetrapod limbs. *Evolutionary Biology* 28:39–85.
Shubin, N., and P. Alberch. 1986. A morphogenetic approach to the origin and basic organization of the tetrapod limb. *Evolutionary Biology* 20:318–90.
Shubin, N., C. Tabin, and S.B. Carroll. 1997. Fossils, genes and the evolution of animal limbs. *Nature* 388:639–48.
Sordino, P., F. van der Hoeven, and D. Duboule. 1995. *Hox* gene expression in teleost fins and the origin of vertebrate digits. *Nature* 375:678–81.
Sordino, P., and D. Duboule. 1996. A molecular approach to the evolution of vertebrate paired appendages. *Trends in Ecology and Evolution* 11:114–19.
Vorobyeva, E., and J.R. Hinchliffe. 1996. From fins to limbs: Developmental perspectives on paleontological and morphological evidence. *Evolutionary Biology* 29:263–11.

FLORAL PROVINCES
See Faunal and Floral Provinces

FORESTS, FOSSIL

There was a time during Earth history when there were no forests. The occurrence of forests such as we know today is the product of the evolution of trees, which began in the Devonian. The tall woody trees characteristic of modern forests did not develop quickly but are the result of long-term evolutionary modifications of plants. The species composition of forests, the nature of the reproductive biology of the trees that make up the forests, and the way in which trees support their height has been reinvented and modified several times and has been subject to continual changes through time. There have been at least five different ways in which structures developed that enabled trees to support their height, and their reproduction has depended upon such variable means as the production of spores, megaspores/microspores (female and male spores), prepollen and seeds, pollen and seeds, and pollen and fruits.

Trees were absent from the Earth during the early colonization of land by plants in the Late Silurian and Early Devonian (Gensel and Andrews 1984; Kendrick and Crane 1997). It was during the early Middle Devonian, about 380 million years ago, that we first find some larger-diameter stems preserved. By the end of the Middle Devonian, quite large diameter stems are found that must have been stems of taller treelike plants that formed forests (Chaloner and Sheerin 1979). These plants had thick stems (10 centimeters to 80 centimeters), probably grew to 5 to 15 meters in height, and reproduced by means of spores rather than seeds. The structures of these trees had some secondary woody tissues, but they were not hard woody trees such as we know today. These early trees are related to today's lycopods (club mosses), sphenopsids (horsetails), and ferns.

By the latest Devonian several plants, including the progymnosperms (ancient ancestors of seed-bearing trees), began to modify their reproductive biology in ways that increased the possibility for plants to cross fertilize. Some descendants of these plants soon began to enclose the newly formed embryo with stored food and a tough covering, thus developing seeds (gymnosperms). The forests of the latest Devonian consisted mainly of lycopod (club moss) and sphenopsid (horsetail) trees, with some shorter tree ferns and some tall progymnosperms such as *Archaeopteris* (Gensel and Andrews 1984). These diverse trees of the later Devonian, along with related shrubs and small trees, were the stock from which the famous Carboniferous forests of the coal ages developed.

Many areas of the Earth were covered by luxuriant, well-developed forests during the Mississippian and Pennsylvanian periods. These often were swamp forests dominated by several species of lycopods (club mosses), such as *Lepidodendron, Lepidophloios,* and *Sigillaria.* These dominant trees of the coal swamp forests had little woody tissue. Instead, they supported their height of 15 to 40 meters by forming massive trunks consisting of thick cylinders of bark. Inside of this stout cylinder were softer tissues and a small amount of woody tissue used to conduct water and nutrients up and down the tall stems between the roots and the leafy shoots. These plants bore spores in cones.

Sphenopsids (horsetails) also were present in these forests, a representative of which was the *Calamites* tree. These were slender trees that looked like tall, leafy bamboo and that also reproduced by spores produced in cones. *Calamites* were supported by secondary woody tissue, much like some trees living today. Several types of ferns also developed a tree habit supported mainly by a massive adventitious root mantel (roots that grew around the main "stem," or trunk) covering the stems. These tree ferns resembled tree ferns living in forests today. Other fernlike plants common in the coal age forests bore seeds on large leaves of fernlike foliage instead of reproducing by spores. These plants were short trees, vines, or shrubs and form a group called "seed ferns" (Pteridosperms), which became extinct in the Cretaceous. Finally, in these forests there were several species of *Cordaites*, an early relative of the seed-bearing conifers. Their wood was most similar to that of living pine trees today, and they reproduced by seeds (Stewart and Rothwell 1993; Taylor and Taylor 1993). Some species of *Cordaites* may have formed some of the earliest known mangrove forests of the world.

The Permian was an important period because it was a time of extensive changes (mountain building and reorganization of continental plates into a single supercontinent called Pangea). These changes affected the biology of both plants and animals (Erwin 1993). The changes were so great that the end of the Permian period marks the end of the Paleozoic era. The composition of fossil forests changed as well at this time. The Late Paleozoic forests consisted of many lycopod and sphenopsid trees in wet areas and some seed ferns and early ancestors of conifers in drier areas, while conifers and other seed plants were common in the upland areas and perhaps dominated them. Numerous plant species became extinct at the end of the Paleozoic. Never again were there forests dominated by lycopod and sphenopsid trees. The earliest evidence of cycads and ginkgos can be traced back to the Permian.

The end of the Paleozoic is marked by the greatest extinction event known in the history of life on Earth (Raup 1986; Erwin 1993). This extinction and death of organisms included forest trees as well, which probably resulted in extensive forests of dead trees around the world. These trees created a tremendous amount of unprotected cellulose, which gave rise to a huge explosion of wood-rotting fungi to consume this forest biomass (Visscher et al. 1996). Sediments deposited at this time contain a huge number of fungal spores that probably came from these wood-rotting fungi.

The Mesozoic is a time of extensive forests around the world. Some remnants of these great forests still can be seen in the petrified forests of the national parks in Arizona; Patagonia, Argentina; Rajasthan, India; and western sections of China. At this time, many forests of the world contained giant trees similar to *Araucaria*, along with cycads, seed ferns, tree ferns, and low-growing ferns. *Ginkgo* became more common and diverse. The fossil record of plants in the Triassic and Jurassic indicates that the conifers were the dominant forest trees. Modern groups of many conifers can be traced back to the Mesozoic (Miller 1971, 1976, 1977). Many of these were seed-bearing trees that often produced cones and had foliage similar to modern *Araucaria*, *Pinus* (pine), *Picea* (spruce), *Taxodium* (bald cypress), and *Sequoia* (redwood).

Fossils of a seed-bearing tree, *Glossopteris*, occur commonly in widely separated areas that once were joined together to form a large Southern Hemisphere landmass known as Gondwana. Permian and Triassic fossils of the *Glossopteris* tree demonstrate that contiguous forests on Gondwana extended across what today are the separated areas of South Africa, southern South America, India, Madagascar, Antarctica, Australia, and New Zealand. Also, an extinct group of cycads, the Cycadoidales (Bennettitales), developed as diverse understory shrubs (those that grow between ground level and the forest canopy) during the Mesozoic and became extinct by the end of the Mesozoic.

The forest assemblage of the Mesozoic was not the same as the forests we know today, because the assembly consisted entirely of conifers or other gymnosperms with an understory of ferns, some lycopods, and other seed-bearing trees. There were also mangrove lycopods, mangrove ferns, and mangrove conifers, which formed thickets along the ocean margins of continents. While conifers dominated some areas of the world during the Mesozoic, other seed plants (gymnosperms) were common, and there was an abundance of ferns. Early forms of the Gnetales and several species of *Ginkgo* are known from this time.

A new group of plants, the flowering plants (angiosperms), probably have a Mesozoic origin and became very common elements in the vegetation of most areas of the Earth during the Late Mesozoic (Cretaceous period). This change in the types of trees, and thus the vegetative structure of the Cretaceous forests, took place during the time of the dinosaurs, but this change in woody vegetation did not seem to have any influence upon the dinosaurs, nor did the dinosaurs appear to influence the angiosperms (Coe et al. 1987). However, at this time, angiosperms and other animals were developing close coevolutionary ties. Flowering plants, including forest trees, began to utilize insects to carry pollen from one plant to another of the same species, resulting in cross pollination (Labandeira et al. 1994). And many insects adapted to certain plants, to the exclusion of other plants. The coevolution of trees and their animal pollinators influenced forest structure profoundly. Insect pollination facilitated the development of forests that contain many diverse species of trees living and mixing together, as is typical of today's tropical forests. In these forests an individual tree of a species may be separated by 100 yards to 1 mile from other individual trees of the same species. Insects, often being faithful pollinators of a particular species, carry pollen great distances between isolated trees. Thus, the monodominant stands of gymnosperms, which relied on wind to distribute pollen in the Early Mesozoic, were replaced by forests rich with complex mixtures of species at the end of the Mesozoic.

During the Early Tertiary, at the same time as the radiation (diversification and geographic spread) of birds and rodents, forest trees began to produce delicious fleshy fruits and nutritious nuts. These fruits and nuts were attractive to animals, served as rich sources of food, and probably were an important factor in the spectacular radiation of these animals. The animals served the plants well, taking their seeds and dispersing them some distance from the parent trees, facilitating the reproduction of these trees and further encouraging cross pollination, a process that enriched the genetic inheritance of each species. Thus, through pollination and fruit and seed dispersal, angiosperms and animals repeatedly have formed special relationships and even dependencies upon each other.

Forests superficially similar to modern forests were widespread around the world by the Middle Eocene. However, many specific elements of these Early Tertiary Age forests became extinct, either regionally or completely. The vegetative zones (areas with generally unified temperature and precipitation characteristics) that we see on the Earth today, extending from the equator north and south towards either pole, begin to be evident during the Tertiary period of the Cenozoic era. Tropical, semi-tropical, and warm temperate climates with more equable seasons than seen today seem to dominate much of the Tertiary. Cooler climates near the poles produced temperate forests in these regions. For example, near the North Pole, there is evidence of a temperate mixed forest of conifers and deciduous hardwoods during the Paleocene and Eocene (Basinger 1986). During this time, the forests of North America indicate a warm temperate climate, perhaps with some frosts in the interior, and more equable, perhaps frost-free areas along the coasts, supporting warm temperate to subtropical forests. During the Paleocene and Eocene, Europe consisted of a series of large islands that contained many elements of flora in common with North America and Asia. In fact, a zone of forest trees that shared several common elements encircled the Northern Hemisphere during the Eocene (Manchester 1994). Remnants of this common forest still can be seen in similar types of plants (genera and/or species) found in southeastern China, the southeastern United States, and Mexico today. The fossil record indicates that these areas shared even more elements of these forests during the Eocene-Miocene. Some examples of such forest plants are *Nyssa, Liriodendron, Carya, Gordonia, Juglans, Liquidambar, Oreomunnea/Engelhardia, Taxodium, Sequoia,* and *Metasequoia.* On the other hand, some forest plants that once lived around the world now only exist as native plants in one small part of their former range. For example, *Ginkgo, Metasequoia,* tree of heaven *(Alianthus),* and *Nypa* (a mangrove palm) now are found growing naturally only in Asia. *Hippomane* (manchineel, a poisonous beach tree) and *Sabal* (a palm) are found naturally only in the Caribbean area, while *Sequoia* and *Taxodium* are restricted to western and southeastern North America respectively. At the end of the Eocene there was a worldwide cooling event; the North and South Poles had deep freezes, and pronounced vegetational zones more similar to today's began to form in the Northern Hemisphere.

During the later Tertiary period, as mountains uplifted and ocean currents changed, large areas of the world became deserts, prairies, or savannas. Close ancestors or modern genera of most forest trees were present by the Middle to Late Oligocene. Climates continued to change through the Oligocene, Miocene, and Pliocene, although a large number of plants still were found all around the globe in the Northern Hemisphere. For example, the Asian *Ginkgo* could be found in Europe and western North America until the close of the Pliocene, when the fluctuations in climate put a great deal of stress on plant distributions. The repeated glaciations of the Pleistocene (Delcourt and Delcourt 1991; Kershaw et al. 1991; Andriessen et al. 1993; Heusser 1995) decimated the diverse

forests of Europe and restricted to a few areas the diverse forests once common across North America and Asia. This persistence was probably true for both the Northern and Southern Hemisphere landmasses but is best documented by the extensive fossil record of the Northern Hemisphere. A few places, such as southeastern Asia (Liu 1998), southeastern North America (Groot 1991), and Mexico, acted as "wildlife" refuges for many of these displaced groups.

The changes in the forest composition of the tropical forests of South America, Africa, and Asia are understood poorly and have been the subject of only limited investigations. What work has been done demonstrates that tropical forests also have responded to fluctuations in world climate, changing the area they cover and some aspects of their composition (Van der Hammen 1982; Bonnefille 1995; Romero 1986; Colinvaux et al. 1996). Some of these changes may have been the result of the disintegration of plant/animal coevolutionary schemes. For example, when the gomphotheres (a four-tusked mastodont) no longer roamed the tropical dry forests of Central America, the fruits and seeds that they ate were no longer dispersed (Jansen and Martin 1982).

The forests that cover the Earth today, or have been cut recently, form a mosaic pattern produced by the evolution of diverse forest trees, each with differing abilities to migrate across moving continental plates, across dry areas, and over mountains. Each species—in fact every unique genotype of each tree—has differing tolerances to changing climates and worldwide atmospheric conditions. Therefore, as the world climate and atmosphere change in the future, each forest and each forest tree will respond in its own unique way. All forests on the Earth are products of their history and hold a key for an understanding of the dynamics of forest trees as individuals and forests as a biological whole, including the interactions of trees with animals. It is important that both fossil and extant forests of the world be studied now in order to be able to relate past Earth history to forest dynamics. This information is necessary because, with continued intervention by humans and as forests are clear cut, in a very short time there will be only refuges and isolated remnants of disturbed forests to study. Forest species are becoming extinct, and undiscovered distributions of forest trees are being lost forever. Therefore, it is important to combine the history of the fossil forests with studies of living forests in order to present a whole view of how forests live and how they change through time.

DAVID DILCHER

See also Angiosperms; Club Mosses and Their Relatives; Coniferophytes; Cycads; Extinction; Faunal and Floral Provinces; Ferns and Their Relatives; Gymnosperms; Horsetails and Their Relatives; Progymnosperms; Sedimentology; Seed Ferns; Terrestrial Environment

Works Cited
Andriessen, P.A.M., K.F. Helmens, H. Hooghiemstra, P.A. Riezebos, and T. van der Hammen. 1993. Absolute chronology of the Pliocene-Quaternary sediment sequence of the Bogota area, Colombia. *Quaternary Science Reviews* 12:483–501.

Basinger, J. 1986. Our tropical Arctic. *Canadian Geographic* 106:28–37.

Bonnefille, R. 1995. Plant reproductive strategies: Using the fossil record to unravel current issues in plant reproduction. *In* P.C. Hoch and A.G. Stephenson (eds.), *Experimental and Molecular Approaches to Plant Biosystematics*. Monographs in Systematic Botany from the Missouri Botanical Garden, 53. St. Louis: Missouri Botanical Gardens.

Coe, M.J., D.L. Dilcher, J.O. Farlow, D.M. Jarzen, and D.A. Russell. 1987. Dinosaurs and land plants. *In* E.N. Friis, W.G. Chaloner, and P.R. Crane (eds.), *The Origins of Angiosperms and Their Biological Consequences*. Cambridge and New York: Cambridge University Press.

Chaloner, W.G., and A. Sheerin. 1979. Devonian macrofloras. *In* M.R. House, C.T. Scrutton, and M.G. Bassett (eds.), *The Devonian System*. Special Papers in Palaeontology, 23. London: Palaeontological Association.

Colinvaux, P.A., P.E. de Oliveira, J.E. Moreno, M.C. Miller, and M.B. Bush. 1996. A long pollen record from lowland Amazonia: Forest and cooling in glacial times. *Science* 273:85–88.

Delcourt, H.R., and P.A. Delcourt. 1991. *Quaternary Ecology, a Paleoecological Perspective*. London and New York: Chapman and Hall.

Erwin, D.H. 1993. *The Great Paleozoic Crisis: Life and Death in the Permian*. New York: Columbia University Press.

Gensel, P.G., and H.N. Andrews. 1984. *Plant Life in the Devonian*. New York: Praeger.

Groot, Johan. 1991. Palynological evidence for Late Miocene, Pliocene, and Early Pleistocene climate changes in the middle U.S. Atlantic coastal plain. *Quaternary Science Reviews* 10:147–62.

Heusser, C.J. 1995. Three late Quaternary pollen diagrams from southern Patagonia and their palaeoecological implications. *Palaeogeography, Palaeoclimatology, Palaeoecology* 118:1–24.

Jansen, D.H., and P.S. Martin. 1982. Neotropical anachronisms: The fruits the Gomphotheres ate. *Science* 215:19–27.

Kenrick, P., and P.R. Crane. 1997. *The Origin and Early Diversification of Land Plants. A Cladistic Study*. Washington, D.C.: Smithsonian.

Kershaw, A.P., D.M. D'Costa, J.R. McEwen Mason, and B.E. Wagstaff. 1991. Palynological evidence for Quaternary vegetation and environments of mainland southeastern Australia. *Quaternary Science Reviews* 10:391–404.

Labandeira, C.C., D.L. Dilcher, D.R. Davis, and D.L. Wagner. 1994. Ninety-seven million years of angiosperm-insect association: Paleobiological insights into the meaning of coevolution. *Proceedings of the National Academy of Sciences USA* 91:12278–82.

Liu, K. 1998. Quaternary history of the temperate forests of China. *Quaternary Science Reviews* 7:1–20.

Manchester, S.R. 1994. Fruits and seeds of the Middle Eocene Nut Beds Flora, Clarno Formation, Oregon. *Palaeontographica Americana* 58:1–205.

Miller Jr., C.N. 1971. Evolution of the fern family Osmundaceae based on anatomical studies. *Contributions of the Museum of Paleontology of the University of Michigan* 23:105–69.

———. 1976. Early evolution of the Pinaceae. *Review of Paleobotany and Palynology* 21:101–17.

———. 1977. Mesozoic conifers. *Botanical Review* 43:218–90.

Raup, D.M. 1986. Biological extinction in earth history. *Science* 231:1528–33.

Romero, E.J. 1986. Paleogene phytogeography and climatology of South America. *Annals of the Missouri Botanical Garden* 73:449–61.

Stewart, W.N., and G.W. Rothwell. 1993. *Paleobotany and the Evolution of Plants*. 2nd ed., Cambridge: Cambridge University Press.

Taylor, T.N., and E.L. Taylor. 1993. *The Biology and Evolution of Fossil Plants*. Englewood Cliffs, New Jersey: Prentice-Hall.

Van der Hammen, T. 1982. Paleoecology of Tropical America. *In* G.T. Prance (ed.), *Biological Diversification in the Tropics*. New York: Columbia University Press.

Visscher, H., H. Brinkhuis, D.L. Dilcher, W.C. Elsik, Y. Eshet, C.V. Looy, M.R. Rampino, and A. Traverse. 1996. The terminal Paleozoic fungal event: Evidence of terrestrial ecosystem destabilization and collapse. *Proceedings of the National Academy of Sciences USA* 93:2155–58.

Further Reading

Fenton, C.L., and M.A. Fenton. 1962. *In Prehistoric Seas*. Garden City, New York: Doubleday; London: Harrap, 1964.

Gould, S.J. 1993. *The Book of Life: An Illustrated History of the Evolution of Life on Earth*. New York: Norton; London: Ebury Hutchinson.

Johnson, K.R., and R.K. Stucky. 1995. *Prehistoric Journey: A History of Life on Earth*. Boulder, Colorado: Roberts Winehart.

Thomas, B. 1981. *The Evolution of Plants and Flowers*. London: Lowe; New York: St. Martin's.

White, M.E. 1986. *The Greening of Gondwana*. French Forest, New South Wales: Reed; 2nd ed., Chatswood, New South Wales: Reed, 1994. 1st ed. as *The Flowering of Gondwana*, Princeton, New Jersey: Princeton University Press, 1990.

FOSSILIZATION PROCESSES

Death, Decay, and Disarticulation

From the moment of an organism's death, the soft parts forming its body start an irreversible process of decay and decomposition. In addition to this, a dead organism is an obvious source of food for other creatures, and therefore scavenging plays an important part in the recycling of an organism's constituents. The chances of an organism surviving these processes is small; hence, of the millions of organisms dying every day, only a minute fraction will have the potential to be fossilized. Organisms with more recalcitrant (durable to decomposition) parts—for example those with a relatively high mineral content such as bones, teeth, or shells—are able to resist decay processes and pass through diagenesis, the physiochemical stages that lead to the preservation of the organism as a fossil.

The actual processes of decay and decomposition have only recently been investigated, and up until the late 1980s paleontological studies of these processes were only observational in nature. More recent studies (e.g., Davis 1997; Davis and Briggs 1995, 1998) have experimentally modeled the decay processes and shed light on the biological and physiochemical nature of decay pathways. These studies have highlighted the role that decay can have in the actual preservation of material; for example, the bacteria that decompose feather keratin produce an exopolysaccharide glue (called a glycocalyx), which attaches them to the feather and acts as an ion exchange resin. This glycocalyx is recalcitrant and actually undergoes diagenesis so as to faithfully retain the outline of the feather (Figure 1).

Modes of Preservation

Mineralization

The most widespread fossilization process is that of mineralization. If a fossil is preserved through a process of mineralization, the fossil may take different forms. For example, if the shell of a bivalve becomes filled with sediment and then dissolves, what is left is an internal mold. Alternatively, a pseudomorph is produced when the original shell is replaced on a molecular level by a different mineral substance. There are many different minerals that can create a pseudomorph or mold; some of the common minerals are listed below.

Calcium carbonate (calcite and aragonite, both $CaCO_3$). Calcite is probably the most common mineral for preserving fossils, in part because many marine organisms build their shells or tests (skeletal body) from the mineral, and also because calcite is often dissolved in pore waters when sedimentary rocks are undergoing diagenesis and is therefore readily available to create pseudomorphs.

Silica (quartz, chalcedony, and opal, all SiO_2). Silica is one of the Earth's most abundant minerals and as such commonly preserves fossils. Flint, a variety of chalcedony, commonly preserves fossils. Flint fossils are exceptionally common throughout the Upper Cretaceous Chalk deposits of Great Britain. For instance, flint is deposited inside the tests of echinoids during diagenesis (the silica in the diagenetic pore waters come from the dissolution of sponge spicules throughout the sediment), while the same diagenesis dissolves the original carbonate test, leaving only an internal mold. Much rarer is the preservation of fossils in opal. Within the Upper Cretaceous sandstones of the Coober Pedy region of Australia, many of the fossils have been replaced by opal pseudomorphs; possibly the most famous of these is Eric, a complete pliosaur (a type of short-necked plesiosaur) skeleton that was saved by the Australian National Museum in Sydney from being broken up and turned into jewelry.

Iron compounds (pyrite and marcasite, FeS_2; limonite FeHO and other iron oxides; vivianite, $Fe_3[PO_4]_2-8H_2O$; and siderite, $FeCO_3$). Iron compounds usually preserve fossils when there is a high iron content in the original sediment. For example, restricted ocean water clay sediments are anoxic and contain finely disseminated iron oxides throughout them. When an organism reaches the sea bed and starts to undergo anoxic decomposition, this changes the iron oxides to iron sulphides in the immediate surrounding area. The fossil then becomes pyritized (i.e., turned into pyrite, FeS_2). Occasionally these conditions occur within fossils themselves; for example, the honeycomb texture inside bones may become highly anoxic during decomposition of the animal. Pyrite then forms inside the bones. Examples of this process include the Lower Cretaceous *Iguanodon* dinosaurs from Bernissart in Bel-

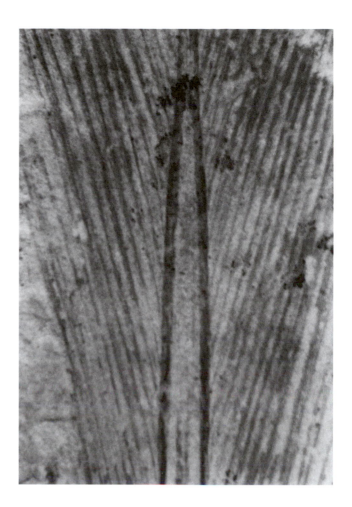

Figure 1. Cretaceous bird feather from the Crato Formation of Brazil. The feather is preserved by the diagenesis of a bacterial exopolysaccharide (a glycocalyx). The central rachis and individual barbs of the feather can be clearly seen.

gium and the ichthyosaurs from the Lower Jurassic rocks of Lyme Regis and Charmouth in Dorset, England.

Phosphates (e.g., apatite, $CaPO_4$). The bones of vertebrates are formed of a calcium phosphate and organic complex. When these undergo diagenesis, the organic matter decays and the phosphatic portion is slowly replaced by apatite. This explains why modern bones are light yet the corresponding fossilized material is much denser.

Impression

Fossils may be preserved as impressions. Often, when the fossil is entombed in a fine-grained sediment, the sediment makes an accurate replica of the organism. If the organism then decays away or if it is removed by diagenesis, this external mold remains. An example of this is the Triassic Elgin sandstones of Scotland. Here the skeletons and bones of fossil reptiles are preserved as external molds, the actual bone having been dissolved away during the diagenesis of the sandstone. Other examples include the preservation of soft-bodied jellyfishes, worms, even feathers in the Jurassic Solnhofen limestone of Germany. The sediments here are exceptionally fine grained, and the action of decomposition by bacteria hardens the sediment before diagenesis. Then, when the soft-bodied organism decays away, an external mold remains and is unaltered during the compaction of the rocks.

Organic Residues and Bacterial Traces

When organisms are buried quickly in fine-grained sediments rich in other organic matter, their volatile organic components are removed during diagenesis. However, these conditions also mean that decay is often retarded and other, less volatile organic components remain. An example of this is the preservation of fossil leaves, for instance vegetation from the Carboniferous Pennsylvanian coal deposits, where leaves, bark, stems, and roots are preserved as black organic residues.

In some special cases the bacteria that were actually consuming the organism are preserved. These rare examples are produced when fossilization is rapid and occurs before the organism's organic tissue is fully decomposed. The skin outlines of the dolphinlike body forms of marine reptiles called ichthyosaurs have been perfectly preserved in this way. Although these outlines look to the naked eye as if they are black carbonlike films, when they are examined under the scanning electron microscope the individual bacteria that were decomposing the skin can be seen. Also, as we have seen in Figure 1, even the organic glycocalyx left behind from bacterial decomposition of organic matter can fossilize.

Exceptional Preservation

Under exceptional circumstances fossils may be preserved intact and whole. The deposits that produce fossils such as these are called *lagerstätten* (from the German mining term for "mother lode"). These deposits often preserve organisms that would not usually survive and become part of the fossil record. Owing to this complete preservation they are of immense interest to paleontologists; they are windows into the past, in which the whole array of past life can be viewed, rather than the snapshot of life that is glimpsed normally. These deposits often produce spectacularly beautiful fossils because they are so well preserved (even organisms

that normally preserve well as fossils may be found here with their soft anatomy, another important reason why paleontologists study these deposits). Examples of these deposits include the Cambrian Burgess Shale of Canada, with its bizarre array of soft-bodied animals from the dawn of multicellular life, and the Carboniferous Mazon Creek of Illinois, with its vast array of soft-bodied animals, including the oddity *Tullimonstrum*.

Preservation of organisms such as insects, lizards, frogs, and mushrooms in amber fall within this category because they are preserved in their entirety, entombed and desiccated with no decomposition. They are so well preserved that even ancient DNA can be extracted from them. Mummification, whether it be in dry conditions such as those of the Aden crater near Deming in New Mexico (where a complete ground sloth, *Nothrotherium shastense,* was found in a cave completely preserved with tendons, claw sheaths, and even the remains of its last meal) or in Arctic conditions such as those of the tundra permafrost of the Indigirka River of Siberia (where a woolly mammoth, *Mammuthus primigenius,* was preserved in its entirety owing to the mummifying conditions created by the severe cold), also counts as exceptional preservation.

PAUL G. DAVIS

See also Fossil Record; Sedimentology; Taphonomy

Works Cited

Davis, P.G. 1997. The bioerosion of bird bones. *International Journal of Osteoarchaeology* 7:388–401.
Davis, P.G., and D.E.G. Briggs. 1995. The fossilization of feathers. *Geology* 23 (9):783–86.
———. 1998. The impact of decay and disarticulation on the preservation of fossil birds. *Palaios* 13 (1):3–13.

Further Reading

Behrensmeyer, A.K., and A.P. Hill (eds.). 1980. *Fossils in the Making: Vertebrate Taphonomy and Paleoecology.* Chicago: University of Chicago Press.
Donovan, S.K. (ed.). 1990. *The Processes of Fossilization.* New York: Columbia University Press.

FOSSIL RECORD

There are more than 1.5 million named and described species of plants and animals on Earth, and probably, many more exist that have never been identified. Some estimates place the total number at approximately 4.5 million species, yet the fossil record preserves only a small fraction of this total and does so in a very selective manner. Some groups of organisms with hard parts (such as shells, skeletons, or wood) tend to fossilize readily; therefore, much is known about their past. Many others are soft-bodied and rarely, if

ever, fossilize, so paleontology has little to say about their history. The study of how living organisms become fossilized is known as taphonomy (Greek for "laws of burial").

The Completeness of the Fossil Record

It is interesting to gain an appreciation of how unlikely the process of fossilization can be. For example, modern biological studies have revealed that the typical sea bottom is often dense with shells. In a study conducted on one-quarter of a square meter of seafloor off the coast of Japan (Thorson 1957), the shell count yielded 25 individuals of a large bivalve *(Macoma incongrua),* 160 of a smaller cockle shell *(Cardium hungerfordi),* and 12 of the tusk shell *(Dentalium octangulatum).* The average age of these molluscs was found to be two years. At this rate of deposit, there would be an accumulation of 1,000 shells in just 10 years, or 100 million shells in a million years—over one-quarter of a square meter thick. If this figure is extrapolated for the entire seafloor over geological time, it suggests that a staggering number of shells could have been fossilized. In fact, the tiny area of seafloor near Japan could produce more fossilized shells than actually are known from the entire fossil record. Clearly, most organisms do not become fossils.

Is it possible to determine in numerical terms the accuracy of the fossil record? We have already estimated that there are 1.5 million described species, or as many as 4.5 million described and undescribed species of organisms alive on Earth today. How many species are known as fossils? There are only about 250,000 described species of fossil plants and animals presently known, translating to just 5 percent of the total number of species living today. But, the present is only one moment in geologic time. If we multiply the present diversity by the 600 million years that multicellular life has existed on the planet, the estimate grows considerably. No matter how one does this calculation, it is clear that the quarter of a million species known as fossils represents only a tiny fraction of a percent of all the species that ever lived.

About half of the 1.5 million described species are insects, which have a poor fossil record and are not useful in estimating the total number of species. Let us just focus on nine well-skeletonized phyla of marine invertebrates and see if we come up with better estimates. These nine phyla are the Protista, Archaeocyatha, Porifera, Cnidaria, Bryozoa, Brachiopoda, Mollusca, Echinodermata, and Arthropoda (excluding insects). Among these groups, there are about 150,000 living species, but more than 180,000 fossil species. To translate these numbers into an estimate of the completeness of the figures, the paleontologist must know the turnover rate of species and the number of coexisting species through time. Different values have been used for each of these variables, but the results of the calculations remain remarkably similar. No matter which values are applied, it appears that 85 to 97 percent of all the species in the nine, well-skeletonized phyla that have ever lived have never been fossilized.

This is a very sobering estimate. It forces us to step back and reassess the limitations of almost any study based on fossil data. However, there is another consideration to bear in mind: The quality of the record depends on the level of detail we require. For a census of all the phyla or classes of invertebrates in a given sample, it would not be hard to get a complete sample. Obtaining every species is much harder, for the simple reason that a higher taxon, like a phylum or class, contains many different genera and species. If we obtain one species in each given phylum or class in a sample, we have a complete sample of phyla or classes with only a few specimens. But we need huge samples to get every species, or even every family or genus, that might have lived in a given time and place.

Fossilization Potential

To understand and interpret the preserved fossil record, the paleontologist must first determine how taphonomic processes have biased a sample. From the moment an organism dies, there is a tremendous loss of information as it decays and is trampled, tumbled, and broken before it is buried. The more of that lost information that we can reconstruct, the more reliable our scientific hypotheses are likely to be. Every paleontologist therefore must act as a coroner–forensic pathologist–detective to determine how the victim died and attempt to reconstruct the events at the "scene of the crime."

Numerous studies have documented the biases inherent in the processes of death and decay and have estimated the preservation potential of various marine invertebrates. For example, three different studies independently concluded that 25 to 30 percent of the species are likely to be preserved in the fossil record, with snails and clams having the highest potential. The soft-bodied groups, such as flatworms, segmented polychaete worms (which may make up 40 percent of the species in modern shallow marine habitats), and other wormlike organisms have very little chance of fossilization. Some arthropods (such as heavy-shelled crabs and barnacles) may fossilize, but other thin-shelled crustaceans, such as shrimp, rarely do. A few thick-shelled echinoderms, such as sea urchins, fossilize, but sea stars and brittle stars have little chance of becoming fossils.

After a death assemblage accumulates, many other factors operate on the hard parts to break them up and scatter them around, so an even smaller percentage ends up buried for future fossilization. These agents of destruction can be biological, mechanical, or chemical.

Among the forces of destruction, biological agents are the most important factor in most environments, both marine and terrestrial. Predators and scavengers are very active in breaking up shells and bones to extract almost all the useful nutrition from them. On the seafloor, a variety of organisms (especially fishes, crabs, and lobsters) are effective in cracking shells to extract their food content. In addition to such activity on the part of predators and scavengers, the shells themselves are subject to other biological agents of destruction. The most important of these are organisms that use the shell as a substrate (surface on which to live) or source of food or nutrients. A variety of organisms—including boring algae, boring sponges, worms, and bryozoans—erode holes and canals in dead shells and eventually weaken them so that they fall apart.

On land, a variety of predators and scavengers work very quickly to break up carcasses or vegetation. Once a tree falls in the forest, a wide variety of organisms—from termites, ants, beetles, and worms, to fungi and bacteria of various kinds—reduce it to organic material that can be recycled back into the food chain. In the African savanna, for example, a wide spectrum of scavengers (from jackals, hyenas, and vultures) and decomposers (insects and bacteria) quickly reduce most carcasses to nutrients that the soil can absorb. The key factor that prevents biological destruction is rapid burial.

Mechanical agents of destruction such as wind, waves, and currents can be very important. These processes are most effective in shallow waters where both waves and storms achieve their greatest force. The densest, most fine-grained shells are the most durable, but skeletons with coarsely crystalline structures (such as oysters) or porous structures (such as corals) are less durable, even if they are relatively thick. The shape, density, and thickness of the bone or shell are the most important factors in determining whether it can withstand the mechanical transport of waves, storms, or river currents.

After burial, a variety of chemical agents and diagenetic changes (i.e., changes after burial) in the rock (especially metamorphism) easily can destroy the shells and prevent their preservation. For example, aragonitic fossils are much more prone to dissolve than calcitic fossils, so fossils that are made primarily of aragonite are discriminated against in the fossil record. One study censused a living oyster bank and found over 303 species (mostly soft-bodied worms). Of the shelly invertebrates, 16 percent (nearly all the snails and many of the bivalves other than oysters) had aragonitic shells. Looking ahead, once these had dissolved, the remaining "oyster community" would appear to be of low diversity, because only these species with calcitic shells would be fossilized. This would be a false conclusion. The original composition and groundwater chemistry are the most important factors in determining whether diagenetic changes are likely to alter or dissolve a fossil.

Finally, only a small portion of all the fossiliferous rocks in the world have been exposed during the last few centuries, when people began to collect them. An even smaller proportion of these outcrops have been seen by a qualified collector before the fossil erodes and is destroyed completely. The chances of a given animal having the extraordinary luck of not only being preserved but also of being collected by a paleontologist are extraordinarily small.

DONALD R. PROTHERO

See also Fossilization Processes; Fossil Resource Management; Geological Timescale; Mortality and Survivorship; Sedimentology; Taphonomy; Trace Fossils

Further Reading

Behrensmeyer, A.K., and A. Hill (eds.). 1980. *Fossils in the Making*. Chicago: University of Chicago Press.

Paul, C.R.C. 1982. The adequacy of the fossil record. *In* K. Joysey and A.E. Friday (eds.), *Problems of Phylogenetic Reconstruction*. New York and London: Academic.

Prothero, D.R. 1998. *Bringing Fossils to Life: An Introduction to Paleobiology*. Boston: Brown/McGraw-Hill.

Raup, D.M. 1976. Species richness in the Phanerozoic: A tabulation. *Paleobiology* 2:279–88.

Shipman, P. 1981. *Life History of a Fossil*. Cambridge, Massachusetts: Harvard University Press.

Thorson, G. 1957. Bottom communities (sublittoral or shallow shelf). *Geological Society of America Memoir* 67:461–534.

FOSSIL RESOURCE MANAGEMENT

In 1990 a skeleton of the dinosaur *Tyrannosaurus rex,* nicknamed "Sue," was collected from a ranch (on Indian land) in South Dakota by the Black Hills Institute of Geological Research, a private company. In 1992 the skeleton was seized by FBI officials and, after a legal battle that went to the U.S. Supreme Court, it was sold at Sothebys auction house in 1997 for $8.3 million to the Field Museum of Natural History in Chicago. This dramatic episode is the most highly controversial instance of conflict in the management of fossil resources, but many other smaller conflicts have taken place since the mid–nineteenth century.

Although primarily a resource management issue, such questions interact with such wider issues as the impact of the popularization of paleontology; the availability and use of new technology for describing, copying, and transmitting information about fossils; the amount and sources of funding for paleontology in academic institutions and museums; and the proper training and ethical standards of businesses, curators, land managers, and paleontologists.

Historical Background

During the nineteenth century, geologists and paleontologists employed by geological surveys, museums, and universities developed sound methods of collection, documentation, and curation of fossils as a necessary tool in support of their work of description, identification, and other research. The few professional collectors and knowledgeable amateurs generally placed their expertise at the service of academic institutions, while the wider public had limited interest in fossils and rarely could afford the time or expense of searching for them. Nevertheless, problems developed, for instance during the close rivalry between paleontologists E.D. Cope and O.C. Marsh, which led to such unethical practices as the destruction of fossils. Purchase and resale of fossils was also commonplace, giving them a financial value that sometimes became extreme. Thus in 1871 English paleontologist John Plant commented that one needed to be a millionaire to pay the "fancy price" then being charged for specimens of the supposed Precambrian fossil *Eozoon.*

In 1913 Earl Douglass attempted unsuccessfully to protect under U.S. mining legislation the important fossil locality that became Dinosaur National Monument. Around the same time fossil collector Barnum Brown was offending local sensibilities in Canada and Europe, and in the twenties the Central Asian expeditions led by Roy Chapman Andrews were brought to an end by nationalist interests attempting to protect their fossils.

Professional paleontologists in the twentieth century saw steadily increasing competition for access to fossil resources from amateur paleontologists, educators, "rockhounds," and commercial collectors anxious to sell their finds at a profit. Governing bodies of regions once indifferent to the removal of their fossil resources now became anxious for them to remain at home, to stimulate local pride and provide opportunities for education and tourism. In recent decades, some museums and universities have come increasingly under financial threat, endangering the care of collections once thought secure.

Management of Fossil Heritage Resources

Historically, fossil resources were managed only after they had been collected, through the practices of museum curatorship. In fieldwork, an informal code of practice developed that left certain sites to the professionals who continued to work them. During the twentieth century, politicians, land managers, and other public servants generally have developed increasing awareness and sophistication in the management of heritage resources, developing legislation and using techniques such as resource inventories and site protection. Practices developed for historic and archaeological resources often have been adapted for fossils, not always appropriately. Few jurisdictions employ professional paleontologists in a full-time management capacity, although Britain has a national program within the Nature Conservancy Council, and some U.S. states have a "state paleontologist" or the equivalent, a civil servant trained in paleontology and entrusted with management of fossil resources. Increasingly other land managers are formally or informally trained in fossil management.

Public pressure often is brought to bear by a variety of interests on local managers and legislators, while professional communities have sometimes, but not always, been consulted. Paleontological interest in management issues generally developed earlier in crowded European countries, where classic sites were more likely to be turned into landfills, golf courses, or housing estates without notice. In North America's generally wider spaces, paleontologists at first did not become concerned until new policies infringed on their own activities. Of late, professional organizations such as the Society for Vertebrate Paleontology have become active in lobbying in support of the interests of professional paleontologists.

Interests in Fossils

Fossils are of interest to many different constituencies. Professional and some amateur paleontologists study fossils scientifically, in increasingly sophisticated ways. A researcher needs to be able to follow a specific scientific inquiry, which may involve study of material from many countries, taxa, and periods. Archaeologists have an interest in Pleistocene and post-Pleistocene fossil remains that may be associated with human remains (compounding the common confusion between archaeology and paleontology). Educators are interested in the accessibility of fossils to students. Geological students need to learn techniques of collection and study, all students of paleontology need class sets of specimens, and the wider public is interested in

seeing fossils in museum displays. Commercial interests seek to collect and sell fossils to make a profit. Fossils particularly sought are those that are large, beautiful, interesting, or portable. Some businesses are ethical and restrict themselves to legal opportunities, while others practice illegal collection (poaching). Sales may be to schools, museums, or private collectors. This business is worth several million dollars per year in the United States alone. Rockhounds collect fossils of interest or beauty and may see them as raw material for polishing and other processing, which may destroy any scientific value they have. Increasingly, high-profile fossils are of interest to a wide public as cultural icons, only indirectly reflecting their greater significance as evidence of the past. Political and business interests increasingly wish to keep fossils in the region in which they are found, as matters of local pride and as significant generators of tourist income.

Although these interests frequently conflict, compromise is often possible. There are also many instances of cooperative relationships (e.g., between amateurs and commercial collectors who will work with the professionals and turn over material of scientific importance to scientists).

Importance of Fossils

A major difficulty in fossil management is that of defining the kinds of fossil that need protection. Some fossils are so abundant that they are routinely burned as fuel or are primary constituents in building stones. At the other extreme are unique specimens of major scientific or interpretive importance. These may be large and spectacular (like Sue), or minute or obscure, with a significance only appreciated after extensive study (as are the Burgess Shale fossils).

Ownership of Fossils

Ownership of fossils is a key legal issue, as it carries both the right of possession and responsibility for management. In laissez-faire situations, that right tends to be with the finder, although landowners also may make a claim. Some jurisdictions have enacted legislation that places all fossils in public ownership, with the rights (and responsibilities) exercised by the appropriate government. Such legislation may include all or only some kinds of fossil and may have a retroactive clause requiring registration of material collected before the act came into force. In some countries, national legislation controls international movement of fossil resources, as in Canada, where the federal government is responsible for the Cultural Property Import and Export Act (1975), while provinces enact other legislation.

In the United States, despite a 1996 poll that "demonstrated that the vast majority of Americans are opposed to the sale of scientifically significant fossils from public lands," there is still (as of 1998) no comprehensive federal legislation. Two recent attempts have been made to create suitable acts, neither of which received the support of many professional paleontologists. A key issue for many paleontologists is the principle that fossils should not be bought and sold for profit, or at least that any "commercial collecting of fossils be undertaken with thorough scientific oversight to ensure that the scientific usefulness of specimens is not impaired" (Society of Vertebrate Paleontologists 1996).

Fossils in the Field

Fossils are found in a wide variety of locations, and discovery may come by chance, by systematic survey, or through excavations for industrial operations. Once found, the potential importance of the material, its vulnerability to destruction through erosion or excavation, the accessibility of the site, and the availability of experienced workers determine the speed with which the material is collected. Inexpert removal usually leads to specimen damage and loss of important data.

Areas with wide exposures of accessible fossiliferous bedrock, such as the Badlands of western North America, are particularly important. Here fossils are periodically exposed through erosion, and if not collected they eventually will be destroyed by the same processes of erosion that reveal them. Regular survey of such areas by experienced collectors is desirable to maximize productivity and minimize loss of important material.

Following the practice applied to archaeological resources, fossils now are often included in environmental impact and mitigation studies for major residential or commercial land developments, sometimes leading to important discoveries. There also may be provision for "stop work" orders when fossils are discovered in the course of excavation.

Site Protection

Sites of importance include type sections, sites with unusual preservation or rarely occurring taxa, and others important to paleontologists. Individual sites noted for their important fossils may be discovered within existing parks (as have new Burgess Shale localities in Yoho National Park, British Columbia, Canada) or may be given special protection specifically for paleontological purposes (as Dinosaur Provincial Park in Alberta, Canada, the first site in the world to be designated a World Heritage Site because of its paleontological resources).

Numerous important paleontological sites, such as Dinosaur National Monument, have been protected in the United States as National Natural Landmarks under the Historic Sites Act. In Britain, sites may be included in National Nature Reserves or (more often) in the approximately 1,500 Sites of Special Scientific Interest (which may be in private ownership, with protection and access established by agreements). Designation of a site may be supplemented by sheltering key fossils from erosion and vandalism with suitable constructions, as the dinosaur footprints in Queens-land's Lark Quarry.

Sometimes important material comes from working quarries (as did the *Archaeopteryx* material from Solnhofen in Bavaria), and no additional material will be produced if work is stopped. Sometimes the site is in demand for other purposes, even though it is no longer being quarried, as was the unique locality at Messel near Frankfurt, which was only saved for science in 1990 after a 20-year struggle against its use for garbage disposal.

Fossil Collecting

Before paleontologists head into the field to collect fossils, they usually must obtain permission both from landowners and appropriate regulatory authorities. Commonly, surface collections may be legal, but excavation is restricted to those qualified and formally authorized. In other jurisdictions, fossil invertebrates and plants may be collected, but vertebrates are protected. Some legislation forbids buying and selling of any fossils or of those fossils not collected commercially under permit. Others require material to be deposited in a designated institution (perhaps after initial study), or the signing of a curatorial agreement acceptable to the appropriate museum. Access may entail a filing fee, bond, or right-of-entry fee.

Since management responsibilities may be exercised by a variety of federal, regional, and local governments, access to fossils in the field is increasingly hedged about with a complex of legislation and regulation. Thus in the United States, national parks, the Forestry Service, and the Bureau of Land Management all have responsibility for fossils found on lands under their care, but those on state-owned or private land may or may not have protection. Depending on the particular jurisdiction, the professional paleontologist, rockhound, or commercial collector may find his projected activities possible only with extensive administrative work; it may even be forbidden altogether. Even with permit in hand, fieldwork may not be easy. Collection may be legal on one site of a boundary but illegal on the other, a trap that has led to professional paleontologists being arrested when boundaries are unmarked. Other paleontologists have deliberately bypassed official procedures, perhaps feeling that their rights supersede those of the management agencies.

Professional paleontologists are equipped to realize the maximum data from fossils in the field. However, if collected by amateurs or professional collectors, fossils may be lost, stored without data, or become unavailable to scientists through sale to collectors. Illegal collection is a widespread problem; some famous sites are frequently raided, with fossils going to private collectors or overseas. Few land managers have the time to catch poachers or the expertise to prosecute them.

Fossils in Museums

When initial study is completed, type specimens (the definitive specimens of a certain group) and other important material must be stored carefully and remain available to the scientific community; new discoveries and theoretical approaches may require restudy of the original material at any time. The material also may be important for display and other educational purposes. The best solution generally has been deposition in a public museum, which may be run by a government or a nonprofit organization or may be connected with an academic institution. Even when placed in a public institution, fossils may be subject to damage, loss, or theft, and some important material has disappeared through acts of war, vandalism, carelessness, or crime. Despite the publication of catalogs of type and figured specimens, interested paleontologists are not always able to track the location of significant material of interest to them. When researchers are not able to travel to see original specimens, provision of casts or loan of original material sometimes is possible. The use of computer technology is making increasing amounts of data available to distant researchers, but it remains to be seen how far, if at all, this will reduce the need to see original specimens.

Recent government downsizing across the western world has led to severe pressures on funding and staff of universities and museums. In the United Kingdom a number of geology departments have disappeared, and in the United States one university has disposed of its fossil collections altogether. Other collecting and research institutions, such as Britain's Natural History Museum, have shifted their priorities so strongly in the direction of popular exhibition that there has been widespread criticism from the academic community.

Conclusion

Fossil resource management is a young and very imperfect art. The many conflicting interests in fossils have made it clear that management is necessary if limited resources are to reach their full potential of usefulness. Numerous successes have shown possible routes to follow, but there is much progress to be made if all parties with legitimate interests are to feel that (as far as possible) their concerns are met adequately.

DAVID A.E. SPALDING

See also Field Techniques

Further Reading

Agnew, N.H., H. Griffin, M. Wade, T. Tebble, and W. Oxnam. 1989. Strategies and techniques for the preservation of fossil tracksites: An Australian example. *In* D.D. Gillette and M.G. Lockley (eds.), *Dinosaur Tracks and Traces.* Cambridge and New York: Cambridge University Press.

Committee on Guidelines on Paleontological Collecting. 1987. *Paleontological Collecting.* Washington, D.C.: National Academy Press.

Feldman, R.M., R.E. Chapman, and J.T. Hannibal. 1989. *Paleotechniques.* Paleontological Society Special Publication, 4. Knoxville, Tennessee: Paleontological Society.

Sarjeant, W.A.S. 1995. Lambert Beverly Halstead (1933–1991): His life, his discoveries and his controversies. *In* W.A.S. Sarjeant (ed.), *Vertebrate Fossils and the Evolution of Scientific Concepts.* Amsterdam: Gordon and Breach.

Schaal, S., and W. Ziegler. 1992. *Messel. An Insight into the History of Life and of the Earth.* Oxford: Clarendon Press; New York: Oxford University Press; as *Messel: Ein Schaufenster in die Geschichte der Erde und des Lebens,* Frankfurt: Kramer, 1991.

Sheets-Pyenson, S. 1996. *John William Dawson: Faith, Hope and Science.* Montreal and New York: McGill-Queens University Press.

Society of Vertebrate Paleontologists. 1996. *News Bulletin of the SPV* 168:10.

Spalding, D. 1993. *Dinosaur Hunters: 150 Years of Extraordinary Discoveries.* Rocklin, California: Prima.

West, R.M. 1991. *State Regulation of Geological, Paleontological and Archaeological Collecting, 1991.* New York: American Museum of Natural History.

Wilson, M.V.H. 1988. Palaeontology in Alberta: A case of excessive regulation. *Alberta Studies in the Arts and Sciences* 1 (1):216–24.

FUNCTIONAL MORPHOLOGY

With the advent of computer-generated graphics and robotic models, we now have an amazing appreciation of how many fossil vertebrates, particularly dinosaurs, may have appeared as living animals. Functional morphology is the area of paleontology that provides much of the structural information for making such restorations. The aim of a functional morphologist is to assess how fossil animals functioned as living machines. What types of food did they eat? Did they filter it, chew it, or swallow it whole? How did they move? Were they specialized for floating in the water or hanging onto rocks, or for running, climbing, digging, swimming, or flying? How did they breathe? Did they have lungs or gills, a combination of both, or some other respiratory apparatus? How did they reproduce? Did they lay eggs or carry live young? What special senses did they have? Could they detect vibrations in water, in air, or from the ground? Did they have a well-developed sense of smell? Were their eyes, if they had any, positioned to give depth perception or a wide field of view? How active were they? Was their metabolism warm- or cold-blooded?

The search for answers to most of these questions describes the field of functional morphology. The main difficulty, or challenge, for the functional morphologist is to come up with scientifically appropriate ways to answer such questions for animals that are known only from preserved parts—usually only of their skeleton or teeth, and occasionally from softer tissues such as feathers—or from trackways (fossilized footprints, often along river banks). Only after these questions have been answered, at least in part, is it possible for the functional morphologist to attempt to restore the appearance, movements, and behavior of animals known only from fossils.

Definitions

Functional Morphology

"Functional morphology" is the study of how an organism uses the various parts of its anatomy to perform the activities of life—feeding, breathing, moving, and reproducing—and of how the parts have been adapted and constructed for that use. It is possible to study the functional morphology of the appropriate parts of any multicellular organism, but this essay focuses on animals and primarily uses vertebrates for examples, since they are more familiar to most readers.

What do we mean by "anatomical parts or structures"? In this context, any organ that acts physically on another organ, such as a muscle, or is acted on by another organ, such as a bone, may be considered an appropriate part. Combinations of these organs that form larger units, such as jaws or legs, are also appropriate parts for functional study. Organs such as the liver, whose functions occur internally at the cellular or tissue level, are not included in studies of functional morphology. Their functions come under the areas of physiology and biochemistry. Often the boundaries between functional morphology and physiology are indistinct. For example, the force a muscle produces defines its function, but the way in which it produces that force—the biological mechanisms—occurs at a physiological level.

The entire field of functional morphology is based on two of the central concepts of evolutionary theory: (1) all organisms are related—they occupy branches on the same evolutionary or phylogenetic tree, and (2) the processes of natural selection tend to adapt organisms to their immediate environment. Most studies of functional morphology have focused on how an anatomical structure currently performs its function rather than how it has evolved as a result of adaptive and other processes. More recent studies deal with change over time as well, using phylogenies (evolutionary histories) to map the changes in structure and function between species over time (Figure 1a) (Lauder 1990).

Straightforward examples of the kinds of adaptation that are studied may be readily found. For example, the teeth of cats are adapted for dealing with prey. Long, spearlike canines are suitable for stabbing and killing, molars and premolars are used for cutting skin, and incisors at the front are adapted to act like scissors to slice meat from bones.

Morphology

Paleontologists use the term "morphology," instead of the simpler term "anatomy," to convey the concepts of phylogenetic interrelation and adaptation, in addition to anatomy. The closer two species are to one another on the evolutionary tree, the more similar their anatomy is likely to be because they have shared much of the same evolutionary history. Not only do the two species have the same organs and tissue types, but these develop in similar ways during embryology and occupy the same relative position in the adult. The species are said to have the same "body plan," or morphology, and all species with a common body plan are put in the same phylum. Parts or structures in related species that develop similarly and share the same position in the adult are said to be "homologous structures" (e.g., the forelimbs of a dolphin, bird, horse, and human). Morphology is sometimes replaced by the simpler, but perhaps more ambiguous term, "form," as in the ubiquitous phrase "form and function," which I will return to below.

Adaptation

"Adaptation" has three possible effects on morphology: divergence, convergence, and neutrality (Rose and Lauder 1996). "Divergent adaptation" can cause all or part of the morphology of closely related species to look very different because the species use their anatomical parts in different ways (e.g., the forelimbs listed in the previous paragraph). It produces anatomical features or characters that are extremely useful in establishing phylogenies. "Convergent adaptation" can cause anatomical structures to look alike superficially because they are put to similar uses. For example, the wings of insects, pterosaurs, birds, and bats are all wide and flat in order to develop lift for flight. Convergent adaptation produces features that may confuse systematic methods because it tends to make unrelated organisms appear closely related. Convergence is of great interest to functional morphologists because it represents different structural solutions to common functional problems. In the case of pterosaurs, birds, and bats, each group independently modified the forelimb, so the bones and muscles within the wings are homologous. But the *ways* in which they are modified for flight are convergent, or analogous. The third possibility, "neutral adaptation," leaves the morphology unmodified. For example, the retention of five digits in the human hand and foot is a holdover from the earliest tetrapods (four-legged terrestrial animals).

Function

In the context of functional morphology, "function" means the specific physical use of an anatomical part (Lauder 1995). It is implicit that the function is dependent on the way in which the part is shaped, constructed, or positioned within a larger unit. The claws of felines are a good example. Their shape, construction, and position help to dispatch prey. The claws would not work as well if they were straight, blunt, and not at the ends of the toes. Studies of this kind of function usually fall into the area of "biomechanics," which describes the movements of animals and the forces associated with those movements. By definition, the main function of mammalian leg bones or of the segments of a crab's leg is to withstand the forces acting on them from muscles and other skeletal structures in supporting and moving the weight of the animal.

Such a narrow definition of the function of a bone may come as a surprise. Often, particularly in older works, the word does carry a broader meaning, including to help support the animal while it stands, chases after prey, or runs away from predators. In most recent works, however, function is narrowly defined, while the broader definition is termed the "biological role" of the structure (Bock and von Wahlert 1965). The function of the bone is to resist force; the biological role is to assist in running after prey. The function of the whole leg is to support and move the animal; its biological role is chasing prey and avoiding predators.

Form, Function, and Adaptation

The characteristic of natural selection—to adapt an organism's anatomical structures to their functions—has led to comparisons with the human process of conscious design. The phrase "form and function" is used by engineers and architects, as well as by biologists, to explicitly convey the link between the design of structures and their functions (Lauder 1995). A bridge is a structure designed to support the weight of road traffic, whereas a car is an automotive vehicle to transport people on wheels. In the case of

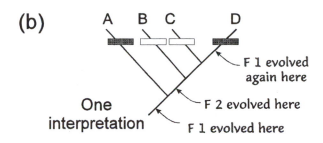

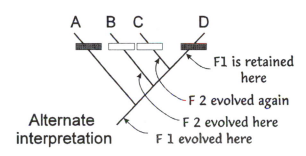

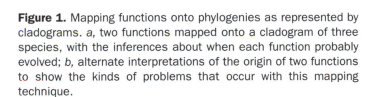

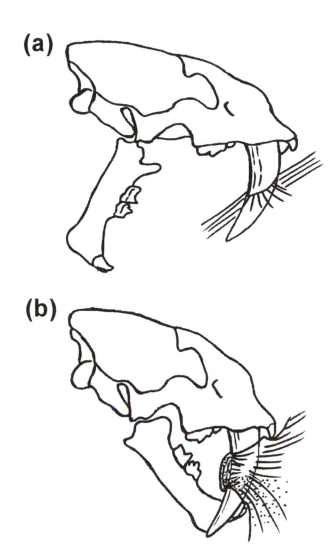

Figure 1. Mapping functions onto phylogenies as represented by cladograms. *a*, two functions mapped onto a cladogram of three species, with the inferences about when each function probably evolved; *b*, alternate interpretations of the origin of two functions to show the kinds of problems that occur with this mapping technique.

Figure 2. Possible canine use in sabertooths. *a*, simple stabbing with the jaw wide open. *b*, biting and slicing through skin and flech using the canine as a scythe blade.

organisms, the processes of adaptation replace those of conscious design. Therefore, a cat's teeth or a lobster's claws are structures that are adapted, rather than designed, for dealing with prey. In this context, the term "functional design" is sometimes used in place of adaptation (Alexander 1974).

The process of design is intended to produce a structure that is perfect or optimal for the function or functions it performs. In the earlier part of this century, many studies of adaptation and functional morphology promoted the same idea: Adaptation produces structures that are perfect for their function. This concept is well embedded in biological literature and teaching and on televised nature shows. Certainly, adaptation is a powerful shaper of living structures, but more and more, recent studies of the functional morphology of living animals are showing that adaptation may not optimize structures to their function (Dudley and Gans

1991). Optimization is currently a major topic of research (Weibel 1998). The following discussion provides a sample of the reasons why adaptation does not "design" optimal structures in the same way as an engineer does (or tries to).

One Structure, Many Functions

A single structure in an organism usually is used for several functions that place opposite demands on it. For example, bones resist force, but they also act as a store for metabolic processes requiring calcium. Where functional demands conflict, it is difficult to produce a structure that performs each individual function optimally. If an optimal solution is reached for all of the conflicting demands together, it is unlikely that any one of them will be performed optimally.

Nonadapted Structures, or "Spandrels"

It is tempting to assume that all anatomical structures have a function. After all, why would they be there if they did not? But, some structures may have arisen for reasons other than adaptation, even if they take on functions later in evolution. Such structures are sometimes called "spandrels" after decorative architectural features of churches that do not serve any mechanical function. In their well-known report, S.J. Gould and R.C. Lewontin (1979) used the example of spandrels to call attention to the nonadaptive formation of some anatomical structures. The sinuses, or air spaces, found in the throats and skulls of many tetrapods and in the limb bones of birds are likely examples of spandrels. Some sinuses act as resonant chambers in vocalization (Weishampel 1981), but many have no apparent function other than to lighten the skull or limb bones (this may be adaptive but can hardly be considered a function). L.M. Witmer (1997) proposed that sinuses may form because certain epithelia (membranes) have a tendency to invade and erode bone and other tissues, creating spaces in them. The results may be adaptive and also may have a function, but the sinuses are not formed initially for that function, so they may be considered spandrels.

Phenotypic Variation and Selection

Individuals in a species do not exhibit exactly the same anatomy, ability, or behavior. This phenotypic variation (variation in the physical manifestation of genetic inheritance) is necessary for the process of natural selection, but it means that individuals are not adapted equally. As a result, the functional morphology of most individuals, or parts of them, is likely to be suboptimal.

Flexibility or Redundancy

Many anatomical structures are complex, and their actions can be varied by nervous control. A structure such as our hand is a complex arrangement of bones, joints, muscles, tendons, ligaments, and nerves. Because of this complexity, the hand can perform many functions and can also perform a single function in more than one way. For example, let us say the function is "hitting keyboard keys in a sequence to produce words." I can achieve this function by using (a) one finger and moving my entire forearm to position the finger over each key, (b) by using all ten fingers and thumbs and keeping my arms still, or (c) by holding a pencil and hitting the keys with it. The end result may be the same, but each action requires different patterns of muscle contraction in my arms and hand and produces different forces on the bones. There are many zoological examples that show similar complexity of structure and flexibility (or redundancy) in the way simple functions may be performed (Lauder 1995). This flexibility may be advantageous in an unpredictable or changing environment, but it also means that the structure may not be optimized for any one function because if that function does not perform well, there are other options.

Phylogenetic Constraint

Because of evolutionary history, major morphological components are shared by animals in the same phylum, so it is very difficult for animals to produce completely new structures (Gould and Lewontin 1979). Usually, adaptation is limited to structures already existing in the body plan. This is called "phylogenetic constraint." A well-known example is the panda's thumb. This structure is simply an extension of a bone in the panda's wrist (humans also have the same bone, but in a smaller version) that forms a projection resembling an extra thumb (Davis 1964; Gould 1980). The panda slides this "thumb" along bamboo shoots to strip off the leaves for eating. It is an effective adaptation, in that the structure performs its function, but it surely cannot represent the perfect or optimal design of a structure for this function because the extra thumb is awkward and vulnerable to fracture.

Functional Morphology of Living Animals

Studies of living animals define how closely animal morphology and function are connected because the function and the structure can be independently observed and then compared. The functional morphologist observes how an animal undertakes a particular activity, notes which anatomical parts are used in the activity, studies the structure of those parts, and then makes appropriate measurements to quantify how each part contributes to or is involved in the activity. In a study of feeding mechanics in sunfishes, G.V. Lauder (1983) dissected their heads to look at the size, shape, and position of the muscles, bones, and other anatomical structures that might be involved with feeding. Next, he took high-speed film of sunfishes feeding to determine how the externally visible parts moved during the extremely rapid feeding movements. Using a technique called electromyography (1983), Lauder also recorded the electrical activity of the muscles thought to be involved in producing the movements; this allowed him to correlate the timing of muscle activity with the observed motion of bones. In this way, Lauder was able to correlate precisely the position and shape of each muscle or bone in the feeding apparatus with its function in the feeding process.

This type of detailed investigation belongs to a hierarchy of studies designed to describe how the animal fits into its environment; this field is called "ecological morphology" or "ecomorphology" (Wainwright 1991; Wainwright and Reilly 1994). The hierarchy includes descriptions or analyses of anatomy, functional morphology, behavior, performance, and interaction with the same and other species, and with the habitat. Studying living communities helps scholars interpret the structure of fossilized ones, while studying fossil communities yields information on how they can and have changed over time (Van Valkenburgh 1994; Janis 1995).

Practical Considerations

Studies of functional morphology often are not completed at one time. Often, the anatomy was described first by one researcher, a preliminary study of function was performed by another at a later date, and further detailed analyses were done by yet others somewhat later—or in many cases, are still waiting to be done (as in the case of cat teeth). Their function in food processing has been described—stabbing, cutting, or slicing—but has not been well quantified. The forces and stresses that the teeth exert on the skin and muscle of the prey, or experience during food processing, have not been measured (Biknevicius and Van Valkenburgh 1996). Such measurements are necessary to determine the function of each tooth type in relation to its shape and construction. Detailed studies of function have lagged behind those of anatomy and morphology because it is often very difficult to investigate function in living animals. Issues of animal rights and welfare preclude many experiments. In other cases, the technology is not yet available: The high-speed camera and electromyographic equipment that Lauder used were not developed much before the 1970s. As more sophisticated methods become available to assess function, scholars can perform more detailed analyses.

As a result of newer studies, it is becoming increasingly evident that the relationship of structure to function in the biological world is often not as close as the expression "form and function" implies. If we attempt to predict how a structure functions, we often receive an incorrect or oversimplified picture. In another study of sunfishes, P.D. Wainwright and colleagues (1991) found two populations, one which included snails in the diet and one which did not. His team dissected specimens of each and found that some feeding muscles were larger in the fishes that ate snails. Wainwright and his colleagues suspected, quite reasonably, that these large muscles were involved in crushing the snails. However, when they conducted electromyographic experiments on live sunfishes, the large muscles were not highly active at the moment when the snails were crushed. The team concluded that this was another example, like the hand, of a complex system having flexibility in performing its function. Because of functional flexibility, spandrels, phenotypic variation, and phylogenetic constraint, it is not always easy to determine which features of a structure are important in the way it functions.

Functional studies of living animals are important to the paleontologist because they determine the limits of confidence we may safely maintain when inferring the function of fossils. The message coming from recent studies is one of caution—the most obvious interpretation may not be the correct one.

Difficulties in Analyzing Functional Morphology in Fossil Animals

Any aspiring functional morphologist must be keenly aware of the many difficulties involved in investigating the function of fossils. The main problem is that function for extinct animals cannot be studied directly since their ability to perform functions died with them (Weishampel 1995). To make matters worse, much of their anatomy disappeared in the process of fossilization. Soft tissues decay quickest, so often only the hard parts—bones and other calcified or calcareous structures, teeth, and shells—are preserved. Occasionally, soft tissues are preserved as well, and these may yield important anatomical and functionally relevant information. The feathers of *Archaeopteryx* are the classic example (Ostrom 1974) because they unequivocally indicate the animal could fly. More recently, the preserved body outline of conodonts (a very primitive vertebrate) has proven to be at least as dramatic in that it indicates the animal's appearance

and use of the conodont structures (toothlike elements) (Briggs et al. 1983; Purnell 1995). Trackways can also be very useful. If they can be confidently matched to a known species, one can infer the manner and speed of locomotion for vertebrates and invertebrates (Brand 1996; McKeever and Haubold 1996; Bennett 1997).

Most often, the functional morphologist is faced with a double dilemma. Not only is it very risky to infer details of the function of most anatomical structures from their appearance, but much of the anatomy is not even present for fossils. In this case, it is important to use as much of the available information as possible to study adaptation in living animals (Lauder 1990).

Modeling approaches treat the animal or the part as a machine, analyzing it by using engineering or physical principles, as exemplified by lever mechanics or hydrostatics. They have been included as part of many comparative analyses, but not yet in many phylogenetic comparisons.

Comparison with Living Animals

Comparing living and fossil animals remains the mainstay in the functional reconstruction of fossils. Such analyses are based on the principles of homology and analogy—and on the fact that most paleontologists have a good knowledge of animal morphology, so they are able to identify fossil remains. Comparison may be direct, where features of a fossil are compared with those of a living animal for which the function has been studied. Or an indirect approach may be used where a living animal's mode of life, or the biological role of parts of it, are correlated with the presence of certain features without studying their function directly. This indirect approach is a powerful tool in paleontology, but it requires imagination and great caution.

Direct Comparison

The first steps in inferring function in fossils can be deceptively easy. Anyone with a firm knowledge of the anatomy and the modes of life of living animals can begin the process. If a limb skeleton is found that has mammalian features and the indication of large claws on its toe bones, the animal can be described as a meat eater with reasonable certainty, and the biological role of the limb can be described as "catching and dispatching prey." If the skull is found as well, and it has teeth resembling those of living cats or dogs, the description becomes more certain. The more closely the fossil is related to a living animal, one can reconstruct, based on homology, in greater detail the biological role and even the function of its parts. If the fossil does not have close living relatives (or is sufficiently different from them, as large dinosaurs are from lizards, birds, or crocodiles), then one can use analogy to infer biological role. *Tyrannosaurus* and *Albertosaurus* had large, sharp teeth and claws that clearly were used in meat eating, either of live prey or by scavenging. Duck-billed dinosaurs had rough-topped teeth resembling those of horses and cows. These teeth almost certainly were used in chewing vegetation, although the mechanism of chewing appears to have been quite different from that of mammalian herbivores (plant eaters) (Weishampel 1984).

As you can see, describing the biological role of parts of a fossil in general terms may not be too difficult. But there are many problem cases for which it is much more difficult to evaluate the detailed function of many parts. Problem cases require imagination. What if different parts of the body appear to have contradictory biological roles? A classic example is the chalicotheres, which resemble ungainly camels in size and shape and have teeth and skulls that appear to be adapted for eating plant matter. The problem is their feet, which bear unmistakable evidence of large claws, not the hooves one might expect. Scholars think chalicotheres used the claws to dig for tubers or roots (Coombs 1983).

Another type of problem occurs when a structure is different from that found in close relatives, such as the large canine teeth of sabertoothed "cats." The canines of sabertooths are so enlarged that it is unlikely that they functioned exactly the same as in those of lions or tigers. Several species of nimravids (an extinct family of carnivorous mammals) and felid have sabers, and paleontologists still are debating how these huge teeth were used (Akersten 1985; Bryant 1996; Anyonge 1996). Did the animals lift the head, open the jaws wide, and use the neck muscles to stab powerfully down (Figure 2a)? Or did they stab, then slice by pulling back their neck and head? Or did they drive the upper teeth in by closing the jaws on a fold of flesh (Figure 2b)? It is also likely that the canines were used for display in mating and dominance behavior, although the wear on them suggests they were not used solely for this purpose (Anyonge 1996). Sabertooths seem to have paid a price for the enlarged teeth because pitting in their skull bones suggests the attachments of their jaw muscle were stressed very heavily during biting (Duckler 1997).

Only in very rare cases may a fossil contain detailed evidence of its function. An example of direct evidence of function is the small scratch marks, or "microwear," that food makes on teeth and that teeth make on each other (Walker and Teaford 1989). These marks give very precise information on the direction the teeth were moving during biting or chewing. In conjunction with studies of feeding in living animals, microwear analyses have described the exact function of the teeth in many fossils, particularly in mammals (Janis 1995). This is one of the main successes of functional reconstruction: the level of detail with which the tooth function can be inferred. Unfortunately, such direct evidence of function is rare and, even if it is present, may be confusing. For example, conodonts also show microwear, which is much more difficult to interpret when there is no living animal on which to base a comparison (Purnell 1995).

Indirect Comparison

Sometimes comparison with living relatives can help identify the biological role of a fossil part without studying its function directly. An example is the shape of the premaxillary bones—bones that are found in the front of the upper jaw—and which support the muzzle in mammals. In giraffes and other ungulates, the premaxillae are shaped differently in browsing (those that eat leaves and twigs) and grazing species (those that eat grass), presumably because the bones have different functions in the two types of feeding. Most giraffes are browsers, but the fossil giraffe

Samotherium was identified as a probable grazer on the basis of its premaxillae (Solounias et al. 1988). Another example of the imaginative use of indirect information is the study of stalk autotomy in *Holocrinus,* a crinoid (sea lily) (Baumiller and Hagdorn 1994). Crinoids have a stalk that attaches to the seabed. "Autotomy" is the animal's ability to sever its stalk and regrow a new type of attachment, an ability that is thought to be important in the animal's ability to grow on both hard and soft seabeds. The anatomy stalk of the fossil *Holocrinus* provides no information on whether autotomy was possible. But T.K. Baumiller and H. Hagdorn (1994) found that fossilized fragments broke primarily at one site, comparable to where the stalk breaks in living, autotomizing crinoids. On the basis of this similarity, they inferred that autotomy was also possible in *Holocrinus*.

Functional Inference from Phylogeny

Phylogenies, or evolutionary trees, can be used to map the occurrence and perhaps predict the origins of functions (Lauder 1990). As a hypothetical example, Figure 1a shows when two separate functions probably evolved among three species, based on knowledge of how they are related and which function they perform. Figure 1b shows the kind of difficulty that animals often present when using this method. At least two interpretations are possible for the distribution of two functions among four species.

The second, and powerful, use of phylogeny is in predicting the possible functions that fossils might have had (Witmer 1995; Bryant and Russell 1992). The method is based on two living species that share a structure that performs the same function in each. These species also must bracket the fossil species on a phylogenetic tree, as shown in Figure 3. If the fossil has the same structure, it is reasonably certain it used it in the same way—or very similarly—as do its living relatives. By using this method, one can infer a function in the fossil without directly investigating it, similar to the example of the giraffe *Samotherium*. The method also is used to reconstruct soft tissues in fossils and can be used to infer the presence of structures and functions for which there is little direct evidence in the fossil. There are difficulties if a fossil does not have close living relatives or if the structure it shares with them is modified. This lowers the level of certainty with which functions can be inferred (Witmer 1995; Bryant and Russell 1992).

Mechanical Modeling

Modeling is used to infer the detailed function of fossil structures, often as a refinement of comparative studies, and comes in many forms. This area is based on engineering principles and methods and has been considerably advanced in recent years by computer technology.

In one modeling approach, the shape of anatomical structures is compared with that of engineering structures designed for specific purposes. The function of the anatomical part is inferred from the known mechanical function of the engineering structure. For example, the vertebral column of the largest sauropod dinosaurs (e.g., "Brontosaurus") has a cross-sectional shape similar to that of I-beams used in many kinds of engineering con-

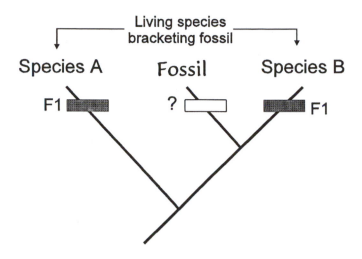

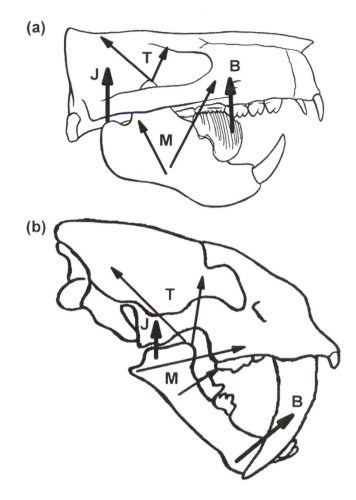

Figure 3. Using phylogenies to predict functions (and/or soft tissues) in fossils. The fossil must be bracketed by living species sharing the same function. After Witmer (1995).

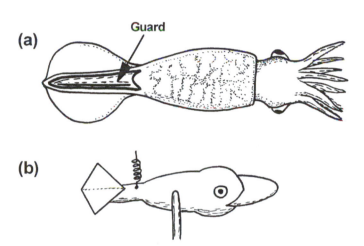

Figure 4. *a,* reconstruction of the belemnite cephalopod *Cylindroteuthis* in dorsal view, showing the calcified guard, and the fins presumed to lie on either side of it. *b,* a wind-tunnel model of *Cylindroteuthis,* which was used to study the lift generated by fins of different shapes. After Monks et al. (1996).

Figure 5. Modeling the jaws as lever systems in mammals. *a,* multituberculate *Ptilodus; b,* sabertoothed felid *Smilodon.* The lines of action of the various parts of the temporalis *(T)* and masseter *(M)* jaw muscles are drawn over a sketch of the skull. The forces of biting *(B)* and at the jaw joint *(J)* can be estimated by making assumptions about the magnitudes of *T* and *M* and by measuring their lever arms about the jaw joint and bite point. Source: *a,* after Wall and Krause (1992); *b,* after Bryant (1996).

struction. I-beams are designed to bear weight efficiently under the downward force of gravity, and the backbone of the dinosaurs served the same function. This approach and variants of it are known as *konstruktionsmorphologie,* or constructional morphology (Schmidt-Kittler and Vogel 1991), and have had a long history in Europe.

One variant on this theme is to use engineering principles to estimate the strength, stiffness, or other mechanical property of a specific fossil structure. For example, the strength of limb bones has been calculated for fossil horses (Thomason 1985), moas

(large, flightless birds) (Alexander 1983), dinosaurs (Alexander 1989), and glyptodonts (large, armadillo-like animals) (Faria 1995). Once you know how much force a bone can withstand, you can begin to rule out functions that might subject it to even greater forces. You can ask questions like: Could the largest sauropod dinosaurs have supported all of their weight on their hind limbs? The answer in this case appears to be yes (Alexander 1989)—which does not mean that they did stand upright, just that their bones were strong enough to allow them to do so.

Modern computer methods can do more than just estimate strength. They allow you to calculate the probable stresses and strains in a fossil structure under load. This approach may lead to more detailed analyses of mechanical function than was previously possible. Y. Song and colleagues (1994) used computer analysis to show how benthic foraminifera (bottom-dwelling microscopic animals) could become large without breaking, while remaining flat and disklike. J.J. Thomason and colleagues (1995) and I. Jenkins (1997) used the same technique to study skull strength in the ancestors of mammals.

Another branch of engineering—hydrostatics—has been used to model buoyancy and swimming in ammonoids (spiral-coiled shelled molluscs) (Chamberlain 1981) and some of the oldest fossil fishes. The theory of aerodynamics has been used to model flying in pterosaurs (Brower 1983) and birds. In studies of swimming or flying, another method is simply to build a working or wind-tunnel model of the animal or the relevant part (e.g., fin or wing). N. Monks and colleagues (1996) used a wind tunnel to show that the long, spearlike guard in belemnite cephalopods probably supported fins for producing lift (Figure 4). C.D. Bramwell and G.R. Whitfield (1970) crafted a radio-controlled model of a pterosaur that actually flew.

The final kind of modeling I will describe is the use of lever mechanics to estimate forces in complex structures. This has been used most often to predict forces of biting and corresponding forces at the jaw joints in mammals (Figure 5). Forces at the jaw joint are of interest because the immediate ancestors of mammals appear to have had weak joints but strong bites. A.W. Crompton and W.L. Hylander (1986) showed that the arrangement of muscles was such that a strong bite with low joint forces was possible in these animals. In this method, you estimate the probable direction and magnitude of forces from each of the jaw muscles and draw them on a side view of the skull. The principles of lever mechanics then allow you to calculate bite and jaw-joint forces. Two examples are given in Figure 5.

JEFF THOMASON

See also Adaptation; Aerial Locomotion; Aquatic Locomotion; Aquatic Reptiles; Biomechanics; Comparative Anatomy; Terrestrial Locomotion in Vertebrates

Works Cited

Akersten, W.A. 1985. Canine function in *Smilodon* (Mammalia; Felidae; Machairodontinae). *Contributions in Science, Natural History Museum of Los Angeles County* 356:1–22.

Alexander, R.McN. 1974. *Functional Design in Fishes*. 3rd. ed., London: Hutchison.

——. 1983. On the massive legs of a moa (*Pachyornis elephantopus*, Dinornithes). *Journal of Zoology, London* 201:363–76.

——. 1989. *Dynamics of Dinosaurs and Other Extinct Giants*. New York: Columbia University Press.

Anyonge, W. 1996. Microwear on canines and killing behavior in large carnivores: Saber function in *Smilodon fatalis*. *Journal of Mammalogy* 77:1059–67.

Baumiller, T.K., and H. Hagdorn. 1994. Taphonomy as a guide to functional morphology of *Holocrinus*, the first post-Paleozoic crinoid. *Lethaia* 28:221–28.

Bennett, S.C. 1997. Terrestrial locomotion of pterosaurs: A reconstruction based on *Pteraichnus* trackways. *Journal of Vertebrate Paleontology* 17:104–13.

Biknevicius, A.R., and B. Van Valkenburgh. 1996. Design for killing: Craniodental adaptations of predators. *In* J.L. Gittleman (ed.), *Carnivore Behavior, Ecology, and Evolution*. Vol. 2. Ithaca, New York and London: Cornell University Press.

Bock, W., and G. von Wahlert. 1965. Adaptation and the form-function complex. *Evolution* 19:269–99.

Bramwell, C.D., and G.R. Whitfield. 1970. Flying speed of the largest aerial vertebrate. *Nature* 225:660–61.

Brand, L.R. 1996. Variations in salamander trackways resulting from substrate differences. *Journal of Palaeontology* 70:1004–10.

Briggs, D.E.G., E.N.K. Clarkson, and R.J. Aldridge. 1983. The Conodont animal. *Lethaia* 16:1–14.

Brower, J.C. 1983. The aerodynamics of *Pteranodon* and *Nyctosaurus*, two large pterosaurs from the Upper Cretaceous of Kansas. *Journal of Vertebrate Paleontology* 3:84–124.

Bryant, H.N. 1996. Force generation by the jaw adductor muscles at different gapes in the Pleistocene sabertoothed felid *Smilodon*. *In* K.M. Stewart and K.L. Seymour (eds.), *Palaeoecology and Palaeoenvironments of Late Cenozoic Mammals—Tributes to the Career of C.S. (Rufus) Churcher*. Toronto and Buffalo, New York: University of Toronto Press.

Bryant, H.W., and A.P. Russell. 1992. The role of phylogenetic analysis in the inference of unpreserved attributes of extinct taxa. *Philosophical Transactions of the Royal Society of London*, ser. B, 337:405–18.

Chamberlain Jr., J.A. 1981. Hydromechanical design of fossil cephalopods. *In* M.R. House and J.R. Senior (eds.), *The Ammonoidea*. Systematics Association Special Volume 18. London: Academic Press.

Coombs, M.C. 1983. Large mammalian clawed herbivores: A comparative study. *Transactions of the American Philosophical Society* 73 (7):1–96.

Crompton, A.W., and W.L. Hylander. 1986. Changes in mandibular function following the acquisition of a dentary-squamosal jaw articulation. *In* N. Hotton III (ed.), *The Ecology and Biology of Mammal-Like Reptiles*. Washington, D.C., and London: Smithsonian Press.

Davis, D.D. 1964. *The Giant Panda: A Morphological Study of Evolutionary Mechanisms*. Fieldiana: Zoological Memoirs of the Chicago Museum of Natural History, Chicago: Field Museum of Natural History.

Duckler, G.L. 1997. Parietal depressions in skulls of the extinct saber-toothed felid *Smilodon fatalis*: Evidence of mechanical strain. *Journal of Vertebrate Paleontology* 17:600–9.

Dudley, R., and C. Gans. 1991. A critique of symmorphosis and optimality models in physiology. *Physiological Zoology* 64:627–37.

Fari a, R.A. 1995. Limb bone strength and habits in large glyptodonts. *Lethaia* 28:189–96.

Gould, S.J. 1980. *The Panda's Thumb: More Reflections on Natural History*. New York: Norton.

Gould, S.J., and R.C. Lewontin. 1979. The spandrels of San Marco and the Panglossian paradigm: A critique of the adaptationist program. *Proceedings of the Royal Society of London*, ser. B, 205:581–98.

Janis, C.M. 1995. Correlations between craniodental morphology and feeding behavior in ungulates: Reciprocal illumination between living and fossil taxa. *In* J.J. Thomason (ed.), *Functional Morphology in Vertebrate Paleontology*. Cambridge and New York: Cambridge University Press.

Jenkins, I. 1997. Cranial dynamics in Permian gorgonopsians. *Journal of Vertebrate Paleontology* 17:55A.

Lauder, G.V. 1983. Functional and morphological bases of trophic specialization in sunfishes. *Journal of Morphology* 178:1–21.

———. 1990. Functional morphology and systematics: Studying functional patterns in an historical context. *Annual Review of Ecology and Systematics* 21:317–40.

———. 1995. On the inference of function from structure. *In* J.J. Thomason (ed.), *Functional Morphology in Vertebrate Paleontology*. Cambridge and New York: Cambridge University Press.

McKeever, P.J., and H. Haubold. 1996. Reclassification of vertebrate trackways from the Permian of Scotland and related forms from Arizona and Germany. *Journal of Palaeontology* 70:1011–22.

Monks, N., J.D. Hardwick, and A.S. Gale. 1996. The function of the belemnite guard. *Paläontologische Zeitschrift* 70:425–31.

Ostrom, J.H. 1974. *Archaeopteryx* and the origin of flight. *Quarterly Review of Biology* 49:27–47.

Purnell, M.A. 1995. Microwear on conodont element and macrophagy in the first vertebrates. *Nature* 374:798–800.

Rose, M.R., and G.V. Lauder (eds.). 1996. *Adaptation*. San Diego, California: Academic Press.

Schmidt-Kittler, N., and K. Vogel. 1991. *Constructional Morphology and Evolution*. Berlin: Springer-Verlag.

Solounias, N., M. Teaford, and A. Walker. 1988. Interpreting the diet of extinct ruminants: The case of a non-browsing giraffid. *Paleobiology* 14:287–300.

Song, Y., R.G. Black, and J.H. Lipps. 1994. Morphological optimization in the largest living foraminifera: Implications from finite element analysis. *Paleobiology* 20:14–26.

Thomason, J.J. 1985. Estimation of locomotory forces and stresses in the limb bones of Recent and extinct equids. *Paleobiology* 11:209–20.

Thomason, J.J., P. Tsui, and A.P. Russell. 1995. Mechanical function of the mammalian secondary palate: A finite element analysis. *Journal of Vertebrate Paleontology* 15:56A.

Van Valkenburgh, B. 1994. Ecomorphological analysis of fossil vertebrates and their paleocommunities. *In* P.C. Wainwright and S.M. Reilly (eds.), *Ecological Morphology: Integrative Organismal Biology*. Chicago: University of Chicago Press.

Wainwright, P.C. 1991. Ecomorphology: Experimental functional anatomy for ecological problems. *American Zoologist* 31:680–93.

Wainwright, P.C, C.W. Osenberg, and G.G. Mittelbach. 1991. Trophic polymorphism in the pumpkinseed sunfish *(Lepomis gibbosus)*. *Functional Ecology* 5:40–55.

Wainwright, P.C., and S.M. Reilly. 1994. *Ecological Morphology: Integrative Organismal Biology*. Chicago: University of Chicago Press.

Walker, A., and M. Teaford. 1989. Inferences from quantitative analysis of dental microwear. *Folia Primatologia* 53:177–89.

Wall, C.E., and D.W. Krause. 1992. A biomechanical analysis of the masticatory apparatus of *Ptilodus* (Multituberculata). *Journal of Vertebrate Paleontology* 12:172–87.

Weibel, E.R. 1998. *Principles of Optimization*. Cambridge and New York: Cambridge University Press.

Weishampel, D.B. 1981. Acoustic analyses of potential vocalisation in lambeosaurine dinosaurs. *Paleobiology* 7:252–61.

———. 1984. Evolution of jaw mechanisms in ornithopod dinosaurs (Reptilia: Ornithischia). *Advances in Anatomy, Embryology, and Cell Biology* 87:1–110.

———. 1995. Fossils, function, and phylogeny. *In* J.J. Thomason (ed.), *Functional Morphology in Vertebrate Paleontology*. Cambridge and New York: Cambridge University Press.

Witmer, L.M. 1995. The extant phylogenetic bracket and the importance of reconstructing soft tissues in fossils. *In* J.J. Thomason (ed.), *Functional Morphology in Vertebrate Paleontology*. Cambridge and New York: Cambridge University Press.

———. 1997. The evolution of the antorbital cavity of archosaurs: A study in soft tissue reconstruction in the fossil record with an analysis of the function of pneumaticity. *Journal of Vertebrate Paleontology*, Supplement Memoir 3:1–73.

Further Reading

Aldridge, R.J. (ed.). 1987. *Palaeobiology of Conodonts*. Chichester: Ellis Horwood; New York: Halsted.

Alexander, R.McN. 1989. *Dynamics of Dinosaurs and Other Extinct Giants*. New York: Columbia University Press.

French, M. 1988. *Invention and Evolution: Design in Nature and Engineering*. Cambridge and New York: Cambridge University Press; 2nd ed., 1994.

McGowan, C. 1983. *The Successful Dragons: A Natural History of Extinct Reptiles*. Toronto and Sarasota, Florida: Stevens; revised and updated as *Dinosaurs, Spitfires, and Sea Dragons*. Cambridge, Massachusetts, and London: Harvard University Press, 1991.

Rayner, J.M.V., and J. Wootton. 1991. *Biomechanics in Evolution*. Society for Experimental Biology, Seminar Series, 36. Cambridge and New York: Cambridge University Press.

Rose, M.R., and G.V. Lauder (eds.). 1996. *Adaptation*. San Diego, California: Academic Press.

Schmidt-Kittler, N., and K. Vogel. 1991. *Constructional Morphology and Evolution*. Berlin: Springer-Verlag.

Thomason, J.J. (ed.). 1995. *Functional Morphology in Vertebrate Paleontology*. Cambridge and New York: Cambridge University Press.

Thompson, D'A.W. 1917. *On Growth and Form*. Cambridge: Cambridge University Press.

Vogel, S. 1988. *Life's Devices*. Princeton, New Jersey: Princeton University Press.

Wainwright, P.C., and S.M. Reilly. 1994. *Ecological Morphology: Integrative Organismal Biology*. Chicago: University of Chicago Press.

Wainwright, S.A., W.D. Biggs, J.D. Currey, and J.M. Gosline. 1976. *Mechanical Design in Organisms*. London: Arnold; New York: Wiley.

FUNGI

The Fungi is one of the most widespread and ecologically important taxa on Earth, with about 65,000 known species. Fossil fungi have received relatively little attention, yet fungi are not uncommon fossils. About 500 fossil species are known (Stewart and Rothwell 1991).

True fungi often grow as filaments, or "hyphae." (Yeasts are an exception; they lack hyphae for most or all of their life cycles.) Hyphae may or may not be partitioned into cells by "septa"; when present, the septa are perforated with fine pores through which the cells interconnect. Hyphae may form masses or networks known as "mycelia" (Figure 1). Hyphae form "spores" by asexual division; these spores may be produced inside specialized sacs, called "sporangia" (Figure 1), or in chains or clusters called "conidia" (Figure 2). Most fungi also have a life cycle that alternates between a "monokaryotic" stage (one haploid nucleus per cell) and a "dikaryotic" stage (two nuclei per cell). (A haploid nucleus contains only one set of chromosomes.) Monokaryotic stages may fuse with each other in a form of sexual reproduction to form a dikaryotic stage. During it, nuclei fuse, undergo meiosis (a type of cell division that segregates characteristics), and produce new monokaryotic stages (Ingold and Hudson 1993).

Several groups of organisms superficially resemble fungi and once were classified with them. Their ultrastructure and gene sequences (information in their DNA), however, show them to be unrelated to true fungi. Water molds, downy mildews, and related organisms are classified in the Oomycota; despite their funguslike appearance, oomycetes are related to diatoms and brown algae, not fungi. Several other funguslike groups, such as the Labyrinthulomycota ("slime nets") and the Plasmodiophorales (clubroot parasites), cause plant diseases. Myxomycetes, or "slime molds," are freeliving amoeboid protists that produce spores from stalked fruiting bodies. Finally, a major group of bacteria, the Actinomycetes, has evolved convergently (independently) funguslike growth patterns. Well-known actinomycetes include *Streptomyces,* which produces the antibiotic streptomycin, and *Mycobacterium,* species of which cause leprosy and tuberculosis. None of these groups has more than a scanty fossil record.

True fungi are classified by their reproductive structures. Chytridiomycotina, the chytrid fungi, reproduce asexually by forming sacs, or "zoosporangia," which burst open and release "zoospores" that are propelled by a long, whiplike structure called a flagellum (plural flagella). Chytrids are the only true fungi to bear flagella at any stage of their life cycle. The Zygomycotina, which include black bread mold, among others, form specialized sporangia on monokaryotic hyphae (Figure 1). In the largest group, the Ascomycotina, sexual spores are formed within saclike structures called "asci." Asci may be borne on or inside protective structures called "ascocarps": truffles and morels are well-known ascocarps. Some ascomycetes, notably the yeasts, do not form ascocarps. Members of the Basidiomycotina form spores on top of club-shaped structures, known as "basidia" (Figure 3). The basidia may be located on "basidiocarps"—examples include mushrooms,

puffballs, and bracket fungi. Rusts and smuts are basidiomycetes that do not form basidiocarps. A fifth grouping, the Deuteromycotina, or Fungi Imperfecti, is a "wastebasket" group for fungi that lack sexual reproduction. Most of these fungi evolved from sexual ascomycete ancestors. Familiar deuteromycetes include the fungi that cause athlete's foot and ringworm—and *Penicillium,* which includes species that produce penicillin and Roquefort cheese (Ingold and Hudson 1993).

Fungi are abundant on land. Some species parasitize plants or animals, causing billions of dollars in damage to crops each year and causing human and animal diseases. Freeliving fungi abound in soils and in plant litters (the broken-up material of dead plants and animals); a gram of soil may contain hundreds of thousands of spores. The mushrooms and puffballs on a forest floor may be only the aboveground tips of vast webs of mycelia, which may live for thousands of years and cover several square kilometers (Smith et al. 1992). Many such fungi are important decomposers, or "saprobes," breaking down dead organic matter. There are even "predatory" fungi, which feed on nematodes (tiny wormlike animals) that the fungi capture with sticky globules or with hyphal "nooses." Fungi exist in fresh water and in the oceans as well.

A noteworthy aspect of fungal ecology is the ability of many species to form symbioses—inter-dependent relationships with other organisms. Lichens, symbiotic associations between fungi and algae, are one type of symbiosis. Fungi also form symbioses with plant roots, supplying the plant with phosphate and other nutrients. These symbiotic fungi, called "mycorrhizae," may grow in sheaths around roots (ectomycorrhizae) or actually penetrate into root cells (endomycorrhizae). About 90 percent of all vascular plants require mycorrhizal symbionts in order to thrive—the fungi supply minerals essential for growth and development. Other fungi form mutualistic symbioses with animals. For instance, the foul-smelling stinkhorn fungus, *Phallus impudicus,* attracts flies, which in turn disperse its spores.

Fungi are thought to have evolved in the Precambrian. Molecular phylogenies (evolutionary histories) show that fungi and animals are each others' closest relatives (Wainright et al. 1993), implying that fungi have been around for at least as long as animals have. A few fungi or funguslike organisms do occur in the Precambrian and early Paleozoic (e.g., Allison 1988; Burzin 1993), but it is hard to tell supposed Precambrian fungi from fossilized empty sheaths that once surrounded filaments of algae or bacteria.

Fossils remain rare and obscure until the Late Silurian, when the oldest known ascomycetes appear in rocks of Gotland, Sweden (Sherwood-Pike and Grey 1985). Land plants, which first become prominent in the fossil record at about this time, may owe their successful colonization of the land to symbiotic fungi (Pirozynski and Malloch 1975). Indeed, fungi are associated with land plants from very early in their history. Some of the oldest known vascular plants, from the Lower Devonian Rhynie Chert, were infected with the fungus *Palaeomyces* (Stewart and Rothwell 1991), and endomycorrhizae also are found in

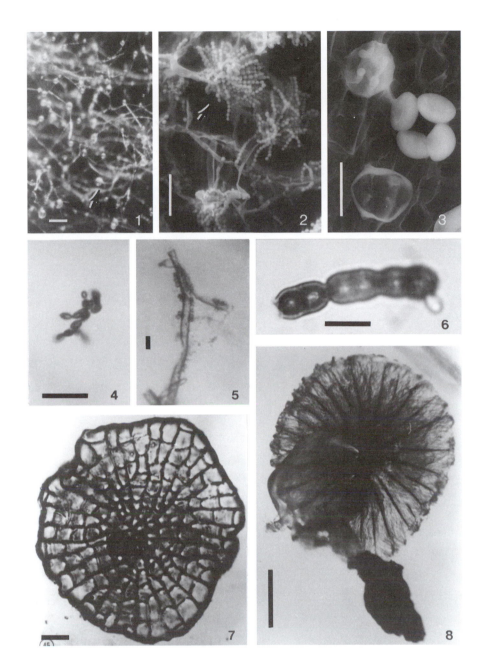

Figure 1. Light micrograph of the mycelium of an unidentified zygomycete. Arrow indicates sporangium; scale bar equals 100 microns. Scanning electron microscopy (SEM) carried out using the University of California Museum of Paleontology (UCMP) Environmental Scanning Electron Microscope (ESEM).

Figure 2. Bread mold (probably *Penicillium*) found on author's lunch. Arrow indicates conidium; scale bar equals 50 microns. Scanning electron microscopy (SEM) carried out using the University of California Museum of Paleontology (UCMP) Environmental Scanning Electron Microscope (ESEM).

Figure 3. Three basidia from the gill of a mushroom. Basidium in center shows four attached basidiospores; scale bar equals 10 microns. Scanning electron microscopy (SEM) carried out using the University of California Museum of Paleontology (UCMP) Environmental Scanning Electron Microscope (ESEM).

Figures 4–6. Miscellaneous fungal spores and hyphae. Late Eocene amber, Baltic region (UCMP collection). Scale bars equal 20 microns. Scanning electron microscopy (SEM) carried out using the University of California Museum of Paleontology (UCMP) Environmental Scanning Electron Microscope (ESEM).

Figure 7. The fungus *Callimothallus* from an Eocene leaf. Scale bar equals 100 microns. From Dilcher (1965).

Figure 8. *Coprinites dominicanus,* a rare instance of a fossil mushroom. Eocene-Oligocene amber, Dominican Republic. Scale bar equals one millimeter. Reprinted with permission from Poinar and Singer (1990). Copyright © 1990 American Association for the Advancement of Science.

plants of the Rhynie Chert in Scotland (Taylor et al. 1995). Recent investigations of Rhynie Chert rocks have revealed additional fungal fossils representative of all living classes of fungi, and even modern genera (Remy et al. 1994; Taylor et al. 1994). Thus, fungi had invaded the land and diversified by the Devonian, well in advance of vascular plants.

Most fossil fungi come from Mesozoic and Cenozoic rocks, and their appearance is much like that of living counterparts. Noteworthy finds include mycorrhizae from Triassic cycads from Antarctica (Stubblefield et al. 1987); bracket fungi from Jurassic and Cenozoic rocks (e.g., Singer and Archangelsky 1958); various fungi from Cretaceous and Cenozoic amber (Figures 4, 5, 6), including a rare instance of a fossil mushroom (Poinar and Singer 1990) (Figure 8); and parasitic fungi on Cenozoic fossil plant leaves (Dilcher 1965) (Figure 7).

BEN WAGGONER

See also Lichens; Plants: Overview

Works Cited

Allison, C.W. 1988. Paleontology of Late Proterozoic and Early Cambrian rocks of east-central Alaska. *U.S. Geological Survey Professional Paper* 1449:1–50.

Burzin, M.B. 1993. Drevnejshij khitridiomitset (Mycota, Chytridiomycetes Incertae Sedis) iz verkhnego Venda vostochno-evropejskoj platformy. *In* B.S. Sokolov and A.B. Iwanowski (eds.), *Fauna i Ekosistemy Geologicheskogo Proshlogo.* Moscow: Nauka.

Dilcher, D.L. 1965. Epiphyllous fungi from Eocene deposits in western Tennessee, U.S.A. *Palaeontographica B* 116:1–54.

Ingold, C.T., and H.J. Hudson. 1993. *The Biology of Fungi.* 6th ed., London and New York: Chapman and Hall.

Pirozynski, K.A., and D.W. Malloch. 1975. The origin of land plants: A matter of mycotrophism. *BioSystems* 6:153–64.

Poinar, G.O., and R. Singer. 1990. Upper Eocene gilled mushroom from the Dominican Republic. *Science* 248:1099–1101.

Remy, W., T.N. Taylor, and H. Hass. 1994. Early Devonian fungi: A blastocladalean fungus with sexual reproduction. *American Journal of Botany* 81:690-702.

Sherwood-Pike, M. 1991. Fossils as keys to evolution in fungi. *BioSystems* 25:121–29.

Sherwood-Pike, M., and J. Grey. 1985. Silurian fungal remains: Probable records of the Class Ascomycetes. *Lethaia* 18:1–20.

Singer, R., and S. Archangelsky. 1958. A petrified basidiomycete from Patagonia. *American Journal of Botany* 45:194–98.

Smith, M.L., J.N. Bruhn, and J.B. Anderson. 1992. The fungus *Armillaria bulbosa* is among the largest and oldest living organisms. *Nature* 356:428–30.

Stewart, W.N., and G.W. Rothwell. 1991. *Paleobotany and the Evolution of Plants.* 2nd ed., Cambridge and New York: Cambridge University Press.

Stubblefield, S.P., T.N. Taylor, and J.M. Trappe. 1987. Vesicular-arbuscular mycorrhizae from the Triassic of Antarctica. *American Journal of Botany* 74:1904–11.

Taylor, T.N., W. Remy, and H. Hass. 1994. *Allomyces* in the Devonian. *Nature* 367:601.

Taylor, T.N., W. Remy, H. Hass, and H. Kerp. 1995. Fossil arbuscular mycorrhizae from the Early Devonian. *Mycologia* 87:560–73.

Wainright, P.O., G. Hinkle, M.L. Sogin, and S.K. Stickel. 1993. Monophyletic origins of the Metazoa: An evolutionary link with the Fungi. *Science* 260:340–42.

Further Reading

Ingold, C.T., and H.J. Hudson. 1961. *The Biology of Fungi.* London: Hutchinson Educational; 6th ed., London and New York: Chapman and Hall, 1993.

Stewart, W.N., and G.W. Rothwell. 1983. *Paleobotany and the Evolution of Plants.* Cambridge and New York: Cambridge University Press; 2nd ed., 1991.

Taylor, T.N., and E.L. Taylor. 1993. *The Biology and Evolution of Fossil Plants.* Englewood Cliffs, New Jersey: Prentice-Hall.

G

GASTROLITHS

Gastroliths are pebbles or stones that have been swallowed by an animal. They usually are made of silicates and are rounded, highly polished, and have a waxy feel—presumably as a result of mechanical or chemical processes within the animal's digestive tract. The term first was coined by Barnum Brown in 1907 and comes from the Greek *gastros,* meaning stomach, and *lith,* meaning stone. Other names include "stomach stones," "(gastric) millstones," and "gizzard stones."

Most modern birds, some modern reptiles (such as alligators, crocodiles, turtles, and certain lizards and snakes), and even a few mammals swallow stones, pebbles, or grit (Gillette 1994; Whittle 1988; Stokes 1987; Hoskin et al. 1970; Baker 1956). Many extinct species of birds, as well as reptiles from as far back as the Permian, also are known to have used gastroliths (Norman 1991; Whittle 1988; Stokes 1987; Hoskin et al. 1970). The extinct giant moa of New Zealand carried up to 5 pounds of gastroliths. Apparently it swallowed only white quartz.

Dinosaur gastroliths long have been controversial (Gillette 1994; Stokes 1987; Baker 1956). However, there are many instances where stones have been found within the rib cage of the fossil remains of a dinosaur. These are clearly gastroliths because of their roundness and polish, their orientation and spatial distribution within the rib cage, and the lack of likely alternate explanations for finding stones having the same characteristics and composition in that layer of rock. Many suspected gastroliths have been found completely unassociated with more fragile fossil bone.

Not all dinosaurs used gastroliths. Dinosaurs for which we have fairly convincing evidence for gastrolith use include a wide variety of prosauropods and sauropods, as well as the ceratopsian *Psittacosaurus,* the hadrosaur *Tenontosaurus,* and certain meat-eating theropods (Cox 1994; Norman 1991; Whittle 1988; Stokes 1987; Baker 1956). Gastroliths are also recorded in *Plesiosaurus,* an extinct aquatic reptile.

Why would an animal swallow stones? There are a number of possible explanations. The most popular explanation is trituration, grinding or crushing food in the gizzard (ventriculus). In modern birds, the gizzard is lined with a hardened material called koilen. Strong muscles surrounding the gizzard generate considerable pressure on the contents of the gizzard to help break down the seeds and plant material eaten by the animal.

Modern birds clearly swallow grit or pebbles deliberately. They can survive without gizzard stones, but if artificially deprived of grit, sand, or pebbles they often search frantically for gastrolith material. Colorful beads, pottery shards, and fragments of brick or ceramics sometimes are used instead of natural materials.

There are other possible reasons why animals might swallow stones. Crocodiles and other aquatic animals probably use gastroliths for ballasts (to help them sink) and for balance. Some gastroliths no doubt are swallowed by accident while eating or drinking. It is also possible that stones could be ingested while eating another gastrolith-using animal, or while eating edible plants or animals that are attached to stones. Animals also might swallow stones because of boredom, aesthetic attraction, to ease hunger pains or stomach atrophy, to help reduce gastric irritation caused by parasites, or as a source of minerals.

Gillette (1994) has speculated that, rather than mechanically grinding food, gastroliths may instead serve to make digestion more efficient by stirring gastric juices in the crop and gizzard, and by keeping their contents from settling. Whatever the explanations for gastroliths, it seems likely that a given animal may swallow stones for more than one reason, and that different species may have different reasons.

In the case of the dinosaurs, we do not know for sure if they even had gizzards. It seems likely, however, that most or all prosauropods and sauropods had gizzards and used gizzard stones. Their relatively small heads, simple teeth, and absence of molars and efficient tooth-to-tooth contact makes it appear that their mouths were more designed for stripping and raking in vegetation than for efficient chewing or grinding (Norman 1991). Gizzard stones would have been useful for breaking down the tough, enzyme-resistant cellulose wall of plant cells to access the inner nutrients. After the food had been ground to a pulp, it probably passed out of the gizzard for further digestion and absorption under the action of fermentation bacteria and enzymes (Gillette 1994; Norman 1991).

The most spectacular and thoroughly documented evidence for sauropod gastroliths was the discovery of *Seismosaurus halli* in New Mexico (Gillette 1994). Over 240 gastroliths were found inside one animal. The silicate stones ranged from peach pit size to grapefruit size. Gastroliths appeared to be in use both in the crop (prior to the stomach) and in the gizzard.

Most dinosaur gastroliths are found in Lower Cretaceous sediments. With the coming of the flowering plants (angiosperms) during the Cretaceous Period, plus the development of more sophisticated dinosaur teeth, the need for gizzard stones may have been reduced greatly (Norman 1991).

Researchers have quantitatively measured the surface polish on gastroliths (Cox 1994; Johnston et al. 1994; Whittle 1988). The goal is to identify gastroliths that are not found with fossil bones, and to distinguish them from rocks polished by wind, flowing water, or ice. Such roughness measurements are complicated, however, by the fact that the gastroliths may have spent different amounts of time inside the living animal, and thus have been polished to different degrees.

There are many potential benefits in studying gastroliths (Gillette 1994; Cox 1994; Norman 1991; Whittle 1988; Stokes 1987; Hoskin et al. 1970). These include tantalizing clues about the anatomy of the digestive tract, the history of a carcass, the size and diet of the gastrolith-using animal, climate and seasonality, population densities and migration, the geological history/identity of a rock layer, and even archaeology—evidence of hunted or domesticated birds at human settlements. In terms of practical applications, the presence of a ruby in the gizzard of a pheasant led to the discovery of the famous Burmese ruby mines (Hoskin et al. 1970).

ROGER G. JOHNSTON AND JANIE A. ENTER

Works Cited

Baker, A. 1956. The swallowing of stones by animals. *Victorian Naturalist* 73:82–95.

Cox, T.D. 1994. The formation of gastrolith derived stone-lines in deep loess upland soils: Mid-continental USA. Master's thesis, University of Illinois.

Gillette, D.D. 1994. *Seismosaurus: The Earth Shaker*. New York: Columbia University Press.

Hoskin, C.M., R.D. Guthrie, and B.L.P.Hoffman. 1970. Pleistocene, holocene, and recent bird gastroliths from interior Alaska. *Arctic* 23:14–23.

Johnston, R.G., W.G. Lee, and W.K. Grace. 1994. Identifying moa gastroliths using a video light scattering instrument. *Journal of Paleontology* 68:159–63.

Norman, D. 1991. *Dinosaur!* London: Boxtree; New York: Prentice Hall; rev. ed., London: Boxtree, 1994; New York: Macmillan, 1995.

Stokes, W.L. 1987. Dinosaur gastroliths revisited. *Journal of Paleontology* 61:1242–46.

Whittle, C.H. 1988. On the origins of gastroliths. *Journal of Vertebrate Paleontology* 8:28A.

Further Reading

Anderson, A. 1989. *Prodigious Birds*. Cambridge and New York: Cambridge University Press.

Brown, B. 1907. Gastroliths. *Science* 25:392.

Lambert, D. 1993. *The Ultimate Dinosaur Book*. London and New York: Dorling Kindersley.

Miller, L. 1962. Stomach stones. *Journal of Zoonooz* 35:10–13.

Norman, D. 1985. *The Illustrated Encyclopedia of Dinosaurs*. London: Salamander; New York: Crescent.

See also Diet

GASTROPODS

The gastropods—the snails and slugs—are a very large and diverse group of molluscs. They include about 4,500 genera and some 90,000 species, known from marine, freshwater, and terrestrial environments on all continents. The first gastropods are known from the Early Cambrian, some 525 million years ago, and they are moderately frequent in the fossil record since the end of the Cambrian period. However, the greatest diversity apparently was achieved in the Cenozoic, including the modern seas. Gastropods are less important as index fossils (used in the identification of geological formations) than most other major invertebrate groups, but they often are useful for the reconstruction of past environments. The smallest gastropods are, as adults, barely larger than one millimeter, whereas fossil shells of the genus *Campanile* (from the Tertiary of Europe) often were longer than 60 centimeters.

Gastropods have an elongate body consisting of a large, generally flat foot and a usually well developed head, known as the head-foot mass (Figure 1). The mouth at the underside of the head bears a tonguelike organ with many rows of minute horny teeth, the radula. This radula allows gastropods to rasp relatively hard organic matter. The number of teeth per row and their arrangement and shape varies considerably between gastropod groups. Radulas are seldom found in the fossil record.

Most gastropods have a dorsal shell that covers at least the dorsally located soft parts. This visceral mass (or visceral hump) consists of various organs such as the digestive gland, heart, gonads, and excretory organs (Figure 2). It is covered by the integument, which is part of the mantle, an organ that secretes the shell. Part of the mantle covers a cavity that is sheltered by the shell and has a narrow opening to the outside at the aperture of the shell. This mantle cavity contains one or two gills (or ctenidia), one or two chemoreceptory organs (sensory organ that responds to chemical stimulae), the osphradia (singular osphradium, an olfactory organ), hypobranchial gland(s) that secrete mucus used to catch particles, and the openings of the digestive tract and the excretory and reproductive systems (Figure 2). The visceral mass is connected to the head-foot mass by a relatively narrow neck that is related to another feature of evolutionary significance: the Gastropoda share as a common feature that the visceral mass is rotated in a counterclockwise direction relative to the head-foot mass. They are characterized as a natural group by this process called torsion.

Torsion is primarily understood as an evolutionary process that separates the Gastropoda from their untorted predecessors, the Class Helcionellida, which have otherwise similar basic body plans (Figure 2A). However, torsion brings about a significant change in functional morphology, and the great number of fossil and extant gastropods suggests that it is of great adaptive significance. The posteriorly positioned mantle cavity of the Helcionellida was supposedly disadvantageous when the shell evolved from limpet-like relatively flat or cap-shaped forms to strongly coiled ones and when the body size increased considerably during the Early Cambrian. The reason for this is most probably an imperfect water current system that brings clean water to the osphradia and gills and transports alimentary and excretory discharges from the mantle cavity with the exhalant water. Torsion at about 180 degrees rotates the mantle cavity together with the visceral mass and the shell so that it comes to lie above the head and improves the water currents into and out of the mantle cavity. However, it also serves for an asymmetry of the body plan that goes hand in hand with a consequent modification of mantle cavity, visceral mass, and shell. As inhalant water in bilaterally symmetric shell-bearing animals tends to enter laterally, the exhalant water current from the mantle cavity flew out over the head in the primordial torted gastropods. One or several slits or apertures on the periphery of the shell enabled better sorted exhalant currents. An improvement was the development of a unidirectional water current in the mantle cavity to enter left of the head and leave at the right side. In such a system, the inhalant water first passes the osphradium and the gill on the left side and then the openings of the excretory, digestive, and reproductive systems. The gill and osphradium on the right-hand side consequently were reduced. Associated with this system is the development of a tubelike inhalant extension of the mantle on the left side, the so-called siphon, which may or may not secrete the siphonal canal of the shell. The position of the siphon may otherwise be marked by an inhalant notch. Special structures on the outer lip of the aperture may indicate the position of the exhalant current.

The nervous system consists of paired ganglia connected by nerve cords similar to a rope ladder. Torsion resulted in a twist of the nerve cords into a figure eight, a condition termed streptoneury.

The greatest group of gastropods, the *Prosobranchia* with about 65,000 species, have retained this torsional state and the basic body plan, and the various subgroups show the trend toward the reduction of gills, right osphradium, righty kidneys, and right auricle of the heart (Figures 2B–2D). The various states of this reduction define the currently distinguished groups of the *Prosobranchia*. The most primordial of these groups, the archaeogastro-

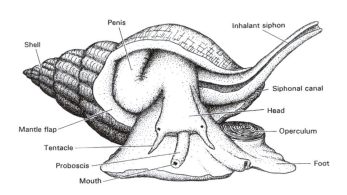

Figure 1. *Buccinum undatum,* a neogastropod; anterior view of animal with protruded head-foot mass. Slightly modified after L.R. Cox in Moore and Pitrat (1960).

pods, have bipectinate gill(s) and a heart with usually two auricles. An inhalant siphon is never developed among them. The shells are either bilaterally symmetrical or form a relatively low spire. The foot is developed for crawling on the floor and can be retracted completely into the helicospirally shell. The members of the group were especially frequent in the Paleozoic and constitute the major part of gastropods during this period. Mesogastropods have a single monopectinate left gill and, as a result, a heart with only one auricle. The shells are usually conispiral and often have a siphonal notch and mostly an operculum (lid) of shell substance that is used to close the aperture when the soft parts are withdrawn into the shell. Although present in the Paleozoic, the mesogastropods did not become frequent and diverse until the Mesozoic. Modern species of this group include periwinkles, turritellas, wendletraps, and cowries. The neogastropods also have a single monopectinate left gill and, as a result, a heart with only one auricle. The shells are conical, often with a high spire, and have a siphonal notch or an often conspicuous siphonal canal. This group is not known from rocks older than Cretaceous and is less diverse than the mesogastropods, although a number of specialized snails belong to this group. Modern species include muricids, whelks, and cones.

Other gastropod groups, however, have undergone secondary modifications. Most important is a detorsion during which visceral mass, mantle cavity, and shell were detorted through some 90 to 110 degrees. As a consequence, the mantle cavity with the retained organs lies on the right-hand. The nerve cords also are detorted, a condition called euthyneury. The second main group of gastropods, the *Opisthobranchia*, including sea slugs and sea hares, typically display this modified body plan (Figure 2E). They also show a marked trend toward a reduction or even total loss of the protective shell and the operculum. This trend allowed a reduction of the mantle cavity as well and opened the way for additional morphologic modifications. Some opisthobranchs are now nearly bilaterally symmetrical externally. The single gill often is displaced posteriorly, or respiration takes place by secondary gills. Many opisthobranchs possess a foot that is modified to enable free swimming.

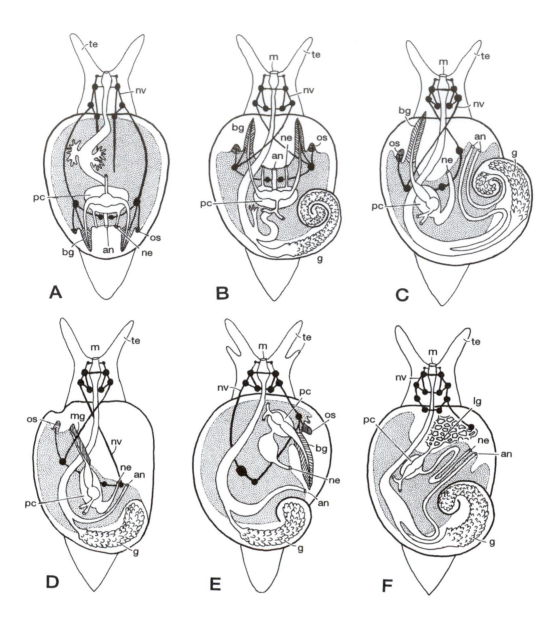

Figure 2. Schematic gastropod mantle cavity structure, soft-part organization, and shell orientation. *A,* helcionelloid; *B,* primitive archaeogastropod; *C,* mesogastropod; *D,* advanced neogastropod; *E,* Opisthobranch; *F,* Pulmonate. Abbreviations: *an,* anus; *bg,* bipectinate gill; *g,* digestive gland; *m,* mouth; *mg,* monopectinate gill; *ne,* opening of nephridial system; *nv,* nervous system with ganglia; *os,* osphradium; *pc,* pericard with heart and aorta; *te,* tentacle.

Another lineage derived from prosobranch gastropods led to a loss of the gill, presumably after detorsion, and to its replacement by a vascularized mantle cavity that permits air breathing (Figure 2F). This evolution of the mantle cavity into a "lung" enabled these *Pulmonata* to colonize terrestrial and freshwater habitats and made them the most successful and abundant gastropods on land. This group includes about 2,500 genera with about 20,000 recent species. The *Pulmonata* commonly retained the shell, but in some (such as slugs) the shell is reduced and sometimes concealed in the mantle.

Other major groups of gastropods with relatively few species were recognized quite recently and are not yet well established.

Many of them show a mixture of prosobranch, opisthobranch, and/or pulmonate features, so that they are best typified by a parallel evolution of a number of "progressive" features.

The most spectacular part of a gastropod is the shell, which shows a wealth of different morphologies. The shell may have a limpet or cap shape, but it is usually coiled. Shells that are coiled in one plane are termed planispiral, but most shells are coiled in three dimesions to form a conical corkscrew helix that differs from low spires to highly conical, needle-shaped shells. The developmentally earliest shell, called the protoconch, is often different in coiling and ornamentation from the later-developing part of the shell (the teleoconch). The surface of the shell is covered with growth lines parallel to the margin of the aperture, and each growth line marks a halt or change in the intensity of successive growth. Periodic halts are commonly marked by prominent transverse ribs or varices (singular varix). Spiral ornaments are parallel to the suture (the line of contact between adjacent whorls). Slits that existed on the periphery of the whorls in primitive archaeogastropods produced during growing a spiral band known as the selenizone. Nonetheless, gastropod higher classification is based on the organization of the soft parts, which are almost never preserved in fossils. The shell bears little direct information on this organization, and the assignment of fossils to the main gastropod groups is based on comparison of fossil shells with those of living species and analysis of functional morphological details such as siphonal canal, siphonal notch (Figure 2D), direction of apertural plane, and apertural shape. However, inferred systematic affinities often are weakly founded. Given the lack of information on soft parts, the higher classification of the Gastropoda is in need of more phylogenetically based approaches and currently in a state of flux (Figure 3).

Subclass Prosobranchia
Archaeogastropods
Caenogastropods*
Mesogastropods*
Neogastropods*
Sublcass Heterobranchia
Opisthobranchia
Gymnomorpha
Allogastropoda
Pulmonata
Basommatophora
Stylommatophora
Systellommatophora
Asterisks indicate traditional groups that describe organizational levels rather than taxa.

Figure 3. Outline classification of the Gastropoda.

Gastropods are generally mobile benthic (seafloor dwelling) animals and occur frequently in marine as well as freshwater and terrestial environments. Prosobranchs are principally marine, but some live in terrestrial or freshwater habitats. Primitive prosobranchs are browsing herbivores (especially the archaeogastropods). Archaeogastropods were abundant shallow-water inhabitants in the Paleozoic, but are rare deep-water species today. Mesogastropods demonstrate various feeding patterns. The majority are marine benthic snails. Many graze on algae but also browse on cnidarians (corals, anemones) and other animals. A number of them are active hunters (on clams, marine worms, or echinoids [sea urchins, sand dollars]). Several are carnivorous and able to bore holes through pelecypod (bivalve) shells to digest soft parts. Mesogastropods already are known from freshwater and terrestrial environments of the Upper Carboniferous (Pennsylvanian). Neogastropods are almost exclusively marine and are generally omnivorous scavengers or carnivorous. Some, called cones, hunt prey such as marine worms, other gastropods, or even fish. They have a poisoned radular tooth that is used for killing the prey. Opisthobranchs are usually marine and live as benthic (deep ocean-dwelling) carnivores or, more rarely, herbivores. An amazing number of different types of ecto- and endoparasitic strategies have been developed among them. However, most of the opisthobranch groups include swimming species (such as the sea hares), and a number of opisthobranchs are pelagic (free-roaming) ciliary feeders, and a few are known as predators. As pulmonates have primarily exploited terrestrial environments, they are primarily herbivores on vascular plants. One group, the basommatophorans, which are the dominant freshwater snails, usually feed by scraping plant matter.

GERD GEYER

Further Reading

Linsley, R.M. 1977. Some "laws" of gastropod shell form. *Paleobiology* 3:196–206.

Moore, R.C., and C.W. Pitrat (eds.). 1960. *Treatise on Invertebrate Paleontology.* Part I, *Mollusca 1.* New York and Lawrence, KS: Geological Society of America and University of Kansas Press.

Peel, J.S. 1987. Class Gastropoda. *In* R.S. Boardman, A.H. Cheetham, and A.J. Rowell (eds.). *Fossil Invertebrates.* Palo Alto, California: Blackwell Scientific.

Pinna, G. 1990. *The Illustrated Encyclopedia of Fossils.* New York, Oxford: Facts on File.

Raup, D.M. 1966. Geometric analysis of shell coiling: general problems. *Journal of Paleontology* 40:1178–90.

Runnegar, B. 1981. Muscle scars, shell form, and torsion in Cambrian and Ordovician univalved molluscs. *Lethia* 14:311–32.

GAUDRY, ALBERT JEAN

French, 1827–1908

Albert Jean Gaudry was born on 15 September 1827 in Saint Germain-en-Laye, France. Through much of his career, Gaudry struggled with contemporaries to reestablish the respectability of evolutionary paleontology and gain acceptance of his theory of evolution. Along the way he published 191 works and was a member of numerous expeditions.

Gaudry's career as a scientist began in 1851, when he entered the Museum d'Histoire Naturelle in Paris. There, he received his Ph.D. in 1852. The following year, Gaudry partook in a geological expedition to the countries of the eastern Mediterranean. During this time, Alcide d'Orbigny (Gaudry's brother-in-law) was appointed to the chair of paleontology at the museum, and he subsequently appointed Gaudry as his assistant.

In 1855 and 1860 Gaudry excavated in Attica, at the Tertiary (Pontian) mammal deposits of Pikermi, Greece. The material from these expeditions not only produced several skeletons of new species, but some fossils exhibited characteristics that may be attributed to "intermediate species." In an article published in 1859, Gaudry interpreted these fossils to be species that "restore the links that were missing in the great chain of beings." This opinion was published nine months prior to Darwin's *Origin of Species,* but Gaudry's concept of biological evolution was the expression of a continuous creation of God: that God did not destroy his creations, but rather, he maintained and improved upon them through time until they were transformed into intelligent human beings. Aside from Gaudry's theory of evolution, Gaudry's work on these expeditions produced the genealogical trees of five large groups of mammals.

From 1866 to 1892, Gaudry continued to take part in expeditions, but his interests shifted toward establishing a new method of paleontological analysis; Gaudry proposed that stratigraphic terrains could be dated according to the evolutionary development of the fossils contained within the strata. This method was successfully applied to the Tertiary mammals recovered from Mont-Leberon (1873). During this time, Gaudry also studied the Lower Permian reptilian and amphibian fossil fauna of Autun at Saone-et-Loire, France. During further excavations in the Quaternary of Saint-Acheul, near Amiens, and Abbeville, Gaudry could attest to the contemporaneity of man with large extinct mammals. Following the latter expedition, Gaudry confirmed that archaic flint chips were associated with the teeth of a large extinct mammal, *Elephas meridionalis.* These findings placed the emergence of human beings further back in time than previously thought.

However, many of Gaudry's findings were revolutionary and thus, not readily accepted by many paleontological colleagues and contemporaries. As a result, Gaudry spent much of his career vindicating evolutionary paleontology and its capacity to establish the reality of biological transformism. Furthermore, by advocating a theory of evolution that espoused a spiritual message, Gaudry presented a message that was quite different from that of Darwin's; to help spread this message, Gaudry did not hesitate to popularize these views in more widely accepted works written in a relaxed style and illustrated with wood engravings.

In 1868 the minister of education assigned Gaudry to teach a course in paleontology at the Sorbonne, but this position only lasted until 1871, when the class was canceled. In 1872 Gaudry was appointed professor of paleontology at the Museum d'Histoire Naturelle, but most of the paleontological collections already had been removed from his laboratory and given to the comparative anatomist. Gaudry would not regain possession of them again until 1878. In 1885, Gaudry began work on a museum of evolution that detailed his theory of evolution. Albert Jean Gaudry died on 27 November 1908 in Paris.

EDOUARD L. BONÉ AND BRIAN CALLENDER

Biography

Born in Saint Germain-en-Laye, France, 15 September 1827. Received Dr.Sc., Museum d'Histoire Naturelle, 1852. Appointed assistant of paleontology, Museum d'Histoire Naturelle, 1853; director of paleontology, Sorbonne, 1868; professor of paleontology, Museum d'Histoire Naturelle, 1872. Fieldwork in the eastern Mediterranean, 1853; Attica at Pikermi, Greece, 1855 and 1860; Saint Acheul, near Amiens, France, 1859; Abbeville, France, 1894. Confirmed contemporaneity of humans with large extinct mammals; establishing an earlier date for the emergence of man; advocated a theory of evolution in which God transformed species into man. Died in Paris, 27 November 1908.

Major Publications

1873. *Animaux fossiles du Mont-Léberon.* Paris: Savy.
1878. Les Reptiles de l'époque permienne aux environs d'Autun. *Bulletin de la Société Géologique de France* 7: 62–77.
1878–90. *Les enchaînements du monde animal dans les temps géologiques.* 3 vols. Paris: Savy.
1876–92. *Matériaux pour l'histoire des temps quaternaires.* Paris: Savy.

Further Readings

Glangeaud, P. 1910. *Albert Gaudry and the Evolution of the Animal Kingdom.* Washington, n.p.

GEOFFROY SAINT-HILAIRE, ÉTIENNE

French, 1772–1844

Étienne Geoffroy was born on 15 April 1772 in Etampes, France. As a child, he received the surname Saint-Hilaire and would later add it to his family name. The youngest of 14 children, Geoffroy displayed the intelligence, imagination, and energy that would win the affection of numerous teachers. Under the guidance of Abbé de Tressan, Geoffroy was headed for a career in the church, but with the outbreak of the French Revolution careers in the church were jeopardized. At his father's insistence, Geoffroy received a degree in law in 1790 but decided to pursue his own interests. He began his medical studies, and in 1792 he was appointed *pensionnaire libre* at the Collège du Cardinal Lemoine in Paris. As a child, Geoffroy was introduced to natural history by Abbé A.H. Tessier in Etampes and later by Brisson and Antoine de Jussieu at the Collège de Navarre in Paris. At the Collège du Cardinal Lemoine, Geoffroy furthered his interest in natural history under the tutelage of Abbé René Just Haüy, a founder of crystallography. Under the tutelage of Daubenton at the Collège de France, Geoffroy also cultivated his interests in mineralogy.

In August 1792, with the outbreak of the Terror, Abbé René Just Haüy was imprisoned because he was a priest. Geoffroy eventually succeeded in freeing him. As a result of his efforts, Geoffroy was appointed demonstrator in zoology at the Jardin des Plants, an appointment made by Geoffroy's former teacher Daubenton, who was a dear friend of Haüy. The following year, in June 1793, the Jardin des Plantes became the Muséum d'Histoire Naturelle, and Geoffroy was subsequently appointed, at the age of 21, professor of quadrupeds, cetaceans, birds, reptiles, and fish. At the same time, Lamarck was appointed to the study of insects, worms, and crustaceans, and given their close association, Geoffroy and Lamarck would become close friends.

Shortly after Geoffroy was appointed professor, Abbé A.H. Tessier, Geoffroy's former teacher, recommended to Geoffroy a young student by the name of Georges Cuvier, who at the time was producing detailed drawings of dissected fishes and invertebrates. Geoffroy happily accepted Cuvier, and they lived and worked together throughout 1795. In this time, they produced five joint publications. In one short work, they claimed that tarsiers are a link between the ape and the bat in the great chain of being. They were also studying the possibility that all species were derived from a single specimen, an idea later rejected by Cuvier. In yet another work, they developed a method for distinguishing characteristics that would allow for the separation of organisms into phyla. This system would later become the basic principle of Cuvier's zoological system. However, the relationship between Geoffroy and Cuvier was not always a productive and peaceful one; in the years to come they would become rivals steeped in intellectual controversy. In 1796 Geoffroy started to research the modification of organisms to their environment. On the contrary, Cuvier persisted in the belief that species were fixed in time.

In 1798 Geoffroy accepted a scientific position accompanying Napoléon on his invasion of Egypt. From 1798 to 1801, Geoffroy traveled through Egypt and up the Nile River as far as Aswan, during which time he collected numerous specimens and made many scientific observations, including examinations of mummified cats from ancient tombs. Although the English were eventually victorious, Geoffroy successfully rescued the scientific collections and brought them back to France. For his part, Cuvier avoided going to Egypt, but he took advantage of Geoffroy's absence and became France's leading naturalist.

Upon his return to France, Geoffroy turned his attentions toward descriptive zoology and classification. From 1802 to 1806, Geoffroy returned to the research on marsupials that he had begun in 1796. During this time, Geoffroy also cataloged the mammal collections of the Muséum d'Histoire Naturelle, producing a rare, unfinished work, of which he stopped the printing in 1803, possibly over contentions with Cuvier. In 1807 Geoffroy was elected into the Academy of Sciences and helped obtain, at Napoléon's request, the collections of Portuguese museums.

The following year, the first of a series of publications on the material collected from Egypt was published. Over the course of 16 years, Geoffroy would contribute to the 24 volumes of *Description de l'Égypte par la Commission des sciences* (1808–24). After examining the mummified cats collected from the ancient tombs, Geoffroy noted that these specimens were identical to extant specimens. For Cuvier, this discovery proved the fixity of species. Lamarck, on the other hand, contested otherwise; that a period of three thousand years is just too short for a perceptible degree of evolution to occur.

The fixity-of-species debate fueled Geoffroy's interests. Believing in the nonfixity of species, Geoffroy set out to prove that, with the passing of time, species were transformed from simpler ones to more complex ones. While the unity of plan of vertebrates was recognized by Aristotle, the idea that different species were derived from a basic anatomical structure was debated in the sixteenth and seventeenth centuries, most notably during Geoffroy's time by Cuvier. Cuvier insisted that each species was a distinct, God-created form, whose parts met functional needs. Over the course of 15 years, from 1806 to 1821, Geoffroy utilized comparative anatomy, teratology (the study of animal malformations), and paleontology to establish the principle of "unity of composition," which states that a simple basic structure is inherent in all animals. In 1818, with the publication of *Philosophie anatomique*, Geoffroy established two fundamental principles of comparative anatomy: (1) the principle of anatomical connections, which states that the same anatomical structural plan exists in all vertebrates, such that one can trace structures from species to species; and (2) the principle of the balance of organs (structures), which claims that when an organ increases in size, the neighboring organ diminishes in size. Inherent in Geoffroy's principle is a kinship among vertebrates, in which more complex species are derivatives of simpler species.

To support his research, Geoffroy proved in 1807 that the pectoral fins of fishes were morphologically and functionally similar to the bones of the front limbs of vertebrates, thus demonstrating that mammals descended from fishes. In later research, Geoffroy proved that the bony flaps covering gill slits in fishes were the equivalent of the auditory bones in mammals. Prior to this research, Cuvier believed he had identified a unique structure of the fish.

During the course of his research, Geoffroy founded experimental embryology and teratology. Following the work of Karl Kielmeyer, who demonstrated that during the course of embryonic life a vertebrate passes through phases homologous to its ancestors, Geoffroy attempted to halt the embryonic development of chicken embryos to maintain the fish stage or demonstrate the transition to the mammalian stage. Although such attempts failed, they were the first of their kind and established Geoffroy as the founder of experimental embryology. Geoffroy was also the first to apply scientific teratology to animals. By studying the malformations of so-called monsters, Geoffroy sought explanations for the sudden transformation of species. During his career, he wrote more than fifty works on the subject, and his *Essai de classification des monstres* represents the debut of scientific teratology.

In 1830 Geoffroy began to apply his principle of "unity of composition" to a wider array of organisms, including invertebrates. He claimed to have evidence that a universal plan was evident in the crustacea, fishes, and molluscs. These claims sparked an ongoing controversy with Cuvier, who believed that all animals were separated into four unchanging groups. This ongoing debate between Geoffroy and Cuvier divided the scientific world and set the stage for Charles Darwin's theory of evolution.

In the following years Geoffroy expanded his research into evolutionary paleontology. He claimed that the Caen, a fossil reptile that he named *Teleosaurus,* displayed characteristics intermediate between those of saurians and mammals. In 1833 Geoffroy examined the fossil mammals of the Perrier bed in the Massif Central and claimed that they were intermediate species. In later work Geoffroy also examined the fossil remains of Saint-Gérand-le-Puy, an Oligocene deposit near Vichy. The following year, in 1834, Geoffroy's work began to focus less on scientific study and more on theory, and as a result, Geoffroy loss respect among his peers.

In July 1840 Geoffroy suffered a stroke that left him blind and paralyzed, and in the years to follow, his mental capacity declined. Étienne Geoffroy Saint-Hilaire died 19 June 1844 in Paris, France.

EDOUARD L. BONÉ AND BRIAN CALLENDER

Biography

Born in Etampes, France, 15 April 1772. Received law degree, 1790; studied medicine, Collège du Cardinal Lemoine, Paris. Appointed demonstrator of zoology, Jardin des Plantes, 1793; appointed professor, Muséum d'Histoire Naturelle, 1793; became professor of zoology, University of Paris, 1809. Traveled through Egypt in conjunction with Napoléon's invasion, 1798–1801. Elected to Académie de Sciences, 1807, became president, 1833. Revitalized comparative anatomy in France; developed the principle of "unity of composition"; founded scientific teratology and experimental embryology; engaged in ongoing scientific debate with Georges Cuvier over the fixity of species. Died in Paris, 19 June 1844.

Major Publications

1803. *Catalogue des mammifères du muséum national d'histoire naturelle.* Paris: Le Muséum.

1807. Considérations sur les pièces de la tête osseuse de vertébrés. *Annales du Muséum d'histoire naturelle* 10:332–65.

1818–22. *Philosophie anatomique.* 2 vols. Paris: Baillière.

1825–26. Sur les déviations organiques provoquées et observés dans un établissement d'incubations artificielles. *Mémoires du Muséum d'histoire naturelle* 13 (1825):289–96; *Archives générales de médecine* 13 (1826):289; *Journal complémentaire des sciences médicales* 24 (1826):256.

1827. Essai de classification des monstres. *In* M. Bory de Saint-Vincent (ed.), *Dictionnaire classique d'histoire naturelle,* vol. 9. Paris: Rey et Gravier.

1830. *Principes de philosophie zoologique discutés en mars 1830 à l'Académie Royale des sciences.* Paris: Pichon et Didier.

1831. *Recherches sur les grands sauriens: Trouvés à l'état fossile vers les confins maritimes de la basse Normandie, attribués d'abord au crocodile, puis déterminés sous les noms de téléosaurus et sténosaurus.* Paris: Firmin Didot.

Further Reading

Appels, T.A. 1987. *The Cuvier-Geoffroy Debate: French Biology in the Decades before Darwin.* New York: Oxford University Press.

Blainville, H.M. Ducrotay de. 1890. *Cuvier et Geoffroy Saint-Hilaire biographies scientifiques.* Paris: Baillière.

Bourdier, F. 1969. Geoffroy Saint-Hilaire versus Cuvier: The Campaign for Paleontological Evolution (1825–1838). *In* C.J. Schneer (ed.), *Toward a History of Geology.* Cambridge, Massachusetts: M.I.T. Press.

Cahn, T. 1962. *La vie et l'oeuvre d'Étienne Geoffroy Saint-Hilaire.* Paris: Presses Universitaires de France.

Flourens, P. 1862. Memoir of Geoffroy Saint-Hilaire. C.A. Alexander (trans). *Smithsonian Institution Annual Report 1861.* Washington, D.C.: Smithsonian Institution.

Salf, E.P.L. 1986. *Un Anatomiste et philosophe français, Étienne Geoffroy Saint-Hilaire (1772–1844): Père de la tératologie morphologique et de l'embryologie expérimentale.* 2 vols. Lyon: Faculté de médecine Lyon Sud.

GEOLOGICAL TIMESCALE

The geological timescale (Figure 1) divides the last 4.6 billion years of Earth history into named intervals of geologic time and provides numerical estimates (usually in millions of years) of the durations of these intervals. Thus, it can be thought of as two timescales—one that is a relative scale of time intervals arranged hierarchically (shorter time intervals are grouped into longer ones), and a second that is a numerical timescale calibrated in millions of years.

The relative geological timescale embodies about 200 years of scientific research aimed at dividing geologic time into intervals that can be recognized and correlated globally. This timescale also is called the standard global chronostratigraphic scale (sgcs). The sgcs is a hierarchy of time intervals, from long (eon, era) to short (period, epoch, age). The name of each time interval has historical significance, reflecting a concept held by the geologist who coined the term. For example, the eon name "Phanerozoic" refers to the interval of Earth history when life was very evident (Greek *phaneros*, evident) on the planet, as proven by an abundance of fossils. During the preceding eon, the Proterozoic, life was in one of its earliest stages of evolution (Greek *proteros*, earlier). The names of the Phanerozoic eras—Paleozoic, Mesozoic, and Cenozoic—were coined by British geologist John Phillips as time intervals of ancient life (Greek *palaios*, ancient; *zöe*, life), intermediate life (Greek *mesos*, intermediate) and recent life (Greek *kainos*, recent), with the Paleozoic-Mesozoic and the Mesozoic-Cenozoic boundaries defined by major, global extinctions.

The names of the periods were coined by European geologists during the nineteenth century. Some refer to a place (e.g., Permian, based on Perm in Russia; Devonian, for Devon in England), others to a kind of rock (e.g., Carboniferous, for coal; Cretaceous, for chalk), and still others are more colorful references to a place (Ordovician and Silurian for ancient Welsh tribes who fought the Romans). Tertiary (third) and Quaternary (fourth) are holdovers from an older geological timescale of the eighteenth century, when Mesozoic rocks were called "Secondary," and pre-Mesozoic rocks were "Primary." There is now a movement to abolish Tertiary and Quaternary and replace them with a more balanced division of Cenozoic time into Paleogene (Paleocene, Eocene, and Oligocene) and Neogene (Miocene, Pliocene, and Pleistocene, including Holocene).

Each period is divided into shorter geologic time intervals, the epochs and ages. Of these, the names of the Cenozoic epochs (e.g., Paleocene, Eocene) are used most commonly. British geologist Charles Lyell originally coined some of these names in 1833, basing them on the observation that fossil mollusc species look more and more like modern species in progressively younger Cenozoic rocks. Thus, in the oldest Cenozoic rocks the fossil molluscs look very little like modern species, but by late Cenozoic time they are quite modern in aspect. As a result, in Lyell's mind, the earliest Cenozoic was termed aptly the "dawn of the recent" (Greek *eos*, dawn; *kainos*, recent). By Miocene time, though, a few molluscs resembled modern forms (Greek *meion*,

less), and by the Pliocene there were many more such molluscs (Greek *pleion*, more). The other epoch names were added later, as the Cenozoic timescale was refined.

Regardless of the term applied to a time interval and the term's derivation, the definition and characterization of the time interval is universal. Thus, suppose a geologist identified a body of rock in a particular place (usually that place is the basis of the name and is referred to as the "type locality") and asserted that the body of rock was formed during a particular time interval. The fossils that the rock contains are of plants and/or animals that lived during that time interval. To assign rocks (and fossils) or events from another place to that time interval requires correlation—the equivalence of age of two rock bodies in separate areas must be determined. One does this by demonstrating that the rock bodies are continuous, are very similar to each other, and/or contain the same fossils. For rocks to be assigned to a given time interval of the relative geological time scale, they must be the same age as at least some of the rocks in the type area.

In the last 50 years, the focus of timescale work has shifted from defining the intervals to defining the boundaries between time intervals precisely. The goal is to define the beginning of a time interval; by default, that defines the end of the preceding time interval. To assign a rock, fossil, or event to a given time interval, we need only demonstrate it is older than the end of and younger than the beginning of that time interval. For example, to place a rock in the Paleocene epoch, it must be older than the end of the epoch (55 million years ago) and younger than the beginning (65 million years ago).

The beginning of a longer time interval in the relative geological timescale (eon, era, period) usually is associated with major physical and/or biological changes on Earth. Thus, the beginning of the Mesozoic is marked by the greatest extinction of life in Earth history, and its end (i.e., the beginning of the Cenozoic) corresponds to the extinction of the dinosaurs and other life forms. Such large-scale events usually provide widespread and easily recognized criteria for the geological time boundary. For example, the last dinosaur fossils herald the beginning of the Cenozoic.

The boundaries of shorter geological time intervals (epochs, ages) usually are not marked by such dramatic events (except in those rare instances where the boundary between shorter time intervals is the same as a boundary between longer time intervals; for instance, the Late Cretaceous-Paleocene boundary is the same as the Mesozoic-Cenozoic boundary). The boundaries of shorter intervals often are identified by a single evolutionary event—the appearance of one or more new species of extinct organism. For example, the appearance of a single species of ammonoid cephalopod (extinct relatives of squid and octopuses) is the principal criterion for identifying the boundary between the Middle and the Late Triassic.

The numerical timescale assigns ages to rocks in thousands, millions, or billions of years, based on radio-isotopic dating. Such numerical ages can be determined only on rocks that contain suffi-

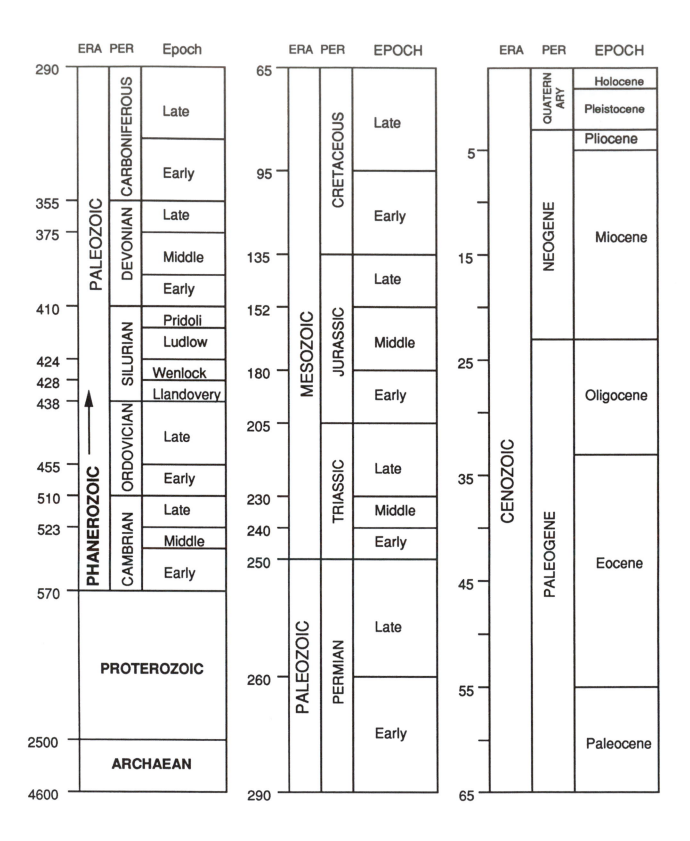

Figure 1. The 1989 geological timescale of the International Union of Geological Sciences. Note that all of the periods and epochs have been further divided into smaller time intervals called ages, not shown here. Eons are in boldface; all numerical ages indicate millions of years.

cient quantities of radioactive elements, usually some form of volcanic ash. This is why it is not possible to determine numerical ages for all rocks. It is also important to remember that the final numbers are approximations based on the best calculated ages, and all these calculated ages have a margin of error. For this reason, as better estimates become available, ages change. Since 1980, for example, the age estimate of the Permian-Triassic boundary changed from 237 to 250 million years.

Refinement of the geological timescale continues, but it faces difficulties in some areas. We usually think of time as a continuum, but the means for dividing and measuring it are episodic. Most of the bodies of rock originally used to define the time intervals of the geological timescale have unconformable boundaries—a hiatus in deposition separates them from older and/or younger rocks. Fossil occurrences are not continuous throughout most rock bodies, and numerical ages are available rather infrequently. For instance, usually they are available only where beds of volcanic rock are present.

These factors make the task of determining the precise ages of many rocks far from straightforward. Furthermore, establishing ideal standards for a global geological timescale that records all of Earth history is not simple. Such ideal standards should involve bodies of sedimentary rock that were produced by continuous (not episodic) deposition, are filled with fossils, and have radioactive minerals (usually in volcanic ash beds). These conditions allow numerical ages to be calculated directly. Furthermore, such ideal rock bodies would be readily accessible to study and restudy, not in extremely remote or dangerous regions. Only such ideal rock bodies can allow timescale researchers to piece together a complete record of Earth history, one with which all rocks and fossils can be correlated. Few sites meet all of these criteria.

Serious problems for the geological timescale are associated with precision and synchroneity (occurring in different places at the same time). The exact ages of most geological and biological events used in correlations are not fixed, and the events are often diachronous (not synchronous over a wide area). Thus, numerical ages calculated for geological phenomena are always approximations, with margins of error in thousands or millions of years. Evolutionary events do not happen simultaneously everywhere. For example, the origination and spread of a new species of animal can take thousands of years. Thus, its fossils do not necessarily indicate the exact same age everywhere they are found. Such phenomena make geologists' efforts to construct, calibrate, and correlate the geological timescale imprecise.

Despite these problems—and in part because of them—the goal of geological timescale research is to produce the most refined, precise, and globally applicable timescale. This timescale is a template for ordering and correlating all events in Earth history.

SPENCER G. LUCAS

See also Dating Methods; Fossil Record; Paleomagnetism; Sedimentology

Further Reading

Berggren, W.A., D.V. Kent, M.P. Aubry, and J. Hardenbol (eds.). 1995. *Geochronology, Time Scales and Global Stratigraphic Correlation.* Society for Sedimentary Geology Special Publication, 54. Tulsa, Oklahoma: Society for Sedimentary Geology.

Berry, W.B.N. 1968. *Growth of a Prehistoric Timescale.* San Francisco: Freeman; 2nd ed., Palo Alto, California: Blackwell Scientific, 1987.

Eicher, D.L. 1968. *Geologic Time.* Englewood Cliffs, New Jersey: Prentice-Hall; 2nd ed., 1976.

Harland, W.B., R.L. Armstrong, A.V. Cox, L.E. Craig, A.G. Smith, and D.G. Smith. 1990. *A Geologic Time Scale 1989.* Cambridge and New York: Cambridge University Press.

GIGANTISM

See Phyletic Dwarfism and Gigantism

GINKGOS

Ginkgo (Maidenhair Tree) belongs to the Division Ginkgophyta.

Prior to the eleventh century, ginkgo does not appear in the literature and is presumed to have been unknown to the ancient Chinese. The first account of ginkgo was reported during the eleventh century Sung Dynasty, when it was described as a plant native to the hilly regions south of the Yangtze River, in southeast China. Because ginkgo did not grow naturally in Kaifeng, the Chinese capital at the time, the tree's "fruit" was considered to be precious rarity and was presented annually to the emperor as a special offering. Eventually ginkgo trees were planted in Kaifeng and regions outside its natural range. Although it is thought that ginkgo was introduced into Japan during the Sung Dynasty, accu-

rate records are limited, and a more precise date is lacking. Nevertheless, its introduction into Japan was fortuitous, for ginkgo was first observed there in cultivation and was brought to the attention of the western world by Engelbert Kaempfer, a Dutch surgeon who worked in Nagasaki, Japan, for the Dutch East India Company between 1690 and 1692. Kaempfer's description of ginkgo did not appear until 1712, and it was not until 1771 that Linnaeus adopted Kaempfer's generic name ginkgo and formally described the only living species, *Ginkgo biloba*.

Ginkgo biloba is a long-lived tree that can be of immense proportions, reaching heights of up to 30 meters (Figure 1). It is deciduous, with its leaves turning a golden yellow in the fall prior

Figure 1. A 645-year-old *Ginkgo biloba* tree from Eihoji Temple, Kokeizan, Tajimi City, Gifu Prefecture, Japan.

to being shed. The leaves are commonly fan-shaped and have two lobes; but scholars have noted considerable variation in the degree of lobing and dissection (splitting), even among the leaves from a single tree (Figure 2). The pattern of veins is open and dichotomous (divides repeatedly into two equal branches) resembling that seen in the seed ferns (Figure 3). Ginkgo is further distinguished from other gymnosperms by possessing both long and short shoots (Figure 4), as well as producing separate male and female trees. Long shoot growth is indefinite, forming the branches of the tree. New long shoots are devoid of short shoots and only bear individually attached leaves arranged in a helical (spiral) pattern. The smaller short shoots are borne only on the long shoots that are more than one year old, have growth limited to only a few millimeters per year, and bear either pollen cones or ovules and a tuft of leaves.

The male trees produce pollen cones that resemble loose, pendulous catkins (Figure 5A); the cones bear several structures called "sporangiophores." Each sporangiophore possesses two pendulous "sporangia," within which the pollen grains (microgametophytes) develop. Aspects of microgametophyte development, including the formation of the pollen-tube (a structure

that delivers sperm to the egg) and growth and the production of large multi-flagellated (many-tailed) sperm closely resembles that seen in the cycads. At maturity, the pollen is released, and wind carries the grains to the pollen droplets that form at the micropylar end (the open end which allows pollen to enter) of the ovules on the female trees (Figure 6). The pollen droplet draws the pollen grains into the pollen chamber, where the pollen grains germinate and produce pollen tubes. Each pollen tube elongates until it enters the archegonial (egg) chamber. Within the pollen tube specialized cells develop into flagellated sperm and are released into the fluid that fills the archegonial chamber. The sperm swim towards the egg nucleus contained within the archegonium. One sperm and one egg unite to form a diploid zygote that will develop into a young embryo and ultimately mature into a seed.

Female trees are distinguished from conifers in that the ovules are produced in pairs (rarely in threes) at the end of short stalks in the axil of the leaves (crook formed by the shoot and the leaf) of the short shoots, rather than in cones (Figures 2, 5B, 5C). The ovules are large, similar to those of the seed ferns and cycads, and develop within a three-layered integument or seed coat (Figure 6). It is the outer fleshy layer ("sarcotesta") that produces a nasty rancid butter smell once the seeds have fallen. The "sclerotesta," which is the middle layer of the seed coat, is the hard nut-like covering that helps protect the ovule. The inner "endotesta" is papery thin and surrounds the nucellus, the structure within which the megagametophyte (the structure that ultimately houses the embryo) develops. Development of the megagametophyte proceeds in a manner similar to that seen in the cycads. Initially, a specialized cell called the megasporocyte undergoes meiosis (a cell division that produces haploid cells) to produce four megaspores. Of the four cells, three degenerate. The remaining megaspore begins to grow rapidly through cell division forming a large multicellular megagametophyte. Embedded within the multicellular tissue of the megagametophyte are two archegonia (each containing an egg cell, a ventral cell, and two or four neck cells). The archegonia develop at the micropylar end (Figure 7). Once fertilization has occurred, the zygote develops and grows into a young embryo and finally into a seed by growing into and feeding on the nutritive megagametophytic tissue surrounding it.

The stalks bearing the ovules are one of the main features that distinguish ginkgo from all other conifers and unite both fossil and living ginkgo as a distinct group, for all ginkgophytes and putative (assumed) ancestors possess ovules borne on stalks. As a group, the ginkgophytes have a long fossil history, with a number of taxa first appearing during the Permian. Probably the oldest genus showing affinity to the ginkgophytes is *Tricopitys*. Specimens of *Tricopitys heteromorpha* possess leaves that are divided into four to eight segments and stalks bearing three to twenty ovules. These specimens, discovered in 1875 by French paleobotanist Gaston de Saporta, were collected from Early Permian (approximately 260 to 280 million years old) sediments from the south of France. Since then, there have been a number of new genera, including those assigned to the Dicranophyllales and Czekanowskiales, described from Permian and younger deposits throughout the world. A summary of these taxa and their possible relationship to the ginkgophytes is provided by Archangelsky and Cúneo (1990) and Taylor and Taylor (1993).

As a group, the ginkgophytes attained prominence not only in the extent of their range of distribution, but also in the number of taxa that appear between the Triassic and Cretaceous, a span of about 165 million years. H. Tralau (1968) indicates that at least 16 genera appeared at this time, and it was during the Jurassic (140 to 195 million years ago) that the ginkgophytes were the most prominent and diverse. However, extensive leaf polymorphism (many and varied shapes and structures) among ginkgophyte fossils has contributed to recognition of a large number of leaf types that have been described as being ginkgolike, and it is not known how many biologically distinct species really existed during the Mesozoic (this era includes the Triassic, Jurassic, and Cretaceous). By the end of the Cretaceous, about 65 million years ago, all genera except for *Ginkgo* became extinct.

The earliest known fossil remains that are unquestionably those of ginkgo appear during the Early Jurassic, and it is for this reason that ginkgo is often referred to as a "living fossil." Throughout the Jurassic, ginkgo was distributed widely throughout Europe and western Asia, and by the end of the Cretaceous the genus had spread

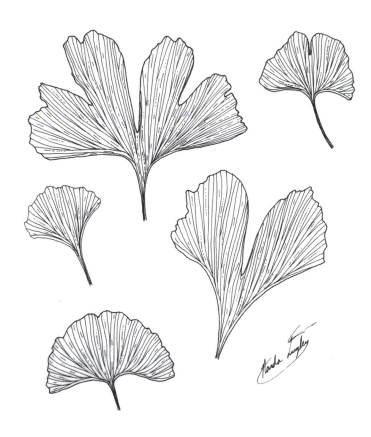

Figure 2. Leaves from a *Ginkgo biloba* tree, showing the natural variability of leaf size and shape. Drawn by Narda Quigley.

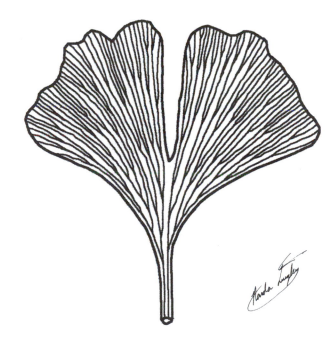

Figure 3. Leaf of *Ginkgo biloba* showing the open and dichotomous pattern in the veins of the leaf. Redrawn by Narda Quigley from Stewart and Rothwell (1993).

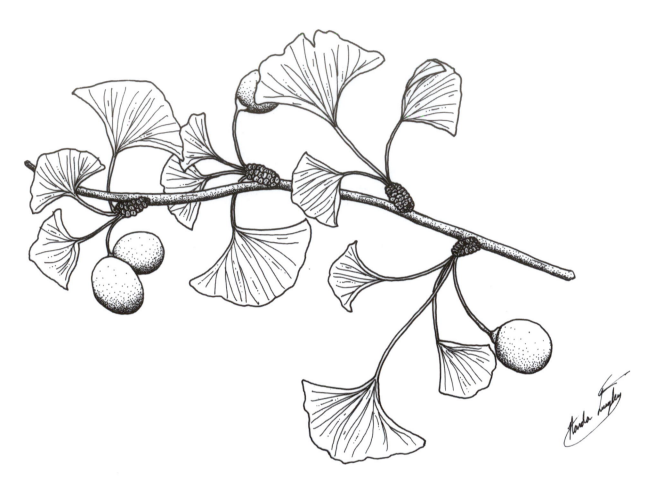

Figure 4. A *Ginkgo biloba* long shoot, bearing short shoots with leaves and ovules. Drawn by Narda Quigley.

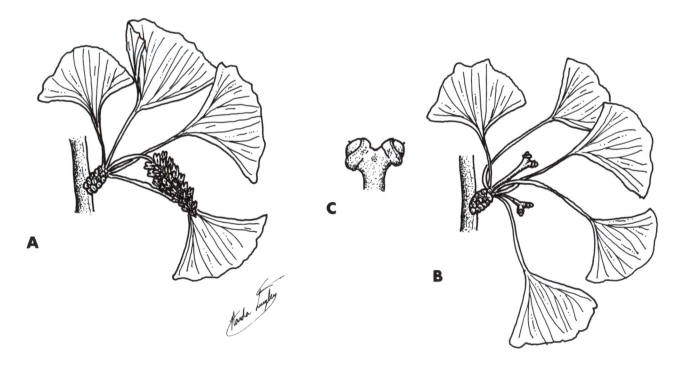

Figure 5. *Ginkgo biloba* cones and ovules. *A*, short shoot bearing leaves and pendulous catkinlike pollen cones; *B*, short shoot bearing leaves and two pairs of ovules on stalks; *C*, closeup of a stalk showing two developing ovules. Drawn by Narda Quigley.

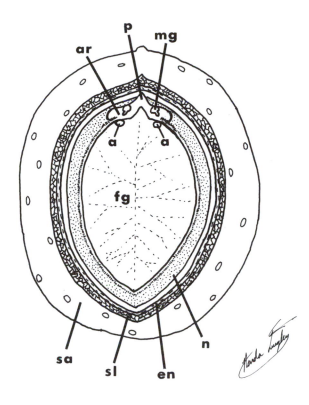

Figure 6. Longitudinal section of a mature ginkgo ovule showing the female gametophyte. Key: *fg,* female gametophyte; *n,* nucellus; *a,* archegonium; *p,* pollen chamber; *ar,* archegonial chamber; *mg,* male gametophyte; *sc,* sclerotesta; *sa,* sarcotesta; *en,* endotesta. Redrawn by Narda Quigley and modified from Foster and Gifford (1974).

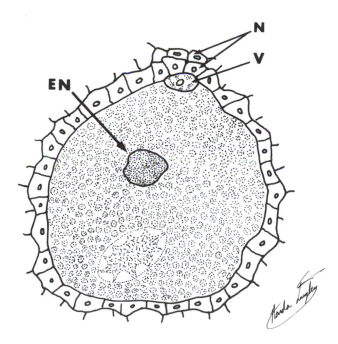

Figure 7. Detailed diagram of an archegonium. Key: *EN,* egg cell; *N,* neck cells; *V,* ventral cell. Redrawn by Narda Quigley from Foster and Gifford (1974).

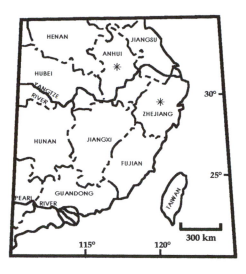

Figure 8. Present—and possibly the last—naturally occurring populations of *Ginkgo biloba* in Anhui and Zhejiang provinces, southeast China. Symbol: *,* location.

to the west and was much more prominent throughout eastern Asia and western North America (Tralau 1968). The global cooling that followed the Cretaceous appears to have fragmented the circumboreal distribution of the two remaining species, *G. biloba* and *G. adiantoides,* into separate North American, European, and east Asian populations. Continued cooling and drying about 33 to 34 million years ago ultimately decimated the North American and European ginkgo populations and forced *G. adiantoides* to go extinct about 10 to 12 million years ago. While there is consensus among botanists that southeast China was the last refuge for *G. biloba,* it is not known whether this species continues to occur naturally in this region. Severe deforestation and population pressures throughout southeast China may have eliminated all natural stands of this once widespread tree. H.-L. Li (1956), however, maintains that naturally occurring trees of *G. biloba* can still be found in Anhui and Zhejiang provinces (Figure 8).

Although the fossil record indicates that the ginkgophytes are ancient, their sudden appearance and apparent lack of potential ancestors have shed little light on the group of plants from which they might have evolved. Based on reproductive structures, ginkgo shows many similarities with the cycads, while wood anatomy appears to be most similar to that seen in the conifers. Alternatively, S.V. Meyen (1984) has suggested that the ginkgophytes evolved from the Peltaspermales, an extinct group of Late Paleozoic/Early Mesozoic seed ferns. While our understanding of ginkgophyte evolution is incomplete, continued study of the fossil record may enable us ultimately to identify the group of plants from which the ginkgophytes evolved, how many species really existed, and provide a suitable explanation for reduction of their former distribution.

BEN A. LEPAGE

See also Cycads; Gymnosperms

Works Cited and Further Reading
Archangelsky, S., and R. Cúneo. 1990. *Polyspermophyllum,* a new Permian gymnosperm from Argentina, with considerations about the Dicranophyllales. *Review of Palaeobotany and Palynology* 63:117–35.
Foster, A.S., and E.M. Gifford Jr. 1974. *Comparative Morphology of Vascular Plants.* 2nd ed. San Francisco: Freeman.
Li, H.-L. 1956. A horticultural and botanical history of *Ginkgo. Morris Arboretum Bulletin* 7:3–12.
Meyen, S.V. 1984. Basic features of gymnosperm systematics and phylogeny as evidenced by the fossil record. *Botanical Review* 50:1–112.
Stewart, W.N., and G.W. Rothwell. 1993. *Peleobiology and the Evolution of Plants.* 2nd ed., Cambridge and New York: Cambridge University Press.
Tralau, H. 1968. Evolutionary trends in the genus *Ginkgo. Lethaia* 1:63–101.
Taylor, T.N., and E.L. Taylor. 1993. *The Biology and Evolution of Fossil Plants.* Englewood, New Jersey: Prentice Hall.

GLIRES

Glires (rodents and lagomorphs) are well known in modern mammalian faunas, where they fill the role of small herbivores that are at the base of many food chains. (Lagomorphs include the rabbits, hares, and pikas while rodents include everything from 40-kilogram capybaras to tiny mice.) The two orders have held this ecological position in many parts of the world for more than 50 million years. Both orders have perfected herbivorous habits through development of enlarged, evergrowing incisors that are used to gnaw a variety of plant foods. It appears that both groups have enlarged the second incisor (out of a primitive complement of three) in each jaw quadrant in both the upper and lower jaw.

Lagomorphs and rodents also share a number of primitive morphological features. Because of these primitive features and the specialized incisor function, lagomorphs and rodents were long united as Glires (gliriform, or gnawing mammals); the lagomorphs, having two pairs of upper incisors, were classified as "Duplicidentata," while the rodents were classified as "Simplicidentata," the latter name reflecting their single pair of upper incisors (Tullberg 1899). Later investigations suggested that these two orders were not closely related because their morphologies did not seem to grow more similar as their fossil records were traced back into the Eocene. Today, an improved fossil record from the Paleocene of Asia, especially from China and Mongolia, has caused scientific opinion to come full circle. The histories of Rodentia and Lagomorpha do indeed converge, and the Glires concept seems to have validity.

The origin of the lagomorphs and rodents can be traced to the Asian order Anagalida, which ranges in time from the Paleocene to the Oligocene. The greatest taxonomic and morphologic variety in this order occurred during the Paleocene. Anagalids were mostly small mammals, with prismatic teeth, some showing hypsodonty (high crowns), but lacking enlarged, ever-growing incisors. Several distinct lineages of gliriform mammals are derived from this Paleocene radiation, including the families Mimotonidae and Eurymylidae. These families represent the initial dichotomy from which the Lagomorpha (sister group of the Mimotonidae) and the Rodentia (sister group of the Eurymylidae) diverged (Li and Ting 1985; Li et al. 1987). The mimotonids retain the third upper incisor (I^3), although it is not as close to I^2 as in the lagomorphs. In contrast, the eurymylids resemble rodents in lacking the third upper incisor.

The Lagomorpha

The lagomorphs include two families, both of which have extinct and extant representatives. The order ranges from the Middle Eocene to the present day. Geologically, lagomorphs occur naturally on all continents except Australia and Antarctica and are also absent from some oceanic islands. The order is characterized by many skeletal and dental features that can be observed in fossil representatives. The dental count on each side of the head is two upper incisors and one lower incisor, no canines, three upper and two lower premolars, and two to three upper and lower molars. As was mentioned earlier, the upper and lower second incisors (I^2 and I$_2$) are enlarged and ever-growing. The enamel on these gnawing teeth is single-layered and restricted to the front surface. There is a long diastema (gap) between the incisors and the premolars. The lateral surface of the maxilla (the main bone of the upper jaw) is fenestrated (riddled with holes) to some degree. There are large incisive foramina (holes) at the front of the hard palate for the passage of nerves and blood vessels. The hard palate itself is unusually short. The glenoid fossa (jaw socket) is transversely expanded (wide from side to side). The coronoid process of the lower jaw, to which temporalis chewing muscles attach, is rudimentary. Cheek teeth are high-crowned, and in some species they are ever-growing. The cheek teeth have mostly lost the triangular shape seen in primitive placental mammals. The upper tooth rows are wider than the lower tooth rows, which is related to the transverse (side-to-side) chewing motion that lagomorphs employ. The auditory bulla (middle ear chamber) develops from an expanded ectotympanic bone (the bone that holds the tympanum, or eardrum). The two lower leg bones (the tibia and the fibula) are fused. The tail is short. While there are still five digits in the hand, there are only four in the foot. The humerus (upper arm bone) lacks an entepicondylar foramen for the passage of the median nerve and brachial artery.

Following their origin in Asia, the lagomorphs show little subsequent morphological diversity. Only two lagomorph families are recognized since the Middle Eocene.

The family Leporidae (rabbits and hares) contains both primitive and more derived taxa. Leporids retain the complete dental count characteristic of the order. Over time, their skulls develop an increased capacity to bend between the face and the skull base. Fenestration of the maxilla also increases. The postcranial skeleton evinces modifications that reflect an increasing com-

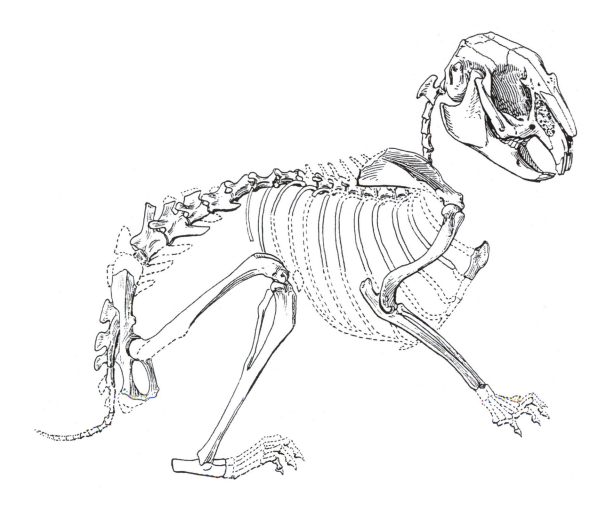

Figure 1. The oligocene leporid *Palaeolagus haydeni*. From Wood (1940).

mitment to a bounding type of locomotion, with a concomitant reduction in lateral trunk flexibility.

The most primitive known leporids occur in the Middle Eocene of Asia. This group made brief forays into western Europe in the Oligocene but did not persist there. Leporids entered North America in the Middle Eocene and rapidly became well established. The Oligocene through Miocene history of the family is largely North American, where a succession of genera show trends through time of increased hysodonty, simplification of the cheek teeth pattern, and some elongation of the hind limb (Figure 1). Leporids occurred only in North America between the Middle Oligocene and Late Miocene. At the end of the Miocene, one or more lines of North American leporids entered Eurasia and flourished there. Recent leporids include such widely distributed genera as *Lepus, Oryctolagus,* and *Sylvilagus.* Also present today are some more primitive genera such as *Pentalagus* (Ryukyu Islands) and *Romerolagus* (Mexico) that are similar to taxa that were present in the Pliocene.

The family Ochotonidae (pikas) is first known from the Middle Oligocene of Asia. The family is characterized a primitive non-molarized upper third premolar, a maxillary premolar foramen, and upper cheek teeth that often have strongly curved roots extending toward the zygomatic bone (cheek bone). Ochotonids reached their peak of diversity and distribution in the Miocene, after which time the family became more restricted taxonomically. Today ochotonids are known only from Asia and western North America.

Ochotonid history includes successful invasions into western Europe, where several lineages became common in the small-mammal faunas of the area. A variety of ochotonid genera flourished during the Miocene. The most long-lived of these was the genus *Prolagus* (Figure 2), whose range shrank to the Mediterranean region late in its history, but which persisted into the Quarternary on the islands of Sardinia and Corsica (Dawson 1967, 1969). During the Miocene, one lineage of ochotonids expanded into eastern Africa, and ochotonids took part in three or four immigration events into North America. The sole surviving ochotonid genus, *Ochotona,* originated in Asia in the later Miocene. It achieved the widest distribution of any genus of the family in the Pleistocene when it expanded its range across the Holarctic realm from western Europe to eastern North America. The modern distribution of the genus represents a small fraction of this former range.

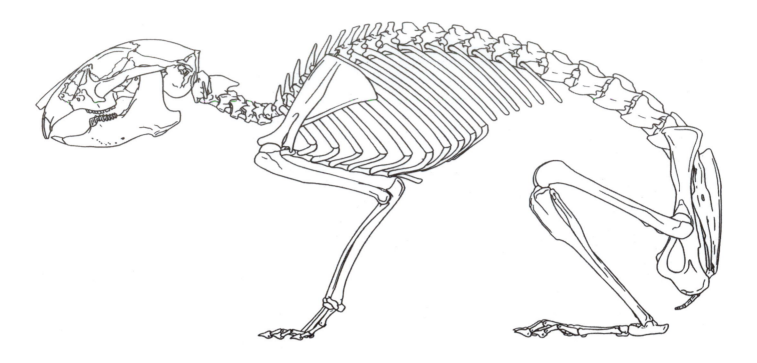

Figure 2. The Pleistocene ochotonid *Prolagus sardus.* From Dawson (1969).

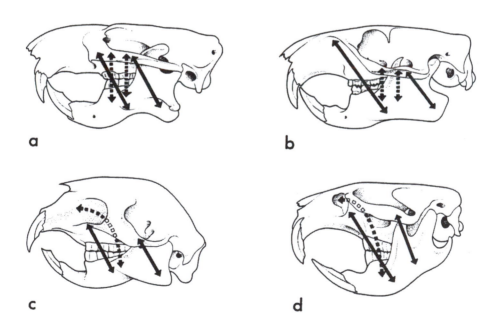

Figure 3. Diagrammatic representation of the origin and insertion of masseter muscles relative to the zyogmatic arch, infraorbital foramen, and lower jaw in mammals. *a,* Protogomorphous (e.g., *Aplodontia*), with masseter muscles originating on the zygomatic arch; *b,* Sciuromorpha *(Marmota); c,* Hystricomorpha *(Hystrix); d,* Myomorpha *(Ondatra). Broken arrows:* internal and anterior masseter medialis muscles; *solid arrows:* external masseter superficialis and masseter lateralis muscles. From Honeycutt (1991). In Sherman, P.W., J.U.M. Jarvis, and R.D. Alexander; THE BIOLOGY OF THE NAKED MOLE-RAT. Copyright © 1991 by Princeton University Press. Reprinted by permission of Princeton University Press.

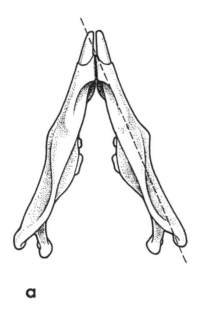
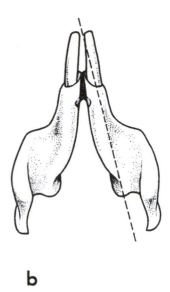

Figure 4. Ventral view of mandible showing the angular process, the key feature used to classify rodents into two major groups: *a*, Sciurognathi (e.g., *Marmota*); b, Hystricognathi (e.g., *Bathyergus*). From Honeycutt (1991). In Sherman, P.W., J.U.M. Jarvis, and R.D. Alexander; THE BIOLOGY OF THE NAKED MOLE-RAT. Copyright © 1991 by Princeton University Press. Reprinted by permission of Princeton University Press.

The Rodentia

The order Rodentia, comprised of diverse and abundant small herbivores with approximately 2,300 extant species, contains about half of all mammalian species living today. The current distribution of the 25 extant families is worldwide except for Antarctica and some oceanic islands. Modern rodents are a diverse group, exhibiting a variety of locomotor adaptations, including quadrupedal scampering and running (rats, mice, voles, guinea pigs, lemmings), gliding (squirrels, anomalurids), climbing (squirrels, dormice), swimming (muskrats, beavers), bipedal jumping (jerboas, pocket mice), and digging (mole rats, marmots, gophers). They exploit most herbivorous food resources, and a few are omnivores or insectivores. Fossil rodents were also successful and diverse, with 27 extinct families currently recognized.

With such diversity, diagnostic ordinal characters are relatively few, but the following skeletal and dental characters have distinguished rodents since their earliest appearance in the Late Paleocene. The dental count in each half of the head consists of one upper and lower incisor, no canines, zero to two upper premolars and zero to one lower premolar, and three upper and lower molars. The incisors have their enamel covering restricted to the front surface, which allows the uneven wear necessary to maintain a chisel-shaped working edge. Incisor enamel is arranged in two layers. Enamel prisms are primitively pauciserial (poorly organized) in orientation, although later forms exhibit stronger and more complex uniserial (stacked) and multiserial (wavy) arrangements. There is a long diastema between the incisors and premolars. In primitive taxa the cheek teeth are still recognizably tribosphenic (having three principal cusps arranged in a triangle), although they are already squared off owing to the loss of the paraconid in the lower molars and the acquisition of a hypocone in the

upper molars. The glenoid fossa (jaw socket) is elongate from front to back, reflecting the primary fore-aft movement of the lower jaw. As in lagomorphs, the auditory bulla is formed from outgrowths of the ectotympanic bone.

Paleocene fossils reveal that rodents originated in Asia. The Eurymylidae, a somewhat primitive anagalid family, is the closest sister group to rodents. The resemblance is so close that one genus, *Heomys*, has been called a rodent by some researchers and a eurymylid by others. *Heomys* has slightly more hypsodont teeth than the earliest true rodents, which excludes it from a more strictly defined Rodentia.

An important character complex in rodents relates to incisor function and the development of muscular and skeletal adaptations to augment fore-aft gnawing motions of the lower jaw. These modifications (Figures 3, 4) involve migration of the masseter muscles (chewing muscles that arise from the face and cheek arch and insert on the outside of the lower jaw) through or around the infraorbital foramen, a hole that primitively transmits blood vessels and sensory nerves. The primitive "protrogomorphous" state characterizes all of the earliest fossil rodents, but the only living protrogomorphous rodent is *Aplodontia*, the "mountain beaver" of western North America. The more derived (specialized) "sciuromorph," "hystricomorph," and "myomorph" conditions involve distinctive methods of shifting the masseter muscle complex farther forward on the face. Hystricomorphous rodents, such as porcupines, greatly enlarge the infraorbital foramen in order to accommodate a portion of the masseter muscle. Hystricomorphy probably preceded myomorphy, since the latter is the most complex arrangement.

The lower jaws of rodents also become modified as the masseter complex grows more complex and powerful. The "sciurogna-

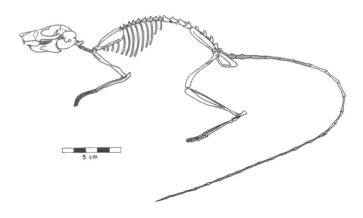

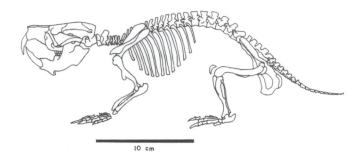

Figure 6. The Miocene burrowing beaver *Palaeocastor fossor*. From Korth (1994).

Figure 5. The Middle Eocene rodent *Protoptychus hatcheri*. From Korth (1994).

thous" condition, typified by squirrels, is the primitive condition for rodents; here the angular process of the mandible (a prong that sticks backward from the "heel" of the lower jaw) is in the same vertical plane as the incisors. In the derived hystricognathous condition, seen, for example, in guinea pigs, the angular process sticks out to the side.

While it is evident that similar derived facial and masseter morphologies have arisen independently several times in rodent history, these traits, together with those of tooth enamel, have proven useful in establishing evolutionary relationships.

The fossil record of rodents can be traced into the Late Paleocene with the appearance of the family Ischyromyidae in North America and the family Alagomyidae in Asia. The alagomyids were tiny rodents that persisted only into the Early Eocene. Of greater importance to rodent evolution were the North American ischyromyids and one or two families of ctenodactyloid rodents that appeared in Asia during the Early Eocene. The first major, long-term division of rodents can be traced to these groups. It led to a predominance of ischyromyids and their relatives in North America and a similar dominance of ctenodactyloids in Asia and Africa. Both ischyromyids and the earliest and most primitive ctenodactyloid family, the Cocomyidae, have protrogomorphous faces and pauciserial incisor enamel, demonstrating that both retain the primitive rodent condition for both characters.

A summary of rodent relationships based on these facts suggests the following: (1) the ctenodactyloids, dentally closest to the eurymylid *Heomys*, were an early branch of rodent development that independently became hystricomorphous in more derived lineages; the ctenodactyloids are probably allied to the south Asian chapattimyids and the African phiomorphs; (2) Eocene ischyromyids are closest to the Sciuravidae of Eocene North America and several other extinct families, as well as to the extant families Aplodontidae, Sciuridae, and Gliridae; all of these evolved during the Eocene; (3) early geomyoids, murioids, and dipodoids share a number of derived characters that suggest a shared common ancestry, but whether this is the Sciuravidae or some Asian lineage remains unclear; (4) hystricognathous rodents, all relatively closely related, are probably of Asian origin.

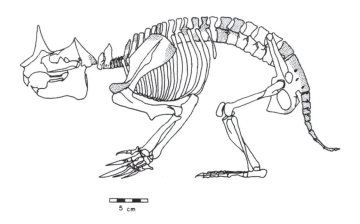

Figure 7. The Miocene mylagaulid rodent *Epigaulus hatcheri*. From Korth (1994).

Endemism (locally restricted geographic distribution) was apparent in rodents even in the Early Eocene. In Asia, cocomyids were joined by other ctenodactyloid families, including the fairly generalized chapattimyids of the Indian subcontinent. Ischyromyids were relatively rare in Asia but dominant in Early Eocene faunas in North America and Europe. European ischyromyids were, at first, mostly represented by microparamyines and later in the Eocene by a group that arose in situ, the theridomorphs. Glirids had evolved from the European microparamyines by the Middle Eocene; they and the theridomorphs evolved in near isolation until the "Grand Coupure" (the "Big Cut"), a major immigration event in the Early Oligocene that brought to Europe cricetids, eomyids, castorids, sciurids, and other rodents of Asian or North American origin.

The earliest Eocene of Africa lacks a good mammalian fossil record, but fossils from later in the Eocene include groups closely related to the phiomorphs. Phiomorphs gave rise to later groups of African rodents, including the Anomaluridae, a family still living in Africa. Affinities of the African rodents and the caviomorphs of South America, both of which have hystricomorphous faces and hystricognathous mandibles, have long been the subject of debate. This is due, in part, to the absence of rodent fossils in South

America prior to the Late Oligocene. When they at last appear in the South American fossil record, caviomorphs are already diversified, with most of the modern families being present. Nonetheless, both the fossil record and the anatomy of living rodents support the thesis that the African hystricomorphs and the South America caviomorphs are closely related.

By the Middle Eocene, several new rodent families with derived facial and mandibular morphologies had appeared. These include the now-extinct hystricomorphous-to-myomorphous family Eomyidae, which appeared more-or-less simultaneously in North America and Asia. This was a successful family that survived into the Pleistocene in Europe. Although many of the eomyids were probably terrestrial, at least one Late Oligocene European eomyid became a glider. Eomyids are closely related to the extant American families Heteromyidae and Geomyidae. The closely related Zapodidae and Cricetidae appeared in the Middle Eocene in Asia. In cricetids, there is a greater reduction of the cheek teeth (three molars in each jaw quadrant) and a greater enlargement of the first molar than in the zapodids. The Muridae, the highly successful rats and mice of modern faunas, were relative latecomers that do not appear until the Middle Miocene in southern Asia.

The rodent fossil record clearly shows that diverse lifestyles developed relatively early in the order's history. The North American Middle Eocene rodent *Protoptychus* (Figure 5), for example, has the enlarged auditory bulla, reduced forelimbs, and elongated hind limbs characteristic of saltatorial (hopping) locomotion. This type of locomotion appeared several times in later lineages, but *Protoptychus* was not closely related to such modern jumpers as the jerboas (family Dipodidae) and kangaroo rats (family Heteromyidae). Among the Castoridae (beavers), the Early Miocene *Palaeocastor* (Figure 6) was not only terrestrial but lived underground. Its remains have been found in huge fossil spiral burrows—a trace fossil named *Daemonelix*—that appear to have been dug by the beavers using their incisors and claws. Another remarkable North American terrestrial beaver was the Pleistocene *Castoroides,* the largest known rodent, which reached a length of about 2.5 meters. Other highly evolved digging rodents are the North American Miocene mylagaulids *Ceratogaulus* and *Epigaulus* (Figure 7). These are unusual for rodents in having bony "horns" on the nasal bones. Mylagaulid skeletons have a number of digging adaptations, and it is presumed that the horns were used as part of this behavior.

Mary R. Dawson

See also Enamel Microstructure

Works Cited

Dawson, M.R. 1967. Lagomorph history and the stratigraphic record. *In* K. Teichert and E.L. Yochelson (eds.), *Essays in Paleontology and Stratigraphy; R.C. Moore Commemorative Volume.* Department of Geology, University of Kansas, Special Publication 2.

———. 1969. Osteology of *Prolagus sardus,* a Quaternary ochotonid (Mammalia, Lagomorpha). *Palaeovertebrata* 2 (4): 157–90.

Honeycutt, R. 1991. Systematics and evolution of the Bathyergidae. *In* P.W. Sherman, J.U.M. Jarvis, and R.D. Alexander (eds.), *The Biology of the Naked Mole-Rat.* Princeton: Princeton University Press.

Korth, W.W. 1994. The Tertiary record of rodents in North America. *Topics in Geobiology* 12:1–319.

Li, C.-K., and S.-Y. Ting. 1985. Possible phylogenetic relationships of Asiatic eurymylids and rodents, with comments on mimotonids. *In* W.P. Luckett and J.-L. Hartenberger (eds.), *Evolutionary Relationships among Rodents.* New York: Plenum.

Li, C.-K., R.W. Wilson, M.R. Dawson, and L. Krishtalka. 1987. The origin of rodents and lagomorphs. *In* H.H. Genoways (ed.), *Current Mammalogy,* vol. 1. New York: Plenum.

Martin, T. 1992. *Schmelzmikrostruktur in den Inzisiven alt- und neuweltlicher hystricognather Nagetiere.* Palaeovertebrata, Memoire extraordinaire, 2. Montpellier: École Pratique Hautes Études, Université de Montpellier.

Tullberg, T. 1899. *Über das System der Nagethiere: Eine phylogenetische Studie.* Nova Acta Reg. Soc. Scient. Upsaliensis 3 (18). Upsala: Die Akademische Buchdruckerei.

Wood, A.E. 1940. The mammalian fauna of the White River Oligocene. Part 3, Lagomorpha. *Transactions of the American Philosophical Society* 28 (3):271–362.

Further Reading

Korth, W.W. 1994. The Tertiary record of rodents in North America. *Topics in Geobiology.* New York: Plenum.

Luckett, W.P., and J.-L. Hartenberger (eds.). 1985. *Evolutionary Relationships among Rodents: A Multidisciplinary Analysis.* Series A, Life Sciences. NATO ASI Series, vol. 92. New York: Plenum.

McKenna, M.C., and S.K. Bell. 1997. *Classification of Mammals above the Species Level.* New York: Columbia University Press.

Wood, A.E. 1962. *The Early Tertiary Rodents of the Family Paramyidae.* Transactions of the American Philosophical Society 52. Philadelphia: American Philosophical Society.

GLOBAL ENVIRONMENT

Global change is a topic of much debate in recent years, but it is important to realize that Earth's environments have been in a constant state of flux since the formation of the planet, more than four billion years ago. Environmental change has been a main driving force in shaping life on this planet. There have been many causes of environmental change through the uncounted millennia of Earth history; most of the agents of change continue unabated to the present time and most likely will persist long into the future. At the root of nearly all significant environmental change is Earth's relationship to the sun. Other than geothermal energy that escapes from the fiery depths beneath the surface of the earth, the sun is the only source of energy for our planet. This is an important concept to keep in mind when one is considering global change. The sun has affected terrestrial environments on all time scales, from today's weather to the uncharted depths of geologic time. Let us consider the sun's role in global change over these varying time scales, moving from longest to shortest lengths of time.

When the Earth was a newly formed planet, its atmosphere was quite unlike that which blankets the planet today. Before the evolution of plant life, there was far less oxygen in the atmosphere. Plants take in carbon dioxide and give off oxygen in photosynthesis. The relatively thin atmosphere of the primordial Earth allowed far more of the sun's ultraviolet radiation to reach the surface of the planet. This radiation is generally harmful to plant and animal life because it damages cells. The ocean waters that covered much of the planet in Precambrian times were the cradle of life, and one of the reasons for this is that water screens out ultraviolet radiation within a few feet of the surface, so one-celled organisms living in Earth's primordial seas were protected from this dangerous radiation. As the seas began to teem with plant and animal life, the exchange of gases between these organisms and the atmosphere (by way of gases dissolved in sea water) began to change the composition of the atmosphere, which in turn led to an increased atmospheric capacity to screen out ultraviolet radiation. Geologists believe that oxygen and carbon dioxide in Earth's atmosphere reached levels roughly equivalent to those of modern times by about 700 million years ago (Garrels et al. 1981). Another critical component of the atmosphere (past and present) is ozone. Ozone is a molecule composed of three atoms of oxygen that forms in the upper atmosphere. As levels of plant-derived oxygen increased in ancient Earth's atmosphere, the ozone layer in the upper atmosphere began to form. This layer effectively screens out much of the ultraviolet radiation coming from the sun. The energy required to form ozone molecules from free oxygen atoms comes from ultraviolet radiation.

The ozone layer in the atmosphere entered in the news as the twentieth century drew to a close because man-made chemicals, such as fluorocarbons, were being produced in such large quantities (largely as lubricants and refrigerants) that they threatened the ozone layer. Fluorocarbons broke down ozone, weakening the ultraviolet "shield" at the top of our atmosphere.

The development of Earth's atmosphere took place on a billion-year time scale. Another element of Earth's history that plays an important part in environmental change is plate tectonics, more commonly called "continental drift," although the latter term is not altogether accurate. Neither the land masses nor the sea floors are fixed, immovable objects. Rather, the Earth's crust is divided into plates that float over a fluid mantle. Movements of heat from greater to shallower depths in the mantle create currents, and these currents are thought to be the driving force in the movement of plates on the crust (Birkeland and Larson 1978). Geologists estimate that the plates move at a rate of 2 to 8 centimeters per year (Bambach et al. 1981). The current configuration of continents and seas is only the latest in an ever-shifting procession of movements. Plate tectonics is an important element of environmental change, because the configuration of continents and seas plays a key role in the solar energy budget of the planet. In other words, even if the total amount of

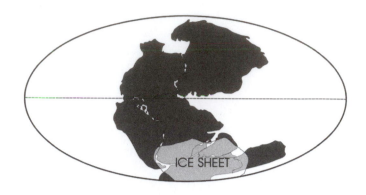

Figure 1. The configuration of continents during Late Carboniferous and Early Permian times, showing the extent of glaciers thought to have developed near the south pole. After Beaty (1981).

insolation (*in*coming *sol*ar radi*ation*) remains constant through time, the ways in which that energy is distributed on the planet can change greatly, depending on how the oceans and continents are aligned. When there are large land masses near the equator, large amounts of solar energy are absorbed by the land, and the creatures living there experience tropical climates. If the land masses break up and move towards the poles, the creatures of the creeping continents will experience colder climates.

In Late Cambrian times (550 to 540 million years ago), there were six major continents, all lying within the tropical and temperate latitudes (between about 40° N and 40° S). By Middle Silurian times (435 to 430 million years ago), some of the land-mass plates (including South America, Africa, Australia, and Antarctica) had come together to form a supercontinent that geologists call Gondwanaland. This continent came together in the high southern latitudes, including the south pole. Toward the end of the Paleozoic era, most of the Earth's land masses were grouped together into another supercontinent called Pangaea. During Late Carboniferous and Early Permian times (about 300 to 280 million years ago), the southern region of Pangaea was located near the south pole (Beaty 1981). The polar regions receive less insolation than the lower latitude regions of the Earth, regardless of the position of continental land masses. There is geologic evidence from the parts of the modern continents that came together in southern Pangaea that these regions were glaciated during the Late Carboniferous and Early Permian interval (Figure 1) .

Plate tectonics has affected Earth's climate in other ways, as well. For instance, the collision of plates has been one of the major factors in mountain building. Large highland regions, such as the Himalayas and the Tibetan Plateau, capture significant amounts of snow from the atmosphere, creating mountain glaciers and ice sheets. As uplift occurs, layers of bedrock that formed in lakes and shallow seas were pushed up and weathered. This erosion of limestone and allied sedimentary rocks released enormous quantities of carbonates, thereby building up the concentration of carbon dioxide in the atmosphere. Also, the move-

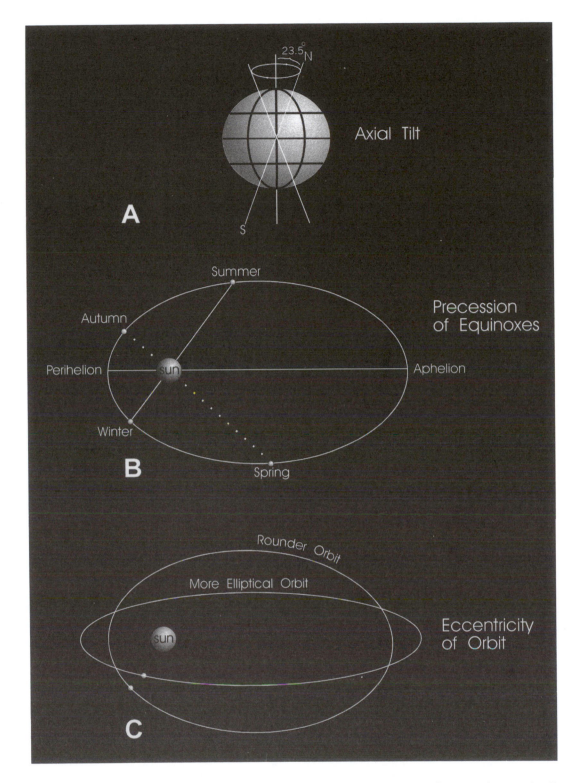

Figure 2. Illustration of the three major components of Earth's orbit about the sun that contribute to changes in climate. After Elias (1997).

ment of continents brought about the opening up of new circulation patterns for ocean currents, transporting cold waters to middle latitudes and warm waters to high latitudes. Such factors as these serve to modulate climate change through long periods of time, even if they are not the primary forcing mechanisms of climate change.

The most recent interval of repeated glaciations, or ice ages, is the Quaternary epoch, the interval spanning the last 2 million years. During the Quaternary the continents have approached their modern configuration, including the positioning of Antarctica over the high southern latitudes and the positioning of major portions of North America and Eurasia over the high northern latitudes. This occurrence of major land masses in high latitudes is thought to be a major factor in the development of the numerous glaciations that occurred in the Pleistocene. The reason for this is relatively straightforward. The high latitude regions receive almost no insolation (solar radiation) during the winter months and receive less insolation than the low latitude regions throughout the year. When land masses exist at high latitudes, they develop ice sheets as the snows of successive years fail to melt completely in the short, cool, high-latitude summers. Large ice sheets do not develop readily over ocean waters, because water circulation between latitudes and the thermal buffering effect of large bodies of water keep ice from forming. Even when sea ice cover can form, ice shelves cannot form except in confined embayments. So glaciations only occur when continents occupy the high latitudes. On the other hand, this is not the only cause of glaciation, and the topic is far from being completely understood (Andersen and Borns 1994).

Another source of climatic variation (and another probable cause of glaciations) concerns Earth's orbit around the sun. Changes in orbital characteristics occur on a time scale of thousands of years. The climatic variations that take place on this time scale include three major components of the Earth's orbit about the sun, as originally described by Milankovitch in 1938 (Berger 1978). These variables do not affect the total amount of insolation reaching the planet during the year, only the way in which insolation is distributed on the planet. The first of these variables concerns the tilt of the Earth's axis in relation to the sun. The Earth's spin on its axis is wobbly, much like a spinning top that starts to wobble after it slows down. This wobble amounts to a variation of up to 23.5 degrees to either side of the axis (Figure 2A). The changing tilt in the Earth's rotation affects the amount of sunlight striking the different parts of the globe. The greater the tilt, the stronger the difference in seasons (i.e., more tilt equals sharper differences between summer and winter temperatures). The range of motion in the tilt (from left-of-center to right-of-center and back again) takes place over a period of 41,000 years.

As a result of a wobble in the Earth's spin, the position of the Earth on its elliptical orbit changes, relative to the time of year. For instance, autumn and winter occur in the northern hemisphere when the Earth is relatively close to the sun, whereas summer and spring occur when the Earth is relatively far from the sun (Figure 2B). This phenomenon is called the precession of equinoxes. The cycle of equinox precession takes 23,000 years to complete. Summer temperatures are probably more important than winter temperatures in the growth of continental ice sheets. Throughout the Pleistocene, high-latitude winters have been cold enough to allow snow to accumulate. When summers are cold, the snows of previous winters do not melt completely. When this process continues for centuries, ice sheets begin to form.

Finally, the shape of Earth's orbit also changes. At one extreme, the orbit is more circular, and each season receives about the same amount of insolation. At the other extreme, the orbital ellipse is stretched, exaggerating the differences between seasons (Figure 2C). The eccentricity of Earth's orbit proceeds through a cycle lasting 100,000 years.

Major glacial events in the Quaternary have coincided when the phases of axial tilt, precession of equinoxes, and eccentricity of orbit align to give the northern hemisphere the least amount of summer insolation. Conversely, major interglacial (warm) periods have occurred when the three factors line up to give the northern hemisphere the greatest amount of summer insolation. The last major convergence of factors giving us maximum summer warmth occurred between 11,000 and 9,000 years ago, at the transition between the last glaciation and the current interglacial, the Holocene. There are other factors involved in climate change, such as volcanic eruptions and large-scale dust storms. For the most part, these phenomena trigger short-term climate change (on a year to decade scale); however, they may interact with orbital factors to draw global climate over the threshold from interglacial to glacial climate.

SCOTT A. ELIAS

See also Atmospheric Environment; Faunal and Floral Provinces; Ocean Environment; Paleoclimatology; Sedimentology; Stable Isotope Analysis; Terrestrial Environment

Works Cited

Andersen, B.G., and H.W. Borns Jr. 1994. *The Ice Age World.* Oslo, Oxford, and New York: Scandinavian University Press and Oxford University Press.

Bambach, R.K., C.R. Scotese, and A.M. Ziegler. 1981. Before Pangaea: The geographies of the Paleozoic world. *In* B.J. Skinner (ed.), *Climates Past and Present.* Los Altos, California: Kaufmann.

Beaty, C.B. 1981. The causes of glaciation. *In* B.J. Skinner (ed.), *Climates Past and Present.* Los Altos, California: Kaufmann.

Berger, A.L. 1978. Long-term variations in caloric insolation resulting from the earth's orbital elements. *Quaternary Research* 9:139–67.

Birkeland, P.W., and E.E. Larson. 1978. *Putnam's Geology.* 3rd ed. New York: Oxford University Press; 1st ed., 1964; 5th ed., 1989.

Elias, S.A. 1997. *Ice-Age History of Southwestern National Parks.* Washington, D.C.: Smithsonian Institution Press.

Garrels, R.M., A. Lerman, and F.T. Mackenzie. 1981. Controls of atmospheric O_2 and CO_2: Past, present, and future. *In* B.J. Skinner (ed.), *Climates Past and Present.* Los Altos, California: Kaufmann.

Further Reading

Birks, H.J.B., and H.H. Birks. 1980. *Quaternary Paleoecology.* London: Arnold; Baltimore, Maryland: University Park.

Bradley, R.S. 1985. *Quaternary Paleoclimatology.* Boston: Allen and Unwin; London: Chapman and Hall.

Elias, S.A. 1997. *Ice-Age History of Southwestern National Parks.* Washington, D.C.: Smithsonian Institution Press.

Goudie, A. 1977. *Environmental Change.* Oxford and New York: Clarendon; 3rd ed., Oxford: Clarendon and New York: Oxford University Press, 1992.

Williams, M.A.J., D.L. Dunkerley, P. De Deckker, A.P. Kershaw, and T. Stokes. 1993. *Quaternary Environments.* London and New York: Arnold.

GNATHOSTOMES

Gnathostomes, or jawed vertebrates, include the first fishes with jaws and teeth (chondrichthyans, acanthodians, placoderms, and osteichthyans) and their evolutionary descendants, the tetrapods (amphibians, reptiles, birds, mammals) (Figure 1). The gills of jawless fishes (agnathans) were supported by bony structures called gill arches. In jawed fishes, the jaws may have first originated by modification of the front gill arch support bones. If so, then the first primitive set of jaws and teeth would have been formed from dermal scales that evolved to have a toothlike structure and shape, then invaded the mouth and pharynx. Supporting this view is the fact that primitive jawless fishes have many more pairs of gill arches than the jawed fishes (up to 20 or more paired gill pouches) and that some agnathans have toothlike scales lining the mouth cavity (e.g., thelodonts). Furthermore, the dermal scales of most jawless fishes are constructed of dentinous tissues that lie under an enamel-like crown, with a bony base. Some jawless fishes, like thelodonts, also have a pulp cavity in the base of the scales. This structure is much like "teeth" in overall form and minute structure.

Recent work by P. Janvier and P.L. Forey (1984) shows that the armored, jawless osteostracan fishes are the closest group to the gnathostomes. Both have perichondral bone (a kind of thin, layered bone that enveloped cartilage) enveloping the braincase, a large median head vein, and true bone with cell sites. In osteostracan fishes, the inside surface of the head shields indicates that the first gill arches were positioned well forward of the eyes and directly above the mouth. Osteostracans presumably had cartilaginous gill arch supports, a theory supported by impressions of gull structures on the head shield's visceral surface. Therefore, the evolution of the front gill arch elements to simple jaws did not necessarily involve large-scale structural reorganization. The hole for the mandibular and maxillary nerves, which serve the jaws, is visible on the first gill ridge in *Scolenaspis* and several other osteostracans (Janvier 1985).

The appearance of jaws in the fossil record should naturally herald the abundant appearance of teeth at the same time. Sharks, for example, have hundreds of teeth in their mouths, and because they grow and shed them continuously through life, the average shark may shed something like 20,000 teeth into the sediments. Shark skin contains thousands of tiny scales, also shed into the sediment after death. Fossilized shark scales are much older than fossilized shark teeth. The oldest sharklike scales are from the Late Ordovician–Lowest Silurian of Mongolia (Karatajute-Talimma 1995), yet the oldest shark's teeth are of lowest Devonian age, some 30 million years later. As the numbers of teeth and scales are both high per individual shark, the absence of teeth in Silurian strata would seem to be a real phenomenon. This suggests that the first sharks had scales that were morphologically similar to modern sharks' scales, but these first sharks probably lacked teeth. The appearance of the first teeth probably correlates with the evolution of jaws in sharks, although scholars are not certain.

Sharks first arose in the Early and Middle Devonian in Gondwana, an ancient continent made up of the landmasses of today's South America, Africa, Antarctica, Australia, and India. The fossilized teeth have been found in a variety of deposits (e.g., Spain, Africa, Australia, Antarctica, South America). The Middle Devonian Aztec Siltstone of Antarctica has an unusually high diversity of sharks in both species numbers and size of teeth, suggesting that Gondwana may well have been the place where toothed sharks first originated and underwent their first major radiation (diversification). By the Lower Carboniferous, sharks were widespread. Some very large forms evolved, such as *Edestus giganteus* from North America, which possessed serrated teeth up to seven to eight centimeters high on a continuous whorl. Such megapredators would have reached six meters or more in length.

The oldest fossil animals with proper jaws and teeth are actually the acanthodian fishes of Early Silurian age. When limestones from this deposit are dissolved, isolated teeth, scales, and fin spines of this group are found in the microscopic residue. In past literature, acanthodians have been likened to "spiny sharks," although their affinities appear to lie close to the higher jawed fishes, such as osteichthyans (true bony fishes), because of their scale structure and the braincase's gross morphology (Denison 1979). The oldest acanthodians include forms with distinct jawbones that have strong teeth ankylosed (fused) onto these bones. This group, the ischnacanthids, were moderately large predators in the early Devonian seas, some reaching sizes of two to three meters, such as *Xylacanthus grandis* from Spitsbergen.

The most successful of all the early jawed fishes were undoubtedly the placoderms. This group appeared in the Early Silurian but flourished during the Devonian, becoming extinct at the end of that period. They take their name from the Greek meaning "plated skin" because the head and trunk of these fishes are enveloped by a mosaic of bony armor plates. The placoderm's tail and overall general anatomy was very sharklike. Some scholars suggest that placoderms were closely allied to bony fishes, but many believe that they are allied to the chondrichthyans. The teeth developed on placoderm jaws are not real teeth, with roots set into a discrete jawbone, like those of the osteichthyan fishes; placoderm "teeth" are well-developed, pointed cusps that protrude from the jawbone itself. There are a multitude of dentition types, revolving around rows of pointed cusps on jawbones or clusters of small denticles or pointed cusps on sheets of bone.

The bony fishes (osteichthyans) first appeared by the Late Silurian, represented by isolated scales and teeth of small ray-finned fishes (lophosteiforms, palaeoniscoids). The Osteichthyes comprise three principal groups: the ray-fins (Actinopterygii), which today form more than 99 percent of all living fishes—over 23,000 species (e.g., trout, salmon); the lungfishes (Dipnoi), with a few living examples in Gondwana countries (Australia, South America, and South Africa); and the Crossopterygii, with one surviving species, the coelacanth *Latimeria chalumnae*. (The latter

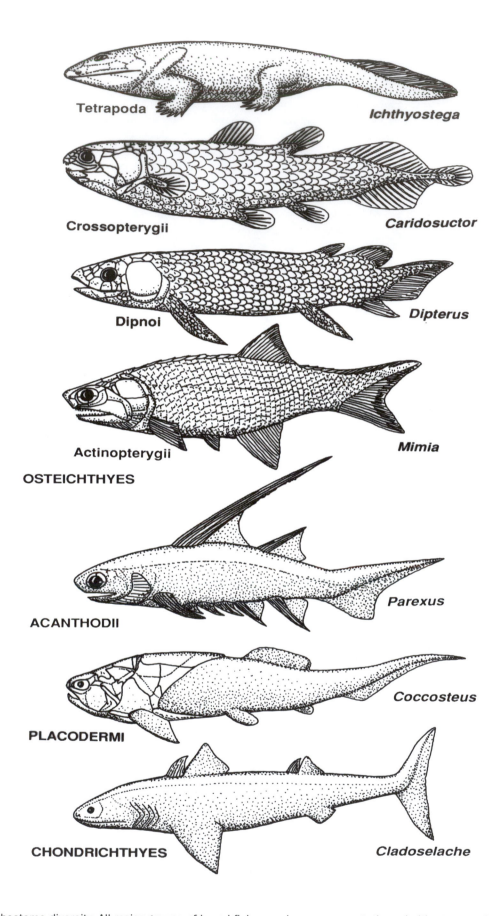

Figure 1. Gnathostome diversity. All major groups of jawed fishes and one representative primitive tetrapod group are shown.

two groups have muscular, fleshy lobed fins and are generally grouped together as the Sarcopterygii.) In the Devonian the ratios were such that the most diverse group of bony fishes were the lungfishes (approximately 45 Devonian genera) and crossopterygians (approximately 50 or more genera), with ray-fins being only a minor component for the fish faunas (under 10 genera). The ability to gulp air and thus cross environmental boundaries only evolved within lungfish in the Middle Devonian and became prominent in the Late Devonian. This adaptation gave lungfish an edge over other groups. Later forms had a further enhanced survival ability, after they gained the ability to become inactive during certain periods of the year (gestivate). Some of the advanced crossopterygians appear to have developed the ability to breathe air independently (also by Middle Devonian times) and possibly gave rise to the first amphibians by the early Late Devonian. One group, the panderichthyid fishes, are believed to be the closest relatives of the first amphibians (Long 1995).

JOHN A. LONG

See also Acanthodians; Chondrichthyans; Feeding Adaptations: Vertebrates; Osteichthyans; Pharyngeal Arches and Derivatives; Placoderms; Respiration; Skull

Works Cited

Denison, R.H. 1979. Acanthodii. *In* H.P. Schultze (ed.), *Handbook of Paleoichthyology*. Vol. 5, New York: Gustav Fisher.

Forey, P.L., and P. Janvier. 1993. Agnathans and the origin of jawed vertebrates. *Nature* 361:129–34.

———. 1994. Evolution of the early vertebrates. *American Scientist* 82:554–65.

Janvier, P. 1985. *Les Céphalaspides du Spitsberg: Anatomie, phylogénie et systématique des Ostéostrachés siluro-dévoniens; révision des Ostéostracés de la Formation de Wood Bay (Dévonien inférieur du Spitsberg)*. Paris: Éditions du Centre National de la Recherche Scientifique.

Karatajute-Talimma, V. 1995. The Mongolepidida: Scale structure and systematic position. *Géobios (mémoire spécial)* 19:35–37.

Long, J.A. 1995. *The Rise of Fishes: 500 Million Years of Evolution*. Baltimore, Maryland: Johns Hopkins University Press.

GNETOPHYTES

Gnetophytes make up a small group of complex seed plants that are considered to be the closest living relatives of flowering plants (angiosperms). There are approximately 90 species of living gnetophytes which belong to three distinctive genera, *Gnetum*, *Ephedra*, and *Welwitschia*. *Gnetum* consists of shrubs, vines, and small trees that have leaves similar to those of many flowering plants and that grow in low-latitude tropics. Species of *Ephedra* are dryland shrubs with narrow leaves and are distributed from equatorial regions into the temperate zone of the Northern Hemisphere. *Welwitschia* has a single species with highly unusual structure and is restricted to extreme deserts on the west coast of Africa.

Modern phylogenetic (evolutionary history) analyses reveal that gnetophytes, angiosperms, cycadeoids (extinct seed plants often referred to the order Bennettitales), and the Jurassic plant *Pentoxylon* are included in a natural group called "anthophytes." These studies show that anthophytes are related more closely to each other than they are to other living groups of seed plants such as conifers (cone-bearing plants), cycads (palmlike tropical trees), and *Ginkgo biloba* (Nixon, et al. 1994; Doyle 1996). *Pentoxylon* is found in Jurassic deposits of India. These plants had branching stems with a rough surface of leaf bases (scale-like structures that remain after leaves drop), and five separate woody cylinders (for transporting materials) surrounding a prominent pith. Leaves were strap-shaped with a prominent midrib and lateral veins (Figure 1A). *Pentoxylon* is unique among anthophytes because it produces either pollen or seeds on modified leaves that occur at the tips of branches (Figures 1B, 1C). At least some species of all other anthophyte groups produce seeds and pollen in the same flower or flowerlike fertile structure (Rothwell and Serbet 1994).

Gnetophyte plants display a unique combination of derived (specialized) characters that have prompted many botanists to consider them to be a natural group. Some of the most distinctive of these characters include the following: oppositely arranged leaves with a network of veins; complex vascular tissues with vessels in the wood and sieve tubes in the phloem (tissue that transports organic compounds); compound cones that produce either pollen or seeds; and specialized features of reproductive biology. Gnetophytes resemble many other gymnosperms—both produce separate cones for female seeds and male pollen—but gnetophyte cones are intriguingly similar to angiosperm flowers because these cones have the potential to produce both seed and pollen. In addition, both the seed- and pollen-producing structures of gnetophytes are surrounded by sterile organs similar to the petals and sepals (leaflife structures below petals in most flowers) of angiosperm flowers.

Fossil evidence shows that the group was once far more diverse and widespread than today's living species (Crane and Lidgard 1989). Distinctive fossil pollen such as that produced by living gnetophytes occurs in sediments that range from Triassic to the Recent. Such pollen becomes common in Triassic sediments of the Northern Hemisphere, diminishes in diversity during the Jurassic, then becomes abundant in low latitudes of both the Northern and Southern Hemispheres during the Cretaceous. Following the highest point in the Mid-Cretaceous, the diversity of gnetalean pollen diminishes rapidly to relatively low levels.

Megafossil evidence (fossilized large structures, such as parts of or complete plants) for gnetophytes is far less common than would be expected from the extensive pollen record for the group. This may be due to the fact that gnetophytes grew in environments where fossilization rarely occurred or extinct gnetophytes

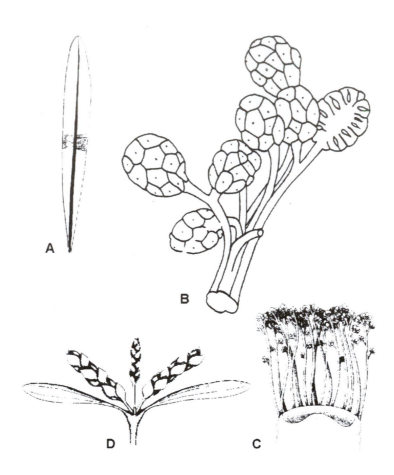

Figure 1. *A*, leaf of the Pentoxylon; *B*, ovulate sporophylls (fertile leaves) of Pentoxylon, with seeds aggregated into conelike groups; *C*, pollen-producing sporophylls of Pentoxylon at the apex of a branch; *D*, fertile shoot of Drewria, showing leaf pair subtending three ovulate cones. From: *A, C*, modified from Crane (1985), courtesy of Peter R. Crane; *B*, modified from Rothwell and Serbet (1994), courtesy of the American Society of Plant Taxonomists and Gar W. Rothwell; *D*, Crane and Upchurch (1987), *American Journal of Botany* 74:1722–1736.

generally may have had herbaceous (nonwoody) shoots that are fossilized far less often than similar organs of woody plants. Because gnetophyte leaves are remarkably similar to those of flowering plants or conifers (Figure 1D), they commonly may be misidentified when discovered as isolated fossilized specimens.

A probable Late Triassic gnetophyte from Arizona includes the seed cone *Masculostrobus clathratus* and associated dispersed organs from northeastern Arizona (Ash 1972) that produce small, oppositely arranged leaves and gnetophyte pollen. The ovulate fertile structure *Piroconites* and associated vegetative (structures not involved in reproduction, such as leaves, stems) and pollen-producing organs from Early Jurassic sediments of Germany are considered convincing evidence of primitive gnetaleans by many scholars (van Konijnenburg-Van Cittert 1992).

The best evidence for an extinct gnetalean plant, *Drewria potomancensis* (Crane and Upchurch 1987) occurs in Lower Cretaceous deposits of Virginia. *Drewria* is an herb or small shrub that bears oppositely arranged leaves with distinctive vein pattern in the leaves similar to that in *Welwitschia*. Cones occur at the tips of branches, immediately above leaves (Figure 1D). Seeds are borne

at the tip of a side branch the in lax (loose) cones and are enclosed by one or two pairs of scale-like leaves just below the seeds. The very end of the seed is elongated into a narrow tip that resembles a micropyle (opening at tip of seed through which pollen enters) of *Welwitschia* seeds. Associated pollen is similar to gnetophyte grains found elsewhere in Cretaceous sediments.

From available fossil evidence, gnetophytes are thought to have originated in the Early Triassic, diversified during the Lower Cretaceous, then rapidly diminished in both diversity and geographical range during the Upper Cretaceous. Whether the decline was due to a failure to compete successfully with the rapidly diverging Cretaceous plants or to a combination of factors has not been determined.

Gar W. Rothwell

Works Cited

Ash, S.R. 1972. Late Triassic plants from the Chinle Formation in northeastern Arizona. *Palaeontology* 15:598–618.

Crane, P.R. 1985. Phylogenetic analysis of seed plants and the origin of angiosperms. *Annals of the Missouri Botanical Garden* 72:716–93.

Crane, P.R., and S. Lidgard. 1989. Paleolatudinal gradients and temporal trends in Cretaceous floristic diversity. Science 246:675–78.

Crane, P.R., and G.R. Upchurch Jr. 1987. *Drewria potomacensis* gen. Et sp. Nov., an Early Cretaceous member of Gnetales from the Potomic Group of Virginia. *American Journal of Botany* 74:1722–36.

Doyle, J.E. 1996. Seed plant phylogeny and evolution of the Gnetales. *International Journal of Plant Sciences* 157:S3–S39.

Nixon, K.C., W.L. Crepet, D. Stevenson, and E.M. Friis. 1994. A reevaluation of seed phylogeny. *Annals of the Missouri Botanical Garden* 81:484–533.

Rothwell, G.W., and R. Serbert. 1994. Lignophyte phylogeny and the evolution of spermatophytes: A numerical cladistic analysis. *Systematic Botany* 19:443–82.

Van Konijnenburg-Van Cittert, J.H.A. 1992. An enigmatic Liassic microsporophyll, yielding *Ephedripites* pollen. *Review of Palaeobotany and Palynology* 71:239–54.

Further Reading

Crane, P.R. 1985. Phylogenetic analysis of seed plants and the origin of angiosperms. *Annals of the Missouri Botanical Garden* 72:716–93.

Friedman, W.E. (ed.). 1996. Biology and evolution of the Gnetales. *International Journal of Plant Sciences* 157:S1–S125.

Gifford, E.M., and A.S. Foster. 1959. *Comparative Morphology of Vascular Plants.* San Francisco: Freeman; 3rd ed., *Morphology and Evolution of Vascular Plants.* New York: Freeman, 1989.

Stewart, W.N., and G.W. Rothwell. 1983. *Paleobotany and the Evolution of Plants.* Cambridge and New York: Cambridge University Press; 2nd ed., 1993.

GRANGER, WALTER WILLIS

American, 1872–1941

Walter Granger demonstrated a keen interest in nature at an early age. As a boy, he spent many hours climbing the rocky hills and wandering through the forests and learning firsthand something of the abundant wildlife of the final decades of the nineteenth century. He was especially interested in birds, an interest that stayed with him throughout his life.

Consequently, when a rather menial position at the American Museum of Natural History became available, Granger boarded the next train from Rutland to New York to embark upon his long career at the museum. His beginnings at the museum were somewhat less than auspicious—although he spent most of his time working in the taxidermy department, he also was assigned the task of cleaning and refilling outdoor oil lamps that lined a sidewalk from the museum entrance to the 81st Street elevated station. As Granger later wrote, it was "a nasty job during a bitterly cold winter, and at the salary of $20 a month."

Soon Granger was well-established in the taxidermy shop—so much so that in 1894 he was asked to join an expedition under the leadership of Jacob Wortman, who in previous years had been an assistant to Edward Drinker Cope. Granger's task was to collect modern mammals, an activity ancillary to the expedition's purpose, which was to collect fossil mammals.

After that trip, Granger decided that his real interest lay within paleontology, so he transferred to the Department of Vertebrate Paleontology, where he came under the influence of its renowned chairman, vertebrate paleontologist Henry Fairfield Osborn. Thus, in 1897 he spent the summer field season at Osborn's famous Bone Cabin site in Wyoming, where the American Museum field party excavated Late Jurassic dinosaurs and early mammals from the Morrison Formation.

From that year to the end of his life in 1941, Granger devoted his energies primarily to the collecting of fossil mammals, especially from the Lower Cenozoic rock strata in the western United States. In 1907, under Osborn's leadership, he also conducted a very successful collecting trip in the Fayum beds of Egypt. He did much of his work in collaboration with William Diller Matthew, curator of Vertebrate Paleontology, and with Albert (Bill) Thomson, preparator, at the American Museum. Granger also joined Matthew in research on the fossils they had collected, producing many important scientific contributions that still stand as classics in their field.

Granger was a superb field paleontologist. Not only did he have a gift for finding fossils, he also kept unusually detailed field notes, neatly recorded, that added immeasurably to the value of the fossils he had excavated. It was only logical, therefore, that he should be designated as second in command to Roy Andrews on a series of paleontological expeditions in Mongolia during the 1920s. These expeditions, renowned in the annals of paleontology, were Granger's last serious efforts in the field. He retained a continuing interest in field paleontology and in his later years joined several American Museum field parties. On one of these trips, he died unexpectedly in his sleep on 6 September 1941.

In 1932, Granger was awarded an honorary doctorate by Middlebury College, Vermont, a source of much satisfaction to him during the last decade of his life.

Walter Granger stands tall in the modern history of vertebrate paleontology, not only because of his legendary fieldwork and his influence upon other paleontologists. He was a sincerely friendly person; he literally had no enemies. He was always ready with wise counsel for those who went to him for advice.

EDWIN H. COLBERT

Biography

Born in Middletown Springs, Vermont, 7 November 1872. Attended high school for two years, Rutland, Vermont; honorary Ph.D., Middlebury College, Vermont, 1932. Worked as taxidermist, expedition member, and expedition leader, 1890–1941; began his association with New York's American Museum of

Natural History, 1890; later promoted at the museum to assistant curator (1909), associate curator (1911), and curator of fossil mammals (1927). Member of such professional and scholarly associations as the Explorer's Club (president, 1935–37), Geological Society, Paleontological Society, and Society for Vertebrate Paleontology. Conducted many fossil collecting trips in North America and abroad; published important research papers devoted particularly to early Cenozoic mammals, frequently in collaboration with William Diller Matthew; second in command to Roy Chapman Andrews during the American Museum expeditions to Mongolia. Died in Lusk, Wyoming, 6 September, 1941.

Major Publications

1910. Tertiary faunal horizons in the Wind River Basin, Wyoming, with descriptions of new Eocene mammals. *Bulletin of the American Museum of Natural History* 28:235–51.

1915. A revision of the Lower Eocene Wasatch and Wind River faunas. Part 3, Order Condylarthra, families Phenacodontidae and Meniscotheriidae. *Bulletin of the American Museum of Natural History* 34:329–62.

1917. With W.D. Matthew. The skeleton of Diatryma, a gigantic bird from the lower Eocene of Wyoming. *Bulletin of the American Museum of Natural History* 37:307–26.

1923. With W.K. Gregory. *Protoceratops andrewsi*, a pre-ceratopsian dinosaur from Mongolia. *American Museum Novitates* 72:1–9.

1929. With W.D. Matthew and G.G. Simpson. Additions to the fauna of the Gashato formation of Mongolia. *American Museum Novitates* 376:1–12.

1932. Palaeontological exploration in eastern Szechwan: Winter Seasons of 1921–22, 1922–23, and 1925–26. *In* Roy Chapman Andrews (ed.), *The New Conquest of Asia.* Natural History of Central Asia, 1. New York: American Museum of Natural History.

1936. With W.K. Gregory. Further notes on the gigantic extinct rhinoceros, *Baluchitherium,* from the Oligocene of Mongolia. *Bulletin of the American Museum of Natural History* 72:1–73.

Further Reading

Simpson, G.G. 1942. Memorial to Walter Granger (1872–1941). *Proceedings Volume of the Geological Society of America.* Annual Report for 1941. 1941:159–72.

GREGORY, WILLIAM KING

American, 1876–1970

William King Gregory, destined to become an internationally recognized authority on all of the vertebrate animals, was one of those rare New Yorkers, born and bred in Manhattan, where he spent almost all the years of a very long life. His life began in Greenwich Village, the son of a printer, George Gregory, and his wife, Jane King Gregory. During Gregory's early years the family lived upstairs in the building that housed the print shop.

For a few years Gregory attended public schools, then enrolled in Trinity School to prepare himself for Columbia University. He enrolled in the School of Mines but after a year he transferred to Columbia College, where the education was more comprehensive than at Mines.

Early in his collegiate career Gregory became a scientific assistant to Henry Fairfield Osborn, an unofficial but important post that Gregory occupied into his middle years. By that time, he was established as an authority in his several fields of research. As such, he frequently opposed Osborn's scientific methods and conclusions, yet he was able to stand up to his famous mentor without arousing serious antagonisms on Osborn's part. This was particularly evident during Osborn's last years, when the two men disagreed most fundamentally on many aspects of human evolution yet remained fast friends.

Gregory's several fields of research established him as a man of many scientific facets. Gregory was basically a comparative anatomist who studied extinct and extant (present-day) vertebrate animals, with much emphasis on form and function. His research studies ranked him, beyond his anatomical work, as an outstanding ichthyologist, paleoherpetologist, mammalogist, and a physical anthropologist who was devoted to the records of primate evolution.

An early indication of the variety of his research interests is evident in the subjects of some of his first publications: in 1903, on the adaptive significance of the shortening of the elephant's skull; in 1904, on the relations of the anterior visceral arches to the chondrocranium (cartilaginous skull base); in 1905, on the weight of *Brontosaurus.* Gregory's doctoral dissertation, "The Order of Mammals," a remarkably penetrating and significant analysis of mammalian relationships and evolution, running to more than 500 pages, was a further indicator of Gregory's ultimate status in paleontology.

Gregory made other outstanding contributions to our knowledge of mammalian evolution through such publications as his monograph on the Eocene lemur, *Notharctus,* and especially on his epochal research on the origins and evolution of mammalian molar teeth, originally conducted in collaboration with Osborn but culminating in his book *The Origin and Evolution of the Human Dentition* (1922).

At the other end of the vertebrate scale, through the years Gregory was devoted to the study of the evolution of fishes. His 1933 monograph *Fish Skulls: A Study of the Evolution of Natural Mechanisms* is a masterful analysis of an extremely complex aspect of cranial evolution. Such a work could only be accomplished by a person with a profound understanding of the vertebrate skull.

With his mastery of vertebrate anatomy, it was inevitable that Gregory would take a comprehensive view of the subject, from the lowest of the backboned animals to the most highly evolved of these organisms; hence, his broad-ranging publications such as *Our Face from Fish to Man* (1929) and his final two-volume masterpiece *Evolution Emerging,* published in 1951. This is his final great effort, a review of all of the vertebrates that occupied many of his later years. Even so, Gregory was probably more widely known for his research on human evolution than for any other aspect of his study. Indeed, much of his attention during his later years was directed to the evolution of man from a primate ancestry.

With all of these research activities, Gregory was also a superb teacher, training an impressive array of students through some four decades. Many of his students became authorities of international repute. William King Gregory died at Woodstock, New York, on 29 December 1970, in his ninety-fifth year.

EDWIN H. COLBERT

Biography

Born in Greenwich Village, New York City, on 19 May 1876. Received B.A. 1900, M.A. 1905, Ph.D. 1910, all from Columbia University. Member, curatorial staff of the American Museum of Natural History, 1911–44; graduate faculty of Columbia University, 1916–45; member of numerous state, national, and international scientific associations, including the New York Academy of Sciences (president, 1932–33); New York Zoological Society; American Association for the Advancement of Science (vice president, section II, 1931); American Society of Naturalists (vice president, 1936); American Association of Anatomists; Geological Society of America; Paleontological Society of America; American Society of Mammalogists; American Philosophical Society; National Academy of Sciences; American Academy of Arts and Sciences; American Association of Physical Anthropology (president, 1941–42); American Society for Ichthyology and Herpetology (president, 1936–38); London Zoological Society; Geological Society of London; Linnean Society of London; Royal Society of Queensland; Royal Society of Upsala; State Russian Paleontological Society, Leningrad. Notable for studies of fossil and recent vertebrates; recognized as an outstanding authority on the evolution and relationships within all of the vertebrate classes; published comprehensive monographs and books on the skulls of teleost fishes, labyrinthodont amphibians, mammal-like reptiles, the evolution of mammalian molar teeth, the orders of mammals, and the evolution of man. Died in Woodstock, New York, 29 December 1970.

Major Publications

1910. *The Order of Mammals.* Bulletin of the American Museum of Natural History, 27. New York: Trustees of American Museum of Natural History.

1920. On the structure and relations of *Notharctus,* an American Eocene primate. *Memoirs of the American Museum of Natural History,* new ser., 3:49–243.

1922. *The Origin and Evolution of Human Dentition.* Baltimore, Maryland: Williams and Wilkins.

1929. *Our Face from Fish to Man: A Portrait Gallery of Our Ancient Ancestors and Kinsfolk Together with a Concise History of Our Best Features.* New York and London: Putnam's.

1933. Fish skulls: A study of the evolution of natural mechanisms. *Transactions of the American Philosophical Society,* new ser., 23:i–vii, 75–481.

1934. A Half Century of Trituberculy: The Cope-Osborn Theory of Dental Evolution, with a Revised Summary of Molar Evolution from Fish to Man. *Proceedings of the American Philosophical Society* 73:169–317.

1951. *Evolution Emerging: A Survey of Changing Patterns from Primeval Life to Man.* 2 vols. New York: Macmillan.

Further Reading

Colbert, E.H. 1975. William King Gregory: May 19, 1876–December 29, 1970. *National Academy of Science Biographical Memoirs* 46:90–133.

Simpson, G.G. 1971. William King Gregory (1876–1970). *American Journal of Physical Anthropology* 35:156–73.

GROSS, WALTER ROBERT

Latvian/German, 1903–74

Walter R. Gross was molded by the region in which he grew up. While still in high school, he systematically began to collect Devonian fish remains, laying the groundwork for what became his doctoral thesis on *Asterolepis,* an antiarch placoderm (an early jawed fish with an armored head and upper body) (1931). Throughout his life, he continued to study Devonian fishes and agnathans from the Baltic region (1933b, 1942, 1956, 1969) and also from Germany (1932, 1933a, 1937, 1947, 1961–63).

Gross' classification of Placodermi (1937) was very influential in subsequent decades. The main placoderm groups—Antiarchi, Arthrodira (restricted to his orders) Euarthrodira, Phyllolepida, Petalichthyida, Ptyctodontida, and Rhenanida—are still used in the discussions of interrelationships of placoderms, with the addition of Acanthothoraci, Pseudopetalichthyida, and sometimes Stensioellida (for Stegoselachii of Gross). Out of favor for a while, even his concept of Brachythoraci (1932) is accepted once again (Goujet and Young 1995). Stranded in western Germany following the erection of the Berlin wall, Gross began a series of reinvestigations of fishes and agnathans from the Hunsrück Slates of Bundenbach (1961–63). Based on this material, he produced the best descriptions of external and internal morphology (shape and structure) of the basal placoderm groups Stensioellida (1962), Pseudopetalichthyida (1962), Rhenanida (1963b), and Petalichthyida (1961), and of the primitive jawless fish *Drepanaspis* (1963a).

Gross utilized histology (study of microscopic structures), or more accurately histomorphology, to characterize fossil vertebrates. In 1934 he showed that the bones of the dinosaur *Brachiosaurus* contain channels called haversian canals, which are canals surrounded by layers of bone. This construction produces a structure that is very strong. Gross then compared the *Brachiosaurus* bone with that of the extinct mammoth elephant. He also found these canals in bones of the large Triassic amphibian *Mastodonsaurus*. He concluded this type of bone to be correlated with body size rather than being a characteristic of any one group or a particular physiology. Enlow and Brown continued this research 20 years later (1956 and following), and Ricqlès did the same even more extensively 30 years later (1968 and following).

Along with T. Ørvig and H. Aldinger, Gross was one of the few paleohistologists of his time. He published important papers on the histology of fossil fish scales (e.g., 1954, 1966–73). Gross utilized histomorphology to characterize scales. He used the distribution of enamel and shape of the pore-canal system in cosmine (a complex of bony and soft tissues) to characterize sarcopterygians (lobe-finned fishes) and cephalaspidomorphs (early jawless fish), and to distinguish between the scales of thelodonts (primitive jawless fishes), acanthodians (spiny sharks, the earliest jawed fishes), and elasmobranchs (primitive sharks, skates, and rays). Gross described the earliest osteichthyans (bony fishes) *Andreolepis* and *Lophosteus* (1968, 1969). *Andreolepis* is the most primitive lungfish known with a substance called ganoine in its scales, whereas *Lophosteus* as the earliest osteichthyan cannot be placed with either lungfish or sarcopterygians. Through his work, small scales became identifiable and the basis for some biostratigraphic correlations (e.g., Karatajuté-Talimaa 1978). The International Geological Correlation Programs (IGCP) continue to build upon Gross' work on scales. His 90th birthday was the focal point of this research, as shown in the Gross symposium of 1993 (special issue of Modern Geology 1996, 1997).

In 1954 Gross used his familiarity with histology to refute the hypothesis that conodonts (an extinct marine invertebrate) are related to vertebrates, demonstrating that conodonts do not have a toothlike structure. Their teeth lack a pulp cavity, dentine, and enamel, and their growth pattern is not comparable with teeth of vertebrates. As a result, he placed conodonts with an unknown chordate group, based on the presence of calcium phosphate in their systems. These arguments are still valid (Schultze 1996). His two papers on conodonts (1954, 1960) established the basis for later discussions on their histology.

Gross also was the first to demonstrate that the majority of early Paleozoic vertebrates were marine animals—they arose in the salty oceans—and that they first entered fresh waters only during the Devonian (1951). That was contrary to prevailing opinion which held that vertebrates originated in fresh water (Romer and Grove 1935), but Gross' conclusion gained strength when it was supported by the work of R.H. Denison (1956) and Robertson (1957).

Although Gross had very few students, he still had great influence on researchers in the Baltic region. Papers dedicated to Gross' 70th birthday reflect his close connection with colleagues working on Devonian vertebrates in the Baltic states, Russia, Germany, Sweden, England, France, and North America (Schultze 1973). Today, biostratigraphers are the ones that use his work most often, even though he wrote only one biostratigraphic paper (1942). To Gross, biostratigraphy was a by-product of good morphological work.

HANS-PETER SCHULTZE

Works Cited

Denison, R.H. 1956. A review of the habitat of the earliest vertebrates. *Fieldiana: Geology* 11:359–457.

Enlow, D.H., and S.O. Brown. 1956. A comparative histological study of fossil and recent bone tissues. Part I. *Texas Journal of Science* 8:405–43.

Goujet, D., and C.C. Young. 1995. Interrelationships of placoderms revisited. *Geobios, Mémoire spécial* 19:89–95.

Karatajuté-Talimaa, V. 1978. Silurian and Devonian thelodonts of the USSR and Spitsbergen. Vilnius: Leidykla, "Mokslas."

Ricqlès, A. de. 1968. Quelques observations paléohistologiques sur le dinosaurien sauropode *Bothriospondylus*. *Annales de l'Université de Madagascar* 6:157–209.

Robertson, J.D. 1957. The habitat of early vertebrates. *Biology Review* 32:156–87.

Schultze, H.-P. (ed.). 1973. Contributions on Devonian fishes by Denison, White, Novitskaya, Karatajuté-Talimaa, Thorsteinsson, Ritchie, Goujet, Mark-Kurik, Miles, Ørvig, Dunkle, Schaeffer, Jessen, Schultze, Thomson, and Worobjewa. *Palaeontographica A* 143:1–229.

———. 1996. Walter R. Gross, a palaeontologist in the turmoil of 20th century Europe. *Modern Geology* 20:209–33.

Special Issue Gross Symposium. 1996. Vol. 1, *Modern Geology* 20:203–401.

Special Issue Gross Symposium. 1996. Vol. 2, *Modern Geology* 21:1–200.

Biography

Born in Katlakaln, near Riga, Livland (today Latvia), province in Imperial Russia, 20 August 1903. Served in the Latvian army, 1923–25; received Ph.D., University of Berlin, 1929; research fellow (Notgemeinschaft der Deutschen Wissenschaft), University of Berlin, 1929–34; assistant professor (1934–35), then associate professor, Institute für Geologie, Universität Frankfurt/Main, 1936–37; associate professor (1937–43), also ausserplanmässiger professor (1943, 1949), full professor, 1950–61, Institut für Geologie und Paläontologie, Humboldt University of Berlin; Germany army, 1943–45; prisoner of war, 1945–46; full professor, University of Munich, 1972; honorary member of the Paläontologische Gesellschaft. Collected Devonian fishes in Latvia and Estonia, 1920–25, 1926–32, 1938, 1939, and in western Germany, 1931–34, 1962. Died in Tübingen, Germany, 9 June 1974.

Major Publications

1931. *Asterolepis ornata* Eichw. und das Antiarchi-Problem. *Palaeontographica A* 74:1–62.

1932. Die Arthrodira Wildungens. *Geologische und Paläontologische Abhandlungen* Neue Folge 19:1–61.

1933a. Die unterdevonischen Fische und Gigantostraken von Overath. *Abhandlungen der preußischen geologischen Landesanstalt*, Neue Folge, 145:41–77.

1933b. Die Fische des baltischen Devons. *Palaeontographica A* 79:1–74.

1934. Die Typen des mikroskopischen Knochenbaues bei fossilen Stegocephalen und Reptilien. *Zeitschrift für Anatomie und Entwicklungsgeschichte* 103:731–64.

1937. Die Wirbeltiere des rheinischen Devons. Teil II. *Abhandlungen der preußischen geologischen Landesanstalt*, Neue Folge, 176:1–83.

1942. Die Fischfaunen des baltischen Devons und ihre biostratigraphische Bedeutung. *Korrespondenz-Blatt des Naturforscher-Vereins zu Riga* 64:373–436.

1947. Die Agnathen und Acanthodier des obersilurischen Beyrichienkalks. *Palaeontographica A* 96:91–161.

1951. Die paläontologische und stratigraphische Bedeutung der Wirbeltierfaunen des Old Reds und der marinen altpaläozoischen Schichten. *Abhandlungen der deutschen Akademie der Wissenschaften zu Berlin, mathematisch-naturwissenschaftliche Klasse* Jahrgang 1949:1–130.

1955. Zur Conodonten-Frage. *Senckenbergiana lethaea* 35:73–85.

1956. Über Crossopterygier und Dipnoer aus dem baltischen Oberdevon im Zusammenhang einer vergleichenden Untersuchung des Porenkanalsystems paläozoischer Agnathen und Fische. *Kungliga svenska VetenskapsAkademiens Handlingar,* 4 serie, 5(6):1–140.

1960. Über die Basis bei den Gattungen *Palmatolepis* und *Polygnathus* (Conodontida). *Paläontologische Zeitschrift* 34:263–73.

1961. *Lunaspis broilii* und *Lunaspis heroldi* aus dem Hunsrückschiefer (Unterdevon, Rheinland). *Notizblatt des hessischen Landesamtes für Bodenforschung Wiesbaden* 89:17–43.

1962. Neuuntersuchung der Stensiöellida (Arthrodira, Unterdevon). *Notizblatt des hessischen Landesamtes für Bodenforschung Wiesbaden* 90:48–86.

1963a. *Drepanaspis gemuendensis* Schlüter. Neuuntersuchung. *Palaeontographica A* 121:133–55.

1963b. *Gemuendina stuertzi* Traquair. Neuuntersuchung. *Notizblatt des hessischen Landesamtes für Bodenforschung Wiesbaden* 91:36–73.

1966. Kleine Schupperkunde. *Neues Jahrbuch für Geologie und Paläontologie, Abhandlungen* 125:29–48.

1967. Über Thelodontier-Schuppen. *Palaeontographica A* 127:1–47.

1968. Fragliche Actinopterygier-Schuppen aus dem Silur Gotlands. *Lethaia* 1:184–218.

1969. *Lophosteus superbus* Pander, ein Teleostome aus dem Silur Oesels. *Lethaia* 2:15–47.

1971. Downtonische und dittonische Acanthodier-Reste des Ostseegebietes. *Palaeontographica A* 136:1–82.

1973. Kleinschuppen, Flossenstacheln und Zähne von Fischen aus europäischen und nordamerikanischen Bonebeds des Devons. *Palaeontographica A* 142:151–55.

Further Reading

Kutscher, F. 1978. Walter Robert Gross und die Fische des Hunsrückschiefers. *Mitteilungen der Pollichia* (Bad Dürkheim/Pfalz) 66:5–10.

Lukesevics, E.B. 1991. [Walter Gross and the investigations of the fossil fishes of the Baltic Devonian.] *Daba muzejs* (Riga) 3:24–27. [In Russian with Latvian and English subtitles]

Schultze, H.-P. 1974. Walter Robert Gross 20.8 1903–9.6.1974. *Paläontologische Zeitschrift* 48:143–48.

———. 1990. Gross, Walter Robert (b. Katakaln near Riga, Latvia, Russia, 20 August 1903; d. Tübingen, Germany, 9 June 1974), vertebrate paleontology. *Dictionary of Scientific Biography.* Vol. 17, Supplement 2:369–71.

———. 1996a. Walter R. Gross, a palaeontologist in the turmoil of 20th century Europe. *Modern Geology* 20:209–33.

———. 1996b. Conodont histology: An indicator of vertebrate relationship? *Modern Geology* 20:275–85.

Seilacher, A. 1974. Walter Gross zum Gedächtnis 20.8.1903–9.6.1974. *Attempto* (Tübingen), Heft 51–52:110–11.

GROWTH, DEVELOPMENT, AND EVOLUTION

Both popular and technical illustrations of evolutionary trees and lineages inevitably show a progression of adult forms. *Hyracotherium* (a primitive four-toed horse) gives rise to a succession of more derived species that feature reduction in toe number, greater tooth height and complexity, and a more elongate muzzle. The adult-to-adult transition is, of course, a convention that arises from both convenience and necessity. Evolutionary change takes place not at the adult stage but in earlier ontogenetic stages (ontogeny refers to both prenatal and postnatal growth and development). In order to create a new kind of adult, the ontogenetic pattern must be altered. Adults are preferentially used in evolutionary analysis because: (1) earlier ontogenetic stages are not as readily preserved in the fossil record, (2) earlier ontogenetic stages may not show diagnostic features that are necessary to distinguish species, (3) larval forms may be drastically different from adults and would greatly confuse analysis, and (4) the adult stage provides a convenient and uniform baseline for analysis.

For a long time in paleontology, the discovery of a larval or juvenile specimen was greeted with less enthusiasm than the discovery of an adult. However, in the past 25 years, studies of development have become a very active area in evolutionary biology. Investigators are no longer interested only in documenting a succession of species as represented by adult forms. They are interested in *how* change occurs and *why* it occurs. Questions are being asked at all levels. What genetic changes underlie morphological change and speciation? What hormonal changes redirect development? How does the timing and rate of development determine adult form? Does natural selection guide evolution exclusively, or do developmental changes spontaneously and continually launch experiments that then seek out niches for which they are equipped? How are larval and juvenile forms themselves adapted to meet unique challenges at their particular stage of life?

Genetics and Regulatory Genes

Tremendous progress has been made in recent years in pinpointing the genetic changes that govern changes in morphology. A cascade of regulatory genes, gene products, and growth factors have been identified, and their effects have been isolated. Foremost among these are the Hox family of genes. Hox genes are involved in the formation of everything from gill arches to limbs. They help determine the fore-aft sequence of body structures, the segmental arrangement of the nervous system and gill arches, and the position of the limb girdles. Acraniate ("headless") chordates such as *Amphioxus* have but one linear cluster of 13 Hox genes. Jawless fishes such as the lamprey have two paralogous ("twin") clusters, and jawed vertebrates (gnathostomes) have four paralogous clusters. These paralogous clusters evidently arose through wholesale duplication of what was originally a single Hox gene cluster. Such duplication events have been implicated in the appearance of jaws and paired fins in gnathostomes. Numerous other regulatory genes and products have been identified, and the interaction between them is at once both complex and highly conservative. It seems that once nature establishes a means of developmental control, it is loathe to abandon it. Identical genes controlling identical body regions and structures are found across vertebrates and even across animal phyla. For example, the Eyeless gene plays a part in eye formation in vertebrates and insects.

One outcome of this research is the realization that major alterations in body structure can be accomplished in an integrated manner through the alteration of regulatory gene function. The difference between a typical fish fin and a lobe fin may simply be a matter of lengthening the time during which the apical epidermal ridge is active. This activity, in turn, would be governed by regulatory genes and their products (so-called morphogens). The difference between a lobe fin and a tetrapod limb with fingers may reflect a shift in Hox gene domains (i.e., area of the body that they affect).

Tissue Interaction and Induction

Teeth are among the earliest hard tissues to have evolved in vertebrates. Dentine and dentinelike tissues arise from amorphous mesenchymal tissue that can trace its origin from populations of migrating neural crest cells. However, in order for the neural crest–derived mesenchyme to differentiate into the odontoblasts that lay down the dentine, there must be an inductive signal from an overlying epithelium (tissue that lines a cavity or external surface; usually ectoderm, but sometimes endoderm, in the case of pharyngeal teeth). These "epithelio-mesenchymal" interactions are essential for the formation of teeth as well as for other mineralized tissues elsewhere in the head and trunk.

Many vertebrates have secondarily lost their teeth (e.g., birds, turtles, rhynchosaurs, oviraptosaurid theropods), which implies the loss of the inductive signal or a lack of sensitivity to the inductive signal. Bird embryos can develop teeth when frog ectoderm is used to induce tooth formation.

The inductive signals necessary for organ formation in model animals such as the frog *Xenopus,* the chick, and the mouse are well known. This knowledge can be used when studying extinct organsims. Presence of structures such as teeth, eyes, and vertebrae testify to the presence of specific inductive processes. Loss or reduction of these structures implies an absence or diminution of these inductive processes. One can thereby reconstruct developmental interactions simply by looking at morphology.

Developmental Rate and Timing

Changes in regulatory gene domain, onset, cessation, and sensitivity are undoubtedly responsible, in a relatively direct way, for all significant changes in morphology. Unfortunately, it is not always possible to pinpoint the genetic basis for evolution. However, development can still be studied at coarser but equally fruitful levels.

It has been realized for some time that major changes in morphology can be effected through alteration of developmental rate and timing (heterochrony). These mechanisms bypass the problem of multiple regions and organs having to adapt independently and simultaneously to new biological roles while maintaining smooth, integrated function. Heterochrony can produce an organism that, relative to its immediate ancestor, looks less mature (juvenilization or pedomorphosis) or more mature (peramorphosis). Each of these end results can be produced by a variety of heterochronic mechanisms. For example, (1) overall developmental rates can be retarded or accelerated; (2) total time devoted to development can be shortened or lengthened; (3) formerly uniform developmental rates can develop spurts or lag periods; (4) the onset of a developmental sequence can be switched on earlier or later; (5) sexual maturity can be delayed or can be precocious—this is important because the onset of sexual maturity generally stops any further development. Each of these heterochronic mechanisms would, in turn, be controlled through a variety of genetic, epigenetic, and hormonal switches. Generally, paleontology is limited to diagnosing nonspecific cases of peramorphosis and pedomorphosis because there is no way to measure the developmental rates of extinct organisms.

Non-heterochronic Developmental Changes

It must be stressed that much of evolutionary change cannot be shoehorned conveniently into one or another heterochronic category. Quite frequently different parts of an organism develop at different rates, resulting in a mosaic of retarded and accelerated features. Mosaic evolution, which ultimately is tied to mosaic development, is far more common in the history of life than uniform ontogenetic change.

Entire developmental stages and sequences can be deleted, inserted, inverted, transposed from one position to another, or added to the beginning or end of a developmental sequence. The insertion of instar stages (i.e., stages between successive molts) in the development of hemimetabolous insects (those characterized by incomplete metamorphosis) and the insertion of drastically different larval stages in holometabolous insects (those characterized by complete metamorphosis) are examples of these extreme changes. The mechanisms behind these kinds of developmental/evolutionary changes are still unclear, but they are relatively common in the history of life.

Allometry

Allometry is the study of changes in body proportion that are simply the result of changes in size. In order for an animal to maintain equivalent function at a drastically altered body size, its proportions have to change. With any linear doubling of body length, surface area increases as length squared (L^2) and mass increases as length cubed (L^3). In other words, an animal twice as long as its ancestor will be eight times as heavy provided all proportions are kept the same. An elephant therefore has to have disproportionately sturdy limbs in order to support its great weight. A shrew has to have a very high metabolism in part because its surface-to-mass ratio is very high and it loses heat quickly. Conversely, an elephant has a low surface-to-mass ratio and a low metabolism because its problem is exactly the opposite: how to dissipate heat.

Some structures, such as the brain and sensory organs, exhibit *negative allometry*. In other words, in larger animals these organs are relatively small compared to total mass. Other structures, such as chewing muscles, tend to exhibit *positive allometry*. The chewing muscles of a tiger are disproportionately large compared with those of a domestic cat. Still other structures maintain a consistent size with respect to body mass and are said to exhibit *isometry*.

In some cases allometry makes physiological sense. The negative allometry of basal metabolism with increasing body size makes intuitive sense because the low surface-to-volume ratio in large animals retains heat effectively. The negative allometry of eyes also makes sense since you would not see any better if your eyes grew at the same rate as your body.

Other allometric relationships are only discovered in hindsight and are neither predictable nor sensible. Why should the antlers of deer exhibit positive allometry? Antlers are physiologically very expensive structures; the massive span of the extinct Irish elk must have been a tremendous drain on the resources of the male. Deer are actually not unusual; there is a general trend toward positive allometry in features that arise through sexual selection and that are used for intraspecific display and competition.

Allometry is typically assessed across species boundaries (interspecific allometry), for example, the famous mouse-to-elephant curve. However, it also can be studied along a growth series within a species (growth allometry) or between adults of differing size within a species (intraspecific allometry). Allometry also can be studied within a temporal series, for example, in the fossil representatives of a rapidly dwarfing lineage. Allometric coefficients (slopes) are often quite different among these varied allometric curves.

Ontogenetic Adaptation

In many animals, early ontogenetic stages are not merely way stations on the path to adulthood. In many cases each stage is exquisitely adapted to a particular set of circumstances. The teeth of adult fruit-eating lizards such as iguanas and tegus are blunt. However, those of their young hatchlings are sharp and reflect a diet of insects. The young of many animals differ from their parents in diet, locomotor pattern, environmental preference, and potential predators. These differing parameters are reflected in morphology, coloration, behavior, physiology, and activity patterns. The fossil record will preserve some evidence of these properties, both direct and indirect. Mass death assemblages of a particular age cohort may reflect schooling behavior or the presence of a rookery. Differential preservation of youngsters in burrows may reflect cryptic behavior designed to avoid predators. Some jawless fishes (e.g., tremataspid and boreaspidid osteostracans) only developed ossified exoskeletons upon reaching adulthood; the young evidently were naked and are not preserved in the fossil record. In this case, negative evidence—the absence of mineralized young—would imply a different lifestyle. Perhaps they lived as filter feeders buried in the sediment, as do modern lamprey larvae. The dramatic cranial ornamentation of ceratopsian dinosaurs and titanotheres

developed only as the animal approached adulthood. These and similar patterns of late ontogenetic appearance of external superstructures is important evidence that these structures were used in interspecific signaling, agonistic displays, intermale combat, or sexual displays. The careful analysis of ontogenetic differences in morphology, taphonomomy, and paleoenvironment yields important clues about the lifestyles of both young and adult individuals.

Growth, Physiology, and Behavior

During the last 30 years, a great deal of effort has been invested in the attempt to correlate growth patterns with physiology, metabolism, thermoregulation, and behavior. Early on it was thought that slow, ectothermic ("cold-blooded") animals should exhibit the following characteristics: (1) indeterminate growth (i.e., they never stop growing), as evidenced by poorly finished articular surfaces, open skull sutures, and lack of peripheral rest lines toward the periphery of long bones; (2) slow growth, as evidenced by lamellar-zonal bone; (3) episodic (interrupted or seasonal) growth, as evidenced by distinct growth lines; (4) relatively few bone cells; (5) poorer blood supply, with blood vessels dispersed erratically through compact bone; (6) lack of epiphyses (separate growth centers) on long bones; (7) lack of internal remodeling of bone (in other words, the bone is not continually resorbed and replaced); (8) hatchlings that are precocial (ready to leave the nest), as evidenced by relatively dense bone in limbs and well-formed articular surfaces.

Fast, endothermic ("warm-blooded"), and metabolically active animals were thought to have these characteristics: (1) terminal growth (i.e., the animal stops growing at a certain point), as evidenced by smooth, finished articular surfaces, closed sutures, and the presence of peripheral rest lines in long bones; (2) fast growth, demonstrated by the presence of fibrolamellar bone; (3) continual growth; (4) abundant bone cells; (5) rich blood supply, with vessels running through the center of osteons (microscopic canals that run longitudinally though dense bone); (6) presence of at least a few epiphyses; (7) internal remodelling of bone (bone tissue is continually replaced); (8) altricial (relatively helpless) young.

These assumptions have taken a beating over the years, and today the picture is rather muddy, especially with regard to such heavily studied groups as dinosaurs and early birds. Some dinosaurs, such as the hadrosaur *Maiasaura,* seem to have produced altricial young, while others, such as the theropod *Troödon,* hatched precocial young. Bone histology (microscopic anatomy) suggests that certain dinosaurs exhibited episodic and indeterminate growth while others exhibited continual and terminal growth patterns. Some evince hybrid patterns that suggest both rapid and episodic growth. Still others have a histological profile that suggests varied growth patterns at different times of their lives. A group of early birds, the enantiornithines, exhibit clear signs of episodic growth, in sharp contrast to modern birds.

While the picture has become quite complex, it should not negate the value of these growth studies, which, if nothing else, clearly show that many extinct taxa defy our predictions and possibly exhibited growth patterns and physiologies unlike anything alive today.

Ontogeny and Adaptation

Ontogenetic trajectories change for many reasons, but natural selection must be included as one of the driving forces that redirect development. In order for an adaptation to manifest itself, ontogeny must change. There are a number of good reasons for a lineage to increase in size over time, but in order to do so one or several of the following changes must occur: an accelerated growth rate, a prolonged growth period, delayed sexual maturity, and new allometric proportions.

MICHAEL K. DIAMOND

See also Allometry; Growth, Postembryonic; Heterochrony; Oceanic Islands; Paleoethology; Phyletic Dwarfism and Gigantism; Reproductive Strategies; Thermoregulation

Further Reading

Arthur, W. 1997. *The Origin of Animal Body Plans: A Study in Evolutionary Developmental Biology.* Cambridge and New York: Cambridge University Press.

Carroll, S.B. 1995. Homeotic genes and the evolution of arthropods and chordates. *Nature* 376:479–85.

Chinsamy, A., and P. Dodson. 1995. Inside a dinosaur bone. *American Scientist* 83 (2):174–80.

Coates, M.I. 1994. The origin of vertebrate limbs. *Development* (Suppl.):69–80.

Damuth, J., and B.J. MacFadden. 1990. *Body Size in Mammalian Paleobiology.* Cambridge and New York: Cambridge University Press.

Gee, H. 1996. *Before the Backbone: Views on the Origin of the Vertebrates.* London and New York: Chapman and Hall.

Hall, B.K. 1992. *Evolutionary Developmental Biology.* London and New York: Chapman and Hall.

Hanken, J., and B.K. Hall (eds.). 1993. *The Skull.* Vols. 1–3. Chicago: University of Chicago Press.

Humphries, C.J. (ed.). 1988. *Ontogeny and Systematics.* London: British Museum (Natural History); New York: Columbia University Press.

Langille, R.M. 1993. Formation of the vertebrate face: Differentiation and Development. *American Zoologist* 33:462–71.

Maderson, P.F.A. (ed.). 1987. *Developmental and Evolutionary Aspects of the Neural Crest.* New York: Wiley.

McKinney, M.L., and K.J. McNamara. 1991. *Heterochrony: The Evolution of Ontogeny.* New York: Plenum.

McNamara, K.J. 1997. *Shapes of Time: The Evolution of Growth and Development.* Baltimore: Johns Hopkins University Press.

Niklas, K.J. 1994. *Plant Allometry: The Scaling of Form and Process.* Chicago: University of Chicago Press.

Raff, R.A. 1996. *The Shape of Life: Genes, Development, and the Evolution of Animal Form.* Chicago: University of Chicago Press.

Schmidt-Nielsen, K. 1984. *Scaling: Why Is Animal Size So Important?* Cambridge and New York: Cambridge University Press.

Shubin, N., C. Tabin, and S. Carroll. 1997. Fossils, genes and the evolution of animal limbs. *Nature* 388:639–48

GROWTH, POSTEMBRYONIC

Our knowledge of extinct animals derives mainly from studying the anatomy and morphology of their fossilized skeletal remains. Most aspects of the biology of the animal cannot be ascertained directly and often are the subject of much speculation. The thermal biology and rate of growth of dinosaurs is a case in point. There is now increasing evidence that studies of fossil bone microstructure allows interpretation of various aspects of the growth of an animal, as well as indirect inferences regarding the physiology of the extinct animal (Chinsamy 1994). Shortly after an animal dies, the organic material (i.e., the skin, muscles, and soft tissue) begins to decompose. This decomposition includes the organic components within bone, such as collagen and mucopolysaccharides. However, even after millions of years, the bones and teeth of the animal can be preserved with their microstructure intact.

Fossil Bone Microstructure

During fossilization, a variety of diagenetic factors (i.e., those converting organic matter into rock) can affect the history of a bone. Besides the loss of the organic components, chemical elements can become incorporated or removed from the bone, and microorganisms such as fungi or bacteria can occupy the bone. Considering the amount of potential damage that can occur, it is surprising that it is more usual than not for the microstructure of fossil bone to be well preserved. Fungal damage to fossil bone or extensive chemical alteration causing total destruction of the microstructure rarely have been reported.

By examining a polished thin section of fossil bone under a microscope, the microstructure (histology) of the bone can be studied. Although the blood vessels are no longer present, the cavities that once housed them are readily recognizable, as are the lacunae (spaces) that the bone cells (osteocytes) occupied in life. Even the lacunae's branching canaliculi, which permitted communication among neighboring cells in the living bone, are distinctly visible. All the natural cavities in the bone, as well as those caused postmortem, generally become infilled by sediments or minerals from the environment during fossilization. The type and extent of infilling depend on the environment in which the remains of the animal became buried.

The compacted bone that makes up the bone wall can be either primary or secondary in origin. Primary compact bone is generally bone formed under the periosteum (surrounding fibrous layer) during appositional growth. Secondary bone, as the name suggests, involves the initial resorption of primary bone and thereafter a redeposition of bone. Both primary and secondary compact bone tissues are observed readily in fossil bone.

Although the collagen has long decomposed, the actual organization of the collagen fibrils that were once present may be assessed by studying the organization of the apatite (calcium phosphate), which, during life, closely followed the collagen fibrillar matrix arrangement. Since the latter is dependent on the rate of bone formation, an examination of the gross textural organization of the apatite can provide insight into the rate of bone formation of the fossil bone.

Two fundamental types of primary compact bone tissues are recognized on the basis of fibrillar arrangement. In quickly deposited bone, the fibrillar matrix has a more haphazard, woven arrangement. This is called fibro-lamellar bone. Lamellar (layered) bone results when bone is formed more slowly, and it typically has a more organized fibrillar matrix. Regardless of whether primary or secondary in origin, compact bone can be vascular or avascular. If vascular, the orientation of the vascular canals are used for further classification of the tissue. The vascular canals themselves can be classified into simple vessels, primary osteons, and secondary osteons. Simple vessels do not interrupt the structure of the bone surrounding them and are distinguished from primary osteons, which have a deposit of lamellar bone around them. Secondary osteons are formed as a result of a process termed secondary or Haversian reconstruction, which involves resorption and subsequent redeposition of bone. Secondary osteons are readily distinguishable from primary osteons by having a cement line that marks the farthest extent of bone resorption. Bone around each secondary osteon is initially primary in origin; however, with continuing secondary reconstruction, the number of secondary osteons increases, and dense Haversian bone can result where even the interstitial bone is a remnant of older secondary osteons.

The usefulness of interpreting various aspects of growth from studies of fossil bone microstructure has been realized. There are an increasing number of researchers entering this field of research, and dinosaur bone in particular has been the focus of much attention. Such studies are used here to illustrate the use of bone histology to determine various aspects of dinosaur growth.

Physiological Significance of Dinosaur Bone Microstructure

Studies of dinosaur bones are showing increasingly that there is no unique dinosaurian type of bone tissue. However, in general, dinosaur bone is very highly vascularized by primary osteons, which usually (particularly in young individuals) are embedded in a woven matrix of a fibro-lamellar type of bone tissue. Pauses in the rate of bone formation, indicated by lines of arrested growth, also appear to be fairly common. In more mature individuals the nature of the primary compact bone can grade into a more slowly formed lamellar type of tissue. Among the dinosaur taxa studied, the extent of secondary reconstruction and amount of secondary osteons formed is highly variable. It ranges from being fairly limited, with just a few isolated secondary osteons, as in *Massospondylus* and *Dryosaurus,* to being extensive as in *Brachiosaurus* and *Pachyrhinosaurus,* where dense Haversian bone results. The extent of secondary reconstruction also can be related to the age of the individual.

A variety of other bone tissue types have been identified in dinosaur bones, for example, endochondral bone, which replaces cartilage; compacted coarse cancellous bone, which results from endosteal infilling of cancellous spaces; metaplastic bone, which is the result of ossification of ligaments or tendons; and pathological bone.

Dinosaur Growth

The nature of the compact bone present in dinosaur bones has provided the greatest insight for interpreting various aspects of their growth. Fibro-lamellar bone and Haversian bone frequently are found in dinosaur bone. These tissues are similar to that found in mammalian bone, and, as such, were cited as evidence of endothermy (warm-bloodedness) in dinosaurs. However, new findings have shown that although fibro-lamellar bone is typical of endothermic mammals, it is now also recognized in known ectotherms, such as juvenile crocodiles, and in mammal-like reptiles from the Permian and Triassic. Haversian bone is also now recognized in reptiles and in some cases can be extensively developed. Thus, fibro-lamellar bone and Haversian bone cannot be considered unique endothermic characteristics.

More recent work on dinosaur bone histology has indicated that some taxa form bone in a cyclical manner, with alternating periods of fast and slow growth. The period of fast growth can be followed or preceded by a line of arrested growth, which marks a cessation of bone deposition. A distinctly stratified compacta, termed zonal bone, results from the alternating periods of slowed and rapid growth. Zonal bone is recognized in a variety of isolated bones of various dinosaur taxa (e.g., *Rhabdodon, Baryonyx, Allosaurus, Tyrannosaurus,* and *Protoceratops*) and appears to be fairly widespread in the Dinosauria (Reid 1990).

Among modern animals, such a cyclical pattern of bone formation is characteristic of reptiles. Experimental analysis using fluorescent dyes on animals of known age has identified such cycles as annual, resulting from an innate biological rhythm synchronized by seasonality. The temporal pattern of the rings cannot be ascertained directly in fossil bones, but since no other cycle in living animals is known to form such rings, it is reasonable to assume that they also represent an annual phenomenon in the extinct animal. Furthermore, examination of individuals of specific dinosaurian taxa at different growth stages have shown that the number of rings increases with size. In the small theropod, *Syntarsus,* at least eight cycles of bone deposition can be recognized (Chinsamy 1994). If one considers that these cycles are annual, then it took about 8 years for this dinosaur to reach a mature body size. Another, smaller theropod, *Troodon,* is considered to have taken about three to five years to reach maximum body size (Varricchio 1993). The prosauropod *Massospondylus* has 15 growth rings in its bone, but no examined specimen appears to have reached maximum body size (Chinsamy 1994). Even if the growth rings were not annual, the occurrence of periodic pauses in the rate of bone deposition is a direct indication that these animals were growing significantly slower than modern mammals and birds. It further suggests that they were unable to maintain a sustained high rate of bone deposition. Lines can result in the bones of mammals as a result of trauma, but such lines are infrequent and are not an integral part of normal growth, as they are in reptiles and these dinosaurs. As in mature mammals, mature individuals of both *Troodon* and *Syntarsus* exhibit closely spaced rest lines in the peripheral region of their bones. These rest lines suggest that they have attained mature body size and that these dinosaurs have a determinate growth pattern. Some dinosaur taxa (e.g., *Massospondylus* and *Dryosaurus*) do not have such terminal deposition, and it is possible that they have an indeterminate growth strategy (like most modern reptiles), or that the largest individual of the species has not yet been examined.

The nature of dinosaur bone is further complicated in that not all dinosaurs have zonal bone. Thirteen femora of different-sized individuals of *Dryosaurus,* a medium-sized ornithopod, showed no growth rings (Chinsamy 1995). This suggests that growth was continuously rapid throughout ontogeny. This is the only described growth series of a dinosaur that apparently grew rapidly throughout its life. *Dryosaurus* was relatively small (70 kilograms); therefore, mass effects could not have played a major role in maintaining a high stable body temperature (homeothermy). Furthermore, studies of modern reptiles living in aseasonal environments still show growth rings in their bones. Thus, the absence of any growth rings in the bones of *Dryosaurus* suggests that it was physiologically capable of growing at a high, sustained rate without any interruptions in the rate of bone deposition. *Dryosaurus* therefore represents the only dinosaur taxon studied that suggests a growth pattern seen in extant endotherms.

Thus, studies of dinosaur bone indicate a combination of both reptilian and mammalian characteristics. This suggests that they were neither typical endotherms nor typical ectotherms. It is quite possible that they represent some intermediate position along the continuum of physiological strategies or were perhaps specialized ectotherms or specialized endotherms.

It is widely held that birds evolved from theropod dinosaurs (i.e., birds are nested phylogenetically within the Dinosauria). For simplicity, in this essay, non-avian dinosaurs are referred to as dinosaurs or theropods while avian theropod dinosaurs are referred to as birds. The histological changes that occurred through the transition from non-avian dinosaurs to birds was explored by examining the bone microstructure of three Late Cretaceous birds from Argentina (Chinsamy et al. 1994). These birds represent the oldest birds ever examined histologically. The results of the study showed that the early birds *Patagopteryx* and two species of Enantiornithines resem-

bled their theropod ancestors in having growth rings in the compacta of their bones. This is quite unlike modern birds, which grow rapidly without any interruptions or pauses in the rate of bone deposition. Thus, it appears that these basal (primitive) birds studied were physiologically different from modern birds and had slower growth rates. The implication is that even halfway through the evolutionary history of birds, these basal birds, like their dinosaurian ancestors, were not classic endotherms. This suggests that endothermy evolved much later in the evolutionary history of birds and was not inherited from their dinosaurian ancestors.

ANUSUYA CHINSAMY

See also Allometry; Growth, Development, and Evolution; Heterochrony; Paleoethology; Phyletic Dwarfism and Gigantism; Reproductive Strategies: Vertebrates; Thermoregulation

Works Cited

Chinsamy, A. 1994. Dinosaur bone histology: Implications and inferences. *In* G.D. Rosenberg and D.L. Wolberg (eds.), *Dinofest*. Paleontological Society Publication, 7. Knoxville, Tennessee: Paleontological Society.

———. 1995. Ontogenetic changes in the bone histology of the Late Jurassic ornithopod *Dryosaurus lettowvorbecki. Journal of Vertebrate Paleontology* 15:96–104.

Chinsamy, A., L. Chiappe, and P. Dodson. 1994. Growth rings in Mesozoic avian bones: Physiological implications for basal birds. *Nature* 368:196–97.

Reid, R.E.H. 1990. Zonal "growth rings" in dinosaurs. *Modern Geology* 15:19–48.

Varricchio, D.J. 1993. Bone microstructure of the Upper Cretaceous theropod dinosaur *Troodon formosus. Journal of Vertebrate Paleontology* 13:99–104.

Further Reading

Chinsamy, A. 1995. Within the bone. *Natural History* 104 (6): 62–63.

Chinsamy, A., and P. Dodson. 1995. Inside a dinosaur bone. *American Scientist* 83:174–80.

GYMNOSPERMS

The gymnosperms—cone-bearing plants such as conifers—share a number of characters, but the singlemost important feature uniting the group is the presence of naked seeds borne on stalks associated with modified leaves or scales. The gymnosperm seed is a an integumented "megasporangium" (an enclosed organ in which spores are formed, often called a "nucellus") that is not enclosed within a carpel (the female reproductive organ seen in the angiosperms), and its evolution is one of the most significant landmarks in the evolution and diversification of terrestrial ecosystems.

Plants go through two stages in their life cycle (alternation of generations), one of which is asexual ("sporophyte") and the other sexual ("gametophyte"). Each stage produces a unique plant structure. The asexual phase produces spores; the sexual phase produces gametes (eggs and sperm). Scholars believe that the evolution of seeds progressed from homospory—a system in which plants produced only one type of spore from which grew a gametophyte stage that produced both male and female reproductive organs—to heterospory—a system in which plants pro-

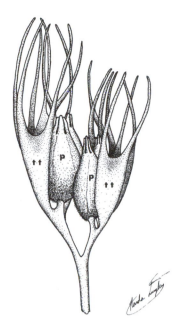

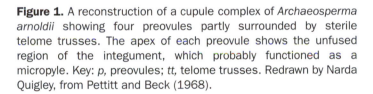

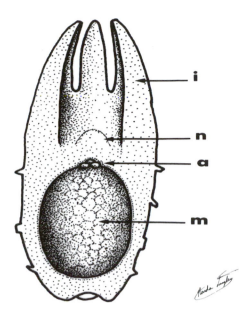

Figure 1. A reconstruction of a cupule complex of *Archaeosperma arnoldii* showing four preovules partly surrounded by sterile telome trusses. The apex of each preovule shows the unfused region of the integument, which probably functioned as a micropyle. Key: *p,* preovules; *tt,* telome trusses. Redrawn by Narda Quigley, from Pettitt and Beck (1968).

Figure 2. A cross section of an *Archaeosperma arnoldii* preovule, showing the integument partly surrounding the nucellus, which contains one large functional megaspore and three abortive megaspores. Key: *i,* integument; *n,* nucellus; *m,* functional megaspore; *a,* abortive megaspores. Redrawn by Narda Quigley from Pettitt and Beck (1968).

duced two types of spores from which grew two different gametophyte stages, one that produced male reproductive structures and one that produced female reproductive structures. After this change, seeds appeared. Because the fossil record has many gaps, the exact timing and progression of these events remain undecided. Nevertheless, prior to the Middle Devonian all vascular plants were homosporous. The discovery of the progymnosperm *Chaleuria* of the Middle Devonian marked a change, for in its "sporangia" (spore-producing structure) it had two different sizes of spores. These have been equated to the male "microspores" and female "megaspores" of modern seed plants, demonstrating that heterospory had evolved. By the Late Devonian and Early Carboniferous, heterospory had evolved independently in a number of unrelated vascular plant groups (Bateman and DiMichele 1994).

The transition from heterospory to the seed production provides a good example of increasingly complex reproductive strategies. Several steps were necessary and include the formation and retention of a single functional megaspore within a nucellus, formation of a specialized structure to receive pollen at the tip of the nucellus, formation of an "integument" (protective covering) and "micropyle" (an opening in the integument that leads to the egg-containing structure), and formation of a "pollen tube" to deliver the microgametophytes to the ovule. The order in which these events occurred is not clear, but the fossil record shows a trend from simple pre-ovule to a structurally more complex seed.

Probably one of the earliest steps in the evolution of the seed habit was the formation and retention of a single functional megaspore (spore that will develop into a female gametophyte) within the nucellus, a feature that evolved independently several times within a number of Paleozoic plant groups. However, in contrast to the lycopsids (club mosses), ferns, and horsetails, which shed their male and female gametophytes into water for fertilization to occur, the gymnosperms retained the female gametophytes on the sporophyte plant and transported the male gametophytes (pollen) to the female. Development of the megaspore is assumed to have proceeded in a manner similar to that seen in modern gymnosperms. That is, the functional megaspore underwent a series of divisions to produce a large multicellular nutritive megagametophyte. Within it was an archegonium (female sex organ) containing the egg nuclei developed at the pollen-receiving end of the megagametophyte. Remains of the Late Devonian *Archaeosperma arnoldii* show integumented preovulate (primitive ovulelike) structures containing one functional and three aborted megaspores within a nucellus (Figures 1 and 2).

The earliest preovulate structure known is that of the *Elkinsia polymorpha*, a Late Devonian seed fern from eastern West Virginia (Rothwell et al. 1989). In *E. polymorpha* (Figure 3) the nucellus is surrounded only partly by the integumentary lobes and the micropyle had not evolved yet, but a specialized pollen-receiving structure (called a hydrasperman pollen chamber) was present (Figure 4). The hydrasperman pollen chamber consists of

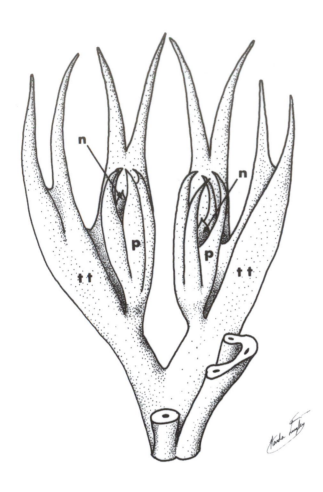

Figure 3. A reconstruction of *Elkinsia polymorpha* cupule showing two preovules surrounded by sterile telome trusses. Note that the more or less unfused integumentary lobes surround the nucellus but that the apex of the nucellus is exposed, indicating that the micropyle had not yet evolved. Key: *p,* preovules; *tt,* telome trusses; *n,* nucellus; Redrawn by Narda Quigley from Rothwell and Scheckler (1988).

a membranous floor and a prominent cone-shaped central column rising from the central part of the floor. The apex of the chamber opens into a modified funnel or cup-shaped structure called a "lagenostome." Wind-blown prepollen (primitive pollenlike structures) is directed into the lagenostome, which then drops into the pollen chamber. Growth of the megagametophyte pushes the apex of the central column into the base of the lagenostome, sealing the pollen chamber, rupturing the thin membranous floor, and allowing the prepollen access to the archegonia embedded near the top of the megagametophyte. After fertilization, the developing embryo, protected from desiccation (drying out) by the integument, fed on the nutritive gametophytic tissue, matured into a seed, and ultimately was shed from the plant.

Although the lack of a micropyle and other structures and functions means that *E. polymorpha* preovules cannot be true seeds, they do provide us with evidence of an intermediate step in ovule evolution and formation of an integument. Hypotheses on

the evolution of the integument are numerous (Stewart and Rothwell 1993; Taylor and Taylor 1993), but the "telome" concept proposed by W. Zimmermann (1952) continues to be the most accepted theory by paleobotanists (Figure 5). Zimmermann posits that one terminal sporangium of a plant became surrounded by other fertile and sterile axes, or "telomes." Continued reduction and ultimate fusion of the telomes ultimately resulted in surrounding the sporangium by an integument. The degree of fusion between integumentary lobes is seen in a number of Lower Carboniferous pteridosperm ovules. The trend from nearly unfused to completely fused integuments strongly supports Zimmermann's telome hypothesis (Figure 6).

As stated earlier, homosporous and heterosporous nonseed plants must have an external source of water for fertilization to occur. While the evolution of a hydrasperman pollen chamber and its replacement, the micropyle, eliminated the need for an external source of water for reproduction, a problem remained: how to deliver the microgametophytes that produce sperm cells to the ovule without water. Based on the rare and fragmentary remains of Carboniferous prepollen and pollen, development of the microgametophyte and the process of fertilization is believed to have proceeded in a manner similar to that seen in gymnosperms today. Remains of pollen droplets and pollen tubes in the pteridosperm *Callospermarion* demonstrate that the problem of sperm delivery in the absence of water had been overcome at least by the Middle Pennsylvanian (Rothwell 1972, 1977).

The evolution of these new and innovative reproductive strategies conferred significant advantages to the gymnosperms, allowing them to evolve and occupy new habitats that previously were unavailable to the vascular plants. Seed-producing plants no longer needed to rely on an external source of water to ensure fertilization, thereby allowing colonization of drier environments. Moreover, the embryo itself now was contained within a protective, desiccation-resistant integument and, embedded within nutritive tissue, could survive unfavorable conditions until such time that germination would favor the survival of the young seedling. Although this discussion has provided only an overview of the significant events in the evolution of the seed habit, comprehensive reviews of heterospory and the evolution of the ovule are provided by J.M. Pettitt (1970) and R.M. Bateman and W.A. DiMichele (1994).

Scholars widely agree that gymnosperms evolved from Devonian progymnosperms. The most pressing question that remains yet to be answered is whether all of the gymnosperms evolved from a common ancestor or whether the various gymnosperm lineages evolved from a number of common ancestors. G.W. Rothwell (1982) suggests that the gymnosperms are monophyletic (have a single ancestor), evolving from the Aneurophytales. On the other hand, C.B. Beck and D.C. Wight (1988) believe that the gymnosperms are polyphyletic (have a number of ancestors), with the seed ferns evolving from the Aneurophytales and the cordaites and conifers evolving from the Archaeopteridales. Alternatively, S.V. Meyen (1984) believes that the gymnosperms evolved from the Archaeopteridales. While cladistic analyses (analysis based upon derived, not ancestral traits) (Crane 1985a, 1985b; Doyle and Donoghue 1986) support the idea of

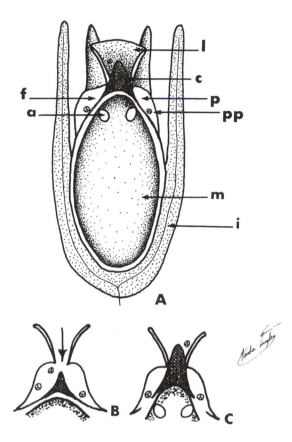

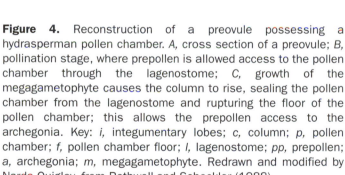

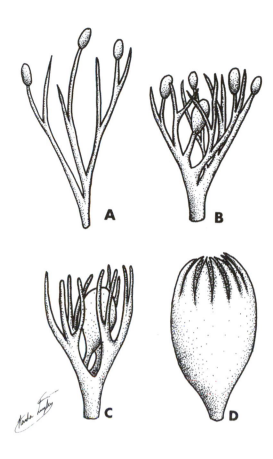

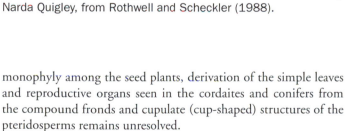

Figure 4. Reconstruction of a preovule possessing a hydrasperman pollen chamber. *A*, cross section of a preovule; *B*, pollination stage, where prepollen is allowed access to the pollen chamber through the lagenostome; *C*, growth of the megagametophyte causes the column to rise, sealing the pollen chamber from the lagenostome and rupturing the floor of the pollen chamber; this allows the prepollen access to the archegonia. Key: *i*, integumentary lobes; *c*, column; *p*, pollen chamber; *f*, pollen chamber floor; *l*, lagenostome; *pp*, prepollen; *a*, archegonia; *m*, megagametophyte. Redrawn and modified by Narda Quigley, from Rothwell and Scheckler (1988).

Figure 5. The Zimmermannian hypothesis of preovule evolution. *A*, a plant bearing terminal isomorphic sporangia; *B*, heterospory occurs and micro- and megasporangia are produced; *C*, one megaspore becomes surrounded by the other fertile and sterile telomes; *D*, reduction and fusion of the telomes results in the sporangium becoming surrounded by an integument. Redrawn by Narda Quigley from Zimmermann (1952).

monophyly among the seed plants, derivation of the simple leaves and reproductive organs seen in the cordaites and conifers from the compound fronds and cupulate (cup-shaped) structures of the pteridosperms remains unresolved.

The problem associated with gymnosperm phylogeny is centered on whether the seed habit evolved once or a number of times (Taylor and Taylor 1993). A growing body of evidence indicates that the seed probably arose independently several times in different lineages throughout geologic time, supporting the notion that the gymnosperms are not a natural grouping of plants. Nevertheless, despite our inability to determine whether the gymnosperms are monophyletic or polyphyletic, the plant groups commonly considered to be gymnospermous include the gingkos, conifers, cycads, gnetophytes, and extinct seed ferns.

Pteridospermophyta

The pteridosperms, or seed ferns, first appeared during the Late Devonian and were prominent constituents of Late Paleozoic forest communities throughout the world. A variety of growth forms are known. Some resembled modern tree ferns, while others were more vinelike or scrambling. Fertile organs were borne on unspecialized fernlike leaves, a feature that differs significantly from the highly modified structures seen in the conifers. The ovules of some pteridosperms were commonly large and resembled those of cycads, or they occurred in elaborate multi-ovulate cupules (cuplike structures) equipped with specialized pollen-receiving structures. The pollen-producing organs were arranged in clusters or fused into a structure called a "synangium," a feature found only in the seed ferns. The type of wood produced among the seed ferns included manoxylic and pycnoxylic types. "Manoxylic

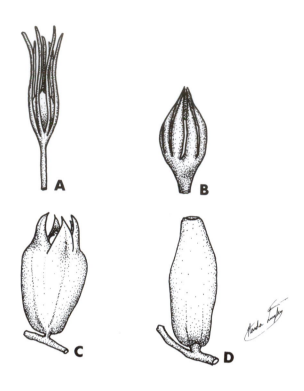

Figure 6. The trend towards increasing fusion of the integumentary lobes, leading to the formation of the micropyle. *A,* the nearly unfused integumentary lobes of *Genomosperma kidstoni; B,* the partly fused lobes of *G. latens; C,* nearly fused lobes of *Eurystoma angulare; D,* complete fusion in *Stamnostoma huttonense,* the first plant to possess a true ovule. Redrawn by Narda Quigley from Stewart and Rothwell (1993).

wood" contains abundant parenchyma (thin-walled cells that form irregularly shaped open spaces) and is common among the cycads; whereas "pycnoxylic wood" is dense, contains little parenchyma, and resembles that seen in the conifers. It was once thought that the seed ferns were an evolutionary intermediate between the ferns and cycads, but anatomical similarities with some of the members of the Aneurophytales indicate that they probably evolved from the progymnosperms. Although the seed ferns ultimately became extinct during the Cretaceous, the fossil record provides evidence that the angiosperms may have evolved from some of the Mesozoic forms.

Coniferophyta

The conifers are a very diverse group of plants represented by some 50 genera and over 500 living species. Most conifers form trees, possess pycnoxylic wood, simple needlelike leaves, and compound ovulate and simple pollen cones. The earliest conifers are represented by the extinct Cordaitales, which were prominent cosmopolitan components of the Late Carboniferous and Permian forests. There is little doubt that the Cordaitales evolved from the

progymnosperms; however, it is not clear whether they arose from the aneurophytes with a lyginopterid seed fern as an intermediate or arose directly from the archaeopteridalean line (Stewart and Rothwell 1993). Scholars' understanding of conifer phylogeny improved greatly following the publication of Florin's (1951) landmark study on cordaitalean and conifer reproductive structures. It was Florin's work that allowed scholars to recognize the Voltziales as transitional between the cordaites and living conifers. Since then, evolutionary relationships among fossil and living conifers have been based primarily on the structure and organization of the ovulate cones. With the exception of a few families, all living conifer families appeared during the Triassic, becoming diverse and widespread mostly during the Late Cretaceous and Tertiary.

Cycadophyta

The cycadophytes include the true cycads and the extinct bennettitaleans, both of which superficially resemble palms. The cycad fossil record extends back to the Carboniferous, and it is believed that they originated from the medullosan group of seed ferns (Stewart 1983). In the past cycads were distributed worldwide, reaching maximum diversity and distribution during the Mesozoic. Today only about 185 species remain, with restricted, disjunct distributions. Living cycads possess two growth forms; those such as *Zamia* are less than one meter in height and possess thick round stems, whereas others, such as *Macrozamia*, reach heights of 18 meters and resemble tree ferns and palms. The leaves, which are made up of individual leaflets arranged on a central stalk like a feather, are unique to this group and distinguish the cycads from all other gymnosperms. The ovulate and pollen-bearing organs are borne on separate plants, on reduced modified leaves that are aggregated into cones.

Throughout the Mesozoic the bennettitaleans were distributed worldwide. Those such as *Cycadeoidea* were unbranched, less than one meter tall, and possessed thick, short, rounded stems, while others such as *Williamsonia* were up to two meters in height and possessed slender, branched stems. Vegetatively and anatomically, the bennettitaleans closely resemble the cycads, but differences in characters of the stomata (openings in leaf surfaces) and reproductive organs facilitate separation of these two groups. The reproductive structures of bennettitaleans have been referred to as being "flowerlike," consisting of cones embedded in the trunk among the leaf bases. These cones produced both pollen and seeds, and it is this feature that appears to unite the bennettitaleans with the gnetales and angiosperms (Doyle and Donoghue 1986; Crane 1988).

Ginkgophyta

The fossil record indicates that the ginkgophyte lineage first appeared during the Triassic and attained prominence and maximum diversity throughout the world by Jurassic time. However, by the end of the Cretaceous, all genera, except for *Ginkgo* became extinct. *Ginkgo* remained widely distributed throughout the Northern Hemisphere during the Cretaceous and Early Tertiary, but as global climate cooled during the later part of the Tertiary, distribution of the genus became extremely restricted. Today only one species, *Ginkgo biloba,* remains. Features that distinguish

Ginkgo from other seed-bearing plants include fan-shaped deciduous leaves that have open and dichotomous (equally branching) venation, long and short shoots, and separate male and female trees. The reproductive structures show similarities with the cycads, and wood anatomy resembles that seen in the coniferophytes. However, the affinity of this group with a Paleozoic progenitor remains speculative.

Gnetophyta

The gnetophytes are a small group of odd plants divided into three extant (present-day) genera that at first glance seem to be unrelated. Features common to *Gnetum, Ephedra,* and *Welwitschia* include compound reproductive structures, vessel elements (specialized structures) in the xylem (transport vessels), and reduced megagametophytes. Affinities of the gnetophytes are uncertain, but recent cladistic analyses indicate that they share a number of features with the bennettitaleans, angiosperms, and another enigmatic gymnosperm, *Pentoxylon* (Crane 1985a, 1985b; Doyle and Donoghue 1986). Gnetophyte fossils are rare, and, at present, there are more questions than answers concerning the ancestry and phylogeny of the group. Nevertheless, gnetalean fossils are known as far back as the Triassic, indicating that the group was distributed much more widely in the past and occupied a diverse range of habitats.

Gymnosperms of Unknown Affinity

Gigantopteridales

Gigantopterid fossils are an extinct group of plants known only from Permian age deposits from North America and southeast and western Asia. The most common gigantopterid fossils are impressions of large leaves, impressions that show dichotomous or pinnate venation patterns with higher-order veins that form a reticulate (netlike) pattern. Reproductive organs are rare but support the notion that the gigantopterids are an obscure group of seed ferns (Li and Yao 1983).

Pentoxylales

The Pentoxylales are known from the Jurassic and Cretaceous of Australia, India, and New Zealand. Anatomically preserved stems of *Pentoxylon* are distinct, revealing five to six triangular vascular segments of pycnoxylic wood enclosed within thin-walled ground tissue (general undifferentiated cells). The stem anatomy indicates that these plants were probably small trees or shrubs, with long, strap-shaped leaves up to 20 centimeters in length and borne on short shoots, which in turn were attached to long shoots. The pollen-bearing organs are arranged in a ring and resemble the pattern in the Bennettitaleans, while the pollen resembles that of the cycads, *Ginkgo,* and some pteridosperms. The seed-bearing organs sometimes have been referred to as flowers or fruits and show similarities to the Bennettitaleans in some features, while the wood is clearly coniferous. Cladistic analyses (Crane 1985a, 1985b; Doyle and Donoghue 1986) indicate that this group is related most closely to the gnetophytes, bennettitaleans, and angiosperms, but affinity to any one of these groups is not particularly strong.

Vojnovskyales

Representatives of this enigmatic group of gymnosperms first were described from the Lower Permian Pechora Basin in Russia. Other specimens since have been described from North America, Argentina, and Africa. The type species (the fossil specimen used to define the group), *Vojnovskaya paradoxa,* is represented by a compression fossil of a branch bearing fan-shaped leaves with parallel veins and fertile organs consisting of branches or cones that are thought to have contained both ovules and pollen-producing organs. The Vojnovskyales are a poorly understood group of plants with proposed affinities to the Cordaitales and angiosperms.

Czekanowskiales

The best-known genus of the Czekanowskiales, *Czekanowskia,* was a prominent component of the Mesozoic forests throughout the Northern Hemisphere. The genus is characterized by persistent leaves that are borne on short shoots surrounded by scale leaves and that superficially resemble those of *Ginkgo.* Details on the classification, history, distribution, and stratigraphic significance of *Czekanowskia* can be found in Samylina and Kiritchkova (1991). The ovulate structure, *Leptostrobus,* has been allied with *Czekanowskia* and consists of an axis bearing spirally-arranged capsules consisting of two valves within which ovules are borne. Although the Czekanowskiales have been allied with the ginkgophytes, seed ferns, and angiosperms, the position of this small group of plants remains poorly understood.

BEN A. LEPAGE

See also Angiosperms; Coniferophytes; Cycads; Ginkgos; Gnetophytes; Progymnosperms; Seed Ferns

Works Cited

Bateman, R.M., and W.A. DiMichele. 1994. Heterospory: The most iterative key innovation in the evolutionary history of the plant kingdom. *Biological Review* 69:345–417.

Beck, C.B. (ed.). 1988. *Origin and Evolution of Gymnosperms.* New York: Columbia University Press.

Beck, C.B., and D.C. Wight. 1988. Progymnosperms. *In* C.B. Beck (ed.), *Origin and Evolution of Gymnosperms.* New York: Columbia University Press.

Crane, P.R. 1985a. Phylogenetic relationships in seed plants. *Cladistics* 1:329–48.

———. 1985b. Phylogenetic analysis of seed plants and the origin of angiosperms. *Annals of the Missouri Botanical Garden* 72:716–93.

———. 1988. Major clades and relationships in the "higher" gymnosperms. *In* C.B. Beck (ed.), *Origin and Evolution of Gymnosperms.* New York: Columbia University Press.

Doyle, J.A., and M.J. Donoghue. 1986. Seed plant phylogeny and the origin of angiosperms: An experimental cladistic approach. *Botanical Review* 52:321–431.

Florin, R. 1951. Evolution in cordaites and conifers. *Acta Horti Bergiani* 15:285–388.

Li, X., and Z. Yao. 1983. Fructifications of gigantopterids from South China. *Palaeontographica* 185B:11–26.

Meyen, S.V. 1984. Basic features of gymnosperm systematics and phylogeny as evidenced by the fossil record. *Botanical Review* 50:1–112.

Pettitt, J.M. 1970. Heterospory and the origin of the seed habit. *Biological Review* 45:401–15.

Pettitt, J.M., and C.B. Beck. 1968. *Archaeosperma arnoldii*—a cupulate seed from the Upper Devonian of North America. *Contributions from the Museum of Paleontology, University of Michigan* 22:139–54.

Rothwell, G.W. 1972. Evidence of pollen tubes in Paleozoic pteridosperms. *Science* 175:772–74.

———. 1977. Evidence for a pollination-drop mechanism in Paleozoic pteridosperms. *Science* 198:1251–52.

———. 1982. New interpretations of the earliest conifers. *Review of Palaeobotany and Palynology* 37:7–28.

Rothwell, G.W., and S.E. Scheckler. 1988. Biology of ancestral gymnosperms. *In* C.B. Beck (ed.), *Origin and Evolution of Gymnosperms*. New York: Columbia University Press.

Rothwell, G.W., S.E. Scheckler, and W.H. Gillespie. 1989. *Elkinsia* gen. nov., a cupulate Devonian gymnosperm with cupulate organs. *Botanical Gazette* 150:170–89.

Samylina, V.A., and A.I. Kiritchkova. 1991. *Rod Czekanowskia: Sistematika, istoriia, rasprostranenie, znachenie dlia stratigrafii.* Leningrad: Leningradskoe otd-nie.

Stewart, W.N., and G.W. Rothwell. 1983. *Paleobotany and the Evolution of Plants*. Cambridge and New York: Cambridge University Press; 2nd ed., 1993.

———. 1993. *Paleobotany and the Evolution of Plants*. 2nd ed., Cambridge and New York: Cambridge University Press.

Taylor, T.N., and E.L. Taylor. 1993. *The Biology and Evolution of Fossil Plants*. Englewood, New Jersey: Prentice-Hall.

Zimmermann, W. 1952. Main results of the "telome theory." *Palaeobotanist* 1:456–70.

Further Reading

Beck, C.B. (ed.). 1988. *Origin and Evolution of Gymnosperms*. New York: Columbia University Press.

Stewart, W.N., and G.W. Rothwell. 1983. *Paleobotany and the Evolution of Plants*. Cambridge and New York: Cambridge University Press; 2nd ed., 1993.

Taylor, T.N., and E.L. Taylor. 1993. *The Biology and Evolution of Fossil Plants*. Englewood, New Jersey: Prentice-Hall.

H

HAECKEL, ERNST HEINRICH

German, 1834–1919

Ernst Haeckel was born in Potsdam, Germany, on 16 February 1834. At an early age, he showed an avid interest in biology, especially botany. In 1849, while still a high school student at Merseburg, he received lessons from M. Schleiden, a botanist at Universität Jena. But in order to please his father, Haeckel entered Universität Berlin in 1852, to study medicine, later moving to Würzburg. It is precisely this conflict of interests in his early academic years that led the young Haeckel to become a student of such renowned German researchers as Koelliker, Leydig, and Virchow, who introduced him to the fascinating world of histology (study of minute structures) and embryology. In April 1856, Haeckel moved back to Universität Berlin, where he continued his medical career under the guidance of Johannes Müller. Müller and Koelliker instilled in Haeckel a strong passion for zoology. In 1859 he abandoned his medical career and traveled to Italy on a collecting trip that became the starting point of a highly productive career. This career continued until shortly before his death, which occurred at age 85, at Jena, on August 9, 1919.

Haeckel's contributions include more than 56 scientific papers and books, as well as many conferences and meetings, on diverse aspects of evolution and morphology (shape and structure), and later in his career, on subjects beyond biology, such as anthropology and theology. He worked on the systematics (classification) of a variety of invertebrate taxa (groups; singular, taxon) such as poriferans (sponges) and cnidarians (corals and more specifically jellyfish). But it is his first work on the Radiolaria (marine protozoans with silicon-based external skeletons) that earned him a zoology professorship at Universität Jena. There he continued his research for more than 47 years, with only brief interruptions to travel to various parts of the world. In this first work, Haeckel used a new geometric method to classify radiolarians that was so practical that scholars still were using it during the first half of the twentieth century. In addition to the numerous new taxa he described (e.g., more than 144 radiolarians in his first work), Haeckel also coined a great variety of scientific terms, some of them still in use in biology, such as phylogeny (genetic history), ontogeny (growth and development), and ecology. After reading Darwin's *Origin of Species* in 1860, Haeckel became one of the most devoted and enthusiastic promoters of this theory and became known as the "apostle of Darwinism in Germany." Interestingly, Haeckel was influenced strongly by the idealistic philosophy of Hegel and Goethe. As a result, Haeckel believed more in evolution as the product of an organism's internal drive for self-perfection, characteristic of its own species, rather than the existence of a mechanism outside the organism's control, such as natural selection. Thus, in some respects, his ideas were not so far from those of Lamarck.

The notion that morphology was the ultimate way to understand the evolution of the organism, and that therefore, embryology (study of an organism before birth) was the key to understanding morphology, was accepted widely during the last part of the nineteenth century. The basis of these ideas can be traced back to the works of von Baer, in the early nineteenth century. Haeckel, like von Baer before him, studied embryonic development in search of the most intimate secrets of the morphology of organisms. According to Haeckel, development and evolution were linked inextricably, and this became the subject of his most influential idea, known as the "Gastræa Theory." This idea, which represents a brilliant synthesis of von Baer's own "law of recapitulation," states that all multicellular organisms were derived from a single common ancestor. Its morphology was equivalent to the morphology of one of the animal's earliest developmental stages: the blastula. This universal archetype represented an ancient Metazoan ancestor, called Gastræa. Adult ancestors, therefore, could be found in the embryological stages of their descendants, and as more and more species evolved, representatives of the evolutionary stages that led to the species were added in order to the developmental stages of embryonic development. (At one stage in humans, for instance, the embryo has gills.) This idea frequently is expressed as "ontogeny recapitulates phylogeny." Haeckel's theory was based on the assumption that a species lineage could be compared with the development of a single individual, thus phylogeny could be studied by looking at ontogeny. Consequently, several authors have interpreted Haeckel's work simply as an extension of von Baer's work. Nevertheless, Haeckel considered himself an opponent of von Baer's ideas.

The Gastræa Theory, as well as the concept of recapitulation, were discredited at the beginning of this century. Experimental research has demonstrated that a direct correspondence between the ontogeny and the phylogeny of the organisms does not exist. However, even though Haeckel's speculative ideas and lack of experimental testing have reduced notably the scientific validity of his work, that work did stimulate further experimental research in embryology and on its relationship with phylogeny.

ROBERTO CIPRIANI

Biography

Born in Potsdam, Prussia, 16 February 1834. Received Doctorate of Medicine, University of Berlin, 1857; private teacher in anatomy, School of Medicine, University of Jena, 1861; extraordinary professor of zoology, University of Jena, 1862; awarded Golden Corthenius Medal, German Leopoldine Academy of Naturalists, 1864; Ph.D., University of Jena, 1865; Prorector Magnificus, University of Jena, 1876; Ph.D., University of Edinburgh, 1884; Golden Swammerdan Medal, 1890; Golden Linnean Medal, Linnean Society of London, 1894; Darwin Medal, Royal Society, 1899; Ph.D., University of Upscale, 1907; Ph.D., Universität Genf, 1909. Died in Jena, Germany, 9 August 1919.

Major Publications

1862. *Die Radiolarien (Rhizopoda radiaria):* Eine Monographie. Part 1, Text 2. Berlin: Reimer.

1866. *Generelle Morphologie der Organismen. 1, Allgemeine Anatomie der Organismen; 2, Allgemeine Entwickelungsgeschichte der Organismen.* Berlin: Reimer.

1874a. *Anthropogenie oder Entwickelungsgeschichte des Menschen: Gemeinverständliche wissenschaftliche Vorträge über die Grundzüge der menschlichen Keimes- und Stammesgeschichte.* Leipzig: Engelmann.

1874b. Die Gastraeatheorie, die phylogenetische Classification des Thierreichs und die Homologie der Keimblätter. *Jenaische Zeitschrift Naturwissenschaften* 8:1–55.

1875. Die Gastrea und die Eifurchung der Thiere. *Jenaische Zeitschrift Naturwissenschaften* 9:402–508.

1894. *Systematische Phylogenie: Entwurf eines natürlichen Systems der Organismen aufgrund ihrer Stammesgeschichte. Vol. 1, Teil: Systematische Phylogenie der Protisten und Pflanzen.* Berlin: Reimer.

1895. *Systematische Phylogenie: Entwurf eines natürlichen Systems der Organismen aufgrund ihrer Stammesgeschichte. Vol. 3, Teil: Systematische Phylogenie der Wirbelthiere (Vertebraten).* Berlin: Reimer.

1896. *Systematische Phylogenie: Entwurf eines natürlichen Systems der Organismen aufgrund ihrer Stammesgeschichte. Vol. 2, Teil: Systematische Phylogenie der Wirbellosen Thiere (Invertebraten).* Berlin: Reimer.

1899. *Kunstformen der Natur.* Leipzig and Vienna: Verlag des Bibliographischen Instituts; as *Art Forms in Nature,* New York: Dover, 1974.

1899. *Die Welträthsel.* Gemeinverständliche Studien über monistische Philosophie. Bonn: Strauss; as *The Riddle of the Universe at the Close of the Nineteenth Century,* New York and London: Harper, 1900.

1923. *The Story of the Development of a Youth: Letters to His Parents 1852–1856.* G. Barry Gifford (trans.). New York and London: Harper, 1923.

Further Reading

Bölsche, W. 1900. *Ernst Haeckel: Ein Lebensbild.* Dresden: Reissner; as *Haeckel, His Life and Work,* London: Unwin; Philadelphia: Jacobs, 1906.

Bowler, P.J. 1984. *Evolution: The History of an Idea.* Berkeley: University of California Press; rev. ed., 1989.

Dose, K. 1981. Ernst Haeckel's concept of an evolutionary origin of life. *Biosystems* 13 (4):253–58.

Hall, B.K. 1992. *Evolutionary Developmental Biology.* London and New York: Chapman and Hall.

Milner, R. 1990. *The Encyclopedia of Evolution.* New York: Facts on File.

Richards, R.J. 1992. *The Meaning of Evolution: The Morphological Construction and Ideological Reconstruction of Darwin's Theory.* Chicago: University of Chicago Press.

HALSTEAD, LAMBERT BEVERLY

English, 1933–91

Beverly Halstead was born 13 June 1933 at Pendleton, Lancashire, England, into comfortable material circumstances, but difficult social ones. His father was an artist; his mother (née Elizabeth Waring) was a militant Communist and atheist in a small-town environment where both beliefs were resented. Halstead's upbringing both stimulated his intellect and isolated him from his peers, an isolation he took long to conquer. Early in Halstead's childhood, his mother divorced his father, moved to Eastbourne (Sussex), and married another fervent Communist, Maurice Tarlo. Halstead was persuaded to adopt his stepfather's name, his first scientific papers being published as "L.B. Tarlo." Later, however, his dislike of his stepfather caused him to shed that name; some papers were published as "L.B. Halstead Tarlo," but after that he signed himself as "Beverly Halstead."

Before gaining a Bachelor of Science with Honors in Geology from the University of Sheffield (1955), Halstead formed a strong friendship with the future sedimentologist John R.L. Allen. They began joint studies of the Old Red Sandstone (Devonian) strata of the Welsh borderland. Halstead was especially interested in the Devonian fishes, an interest that increased when his Communist affiliations enabled him to travel in Poland and visit its classic fossil localities. He undertook extensive researches on the Polish Devonian fishes, culminating in two monographs (1964, 1965).

However, when Halstead first began doctoral studies at the University of London, he concentrated upon fossil marine reptiles (pliosaurs). Discovering a little-used regulation that allowed him to submit published papers instead of a thesis, he did so and, even before gaining his doctorate (1959), resumed work on the ancient fishes. This continued under support of a Senior Research Fellowship at the British Museum (Natural History). In particular, Halstead examined the dermal armor of the ostracoderms (ancient jawless fishes) and its relation to the origin of teeth. A Nuffield Research Fellowship, held jointly at the University of Oxford and Royal Dental Hospital (1961–63), allowed him to expand this study, enabling him to visit collections in Moscow and Estonia. His work on scales and teeth led to many papers, culminating in his book *Vertebrate Hard Tissues* (1974).

In 1963, Halstead secured a joint appointment in zoology and geology at the University of Reading, which he was to hold for 27 years. He was an excellent lecturer to both students and public; several of his students—among them Susan Turner, David Unwin, and T. Lingham-Soliar—went on to distinguished careers in vertebrate paleontology. Halstead himself was developing a fascination with Africa. He visited Nigeria in 1967, Tunisia in 1968, and Rhodesia and South Africa in 1969. (He was expelled from the latter country because of what were considered transgressions of its apartheid laws.) During three years' leave-of-absence from Reading, Halstead served temporarily as chair of the Biological Sciences Department at the University of Ile-Ife, Nigeria (1971–74), a highly productive time during which he married the biological artist Jennifer Middleton. She went on to illustrate or coauthor a number of books with Halstead, notably *Bare Bones* (1972) and a series of fictional lives of extinct animals for children (e.g., *Terrible Claw* 1983). A first expedition to the Sokoto region of northwestern Nigeria (1974) brought spectacular discoveries of extinct crocodiles and whales, but a subsequent expedition (1977) was marred by political difficulties. Halstead's fourth return to Nigeria (1983) brought a frightening spell of imprisonment that ended his enchantment with Africa.

By this time, Halstead's flirtation with Communism, strained early on by the Soviet invasion of Hungary in 1956, had ended altogether. However, he remained passionate in all his involvements, whether scientific, academic, or social—a quality that, although gaining him fame and affection among many, provoked jealousy and dislike in certain quarters. Not until his last years, when he served as president of the Geologists' Association and as president of the Geological Section of the British Association for the Advancement of Science, did Halstead attain a measure of acceptance. By then, there had been a stormy severance from Reading University, and he was attached instead to Imperial College, London.

The diversity of Halstead's concerns virtually defies characterization. They included head-on confrontations with Creationists, cladists, and the theories of Imanishi and Karl Popper; writings on the Piltdown skull and the Loch Ness Monster; accounts of the behavior of West African mammals; the description of what he considered (wrongly) to be the earliest whale; a defense of the British Museum (Natural History) against research-budget cuts; a much-publicized (and justified) dismissal of the idea of cold nuclear fusion in a test-tube; early recognition of the threat to humanity represented by the AIDS virus; and the advocation of new methods for awarding doctoral degrees. While editing *Modern Geology* (from 1983), he published an article on "Geoscience and the feasibility of cheating on test ban treaties," which provoked a major political controversy.

Halstead was especially adept at interesting the public—children, in particular—in science, through lectures, newspaper articles, and such popular books as *The Pattern of Vertebrate Evolution* (1968), *The Evolution of the Mammals* (1978), and *The Search for the Past* (1982). In consequence, he became one of the best-known British scientists, while his willingness to express colorful opinions made him a darling of the media.

Nonetheless, Beverly Halstead never ceased to be a serious scientist. He was a major contributor to such important compilative works as *The Fossil Record* (1967, 1993), *The Encyclopaedia of Prehistoric Life* (1979), and the *Handbuch der Paläoherpetologie* (1985). A visit to China (1979) led to the discovery not only of the first galeaspid fishes (a rare ostracoderm) but also of the remarkable mineralized replica of the brain, nerves, blood vessels, and inner ear of a Devonian fish. His last writings included a study of palaeopathology and thoughtful critiques of two currently fashionable theories—the concept of punctuated equilibria in evolution and of a cataclysmic extinction of the dinosaurs. Beverly Halstead's death in a car accident near Bath, on 30 April 1991, prematurely ended a career characterized by high energy, versatility, and humanity.

WILLIAM A.S. SARJEANT

Biography

Born in Pendleton, Lancashire, 13 June 1933. Received B.Sc., University of Sheffield, 1955; Ph.D., University of London, 1959. Recipient, Senior Research Fellowship, British Museum (Natural History), 1958–61; Nuffield Research Fellowship, University of Oxford and Royal Dental Hospital, 1961–63; assistant lecturer, lecturer, and reader, University of Reading, 1963–1991; chair, Biological Sciences Department, University of Ile-Ife, Nigeria, 1971–74; professor, Imperial College, London, 1990–1991. President, Geologists' Association; president, Geological Section of the British Association for the Advancement of Science, 1990. Made scientific visits to Eastern Europe, China, North America, and especially Africa, where he led expeditions to Sokoto (Nigeria); writings included studies of Paleozoic fishes and the origin of bones and teeth, the evolution and swimming behavior of pliosaurs, the processes of evolution and extinction; prominent popularizer of paleontology through books and public lectures. Died near Bath, 30 April 1991.

Major Publications

1964–65. Psammosteiformes (Agnatha): A review with descriptions of new material from the Lower Devonian of Poland. *Palaeontologia Polonica* 13:1–133; 14:1–168.

1972. With J. Middleton. *Bare Bones: An Exploration in Art and Science.* Edinburgh: Oliver and Boyd.

1973. Hunting pre-historic reptiles in Nigeria. *Nigerian Field* 38:4–14.

1974. *Vertebrate Hard Tissues.* London and New York: Wykeham.

1975. *The Evolution and Ecology of the Dinosaurs.* Giovanni Caselli (illus.). London: Lowe; as *The World of Dinosaurs*, New York: Derrydale.

1978. *The Evolution of Mammals.* Sergio (illus.). London: Lowe.

1982. *The Search for the Past.* Garden City, New York: Doubleday; as *Hunting the Past*, London: Hamilton.

Further Reading

Dietz, L.F., and W.A.S. Sarjeant. 1993. L.B. Halstead: A bibliography of his published writings. *Modern Geology* 18 (1) [Halstead Memorial Volume]:61–81; also published in W.A.S. Sarjeant (ed.), *Vertebrate Fossils and the Evolution of Scientific Concepts: Writings in Tribute to Beverly Halstead, by Some of His Many Friends.* Amsterdam: Gordon and Breach, 1995.

Janvier, P., and A. Blieck. 1993. L.B. Halstead and the heterostracan controversy. *Modern Geology* 18 (1) [Halstead Memorial Volume]:89–105; also published in W.A.S. Sarjeant (ed.), *Vertebrate Fossils and the Evolution of Scientific Concepts: Writings in Tribute to Beverly Halstead, by Some of His Many Friends.* Amsterdam: Gordon and Breach, 1995.

Kielan-Jaworowska, S. 1993. Remembrance of L. Beverly Halstead in Poland. *Modern Geology* 18 (1) [Halstead Memorial Volume]:83–87; also published in W.A.S. Sarjeant (ed.), *Vertebrate Fossils and the Evolution of Scientific Concepts: Writings in Tribute to Beverly Halstead, by Some of His Many Friends.* Amsterdam: Gordon and Breach, 1995.

Sarjeant, W.A.S. 1993. Lambert Beverly Halstead (1933–1991): His life, his discoveries and his controversies. *Modern Geology* 18 (1) [Halstead Memorial Volume]:5–59; also published in W.A.S. Sarjeant (ed.), *Vertebrate Fossils and the Evolution of Scientific Concepts: Writings in Tribute to Beverly Halstead, by Some of His Many Friends.* Amsterdam: Gordon and Breach, 1995.

HEARING AND POSITIONAL SENSE

All living vertebrates have an "inner ear" that senses head position and movements. The inner ear usually also serves an important auditory role, but probably did not do so in the earliest vertebrates. These vertebrates would have had some capacity to detect low frequency vibrations generated when nearby moving objects displace water (sometimes called "near-field sound"), but very little capacity to detect propagated pressure waves (sometimes called "far-field sound" or "conventional sound"). Many vertebrates have additional specializations for sound reception: a sound-gathering "outer ear" and a "middle ear" that converts pressure fluctuations of far-field sound into vibratory displacements of ear ossicles. These small bones amplify the force of the original far-field sound and transmit their vibrations to the fluid-filled inner ear.

Receptors in the inner ear are exquisitely sensitive to displacement but insensitive to pressure as such. The receptors in the inner ear consist of clusters of "hair cells"; hair cells consist of tiny processes ("hairs") that project into the interior of a membranous labyrinth. This set of interconnected tubes and sacs is filled with watery liquid (endolymph). When a stimulus bends the hairs, whether sound or head movement, the movement activates the hair cells to signal neurons of the eighth cranial nerve as to the amount and direction of bending. The membranous labyrinth is enclosed within a skeletal labyrinth, part of a protective otic capsule that is composed of cartilage and (usually) bone.

In the primitive chordate ancestor of the vertebrates, the precursor of the membranous labyrinth was probably an area on the surface of the head with hair cells that sensed movements of the animal in relation to the surrounding water. (Other similar areas sensed movements of the water itself; these became the receptors of the lateral line system.) This area then sank into the skin (inpocketed) to form a hollow sac, the primitive membranous labyrinth, which became enclosed in a skeletal capsule. These changes allowed the animal to sense movements of the head without reference to the aquatic environment. Inertia of the liquid within the labyrinth caused the liquid to lag as the head turned, activating certain hair cells; this ability was enhanced by "pinching off" first one, then two, then three semicircular ducts (enclosed within skeletal semicircular canals) in planes at right angles to one another. The labyrinth generated sand grains (later replaced by calcium carbonate crystals, called "otoliths") that adhered to other hair cells; the heavy crystals descended or lagged as the head moved, allowing the animal to sense gravity and acceleration. The ability of hair cells to respond to vibration made hearing possible. As animals evolved, this capacity was enhanced in various ways.

Agnathan (Jawless) Fishes

The living jawless fishes have a cartilaginous otic capsule enclosing a single semicircular canal (hagfishes) or two canals (lampreys), plus a simple lower chamber. In heterostracan ostracoderms (ancient armored agnathans), the otic capsule also was composed of cartilage and did not fossilize, but impressions on the underside of the bony skull roof show that two vertical semicircular canals were present. There was probably no horizontal canal. Galeaspid and osteostracan ostracoderms, which had a layer of bone lining the cavities of their cartilaginous labyrinth, definitely had two vertical canals and no horizontal canal. In addition, some cephalaspid ostracoderms had remarkable tubular extensions from their bony labyrinth. These extensions led to three large chambers on the upper side of the head, roofed by many small bone plates; perhaps these were devices to monitor vibration or other mechanical forces (Hanken and Hall 1993).

Gnathostome (Jawed) Fishes

All gnathostomes, even the earliest known, have three semicircular canals. Some chondrichthyan fishes (sharks and their relatives) are unique among living vertebrates in retaining throughout life a tubular connection between the membranous labyrinth and the surrounding sea water; these animals pick up sand grains to serve as otoliths. Gnathostomes generally have three patches of hair cells that are associated with otoliths. (They are found in subdivisions of the membranous labyrinth called the sacculus, utriculus, and lagena). In acanthodians ("spiny sharks") and osteichthyans (bony

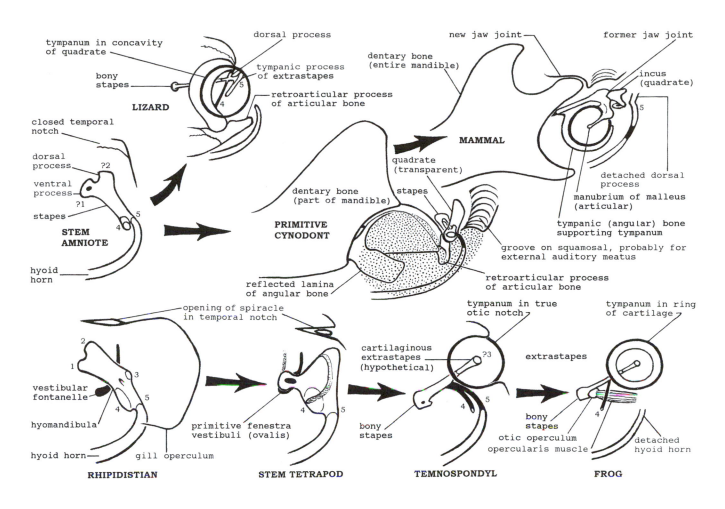

Figure 1. Evolution of tympanic ears in amphibians, sauropsids, and synapsids. Numbers indicated processes of the rhipidistian hyomandibula. Key: *1,* ventral; *2,* dorsal; *3,* opercular; *4,* quadrate; *5,* hyoid. Symbol: *stippling,* possible sound-receptive area (functional tympanum).

fishes), each of these three organs has a single large otolith, rather than numerous tiny ones. These large otoliths may show growth rings and often are uniquely shaped in different species.

Chondrichthyans do not show conspicuous specializations for hearing, yet some sharks can detect low frequency waterborne sounds over a distance of many meters. Unlike chondrichthyans, many osteichthyans have gas-filled swimbladders, and a few have lungs or gulp air. Underwater, a gas-filled chamber is set into vibration by far-field sound. Some bony fishes use this mechanism to increase auditory sensitivity, notably two major groups of teleosts, the clupeoids (e.g., herrings) and ostariophysans (e.g., catfishes). The former have extensions of the swimbladder into spherical bullae of the otic capsule, and the latter have a chain of small modified ribs (weberian ossicles) that transmit vibrations from the swimbladder to the inner ear. Late Mesozoic clupeomorphs and Early Tertiary ostariophysans already had these specializations (L. Grande, personal communication).

Some scholars have hypothesized that certain lobe-finned Paleozoic fishes, the rhipidistian crossopterygians, had an air-filled pocket in their spiracular passage (reduced first gill opening) and

that waterborne sound waves set up vibrations that were transmitted to the inner ear by the adjacent hyomandibula. This large jaw-supporting strut is attached to the otic capsule (Thomson 1966) (Figure 1). Their tetrapod (four-limbed) descendants may have modified this mechanism to evolve a middle ear capable of receiving airborne sound efficiently. The crossopterygian hyomandibula is the homolog of the sound-transmitting stapes of tetrapods. The hyomandibula has five processes, or attachments, all of which are thought to have persisted (in modified form) in early tetrapods (Romer 1941): dorsal and ventral processes to articulate with the otic capsule, an opercular process to support a thin bone plate in the gill cover (operculum), a hyoid process to support the lower part of the hyoid arch skeleton, and a quadrate process to articulate with the posterior portion of the palatoquadrate (original gnathostome upper jaw). The rhipidistian hyomandibula resembles the stapes of ancient amniotes. (Amniotes are tetrapods that lay shelled eggs, or did so at one stage of their history; living ones are the reptiles, birds, and mammals.) This stapes, long thought to retain the primitive morphology for tetrapods, is a sturdy structure with dorsal and ventral processes as well as strong hyoid and quadrate attachments. It has no structure that corresponds to the bony opercular process, but this was inferred to have been present in life as a cartilaginous tympanic process running to an eardrum derived from the upper part of the gill cover. However, this reasoning no longer seems secure, in part because the recently described stapes of the earliest known tetrapods bears less resemblance to the hyomandibula than does that of early amniotes.

The Tympanic Ear

Living terrestrial vertebrates that are most sensitive to airborne sound have what often is called a "tympanic ear" or "impedance-matching ear"; it is characterized by a thin tympanic membrane (eardrum or tympanum), an air-filled middle ear cavity, and a delicate conducting mechanism consisting of a single skeletal structure (stapes or columella) or, in the care of mammals, three small bones (middle ear ossicles: malleus, incus, and stapes). Pressure oscillations of far-field sound cause displacements of the light tympanum, and the sound energy is concentrated from the eardrum to the much smaller base (footplate) of the stapes. Some additional amplification is generally provided by the conducting apparatus through a leverage mechanism. To allow vibrations of the stapes to reach the inner ear efficiently, its footplate occupies an opening in the wall of the otic capsule, the fenestra vestibuli (commonly termed fenestra ovalis or oval window, although it is not always oval). To allow the liquids of the inner ear to move there is a pressure release mechanism, usually a fenestra rotunda (round window) where perilymph (liquid external to the membranous labyrinth) can cause a membrane to bulge outward toward the middle ear cavity when the stapes moves inward.

When and how a middle ear of this nature evolved, and whether or not this occurred more than once, are major issues. For many years it was generally thought that the early tetrapod, from which all surviving tetrapods descended, already had a tympanic ear, with a tympanic membrane spanning an embayment of the posterior margin of the skull (otic notch) between the squamosal and tabular bones. The hyomandibula was thought to have essentially lost its jaw-supporting function, having been transformed into a stapes with a cartilaginous tympanic process that extended to the eardrum. It was assumed that all tympanic ears of extant vertebrates are derived from this original version, all eardrums being homologous. The fenestra vestibuli was believed to have formed by thinning and eventual disappearance of the part of the otic capsule subjacent to the ventral process of the hyomandibula (now the base or footplate of the stapes). Now, for a number of reasons, it is believed widely that tympanic ears evolved independently at least three times (in the ancestors of frogs, living reptiles plus birds, and mammals), and that the stapedial tympanic process of living amphibians is not homologous with that of reptiles and birds. Also, the fenestra vestibuli may have originated differently than had been supposed (Figure 2).

The Earliest Tetrapods

New information on Devonian tetrapods suggests that they were entirely aquatic, retaining internal gills but no longer having large bony plates in their gill cover. The notch in the posterior skull margin may have contained an open spiracle rather than an eardrum; if so, the structure is better termed a temporal notch than an otic notch. The stapes of the most primitive known tetrapod, *Acanthostega,* is somewhat smaller than the rhipidistian hyomandibula and is very different in shape; it has a single proximal process in place of dorsal and ventral ones (perhaps formed by their fusion), and is platelike distally (Clack 1989) (Figure 1). This stapes probably continued to provide a major brace between the braincase and upper jaw and seems ill-suited to aerial sound reception. It is termed a "stapes" rather than a "hyomandibula" only because *Acanthostega* is a tetrapod. Its distal margin is unfinished, indicating that it was continued in cartilage, and any additional processes that were present were also cartilaginous. A similar stapes is known in three other very primitive tetrapods, which may indicate that it represents the configuration of the original tetrapod stapes. If so, the dorsal process of the stapes found in amniotes is probably a new development, not homologous with the dorsal process of the hyomandibula.

The base of the stapes of *Acanthostega* occupies a large fenestra vestibuli that, at least in part, appears to correspond to the lower portion of the vestibular fontanelle of crossopterygians (an opening between the otic capsule and the occipital region, i.e., the rear of the skull). Thus, the hyomandibula, as a stapes, had come to occupy a preexistent aperture (Clack 1994, 1997), perhaps in conjunction with a new opening between the anterior and posterior ossification centers (prootic and opisthotic bones) of the otic capsule, where cartilage had formerly existed. It is not clear whether the latter opening had been fully established in *Acanthostega,* but in advanced tetrapods it forms the entire fenestra vestibuli.

True Amphibians and Early Tetrapods of Uncertain Affinities

There is little doubt that a tympanic ear was present in typical Paleozoic temnospondyls, the dominant early nonamniote tetrapods. Their bony stapes is a rather slender rod projecting toward a large, rounded temporal notch (sometimes a foramen, as in *Cacops*) (Bolt and Lombard 1985) that confidently can be called "otic" (Figure 1). Only one proximal process of the stapes is present in most temnospondyls, an exception being *Trimerorhachis,* in which it is subdivided into dorsal and ventral parts. The dorsal one (probably not homologous with the dorsal process of the hyomandibula) occupies the fenestra vestibuli (Fritzsch et al. 1988). There is no temporal notch in colosteids (very primitive relatives of temnospondyls), one of which *(Greererpeton)* is known to have a stapes like that of *Acanthostega.*

In general, lissamphibians (living amphibians and their antecedents) are thought to be descended from a lineage of Paleozoic temnospondyls (this is disputed by Laurin and Reisz 1997). Most anurans (frogs and toads) have a well-developed tympanic ear, but some have no eardrum or middle ear cavity, and this is also true for all other surviving amphibians, the urodeles (salamanders and newts) and the caecilians (limbless burrowing forms). It seems probable that ancestral lissamphibians inherited a tympanic ear,

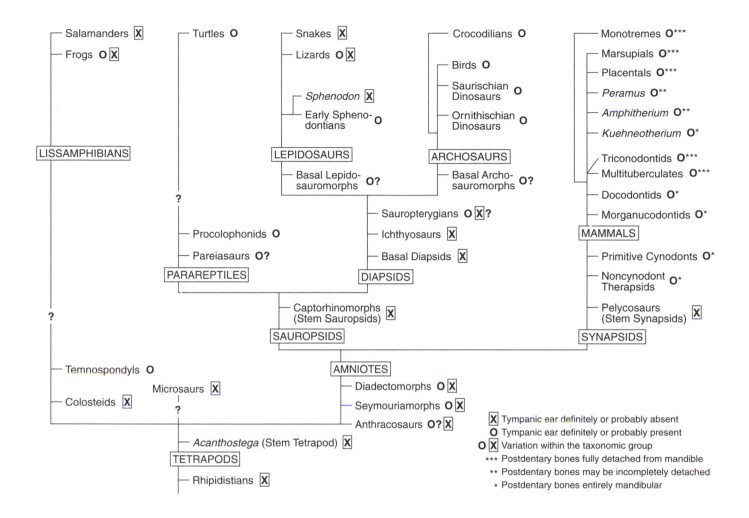

Figure 2. Caldogram of tetrapods, showing presence and absence of a tympanic ear. A true impedance-matching middle ear probably originated independently at least three times, in amphibians, sauropsids, and mammals. This structure also was lost independently in several lineages. Illustration by Catherine P. Sexton.

but this was lost in several groups. A few anurans have a stapes similar to that of *Trimerorhachis*. In mature anurans, the rear of the fenestra vestibuli embraces a cartilage plate with a small opercularis muscle running from it to the shoulder girdle (Figure 1). This "opercularis system" may serve to attenuate sound transmission when the animal generates loud mating calls; it also may serve to receive ground vibrations and airborne sounds of very low frequencies, while the eardrum and stapes serve primarily for receiving mating calls of higher pitch. Salamanders have an opercularis system but caecilians do not, and in both groups the stapes connects to the squamosal or quadrate bone of the skull. Whether any Paleozoic temnospondyls had this unique system is uncertain.

Some other early tetrapods, usually considered closer to the amniotes than to the true amphibians (various groups called anthracosaurs, seymouriamorphs, and diadectomorphs) also appear to have had tympanic ears. Although their stapes is poorly known, these animals have a large temporal notch similar to that of temnospondyls. In *Diadectes* it is especially large and is spanned by a thin

plate that is either an ossified tympanic membrane or an expanded, calcified tympanic process of the stapes. Not all seymouriamorphs have such a narrow notch, and the primitive anthracosaur *Pholiderpeton* has a notch, its stapes is much like that of *Acanthostega*; thus, a true tympanic ear may have evolved independently in two or more of these lineages. Also, the microsaurs (small reptilelike Paleozoic amphibians) show no hint of having had an impedance-matching ear; its stapes is massive, and it lacks a temporal notch.

Early Amniotes

Two great clades of amniotes are recognized, the sauropsids (living reptiles and birds plus all of their earlier relatives back to their last common ancestor) and the synapsids (mammals and their antecedents, the "mammal-like reptiles"). The earliest sauropsids and synapsids have neither a temporal notch nor any other evident attachment site for an eardrum. Also, their stapes is quite massive and runs directly toward a strong articulation with the quadrate bone (which forms the upper part of the jaw joint). There is a ventral process with a large footplate in the fenestra vestibuli and a dorsal process close to it. In captorhinomorphs (very primitive sauropsids) and early synapsids, there is strong evidence that a large hyoid horn (ceratohyal) was attached to the stapes. No stapedial tympanic process is preserved in any early amniote, and it seems improbable that a tympanic membrane existed (Watson 1953) (Figure 1). However, living sauropsids that lack a tympanic membrane and middle ear cavity, such as snakes, still can hear moderate-intensity airborne sound below 1,000 Hz (Hertz, or cycles per second), and the same would almost certainly have been true for ancestral amniotes, even if they did not possess a tympanic ear.

Sauropsids

Before proceeding, major groups of sauropsids must be defined: (1) All descendants of the last common ancestor of crocodiles and birds are archosaurs; this group includes dinosaurs and pterosaurs. (2) All descendants of the last common ancestor of lizards and the lizardlike *Sphenodon* are lepidosaurs; this group includes snakes and the snakelike amphisbaenians. (3) Diapsids are archosaurs and lepidosaurs plus some early relatives. Two extinct marine groups, the sauropterygians (e.g., plesiosaurs) and ichthyosaurs (superficially fishlike forms) are now thought to be highly specialized diapsids. (4) Turtles and their early relatives are also sauropsids.

Living sauropsids with tympanic ears have a tympanic membrane supported in a concave area on the posterior side of the quadrate and a slender, light stapes (Figure 1). The proximal part of the stapes is composed of bone, while the distal part (extrastapes) is cartilaginous. The extrastapes usually has a dorsal process that attaches to the skull, a slender process or ligament that connects to the quadrate, and a tympanic process that attaches to the eardrum. During embryonic development the extrastapes is continuous with the hyoid horn, but this continuity is later lost. Living sauropsids with the most refined tympanic ears and acute hearing (gecko lizards, crocodilians, and birds) communicate vocally, are able to hear frequencies up to at least 10,000 Hz, and have a relatively long auditory region of the inner ear (cochlea).

The earliest turtles, archosaurs, and lepidosaurs (all Triassic) have a conspicuous concave region in the quadrate and a slender stapes, strong evidence that all had a true tympanic ear. However, the earliest diapsids do not have these features, so the tympanic ear may have evolved independently in turtles and later diapsids. A tympanic ear modified for aquatic hearing was present in mosasaurs (giant Cretaceous marine lizards), which had an expanded, calcified extrastapes cupped in a deeply excavated quadrate that would have prevented the extrastapes from being driven inward by water pressure. Most lizards retain a tympanic ear, but no other living lepidosaurs do. Primitive sauropterygians appear to have had a tympanic ear, but some plesiosaurs may have lost it. Ichthyosaurs probably did not have a tympanic ear, and there is no evidence that their ancestors did either. Their stapes is a robust brace between the otic capsule and the quadrate.

Whereas in anurans the internal mandibular (chorda tympani) branch of the seventh cranial nerve passes below the eardrum, in sauropsids it passes above. This, along with paleontologic and other evidence, supports an independent evolutionary origin of the tympanic ears of amphibians and sauropsids. In early amniotes, it is probable that low frequency aerial sound caused tissues external to the cavity of the mouth and pharynx (gullet) to vibrate, and the hyoid horn transmitted these vibrations to the stapes. Subsequent specializations in sauropsids enhanced sensitivity and extended the frequency range upward, resulting in formation of a true tympanic membrane, a deeply excavated quadrate, and a delicate stapes with a tympanic process that was formed by modification of the hyoid attachment (corresponding to the hyoid process of the rhipidistian hyomandibula).

Like anurans, living lizards have a wide connection (eustachian opening) between the pharynx and the middle ear cavity (the primitive configuration). Archosaurs, both ancient and recent, have long tubular eustachian tubes that are enclosed within bony grooves or canals and meet at an unpaired midline passage anteriorly. They also have air-filled extensions from the middle ear cavity into adjacent bones.

In some living sauropsids the tympanum is flush with the surface of the head, but in most there is a shallow depression (an external auditory meatus), and a few lizards and birds have a tubular meatus like that of mammals. Crocodilians have a closeable meatal valve (earlids) to protect the drum when the animal is submerged.

Synapsids (Mammals and Their Antecedents)

Until fairly recently, it was conventional to call the early relatives of mammals "synapsid reptiles" or "mammal-like reptiles." Archaic ones (such as *Dimetrodon*) were classed as "pelycosaurs"; later ones were "therapsids." The latter included the "cynodonts," from which mammals arose, but did not include mammals. Current cladistic terminology is more meaningful but cumbersome; mammals are now included in the Cynodontia, Therapsida, and Synapsida. Pelycosaurs are now termed "nontherapsid synapsids," and one must speak of mammalian and nonmammalian cynodonts. For convenience, the older usage will be adhered to in the following account, except that mammals will be included in the Synapsida.

For an extensive discussion of ear evolution in synapsids, see Allin and Hopson 1992. Pelycosaurs probably did not have a tympanic middle ear but could hear low-frequency airborne sound, with transmission from hyoid horn to stapes (in part). Unlike sauropsids, direct articulation of the stapes with the quadrate persisted in all synapsid lineages, including mammals (the incus being a modified quadrate). Also, the stapes remained relatively large in all but the most advanced ones. Its dorsal process shifted distally, as in advanced sauropsids, and in mammals it and the hyoid attachment separate from the stapes during embryonic life. There is no convincing evidence for a tympanic process in any synapsid, and the quadrate is not excavated to provide support for a tympanum. On the outer side of the squamosal bone, therapsids have a depression or groove that ends behind the quadrate. Researchers usually posit that it was occupied by a large, tubular external auditory meatus that ran to an eardrum supported mainly by the squamosal and that this eardrum was reached by a cartilaginous tympanic process of the stapes. It is possible that the groove housed a jaw-opening muscle that inserted on the articular bone and that no tympanum existed behind the quadrate. If a meatus was present, it may have been a depression rather than a tube.

Nonmammalian synapsids have a mandible (lower jaw) consisting of the tooth-bearing dentary bone and several other bones, four of which are termed "postdentary": the articular, prearticular, angular, and surangular. The angular bone of some pelycosaurs and all therapsids has a thin flange (the reflected lamina), seen in no other vertebrates. On the outer side of the angular bone is a smooth depression, partially covered by the reflected lamina. Some investigators think a jaw-closing muscle wrapped around the lower border of the mandible to insert in the depression. Others think an air-filled outpocketing of the pharynx (a recessus mandibularis) occupied the depression (Shute 1956; Westoll 1945). The articular bone of therapsids has a downward-projecting prong (the retroarticular process). Among living vertebrates, mammals are unique in having homologues of the postdentary bones and quadrate as components of their middle ear. The C-shaped tympanic bone that supports the eardrum is a modified angular bone, including the reflected lamina. The surangular has disappeared but the articular and prearticular persist, fused together as the malleus, and the quadrate persists as the incus. Elongation of the retroarticular process has formed the slender handle of the malleus (manuorium) that runs to the center of the eardrum. The dentary bone has become the entire mandible, and a new jaw joint has formed between it and the squamosal. The original jaw joint persists as the articulation between malleus and incus. These seemingly implausible homologies were recognized long ago on the basis of embryological evidence and have since been abundantly confirmed by paleontological evidence.

Unlike pelycosaurs, primitive therapsids have a broad reflected lamina and have postdentary bones that form a distinct unit, flexibly articulated with the dentary. The quadrate is also much reduced in size and is articulated more flexibly with the skull. At least four cynodont lineages showed parallel changes that continued in the one that led to mammals, resulting in the mammalian middle ear (Figure 1). The dentary enlarged and developed a process that projected backward as a brace above the postdentary unit until, in mammals, it met the squamosal bone to form a new jaw joint. The postdentary unit became reduced in size, especially in height, becoming nestled in a smooth trough in the dentary. The original jaw articulation became greatly reduced in size, even before the new jaw joint appeared, while the size of the jaw muscles and bite forces increased progressively. In the earliest mammals (sometimes called mammaliamorphs), such as *Morganucodon*, both jaw joints coexist, yet the quadrate is incuslike in shape, and the postdentary bones resemble their homologues in Recent mammals. The reflected lamina is long and slender.

By one line of reasoning (Hopson 1966), these changes took place for reasons unrelated to hearing, such as improvements in chewing. Once the new jaw joint had appeared, the postdentary bones and quadrate became superfluous, dwindled in size, and became moored even more loosely. Serendipitously, they were rescued from oblivion when the postquadrate ("reptilian") eardrum

became attached to the retroarticular process; the articular and quadrate then became sound-transmitting structures, replacing the tympanic process of the stapes and providing some sort of auditory advantage. The angular bone was later recruited to support the eardrum.

An alternative line of reasoning (Allin 1975) holds that a recessus mandibularis was present in therapsids, and the thin tissues superficial to this air space, including the reflected lamina, served as a functional tympanum. Its vibrations were transmitted to the stapes via the articular and quadrate. This postdentary tympanum gave rise to the tympanic membrane in mammals (Figure 1). The recessus mandibularis may have originally served as a vocal resonator (Westoll 1945). Auditory adaption is seen as an important element in explaining the trends observed. Reduction in mass of the postdentary unit and quadrate, loosening of their attachments to adjacent bones, and transferring jaw muscle insertions from the postdentary bones to the dentary—all these changes increased auditory sensitivity and extended the frequency range upward. Remodeling the dentary to better brace the postdentary unit and reorienting muscle forces to reduce stress on the jaw joint (Crompton 1963) made these changes possible. If a "reptilian" tympanum behind the quadrate existed in synapsids, presumably it initially would have received higher frequencies than the postdentary tympanum and eventually lost its utility. It is possible that a single functional tympanum was present, having postdentary and postquadrate fields (the latter transmitting vibrations via the hyoid connection to the stapes). This line of reasoning fits with embryological evidence, which indicates that the eardrums of mammals and sauropsids are not homologous, and it makes sense of some otherwise puzzling matters, such as why the stapes would persistently abut the quadrate rather than separating (as in sauropsids and anurans) and why the eardrum of mammals is attached to former jaw parts. The postdentary bones and quadrate would have been middle ear components long before mammals emerged.

In all known mammals that survived beyond the Middle Jurassic (except for the Late Jurassic docodonts and perhaps the Paleocene mammal or cynodont *Chronoperates*), the postdentary bones appear to have separated from the mandible. For most Mesozoic mammals this is an inference based on the absence of a trough on the dentary bone for their attachment, the postdentary bones themselves not being preserved. In two extinct groups of Mesozoic mammals, multituberculates and advanced triconodonts, these bones definitely persisted as ear ossicles. A tympanic bone, malleus, and incus are preserved in a few multituberculates (Rougier et al. 1996), and cranial specimens of triconodontids show clear indications that these bones were present in life. It is possible that freeing of the postdentary bones and quadrate from the jaws as purely auditory structures occurred independently in more than one lineage of mammals.

The tympanic bone remained loosely suspended from the skull in Cretaceous marsupials and placentals, and this is still true in such living mammals as opossums, hedgehogs, and monotremes (the egg-laying platypus and echidnas) (Figure 3). In monotremes the tympanic bone may vibrate with the malleus and incus, functioning as, in effect, a fourth ossicle. In various other mammals this bone fuses to the squamosal and petrosal (otic capsule) as part

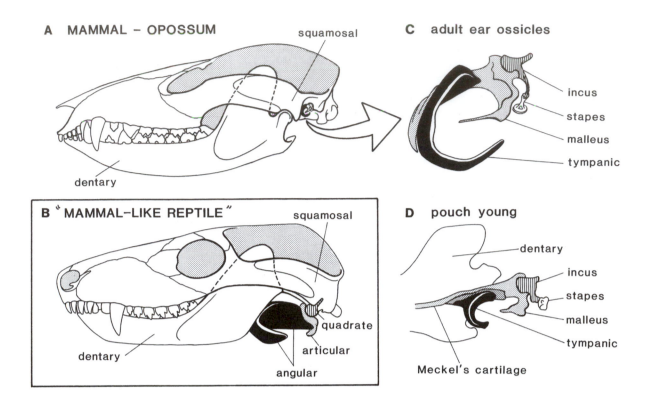

Figure 3. *A,* skull of an opossum; *B,* skull of a primitive cynodont, *Thrinaxodon; C,* middle ear bones of an adult opossum (lateral view); *D,* lower jaw of a pouch-young opossum (medial view), showing that the middle ear elements are mandibular components in early development. From Allin and Hopson (1992), with permission of Springer-Verlag.

of a composite temporal bone. It may extend inward to provide a bony floor for the middle ear cavity as protection against injury and pressure (this is one form of auditory bulla; others involve various skull bones). No bulla is present in monotremes, Mesozoic mammals, or therapsids.

Cynodonts, the earliest mammals, and multituberculates have grooves on the lower surface of the skull that appear to be for eustachian passages leading toward the internal nasal openings. These grooves disappear in later mammals; they usually are replaced by cartilaginous tubal walls.

Except for monotremes, living mammals can hear sound frequencies far above the range of all other vertebrates. Those that use sonar (echolocation)—toothed whales and bats—hear the highest frequencies of all. The auditory part of the inner ear (the cochlea) of marsupial and placental mammals is far longer than in other vertebrates, enabling them to discriminate a broader range of frequencies, and the cochlea runs a uniquely spiral course. Even in Cretaceous marsupials and placentals, the cochlea is coiled, making 1.25 to 1.5 turns (Meng and Fox 1995). The cochlea of monotremes is shorter, curved but not coiled, and ends in a lagena (a structure lost in other living mammals). Working backward in evolutionary history, the cochlea of multituberculates and advanced triconodonts is somewhat shorter and straighter, that of *Morganucodon* (a mouse-sized insect-eater) shorter still, and that of cynodonts even shorter. It is likely that *Morganucodon* could

hear higher frequencies than previous synapsids (and most other vertebrates) but not as high as later mammals.

Marsupials and placentals have two parallel bony spiral ridges in the part of the cochlea that is nearest to the fenestra vestibuli; these ridges support between themselves a ribbon of auditory hair cells and connective tissue (the organ of Corti and basilar membrane). The narrower the gap between ridges, the higher the frequencies that can be heard. There are no bony ridges in other mammals (or other vertebrates), so no reliable estimate can be made of the highest frequencies they could hear. The gap is extremely narrow in living bats and toothed whales (odontocetes) but much wider in baleen whales (mysticetes), which do not echolocate. Very primitive whales (archaeocetes) and early mysticetes also have a rather wide gap, but early odontocetes already have a very narrow one (Geisler and Luo 1996). The petrosal and tympanic of all odontocetes and mysticetes are large, exceedingly dense bones, that are firmly attached to one another but which are acoustically isolated from the rest of the skull (by spaces filled with aerated foam). They are common fossils. Bats also have isolated petrosals.

It is not known whether early mammals or their antecedents had projecting external ears (pinnae). For a small animal such as *Morganucodon,* which probably hunted in dim light, the ability to locate prey by hearing would have been valuable. This animal might have had pinnae large enough to diffract and therefore localize sounds above about 10,000 Hz, including many sounds generated by insects. However, the ears may not have been large enough for lower frequencies. It seems likely that early mammals could hear frequencies above 10,000 Hz, given their rather elongate cochlea and diminutive postdentary bones and quadrate.

EDGAR F. ALLIN

See also Pharyngeal Arches and Derivatives; Sensory Capsules; Skull

Works Cited

Allin, E.F. 1975. Evolution of the mammalian middle ear. *Journal of Morphology* 47:403–37.

Allin, E.F., and J.A. Hopson. 1992. Evolution of the auditory system in Synapsida ("mammal-like reptiles" and primitive mammals) as seen in the fossil record. *In* D.B. Webster, R.R. Fay, and A.N. Popper (eds.), *The Evolutionary Biology of Hearing.* New York: Springer-Verlag.

Bolt, J.R., and R.E. Lombard. 1985. Evolution of the amphibian tympanic ear and the origin of frogs. *Biological Journal of the Linnean Society* 24:83–99.

Clack, J.A. 1989. Discovery of the earliest known tetrapod stapes. *Nature* 342:425–27.

———. 1994. Earliest known tetrapod braincase and the evolution of the stapes and fenestra ovalis. *Nature* 369:392–94.

———. 1997. The evolution of tetrapod ears and the fossil record. *Brain, Behavior, and Evolution* 50:198–212.

Crompton, A.W. 1963. On the lower jaw of *Diarthrognathus* and the origin of the mammalian lower jaw. *Proceedings of the Zoological Society of London,* ser. B, 140:697–753.

Fritzsch, B., M.J. Ryan, W. Wilczynski, T.E. Hetherington, and W. Walkowiak (eds.). 1988. *The Evolution of the Amphibian Auditory System.* New York: Wiley.

Geisler, J.H., and Z. Luo. 1996. The petrosal and inner ear of *Herpetocetus sp.* (Mammalia, Cetacea) and their implications for the phylogeny and hearing of archaic mysticetes. *Journal of Paleontology* 70:1045–66.

Hanken, J., and B.K. Hall. 1993. *The Skull.* 3 vols. Chicago: University of Chicago Press.

Hopson, J.A. 1966. The origin of the mammalian middle ear. *American Zoologist* 6:437–50.

Laurin, M., and R.R. Reisz. 1997. A new perspective on tetrapod phylogeny. *In* S.S. Sumida and K.L.M. Martin (eds.), *Amniote Origins.* San Diego, California: Academic Press.

Meng, J., and R.C. Fox. 1995. Therian petrosals from the Oldman and Milk River Formation (Late Cretaceous), Alberta, Canada. *Journal of Vertebrate Paleontology* 15:122–30.

Romer, A.S. 1941. Notes on the crossopterygian hyomandibular and braincase. *Journal of Morphology* 69:141–60.

Rougier, G.W., J.R. Wible, and M.J. Novacek. 1996. Middle-ear ossicles of the Multituberculate *Kryptobaatar* from the Mongolian Late Cretaceous: Implications for Mammaliamorph relationships and the evolution of the auditory apparatus. *American Museum of Natural History Novitates* 3187:1–43.

Shute, C.D. 1956. The evolution of the mammalian eardrum and tympanic cavity. *Journal of Anatomy* 90:261–81.

Thomson, K.S. 1966. The evolution of the tetrapod middle ear in the rhipidistian-amphibian transition. *American Zoologist* 6:379–97.

Watson, D.M.S. 1953. The evolution of the mammalian ear. *Evolution* 7:159–77.

Westoll, T.S. 1945. The mammalian middle ear. *Nature* 155:114–15.

Further Reading

Henson, O.W. 1974. Comparative anatomy of the middle ear. *In* W.D. Keibel and W.D. Neff (eds.), *Auditory System: Anatomy, Physiology (Ear).* Handbook of Sensory Physiology, vol. 1. Berlin and New York: Springer-Verlag.

Lombard, R.E., and J.R. Bolt. 1979. Evolution of the tetrapod ear: An analysis and reinterpretation. *Biological Journal of the Linnean Society* 11:19–76.

Webster, D.B., R.R. Fay, and A.N. Popper (eds.). 1992. *The Evolutionary Biology of Hearing.* New York: Springer-Verlag.

HEMICHORDATES

Hemichordates, or stomochordates, are a minor group that has figured prominently in theories of animal evolution. As their name suggests, hemichordates possess half of the chordate features, especially the stomochord (a rodlike structure near the front of the animal) in the anterior part of the body and the pharyngeal gill slits in the trunk. Together with cephalochordates and urochordates, the hemichordates were included within the Chordata as protochordates, or "first chordates." However, scholars now believe that the stomochord, which was the key reason for assigning them into the chordates, is actually a small branch of the gut rather than a real notochord. Since their general body structure is also quite different from that of the chordates, the hemichordates have been removed from the Chordata and now comprise an independent group, Hemichordata. Nevertheless, since hemichordates possess pharyngeal gill slits, the characteristic feature of chordates, the group generally is considered to be closely related to chordates and to form an important intermediate stage between nonchordates (or invertebrates) and chordates (chiefly vertebrates).

On the other hand, hemichordates also are linked to echinoderms (marine animals, including sea stars, sea urchins, sea cucumbers) because both share extremely similar larvae and the same body plan, consisting of three pairs of coeloms (body cavities). In fact, the process of gastrulation, an early stage in the development of a fertilized egg (ontogeny), produces a saclike embryo with a single opening into the cavity; this opening becomes the gut. In the hemichordates, chordates, and echinoderms (unlike all other groups), this opening becomes the anus, while a new opening, formed later, becomes the mouth. As a result, it generally is held that

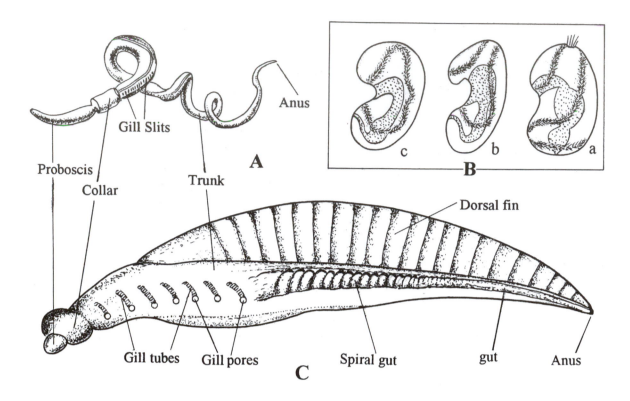

Figure 1. *A*, *Balanoglossus*, a typical living enteropneust. *B*, enteropneust larvae (side view) and larva of two echinoderm classes: *a*, tonaria, the early larva of enteropneusts; *b*, starfish larva; *c*, sea cucumber larva; *C*, *Yunnanozoon*, reconstruction.

the three phyla form a natural group, named "deuterostomes," which means "the mouth forms later." However, the exact evolutionary relationship between the three phyla is still unknown. The chordates may not originate directly from the hemichordates. In fact, the earliest known chordate is as old as the earliest known hemichordate (Shu et al. 1996a).

All hemichordates inhabit the sea. Their bodies are divided into three regions—a moveable lobe in front of the "mouth" opening, called a proboscis; a short collar; and a trunk—reflecting an underlying tricoelomate organization. The basic concentration of nerve structures occurs at the "back" (dorsally), in the collar region, and, in some forms, is hollow. A pharynx (throat) bearing one or more pairs of gill openings, is located in the anterior part of the trunk. On the basis of distinction in principal morphological and behavioral features—such as being solitary or colonial, mobile or sedentary—biologists generally divide the hemichordates into two groups, enteropneusts and pterobranchs (Ruppert and Barnes 1994); paleontologists refer to three classes: Enteropneusta, Pterobranchia, and Graptolithina, the last of which is an extinct group of the Paleozoic (Berry 1987).

Class Enteropneusta

Enteropneusts, the best-known hemichordates, are a large worm-like animals called "acorn worms," the majority ranging between

9 and 45 centimeters in length. The largest known specimen of *Balanoglossus gigas* can be as long as 2.5 meters. Some 70 species are distributed widely in the world. They are found primarily as benthic (bottom-dwelling) inhabitants of shallow water, but some appear in the deep sea and in association with hydrothermal vents. Some live under stones and shells, and many common forms construct mucus-lined burrows in mud and sand. Exposed tidal flats usually are dotted with the coiled, ropelike castings of these creatures.

The cylindrical and flaccid organisms display the typical tripartite deuterostome body plan. The proboscis is usually conical, giving rise to the common name acorn worm, and is connected to the collar by a narrow stalk. The collar is a short cylinder that anteriorly overlaps the proboscis stalk and ventrally (on the "belly" side) contains the mouth. The long trunk comprises the major part of the body. It is subdivided into a branchial (gill) region anteriorly and an intestinal region posteriorly, with an anus at the end of the body. The sides of the branchial region are open to the exterior by pairs of gill slits or pores (Figure 1A).

Generally, acorn worms are sluggish organisms that move slowly via contractions that move in waves down the proboscis, where the musculature is best developed. The proboscis advances and anchors the organism to the bottom, then pulls the trunk and collar forward. These animals may feed upon materials on the sea-floor (deposit feeders), suspended in the water (suspension feed-

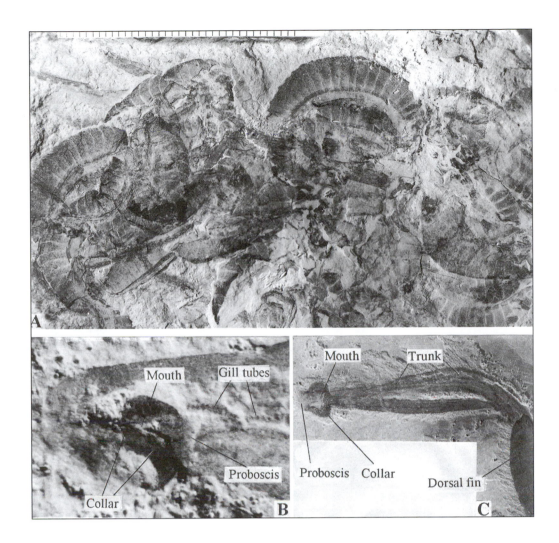

Figure 2. *Yunnanozoon.* *A,* unusual preservation of a population of more than 20 individuals; *B,* individual whose collar with proboscis inside and the foremost part of the trunk are bent backwards; *C,* individual with a dorsal fin detached from trunk.

ers), or both. The gill slits are assumed to be gas exchange structures. After the water with food particles is transported into the mouth by cilia (shorter, continually beating, hairlike structures) on the proboscis, the water is separated from the particles in the pharynx and expelled out via gill slits, while the food particles run through the gut for digestion and absorption.

Acorn worms are very fragile and may be damaged under natural conditions. Fortunately, they can heal the wound and regenerate missing parts. Not surprisingly, asexual reproduction by fragmentation has been reported for several species, including members of *Balanoglossus.* On the other hand, the enteropneusts are all dioecious—that is, individuals have either male or female reproductive organs, not both. They release sperms and eggs into the seawater, where fertilization occurs. Most acorn worms have a planktotrophic larva called "tornaria." Its organization closely resembles that of some echinoderm larvae. This similarity provides the main evidence for assuming a close evolutionary relationship between hemichordates and echinoderms (Figure 1B).

All the enteropneusts are soft-bodied, which means that they leave few fossil records, except the Lower Jurassic body fossil *Megaderaion* (Arduini et al. 1981) and some possible burrows (Kazmierczak and Pszczolkowski 1969). Recently, there was a significant discovery in the celebrated Early Cambrian Chengjiang fossil deposits of South China. X. Hou and colleagues first described a strange, segmented wormlike animal called *Yunnanozoon* but left it in uncertain taxonomic position (1991). Later, the animal was placed in chordates (Chen et al. 1995). Careful restudy by D. Shu and colleagues has revealed that although *Yunnanozoon* has characteristics shared by chordates and hemichordates—pairs of gill pores, associated gill tubes in the anterior part of the trunk, and a spiral intestine in its posterior part—this creature has a typical tripartite proboscis–collar–trunk body plan with a possible stomochord in the collar area. These characteristics are found only in hemichordates. Moreover, the supposed notochord found in *Yunnanozoon* turned out to be the alimentary canal with gut contents in it, and the so-called myomeres are actually a bladelike structure

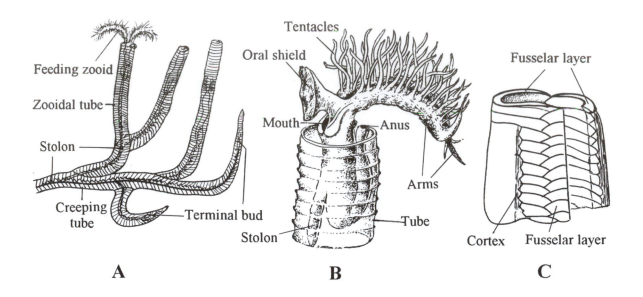

Figure 3. Pterobranch *Rhabdopleura* and a graptolite. *A, B, Rhabdopleura; A,* colonial organization; *B,* feeding position of a zooid; *C,* Part of a graptolite tube; note the resemblance to the *Rhabdopleura* tube.

along the back, which most probably functioned as a fin. In addition, unlike the case in chordates, the anus is located at the extreme end of the body. All these facts strongly support the affinities of *Yunnanozoon* with enteropneust hemichordates, not the chordates, which means it should be considered the earliest known hemichordate (Shu et al. 1996b) (Figures 1C and 2).

The major distinction between *Yunnanozoon* and the modern acorn worms is that the Early Cambrian creature bears a segmented dorsal fin. This fact has at least two implications. First, the fin would allow the animal to be an active swimmer to some extent. And second, the enteropneusts might originate from certain segmented ancestral worms. It appears reasonable that as the enteropneusts evolved from a swimmer into an epibenthic form (one that lives on the seafloor) or burrowed beneath it, the segmented fin was lost, and the proboscis as the chief locomotory organ became much more developed (Figures 1A, C).

Some giant larvae (up to 22 millimeters in diameter), whose general form resembled that of enteropneusts, have been gathered by plankton tows in the Atlantic Ocean since the early 1930s. As yet the adult forms of these larvae are still unknown, so their status and affinities remain uncertain. Nevertheless, some biologists have erected a new class Planctosphaeroidea to house these larvae (Barnes et al. 1993).

Class Pterobranchia

The pterobranchs are colonial, tube-dwelling, epibenthic hemichordates that superficially resemble hydroids. Individuals, called "zooids," are very small, usually only a few millimeters or less in length. Pterobranchs are a small group, embracing only three genera: *Rhabdopleura, Cephalodiscus,* and *Atubaris*. Although widespread in both warm and cold seas, they are encountered in

shallow water rarely. More often, they are dredged from deep water and are best known from the seas around Antarctica, though some forms can be found in the North Hemisphere (e.g., Florida, Bermuda, and Japan).

Both the tiny colonial zooids and their large, solitary enteropneust relatives share a similar tripartite body structure. However, pterobranchs differ from enteropneusts in several ways (Figure 3A, B). The proboscis is modified into an oral shield, which functions in creeping up the inner side of the tube as well as in secreting the tube. The gut in their trunk is not straight but U-shaped, which brings the mouth and anus close together. The trunk bears a long, fleshy stolon (stalk) that unites zooids together into a colony. More conspicuously, the short collar region arches dorsally over the oral shield and bears two or more arms and featherlike tentacles.

Pterobranchs are filter-feeders. Cilia on the sides of the tentacles create a flow of water and food particles over the front surfaces of the tentacles and arms. Once captured on the surface, the particles are transported by cilia along the length of the arms to a ciliated groove and finally into the mouth. Pterobranch colonies are thought to be dioecian—the male and female zooids show sexual dimorphism, which means male and female individuals are apparently different in morphology (shape and structure). The details of fertilization are not known fully but males probably release sperm or spermatophores into the water. Fertilization is internal, and development also begins in the body of the female. The embryos develop into uniformly ciliated larvae, which then are released into the sea. After settling on the sea floor, a larva gradually develops into an ancestrula, an intermediate form that later produces a colony asexually, by budding (Figure 3A).

Rhabdopleura is a "living fossil"—a present-day species that has existed in its present form essentially unchanged, since it first evolved. Fossils of it have been discovered in the Middle Cambrian strata and are recognized as one of the earliest known ptero-branchs, which indicates its remarkably conservative nature (Dur-man and Sennikov 1993). This important discovery also provides some evidence for preservation of zooid material. The only other record of a pterobranch from the Middle Cambrian is *Rhabdotu-bus* from Sweden and Norway (Bengtson and Urbanek 1986). Other fossil pterobranchs have been found in the Ordovician, Silurian, and other periods (Chapman et al. 1995). All fossil spe-cies clearly resemble modern forms in growth habits and in the gross aspects of shape and structure of tubular outer coverings.

Class Graptolithina

Graptolites flourished in the Lower Paleozoic but were extinct in the Carboniferous. They are a very important fossil group in pale-ontology and stratigraphy, especially in the Ordovician and Silu-rian biostratigraphy and ecology, as well as biogeography. Because graptolites are the remains of long-extinct organisms, and all that is available from them is certain hard skeletal materials, scholars have placed them in many phyla, particularly in Bryozoa and Coe-lenterata. However, some graptolites that lived by encrusting rocks and shells (instead of floating in the water column) have yielded fossil remains so similar to the hard parts secreted by rhabdopleu-rans that the two groups now are believed to be closely related to the pterobranchs (Figure 3C) (Kozlowski 1949; Bulman 1970; Durman and Sennikov 1993).

Graptolites appear to have exploited many different benthic habits, but the major group floated in seawater, much like plankton. Although many graptoloid species had worldwide distribution, they were distributed in certain provinces and regions at certain geological times. The major influence on grap-toloid regionalism seems to be temperature. Graptolite provin-cialism was marked during the Ordovician, when two distinct faunas occupied different parts of the world's oceans. The Pacific Faunal Region was within a belt of tropical environments and is characterized by the presence of certain genera, especially *Cardi-graptus* and *Isograptus*. On the other hand, the Atlantic Faunal region was within cold areas and was marked by certain tuning-fork-shaped *Didymograptus*. Since the life spans of many floating or drifting species are short geologically, and they are distributed worldwide, these organisms have been used frequently as one of the major biostratigraphic tools, particularly in the Ordovician, Silurian, and Early Devonian (Bulman 1970). That is, when a particular graptolite is found in a rock sample, the excavator can use this biological clue to determine the general age of the rock sample. Graptolites are found in many metamorphic rock ter-rains, and they have proven to be a valuable tool to structural geologists, not only in dating rocks in such terrains but also in making correlations between sequences of metamorphosed and nonmetamorphosed rock strata.

DEGAN SHU

See also Cephalochordates; Chordates; Echinoderms; Superphyla; Urochordates

Works Cited

Arduini, P., G. Pinna, and G. Teruzzi. 1981. *Megaderaion sinemuriense* n. gen. n. sp., a new fossil enteropneust of the Sinemurian of Osteno in Lombardy. *Atti della Società Italiana di Science Naturali e del Museo Civico de Storia Naturali de Milano* 122:104–8.
Barnes, R.S.K., P. Calow, and P.J.W. Olive. 1993. *The Invertebrates: A New Synthesis.* 2nd ed., Oxford and Boston: Blackwell Scientific.
Bengtson, S., and A. Urbanek. 1986. *Rhabdotubus,* a Middle Cambrian rhabdopleurid hemichordate. *Lethaia* 19:293–308.
Berry, W.B.N. 1987. *In* R. Boadman, A. Cheethan, and A. Rowell (eds.), *Fossil Invertebrates.* Palo Alto, California: Blackwell Scientific.
Bulman, O.M.B. 1970. Graptolithina. *In* C. Teichert (ed.), *Treatise on Invertebrate Paleontology.* Part 5. 2nd ed., Lawrence: University of Kansas Press; Boulder, Colorado: Geological Society of America.
Chapman, A.J., P.N. Durman, and R.B. Rickards. 1995. Rhabdopleuran hemichordates: New fossil forms and review. *Proceedings of the Geologists' Association* 106:293–303.
Chen, J., J. Dzik, G.D. Edgecombe, L. Ramsköld, and G. Zhou. 1995. A possible Early Cambrian chordate. *Nature* 377:720–22.
Durman, P.N., and N.V. Sennikov. 1993. A new rhabdopleurid hemichordate from the Middle Cambrian of Siberia. *Palaeontology* 36:283–96.
Hou, X., L. Ramsköld, and J. Bergström. 1991. Composition and preservation of the Chengjiang fauna: A Lower Cambrian soft-bodied biota. *Zoologica Scripta* 20:395–411.
Kazmierczak, J., and A. Pszczolkowski. 1969. Burrows of Enteropneusta in Muschelkalk (Middle Triassic) of the Holy Cross Mountains, Poland. *Acta Palaeontologica Polonica* 14:299–324.
Kozlowski, R. 1949. *Les graptolithes et quelques nouveaux groupes d'animaux du Trémadoc de la Pologne.* Palaeontological Polonica, 3. Warsaw: n.p.
Ruppert, E.E., and R.D. Barnes. 1994. *Invertebrate Zoology.* 6th ed., Fort Worth, Texas: Saunders College Publishing.
Shu, D., S. Morris, and X. Zhang. 1996a. A *Pikaia*-like chordate from the Lower Cambrian of China. *Nature* 384:157–58.
Shu, D., X. Zhang, and L. Chen. 1996b. Reinterpretation of *Yunnanozoon* as the earliest known hemichordate. *Nature* 380:428–30.

Further Reading

Barnes, R.D. 1963. *Invertebrate Zoology.* Philadelphia: Saunders College Publishing; 6th ed., E.E. Ruppert and R.D. Barnes (eds.), Fort Worth, Texas: Saunders College Publishing; 1994.
Barnes, R.S.K., P. Calow, and P.J.W. Olive. 1988. *The Invertebrates: A New Synthesis.* Oxford and Boston: Blackwell Scientific; 2nd ed., 1993.
Berry, W.B.N. 1987. *In* R. Boadman, A. Cheethan, and A. Rowell (eds.), *Fossil Invertebrates.* Palo Alto, California: Blackwell Scientific.
Bulman, O.M.B. 1969. Graptolithina. *In* C. Teichert (ed.), *Treatise on Invertebrate Paleontology.* Part 5. Lawrence: University of Kansas Press; Boulder, Colorado: Geological Society of America; 2nd ed., 1970.

HETEROCHRONY

The term heterochrony comes from Greek roots meaning "of different time." As an evolutionary concept, it has had a long history linked to one of biology's fundamental and recurrent organizing principles: the frequent parallel evolution of morphological features and transformations observed during ontogeny (an organism's development) and phylogeny (evolutionary history). This patterning served as the basis for Ernst Heinrich Haeckel's famous "biogenetic law," which states that "ontogeny recapitulates phylogeny." The primary evidence in support of this organizing principle came from the fields of comparative embryology, anatomy, and paleontology. Haeckel's usage of heterochrony actually identified changes in developmental timing of one organ or structure relative to others within a given organism. Only subsequently did Gavin DeBeer and others provide the foundation for our current usage of the term heterochrony, rooting it in shifts in timing of a given structure in different organisms that are hypothesized to be related phylogenetically. Paleontology has yielded many of the classic examples of purported heterochronic transformations, but a few selected cases include trends of "hypermorphic overgrowths"—such as antler size in the Irish Elk, horn length in titanotheres, and certain proportions of crests in the skulls in various dinosaur taxa (groups; singular, taxon)—in addition to "paedomorphic reductions" of fossil sea urchins and salamanders, seen also in living forms.

Following S.J. Gould's 1977 landmark treatise *Ontogeny and Phylogeny*, evolutionary change via heterochrony has become one of the most discussed topics in the resurgent synthesis of development and evolution that has characterized the 1980s and 1990s. In its traditional usage, phylogenetic heterochrony is defined as "changes in the relative time of appearance and/or rate of development of characters already present in ancestors" (Gould 1977). Heterochronic characters typically have been qualitative morphological features or quantitative proportions. Evolution via heterochrony is largely the stuff of minor variations on existing themes, rather than major transitions to novel features. While the latter of course also are produced through changes in ancestral developmental processes and program, they do not yield obvious parallels between ontogeny and phylogeny. It is therefore easy to understand that whether an evolutionary transformation is deemed "heterochronic" or not is often a matter of definition and scale; in fact, as the molecular genetics of developmental processes are further probed, the traditional definitions, classifications, and applications of heterochrony will undoubtedly undergo much change.

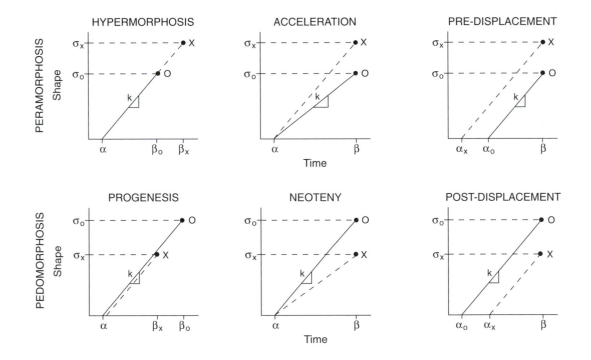

Figure 1. Three types of peramorphosis (top) and three types of pedomorphosis (bottom). The vertical axis represents shape and the horizontal axis represents time. Steeper, more vertical slopes (k) represent faster growth rate or faster shape change. Code: alpha (α), onset of growth; beta (β), cessation of growth; β_o, cessation of growth in ancestor; β_x, cessation of growth in descendant; sigma (σ) final shape; σ_o, shape of ancestor; σ_x, shape of descendant; O, ancestral growth trajectory; X, descendant's growth trajectory. Redrawn by Catherine P. Sexton, after Kluge 1988.

Most current scholars agree in viewing and depicting heterochrony as an evolutionary displacement in descendants of a specific ancestral feature (or "shape") relative to a common standard of size, age or developmental stage. This focus on changes in shape ties heterochrony to the evolutionary biologist's notion of true morphology; simple transformations in size (e.g., geometric or isometric shifts—changes in size that retain overall proportions) or age are not typically interpreted as resulting from heterochrony, although of course these are still evolutionary changes. In order to best establish comparative standards of true developmental timing, studies of heterochrony have optimally sought criteria such as birth, fusion of growth plates in bones, eruption of a tooth, and sexual maturity. When size (as in some studies of allometry, the relative growth of a part in relation to an entire organism) or chronological age (as in studies of growth-in-time) are substituted for such qualitative developmental standards, heterochronic comparisons of shape transformations are still possible but are not as complete as when all information is available. A key point not fully appreciated in much of the current pedantic bickering over heterochronic labels is that characterizations of heterochrony are inherently relative and dependent on both the standardization framework and the shape depiction utilized. This is inevitable and even desirable.

Figures 1 and 2 provide summaries of the primary categories of heterochronic transformation currently in use. Several factors can cause pedomorphism, the retention in adults of juvenile morphological features or shapes relative to common ancestral developmental standards: (1) time hypomorphosis (progenesis), the early cessation of growth and morphogenesis; (2) rate hypomorphosis, the reduction of rates of growth-in-time and size; (3) neoteny, the retardation in rates of shape change; and (4) predisplacement, the delayed onset of growth. Conversely, morphological features or shapes may be peramorphic (meaning "shapes beyond") or recapitulatory in descendants relative to common ancestral developmental standards as a result of the opposite trends: (1) time hypermorphosis, the extension of periods of growth and morphogenesis; (2) rate hypermorphosis, the increase in rates of growth-in-time and size; (3) acceleration, the increase in rates of shape change; and (4) postdisplacement, the premature onset of growth.

An example of time hypomorphosis or progenesis is provided by the wingless and parthenogenetic aphids, an adaptation that permits the rapid production of large numbers of offspring to utilize temporarily superabundant resources. Human pygmies provide a microevolutionary case of rate hypomorphosis for those features in which they exhibit pedomorphosis through reduced rates of growth-in-time, smaller terminal body size, and retention of ancestral patterns of allometric shape change. Gould provides a classic paleontological example of pedomorphosis via neoteny in Bermudian land snails, which attain ancestral sizes but retain juvenilized morphology (in shell coiling, proportions, and color banding) through dissociation and retardation of the ancestral patterns of morphogenesis. A well-known example from the fossil record of peramorphosis via hypermorphosis is the recapitulatory relative enlargement of antler size in the extinct giant Irish Elk, *Megaloceros giganteus*. (Because we do not have the necessary information

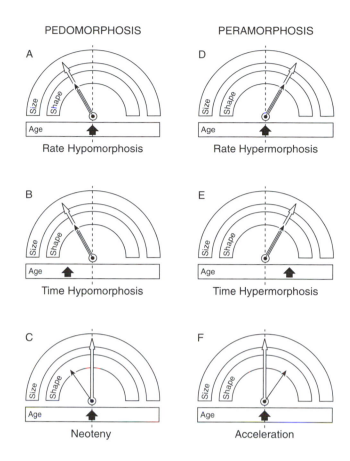

Figure 2. Another way of depicting heterochrony. The clock diagrams represent three types of pedomorphosis and three types of peramorphosis that partly overlap the types depicted in Figure 1. In these diagrams size and shape are decoupled, refining the diagnosis. The dashed line bisecting the clock represents the ancestral ontogenetic pattern. The open arrow represents changes in size of the descendant. The thin solid arrow represents changes in shape of the descendant. The thick solid arrow represents the point at which ontogeny ceases. Redrawn by Catherine P. Sexton, after Shea 1983.

on absolute age chronologies, we cannot differentiate between rate and time hypermorphoses in such cases—this is a common problem with such paleontological cases). Gorillas provide an example of rate hypermorphosis relative to chimpanzees, since they exhibit increased rates of growth-in-time and larger terminal size, but they share absolute age chronologies and many underlying allometric patterns of morphogenesis. Thus, as subadults gorillas attain the proportions observed in adult chimpanzees for myriad comparisons. Finally, peramorphosis via acceleration is clearly exhibited among some Paleozoic ammonoids (a kind of shelled cephalopod), where ancestral adult suture (lines marking the position of internal partitions) lengths are reached at progressively smaller shell sizes in descendants.

Paleontologists and other evolutionary biologists have tried to move beyond cataloging the morphological patterning produced by heterochrony to understanding two key aspects of such phenomena. One aspect is the ecological context of heterochronic change, and here growth rates and life history features (such as truncated or prolonged maturation) have played central roles. Such studies indicate that it is often the developmental parameters themselves, rather than specific morphological configurations, that are the target of selective change. Another aspect is the genetic basis of heterochronic transformations, and efforts in this regard have focused on gene products controlling both local and regional differentiation and growth, as well as the timing of developmental transitions. Future work in developmental genetics will undoubtedly prove very significant for our understanding of heterochrony.

BRIAN T. SHEA

See also Allometry; Evolutionary Novelty; Evolutionary Trends; Growth, Development, and Evolution; Phyletic Dwarfism and Gigantism; Speciation and Morphological Change

Works Cited

Gould, S.J. 1977. *Ontogeny and Phylogeny*. Cambridge, Massachusetts: Harvard University Press.
Kluge, A.G. 1988. The characteristics of Ontogeny. *In* C.J. Humphries (ed.), *Ontogeny and Systematics*. New York: Columbia University Press.
Shea, B.T. 1983. Allometry and heterochrony in African apes. *American Journal of Physical Anthropology* 62:275–89.

Further Reading

Alberch, P., S.J. Gould, G.F. Oster, and D.B. Wake. 1979. Size and shape in ontogeny and phylogeny. *Paleobiology* 5:296–317.
Levinton, J.S. 1988. *Genetics, Paleontology and Macroevolution*. Cambridge and New York: Cambridge University Press.
McKinney, M.L. (ed.). 1988. *Heterochrony in Evolution*. New York: Plenum.
McKinney, M.L. and K.J. McNamara. 1991. *Heterochrony: The Evolution of Ontogeny*. New York: Plenum.
Raff, R.A. 1996. *The Shape of Life: Genes, Development and the Evolution of Animal Form*. Chicago: University of Chicago Press.

HIBBARD, CLAUDE W.

American, 1905–73

The prairie farmer background has been a potent tradition in American vertebrate paleontology. The abundance of fossils on the Great Plains attracted many youths who had internalized knowledge of climatic forces as causes of death and regulators of births and food. Claude W. Hibbard, for example, was virtually a complete naturalist as a young man, extending his Kansas farm background to a thorough knowledge of local plants, invertebrates, and the interactions among these through seasons. Modern research interest in the Pliocene and Pleistocene faunas and climates of North America owes much to his influence. Integration of faunal and floral change as a response to climate and habitat change through time was the central theme of Hibbard's career. He was a vertebrate paleontologist who saw faunas and sedimentary environments as inseparable; he collected outcrops and he interpreted ecosystems. The wet-screening technique for recovering microvertebrates and molluscs from massive sediment samples was largely developed by him in his all-consuming drive to know what once lived on the prairie and in what sequence. Hibbard's technical expertise was biostratigraphy of morphological changes in rodent teeth. He developed the chronological context for the numerous faunas that he collected on the Great Plains, especially Kansas, Oklahoma, and Nebraska. Understanding effects of seasonality and climate change on ecology and evolution on the prairie was his life-long passion. He avoided abstract theories, focusing instead on morphological variation, paleoecological associations, and geologic time.

It is clear that his agricultural background dominated his understanding of natural history, his practical approach to collecting fossils, and his influential teaching, not to mention his colorful speech. After high school and a summer of study to gain a teaching certificate at Emporia State (Kansas) Teachers College, Hibbard became principal of the grade school in Thrall, Kansas, a roughneck oil town. As retold by Semken and Zakrzewski (1974), "If the children were lacking in formal education, they compensated for it in age, many being as old or older than their green principal. Order was established rapidly behind the outhouse by effective but currently out-of-vogue methods." He went on to the University of Kansas, where he became a museum assistant as a junior, a fossil collector in the summers, and an actively publishing scientist by the time he graduated with his bachelor's degree in zoology in 1933. This background helps explain his intensity and single-mindedness of purpose. His field camps were remarkable for the crews' predawn readiness on the outcrops and unusually hard labor, hauling tons of matrix in burlap bags to the washing stream. Then came long afternoons preparing matrix, washing, picking, and sorting fossils in the relentless search for diagnostic vertebrates (Semken and Zakrzewski 1974). In this labor no one worked harder than Hibbard. Inspiration by example was the secret of his success with students and peers, as understanding of the land was the basis for his scientific success. In 1935, he became the assistant curator of vertebrate paleontology at the University of Kansas and began his 39 field seasons, leading to huge collections of microvertebrate fossils at Kansas and later at the University of Michigan. He published 154 papers in zoology, paleontology, and geology, but he was first and foremost a forceful and respected teacher.

Four significant advancements in paleontology were strongly influenced by Hibbard's research. First was the necessity to integrate as much faunal and floral data as possible to answer paleoecological questions. He collected molluscs and pollen as well as all vertebrates from his quarries and invited students and colleagues to study these collections and make independent paleoecological and biogeographic inferences (e.g., Hibbard and Taylor 1960). This eclectic approach has since become fundamental to paleontology and geochemistry of cores and other research programs in Earth history. Second, he recognized the significance of nonanalog faunas—sympatric mixtures of cool and warm fauna brought together by equable climates that permitted northward extension of cold-intolerant organisms and southern extension of summer heat-tolerant organisms in the Pliocene and Pleistocene (Hibbard 1955, 1960). Third, Hibbard was among the first to recognize the correct position of the Pliocene-Pleistocene boundary in continental deposits of North America, with the Blancan faunas recognized as Pliocene and with evidence for pre-Wisconsin glaciation in North America (Skinner and Hibbard 1972). Fourth, Hibbard was a leader among the paleomammalogists who established the North American mammal biostratigraphy based on high-resolution correlations of rodent, horse, elephant, and other mammal teeth from the Great Plains states, western North America, and Eurasia. These, in conjunction with paleomagnetics, tephra stratigraphy, and potassium/argon dating, resulted in today's remarkably resolved chronological system for continental deposits of the Late Cenozoic (Woodburne 1987).

GERALD R. SMITH

Works Cited

Semken Jr., H.A., and R.J. Zakrzewski. 1974. Obituary, Claude W. Hibbard. *Journal of Mammalogy* 56:275–79.

Woodburne, M.O. (ed.). 1987. *Cenozoic Mammals of North America, Geochronology and Biostratigraphy.* Berkeley: University of California Press.

Biography

Born in Toronto, Kansas, 21 March 1905. Received B.A. (1933) and M.A. (1934), University of Kansas; Ph.D., University of Michigan, 1941. Museum assistant (1928–34), assistant curator of vertebrate paleontology (1935–41), curator of vertebrate paleontology (1941–46), and assistant professor of zoology (1941–46), University of Kansas; professor of geology and curator of vertebrate paleontology, University of Michigan, 1946–73. President of numerous scholarly societies, such as the Society of Vertebrate Paleontology, Kansas Academy of Science, Michigan Academy of Science, and Michigan Geological Society; fellow, Geological Society of America; member, board of governors, American Society of Ichthyologists and Herpetologists; member, board of directors, American Ornithological Union and American Society of Mammalogists. Developed wet screen-washing methods for recovering large samples of microvertebrate fossils from compacted sediments; established early mammalian biostratigraphy for Pliocene and Pleistocene of southern Great Plains; originated the concept of nonanalog faunas as evidence for climatic equability in the Late Cenozoic. Died in Ann Arbor, Michigan, 9 October 1973.

Major Publications

1941. Paleoecology and correlation of the Rexroad fauna from the Upper Pliocene of southwestern Kansas, as indicated by the mammals. *Kansas University Bulletin* 27:79–104.

1944. Stratigraphy and vertebrate paleontology of Pleistocene deposits in southwestern Kansas. *Geological Society of America Bulletin* 55:707–54.

1950. Mammals of the Rexroad formation from Fox Canyon, Meade County, Kansas. *University of Michigan Museum of Paleontology Contributions* 8 (6):113–92.

1955. The Jinglebob interglacial (Sangamon?) fauna from Kansas and its climatic significance. *University of Michigan Museum of Paleontology Contributions* 12 (10):179–228.

1960. With D.W. Taylor. Two Late Pleistocene faunas from southwestern Kansas. *University of Michigan Museum of Paleontology Contributions* 16:1–223.

1960. An interpretation of Pliocene and Pleistocene climates in North America. *President's Address, Michigan Academy of Science, Arts and Letters Annual Report* 62:5–30.

1965. With C.E. Ray, D.E. Savage, D.W. Taylor, and J.E. Guilday. Quaternary mammals of North America. *In* H.E. Wright and D.G. Frey (eds.), *The Quaternary of the United States.* Princeton, New Jersey: Princeton University Press.

1972. Wuth M.F. Skinner. Early Pleistocene preglacial and glacial rocks and faunas of north-central Nebraska. *American Museum of Natural History Bulletin* 148:1–148.

Further Reading

Dorr Jr., J.A. 1974. Obituary, Claude W. Hibbard. *Society of Vertebrate Paleontology Bulletin* 100:59–60.

McKenna, M.C. 1962. Collecting small fossils by washing and screening. *Curator* 3:221–35.

Semken Jr., H.A., and R.J. Zakrzewski. 1974. Obituary, Claude W. Hibbard. *Journal of Mammalogy* 56:275–79.

Smith, G.R., and N.E. Friedland (eds.). 1975. Studies on Cenozoic paleontology and stratigraphy in honor of Claude W. Hibbard [with a biography and bibliography by G.R. Smith, and a biographical letter by C.W. Hibbard]. *University of Michigan Museum of Paleontology Papers on Paleontology* 12:1–143.

Wilson, J.A. 1974. Claude William Hibbard, 1905–1973. *Geological Society of America Memorial and Bibliography* 1974:1–8.

Woodburne, M.O. (ed.). 1987. *Cenozoic Mammals of North America, Geochronology and Biostratigraphy.* Berkeley: University of California Press.

HOAXES AND ERRORS

The issue of hoaxes, frauds, and errors in paleontology is a difficult and multifaceted subject. Genuine fossils found in context can be misinterpreted by legitimate paleontologists. Indeed, one could argue that the history of paleontology is in large part the correction of errors or misinterpretations promulgated by earlier scientists; this is the nature of science. But there are "errors" that are not simply the result of misinterpretation. Unfortunately, "fossils" have been fabricated with the intention of deceiving unsuspecting paleontologists, or in some cases were fabricated by the discoverer as a way of promoting his or her own career. Another area of error occurs when fossils are placed in the wrong context, perhaps unintentionally through sloppy note taking and recording, or in some cases intentionally when fossils from one geographic locale or stratum are planted in another locale or stratum with the purpose to deceive.

Hoaxes and errors in paleontology can have wider implications beyond simply the subfield or specialty in which they occur, especially when it comes to topics of wide general interest, such as human evolution. Creationists and other anti-evolutionists sometimes latch onto infamous frauds and misinterpretations, such as "Piltdown Man" and "Nebraska Man" (both discussed below), to argue that all fossil evidence is unreliable and thus should be dismissed in toto as supporting evidence for an evolutionary point of view.

Piltdown Man (*Eoanthropus,* "dawn man," as it formally was named) is undoubtedly the best known of all major paleontological frauds. Today this obvious fraud is known to be a composite of recent (probably no older than medieval in age) human skull fragments, an orangutan lower jaw and canine tooth that were filed to crudely imitate dental wear patterns and artificially colored to look old, and various prehistoric bones (mastodon, stegodon, hippo, and beaver) and flint and bone implements that were claimed to be found in association with Piltdown Man. Yet, for over 30 years Piltdown Man was accepted by some scientists as a genuine human ancestor, perhaps half a million years old, although from the start there were questions surrounding the authenticity of the finds.

Piltdown Man first came to attention in 1912 when amateur archaeologist, fossil collector, and professional lawyer, Charles Dawson approached Arthur Smith Woodward, Keeper of the Geological Department at The British Museum (Natural History), with human cranial fragments and apparently associated prehistoric animal fossils and flint implements said to come from a gravel pit in Piltdown, England. Dawson stated that he had first received some skull fragments from workmen digging at the pit in 1908, and since then he had visited the site and found more skull fragments and the associated materials. Smith Woodward's interest was sparked, and he, along with Dawson and the young Jesuit paleontologist Pierre Teilhard de Chardin, searched the Piltdown site further, and Smith Woodward found a lower jaw that supposedly belonged to the skull. Over the next several years Dawson and Teilhard de Chardin recovered more material that appeared to belong to Piltdown Man.

The formal scientific announcement of Piltdown Man was made in December 1912 by Smith Woodward before the Geological Society of London. It was interpreted as a prehistoric human with an expanded braincase (indicating that it had a brain nearly as large as that of a modern human) but retaining an apelike lower jaw (and therefore, it was assumed, an apelike face). This fossil seemed to confirm the theories of some paleontologists that the distinguishing human attribute is the large brain, and that, therefore, the large brain evolved first, subsequently followed by other human features. (In hindsight, we know that in fact the large brain was one of the last features to fully evolve in the human lineage. Our early ancestors stood upright but still had relatively small brains.) Piltdown Man also fed the chauvinistic prejudices of some Englishmen that the true ancestors of modern humans were not to be found in Java *(Pithecanthropus)* or in France or Germany (Neanderthals), but in Britain.

From the beginning some paleontologists questioned Piltdown Man. The skull fragments, lower jaw, and important isolated canine tooth had not been found together in direct association, and there was no way to prove that they all came from the same individual or even species. Perhaps, it was suggested, Piltdown Man was based on several different individuals, representing different species, that had been mixed together in the gravel pit. It might even be a matter of a prehistoric ape jaw being incorrectly associated with human skull bones derived from an ancient Roman or medieval grave. Although ultimately accepted by many paleontologists at the time as genuine, doubts persisted concerning Piltdown Man.

In 1949 the new method of fluorine dating was applied to the Piltdown skull, with the unexpected result that it was only about 50,000 years old (subsequent analysis indicates that it is even younger, no older than a thousand years or so). The same dating techniques applied to the Piltdown jaw indicated clearly that it was modern. Subsequent close inspection of the jaw and teeth indicated that the teeth had been filed (to produce wear patterns typical of truly human teeth), painted, and stained to look old. By 1953 it was patently obvious the Piltdown Man was an outright fraud. The only real question that remained was the identity of the perpetrator(s).

It has never been seriously suggested that Smith Woodward was the hoaxer; rather, he appears to have been taken in completely by the fraud. In many people's opinions, Charles Dawson is the most likely candidate. Dawson found many questionable, and downright spurious, items during his career (he died in 1916), including a "Roman" tile supposedly from the late fourth or early fifth century A.D. that in 1972 was dated to the late nineteenth or early twentieth century by thermoluminescence dating. It has also been proposed that Teilhard de Chardin may have been part of the hoax, although he lived to see Piltdown Man exposed and never admitted to any part in the fraud.

Most recently it has been suggested the perpetrator of the Piltdown fraud was Martin A.C. Hinton, keeper of zoology at the British Museum from 1936 to 1945. Hinton was a museum volunteer at the time of the Piltdown discovery. His motive for the fraud may have been to embarrass Woodward Smith; Woodward Smith had recently turned down Hinton's request for a salary. Linking Hinton to the fraud are bones, discovered in 1975 in an old steamer trunk that had belonged to Hinton, that had been "aged" in the same manner as the Piltdown remains. It is possible that Hinton created the actual Piltdown remains, but that Dawson and/or Teilhard de Chardin were also in on the hoax.

Another well-known paleontological error was the so-called Nebraska Man, for a short time thought to be an early human ancestor indigenous to North America. This was in the early 1920s, at the height of some of the arguments between creationists and evolutionists (the John Scopes "monkey trial" concerning the teaching of evolution in schools took place in Tennessee in 1925). Some fossilized teeth recovered from deposits in Nebraska, thought at the time to be at least 2 million years old, made their way to Henry Fairfield Osborn, then director of the American Museum of Natural History in New York. Osborn interpreted the newly discovered fossil to be extremely humanlike, dubbed it *Hesperopithecus* ("western ape"), and interpreted it as evidence for the descent of humans from apelike ancestors. It later was realized, however, that *Hesperopithecus* was actually based on worn teeth of an extinct peccary (a mammal resembling a pig), and Nebraska Man faded away.

An early eighteenth-century hoax was the case of "Beringer's fossils." J.B.A. Beringer was professor of medicine at Wurzburg University, Bavaria. In the country around the university, local children collected various rocks that had odd forms on them resembling organisms and even, apparently, letters of the Hebrew alphabet. Through the children Beringer amassed a collection of about two thousand of these mysterious stones and undertook a study of them that he published as the 1726 monograph *Lithographiae Wirceburgensis*. Beringer's basic conclusion was that the "fossils" (or "formed stones" as they were called) represented a natural phenomenon, and he advanced several theories to explain their origins, including the notion that the forms could have been imprinted on the rocks by the solar particles that make up light after being reflected off or passing through other substances (somewhat similar to a shadow). In this manner the Hebrew letter might have been impressed upon certain stones by light coming from an ancient Jewish cemetery located near the locality where many of the "fossils" were found.

Today it is clear that "Beringer's fossils" were carved by human hands with the intent to deceive, and even in the 1720s there were allegations that the credulous Beringer was being victimized by hoaxers. In fact, an official inquiry was made at the time, and it was suggested that the perpetrators were two colleagues at the university who harbored personal animosity and jealousy toward Professor Beringer: J.J. Roderich, a professor of mathematics, and G. von Eckhart, a librarian.

A classic, if extreme, error of misinterpretation that involved no hoax or fraud per se was the "nummulosphere" theory propounded by Randolph Kirkpatrick, assistant keeper of lower invertebrates at the British Museum from 1886 to 1926. After an early career devoted to the taxonomy of living and extinct sponges, in approximately 1912 Kirkpatrick discovered what he interpreted to be shells of the single-celled organism *Nummulites* (a type of foraminifera) embedded in the volcanic rocks of the island of Porto Santo (west of Morocco). This set Kirkpatrick on a quest to examine igneous rocks (normally thought to have formed from hot, molten magma and to be totally devoid of any fossil remains) from around the world. In all of the rocks he examined, Kirkpatrick found what he interpreted to be the remains of nummulitic-type organisms. He then studied meteorites and found nummulitic organisms in them as well. Kirkpatrick concluded that all rocks are formed from fossils, and furthermore that the spiral-shaped nummulite is the expression of the fundamental structure of life, and indeed of all matter. Needless to say, other researchers have not been able to confirm the presence of nummulites in igneous rocks. Kirkpatrick's nummulosphere theory has been rightfully dismissed as eccentric (to put it mildly).

A recent alleged hoax involves fossil ammonoids and condonts reported by Indian geologist V.J. Gupta from the Himalayas. Previously the varieties of fossils involved were known only from Morocco and New York; their discovery in the Himalayas was quite exciting. Now it has been suggested by some authorities that Gupta may have salted various Himalayan exposures with imported fossils. As of this writing, Gupta continues to assert that his discoveries are genuine.

ROBERT M. SCHOCH

Further Reading

Blinderman, C. 1986. *The Piltdown Inquest*. Buffalo, New York: Prometheus.

Gould, S.J. 1980. *The Panda's Thumb: More Reflections in Natural History*. New York: Norton; Harmondsworth, Middlesex: Penguin.

Hitching, F. 1982. *The Neck of the Giraffe: Where Darwin Went Wrong*. London: Pan; New Haven, Connecticut: Ticknor and Fields.

Jones, M. (ed.). 1990. *Fake? The Art of Deception*. London: British Museum Publications; Berkeley: University of California Press.

Menon, S. 1997. The Piltdown Perp. *Discover*. January 1997:34.

Romer, A.S. 1933. *Man and the Vertebrates*. Chicago: University of Chicago Press; 3rd ed., 1941; Harmondsworth, Middlesex: Penguin, 1954.

Weiner, J.S. 1955. *The Piltdown Forgery*. London and New York: Oxford University Press.

HOMINIDS

Hominids are members of the zoological family Hominidae, superfamily Hominoidea (together with the apes), suborder Anthropoidea (together with the monkeys and apes), order Primates, class Mammalia, phylum Chordata, and kingdom Animalia. *Homo sapiens* is the only living hominid species.

Athough modern paleoanthropological research has provided abundant data about human evolution, there are still notable gaps in knowledge. During the past century a trove of fossil human and humanlike creatures has been collected in Africa, Eurasia, and Australia. Paleoanthropologists use them to model when and how we acquired our peculiar morphology (shape and structure) and behavioral characteristics. Unfortunately, novel fossil discoveries often generate new speculation and controversy instead of solving existing puzzles.

Before the 1960s the inability to date ancient sites geochemically confounded theories on the timing of hominid evolutionary events. Moreover, fossil hominid discoveries did not proceed according to the chronological sequence of hominid evolution. Accordingly, the early history of paleoanthropology is punctuated by exaggerated claims for the importance of individual specimens and by oversimplified phylogenetic (evolutionary) models of the Hominidae.

Neanderthalian specimens were the first exotic hominid specimens to tease Western minds. Although remains from Belgium (1829–30) and Gibralter (1848) received little fanfare, a partial skeleton from the Neander Valley, Germany (1856), sparked notable discussion among nineteenth-century scientists and the lay public. Opinions ranged from it being a pathological freak to representing a barbarian race of humanity or an extinct species, *Homo neanderthalensis* (King 1864). Growing acceptance that Darwin's theory of descent with modification could apply to human origins and the discovery of even less humanoid, ancient *Homo erectus* in Java (1890–1900) and China (1923–38) made Neanderthalians more acceptable as ancestors of *Homo sapiens*.

The battle for acceptance of very apish hominids in our family tree was more prolonged and difficult to win among the scientific community. In 1924 Raymond Dart recognized that a fossil child's skull (*Australopithecus africanus*) from Taung, South Africa, represented a bipedal creature (one that walked on two feet) that was much closer to hominid beginnings than *Homo erectus*. The scientific establishment generally rejected Dart's claims in favor of their own candidate from Down, England—the Piltdown fabrication (1912–15). Although Piltdown was not debunked until 1953–55, additional specimens of *Australopithecus,* including locomotor skeletal remains from four sites in the Transvaal, South Africa (1936–58), increasingly persuaded experts that *Australopithecus* belonged near the root of the Hominidae.

The modern era of paleoanthropological research began in 1959 with the discovery of 1.8-million-year-old *Australopithecus (Paranthropus) boisei* by Mary and Louis Leakey in Olduvai Gorge, northern Tanzania. Because this hominid was associated with datable minerals, artifacts, and many other animal bones, paleontolo-

gists could make inferences about its geochronological age and behavior. Expert geologists, geochemists, paleontologists, prehistoric archaeologists, human biologists, and other specialists were drawn to Olduvai Gorge, where they worked as teams to interpret the many hominid specimens that followed, including *Homo habilis* and African representatives of *Homo erectus.* In the minds of scientists, Africa began to replace Asia as the primary continent where new hominid species had arisen.

Between 1967 and 1997, similar paleoanthropological teams achieved even more spectacular results in the Omo River Valley, Afar Depression, and Awash River Valley of Ethiopia, at localities around the Kenyan shores of Lake Turkana, and at Laetoli, near Olduvai Gorge in northern Tanzania.

Despite stunning past and prospective successes in the field, the art of tracing human phylogeny will always be difficult and in flux. Even if accurately dated fossil bones alone could inform us definitively about morphology, behavior, and phylogeny, the brutal truth is that full documentation probably has not been preserved. Myriad telltale bits of evidence have been smashed and pulverized beyond recognition by natural processes and human-mediated processes. Furthermore, for a variety of practical and political reasons, we may never be able to salvage enough of the fossils that are buried in Africa and Eurasia.

Although we are now blessed with a variety of geochemical dating methods, prized hominid fossils are not always found with minerals that provide precise chronological dates, and the taphonomy of the site may be ambiguous regarding the temporal relationship of a focal fossil with datable minerals and associated faunal and floral remains.

Living animals, particularly the apes, also provide clues to our past, but because they have followed their own evolutionary paths, they do not represent the actual forms through which our ancestors evolved. Recent comparisons of DNA and other molecular biological studies suggest that humans and the African apes—chimpanzees *(Pan troglodytes),* bonobos *(Pan paniscus),* and gorillas *(Pan gorilla)*—are related more closely to one another than any of them is related to Asian apes—orangutans *(Pongo pygmaeus)* and gibbons *(Hylobatidae)*—or to monkeys (Ceboidea and Cercopithecoidea). Accordingly, molecular anthropologists are inclined to place the African apes with humans in the Hominidae. On the other hand, morphologists and behavioralists, who stress the bodily and behavioral differences between people and apes, continue to reserve the Hominidae for humans and fossil species that have humanoid physical characteristics.

Scientists and humanists vigorously debate how closely apes emulate human behaviors and the biological bases of those behaviors; nonetheless, living apes stimulate many ideas among theorists about the adaptations of our apish and ancient humanoid ancestors.

The chief trait shared by all the Hominidae is obligately terrestrial, fully upright bipedal posture and gait. Some anthropologists further consider all fossil members of the Hominidae to be human. Others restrict humankind to hominids that are and were dependent on culture, as represented archaeologically by stone tool technologies and later by control of fire (hearths), fabricated shelters, intentional burial of the dead, bodily adornment, rock art, and figurines. Given this perspective, mere evidence of bipedalism is not sufficient for a fossil hominoid to be human. Behavioral traits that first appear with hominids and were elaborated by later hominids with expanded brains and reduced faces and dentitions—which we use to identify genus *Homo* anatomically—are the chief critera for humankind. In brief, because humanity began with *Homo,* all humans are hominids, but not all hominids are humans.

By 4.4 million years ago, hominids with many apelike dental and upper limb features inhabited Africa, as evidenced by *Ardipithecus ramidus* at Aramis, Ethiopia. Although a crushed partial skeleton was recovered, it has not been reassembled and studied sufficiently to determine its method of locomotion. *Ardipithecus ramidus* lived in a closed woodland. If it was not an obligately terrestrial biped (i.e., if it also was arboreal), it could be grouped with apes instead of the hominids.

Two major adaptive radiations of Hominidae followed *Ardipithecus:* one of *Australopithecus*—between 4.1 and 1 million years ago— and a second of *Homo* between 2.5 million years ago and 100 thousand years ago. Global climatic changes reduced African forests, which allowed open woodlands and grasslands to become more extensive. These areas provided novel habitats for new species and greater numbers of antelopes, pigs, monkeys, giraffes, elephants, and other animals that adventurous hominids could scavenge and perhaps kill. Tubers, seeds, and grasses also may have become more common in the diets of hominids that foraged in the open areas. Large cats, dogs, and hyenas also flourished in the new environments. They not only provided meat for alert scavengers but also posed a threat to hominids with whom they competed and upon whom they probably preyed.

The initial radiation of *Australopithecus* probably occurred in forests or in mosaic localities of riverine forest with adjacent woodlands and more open areas. *Australopithecus* includes at least seven species, distinguished chiefly by differences in their teeth, jaws, and other cranial parts (when available): *Australopithecus anamensis* (4.1 to 3.5 million years ago) in northern Kenya; *Australopithecus afarensis* (3.9 to 3.0 million years ago) in Ethiopia and perhaps northern Tanzania; *Australopithecus bahrelghazali* (3.5 to 3.0 million years ago) in Chad; *Australopithecus africanus* (3.0 to 2.3 million years ago) in northeastern South Africa; *Australopithecus (Paranthropus) aethiopicus* (2.6 to 2.2 million years ago) in Ethiopia and northern Kenya; *Australopithecus (Paranthropus) boisei* (2.6 to 1.0 million years ago) in northern Kenya and northern Tanzania; and *Australopithecus (Paranthropus) robustus* (2.0 to 1.2 million years ago) in northeastern South Africa.

Australopithecus is characterized by ape-sized brains (400 to 500 cubic centimeters) and large molar teeth with thick enamel. The early species and *Australopithecus africanus* have protruding jaws, but the faces of *A. robustus* and *A. boisei* are more vertical. The latter two species are also characterized by relatively small incisors and canine teeth, particularly when compared to their enormous cheek teeth and molarized bicuspids. *A. afarensis* and species of *Paranthropus* also commonly have sizeable bony crests

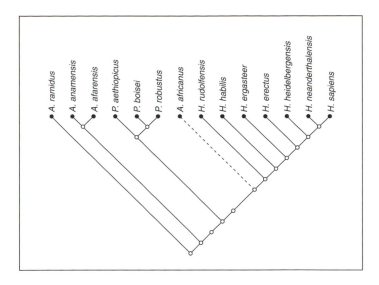

Figure 1. Cladogram of human evolution. Illustration by Catherine P. Sexton, after Johanson and Edgar (1996).

on the top and the back of the skull, to which powerful chewing and neck muscles attached.

For half a century, the species of *Paranthropus* were known as "robust australopithecines," while *Australopithecus africanus* were called "gracile australopitheines." When sufficient noncranial skeletal parts were found, it became clear that the names are unwarranted since their bodily size ranges overlapped notably. Females were smaller than the males in species of *Australopithecus,* for which there are quantities of specimens. The robustly skulled species of *Australopithecus (Paranthropus)* may have eaten tougher foods than those of the more gracile-skulled *Australopithecus.* Indeed, John T. Robinson suggested that *Paranthropus* were vegetarians, while *Australopithecus africanus* had more meat in their diet. Tooth wear patterns in *Australopithecus afarensis* indicate that they may have stripped vegetation by manually pulling it across their front teeth. Locomotor skeletal remains of *Australopithecus* sport apish features that are related to arboreal activity, so it is reasonable to conclude that they continued to climb trees to forage, rest, sleep, and escape from terrestrial predators, rivals, and pests.

The phylogenetic relationships among the seven species of *Australopithecus* and the direct ancestors of *Homo,* which presumably arose from one of them, are all unknown. *Australopithecus (Paranthropus) aethiopicus* may have evolved from *Australopithecus afarensis,* which then gave rise to *Paranthropus boisei* and *P. robustus.* Alternatively, *Australopithecus africanus* may be ancestral to *P. robustus* in southern Africa, and only *P. boisei* descended from *P. aethiopicus* in eastern Africa. In any event, species of *Paranthropus* are unlikely to be ancestors to *Homo,* and it is arguable whether *Homo* arose directly from *Australopithecus afarensis* or from a smaller-toothed variant of *A. africanus.*

Although there is no consensus on which specimens belong in each species, the radiation of *Homo* is thought to have produced the following: *Homo habilis* (2.5 to 1.6 million years ago) at Olduvai Gorge, Tanzania, and perhaps several localities in

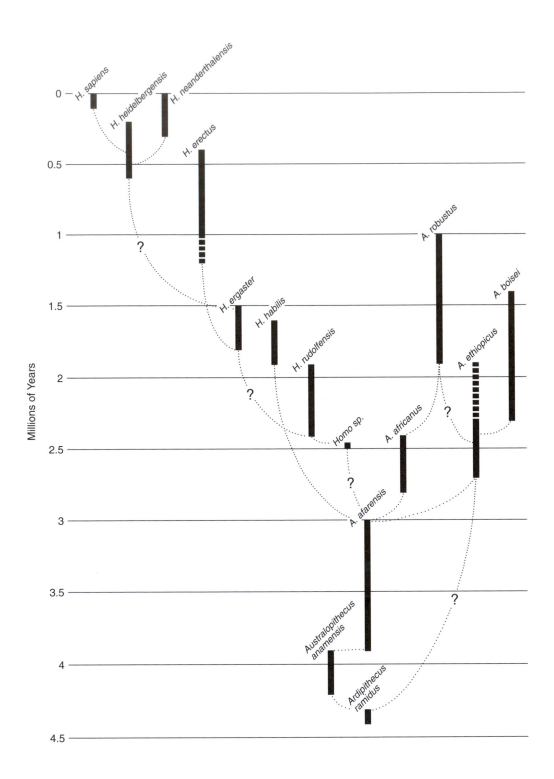

Figure 2. Phylogenetic tree of human evolution. Illustration by Catherine P. Sexton, after Johanson and Edgar (1996).

Kenya and South Africa; *Homo rudolfensis* (2.5 to 1.9 million years ago) in northern Kenya and perhaps Malawi; *Homo ergaster* (1.8 to 1.4 million years ago) in northern Kenya; *Homo erectus* (1.8 million years ago to 400 thousand years ago) in Africa, Asia, and perhaps Europe; *Homo antecessor* in northern Spain (800 thousand years ago); *Homo heidelbergensis* (600 to 200 thousand years ago) in Europe and possibly Ethiopia and South Africa; *Homo neanderthalensis* (300 to 30 thousand years ago) in Europe and western Asia; and *Homo sapiens* (100 thousand years ago to the present) globally.

Although there is no agreement about which of the three early species of *Homo*—*H. rudolfensis, H. habilis, H. ergaster*—gave rise to the four younger species, the candidacy of African *Homo ergaster* is gaining popularity among paleoanthropologists, who accept it as a species distinct from *Homo erectus. Homo heidelbergensis* may have arisen from *Homo ergaster, Homo erectus,* or *Homo antecessor.* And any or none of them could have been ancestral to the two latest species of *Homo: Homo neanderthalensis* and *Homo sapiens.* Neanderthalian populations, particularly as represented by specimens from Western Europe, are generally thought not to be ancestral to modern humans.

Species of *Homo* have smaller molars and bicuspids and larger brains (from over 600 to 2400 cubic centimeters) than those of *Australopithecus.* Apish features in the locomotor skeletons of *Homo habilis* suggest regular arboreal activity, though they were limited to bipedal locomotion when moving on the ground. Although foot bones from *Homo erectus, Homo ergaster, Homo antecessor,* and *Homo heidelbergensis* are precious few, other skeletal parts indicate that, like *Homo neanderthalensis,* they were basically adapted to a human pattern of bipedal locomotion.

Many scenarios have been suggested for the development of bipedalism, and the selective factors stressed in each scenario are not mutually exclusive, particularly if one introduces them at different times in the hominid career. A prior history of bipedal movement, foraging on branches, and climbing vertically on tree trunks and vines would prepare the earliest hominids for bipedal terrestrial foraging on shrubs and low tree branches and traveling for short distances in open woodland habitats. Experiments show that gibbons, which naturally run bipedally on large branches, expend more energy in bipedal branch walking and climbing vertical supports than when running bipedally on the ground. Bipedal foraging, crouching, and squatting would select for robust heels and perhaps short toes and the unique arch of the foot that serve *Homo* so well in running and trekking.

Bipedalism is advantageous over quadrupedism in open tropical areas because less bodily surface is exposed to direct sunlight and because the delicate brain is kept away from the ground and higher up, where the air is cooler because of greater circulation. Reduction of bodily hair and the proliferation of sweat glands in areas that benefit most from moving air also developed during eras of routine vigorous activity in hot open areas. These physiological refinements probably occurred sometime after 2 million years ago, during the period of brain enlargement, elaboration of technology, and the deployment of *Homo* out of Africa.

We do not know when our ancestors essentially quit the trees. Until they had innovated secure technological defenses—control of fire, formidable weapons, secure ground shelters—they probably used tree platforms for nightly repose, and there they may have conducted other activities, such as food collection and processing, grooming, play, and defensive maneuvers. The earliest record of stone artifacts is 2.5 million years ago in Ethiopia. These crude flakes and chipped nodules could assist food processing. However, they (and tree branches) would not be effective defensive weapons against large individual predators and groups of smaller social carnivores unless launched from above—from trees.

Heavier stone tools and more diversified tool kits are associated with *Homo erectus* and especially with *Homo heidelbergensis, Homo neanderthalensis,* and *Homo sapiens.* Although hearths are rare until 100 thousand years ago, concentrations of charcoal, burnt bones, seeds, and artifacts occur in China and France as early as 460 thousand years ago. They indicate that *Homo erectus, Homo heidelbergensis,* or members of both species used fire. If claims that hominids controlled fire in South Africa 1 million years ago are confirmed, *Australopithecus robustus* or *Homo habilis* could be added as fire keepers.

Archaeological traces of human-made shelters appear rarely in Middle Paleolithic Europe 60 thousand years ago, and become common in the Upper Paleolithic (40 to 10 thousand years ago), particularly in regions with notable seasons of inclement weather. Although some Neanderthalians buried their dead, there is little evidence of mortuary ceremony in their graves. During the Upper Paleolithic, there flourished many other features and artifacts that characterize the modern human condition: stylized burial of the dead; sewn, decorated clothing and other bodily adornment; elegant realistic and abstract paintings, engravings, and figurines; and a greater variety of tools in materials other than stone.

The first appearances and development of symbolically based speech and spirituality are highly elusive to paleoanthropologists because they leave no morphological or unarguable archaeological trace before the innovation of writing and ritual paraphernalia. Some paleoanthropologists believe that cerebral regions associated with human speech—Broca's area and Wernicke's area—can be detected on the inner surface of fossil hominid braincases and that flexion of the base of the skull indicates a roomy humanoid vocal tract. Moreover, some experts interpret Upper Paleolithic cultural remains to indicate religious beliefs among their makers. Actually, too little is known about the neurological speech structures, symbolic capabilities, and other markers of the several human intelligences to presume to detect them from inside battered fossil braincases, models of ancient hominid vocal tracts, or Pleistocene (1.6 million years ago to 10 thousand years ago) remnants of technology and art.

RUSSELL H. TUTTLE

Works Cited and Further Reading

Campbell, B.G., and J.D. Loy. 1996. *Humankind Emerging.* 7th ed., HarperCollins, New York.

Dart, R.A. 1925. *Australopithecus africanus:* The man-ape of South Africa. *Nature* 115:195–99.

Gore, R. 1997a. Expanding worlds. *National Geographic Magazine* 191 (5):84–109.

———. 1997b. The first steps. *National Geographic Magazine* 191 (2):72–99.

Johanson, D., and B. Edgar. 1996. *From Lucy to Language.* New York: Simon and Schuster; London: Weidenfeld and Nicolson.

King, W. 1864. The reputed fossil man of the Neanderthal. *Quarterly Journal of Science* 1:88–97.

Robinson, J.T. 1963. Adaptive radiation in australopithecines and the origin of man. *In* F.C. Howell and F. Bourlière (eds.), *African Ecology and Human Evolution.* New York: Wenner-Gren Foundation for Anthropological Research; London: Methuen.

Tuttle, R.H. 1994. Up from electromyography: Primate energetics and the evolution of human bipedalism. *In* R.S. Corruccini and R.L. Ciochon (eds.), *Integrative Paths to the Past: Paleoanthropological*   *Advances in Honor of F. Clark Howell*. Englewood Cliffs, New Jersey: Prentice-Hall.

HOMOLOGY

The term "homology" comes from the Greek *homos* meaning "same," and in its simplest form is used to describe an evolutionary relationship between biological features (e.g., organs, molecules, etc.). Although the concept of "sameness" has been recognized since the time of Aristotle, it was not until the early nineteenth century that scholars sought a precise definition. Homology is an essential component of—and, arguably, the central concept in—evolutionary biology, and it remains a very contentious issue. Aristotle, recognizing a "unity of plan" among groups of animals, developed the first classification of animals based upon the shared presence or absence of certain structural features. From the late eighteenth to the early nineteenth century, identification of such "equivalent" structures preoccupied the well-known morphologists of the day. (Morphology is the study of biological structures.) They sought to identify structures in different organisms that corresponded to the same archetype. In other words, they searched for structures that could be simple or complex, but that were constructed on the same ground plan. The goal was to discover the "natural hierarchy" among these organisms.

Competition between morphologists and their different theories was fierce, culminating in 1830 in the famous debates between Georges Cuvier and Etienne Geoffroy Saint-Hilaire before the Académie Royale des Sciences (Appel, 1987). Cuvier had proposed a division of the animal kingdom into four unrelated embranchements (groups, phyla)—the articulata, mollusca, vertebrata, and radiata—based on their conceived unity of body plan. He regarded these body plans as incompatible across groups. Saint-Hilaire, however, believed in a philosophy of a universal, idealistic animal morphology; he recognized that there were equivalent organs, organ systems, and even regions of animals, not only within different groups (phyla) but also across them.

However, although scientists had been using such terms as "equivalent" and "unity of plan," there was, as yet, no explicit definition of these terms. This changed in 1843, when the British scientist Richard Owen provided his famous definition of homology: "the same organ in different animals under every form of variety and function." In other words, organs could be homologous even if they didn't look identical. He also made the essential distinction between homology and analogy, defining analogous parts or organs as those that "had the same function as another part or organ in another species." Owen also identified homologous structures between extant and fossil taxa but still believed that such homology existed because the different taxa represented construction on the same rational plan, an archetype that had been designed by God.

At this time then, even with Owen's definition, homology was still an idealistic concept. It was left to Owen's great adversary, Charles Darwin, in *The Origin of the Species* (1859) to provide homology with its mechanism of action, that of evolution. He added to Owen's definition by stating that a structure found in two or more species could be considered homologous if it had evolved from a structure present in the ancestor of the two species. Descent by modification from a common ancestor represents "divergent evolution." Analogous structures, those structures that only superficially resemble one another, are those that arise from "convergent evolution." They originate from different ancestral structures in response to similar environmental pressures. This definition of homology based on common origin became known as "historical homology," and it came to be used as evidence of common ancestry rather than common rational plan.

Defining homology, however, is easier than actually recognizing truly homologous features. Until the discovery and popularization of molecular techniques, morphologists usually used three main anatomical criteria to distinguish between homologous and analogous features (Riedl 1978). Applying these criteria, however, often results in conflicting evidence for and against homology, making it difficult, even impossible, to weigh different criteria against one another. The first criterion involves comparing the relative position of the feature (e.g. its position in relation to other features along the various axes of the body); the second, its actual formation (e.g., its embryonic development, constituent cell types, and correspondence in fine detail); and the third, identification of transition states of the feature during its evolution. Of course, determining homology is even more difficult if two daughter species develop very similar structures independently, when such a structure is not present in the last common ancestor.

The fossil record has proved invaluable for the third criterion, that of transitionary states, as it provides us with examples of speciation, extinctions, and patterns of morphological change in a measurable direction, that of time. Difficulties can arise, however, in the interpretation of some fossil remains. Nevertheless, one can follow transitionary forms between at least some anatomical states through the fossil record and construct a directional series of homologous character states. In this way, one can identify the ancestral forms of certain features; the classification of such shared ancestral or "primitive" characters versus "newly acquired" or derived characters is the basis of phylogenetic analysis. In this type of analysis, attempts are made to reconstruct an evolutionary tree (a phylogeny), showing the branching order of living (and extinct) taxa (groups; singular, taxon), through evolutionary time. Morphologists compare structure, embryology, and the fossil record in order to try to differentiate between homologous and analogous features. A.W. Crompton and P. Parker (1978) showed the importance of the fossil record in ascertaining ancestral and transitory states of features in their investigation of the origin of the bones of the middle ear in mammals. Crompton and Parker used the fossil record to show that during evolution these bones had arisen by modification of elements of the jaw in a reptilian ancestor. Thus, the bones of the mammalian middle ear are homologous with the reptilian jaw support.

In applying the three criteria of homology, one must also take care to differentiate between different levels of homology. For example, consider the classic example of the wings of birds and bats. The wings of birds and bats are homologous as forelimbs yet they are analogous as wings. That is, their last common ancestor possessed forelimbs but not wings. Wings have arisen in both groups independently, as a result of convergent evolution. Thus, homology can be present at some levels but absent at others, even when considering the same structure.

In more recent times, the concept of historical homology has been expanded to that of biological homology. Biological homology includes a new, fourth criterion of homology: the sharing of common developmental pathways. This expanded concept was necessary once the biologists in the new, molecular era began to elucidate the genetic basis of the origin and differentiation of characters/features. The widely used techniques of gene cloning and the identification of these genes' sites of expression (and putative—generally assumed—functions) have identified further possible lines of evidence of homology of features across taxa. The DNA sequence and protein sequence encoded by a gene can be compared to that of genes isolated from other, often quite distantly related species. Mathematical analysis reveals that particular genes cloned from different species can be shown to have arisen from a single, common, ancestral gene. That gene must have been present in the common ancestor of the two species. Such genes present in a single copy in different taxa are said to be homologous, and molecular biologists have begun to use the expression sites of such genes as markers of spatial or structural homology. Note that the three criteria previously applied to anatomical features can also be applied to gene sequences or expression data.

Elucidation of the genetic basis of developmental processes adds a further dimension to understanding and identifying homology. However, many complications have arisen when considering molecular data as evidence of homologous or analogous processes/features. Not least of these problems is gene duplication. During evolution, independent gene duplications have occurred in different lineages. Sometimes these new genes are retained in the genome and be "co-opted" (taken over) for a new function. Such duplication within a lineage produces what are known as paralogous genes (i.e., homologous genes that have resulted from a duplication event). Splitting of lineages produces orthologous genes (i.e., homologous genes that have resulted from a speciation event) (Fitch 1970). Sometimes large regions of DNA, chromosomes, or even most of the genome may be duplicated, resulting in

duplication of whole interacting genetic pathways. This produces raw material for the processes of natural selection and random changes. More evidence is being obtained showing that once integrated into the genome, such genes or gene networks can be used in many different, not necessarily homologous, processes. Obviously this presents problems when trying to determine the ancestral condition of a gene (or gene family) and when trying to homologize features based upon the genes involved in its formation.

Clearly, a modern, inclusive, working definition of homology is still proving elusive. We apply various criteria in order to identify homology, and yet we still have problems differentiating between homology and analogy, whether it relates to anatomical, biochemical, developmental, or even behavioral processes and structures. Different, hierarchical levels of homology exist, even within single features, and we must take care to distinguish between such levels, especially when considering only a fraction of the available data.

NIC A. WILLIAMS

See also Comparative Anatomy; Evolutionary Novelty; Growth, Development, and Evolution; Speciation and Morphological Change; Systematics

Works Cited

Appel, T.A. 1987. *The Cuvier-Geoffroy Debate: French Biology in the Decades before Darwin.* Oxford and New York: Oxford University Press.

Compton, A.W., and P. Parker. 1978. Evolution of the mammalian masticatory apparatus. *American Scientist* 66:192–201.

Darwin, C.R. 1859. *The Origin of Species by Means of Natural Selection.* London: J. Murry; Darby, Pennsylvania: Arden.

Fitch, W.M. 1970. Distinguishing homologous from analogous proteins. *Systemic Zoology* 19:99–113.

Owen, R. 1843. *Lectures on the Comparative Anatomy and Physiology of the Invertebrate Animals.* London: Brown, Green and Longmans.

Riedl, R. 1978. *Order in Living Organisms: A Systems Analysis of Evolution.* Chichester and New York: Wiley; as *Die Ordnung des Lebendigen,* Hamburg and Berlin: Parey, 1975.

Further Reading

Dickinson, W.J. 1995. Molecules and morphology: Where's the homology? *Trends in Genetics* 11:119–21.

Hall, B.K. (ed.). 1994. *Homology: The Hierarchical Basis of Comparative Anatomy.* San Diego, California: Academic Press.

Hennig, W. 1979. *Phylogenetic Systematics,* D.D. Davis and R. Zangerl (trans.). Urbana: University of Illinois Press; as *Grundzüge einer Theorie der Phylogenetischen Systematik,* Berlin: Deutscher Zentralverlag, 1950.

Roth, V.L. 1984. On homology. *Biological Society of the Linnaean Society* 22:13–29.

HOOIJER, DIRK ALBERT

Dutch, 1919–93

Perhaps the most prolific of workers on Pleistocene mammal faunas of southeast Asia in the decades following World War II, Hooijer was a Dutch vertebrate paleontologist and foremost mammalian specialist, especially on young Tertiary and Quaternary rhinoceroses and elephants (especially pygmy stegodonts) in the Netherlands, Africa, Antilles, Near East, China, India, and Indonesia. He also studied langurs, macaques, gibbons, orangutans, humans, sabre-tooth cats, panthers, porcupines, hyenas, hippos, bantengs (a type of cattle), and giant sloths. He tackled subjects as widely separated in time and space as Dutch Middle Triassic tetrapods and Neolithic prehistoric and semidomesticated assemblages in Syrian tells (debris mounds), producing more than 270 publications. During his career he named six new genera and 47 new species. He utilized his knowledge of mammalian comparative anatomy (gained under his supervisor and director of the Leiden Museum, systematic zoologist H. Boschma) to shed light on topics such as the dating of rocks to the evolution of the dentition and shedding of elephant teeth (1979). In all he described over 50 new taxa; in turn he has only one genus, *Hooijeromys* 1981, named for him.

In 1941 Hooijer was entrusted with the responsibility for the Eugène Dubois vertebrate collection in what was then known as the Rijksmuseum van Natuurlijke Historie in Leiden, assembled during the extensive excavations in the search for *Pithecanthropus erectus* near Trinil on the River Solo in Java at the end of the nineteenth century. Hooijer planned a doctoral thesis on Cainozoic stratigraphy under Van der Vlerk, but World War II prevented this. Instead, he studied under systematic zoologist Boschma, his thesis dealing with fossil rhinoceratids. Hooijer's subsequent body of work has greatly contributed to our understanding of the animal life that flourished on the Sunda Islands of one-half to one million years ago. The vertebrate remains helped to date more rigorously the hominids; in the process there were some disputes about dating with G. von Koenigswald, who had worked in the East Indies in the 1930s. Turtles in Dubois' collection also had an impact on Hooijer, and he later devoted time to plotting the course of tortoise gigantism in the Indo-Australian region. At the same time he began working on the H.R. van Heekeren collections made in Indonesia from the 1940s, especially elephantid remains found with hominid tools on Celebes (Bartstra 1997), and giant rats in Flores/Timor.

In the 1950s Hooijer's work was dominated by southeastern Asiatic fossil mammals; the Bovidae of the Dubois collection from Borneo, Java, Sumatra, and the Punjab were among these. By 1952 he had made useful comparative faunal lists for Villafranchian and Middle Pleistocene sites in Burma (Upper Irrawaddy), Java (Cijulang and Kaliglagah), China (Ma Kai Valley in Yunnan), and Vietnam. He was coming to grips with proboscideans: The discovery of a tooth of *Palaeoloxodon* in Teyler's Museum at Haarlem increased the East Indies taxa by 100 percent. In 1958 he identified a fossil *Stegodon* from Flores, the first of its kind from the Lesser Sunda Islands, and he realized that, as the Flores stegodont is only slightly different from *Stegodon trigonocephalus* Martin from the Pleistocene of Java, it must have been quite easy for this species to cross "Wallace's Line" between Bali and Lombok during Pleistocene glaciation. This proposal was in harmony with findings of contemporary zoogeographers that the fauna of the Lesser Sunda Islands was predominantly oriental, becoming impoverished eastward along the island chain. He hoped to find more oriental fossil mammals in Flores; if *Stegodon* got there, other herbivores (and carnivores) also may have. Then in 1964 *Stegodon* from the island of Timor was collected. Hooijer found it a very small creature, geographically as well as morphologically "the end" in stegodontines. With it was associated a huge varanid, which he saw as greatly surpassing the Komodo dragon lizard in size, and apparently of Australian origin. Finally, in 1970, he saw for himself for the first time the Pleistocene fossil localities in Sulawesi (Celebes), Flores, and Timor, about which he had written so much. He now concluded also that the giant land tortoises from Timor and Sulawesi belonged to one species—*Geochelone atlas* (F and C)—and is the same taxon as in Upper Siwaliks of India. On the other hand, pygmy stegodonts of Flores and Timor seemed identical but widely different from those of Sulawesi, where there is a normal-sized stegodont and a pygmy. Presumably they had been separated by rising sea levels in the former "Stegoland," a zoogeographic entity between Sundaland and Sahulland coined by Hooijer (1975; van Oosterzee 1997). In all subsequent work he upheld endemism of the pygmy elephants and proclaimed the correlation with gigantism in rodents, several of which he described. In later life he seriously suggested that a search be made for dwarf elephants in northern Australia (e.g., 1967). In 1971 he visited San Miguel Island in California, where he observed pygmy elephants *in situ* rather than having them sent to him.

Hooijer bridged the gap between paleontology and archaeology; his paleontological detective work in the Levant (Middle East) epitomized both his efforts in the field and in searching museum drawers: a Villafranchian fauna comprising a fossil giraffe, but lacking deer, from Bethlehem, proved interesting to him because it showed that the area had been a "halfway house" between Eurasia and Africa; on the other hand, it contained typical Pleistocene mammals never found in Africa. During work in the National Museum in Damascus (Syria)—on Pleistocene mammals of the Orontes Valley—he found an antiquoid variety of *Elephas trogontherii*, and the tooth of a cave hyena thus far known only from coprolites.

He began work on African material, gaining grants to visit Cape Town in 1958, where he worked with Ronald Singer on the Hopefield fauna. They discovered a new Late Pliocene locality that yielded *Stegolophodon* and other elements never found in Africa before except in Cyrenaica; over 1,000 specimens of one taxon were excavated. The Makapan rhinos at the Bernard Price Institute in Johannesburg provided a new direction. After examining the classic australopithecine sites and material, he concluded that, in his opinion, *Meganthropus palaeojavanicus* is a *Paranthropus* and not simply a large *Pithecanthropus erectus.* Taking up work on African rhinos, equids, and hippos at the behest of the Leakeys, he returned again to South and East Africa in 1971. In the late 1960s he began to consider Miocene forms, conducting pioneer work on rhino faunas. He also worked with the EAGRU team organized by Bedford College's "Bill" Bishop, noting that the Plio-Pleistocene Baringo material make "more pieces fall into line of what is still largely a puzzle: the phylogeny of the rhinoceroses of Africa." He completed analyses of faunal assemblages of many East African (Kenyan and Ethiopian) Tertiary sites in the major push to understand hominid and mammalian evoulution led by Louis Leaky and Bryan Patterson, becoming part of a team of specialists who assessed over 20,000 mammalian remains in the Lower Omo Valley, including rhinoceros, *Hipparian,* and in the Lake Rudolf Basin. In the mid–1970s and early 1980s, Mary Leakey sent him the interesting hipparians, from beds over a million years older than the amazing 3.8-million-year-old Laetoli site in northern Tanzania, where hipparion footprints are associated with those of hominids at a time pivotal in the history of these equids. He maintained the separate evolution of the African elephant and went on to deduce that the Miocene rhinos of East Africa were generically the same as those of the Miocence of Eurasia, but different specifically with four or five taxa.

G.J. Boekschoten (1994) wrote "Hooijer was an excellent paleontologist, an enthusiastic expert who aimed at perfection. His intense commitment and sensitive nature sometimes made him sharp and fierce. Hooijer was often difficult for younger colleagues. Those who knew him well enjoyed his fabulous erudition and will remember him as a passionate scientist." Until quite late in life he was isolated to a certain extent, and his life was not easy, partly for this reason. Gaining a Rockefeller fellowship he went to New York for a year and a half to work in the American Museum of Natural History on the Pleistocene mammalian fauna from Yenchingkou, a joint project with E.H. Colbert. In 1951 he joined the staff of the Royal Ontario Museum, Canada, as Curator of Vertebrate Paleontology, where he planned to work on Canadian vertebrates, but he was back in Holland before the year was out. He had been disappointed with the museum facilities (there was but a minor library and no laboratory); fortunately, he still could find a place at the Leiden museum. Hooijer wrote infrequently with other people; these included Ned Colbert, Ronald Singer, Bryan Patterson, Vince Maglio, Rufus Churcher, and G.-J. Bartstra. Hooijer's scientific career was marred by tragedy and circumstances often beyond his control. In the 1940s it was the German occupation, which prevented him from properly embracing his studies, leaving, as with others, scars and bitter memories. Illness resulted, which dominated his personal and professional relationships. However, he later relished his chance to teach at a budding American university, the University of California at Irvine, and to be present during the spring 1970 campus events. He left the museum in 1979 under a cloud, but his retirement was made happier by collaboration with the editorial group in the venture *Museologia,* a journal devoted to the Muse. An invitation to lecture at an international conference at Leiden, "Human Evolution in Its Ecological Context," gave him great satisfaction.

Most interested in the philosophical implications of his work, he wrote in a serious and sometimes a not-so-serious vein about elephant teeth and tusks and rhino horns and the efficacy of people's beliefs in such appendages. One brilliant lecture concerned the relic of a saint housed in a Tibetan monastery, which was supposed to give the possessor absolute immunity from death; he proposed to test this by walking out into a busy Edinburgh road. But the specimen was in fact the juvenile tooth of an Argali (a wild sheep), which exhibited about 64 dental or enamel pearls—proof that the mother goat at least had survived many traumatic experiences, a phenomenon also noted by Hooijer in one fossil rhino.

Hooijer was not a cladist (a proponent of cladistics, the current dominant school of systematics); he studied and described the specimens in his care to the best of his ability. He exhorted his colleagues to handle ample collections especially of pre- or protohistoric remains of living species and to study this valuable material as intensively as possible, with the help of adequate series of recent material and all sorts of statistical methods. "The study of variation is the basic task for the paleontologist" (1950c).

SUSAN TURNER

Works Cited

Bartstra, G.J. 1997. A fifty-years commemoration of fossil vertebrates and stone tools in the Walanae valley, South Sulawesi, Indonesia. *Quartär* 47/48:29–50.

Boekschoten, G.J. 1994. Dr. Dirk Hooijer (1919–1993). *Newsletter of the Koninklijk Nederlands Geologisch en Mijnbouwkundig Genootschap* 1994 (1): 7–8.

van Oosterzee, P. 1997. *Where Worlds Collide: The Wallace Line.* Kew, Victoria: Reed; Ithaca, New York, and London: Cornell University Press.

Biography

Born in Medan, Sumatra, 30 May 1919. Received degrees of candidaat (1940), doctorandus (1945), and Ph.D. (1946), Leiden University. Became assistant curator, Eugène Dubois Collection, Rijksmuseum van Natuurlijke Historie, Leiden, 1941; full curator of Pleistocene fossils, Rijksmuseum van Natuurlijke Historie, Leiden, 1946; curator, Eugène Dubois Collection, Rijksmuseum van Natuurlijke Historie, Leiden, 1947; Rockefeller Fellow, American Museum of Natural History, New York, 1950–51; named Curator of Vertebrate Palaeontology, Royal Ontario Museum of Zoology and Palaeontology, 1951 (but returned to post as curator in Leiden in November); visited southern and eastern Africa under the auspices of the Netherlands Organization for Pure Research (Z.W.O.), 1958; lectured on evolution to the International School of Philosophy at Amersfoort, Holland, 1967; Regent's Professor, University of California, Irvine, 1970; taught graduate courses, Princeton University, 1973; delivered Staring lecture at the Hague for the Koninklijk Nederlands Geologisch en Mijnbouwkundig Genootschap, 1975; retired from Rijksmuseum, 1979. Member, editorial board, *Museologia,* 1973–80. Elected to Society of Vertebrate Paleontology, 1947; received Akzo Prijs, Hollandsche Maatschappij van Wetenschappen [Holland Society of Sciences], 1971. Died in Leiden 26 November 1993.

Major Publications

1942. On the nomenclature of some fossil hippopotami. *Arches Néerlandaises de Zoologie* 6:279–82.

1946. *Prehistoric and Fossil Rhinoceroses from the Malay Archipelago and India.* Leiden: Brill.

1947. On fossil and prehistoric remains of *Tapirus* from Java, Sumatra and China. *Zoologische Mededelingen Leiden* 27:253–99.

1948. Prehistoric teeth of man and the orang-utan from central Sumatra, with notes on the fossil orang-utan from Java and southern China. *Zoologische Mededelingen Leiden* 29:175–305.

1949a. Mammalian evolution in the Quaternary of southern and eastern Asia. *Evolution* 3 (2):125–28.

1949b. Pleistocene vertebrates from Celebes. Part 4, *Archidiskodon celebensis* nov. spec. *Zoologische Mededelingen Leiden* 30 (14):205–26.

1950a. The fossil Hippopotamidae of Asia, with notes on the Recent species. *Zoologische verhandelingen uitgegeven door het Rijksmuseum van Natuurlijke Historie te Leiden* 8:1–124.

1950b. Man and other mammals from Toalian sites in south-western Celebes. *Verhandelingen de Koninklijke Nederlandsche Akademie von Wetenschappen, Afd. Natuurkunde,* 46 (2). Amsterdam: North Holland.

1950c. The study of subspecific advance in the Quaternary: Notes and comments. *Evolution* 4 (4):360–61.

1951a. Fossil evidence of Austromelanesian migrations in Malaysia? *Southwestern Journal of Anthropology* 6 (4): 416–22.

1951b. On the supposed evidence of early man in the Middle Pleistocene of southwest China. *Southwestern Journal of Anthropology* 7 (1):77–81.

1951c. Pygmy elephant and giant tortoise. *Scientific Monthly* 72 (4):3–8.

1951d. Questions relating to a new large anthropoid ape from the Mio-Pliocene of the Siwaliks. *American Journal of Physical Anthropology,* new ser., 9 (1): 79–94.

1953. With E.H. Colbert. Pleistocene mammals from the limestone fissures of Szechwan, China. *Bulletin of the American Museum of Natural History* 102:1–134.

1954. Pleistocene vertebrates from Celebes. Part 8, Dentition and skeleton of *Celebochoerus heekereni* Hooijer. *Zoologische verhandelingen uitgegeven door het Rijksmuseum van Natuurlijke Historie te Leiden* 24:1–46.

1955. Fossil Proboscidea from the Malay Archipelago and the Punjab. *Zoologische verhandelingen uitgegeven door het Rijksmuseum van Natuurlijke Historie te Leiden* 28:1–146.

1960. With Ronald Singer. Fossil rhinoceroses from Hopefield, South Africa. *Zoologische Mededelingen Leiden* 37 (8):113–28.

1961. With Ronald Singer. The fossil Hippopotamus from Hopefield, South Africa. *Zoologische Mededelingen Leiden* 37 (10):157–64.

1964. Pleistocene vertebrates from Celebes. Part 12, Notes on pygmy stegodonts. *Zoologische Mededelingen Leiden* 40 (7):37–44.

1966. Fossil Mammals of Africa. No. 21, Miocene rhinoceroses of East Africa. *Bulletin of the British Museum of Natural History, Geology,* 13 (2):117–90.

1967. Indo-Australian Insular Elephants. *Genetica* 38 (2):143–62.

1970. Pleistocene south-east Asia pygmy stegodonts. *Nature* 225 (5231):474–75.

1973. With M.G. Audley-Charles. Relation of Pleistocene migrations of pygmy Stegodonts to island arc tectonics in eastern Indonesia. *Nature* 241 (5386):197–98.

1974. With V.J. Maglio. Hipparions from the Late Miocene and Pliocene of northwestern Kenya. *Zoologische verhandelingen uitgegeven door het Rijksmuseum van Natuurlijke Historie te Leiden* 134:1–34.

1975. Quaternary mammals west and east of Wallace's Line. *In* G.J. Bartstra and W.A. Casparie (eds.), *Modern Quaternary Research in Southeast Asia.* Rotterdam: Balkema.

1979. Opmerkingen over het gebit en de tandwisseling bij olifanten. *Museologia* 12 (13):29–34.

1982. The extinct giant land tortoise and the pygmy stegodont of Indonesia. In G.-J. Bartstra (ed.), A Volume in Memory of Prof. Dr. G.H.R. von Koenigswald. *Modern Quaternary Research of Southeast Asia* 7:171–76.

1995. With G.J. Bartstra. Fossils and artifacts from southwestern Sulawesi (Celebes). *In* J.R.F. Bower and S. Sartono (eds.), *Human Evolution in Its Ecological Context.* Vol. 1, *Paleoanthropology: Evolution and Ecology of* Homo erectus. Leiden: Leiden University Press.

Further Reading

Bartstra, G.J. 1997. A fifty-years commemoration fossil vertebrates and stone tools in the Walanae valley, South Sulawesi, Indonesia. *Quartär* 47/ 48:29–50.

Boekschoten, G.J. 1994. Dr. Dirk Hooijer (1919–1993). *Newsletter of the Koninklijk Nederlands Geologisch en Mijnbouwkundig Genootschap* 1994.

Davis, A.M., F.S. Eames, and R.J.G. Savage. 1975. *Tertiary Faunas: A Text-Book for Oilfield Palaeontologists and Students of Geology.* Vol. 2. London: Allen and Unwin.

van Oosterzee, P. 1997. *Where Worlds Collide: The Wallace Line.* Kew, Victoria: Reed; Ithaca, New York, and London: Cornell University Press.

Turner, S. 1996. Dr. Dirk Hooijer (1919–1993). *Introduction to* G.J. Boekschoten (author), J.M.J. Vergoossen (trans.), In Memorian. *SVP News Bulletin* 167:79–80.

HORSETAILS AND THEIR RELATIVES

Equisetum, or "horsetails" as they more often are called, are the only survivors of the sphenophytes, the oldest living group of vascular plants. The Sphenophyta includes three orders—Pseudoborniales, Sphenophyllales, and Equisetales.

Today, species of *Equisetum* are found all over the world except Australia and New Zealand. Altogether, 15 species plus some hybrids of *Equisetum* are known from subtropical to polar areas. Today's species of *Equisetum* (Figure 1) are herbaceous perennials (short plants that regrow yearly) that grow in sand and gravelly soils close to water, or even within shallow water. However, from the fossil record we know that sphenophytes were both perennials and huge woody trees that formed forests in swampy areas. Their golden age was some 300 million years ago.

The stem of a recent *Equisetum* is very rough and has longitudinal grooves. The rough surface is formed by silica. The leaves and branches emerge in a whorl at regularly spaced nodes, as do the roots and rhizomes (horizontal rootlike structures). The toothlike leaves around the stem are small and lack chlorophyll; therefore photosynthesis is conducted within the green stems. *Equisetum* has both sterile and fertile shoots. Some species have fertile shoots that lack chlorophyll, whereas others have it (Figure 1).

Stems terminate with a "strobilus," a conelike reproductive structure that consists of whorls of "sporangiophores" (Figure 2). Each sporangiophore consists of several "sporangia," small sacs or cases in which spores develop. A "spore" consists of a spore body and four extensions called "elaters." Under arid conditions elaters remain coiled, but under humid conditions they uncoil and help disperse the spores in small clusters. The spore can survive a few days and, under moist conditions, germinates into a simple, green plant body called a "gametophyte." This structure, less than one centimeter in diameter, has no roots, stems, or leaves. Small rootlike rhizoids attach it to the earth. Upon the upper surface develop "antheridia" (male sex organs, which produce male sperm) and "archegonia" (the female sex organ, which develops the egg). Each antheridium produces many sperm, spirally coiled structures with many tails. They swim over to the archegonium and fertilizes the egg, which then develops into the second structure in the plant's life cycle, the sporophyte (Figure 2).

Before we begin a review of horsetails, we need to discuss the concept of "form genera." It is rare when scholars find a fossil of an entire plant, including stem, leaves, roots, and reproductive structures. Instead, paleobotanists often face an aggregation of pieces. In order to keep other scholars informed about the latest discoveries, paleobotanists group plant parts into classifications called "form genera" (groups; singular, genus). As a result, once a plant's entire system is learned, the leaves will be known by one name, the stems another, and so on.

The first occurrence of sphenophytes is from Upper Devonian rocks found on Bear Island, south of Spitsbergen, Norway, where A.G. Nathorst collected *Pseudobornia ursina* in 1894 (Figure 3). The stem of *P. ursina* consists of nodes separated by internodes (the part of the plant between the nodes), and is estimated to have been 15 to 20 meters tall. Branches were produced at the nodes, and leaves were arranged in whorls of four. The fertile branches carried approximately 30 sporangia each. *P. ursina* belongs to the order Pseudoborniales.

From the order Sphenophyllales, *Sphenophyllum* is known from Late Devonian until Triassic times (Figure 4). The genus name *Sphenophyllum* is used for leaves, stems, and roots. Species of *Sphenophyllum* were very abundant in Carboniferous times, when they formed part of the forest understory, the zone just above the ground. They were herbaceous plants with thin, ribbed stems, standing approximately a meter high. The leaves are found in whorls of 6 to 18 at the nodes and were from 9 to 20 millimeters long (Figure 5). Some leaves are deeply cleft, and others are whole and triangular in shape (Figures 4, 5). The slender cones are formed at the ends of branches. The sporangiophores are arranged in whorls, and each bears small terminal sporangia. The most frequently occurring form genera for the cones are *Sphenophyllostachys* or *Bowmanites*. The sporangia contain uniform spores (homosporous) except for one heterosporous species which, by definition, has two sizes of spores: microspores, which are male,

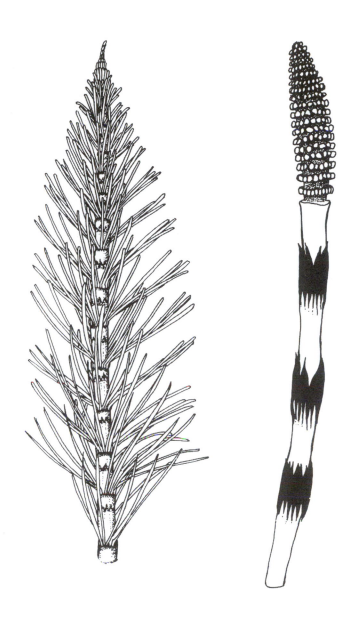

Figure 1. Recent *Equisetum*. Illustration by Brenda Middagh.

and megaspores, which are female. The spores are smooth, approximately 65 millimeters in diameter, and develop both antheridia and archegonia.

The order Equisetales includes calamites and equisetaleans, which share characteristics such as elaters to disperse the spores. *Archaeocalamites,* from Devonian and Carboniferous times, had a meter-long stem that was up to 16 centimeters in diameter (Figures 6, 7). The stem has grooves, but the grooves do not alternate at the internodes as in *Equisetum* (Figure 1). The leaves, branches, and roots emerge from the nodes. The leaves are slim, only one millimeter wide yet up to 10 centimeters long, and they dichotomize (split) several times (Figure 8). The cones were borne on branches, where they replaced several whorls of leaves. There were several whorls in each cone, and 8 to 10 sporangiophores devel-

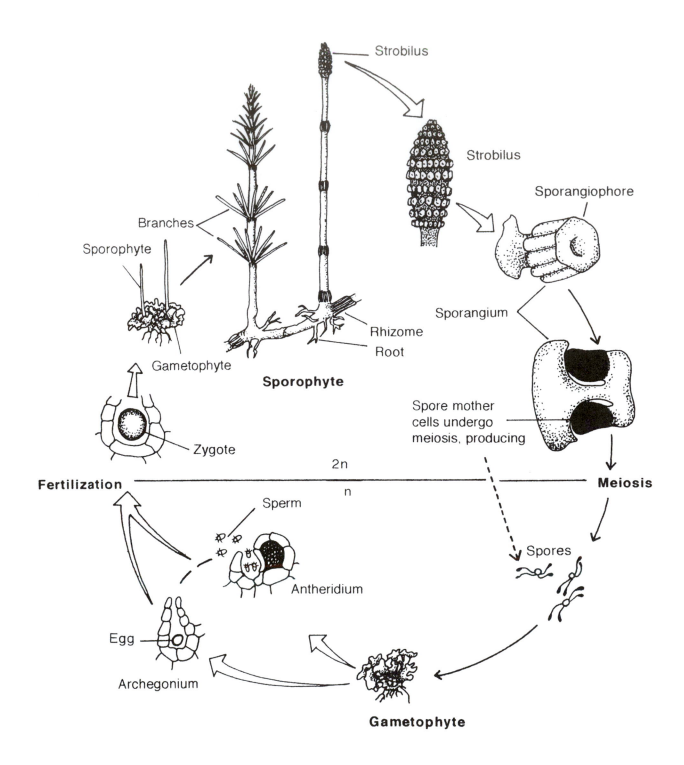

Figure 2. Life history of *Equisetum*. Illustration by Brenda Middagh.

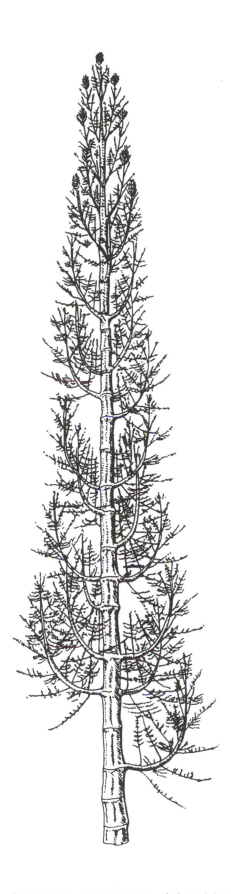

Figure 3. Suggested reconstruction of *Pseudobornia ursina*. Illustration by Brenda Middagh.

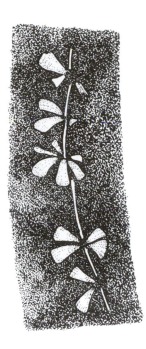

Figure 4. Leaves and stem of *Sphenophyllum* sp. Scale, one centimeter. Photograph by Rasmus B. Koppelhus from the collection at the University of Copenhagen, with permission.

Figure 5. *Sphenophyllum* sp. Scale, one centimeter. Photograph by Rasmus B. Koppelhus from the collection at the University of Copenhagen, with permission.

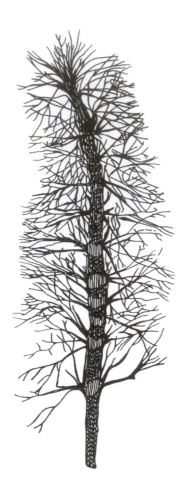

Figure 6. *Archeocalamites radiatus* reconstruction of shoot with sterile appendages. From Lower Carboniferous. Illustration by Brenda Middagh.

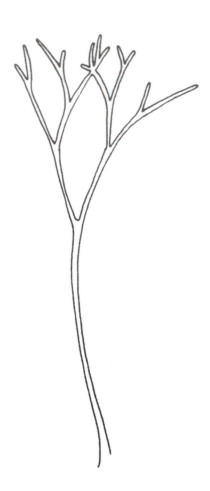

Figure 8. *A. radiatus* foliar appendage enlarged. From Lower Carboniferous. Illustration by Brenda Middagh.

Figure 7. Cast of *Archeocalamites.* Scale, one centimeter. Photograph by Rasmus B. Koppelhus from the collection at the University of Copenhagen, with permission.

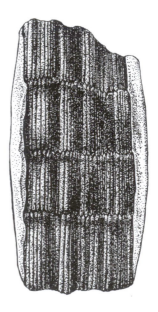

Figure 9. Impression of *Calamites suckowi* from cast. Illustration by Brenda Middagh.

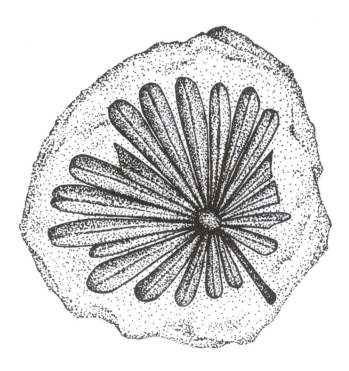

Figure 10. Leaves of *Annularia*. Illustration by Brenda Middagh.

Figure 12. Cast of *Calamites* sp. Scale, one centimeter. Photograph by Rasmus B. Koppelhus from the collection at the University of Copenhagen, with permission.

Figure 11. Leaves and stem of *Annularia*. Scale, one centimeter. Photograph by Rasmus B. Koppelhus from the collection at the University of Copenhagen, with permission.

oped per whorl. A sporangiophore has four sporangia. The spores are called trilete because they have a triradiate (three grooves diverging from a common center) scar: The spore wall is composed of two layers, an outer (perispore) and an inner (endospore). The diameters of the spores range from 82 to 104 millimeters, and they are called *Calamospora*.

Calamites (Figure 9) from the Carboniferous is one of the biggest and most fascinating trees, with trunks 20 to 30 meters in height and 30 centimeters in diameter. It first appeared in the Middle Carboniferous and became extinct during the Early Permian. The leaves and branches are arranged in dense whorls at the nodes. In each whorl, there are from 4 to 60 simple leaves, each with one vein. The form genus for the linear leaves is *Asterophyllits,* and the spatulate (spoon-shaped) or deltoid (triangular) forms are called *Annularia* (Figures 10, 11). The leaf length varies from 0.5 centimeters to more than five centimeters. The cones are most commonly situated at the top of the main shoot. Each cone has whorls of sporangiophores alternating with whorls of sterile bracts (small leaves). Most of the cones are placed in the form genera *Calamostachys* and *Palaeostachya.* When roots have been found attached to *Calamites,* they have been assigned to the form genus *Pinnularia,* whereas isolated roots are referred to the form genus *Astromyelon.* Trunks of *Calamites* were preserved because the soft

internal fillings, forming pitch casts, deteriorated and the hollow central canal was filled with sediments before microorganisms could break down the stem tissues. The pitch casts lack branches, which apparently had already disappeared before the plant could be fossilized (Figure 12).

There is still uncertainty about the origin of sphenophytes. However, there are interesting similarities between lycopods (club mosses) and Equisetales. Both groups are known to have produced abundant, large trees during the Carboniferous but in recent times are only represented by herbaceous forms.

EVA BUNDGAARD KOPPELHUS

Further Reading

Foster, A.S., and E.M. Gifford. 1959. *Comparative Morphology of Vascular Plants.* San Francisco: Freeman; 2nd ed., 1974.
Stewart, W.N. 1983. *Paleobotany and the Evolution of Plants.* Cambridge and New York: Cambridge University Press; 2nd ed., with G.W. Rothwell, 1993.
Taylor, T.N., and E.L. Taylor. 1993. *The Biology and Evolution of Fossil Plants.* Englewood Cliffs, New Jersey: Prentice-Hall.
Tryon, R.M., and A.F. Tryon. 1982. *Ferns and Allied Plants.* New York: Springer-Verlag.

HUENE, FRIEDRICH FREIHERR VON

German, 1875–1969

Friedrich Freiherr von Huene was one of the most important and influential paleoherpetologists of the twentieth century. He was mainly concerned with the phylogeny (evolutionary history) and systematics (evolutionary relationships) of fossil reptiles and amphibians, as documented by more than 300 technical publications on almost every group of fossil lower tetrapods (limbed vertebrates), from temnospondyls to therapsids.

Von Huene started his scientific career as an invertebrate paleontologist, soon becoming a well-known expert on Silurian inarticulate brachiopods (bivalved marine invertebrates), on which he published several monographs (e.g., 1899). Throughout this time von Huene was in continuous scientific exchange with authorities like C.D. Walcott. Soon von Huene shifted to vertebrate paleontology, first placoderms (early armored marine fishes), then, following a suggestion of his teacher, von Koken, fossil reptiles. His habilitation (thesis, 1902) presented a comprehensive overview of the Triassic reptiles, a theme that later on played a major role in his work.

Throughout the following years, von Huene mainly was concerned with a revision of the Triassic dinosaurs of the world, which appeared in two parts (1906, 1907–8). The latter publication in particular is a classic work, the most voluminous and probably the most beautifully illustrated dinosaur monograph of all time. With these contributions, von Huene established himself as the world's leading authority on early dinosaurs. In subsequent years, he extended his studies to a large number of fossil reptile groups, including studies on fossil amphibians. Alongside Samuel

W. (Wendell) Williston in the United States, with whom he did fieldwork in the American southwest in 1911, von Huene eventually became the most renowned expert of his time on fossil lower tetrapods, a reputation he would enjoy until his death. From 1914 to 1918, von Huene served in the German army. After World War I, he began to work out new and revolutionary mounting techniques for fossil vertebrate skeletons, resulting in the exhibition of a large number of beautiful specimens of fossil reptiles and mammals in the Tübingen Museum, in Tübingen, Germany. From 1921 to 1923, von Huene carried out a successful excavation of Upper Triassic dinosaurs at Trossingen in a joint venture with the American Museum.

In 1924, von Huene traveled to Argentina, where he excavated and studied Cretaceous dinosaurs and, on cursory inspection, discovered the now world-famous Valle de la Luna, where later the oldest dinosaurs were found. He also visited the southern tip of Africa, studying the geology of the Karroo region and excavating numerous excellent fossil reptiles. From 1928 to 1929, von Huene worked in Brazil, digging for Middle Triassic tetrapods. As in all of his field campaigns, this expedition was extremely successful and resulted in the discovery of many fine specimens, most of which belonged to genera or even families previously unknown to science. A 1933 expedition to Australia failed because of the bad economic situation in Germany. In 1936 he described the miraculously strange placodont *Henodus,* a turtlelike marine reptile that lived along the shorelines of early seas. Early in the years of the Nazi regime, von Huene recognized the inhumanity of fascism and refused cooperation and collaboration as far as possible. After World War II, he was appointed as the commissionary director of the Geological-Paleontological Institute of Tübingen University from 1946 until 1948. In 1957, von Huene was invited to Russia, one of the first German scientists to visit that country after the war. His collaboration with Russian colleagues, which had begun in the 1920s, lasted until his death and resulted in important publications on fossil reptiles from eastern Europe. In 1956, von Huene's influential and important textbook on fossil amphibians and reptiles appeared. It remains a unique text today, because of its erudition and its original approach.

Throughout his life, von Huene was a deeply religious person and never adopted the view that natural selection played a major role in large-scale evolutionary events, although he admitted that it might be important at the species level. Instead, he strived to combine his Christian beliefs and the paleontological results into a rather unusual view of evolution. In it, he regarded the phylogeny of the vertebrates as a singular historical process under divine influences, with the ultimate aim to produce *Homo sapiens* as the peak of creation. This view did not hamper him in becoming one of the most prolific students of vertebrate phylogeny. The numerous descriptions of new groups and revisions of faunas from all continents served as a sound database for his quite modern phylogenetic approach, which in some ways antedated today's modern cladistic methodology. His study on Liassic (Lower Jurassic) ichthyosaurs (1931) is notable as one of the first attempts to document speciation and microevolution in a lineage of extinct vertebrates.

Von Huene's main influence on today's paleoherpetological research is found in his extensive contributions to the systematics and morphology of fossil reptiles. To a large extent, today's generally accepted systematics of several major groups, such as dinosaurs, early archosaurs, and ichthyosaurs, is based on his results. Some of his osteological studies on fossil reptiles rank among the best of their time and still provide a reliable database for modern morphological research. Most notable are his contributions on dinosaurs, especially saurischians (1906, 1907–8, 1926, 1929, 1932, 1933) as well as ichthyosaurs (1922), sauropterygians (1921), early archosaurs (1911, 1935–42), therapsids (1935–42, 1950), and rhynchosaurs (1938, 1935–42), to mention only a few. All of these were largely ground-breaking, pioneer studies. Von Huene was the first to publish extensively on the fossil reptile faunas of South America, India, and the African Karroo. In terms of rock strata, his original descriptions of fossil vertebrates reach from the Middle Devonian to the Pliocene; geographically they reach from Greenland to Timor; and systematically they reach from early fishes to mammals. However, the reptiles—particularly the Permian and Triassic forms—always played the major role. One of the most severe shortcomings of his work is the fact that in many instances he published his results extremely hastily, leading to a number of serious misidentifications.

Colleagues who knew von Huene personally were greatly impressed by his friendly and modest behavior and his immense scientific knowledge. He established long-lasting friendships with most vertebrate paleontologists of his time, making Tübingen an international center of paleoherpetological research. The importance of both his enormous collections at the Tübingen Museum and his scientific contributions can hardly be overestimated. They remain a lasting monument of an outstanding scientist's deep devotion to his subject.

MICHAEL W. MAISCH

Biography

Born in Tübingen, Germany, 22 March 1875. Received Ph.D., Tübingen University, 1898; habilitation (qualifying essay) Tübingen University, 1902; assistant professorship, Tübingen University, 1908; member, German Academy of Natural Scientists, Leopoldina, 1944; commissionary director, Geological-Paleontological Institute, Tübingen University, 1946–48; honorary member, Paleontological Society, 1956; recipient, Buch Plaque of the German Geological Society, 1956. Excavations in Trossingen dinosaur quarry, 1921–23; expeditions to South Africa and Argentina, discovered Ischigualasto formation, 1924; expedition to Brazil and Uruguay, new Triassic reptile faunas, 1928–29; described extraordinary placodont *Henodus*, 1936. Died in Tübingen, 4 April 1969.

Major Publications

1899. Die silurischen Craniaden der Ostseeländer mit Ausschluß Gotlands. *Verhandlungen der Kaiserlich Russischen Mineralogischen Gesellschaft* 36:181–359.

1902. Übersicht über die Reptilien der Trias. *Geologische und Paläontologische Abhandlungen,* Neue Folge, 6 (1):1–84.

1906. Über die Dinosaurier der außereuropäischen Trias. *Geologische und Paläontologische Abhandlungen,* Neue Folge, 8 (2):99–156.

1907–8. Die Dinosaurier der europäischen Triasformation mit Berücksichtigung der außereuropäischen Vorkommnisse. *Geologische und Paläontologische Abhandlungen,* Supplement-Band, 1:1–419.

1911. Beiträge zur Kenntnis und Beurteilung der Parasuchia. *Geologische und Paläontologische Abhandlungen,* Neue Folge, 10 (1):61–122.

1921. Neue Beobachtungen an *Simosaurus. Acta Zoologica* 1921:201–39.

1922. *Die Ichthyosaurier des Lias und ihre Zusammenhänge.* Monographien zur Geologie und Paläontologie, 1 (6). Berlin and Leipzig: Borntraeger.

1926. Die vollständige Osteologie eines Plateosauriden aus dem Schwäbischen Keuper. *Geologische und Paläontologische Abhandlungen,* Neue Folge, 15 (2):1–45.

1929. Los Saurisquios y Ornitisquios del Cretaceo Argentino. *Anales del Museo de la Plata* 3 (2):1–196.

1931. Neue Studien über Ichthyosaurier aus Holzmaden. *Abhandlungen der Senckenbergischen Naturforschenden Gesellschaft* 42 (2):345–82.

1932. *Die fossile Reptilordnung Saurischia, ihre Entwicklung und Geschichte.* Monographien zur Geologie und Paläontologie 1 (4). Berlin and Leipzig: Borntraeger.

1933. With C.A. Matley. The Cretaceous Saurischia and Ornithischia of the Central Provinces of India. *Geological Survey of India: Palaeontologia India* 21 (1):1–74.

1935–42. *Die fossilen Reptilien des südamerikanischen Gondwanalandes.* Munich: Beck.

1936. *Henodus chelyops,* ein neuer Placodontier. *Palaeontographica,* Abteilung A. 84:97–148.

1938. *Stenaulorhynchus,* ein Rhynchosauride der ostafrikanischen Obertrias. *Nova Acta Leopoldina,* Neue Folge, 6 (36):83–121.

1950. Die Theriodontier des ostafrikanischen Ruhuhu-Gebietes in der Tübinger Sammlung. *Neues Jahrbuch für Geologie und Paläontologie,* Abhandlungen 92:47–136.

1956. *Paläontologie und Phylogenie der niederen Tetrapoden.* Vol. 7. Jena: Fischer.

Further Reading

Colbert, E.H. 1968. *Men and Dinosaurs.* New York: Dutton; London: Evans.

Hoelder, H. 1977. Geschichte der Geologie und Paläontologie an der Universität Tübingen. In *Mineralogie, Geologie und Paläontologie*

an der Universität Tübingen von den Anfängen bis zur Gegenwart. Tübingen: Mohr.

Huene, F. v. 1944. Arbeitserinnerungen. *Selbstbiographien von Naturforschern* 2:1–52.

Reif, W.-E., and W. Lux. 1987. Evolutionstheorie und religiöses Konzept im Werk des Wirbeltierpaläontologen Friedrich Freiherr von Huene (1875–1969). *Werkschriften des Universitätsarchivs Tübingen* 1 (12):91–140.

Seilacher, A., and F. Westphal. 1969. Friedrich Freiherr von Huene, 22 März 1875–4 April 1969. *Jahresberichte und Mitteilungen des Oberrheinischen Geologischen Vereins,* Neue Folge 51:25–30.

HÜRZELER, JOHANNES

Swiss, 1908–95

Born in Gretzenbach (Canton Solothurn, Switzerland) 1 February 1908, Johannes Hürzeler belongs to the exceptional cohort of Swiss vertebrate paleontologists of the nineteenth and twentieth centuries. He may be considered as the heir of the great tradition built in Basel and Zurich by Rütimeyer, Stehlin, Helbing, Schaub, Peyer, and Kuhn-Schnyder. His career in the field of paleontology started very early; as a 12-year-old boy, playing in the heaps of excavated sediments, he discovered teeth and jaws of mammals of an Eocene fauna (Obergösgen), the scientific value of which he intuitively recognized. Developing his interest for fossil life, the young man went on collecting at Swiss localities such as Egerkingen, Rickenbach, Küttingen, Wynau, and Aarwangen. After completing secondary education at the Cantonal Technical School of Aarau, Hürzeler matriculated at Basel University and studied geology with August Buxtorf. Under the direction of H.G. Stehlin, he wrote a thesis on the osteology and odontology of the Caenotheridae (1936). This monograph laid the foundation of Hürzeler's scientific reputation.

Conservator (1937) and director (1957–73) of the osteological section of the Natural History Museum of Basel, he was particularly instrumental in assembling one of the most complete libraries in the field of mammalian paleontology.

The outstanding scientific environment of Basel and Hürzeler's complete dedication are responsible for his many important publications on fossil artiodactyls, carnivores, insectivores, and primates, which, on different occasions, were praised by the great Alfred S. Romer as "the best monograph ever written on the subject." His revisions of the European Hemicyonidae (a carnivoran family) and the Dimylidae (an insectivoran family) and on the phylogeny of the Necrolemuridae (a primate family) are exemplary for clarity and careful formulation.

In 1949 Hürzeler developed special interest in a strange endemic Miocene, almost forgotten, primate, *Oreopithecus.* The fossil fragments had been discovered in Italy and studied by Gervais in 1872, but they subsequently had remained practically unknown. Contrary to traditional opinion, Hürzeler took the view that *Oreopithecus* was not an ape, but an early hominid. Excavations in the lignite mine of Baccinello (southern Tuscany, Italy) provided jaws, bone fragments, and even a complete skeleton of *Oreopithecus* (1958). The finds made headlines all over the world

and raised considerable discussion. The scientific community was divided into two camps: personal and sometimes unfair attacks prevented Hürzeler from continuing to publish about *Oreopithecus.* However, he continued to collect more material from Baccinello and to write important papers on the suids (pigs), alcelaphine bovids (antelopes), and lutrines (otters).

Hürzeler managed to document more than 600 Tertiary mammal localities of Switzerland. As "one of the last scholars of a generation of vertebrate paleontologists with universal knowledge" (so writes Burkart Engesser), Hürzeler developed a very open and generous collaboration with colleagues all over the world. He carried out major excavations in France (e.g., with Jean Viret, from Lyons, in Estrepouy, Vieux Collonges, Saint-Vallier, and Sansan) and during World War II in Switzerland: These last activities are the basis of some important papers on the biostratigraphy of the Swiss Molasse.

EDOUARD L. BONÉ

Biography

Born in Gretzenbach (Canton Solothurn, Switzerland), 1 February 1908. Received Ph.D., Basel University, 1936. Named conservator (1937) and director (1957–73), Osteology Section, Natural History Museum, Basel. Awarded Scientific Prize, City of Basel, 1960; honorary lecturer, Basel University; honorary citizen of the community of Scransano (Tuscany); commander of the Order of St. Gregory the Great (Rome); member of many honorary societies, including Paris Academy of Sciences (corresponding member), Society of Vertebrate Paleontology (honorary member). Died in Basel, 24 July 1995.

Major Publications

1944. Beiträge zur Kenntnis der Dimylidae. *Schweizerische paläontologische Abhandlungen* 65:1–44.

1948. Zur stammesgeschichte der necrolemuriden. *Schweizerische paläontologische Abhandlungen* 66:1–46.

1949. Neubeschreibung von Oreopithecus bambolii Gervais. *Separatabdruck aus Schweizerischen paläontologischen Abhandlungen* 66:1–20.

1969. Catalogo comentado de los Pongidos fosiles de España. *Acta Geologica Hispanica* 4 (2):44–48.

HUXLEY, THOMAS HENRY

English, 1825–95

Thomas Henry Huxley was born 4 May 1825 in Ealing, near London, and died 29 June 1895 in Eastborne, England. As the youngest surviving child of a schoolmaster with an unstable disposition, he received a minimal amount of formal instruction. From an early age, however, he demonstrated great precocity, and as a teenager he taught himself German and French. Two of his sisters' husbands were practicing physicians, and the young Huxley served as an apprentice to one of them. Using this background as a springboard, he began a rapid rise upward with receipt of scholarships and medals for his academic achievements, including a scholarship at the Charing Cross Hospital. In 1845 Huxley finished his medical studies, and then immediately began service in the Royal Navy. He spent the next four years traveling the seas of the Southern Hemisphere as a medical officer on board the H.M.S. *Rattlesnake.*

Huxley devoted himself to problems of comparative anatomy during extended periods of free time on board the ship. He concentrated on dissecting and understanding the fragile invertebrates that were caught in the ship's nets every day. The papers he wrote and sent back to England concerning jellyfish—in which he revised and clarified some of the suggestions of French theorist Georges Cuvier—earned Huxley a formidable reputation by the time the *Rattlesnake* returned to London. Shortly thereafter, he was elected to the Royal Society of London and in 1852 was awarded their Royal Medal. It was not until several years later, however, that Huxley gained employment as a practicing scientist. (He once wrote to his sister that his activities brought "much praise, but no pudding.") In 1854 he finally was appointed lecturer in natural history at the Government School of Mines in London. Soon after, he received the additional appointment of naturalist with the Geological Survey. With his career in order, Huxley was ready to marry Henrietta Heathorne, a young woman to whom he had become engaged while visiting in Australia. Their oldest surviving son, Leonard, was the father of Julian Huxley, the biologist; Aldous Huxley, the well-known novelist; and Andrew Fielding Huxley, the physiologist.

Early in his career, Huxley was an ardent critic of evolutionary theory, penning a savage review of a late edition of *Vestiges of the Natural History of Creation,* the evolutionary tract by Robert Chambers, the then-anonymous Scottish publisher. However, Huxley gradually began to accept the idea of evolution, in large part because of a dispute with Richard Owen, the most established British biologist of the day. Although the two men were initially on good terms, Huxley grew to abominate the older scientist's idealistic world system. His friendship with the English biologist, philosopher, and sociologist, Herbert Spencer, who was an ardent evolutionist by the 1850s, bore some influence on Huxley's position. The key influence, however—sociologically, psychologically,

Further Reading

Haag, H. 1962. *Evolution und Bibel.* Lucerne and Munich: Rex Verlag.

and intellectually—was Huxley's friendship with the older Charles Darwin, and his reading of *The Origin of Species by Means of Natural Selection* (1859). While Huxley never became a proponent of natural selection, he embraced other arguments from the *Origin* and benefited from the security within the Darwinian circle. With the enthusiasm of a recent convert, Huxley became one of evolution's most fervent champions—a role that the ailing Darwin was likely glad to assign to someone else.

Huxley, more than any other figure, can be credited with making biology in Victorian Britain into a professional science replete with academic posts, curricula, and a student body. While physiology and morphology had their place in this program, evolution did not. Evolution seemed to serve no practical purpose in the scientific community. It was deemed to be progressive, an idea that was presented more appropriately in museums and places of public entertainment and instruction than in academia. Evolution became a source of inspiration, moral insight, legend, and myth. The theory was conferred the role of a religion, and Huxley assumed a leadership position in this movement. After the publication of Darwin's *Origin,* Huxley increasingly devoted himself to lecturing popular audiences on the theory of evolution, leaving his ongoing work in morphology to his students and other professionals.

Despite his fervor for the theory of evolution, Huxley was not convinced that the fossil record offered enough evidence in its favor. Initially, he maintained that the record was insufficiently complete to render a judgment. However, in the decade after pulication of the *Origin,* many more fossil finds came to light and Huxley altered his assessment accordingly. He felt that, despite many qualifications, the record did support the theory of evolution, although the actual mechanism by which it occurred was not something revealed by the rocks and the fossils they contained. (Huxley favored "saltations," jumps in the fossil record from one organic form to another, for example, a fox into a dog.)

Huxley's new regard for the fossil evidence was more than passive acceptance. During the 1860s, Huxley concentrated on paleontological issues, particularly on the origin and evolution of birds. His interest was stimulated by the first discoveries of that peculiar hybrid *Archaeopteryx.* It was Huxley's claim that the evidence suggests that birds evolved from dinosaurs. This view long was dismissed as untenable; however, in recent years, it has once again gained prominence in the scientific community and is, in fact, very well supported.

Huxley was also greatly interested in the evolution of humankind. It is significant, given that he was to assign evolution to the status of a secular religion, that he, perhaps more than Darwin, seized on the implications of evolutionism for the origin of the human species. Huxley recognized the profound change in the status of humans in the overall cosmic scheme if evolution was found to be true. As an advocate of a secular society, it was natural and important for Huxley to concern himself with human evolution. In a like manner, his old adversary, Richard Owen, had focused on humans as the critical case, arguing that significant and unbridgeable gaps existed between the human brain and that of our nearest relatives, the apes. In Huxley's first full publication on evolution, *Evidence as to Man's Place in Nature,* he explored all of the empirical facts relating humans to the organic world. He was especially interested in the newly discovered Neanderthal remains from Germany. He interpreted them to be an important aspect of human evolution, as a significant link to the past. In the end, however, he decided that Neanderthal man should be considered a subspecies of *Homo sapiens,* as opposed to a separate species.

Huxley's interests in the fossil record continued through the 1870s, although his various administrative and teaching duties took him increasingly from the forefront of scientific research. He became greatly interested in the evolution of the horse, which he considered to be an exemplar of the manner in which life developed. The horse also served as a striking example for his public lectures on evolutionism. In 1876 Huxley visited America, where there had been significant discoveries of fossil equines. After examining the specimens obtained by O.C. Marsh, Huxley revised his treatment of the horse lineage and went so far as to predict that a very generalized early form with five toes was likely to have existed. Approximately two months later, Marsh discovered *Eohippus,* a discovery that matched Huxley's prediction and became a feature in his lectures on the validity of evolution.

Although Huxley was a man of great brilliance and scientific understanding, he is not remembered as a creative scientist of the first rank. His writings are not laden with discoveries of the order found in the work of Darwin or others, but as a general science administrator and teacher, his influence cannot be underestimated. Even though some scholars now blame Huxley's influence for condemning evolutionary studies to second-class status for generations, as a general proponent of evolution, his importance was vast.

MICHAEL RUSE

Biography

Born in Ealing, west London, 4 May 1825. Early education in Ealing School, 1833–35; began medical apprenticeship, Rotherhithe, London, 1841; studied medicine, Charing Cross Hospital Medical School, 1842–45. Assistant surgeon, H.M.S. *Rattlesnake,* 1846–50; elected as fellow (1851), council member (1852), secretary (1872–81), and president (1883–85), Royal Society; fellow (1859), secretary (1859–63), and president (1868–70), Geological Society of London; naturalist, Geological Survey, 1854; lecturer (1854–55) and professor in natural history (1855–85), Government School of Mines, London [later called the Normal School of Science, then the Royal College of Science]; Fullerian Professor, Royal Institution, 1856–58, 1865–68; Croonian Lecturer, Royal Society, 1858; Hunterian Professor, Royal College of Surgeons, 1862–69; governor, International College, 1865; president, Ethnological Society, 1868; governor, Owens

College, 1870–75; rector, Aberdeen University, 1872–74; governor, Eton College, 1879–88; senator, University of London, 1883–95. Science columnist, *Westminster Review* and *Saturday Review.* Sat on numerous royal commissions and boards, most notably the First Royal School Board, 1870–72. Awarded Royal Medal, Royal Society, 1852; Wollaston Medal, Geological Society of London, 1876; Copley Medal, Royal Society, 1888; Darwin Medal, Royal Society, 1894. Honored by more than 50 foreign scientific societies and recipient of honorary degrees from numerous universities, including those at Bologna, Breslau, Dublin, Cambridge, Edinburgh, Erlangen, Oxford, and Würzburg. Died in Eastbourne, England, 29 June 1895.

Major Publications

1853. On the morphology of the Cephalus Mullusca, as illustrated by the anatomy of certain heteropoda and pteropoda collected during the voyage of the HMS *Rattlesnake* in 1846–50. *Philosophical Transactions of the Royal Society* 143 (1):29–66.

1863. *Evidence as to Man's Place in Nature.* London and Edinburgh: Williams and Norgaten; New York: Appleton.

1866. *Lessons in Elementary Physiology.* London: Macmillan; New York: Macmillan, 1890.

1868. Remarks upon the Archaeopteryx Lithographica. *Proceedings of the Royal Society of London* 16:243–48.

1869. *An Introduction to the Classification of Animals.* London: Churchill.

1870a. *Lay Sermons, Addresses and Reviews.* London: Macmillan; New York: Appleton; 3rd edition, rev. and enlarged, 1887.

1870b. Paleontology and the doctrine of evolution. *Quarterly Journal of the Geological Society of London* 26:42.

1871. *A Manual of the Anatomy of Vertebrated Animals.* London: Churchill; New York: Appleton, 1872.

1872. *More Criticism on Darwin, and Administrative Nihilism.* New York: Appleton.

1873. *Critiques and Addresses.* London: Macmillan; New York: Appleton.

1877a. *American Addresses.* London: Macmillan; New York: Appleton.

1877b. *A Manual of the Anatomy of Invertebrated Animals.* London: Churchill; New York: Appleton.

1880. *The Crayfish: An Introduction to the Study of Zoology.* London: Kegan Paul; New York: Appleton.

1881a. *Science and Culture, and Other Essays.* London: Macmillan; New York: Appleton, 1882.

[1881b.] The rise and progress of paleontology. First published in book form, *In Science and the Hebrew Tradition,* London: Macmillan, 1893; Appleton, 1893.

1892. *Essays on Some Controverted Questions.* London and New York: Macmillan.

1893b. *Evolution and Ethics: The Romanes Lectures, 1893.* London and New York: Macmillan.

1893–94. *Collected Essays.* 9 vols. London: Macmillan; New York: Appleton.

1894. *Discourses: Biological and Geological.* London: Macmillan; New York: Appleton, 1895.

1898–1903. M. Foster and E.R. Lankester (eds.). *Scientific Memoirs of Thomas Henry Huxley.* 5 vols. London: Macmillan; New York: Appleton, 1898.

1935. J. Huxley (ed.). *T.H. Huxley's Diary of the Voyage of H.M.S. Rattlesnake: Edited from the Unpublished Manuscript by Julian Huxley.* London: Chatto and Windus; New York: Doubleday, 1936.

Further Reading

Desmond, A. 1994. *Huxley, the Devil's Disciple*. London: Michael Joseph; New York: Viking Penguin.

———. 1997. *Huxley: Evolution's High Priest*. London: Michael Joseph; New York: Viking Penguin.

DiGregorio, M. 1984. *T.H. Huxley's Place in Natural Science*. New Haven, Connecticut: Yale University Press.

Ruse, M. 1996. *Monad to Man: The Concept of Progress in Evolutionary Biology*. Cambridge, Massachusetts: Harvard University Press.

HYATT, ALPHEUS

American, 1838–1902

Although a tenacious antagonist of Darwin's idea that natural selection guided evolutionary change, Alpheus Hyatt devoted his career to documenting and describing the process of evolution. In 1866, only seven years after Darwin's *Origin,* Hyatt presented a paper to the Boston Society of Natural History—an organization over which he later would preside—in which he outlined some of the basic principles of what would become known as the "American neo-Lamarckian movement." In the paper "On the parallelism between the different stages of life in the individual and those in the entire group of the molluscous order Tetrabranchiata," Hyatt argued that species and other biological groups have life histories that are analogous to those of individual organisms. Each group had a birth, growth period, adulthood, old age, and death. Hyatt was particularly interested in the concept of "racial senescence," or the decline and degeneration of a group. That, he argued, was the cause of extinction. For Hyatt, evolutionary change was driven not by competition and chance, as in the Darwinian view, but by the same principles of growth and aging that usher an individual through its life. It did not matter how fit and robust a species was in its youth; its natural fate was decline and extinction.

For Hyatt and his colleague Edward Drinker Cope, a fellow vertebrate paleontologist, Darwin's theory of natural selection could only explain the evolution of superficial features, such as hair color, but not the origin of structural features, such as bones or teeth (Bowler 1988, 1989). Instead, Hyatt and Cope advocated a complex theory of evolution centered around the principles of growth and development (Pfeifer 1965; Dexter 1979). Repeated actions, they argued, caused the concentration of an unknown growth force—Cope speculated that it might be electrical in nature—that resulted in the growth and perfection of the exercised structures. Over generations, new structures would arise and evolve in this manner. In contrast, disuse resulted in the atrophy (wasting away) and loss of features on an evolutionary time scale. These two processes were known respectively as "acceleration" and "retardation" (Cope 1866; Gould 1977; Richardson and Kane 1988).

Hyatt spent his career popularizing his theoretical work, supporting it with paleontological studies of cephalopods (marine animals such as squids and octopuses) and other molluscs (boneless, unsegmented animals, such as snails and slugs). His papers included works on evolution, taxonomy, and development. Among the most famous of these was "Transformations of *Planorbis* at Steinheim, with remarks on the effects of gravity upon the forms of shells and animals." In it, Hyatt used the small fossil snails found in the Miocene Steinheim meteor crater in Germany to argue that changes in general habits resulted in evolutionary transformations. In 1867 Hyatt (along with A.S. Packard, E.S. Morse, and F.W. Putnum) founded the *American Naturalist,* a journal that was subsequently purchased by E.D. Cope in 1877. It became the primary forum for American evolutionists, particularly neo-Lamarckians.

Hyatt and Cope gained a great following in the United States during the nineteenth century, including the geologists Clarence King and Joseph Le Conte, the zoologists Alpheus Packard and Joel Allen, and the paleontologists William Dall and Henry Osborn. In America their influence was so pervasive that in 1907 (five years after Hyatt's death) Vernon Kellogg pronounced that Darwin's theory of natural selection was dead (Kellogg 1907; Bowler 1988). But the Americans were misunderstood or ignored in Europe. In a letter to Hyatt in 1872, Charles Darwin wrote, "I confess that I have never been able to grasp fully what you wish to show" (in Darwin and Seward 1903). In the early twentieth century the influence of Hyatt and the neo-Lamarckians waned (Bowler 1988, 1989). Geneticists such as T.H. Morgan began to demonstrate that characteristics acquired during the life of an individual were not passed on to the next generation. This new genetics was combined with population biology and studies of variability in the neo-Darwinian system called the Modern Synthesis (Provine 1971; Bowler 1989). The death of Darwinism had been announced prematurely, and, after the 1940s, the neo-Lamarckians, including Hyatt, were largely forgotten.

PAUL DAVID POLLY

Works Cited

Bowler, P.J. 1988. *The Non-Darwinian Revolution: Reinterpreting a Historical Myth*. Baltimore: Johns Hopkins University Press; London: Johns Hopkins University Press, 1992.

———. 1989. *Evolution: The History of an Idea*. Rev. ed., Berkeley: University of California Press.

Cope, E.D. 1866. On the origin of genera. *Proceedings of the Academy of Natural Sciences of Philadelphia* 272–73.

Darwin, F., and A.L. Seward (eds.). 1903. *More Letters of Charles Darwin*. Vol. 1, London: Murray; New York: Appleton.

Dexter, R.W. 1979. The impact of evolutionary theories of the Salem group of Agassiz Zoologists (Morse, Hyatt, Packard, Putnum). *Essex Institute Historical Collections* 115:144–71.

Gould, S.J. 1977. *Ontogeny and Phylogeny*. Cambridge, Massachusetts: Belknap.

Kellogg, V.L. 1907. *Darwinism Today: A Discussion of Present Day Scientific Criticism of the Darwinian Selection Theories*. New York: Holt; London: Bell.

Pfeifer, E.J. 1965. The genesis of American Neo-Lamarckism. *ISIS* 56:156–67.

Provine, W.B. 1971. *The Origins of Theoretical Population Genetics.* Chicago: University of Chicago Press; London: University of Chicago Press, 1987.

Richardson, R.C., and T.C. Kane. 1988. Orthogenesis and evolution in the 19th century: The idea of progress in American Neo-Lamarckism. *In* M.H. Nitecki (ed.), *Evolutionary Progress.* Chicago: University of Chicago Press.

Biography

Born in Washington, D.C., 5 or 6 April 1838. Received B.S. in geology, Lawrence Scientific School, Harvard University, 1862; studied cephalopods, Harvard University, with Agassiz. Appointed curator, Essex Institute (Salem, Massachusetts), 1867; founder and editor (1867–71), *American Naturalist;* appointed custodian (1870) then curator (1881–1902), Boston Society of Natural History; elected to the National Academy of Sciences, 1875; director, Teacher's School of Science, Boston Society of Natural History, 1870–1902; appointed chairs of zoology and paleontology, Massachusetts Institute of Technology, 1870; chair of biology, Boston University, 1877–1902; founder and first president, American Society of Naturalists, 1883; appointed assistant for paleontology, Cambridge Museum of Comparative Anatomy, 1886; appointed paleontologist with U.S. Geological Survey, 1889; helped found Marine Biology Laboratory, Annisquam, Massachusetts (later moved to Woods Hole, Massachusetts); member, American Academy of Arts and Sciences; member, Geological Society of London. Died in Cambridge, Massachusetts, 15 January 1902.

Major Publications

1866. On the parallelism between the different stages of life in the individual and those in the entire group of the molluscous order Tetrabranchiata. *Memoirs of the Boston Society of Natural History, 1866–69* 1:193–209.

1871. On natural selection. *Proceedings of the Boston Society of Natural History* 14:146–48.

1875–77. Revision of the North American Poriferae. *Memoirs of the Boston Society of Natural History* 2 (2): 399–408; 2(5):481–554.

1880. Transformations of *Planorbis* at Steinheim with remarks on the effects of gravity upon the forms of shells and animals. *Proceedings of the American Association for the Advancement of Science* 29:527–50.

1884. The evolution of the Cephalopoda. *Science* 3:122–27, 145–49.

1888. Values in classification of the stages of growth and decline with propositions for a new nomenclature. *Proceedings of the Boston Society of Natural History* 23:396–408.

1893. Phylogeny of an acquired characteristic. *American Naturalist* 27:865–77.

1894. Phylogeny of an acquired characteristic. *Proceedings of the American Philosophical Society* 32:349–647.

Further Reading

Bowler, P.J. 1984. *Evolution: The History of an Idea.* Berkeley: University of California Press; rev. ed., 1989.

———. 1988. *The Non-Darwinian Revolution: Reinterpreting a Historical Myth.* Baltimore: Johns Hopkins University Press; London: Johns Hopkins University Press, 1992.

Crosby, W.O. 1904. Memoir of Alpheus Hyatt. *Bulletin of the Geological Society of America* 14:504–12.

Jackson, R.T. 1913. Alpheus Hyatt and his principles of research. *The American Naturalist* 47:195–205.

Winsor, M.P. 1991. *Reading the Shape of Nature: Comparative Zoology at the Agassiz Museum.* Chicago: University of Chicago Press.

HYRAXES

The living species of hyraxes represent a tiny fraction of the diversity once present within the order Hyracoidea. During the Early Tertiary, hyracoids were the dominant herbivores of Africa, both in terms of abundance and adaptive diversity. The early fossil forms ranged in size from animals as small as rabbits to ones as large as modern Sumatran rhinos (Schwartz et al. 1995). The skeletons of the smallest forms indicate that they were generalized quadrupeds (had no specialized structures for locomotion), while some of the larger species were runners and leapers. Some early hyracoids were specialized browsers (had a diet based upon leaves and twigs) whose teeth were capable of slicing up fibrous leafy material, while others possessed heavy, bunodont teeth (teeth with low bulbous cusps, or points) used to crush and grind pulpy fruits or roots. The order Hyracoidea represents a classic case of a spectacular adaptive radiation (diversification and geographic spread) on an isolated continent, now reduced to a few remnant living taxa (groups; singular, taxon) (Rasmussen 1989).

The modern hyraxes include approximately 7 to 12 species (the exact number is unclear) divided among three genera—*Procavia, Heterohyrax,* and *Dendrohyrax*—that are placed within a single family, Procaviidae. They are distributed in sub-Saharan Africa and parts of the Middle East; *Dendrohyrax* is an arboreal climber in equatorial tropical forests, while *Procavia* and *Heterohyrax* live on rocky outcrops in arid brush country or desert (Sale 1960; Turner and Watson 1965). Among the distinctive, shared specializations of the group are curved, continuously growing upper incisors; mammary glands located on the chest rather than low on the abdomen; testes that remain in the body cavity rather than descending into a scrotum during development; and a peculiar linear arrangement of the small bones in the wrist and foot.

Both morphological (structural) and molecular lines of evidence indicate that hyraxes are close relatives of elephants (order Proboscidea) and manatees and dugongs (order Sirenia). Linking the small hyraxes with giant elephants may seem counterintuitive, but these two orders share several peculiar specializations, including the continuously growing "tusks," the pectoral mammary glands, the arrangement of foot and wrist bones, and some details of cranial (skull) morphology. Molecular studies of blood proteins and proteins that make up the eye lens further support this evolutionary relationship. Because of these similarities, the orders Hyracoidea, Proboscidea, and Sirenia are best classified together in the Superorder Paenungulata (Rasmussen et al. 1990).

This would be all that was known of hyracoids if a rich fossil record were not available for study. The earliest hyracoids are found at several Eocene and Oligocene sites across North Africa, at a time when Africa was an island continent, similar to today's Australia. Further research is needed to date Eocene sites precisely, but for now it appears that the oldest known hyraxes come from two sites, Chambi, Tunisia, and El Kohol, Algeria, both apparently of about Middle Eocene age. Among several hyraxes known from these sites—all represented only by teeth and jaws—the morphologically most primitive one may be *Seggeurius* from El Kohol, a relatively small, bunodont genus. Other Eocene genera from Algeria include *Microhyrax, Megalohyrax,* and *Titanohyrax.* (The names alone testify to how impressed paleontologists have been by the size range of the early forms.) These fragmentary records are important because they show that well before any artiodactyls (even-toed ungulates) or perissodactyls (odd-toed ungulates) arrived in Africa, hyraxes were already present, abundant, diverse, and filled a great variety of ecological niches alongside the earliest known fossil proboscideans (animals with a flexible trunk) (Mahboubi et al. 1986).

The best paleontological view of early hyracoids comes from a region of Egypt called the Fayum. Fossil hyracoids and other mammals were first found in the Fayum early in the century by C.W. Andrews (1906). He described several different genera (groups of species; singular, genus), some of which he recognized as being related to modern hyraxes, but one, *Geniohyus,* he misclassified in the modern pig family, Suidae. After an initial flurry of paleontological activity, fieldwork in the Fayum was abandoned until the early 1960s, when E.L. Simons began a series of expeditions that are still ongoing in the late 1990s. Many thousands of mammalian fossils have been found in the Fayum deposits, including skulls and skeletal remains of several hyracoid taxa.

The earliest important locality in the Fayum is quarry L-41, of Late Eocene age (35 million years ago). This is one of the richest fossil mammal localities in the world, and about 90 percent of the fossils recovered from this quarry are hyracoids (Rasmussen and Simons 1991). The most common are small species belonging to the genera *Saghatherium* and *Thyrohyrax.* They differ from procaviids in retaining a tooth pattern common in placental animals, but in most respects they probably already had many of the adaptations seen in modern hyraxes. Quarry L-41 also preserves a pig-like geniohyine, and two very large species of the genera *Titanohyrax* and *Megalohyrax.* A final, unique genus from quarry L-41 (still unnamed) is a superficially antelope-like animal about the size of a springbok, with cresty teeth for leaf eating and slender hind limbs in which the lower leg bones (tibia and fibula) are fused to accommodate leaping.

Throughout the younger Fayum sediments hyracoids continue to dominate the mammalian faunas. The youngest strata (Early Oligocene, approximately 32 million years ago) preserve teeth of the largest known hyracoid, *Titanohyrax ultimus,* with an estimated body mass of over 2,000 kilograms. Other common genera of the Early Oligocene are *Thyrohyrax, Megalohyrax,* and *Pachyhyrax.* Our knowledge of hyracoid evolution younger than the upper Fayum strata is thwarted by a major gap in the African fossil record, a gap that spans the time from 32 to 20 million years ago. When fossil hyracoids are found again, after 20 million years ago, it is in Early Miocene deposits of East Africa, by which time these animals were much less common and considerably less diverse. Miocene faunas are dominated instead by hoofed mammals (orders Artiodactyla and Perissodactyla), recent arrivals from the northern continents that had traveled south along newly established land areas. The only reasonably well-known Early Miocene species is *"Megalohyrax" championi,* a tapir-sized cursorial (running-adapted) species (Whitworth 1954). Two other Miocene genera, *Prohyrax* and *Parapliohyrax,* are apparently the earliest representatives of a radiation that occurred later in Eurasia (Pickford and Fischer 1987).

The land contact established between Africa and Eurasia by the earliest Miocene not only allowed northern artiodactyls and perissodactyls to flood into Africa, it also provided a route for hyracoids to move south and east to enter Europe and Asia. The Late Miocene and Pliocene of Eurasia witnessed a radiation of large-bodied, semiaquatic hyracoids called "pliohyracines," which were distributed in a broad band from Spain to China (Rasmussen 1989). The best known and most wide ranging of these was *Pliohyrax;* other genera include *Kvabebihyrax* and *Sogdohyrax.* The youngest pliohyracines from China, including the hypsodont-toothed (those with high-crowned molars) *Postschizotherium,* survived up to the latest Pliocene (approximately 2 million years ago).

Meanwhile, the radiation of modern hyraxes of the family Procaviidae was underway in Africa. The earliest fossil record of a true procaviid is from Late Miocene deposits in Namibia, where expeditions led by G.C. Conroy have unveiled a tropical mammal fauna in rocks initially formed in caves, including an early procaviid named *Heterohyrax auricampensis.* This early procaviid lacks arboreal (tree-dwelling) specializations of the forearm and foot found today in *Dendrohyrax,* and it lacks the high-crowned lophodont molars (characterized by ridges arranged in folds) found today in the grazing rock hyraxes, *Procavia.* This suggests that generalized terrestrial (land-based) scrambling and an eclectic plant diet characterized early members of Procaviidae (Rasmussen et al. 1996). Other fossil hyracoids are found in Pliocene and Pleistocene sediments in eastern and southern Africa, including the remains of a large genus, *Gigantohyrax* (Churcher 1956; Kitching 1965). Extinct species of *Procavia* are among the most abundant mammals in the famous Plio-Pleistocene caves of South Africa, which indicates that by then they had evolved the key morphological attributes and habitat preferences of the currently living species.

D. Tab Rasmussen

Works Cited

Andrews, C.W. 1906. *A Descriptive Catalogue of the Tertiary Vertebrata of the Fayum, Egypt.* London: British Museum of Natural History.

Churcher, C.S. 1956. The fossil Hyracoidea of the Transvaal and Taungs deposits. *Annals of the Transvaal Museum* 22:477–501.

Kitching, J.W. 1965. A new giant hyracoid from the Limeworks Quarry, Makapansgat, Potgietersuas. *Paleontologica Africana* 8:91–96.

Mahboubi, M., R. Ameur, J.Y. Crochet, and J.J. Jaeger. 1986. El Kohol (Saharan Atlas, Algeria): A new Eocene mammal locality in northwestern Africa: Stratigraphical, phylogenetic and paleobiological data. *Palaeontographica Abteilung A. Paläozoologie-Stratigraphie* 192:15–49.

Pickford, M., and M.S. Fischer. 1987. *Parapliohyrax ngororaensis,* a new hyracoid from the Miocene of Kenya, with an outline of the classification of Neogene Hyracoidea. *Neues Jahrbuch für Geologie und Paläontologie, Abhandlung* 175:207–34.

Rasmussen, D.T. 1989. The evolution of the Hyracoidea: A review of the fossil evidence. *In* D.R. Prothero and R.M. Schoch (eds.), *The Evolution of Perissodactyls.* New York: Oxford University Press.

Rasmussen, D.T., and E.L. Simons. 1991. The oldest Egyptian hyracoids (Mammalia: Pliohyracidae): New species of *Saghatherium* and *Thyrohyrax* from the Fayum. *Neues Jahrbuch für Geologie und Paläontologie, Abhandlung* 182:187–209.

Rasmussen, D.T., M. Gagnon, and E.L. Simons. 1990. Taxeopody in the carpus and tarsus of Oligocene Pliohyracidae (Mammalia: Hyracoidea) and the phyletic position of hyraxes. *Proceedings of the National Academy of Sciences USA* 87:4688–91.

Rasmussen, D.T., M. Pickford, P. Mein, B. Senut, and G.C. Conroy. 1996. Earliest known procaviid hyracoid from the late Miocene of Namibia. *Journal of Mammalogy* 77:745–54.

Sale, J.B. 1960. The Hyracoidea: A review of the systematic position and biology of the hyrax. *Journal of the East African Natural History Society* 23:185–88.

Schwartz, G.T., D.T. Rasmussen, and R.J. Smith. 1995. Body size diversity and community structure of fossil hyracoids. *Journal of Mammalogy* 76:1088–99.

Turner, M.I.M., and R.M. Watson. 1965. An introductory study on the ecology of hyrax (*Dendrohyrax brucei* and *Procavia johnstoni*) in the Serengeti National Park. *East African Wildlife Journal* 3:49–60.

Whitworth, T. 1954. The Miocene hyracoids of East Africa, with some observations on the order Hyracoidea. *British Museum of Natural History, Fossil Mammals of Africa* 7:1–58.

Further Reading

Andrews, C.W. 1906. *A Descriptive Catalogue of the Tertiary Vertebrata of the Fayum, Egypt.* London: British Museum of Natural History.

Kingdon, J. 1971–74. *East African Mammals: An Atlas of Evolution in Africa.* 2 vols. London and New York: Academic Press.

Rasmussen, D.T. 1989. The evolution of the Hyracoidea: A review of the fossil evidence. *In* Prothero and R.M. Schoch (eds.), *The Evolution of Perissodactyls.* New York: Oxford University Press.

I

ICHTHYOSAURS

Ichthyosaurs are fishlike reptiles that were important marine predators throughout most of the Mesozoic Era. They first appeared in the Early Triassic, before the first dinosaurs. Ichthyosaurs reached their peak diversity in the Early Jurassic when they were the largest predators in the oceans. Ichthyosaur diversity declined rapidly from the Middle Jurassic onward. By the Cretaceous, ichthyosaurs were represented by a single genus, *Platypterygius,* found worldwide. Ichthyosaurs persisted at a very low diversity until the early part of the Late Cretaceous (Cenomanian), becoming extinct well before the demise of the dinosaurs (Bardet 1994).

Ancestry and Evolutionary Relationships

Of all of the Mesozoic marine reptiles, the ichthyosaurs were the most highly specialized for an aquatic environment. Their name, meaning "fish lizard," reflects the confusion of scholars in determining whether ichthyosaurs were fish or reptiles. By the mid-1800s, ichthyosaurs were recognized unequivocally as reptiles, but their evolutionary relationships with other reptiles continue to be debated. Although the ancestors of ichthyosaurs were probably terrestrial, ichthyosaurs retain few traces of this heritage. Even the earliest ichthyosaurs are highly adapted to an aquatic habitat and show no close morphological resemblance to any other reptiles. Their uniqueness has made it difficult to determine evolutionary relationships.

The ichthyosaurs have been placed in the order Ichthyosauria. The current consensus is that the Ichthyosauria belong to the subclass Diapsida (Callaway 1997; Caldwell 1996). This assignment, however, remains problematic. The diapsids evolved along two main branches, the Lepidosauromorpha (lizards, snakes, and their relatives) and the Archosauromorpha (dinosaurs, pterosaurs, and crocodiles). The Younginiformes, small reptiles similar to lizards in their overall body plan, diverged from the main line of diapsid evolution before the split occurred between lepidosauromorphs and archosauromorphs (Laurin 1991). Ichthyosaurs seem to be related to the Younginiformes, perhaps sharing a common ancestor with them (Massare and Callaway 1990). This relationship would place ichthyosaurs toward the base of the diapsid tree, before the split between the Lepidosauromorpha and the Archosauromorpha (Callaway 1997). This hypothesis, however, has not been tested rigorously. Other recent hypotheses suggest that ichthyosaurs fall within the lepidosauromorphs (Caldwell 1996; Massare and Callaway, 1990).

Morphology and Adaptations to a Marine Environment

Ichthyosaurs ranged in size from about 1 meter for the Early to Middle Triassic *Mixosaurus,* to almost 14 meters for the Late Triassic *Shonisaurus.* A more typical size, however, was 2–3 meters, about the size of a living dolphin.

The best known ichthyosaurs—and the first ones studied—are from the Early Jurassic of England and southern Germany. Nearly complete skeletons show that ichthyosaurs were deep-bodied. Their streamlined bodies were deepest in the pectoral (chest) region and tapered posteriorly (toward the rear). An unusual feature is the presence of three or more wedge-shaped vertebrae (McGowan 1989) causing a downward bend of the vertebral column toward the end of the tail. Carbonized skin impressions on some specimens from the slate quarries of Holzmaden, Germany, reveal that the down-turned bend supported a nearly symmetric, crescent-shaped tail fluke. Many of these specimens also display a dorsal fin along the back.

Ichthyosaurs demonstrate a number of other adaptations to an aquatic environment. The vertebrae are simple: The centrum (the main portion) is a biconcave disk, the dorsally projecting neural spine is not fused to the centrum, and the vertebrae lack complex projections that stiffen and strengthen the vertebral column in terrestrial vertebrates. Ichthyosaurs do not possess a sacrum, the bony connection between the vertebral column and the pelvis, typical of all terrestrial tetrapods. Like whales, these reptiles lost the ability to support themselves on land. Ichthyosaur limbs were stiff fins, quite unlike the walking limbs of a terrestrial reptile. The bones of the limbs were flat rather than cylindrical. The distal bones of the limbs—that is, the fingers and toes, wrist and ankle—were polygonal disks that fit together tightly along straight, immobile joints. The limb moved from the shoulder or hip as a single unit, with no bending at the joints. It was much less flexible than the flipper of a seal or sea lion.

A surprising adaptation that may have allowed ichthyosaurs to become so fishlike was their mode of reproduction. They did not lay eggs, which is the typical reproductive strategy of reptiles. Instead, the egg was retained within the female's body, where the embryo developed—a mode of reproduction called "ovovivipary." Young ichthyosaurs were born fully developed. The first evidence of this was reported in 1846, when small vertebrae accompanied by skull and jaw pieces were found within the pelvic region of an adult ichthyosaur from southern England. Since that time, many skeletons with embryos have been discovered in the Holzmaden quarries, enough to confirm the observation (Massare 1994; McGowan 1979). Ichthyosaurs evidently acquired this adaptation early in their evolution. An embryo has been reported from a *Mixosaurus* specimen from the Middle Triassic of Switzerland. Oviparous reproduction freed ichthyosaurs from the necessity of returning to land to lay eggs, as do present-day aquatic reptiles such as sea turtles and crocodiles. In this respect, ichthyosaurs are similar to the lepidosauromorph branch of the diapsid tree (Tarsitano 1982, 1983). Many living species of lizards and snakes give birth to live young. Archosauromorphs and their bird descendants, on the other hand, only lay eggs. There is no instance of live birth among living birds or crocodiles.

Not all ichthyosaurs had a compact, streamlined shape. Many Triassic ichthyosaurs had narrower, more elongate bodies. One of the most common and widespread ichthyosaurs of the Middle Triassic, *Mixosaurus,* had a length/depth ratio just under seven—its length was seven times greater than its depth. This meant that *Mixosaurus* had a longer body shape than that of most Jurassic ichthyosaurs (Massare 1988). *Mixosaurus* most likely had a broader, more asymmetric tail as well. It lacked a bend in the vertebral column, having instead elongate neural spines positioned at approximately the tail bend in later ichthyosaurs. These spines could have broadened the tail, or they could have supported the upper lobe of a very asymmetric tail fluke. An even more elongate form was the Middle Triassic *Cymbospondylus,* a large ichthyosaur reaching nine meters in length. It had a very shallow tail bend, suggesting that the tail fluke was asymmetric, with a small upper lobe. *Cymbospondylus* had 65 vertebrae between its head and pelvis as compared to approximately 50 in most Early Jurassic ichthyosaurs. The additional vertebrate gave *Cymbospondylus* a more flexible spine. One of the earliest ichthyosaurs, *Chensaurus,* although less than one meter long, was similarly elongated (Motani et al. 1996).

Swimming

The crescent-shaped tail fluke is a good indication that ichthyosaurs propelled themselves by using their tail. The resemblance of ichthyosaurs to the fastest swimmers in today's oceans—dolphins, thunniform fishes (tuna, marlin), and pelagic sharks (mako, great white)—has led to the assumption that ichthyosaurs were also fast, efficient swimmers. Jurassic ichthyosaurs display many adaptations for minimizing drag, the resistance of water to movement through it. The streamlined body of many Jurassic ichthyosaurs had a length/depth ratio between four and five, the optimum

shape for reducing the total drag on a swimming animal (Massare 1988). Additionally, the ichthyosaurs' tail was tall and crescent shaped, with a narrow base. These features, also found in tuna, mako sharks, dolphins, and other fast swimmers, are adaptations to reduce the amount of energy lost in creating a wake while swimming. Ichthyosaurs also had a dorsal fin, presumably to prevent rolling at high speeds. All in all, these characteristics create similarities between ichthyosaurs and today's dolphins and tuna: All share similar adaptations to reduce drag during swimming. Therefore, we can safely infer that ichthyosaurs were also pursuit predators, capable of efficient sustained swimming. How fast were they? One estimate suggests that a two meter–long ichthyosaur could swim at a speed of just under five meters per second (Massare 1994). For a given size, they were faster than their reptilian contemporaries, the plesiosaurs and marine crocodiles. But, because of their lower, reptilian metabolism, ichthyosaurs were probably not as fast as living marine mammals of comparable size.

The Triassic ichthyosaurs, on the other hand, were probably not fast, sustained swimmers. With longer bodies and higher vertebral counts, they may have used a more undulatory mode of propulsion, swimming like a crocodile or eel, which move the whole body and tail in a large wave. The elongate shape did not minimize the drag. Propulsion was less efficient than in the deeper-bodied forms, which oscillated mainly their tails. A broad tail and an elongate body, however, are better suited for acceleration than for high-speed endurance. Thus, Triassic ichthyosaurs may have been ambush predators, lying in wait for a prey species to swim by, then lunging at them with a short burst of speed (Massare 1988, 1992).

The limb girdles were small, suggesting that ichthyosaurs did not use their limbs for propulsion. Instead, limbs probably were used for stabilizing and maneuvering in the water. Some ichthyosaurs, such as *Eurhinosaurus* and *Shonisaurus,* had long, narrow forelimbs and hind limbs that were about equal in size. Others such as *Ophthalmosaurus* and *Ichthyosaurus,* had shorter, wider forelimbs that were much larger than the hind limbs. Still others, such as *Platypterygius,* had very broad forelimbs with 10 fingers on each. So, it is likely that various species of ichthyosaurs used their limbs in different ways.

Food and Feeding

Ichthyosaurs were predators, and they probably captured their prey in mid-water. The prominent eyes on most species suggest that they relied on vision to recognize and catch their prey. Their elongate snout and jaw held long rows of simple, conical teeth. Most ichthyosaurs have only one form of tooth in the jaws, a condition called "homodonty." Like most reptiles and living toothed whales, ichthyosaurs probably swallowed their prey whole, without chewing it. Ichthyosaurs used their teeth to catch and immobilize their prey. They could choose from such prey items as fishes, sharks, squidlike cephalopods, belemnoids (a type of cephalopod), thin-shelled ammonoids (another type of cephalopod), and even other marine reptiles. The kind of prey was determined by the size of the ichthyosaur's gullet (esophagus) and by the form of the teeth.

As a group, ichthyosaurs display several different tooth forms (Massare 1987). The largest ichthyosaurs had sharp, robust teeth that show the same kind of wear as those of a killer whale. These ichthyosaurs probably devoured large prey, including other marine reptiles. Other ichthyosaurs were more like dolphins in their preference for squidlike cephalopods. The teeth of this ichthyosaur group were small and cone-shaped, with a rounded tip. The teeth were used for grasping prey, not piercing them. Some ichthyosaurs with this tooth form have been found with the remains of cephalopod hooklets in their stomach region, confirming their prey preference. Other ichthyosaurs had a more robust, probably stronger, version of this tooth. The apex was blunt, and on many specimens it is polished, probably from abrasion with the prey. The prey may have had a hard exterior, such as the bony scales of some fishes or the thin shells of ammonoids. Still other ichthyosaurs, especially those with very long, narrow snouts, had longer, more sharply pointed teeth that may have been used for piercing soft or small prey. Overall, ichthyosaurs as a group displayed a wide range of tooth forms and, by inference, prey preferences, reaching their greatest diversity of feeding types in the Early Jurassic (Massare 1987).

Some Triassic ichthyosaurs, such as *Phalarodon* and *Mixosaurus,* had several kinds of teeth within a single individual, a condition called "heterodonty." The front teeth are sharply pointed, but the back teeth are very blunt and robust. These Triassic forms may have been more generalized in their choice of prey (Massare and Callaway 1990), although the function of heterodont teeth in ichthyosaurs has not been explained adequately.

Important Localities

Most of our information and specimens of ichthyosaurs come from a relatively small number of locations, mainly in Europe. Four localities stand out for their quality of preservation and for the number of specimens that have been collected over the years (Massare 1997). The Middle Triassic black shales of the Monte San Giorgio region of Switzerland and the adjacent Besano region of Italy have yielded many skeletons of *Mixosaurus.* The fauna also includes the ichthyosaur *Cymbospondylus,* two placodonts (turtlelike reptiles), five nothosaurs (long-necked marine reptiles), and a few other reptiles (Bürgin et al. 1989). Another fauna, from the dark shales and limestones in and around Lyme Regis, in southern England, is Early Jurassic in age. The genera *Ichthyosaurus, Temnodontosaurus, Excalibosaurus,* and *Leptopterygius,* representing more than a half-dozen species, are known from this area. Although plesiosaurs (long-necked marine reptiles with paddlelike limbs) were also present, the fauna is dominated by a high diversity of ichthyosaurs, not only in terms of the number of species, but also in terms of the range of feeding types (Massare 1997).

The black Posidonia Shale of Holzmaden, Germany, is slightly younger, but its fauna shows a similar high diversity of ichthyosaurs. Nearly a dozen species from the genera *Stenopterygius, Leptopterygius,* and *Eurhinosaurus* have been identified (McGowan 1979). Skeletons are very complete, and some show carbonized impressions of skin. Three species of plesiosaurs and three of marine crocodiles complete the fauna. The Holzmaden fauna gives us a glimpse at the peak of ichthyosaurian diversity.

Between the time of the Posidonia Shale and that of the next well-preserved fauna, a major crisis in the marine ecosystem caused a change in the types of marine predators (Massare 1997; Bardet 1994). When we next see a well-preserved marine reptile fauna, in the late Middle Jurassic Oxford Clay of Peterborough, England, ichthyosaur diversity had been reduced to a single species of *Ophthalmosaurus.* However, the fauna does include 10 species of plesiosaurs and at least four species of crocodiles (Martill et al. 1994). Thus, the decline of the ichthyosaurs already had begun by the latter part of the Middle Jurassic.

Late Jurassic and Cretaceous records of ichthyosaurs are fragmentary. Although well-preserved, fairly complete specimens have been discovered, as of yet we do not have a well-preserved, extensively collected fauna of Late Jurassic or Early Cretaceous age that compares to the four earlier faunas. The fauna of the Late Jurassic of the Neuquén Basin of west-central Argentina, however, is helping to fill in the gap (Gasparini and Fernandez 1997). The composition of this fauna is similar to that of the Oxford Clay, confirming that the decline of the ichthyosaurs was a worldwide occurrence. Although the Late Cretaceous Niobrara Chalk and Pierre Shale of the United States also have well-preserved marine reptile faunas, these strata were deposited long after the ichthyosaurs became extinct.

Other North American localities are helping to fill in our picture of ichthyosaur evolution. One problem, for example, is that most Triassic ichthyosaurs have few features in common with the better-known Jurassic genera. The relationships between Triassic ichthyosaurs and their Jurassic descendants are unknown. Some information about this transitional period is coming from the Late Triassic calcareous shales and siltstones of the Williston Lake region of northern British Columbia, which are yielding new species from the time bridging the Triassic and the Jurassic (McGowan 1996, 1997). At another locality in British Columbia, specimens of Early and Middle Triassic ichthyosaurs have been discovered near Wapiti Lake. These specimens are revealing more information on the earliest ichthyosaurs and their contemporaries (Brinkman et al. 1992; Nicholls and Brinkman 1993, 1995). With the renewed interest in ichthyosaurs over the last decade, new discoveries in the United States and elsewhere are continuing to expand our knowledge and understanding of these unusual reptiles.

JUDY A. MASSARE AND JACK M. CALLAWAY

See also Aquatic Locomotion; Aquatic Reptiles

Works Cited

Bardet, N. 1994. Extinction events among Mesozoic marine reptiles. *Historical Biology* 7:313–24.

Brinkman, D.B., X. Zhao, and E.L. Nicholls. 1992. A primitive ichthyosaur from the Lower Triassic of British Columbia, Canada. *Paleontology* 35:465–74.

Bürgin, T., O. Rieppel, P.M. Sander, and K. Tschanz. 1989. The fossils of Monte San Giorgio. *Scientific American* 260 (6):74–81.

Caldwell, M.W. 1996. Ichthyosaur: A preliminary phylogenetic analysis of diapsid affinities. *Neues Jahrbuch für Geologie und Paläontologie, Abhandlungen* 200:361–86.

Callaway, J.M. 1997. Introduction to Ichthyosauria. *In* J.M. Callaway and E.L. Nicholls (eds.), *Ancient Marine Reptiles.* San Diego, California: Academic Press.

Gasparini, Z., and M. Fernandez. 1997. Tithonian marine reptiles of the eastern Pacific. *In* J.M. Callaway and E.L. Nicholls (eds.), *Ancient Marine Reptiles.* San Diego, California: Academic Press.

Laurin, M. 1991. The osteology of a Lower Permian eosuchian from Texas and a review of diapsid phylogeny. *Zoological Journal of the Linnean Society* 101:59–95.

Martill, D.M., M.A. Taylor, and K.L. Duff. 1994. The trophic structure of the biota of the Peterborough Member, Oxford Clay Formation (Jurassic) U.K. *Journal of the Geological Society, London* 151:173–94.

Massare, J.A. 1987. Tooth morphology and prey preference in Mesozoic marine reptiles. *Journal of Paleontology* 7:121–37.

———. 1988. Swimming capabilities of Mesozoic marine reptiles: Implications for mode of predation. *Paleobiology* 14:187–205.

———. 1992. Ancient mariners. *Natural History* 101:48–53.

———. 1994. Swimming capabilities of Mesozoic marine reptiles: A review. *In* L. Maddock, Q. Bone, and J.M.V. Rayner (eds.), *Mechanics and Physiology of Animal Swimming.* Cambridge and New York: Cambridge University Press.

———. 1997. Introduction to faunas, behavior, and evolution. *In* J.M. Callaway and E.L. Nicholls (eds.), *Ancient Marine Reptiles.* San Diego, California: Academic Press.

Massare, J.A., and J.M. Callaway. 1990. The affinities and ecology of Triassic ichthyosaurs. *Geological Society of America Bulletin* 102:409–16.

McGowan, C. 1979. A revision of the Lower Jurassic ichthyosaurs of Germany, with descriptions of two new species. *Palaeontographica A* 166:93–135.

———. 1989. The ichthyosaurian tailbend: A verification problem facilitated by computed tomography. *Paleobiology* 15:429–36.

———. 1996. A new and typically Jurassic ichthyosaur from the Upper Triassic of British Columbia, representing a new genus and species. *Canadian Journal of Earth Sciences* 33:24–32.

———. 1997. A transitional ichthyosaur fauna. *In* J.M. Callaway and E.L. Nicholls (eds.), *Ancient Marine Reptiles.* San Diego, California: Academic Press.

Motani, R., H. You, and C. McGowan. 1996. Eel-like swimming in the earliest ichthyosaurs. *Nature* 382:347–48.

Nicholls, E.L., and D.B. Brinkman. 1993. A new specimen of *Utatsusaurus* (Reptilia: Ichthyosauria) from the Lower Triassic Sulphur Mountain Formation of British Columbia. *Canadian Journal of Earth Sciences* 30:486–90.

———. 1995. A new ichthyosaur from the Triassic Sulphur Mountain Formation of British Columbia. *In* W.A.S. Sarjeant (ed.), *Vertebrate Fossils and the Evolution of Scientific Concepts.* Amsterdam and Australia: Gordon and Breach Publishers.

Tarsitano, S. 1982. A model for the origin of ichthyosaurs. *Neues Jahrbuch für Geologie und Paläontologie, Abhandlungen* 164:143–45.

———. 1983. A case for the diapsid origins of ichthyosaurs. *Neues Jahrbuch für Geologie und Paläontologie, Monatshefte* 1983:59–64.

Further Reading

Callaway, J.M., and E.L. Nicholls (eds.). 1997. *Ancient Marine Reptiles.* San Diego, California: Academic Press.

Carroll, R.L. 1988. *Vertebrate Paleontology and Evolution.* New York: Freeman.

Massare, J.A. 1991. *Prehistoric Marine Reptiles.* New York: Franklin Watts.

———. 1992. Ancient mariners. *Natural History* 101:48–53.

McGowan, C. 1983. *The Successful Dragons: A Natural History of Mesozoic Reptiles.* Toronto and Sarasota, Florida: Stevens; 2nd ed. as *Dinosaurs, Spitfires, and Sea Dragons,* Cambridge, Massachusetts, and London: Harvard University Press, 1991.

INDIAN SUBCONTINENT

A century and a half ago, British-India Army officers discovered cartloads of fossil bones from the rich sedimentary deposits of Baluchistan (Vickary 1846). Even before that, European scientists began to publish notes and descriptions on fossils found in what is now Pakistan and India. Clearly, too, the people of the Indian subcontinent felt the prevalence of fossil vertebrates at least 700 years ago; E.H. Colbert (1935) notes that Moghul emperors were aware of the bones of giants encountered when digging.

Indeed, paleontology in the Indian subcontinent is best known for its record of vertebrate fossils. This is because vast wedges of terrestrial sediments were shed from the highlands to the north and the Himalaya, Hindu Kush, and other ranges. These sediments are mainly Neogene in age, dating since Early Miocene time, and are preserved today as the famous Siwalik Group and other rock formations. The Siwaliks, a deposit that is several kilometers thick and is exposed through Pakistan, Nepal, and India, has produced a marvelously rich fossil record of land vertebrates. This record is especially important because it includes many rich fossil horizons spanning the last 25 million years. This series of faunas offers modern science many avenues of productive research on paleobiological questions by virtue of the fact that scholars can study community evolution and patterns of change in one area.

Yet, the robust Neogene fossil record is not the only paleontological resource in the Indian subcontinent. The key to understanding the geology and paleontology of this area lies in plate tectonics. The Indian subcontinent was not always part of the underbelly of Asia. Formerly, the region was attached on the eastern edge of the African plate. During the Mesozoic era, the Indian plate sheared away from the Africa-Madagascar landmass and moved northward. It came into oblique contact with Asia in the Late Cretaceous period and rotated counterclockwise as it drove northward.

As a consequence of this history, the Paleozoic and Mesozoic rocks of the Indian subcontinent are of marine origin and contain a record of invertebrate evolution. There is a fine biostratigraphic sequence (a sequence of characteristic fossils that is used to date rock layers) of Permian brachiopod and other invertebrates in the Salt Range of Pakistan, making the region a world-class reference for biochronology of the Paleozoic/Mesozoic transition. Local Mesozoic biozonations are also based on ammonoids (a type of cephalopod molluscs) and conodonts (jawless vertebrates with toothlike elements in their pharynx). In peninsular India, a thick sequence of lava flows includes interbedded and superposed sediments that have been found in recent years to produce fossil vertebrates. Important clues about the evolution of Cretaceous mammals can be found among microvertebrates (Khajuria and Prasad 1998).

As the Indian subcontinent sutured with Asia, Early Cenozoic era deposits on its northern edge emerged more and more. Eocene sequences of rock strata contain shallow water marine invertebrates and some terrestrial beds. It is with great excitement, if not surprise, that paleontologists have begun to find the remains of primitive whales, including specimens that record the loss of hind legs and the evolution of underwater physiology. These remains document the transition from land to marine life (Gingerich et al. 1994; Bajpai et al. 1996).

Multinational teams of scientists have been developing microvertebrate sites in the Eocene deposits of Pakistan, finding a largely endemic (unique to a region) assemblage of rodents. These fossils indicate common ancestry with other rodents dating from the origin of this mammalian order. Many are assignable to an indigenous family, Chapattimyidae, and are the closest known relatives to rodents 20 million years younger. These latter, the Baluchimyinae, come from the earliest Miocene pre-Siwalik deposits of Pakistan and India (Flynn et al. 1986). They attest to long-term endemic evolution of the microvertebrate fauna.

Pre-Siwalik Oligocene/Miocene deposits are partly marine but become fully terrestrial in the upper zone. Here are the rocks yielding the famous cartloads of bones from the region around Bugti, Baluchistan. The large mammals include giant rhinoceroses, early Asian proboscideans (elephant order), archaic creodont carnivores, and piglike anthracotheres. Some of these animals foreshadow the Siwalik large mammal fauna, but not the rodents. The succeeding Siwalik small mammal fauna is composed of different rodent families of African and Asian origin; the period of endemism came to an abrupt end about 20 million years ago.

Siwalik mammal faunas were established by the time sedimentation north of the Salt Range in Pakistan commenced, more than 18 million years ago. Likely, they were established before that, as evidenced by the few assemblages of fossils recovered from the Murree Formation. In the region around Chinji Village, north of the Salt Range, the lowest terrestrial deposits are assigned to the Kamlial Formation, a thick sequence of deep red to blue-gray clays and sands that sporadically produces fossil elephantoids, deinotheres (a proboscidean family), creodonts, amphicyonids (bear-dogs) and feloid (catlike) carnivores, anthracotheres (piglike ungulates), pigs, tragulids (primitive ruminants), early bovids (antelopes, cattle, etc.), giraffes, rhinos, and chalicotheres (clawed perissodactyls). Siwalik rocks and faunas are the subject of Colbert's landmark monograph (1935) and a 1995 assemblage of modern studies edited by Badgley and Behrensmeyer.

The overlying Chinji Formation is dominated by red silts and produces fossils from numerous levels. Families of mammals present in the preceding Kamlial Formation continue into it and others appear. Some appearances, such as aardvarks, reflect greater productivity; others, like dormice, are immigrants. A notable addition to the Siwalik fauna in the Chinji Formation is large-bodied hominoid primates. The famous *Sivapithecus* appears shortly after 13 million years ago; this hominoid has great implications for the evolution of large primates in general, and of orangutans in particular. The importance of this find highlights the need to continue research on these productive beds—to determine just how these organisms interacted and coevolved during the Miocene epoch.

The succeeding Nagri Formation is dominated by massive sandstones. Occasional fossil concentrations represent a continued history of mammalian evolution in the Indian subcontinent. The most notable addition to the Siwalik fauna is the horse. Hipparionine (three-toed grazer) equids are distinct markers of later Miocene time and appear abruptly about 10.7 million years ago. Yet, they seem to fit right into the Siwalik fauna, rather than causing faunal reorganization.

The Dhok Pathan Formation contains a lesser amount of sandstone. Some levels are very fossiliferous. The "U" level, dated to about 9 million years ago, includes many sites yielding *Sivapithecus* associated with a rich fauna. Toward the top of the formation, new appearances indicate a changing environment, probably increasing seasonality in the climate. These higher levels are more noted for disappearances, in particular the last hominoids and tree shrews.

Younger rock units are less homogeneous throughout the region. The famous Tatrot and Pinjor beds are in Pakistan and India, respectively. They record modernization of the Siwalik fauna: archaic groups disappear; elephants, hippos, deer, camels, and *Equus* appear. The Plio/Pleistocene record is more complete in northern India and contains true cold-fauna elements.

The small mammal faunas are a rich component to the history of the Siwaliks. These faunas document evolutionary trends and patterns on a fine scale because of the density of good data through time. Siwalik Rodentia include squirrels, gundis, thryonomyoids, rhizomyids, cricetids (hamsters and their relatives), and murids (true rats and mice). Some of these are diverse and well-documented, especially certain muroid lineages. On the global scale, most of the evolutionary story of some groups, such as Rhizomyidae (moles), is to be found in the Indian subcontinent. Deposits here chronicle the period when these interesting herbivores invaded the subterranean (burrowing) habitat that they exploit today. This happened in the Late Miocene, between 10 and 9 million years ago, before the more general faunal change seen in various groups. The appearance of other small mammals indicate the increasing seasonality of the Late Miocene climate. Among these are hares and the porcupine, which appear about 8 million years ago. Taken as a whole, the fossil record shows the evolution of the modern biota in southern Asia and the complex interactions of organisms that led to origins of living taxa (groups; singular, taxon), including hominids.

The rich mammalian history of the Indian subcontinent continues to be mined by scientists from many nations. It is a treasure that grows with the international exchange of knowledge, and its potential expands in a synergistic fashion. It is a fine example of how science progresses as we learn, and how paleontology enriches human understanding of our role in the natural world.

LAWRENCE J. FLYNN

Works Cited

Badgley, C., and A.K. Behrensmeyer. 1995. Long records of continental ecosystems. *Palaeogeography, Palaeoclimatology, Palaeoecology* 115:1–340.

Bajpai, S., J.G.M. Thewissen, and A. Sahni. 1996. *Indocetus* (Cetacea, Mammalia) endocasts from Kachchh (India). *Journal of Vertebrate Paleontology* 16 (3):582–84.

Colbert, E.H. 1935. Siwalik mammals in the American Museum of Natural History. *Transactions of the American Philosophical Society*, new ser., 26:1–401.

Flynn, L.J., L.L. Jacobs, and I.U. Cheema. 1986. Baluchimyinae, a new ctenodactyloid rodent subfamily from the Miocene of Baluchistan. *American Museum Novitates* 2841:1–58.

Gigerich, P.D., S.M. Raza, M. Arif, M. Anwar, and X. Zhou. 1994. New whale from the Eocene of Pakistan and the origin of cetacean swimming. *Nature* 368:842–44.

Khajuria, C.K., and G.V.R. Prasad. 1998. Taphonomy of a Late Cretaceous mammal-bearing microvertebrate assemblage from the Deccan inter-trappean beds of Naskal, peninsular India. *Palaeogreography, Palaeoclimatology, Palaeoecology* 137:153–72.

Vickary, N. 1846. Geological report on a portion of the Baluchistan Hills. *Quarterly Journal Geological Society London* 2:260–65.

INSECTIVORANS

Many different kinds of animals throughout the 200-odd million years of mammalian history have been classified as "Insectivora"—so many, in fact, that few contemporary scientists believe that this group represents a biologically coherent taxon (group; plural, taxa), that is, one descended from a single common ancestor. A much more manageable—and scientifically valid—concept of the "Insectivora" includes just five families with modern representatives: the Erinaceidae (hedgehogs), Tenrecidae (tenrecs), Soricidae (shrews), Talpidae (moles), and Chrysochloridae (golden moles). Two animals from the Caribbean—*Solenodon* and *Nesophontes*—are included in this group as well. Based on the simplified intestinal anatomy of these mammals (they lack a blind pocket at the beginning of the large intestine, called the "cecum"), the German anatomist Ernst Haeckel named this group the "Lipotyphla" in 1866. The fossil record of these and a few other closely related animals will be the focus of this essay.

Erinaceids have the best documented fossil record of all of the Insectivora families. Fossil hedgehogs and their relatives are as old as the Paleocene and are found in North America, Europe, Asia, and Africa. One of the more spectacular sites is Grube Messel, near Frankfurt, Germany. This Middle Eocene locality has produced not only complete skeletons, but also impressions of soft tissues (e.g., hair, claws, and stomach contents) from animals such as *Pholidocercus* and *Macrocranion* (Figure 1). Although erinaceids have been absent from North America since the end of the Miocene, their teeth and jaws are fairly common in Early Tertiary deposits throughout the North American West; particularly well-preserved forms include the Miocene fossils *Brachyerix* and *Metechinus* (Figure 2). These and other erinaceids are recognizable based on their low-crowned teeth, relatively large first lower molar, and reduced paraconids (front-most cusp) on their lower molars. Most fossil erinaceids share characters with other lipotyphlans, such as a maxilla (upper jaw) that extends well into the medial wall of the orbit (eye socket), and an auditory bulla (middle ear chamber) that is comprised partially of the basisphenoid, a midline bone of the cranial base.

Soricids have a long history on all northern continents and in Africa. The earliest undisputed members of this group are from the Middle Eocene of North America and include such forms as *Domnina* (Figure 3) and *Trimylus*. Soricids may have radiated (diversified and spread geographically) into the two major groups today—soricines and crocidurines—at some point during the Early Oligocene. This radiation of shrews possesses a unique adaptation among mammals: the double jaw-joint. That is, in soricids, the structure on the lower jaw (mandible) that is part of the hinge of the jaw is divided into two distinct articular facets (faces), each having its own articulation (joint) with the skull.

Talpids first appear in the Late Eocene of Europe and soon after appear in North America and Asia. Living moles are found on all northern continents, and are characterized by a soricid-like dentition (i.e., prominent cusps on their upper molars, giving these teeth a "W"-shaped appearance known as "dilambdodont"), and have greatly modified shoulders and forelimbs due to their famous subterranean habitat. A European group best known from the Late Oligocene, the Dimylidae, is thought to be closely related to talpids (Figure 4). Tenrecids and chrysochlorids are the only insectivorans with an extant (present-day) distribution and fossil record restricted to Africa. Although nearly all living tenrecids exist on the island of Madagascar (off the southeast African coast), their earliest undisputed fossil remains are from the Early Miocene of Kenya, in East Africa. The oldest unquestionable chrysochlorids are also from the Early Miocene of Kenya. Both of these families have a distinctive tooth structure, in which the upper molars have some absent (or highly reduced, in some cases) cusps, contributing to a "V" shaped morphology referred to as "zalambdodont."

The larger of the two Caribbean insectivorans, *Solenodon*, is known from Cuba and the island of Hispaniola (home of Haiti and the Dominican Republic). Fossils of this taxon, known from cave deposits on those islands, are probably no older than the Pleistocene. *Nesophontes*, believed to have lived into the early years of the twentieth century, is now extinct and known from Pleis-

Figure 1. *Pholidocercus hassiacus* from the Middle Eocene of Germany. From MacPhee et al. (1988), photograph courtesy of Dr. Gerhard Storch.

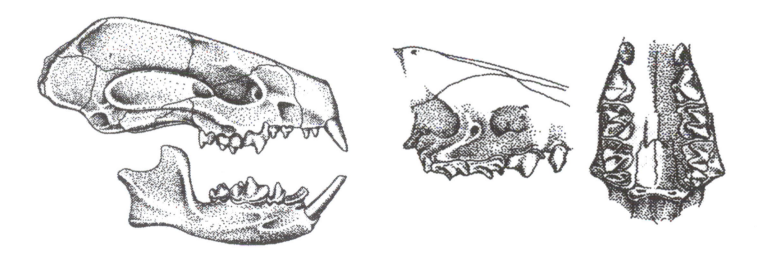

Figure 2. Skull and jaws of *Brachyerix macrotis* from the Miocene of Montana. From VERTEBRATE PALEONTOLOGY AND EVOLUTION by Robert L. Carroll, ©1988 by W.W. Freeman and Company, Used with permission.

Figure 3. *Dominina gradata* from the Late Eocene of Montana. From VERTEBRATE PALEONTOLOGY AND EVOLUTION by Robert L. Carroll, ©1988 by W.W. Freeman and Company, Used with permission.

tocene to Recent fossils from Cuba, Hispaniola, and Puerto Rico. The relationships of both of these animals to other lipotyphlans is unclear. Based partly on their teeth, some scientists have argued that *Solenodon* is a close relative of tenrecids and that *Nesophontes* is related to soricids. Other researchers have regarded the Caribbean taxa to form a group unto themselves that is, in turn, related to the Soricidae.

From Paleogene deposits in North America, several extinct lipotyphlans almost certainly are related closely to one of the above families, but it is not clear to which. One of the most conspicuous such groups is the Apternodontidae (Figure 5), best known from the Late Eocene and Early Oligocene of Wyoming and Montana. Various scholars have argued that these are relatives of tenrecids, soricids, and/or *Solenodon*. Larger species of apternodontids possess a bizarre

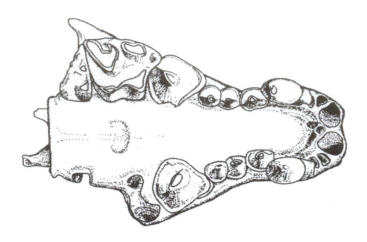

Figure 4. *Dimyloides stehlini* from the Late Oligocene of Germany. From Savage and Long (1986), courtesy of the Natural History Museum, London.

Figure 5. *Apternodus mediavevus* from the Late Eocene of Montana. Photograph by C. Tarka.

Figure 6. *Leptictis dakotensis* from the Late Eocene of South Dakota. From Novacek (1986), courtesy of the Department of Library Services, American Museum of Natural History.

chewing mechanism, in which the front teeth (i.e., canines and some incisors) are large and bulbous, contributing more surface area for mastication than their entire molar toothrow. Jaw muscle attachments on the rear of the skull are correspondingly unique, giving the skull a strange, boxlike appearance.

The Geolabididae is another extinct group of insectivorans known to have been most diverse at roughly the same times and places as the Apternodontidae. The geolabidid *Centetodon* is not quite as strange an animal as *Apternodus,* however. *Centetodon* retains fairly primitive-looking teeth, a gracile skull, and a robust zygomatic arch (cheekbone). As is the case for apternodontids, exceedingly little is known about this animal's postcranial (body) skeleton.

All of the above animals are believed to share important anatomical similarities—such as a simplified gut, extension of the maxilla in the orbital wall, and reduced pubic symphysis (area of contact between the pubic bones). These similarities are believed to have arisen from a single, common ancestor, but such an ancestor has yet to be identified. The choice is made particularly difficult since most insectivorans of the Cretaceous—presumably the time at which the first lipotyphlans appeared—are known primarily from just teeth and jaws.

Nevertheless, one possible ancestor is worth mentioning here: the Leptictidae (Figure 6). Although the most complete leptictid specimens are rather young (dating from Late Eocene/Early Oligocene times, at which time the Lipotyphla was already quite diverse), several scholars have discussed the group as a potential "sister group" (i.e., stemming from the same common ancestor) to the Lipotyphla. *Leptictis* is a hedgehog-sized animal that was probably adept at the same niche, generalized land-based diet called "omnivory," which includes plants and animals. The maxilla of leptictids protrudes slightly into its orbital wall, a similarity in kind, but not degree, with lipotyphlans.

Not all scientists agree that the Lipotyphla forms a biologically unified group. One recent study of lipotyphlan evolution based on DNA sequences in five different genes argued that chrysochlorids are not lipotyphlans at all. Until some of these animals (particularly chrysochlorids, tenrecids, and Caribbean lipotyphlans) have a better fossil record, it will remain difficult to understand their evolutionary history and how they relate to other mammalian groups.

ROBERT ASHER

Works Cited

Carroll, R.L. 1988. *Vertebrate Paleontology and Evolution.* New York: Freeman.

Savage, R.J.G., and M.R. Long. 1986. *Mammal Evolution: An Illustrated Guide.* London: British Museum (Natural History); New York: Facts on File.

MacPhee, R.D.E., M.J. Novacek, and G. Storch. 1988. *Basicranial Morphology of Early Tertiary Erinaceomorphs and the Origin of Primates.* American Museum Novitates, 2921. New York: American Museum of Natural History.

Novacek, M.J. 1986. The skull of leptictid insectivorans and the higher level classification of eutherian mammals. *Bulletin of the American Museum of Natural History* 183:1–111.

Further Reading

Butler, P.M. 1956. The skull of *Ictops* and the classification of the Insectivora. *Proceedings of the Zoological Society of London* 126:453–81.

———. 1972. The problem of insectivore classification. *In* K.A. Joysey and T.S. Kemp (eds.), *Studies in Vertebrate Evolution.* New York: Winchester.

———. 1984. Macroscelidea, Insectivora, and Chiroptera from the Miocene of East Africa. *Palaeovertebrata* 14:117–200.

———. 1988. Phylogeny of the insectivores. *In* M.J. Benton (ed.), *The Phylogeny and Classification of the Tetrapods,* vol. 2. Systematics Association Special, vol. 35-B. Oxford: Clarendon Press; New York: Oxford University Press.

Carroll, R.L. 1988. *Vertebrate Paleontology and Evolution.* New York: Freeman.

MacPhee, R.D.E., and M.J. Novacek. 1993. Definition and relationships of Lipotyphla. *In* F.S. Szalay, M.J. Novacek, and M.C. McKenna (eds.), *Mammal Phylogeny.* Vol. 2, *Placentals.* London and New York: Springer-Verlag.

MacPhee, R.D.E., M.J. Novacek, and G. Storch. 1988. *Basicranial Morphology of Early Tertiary Erinaceomorphs and the Origin of Primates.* American Museum Novitates, 2921. New York: American Museum of Natural History.

McDowell, S.B. 1958. The Greater Antillean insectivores. *Bulletin of the American Museum of Natural History* 115:117–213.

McKenna, M.C., and S.K. Bell. 1997. *Classification of Mammals above the Species Level.* New York: Columbia University Press.

Novacek, M.J. 1986. The skull of leptictid insectivorans and the higher level classification of eutherian mammals. *Bulletin of the American Museum of Natural History* 183:1–111.

———. 1992. Mammalian phylogeny: Shaking the tree. *Nature* 356:121–25.

Repenning, C.A. 1967. Subfamilies and genera of the Soricidae. *United States Geological Survey Professional Paper* 565:1–74.

Savage, R.J.G., and M.R. Long. 1986. *Mammal Evolution: An Illustrated Guide.* London: British Museum (Natural History); New York: Facts on File.

Springer, M.S., G.C. Cleven, O. Madsen, W.W. de Jong, V.G. Waddell, H.M. Amrine, and M.J. Stanhope. 1997. Endemic African mammals shake the phylogenetic tree. *Nature* 388: 61–64.

INSECTS AND OTHER HEXAPODS

Hexapods are a distinctive group of six-legged arthropods that possess tracheae (branching tubes) as breathing organs and bodies that are subdivided into an identifiable head, thorax, and abdomen. They are differentiated from other arthropods by the presence on the head of a single pair of antennae, three pairs of externally visible, mouthpart appendages, a three-segmented thorax, an abdomen of 12 or fewer evident segments, and an elongate terminal filament originating from the last abdominal segment. Hexapods inhabit virtually all terrestrial and freshwater environments and have been the most species-rich and ecologically wide-ranging group of macroscopic life since the spread of Carboniferous forests. The origin and early evolution of hexapods is poorly understood, principally because of uncertain relationships to other major clades of arthropods, and a poorly documented Devonian and Early Carboniferous record shrouded by the absence of forms connecting ancestral marine and subsequent terrestrial lineages. Traditionally thought to be closely related to myriapods such as centipedes and millipedes (Snodgrass 1935; Boudreaux 1987), recent biomolecular studies indicate that hexapods are derived from an unspecified lineage of crustaceans (Wägele 1993). This proposed placement reestablishes an older view of a close Crustacea + Hexapoda relationship and the erection of a broader clade, the Mandibulata, perhaps with inclusion of the Myriapoda as an early evolutionary lineage. Fossil evidence indicates that myriapods are an older mandibulate group whose similarities to hexapods may have arisen in parallel by convergent evolution resulting from the similar functional demands of a land existence. Nevertheless, the issue of hexapod origins remains unsettled; several basic features of the head are shared by myriapods and hexapods, providing evidence for descent from a non-crustacean ancestor.

Hexapod Structure

Hexapods primitively consist of probably 21 or 22 segments. These segments are organized during early development into three body regions, or tagmata: the head, responsible for sensory perception of the environment and procurement and ingestion of food; the thorax, bearing the organs of locomotion; and the abdomen, housing the reproductive organs and much of the digestive tract (Figure 1). These regions have been externally altered in diverse ways, principally by embryonic rearrangement of the fundamental exoskeletal elements, the sclerites, into a shifted, secondary segmentation (Gillott 1995). Because hexapod internal anatomy is rarely preserved as fossils, this discussion will emphasize external structure.

Head

The hexapod head is a sclerotized, or stiffened, spheroidal capsule whose anatomically ventral aspect houses the mouthparts (Figure 2). The head capsule typically has an internal skeleton, the tentorium, possessing rigid processes that attach to numerous muscles involved in movement of mouthparts and other structures. These tentorial processes originate on the head capsule at important anatomic landmarks—the anterior and posterior tentorial pits. In a generalized mandibulate (chewing) insect such as the grasshopper, compound eyes occur dorsolaterally on the top and to the side of the head, and three ocelli face anteriorly and frontally, two between the compound eyes and a median ocellus located on an anterior triangular sclerite, the frons. The single pair of segmented sensory antennae are inserted typically below the ocelli, adjacent to the compound eyes. The area between the compound eye and the mouthparts is the gena. The head capsule is often divided by posterior, dorsal, and frontal sutures, which are lines of juncture between sclerites. The

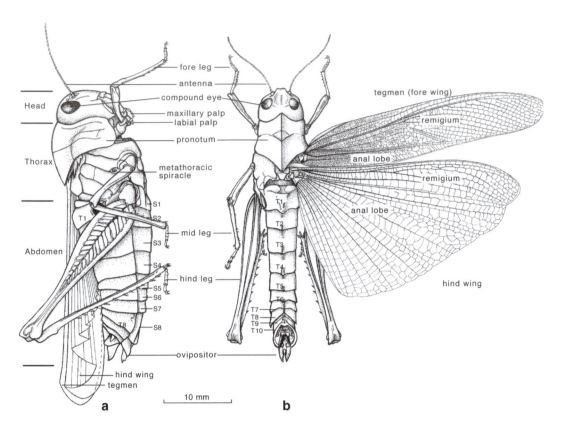

Figure 1. Major structural divisions and landmarks of a generalized female insect, the common locust. Key: *S*, sternum; *T*, tergum, Modified from Lawrence et al. (1991). Copyright © Commonwealth Scientific and Industrial Research Organization 1991. Used by permission of the American Publisher, Cornell University Press.

medial epicranial suture, which splits during molting, may bifurcate anteriorly and terminate at the transverse clypeal suture. The grasshopper has mouthparts that are ventrally attached, whereas insects such as cicadas have mouthparts angulated posteriorly; other insects such as ground beetles have mouthparts that are forwardly directed.

Hexapods have five major mouthpart regions, the posterior three of which correspond to primitive segment divisions (Snodgrass 1935). The anterior-most labrum, or "upper lip" (Figure 2a), is a medially located, movable, and enclosing flap that bears gustatory (taste) and other sensory receptors on its inner surface, the epipharynx. The hypopharynx (Figure 2d) is a typically fleshy, medially positioned (mesal) lobe that divides the preoral cavity into a dorsal mouth and a ventral salivarium; it usually bears a complement of sclerites in primitive lineages. The mandibles are paired, generally triangular, and highly sclerotized jaws that generally contact the clypeus anteriorly by an articulatory hinge, and the gena posteriorly by an exoskeletal process (condyle) and associated head cavity (Figure 2b, d). Posterior and ventral to the mandibles are the paired maxillae that consist of medial and lateral elements (Figure 2b, c). A basal sclerite attaches each maxilla to a head cavity, whereas a longer, distal segment bears all the appendages. These include a mesal, often spinose (spiny) or toothed lobe, the lacinia, and a generally fleshy lateral galea, in addition to a one- to seven-segmented palp. The labium, or "lower lip," is a medial structure representing fusion of two maxilla-like structures membranously connected to the posterior and ventral margin of

the head capsule. This structure is divided into proximal and a distal sclerites, the latter which supports two pairs of lobes—mesal glossae and lateral paraglossae—and a pair of lateral, one- to four-segmented palps.

Mouthparts are modified into major, diverse, multielement organs used for consuming fluid and particulate food (Snodgrass 1935). Piercing-and-sucking mouthparts are formed by transformation of various combinations of mandibles, maxillary laciniae, hypopharynx, and other mouthpart elements into stylets, often housed in a closed sheath or an open channel. Feeding on surface fluids is accomplished by modification of mouthparts into various mechanisms such as a siphon formed by conjoined galeae, or a sponging organ resulting from expansion of the labium into a fleshy structure. Relatively minor modifications of individual mouthpart elements can result in pronounced mouthpart asymmetry, co-optation of adjacent regions such as the labium and hypopharynx in the formation of silk-producing spinneret organs in certain larvae such as caterpillars, and transformation of mandibles and maxillary lobes into rakes and brushes as filtering or sieving devices for consumption of water-suspended detritus.

Thorax

The thorax consists of three segments: an anterior prothorax, middle mesothorax, and posterior metathorax. Each thoracic segment is divided into a dorsal tergum, two lateral pleura, and a ventral

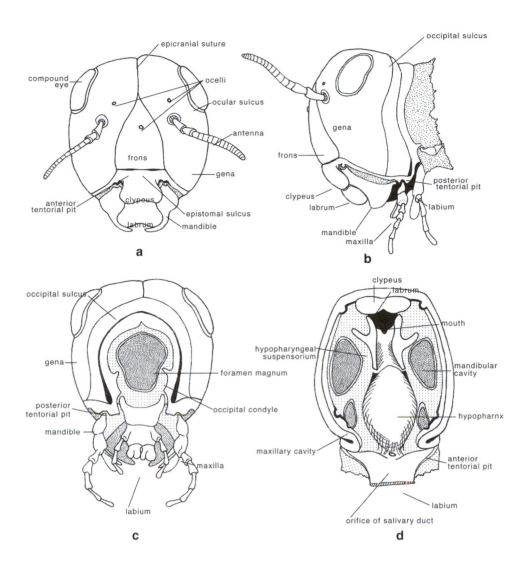

Figure 2. Head and mouthpart structures of a generalized pterygotan insect. *a*, anterior; *b*, lateral; *c*, posterior; *d*, ventral. Modified from Gillott (1995).

sternum, which respectively bear tergites, pleurites, and sternites. These sclerites are arranged in a complex series of exoskeletal plates of varying sizes and shapes, connected by intersegmental membranes (Figure 1). In winged insects thoracic segments are structured to meet the biomechanical forces induced by wings, and the segments can accommodate a significant volume of flight muscle. The anchoring and movement of legs also determine sclerite size, shape, and robustness. Although the archetypal hexapodan leg is used for walking or climbing, specializations include jumping, swimming, and impaling prey. The number of fundamental segments in the hexapod leg is debated, but it is likely that Paleozoic insects bore additional free segments that later became fused in more modern formal taxonomic groups, or taxa (Kukalová-Peck 1991). Modern taxa have, from proximal to distal, the following segments: a coxa, the functional leg base articulating with the thoracic pleurite; a trochanter that is often rigidly attached to the

femur; a femur that is the most conspicuous part of the leg; a generally elongate tibia; a slender tarsus, which is subdivided into a musculated basitarsus and two to four nonmusculated subsegments known as the eutarsus, and the pretarsus, which in most forms bears one to three lobes and a pair of lateral claws.

Apterygote hexapods are defined as primitively lacking wings, whereas modern pterygotes bear two pairs of lateral wings that articulate to the meso- and metathoracic segments by a complex system of articular sclerites (Gillott 1995). The prothoracic segment of some Paleozoic insects bore movable, lateral lobes with veins that indicate a parallel developmental path (serial homology) with functional wings. In other insects the prothorax elongated as a feeding specialization, or became spinose to deter predation. Both pairs of wings are primitively similar in general form and construction, and they are fluted into a system of alternating convex and concave veins to impart structural rigidity to the wing membrane. Often there is a distinctive, often pigmented spot, the pterostigma, on the distal end of the anterior margin of both wing pairs. In many lineages the anterior pair became modified into leathery or rigid wing covers such as tegmina in grasshoppers or the elytra of beetles, whereas the hind wing remained membranous, stored in a pleatlike fashion over the abdomen by a system of wing folds (Figure 3). Some insects, such as true flies (Diptera) and adult male scale insects, have modified one of the pairs of metathoracic wings into small, spoon-shaped balance organs, or halteres. Similar structures, arising through the modification of wing covers, occur on the mesothorax of adult male twisted-wing parasites (Strepsiptera). Some parasitic insect groups have lost all external evidence of wings, such as the Phthiraptera (lice) and Siphonaptera (fleas).

The primitive insect wing is a double-walled membrane supported by a network of radiating, bifurcating veins that commonly connect by short crossveins that define enclosed areas called cells (Figure 3). From the anterior to the posterior wing margin, the principal veins and their abbreviations are the following, with raised convex veins designated as (+) and depressed concave veins as (–): costa, C (+); subcosta, Sc (–); radius, R (+); media, M (–); cubitus, Cu (–); first anal, 1A (+); second anal, 2A (– or +); third anal, 3A (+) (nomenclature after Kukalová-Peck 1991). Each of these veins, with the exception of the costa, bifurcate once to several times and support increasing surface area toward the distal wing membrane. In the case of plecopteroid and orthopteroid insects, the hind wing anal veins are arranged into an anal fan that is distinguished from the wing proper (remigium) by a characteristic claval fold; for blattoid, hemipteroid, and holometabolous insects, the anal lobe starts with the anal fold. The nomenclature of these veinal branches has been standardized, although there are difficulties in applying these names homologously across some insect orders. A few important primary branches are the anterior branch of the radius, designated as RA, and the posterior branch, designated as RP (also known as the radial sector); the anterior media, MA, and the posterior media, MP; and the anterior and posterior branches of the cubitus, which are CuA and CuP, respectively (Figure 3). Modification of this fundamental venation has occurred principally by reduction of veins, especially in hemipteroid and holometabolous lineages. In forms possessing generalized venation, especially primitive palaeodictyopteroids, orthopteroids, and blattoids, a characteristic archedictyon occurs between major veins, consisting of an intricate meshwork of venules. Derived from a few selected veins of this archedictyon are major crossveins (Figure 3), which are diagnostic features, particularly among holometabolous insects. Primitively the fore- and hind wing pairs moved independently, although in derived lineages there were parallel tendencies to couple adjacent fore- and hind wings for synchronized motion during flight (Brodsky 1994). Various wing-coupling devices included mutual overlap of interdigitating lobes and interconnecting bristles or hooks.

Abdomen

Evidence from developmental genetics indicates that the hexapod abdomen primitively consists of 12 segments (Raff 1996). Unlike

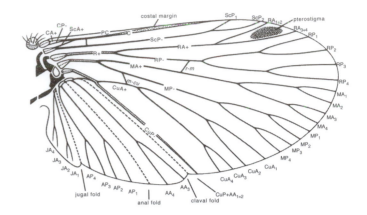

Figure 3. Nomenclature of wing venation in a hypothetical generalized insect. Crossveins: *r-m*, radio-medial; *m-cu*, medio-cubitus; see text for key to other abbreviations. From Lawrence et al. (1991). Copyright © Commonwealth Scientific and Industrial Research Organization 1991. Used by permission of the American Publisher, Cornell University Press.

the thorax, which has been extensively remodeled to accommodate the demands of locomotion, the abdomen consists of series of segments with relatively simple, mostly undivided terga and sterna. The anatomically dorsal terga are connected to anatomically ventral sterna either by a rigid pleuron or by a pleural membrane. Major changes have occurred anteriorly, where the first abdominal segment has been reduced or incorporated with the metathorax in some insects, and in the eighth to tenth segments, which have been significantly modified for appendicular genitalia. The 11th segment almost always occurs in the embryonic stage, and its appendages are externally evident as the cerci of many basal insect groups, transformed into forceps in diplurans and earwigs. Primitive insects bear abdominal appendages known as styli, which are developmentally equivalent, or homologous, to walking limbs (Raff 1996). Additional evidence from studies of early insect development (Raff 1996) indicate that appendages positioned above the styli, such as gills in mayfly naiads and prolegs of some holometabolous caterpillars, are homologous to wings.

There is considerable confusion regarding homologies of external hexapod genitalia across the taxonomic orders. However, a generalized description of basic structures is useful for male genitalia and the female ovipositor. The male genitalia originate from the ninth segment, are highly variable structurally, and frequently are comprised of a pair of claspers, originating from modified styles to grasp the female during copulation, and a median intromittent organ. The claspers are well developed on modern mayflies, although Paleozoic mayflies displayed more generalized and larger structures. The intromittent organ consists of a penis, sometimes paired as hemipenes, and lateral structures variously termed parameres or gonapophyses. In the female the leg appendages of the eighth and ninth segments provide the first (ventral) and second (dorsal) valves of a compound organ, the ovipositor (Figure 4), which deposits eggs through an egg canal on or into various substrates. A third valve or sheath occurs in many insects as a posterior process originating from the gonocoxite of the ninth segment (Gullan and Cranston 1994). The ovipositor can range from a barely protruding stub to an impressively long organ that is used to insert eggs into substrates as diverse as soil, wood, plant tissues, or other animals such as insects and vertebrates. In paleodictyopteroids, grasshoppers, and sawflies, ovipositor valve cuticle is often modified into sawtooth structures and is primarily involved in piercing fleshy plant tissues. In some ichneumonid wasps a terminal "drill" bores through wood for oviposition in wood-boring larvae. Departures from typical egg-laying include formation of egg cases known as oöthecae in cockroaches and mantids, egg retention and live birth in aphids and some parasitic flies, and indiscriminate ejection by walkingsticks.

Characterization and Fossil History of Major Hexapod Groups

Recently, anatomic and morphologic features have been used to differentiate the most basal (primitive) lineages from "typical" insects (Figure 5). With this fundamental distinction, the term "Hexapoda" is now used to characterize all terrestrial arthropods with three independent tagmata and three walking legs. The Hexapoda, in turn, are formally subdivided by some into the Parainsecta and Insecta (Figure 5). (In the following discussion, Table 1 lists the geochronological duration of major insect clades.)

Parainsecta

The Parainsecta are defined by several major features, principally entognathy, or an overgrowth of the lateral head wall to form an oral cavity that surrounds often attenuated mouthparts. Degenerate to absent compound eyes and unpaired pretarsal claws are also diagnostic features. The Parainsecta consists of two taxa: the Collembola (springtails), which have a fossil record extending to the Early Devonian; and the rarely encountered Protura (proturans), lacking a fossil record. The Insecta comprise all other hexapods and are characterized by a transverse bar in the posterior part of tentorium, leg-articulating coxae that do not include the sternum, and an ovipositor formed by limb-base endites on segments eight and nine. Although the position of the Diplura was previously unresolved (Kristensen 1991), several lines of evidence indicate that they are true insects (Kukalová-Peck 1987; Raff 1996).

Archaeognatha and Zygentoma

Within the Insecta, the primary subdivision is between the Archaeognatha (bristletails) and all other insects. Archaeognatha possess the derived characteristics of medially abutting compound eyes and the absence of spiracles on the first thoracic segment. They are the only true insect clade that primitively bear mandibles that articulate with the head capsule by a single condyle. The fossil Monura are now known to be a Late Paleozoic subgroup of the Archaeognatha. The more-derived Zygentoma by contrast evolved mandibles with a secondary, anterior condyle (Kukalová-Peck 1991) and thus define the insect clade Dicondylia. Fossil archaeognathans first appear during the Early Devonian, whereas

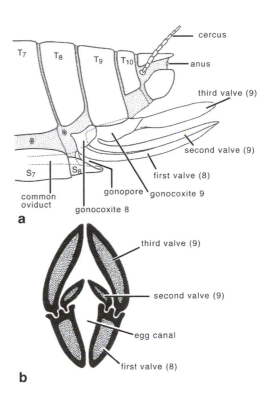

Figure 4. Terminal aspect of a female insect abdomen and associated ovipositor. *a*, Lateral view of a generalized orthopteroid ovipositor; *b*, Transverse section of a katydid (Orthoptera) ovipositor. Parenthetical insertions refer to segment number origin. Key: *S*, sternum; *T*, tergum. From Gullan and Cranston (1994).

zygentomans are known from the Late Carboniferous; both have a sporadic fossil record to the Recent.

Pterygota

Within the Dicondylia, the vast clade Pterygota, or winged insects, is defined primarily by the presence of two pairs of wings on the second (mesothoracic) and third (metathoracic) segments and by a remodeled thorax associated with flight. The Pterygota also is characterized by fusion of major elements of the head endoskeleton and by suppression of eversible sacs, which are small and ventral abdominal structures that presumably absorb water. The Pterygota consists of two major clades, the Neoptera and probably the Palaeoptera. Fossils of these taxa first appear at the Early to Late Carboniferous boundary and are represented by ten orders of insects. This suggests that the Pterygota had an appreciably earlier origin.

PALAEOPTERA. With one Paleozoic exception, the Palaeoptera is characterized by wings that are held outstretched from the body, incapable of being folded over the abdomen. Additionally the Paleoptera bear homonomous wings, in which fore- and hind wings appear similar and have identical wing venation. The Palaeoptera is comprised of the extant Ephemeroptera (mayflies) and Odonatoptera (dragonflies), and the Paleozoic Palaeodicty-

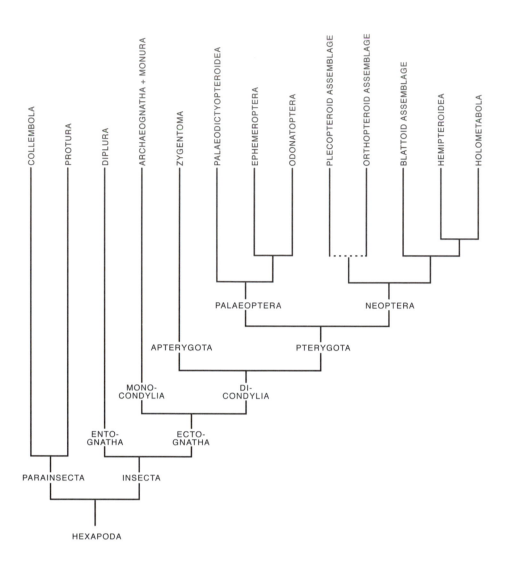

Figure 5. Phylogeny of major groups of hexapods, as proposed by Kukalová-Peck (1991). Symbols: *dashed lines,* less assured relationships.

opteroidea. The Palaeoptera is considered by many as a monophyletic group, in which all lineages originate from a common ancestor. For modern taxa, features, particularly wing venation and articulation structures, convincingly indicate that the Odonatoptera + Ephemeroptera jointly have a sister-group relationship with the Neoptera. Other features, such as loss of certain muscles in the thorax and absence of the molt in the fully winged stage, have been used to suggest that the Odonata alone may bear a sister-group relationship with the remaining Neoptera (Kristensen 1991). The third possible combination—a sister-group relationship between the Ephemeroptera and Neoptera—has been supported by the presence of direct sperm transfer during copulation in the two groups, contrasting with the indirect and external mode used by the Odonata.

Palaeodictyopteroidea. The Palaeodictyopteroidea constituted a majority of Late Carboniferous taxa and is distinguished from other paleopterous insects by the presence of unique stylate-

nonhaustellate mouthparts characterized by exposed piercing stylets lacking an encompassing sheath. The Palaeodictyopteroidea is subdivided into four orders, the Diaphanopterodea, Palaeodictyoptera, Megasecoptera, and Permothemistida (Kukalová-Peck 1991). The Palaeodictyopteroidea, the only extinct supraordinal taxon of insects, was a structurally diverse clade; wingspans, for example, ranged by more than an order of magnitude, from mosquito-like permothemistids at 0.9 centimeters to giant paleodictyopterids at 56 centimeters. The strongly fluted, stiff, archedictyon-rich wings of large paleodictyopteroids were modified into the streamlined, petiolate shapes of the Megasecoptera, or they were significantly reduced as hind wings in the Permothemistida. The Diaphanopterodea independently evolved a non-neopteran mechanism of abdominal wing folding. Major differences in beak shape also occurred among these orders.

Odonatoptera. The shared ancestry of the Protodonata and Odonata is indicated by the presence of distinctive intercalary

Table 1. Geochronologic distribution of hexapod orders

Order[2]	Common name	First occurrence[3]	Last occurrence[3]
Collembola	springtails	Devonian (Lochkovian)	Recent
Diplura	telsontails	Carboniferous (Moscovian)	Recent
Archaeognatha	bristletails	Devonian (Pragian)	Recent
Monura	monurans	Carboniferous (Bashkirian)	Permian (Artinskian)
Zygentoma	silverfish, firebrats	Carboniferous (Moscovian)	Recent
Ephemeroptera	mayflies	Carboniferous (Moscovian)	Recent
Odonata	dragonflies, damselflies	Carboniferous (Bashkirian)	Recent
Palaeodictyoptera	paleodictyopterans	Carboniferous (Serpukhovian)	Permian (Wordian)
Diaphanopterodea	diaphanopterodeans	Carboniferous (Bashkirian)	Permian (Capitanian)
Megasecoptera	megasecopterans	Carboniferous (Bashkirian)	Permian (Longtanian)
Permothemistida	permothemistidans	Carboniferous (Bashkirian)	Permian (Wordian)
"Protorthoptera"[4]	protorthopterans	Carboniferous (Bashkirian)	Triassic (Anisian)
Blattodea	cockroaches	Carboniferous (Bashkirian)	Recent
Mantodea	mantids	Cretaceous (Hauterivian)	Recent
Isoptera	termites	Cretaceous (Valanginian)	Recent
Protelytroptera	protelytropterans	Carboniferous (Kasimovian)	Recent
Dermaptera	earwigs	Jurassic (Sinemurian)	Recent
Orthoptera	grasshoppers, katydids, crickets	Carboniferous (Moscovian)	Recent
Phasmatoptera[5]	walkingsticks, leaf insects	Triassic (Ladinian)	Recent
Titanoptera	titanopterans	Triassic (Anisian)	Jurassic (Hettangian)
Embioptera	webspinners	Permian (Wordian)	Recent
Grylloblattodea	rock crawlers	Carboniferous (Gzelian)	Recent
Plecoptera	stoneflies	Carboniferous (Gzelian)	Recent
Caloneurodea	caloneurids	Carboniferous (Moscovian)	Permian (Capitanian)
Hypoperlida	ancestral hemipteroids	Carboniferous (Bashkirian)	Triassic (Anisian)
Zoraptera	angel insects	Paleogene (Chattian)	Recent
Psocoptera	booklice, psocids	Permian (Sakmarian)	Recent
Phthiraptera	lice	Paleogene (Priabonian)	Recent
Thysanoptera	thrips	Permian (Sakmarian)	Recent
Hemiptera	bugs, cicadas, hoppers, aphids, whiteflies, scales	Carboniferous (Moscovian)	Recent
Miomoptera	miomopterans	Carboniferous (Bashkirian)	Recent
Glosselytrodea	glosselytrodeans	Carboniferous (Bashkirian)	Jurassic (Sinemurian)
Megaloptera	alderflies, dobsonflies	Permian (Kungurian)	Recent
Raphidioidea	snakeflies	Permian (Wordian)	Recent

Order[2]	Common name	First occurrence[3]	Last occurrence[3]
Planipennia[6]	lacewings, antlions, owlflies	Permian (Sakmarian)	Recent
Coleoptera[7]	beetles	Permian (Sakmarian)	Recent
Strepsiptera	twisted-wing parasites	Paleogene (Lutetian)	Recent
"Paratrichoptera"[4]	paratrichopterans	Permian (Sakmarian)	Cretaceous (Berriasian)
Mecoptera	scorpionflies	Permian (Asselian)	Recent
Siphonaptera	fleas	?Cretaceous (Aptian)	Recent
Diptera	flies	?Permian (Ufimian)	Recent
Trichoptera	caddisflies	Triassic (Ladinian)	Recent
Lepidoptera	moths, butterflies	Jurassic (Sinemurian)	Recent
Hymenoptera	sawflies, wasps, ants, bees	Triassic (Ladinian)	Recent

Notes 1. This list is modified slightly from Labandeira (1994).
      2. The Protura lack a fossil record.
      3. Epoch and stage names from Harland et al. (1990).
      4. An informal, paraphyletic designation.
      5. Includes the Early Mesozoic Chresmodidae, Aeroplanidae, and related families.
      6. Also known as Neuroptera *sensu stricto*.
      7. Includes the Protocoleoptera of several authors.

wing veins, the oblique orientation of thoracic segments (Hennig 1981), and a raptorial and protractile labial mask in the aquatic nymph (Kukalová-Peck 1991). The Protodonata, including the gigantic Meganeuridae, are distinguished from the Odonata by absence of or an incomplete nodus, costal triangle, and pterostigma on the wing, and by serrate anterior wing margins, a sinuous CuP vein, and unreduced male genitalia. The Protodonata and Odonata generally have often been considered distinctive at the ordinal level; however, there now is evidence for a third order, the Paleozoic Geroptera (Bechley 1996). The Protodonata and Odonata have a rich fossil record, attributable to their large size and sturdy wing construction. Late Carboniferous members of the Meganeuridae that achieved wingspans of 70 centimeters are the largest known insects.

Ephemeroptera. The most compelling derived feature (autapomorphy) of the Ephemeroptera is a vein known as the "subcostal brace." The Paleozoic Syntonopterodea resembled protodonatan dragonflies and palaeodictyopteroids, with hind wings broader than forewings and a shorter subcostal brace—as opposed to modern mayflies, which possess reduced hind wings and elongate male forelegs (Kristensen 1991). Paleozoic adult mayflies had robust, functional mouthparts and probably were active feeders (Shear and Kukalová-Peck 1990); by contrast, post-Paleozoic adults had strongly reduced, nonfunctional mouthparts. Ephemeropteran nymphs, however, were aquatic detritus feeders that had a mandibular articulation with the head capsule unique among extant insects. Some Paleozoic ephemeropterans were frequently large, one species reaching 45 centimeters in wingspan.

NEOPTERA. The fundamental defining feature of the Neoptera is a distinctive wing-articulation mechanism resulting in rotation, flexing, and locking of the wings over the abdomen. Of the five major neopteran assemblages that encompasses 33 conventional orders, the best-circumscribed is the Holometabola. The Hemipteroidea is less well defined, but their unity is widely accepted. The Hemipteroidea and the Holometabola together have been termed the "higher" Neoptera, and probably are sister groups, constituting the Eumetabola (Kristensen 1991). The three assemblages of "lower" Neoptera are broadly termed the plecopteroid, orthopteroid, and blattoid assemblages. Collectively these taxa have been placed in the presumably polyphyletic lower Neoptera, in which descent has proceeded from multiple unrelated ancestors (Kristensen 1994).

Plecopteroid Assemblage. Autapomorphies of the Plecoptera include males lacking gonostyli, intromittent organs on the ninth abdominal segment, and presence of a common medial stem to the MA and MP veins (Kristensen 1991; Kukalová-Peck 1991). Recognition of plecopteran vein characters in some members of the extinct "Protorthoptera" has resulted in extension of stem-group plecopteroids into the Late Carboniferous (Kukalová-Peck 1991). Most of these taxa are woefully incomplete and are based principally on wings, although near-complete bodies are known for many. The nymphs of Permian plecopteroids were aquatic, although A.G. Sharov (1966) indicated that some were probably terrestrial and capable of flight. Modern Plecoptera are among the least derived of Neoptera and may be the sister group to all other Neoptera (Hennig 1981). The presently relict Grylloblattida (rock crawlers) also may be members (Rohdendorf and Rasnitsyn 1980).

Orthopteroid Assemblage. The most taxonomically confusing of all lower Neoptera is the orthopteroid assemblage. Orthopteroids have generalized mandibulate mouthparts and an enlarged anal fan in the hind wing. Members of this group are the Orthoptera (grasshoppers and crickets), Phasmatoptera (stick insects), the extinct Titanoptera, probably the Embioptera (webspinners), and possibly the Zoraptera (angel insects). Orthopterans with leathery, rooflike folded forewings (tegmina) and jumping hind legs are known from the Middle Pennsylvanian; forms with stridulatory organs are documented for the Lower Permian, although the earliest members of the cricket lineage are Late Triassic to Early Jurassic (Hennig 1981). Phasmatopterans have a poor fossil record, although modern-aspect taxa are known from the Late Jurassic. The Titanoptera are exclusively a Mid-Mesozoic clade of structurally derived and apparently predaceous insects with raptorial forelegs, incisiform mandibles, and wings with spans up to 36 centimeters that were folded flat over their abdomen. Embiopterans, characterized by absence of a hind wing anal fan, are reported from the Late Permian of Russia. Modern Zoraptera are poorly known anatomically and have a single occurrence in the Mid-Cenozoic (Poinar 1992).

A vexing issue in insect paleobiology is taxonomic characterization and phylogenetic relationships of the diverse, abundant, and undoubtedly polyphyletic "Protorthoptera" (Hennig 1981). Because of the very generalized structure and the consequent absence of identifiable, derived features in this Paleozoic group, paleoentomologists have found definition of this group difficult. Many protorthopterans exhibit features of primitive hemipteroids, whereas others are taxonomically isolated because of very incomplete knowledge regarding head, mouthpart, and reproductive structures. As knowledge of these features and interpretation of wing venation advances, definable groups will be segregated and allocated to other neopteran clades (Kukalová-Peck 1991).

Blattoid Assemblage. As in the plecopteroid and orthopteroid assemblages, debate surrounds whether the blattoid assemblage is separable from the rest of the lower Neoptera as an identifiable clade. Nevertheless, an intact group of Mantodea + (Blattodea + Isoptera) has been established, and other, more distant members of this group probably include the extinct Protelytroptera and its modern descendants, the Dermaptera (earwigs). As a major clade, the Blattodea (cockroaches) is a ubiquitous and persistent element in equatorial Paleozoic localities (Wootton 1981). Numerically they are the most frequently encountered insect and occur overwhelmingly as isolated tegmina or hind wings in many deposits. During the Paleozoic, as now, cockroaches were dorsoventrally flattened, had an inconspicuous head that bore ventrally deployed mouthparts, and were covered dorsally by a pronotal shield. At least some Paleozoic and Mesozoic cockroaches possessed prominent, external ovipositors capable of penetrating firm substrates (see Hennig 1981 for an alternative view). Modern cockroaches lack external ovipositors and produce eggs that occur in an oötheca, a leathery egg case that is dropped from the body. Although most studies cite a sister-group relationship between the Blattodea and the Isoptera, there is recent evidence that termites may be derived from within the cockroach clade. Supporting the view that termites are modified cockroaches is the absence of pre-Cretaceous

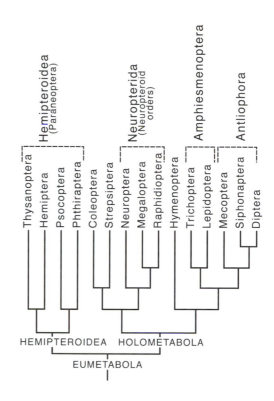

Figure 6. Possible phylogeny of the Hemipteroidea and Holometabola. Modified from Gullan and Cranston (1994).

termite body-fossils and trace-fossils, suggesting a Mid-Mesozoic origin. Mantids have a sporadic and poor fossil record that begins during the Early Cretaceous.

Hemipteroidea (Paraneoptera). The Hemipteroidea (Figure 6) are principally characterized by head and mouthpart specializations, such as an enlarged segment of the clypeus, the postclypeus, with mouth-cavity dilator muscles, and a detached and slender maxillary lacinia (Kukalová-Peck 1991). They also bear six or fewer Malpighian excretory tubules and have abdominal ganglia consolidated into one mass. Included in this group are certain Paleozoic taxa, long considered as "Protorthoptera" and taxonomically segregated by Russian paleoentomologists, that bore head and mouthpart modifications similar to modern Psocoptera (psocids) and Hemiptera (cicadas, aphids, scale insects, and bugs). Modern Hemipteroidea is divisible into four clades, the Psocoptera (booklice) + Phthiraptera (lice), and the Thysanoptera (thrips) + Hemiptera (aphids, bugs, and relatives). The relationship of the Phthiraptera to the Psocoptera is contentious; the two major proposals are either a sister-group relationship or gradual paraphyletic branching of multiple phthirapteran lineages from within the Psocoptera. By contrast the sister-group relationship of the Thysanoptera and Hemiptera is better established. Ancestral hemipteroids were common in Late Paleozoic insect faunas; all modern hemipteroid lineages except the Phthiraptera are known from the Early Permian (Labandeira 1994).

The evolution of mouthparts in the Hemipteroidea parallels that of the Palaeodictyopteroidea. In both clades there was a transformation of mandibulate mouthparts associated with solid-food feeding into highly integrated, multielement structures capable of piercing tissue and imbibing deep-seated fluid food. The Permian demise of paleodictyopteroids was probably a consequence of extinction of their food plants and competition from the hemipteroid diversification that resulted in occupation of earlier paleodictyopteroid feeding niches (Labandeira and Phillips 1996). This radiation produced early, plant-feeding, homopterous hemipterans that included taxa superficially resembling modern cicadas and jumping lice. During the Late Permian, heteropterous hemipterans were established, although the earliest modern lineages are recorded from Late Triassic strata.

Holometabola (Endopterygota). The Holometabola consists of 11 orders united by the well-accepted feature of holometabolous development (Figure 6). The holometabolous life cycle is characterized by an egg→larva→pupa→adult sequence rather than the nonholometabolous egg→nymph→adult sequence. Holometabolous insects have an active juvenile stage, termed a larva, that is separated from a morphologically and ecologically differentiated adult stage by a typically quiescent pupal stage. Related to this unique life cycle are several other distinctive features of the eyes, genitalia, and wings. Larvae lack true ocelli and instead have lateral stemmata, whereas adults have structurally different compound eyes. Wings and genitalia occur as rudiments in larvae, namely inpocketings under the body wall, which subsequently become everted externally during the pupal stage.

The Holometabola, comprising 90 percent of hexapod species, is probably divisible into two major assemblages (Kristensen 1991). One is the Coleoptera + the neuropteroid orders, consisting of the Coleoptera (beetles) and their sister group, the three neuropteroid orders of Planipennia (lacewings, antlions, owlflies), Raphidioidea (snakeflies), and Megaloptera (dobsonflies and alderflies). The second assemblage is the Hymenoptera (sawflies, wasps, ants, and bees) and the five orders of the panorpoid complex—the Mecoptera (scorpionflies), Diptera (flies), Siphonaptera (fleas), collectively designated as the Antliophora, and the Trichoptera (caddisflies) and Lepidoptera (moths, butterflies) which form the Amphiesmenoptera.

The Coleoptera + neuropteroid assemblage is poorly defined, but it is based on valvular modifications of the ovipositor and reduction of terminal abdominal cerci to short and nonarticulated structures, among other features (Kristensen 1994). While true beetles do not appear until the Late Permian, their stem group, known as the Protocoleoptera, occur in earliest Permian deposits from Europe. The distinction between these two groups is that the Protocoleoptera bore a unique elytral locking mechanism, a significantly long external ovipositor rather than one retracted internally, 13- rather than 11-segmented antennae, and wing venation with primitive cross-veins that are lacking in true beetles. Within the neuropteroid orders, several structures provide links among taxa, including a medially divided dorsal thoracic sclerite, the metapostnotum, and fused third valves of the ovipositor. Basal lineages of Coleoptera, Planipennia and Mecoptera, are the earliest documented fossil holometabolous insects, occurring in earliest Permian riparian (river) and lacustrine (lake) environments.

Features linking the Hymenoptera to the Mecopterida are larval silk production from a labial spinneret and unpaired pretar- sal claws, among others (Kristensen 1991). The Hymenoptera is defined by several derived characters, including considerable reduction of the hind wing, coupling of the hind wing to the forewing by hooks, major flight musculature located in the mesothorax rather than metathorax, and haplodiploid sex determination. The Hymenoptera undoubtedly originated considerably earlier than their Middle Triassic fossil appearance would indicate, but it is noteworthy that the earliest fossil representatives of Hymenoptera are closely related to the Xyelidae, considered to be the most basal extant hymenopteran lineage.

The Mecopterida is an ecologically varied and taxonomically diverse clade, united by loss or extreme reduction of the ovipositor and certain mouthpart losses. Within this clade, two groupings are evident: the Antliophora consisting of Mecoptera + (Diptera + Siphonaptera), and the Amphiesmenoptera comprising the well-corroborated Trichoptera + Lepidoptera. The Antliophora are defined by structures such as larval mouthparts. The Nannochoristidae, a basal mecopteran lineage with a Late Permian record, have been considered by some as ordinally distinct and perhaps the most primitive extant antliophoran. Adult nannochoristids, unlike other mecopterans, possess a few mouthpart specializations similar to some basal Diptera and have a unique, aquatic larva. Nannochoristids notwithstanding, the earliest body-fossil representatives of the Mecopterida are Early Permian stem-group lineages historically designated as "Paramecoptera" (Hennig 1981). The enigmatic Miomoptera, including Late Carboniferous taxa that bear mecopterid wing venation, may be such a lineage. True Mecoptera and the earliest Diptera, the latter with vestigial but veined hind wings, appear during the Late Permian. The Mecoptera experienced a major taxonomic radiation during the Early Mesozoic and achieved a diversity considerably greater than its collective modern descendants, many of which now have relict geographical distributions. The earliest documented Siphonaptera are Late Eocene, although Early Cretaceous specimens from Australia may be primitive fleas. Some recent molecular studies, however, have relegated fleas to a clade within the Mecoptera.

Approximately 20 discrete characters unite the Trichoptera and Lepidoptera into the Amphiesmenoptera, of which the most prominent are looped anal veins in the forewing and fusion of the prelabium with the hypopharynx to form a projecting silk gland with an apical aperture (Kristensen 1991). The Amphiesmenoptera are probably represented in the Permian, and by the Middle Triassic the Trichoptera and Lepidoptera probably had emerged as distinct lineages. The earliest fossil trichopterans are from the Middle Triassic of Asia and include the extant family Philopotamidae. Many Recent trichopteran families can be recognized as body fossils in Jurassic deposits. There also is a parallel trace-fossil record in later Mesozoic strata of distinctive caddisfly cases, though they are not associated with respective body fossils.

Unlike aquatic trichopteran larvae, lepidopteran larvae are terrestrial, with primitive lineages inhabiting bryophyte foliage or commonly are endophytic herbivores as miners, borers, or gallers. Even though the Lepidoptera are characterized by approximately 25 derived characters, much debate has surrounded the age of the oldest Lepidoptera (Hennig 1981). Spec-

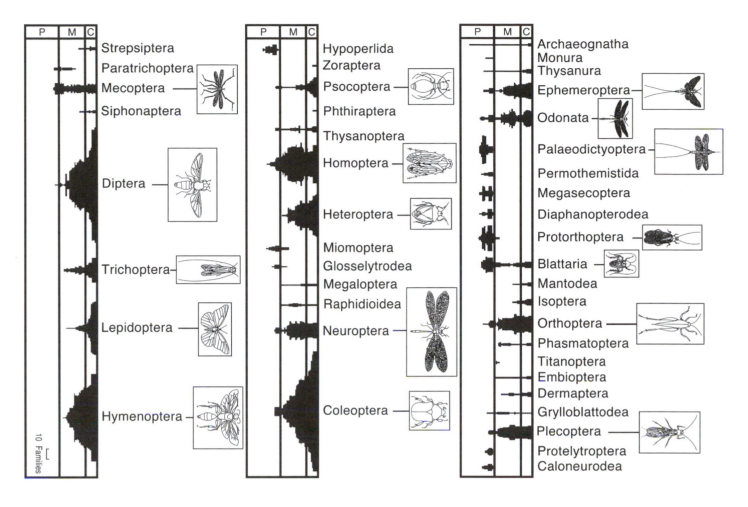

Figure 7. Family-level diversity of major insect clades through time. (Homoptera, an apparently paraphyletic assemblage, and Heteroptera are now combined into a composite clade, the Hemiptera.) Reprinted from Labandeira and Sepkoski (1993). Copyright © 1993 American Association for the Advancement of Science.

imens from the Middle and Upper Triassic were initially described as lepidopterans, although they subsequently have been reassigned to early trichopteran lineages or to the undifferentiated Amphiesmenoptera. The earliest lepidopteran is a Lower Jurassic moth. By the Mid-Cretaceous, there was a radiation of primitive phytophagous lineages (Labandeira et al. 1994). More derived, externally feeding clades, such as butterflies, are present during the earliest Cenozoic.

Diversity

Hexapod diversity can be gauged by three measures. "Taxonomic diversity" documents the breadth of unique and cumulative speciation events produced by the evolutionary process. "Morpho-ecologic diversity" refers to the modes by which hexapods interact with their environment, as determined by associated structural adaptations evolved to meet ecologic demand. "Behavioral diversity" reveals the repertoire of sexual, social, parental, feeding, and defensive strategies of a particular life history. All three assessments express the different ways that hexapods have subdivided their environment and achieved dominance on land and in fresh water.

Taxonomic

Estimates of modern insect taxonomic diversity range from a low of approximately 5 million to a high of 80 million species, although there is much uncertainty. Regardless, only 876,000 extant species are taxonomically named or otherwise known, compared to approximately 20,000 identified insect fossil species, relegating the insect fossil record to less than 1 percent of inferred modern species diversity (Carpenter 1992). At the genus level, the record is better, with the fossil record representing 11 percent of extant generic diversity. However, because of the omnipresence of insect species and the prevalence of well-preserved fossil insect deposits, the family-level representation of insects is high: 63 percent of the approximately 1,000 extant families of insects are represented as fossils (Labandeira 1994). Additionally, many of these families have long geologic durations. These features show that gross aspects of the insect fossil record are well documented (Fig-

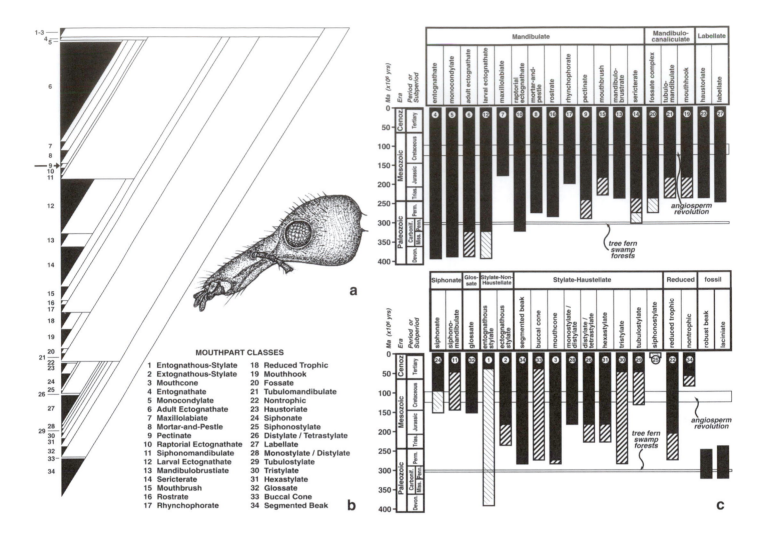

Figure 8. The geochronological extension of modern mouthpart classes for an assessment of mouthpart diversity through time. *a,* Head and mouthparts of a weevil, corresponding to dendrogram cluster 9 in *b* (indicated by *arrow*). *b,* Dendrogram resulting from a cluster analysis of recent hexapod mouthparts; for details of dataset structure and methods of analysis, see Labandeira (1997). *c,* Extension of basic mouthpart types in *b* into the fossil record. Symbols: *solid black segments,* solid evidence; *heavy slashed segments,* based on sister-group relationships; *lightly slashed segments,* more indirect evidence, based on trace fossils or presence of conspecific but alternate life stage of the life stage pertaining to the mouthpart class under consideration. Abbreviations: *Devon.,* Devonian; *Carbonif.,* Carboniferous; *Miss.,* Mississippian; *Penn.,* Pennsylvanian; *Perm.,* Permian; *Trias.,* Triassic; *Cenoz.,* Cenozoic. From Labandeira (1997). With permission from the *Annual Review of Ecology and Systematics,* volume 28, © 1997, by Annual Reviews, Inc.

ure 7), driven principally by exceptional fossil deposits (Labandeira and Sepkoski 1993).

Morphoecologic

Since securing and consuming food is central to an insect's existence, an evaluation of mouthpart structure (Figures 2, 8a) is an important measure of morphoecologic diversity. In a recent study it was found that there are 34 fundamental mouthpart classes among extant hexapods and two additional classes that are extinct (Figure 8b), of which all but three can be tracked with some certainty in the fossil record (Labandeira 1997). When the geochronologic ranges of these mouthpart classes are integrated over

geologic time (Figure 8c), there is a characteristic pattern of logistic increase with a rapid rise during the Late Carboniferous to Late Triassic, followed by an essentially modern level after the Mid-Jurassic (Figure 9). Superimposed on this pattern are five discrete episodes of mouthpart class origination (Labandeira 1997), the first consisting of approximately five mandibulate (chewing) and stylate (piercing-and-sucking) types for penetrating dead and live plant tissue by early hexapod colonists of land. The second expansion of mouthpart types is evident during the Late Carboniferous, perhaps earlier, with additions to existing mandibulate and stylate classes. A third phase during the Early Permian is associated with the early radiation of stylate-haustellate mouthpart types—piercing mouthparts surrounded by a labial sheath—in

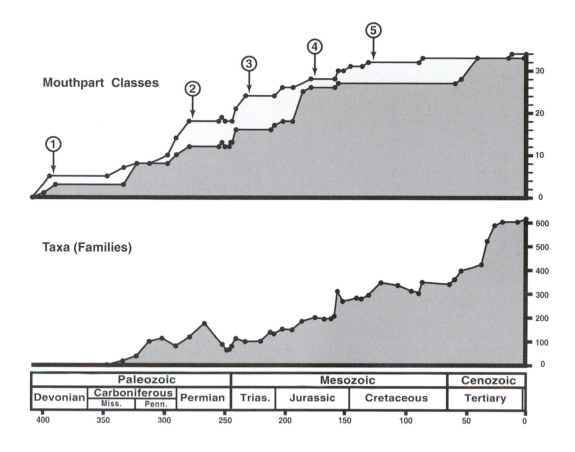

Figure 9. A comparison of mouthpart class diversity *(top)* and family-level taxonomic diversity *(bottom)* for the past 400 million years. Data is resolved to stage level. Key: *light grey*, less reliable evidence (as indicated by the slashed segments in Figure 8c). Abbreviations: *Miss.*, Mississippian; *Penn.*, Pennsylvanian; *Trias.*, Triassic. From Labandeira (1997). See Labandeira and Sepkoski (1993) and Labandeira (1997) for additional details.

basal hemipteroids and modified mandibulate mouthpart types associated with early holometabolous lineages. During the Late Triassic to Early Jurassic the radiation of several holometabolous clades, especially Diptera, resulted in a major addition of stylate-haustellate mouthpart types for extracting tissue-embedded and surface-exposed fluid, including blood and nectar. Contemporaneously in freshwater habitats there was exploitation of the thin neuston zone just below the water surface, the water column itself, and the benthos by immatures of dipteran, trichopteran, and coleopteran lineages. The last phase, during the Late Jurassic to Early Cretaceous, documents further partitioning of vascular-plant resources by the addition of the labellate (sponging), glossate (lapping), and siphonate (siphoning) mouthpart classes. These surface-fluid-feeding mouthparts subsequently became highly integrated with angiosperms as pollinators.

Several conclusions are obvious from an ecomorphic analysis of mouthpart design through geologic time. A major trend has been the conversion of primitive mandibulate mouthparts from the coordination of structurally independent elements borne on separate mouthpart regions, to mouthpart types consisting of functionally integrated ensembles of fused elements. The evolution of these derived mouthpart types was directed into three

broad directions: (1) transformation into stylate-nonhaustellate and stylate-haustellate mouthparts during the Late Carboniferous and Early Permian, followed by an additional wave of stylate-haustellate mouthparts during the Late Triassic to Early Jurassic; (2) modifications for capturing fine particulate matter, both in the water by sieving and filtering devices and on land by investing mouthpart element surfaces with hairs or spines to form brushes or rakes; and (3) integration of elements within and between the maxilla and labium for siphoning, lapping, and sponging exposed surface fluids. A relevant feature of these patterns is that there has been considerable convergence on particular mouthpart designs by unrelated lineages of insects; in some cases a particular mouthpart class originated independently at least seven times (Labandeira 1997). Evidently there was significant early dietary partitioning of ecologic resources, judging from the comparatively early occurrence of major mouthpart types when compared to subsequent rises in hexapod taxonomic diversity (Figure 9).

Behavioral

The behavioral diversity of hexapods is difficult to characterize. This is because, unlike most morphological characters, behavioral traits are difficult to define, have been neglected historically in classification and phylogeny, and exhibit considerably more rampant and independent origination than most structural features. However, five types of behavior—sexual, egg-laying, defensive, parental care, and feeding (Preston-Mafham and Preston-Mafham 1993)—categorize most of hexapod behavioral diversity. Diversity in sexual behavior includes courtship and prenuptial offerings and displays, notably sound and light emission, and secretions of various volatile chemicals that promote eventual copulation. Particular egg-laying behaviors determine the location and microhabitat for developing eggs, although insects with ovipositors accurately insert eggs into substrates that are otherwise behaviorally inaccessible. With the exception of feeding, perhaps the most studied insect behavior has been parental care, particularly the role of nest construction and provisioning among social insects. A variety of insect-fashioned substrates are used for housing immatures, including subterranean chambers, brood balls constructed of dung, and nests fabricated from resin, wax, mud, and carton. Some of these nest types have a fossil record; subterranean chambers are known from the Mid-Mesozoic, and bee nests have been identified in Late Cretaceous and Cenozoic deposits.

There are several hard-wired behaviors associated with the securing, processing, and consumption of food that extend what is only physically possible with mouthparts. Foraging patterns can occur as a solitary or a colonial effort, as passive or active pursuit of food, or the seeking of a species-specific host substrate. Behavioral preludes to feeding can employ latex vein cutting, mowing of trichomes, or avoidance of tissues that are difficult to process. During feeding, the use of noxious pheromones, silk shelters, mimicry, frightening displays, or disruptive coloration effectively deters predation. Of these attributes, the fossil record is best for various patterns of coloration to protect insect herbivores. Examples of Batesian mimicry, where a mimic resembles a conspicuous but less palatable model to evade a predator, is known for a Late Eocene solder fly bearing a conspicuous color-barred abdomen mimicking an aculeate wasp. Similarly, crypsis—where there is confusion to a potential predator based on disruptive coloration—occurs in Paleozoic Paleoptera (Carpenter 1971). The wings of some Carboniferous protorthopterans and Jurassic kalligrammatid planipennians record the presence of large, "frightening" eyespots that were predator deterrents, based on identical patterns in modern insects.

Geographic Distribution

Known fossil insect deposits have an uneven distribution on modern continents (Figure 10). Major reasons for this concentration of fossil insect sites are the vagaries of sediment preservation and the elevated intensity of paleoentomological effort in Europe and to a lesser degree in North America. These deposits record a 400-million-year interval that began as several major Late Paleozoic continents were separated by major deep-ocean barriers, namely Laurussia and the North China and South China terranes at low latitudes, Siberia and Kazakhstania to the north, and Gondwanaland to the south. With the possible exception of China, consolidation of these major continents into a major land mass, Pangaea,

occurred during the Late Permian and resulted in a pole-to-pole supercontinent that persisted into the Early Jurassic. During the Jurassic, Pangaea fragmented into a northern Laurasia and a southern Gondwanaland, followed by renewed fragmentation within Laurasia and Gondwanaland during the Early Cretaceous into the dispersed continental configuration of today.

Paleozoic Continents

The earliest evidence for hexapod fossils occurs in Lower Devonian environments adjacent marine deposits approximately 30° south of the paleoequator of Laurussia, a paleocontinent consisting of most of Europe and North America. After a 50-million-year hiatus, relatively diverse assemblages of earliest Late Carboniferous insects are known from Laurussia and, to a much lesser extent, Siberia, the North China and South China terranes, and southern Gondwanaland. Overwhelmingly, knowledge of Paleozoic insect faunas originates from the broad, warm, and humid equatorial belt of Laurussia typically consisting of lowland, wetland environments during the Late Carboniferous (Wootton 1981), incorporating some better-drained, riparian, and lacustrine environments of the Early Permian. Although insect faunas from these paleocontinents have not been analyzed biogeographically, they appear distinctive at the highest taxonomic levels. This regional intercontinental endemism probably persisted until the end-Permian mass extinction. Martynov recognized lower-level taxonomic similarities between Lower Permian insect taxa from Kansas and the central Urals, widely separated localities within Laurussia. This distinctive, Late Paleozoic insect fauna suffered a major extinction at the end of the Permian. It was replaced during the Triassic by a modern insect fauna characterized by taxonomic orders and many families that occur today (Figure 7).

Gondwanan Distributions

Many insect clades that occurred on Gondwanaland during the Early to Middle Mesozoic currently have distributions, relict or otherwise, on some of the Southern Hemisphere continents (Briggs 1995). The earliest separation event was probably South America plus Africa from the rest of Gondwanaland, both of which contain unique subfamilies of earwigs, vespid wasps, and fideliid bees, among others. South America and Australia, but occasionally New Zealand and presumably interconnecting Antarctica in the past, harbor many insect groups that indicate a more recent, Mesozoic connection. These include belid and nemonychid weevils occurring in South America and Australia, most which are associated with the primitive seed-plant families Araucariaceae and Podocarpaceae. Similarly, although the beetle family Boganiidae incorporates one subfamily feeding on angiosperms in South Africa and Australia, a second cycad-feeding subfamily also occurs in these two regions. These associations of basal lineages of insects that are coevolved with nonangiospermous seed plants probably represent ancient associations that extend to the Middle Mesozoic (Labandeira 1997). Ancient nonphytophagous lineages with extant Gondwanan distributions include nannochoristid scorpionflies, the corydalid megalopteran *Archichauliodes,* and stilbopterygine antlions (Briggs 1995). One analysis of Gondwanan

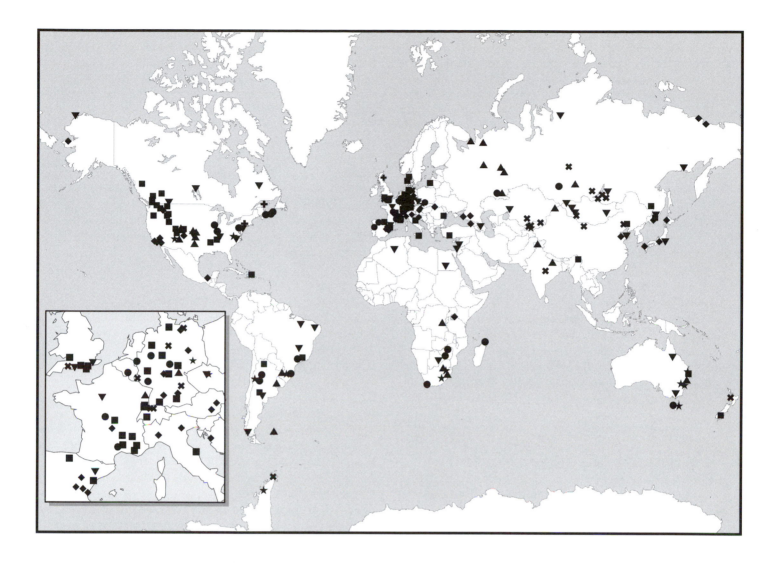

Figure 10. Geographic distribution of major fossil insect deposits from which taxa have been documented in the primary literature. Inset at lower left depicts an enlarged western Europe to resolve site overlap. Symbols: **+** = Devonian, **●** = Carboniferous, **▲** = Permian, **✳** = Triassic, **✕** = Jurassic, **▼** = Cretaceous, **■** = Paleogene, **◆** = Neogene. This map does not depict all known localities, and Quaternary and extreme polar localities are not recorded (see Elias 1994); it is representative of the pre-Quaternary fossil insect record.

insect distributions is Brundin's biogeographic study of midges, which demonstrates that several Gondwanan landmasses were colonized successively in a vicariant fashion. Brundin's conclusions subsequently have been supplemented by studies of other Early Mesozoic aquatic clades, including leptophlebiid and siphlonurid mayflies, petalurid dragonflies, and anarctoperlian stoneflies.

Some modern, primitive Gondwanan taxa occur as fossils only in Laurasia (Grimaldi 1990). For example, the primitive, cycad-feeding chrysomelid beetle *Aulacoscelis* of Central America and Andean South America is virtually identical to the Upper Jurassic *Protoscelis* of Kazakhstan. Early Cretaceous examples are the snakefly *Baissoptera,* known as a fossil from northeastern Brazil but congeneric with penecontemporaneous specimens from northern Asia, and the termite *Meiatermes,* also from the same deposit in Brazil but congeneric with similarly aged specimens from northern

Spain. The extant primitive termite from Australia, *Mastotermes,* occurs in the fossil record of only northern continents, and the primitive Australian moth-lacewing family Ithonidae has its closest relatives in southwestern North America. These distributions indicate that some modern relict occurrences are the result of significant extinction in regions formerly occupied, rather than past vicariant events separating continental faunas.

Subsequent Events

Important biogeographic events during the Cenozoic include faunal movements promoted by filter bridges such as island arcs and intercontinental isthmuses, and colonization of oceanic islands followed by often spectacular radiations of taxa. For the former, the Bering island arc has been invoked to explain the Asian origins of North American ground beetles and certain ichneumonid wasps. The intercontinental dispersal of insects across the Panamanian isthmus has resulted in more direct, two-way traffic since a permanent land connection was established during the Pliocene. One of the most spectacular radiations on an island chain has been pomace flies on Hawai'i, which comprise approximately 700 species from two north-subtropical introductions within the last 5 to 6 million years. Other examples are several groups of insects, particularly cryptorhynchine weevils and sphinx moths, that have colonized the southeastern Pacific from sources in Indonesia, New Guinea, and northern Australia through a series of island archipelagos that extend as far west as Samoa. A modest radiation has occurred on Rapa, a small south-central Pacific island, where 67 species of *Miocalles* weevils have radiated on a variety of host plants, including many ferns.

Functional Morphology

Two of the most important organs for insects are wings for flight and mouthparts for obtaining food. Tentative inferences regarding the origin of flight are based on biomechanical models of modern primitive insects and knowledge of the wing structure in early fossils. For mouthparts, there are a few instances where specific structures and function have been used to determine ancient feeding habits.

The Origin of Insect Wings and Flight

Perhaps the most controversial topic in paleoentomology is the origin of insect wings and flight. Several theories have been proposed (Gillott 1995), only two of which retain currency. The paranotal theory historically is the older view. It proposes that wings originated from rigid, lateral projections of thoracic terga that became enlarged, flattened, supplied with a regularized system of veins, and eventually articulated with the thorax to produce flapping flight. However, the paranotal theory suffers from several deficits, including absence of evidence for an articulatory wing hinge characterizing the attachment of paranotal lobes to an associated thorax, thus disallowing flapping flight. Nevertheless, the use of paranotal lobes as airfoils to guide takeoff from elevated perches onto horizontal air currents has been experimentally modeled (Brodsky 1994).

An alternative to the paranotal theory is Kukalová-Peck's epicoxal exite theory. Accordingly, serially homologous protowings originated in semiaquatic insects from small appendages located above the leg bases, known as epicoxal exites, initially for purposes other than aerial flight. Subsequently protowings developed laterally on thoracic and abdominal segments from these exites, which were initially articulated to the pleurae, a condition different from the initially rigid attachment proposed by the paranotal theory. This theory is consistent with much embryological, genetic, and fossil evidence, although these structures initially may have functioned on the abdomen as coverlets for tracheal openings to retard water loss in terrestrial insects or to prevent water entry in aquatic forms. Nevertheless, an intermediate stage by which gills or other homologous lateral structures could have been converted to functional aerial wings has always been challenging. One plausible proposal involves an insect dwelling on the water surface in which its winglike gills flapped to provide forward thrust and modest lift while its abdomen was supported by water surface tension. Such a locomotory mechanism has been documented in modern primitive stoneflies (Marden and Kramer 1994) as the surface skimming hypothesis and may represent a modern analog for how fully aerial flight originated. Another proposal potentially linking gills or its homologues to fully developed wings is the thermoregulatory hypothesis proposed by Kingsolver and Koehl (1985) and others. Initially envisaged as pertaining to paranotal lobes, wings increased in size and changed their angle to intercept incident solar radiation; such a function could have occurred on any lateral, flat organ supplied by blood, such as abdominal gills. Later, such thermoregulatory structures could have been functionally transformed into flight organs.

Feeding Habits of Some Late Cretaceous Flies

From Late Cretaceous amber deposits of Alberta, Canada, certain dipterans with piercing-and-sucking mouthparts—biting midges—are commonly preserved with good resolution of external body structures. In many specimens, structures such as antennae, maxillary palps, mouthpart stylets, and other head-associated structures are exquisitely preserved and include detail of trichomes, sensillae, and surface ornamentation (Borkent 1995). Depending on the species, biting midges imbibe the internal fluids of other insects, vertebrate blood, nectar, and rarely other substances. In modern female biting midges, there is a strong correlation between serrated mandibular stylets and the blood-sucking habit. Within blood-sucking species, females that imbibe vertebrate blood have coarsely toothed mandibles, recurved-toothed lacinial stylets, and generally a toothed labrum and hypopharyngeal stylet (Figure 11a, b), as opposed to species not feeding on blood that lack these features. Additionally, patterns of sensilla number, size, and placement on the antennae, and the third maxillary palp segment are important for distinguishing between species feeding on small birds or large mammals. Modern *Culicoides* species feeding on large mammals bear from 9 to 24 capitate palpal sensilla, whereas those feeding on birds have 29 to 75 such sensilla (Borkent 1995). Species feeding on larger vertebrates need considerably fewer sensillae to detect elevated CO_2 levels in the downwind plume of large hosts. Isolated exceptions to these robust associations are species that possess other mouthpart and antennal features that identify them as nonblood feeders.

Two, perhaps three, Canadian amber species of *Culicoides* fit the mouthpart morphological criteria for feeding on large vertebrates. Both birds and mammals were relatively small during the Late Cretaceous. The likely candidate hosts for these *Culicoides* species were hadrosaurian dinosaurs (Figure 11c), which are recorded in the same deposits. The site of host attack was probably exposed, blood-filled membranes such as eyelids (Figure 11d) or membranous zones between much thicker dermal scales or scutes.

Relationships to Other Organisms

Hexapods interact with virtually all terrestrial and freshwater organisms in some way. For many, these interactions provide reciprocal benefit, such as the mutually beneficial gut symbioses of termites or the pollination mutualisms between butterflies and flowering plants. Others result in an advantage provided to the insect at the expense of its live host, which may be a herbivorized plant or an insect attacked by a parasitoid larva. Such associations are the result of adaptive and other reciprocal processes occurring on large numbers of individuals and populations at geologically long intervals.

Microorganisms

Insects interact with five major types of organisms, generally with negative consequences to the plant and animal world. They are viruses, rikettsias, bacteria, protozoans, and fungi. Additionally macroscopic internal parasites, principally nematodes and cestodes, are transmitted to plants, fungi, and animals by insect vectors. Many bacteria are important as gut symbionts in rendering wood digestively available for wood-consuming insects, but other interactions are expressed as diseases that are debilitating to crop plants, livestock, and humans. A few examples are known where insect vector species have been tracked in the fossil record. One involves a bark beetle species responsible for Dutch elm disease, which apparently experienced a dieback in northern Europe during the Holocene. More ancient examples are particular mosquito and tsetse taxa with Cenozoic fossil records that are highly associated with diseases such as malaria and sleeping sickness (both protozoans), yellow fever (a virus), and filiariasis (a worm). These diseases probably originated on mammals and birds during the Early Cenozoic and colonized early hominid populations during the Pliocene.

Fungi

Hexapods interact with fungi in diverse ways. Beetles and flies dietarily partition ephemeral fruiting bodies such as polypores and gilled mushrooms in an intricate fashion. Other insects such as leaf-cutting ants and macrotermitine termites culture fungi in underground galleries that contain decomposing plant substrates. Nonmutualistic consumption of macrofungi, in which one participant does not benefit, is accomplished principally by specialists on spores and hyphae. This feeding mode is known extensively for beetles and flies, and to a lesser extent for thrips, bugs, moths, and wasps. Nonmutualistic interactions of hexapods and fungi probably extends to the Devonian, supported by two occurrences of unattributed arthropod borings with reaction tissue in a large, enigmatic, Devonian fungus. Limited occurrences in anatomically preserved coprolites of the Late Carboniferous of Laurussia also hint at fungivory, although it is not until the Lower Jurassic that insectan wood-borings are known with fungal contents. Several modern lineages of fungus-associated insects are known from the Early Cretaceous, including bark beetles, which have their borings preserved in conifer wood.

Plants

Plants contribute the most intensively examined and wide-ranging spectrum of interactions that insects have with any major organismic group. These myriad associations include seed preda-

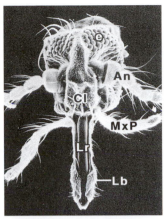
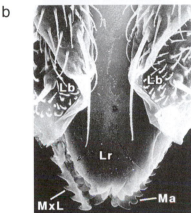
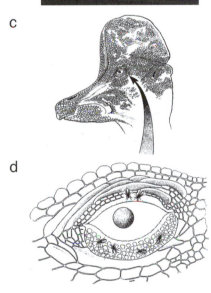

Figure 11. Female ceratopogonid midge mouthpart structure and blood-feeding on Late Cretaceous hadrosaurs. *a*, extant blood-feeding species of *Culicoides*; frontal (dorsal) view of head and mouthparts; *b*, dorsal, distal view of labrum, mandibular and lacinial stylets, and labellum, with serrated teeth; *c*, the Late Cretaceous hadrosaur *Corythosaurus*; with *d*, *Culicoides* blood-feeding on eye membrane tissue. See Borkent (1995) for additional details. *a*, *b*, reprinted by permission of the Entomological Society of America; *c*, *d*, from Borkent (1995), permission to reproduce kindly granted by Backhuys Publishers, Leiden, The Netherlands.

tion, pollinator mutualisms, and consumption of externally and internally accessible tissues by modes as distinctive as external foliage feeding, leaf-mining, galling, stem boring, and piercing-and-sucking. Many of these interactions are performed by more eclectic-feeding generalists; others are host specific and represent intricate and intimate codependence through long stretches of geologic time (Labandeira et al. 1994). Examination of insect-mediated plant damage from well-preserved plant deposits indicates that significant insect herbivory began during the Late Carboniferous to Early Permian, providing evidence for a distinctive Paleozoic herbivore fauna preceding the post-Paleozoic herbivore fauna of today.

A trace-fossil record, parallel to and independent of the body-fossil record, exists for the varied effects of hexapods on plants, notably damage resulting from herbivory (Labandeira 1997). The earliest documented examples of hexapod-mediated plant damage are rare Early Devonian herbivory, principally external feeding and stylet penetration of stem tissues. By the Late Carboniferous, leaf margins were consumed by external feeders, internal petiolar parenchyma was galled (Figure 12b), petiolar vascular tissue was targeted by piercer-and-suckers, and pith borers were tunneling through softer stem tissues. During the Early Permian, external foliage feeders expanded their repertoire to include hole-feeding, skeletonization, and consumption of near-entire leaves. Pollinivory is first documented from the Late Carboniferous but expanded during the Early Permian. The earliest evidence for leaf mining is on a Late Triassic seed fern, although this herbivory type was well established on another seed-fern lineage by the latest Jurassic. Leaf mining subsequently diversified during the Mid-Cretaceous on basal angiosperm clades (Figure 12d, e; Labandeira et al. 1994). Recently, galls have been identified from Triassic conifers, especially on the terminal branchlets and reproductive organs. Although earlier Permian borings are known from glossopterid wood, there are beetle borings in heartwood, developing cambial tissue, and reproductive organs of conifers and cycadeoids that occur throughout the Late Triassic to Early Cretaceous. By the Late Jurassic, beetles were pollinating cycadophytes; some of these associations persist today. As angiosperms expanded ecologically during the Middle to Late Cretaceous, some major pollination syndromes became fine-tuned mutualisms.

Animals

Hexapod consumption of dead animal tissue, together with plant and fungal detritivory, is an ancient feeding habit that undoubtedly extends to the Early Devonian. Predation upon live insect tissue was present during the Late Carboniferous, evidenced by protodonatan dragonflies with robust, incisiform mandibles and raptorial forelegs. It is unclear whether any fluid-feeding paleodictyopteroid consumed other insects or vertebrate blood, but the exceptionally small size of some dipterous Permian taxa suggest functional comparisons to mosquitos (Shear and Kukalová-Peck 1990). During the Late Triassic to Early Jurassic, the radiation of lower Diptera resulted in a significant expansion of piercing-and-sucking mouthpart types that included blood- and insect-feeding (Labandeira 1997). In the Jurassic there was a significant radiation

of the hymenopteran parasitoid guild. More modern lineages of insects feeding on vertebrate blood, integument, hair, lymph, and other substances expanded during the Late Cretaceous and Early Cenozoic, principally fleas, several clades of brachycerous flies and lice, but also bugs and earwigs. Contemporaneously there was expansion of carnivorous and predatory insect clades, possibly responding to increases in phytophagous insect diversity associated with the ecological expansion of seed plants.

The Fossil Record and Paleoentomology

The common perception is that the insect fossil record is poor when compared to other fossil groups such as vascular plants and vertebrates. However, it is well represented at the family level (Labandeira 1994). Additionally, a strong association exists between those orders that are currently the most diverse (Hemiptera, Coleoptera, Diptera, and Hymenoptera) and their diversities in the fossil record (Figure 7). The greatest deficit of the insect fossil record is representation of the lowest taxonomic levels and the Lepidoptera. Figure 12 illustrates several typical occurrences of fossil insects in commonly encountered deposits.

Types of Deposits

The hexapod fossil record is characterized by ten major deposit types (Figure 13), ranging in age from Early Devonian to Quaternary. Some of these deposits are restricted paleolatitudinally and reveal the vagaries of sediment cover preservation during the past 400 million years. Others are restricted spatiotemporally and document unique, often geologically unusual environments for entombing insects.

The earliest hexapods are from the Early to Middle Devonian of equatorial Laurussia. The Rhynie Chert in Scotland, Gaspé in Québec, and Gilboa in New York share a common feature of being deposited marginally above sea level adjacent to major ocean basins, rather than by lithological uniformity. Similar earlier deposits containing myriapods and land plants extend to the Late Silurian. From the Carboniferous, characteristic ironstone concretions are known for several sites in clastic-dominated swamps in the interior of Laurussia. Occurring at about the same time but extending into the Early Permian at some localities are coal-ball deposits that represent three-dimensional permineralizations of plant tissue that reveal considerable evidence for vascular plant/insect interactions. These deposits are best developed in equatorial, peat-dominated swamps of Laurussia and China. Succeeding typically black, Late Carboniferous strata are Early Permian redbed deposits that represent better-drained, higher elevated, and riparian habitats. Redbed deposits occur in extratropical latitudes in Laurussia and Gondwanaland, extending to the Triassic in many stratigraphic sequences.

Distinct from previous and succeeding deposit types, fine-grained lacustrine deposits represent the persistence of a sediment type for the past 280 million years. Lake basin sediments and associated fine-grained deposits provide the single most important source for the fossil insect record. A variant of lacustrine deposits, but lithologically distinctive and confined to basins with some

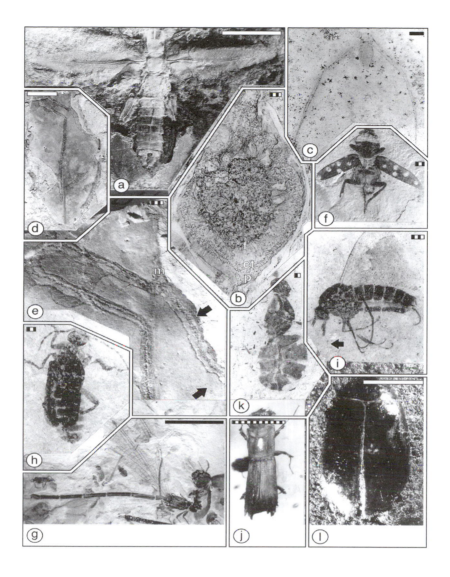

Figure 12. Fossil insects occurring in several commonly encountered depositional environments (see also Figure 13). *a,* a protortho-pteran insect (Family Eucaenidae) in an ironstone concretion (Middle Pennsylvanian; Carbondale Formation, Mazon Creek, north-central Illinois) (FMNH-PE967). *b,* a primitive gall of an early holometabolous insect in the frond rhachis of the tree fern *Psaronius;* from a coal-ball permineralization (Late Pennsylvanian, Mattoon Formation of east-central Illinois) (NMNH-483990); key: *p,* normal parenchyma; *ct,* callus tissue created as a response to insect-induced trauma; *f,* insect frass. *c,* member of an extinct clade of aquatic, surface-dwelling insects (Order Phasmatoptera) in lithographic limestone (Late Jurassic Solnhofen Formation, southern Germany) (USNM-33067). *d,* a leaf mine of a moth larva (Lepidoptera) and external foliage feeding by a mandibulate insect on a primitive angiosperm leaf (Middle Cretaceous Dakota Formation of Kansas) (UF-14881). *e,* Enlargement of leaf mine in *D,* showing central frass trail of mine *(lower arrow),* avoidance of leaf midrib *(m),* and chewed leaf edge *(upper arrow). f,* Longhorn beetle (Coleoptera: Cerambycidae) from a lacus-trine shale (Middle Eocene Green River Formation, Colorado) (USNM-497410). *g,* A narrowwing damselfly (Odonata: Coenagrionidae) (Green River Formation) (USNM-497411). *h,* Beetle (Coleoptera: ?Meloidae) from a lacustrine shale (Early Oligocene Antero Formation, Florissant, Colorado) (USNM-90535). *i,* bee fly (Diptera: Bombyliidae) (Antero Formation) (USNM-127677); key: *arrow,* elongate mouth-parts for imbibing floral nectar. *j,* pinhole borer (Coleoptera: Platypodidae) entombed in amber (Early Miocene, Dominican Republic) (USNM-497409). *k,* A giant ant (Hymenoptera: Formicidae) (Late Miocene lacustrine shales at Oeningen, northern Switzerland) (USNM-38549). Body length, excluding appendages: 2.2 centimeters. *l,* a predaceous diving beetle (Coleoptera: Dytiscidae) (Late Pleistocene, McKittrick asphalt deposit, south-central California) (USNM-33879). Scale bars: *solid,* 1 centimeters; *striped,* 0.1 centimeters. Reposi-tory abbreviations: *A,* Field Museum of Natural History (FMNH); *B, C, F, G, H, I, J, K, L,* National Museum of Natural History (USNM); *D, E,* University of Florida (UF).

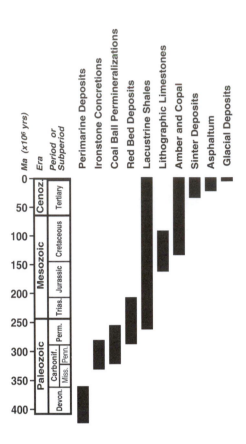

Figure 13. Geochronologic distribution of major types of insect-bearing deposits. Abbreviations: *Devon.,* Devonian; *Carbonif.,* Carboniferous; *Miss.,* Mississippian; *Penn.,* Pennsylvanian; *Perm.,* Permian; *Trias.,* Triassic; *Cenoz.* Cenozoic.

marine input, are Mid-Mesozoic lithographic limestones. By contrast, amber represents the accumulation of tree resins generally in forested habitats (Poinar 1992). Although Late Triassic amber is known, insect inclusions are traceable only to the Early Cretaceous. Subsequently, more geologically ephemeral, insect-bearing deposits are those confined to sites of minimal areal extent, namely sinter and asphaltum traps. These Late Cenozoic deposits trap insects, respectively, in pools of highly mineralized water and viscous tar. The most geologically fleeting of all deposits are Quaternary glacial deposits. These deposits document the advances and retreats of the most recent glacial episodes and are confined to high latitudes of the Northern and Southern Hemispheres and to higher elevations at lower latitudes (Elias 1994).

History of Paleoentomology

Twentieth-century paleoentomology has been dominated by two countries, Russia and Germany. Both countries have had strong academic traditions and institutions capable of supporting several to as many as 20 paleoentomologists simultaneously in various academic institutions. Unlike other national traditions, a strong tendency of the Russian school of paleoentomology is investigator specialization on particular taxonomic groups, usually at the ordi-

nal level, during the course of a career (Rohdendorf 1973). Less well-established traditions occur in France, the United Kingdom, the United States, and more recently Poland and China, where a few to several full-time researchers simultaneously have devoted major responsibilities to paleoentomology. Beyond this second tier, several other countries periodically have supported one or a few paleoentomologists, including Australia, Brazil, Canada, South Africa, and Spain. The paleoentomological histories of Russia and Germany will be emphasized in this brief sketch; the reader is referred to Rohdendorf's (1973) comprehensive, albeit dated, article on this topic.

The most coordinated and extensive enterprise in the study of fossil insects has been the paleoentomology group at the Paleontological Institute of the Soviet (now Russian) Academy of Sciences (Rohdendorf 1973). A.V. Martynov provided the major impetus to the Soviet school during the mid-1920s with description of Upper Jurassic material from Karatau in Kazakhstan, followed by discovery and documentation of Mid-Permian insects at Chekarda and other localities in the central Urals, and eventual investigation of Lower Jurassic material from Fergana in Kirghizstan. During the mid-1920s to 1950s, additional taxa from the central Urals and new Late Carboniferous to Mid-Permian material from the Kaltan locality of the Kuznetsk Basin was extensively studied. After Martynov's death in 1938 and particularly after World War II, O.M. Martynova continued paleoentomological investigations in these deposits. During the 1950s additional paleoentomologists joined the Paleontological Institute. Their first major work was a monograph on the insects of the Kuznetsk Basin, published in 1961. Approximately 20 major monographic studies appeared from the 1960s to the late 1990s, either focusing on comprehensive and systematic accounts of major insect taxa by single authors or multiauthored works describing fossil insect taxa and the geological context of a diverse, well-preserved, and intensively collected fossil deposit. An important volume was *Historical Development of the Class Insecta,* a comprehensive survey of the evolutionary biology and ecology of all well-documented fossil insect lineages, edited by B.B. Rohdendorf and A.P. Rasnitsyn in 1980. During this flowering of paleoentomology in the Soviet Union, paleoentomologists representing a broad spectrum of specialities were added to the Paleontological Institute and other academic institutions. Recently, the direction of research has included examination of extensive Baltic Amber collections, although several important sites in central Asia are still being intensively explored.

In Germany the earliest major monographer of fossil insects was O. Heer, who described from the mid-1840s to mid-1860s insect faunas from the Early Miocene of Radaboj in Croatia and Late Miocene of Oeningen in Switzerland. Although subsequent German and British researchers described additional European insect faunas and occasional specimens, it was A. Handlirsch who, from 1906 to 1908, provided a comprehensive taxonomic synthesis of all known fossil insect material in his classic *Die Fossilien Insekten,* which remained the only major taxonomic compendium of the fossil insect record until B.B. Rohdendorf's (1962; English translation, 1991) and F.M. Carpenter's (1992) treatises. From the 1930s to 1960s, P. Guthörl described in a series of articles Upper

Carboniferous to Lower Permian Rothliegende strata in Thuringia. A. Bode in 1953 monographed Early Jurassic insects from the Posidonschiefer of Dobbertin and O. Kuhn did likewise in 1961 for the Late Jurassic Solnhofen Limestone in Bavaria. Meanwhile W. Hennig had established a research program at Stuttgart, focusing on examination of fossil Diptera, particularly material from Baltic and Lebanese amber. Hennig also provided an extensive treatise on the phylogenetic systematics and fossil history of insects that culminated in his much-cited work, *Die Stammesgeschichte der Insekten* (English translation, 1981). Recently, C. Brauckmann, W. Zessin, J. Schneider, and others have explored intensively Paleozoic insect faunas in northern Europe, including description of the earliest known pterygote insects.

J. Kukalová-Peck of Canada and F.M. Carpenter of the United States have provided significant perspectives in interpreting the fossil insect record, invigorating recent biological interest in Paleozoic insects (e.g., Brodsky 1994; Bechley 1996; Raff 1996). Both have documented extensive structural detail in Paleozoic insects that was previously unexplored. Kukalová-Peck's notable contributions to paleoentomology include the development of a homologizable, universal system of veinal nomenclature and in particular the assembly of multidisciplinary evidence—including the fossil record, developmental genetics, embryology, and the morphology of modern forms—for inferring patterns of early insect evolution.

Recent Discoveries

From 1980 to 1990, newly reported insect deposits enlarged considerably the stratigraphic, geographic, and taxonomic scope of the fossil insect record. Most notable are six mostly Lower Cretaceous compression deposits from widely scattered regions. They are, approximately from oldest to youngest, Montsec in Spain, Baissa in Transbaikalian Russia, Gurvan and associated sites in northwestern Mongolia, Santana in Brazil (Grimaldi 1990), Koonwarra in Australia, and Orapa in Botswana. These deposits have extended the stratigraphic ranges of many Cenozoic taxa to the Lower Cretaceous, enlarged our knowledge of the past and present biogeographic distributions of Gondwanan taxa, and have provided data for paleoenvironmental settings that contrast with amber deposits of the Late Cretaceous.

There are other recently discovered but important deposits. The documentation of paleodictyopteroid, protodonatan, and "protorthopteran" insects at Hagen-Vorhalle in Germany now contains some of the earliest known winged insects. Initially described in 1978, the Newark Basin insect fauna of Virginia has confirmed the earliest occurrences of several modern insect families, supporting the unusually long family durations documented by Labandeira and Sepkoski (1993). Although the Middle Eocene Messel deposits have been known since the earlier 1900s, recent discoveries have revealed exquisitely preserved insects that have retained external color patterns and internal gut contents. A flurry of recently described taxa from the Early Miocene Dominican amber now ranks this deposit as the second most abundant amber fauna, revealing examples of arthropod parasitism on insects rarely preserved in the fossil record.

Acknowledgments

Special appreciation is provided to Finnegan Marsh, who formatted the figures accompanying this article. Niels Kristensen and Jarmila Kukalová-Peck provided insightful comments on earlier drafts of this manuscript. This is contribution No. 57 of the Evolution of Terrestrial Ecosystems Consortium at the National Museum of Natural History. Support for this article was provided by the Scholarly Studies Program of the Smithsonian Institution.

CONRAD C. LABANDEIRA

Works Cited

Bechley, G. 1996. Morphologische Untersuchungen am Flügelgeäder der rezenten Libellen und deren Stammgruppenvertreter (Insecta; Pterygota; Odonata). *Petalura* Special volume, 2:1–402.

Boudreaux, H.B. 1987. *Arthropod Phylogeny with Special Reference to Insects.* Malabar, Florida: Krieger.

Borkent, A. 1995. *Biting Midges in the Cretaceous Amber of North America (Diptera: Ceratopogonidae).* Leiden: Backhuys.

Briggs, J.C. 1995. *Global Biogeography.* Amsterdam and New York: Elsevier.

Brodsky, A.K. 1994. *The Evolution of Insect Flight.* Oxford and New York: Oxford University Press.

Carpenter, F.M. 1971. Adaptations among Paleozoic insects. *In* E.L. Yochelson (ed.), *Proceedings of the First North American Paleontological Convention.* Lawrence, Kansas: Allen Press.

———. 1992. *Superclass Insecta. In* R.C. Moore, R.L. Kaesler, E. Brosius, J. Kiem, and J. Priesner (eds.), *Treatise on Invertebrate Paleontology,* vol. 3, part R, *Arthropoda 4.* Boulder, Colorado, and Lawrence, Kansas: Geological Society of America and University of Kansas.

Elias, S.A. 1994. *Quaternary Insects and Their Environments.* Washington, D.C.: Smithsonian Institution Press.

Gillott, C. 1995. *Entomology.* 2nd ed., New York: Plenum.

Grimaldi, D.A. (ed.). 1990. Insects from the Santana Formation, Lower Cretaceous, of Brazil. *Bulletin of the American Museum of Natural History* 195:1–191.

Gullan, P.J., and P.S. Cranston. 1994. *The Insects: An Outline of Entomology.* London and New York: Chapman and Hall.

Harland, W.B., R.L. Armstrong, A.V. Cox, L.E. Craig, A.G. Smith, and D.G. Smith. 1990. *A Geologic Time Scale: 1989.* Cambridge and New York: Cambridge University Press.

Hennig, W. 1981. *Insect Phylogeny.* New York and Chichester: Wiley.

Kingsolver, J.G., and M.A.R. Koehl. 1985. Aerodynamics, thermoregulation, and the evolution of insect wings: Differential scaling and evolutionary change. *Evolution* 39:488–504.

Kristensen, N.P. 1991. Phylogeny of extant hexapods. *In* I.D. Naumann, P.B. Carne, J.F. Lawrence, E.S. Nielsen, J.P. Spradbery, R.W. Taylor, M.J. Whitten, and M.J. Littlejohn (eds.), *The Insects of Australia: A Textbook for Students and Research Workers.* 2 vols. 2nd ed., Ithaca, New York: Cornell University Press; Carlton, Victoria: Melbourne University Press.

———. 1994. Forty years' insect phylogenetic systematics. Hennig's "Kritische Bemerkungen. . . ," and subsequent developments. *Zoologische Beiträge* 36:83–124.

Kukalová-Peck, J. 1987. New Carboniferous Diplura, Monura, Thysanura, the hexapod ground plan, and the role of thoracic side lobes in the origin of wings (Insecta). *Canadian Journal of Zoology* 65:2327–45.

———. 1991. Fossil history and the evolution of hexapod structures. *In* I.D. Naumann, P.B. Carne, J.F. Lawrence, E.S. Nielsen, J.P. Spradbery, R.W. Taylor, M.J. Whitten, and M.J. Littlejohn (eds.), *The Insects of Australia: A Textbook for Students and Research Workers.* 2 vols. 2nd ed., Ithaca, New York: Cornell University Press; Carlton, Victoria: Melbourne University Press.

Labandeira, C.C. 1994. A compendium of fossil insect families. *Milwaukee Public Museum Contributions in Biology and Geology* 88:1–71.

———. 1997. Insect mouthparts: Ascertaining the paleobiology of insect feeding strategies. *Annual Review of Ecology and Systematics* 28:153–93.

Labandeira, C.C., D.L. Dilcher, D.R. Davis, and D.L. Wagner. 1994. Ninety-seven million years of angiosperm-insect association: Paleobiological insights into the meaning of coevolution. *Proceedings of the National Academy of Sciences USA* 91 (12):278–82.

Labandeira, C.C., and T.L. Phillips. 1996. Insect fluid-feeding on Upper Pennsylvanian tree ferns (Palaeodictyoptera, Marattiales) and the early history of the piercing-and-sucking functional feeding group. *Annals of the Entomological Society of America* 89:157–83.

Labandeira, C.C., and J.J. Sepkoski Jr. 1993. Insect diversity in the fossil record. *Science* 261:310–15.

Lawrence, J.F., E.S. Nielsen, and I.M. Mackerras. 1991. Skeletal anatomy and key to orders. *In* I.D. Naumann, P.B. Carne, J.F. Lawrence, E.S. Nielsen, J.P. Spradbery, R.W. Taylor, M.J. Whitten, and M.J. Littlejohn (eds.), *The Insects of Australia: A Textbook for Students and Research Workers.* 2 vols. 2nd ed., Ithaca, New York: Cornell University Press; Carlton, Victoria: Melbourne University Press.

Marden, J.H., and M.G. Kramer. 1994. Surface-skimming stoneflies: A possible intermediate stage in insect flight evolution. *Science* 266:427–30.

Poinar Jr., G.L. 1992. *Life in Amber.* Stanford, California: Stanford University Press.

Preston-Mafham, R., and K. Preston-Mafham. 1993. *Encyclopedia of Land Invertebrate Behavior.* Cambridge, Massachusetts: MIT Press; London: Blandford.

Raff, R.A. 1996. *The Shape of Life.* Chicago: University of Chicago Press.

Rohdendorf, B.B. (ed.). 1973. The history of paleoentomology. *In* R.F. Smith, T.E. Mittler, and C.N. Smith (eds.), *History of Entomology.* Palo Alto, California: Annual Reviews.

———. 1991. Arthropoda, Tracheata, Chelicerata. *In* Y.A. Orlov (ed.), *Fundamentals of Paleontology.* S. Viswanathan (trans.) 9:1–894.

Rohdendorf, B.B., E.E. Becker-Migdisova, O.M. Martynova, and A.G. Sharov. 1961. Paleozoic insects from the Kuznetsk Basin. *Transactions of the Paleontological Institute* 85:1–705. [in Russian]

Rohdendorf, B.B., and A.P. Rasnitsyn. 1980. Historical development of the class Insecta. *Transactions of the Paleontological Institute* 175:1–270. [in Russian]

Sharov, A.G. 1966. *Basic Arthropodan Stock, with Special Reference to Insects.* Oxford and New York: Pergamon.

Shear, W.A., and J. Kukalová-Peck. 1990. The ecology of Paleozoic terrestrial arthropods: The fossil evidence. *Canadian Journal of Zoology* 68:1807–34.

Snodgrass, R.E. 1935. *Principles of Insect Morphology.* New York and London: McGraw-Hill.

Wägele, J.W. 1993. Rejection of the "Uniramia" hypothesis and implications of the Mandibulata concept. *Zoologisches Jahrbuch, Systematik* 120:253–88.

Wootton, R.J. 1981. Palaeozoic insects. *Annual Review of Entomology* 26:319–44.

Further Reading

Boudreaux, H.B. 1987. *Arthropod Phylogeny with Special Reference to Insects.* Malabar, Florida: Krieger.

Brodsky, A.K. 1994. *The Evolution of Insect Flight.* Oxford and New York: Oxford University Press.

Carpenter, F.M. 1992. *Superclass Insecta. In* R.C. Moore, R.L. Kaesler, E. Brosius, J. Kiem, and J. Priesner (eds.), *Treatise on Invertebrate Paleontology,* vol. 3, part R, *Arthropoda 4.* Boulder, Colorado, and Lawrence, Kansas: Geological Society of America and University of Kansas.

Gillott, C. 1980. *Entomology.* New York: Plenum; 2nd ed., 1995.

Gullan, P.J., and P.S. Cranston. 1994. *The Insects: An Outline of Entomology.* London and New York: Chapman and Hall.

Hennig, W. 1981. *Insect Phylogeny.* New York and Chichester: Wiley.

J

JAWLESS FISHES

"Fishes" is a vernacular term for cold-blooded, gill-breathing, aquatic vertebrates (having a vertebral column) or craniates (having a cranium that encloses the brain). All possess a stiffening rod (notochord) and a branchial (gill arch) system. These animals also have some sort of stabilizing device—tail, sets of fins, or flaps—and a sensory system, usually located anteriorly (at the front) in the form of a three- or four-part brain, semicircular canals, and often a pore-canal or lateral line system. There are two groups, the Agnatha (agnaths or agnathans)—literally "jawless fishes"—represented by extant (present-day) lampreys and hagfishes, and the Gnathostomata (jawed fishes).

The jawless fishes dominated the first 150 million years or so of vertebrate history, and their total history spans some 500 million years. Unlike gnathostomes, the agnathan fishes did not possess true jaws, and a fully ossified vertebral column is rare, although the notochord and surrounding cartilaginous supports are seen. Both paired and median fins with a stiffening skeleton and/or fin rays called "lepidotrichia" have been claimed. Some researchers argue that vertebrates arose from echinoderms (starfish and their relatives). The larval stage of echinoderms is similar in some respects to that of vertebrates. Others champion the tunicates and other "protochordates" as our closest relatives (e.g., Long 1995).

Recent phylogenetic and systematic frameworks were given by P. Janvier (1996a, 1996b) and J.G. Maisey (1996). Janvier surmised that jawless fishes are not a clade (a group that consists of all the descendants of a common ancestor) but a paraphyletic group of related forms, one of which gave rise to jawed fishes. The Recent agnathans are highly specialized (or degenerate, depending on your point of view), being scavengers and parasites on other fishes (e.g., Hardisty and Potter 1971). Paleozoic agnathans from Ordovician, Silurian, and Devonian times (Figure 1) were also weird-looking fishes that seem only distantly related to lampreys and hagfishes.

Paleozoic agnathans are found worldwide. G.C. Young (1981) discussed their biogeography and proposed a series of biogeographic provinces (Figure 2). In the process he explained why some agnathans have not been found in former Gondwana coun-

tries, despite their widespread occurrence in Europe, Siberia, and America (the Osteostraci, Heterostraci, and possibly Anaspida), and endemism (local occurrence) in China (the Galeaspida). (Gondwana was one of two supercontinents; it was made up of today's South America, Africa, Antarctica, Australia, and India.)

Fossil Hagfishes (Hyperotreti)

Hagfish, an exclusively marine group, possess 1 to 15 pairs of gill openings. The extant *Myxine* possesses a common branchial opening, as in extinct Heterostraci. Fossil hagfishes to date include *Myxinikela* from Late Carboniferous near-shore marine, anoxic (oxygen-free) carbonaceous shales of Mazon Creek, Illinois, an environment that preserved soft tissues. *Myxinikela* is around 50 millimeters long, with tentacles and a long prenasal sinus characteristic of Recent hagfishes (Janvier 1996b). Another purported hagfish, *Gilpichthys* (also from Mazon Creek), has hagfishlike non-mineralized teeth. Current thinking places hagfish as the nearest living relative (sister group) to true vertebrates. If the affinities of the conodonts (see below) are with hagfishes (Janvier 1996b; Pridmore et al. 1997), as some scholars hypothesize, then the stratigraphical range of the group would extend to the Cambrian.

Fossil Lampreys (Hyperoartia, Petromyzontiformes)

Fossil lampreys are also known from marine Carboniferous deposits; they are small (about five centimeters), suggesting that they are juveniles. However, since possible piston cartilage and oral suckers exist, this suggests that they were already becoming parasitic, prompting Janvier (1996b) to regard them as adults. The best example is *Mayomyzon* (Janvier 1996b) from Mazon Creek, which shows imprints of a lampreylike cartilaginous endoskeleton. This fish has five or six small, closely set gill pouches situated close to the eyes, instead of the seven found in living taxa. *Mayomyzon* also has a continuous finweb from head to tail. A continuous finfold was once thought to be a primitive vertebrate character. A second form, *Pipiscius*, has possible horny plates embedded in an oral sucker (Janvier 1996b). *Hardistiella* from mid-Carboniferous Bear

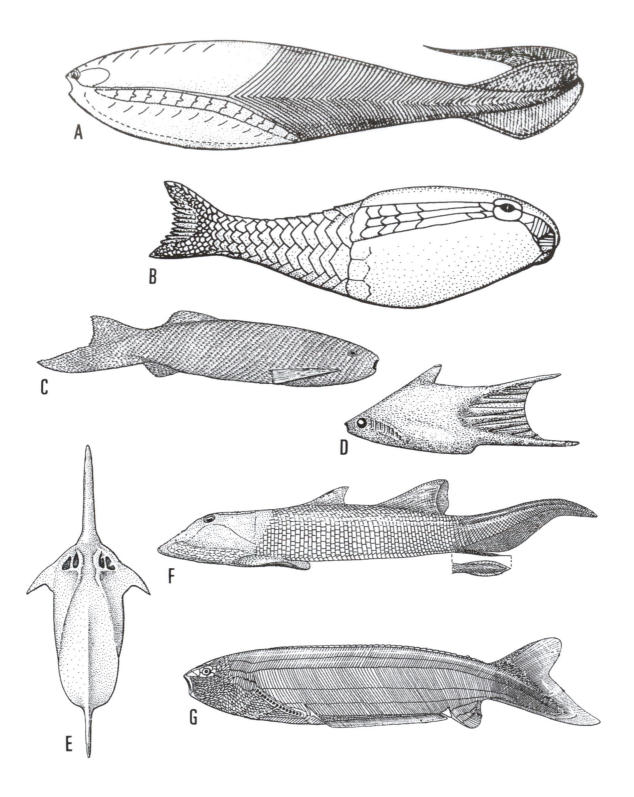

Figure 1. Paleozoic agnathans from Ordovician, Silurian, and Devonian times. *A, Sacabambaspis,* an arandaspid (Early Ordovician, Bolivia); *B, Athenaegis,* a heterostrachan (Early Silurian, Canada); *C, Phlebolepis,* a thelodont (Silurian of Estonia); *D,* unnamed Early Devonian thelodont (Canada); *E, Pituariaspis,* a pituriaspid (Early Mid-Devonian, Queensland); *F, Ateleaspis,* an osteostracan (Early Silurian, Scotland); *G, Pharyngolepis,* an anaspid (Early Silurian, Norway). From: *A, B,* Long (1995), by permission of John Long, W.A. Museum, Perth; *C,* Moy-Thomas and Miles (1971); *D–G,* after Janvier (1996b), by permission of Oxford University Press.

Gulch in Montana is less well preserved, with what is claimed to be a slightly hypocercal tail (one in which the notochord angles down) and a small anal fin.

Conodont Animals, Conodont Elements

The fossil record of conodonts, first described by Pander in 1856, consists almost entirely of the dissociated comblike parts. Fossils that show these elements in their approximate life position are comparatively rare and represent the only direct evidence of the three-dimensional architecture of the conodont apparatus. In the last decade actual conodont animals have been found (Figure 3) and are claimed by some (e.g., Aldridge et al. 1994) to be true craniates, if not vertebrates. Such interpretations have led to one of the hottest modern debates on the evolution of early vertebrates and what constitutes the group; some scholars now place the Conodonta as vertebrates within a "paraphyletic" Agnatha and regard conodont elements as teeth capable of occlusion and thus exhibiting "tooth wear" (Aldridge and Purnell 1996). S. Kivett and colleagues (1996), A. Kemp and R.S. Nicoll (1996), P.A. Pridmore and colleagues (1997), and others reject that hypothesis because conodont elements and apparatuses differ radically from vertebrate teeth in their composition, organization, and histology, which precludes a toothlike function. Accepting conodont elements as teeth and including conodont animals in Vertebrata, despite fundamental differences, would require a dramatic and for many, unacceptable revision of current hypotheses of vertebrate phylogeny (evolutionary history) and reconstructed primitive character states. Based on the divergence of opinion on the interpretation of hard tissues, notochord, vertebrate pattern, eyes, and the lack of any sign of a branchial basket or brain, it probably is best to regard the conodonts for the time being as "protochordates."

The Earliest Known Vertebrate and Chordate Remains

Rare contenders for the earliest prevertebrates include the new discovery by D.G. Shu and colleagues (1996) of *Cathaymyrus diadexus* (Figure 4 bottom) from the Early Cambrian of south China (which dates back 535 million years ago). This form is about 2.5 centimeters long, with apparent notochord, V-shaped musculature, and pharynx with "gill" slits. Also Early Cambrian is *Pikaia gracilens* (Figure 4 top) from the Burgess Shale of Canada (which dates back 527 million years), which has long been regarded as a cephalochordate. From the later Cambrian Gola Beds of western Queensland, Australia, come ornamented hard tissues interpreted as vertebrate by Young and colleagues (1996). Another possible early vertebrate, with phosphatic bonelike tissue with tubercles, is *Fenhsiangia* from the early Ordovician of China (Long 1995).

Anatolepis is another vertebrate cinderella. Fragments occur from Late Cambrian to Ordovician and have been regarded as possible vertebrate remains for two decades. The small phosphatic carapace and spine fragments are ornamented with minute tubercles, the structure of which recalls vertebrate exoskeletal dentine. The structure of *Anatolepis* is different from that of typical vertebrate dentine and aspidine (an acellular form of bone) (Ørvig 1989), but it is equally different from that of any arthropod. Some specimens clearly show a three-layer organization of hard tissue: a basal laminated layer, a cancellar (porous) layer, and a superficial layer. This is a familiar pattern among agnathans. M.P. Smith (1946) and colleagues claimed new evidence for the vertebrate affinities of these hard tissues, and *Anatolepis heintzi* appears to represent a single distinct species that lived around the margins of the land mass called Laurentia.

A number of other enigmatic fossils made of apatite (calcium phosphate) have been recorded from the Cambrian (Figure 5 top) and Lower Ordovician and referred to vertebrates or craniates. These remains were considered by A. Blieck (1992), who referred most to nonvertebrate groups.

Extinct Agnathan Groups

The extinct forms formerly called "ostracoderms" by E.D. Cope (because of their calcium phosphate–based exoskeleton) comprise eight main and rather disparate types. These are the pteraspidomorphs (including Ordovician arandaspids), astrapids, heterostracans, thelodonts, osteostracans (cephalaspids), anaspids, galeaspids, and pituriaspids. These agnathans range from possibly the Upper Cambrian to the Late Devonian (Late Frasnian). Recent reviews include those of P.F. Forey and Janvier (1994), P.-Y. Gagnier (1995), Janvier (1996a, 1996b), J.A. Long (1995), Maisey (1996), and S. Turner (1991), who discuss debated relationships and monophyletic status (Figure 6). The "Agnatha" is no longer regarded as monophyletic. Current arguments place one or another group of agnathans nearest to the jawed fishes: Janvier (e.g., 1996b) favors Osteostraci; others consider Thelodonti as possible stem chondrichthyans (sister taxon and possible ancestor to jawed cartilaginous fishes) (Turner 1985; Mallatt 1996; Zimmer 1996).

In general, agnathans are streamlined in shape with an armored head and trunk. Most probably swam with side-to-side movements of the trunk and tail or by muscle contractions to produce a series of waves traveling down the body and pushing the fish through the water. Others had an exoskeleton of discrete tesserae or scales and were more flexible. The tail form varied, some with an enlarged upper or lower lobe, some more symmetrical. Some had hydrofoil-shaped pectoral fins or flaps, which could generate lift.

Each group of fishes has distinctive hard parts that can be preserved as macro- or microfossils. The different morphologies and microornaments help identify the fossils. Scales, the characteristic covering of fishes, may have originated as a means of excreting calcium salts and later may have acted as a means of storing phosphate. In many agnathans these scales eventually became protective bony armor with a sensory function.

Ordovician Vertebrates

Worldwide, pteraspidomorphs have a bimodal distribution in the Ordovician, with an older Gondwana group, the arandaspids, and a younger group from the northern hemisphere (Laurasian) (see e.g., Elliott et al. 1991; Gagnier and Blieck 1992).

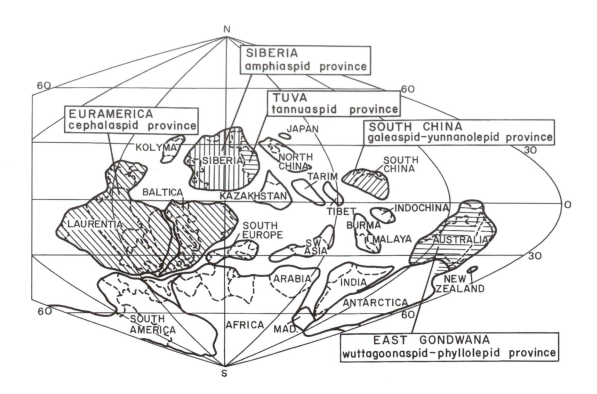

Figure 2. Five biogeographic provinces in the early Devonian; East Gondwana has turiniid thelodonts. From Young (1981).

Figure 3. *Clydagnathus,* the first conodont body fossil to be discovered (Lower Carboniferous, Scotland). From Brigs et al. (1983), by permission of Scandinavian University Press.

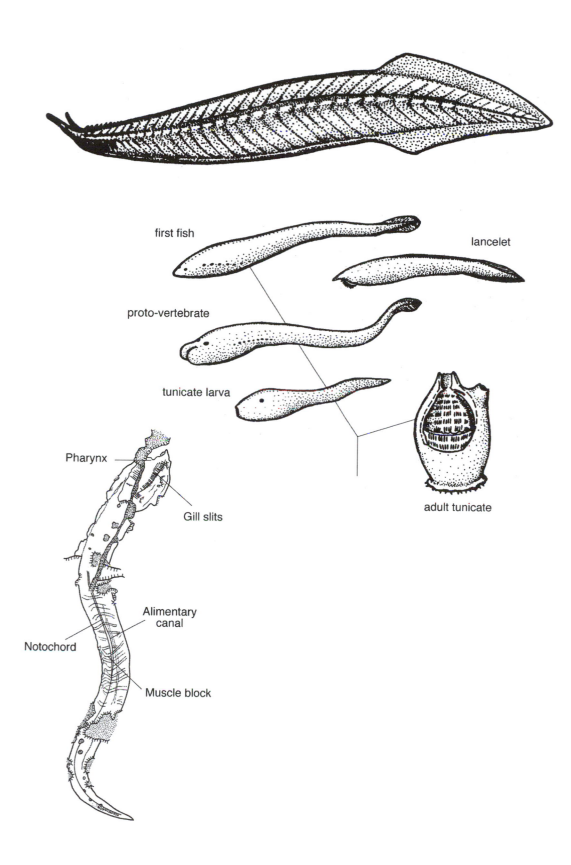

Figure 4. Prevertebrate history. *Top,* reconstruction of *Pikaia,* chordate (Middle Cambrian of Canada); *middle,* diagrammatic representation of evolution of fishes from protochordate ancestors; *lower left, Cathaymyrus* (Lower Cambrian of China). From: *top, middle,* Long (1995) by permission of John Long, W.A. Museum, Perth; *lower left,* Shu et al. (1996).

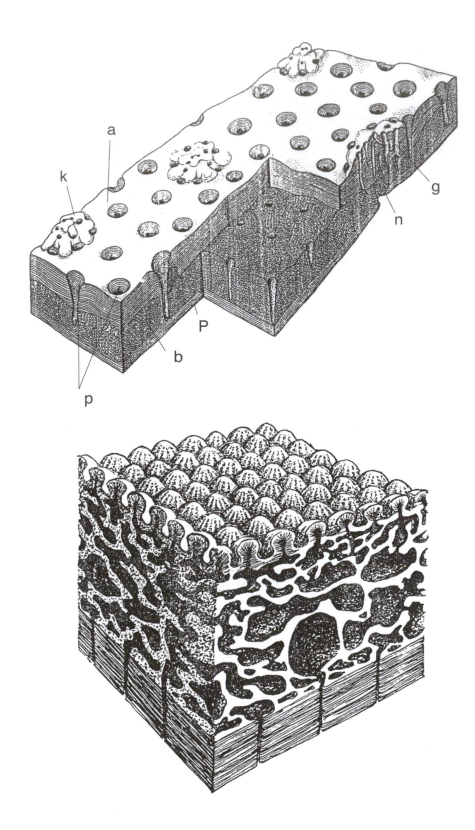

Figure 5. Vertebrate hard tissues with typical three-layered structure. *Top,* block diagram of unnamed Cambrian vertebrate; *bottom,* block diagram of heterostracan armor with upper layer with orthodentine tubercles, middle cancellar layer, basal laminated aspidine layer. Key: *a,* upper layer; *b,* middle layer; *c,* lower layer; *g,* vascular canals below tubercle; *k,* surface tubercles; *n,* basal vascular canal opening; *p,* large funnel-shaped pores. From: *top,* Halstead (1974); *bottom,* Karatajuté-Talimaa (1996).

Arandaspida

Undoubted vertebrate remains occur in the Ordovician, and the earliest known articulated vertebrates are *Arandaspis* and *Porophoraspis* from the Amadeus Basin in the Northern Territory of Australia (Figure 1A), now dated as Early Llanvirn (dating back 470 million years) (e.g., Long 1995). Arandaspid remains occur there up to the Late Ordovician (Ashgill). Somewhat earlier (about 485 million years ago) arandaspid-like dermal fragments are known from the Pacoota Sandstone from the Amadeus Basin in Australia (Young 1997). Knowledge of the early Gondwanan vertebrates was increased greatly by Gagnier's 1989 discovery of quite abundant, almost-complete specimens of *Sacabambaspis,* along with fossilized marine invertebrates from the Anzaldo Formation of central Bolivia of Llanvirn or Caradoc age (around 450 million years ago). This genus, as well as a poorly known genus, *Andinaspis,* are very similar to Australian arandaspids (Gagnier 1992, 1995), and *Sacabambaspis*-like fragments even occur at some levels of the Amadeus Basin (Stokes Siltstone, Llanvirn-Caradoc) (Young 1997).

The Arandaspida all apparently had eyes at the tip of the head (Janvier 1996b). The head armor, known particularly from *Sacabambaspis* (Janvier 1996b), consists of two large, roughly oval median plates, or shields, the dorsal one more flattened and the ventral one more convex. Both are ornamented with minute, closely set, drop-shaped or oak-leaf-shaped tubercles. The shields are separated by diamond-shaped lateral branchial plates lined along the side toward the back with an elongated marginal, or epibranchial, plate. Behind the anterior area containing the eyes and nostrils, the dorsal shield is pierced by a pair of closely set foramina (openings) that are regarded as the pineal and parapineal "eyes." The co-occurrence of both openings is unique to these vertebrates (Janvier 1996b). On the lower "lip" of the median plate was a fan-shaped bundle of minute scale rows that probably could expand as the mouth opened. The post-pectoral scales (behind the head shield) of arandaspids are elongate, rod-shaped, and arranged in chevrons on each flank, an arrangement that probably reflects underlying muscle blocks. The tail consists of a quite large web covered with minute scales and has a strange median (axial) extension. The lateral-line system was well developed and housed in narrow grooves lined with rows of minute tubercles. There were probably at least 10 branchial units or pouches—they could have numbered as many as 20, if the number of branchial plates reflects the branchial openings. The latter opened between the branchial plates, through a minute foramen.

The structure of the exoskeleton is poorly known but is three-layered, with a superficial spongy layer topped with tubercles, a middle cancellar layer, and a basal laminar layer (Janvier 1996b). Whether the exoskeleton is made of cellular bone or aspidine is still uncertain. The cancellar layer is honeycomb-like, as in heterostracans, but the walls are paired between the adjacent dermal units, or tesserae. Each tessera bears a single tubercle apparently not made of dentine, a characteristic vertebrate hard tissue.

Astraspida

The Ordovician astrapids of North America, first discovered in the nineteenth century, are now regarded as a distinct group (Janvier 1996 a, b). It includes *Astraspis* (Figure 7, bottom), possibly *Tesakoviaspis* (Karatajuté-Talimaa 1978), and several forms from Timan, Siberia, and Tuva. This group is mainly of Caradoc age, extending into the Early Llandovery. The Harding Sandstone Formation and contemporaneous formations from near Canyon City, Colorado, and adjoining states in North America are the main sources of astraspids and other forms of primitive agnathans claimed by I.J. Sansom and colleagues (1996).

The Harding Sandstone Formation consists of thick red sandstone series in which scattered vertebrate remains can be found in great abundance, in the form of scales and platelets ornamented with large rounded tubercles. In 1892, C.D. Walcott found one partly articulated head-shield of *Astraspis* (Janvier 1996b) and remains he called *Eriptychius*. *Astraspis* is now known from other partly articulated specimens, including the tail. Astraspids are characterized by dermal head armor of loosely attached polygonal units (tesserae) of spongy aspidine that bear numerous small tubercles surrounding a larger median one (Janvier 1996b). The tubercles bear a thick, glassy enameloid-like cap. The armor is similar to that in arandaspids, with branchial plates that separate at least eight horizontally aligned external gill openings (Sansom et al. 1997). Unlike arandaspids, the gill openings are relatively large and separate and have no cover. The sensory-line grooves are difficult to find and pass through the center of some of the tesserae. The scales of *Astraspis* are large, diamond-shaped, and ornamented with tubercles. There is no evidence of a median fin or paired fins, and the shape of the tail is still uncertain. *Eriptychius* is also poorly known; T. Ørvig (1989) regarded the histology of its very large dentine tubules as similar to heterostracan armor.

The late nineteenth century discovery of astraspids was the first evidence of vertebrates older than the classical (Silurian-Devonian) Old Red Sandstone fauna. Most subsequent authors (e.g., Gagnier 1995) agree that the affinities of the Ordovician forms are with the Silurian and Devonian heterostracans because their dermal skeletons were made up of acellular bone (aspidine). Since then, *Astraspis* and *Eriptychius* have been found in the Ordovician of most of the United States and Canada. Conodonts from the Harding Sandstone Formation clearly indicate a Middle Caradoc age and a marine environment. In addition to the above genera, Ørvig (1989) described a third, *Pycnaspis,* from Wyoming, which differs in its histological structure but is now regarded as a variant of *Astraspis*.

As noted above, the rich bone beds of the Harding Sandstone undoubtedly contain a more diverse vertebrate fauna, but the affinities of those remains are still uncertain. As early as 1902, Vaillant confirmed bone fragments with clear cell spaces in thin sections of Harding Sandstone (Janvier 1996). Karatajuté-Talimaa (1978) associated this cellular bone with tubercles of a specialized dentine called "mesodentine," which is found in Silurian and Devonian osteostracans and acanthodians. Fragments of globular calcified cartilage from the Harding Sandstone are also found with *Eriptychius* (Janvier 1996).

Towards the end of the Ordovician a major glaciation occurred, and the subsequent time was one of crisis for vertebrates. Very little is known of Late Ordovician forms except for the work of Karatajuté-Talimaa (e.g., 1997), who has found thelodonts and

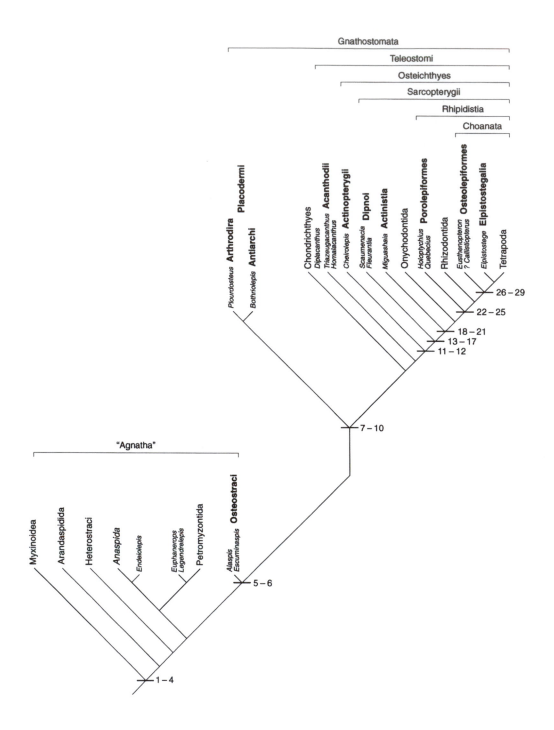

Figure 6A.

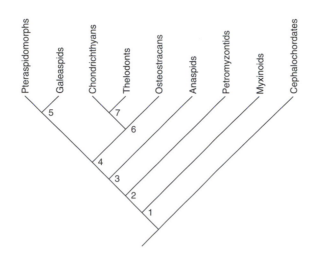

Figure 6B.

Figure 6. Contrasting schema for comparison. **6A** (at left), phylogenetic relationships of vertebrates with a paraphyletic "Agnatha." Key to characters: *1–4 Vertebrata: 1,* regionalization (head, trunk, tail); *2,* two-chambered heart; *3,* sensory capsules; *4,* neural crest. *5–6 Osteostraci + Gnathostomata: 5,* epicercal lobe in tail; *6,* sclerotic ossifications. *7–10 Gnathostomata: 7,* mandibular arch (biting jaws); *8,* two paired fins with girdles; *9,* three semicircular canals (addition of horizontal canal); *10,* gills outside gill arches. *11–12 Teleostomi: 11,* dermal branchiostegal rays; *12,* stylohyal. *13–17 Osteichthyes: 13,* dermal skull bones with descending laminae attaching to the endocranium; *14,* marginal teeth on dermal bones of upper and lower jaw; *15,* dermal shoulder girdle formed of posttemporal, supracleithrum, cleithrum, clavicle, and unpaired interclavicle; *16,* rhombic scales with peg-and-socket articulation; *17,* lepidotrichia. *18–21 Sarcopterygii: 18,* cosmine; *19,* true enamel; *20,* anocleithrum; *21,* archipterygium (= axial endoskeleton of paired fins). *22–25 Rhipidistia: 22,* plicidentine; *23,* tusks on vomers; *24,* co-occurrence of four infradentaries and three coronoids; *25,* postparietals flanked by two bones (tabular and supratemporal). *26–29 Choanata: 26,* only one external nasal opening; *27,* only anterior external nasal opening opens in lateral rostral; *28,* cheek formed by five bones (jugal, postorbital, squamosal, quadratojugal, and reduced preoperculum); *29,* convex head of the proximal element of the paired appendages articulates in a socket of the girdle.
6B (above), hypothesis of phylogenetic relationships among craniates. Key to characters: *1,* neural crest and its derivative, horny teeth; *2,* nervous regulation of the heart, arcualia, oculomotor musculature, caudal fin with rays; *3,* branchial chambers transversally elongated, (phosphatic) acellular bone; *4,* mouth with inferior lip covered by articulated scales or tesserae, sensory-line system enclosed in canals; *5,* ventral shield; *6,* branchial openings covered with individual gill covers, heterocercal caudal fin, pectoral fin, cellular dermal bone with non-lamellar but cancellar base or with pulp cavity openings, bone covered with superficial dentinous tissue (mesodentine, metadentine, or orthodentine); *7,* micromeric dermal skeleton without differentiation between cranial and postcranial skeleton, two anterior nostrils (diplorhiny), anal fin. From: *A,* Schultze and Cloutier (1996); *B,* Gagnier (1995).

astraspids in Timan, Estonia. Ørvig (1989) posited that certain conodonts *(Evencodus, Stereoconus)* from the Ordovician of the Siberian Platform resembled thelodont scales (Janvier 1996), but the histological structure of these conodonts has not been studied yet.

Post-Ordovician

Agnathans—heterostracans and thelodonts and then cephalaspidomorphs—reappear in the Early Silurian and are found in strength in Mid-Silurian times, being found in Timan, Siberia, Mongolia, Britain, Maritime Canada, the Michigan Basin, and Arctic regions.

Heterostraci

The heterostracans are characterized by a pair of common external branchial openings on either side of the head armor, a feature first

pointed out by E.R. Lankester in 1864 (Janvier 1996a). Some fossilized heterostracans had been discovered earlier, in the nineteenth century, based on isolated plates, and their vertebrate nature was not recognized at first; they were thought to be crustaceans or squids. Eventually, based on the histological structure of their peculiar honeycomb-like layers with dentine and aspidine, T.H. Huxley suggested that they were fishes.

Heterostracans proper are known from North America, northern Europe, Russia (including Siberia), and the Ukraine. No heterostracan is known from the southern hemisphere or from Southeast Asia. Most heterostracans lived in shallow seas, but some could live in deltas or rivers. While most were small, around 100–150 millimeters long, Late Devonian psammosteids, such as *Pycnosteus, Psammolepis, Schizosteus,* or *Tartuosteus,* reached widths of 1.5 meters (Obruchev and Mark-Kurik 1965).

The earliest known described heterostracans are Early Wenlock (430 million years) in age, and the youngest ones are Late

Frasnian (367 million years). Janvier (1996b) depicts the interrelationships of heterostracans, with *Athenaegis* (Figure 1B) (or all tolypelepids) regarded as the sister group of the "higher heterostracans" (pteraspids, psammosteids), which are not found before the Late Silurian. Other Silurian forms, such as Traquairaspidiformes, are left undecided. By Early Devonian times, the more primitive cyathaspidiforms were less numerous, and pteraspidiforms took over, except in western Siberia, where amphiaspidids survive until the Pragian. By the end of Middle Devonian times, the only survivors are psammosteids.

As in Ordovician agnathans, heterostracans exhibit an oblong, fusiform (tapered at both ends) overall body shape, large median ventral and dorsal shields covering the head, and the fan-shaped arrangement of the oral plates, which probably protected the ventral lip of the mouth or even could scrape or grasp food (Janvier 1996b). In several early heterostracans (e.g., traquairaspids), the oak-leaf-shaped tubercles of the dermal ornament are again characteristic.

The question of the affinities of heterostracans with other vertebrate taxa is still much-debated (e.g., Janvier 1996b) (Figure 7). First they were referred to as chondrichthyans, then recognized as "agnathans," and they have been considered as ancestral either to hagfishes or to gnathostomes. The current classification recognizes two divisions, the Cyathaspidiformes (e.g., *Poraspis, Anglaspis*) and the Pteraspidiformes (e.g., *Pteraspis, Errivaspis*), and other minor groups of uncertain affiliation—Lepidaspidida, Tesseraspidida, Traquairaspidiformes, Corvaspidida, Cardipeltida, and Tolypelepidida (e.g., Janvier 1996b). Exceptions to the normal plan include the Amphiaspidida and the genus *Boothiaspis*, both of which have all the plates of the armor fused into a rigid "box," and *Cardipeltis*, in which the ventral shield is replaced by numerous platelets.

Most ideas about affinities come from the exoskeleton. The dermal armor is composed of several plates containing sensory-line canals (Janvier 1996b). The trunk is covered with large platelets; the tail, which is either blunt but still hypocercal (that is, the lobe containing the notochord points down), diphycercal, or lobed, is covered with smaller scales arranged in radial rows. There is always a series of large median dorsal and ventral ridge scales. There is no median fin, except the caudal (tail), and no paired fins. The head shield may be fusiform, flattened, or bulge ventrally, and it may bear dorsal or lateral expansions, some very long (e.g., in *Doryaspis, Unarkaspis*; Janvier 1996b).

Some well-preserved heterostracans exist, particularly in the Early Silurian of Canada (e.g., *Athenaegis*; see Long 1995), in the Early Devonian Hunsrück Shale of Germany *(Drepanaspis),* and in the Welsh Borderland. In rare cases, the cartilaginous endoskeleton is preserved as impressions on the internal surface of dermal plates; two vertical semicircular canals, the brain, spinal cord, and possible arcualia (cartilaginous neural arches) of the vertebral column, small eyes, the pineal organ, olfactory organs (paired and connected to the brain impression by two convergent grooves, which may correspond to the olfactory tract), branchial pouches, and myomeres (muscle blocks) have been interpreted (e.g., Blieck and Janvier 1993) (Figures 8A, 8B). The position of the branchial apparatus often is indicated by a series of eight to ten paired impressions, sometimes with parallel longitudinal grooves left by the gill lamellae (Janvier 1996b). Lateral to these "gill-pouches" are U- or Y-shaped impressions (Figures 8A, 8B), which could be the external component of the gill arches or the extrabranchial atria (chambers).

Silurian cyathaspidids have a fusiform (some almost cigar-shaped) head armor (*Irregulareaspis, Anglaspis, Poraspis, Nahanniaspis,* and *Torpedaspis*) and have deep, vertical or angled flange scales (Janvier 1996b). In other forms, such as corvaspids and tolypelepids, the shields are made up of a single unit, but their ornamentation seems to consist of many overlapping, separate scales. In the unusual Siberian amphiaspidids (Novitskaya 1971), the head armor is fused and flattened, suggesting benthic (bottom-dwelling) or even burrowing habits. In some, the mouth, eyes, and olfactory organs are at the end of a long tube far in front of the pineal (Figure 7), or the eyes disappear (e.g., *Eglonaspis*). In others (e.g., *Gabreyaspis*), there is a larger kidney-shaped opening beside the eye which has been interpreted as a prenasal sinus, a spiracle, a pre-spiracle, or a dorsally displaced nostril. Janvier (1996b) considers that the opening probably had an inhalant respiratory function because amphiaspids probably lived half-buried in sediment, like many living rays.

The heterostracan exoskeleton generally consists of three layers (Figure 5 right): a basal laminar layer, a middle cancellar layer with honeycomb-shaped cavities, and a superficial layer of dentine ridges or tubercles (e.g., Halstead 1974). The middle and basal layers are made up of aspidine, an acellular hard tissue with growth zones. In the advanced psammosteids (e.g., Halstead-Tarlo 1964), there is only a thick layer of spongy aspidine. One attribute of this histology is its ability to heal after damage (e.g., Long 1995).

Several Silurian and Early Devonian forms, the "tessellate heterostracans," are regarded as the most primitive heterostracans. This includes *Tesseraspis, Oniscolepis,* and *Kallostracon,* known from fragment remains, and *Lepidaspis* or "Heterostracan indet. Type 5" with elongated tesserae with oak-leaf-shaped tubercular ornament (Dineley and Loeffler 1976). There is no clear evidence of a common branchial opening in these forms.

The Pteraspidiformes, which flourished in the Early Devonian, are characterized by several independent dorsal plates, ornamented with concentric, laterally serrated ridges made of dentine. The body scales are relatively small and diamond-shaped (Janvier 1996b); Janvier thinks this is the plesiomorphous (primitive) condition, since it also occurs in non-pteraspidiforms such as *Athenaegis*. The related Psammosteidae, however, have secondarily tuberculate ornamentation and body scales (Mark-Kurik 1993). The best-known form is the Early Devonian *Drepanaspis* (e.g., Long 1995). In young psammosteids the larger plates apparently were separated by joints, and as individuals grew to adulthood the plates became separated by fields of smaller polygonal platelets that also could grow.

Thelodonti

Contrary to the view of Janvier (1996a, 1996b, in Schultze and Cloutier 1996), most thelodont scholars consider thelodonts to be a monophyletic group (Turner 1991; Karatajuté-Talimaa 1997) united by their specialized squamation (scale cover) of highly vari-

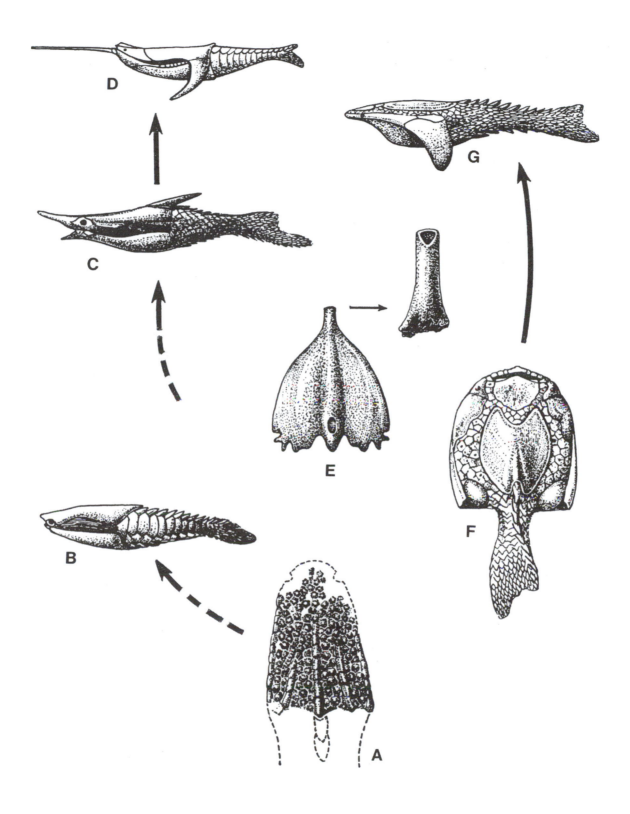

Figure 7. Heterostracan types. *A*, pteraspidomorph Ordovician ancestor (?), *Astraspis* head shield; *B*, cyathaspidiform *Anglaspis; C,* pteraspidid *Pteraspis; D,* advanced pteraspidid *Doryaspis; E,* amphiaspidid *Eglonaspis; F,* basal psammosteid *Drepanaspis; G,* advanced psammosteid *Pycnosteus.* After Halstead-Tarlo (1968).

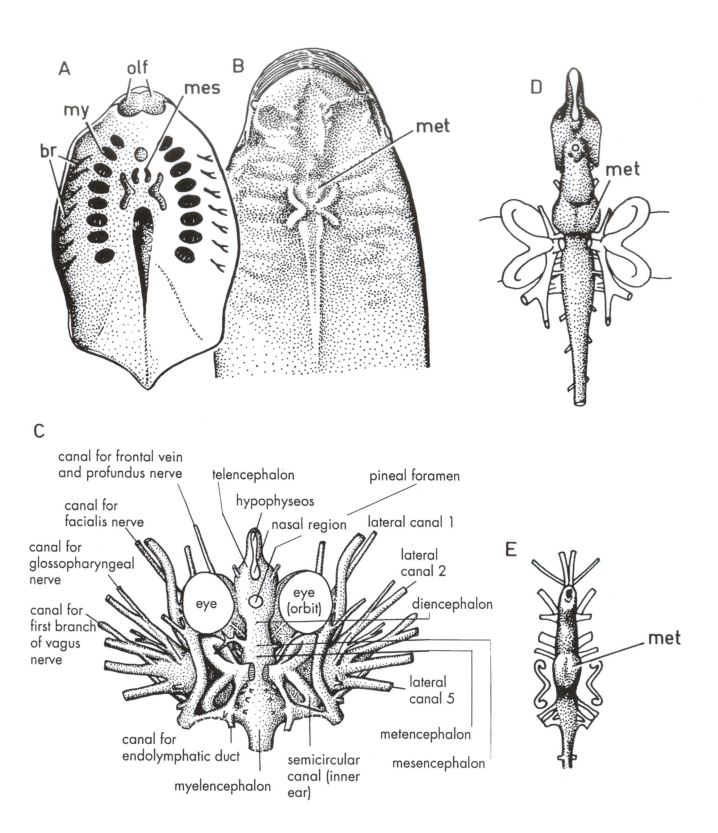

Figure 8. Examples of brain impressions *(B)* and interpretations thereof *(A, C–E)*. *A*, general heterostracan pattern as interpreted by Halstead-Tarlo and Whiting; *B*, heterostracan *Poraspis*; *C*, brain reconstruction of advanced osteostracan *Benneviaspis*; *D*, osteostracan *Boreaspis*; *E*, galeaspid *Changxingaspis*. Key: *br*, branchial arches; *mes*, mesencephalon; *met*, metencephalon (cerebellum); *my*, "myotomes"; *olf*, olfactory tract. From: *A, B, D, E*, after Blieck and Janvier (1993), copyright © 1993 by Gordon and Breach Publishers; *C*, Long (1995), by permission of John Long, W.A. Museum, Perth.

able placoidlike (toothlike) scales and possibly by possession of only seven or eight pairs of branchial structures and a stomach. Thelodont fish (Figures 1C, 1D, 9) were covered with an exoskeleton of minute (around 0.1–3.0 millimeters in length) dentine scales which have a structure much like that of mammalian teeth, hence the name *Thelodus* given to the type genus (the first accepted example of this fish) by Louis Agassiz in 1838. They strongly resemble modern sharks in that both have an external covering of shagreen (skin studded with placoid scales) that continues on into the mouth and throat to form either abrasive fields (thelodonts) or tooth rows (sharks). Also, both lack a bony endoskeleton.

Only a few taxa are known from complete body fossils. When they are found, as with *Loganellia scotica* from the Lower Silurian of Scotland, *Phlebolepis elegans* (Figure 1C) and the new Silurian and Early Devonian taxa from the Northwest Territories of Canada (Figure 1D) (e.g., Long 1995), a great deal of morphological information is preserved. Turner (1994) and Turner and W. van den Brugghen (1993) recently have discussed the thelodont endoskeleton and internal squamation. Thelodont scales are one millimeter^3 on average and with their cosmopolitan geographic and facies distribution (i.e., distribution in different sediment types), make excellent microfossils for biostratigraphy (e.g., Karatajuté-Talimaa 1978; Turner 1997). Generally, the scales from the head, mid-thorax, and body are differently shaped and can be recognized for each species by associating similar morphology and histology.

Thelodonts have a worldwide range of at least late Ordovician to Early Frasnian (Late Devonian), and they occur in rocks formed in both marine and nonmarine environments, including (presumably) freshwater. The simple placoidlike scales are some of the most common Paleozoic fossils; an individual that was 200 millimeters long had around 20,000 scales at any one time, and these could be shed throughout its lifetime. Extensive bonebeds are rich in these scales. Taxa from the Late Ordovician to the Early Silurian are restricted to the Northern Hemisphere in North America, Europe, and Russia. The Late Ordovician thelodont *Sandivia* from Timan (Karatajuté-Talimaa 1997) appears closely related to *Valyalepis* from the Early Silurian of Quebec and to a new Aeronian taxon from the Michigan Basin.

In general, primitive thelodonts grouped together as "Loganiids" dominate until the Mid-Silurian, when a major split appears, the Katoporodids and Thelodontidids. The former continue only into the earliest Devonian, while the advanced thelodontidids— *Turinia* (Figure 9), *Nikolivia,* and relatives—continue to flourish until their final demise sometime before the Frasnian-Fammenian extinction events of 364 million years ago. In the Northern Hemisphere, however, the last fling was a little earlier, in the early Mid-Devonian, where *Amaltheolepis* is found in the Baltic, Spitsbergen (Norway), and Arctic regions. In many parts of the world, especially those that were once part of the Gondwana supercontinent, thelodonts are known only from scales. These meager remains testify to the presence of the thelodonts in Australia, Antarctica, China, and South America. Gondwanian thelodonts first appear in the Late Silurian (in Iran and Irian Jaya), and turiniids are common in the Devonian. The very last thelodont anywhere in the world is *Australolepis* from the Late Devonian (Frasnian) of western Australia.

Thelodonts usually were small, less than 200 millimeters long, but the largest estimated size is about one meter in *Thelodus parvidens*. Most thelodonts possessed a large head and pharyngeal region, lateral triangular pectoral flaps, a slim trunk, dorsal and anal fins, and a large, usually hypocercal, tail (Figure 9) (Turner 1991). They had an external skeleton of discrete dermal denticles—some overlapping, some not. The internal skeleton was cartilaginous, with rings of cartilage supporting the mouth, paired branchial structures, and possible perichondral endocranium (Turner 1991). Recent work on the Silurian lagerstätte of Scotland and Canada (in which soft tissue outlines are preserved) is yielding new data on the thelodont morphology (Turner and van den Brugghen 1993; Wilson and Caldwell 1993; Märss and Ritchie in press). The nature of the branchial apparatus has been clarified, including evidence for cartilaginous supports for the mouth, throat, and gills. Additionally, whorl-like denticles, probably associated with the gill arches, have been identified. The tails of these exquisitely preserved fishes show a great deal of diversity. Some are hypocercal (with a downward-pointing notochordal lobe and a dosally directed fin-fold) as in *Lanarkia;* others are lobed, as in *Loganellia scotica,* and still others are forked, as in the new Canadian forms (Wilson and Caldwell 1993). In addition, it is possible that one thelodont exhibits pelvic fins (Märrs and Ritchie in press).

Even a small, 200 millimeters–long thelodont was covered with myriad scales at any one time. Each scale had a dentinous, nongrowing crown and neck, with a growing base of aspidine-like tissue. An enameloid outer layer has not been confirmed yet in thelodont scales. The base was held in the dermis by partially mineralized collagen fibers and routinely develops specialized processes and outgrowths that unify the thelodonts as a natural group (Turner 1991). Dentine types exhibited in thelodont scales range from orthodentine to a tissue similar to mesodentine. Modern classification relies on the histological differences—Katoporodids have many basal dentine canal openings, while thelodontidids have one or few pulp canal openings on the base. The scales show great morphological variation from one taxon to another and from region to region across the body of an individual animal (with distinctive head, transitional, and body scales, plus areas with special scales such as sensory pore canals and orbital scales. Karatajuté-Talimaa (1978) and Märss and Ritchie (in press) have refined the mapping of scale patterns. There is also known to have been ontogenetic changes (changes during development) in the form of the scales (e.g., Turner 1991).

Anaspida

Anaspids (e.g., Birkeniids, *Lasanius, Pharyngolepis*) are among the few early jawless vertebrates that do not possess a platelike dermal head armor; hence their name, which means "shield-less." They are small, slender in shape, laterally compressed, and characterized by one or several triradiate "postbranchial" spines (Janvier 1996b) behind a series of external branchial openings (Figure 1G). There is a strongly hypocercal tail. There are a few atypical "anaspids"— *Jamoytius* (Lower Silurian: Scotland); *Endeiolepis, Euphanerops,* and *Legendrelepis* (Late Devonian: Miguasha, Quebec)—that have

Figure 9. Thelodont *Turinia* (Lower Devonian of Scotland), showing scales and various soft tissue impressions. © The Trustees of the National Museum of Scotland, 1999.

been referred to this taxon, although they do not appear to possess postbranchial spines (e.g., Janvier in Schultze and Cloutier 1996). The lampreylike *Jamoytius* continues to be enigmatic, and dispute continues on whether it is a true anaspid.

The Anaspida occur from the Early Silurian to the latest Silurian in North America and Europe. There is a single record of a "birkeniid" squamation from the Silurian of China. *Jamoytius* is Clandovery (Early Silurian) in age but *Jamoytius*-like forms occur in the Early Devonian of the United States. The best-preserved material described to date—*Pharyngolepis, Pterygolepis,* and *Rhyncholepis*—comes from the Early Silurian of Ringerike (Norway), although some anaspid "giants" of over 200 millimeters have been found by Ray Thorsteinsson (Canada) in the Early Silurian of Cornwallis Island. All known anaspids, including the atypical Late Devonian forms, were most probably epipelagic animals seeming to prefer shallow-water marginal marine or freshwater habitats.

The head of anaspids is fusiform and usually is covered with minute scales or a few larger dermal plates. The eyes are large, laterally placed, and surrounded by a ring of dermal plates, which Janvier (1996b) insists is not a sclerotic ring. The pineal foramen opens midway between the eyes, and in front of it is a T-shaped or keyhole-shaped opening, which currently is interpreted as a dorsal nasohypophyseal opening, similar to that of lampreys and osteostracans (Janvier 1996b). The mouth seems to have been more-or-less oval with upper and lower lips supported by an annular cartilage and armed with dermal oral plates that probably could bite vertically against each other, much like gnathostome jaws. Behind the eyes is a series of six to fifteen external branchial openings (up to 30 in *Legendrelepis*), arranged in slanting lines (Long 1995) that either pierce a single branchial plate or are lined with crescentic scales. The trunk bears elongate, rod-shaped scales arranged in chevrons and there is always a median dorsal series of large ridge scales.

Paired fins, known only in *Pharyngolepis* and *Rhyncholepis,* extend along the ventrolateral side of the body, from behind the postbranchial spines to the anal region; their length depends on the position of the latter. In *Pharyngolepis* they are almost ribbon-like; in *Rhyncholepis,* however, there is a very short preanal region, producing rather short fins. The paired fins are covered with minute scales arranged in thin rows, suggesting the presence of numerous underlying radials. There is no dorsal fin. Unpaired fins are the dorsal (epichordal) lobe of the tail and the anal fin, which is reduced or lacking in several genera.

Very little is known of the internal anatomy of anaspids except for vague imprints of soft structures preserved under unusual conditions (i.e., postmortem decalcification or transformation) in the four questionable anaspids, *Jamoytius, Endeiolepis, Euphanerops,* and *Legendrelepis.* These forms may have had nonmineralized, or "horny," scales, but clearly had cartilage around the mouth and cartilaginous branchial baskets (Janvier in Schultze and Cloutier 1996). *Jamoytius* is an eel-shaped form, some specimens of which show imprints of the eyes, a possible olfactory organ or surrounding cartilaginous ring, and a branchial "basket" with about 20 branchial units or openings (Janvier 1996b). *Jamoytius* was first regarded as a very primitive craniate, but it is currently interpreted either as a primitive lamprey or as a "naked" anaspid. Some specimens of

Endeiolepis from Miguasha display traces of the myomeres and the imprint of either the intestine or the stomach, another feature this animal has in common with thelodonts. All the plates and scales are formed of acellular, laminar bone that strongly resembles aspidine. There is no dentine, not even in the tubercles of scales.

The Anaspida often are regarded as the sister group of lampreys because of the dorsal nasohypophyseal opening, a slender body shape, and gill openings arranged in a slanting line—the latter now known in the new thelodonts from Canada. In addition, if the arrangement of the body scales reflects that of the underlying myomeres, then, as in lampreys, the body musculature extended above—and perhaps beneath—the branchial apparatus. *Jamoytius* has been regarded as a possible link between the anaspid and lamprey morphologies because of its naked skin, slender body shape, and possible circular cartilage. All these features might be parallelisms. Maisey (1986), however, placed anaspids as the closest relatives to the gnathostomes because their body musculature suggests the presence of a horizontal septum and their paired fins extend to the anal region (a prerequisite for the formation of pelvic fins). Janvier (1996b) regards this argument as tenuous and presents a classification that supports the lamprey connection (Table 4.2).

Osteostraci

Osteostracans (Figure 1F) occur exclusively in the Silurian to early Devonian of the Northern Hemisphere (Young 1981): North America, Europe, the Ukraine and Russia, and in the form of the tannuaspids from Tuva in Central Asia. Several appear endemic. Thyestiids, for example, come only from Britain, the Baltic, Timan, and the Urals. The Boreaspididae occur only in Spitsbergen and Severnaya Zemlya. The earliest known osteostracans are Early Silurian (Wenlockian) in age. They comprise generalized, primitive forms, like *Ateleaspis,* as well as derived cornuate forms, like tremataspids. Osteostracans remain rare until the Early Devonian, when a wide range of forms suddenly appears, in association with the extension of the Old Red Sandstone facies around Laurentia. By Middle Devonian times, most of the major cornuates have disappeared, and only cephalaspidid or zenaspidid-related forms survive until the Frasnian. The last known osteostracan is *Escuminaspis* from Miguasha, Quebec.

Osteostracans had an exoskeleton of cellular bone and an endoskeleton that was perichondrally ossified (i.e., only the outermost zone of cartilage was converted to bone). On the dorsal head shield were unusual median and lateral shallow depressions called cephalic fields. These fields are covered by polygonal platelets and are connected to the internal labyrinth cavity ("inner ear") by means of large branching canals that may have housed either electric organs or some other sensory organ linked to the lateral line system (Janvier 1996b). The perichondrally ossified brain case of osteostracans preserves natural casts of the brain, cranial nerves, and cerebral vessels as well as impressions of the underlying pharyngeal soft tissues. These are best seen in Late Silurian material from Saaremaa, Estonia, and in Early Devonian material from Spitsbergen. Eric Stensiö first revealed these structures by serially sectioning whole heads using the painstaking grinding method pioneered by W.J. Sollas. Janvier (e.g., 1996b) has since added to this work. The sensory line system, which is fairly constant in osteostracans, consists of canals and grooves in the head-shield exoskeleton, but as yet no sensory lines have been recognized on the trunk.

Most osteostracans have a horseshoe-shaped head with a pair of pectoral fins. Various modifications include development of processes, reduction of cephalic fields, or loss of paired fins (Janvier 1996b). Another peculiarity of some osteostracans is a horizontal lobe ventral to the caudal fin, which may have been a modified anal fin (Figure 1F). The trunk shape is more conservative, but dorsal fins may be reduced and the unusual horizontal lobe of the tail may be lost. The dominant group of Osteostraci is the Cornuata (Janvier 1996b), which has cornual (horn-shaped) processes in front of the paired fins. The group is divided into (1) the Cephalaspidida, with a long prehypophyseal region and broad cornual processes; (2) the Zenaspidida, with narrow and thick cornual processes, posteriorly enlarged lateral fields, and enlarged hypophyseal division of the nasohypophyseal opening; (3) the Benneviaspidida, with no radiating canals in the exoskeleton and a depressed shield; (4) the Kiaeraspidida, with reduced cornual processes and enlarged supraoral field; and (5) the Thyestiida. There are also five or six genera of "noncornuate" osteostracans.

Janvier discerns three main stages in osteostracan evolution. The most generalized form is in the Early Silurian (Wenlock) *Ateleaspis* from Scotland; it is primitive in its retention of a micromeric scale covering behind the head shield. The most primitive cornuate is *Zenaspis* from the Early Devonian of Europe and Spitsbergen; it displays the characteristic cornua extending from the rear corners of the head shield in front of the pectoral fins. The most derived group of cornuates appear to be the thyestiids, with one of its best-known members being *Tremataspis*, from Estonia. Thyestiids have many unique characters embedded in a secondarily simplified body. Paired fins and cornual processes are absent, and the head shield extends over the abdominal region (Janvier 1996b). The exoskeleton of *Tremataspis* is also unique, having a shiny layer of mesodentine covered with enameloid and containing a network that may have included electrosensory organs. Thyestiids, like today's rays, may have been adapted for a burrowing lifestyle.

The osteostracan brain is well-known, thanks to Janvier's work (Figures 8C, 8D); the telencephalon (forebrain), mesencephalon (midbrain), metencephalon (hind brain), and medulla oblongata (brain stem) have been distinguished. Beneath the brain cavity is a thin median canal for the notochord, which ends anteriorly just behind the hypophyseal (pituitary) region. At the back of the occipital region, this canal becomes much enlarged, showing that posteriorly the notochord must have been as large as in hagfishes and lampreys. A number of canals branched off for cranial nerves, cerebral veins, and arteries. The eyes are ossified in some osteostracans (e.g, *Tremataspis*) with a cup-shaped ossification and a dermal sclerotic ossification (Janvier 1996b). The most intriguing features of the osteostracan labyrinth are the canals that send branches into the lateral and dorsal fields. Janvier (1996b) debates whether these "sel" canals might have housed electromotor nerves (as in modern torpedo rays), performed a sensory function, or housed extensions of the labyrinth, similar to the ciliated chambers of the lamprey labyrinth, which transmit vibrations.

The histology of osteostracans is more complicated than that of other jawless vertebrates (Janvier 1996). The scales and the tesserae are formed of true bone, and the exoskeleton is covered with a dentinous tissue, mesodentine, which sometimes (e.g., in thyestidians) is lined with a thin layer of enameloid. The middle layer of the osteostracan exoskeleton is bony and contains a horizontal network of canals that form a polygonal pattern along the limits of the tesserae and smaller intra-areal canals within the tesserae. In osteostracans that have a reduced or missing dentinous layer, these canals become "mucous" grooves, which might be part of the lateral sensory-line system (Janvier 1996b). There is a basal laminar layer of bone that rests on the endoskeleton, and between the exo- and endoskeleton there is an intervening network of vascular canals, from which arise the vessels that supply the exoskeleton. Cartilage lined with perichondral bone and globular calcified cartilage also occur in osteostracan endoskeletons. A secondarily acellular exoskeleton occurs in the Late Devonian osteostracan *Escuminaspis* (Janvier in Schultze and Cloutier 1996).

Tessellate osteostracans could grow until the shield became solid, depending on the species, and probably also on the age of the individual. In a single population of *Zenaspis*, the size difference among individuals ranges up to 200 per cent. Nevertheless, there are instances where determinate growth (adult growth stoppage) in osteostracans may have existed. In the boreaspidids or tremataspidids, however, Janvier (1996b) thinks that the entire shield became ossified once the animal reached a definitive size. (Prior to this, the animal would have been naked.) Developmental stages in *Tremataspis* show that the superficial dentinous layer formed first, and then the rest of the exoskeleton followed.

Most osteostracans lived in quiet nearshore marine environments—lagoons, tidal flats, deltas—but some may have lived in rivers. Osteostracans were microphagous (eating small organisms) and, possibly suspension feeders; some probably burrowed, but without a dorsal opening for water intake; they could not live under the surface for too long without damaging their gills (Janvier 1996b).

Galeaspida

Galeaspids are also armored with a massive endo- and exoskeletal head shield (Figure 10). They are characterized by a large median dorsal opening in the front part of the head shield, which connects ventrally with the underlying mouth and gill cavity (Janvier 1996b). Also characteristic is the dorsal pattern of lateral line canals on the head shield (Janvier 1996b). The entire exoskeleton of galeaspids consist of minute semifused units.

Galeaspids range from Early Silurian to Late Devonian and appear endemic to China, including Xinjiang, and northern Vietnam. The earliest known is *Dayongaspis* from the Early Silurian (Clandovery) of Hunan. *Hanyangaspis, Xiushuiaspis,* and *Sinogaleaspis* occur in the Wenlock of Wuhan and Jiangxi. Most other galeaspids are from the Early Devonian of Yunnan, Guizhou, Guangxi, and Sichuan in China and the Bac Bo (Tonkin), Vietnam. The youngest known is a large, unnamed eugaleaspid from the Zhongning Formation in Ningxia, northern China, found with the antiarch *Remigolepis* and of probable Frasnian age (Wang 1993).

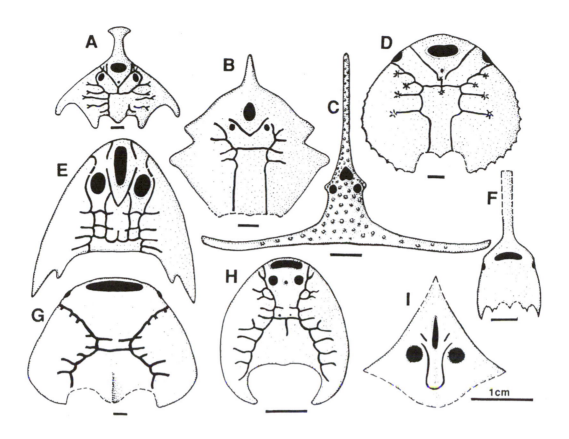

Figure 10. Weird endemic galeaspid head shields from the Silurian and Devonian of China. These are among the strangest fish ever to have evolved. *A, Sanchaspis; B, Nanpanaspis; C, Lungmenshanaspis; D, Cyclodiscaspis; E, Sinogaleaspis; F, Sanqiaspis; G, Hanyangaspis; H, Changxingaspis; I, Tridenaspis.* Scale bar, 10 millimeters. From Wang (1993).

Most galeaspids were benthic forms, living on sandy or muddy substrates in marginal marine environments (deltas, lagoons). Some forms *(Duyunolepis, Paraduyunaspis)* occur in brachiopod-rich marine deposits (Wang 1993). Janvier (1996b) interprets the shape of the shield in some hunanaspidiforms, such as *Sanqiaspis* or *Lungmenshanaspis,* as similar to that in boreaspid osteostracans; this shape suggests more nektonic (open water) habits.

Galeaspid head shields can be elongate and oval, horseshoe-shaped like osteostracans, or have long rostral (snout) and cornual processes (Figure 10). Janvier (1996b) regards *Hanyangaspis* (Silurian, Wuhan Province) as the most generalized galeaspid because of its almost terminal and transversally elongated dorsal opening and laterally placed eyes. Based on this assumption, Janvier defines two major groups, the Eugaleaspidiformes and the Huananaspidiformes, with a remaining paraphyletic group, the Polybranchiaspidiformes (Janvier 1996b). His cladogram (family tree) is based on the assumption that homoplasy (parallelism) is more likely to affect the cornual process of eugaleaspidiforms and huananaspidiforms than the "polybranchial" condition, which necessitates

important modification in the branchial blood circulation and innervation. Therefore, Janvier unites "polybranchiaspidiforms" and huananaspidiforms in one larger group, the Polybranchiaspidida (with more than 10 branchial fossae). The dorsal surface of the galeaspid shield is ornamented with uniform stellate (star-shaped) tubercles. The rest of the body was covered with minute, button-shaped scales that had bulging bases and single external tubercles. The seven pairs of branchial openings are arranged in a semicircle ventrally at the junction between the large posterior plate and the rim of the shield. There were no paired fins, but a ventrolateral ridge of scales, as in osteostracans. The tail is rarely preserved (e.g., *Sanqiaspis*), but when it is, it displays large overlapping scales like those of heterostracans.

Polybranchiaspis (Early Devonian: South China, northern Vietnam) has a roughly oval head shield, with a kidney-shaped median dorsal opening, dorsally placed eyes, and a small, rounded pineal opening (Janvier 1996b). Ornament consists of minute, closely set tubercles arranged in radiating rows. As with other galeaspids, the sensory-line canals are large and open to the exterior through a few large slits or pores at the end of canals. The orobranchial chamber is closed by a large median plate surrounded by minute scales. Polybranchiaspids have around 13 to 24 pairs of branchial structures.

The internal anatomy is known in only a few genera (e.g., *Polybranchiaspis, Duyunolepis, Xiushuiaspis*). The poorly known brain structure (Figure 8E) is roughly similar to that in osteostracans, with a paired dorsal swelling representing a possible metencephalon (Janvier 1996b). In some Silurian forms the large orobranchial cavity seems to be completely closed at the rear by a postbranchial wall (Janvier 1996b). The nature of the median dorsal opening and the duct by which it communicated with the orobranchial cavity remain enigmatic. The dorsal position of the opening suggests it was a nasohypophyseal opening, and this is how it was first interpreted, before details of its internal structure were known. Janvier (1996b) now thinks it was similar to the nasopharyngeal duct of hagfishes, which it communicates with the gill chamber. The surface of the dorsal duct in galeaspids is covered with minute sharp tubercles that point toward the exterior (Janvier 1996b), against the presumed main flow of inhaled water. Thus he considers that galeaspids have a prenasal sinus, since the olfactory organs open into its posterior wall.

The galeaspid exoskeleton bears no dentine but is made of aspidine-like acellular bone. In some forms the center of the external tubercles is covered with a thin layer of transparent tissue that looks like enameloid (Janvier 1996b). This histology closely resembles that of *Astraspis*. In some (e.g., *Polybranchiaspis*), the exoskeleton has large, polygonal cavities similar to those found in heterostracans, but overall the structure of the endoskeleton seems identical to that of osteostracans; for instance, the cartilage was lined with a thin layer of perichondral bone (Janvier 1996b).

Pituriaspida

Young described this poorly known group of agnathans in 1991, on the basis of a few (two or three) specimens preserved as impressions in sandstone from a single locality in the Cravens Peak Beds of the Georgina Basin of Queensland (Late Early or early Middle Devonian age). Named from an aboriginal word for a hallucinogenic plant, the fossils are quite weird (Figure 1E). They appear to have good pectoral fins and a tubelike exoskeleton that extends into a long rostrum. Young referred them to two different genera, the better known *Pituriaspis* (see reconstruction, Long 1995) and *Neeyambaspis* (Janvier 1996). The composition of the external and internal skeletons remain unknown. The sutureless (seamless) armor bears tuberculate ornament, a long narrow rostral process and posterior spine, anterior cornuate processes, oval pectoral fenestrae (openings for the pectoral fins), and anteroventral branchial opening. Janvier (1996b) predicted that pituriaspids had galeaspid-like scales but none have been found to date in Australian samples.

The Pituriaspids are assumed to have lived in deltaic or freshwater deposits, in association with placoderms (e.g., *Wuttagoonaspis*) and thelodonts; Turner (1997), however, has suggested that some of the Cravens Peak Beds are shallow-water marine deposits.

Pituriaspis apparently shares with the osteostracans and gnathostomes well-defined pectoral fins and shares with the lat-

ter two and the galeaspids the perichondrally ossified endoskeleton. Young (1991) placed the pituriaspids at the base of the radiation containing osteostracans and galeaspids. Janvier (1996a) placed pituriaspids close to these three groups.

SUSAN TURNER

See also Brain and Cranial Nerves; Craniates; Fins and Limbs, Paired; Gnathostomes; Lateral Line System; Skeleton; Skull

Works Cited

Aldridge, R.J., and M.A. Purnell. 1996. The conodont controversies. *Trends in Ecology and Evolution* 11 (11):463–68.

Aldridge, R.J., D.E.G. Briggs, I.J. Sansom, and M.P. Smith. 1994. The latest vertebrates are the earliest. *Geology Today* 10:141–45.

Blieck, A. 1992. At the origin of chordates. *Géobios* 25 (1):101–13.

Blieck, A., and P. Janvier. 1993. L.B. Halstead and the heterostracan controversy. *Modern Geology* 18:89–105.

Briggs, D.E.G., E.N.K. Clarkson, and R.J. Aldridge. 1983. The conodont animal. *Lethaia* 16:1–14.

Dineley, D.L., and E.J. Loeffler. 1976. Ostracoderm fauna of the Delorme and associated Siluro-Devonian formations, North West Territories, Canada. *Special Papers in Palaeontology* 18:1–218.

Elliott, D.K., A. Blieck, and P.-Y. Gagnier. 1991. Ordovician vertebrates. *In* C.R. Barnes and S.H. Williams (eds.), *Geological Survey of Canada Paper* Proc. VIntern. Symp. Ordovician System (St. John's, Newfoundland, 1988) paper 90-9:93–106.

Forey, P.F., and P. Janvier. 1994. Evolution of the early vertebrates. *American Scientist* 82:554–65.

Gagnier, P.-Y. 1992. Ordovician vertebrates from Bolivia: Comments on *Sacabambaspis janvieri* and description of *Andinaspis suarezorum* nov. gen. et sp. *In* R. Suarez-Soruco (ed.), *Fossiles y Facies de Bolivia*. Vol. 1, *Vertebrados. Revista Técnica de YPFB* 12 (3–4):371–79.

———. 1995. Ordovician vertebrates and Agnathan phylogeny. *In* M. Arsenault, H. Lelièvre, and P. Janvier (eds.), *Études sur les vertébrés inférieurs* (VIIᵉ Symposium international, Parc de Miguasha, Québec, 1991). *Bulletin du Muséum National d'Histoire Naturelle*, sectn. C, 4 ser., t. 17, 1995 (1–4), 1–38.

Gagnier, P.-Y., and A. Blieck. 1992. On *Sacabambaspis janvieri* and the vertebrate diversity in Ordovician seas. *In* E. Mark-Kurik (ed.), *Fossil Fishes as Living Animals. Academia* (Tallinn) 1:9–20.

Halstead, L.B. 1974. *Vertebrate Hard Tissues*. Wykeham Science Series. London: Wykeham; New York: Springer-Verlag.

Halstead-Tarlo, L.B. 1964. Psammosteiformes (Agnatha) a review with descriptions of new material from the Lower Devonian of Poland. General part. *Palaeontologia Polonica* (13):1–135.

———. 1968. The first vertebrates. *Spectrum* 49:1–5.

Hardisty, M.W., and I.C. Potter (eds.). 1971. *The Biology of Lampreys*. London and New York: Academic Press.

Janvier, P. 1996a. The dawn of vertebrates: Characters versus common ascent in the rise of current vertebrate phylogenies. *Palaeontology* 39 (2):259–87.

———. 1996b. *Early Vertebrates*. Oxford Monographs on Geology and Geophysics, 33. Oxford: Clarendon; New York: Oxford University Press.

Karatajuté-Talimaa, V.N. 1978. *Telodonti Siluri i Devona SSSR i Shpitsbergena*. [Silurian and Devonian Thelodonts of the U.S.S.R. and Spitsbergen]. Vilnius: Mosklas.

———. 1996. Stuburiniu isorinio sarvo mikroliekanos surastos velyvojo Kambro uolienose. (Vertebrate outside micro-remains found in Late Carboniferous [Late Cambrian] rocks.) *Geologijos Akiraciai* 1 (97):48–50. [In Lithuanian with English summary.]

———. 1997. Taxonomy of Loganiid Thelodonts. *Modern Geology* 21(1–2):1–15.

Kemp, A., and R.S. Nicoll. 1996. A histochemical analysis of biological residues in conodont elements. *Modern Geology* 20 (3–4):287–302; 21 (1–2):197–213.

Kivett, S., G.K. Merrill, and C.R. Cunningham. 1996. Problematic implications of an acceptance of Conodonta as vertebrates and conodonts as teeth. *Journal of Vertebrate Paleontology*, supplement to no. 3, 16:45–46.

Long, J.A. 1995. *The Rise of Fishes: 500 Million Years of Evolution*. Sydney: University of New South Wales Press; Baltimore, Maryland: Johns Hopkins University Press.

Maisey, J.G. 1986. Heads or tails: A chordate phylogeny. *Cladistics* 2:201–56.

———. 1996. *Discovering Fossil Fishes*. New York: Holt.

Mallatt, J. 1996. Ventilation and the origin of jawed vertebrates: A new mouth. *Zoological Journal of the Linnean Society* 117:329–404.

Mark-Kurik, E. 1993. Notes on the squamation in psammosteids. Beverly Halstead Memorial volume. *Modern Geology* 18 (1):107–14.

Märss, T., and A. Ritchie. In press. Scottish Silurian and Devonian thelodonts. *Transactions of the Royal Society, Edinburgh.*

Moy-Thomas, J.A., and R.S. Miles. 1971. *Palaeozoic Fishes*. 2nd ed., London: Chapman and Hall; Philadelphia: Saunders.

Novitskaya, L.A. 1971. *Les Amphiaspides (Heterostraci) du Dévonien de la Sibérie*. Cahiers de Paléontologie CNRS. Paris: CNRS.

Obruchev, D.V., and E.U. Mark-Kurik (with L.I. Novitskaya on histology). 1965. *Psammosteidi (Agnatha, Psammosteidae) of the Devonian of the USSR*. Tallinn: Eesti NSV Teaduste Akademia Geoologigia Instituut.

Ørvig, T. 1989. Histologic studies of ostracoderms, placoderms and fossil elasmobranchs. Part 6, Hard tissues of Ordovician vertebrates. *Zoologica Scripta* 18:427–46.

Pridmore, P.A., R.E. Barwick, and R.S. Nicoll. 1997. Soft tissue anatomy and the affinities of conodonts. *Lethaia* 29:317–28.

Sansom, I.J., M.M. Smith, and M.P. Smith. 1996. Scales of thelodont and shark-like fishes from the Ordovician of Colorado. *Nature* 379:628–30.

Sansom, I.J., M.P. Smith, M.M. Smith, and P. Turner. 1997. *Astraspis*: The anatomy and histology of an Ordovician fish. *Palaeontology* 40:625–43.

Smith, M.P., I.J. Sansom, and J.E. Repetski. 1996. Histology of first fish. *Nature* 380:702–4.

Shu, D.G., S. Conway Morris, and X.L. Xhang. 1996. A *Pikaia*-like chordate from the Lower Cambrian of China. *Nature* (November):157–58.

Schultze, H.-P. 1996. Conodont histology: An indicator of vertebrate relationship? *Modern Geology* 20 (3):275–86.

Schultze, H.-P., and R. Cloutier (eds.). 1996. *Devonian Fishes and Plants of Miguasha, Quebec, Canada*. Munich: Pfeil.

Turner, S. 1985. Remarks on the early history of chondrichthyans, thelodonts, and some "higher elasmobranchs." AAP Hornibrook Symposium. *Recordings of the New Zealand Geological Survey* 9:93–95.

———. 1991. Monophyly and interrelationship of the Thelodonti. *In* M.-M. Chang, Y.-H. Liu, and G.R. Zhang (eds.), *Early Vertebrates and Related Problems of Evolutionary Biology: Symposium on Early Vertebrates, September 1987*. Beijing: Science Press.

———. 1994. Thelodont squamation. *Ichthyolith Issues* 13:12–15.

———. 1997. Sequence of Devonian thelodont scale assemblages in East Gondwana. *In* G. Klapper, M.A. Murphy, and J.A. Talent (eds.), *Paleozoic Sequence Stratigraphy, Biostratigraphy, and Biogeography: Studies in Honor of Dr. J. Granville ("Jess") Johnson*. Geological Society of America Special Paper, 321. Boulder, Colorado: Geological Society of America.

Turner, S., and W. Van der Brugghen. 1993. The Thelodonti, an important but enigmatic group of fishes. *Modern Geology* 18:125–40.

Wang, S.-T. 1993. Vertebrate biostratigraphy of the Middle Palaeozoic of China. *In* J.A. Long (ed.), *Palaeozoic Vertebrate Biostratigraphy and Biogeography*. London: Belhaven; Baltimore, Maryland: Johns Hopkins University Press, 1994.

Wilson, M.V.H., and M.W. Caldwell. 1993. New Silurian and Devonian fork-tailed thelodonts are jawless vertebrates with stomachs and deep bodies. *Nature* 361:442–44.

Young, G.C. 1981. Biogeography of Devonian vertebrates. *Alcheringa* 5:225–43.

———. 1991. The first armoured agnathan vertebrates from the Devonian of Australia. *In* M.-M. Chang, Y.-H. Liu, and G.R. Zhang (eds.), *Early Vertebrates and Related Problems of Evolutionary Biology: Symposium on Early Vertebrates, September 1987*. Beijing: Science Press.

———. 1997. Ordovician microvertebrate remains from the Amadeus Basin, central Australia. *Journal of Vertebrate Paleontology* 17:1–25.

Young, G.C., V.N. Karatajuté-Talimaa, and M.M. Smith. 1996. A possible Late Cambrian vertebrate from Australia. *Nature* 383:810–12.

Zimmer, C. 1996. Breathe before you bite. *Discover* 17 (3):34.

Further Reading

Gagnier, P.-Y. 1995. Ordovician vertebrates and Agnathan phylogeny. *In* M. Arsenault, H. Lelièvre, and P. Janvier (eds.), *Études sur les vertébrés inférieurs* (VIIᵉ Symposium international, Parc de Miguasha, Québec, 1991). *Bulletin du Muséum National d'Histoire Naturelle*, sectn. C, 4 ser., t. 17, 1995 (1–4), 1–38.

Janvier, P. 1996. *Early Vertebrates*. Oxford Monographs on Geology and Geophysics, 33. Oxford: Clarendon; New York: Oxford University Press.

Long, J.A. 1995. *The Rise of Fishes: 500 Million Years of Evolution*. Sydney: University of New South Wales Press; Baltimore, Maryland: Johns Hopkins University Press.

K

KOWALEVSKY, VLADIMIR (WOLDEMAR) ONUFRIEVICH

Russian, 1842–83

Impressed and greatly influenced by Darwin's work on evolution (he translated two books on the subject into Russian), Kowalevsky applied Darwinian ideas in his work on the osteology (structure and biology of bones) of fossil ungulates. Before him, zoologists and paleontologists generally had regarded animal species as static and unchanging. Over the ages, species that made up successive fossil faunas did show changes, but such changes were explained as the result of new creations. Kowalevsky introduced ideas of evolution, which held that animals change due to functional demands and that competition determines the extinction or survival of species.

According to Kowalevsky, a central tendency in the evolution of vertebrate animals is the reduction of the skeleton, especially of the limbs that function mainly as props, as in the ungulates. Developing, maintaining, and repairing parts (such as limbs) requires energy. If a part is not useful in an animal or for a function, the energy is wasted, dictating reduction. In ungulates, Kowalevsky believed, changes in limb structure would follow this principle. Limbs with only one (horses) or two fused (cattle, sheep) functional fingers or toes cost less to maintain than limbs with several (rhinoceroses, hippopotamus). Kowalevsky went on to trace the reduction of the limbs and to discuss their function in fossil ungulates, including the horse (1873a, 1873b, 1873–74, 1875, 1876).

On the basis of European finds of fossil horses, Kowalevsky believed horse evolution proceeded from *Palaeotherium* to *Anchitherium* and through *Hipparion* on to *Equus*. He showed that each stage was characterized by the reduction and functional modernization of the "feet," ankles, and lower legs and by changes in the teeth. He interpreted the dental changes (e.g., the increase in size of the premolars and increase in tooth height), as due to environmental demands—mainly to the spread of grassland. Grass mingled with sand was abrasive, causing increased tooth wear. The changes in shape and size was an adaptation that compensated for such wear.

Although the horse genera listed above do not represent a true ancestor-descendant line, as Kowalevsky believed, but instead side branches or stages of evolution (Simpson 1953), that does not detract from the brilliance of Kowalevsky's work. His careful observation and comparison enabled him to answer questions regarding relationships. In his hands, paleontology became a truly historical and evolutionary science.

Kowalevsky's evolutionary ideas differ from those of Darwin. Kowalevsky put less emphasis on environmental selection of hereditary variation (differential reproduction) as the basis for adaptation. Instead he stressed competition (differential survival) as the selective force in the reduction of limbs. Without considering the ecosystem of which each group is a part and to which each is adapted, he theorized, ungulates with unreduced fingers/ toes should be condemned to speedy extinction in the struggle for existence with more reduced groups. There is here a touch of finalism in Kowalevsky's work: he considered reduction of the ungulate limbs almost a necessity, a goal toward which evolution strives. Kowalevsky also believed that, because of the presence of man, evolution has now ceased in most animal groups, with the possible exception of the rodents, but he provided no support for these ideas.

ANN FORSTEN

Works Cited

Borisyak, A.A. 1928. V.O. Kovalevskii, ego zhizn i nauch nye trudy. *In Trudy Komissii po Istorii Znanaii.* Leningrad: ANSSSR.
Simpson, G.G. 1953. *The Major Features of Evolution.* New York: Columbia University Press.

Biography

Born in Vitebsk, Russia, October 1842. Educated in St. Petersburg as a lawyer; worked as a translator and book publisher; studied geology and paleontology in Germany, 1869–74; Ph.D., in Jena, Germany, 1872; M.S., 1875. Defended and promoted Darwinian approach; museum studies in France, Germany, and England resulted in a series of monographs on the osteology of fossil ungulates, 1873–76; docent, University of Moscow, 1881–83. Died in Moscow, 15/16 April 1883.

Major Publications

1873a. Sur l'*Anchitherium aurelianese* Cuv., et sur l'histoire paléontologique des chevaux. *Mémoires de l'Académie Impériale des Sciences St. Pétersbourg* 20 (5):1–73.

1873b. On the osteology of the Hyopotamidae. *Philosophical Transactions of the Royal Society of London* 163:19–94.

1873–74. Monographie der Gattung *Anthracotherium* Cuv. und Versuch einer natürlichen Classification der fossilen Hufthiere. *Palaeontographica*, new folio, 3 (22):131–346.

1875. Osteologya dvukh iskopaemykh vidov iz gruppy kopytnykh *Entelodon i Gelocus Aymardi*. *Izvestiya Imperatorskago obshchestva Lyubitelei Estestvoznaniya, Antropologii i Etnografii* 16 (1):1–62.

1876. Osteologie des Genus *Entelodon* Aym. *Palaeontographica*, new folio, 7 (22):415–50.

Further Reading

Borissiak, A. 1930. W. Kowalevsky, sein Leben und sein Werk. *Palaeobiologica* 3:131–256.

Franzen, J.L. 1984. Die Stammesgeschichte der Pferde in ihrer wissenschaftshistorischen Entwicklung. *Natur und Museum* 114 (6):149–62.

Strelnikov, I., and R. Hecker. 1968. Vladimir Kowalevsky's sources of ideas and their importance for his work and for Russian evolutionary palaeontology. *Lethaia* 1:219–29.

KUHN-SCHNYDER, EMIL

Swiss, 1905–1994

One of the most renowned European vertebrate paleontologists of the twentieth century was Emil Kuhn-Schnyder, whose name is most intimately connected to the Middle Triassic vertebrate fauna of the world-famous Fossillagerstätte of Monte San Giorgio in Tessin, Switzerland.

Early in his studies at Zurich, Kuhn-Schnyder became interested in fossil vertebrates through his teacher, the zoologist Karl Hescheler. Initially, his main field of research was the quaternary mammals of Switzerland, with which his Ph.D. dissertation (1932) was concerned. After finishing his studies, Kuhn-Schnyder worked as a school teacher in Bremgarten, publishing several important contributions on fossil mammals. Not until 1940 did Kuhn-Schnyder start his second career as a professional full-time paleontologist. In 1943 his teacher and friend Bernhard Peyer (who pioneered studies of the Triassic vertebrates of Monte San Giorgio) made Kuhn-Schnyder his assistant at the University Museum at Zurich in 1943. There Kuhn-Schnyder was mainly concerned with the Triassic reptiles, choosing the enigmatic thalattosaur *Askeptosaurus italicus,* an animal poorly understood at the time, as a topic for his habilitation (qualifying essay, published 1952). In 1955, following Peyer's footsteps, Kuhn-Schnyder rose to the position of extraordinary professor for vertebrate paleontology in Zurich.

Due to his extraordinary abilities as teacher and supervisor and his wide-reaching knowledge in all fields of zoology and paleontology, Kuhn-Schnyder became very influential in European vertebrate paleontology. He published two important textbooks, one on vertebrate paleontology (1953) and one on paleozoology (1984, with H. Rieber). The latter is still widely used at universities in all German-speaking countries and in 1986 was translated into English. The collecting campaigns in the Anisian/Ladinian Grenzbitumenzone, initiated by Bernhard Peyer in 1924, were successfully continued under Kuhn-Schnyder's direction. Painstaking documentation of stratigraphic (sequence and type of rock strata) and taphonomic (study of fossilization process) data and development of new preparation techniques under Kuhn-Schnyder's direction made this collection the best on Middle Triassic marine vertebrates in the world. His work made the Zurich Museum and Institute one of the world's centers for paleoichthyological and paleoherpetological research.

The main importance of Kuhn-Schnyder's work lies in his far-reaching and detailed morphological studies on various groups of Triassic reptiles. His three central points of interest were the relationships and evolution of early diapsids (a major group of amniotes), the phylogeny and taxonomy (evolutionary history and classification) of Triassic sauropterygians (plesiosaurs and their close relatives), and the morphology and origin of the placodonts (a group of bottom-dwelling, shellfish-eating, marine reptiles). His 1962 and 1967 papers on the skull of the archosauromorph *Macrocnemus* and on the Euryapsida-problem, in which he demonstrated the diapsid origin of the Sauropterygia, rank among his most important contributions to paleoherpetology.

Being concerned with phylogenetically enigmatic groups such as the placodonts, Kuhn-Schnyder always was interested in the general aspects of paleoherpetology and systematics (evolutionary relationships). Consequently, he published several review papers tracing the different, and often contradictory, phylogenetic ideas and systematic concepts of paleoherpetology through time (e.g., 1963, 1980). His contributions on pioneers of zoology and paleontology, such as Georges Cuvier (1969), Karl Ernst von Baer (1976), and Louis Agassiz (1973), are excellent examples of Kuhn-Schnyder's abilities as writer, historian, and scientist. His almost pedantic accuracy and scholarly approach, combined with the unusual mastery of the German language that characterizes these publications, are also found in his technical writings. The studies on the skulls of *Simosaurus* (1961) and *Cyamodus* (1965) are probably the most excellent examples of his abilities as morphologist. Despite concentrating his research program on Middle Triassic marine reptiles, Kuhn-Schnyder was far from being a narrowminded specialist. His more than 130 publications include numerous contributions on fossil fish and several other fossil reptile groups, such as crocodiles, turtles, and ichthyosaurs. And he never abandoned his initial interest in quaternary mammals.

Kuhn-Schnyder was not only a historian of nature but also of paleontology, and his extensive knowledge of mistakes of the past made him cautious of new ideas. He became a great skeptic in his later years and did not easily accept modern views on reptile phylogeny or new methods such as pattern cladistics. However, he himself was not immune to major misconceptions, such as his erroneous attempt to show that the nothosaurs (now recognized as a group of sauropterygians) arose directly from labyrinthodont amphibians (1962b). In losing the critical, humorous voice of Emil Kuhn-Schnyder, the field has lost one of the last living witnesses of the glorious paleontological pioneering days of the early twentieth century and one of the most thoughtful and experienced representatives of what Kuhn-Schnyder himself called the "most beautiful of all sciences."

MICHAEL W. MAISCH

Biography

Born in Zurich, Switzerland, 29 April 1905. Received Ph.D., Zurich University, 1932; habilitation (qualifying), Zurich University, 1947. Extraordinary professorship, Zurich University, 1955; directorship of the paleontological institute and museum, Zurich University, 1956; ordinary professorship, Zurich University, 1962. Excavations of Monte San Giorgio fossil vertebrates, 1950–68; monographic description of *Askeptosaurus*, 1952; reptile systematics; history of paleontology. Died in Zurich, Switzerland, 30 July 1994.

Major Publications

1952. *Askeptosaurus italicus* NOPCSA. *Schweizerische Paläontologische Abhandlungen* 69:1–73.
1953. *Geschichte der Wirbeltiere*. Basel: Schwabe.
1961. *Der Schädel von Simosaurus. Paläontologische Zeitschrift* 35:95–113.

1962a. Ein weiter Schädel von *macrocnemus bassanii* NOPCSA aus der anisischen Stufe der Trias des Monte San Giorgio (Kt. Tessin, Schweiz). *Paläontologische Zeitschrift* Festband H. Schmidt:110–33.
1962b. La position des nothosauridés dans le système des reptiles. *Problèmes actuals de paléontologie (Évolution des Vertébrés), CNRS Colloque International* 104:135–44.
1963. Wege der Reptiliensystematik. *Paläontologische Zeitschrift* 37:61–87.
1965. Der Typus-Schädel von *Cyamodus rostratus (Muenster 1839). Senckenbergiana lethaea* 46:257–89.
1967. Das Problem der Euryapsida. *Problèmes actuals de paléontologie (Évolution des Vertébrés), CNRS Colloque International* 163:336–48.
1969. Georges Cuvier 1769–1832. *Jahreshefte der Gesellschaft für Naturkunde in Württemberg* 124:65–105.
1973. Louis Agassiz als Paläontologe. *Denkschriften der Schweizerischen Naturforschenden Gesellschaft* 89:21–113.
1976. Karl Ernst Von Baer, Begründer der modernen Embryologie (1792–1876). *Acta Tielhardiana* 13:1–32.
1980. Observations on the temporal openings of reptilian skulls and the classification of reptiles. *In* L.L. Jacobs (ed.), *Aspects of Vertebrate History, Essays in Honour of Edwin H. Colbert*. Flagstaff: Museum of Northern Arizona Press.
1984. With H. Rieber. *Paläozoologie: Morphologie und Systematik der ausgestorben Tiere*. Stuttgart: Thieme.

Further Reading

Adam, K.-D. 1995. Emil Kuhn-Schnyder. *Jahreshefte der Gesellschaft für Naturkunde in Württemberg* 151:517–23.
Kuhn-Schnyder, E. 1974. Die Triasfauna der Tessiner Kalkalpen. *Neujahrsblatt der Naturforschenden Gessellschaft in Zürich* 176:1–119.
Rieber, H. 1994. Emil Kuhn-Schnyder. *Paläontologische Zeitschrift* 69:313–20.

KURTÉN, BJÖRN

Finnish, 1924–88

Kurtén was born in Vasa, Finland, a member of the Swedish-speaking minority of that country. Early in his life he developed an interest in writing and published his first novel in Swedish at the age of 17, to be followed by two more. After the war he studied zoology at the University of Helsinki, with special interests in paleontology and functional morphology. Since no formal training in vertebrate paleontology existed in Finland at the time, he received informal tutelage from Birger Bohlin in Uppsala, Sweden, and the famous Lagrelius collection of Chinese fossil mammals remained one of his research foci until his death. Kurtén received his Ph.D. from the University of Helsinki in 1954, and subsequently held a variety of positions. In 1972, he became Personal Professor of Paleontology at the University of Helsinki, a position he held until his death.

Right from the start of his research career, Björn Kurtén was a leading proponent of the "Modern Synthesis" as applied to paleontological material and issues. His thesis was entitled "On the Variation and Population Dynamics of Fossil and Recent Mammals" and its uncompromisingly actualistic view of fossil mammals and innovative use of methods derived from population

biology catapulted him to instant international recognition. During the 1950s he became a leader in, among other fields, the study of the age structure of fossil mammal populations, the study of the longevity of taxa (groups; singular, taxon) in geological time, and the study of microevolution and the history of mutations in fossil mammals. He also provided a seminal analysis of the functional morphology of the sabertooth jaw apparatus and was one of the first scholars to explore the significance of the (then) new theory of plate tectonics for vertebrate biogeography in the Phanerozoic. Just before his death, a collection of some of his older papers was published by Columbia University Press as *On Evolution and Fossil Mammals* (1988), in the foreword to which the late George Gaylord Simpson called him "a paleontologist's paleontologist."

In the 1960s Kurtén's main research focus shifted toward Pleistocene mammals, especially carnivores, and he also became a great compiler and organizer of information on Pleistocene mammals from other sources, both published and unpublished. During this time he published many taxonomic studies of a wide variety of carnivores in which he was very concerned to use a combination of morphological observation and statistical analysis to support his viewpoint. These and other studies laid the foundation for Kurtén's great compilations: *Pleistocene Mammals of Europe* (1968) and *Pleistocene Mammals of North America* (1980; with Elaine Anderson). These works collate an enormous amount of scattered data in their respective areas and have been and continue to be of great value to generations of paleontologists.

Kurtén was also a prolific popularizer of science, contributing numerous articles to newspapers and magazines, as well as writing a number of successful books, including *The Age of Mammals* (1972), *The Cave Bear Story* (1976), and *How to Deep-Freeze a Mammoth* (1986). In all, his popular science books have been translated into 14 languages. Late in life Kurtén also resurrected his career as a novelist, publishing two popular novels with Ice Age themes, *Dance of the Tiger* (1980) and *Singletusk* (1986), in which he used his professional knowledge of the Pleistocene world to full effect. As was the case with so much of his research work, he was ahead of his time in writing novels about the life and times of early humans.

LARS WERDELIN

Biography

Born in Vasa, Finland, 19 November 1924. Received Ph.D., University of Helsinki, 1954. Docent (lecturer) in paleontology, University of Helsinki, 1954–72; docent, University of Stockholm, 1959; visiting faculty member, University of Florida, 1963–64; visiting faculty member, Harvard University, 1970–71; personal professor of paleontology, University of Helsinki, 1972–88. Received Finnish state award for the popularization of science, 1969 and 1980; received UNESCO Kalinga Prize for the popularization of science, 1988. Died in Helsinki, Finland, 28 December 1988.

Major Publications

1953. On the variation and population dynamics of fossil and recent mammal populations. *Acta Zoologica Fennica* 76:1–122.

1966. *Pleistocene Mammals of Europe*. Helsinki: Societas Scientiarum Fennica; London: Weidenfeld and Nicholson, 1968; Chicago: Aldine, 1968.

1969. *Istiden*. Stockholm: Forum; as *The Ice Age*, New York: Putnam's, 1972; London: Hart-Davis, 1972.

1971. *The Age of Mammals*. New York: Columbia University Press; London: Weidenfeld and Nicholson.

1976. *The Cave Bear Story: The Life and Death of a Vanished Animal*. New York and Chichester: Columbia University Press.

1978. *Den svarta tigern*. Stockholm: Alba; as *Dance of the Tiger: A Novel of the Ice Age,* New York: Pantheon, 1980; London: Abacus, 1982.

1980. With E. Anderson. *Pleistocene Mammals of North America*. New York: Columbia University Press.

1981. *Hur man fryser in en mammut*. Stockholm: Alba; as *How to Deep-Freeze a Mammoth,* New York: Columbia University Press, 1986.

1984. *Mammutens rådare*. Stockholm: Alba; as *Singletusk: A Novel of the Ice Age,* New York: Pantheon, 1986.

1986. *Våra äldsta förfäder*. Stockholm: Liber; as *Our Earliest Ancestors,* New York: Columbia University Press, 1993.

1988a. *Before the Indians*. New York and Guilford: Columbia University Press.

1988b. *On Evolution and Fossil Mammals*. New York: Columbia University Press. [Includes "On the variation and population dynamics of fossil and recent mammal populations."]

1991. *De skuldlöse mördarna*. Stockholm: Alba; as *The Innocent Assassins: Biological Essays on Life in the Present and Distant Past,* New York: Columbia University Press, 1991.

Further Reading

Anderson, E. 1992. Björn Kurtén, an eminent paleotheriologist. *In* A. Forster, M. Fortelius, and L. Werdelin (eds.), *Björn Kurtén: A Memorial Volume*. Helsinki: Finnish Zoological Publishing Board.

Gould, S.J. 1980. Introduction to *Dance of the Tiger*. New York: Pantheon; London: Abacus, 1982.

Leikola, A. 1992. Björn Kurtén, scientist and writer. *In* A. Forster, M. Fortelius, and L. Werdelin (eds.), *Björn Kurtén: A Memorial Volume*. Helsinki: Finnish Zoological Publishing Board.

L

LAGOMORPHS

See Glires

LAPWORTH, CHARLES

English, 1842–1920

Charles Lapworth was a schoolmaster who trained himself to make detailed observations of successive layers in sedimentary rocks and to find and collect fossils from them. In the Southern Uplands of Scotland, these fossils were predominantly of single-celled organisms called graptolites, which were organized in colonies and existed during the Paleozoic era. In a series of papers, Lapworth drew and described graptolites, recording precisely the thickness of rocks in which they occurred. To correlate these discoveries with those from areas elsewhere in Britain, he also studied graptolites from south Wales, the Lake District, and Ireland. In 1879–80, Lapworth brought together this work in a masterly summary, in which he distinguished 20 zones (thicknesses of rocks containing a distinctive assemblage of graptolite species) in Ordovician and Silurian strata. Many of these zones were also found in Europe and North America, and one was found in Australia. These results, and Lapworth's graptolite collection, formed the basis for the great monograph (1901–18) by G.L. Elles and E.M.R. Wood, written under Lapworth's editorship. Most of Lapworth's zones, modified and refined, remain in use today.

When Lapworth began his work, graptolites were little understood, and their stratigraphical value was not appreciated. His observations provided a more exact understanding of their morphology (shape and structure), and he defined species much more precisely than before. Above all, he showed that these organisms could be used like fossil "clocks," enabling scholars to subdivide and correlate Ordovician and Silurian rocks in a manner quite as precise as that in which ammonites, a group of extinct, shelled animals, had been shown to do in Mesozoic rocks. Lapworth's experience made it quite clear to him that the older Paleozoic rocks (those laid down before the Devonian period) could be divided naturally into three portions of roughly equal duration, each portion with its distinctive fauna. He therefore proposed (1879) the Ordovician System of rocks to intervene between Sedgwick's Cambrian and Murchison's Silurian systems. By the early part of this century, this proposal had become generally acceptable.

Fundamental to Lapworth's fieldwork was (1) his accurate and detailed portrayal of the layers of rock and their attitude (the angle at which the layers lay), in vertical sections exposed along valleys in the Southern Uplands, and (2) the preparation of large-scale maps that traced the layers across the country. The quality of his work is shown in his classic memoir (1878) on the Moffat Series, which also contains vertical sections showing the color, texture, and rock type of individual layers. Prior to Lapworth's work, the Southern Uplands had been thought to be underlain by a continuous sequence of Paleozoic strata some 8 kilometers thick, arranged in alternating layers of black shale and sandstones, all inclined steeply downward to the north. The graptolites in the black shale had appeared to be much the same through the thick sequence, and apparently of little value in subdividing the rocks. Lapworth showed that there was only one sequence of black shale containing Ordovician and early Silurian graptolites, some 150 to 180 meters thick. This layer could be traced from west to east across the Uplands but was repeated many times from south to north because the rocks had undergone tight, concertina-like folding. Thus, graptolites could be used not only to distinguish zones in the sequence, but to reveal how the strata had been folded and frequently turned upside-down, owing to intense deformation.

As a result of his work, Lapworth pioneered the discrimination between types of graptolites and their use in recognizing zones which could be used to correlate sequences between continents. Also, he showed how these colonial animals grew and how the forms of the colonies, the numbers of branches, and the directions in which they grew changed with time. Lapworth was well aware of how thin the Ordovician sequence in the Moffat area was in comparison to the far thicker sequences of Ordovician rocks in other areas such as Wales. He ascribed the abundance of graptolites in black shale sequences to their being a type of plankton. The remains of such organisms would be covered over and ultimately entombed in fine-grained deposits typical of shale. Such deposits had accumulated slowly in areas away from land.

Lapworth's genius in shedding light upon hitherto intractable problems led to his rapid recognition. From being a school teacher in Scotland, he was appointed to be the first professor and head of the Geology Department in the new Mason College (1881), which later became the University of Birmingham, England. An inspiring and sympathetic teacher, Lapworth's audiences included mining and engineering students, as well as geologists. He ended his work in Scotland but continued mapping and collecting, adding much to knowledge of the Paleozoic rocks in the Birmingham area and Welsh borders. Notable was his discovery of the *Olenellus* fauna in Lower Cambrian rocks in Shropshire (1888). He died in Birmingham, on 13 March 1920.

H.B. WHITTINGTON

Biography

Born in Faringdon, Berkshire, on 20 September 1842. Received government certificate, teachers training college, Culham, Oxfordshire, 1864. Became school teacher, Galashiels, Southern Uplands, Scotland, 1864; professor and head of Geology Department, Mason College, 1881; fellow, Royal Society of London, 1888; recipient, Royal Medal, Royal Society, 1891; president, Geological Section, British Association, 1892; recipient, Wollaston Medal, Geological Society of London, 1899; president, Geological Society of London, 1902–4; member, Royal Coal Commission, 1902–5; recipient, Wilde Medal, Manchester Philosophical Society, 1905. Delineated graptolite zones in Ordovician and Silurian black shales and demonstrated their use in revealing the structure of the Southern Uplands, 1864–78; proposed Ordovician System, 1879; proposed 20 graptolite zones in Ordovician and Silurian rocks and revealed their value in intercontinental correlation, 1879–80; field work on Paleozoic rocks in the Birmingham area and Shropshire, discovered early Cambrian fauna, 1888; directed work on monograph of British graptolites, 1888. Died in Birmingham, 13 March 1920.

Major Publications

1878. The Moffat Series. *Quarterly Journal of the Geological Society of London* 34:240–346.

1879. On the tripartite classification of the Lower Palaeozoic Rocks. *Geological Magazine,* new ser., decade 2, 6:1–15.

1879–80. On the geographical distribution of the Rhabdophora. *Annals and Magazine of Natural History,* ser. 5, 3 (1879):245–57, 449–55; 4 (1879):333–41, 423–31; 5 (1880):45–62, 273–85, 359–69; 6 (1880):16–29, 185–207.

1882. The Girvan Succession. *Quarterly Journal of the Geological Society of London* 38:537–666.

1883. The secret of the Highlands. *Geological Magazine* Decade 2, 10:120–28, 193–99, 337–44.

1885. On the close of the Highland controversy. *Geological Magazine* Decade 3, 10:97–106.

1888. On the discovery of the *Olenellus* fauna in the Lower Cambrian rocks of Britain. *Geological Magazine,* new ser., decade 3,5:484–86.

1889. On the Ballantrae rocks of the south of Scotland and their place in the Upland Sequence. *Geological Magazine* Decade 3, 6:20–24, 59–69.

1894. With W.W. Watts. The geology of South Shropshire. *Proceedings of the Geologists' Association* 13:297–355.

1898. A sketch of the geology of the Birmingham district. *Proceedings of the Geologists' Association* 15:313–416.

1901–18. With G.L. Elles and E.M.R. Wood. *A Monograph of British Graptolites.* 5 vols. London: London Palaeontographical Society.

Further Reading

Watts, W.W. 1921. *The Geological Work of Charles Lapworth.* Proceedings of the Birmingham Natural History and Philosophical Society, 14, Supplement. Birmingham: Birmingham Natural History and Philosophical Society.

Fortey, R.A. 1993. Charles Lapworth and the biostratigraphic paradigm. *Journal of the Geological Society, London* 150:209–18.

LATERAL LINE SYSTEM

All fishes and many amphibians possess a series of specialized sense organs, the "lateral line system," distributed along the length of the body. The lateral line system is clearly an important sensory system to those animals that possess it, and the evolution of this system has resulted in a huge range of specializations and variety. This variation and the obvious importance of the lateral line system has made it a subject of intense study, yet the functions and evolutionary history of the system remain obscure. Typically, lateral line organs form complex arrays on the surface of the body and in pits or canals embedded within the deeper layers of the skin (Figure 1). Lateral line canals typically open to the exterior through "pores," and the morphology (shape and structure) of the canals and the spacing of these pores has been used widely in systematic studies and may also have functional importance. Although each group of extinct and extant (present-day) fishes and amphibians exhibit a wide range of variation in the distribution of these sensory arrays (Figure 2), the phylogenetic (evolutionary) and functional implications of this variation are still under investigation. Recent developmental, functional, and morphological studies have made it clear, however, that the lateral line system frequently consists of two distinct morphological and functional classes of sensory receptors: "mechanoreceptive neuromasts" (Figure 3A) and "electroreceptive ampullary organs" (Figure 3B).

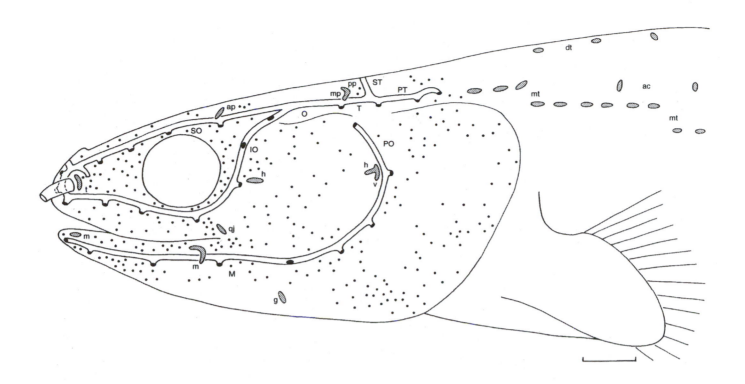

Figure 1. A line drawing of the lateral surface of the head and rostral trunk of a generalized living bony fish, a juvenile Senegal bichir *(Polypterus senegalus)*, illustrating the complex nature of the lateral line system of many extinct and living fishes and amphibians. Like many of these animals, *Polypterus* possesses mechanoreceptive neuromasts enclosed in cartilaginous or bony canals that open to the surface through pores *(black elipsoids)*. Superficial neuromasts are also found in short lines termed pit lines *(oval or ellipsoidal stippled areas* adjacent to or overlying the canals). While neuromasts generally occur in lines, electroreceptive ampullary organs occur as clusters of individual receptors located within the skin *(small black dots)*. Key: *ac*, accessory neuromast line; *ap*, anterior pit line; *dt*, dorsal trunk neuromast line; *g*, gular pit line; *h*, horizontal pit line; *IO*, infraorbital sensory canal; *M*, mandibular sensory canal; *m*, mandibular pit line; *mp*, middle pit line; *mt*, main trunk neuromast line; *O*, otic sensory canal; *pp*, posterior pit line; *PO*, preopercular sensory canal, *PT*, post-temporal sensory canal; *qj*, quadratojugal pit line; *SO*, supraorbital sensory canal; *ST*, supratemporal sensory canal; *t*, tectal pit line; *T*, temporal sensory canal; *v*, vertical pit line. Scale, *bar*, two millimeters. Drawing from T. Piotrowski and R.G. Northcutt. 1996. The cranial nerves of the Senegal bichir, *Polypterus senegalus* [Osteichthyes: Actinopterygii: Cladistia]. *Brain, Behavior and Evolution* 47:55– 102. Permission granted by Karger, Basel.

Neuromasts are multicellular organs composed of a centrally elongate strip of hair cells (Figure 3A), similar to those that occur within the sensory organs of the inner ear. The apical surface (that of the tip) of each hair cell within this strip consists of a ramp of short microvilli (fine cellular "fingers"; not illustrated in Figure 3A) and an elongate single cilium ("kinocilium"), which is a long, hair-like structure. The kinocilia of the hair cells are embedded in a gelatinous "cupula," probably secreted by the support cells. The cupula unifies the kinocilia of a neuromast, coupling their movements to the drag forces of water moving across the neuromast. Each hair cell is said to be a "polarized receptor," because bending of the microvilli toward the kinocilium depolarizes the hair cell, causing the cell to be excited, whereas bending in the opposite direction hyperpolarizes the hair cell and inhibits the cell. These changes in the resting activity of the hair cells are transmitted to sensory ganglion cells and from there on to the brain. Most of the hair cells within a neuromast form pairs, the kinocilia of which face in opposite directions and generally are aligned with the long axis of the sensory strips of the neuromasts.

Thus, neuromasts are polarized, responding in proportion only to the strength of the flow of the fluid in this axis of sensitivity. This polarization and the multiple linear arrays of neuromasts provides the animal with a complex representation of the pattern of water movements across its body surface.

The location of neuromasts, whether on the body surface or within a canal, has important mechanical effects on neuromast function. Recent theoretical (Kalmijn 1989) and experimental studies in teleosts (higher bony fishes) (Kroese and Schellart 1992; Montgomery et al. 1997) suggest that superficial neuromasts (those closest to the surface) are most sensitive to the velocity of local water flow and provide clues needed for fishes and amphibians to orient to water currents ("rheotaxis"). Canal neuromasts, on the other hand, are sensitive to local *changes* in velocity (e.g., accelerations), which accompany the movements of animals, allowing animals to locate prey or avoid predators. Canals also may have substantial filtering properties, and affect the frequency range and spatial resolution of the neuromasts within them. Scholars are only

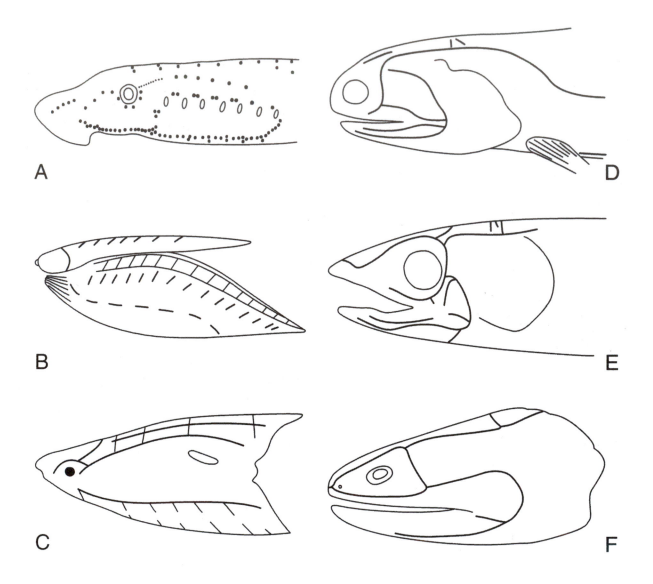

Figure 2. Line drawings of lateral views of the heads of a number of vertebrates illustrating some of the variation that occurs in the distribution of neuromast lines among different groups of *A,* extant, and *B–F,* extinct vertebrates. *A,* living jawless vertebrates such as lampreys possess only superficial lines of neuromasts *(solid dots). B,* some of the earliest jawless fishes, such as the Early Ordovician arandaspid *Sacabambaspis,* appear to have possessed neuromasts located in the floor of open grooves. *C,* other jawless fishes, such as *Poraspis,* probably had neuromasts situated in both open grooves and canals. Although it is very difficult to recognize identical neuromast lines across jawless fishes, their distribution becomes more conservative within jawed fishes. A number of homologous neuromast lines can be recognized in Devonian acanthodians like *D, Euthacanthus, E,* Devonian lungfishes such as *Dipterus,* and *F,* Devonian lobe-finned fishes, such as *Eusthenopteron.* Most of these neuromast lines can be homologized to lines found in modern bony fishes such as *Polypterus* (see Figure 1), but there are still difficulties in accurately identifying some homologous neuromast lines.

beginning to understand the functional implications of lateral line morphology, so it is too early to extend the conclusions drawn from a few teleosts to all other groups of fishes and amphibians. These results, however, do suggest that neuromast patterns and their orientations are highly adaptive.

The phylogenetic origin of neuromasts and the history of homologous groups of neuromasts are also only minimally understood. Hagfishes—probably the most distant relative (outgroup)

to all other vertebrates—do possess a lateral line system but do not possess distinct neuromasts. Of the two groups of living hagfishes, only the eptatretid hagfishes possess a small number of shallow trenches or grooves lined by a single class of flask-shaped receptor cells. These cells are more similar to the ciliated mechanoreceptive cells (those that respond to mechanical stimuli, such as changes in pressure) of other chordates than to the hair cells of neuromasts (Braun and Northcutt 1997). The distribution of the lateral line

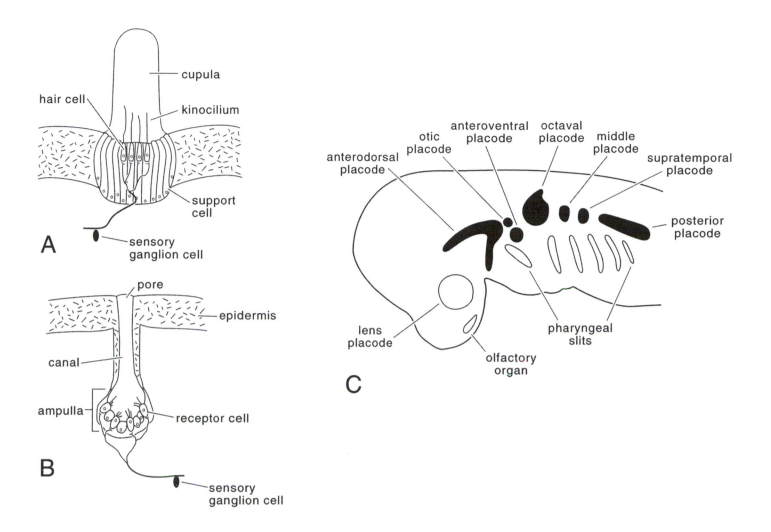

Figure 3. *A*, the mechanoreceptive neuromasts and *B*, the electroreceptive ampullary organs. *C*, in vertebrate embryos, both types of structures, along with the cranial nerves that innervate them, arise from a dorsolateral series of localized patches of ectoderm termed "placodes" (indicated in *black*). Most extant jawed fishes and many amphibians form a series of seven placodes on each side of the embryonic head. The eighth, or octaval, placode invaginates to form the inner ear and the octaval cranial nerve. Three additional dorsolateral placodes (the anterodorsal, anteroventral, and otic placodes, collectively called the "preotic" or "preoctaval placodes") give rise to the lateral line receptors on the rostral half of the head. The "anterodorsal placode" elongates to form the supraorbital and infraorbital lateral lines and generates the electroreceptors associated with these neuromast lines (see Figure 1). The "anteroventral placode" elongates to form the lateral lines located on the cheek and lower jaw (mandibular, oral, and preopercular neuromast lines) and their associated electroreceptors. The "otic placode" forms a short lateral line that frequently consists of only one or two neuromasts; they pass around the lateral surface of the inner ear. The remaining dorsolateral placodes located to the rear of the inner ear constitute a "postotic series" (middle, supratemporal, and posterior placodes). The middle and supratemporal placodes form the neuromast lines and associated electroreceptors on the caudal roof of the head, while the posterior placode migrates caudally onto the trunk to form two to three neuromast lines.

system within hagfishes and other features of their structure, however, indicate that the lateral line system of hagfishes may be degenerate and secondarily simplified from the ancestral condition. Lampreys—which appear to be the outgroup to all of the remaining extinct jawless fishes and jawed fishes (Janvier 1996)—do possess superficial lines of neuromasts (Figure 2A), but their neuromasts lack cupulae. If our current view of craniate phylogeny is valid, neuromasts must have arisen in the common ancestor of lampreys and other vertebrates, or earlier, in the ancestor of hagfishes and the vertebrates, and then were simplified or lost altogether in some hagfishes. The earliest neuromasts may have formed superficial lines as in living lampreys, or they may have been located in open grooves like those that occur in the Early Ordovician arandaspids (Gagnier 1993) such as *Sacabambaspis* (Figure 2B). The neuromasts in other jawless fishes, however, such as the osteostracan *Ateleaspis,* were located in both grooves and canals, and the neuromasts in some cyathaspidiform heterostracans, such as *Poraspis* (Figure 2C), were enclosed completely in canals (Janvier 1996). Hypotheses of the exact nature of the earliest lateral line system depend on assumptions about the phylogeny of the earliest fishes, but it is clear that a wide range of morphologies was present very early in vertebrate history.

The lateral lines of most extinct (Figures 2D–2F) and extant jawed vertebrates exhibit a more conservative (primitive) pattern of organization than those of extinct jawless fishes. Most groups of jawed fishes possess neuromasts organized into superficial pit lines and deep canals. In addition, some groups of jawed fishes, such as the extinct placoderms (fishes with an armored head and shoulders) and some extant cartilaginous fishes (e.g., sharks), exhibit large numbers of superficial or grooved neuromast lines as well as neuromasts enclosed in pits and canals. Although in the earliest lungfishes (Figure 2E) and in lobe-finned fishes such as *Eusthenopteron* (Figure 2F), as well as the earliest amphibians (Jarvik 1980, 1996), the dominant pattern appears to have been neuromasts enclosed in canals, most neuromast lines in the living lepidosirenid lungfishes occur in open grooves, and the neuromasts in living amphibians that possess these organs are always arrayed in superficial lines (Northcutt 1989, 1997). The reduction and/or loss of neuromasts within canals in lepidosirenid lungfishes and living amphibians strongly indicates that profound heterochronic changes (i.e., changes in developmental timing), involving the truncation of the ancestral pattern of lateral line development (Figure 4), have occurred independently in both living lungfishes and amphibians (Northcutt 1997).

Electroreceptive ampullary organs comprise the second distinct morphological and functional class of lateral line sensory receptors. "Electroreceptors" (Figure 3B) can be recognized in living cartilaginous and bony fishes, such as the chondrosteans (e.g., sturgeons), lungfishes, and *Latimeria* (the living coelacanth), as well as in some apodan (frogs) and urodele (salamander) amphibians (Northcutt 1986). Typically, these organs are restricted to the head. A single organ consists of a small pore leading into a canal; it passes into the dermis to end in a spherical sac termed an "ampulla" (Figure 3B). Like neuromasts, ampullae consist of support cells and hair cell–like receptors that may or may not possess kinocilia. While these receptors are sensitive to changes in temperature and mechanical distortions, they are most sensitive to low-frequency electric fields generated by biological and inanimate sources. Such low-frequency fields are generated by the muscular activities of small animals and by the movements of seawater through the Earth's magnetic field. A breathing flatfish, for instance, generates a voltage gradient of two microvolts per centimeter at a distance of five centimeters above their head. This weak field is clearly below the threshold of many marine fishes, some of whom are able to detect electric fields as weak as five nanovolts per centimeter (Kalmijn 1988). Due to the decreased conductance of fresh water, fresh water

fishes are not as sensitive, but are still able to detect fields as weak as one to five microvolts per centimeter.

In living fishes and amphibians, ampullary electroreceptors may occur as a few scattered single receptors, as in the genus (groups; plural, genera) bichirs, or they may form extensive fields of thousands, as in many sharks and chondrosteans such as the sturgeons and paddlefishes. *Latimeria,* the single living lobe-finned actinistian (coelacanth), possesses the most unique array of ampullary organs, the rostral organ. The rostral organ is a large medial (near the midline) cavity deep within the snout; the organ is lined with ampullary organs and is connected to the external environment by three pairs of canals (Millot and Anthony 1956; Bemis and Hetherington 1982).

A number of unanswered questions also plague our understanding of the phylogenetic origin and homology of electroreceptors. Hagfishes lack electroreceptors, but lampreys have them, although they differ from typical ampullary organs. Lamprey electroreceptors, traditionally termed "end buds," are small collections of goblet-shaped organs embedded within the epidermis rather than being housed in ampullae located deep within the dermis. In spite of these differences, the physiological properties and pattern of innervation of lamprey electroreceptors suggest that they are homologous to the electroreceptors of other vertebrates, not including the independently evolved electroreceptors of several orders of teleost bony fishes (see below, Ronan 1986; Northcutt 1986). Thus, it is likely that electroreceptors arose in the common ancestor of lampreys and other vertebrates.

At present, it is unclear which groups of extinct jawless or jawed fishes possessed electroreceptors. It is possible that many jawless groups possessed intraepidermal electroreceptors similar to living lampreys, as these electroreceptors would leave no trace in the fossil record. Clear evidence of ampullary organs, in the form of appropriately sized pores scattered on the head, or centered around the canals of the lateral line, is found only in ptyctodontid placoderms (Ørvig 1971), in early lobe-finned fishes such as *Eusthenopteron,* and the dipnoan *Dipterus* (Jarvik 1950; Bemis and Northcutt 1992). Among extant groups, all cartilaginous fishes, chondrosteans, lungfishes, *Latimeria,* and many apodan and anuran amphibians possess true ampullary organs. Given this distribution, it is likely that electroreception evolved early in vertebrate history, at least as early as the common ancestor of lampreys and gnathostomes (jawed fishes). True ampullary organs, however, may not have arisen until the dawn of the gnathostomes.

A pore-canal system, often regarded as related to electroreception, is more widespread, and has been advanced as evidence of electroreceptors (Thomson 1977; Northcutt and Gans 1983; Meinke 1987) in osteostracans (a class of jawed fishes), acanthodians (spiny sharks), and several groups of ancient sarcopterygians, including porolepiformes and lungfishes. All these fishes exhibit an extensive series of small pores that open onto the surface of the dermal bones of the head (Figure 5A) and the surface of the trunk scales. These pores form the superficial openings of flask-shaped cavities that are frequently interconnected by a complex series of horizontal canals (Figure 5B); these canals, in turn, may connect with the lateral line canals. The dentine that contains this pore-canal system is often referred to as cosmine.

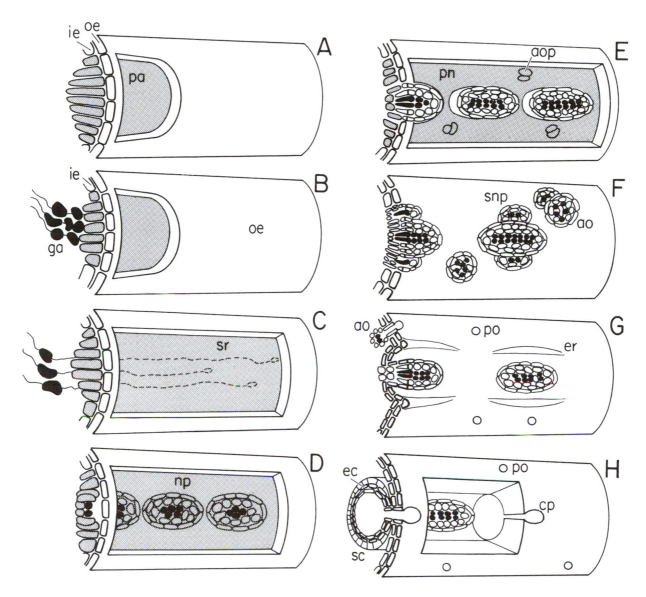

Figure 4. Schematic representation of sequential stages in the development of many lateral line placodes in jawed fishes and those of amphibians that retain primitive electroreceptive ampullary organs. *A*, placodes *(pa)* initially form as a result of the elongation of a localized patch of cells in the inner layer *(ie)* of the ectoderm. *B*, presumptive sensory ganglionic cells *(ga)* then migrate out of the placode and extend their axons toward the brain. *C*, by the time these axons reach and enter the brain, the placode begins to elongate or migrate to form a sensory ridge *(sr)* beneath the outer layer of the ectoderm *(oe)*. *D*, as the placode elongates, peripheral processes of the developing ganglion cells also keep pace with the elongating placode and may be responsible for the induction of the neuromasts primordia *(np)* that form within the central zone of the elongated sensory ridge. *E*, electroreceptive ampullary primorida *(aop)* subsequently form from the more lateral zones of the sensory ridge. *F*, neuromasts become exposed to the surface as superficial lines of sensory organs when the cells of the outer layer of the ectoderm *(oe)* retract from over the developing neuromast primordia. The initial neuromasts may give rise to secondary neuromasts *(snp)* which may remain adjacent to the initial (primary) neuromasts *(pn)* or may migrate some distance from their origin. At this same time or shortly later, the cells of the outer ectoderm also retract from over the ampullary organ primordia *(aop)*. These primordia may also give rise to secondary ampullary organs; these may form clusters adjacent to the neuromast lines, or they may become widely scattered over the head as in bichirs (Figure 1). *G*, following their origin, all ampullary organs invaginate into the underlying skin to form ampullary canals *(ao)*, which open to the surface as an ampullary pore *(po)*. *G–H*, in living amphibians, development terminates at this stage, but in most bony and cartilaginous fishes, many of the superficial lines of neuromasts subsequently are enclosed within canals *(ec, sc)* that open to the surface of the skin through pores *(cp)*. These canals may remain simple, or they may further develop into a pattern of secondary or even tertiary branching canals. In bony fishes, canals form as ectodermal ridges *(er)* parallel to the neuromasts and rise up and enclose the neuromasts within a primary canal. The epithelium of the canal *(ec)* appears to arise from placodal cells, but the bony or cartilaginous secondary connective tissues of the canals *(sc)* appear to arise from other embryonic tissues. Drawing from Northcutt et al. (1994). Copyright © 1994 John Wiley and Sons, Inc., reprinted by permission of John Wiley and Sons, Inc., and R. Glenn Northcutt.

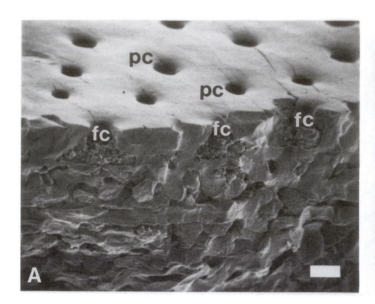
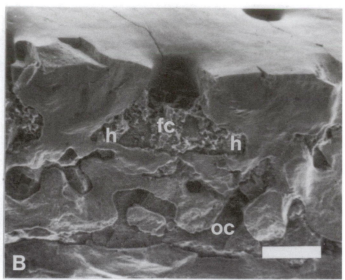

Figure 5. Scanning electron micrographs of the dermal surface of the snout of a Devonian lungfish *Dipterus valenciennesi*. A, the snout has been broken to show the relationship between the superficial pore canal openings *(pc)* and the deeper flask cavities *(fc)* that lie within the dermal exoskeleton. B, a view of the fractured surface at higher magnification shows that the flask cavity is interconnected by a series of horizontal *(h)* and oblique *(oc)* canals. The flask cavities have been interpreted as places to house ampullary organs (Thomson 1977), but are better interpreted as housing a vascular complex involved in the deposition of the surrounding mineralized tissues (Bemis and Northcutt 1992). Scale, *bar,* 100 micrometers. From Bemis and Northcutt (1992).

The pores of this system, however, are smaller in diameter than the ampullary pores of any living group of electroreceptive fishes. More importantly, the density of these pores in extinct fishes is several orders of magnitude higher than the density of ampullary pores reported for the most highly developed electroreceptive living fishes, such as the sturgeons and paddlefishes (Northcutt 1986). Furthermore, the histological (microscopic) organization of the snout of adult Australian lungfish, *Neoceratodus forsteri,* reveals a series of horizontal vascular plexuses and vertical capillary loops that closely resemble the size, structure, and density of the pore-canal system of extinct fishes. These characteristics suggest that this system was not an electrosensory system but was part of a complex cutaneous vasculature system that may have been involved in the deposition and remodeling of the mineralized exoskeleton (Bemis and Northcutt 1992).

In another riddle in the history of electroreception, ampullary organs appear to have been lost with the origin of neopterygian bony fishes, and the vast majority of living neopterygians (gars, bowfins, and teleosts) are not electroreceptive. The majority of the approximately 35 orders represented by some 23,000 species of teleost fishes, the most successful group of living fishes, have no trace of an electroreceptor system. Approximately five orders of teleosts, however, are electroreceptive, and appear to have independently re-evolved at least two different new functional classes of electroreceptors. Many of these electroreceptive teleosts are also electrogenic, capable of creating weak electric fields used for communication, courtship, and electrosensory imaging (in a manner analogous to sonar or echolocation).

This loss and re-evolution of electroreceptors constitutes one of the most fascinating puzzles in the evolution of vertebrate sensory systems. This puzzle and the many other unanswered questions regarding the origin and evolution of neuromast lines and the presence or absence of particular fields of electroreceptors will require re-examination of fossil material presently in museum collections. Also needed is the discovery and description of new material, using more modern methods of preparation and three-dimensional computer reconstructions, both of which were not available when much of the presently available museum material was described initially. Reinterpretation of the fossil material will also be greatly enhanced by the renaissance of the role of development in evolution. We now know that six placodes (Figure 3C) form the basic developmental unit for the formation of both electroreceptors and neuromasts, and of the cranial nerves that innervate these receptors. The critical developmental stages in the formation of neuromasts and primitive electroreceptors has been elucidated in jawed fishes (Figure 4), but an understanding of the generation of specific patterns of neuromast lines and which placodes generate electroreceptors in each vertebrate radiation remains to be elucidated. New studies on the genetic control of the development of the placodes and the extracellular matrix molecules that are involved in their elongation and/or migration will almost certainly provide critical insights into the staggering variation in this system that has occurred over the last 400 million years.

R. GLENN NORTHCUTT

See also Brain and Cranial Nerves; Hearing and Positional Sense; Sensory Capsules

Works Cited

Bemis, W.E., and T.E. Hetherington. 1982. The rostral organ of *Latimeria chalumnae:* Morphological evidence of an electroreceptive function. *Copeia* 2:467–71.

Bemis, W.E., and R.G. Northcutt. 1992. Skin and blood vessels of the snout of the Australian lungfish, *Neoceratodus forsteri* and their significance for interpreting the cosmine of Devonian lungfishes. *Acta Zoologica* 73:115–39.

Braun, C.B., and R.G. Northcutt. 1997. The lateral line system of hagfishes (Craniata: Myxinoidea). *Acta Zoologica* 78:247–68.

Gagnier, P.-Y. 1993. *Sacabambaspis janvieri,* Vertébré Ordovicien de Bolivie. Part 1, Analyse morphologique. *Annales de Paléontologie* 79:19–57.

Janvier, P. 1996. *Early Vertebrates.* Oxford: Clarendon; New York: Oxford University Press.

Jarvik, E. 1950. Middle Devonian vertebrates from Canning Land and Wegeners Halvø (East Greenland). Part 2, Crossopterygii. *Meddelser om Grønland* 96:1–132.

———. 1980. *Basic Structure and Evolution of Vertebrates.* Vol. 1. London and New York: Academic Press.

———. 1996. *The Devonian Tetrapod Ichthyostega.* Oslo and Boston: Scandinavian University Press.

Kalmijn, A.J. 1988. Detection of weak electric fields. *In* J. Atema, R.R. Fay, A.N. Popper, and W.N. Tavolga (eds.), *Sensory Biology of Aquatic Animals: Neurobiology and Evolution.* New York: Springer-Verlag.

———. 1989. Functional evolution of lateral line and inner ear sensory systems. *In* S. Coombs, P. Görner, and H. Münz (eds.), *The Mechanosensory Lateral Line.* New York: Springer-Verlag.

Kroese, A.B.A., and N.A.M. Schellart. 1992. Velocity-sensitive and acceleration-sensitive units in the trunk lateral line of the trout. *Neurophysiology* 68:2,212–21.

Meinke, D. 1987. Morphology and evolution of the dermal skeleton in lungfishes. *In* W.E. Bemis, W.W. Burggren, and N.E. Kemp (eds.), *The Biology and Evolution of Lungfishes.* New York: Alan Liss.

Millot, J., and J. Anthony. 1956. L'organe rostral de *Latimeria* (Crossoptérygien Coelacanthide). *Annals of Scientific Natural Zoology* 18:381–87.

Montgomery, J.C., C.F. Baker, and A.G. Carton. 1997. The lateral line can mediate rheotaxis in fish. *Nature* 389:960–63.

Northcutt, R.G., and C. Gans. 1983. The genesis of neural crest and epidermal placodes: A reinterpretation of vertebrate origins. *Quarterly Review of Biology* 58:1–28.

———. 1986. Electroreception in nonteleost bony fishes. *In* T.H. Bullock and W.F. Heiligenberg (eds.), *Electroreception.* New York: Wiley.

———. 1989. The phylogenetic distribution and innervation of craniate mechanoreceptive lateral lines. *In* S. Coombs, P. Görner, and H. Münz (eds.), *Mechanosensory Lateral Line: Neurobiology and Evolution.* New York: Springer-Verlag.

———. 1997. Evolution of gnathostome lateral line ontogenies. *Brain, Behavior and Evolution* 50:25–37.

Northcutt, R.G., K.C. Catania, and B.B. Criley. 1994. Development of lateral line organs in the axolotl. *Journal of Comparative Neurology* 340:480–514.

Ørvig, L. 1971. Comments on the lateral line system of some brachythoracid and ptyctodontid arthrodires. *Zoologica Scripta* 1:5–35.

Piotrowski, T., and R.G. Northcutt. 1996. The cranial nerves of the Senegal bichir, *Polypterus senegalus* [Osteichthyes: Actinopterygii: Cladistia]. *Brain, Behavior and Evolution* 47:55–102.

Ronan, M. 1986. Electroreception in Cyclostomes. *In* T.H. Bullock and W. Heiligenberg (eds.), *Electroreception.* New York: Wiley.

Thomson, K.S. 1975. On the biology of cosmine. *Bulletin of the Peabody Museum of Natural History* 40:1–59.

———. 1977. On the individual history of cosmine and possible electroreceptive function of the pore canal system in fossil fishes. *In* S.M. Andres, R.S. Miles, and A.D. Walker (eds.), *Problems in Vertebrate Evolution.* Linnean Society Symposium Series 4. London and New York: Academic Press.

Further Reading

Atema, J., R.R. Fay, A.N. Popper, and W.N. Tavolga (eds.). 1988. *Sensory Biology of Aquatic Animals.* New York: Springer-Verlag.

Bleckmann, H. 1994. *Reception of Hydrodynamic Stimuli in Aquatic and Semiaquatic Animals.* Stuttgart and New York: Fischer.

Bullock, T.H., and W. Heiligenberg (eds.). 1986. *Electroreception.* New York: Wiley.

Coombs, S., P. Görner, and H. Münz (eds.). 1989. *The Mechanosensory Lateral Line: Neurobiology and Evolution.* New York: Springer-Verlag.

New, J.G. 1997. The evolution of vertebrate electrosensory systems. *Brain, Behavior and Evolution* 50:244–52.

LEAKEY, LOUIS SEYMOUR BAZETT

Kenyan/British, 1903–72

Louis Leakey was born prematurely on 7 August 1903 at the Kabete Mission Station, Kenya, which consisted of a few tents and a mud-walled thatched house that was the home of the Reverend Harry Leakey and his wife Mary; the infant's survival was little short of a miracle. His childhood companions were mainly Kikuyu boys, and he soon absorbed their culture and language as well as acquiring skills in hunting and tracking and an abiding interest in wildlife and the environment. He became a collector of bird eggs and skins and stone tools, encouraged and inspired by the assistant curator of the museum in Nairobi, Arthur Loveridge. Leakey was initiated in the Kikuyu tribe and built himself a Kikuyu-style house in which he lived and stored his collections. By age 13 he had embarked on a study of the Stone Age in East Africa, which became his life work.

Leakey was educated by his parents and a series of governesses until, at 16, he entered his first proper school, Weymouth College in England, from which he gained entrance to Cambridge University in 1922 to study archaeology and anthropology. Following a football injury he took a year off in 1924 to act as adviser and assistant to William Cutler of the British Museum of Natural History in excavating dinosaur remains at Tendaguru in Tanganyika Territory (now Tanzania). There he learned from this expert the techniques of extracting and preserving fossil bones and developed an enthusiasm for paleontology. After returning to Cambridge, he spent the Christmas vacation visiting some of the principal museums in Europe and in Berlin he met Dr. Hans Reck, who had excavated at Tendaguru and who now told Leakey about the exciting potential of Oldoway (Olduvai) Gorge. Leakey earned his bachelor's degree with first class standing and immediately gathered funding for his high-sounding 1926 First East African Archaeological Expedition.

Many prehistoric skulls and skeletons were found as well as stone tools that proved the rich potential of East Africa, hitherto neglected. The animal bones and human skeletons were studied at the British Museum of Natural History by A. Tindall Hopwood, who later worked with Leakey in the field and studied other fossil collections. The stone tools were taken to St. John's College, where Leakey had a research fellowship, but in 1928 he organized another expedition that extended and reinforced his earlier studies. In 1929 he drove 3,000 miles to Johannesburg, on appalling roads, to outline his discoveries at the gathering of the British Association for the Advancement of Science, meeting many eminent scientists, several of whom were impressed enough for them to visit East Africa on their way back to England to see some of the new sites.

For his researches, Leakey was awarded his doctorate at Cambridge in 1930, and in the following year his first major book, *The Stone Age Cultures of Kenya Colony,* was published, to be followed five years later by the companion volume *The Stone Age Races of Kenya.* They formed the framework on which later research was built. In 1931 he organized his Third East African Archaeological Expedition and, accompanied by Hans Reck, explored Olduvai Gorge and revealed a treasure-house of stone tools and fossil remains. Leakey also explored the Kavirondo Gulf area on Lake Victoria and at Kanam and Kanjera found fossil human remains for which he claimed great antiquity, but unfortunately the dating proved somewhat controversial. He also explored the Miocene deposits on Rusinga Island, which became the focal point of much additional work in later years.

Back in Cambridge, he wrote a book entitled *Adam's Ancestors* and asked Mary Nicol to illustrate the stone tools with her superb drawings. He was immediately attracted to her, and in 1936 she became his second wife and close collaborator to the extent that their later roles in new discoveries were virtually inseparable. On the outbreak of the Second World War, they returned to Kenya, where Leakey's diverse talents were employed as head of the African section of the Special Branch of the Criminal Investigation Department (CID) in Nairobi, and he continued to be consulted as a handwriting expert until 1951. During periods of leave, he and Mary discovered the site of Olorgesailie, rich in Acheulean hand axes. They worked most evenings at the Coryndon Memorial Museum and in 1940, with the resignation of the curator, Leakey became honorary curator while continuing to work for the CID; in 1946 he became full-time curator. One of his earliest activities was to organize the First Pan-African Congress on Prehistory, which was held in Nairobi in 1947 and attended by leading prehistorians, geologists, and anthropologists from many countries. At this meeting, Wilfrid Le Gros Clark of Oxford announced his unstinting endorsement of the status of the South African fossil ape-men—the Australopithecinae—as truly

members of the hominid clan and not just aberrant apes. The conference set in motion an invaluable cycle of interchange of information and collaboration between different specialists and represented a great stride forward.

Louis and Mary were working at Rusinga in 1948 when Mary found in the 20-million-year-old beds an almost complete skull and lower jaw of Proconsul, then thought to be close to the branching point between ape and human lineages, and the discovery received great publicity. It still is one of the most complete skulls of a hominoid ever found and remains of great significance as the earliest member of the family that separated from the monkeys and was ancestral to both apes and man. Later another interesting early ape was found in 14-million-year-old beds at Fort Ternan, which Leakey named *Kenyapithecus wickeri.*

Although very busy running the museum, he and Mary spent as much time as they could at Olduvai Gorge, where stone tools were found throughout the 100-meter thickness of sediments and large numbers of fossils emerged over the years. Research funds were scarce until, in 1959, Mary came across some teeth that looked human, and, rousing Leakey from his sickbed at the camp, they carefully excavated from the lower layers of the sequence what proved to be the greater part of a hominid skull clearly allied to the ape-man of South Africa, *Australopithecus,* which was then not known outside that country. The large teeth and wide cheekbones led Leakey to call it "Nutcracker Man"; he named it *Zinjanthropus boisei* (*Zinj* being an old Arab name for the coast of East Africa) but the genus is now absorbed into *Australopithecus.* This sensational discovery was publicized widely and, after decades of work with little money, research funds soon were forthcoming. The additional funding made possible more extensive exploration and excavation. The lower jaw of a juvenile and pieces of its cranium and hand bones were found close to the same horizon as *Zinj,* and nearby was found an almost complete foot, the earliest hominid foot yet recorded. In 1961 came the astonishing news that a laboratory at the University of California had determined these lower deposits to be close to 1.75 million years old, almost three times as great as previous estimates. A little higher in the sequence was found a braincase so similar to specimens from Java that it clearly belonged to *Homo erectus,* with an estimated age of about 1.4 million years. The juvenile had a braincase larger than that of the adult *Zinj,* and in the next couple of years other specimens were found so that in 1964 these were placed in a new species, named *Homo habilis,* or handy man—the toolmaker—probably the earliest representatives of ancestral man. These discoveries of three different hominids within the Olduvai sequence, and their great antiquity, revolutionized the whole concept of human evolution.

Leakey was extremely interested in learning more about the behavior of primates and in 1958 set up the Tigoni Primate Research Centre not far from Nairobi, where captured monkeys could be studied. Jane Goodall came to see him, and in 1960, after studying primate behavior in England, she started her celebrated and productive long-term observation of the wild chimpanzees in the Gombe Stream Chimpanzee Reserve in Tanzania. Six years later Dian Fossey was recruited to study the mountain gorillas in the volcanic region on the borders of Rwanda and Zaire, where her work and life were ended by poachers. Shortly before his death, Leakey managed to secure funds to enable Birute Galdikas and her husband to begin a productive long-term study of the orangutans in Malaysia.

Although the excitement engendered by all the new discoveries was a great stimulus to him, Leakey took on far too many commitments and in 1961 resigned as curator of the museum, although remaining a trustee, and worked hard to get approval for the construction of a Centre for Prehistory and Paleontology on vacant space on the museum grounds. He was successful and in 1962 the new squat buildings were filled with the rapidly accumulating collections and Leakey moved into his new office as director. Soon the new Centre became the mecca for a succession of scientists anxious to study at first hand the valuable collections of stone tools, fossil animals, and, of course, the hominid remains. Leakey was an outstanding speaker and spent a great deal of time abroad giving lectures to raise funds for the Centre and for work in the field. His health suffered, and he endured several minor heart attacks. In January 1971, while he was on the coast at Malindi, he was attacked and stung by several hundred bees, almost dying from their toxins. He fell and was partially paralyzed as a result of a severe head injury; brain surgery later removed the clots from his brain and he resumed his hectic life. On 1 October 1972, he collapsed and died in London on the eve of another trip to the United States of America for fund raising. He received many honorary doctoral degrees, medals, and other awards during his intense and productive lifetime. After his death the Kenya authorities established the Louis Leakey Memorial Institute for African Prehistory to commemorate his immense contribution to knowledge of early man and his ancient culture.

H.B.S. COOKE

Biography

Born in Kabete, Kenya, 7 August 1903. Ph.D., St. John's College, Cambridge University, 1930. Research fellow, St. John's College, Cambridge University, 1930–35; honorary curator (1940–45) and curator (1945–61), Coryndon Memorial Museum, Nairobi, Kenya; founder (1947), general secretary (1947–51), and president (1955–59), Pan-African Congress on Prehistory; founder Tigoni Primate Research Centre, Kenya, 1958; founder and director, Centre for Prehistory and Paleontology, Nairobi, Kenya, 1962–72; honorary fellow, Cambridge University, 1966; fellow, British Academy; recipient, Royal Medal; trustee, National Parks of Kenya; trustee, Kenya Wild Life Society. Led many expeditions in Kenya, excavating Stone Age caves and open sites, particularly in Olduvai Gorge and on Rusinga Island; described many new species of fossil mammals and hominoids, including *Kenyapithecus wickeri*, *Australopithecus (Zinjanthropus) boisei,* and *Homo habilis.*

Major Publications

1931. *The Stone Age Cultures of Kenya Colony.* Cambridge: Cambridge University Press.
1934. *Adam's Ancestors: An Up-to-Date Outline of What is Known about the Origin of Man.* London: Methuen; 4th ed., 1953; New York, Harper and Row.
1935. *The Stone Age Races of Kenya.* London: Oxford University.
1936a. *Kenya: Contrasts and Problems.* London: Methuen Press; Cambridge, Massachusetts: Schenkman, 1966.
1936b. *Stone Age Africa: An Outline of Prehistory in Africa.* London: Oxford University Press.
1937. *White African.* London: Hodder and Stoughton; subtitled *An Early Biography,* Cambridge, Massachusetts: Schenkman, 1966.
1951a. *Olduvai Gorge: A Report of the Evolution of the Hand-Axe Cultures in Beds I-IV.* Cambridge: Cambridge University Press.
1951b. With W.E. Le Gros Clark. *The Miocene Hominoidea of East Africa.* London: British Museum (Natural History).
1952. *Mau Mau and the Kikuyu.* London: Methuen; New York: Day.
1959. A new fossil skull from Olduvai. *Nature* 184:491–93.
1964. With P.V. Tobias and J.R. Napier. A new species of the genus *Homo* from Olduvai Gorge. *Nature* 202:5–7.
1965. *Olduvai Gorge: 1951–1961.* Vol. 1, *A Preliminary Report on the Geology and Fauna.* Cambridge: Cambridge University Press.
1969a. *Animals of East Africa: The Wild Realm.* Washington, D.C.: National Geographic Society.
1969b. With V.M. Goodall. *Unveiling Man's Origins: Ten Decades of Thought about Human Evolution.* Cambridge, Massachusetts: Schenkman; London: Methuen, 1970.
1974. *By the Evidence: Memoirs, 1932–51.* New York: Harcourt Brace Jovanovich.

Further Reading

Cole, S. 1975. *Leakey's Luck.* London: Collins; New York: Harcourt Brace Jovanovich.
Isaac, G.Ll., and E.R. McCown (eds.). 1976. *Human Origins: Louis Leakey and the East African Evidence.* Menlo Park, California: Benjamin.
Morell, V. 1995. *Ancestral Passions: The Leakey Family and the Quest for Humankind's Beginnings.* New York and London: Simon and Schuster.

LEIDY, JOSEPH

American, 1823–91

Joseph Leidy generally is considered to be one of the founders of vertebrate paleontology in the United States. But he was a man of wide-ranging interests, and his contributions to paleontology are only a part of his scientific work, which also encompassed zoology, protistology (studies of single-celled organisms), parasitology (the study of parasites such as ringworm), and anatomy. He was trained as a physician but practiced medicine for only two years. Then he devoted himself to scientific research while teaching anatomy at the University of Pennsylvania, and, from 1871, natural history at Swarthmore College. Served by his excellent knowledge of anatomy, he soon became an authority in the field of vertebrate paleontology.

Since he was based in Philadelphia, Leidy was naturally interested in the fossils from the East Coast of the United States, but he soon became deeply involved in the study of the fossil vertebrates that explorers were collecting in the Western Territories. Although he published several papers on Paleozoic fishes, Leidy's main interests were in fossil reptiles and mammals. In the field of paleoherpetology (ancient reptiles), he described a number of plesiosaurs and mosasaurs (two large marine reptiles), turtles, and crocodilians from the Upper Cretaceous of the East Coast, notably in a large monograph published in 1865.

Leidy is mainly remembered, however, for being the first to have described dinosaur remains from North America. In 1856, he described a small collection of fossil vertebrates that F.V. Hayden collected during his exploration of the Judith River area in what is now Montana. On the basis of isolated teeth, Leidy erected several new genera (categories; singular, genus), four of which turned out to be dinosaurs: *Trachodon* (a hadrosaur), *Deinodon* (a tyrannosaur), *Troodon* (a troodontid), and *Palaeoscincus* (an ankylosaur). In 1858, he described a partial skeleton of a dinosaur from the Upper Cretaceous rock strata of Haddonfield, New Jersey, and named it *Hadrosaurus foulkii*. This was the most complete dinosaur skeleton known at the time, and Leidy concluded that it could adopt a bipedal stance, contrary to current restorations of dinosaurs at that time, which showed them as heavily built quadrupeds. Working with the sculptor Waterhouse Hawkins, who previously had produced the famous Crystal Palace dinosaurs under Richard Owen's supervision, Leidy restored the skeleton in a kangaroo-like posture. Leidy's new interpretation of the possible dinosaur posture was to have a lasting influence on dinosaur reconstructions.

In the 1850s and 1860s, Leidy was acknowledged as the leading authority in the field of vertebrate paleontology in the United States, so the abundant vertebrate fossils that exploring surveys found in the Western Territories were usually sent to him for study. This resulted in the publication of a first monograph on *The Ancient Fauna of Nebraska* in 1853, in which he described a number of new genera of mammals (notably oreodonts, which were woodland and grassland browsers), as well as large tortoises. In 1869, a larger monograph appeared, on *The Extinct Mammalian Fauna of Dakota and Nebraska,* in which Leidy described all kinds of Tertiary mammals, from carnivores to horses, titanotheres (very large rhinoceros-like animals), oreodonts, and proboscideans (large elephant-like mammals with long snouts). He also included a synopsis of the fossil mammals known from North America at that time. This book ranks as one of Leidy's major contributions to vertebrate paleontology.

During the 1870s, Leidy's access to fossil vertebrate specimens from the West became more difficult, largely because at that time a raging competition arose between two fossil hunters, E.D. Cope (who had studied anatomy under Leidy at the University of Pennsylvania) and O.C. Marsh. Both men were associated with some of the surveys and headed their own expeditions to the fossil localities of the West. Although Leidy had closer ties with Cope than with Marsh (he even joined one of Cope's expeditions to the West in 1872), he could not compete financially with his wealthy colleagues, and the increasingly bitter rivalry between Cope and Marsh was clearly not to his taste. It is often said that Leidy was so disgusted by the situation that he stopped doing research on fossil

vertebrates early in the 1870s, turning instead to the fields of protistology and parasitology, in which he made important discoveries. While it is true that his paleontological activity slowed after the publication of his 1873 monograph on fossil vertebrates from the Western Territories, Leidy continued to publish on fossil vertebrates, especially fossil mammals from the southeastern United States, until 1890, the year before he died.

Joseph Leidy was one of the last great naturalists, whose writings could encompass more or less all aspects of natural history, but he can also be considered as the first professional vertebrate paleontologist in the United States. Before him, research on fossil vertebrates had been carried out by gifted amateurs, whose professional avocations were not paleontological research. They were politicians (such as Thomas Jefferson), physicians (such as Richard Harlan or James Ellsworth De Kay), or artists (such as Rembrandt Peale). Leidy, active at a time when professional science was emerging, could afford to abandon his medical practice to devote all his energy to scientific research and education, both in paleontology and in the various domains of biological science in which he was interested. He was among the first paleontologists to describe fossil vertebrates from the Western Territories, and the collaboration he established with the Hayden survey set the pace for other paleontologists, among whom were Marsh and Cope. Eventually, he no longer could compete with his younger, wealthier, and more ambitious colleagues, but the quality and diversity of his work on fossil vertebrates gained him a lasting and important position in the history of American paleontology.

ERIC BUFFETAUT

Biography

Born in Philadelphia, Pennsylvania, 9 September 1823. Received M.D., University of Pennsylvania, 1844; appointed demonstrator of anatomy, Franklin Medical College, 1846; elected member (1848) and later president (1881–91), Academy of Natural Sciences of Philadelphia; appointed professor of anatomy, University of Pennsylvania, 1853; appointed professor of natural history, Swarthmore College, 1871; elected president, Wagner Free Institute of Science, 1885. Described *Poebrotherium wilsoni,* 1848; *Oreodon gracilis,* 1852; *Merychippus insignis,* 1856; *Palaeoscincus costatus, Trachodon mirabilis, Troodon formosus,* and *Deinodon horridus,* 1856; *Hadrosaurus foulkii,* 1858. Died in Philadelphia, 30 April 1891.

Major Publications

1853. *A Flora and Fauna within Living Animals.* Smithsonian Contributions to Knowledge, 5. Washington, D.C., Smithsonian Institution.
1854. *The Ancient Fauna of Nebraska; or, A Description of Remains of Extinct Mammalia and Chelonia, from the Mauvaises Terres of Nebraska.* Smithsonian Contributions to Knowledge, 6. Washington, D.C.: Smithsonian Institution.
1855. *A Memoir on the Extinct Sloth Tribe of North America.* Smithsonian Contributions to Knowledge, 7. Washington, D.C.: Smithsonian Institution.
1856. Notices of remains of extinct reptiles and fishes, discovered by Dr. F.V. Hayden in the Bad Lands of the Judith River, Nebraska

Territory. *Proceedings of the Academy of Natural Sciences of Philadelphia* 8:72–73.

1858. Remarks on *Hadrosaurus foulkii*, a new saurian from the Cretaceous of New Jersey. *Proceedings of the Academy of Natural Sciences of Philadelphia* 10:215–18.

1865. *Cretaceous Reptiles of the United States.* Smithsonian Contributions to Knowledge, 14. Washington, D.C.: Smithsonian Institution.

1869. *The Extinct Mammalian Fauna of Dakota and Nebraska, Including an Account of Some Allied Forms from Other Localities, Together with a Synopsis of Mammalian Remains of North America.* Journal of the Academy of Natural Sciences of Philadelphia, 2nd ser., 7. Philadelphia: Academy of Natural Sciences.

1873. *Contributions to the Extinct Vertebrate Fauna of the Western Territories.* Report of the United States Geological Survey of the Territories, 1. Washington, D.C.: U.S. Government Printing Office.

1879. *Fresh-Water Rhizopods of North America.* Report of the United States Geological Survey of the Territories, 1. Washington, D.C.: U.S. Government Printing Office.

Further Reading

Chapman, H.C. 1891. Memoir of Joseph Leidy, M.D., L.L.D. *Proceedings of the Academy of Natural Sciences of Philadelphia* (30 June):1–49.

Colbert, E.H. 1968. *Men and Dinosaurs.* New York: Dutton; London: Evans; 2nd ed., *The Great Dinosaur Hunters and Their Discoveries,* New York: Dover, 1984.

Howard, R.W. 1975. *The Dawnseekers.* New York: Harcourt Brace Jovanovich.

Lanham, U. 1973. *The Bone Hunters.* New York: Columbia University Press; rev. ed., New York and London: Constable, 1991.

Ritterbush, P.C. 1973. Leidy, Joseph. *In* C.C. Gillispie (ed.), *Dictionary of Scientific Biography.* Vol. 2, New York: Scribner's.

Spamer, E.E., E. Daeschler, and L.G. Vostreys-Shapiro. 1995. *A Study of Fossil Vertebrate Types in the Academy of Natural Sciences of Philadelphia: Taxonomic, Systematic and Historical Perspectives.* Academy of Natural Sciences of Philadelphia Special Publication, 16. Philadelphia: Academy of Natural Sciences.

LEPIDOSAUROMORPHS

Ever since S.W. Williston's (1917) classical study, reptile classification traditionally has been based on the pattern of fenestration (openings in the bone) of the temporal region of the skull. The primitive (anapsid) condition, with a complete bony roofing of the cheek region of the skull, characterizes the Anapsida, Paleozoic stem reptiles. The Diapsida are reptiles that show a single opening in the upper temporal region or two (upper and lower) openings between the bones of the temporal region. Although the presence, and pattern, of temporal fenestration has been considered an important character for reptile classification, the functional significance of temporal fenestration remains poorly understood. More recently, with the application of cladistic methods of classification, scholars have shifted their emphasis away from patterns of temporal fenestration and toward a host of additional characters, both cranial and postcranial, in the reconstruction of reptile phylogeny (evolutionary history).

The Diapsida can be divided into primitive representatives (stem group taxa), Late Paleozoic and Early Mesozoic fossils, and more derived (crown-group) taxa, such as modern crocodiles, lizards, amphisbaenians, snakes, and their fossil relatives. Indeed, crown-group diapsids, known as Sauria, comprise two distinctive evolutionary lineages (clades): the Archosauromorpha (including such diverse groups as crocodiles, pterosaurs, dinosaurs, and birds) on the one hand, and the Lepidosauromorpha (including lizards and snakes) on the other. This essay will review the diversity, evolutionary history, and biogeography of the Lepidosauromorpha.

Lepidosauromorpha

Lepidosauromorphs originally were defined as *"Sphenodon"* (the Tuatara), and squamates (lizards, amphisbaenians, and snakes) and all saurians sharing a more recent common ancestor with them than they do with crocodiles and birds (Gauthier et al. 1988).

Defined as such, the Lepidosauromorpha would include the Younginiformes, *Palaeagama, Saurosternon, Paliguana,* the Kuehneosauridae, Rhynchocephalia, and Squamata (Figure 1).

The Younginiformes include the poorly known stem-taxon *Acerosodontosaurus* (Currie 1980), the well-known genus *Youngina* (Figure 2A) from the Upper Permian of South Africa, and a number of aquatic forms (the tangasuaurids) from the Permo-Triassic of Madagascar. *Youngina* was a lightly built, long-limbed, lizardlike creature occupying semiarid environments (Figure 3A). A spectacular recent find documents the way that juvenile *Youngia* kept together in groups to protect themselves from adverse climatic conditions (Smith and Evans 1996), a behavior also observed in some of today's lizard species living in comparable environments (Shine 1994). The tangasaurids (*Hovasaurus, Kenyasaurus, Thadeosaurus,* and *Tangasaurus;* Currie 1981, 1982), preserved in large numbers and different sizes, provide an excellent model for studying growth and development (Caldwell 1994), as well as aquatic adaptations in early lepidosauromorphs (Figure 3B). Notable are the gastroliths (stomach stones) of *Hovasaurus* (Currie 1981), which, like some modern aquatic animals, such as crocodiles (Cott 1961), voluntarily ingested pebbles of various sizes to serve as ballast, in order to achieve negative buoyancy in diving.

More recent studies (Zanon 1990; Laurin 1991) of reptile phylogeny suggest, however, that Younginiformes belong outside the Sauria (lepidosaurs and archosaurs). In this arrangement, the Lepidosauriformes become the sister group of the Archosauromorpha (Figure 4). Similarly, the three genera *Palaeagama, Saurosternon,* and *Paliguana,* from the Permo-Triassic of South Africa, collectively referred to as "Paliguanidae" (Carroll 1975), are known from very incomplete specimens only, so their phylogenetic position within the Diapsida has remained a matter of debate.

On the other hand, cladistic analysis recently has shown that the Sauropterygia are lepidosauromorphs (Rieppel 1994).

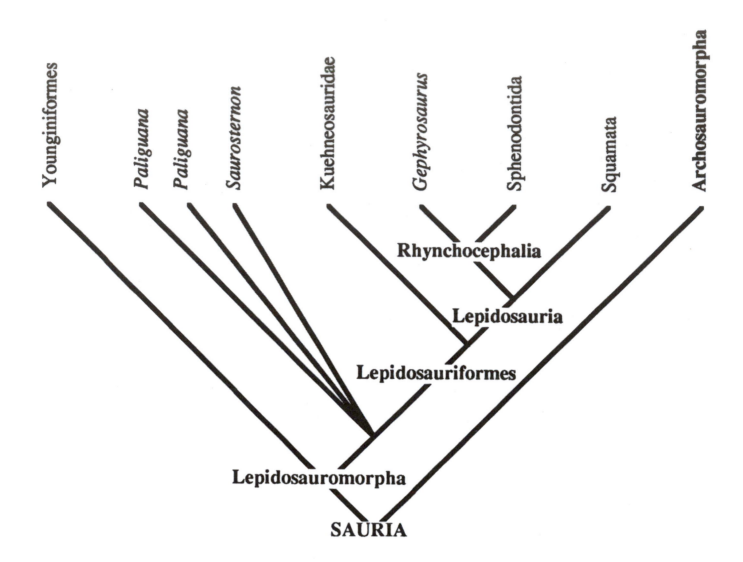

Figure 1. Conventional relationships of the Lepidosauromorpha. With the classification of Younginiformes outside the Sauria, the Lepidosauromorph clade collapses, and the Lepidosauriformes become the sister group of Archosauromorpha.

The Sauropterygia are a major group of secondarily marine reptiles (i.e., their ancestors were terrestrial) that invaded shallow interior continental seas and coastal habitats during the early Middle Triassic. Later, large pelagic (open ocean) forms evolved including the plesiosaurs, pliosaurs, and elasmosaurs of the Jurassic and Cretaceous.

An unexpected result of the cladistic analysis of Sauropterygia was to place turtles, universally accepted as the only surviving anapsids, as sister group of the Sauropterygia. Together, the two formed the sister group of the lepidosauriform clade (Rieppel 1994). This interpretation has been supported (Figure 4) by a global phylogenetic analysis of interrelationships among amniotes (tetrapods that lay shelled eggs, or whose ancestors did) (Rieppel and deBraga 1996). Again, the study shows turtles as the sister group of the lepidosauriform clade even after deleting the Sauropterygia from the analysis. Such disagreements show that reptile

phylogeny is still very much in flux, and that changes in our understanding are still to come.

Lepidosauriformes

The Lepidosauriformes have been defined as "*Sphenodon* and squamates and all organisms sharing a more recent common ancestry with them than they do with younginiforms" (Gauthier et al. 1988). As such, the Lepidosauriformes include the Kuehneosauridae, Rhynchocephalia, and Squamata.

The Kuehneosauridae contain a fascinating diversity of small, lizardlike creatures from the Upper Triassic, with greatly elongated ribs that support a wing membrane. Kuehneosaurs are known from three species, *Kuehneosuarus latus* (Robinson 1962) and *Kuehneosuchus latissimus* (Robinson 1962; see also Robinson 1967), both from the Upper Triassic of England, and *Icarosaurus siefkeri* (Colbert

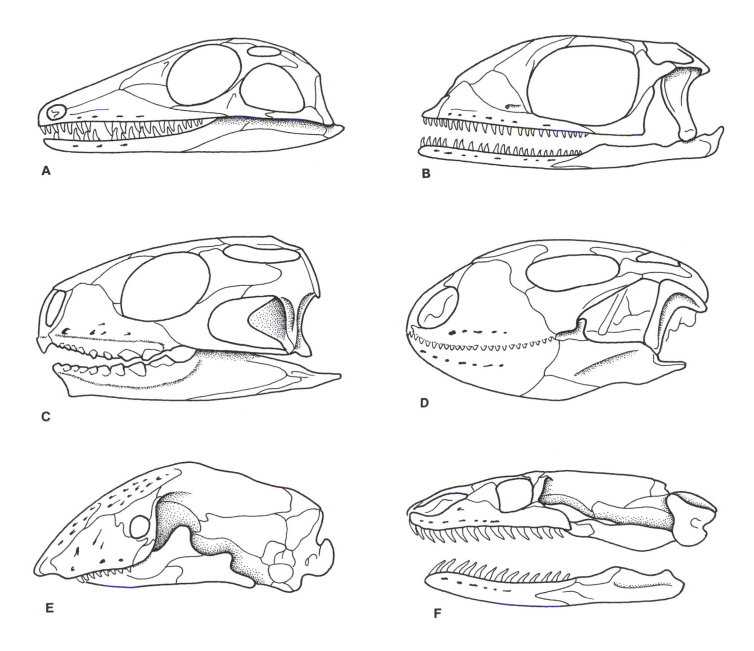

Figure 2. The skull of lepidosauromorph reptiles in left lateral view. *A*, the younginiform *Youngina capensis; B,* the kuehneosaur *Kuehneosaurus* sp.; *C,* the sphenodontian *Clevosaurus hudsoni; D,* the teiid *Macrocephalosaurus chulsanensis; E,* the amphisbaenian *Dyticonastis rensbergeri; F,* the snake *Dinilysia patagonica.* Redrawn, *A,* after Carroll (1951); *B,* after Colbert (1970); *C,* after Fraser (1988); *D,* after Sulimski (1975); *E,* after Berman (1976); *F,* after Frazzetta (1970).

1966, 1970) from New Jersey (Figure 5). Gliding by means of a wing membrane supported by drastically elongate ribs provides one of the most striking examples of convergent (independent) evolution among tetrapods, as it evolved independently in reptiles twice: first in the Upper Triassic kuehneosaurs and second in modern *Draco,* found in the indoaustralian archipelago. Convergence is indicated because there are a large number of detailed skeletal differences in these two groups. These are apparent in aspects of the flight apparatus including the number of thoracic (trunk) vertebrae and their articulation with the elongated ribs. In the resting position, the wing apparatus of the modern *Draco* is folded back along the body flanks.

It is extended for use in a gliding flight from the branch of one tree to the foot of another, both to escape and to search for food. The gliding apparatus probably functioned in the same way for the fossil kuehneosaurids.

Rhynchocephalia

The only surviving rhynchocephalian is the genus *Sphenodon,* including two species—*S. punctatus* and *S. guentheri* (Daugherty et al. 1990). Called "tautaras," these lizards are found only on isolated islands off the coast of New Zealand. Originally described

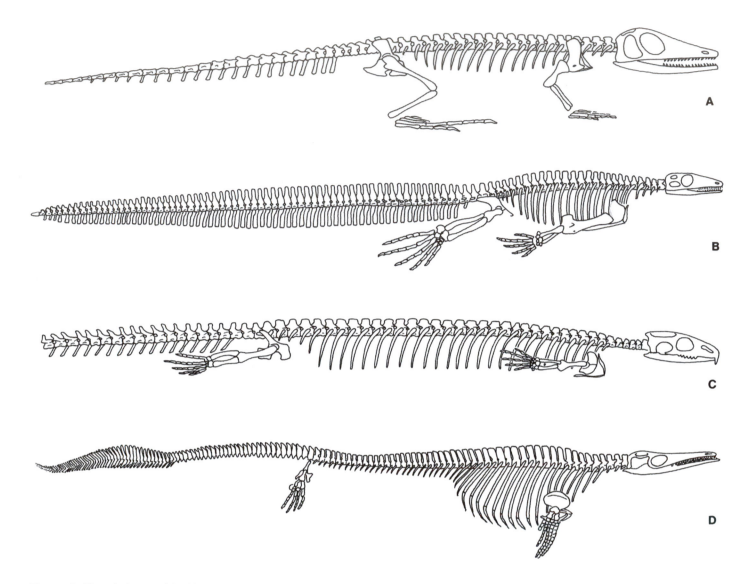

Figure 3. The skeleton of lepidosauromorph reptiles. *A*, the younginiform *Youngina capensis* (×0.7); *B*, the tangasaurid *Hovasaurus boulei* (×0.25); *C*, the pleurosaur *Palaeopleurosaurus posidoniae* (×1.2); *D*, the mosasaur *Plotosaurus* (×0.025). Redrawn, *A*, after Gow (1975); *B*, after Currie (1981); *C*, after Carroll (1985); *D*, after Russell (1967).

as an agamid lizard, its special status was recognized by A. Günther (1867) due to its complete lower temporal arch, which closes the bottom of the lower temporal fenestra. He thus formed the category of Rhynchocephalia, while nevertheless still advocating the inclusion of *Sphenodon* within the Squamata. As defined by J.A. Gauthier and colleagues (1988), the Rhynchocephalia includes *Gephyrosaurus* and its sister group, the Sphenodontida. Including Triassic rhynchosaurs (which are now known to be archosauromorphs) within the Rhynchocephalia (Owen 1859; Huxley 1869; Zittel 1887–90; Boulenger 1891) was shown to be unjustified (Carroll 1977).

Sphenodon—as indeed all sphenodontids—is characterized by a peculiar dentition (Figure 2C). The single row of teeth on the dentary bone of the lower jaw fits between two parallel rows of teeth in the upper jaw. The teeth of the inner row, which are attached to the palatine bone, are enlarged. Experimental investigation of jaw mechanics in *Sphenodon* revealed chewing movements that are unique among living reptiles: the lower jaw slides forward and back, creating a highly efficient sawlike action between the teeth of the upper and lower jaws (Gorniack et al. 1982). This specialized tooth arrangement is shared with *Gephyrosaurus*, a lepidosaur from the Lower Jurassic of Britain (Evans

1980, 1981). Recognition of a sister-group relationship between *Gephyrosaurus* and sphenodontians forced reinterpretation of a number of characters previously thought to be primitive for sphenodontians relative to squamates.

The teeth of sphenodontians are generally ankylosed (fused) directly to the outermost rim of the tooth-bearing bones, a condition known as "acrodonty." Tooth implantation in *Gephyrosaurus* is of the pleurodont type, in which the teeth are ankylosed to the internal sloping surface of the tooth-bearing bones. Pleurodont tooth implantation is also retained in the back of the upper jaw and dentary in *Diphydontosaurus,* a sphenodontian from the uppermost Triassic or lowermost Jurassic of Britain. This distribution of tooth implantation types suggests that the shift from pleurodonty to acrodonty occurred within sphenodontidans.

Sphenodon was recognized to be different from lizards—indeed a representative of an otherwise extinct group—because its lower temporal bar is complete, closing the lower temporal fenestra. This is another supposedly primitive feature that is universally lost in squamates. However, the lower temporal bar is incomplete in *Gephyrosaurus* (Evans 1980), as well as in some (perhaps juvenile) specimens of several other sphenodontid genera: *Diphydontosaurus* (Whiteside 1986), *Planocephalosaurus* from the Upper Triassic of Britain (Fraser 1982), *Clevosaurus* (Figure 2C) from the late Triassic of Britain (Fraser 1988), and in the marine sphenodontids *Palaeopleurosaurus* (Figure 3C) and pleurosaurs (Carroll 1985). This, together with information gleaned from the embryonic development of *Sphenodon* (Howes and Swinnerton 1901), suggests that in sphenodontids the complete lower temporal bar is a secondary development (Whiteside 1986). This conclusion is supported by the cladogram (evolutionary tree) that places kuehneosaurs (characterized by an incomplete lower temporal bar; Figure 2B) as sister group of the Lepidosauria. The redevelopment of a complete lower bar in sphenodontids may be correlated to their unique jaw movements, which may require stabilization of the jaw suspension.

The Sphenodontia are a moderately diversified group, undoubted representatives of which are first found in the Upper Triassic of England and Scotland (*Clevosaurus:* Robinson 1973; *Brachyrhinodon:* Fraser and Benton 1989). Another early sphenodontid is *Polysphenodon,* found in the middle Keuper (Upper Triassic) of Hoffmannsthal near Hannover (Fraser and Benton 1989). Indeed, sphenodontids quickly became distributed widely throughout the northern hemisphere at the end of the Triassic and during the Jurassic. An incomplete skull from the Upper Triassic (Norian) of Connecticut represents the first record of a sphenodontian of North America (Sues and Baird 1993). Three species of *Clevosaurus* date from the Late Triassic to Early Jurassic of southwestern China (Wu 1994). The first report of a sphenodontian in the southern hemisphere is *Clevosaurus,* from the Lower Jurassic of South Africa. The specimen appears to be most closely related to *Clevosaurus bairdi* from the Lower Jurassic of Nova Scotia (Sues et al. 1994) and *Clevosaurus mcgilli* from Lower Lufeng formation of Yunnan (Wu 1994). *Clevosaurus,* together with other terrestrial fauna, documents a surprising global uniformity of continental tetrapod communities during the early Jurassic, in spite of the fact that the fragmentation of Pangaea had already begun (Sues and Reisz 1995).

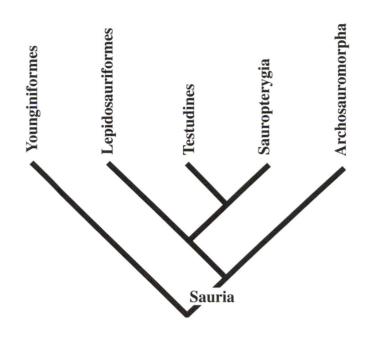

Figure 4. Lepidosauriform interrelationships as reconstructed in recent cladistic analyses.

Marine sphenodontids include the genera *Palaeopleurosaurus* (Figure 3C) from the Lower Jurassic of southwestern Germany and *Pleurosaurus* from the Upper Jurassic and Lower Cretaceous of Europe. *Palaeopleurosaurus* had a somewhat elongate trunk consisting of 37 vertebrae, a slightly elongate skull, a beaklike premaxilla at the front of the upper jaw (typical of sphenodontians of that time), and well-developed limbs. *Palaeopleurosaurus* had a body plan that is intermediate between the more terrestrial sphenodontids and the highly derived *Pleurosaurus.* This animal had an even more elongate trunk with 57 vertebrae, a long tail, reduced limbs (especially forelimbs) in adaptation to eel-like swimming, a very elongate skull with a pointed snout, and retracted external nasal openings. Derived from terrestrial sphenodontids, pleurosaurs fall within the sphenodontian group. However, their precise position remains a matter of debate—should they be placed with derived (specialized) sphenodontids, based on a narrow, crested rear skull roof *Palaeopleurosaurus* (Fraser and Benton 1989; Sues et al. 1994), or nearer the base of the sphenodontian tree (Wu 1994)?

Indeed, general phyletic resolution among crown-group sphenodontids remains a matter of debate, in part because of different interpretations of anatomical characters (Sues et al. 1994). The most completely resolved hypothesis for rhynchocephalian interrelationships (Figure 6) was developed by X.-C. Wu (1994), whose arrangement was recently corroborated by V.-H. Reynoso (1996).

Squamata

The Squamata is a diverse group of reptiles distributed worldwide, including the extant "lizards," amphisbaenians, and snakes. In contrast to all other extant reptile groups, the Squamata (with approximately 3,000 species of lizards and 2,500 species of snakes)

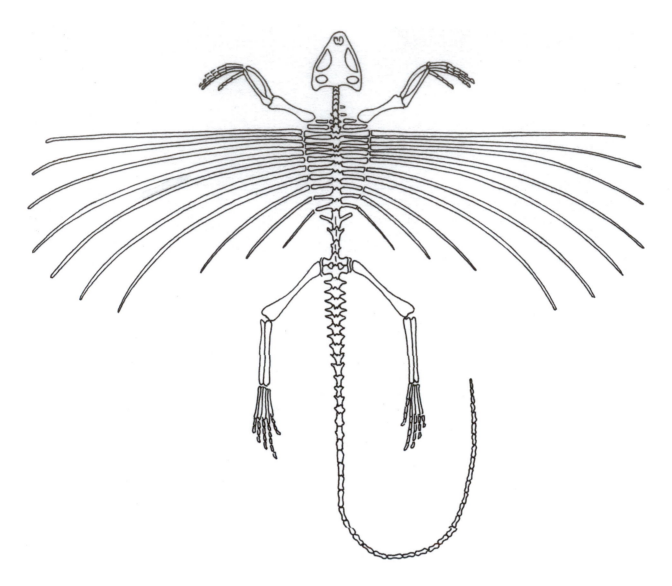

Figure 5. The skeleton of the kuehneosaur *Icarosaurus siefkeri* (×1). Redrawn, after Colbert (1970).

are at the peak of their evolution and diversity in modern biotas. The group's evolutionary success may be related to the adaptability of their system of movement and structural modifications in ways of eating. Starting from a generalized tetrapod pattern, lizard diversity covers body plans from highly arboreal chameleons with opposable digits, to occasionally bipedal agamids or iguanids, to all stages of reduced limbs and elongate bodies of fossorial (burrowing) forms. The skulls of all squamates have lost the lower temporal arch, freeing the lower end of the quadrate bone from which the lower jaw is suspended (Figure 7). A joint develops at the upper edge of the quadrate, so the lower end of the quadrate moves forward when the jaw opens, backward when the jaw closes. This movement, called "streptostyly," appears to increase the amount of force applied by the jaw-closing muscles (Rieppel 1978) and may be correlated with additional complex movements in the lizard skull known as "amphikinesis," which improved the mechanical grip of the jaws on prey (Frazzetta 1962, 1986).

Burrowing lizards retain streptostyly, but amphikinesis tends to get lost because of a consolidation of the skull. The highest degree of consolidation is observed in the amphisbaenians, limbless burrowing squamates in which the skull is transformed into a rigid, sometimes even chisel- or shovel-shaped tunneling device (Gans 1960, 1974; Figure 2E).

Snakes, in general, have an elongate body without limbs, which may be a superior means of movement in complex (cluttered) habitats (Goldspink 1977). Again, the snake skull is highly modified as compared to generalized lizards: both upper and lower temporal arches are lost, and the skull is consolidated into a solid, closed braincase from which both the snout (prokinesis) and the jaws (streptostyly) are movably suspended. Because a solid tie is lost between the two halves of the upper jaw, the two sides of the upper jaw can move independently. Alternate movements of the upper jaws, generated by muscles that extend and retract them, result in a "pterygoid walk," a successive shifting of the jaws across the surface of a previously killed prey item. Muscles that control the pterygoid walk arise from the undersurface of the braincase and insert into bones of the palate. Loosely connected and independently mobile halves of both the upper and lower jaw allow at least advanced snakes (macrostomatan) (Rieppel 1988) to swallow prey with a diameter much larger than the diameter of the snake's head.

Dealing with the Squamata as a strictly monophyletic group (a group comprising the ancestor and all of its descendants) raises some problems with respect to the common use of the term "lizards." Commonly known as small- to medium-sized tetrapod squamates (rarely reaching large body size, such as the Komodo dragon, *Varanus comodoensis*), the lizards divide into four major clades: the Iguania (iguanas, agamids, and chameleons), the Gekkota (geckos and pygopodids), the Scincomorpha, or skinks (xantusiids, lacertids, teiids, cordyloids, and scincoids), and the Anguimorpha (anguioids including anguids, anniellids, xenosaurids, and varanoids, including helodermatids and varanids). The non-iguanian clades (Gekkota, Scincomorpha, and Anguimorpha) are grouped together as Scleroglossa (with Iguania as their sister group); the Scincomorpha and Anguimorpha together form the Autarchoglossa, a subgroup of the Scleroglossa (Figure 8). The Dibamidae is a family of highly specialized, fossorial, limbless lizards (two genera, *Dibamus* and *Anelytropsis*) that are difficult to place within lizards. Most authors agree that dibamids are to be placed within the Scleroglossa (Estes et al. 1988), perhaps close to the Scincomorpha.

Amphisbaenians are essentially limbless lizards with a highly specialized anatomy, particularly in the skull, an adaptation to their permanently burrowing mode of life. Although it is beyond doubt that the Amphisbaenia share a common ancestry with all these groups (monophyly), the relationship of amphisbaenians to lizards remains ambiguous. Over time, amphisbaenians have been included within "lizards" (related to scincomorphs, gekkotans, and dibamids), or they have been considered as sister group of "lizards" as opposed to snakes, or as sister group of snakes as opposed to lizards (see Rage 1992). The most recent analysis, based on molecular (mitochondrial and ribosomal DNA) and morphological data, places amphisbaenians as the sister group of a clade composed of snakes and dibamids. All three define a larger clade whose sister taxon is the Scleroglossa (Reeder 1995). The Iguania remain the sister group to all other squamates.

The relationships of snakes are even more controversial. Again, the monophyly of Serpentes is beyond doubt, but their relationships to lizards continue to be debated. Based on the fossil record and on skeletal anatomy, snakes have traditionally been related to varanoid lizards in particular their Mesozoic marine relatives such as dolichosaurs and aigialosaurs (Cope 1869; McDowell and Bogert 1954; Rieppel 1988). Specifically, these groups share an elongate body, reduced limb size, and important features of the cranial anatomy, such as a hinge joint in the lower jaw. The notion that snakes derive from Cretaceous marine varanoids has been reinforced by the discovery of snake-like fossils *(Pachyrhachis)* in the lower Cenomanian of Ein Jabrud, Israel (Haas 1979, 1980a, 1980b). R.L. Carroll (1988) considered the Ein Jabrud fossils almost ideal intermediates between dolichosaurs and snakes (see also Caldwell and Lee 1997).

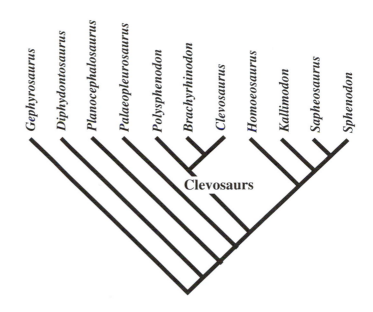

Figure 6. Cladogram for sphenodontian interrelationships of Wu (1994). See Reynoso (1996) for corroboration of this cladogram.

However, some of the sensory systems—such as the optic system (Walls 1940) and the associated central nervous system (Senn and Northcutt 1973)—point toward a relationship between snakes and fossorial lizards (Bellairs and Underwood 1951). That would also explain some fundamental structural changes in snake skeletal morphology (Rieppel 1988). Accordingly, snakes have been classified with fossorial gekkotans (Underwood 1957), fossorial scincomorphs (Brock 1941; Senn and Northcutt 1973), or amphisbaenians (Rage 1982). The most comprehensive analysis of snake relationships to date is that of T.W. Reeder (1995), based on morphological and molecular data. Separate analysis of the molecular data placed snakes as sister group to varanids; separate analysis of the morphological data placed snakes as sister group of amphisbaenids. The analysis of the combined data set resulted in seeing snakes and dibamids as one group, relating that group to amphisbaenians, and seeing this combination as the sister group of scleroglossan (non-iguanian) lizards. With these phylogenetic relationships, lizards are only monophyletic if they include amphisbaenians and snakes. Hence, the term "lizards" becomes synonymous with Squamata (Figure 8).

Owing to their predominantly terrestrial habits and their often fragile skeletons, the fossil record of the Squamata is remarkably poor. Although the sister group relationship with rhynchocephalians indicates that squamates must go back at least to the early Upper Triassic, the first unambiguous squamate fossils come from the Middle Jurassic of Britain. They include jaw elements of the scincomorph *Paramacellodus* (Waldman and Evans 1994) and scattered skeletal remains of the anguimorph *Parviraptor* (Evans 1994a). By the Upper Jurassic, at least three of the four major groups of lizards (the Scincomorpha, Anguimorpha, and Gekkota) are found in Europe, Kazakhstan, China, and the United States. Notable is a gap in the fossil record of lizards in the

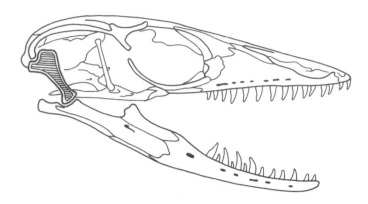

Figure 7. The skull of a monitor lizard *(Varanus salvator)* showing the movably suspended (streptostylic) quadrate bone (hatched).

Lower Cretaceous. Interestingly, the lizard group judged most plesiomorphic (primitive) on the basis of skeletal anatomy—the Iguana—does not appear in these early fossil assemblages. The first unequivocal iguanian fossils are *Pristiguana* from the Late Cretaceous of South America (Estes and Price 1973) and iguanids and agamids from the upper Cretaceous of Mongolia (Borsuk-Bialynicka and Moody 1984; Kequin and Lianhai 1995). The supposed iguanian *Euposaurus* (Cocude-Michel 1963) from the Late Jurassic of France was later shown to be based on a juvenile sphenodontian fossil and on an indistinct squamate that preserved no evidence of iguanian affinities (Evans 1994b). The late appearance of unequivocal iguanians in the fossil record is a remarkable mismatch of stratigraphic distribution (distribution in the rock strata) and the phylogenetic position of the Iguania as the first major offshoot in squamate phylogeny. By the Early Cenozoic, however all major extant iguanid groups were diversified (Estes 1983a, 1983b). The chances for arboreal lizards to get fossilized are naturally small, but spectacular fossil chameleons are known from the Miocene of Kenya, with one specimen having its skull and parts of its skin cast in calcite.

The famous Upper Jurassic lithographic limestone of Solnhofen in Bavaria (Germany), which yielded *Archaeopteryx,* also was believed to have yielded a lizard assemblage dominated by the earliest gekkotans (Hoffstetter 1964). Recent revisions of the fauna (Evans 1993, 1994c) consider gekkotan affinities possible for *Eichstaettisaurus,* but not for *Bavarisaurus,* an autarchoglossan lizard. The earliest unequivocal gekkotan is *Hoburogecko* from the late Lower Cretaceous of Mongolia (Alifanov 1989). Fossil egg shells from the Lower Cretaceous of the Cuenca Province, Spain, share the gekkonid microstructure (Kohring 1991).

The Scincomorpha are the dominant fauna in early lizard assemblages. Early scincomorphs include *Sharovisaurus* from the Kimmeridgian of Kazakhstan (Hecht and Hecht 1984) and *Mimbobecklesisaurus* from the Upper Jurassic of China (Li 1985). The most successful and widespread group is the cordyloid paramacellodids, characterized (as are modern cordylids, or skinks) by sturdy dermal armor composed of small rectangular osteoscutes (embedded bony scales). Paramacellodids are known from the Jurassic of

England, Spain, and North America. Teiids go back to the Upper Cretaceous of North America and Central Asia (Figure 2D); lacertids first appear in the Paleocene of Europe (Estes 1983a, 1983b). In spite of their current abundance and cosmopolitan distribution, the fossil record of scincoids is surprisingly poor. An interesting pairing of fossil lizards was recently described from the Lower Cretaceous of Morocco, comprising a paramacellodid along with a miniaturized, fossorial scincomorph, comparable to acontine skinks or dibamids (Broschinski and Sigogneau-Russell 1996).

The Anguimorpha have a very rich Late Cretaceous and Early Cenozoic fossil record throughout the Northern Hemisphere and are present (but less frequently than scincomorphs) in most early lizard assemblages. The Anguimorpha subdivide into two clades, Anguioidea and Varanoidea. This dichotomy may go back to the Middle Jurassic, as indicated by the description of *Parviraptor* from the Jurassic and Early Cretaceous of Britain (Evans 1994a). *Dorsetisaurus* is widespread in the Upper Jurassic of Portugal, Britain, and North America and appears to be more closely related to anguids than to xenosaurids, indicating that these two lineages may have split before the Late Jurassic (Estes 1983b). An extensive Early Cenozoic radiation of angioids is represented by the omnivorous glyptosaurs, known from North America and Europe, with a possible specimen in the Canadian Arctic Archipelago (Estes 1983a, 1983b). Glyptosaurs are characterized by a heavy armor composed of thick osteoscutes that lay just below thin epidermal scales (Figure 9). As a consequence, glyptosaurs fossilize very well, often as exquisite specimens.

Necrosaurs are a group of extinct varanoids. Fossils date from the Upper Cretaceous of Central Asia (Mongolia), from the Late Cretaceous and Early Cenozoic of North America, and from the Early Cenozoic of Europe. Helodermatids (e.g., gila monster) may date back to the North American Upper Cretaceous (Estes 1964), whereas varanids achieved a wide distribution by the Late Cretaceous (North America and central Asia) and Early Cenozoic (Europe). Most notable is a diverse and widespread group of marine squamates that existed in the upper Cretaceous, the Mosasauroidea. Usually classified with the Varanoidea, there is some evidence that the observed similarities might be a result of convergent evolution (J. Gauthier, quoted in Estes 1983b). Mosasauroids might, in fact, be the sister group of Scleroglossa. Mosasauroids can be divided into primitive stem groups from the Cenomanian-Turonian, and advanced groups from the Upper Turonian through to Maastrichtian. Primitive mosasauroids include aigialosaurs, dolichosaurs, and related forms that inhabited coastal marine habitats and interior (epicontinental) seas. Advanced groups, the mosasaurs proper, enjoyed a global distribution during the Upper Cretaceous. They were completely aquatic, their limbs transformed into paddles (Figure 3D).

Nearly 20 genera of mosasaurs are recognized. Dinosaurs among "lizards," some mosasaurs exceeded 10 meters in length and were the top carnivores in their near-shore habitats. Their teeth are large, robust, and conical. Tooth implantation is of the thecodont type—each tooth is set in a deep socket. No other lepidosaur group evolved this implantation style. Although hundreds of well-preserved specimens exist, juvenile mosasaurs are extremely rare, which may suggest that mosasaurs laid their eggs on land,

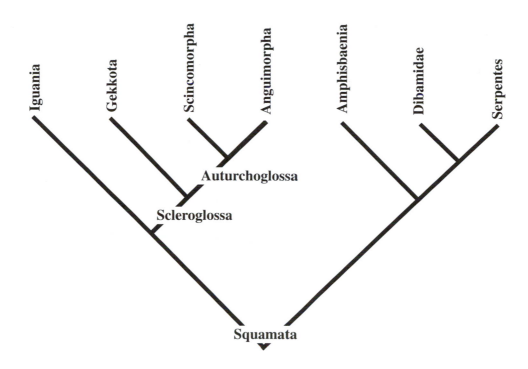

Figure 8. Phylogenetic relationships of major groups of Squamata.

although it is difficult to imagine how females would have moved out onto the beach with limbs shaped like paddles. Both hands and feet developed extra phalanges (hyperphalangy), but in contrast with other marine reptiles such as ichthyosaurs, the mosasaurs did not develop additional digits (hyperdactyly).

In view of their burrowing mode of life, it is a little surprising that the early fossil record of amphisbaenians (Figure 2E) is very scarce and incomplete. The oldest fossil that may be an amphisbaenian, *Oligodontosaurus,* is represented by a jaw from the Upper Paleocene of Wyoming (Estes 1965). The oldest positively identified amphisbaenian, *Ototriton,* is represented by more complete material, including a skull that differs little from today's amphisbaenians. This fossil is from the Lower Eocene of Wyoming (Gilmore and Jepsen 1945). More recently, a spectacular specimen from the Upper Cretaceous of Inner Mongolia was described as an amphisbaenian *(Sineoamphisbaena),* with a skull that differs significantly from the highly modified shape seen in living forms (Wu et al. 1995).

The earliest snake (only recently described) dates from the Lower Cretaceous (Barremian) of Spain. It was classified on the basis of an isolated vertebra; other early, isolated snake vertebrae come from the Late Albian of Algeria, North Africa (Rage and Richter 1994). *Pachyrhachis* (which is presumed to have some affinities with mosasaurs) from the lower Cenomanian of Israel was recently postulated to represent the sister group to all other snakes (Caldwell and Lee 1997). Unlike modern snakes, it retained hind limbs. *Dinilysia* (Figure 2F) from the Upper Cretaceous of Patagonia, is known from an almost complete skull (Estes et al. 1970) and a number of vertebrae (Hecht 1982). The skull

combines some distinctly lizardlike features, such as the rudiment of a jugal bone, with typical snakelike characteristics, such as the lack of sutural contact of maxilla and premaxilla. Although all scholars agree that *Dinilysia* is a snake, its position within the Serpentes remains controversial.

The fossil record of squamates indicates that much of the early diversification of "lizards" occurred while the supercontinent of Pangaea was still intact. R. Estes (1983b) identified an initial division in lizard evolution that correlates with the separation of Pangaea into the two landmasses, Laurasia and Gondwana in the Middle Jurassic. The Gondwana biotas would have retained early iguanians, and Laurasia would have been home to a gekkotan-scincomorph-anguimorph (i.e., scleroglossan) assemblage. This scenario recently has been challenged by the rich fossil record of iguanids and agamids from the Upper Cretaceous of the Gobi Desert (Kequin and Lianhai 1995). According to Estes (1983b), the agamid-chamaeleonid clade continued to evolve in northwestern Gondwana in response to intracontinental factors. Iguanids disappeared from the African continent after it became isolated, resulting in their present-day distribution in the Americas and in Madagascar. Habitat fragmentation in Laurasia from such factors as the invasion of epicontinental seas was probably responsible for the later disjunct distribution and diversification of scleroglossans. The split between gekkotans and scincomorphs came first, the gekkotans evolving in the east, and the scincomorphs evolving in the west. Later the anguimorphs branched off from scincomorph stock. The anguimorphs dominated in the north while the scincomorphs dominated in the south of Laurasia.

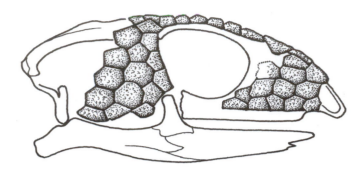

Figure 9. The skull of *Glyptosaurus montanus,* encrusted with osteoscutes. Redrawn, after Gilmore (1945).

Conclusions

The fossil record for sphenodontians is relatively rich in the Upper Triassic and Lower Jurassic, specimens having been reported from North America, Europe, Central Asia, and South Africa. However, no fossils of their sister group, the Squamata, have been collected at the same localities. During the Jurassic, localities yielding much sphenodontian material produced relatively few squamates, and vice versa. Summarizing these patterns, S.E. Evans (1995) observed that a preponderance of drier upland localities may distort our knowledge of the early history of the Lepidosauriformes. Perhaps the ecological niches occupied by early sphenodontians and squamates also overlap, resulting in some mutual exclusion within any given habitat. The diversity of squamates increases as that of sphenodontians declines. For squamate evolution Estes (1983b) identified a series of successive evolutionary phases: an early phase of experimentation within the insect-eating niche that left virtually no fossil traces, the subsequent diversification of all major lizard lineages by the end of the Jurassic (catalyzed by the Middle Jurassic separation of Gondwana from Laurasia), a Cretaceous phase of diversification and individualization of family groups (which persist into modern biotas), and finally a Cenozoic phase of restriction of lizard diversity and distribution, perhaps as a result of the rise of colubroid snakes.

OLIVIER RIEPPEL

See also Aquatic Reptiles

Works Cited

Alifanov, V.R. 1989. The oldest gecko (Lacertilia: Gekkonidae) from the Lower Cretaceous of Mongolia. *Paleontological Journal* 23:128–31.

Bellairs, A. d'A., and G. Underwood. 1951. The origin of snakes. *Biological Reviews* 26:193–237.

Berman, D. 1976. A new amphisbaenian (Reptilia: Amphisbaenia) from the Oligocene-Miocene John Day Formation, Oregon. *Journal of Paleontology* 50:165–74.

Borsuk-Bialynicka, M., and S.M. Moody. 1984. Priscagamidae, a new subfamily of the Agamidae (Sauria) from the late Cretaceous of the Gobi Desert. *Acta Paleontologica Polonica* 29:51–81.

Boulenger, G.A. 1891. On British remains of *Homeosaurus,* with remarks on the classification of the Rhynchocephalia. *Proceedings of the Zoological Society of London* 1891:167–72.

Brock, G.T. 1941. The skull of *Acontias meleagris,* with a study of the affinities between lizards and snakes. *Journal of the Linnean Society (Zoology)* 41:71–88.

Broschinski, A., and D. Sigogneau-Russell. 1996. Remarkable lizards from the Lower Cretaceous of Anoual (Morocco). *Annales de Paléontologie* 82:147–75.

Caldwell, M.W. 1994. Developmental constraints and limb evolution in Permian and extant lepidosauromorph diapsids. *Journal of Vertebrate Paleontology* 14:459–71.

Caldwell, M.W., R.L. Carroll, and H. Kaiser. 1995. The pectoral girdle and front limb of *Carsosaurus marchesetti* (Aigialosauridae), with a preliminary phylogenetic analysis of varanoids and mosasauroids. *Journal of Vertebrate Paleontology* 15(3):516–31.

Caldwell, M.W., and M.S.Y. Lee. 1997. A snake with legs from the marine Cretaceous of the Middle East. *Nature* 386:705–9.

Carroll, R.L. 1975. Permo-Triassic "lizards" from the Karroo. *Paleontographica Africana* 18:71–87.

———. 1977. The origin of lizards. *In* S. Andrews, R. Miles, and A. Walker (eds.), *Problems in Vertebrate Evolution.* New York and London: Academic Press.

———. 1981. Plesiosaur ancestors from the Upper Permian of Madagascar. *Philosophical Transactions of the Royal Society of London,* ser. B, 293:315–83.

———. 1985. A pleurosaur from the Lower Jurassic and the taxonomic position of the Sphenodontida. *Palaeontographica A* 189:1–28.

———. 1988. *Vertebrate Paleontology and Evolution.* San Francisco: Freeman.

Carroll, R.L., and R. Wild. 1994. Marine members of the Sphenodontia. *In* N.C. Fraser and H.D. Sues (eds.), *In the Shadow of the Dinosaurs.* Cambridge and New York: Cambridge University Press.

Cocude-Michel, M. 1963. Les rhynchocéphales et les sauriens des calcaires lithographiques (Jurassicque supérieur) d'Éurope occidentale. *Nouveaux Archives du Muséum d'Histoire Naturelle, Lyon* 7:1–187.

Colbert, E.H. 1966. A gliding reptile from the Triassic of New Jersey. *American Museum Novitates* 2246:1–23.

———. 1970. The Triassic gliding reptile *Icarosaurus. Bulletin of the American Museum of Natural History* 143:85–142.

Cope, E.D. 1869. On the reptilian orders Pythonomorpha and Streptosauria. *Proceedings of the Boston Society of Natural History* 12:250–67.

Cott, H.B. 1961. Scientific result of an inquiry into the ecology and economic status of the Nile Crocodile *(Crocodylus niloticus)* in Uganda and Northern Rhodesia. *Transactions of the Zoological Society of London* 21:211–356.

Cundall, D. 1987. Functional morphology. *In* R.A. Seigel, J.T. Collins, and S.S. Novak (eds.), *Snakes: Ecology and Evolutionary Biology.* New York: Macmillan.

Currie, P.J. 1980. A new younginid (Reptilia: Eosuchia) from the Upper Permian of Madagascar. *Canadian Journal of Earth Sciences* 17:500–11.

———. 1981. *Hovasaurus boulei,* an aquatic eosuchian from the Upper Permian of Madagascar. *Paleontologia Africana* 24:99–168.

——. 1982. The osteology and relationships of *Tangasaurus mennelli* Haughton (Reptilia; Eosuchia). *Annals of the South African Museum* 86:247–65.

Daugherty, C.H., A. Cree, J.M. Hay, and M.B. Thompson. 1990. Neglected taxonomy and continuing extinctions of the tautara (Sphenodon). *Nature* 347:177–79.

Estes, R. 1964. Fossil vertebrates from the late Cretaceous Lance Formation, Wyoming. *University of California Publications in Geological Sciences* 49:1–180.

——. 1965. Notes on some Paleocene lizards. *Copeia* 1965:104–6.

——. 1983a. *Sauria terrestria, Amphisbaenia.* Vol. 10A, Encyclopedia of Paleoherpetology. Stuttgart and New York: Fischer.

——. 1983b. The fossil record and early distribution of lizards. *In* A.G.J. Rhodin and K. Miyata (eds.), *Advances in Herpetology and Evolutionary Biology.* Cambridge, Massachusetts: Museum of Comparative Zoology.

Estes, R., K. de Queiroz, and J.A. Gauthier. 1988. Phylogenetic relationships within Squamata. *In* R. Estes and G. Pegill (eds.), *Phylogenetic Relationships of the Lizard Families.* Stanford, California: Stanford University Press.

Estes, R., T.H. Frazzetta, and E.E. Williams. 1970. Studies on the fossil snake *Dinilysia patagonica* Woodward. Part 1. Cranial morphology. *Bulletin of the Museum of Comparative Zoology* 140:25–74.

Estes, R., and L. Price. 1973. Iguanid lizard from the Upper Cretaceous of Brazil. *Science* 180:748–51.

Evans, S.E. 1980. The skull of a new eosuchian reptile from the Lower Jurassic of South Wales. *Zoological Journal of the Linnean Society* 70:81–116.

——. 1981. The postcranial skeleton of the Lower Jurassic eosuchian *Gephyrosaurus bridensis. Zoological Journal of the Linnean Society* 73:81–116.

——. 1988. The early history and relationships of the Diapsida. *In* M.J. Benton (ed.), *The Phylogeny and Classification of the Tetrapods.* Vol. 1. Oxford: Clarendon; New York: Oxford University Press.

——. 1993. Jurassic lizard assemblages. Second Georges Cuvier Symposium. *Revue de Paléobiologie, Volume Spécial* 7:55–65.

——. 1994a. A new anguimorph lizard from the Jurassic and Lower Cretaceous of England. *Palaeontology* 37:33–49.

——. 1994b. A reevaluation of the late Jurassic (Kimmeridgian) reptile *Euposaurus* (Reptilia, Lepidosauria) from Cerin, France. *Geobios* 27:621–31.

——. 1994c. The Solnhofen (Jurassic: Tithonian) lizard genus *Bavarisaurus:* New skull material and a reinterpretation. *Neues Jahrbuch für Geologie und Paläontologie, Abhandlungen* 192:37–52.

——. 1995. Lizards: Evolution, early radiation and biogeography. *In* A. Sun and Y. Wang (eds.), *Sixth Symposium on Mesozoic Terrestrial Ecosystems and Biota, Short Papers.* Beijing: China Ocean.

Fraser, N.C. 1982. A new rhynchocephalian from the British Upper Trias. *Palaeontology* 25:709–25.

——. 1988. The osteology and relationships of *Clevosaurus* (Reptilia: Sphenodontida). *Philosophical Transactions of the Royal Society of London,* ser. B, 321:125–78.

Fraser, N.C., and M.J. Benton. 1989. The Triassic reptiles Brachyrhinodon and Polysphenodon and the relationships of the sphenodontids. *Zoological Journal of the Linnean Society* 96:413–45.

Frazzetta, T.H. 1962. A functional consideration of cranial kinesis in lizards. *Journal of Morphology* 111:287–319.

——. 1986. The origin of amphikinesis in lizards. *Evolutionary Biology* 20:419–61.

——. 1970. Studies on the fossil snake *Dinilysia patagonica* Woodward. Part 2, Jaw machinery in the earliest snakes. *Forma et Functio* 3:205–21.

Gans, C. 1960. Studies on amphisbaenids (Amphisbaenia, Reptilia). 1. A taxonomic revision of the Trogonophinae and a functional interpretation of the amphisbaenid adaptive pattern. *Bulletin of the American Museum of Natural History* 134:185–260.

——. 1974. *Biomechanics: Approach to Vertebrate Biology.* Philadelphia: Lippincott.

Gauthier, J.A. 1984. A cladistic analysis of the higher systematic categories of the Diapsida. Ph.D. diss., University of California, Berkeley.

Gauthier, J.A., R. Estes, and K. de Queiroz. 1988. A phylogenetic analysis of Lepidosauromorpha. *In* R. Estes and G. Pegill (eds.), *Phylogenetic Relationships of the Lizard Families.* Stanford, California: Stanford University Press.

Gilmore, C.W. 1928. The fossil lizards from North America. *Memoirs of the National Academy of Sciences* 22:1–197.

Gilmore, C.W., and G. Jepsen. 1945. A new Eocene lizard from Wyoming. *Journal of Paleontology* 19:30–34.

Goldspink, G. 1977. Energy cost of locomotion. *In* R.McN. Alexander and G. Goldspink (eds.), *Mechanics and Energetics of Animal Locomotion.* London and New York: Chapman and Hall.

Gorniack, G.C., H.I. Rosenberg, and C. Gans. 1982. Mastication in the Tuatara, *Sphenodon punctatus* (Reptilia; Rhynchocephalia): Structure and activity of the motor system. *Journal of Morphology* 171:321–53.

Gow, C. 1975. The morphology and relationships of *Youngina capensis* Broom and *Prolacerta broomi* Parrington. *Paleontologica Africana* 18:89–131.

Greene, H.W. 1983. Dietary correlates of the origin and radiation of snakes. *American Zoologist* 23:431–41.

Günther, A. 1867. Contribution to the anatomy of *Hatteria* (*Rhynchocephalus,* Owen). *Philosophical Transactions of the Royal Society of London* 157:595–629.

Haas, G. 1979. On a new snake-like reptile from the Lower Cenomanian of Ein Jabrud, near Jerusalem. *Bulletin du Muséum National d'Histoire Naturelle* 4 (1C):51–64.

——. 1980a. Remarks on a new ophiomorph reptile from the Lower Cenomanian of Ein Jabrud, Israel. *In* L.L. Jacobs (ed.), *Aspects of Vertebrate History.* Flagstaff, Arizona: Museum of Northern Arizona Press.

——. 1980b. *Pachyrhachis problematicus* Haas, snakelike reptile from the Lower Cenomanian: Ventral view of the skull. *Bulletin du Muséum National d'Histoire Naturelle* 4 (2C):87–104.

Hecht, M.K. 1982. The vertebral morphology of the Cretaceous snake *Dinilysia patagonica* Woodward. *Neues Jahrbuch für Geologie und Palaeontologie, Monatshefte* 1982:523–32.

Hecht, M.K., and B.M. Hecht. 1984. A new lizard from the Jurassic of Middle Asia. *Paleontological Journal* 3:135–38.

Hoffstetter, R. 1964. Les Sauria du Jurassique supérieur et spécialement les Gekkota de Bavière et de Mandchourie. *Senckenbergiana Biologica* 45:281–324.

Howes, G.B., and H.H. Swinnerto. 1901. On the development of the skeleton of the Tuatara, *Sphenodon punctatus;* with remarks on the egg, on the hatchling, and on the hatched young. *Transactions of the Zoological Society of London* 16:1–86.

Huxley, T.H. 1869. On *Hyperodapedon. Quarterly Journal of the Geological Society of London* 25:138–52.

Kequin, G., and H. Lianhai. 1995. Iguanians from the Upper Cretaceous Djadochta Formation, Gobi Desert, China. *Journal of Vertebrate Paleontology* 15:57–78.

Kohring, R. 1991. Lizard egg shells from the Lower Cretaceous of Cuenca Province, Spain. *Palaeontology* 34:237–40.

Laurin, M. 1991. The osteology of a Lower Permian eosuchian from Texas and a review of diapsid phylogeny. *Zoological Journal of the Linnean Society* 101:59–95.

Li, J. 1985. A new lizard from Late Jurassic of Subei, Gansu. *Vertebrata PalAsiatica* 23:13–18.

McDowell, S.B. 1974. A catalogue of the snakes of New Guinea and the Solomons, with special reference to those in the Bernice P. Bishop Museum, Part 1: Scolecophidia. *Journal of Herpetology* 8:1–57.

McDowell, S.B., and C.M. Bogert. 1954. The systematic position of *Lanthanotus* and the affinities of anguinomorphan lizards. *Bulletin of the American Museum of Natural History* 105:1–142.

Owen, R. 1859. Note on the affinities of *Rhynchosaurus*. *Annals and Magazine of Natural History* 4(3):237–38.

Rage, J.-C. 1982. La phylogénie des Lépidosauriens (Reptilia): Une approche cladistique. *Comptes Renduz de l'Académie des Sciences Paris* 294 (2):563–66.

———. 1984. *Serpentes*. Vol. 11, Encyclopedia of Paleoherpetology. Stuttgart and New York: Fischer.

———. 1992. Phylogénie et systématique des lépidosauriens: Où en sommes-nous? *Bulletin de la Société Herpétologique de France* 62:19–36.

Rage, J.-C., and A. Richter. 1994. A snake from the Lower Cretaceous (Barremian) of Spain: The oldest known snake. *Neues Jahrbuch für Geologie und Palaeontologie, Monatshefte* 1994 (9):561–65.

Reeder, T.W. 1995. Phylogenetic placement of snakes within the Squamata: Evidence from molecules and morphology. *Program and Abstracts, Seventy-fifth Annual Meeting of the American Society of Ichthyologists and Herpetologists*. Edmundton: University of Alberta.

Reynoso, V.-H. 1996. A Middle Jurassic *Sphenodon*-like sphenodontian (Diapsida: Lepidosauria) from Huizachal Canyon, Tamaulipas, Mexico. *Journal of Vertebrate Paleontology* 16:210–21.

Rieppel, O. 1978. Streptostyly and muscle function in lizards. *Experientia* 34:776–77.

———. 1988. A review of the origin of snakes. *In* M.K. Hecht, B. Wallace, and C.T. Prance (eds.), *Evolutionary Biology*. New York: Plenum.

———. 1994. Osteology of *Simosaurus gaillardoti* and the relationships of stem-group Sauropterygia. *Fieldiana (Geology)*, new series, 28:1–85.

Rieppel, O., and M. deBraga. 1996. Turtles as diapsid reptiles. *Nature* 384:453–55.

Robinson, P.L. 1962. Gliding lizards from the Upper Keuper of Great Britain. *Proceedings of the Geological Society of London* 1601:137–46.

———. 1967. The evolution of the Lacertilia. *Colloques internationaux du Centre National de la Recherche Scientifique* 163:395–407.

———. 1973. A problematic reptile from the British Upper Trias. *Journal of the Geological Society of London* 129:457–79.

Russell, D.A. 1967. Systematics and morphology of American mosasaurs. *Peabody Museum of Natural History, Yale University, Bulletin* 23:1–240.

Senn, D.G., and R.G. Northcutt. 1973. The forebrain and midbrain of some squamates and their bearing on the origin of snakes. *Journal of Morphology* 140:135–52.

Shine, R. 1994. Young lizards can be bearable. *Natural History* 1994 (1):34–39.

Smith, R.M.H., and S.E. Evans. 1996. New material of *Youngina*: Evidence of juvenile aggregation in Permian diapsid reptiles. *Palaeontology* 39:289–303.

Sues, H.-D., and D. Baird. 1993. A skull of sphenodontian lepidosaur from the New Haven Arlose (Upper Triassic: Norian) of Connecticut. *Journal of Vertebrate Paleontology* 13:370–72.

Sues, H.-D., and R.R. Reisz. 1995. First record of the Early Mesozoic sphenodontian Clevosaurus (Lepidosauria: Rhynchocephalia) from the southern hemisphere. *Journal of Vertebrate Paleontology* 63:123–26.

Sues, H.-D., N.H. Shubin, and P.E. Olsen. 1994. A new sphenodontian (Lepidosauria: Rhynchocephalia) from the Mccoy Brook Formation (Lower Jurassic) of Nova Scotia. *Journal of Vertebrate Paleontology* 14:327–40.

Sulimski, A. 1975. Results of the Polish-Mongolian Palaeontological Expeditions. Part 6, Macrocephalosauridae and Polyglyphanodontidae (Sauria) from the Late Cretaceous of Mongolia. *Palaeontologia Polonica* 33:25–102.

Underwood, G. 1957. On lizards of the family Pygopodidae: A contribution to the morphology and phylogeny of the Squamata. *Journal of Morphology* 100:207–68.

Waldman, M., and S.E. Evans. 1994. Lepidosauromorph reptiles from the Middle Jurassic of Skye. *Zoological Journal of the Linnean Society* 112:135–50.

Walls, G. 1940. Ophthalmological implications for the early history of snakes. *Copeia* 1940:1–8.

Whiteside, D.I. 1986. The head skeleton of the Rhaetian sphenodontid *Diphydontosaurus avonis* gen. et sp. nov. and the modernizing of a living fossil. *Philosophical Transactions of the Royal Society of London*, ser. B, 312:379–430.

Williston, S.W. 1917. The phylogeny and classification of reptiles. *Journal of Geology* 25:411–21.

Wu, X.-C. 1994. Late Triassic-Early Jurassic sphenodontians from China and the phylogeny of the Sphenodontia. *In* N.C. Fraser and H.D. Sues (eds.), *In the Shadow of the Dinosaurs*. Cambridge and New York: Cambridge University Press.

Wu, X.-C., D.B. Brinkman, and A.P. Russell. 1995. *Sineoamphisbaena hexatabularis*, an amphisbaenian (Diapsida: Squamata) from the Upper Cretaceous redbeds at Bayan Mandahu (Inner Mongolia, People's Republic of China), and comments on the phylogenetic relationships of the Amphisbaenia. *Canadian Journal of Earth Sciences* 33:541–77.

Zanon, R.T. 1990. The sternum of *Araeoscelis* and its implications for basal diapsid phylogeny. *Journal of Vertebrate Paleontology* 9:51A (abstract).

Zittel, A. 1880–93. *Handbuch der Palaeontologie, 1. Abt. Palaeozoologie.* Vol. 3, *Vertebrata*. Munich and Leipzig: Oldenbourg.

Further Reading

Bellairs, A. d'A., and R. Carrington. 1966. *The World of Reptiles*. New York: American Elsevier; London: Chatto and Windus.

Carroll, R.L. 1988. *Vertebrate Paleontology and Evolution*. New York: Freeman.

Estes, R. 1983a. *Sauria Terrestria, Amphisbaenia*. Vol. 10A, Encyclopedia of Paleoherpetology. Stuttgart and New York: Fischer.

Estes, R., and W. Pregill. 1988. *Phylogenetic Relationships of the Lizard Families*. Stanford, California: Stanford University Press.

Rage, J.-C. 1984. *Serpentes*. Vol. 11, Encyclopedia of Paleoherpetology. Stuttgart and New York: Fischer.

Romer, A.S. 1956. *Osteology of the Reptiles*. Chicago: University of Chicago Press; 2nd ed., Chicago and London: University of Chicago Press, 1968.

LEPOSPONDYLS

Several orders of late Paleozoic aquatic, amphibious, and terrestrial tetrapods (four-legged animals) are referred to collectively as lepospondyls. Except for one record from the Permian of North Africa, all occur in the Carboniferous and Permian equatorial belt of the Laurasian supercontinent. (Laurasia was one of two supercontinents at this time; it included today's North America, Europe, and Asia except for India.) Lepospondyls are much more diverse in morphology and habits than their contemporaries, the labyrinthodonts, the first group of amphibians. Lepospondyls occupied a range of habitats comparable with those filled today by salamanders, caecilians, snakes, and lizards. Some were fully aquatic swimming forms; others were adapted to a terrestrial (land-based) existence, including burrowing.

Lepospondyls show great variability in the numbers of presacral (in front of the pelvic region) vertebrae, from as few as 14 to more than 200. Some had well-developed limbs, others show limb reduction, and still others were completely limbless. These two trends—great trunk elongation and limb reduction—occurred in several lineages and in modern amphibians and reptiles are associated with small body size and terrestrial locomotion. The number of bones in the skull roof is usually reduced, and their patterns may be much more specialized than those of labyrinthodonts. Despite these differences between various subgroups, lepospondyls often have been assumed to belong to a single evolutionary group because they all share a number of common features that set them apart from labyrinthodonts. Lepospondyl features include the structure of the teeth, the lack of large fangs in the roof of the mouth, and a relatively straight edge to the back of the skull (whereas labyrinthodonts have a pair of notches associated with the ear region).

The most distinctive feature shared by lepospondyls is the form of their vertebrae. In at least part of the vertebral column, each vertebra consists of a single spool-shaped centrum (vertebral body); this style is called "holospondylous." A one-piece vertebral element forms the joint between the skull and the trunk. In the labyrinthodonts, each centrum is composed of three elements.

In 1881 Karl Zittell grouped together three orders—Aïstopoda, Nectridea, and Microsauria—in the Subclass Lepospondyli on the basis of their vertebral structure. Other groups that share the same features are lysorophids, which were once classified as microsaurs, and adelogyrinids. Although the lepospondyl groups apparently have characters in common, each may have evolved as separate lineages from earlier, more primitive tetrapods. The question of origins is unclear because each lepospondyl group shows very distinctive and specialized features at its earliest known occurrence in the fossil record. This implies that all may have a separate evolutionary history extending back through the Early Carboniferous, a history about which nothing is currently known. No group can be identified as more primitive or related more closely to the labyrinthodonts than any other, nor does any group show features that support a single common origin. Thus the term "lepospondyl" cannot be demonstrated to be a natural monophyletic group (a group with a single common ancestor) containing closely related forms, although it is a useful descriptive term to cover "holospondylous" Paleozoic tetrapods.

Aïstopoda

The aïstopods are a group of very specialized limbless tetrapods with very long bodies and short tails (Figure 1A). The aïstopod trunk contains up to 200 vertebrae, and this, in combination with a short, almost rudimentary tail, suggests that these animals lived a snakelike lifestyle and that aïstopods were primarily terrestrial animals (Milner et al. 1986). The largest aïstopods, belonging to the genus (division; plural, genera) *Ophiderpeton*, were up to a meter long but most were less than half that length. They range from the Viséan (Early Carboniferous, 342 to 325 million years ago) to the Lower Permian in Euramerica.

The extreme specialization of the group at its earliest occurrence implies that it differentiated from the tetrapod stem very early (Baird 1964; Wellstead 1982). The relationships of aïstopods to other early tetrapods are problematic; the search for shared derived (specialized) characters in these forms is complicated by the specialization of both the skull and the postcranial skeleton, not least because they lack any trace of limbs or limb girdles. With respect to the basic tetrapod pattern, aïstopod skulls are highly derived, with emargination and loss of bones in the snout, cheek, and skull table. Their teeth were sharp, with backwardly curved and sometimes chisel-like tips. In the most specialized forms, the phlegethontiids, the skull is reduced to a series of struts that support the lower jaws against the braincase, a condition analogous (comparable) to that found in snakes (McGinnis 1967; Lund 1978). This may have allowed them to open the jaws unusually wide, again in a manner similar to snakes.

The oldest aïstopod, *Lethiscus stocki* (Wellstead 1982), is represented by a single specimen found in the Middle Wardie shales (late Early Carboniferous/Mississippian), near Edinburgh in Scotland. The second oldest fossil, also from Scotland, is from East Kirkton, near Bathgate, where *Ophiderpeton* is a rare member of the earliest known terrestrial assemblage of late Viséan age (Milner 1994). The lack of a lateral-line system (a sensory system in aquatic tetrapods, detectable in fossils by a pattern of grooves on the skull and jaw bones) is consistent with the interpretation of aïstopods as primarily terrestrial animals. Only seven genera of aïstopods are recognized. They occur in coal-swamp assemblages in the Late Carboniferous (Pennsylvanian)—principally Newsham, England; Jarrow, Ireland; Nýřany, Czech Republic; and Linton, Ohio—probably not as specialized water-dwellers but as accidental occurrences from the surrounding swamps or as adults that had returned to water to breed.

Adelogyrinids are known only from Viséan and Namurian localities in the Scottish midland valley. Three genera have been described, all of which conform to a similar body plan, although no complete articulated (intact) specimen is known. In contrast to aïstopods, adelogyrinids have a complete skull roof and a unique pattern of bones, with one large element making up most of the cheek. The jaws are fringed with closely packed, tiny teeth. They have a well-ossified hyoid apparatus (bones that support the tongue and its muscles), which strongly suggests that they were aquatic animals. The trunk is long, containing at least 70 vertebrae. The shoulder skeleton is fully formed, but there is no trace of bony forelimbs, nor of any pelvis or hind limb. Adelogyrinids were at least mainly aquatic and perhaps were rather eel-like. Their closely spaced, small, sharp teeth may have been used for gripping soft-bodied prey or as part of a gape-and-suck feeding system, with the teeth straining small prey as mouthfuls of water were squirted through them (Andrews and Carroll 1991).

Nectridea

Most nectrideans were specialized for an aquatic mode of life. All possessed limbs, although they were generally small in relation to body size. Nectrideans are immediately recognizable and clearly defined by their distinctive vertebrae. They are holospondylous throughout the column with no dividing sutures—the neural dorsal and haemal (ventral) arches are fused to the centra. The neural arches bear unique bony extensions that form a system of extra interlocking tabs between adjacent vertebrae to minimize risk of disarticulation. In the tail the expanded, often fan-shaped neural and haemal spines are also unique among Paleozoic tetrapods. The long, deep, flat-sided tail—taking up to two-thirds of the total length of the animal—moved from side to side to propel the animal through the water.

Nectrideans range from the Late Carboniferous (Westphalian/Pennsylvanian), where they are an important element of coal swamp faunas of North America and Europe, to the basal Upper Permian redbeds (named for their color) in North America, Europe, and Africa. The diversification of nectrideans at their first appearance in the fossil record suggests that they probably originated, at the latest, in the Lower Carboniferous. Shared derived characters clearly demonstrate that they form a clade (a natural evolutionary group) (Milner 1980a, 1996).

Three families of nectrideans are recognized. The Urocordylidae consist of newtlike forms (Figure 1B); with some exceptions the skull is short-snouted but always relatively high-sided, with the jaw articulation behind (posterior to) the occiput (the hind end of the skull, which joins the trunk). The skull is highly kinetic (mobile)—some of the bones of the snout and cheek could move to accommodate a wide-opening mouth (Bossy and Milner 1997). In the Diplocaulidae (Milner 1994) the skull is akinetic (immobile), comparatively broad and flattened, and has a short, blunt snout. The jaw articulation is usually in front of (anterior to) the occiput so those animals had a smaller gape.

The bones at the back corners of the urocordylid skull are drawn out backward or backward and sideways into large "horns." In the Carboniferous forms, the horns pointed backward and were linked to the shoulder girdle. This bizarre condition may have helped to dampen side-to-side oscillation produced by the tail's undulation and kept the head moving in a straight line through the water (Milner 1980a; Bossy and Milner

1997). The horns of the Permian *Diplocaulus* and *Diploceraspis* were expanded dramatically to produce a boomerang-shaped skull in adults (Figure 1B). Biomechanical tests on models of the head of *Diplocaulus* have shown that its shape acts as a hydrofoil, providing lift even in very slow flowing water (Cruickshank and Skews 1980). The long-horned diplocaulids may have been bottom dwellers in flowing streams or still water bodies, able to rise up to feed either by swimming actively or by passively using water currents. It is unlikely they could have fed while resting on the bottom—their horns were too long to permit jaw opening. Body traces of a long-horned diplocaulid imprinted on a muddy substrate in the Lower Permian of Germany lend support to this idea (Walter and Werneberg 1988) (Figure 1C). *Diplocaulus* is the only lepospondyl recorded from outside Euramerica. Fragmentary remains have been reported from the Permian of Morocco (Dutuit 1988).

The Scincosauridae lack the skull specializations of the other nectridean families and are considered to be more terrestrial, perhaps reflecting the primitive condition for the order. More than 60 similarly sized individuals of *Scincosaurus*, between 120 and 140 millimeters long, are known from the famous Late Carboniferous (Westphalian D) coal-swamp lake locality at Nýřany in the Czech Republic. *Scincosaurus* has a robust skeleton with ossified wrist and ankle bones; a heavy, shieldlike shoulder girdle; and a rounded, rather than flat-sided, tail. All these features suggest life on land (Bossy and Milner 1997). The concentration of individuals in the Nýřany lake deposit may represent a single age-class of individuals that had returned to the water to breed and been overcome by some natural disaster (Milner 1980b).

Microsauria

The Microsauria is the largest and most diverse lepospondyl group, containing at least 26 genera. All microsaurs are united by the specialized connection between the skull and the neck. The first trunk vertebra includes a forward-facing convex "peg" that articulates with a broad, strap-shaped occiput (bone at the rear of the skull), similar to a ball-and-socket joint.

Microsaurs are known from deposits that reflect a range of environments: shallow ponds, coal swamps, streams, and deltas. None is found in deposits from deep water bodies. The oldest microsaur is from the basal Late Carboniferous (Namurian A) near Goreville, Illinois (Lombard and Bolt 1997), although it has not been named yet. Microsaurs belonging to four or five species occur in the famous Lower Pennsylvanian (Westphalian A) lycopod tree stump locality at Joggins, Nova Scotia. The hollow stumps apparently acted as traps or natural refuges for small terrestrial animals, including microsaurs and the earliest unequivocal amniote, *Hylonomus* (Carroll 1964). (The amniotes include all animals that lay eggs; these include mammals, birds, and reptiles.) The terrestrial nature of these early microsaur occurrences suggests that their early radiation was terrestrial rather than aquatic.

Microsaurs have been divided into two suborders, Tuditanomorpha and Microbrachiomorpha (Carroll and Gaskill 1978). Tuditanomorphs all possess a four-fingered hand and were mainly terrestrial; some of the early Permian forms were short-bodied and

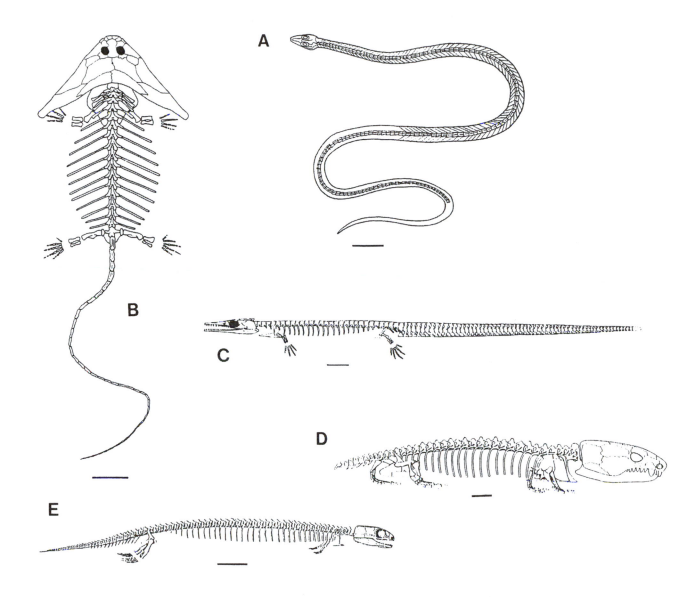

Figure 1. Skeletal reconstructions of representative lepospondyls. *A*, the aïstopod *Aornerpeton* (scale, 100 millimeters); *B*, the diplocaulid nectridean *Diplocaulus* (scale, 120 millimeters); *C*, the urocordylid nectridean *Sauropleura* (scale, 200 millimeters); *D*, the tuditanomorph microsaur *Pantylus* (scale, 10 millimeters); *E*, the microbrachomorph microsaur *Microbrachis* (scale, 10 millimeters). Source: *A*, from Lund (1978), courtesy Carnegie Museum of Natural History, Pittsburgh, PA; *B*, courtesy of Angela C. Milner; *C*, from Milner (1980a); *D*, from Carroll and Gaskill (1978); *E*, from Carroll and Gaskill (1978).

stoutly built (e.g., *Pantylus*) and have robust crushing and puncturing teeth (Figure 1D). The Permian ostodolepids were the largest and most spectacular microsaurs. They reached lengths of up to 750 millimeters and were proportioned rather like a gila monster with shovel-shaped skulls, long fat trunks, stout limbs, and a stubby tail—all adaptations to a burrowing habit. Microbrachomorphs were relatively long-bodied aquatic forms, with small limbs and a hand with three fingers only. *Microbrachis* (Figure 1E) from Nyřany shows lateral line grooves on the surface of the skull and external gills, suggesting that it was an aquatic member of the coal swamp faunas, probably feeding on small invertebrate prey.

Lysorophids

Lysorophids are very long-bodied lepospondyls, with tiny limbs and between 69 and 97 trunk vertebrae. Their skulls were open-sided, and they had short jaws with robust conical teeth. The form of the skull-trunk articulation is similar to that of microsaurs, the group to which lysorophids might be related most closely. They have a prominent hyoid skeleton, which confirms an aquatic habit. Lysorophids occur in the Late Carboniferous coal-swamp assemblages, the earliest from the Westphalian A at Jarrow, Republic of Ireland. These animals are found also in Permian redbed localities in the southeastern United States, where specimens are characteristically found coiled inside nodules. The coiled attitude has been interpreted as a behavioral adaptation to resist desiccation (drying out) in drying ponds (Wellstead 1991), analogous to the aestivating behavior (a type of hibernation that occurs in summer) shown by some living lungfishes.

ANGELA C. MILNER

See also Lissamphibians; Tetrapods

Works Cited

Andrews, S.M., and R.L. Carroll. 1991. The Order Adelospondyli: Carboniferous lepospondyl amphibians. *Transactions of the Royal Society of Edinburgh: Earth Sciences* 82:239–75.

Baird, D. 1964. The aïstopod amphibians surveyed. *Breviora* 206:1–17.

Bossy, K.A., and A.C. Milner. 1997. Order Nectridea Miall 1875. *In* R.L. Carroll, K.A. Bossy, A.C. Milner, S.M. Andrews, and C.F. Wellstead (eds.), *Handbuch der Paläoherpetologie. Teil 1, Lepospondyli (Microsauria, Nectridea, Lysorophia, Aïstopoda, Acherontiscidae)*. Munich: Pfeil.

Carroll, R.L. 1964. The earliest reptiles. *Zoological Journal of the Linnean Society* 45:61–83.

Carroll, R.L., and P. Gaskill. 1978. *The Order Microsauria*. Memoirs of the American Philosophical Society, 126. Philadelphia: American Philosophical Society.

Cruickshank, A.R.I., and B.W. Skews. 1980. The functional significance of nectridean tabular horns. *Proceedings of the Royal Society of London*, ser. B, 209:513–37.

Dutuit, J.-M. 1988. *Diplocaulus minimus* n.sp. (Amphibia: Nectridea) Lepospondyl of the Argana Formation (Moroccan Occidental Atlas). *Compte rendu de l'Académie des Sciences, Paris* (2) 307:851–54.

Lombard, R.E., and J.R. Bolt. 1997. The oldest microsaur. *Journal of Vertebrate Paleontology* 17:60.

Lund, R. 1978. Anatomy and relationships of the family Phlegethontiidae (Amphibia, Aïstopoda). *Annals of the Carnegie Museum* 47:53–79.

McGinnis, H.J. 1967. The osteology of *Phlegethontia*, a Carboniferous and Permian aïstopod amphibian. *University of California Publications in Geological Sciences* 71:1–46.

Milner, A.C. 1980a. A review of the Nectridea (Amphibia). *In* A.L. Panchen (ed.), *The Terrestrial Environment and the Origin of Land Vertebrates*. London and New York: Academic Press.

———. 1980b. The tetrapod assemblage from Nýřany, Czechoslovakia. *In* A.L. Panchen (ed.), *The Terrestrial Environment and the Origin of Land Vertebrates*. London and New York: Academic Press.

———. 1994. The aïstopod amphibian from the Viséan of East Kirkton, West Lothian, Scotland. *Transactions of the Royal Society of Edinburgh* 84:363–69.

———. 1996. A juvenile long-horned nectridean (Amphibia) from the Lower Permian of the southeastern USA and the status of the family Diplocaulidae. *Special Papers in Palaeontology* 52:29–38.

Milner, A.R., T.R. Smithson, A.C. Milner, M.C. Coates, and W.D.I. Rolfe. 1986. The search for early tetrapods. *Modern Geology* 10:1–28.

Walter, H., and R. Werneburg. 1988. Über Liegespuren (Cubichnia) aquatischer Tetrapoden (?Diplocauliden, Nectridea) aus den Rotteröder Schichten (Rotliegendes, Thüringer Wald/DDR). *Freiberger Forschungsheft* (C) 419:96–105.

Wellstead, C.F. 1982. A Lower Carboniferous aïstopod amphibian from Scotland. *Palaeontology* 25:193–208.

———. 1991. *Taxonomic Revision of the Lysorophia, Permo-Carboniferous Lepospondyl Amphibians*. Bulletin of the American Museum of Natural History, 209. New York: American Museum of Natural History.

Further Reading

Carroll, R.L. 1988. *Vertebrate Paleontology and Evolution*. New York: Freeman.

———. 1992. The primary radiation of terrestrial vertebrates. *Annual Reviews of Earth and Planetary Science* 20:45–84.

Carroll, R.L., K.A. Bossy, A.C. Milner, S.M. Andrews, and C.F. Wellstead. 1997. *Handbuch der Paläoherpetologie. Teil 1, Lepospondyli (Microsauria, Nectridea, Lysorophia, Aïstopoda, Acherontiscidae)*. Munich: Pfeil.

Milner, A.R. (ed.). 1996. Studies on Carboniferous and Permian vertebrates. Proceedings of the fourth International Symposium on Permo-Carboniferous Continental Faunas. *Special Papers in Palaeontology* 52:148.

Panchen, A.L. (ed.). 1980. *The Terrestrial Environment and the Origin of Land Vertebrates*. London and New York: Academic Press.

LICHENS

A lichen is not an individual organism; it is two or more very different organisms, usually a photosynthetic alga (the phycobiont) and a non-photosynthetic fungus (the mycobiont), intimately connected and interdependent. This dual nature was not demonstrated until 1869 by the Swiss botanist Simon Schwendener; before that, lichens had been classified as simple plants.

The photosynthetic "partner" of a lichen is usually a single-celled green alga but is sometimes a cyanobacterium (blue-green alga). The fungus partner is usually an ascomycete (sac fungus), but a few basidiomycetes (club fungi) and deuteromycetes (imperfect fungi) also form lichens. A few lichens may contain two different fungi, or may have both a green alga and a cyanobacterium. In all, about 13,500 species of fungi—roughly 20 percent of all known fungi—form lichens. Most of these fungi are rarely, if ever, found growing independently. There are cases of fungi living in the tissues of apparently healthy marine seaweeds, as well as symbioses between algae and actinomycetes (filamentous bacteria that superficially resemble fungi) or myxomycetes (slime molds). Whether these should be called lichens or not is debatable (Hawksworth and Hill 1984; Smith and Douglas 1987).

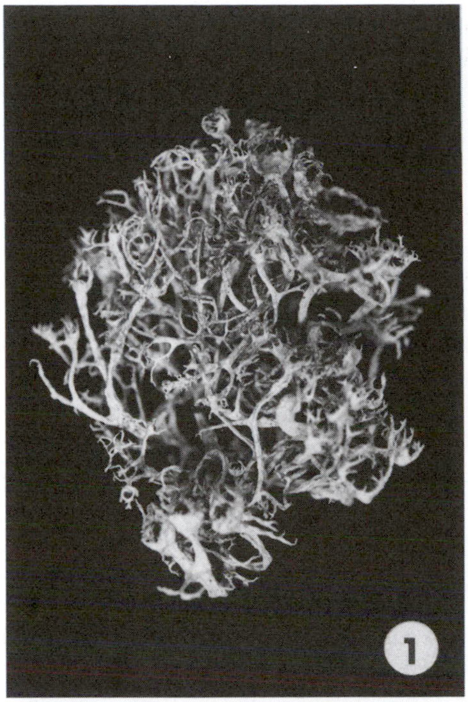

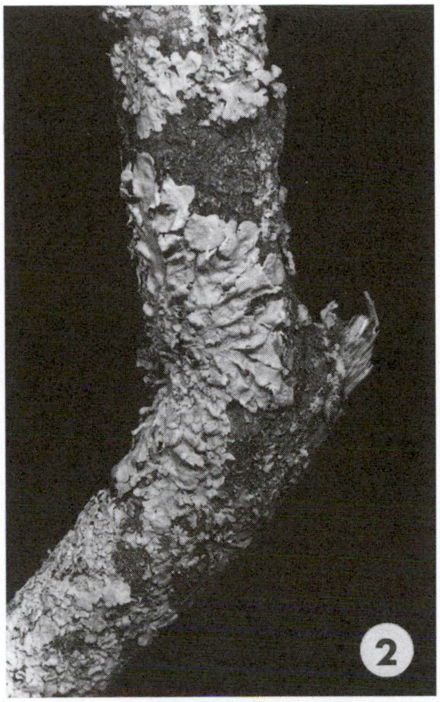

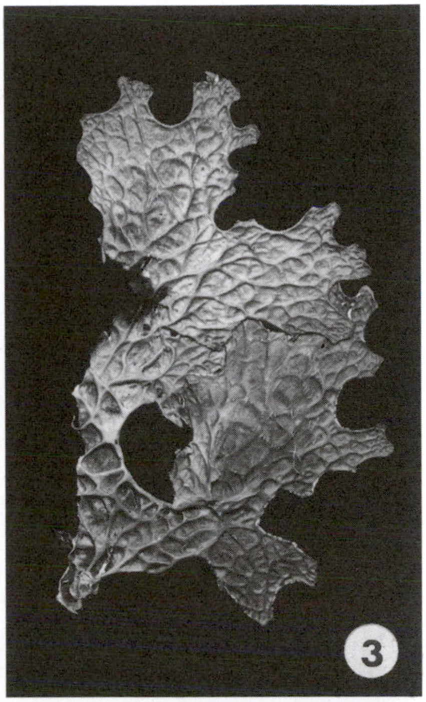

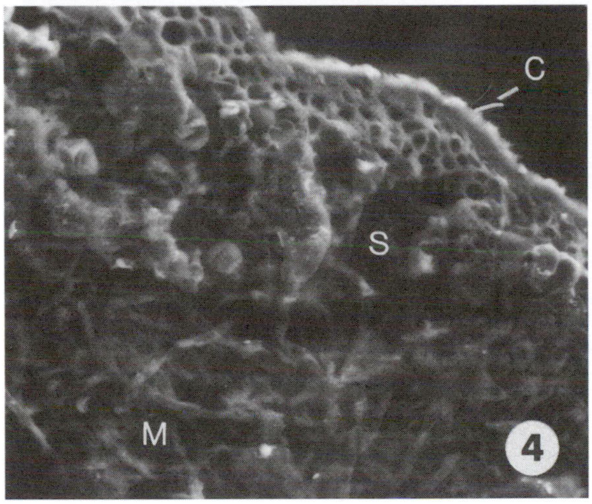

Figure 1. A fruticose lichen, *Letharia columbiana,* collected in Placer County, California. From the University of California and Jepson Herbarium Collection; thanks to Brian R. Speer.

Figure 2. Tree branch with a foliose lichen, *Flavoparmelia caperata,* collected in Alameda County, California. From the University of California and Jepson Herbarium Collection; thanks to Brian R. Speer.

Figure 3. A foliose lichen, *Lobaria pulmonaria* ("lungwort"); collected in Skamania County, Washington; compare with Figure 5. From the University of California and Jepson Herbarium Collection; thanks to Brian R. Speer.

Figure 4. Cross section of *Flavoparmelia* under the electron microscope. *C,* cortex; *S,* symbiont layer; *M,* medulla. From the University of California Museum of Paleontology; image taken with UCMP Environmental Scanning Electon Microscope; thanks to Brian R. Speer.

Figure 5. Fossil lichen, *Lobaria* sp. Miocene; Redding Creek, California. From the University of California Museum of Paleontology, paleobotany type collection, specimen #1014; thanks to Brian R. Speer.

The body of a lichen, or thallus, may be described generally as leprose (powdery), filamentous, crustose (crustlike), squamulose (scaly), foliose (leafy), or fruticose (branching, shrubby); (Figures 1–3). A typical crustose lichen is layered in cross section (Figure 4). The outer layer, the cortex, is made of tightly packed fungal hyphae (threads) and serves a protective function. Below the cortex is a zone where the algal symbionts are concentrated. Special hyphae, called haustoria, penetrate the algal cells and absorb the carbohydrates that the algae make. Finally, the lowest zone, the medulla, is made up of more loosely packed fungal hyphae. It may include rhizoids, filaments by which the lichen is attached to the substrate.

Almost all true lichens live on land, although a few can be found in fresh water or in the intertidal zone of the ocean. Lichens can be incredibly tough; they dominate the rocks and soils of harsh environments such as deserts, mountain tops, and tundra. Lichens are also common in less extreme environments and in fact may be found wherever there is a stable place for them to grow. Able to grow on bare rock, lichens may be important in initiating the formation of soil; they secrete organic acids that weather the rock. Lichens also harbor small animals such as insects and mites, and may be an important food source for insects, mites, and snails. Some, such as the "reindeer moss" of northern Europe (*Cladonia rangifera)*, are important food for reindeer and caribou, especially in the winter.

The hardiest lichens of all are found in the snow-free "dry valleys" of Victoria Land, Antarctica. Almost nothing else can live here: temperatures drop to −60 degrees Celcius in winter, dry freezing winds scour the bare rocks, humidity may fall as low as 16 percent, and what little snow there is evaporates so rapidly that there is very rarely any liquid water. Lichens survive here, as do some bacteria, by growing in layers a few millimeters inside sandstone rocks. Enough light penetrates the quartz grains of the rock to allow photosynthesis, and the rock protects the lichens and traps what little moisture there is. These so-called cryptoendolithic lichens have been proposed as models for what microbial life on Mars might be like (Friedmann 1982; Friedmann and Ocampo-Friedmann 1984).

Lichens are of little economic importance. A few are used as food, fodder, folk medicine, and sources of dyes, including the well-known litmus dye used by chemists (Smith 1921). The potential uses of lichens are far greater: over 550 natural compounds have been isolated from lichens, including some that kill bacteria or cancer cells (Hawksworth and Hill 1984). Lichens do not tolerate air pollution, in particular sulfur dioxide; on the other hand, many can concentrate and retain heavy metals and radioactive elements from the environment. Thus, lichens often are used as indicators of local pollution or fallout. The size of slow-growing lichen colonies can sometimes be used to estimate the age of stone monuments and buildings, as well as natural features such as rock slides, that are within a few hundred years old (Hawksworth and Hill 1984).

Lichens have a sparse fossil record—in many habitats that they dominate, such as deserts and tundra, the chances of forming fossils are very low. Some filamentous microfossils from South Africa, dated between 2.2 and 2.7 billion years old, have been interpreted as lichenlike associations between two different microbes (Hallbauer and van Warmelo 1974). However, similar microstruc-

tures can be produced in the laboratory, and some paleontologists doubt that these are real fossils (Cloud and Pierce 1977). Retallack (1994) theorized that the Late Precambrian "Ediacara fossils," usually thought to be early animals, were lichens or lichenlike organisms. There are a number of problems with this theory (Waggoner 1995), and it has not found wide acceptance. Some botanists have proposed that vascular plants, which first appear as recognizable fossils in the Late Silurian, evolved from a lichenlike ancestor in which fungal and algal genes were mixed (e.g., Pirozynski and Malloch 1975, Atsatt 1988). This idea remains controversial at best, and there is no real fossil evidence for it.

The oldest certain fossil lichen is Early Devonian (about 400 million years old) from the Rhynie Chert of northeast Scotland (Taylor et al. 1995). Several unusual plantlike land organisms lived at about this time, including the crustlike spongiophytes, matlike nematophytes, and the huge, loglike *Prototaxites*. These are composed of intertwining filaments and have been proposed as lichens or lichenlike symbioses (e.g., Retallack 1994). Spongiophytes may plausibly be lichens (Stein et al. 1993), but nematophyte and *Prototaxites* filaments lack the typical branching patterns of fungal hyphae. They probably represent unsuccessful experiments in colonizing the land, isolated offshoots of an algal lineage that left no descendants. A few lichen fossils are known from Mesozoic and Cenozoic rocks (Figure 5), including at least two species from Oligocene Baltic amber (Larson 1978; Garty et al. 1982).

BEN WAGGONER

See also Algae; Fungi

Works Cited

Atsatt, P.R. 1988. Are vascular plants "inside-out" lichens? *Ecology* 69: 17–23.

Cloud, P., and D. Pierce. 1977. Experimental production of pseudomicrofossils. *GSA Abstracts with Programs* 9:102.

Friedmann, E.I. 1982. Endolithic microorganisms in the Antarctic cold desert. *Science* 215:1045–53.

Friedmann, E.I., and R. Ocampo-Friedmann. 1984. The Antarctic cryptoendolithic ecosystem: Relevance to exobiology. *Origins of Life* 14:771–76.

Garty, J., C. Giele, and W.E. Krumbein. 1982. On the occurrence of pyrite in a lichenlike inclusion in Eocene amber (Baltic). *Palaeogeography, Palaeoclimatology, Palaeoecology* 39:139–47.

Hallbauer, D.K., and K.T. van Warmelo. 1974. Fossilized plants in thucholite from Precambrian rocks of the Witwatersrand, South Africa. *Precambrian Research* 1:199–212.

Hawksworth, D.L., and D.J. Hill. 1984. *The Lichen-Forming Fungi.* Glasgow and New York: Blackie.

Larson, S.G. 1978. *Baltic Amber: A Palaeobiological Study.* Entomonograph 1. Klampenborg, Denmark: Scandinavian Science Press.

Pirozynski, K.A., and D.W. Malloch. 1975. The origin of land plants: A matter of mycotrophism. *BioSystems* 6:153–64.

Retallack, G.J. 1994. Were the Ediacaran fossils lichens? *Paleobiology* 20: 523–44.

Smith, A.L. 1921. *Lichens.* Cambridge: Cambridge University Press.

Smith, D.C., and A.E. Douglas. 1987. *The Biology of Symbiosis.* London and Baltimore, Maryland: Arnold.

Stein, W.E., G.D. Harmon, and F.M. Hueber. 1993. *Spongiophyton* from the Lower Devonian of North America reinterpreted as a lichen. *American Journal of Botany* 80 (6):93.

Taylor, T.N., H. Hass, W. Remy, and H. Kerp. 1995. The oldest fossil lichen. *Nature* 378:244.

Waggoner, B.M. 1995. Ediacaran lichens: A critique. *Paleobiology* 21: 393–97.

Further Reading

Hawksworth, D.L., and D.J. Hill. 1984. *The Lichen-Forming Fungi.* Glasgow and New York: Blackie.

Taylor, T.N., and E.L. Taylor. 1993. *The Biology and Evolution of Fossil Plants.* Englewood Cliffs, New Jersey: Prentice-Hall.

LIMBS, PAIRED

See Fins and Limbs, Paired

LINNAEUS, CAROLUS (CARL VON LINNÉ)

Swedish, 1707–78

During his lifetime, Carolus Linnaeus produced an impressive body of work that was both revolutionary and influential in its scope and ambition. Through his work, Linnaeus developed and refined a taxonomic system that introduced binomial nomenclature to the scientific classification of the natural world. While certainly influential during his lifetime, the greatest testimony to Linnaeus' influence on and contribution to science is the fact that the Linnaean system remains the basis on which animals, plants, and minerals are classified.

Linnaeus was born in Rashult, Smaland, Sweden on 23 May 1707. As the son of a clergyman interested in gardening, Linnaeus expressed a childhood interest in botany while attending the Latin school in the cathedral city of Växjö. However, at his father's urging, Linnaeus matriculated at the University of Lund to study medicine in 1727. Supposedly disappointed with his education there, Linnaeus transferred to the University of Uppsala the following year. Here Linnaeus began to cultivate his interest in botany and develop the taxonomic system that would revolutionize the way the natural world is classified.

In 1730 Linnaeus was appointed lecturer in botany at Uppsala and subsequently took over Olof Rudbeck's lectures and the neglected botanical garden of the university. During this time Linnaeus was researching the newly proposed theory that plants display sexuality, and from this research he began formulating a taxonomic system of plants based upon their sexual organs, stamens and pistils. This theory, although incomplete at the time, was first presented in *Hortus uplandicus* (1730). Although not published until later in his career, Linnaeus was also busy working on a series of manuscripts for future botanical works: *Bibliotheca botanica, Classes plantarum, Critica botanica,* and *Genera plantarum.*

In 1732, on a trip sponsored by the Uppsala Society of Science, Linnaeus traveled through Lapland and Finland, discovering a hundred new plant species and studying the animal life of the region. Two years later Linnaeus journeyed through Dalecarlia, and in 1735 he traveled through Lübeck, Hamburg, and Amsterdam. Later that year, deciding to complete his medical training, Linnaeus left Sweden for Holland, where he would receive his M.D. from the University of Harderwijk.

In 1735 Linnaeus published his influential work, *Systema Naturae,* in which he presented his methodical arrangement of the animal, plant, and mineral kingdoms. In this work Linnaeus drew upon his earlier research to divide plants into classes depending upon their number and arrangement of stamens and into orders depending upon the number of pistils. However, while this system was convenient, it was not, as Linnaeus himself recognized, based upon the natural relationships of plants and was, thus, an artificial system. Nonetheless, this system was quickly adopted as the standard system of classification and implemented until one conveying more natural relationships was developed. In this work Linnaeus also placed whales with mammals and noted human's affinity to the apes.

Linnaeus remained in Holland until 1738, during which time he published an impressive array of botanical works. In 1736 *Bibliotheca botanica* and *Fundamenta botanica* were published. In *Bibliotheca botanica* Linnaeus systematically listed the botanical literature of the time, and in *Fundamenta botanica* he presented his theory of systematic botany. The following year he published three more works: *Flora lapponica, Critica botanica,* and most importantly, *Genera plantarum.* In the former two, Linnaeus presented, respectively, his descriptions of flora collected from his journey to Lapland and his guidelines for botanical nomenclature. *Genera plantarum* contains descriptions of the 935 known plant genera. In 1738 *Classes plantarum,* a review of prior plant systems, and *Hortus Cliffortianus,* a description of the plants found in a wealthy merchant's garden, were published.

In the early summer of 1738, Linnaeus returned to Sweden and took up practice as a physician in Stockholm. The following year he helped found the Academy of Sciences and subsequently was chosen as its president. In 1741 Linnaeus was appointed professor of theoretical and practical medicine at the University of Uppsala, but a year later he gave up this position for a more suitable position as chair of botany and supervisor of the botanical gardens. For Linnaeus, this period of his life was marked by his dedication to teaching and his students. As a teacher and mentor, Linnaeus was well liked by his students and enthusiastic about sending them out on botanical excursions throughout the world, and although his fame would grow, he would remain as a professor at Uppsala for the rest of his life.

In 1744 Linnaeus was appointed secretary of the Royal Society of Sciences in Uppsala. The following year Linnaeus published two works, *Ölandska och Gothländska resa 1741* and *Flora suecia,* which were followed by a series of works including *Fauna suecia* (1746), *Wästgöta-resa 1746* (1747), *Hortus Upsaliensis* (1748), and *Materia medica* (1749).

Upon his return from a journey through Skåne, Linnaeus was appointed rector of the University of Uppsala in 1749. In 1751 Linnaeus published two more works, *Skånska resa 1749* and *Philosophia botanica,* in which he presented his theory of botanical classification and the laws and rules that botanists should follow when naming and describing plants. During this time Linnaeus was continuing his work on the classification of botany, but he struggled with finding a simple and efficient system. Prior to Linnaeus' work, plants were scientifically catalogued by a name followed by a short Latin description of the plant. This system was unsatisfactory owing to both its lengthy names and incomplete descriptions. With the publication of *Species plantarum* in 1753, however, Linnaeus simplified this system and in doing so, made his most lasting contribution to science: binomial nomenclature. In this work, Linnaeus identified 8,000 plant species by a generic name and a specific name and became the first person to uniformly apply such a system. In contrast to prior naming systems, binomial nomenclature was short, simple, and accommodated the rapid discovery of plants and (eventually) the introduction of evolutionary principles to taxonomy.

In the following years, Linnaeus continued teaching at the university and updating previous works. In 1758 *Systema naturae, Animalia,* a tenth edition, was published, in which Linnaeus applied binomial nomenclature to the animal kingdom. The following year, *Systema naturae, Vegetablia,* tenth edition, was published. That same year, Linnaeus was again appointed rector of the University, a position he would be appointed to for a third time in 1772.

For his ambitions and dedication to his work, however, Linnaeus' health suffered, and as a result, his workload declined. In 1763 he was relieved of his teaching duties but continued to revise his previous works. In 1766 *Systema naturae,* twelfth edition, Part 1 was published, followed by Parts 2 and 3 in 1767 and 1768, respectively. Other works of this time include *Genera morborum* (1763), *Clavis medicinae* (1766), and *Systema vegetabilium* (1774).

During his lifetime, Linnaeus was recognized for his invaluable contribution to science. As one of the world's leading botanists, Linnaeus received botanical samples from around the world. He was also a member of numerous scientific societies, including the Paris Academy and the Academy of Sciences. In 1752 he was honored as a Knight of the Order of the Polar Star, and in a royal decree antedated to 1757, Linnaeus was granted nobility as Carl von Linné.

In 1774 and 1776 Linnaeus suffered strokes that left him permanently disabled, both physically and mentally. On 10 January 1778, Carolus Linnaeus died in Uppsala.

Following Linnaeus' death, his botanical collections and manuscripts were sold by his widow to English naturalist James Edward Smith, who founded the Linnaean Society in 1788 and served as the society's first president. Today, they are housed in Burlington House, London.

EDOUARD L. BONÉ AND BRIAN CALLENDER

Biography

Born in Råshult, Småland, Sweden, 23 May 1707. Received M.D., University of Harderwijk, 1735. Appointed lecturer, University of Uppsala, 1730; appointed president, Academy of Sciences, 1739; professor of medicine, University of Uppsala, 1741; professor of botany, University of Uppsala, 1742; secretary, Royal Society of Sciences, 1744; rector, University of Uppsala, 1749, 1759, 1772. Raised to nobility, 1762. Traveled extensively through Lapland and Finland, 1732; Dalecarlia, 1734; Lübeck, Hamburg, and Amsterdam, 1735; England, 1736; Öland and Gotland, 1741; Västergötland, 1746; Skåne, 1749. Presented theory of botanical classification based on plant sexuality, *Systema naturae,* 1735; introduced binomial nomenclature, *Species plantarum,* 1753. Died in Uppsala, 10 January 1778.

Major Publications

1735. *Systema naturae* [System of Nature]. Leyden; 12th ed., pts. 1–3, Stockholm: Salvii, 1766–68.

1736a. *Bibliotheca botanica* [The Botanical Library]. Amsterdam: Schouten.

1736b. *Fundamenta botanica* [Fundamentals of Botany]. Amsterdam: Schouten.

1737a. *Critica botanica* [Rules for Botanical Naming]. Leyden: Wishoff.

1737b. *Flora Lapponica* [Flora of Lapland]. Amsterdam: Schouten.

1737c. *Genera plantarum* [Genera of Plants]. Leyden: Wishoff.

1738. *Classes plantarum* [Classes of Plants]. Leyden: Wishoff.

1745. *Flora suecia* [Flora of Sweden]. Stockholm: Wishoff.

1746. *Fauna suecia* [Fauna of Sweden]. Stockholm: Wishoff and Salvii.

1751. *Philosophia botanica* [Botanical Philosophy]. Stockholm: G. Kisewetter.

1753. *Species plantarum* [Species of Plants]. 2 vols. Stockholm: L. Salvii.

Further Reading

Anderson, M.J. 1997. *Carl Linnaeus: Father of Classification.* Springfield, New Jersey: Enslow Publishers.

Blunt, W. 1971. *The Compleat Naturalist: A Life of Linnaeus.* New York: Viking; London: Collins.

Frangsmyr, T., S. Lindroth, G. Eriksson, and G. Broberg. 1983. *Linnaeus, the Man and His Work.* Berkely: University of California Press.

Fries, T.M. 1903. *Linné, lefnadsteckning.* 2 vols. Stockholm: Fahlerantz.

———. 1923. *Linnaeus: The Story of His Life.* B.D. Jackson (trans). London: Witherby; as *Linné, lefnadsteckning,* 2 vols., Stockholm: Fahlerantz.

Goerke, H. 1973. *Linnaeus.* D. Lindley (trans.). New York: Scribner's; as *Carl von Linné,* Stuttgart: Wissenschaftliche Verlagsgesellschaft, 1966.

Gourlie, N. 1953. *The Prince of Botanists: Carl Linnaeus.* London: Witherby.

Hulth, J.M. 1907. *Bibliographia Linnaeana.* Uppsala: Almqvist and Wiksells.

Hagberg, K. 1939. *Carl Linnaeus.* Stockholm: Naturoch Fultur; London: Jonathon Cape, 1952. New York: Dutton, 1952; 2nd ed. Stockholm: Natur och Fultur, 1957.

Lindroth, S. 1966. Two Centuries of Linnean Studies. *In* T. Buckman (ed.), *Bibliography and Natural History.* Lawrence: University of Kansas Libraries.

Silverstein, A., and V. Silverstein. 1969. *Carl Linnaeus: The Man Who Put The World of Life in Order.* New York: Day.

Soulsby, B.H. 1933. *A Catalogue of the Works of Linnaeus.* London: British Museum of Natural History; 2nd ed., 1936.

Stafleu, F.A. 1971. *Linnaeus and the Linnaeans: The Spreading of Their Ideas in Systematic Botany.* Utrech: Osthoek.

LISSAMPHIBIANS

The Lissamphibia include all living amphibians (and fossils associated with them) and an extinct group, the Albanerpetontidae. Living amphibians are subdivided into three groups, often regarded as orders: Salientia, Caudata, Gymnophiona. Among the major groups (classes) of vertebrates, lissamphibians represent, by far, the smallest one; about 4,500 living species only are known, and fossil species are not numerous. Nevertheless, two of the most remarkable "intermediate" fossils belong to the Lissamphibia (*Triadobatrachus massinoti* and *Eocaecilia micropodia*). The concept of Lissamphibia, which implies that the group is monophyletic (having a single common ancestor) generally is agreed upon today. However, some paleontologists have believed that lissamphibians are polyphyletic (see below).

Salientia

The Salientia comprise the Anura (e.g., frogs and toads) and one fossil, *Triadobatrachus massinoti,* which sometimes is placed in its own group, the Proanura. Salientians are small tetrapod vertebrates whose skull is broad, flat, and widely fenestrate (composed of thin struts separated by large openings) and whose trunk is short. They share four significant characters that are diagnostic: (1) the frontal and parietal bones are fused, making up a single bone, the frontoparietal; (2) the palatine (a bone on the roof of the mouth) is a single rod that lies in an unusual transverse (sideways) position; (3) the parasphenoid (a bone underlying the braincase) appears as an inverted T, because of the presence of posterolateral wings; (4) the ilia (dorsal hip bones) are markedly elongate anteriorly. Moreover, except for one living species, they lack mandibular teeth (teeth on the lower jaw).

Anura

The anurans are nearly cosmopolitan (enjoying a world-wide distribution); they make up the largest group of lissamphibians (almost 4,000 living species and a number of fossil species currently under revision). They are salientians that have achieved a saltatorial (hopping) mode of locomotion (although secondarily reduced in various forms). Their morphology and anatomy are quite homogeneous. Their trunk is strongly shortened, they lack a tail, and their hind limbs are clearly longer than the forelimbs (more specifically, the tarsus—footbones belonging to, and just in front of, the ankle—is elongated, and it forms an additional segment).

Prosalirus bitis and Vieraella herbstii represent the earliest fossil record for the anurans; they are nearly coeval (contemporary). P. bitis apparently is slightly older than V. herbstii. It was found among fossils collected in the presumed Pliensbachian (late Early Jurassic, 194–187 million years ago) of Arizona by N.H. Shubin and F.A. Jenkins Jr., two paleozoologists, in 1982. This rather small anuran (with snout-vent length about 5 centimeters) is known by various remains of at least two individuals. It has been placed in its own family, the Prosaliridae (Shubin and Jenkins 1995). V. herbstii comes from the late Early Jurassic or the earliest Middle Jurassic. It is represented by a single specimen whose dorsal and ventral impressions are known. The dorsal impression was recovered in 1961 by a paleobotanist, R. Herbst, in southern Argentina. R. Casamiquela, a paleovertebrist, found the ventral impression later, in 1965. This fossil has been revised recently (Báez and Basso 1996). *Vieraella* is a small anuran (with snout-vent length about 2.2 centimeters). It might have had eleven vertebrae, more than in all other anurans. The 11th vertebra apparently formed the sacrum (part of the spine to which the hip is attached). The most primitive living anurans, Ascaphidae (from North America) and Leiopelmatidae (from New Zealand) have 10 vertebrae; this number decreases in more advanced forms. *Vieraella* is regarded as the most primitive anuran, but its family assignment is unknown. The modern anuran pattern emerged as early as the Middle Jurassic (167–160 million years ago) when the Discoglossidae, a living family, appeared.

Triadobatrachus Massinoti

Triadobatrachus is a celebrated fossil known by only one specimen from the earliest Triassic of Madagascar (245–240 million years ago). The fossil lies in a nodule that, split open, shows the dorsal and ventral faces of the specimen. The skeleton has disappeared but a sharply defined mold remains. It was found by an amateur and first described by J. Piveteau. It was revised by J.C. Rage and Z. Roček (1989). *Triadobatrachus* is a medium-sized salientian (with snout-vent length less than 10 centimeters). The four derived (adapted) features that define the salientians are obviously present in *Triadobatrachus,* and they ally it to the anurans. Its skull is very similar to that of anurans, but *Triadobatrachus* is more primitive than the latter: its trunk is less shortened and its hind limbs are less elongate than in anurans; moreover, it retains a tail (Figure 1). In other words, the skull of *Triadobatrachus* is that of an anuran, whereas the postcranial skeleton is that of a more generalized tetrapod. Because of various postcranial features, *Triadobatrachus* was not a true and efficient jumper. It is not possible to establish definitely whether *Triadobatrachus* belongs to the ancestry of the anurans or represents the sister group of the latter.

Anurans are rather peculiar tetrapods adapted to saltatorial habits. Therefore, it may be presumed that saltation was the impetus that caused the emergence of anurans. But *Triadobatrachus,* which represents a "structural connecting link" between general-

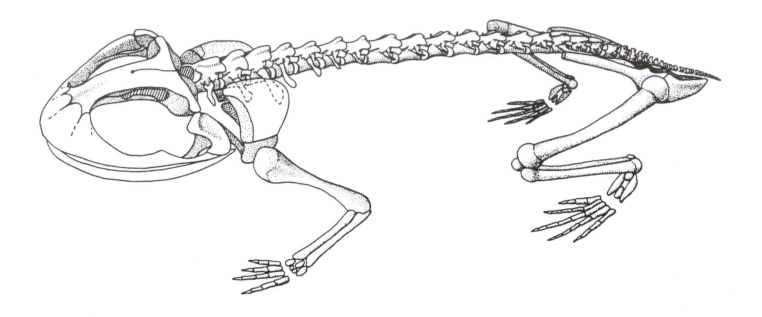

Figure 1. *Triadobatrachus massinoti* from the Early Triassic of Madagascar; reconstruction of skeleton. After Rage and Roček (1989, modified).

ized tetrapods and anurans, was not a good jumper; it shows only incipient specializations toward saltation. On the other hand, its skull already was anuran-like. Therefore, surprisingly, the earliest evolutionary changes toward anurans affected the skull, not the locomotory apparatus (Rage and Roček 1989); improvement toward a saltatory mode of locomotion only followed later. Full saltatorial capabilities were established by the early Jurassic (Shubin and Jenkins 1995).

Gymnophiona

The Gymnophiona include the Apoda (which are Caecilians, or limbless amphibians) and one fossil, *Eocaecilia micropodia*. They are diagnosed by the presence of four features: (1) a chemosensory tentacle sheltered in a fossa (depression) located, on each side, between the eye and the nostril; (2) an "os basale" (basal bone) formed by the coalescence of several bones of the posterior part of the skull; (3) a long internal process on each mandible; and (4) the marked elongation of the part (retroarticular process) of the mandible that is posterior to its articulation with the skull.

Apoda

The Apoda comprise about 160 living species. They are distinguished rather easily from other amphibians by their elongate and limbless, snakelike body that exhibits annuli (rings), their reduced eyes concealed beneath the skin or even beneath the skull bones, the presence of the chemosensory tentacle, and their almost terminal vent (uro-genito-excretory opening). With the exception of the aquatic Typhlonectidae, they are fossorial (burrowing), or at least

secretive animals that essentially inhabit forest and are nearly restricted to the intertropical belt.

The fossil record of apodans is very poor. They are represented only by disarticulated vertebrae. The oldest apodan is found in the late Cretaceous (presumed Cenomanian; about 96–91 million years ago) of Sudan (Evans et al. 1996). Apodans also are reported from the latest Cretaceous (Maastrichtian) and early Paleocene of Bolivia. These fossils were not named. The only named fossil apodan is *Apodops pricei* from the Middle Paleocene of Brazil.

Eocaecilia micropodia

This astonishing fossil may be labeled an "apodan with limbs." It is represented by 38 specimens dating from the Early Jurassic of Arizona (194–187 million years ago). Recently, F.A. Jenkins Jr. and D.M. Walsh (1993) described them. *Eocaecilia* is elongate (about 15 centimeters) but less elongate than apodans; it has four short but well-formed limbs, and a true tail is present (Figure 2).

Eocaecilia exhibits the four features that characterize the Gymnophiona (the tentacular fossa is particularly apparent). This demonstrates that *Eocaecilia* and the Apoda belong to the same monophyletic group, the Gymnophiona. However, *Eocaecilia* displays several primitive features that have been lost in apodans, among them the rather large size of the orbits (which shows that the eyes were not yet reduced in *Eocaecilia*), the presence of a rather long tail, and obviously the presence of four limbs. On the other hand, *Eocaecilia* displays a feature that is unique: the stapes articulates with the retroarticular process of the mandible. The stapes is the bone of the middle ear that, in tetrapod vertebrates,

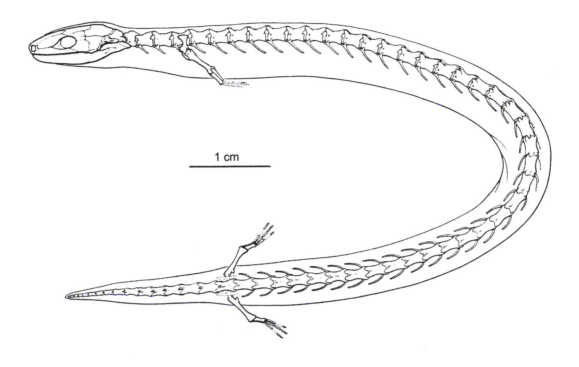

Figure 2. *Eocaecilia micropodia* from the Early Jurassic of the USA; reconstruction. After Jenkins and Walsh (1993), with permission, copyright © 1993 Macmillan Magazines Limited.

transmits the airborne vibrations to the inner ear. Normally, that is in all tetrapods except *Eocaecilia,* the lateral extremity of the stapes contacts an immovable structure that is either a tympanum (eardrum) or a superficial bone. The condition in *Eocaecilia* is quite puzzling: what could have been the role of a stapes that contacted a highly mobile bone? Whatever the role of this stapes, this articulation represents a peculiar derived character. As a result, *Eocaecilia* cannot belong to the ancestry of Apoda; this fossil is the sister group of the latter.

Caudata

The Caudata usually have four limbs of equal length; they also have a long tail. Externally, such caudates resemble primitive amphibian types: basal tetrapods. However, some neotenic (juvenilized) forms are elongate and their limbs are reduced. Caudates are characterized by peculiar rib-bearing processes: on either side of at least the anterior trunk vertebrae, an elongate outgrowth supports the rib; this outgrowth comprises a dorsal and a ventral process that provide a double articular surface for the rib.

Caudates are primarily Laurasian (Northern Hemisphere) in distribution, but they rather recently (perhaps during the late Tertiary) entered Gondwanan areas (South America and northernmost Africa). The Caudata are subdivided into two groups, the Urodela (which include all living forms and various fossils) and the extinct Karauridae.

Urodela

The Urodela (such as salamanders, newts, and sirens) include about 400 living species and a number of fossil species. They are characterized mainly by the posterodorsal stretch of the adductor muscles of the mandible (the muscles that close the mouth), a part of which extends to the occipital area of the skull or even to the first vertebrae.

The earliest remain of a urodele is a fragment of mandible from the latest Jurassic (Tithonian; 140–135 million years ago) of England. This fossil was referred to the Batrachosauroididae, an extinct family, and it remains unnamed. The oldest named urodele is *Horezmia gracile* from the mid-Cretaceous (Albian; 108–95 million years ago) of Uzbekistan. This fossil, which is assigned to the extinct family Scapherpetontidae, is represented by a few isolated bones. Extant families are known first from the latest Cretaceous (76–65 million years ago), when Sirenidae and Amphiumidae appeared.

Karauridae

The Karauridae comprise *Kokartus honorarius* from the Middle Jurassic (Bathonian; 167–160 million years ago) of Kirghizia, and *Karaurus sharovi* from the Late Jurassic (Kimmeridgian; 146–140 million years ago) of Kazakhstan. *Karaurus* is represented by a complete skeleton described by M.F. Ivakhnenko (1978). The posterior part of the *Karaurus* skull exhibits dermal sculpture, which

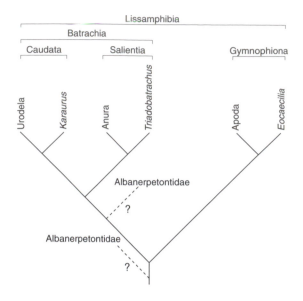

Figure 3. Interrelationships within Lissamphibia.

shows that the adductor muscles of the mandible neither originated there nor crossed this area (that is, they did not reach the first vertebrae). Therefore, *Karaurus* lacked the derived condition present in urodeles. The Karauridae might represent the sister group of the Urodela, but this cannot be demonstrated; therefore, it is not impossible that they are primitive urodeles.

Caudata of Unknown Relationships
Marmorerpeton is a genus from the Bathonian of England; it includes two species, *M. kermacki* and *M. freemani,* both represented by disarticulated bones. They are coeval with the karaurid *Korkatus honorarius;* these three species represent the oldest caudates. The vertebrae of *Marmorerpeton* appear to be more primitive than those of other caudates, but the condition of the adductor muscles of the mandible is unknown. The relationships of *Marmorerpeton* within Caudata cannot be determined.

Albanerpetontidae
The Albanerpetontidae are an extinct group of terrestrial salamanderlike amphibians from North America, Europe, and Central Asia. They range from the Middle Jurassic (167–160 million years ago) to the Middle Miocene (16–15 million years ago). They include two genera, *Celtedens* (Early Cretaceous) and *Albanerpeton* (Late Cretaceous–Middle Miocene). Fossils from the Jurassic remain unnamed. Albanerpetontids are characterized by a peculiar atlas (first vertebrae)-second-and-third-vertebrae complex and by an interlocking mandibular symphysis (intermandibular joint). *Celtedens ibericus,* represented by a complete specimen from Spain, apparently had epidermal scales on the body, while the skin of the

head, including the eyelids, contained thin dermal ossifications (osteoderms). The Albanerpetontidae originally were referred to the Caudata, but a recent analysis has shown that they probably represent a distinct group (see below), although they appear to have rib-bearers similar to those of Caudata.

Origin and Interrelationships of the Lissamphibia
It has been suggested that Lissamphibia are polyphyletic. According to the Swedish scholars Nils Holmgren and Gunnar Säve-Söderbergh, the Caudata originated from dipnoan ancestors, whereas Salientia and other tetrapods are derived from "crossopterygian" fishes. This point of view has been superseded by the theory of Erik Jarvik, another Swede, who suggested that the Caudata are derived from porolepiform "crossopterygians" while Salientia and other tetrapods are descended from osteolepiform "crossopterygians" (Gymnophiona were not considered in these studies). This theory has achieved little acceptance. On the other hand, various paleontologists have proposed the origins of the three extant groups from two or three different groups of palaeozoic amphibians. From this point of view, the lepospondyls (Early Carboniferous–Early Permian; 350–260 million years ago) often are considered as the ancestors of the Caudata and Gymnophiona, whereas the temnospondyls (Early Carboniferous–Early Cretaceous; 325–130 million years ago) would be the stem group of the Salientia.

However, an almost general agreement emerged during the last two or three decades of the twentieth century: Lissamphibia are a monophyletic group nested among the dissorophoid temnospondyls. The Dissorophoidea are known from deposits of Late Carboniferous to Late Permian age (310–250 million years ago). Among the dissorophoids, two families appear to be especially close to the Lissamphibia: the Branchiosauridae and the Amphibamidae (Milner 1993), both from the Late Carboniferous and Early Permian (310–265 million years ago). The Branchiosauridae were small lacustrine (lake-dwelling) carnivores and were regarded as larvae of various temnospondyls for many years; they are in fact pedomorphic (juvenilized) adults, and they now are recognized as a group of dissorophoids. The terrestrial Amphibamidae are perhaps closer to the Lissamphibia than are the Branchiosauridae.

Assuming that the Lissamphibia are monophyletic, it generally is agreed that the Salientia and Caudata are sister groups (they make up the Batrachia), and that, if only living forms are considered, the Gymnophiona represent the sister group of the Batrachia (Figure 3). According to an alternative view, Caudata and Gymnophiona might be sister groups. As far as the Albanerpetontidae are concerned, G. McGowan and S.E. Evans (1995) have shown that the group would be the sister group of the Batrachia, but they do not rule out a sister group relationship between Albanerpetontidae and all other Lissamphibia. If the latter hypothesis proves correct, then the Albanerpetontidae might be excluded from the Lissamphibia. As the earliest lissamphibian, *Triadobatrachus,* is from the base of the Triassic, it may be inferred that Lissamphibia originated during the latest Paleozoic.

JEAN-CLAUDE RAGE

Works Cited

Báez, A.M., and N.G. Basso. 1996. The earliest known frogs of the Jurassic of South America: Review and cladistic appraisal of their relationships. *In* G. Arratia (ed.), *Contributions of Southern South America to Vertebrate Paleontology. Münchner Geowissenschaftliche Abhandlungen*, A, 30. Munich: Pfeil.

Evans, S.E., A.R. Milner, and C. Werner. 1996. Sirenid salamanders and a gymnophionan amphibian from the Cretaceous of the Sudan. *Palaeontology* 39:77–95.

Ivakhnenko, M.F. 1978. Urodelans from the Triassic and Jurassic of Soviet Central Asia. *Paleontological Journal* 12:362–68.

Jenkins, Jr., F.A., and D.M. Walsh. 1993. An early Jurassic caecilian with limbs. *Nature* 365:246–50.

McGowan, G., and S.E. Evans. 1995. Albanerpetontid amphibians from the Cretaceous of Spain. *Nature* 373:143–45.

Milner, A.R. 1993. The Paleozoic relatives of Lissamphibians. *Herpetological Monographs* 7:8–27.

Rage, J.C., and Z. Roček. 1989. Redescription of *Triadobatrachus massinoti* (Piveteau, 1936) an anuran Amphibian from the early Triassic. *Palaeontographica*, ser. A, 206:1–16.

Shubin, N.H., and F.A. Jenkins Jr. 1995. An early Jurassic jumping frog. *Nature* 377:49–52.

Further Reading

Milner, A.R. 1988. The relationships and origin of living amphibians. *In* M.J. Benton (ed.), *The Phylogeny and Classification of the Tetrapods, Volume I: Amphibians, Reptiles, Birds.* Oxford: Clarendon Press; New York: Oxford University Press.

Schultze, H.P., and L. Trueb (eds.). 1991. *Origins of the Higher Groups of Tetrapods: Controversy and Consensus.* Ithaca, New York: Cornell University Press.

LOCOMOTION

See Aerial Locomotion; Aquatic Locomotion; Terrestrial Locomotion in Vertebrates

LYCOPODS

See Club Mosses and Their Relatives

LYELL, CHARLES

Scottish, 1797–1875

Charles Lyell, the geologist, was born 14 November 1797 in Kinnordy, Scotland, and died 22 February 1875 in London, England. He was raised in the south of England as the oldest child of a Scottish laird and was sent to Oxford University, where he received the usual classical education. He was first introduced to geological issues while at Oxford in a lecture course on mineralogy taught by William Buckland, the then-Reader in the subject.

The intention had been that Lyell would pursue a career in law, and indeed, he qualified as a barrister (that is, one who pleads the cases in court). Over the following years, however, he developed severe eye problems which interfered with his professional capabilities. By the time he was thirty years old, Lyell had ceased practicing law and was chiefly engaged in writing reviews for major journals, particularly for the conservative *Quarterly Review.* As his interest in law declined, his interest in geology increased. Lyell's initial study of the rock strata beneath the chalk formations in the south of England and on the Isle of Wight in the English Channel convinced him of the validity of dating rocks relatively according to their composition and, in particular, their fossil content. He did not, however, publish these particular findings.

In 1823 Lyell spent some time in Paris, where his interest in geology was strengthened while his thinking, overall, turned to broader perspectives. Lyell continued to investigate geologic history as revealed by rock strata on the continent throughout the decade, either alone or in the company of other scientists, particularly the geologist, Roderick Murchison. His examination of rocks containing fossil shells on the Isle of Ischia, off the coast of Naples, provided a major revelation and inspiration for future work. From this study, Lyell conceived of a system of dating rocks all over the world on the basis of their fossil evidence. He also noted the similarity between such fossils and living organisms.

Lyell's recognition of the significance of rock stratigraphy was reinforced on a visit to Sicily, where he had the opportunity to climb the volcano Mt. Etna. While he was impressed by the size of the mountain, his visit confirmed his belief that modern, active phenomena, such as the volcano, can provide invaluable insight to past events. While studying the rocks of Sicily, he found further evidence in the local strata to support his belief by observing the repetition of events preserved in the geological record and still occurring today.

As the decade drew to a close and his law activities ceased completely, Lyell experienced financial pressures. He initially planned to write a popular book on geology in the format of a series of conversations directed at the general public. As he began writing, however, his project rapidly developed into something far greater, although it always retained the air of a tome written for the nonprofessional (like Charles Darwin's *Origin of Species,* [1859] written some thirty years later). His project developed eventually into a massive three-volume work, *The Principles of Geology,* published between 1830 and 1833.

For a brief time in the early 1830s, Lyell assumed the position of professor of geology at the newly founded Anglican King's College in London. After the publication of the *Principles,* however, he was able to earn a living from his writings. Essentially, his later writings were variations on this one work. He revised and augmented the *Principles* over 12 editions, the last of which appeared posthumously. Lyell also wrote a simpler version of the *Principles,* the *Elements of Geology,* in the style of a textbook. The scholastic nature was noted by the third edition (1851) and the book was retitled as *A Manual of Elementary Geology.* (Other works by Lyell include two travel books about North America, published in the 1840s, and an expansion of his views about humankind, *The Antiquity of Man,* published in 1863.)

When Lyell began publishing the *Principles* in 1830, the prevailing geological theory was what the philosopher William Whewell labeled "catastrophism," a view much indebted to the thinking of Georges Cuvier in France. Proponents of this theory believed that the Earth's history was limited. Although the exact time span could not be specified, all agreed that it was considerably longer than the Bible's attribution of 6,000 years. It was believed that the Earth was "directional," meaning that it had progressed from its initial hotter state to its present cooler condition. Most importantly, these theorists maintained that the Earth was subject to periodic cataclysms, or upheavals, of a kind not known or experienced today. Generally, it was believed that these catastrophes (the last of which was associated with Noah's flood) were of natural origin as opposed to divine intervention. Each catastrophe purged the existing organic forms, after which the Earth was restocked. Not only was this restocking process believed to be divinely caused, it was also thought that God progressively restocked the earth from simple to more complex life-forms. The progressive stocking explained why the most primitive organisms were found in the lowest levels of the fossil record while the most sophisticated forms were found in the highest, more recent levels, culminating in humans as the last to be created.

Lyell adopted the rival position, "uniformitarianism," as coined also by Whewell, which challenged all aspects of catastrophism. In a view that clearly owes much to the eighteenth-century Scottish geologist James Hutton, Lyell argued that the Earth exists in a very old state and is moving toward the future in much the same way that it has arrived. As Hutton stated, the Earth has "no trace of a beginning, no prospect of an end." Lyell did not deny that there have been variations of the Earth throughout its history, but he argued that, over time, these changes have balanced out. The fluctuations occur within bounds, so that, overall, the Earth essentially exists in a "steady state." Lyell challenged the need for catastrophes—miraculous or material—in his explanation of the history of the Earth. He insisted that the causes of the past are of the same kind and intensity as those of the present. Natural phenomena, such as rain, wind, erosion, and deposition, coupled with a large time factor, are enough to account for all.

In order to defend his theory that the Earth exists in a steady state, Lyell had to counter the evidence for directionality. For example, the fossil plants found around Paris, which are tropical-like (palms and so forth), were interpreted traditionally as an indication of the area's previous warm climate. Instead of challenging the fossil evidence, Lyell argued that it supported his theory within the limits he set. In his "grand theory of climate," proposed in volume 1 of the *Principles,* Lyell proposed that the temperature variations among different parts of the Earth are less a function of distance from the equator as they are determined by the relative distributions of land and sea. The distribution patterns affect thermal currents and other natural factors. Lyell used the Gulf Stream, the body of water from the West Indies that keeps Britain and surrounding areas much warmer than other places at the same latitude, as contemporary evidence for the kind of phenomenon that

was significant in the past. According to Lyell, it is impossible to determine the warmth of a place by its geographic position unless the land and sea distributions are known. He envisioned the Earth as rather like a grand water bed. As one part of the earth subsides, perhaps owing to the deposition of silt carried downstream by rivers, other parts will rise. Lyell was determined to document evidence of the land-water relationship in the *Principles.* This subject became the young Charles Darwin's first major research project as he embarked on his five-year voyage aboard the *H.M.S. Beagle* in 1831 with volume 1 of Lyell's *Principles* in his library.

In the *Principles,* Lyell's presentation of geological history is intended less to inform the reader than it is to disqualify rival theories. Part of Lyell's lawyerlike strategy was to portray the catastrophists as being unduly influenced by theological considerations. This may or may not have been the case. Nevertheless, the theology underlying Lyell's thinking should not be underestimated. Lyell was clearly not a conventional "theist"—he did not believe in a providential God who intervenes miraculously in His Creation. Like others before him, however (particularly J. Hutton and other Scottish Enlightenment figures), Lyell maintained a belief in some form of "deism." That is, he endorsed a notion of God as "Unmoved Mover": a god who set the universe in motion and then let the laws of nature function without interference. (It is significant that Lyell worshipped for many years with the Unitarians, the Christian denomination that most closely approximates a deistic church.) Lyell's theory that the world existed in a steady state, subject only to unbroken law, was as much a confirmation of his theology as it was of his geology.

Lyell's break from strict deism occurred regarding his belief concerning the origin of humans. He maintained that the geologist's task includes accounting for the nature of the fossil record and, indeed, of the world of organisms reflected in that record. In the *Principles,* particularly in volume 2, Lyell demonstrates at great length how extinction can be expected to occur at a steady rate, strictly according to natural phenomena, as seen today, without invoking cataclysmic events. Although he fails to address the issue explicitly, Lyell apparently believed that new species come into existence on a regular rate through natural, as opposed to supernatural, causes. The only exception, however, was *Homo sapiens.* Lyell clearly asserts that with respect to this species, and this species alone, God must have intervened directly, in a nondeistic manner, to create man.

Although Lyell was careful to cover his tracks, this belief regarding humans probably explains his opposition to evolutionism. In the second volume of the *Principles,* Lyell discusses in some detail the evolutionary theory of the French biologist, Jean Baptiste de Lamarck. Lyell undermines Lamarck by demonstrating how the biologist's views contradict the world picture of uniformitarianism, particularly its steady-state aspects. Evolution, which Lyell understood to be necessarily progressive, inherently contradicts the nonprogressive nature of rocks. Ironically, Lamarck held that the fossil record is of little importance with respect to evolution, whereas Lyell presented evolution as an answer to the nature of the fossil record. However, after publication of the *Principles,* the fossil record and the theory of evolution were forever fused together as question and answer.

Lyell perceived more to be at stake than a simple matter of paleontological interpretation. He regarded evolution, particularly a Lamarckian progressivist evolution, as having humankind as its apotheosis. In other words, if evolution is accepted as a natural, law-bound process, the creation of man would follow as a natural, law-bound consequence. Although he had been almost sympathetic to evolution in his earlier writings in the 1820s, Lyell argued vehemently against it once he recognized the consequences. He debated evolutionary theory from uniformitarian grounds rather than from the religious grounds for which he criticized his contemporaries. For instance, he borrowed a leaf from George Cuvier's book and attempted to refute the possibility of artificially creating new species, as the failure of contemporary animal and plant breeders demonstrated. In many respects, however, Lyell was more successful in explaining Lamarck's ideas than in refuting them. Several people, most notably the British philosopher Herbert Spencer, read Lyell's refutation of Lamarck and were at once convinced of the validity of evolutionism.

The first two volumes of *The Principles* are devoted to general questions. The third volume opens with a defense of uniformitarianism versus some of the previously raised criticisms. The primary purpose of the volume is to use the general, scientific-cum-philosophical position as a working tool. To this end, Lyell turned to questions regarding the fossil record in the Tertiary period (65 to 1.6 million years ago). Using terms supplied by Whewell, Lyell divided the Tertiary into successive epochs—including the Eocene, the Miocene, and the Pliocene—and argued that a comparative analysis of the fauna fossils is the best method for assigning a newfound stratum to a particular epoch. Bearing in mind that uniformitarians expect various species to appear and become extinct at a regular rate, then the assignment of a stratum to a particular epoch depends on a ratio of living forms to fossilized, extinct ones preserved in the layer.

Later in the decade, Lyell became much involved in a controversy with one Edward Charlesworth over the classification of the crag (a Tertiary formation found in the east England county of Norfolk). Charlesworth argued that the crag represents an exception to Lyell's claims about fossil formation. However, detailed studies confirmed Lyell's conclusion that the older the formation, the smaller the proportion of extant species to extinct forms to be found. This was triumphant confirmation of his position, although one should emphasize that for Lyell the real strength of his position lay less in the empirical evidence than in the way in which it followed from his fundamental geological and philosophical presuppositions.

Lyell's greatest and most enthusiastic supporter was the young Charles Darwin. On Darwin's return from the *Beagle* voyage, the two men began a lifelong friendship. Darwin remained silent about his unorthodox views on species creation, until just before *On the Origin of Species* (1859) was published. Although Lyell (together with the botanist Joseph Hooker) arranged for the expeditious publication of Darwin's ideas when his hand was forced by the arrival of an evolutionary essay from the young naturalist Alfred Russel Wallace, the older geologist was not yet a convert. It was only toward the end of the following decade that Lyell finally conceded that perhaps origins, even human origins, may be evolutionary. Despite his concession, he remained reticent to accept natural selection. To Darwin's chagrin, Lyell continued to maintain that Lamarckian inheritance of acquired characters might be the real key to change.

Lyell's eventual conversion to evolutionism was hard fought. Although Darwin was less than appreciative of the effort such a dramatic change in thinking required, it demonstrates Lyell's position as a great scientist—one who merits his final resting place in Westminster Abbey, just down the aisle from where Charles Darwin was soon to join him.

MICHAEL RUSE

Biography

Born in Kinnordy, Forfarshire, Scotland, 14 November 1797. B.A., Exeter College, Oxford University, 1819; M.A., 1821; studied law, Lincoln's Inn, 1819–20; called to the bar, 1825. Appointed professor of geology, King's College, London, 1831. Elected member (1819), secretary (1823–26), president (1835–37, 1849–51), Royal Geological Society of London; elected to Linnean Society, 1819; elected fellow, Royal Society of London, 1826; received honorary M.H., Cambridge University, 1831; awarded Royal Medal of the Royal Society of London, 1834; knighted, 1848; royal commissioner, Great Exhibition of 1851; awarded Copley Medal of the Royal Society of London, 1858; president, British Association for the Advancement of Science, 1864; created a baronet, 1864; awarded Wollaston Medal of the Geological Society, 1866; member of numerous foreign scientific associations, including the American Philosophical Society, the Royal Academy of Sciences at Berlin, and the French Académie des Sciences. Died in London, 22 February 1875.

Major Publications

1830–33. *Principles of Geology*. 3 vols. London: Murray; 1st U.S. ed. [5th U.K. ed. in 4 vols.], Philadelphia: Kay, 1837; 11th ed. in 2 vols., London: Murray, 1872; New York: Appleton, 1872.

1838. *Elements of Geology*. London: Murray; Philadelphia: Kay, 1839; 6th ed., London: Murray, 1865; New York: Appleton, 1866.

1863. *The Geological Evidences of the Antiquity of Man*. London: Murray; Philadelphia: Childs; 4th ed., London: Murray, 1873.

Further Reading

Rudwick, M.J.S. 1970. The strategy of Lyell's *Principles of Geology*. *Isis* 61:5–33.

Wilson, L.G. (ed.). 1970. *Sir Charles Lyell's Scientific Journals on the Species Question*. New Haven, Connecticut: Yale University Press.

———. 1972. *Charles Lyell, the Years to 1841: The Revolution in Geology*. New Haven, Connecticut: Yale University Press.

Ohmer